The Renaissance & Early Modern Era

1454 - 1600

Great Lives from History

The Renaissance & Early Modern Era

1454 - 1600

Volume 1
Isaac ben Judah Abravanel-Leo X

Editor
Christina J. Moose

Editor, First Edition
Frank N. Magill

SALEM PRESS
Pasadena, California   Hackensack, New Jersey

Editor in Chief: Dawn P. Dawson   *Production Editor:* Joyce I. Buchea
Acquisitions Editor: Mark Rehn   *Graphics and Design:* James Hutson
Research Supervisor: Jeffry Jensen   *Editorial Assistant:* Dana Garey
Manuscript Editors: Desiree Dreeuws, Andy Perry   *Layout:* Eddie Murillo
Assistant Editor: Andrea E. Miller   *Photograph Editor:* Philip Bader

Cover photos: Library of Congress
(Pictured left to right, top to bottom: Montezuma II, Henry VIII, Francis Bacon, Elizabeth I, African sculpture from Benin Empire, Süleyman the Magnificent, Wang Yangming, William Shakespeare, Catherine Parr)

Some of the essays in this work originally appeared in the following Salem Press sets: *Dictionary of World Biography* (© 1998-1999, edited by Frank N. Magill) and *Great Lives from History* (© 1987-1995, edited by Frank N. Magill).

Library of Congress Cataloging-in-Publication Data

Great lives from history. The Renaissance & early modern era, 1454-1600 / editors, Christina J. Moose, Frank N. Magill.— 1st ed.
     p. cm.
     Includes bibliographical references and indexes.
     ISBN 1-58765-211-0 (set : alk. paper) — ISBN 1-58765-212-9 (v. 1 : alk. paper) — ISBN 1-58765-213-7 (v. 2 : alk. paper)
     1. Biography—15th century. 2. Biography—16th century. 3. Renaissance. I. Title: Renaissance & early modern era, 1454-1600. II. Moose, Christina J., 1952- . III. Magill, Frank Northen, 1907-1997.
     CT115.G74 2005
     909'.5'0922—dc22

2004028875

First Printing

CONTENTS

Contents

PUBLISHER'S NOTE

Great Lives from History: The Renaissance & Early Modern Era, 1454-1600 is the third installment in the revised and expanded *Great Lives* series, initiated in 2004 with *The Ancient World, Prehistory-476 C.E.* (2 vols.) and followed in Fall 2004 with *The Middle Ages, 477-1453* (2 vols.). It will be joined by *Great Lives from History: The Seventeenth Century, 1601-1700*, planned for Fall 2005, and later by volumes covering *The Eighteenth Century*, *The Nineteenth Century*, and *The Twentieth Century*. The entire series, when complete, is expected to cover more than 2,500 lives in essays ranging from 3 to 5 pages in length.

EXPANDED COVERAGE

This ongoing series is a revision of the 10-volume *Dictionary of World Biography* (*DWB*) series (1998-1999), which in turn was a revision and reordering of Salem Press's 30-volume *Great Lives from History* series (1987-1995). The expanded *Great Lives* differs in several ways from *DWB*:

- The original essays are enhanced by the addition of new entries covering a wider geographical area and including many more women. The coverage of each set has been increased significantly. In the current two volumes on *The Renaissance & Early Modern Era*, for example, 141 new essays have been added to the original 192 for a total of 333 essays covering 338 historical figures (5 essays address more than one person).

- In an effort to align coverage with curriculum, the new series provides more logical breaks between eras. For example, *The Ancient World* ends at 476 C.E. (the fall of Rome), *The Middle Ages* ends at 1453 (the end of the Hundred Years' War and the fall of Constantinople), and the current *Renaissance* volumes cover the peak of the transition between the late medieval period and the early modern era, 1454-1600. Subsequent volumes will cover centuries.

- Tables and dynastic lists have been added to enhance and supplement the text throughout.

- A section of maps has been added to the front matter of each volume to allow students to locate personages geographically.

- Essays from the original *DWB* on all personages falling into the new time frame are reprinted in this new series with updated and annotated bibliographies.

SCOPE OF COVERAGE

The geographic and occupational scope of the individuals covered in *Great Lives from History: The Renaissance & Early Modern Era, 1454-1600* is broad. Coverage is worldwide, with individuals identified with one or more of the following areas: Africa (10), Austria (6), Belgium and Flanders (6), Bohemia (2), Caribbean (1), China (4), Denmark (2), Egypt (1), England (68), France (34), Germany (12), Hungary (3), India (6), Ireland (1), Italy (72), Japan (7), Mesoamerica (4), Netherlands (10), North America (6), Palestine (2), Poland (4), Portugal (12), Romania (1), Russia (5), Scotland (6), South America (3), Spain (35), Sweden (1), Switzerland (3), Ottoman Empire (5), and Vietnam (1).

The editors have sought to provide coverage that is broad in areas of achievement as well as geography, while at the same time including the recognized shapers of history essential in any liberal arts curriculum. Major world leaders appear here—emperors, conquerors, kings, queens, and khans—as well as the giants of religious faith who were central to the Renaissance world: popes, monks, and saints who left their imprint on political as well as spiritual institutions. The set also includes figures who have received little or no attention in the past—from the queen of Hausaland Amina Sarauniya Zazzua, to the composer Thomas Tallis, and even such notorious figures as Irish pirate Grace O'Malley and Hungarian nobelwoman Elizabeth Báthory. By category, the contents include figures who belong to one or more of the following categories: Architecture (7), Art (28), Astronomy (4), Chemistry (1), Church Reform (12), Crime (1), Diplomacy (5), Education and Library Science (4), Exploration (27), Geography and Cartography (6), Government and Politics (108), Historiography (4), Law (5), Literature (26), Mathematics (6), Medicine (4), Military and Warfare (13), Music (10), Patronage of the Arts (5), Philosophy (9), Religion and Theology (32), Scholarship (2), Science and Technology (7), Social Reform (2), and Theater (5). Among these architects of civilization are 47 women, including writers, scholars, scientists, and national leaders.

Essay Length and Format

Each essay ranges from 1,500 to 3,000 words in length (roughly 3 to 5 pages).

Each essay displays standard ready-reference top matter offering easy access to biographical information:

- The essay title is the name of the individual; editors have chosen the name as it is most commonly found in Western English-language sources.

- The individual's *nationality or ethnicity* and *occupation or historical role* follow on the second line, including reign dates for rulers.

- A *summary paragraph* highlighting the individual's historical importance indicates why the person is studied today.

- The *Born* and *Died* lines list the most complete dates of birth and death available, followed by the most precise locations available, as well as an indication of when these are unknown, only probable, or only approximate; both contemporary and modern place-names (where different) are listed.

- *Also known as* lists all known versions of the individual's name, including full names, given names, alternative spellings, pseudonyms, and common epithets.

- *Area(s) of achievement* lists all categories of contribution, from Architecture and Art through Social Reform and Theater.

The body of each article is divided into three parts:

- *Early Life* provides facts about the individual's upbringing and the environment in which he or she was reared, as well as the pronunciation of his or her name, if unusual. Where little is known about the individual's rearing, historical context is provided.

- *Life's Work*, the heart of the article, consists of a straightforward, generally chronological, account of the period during which the individual's most significant achievements were accomplished.

- *Significance* is an overview of the individual's place in history.

- *Further Reading* is an annotated bibliography, a starting point for further research.

- *See also* is a list of cross-references to essays in the set covering related personages.

- *Related articles* lists essays of interest in Salem's companion publication, *Great Events from History: The Renaissance & Early Modern Era, 1454-1600* (2 vols., 2005).

Special Features

Several features distinguish this series as a whole from other biographical reference works. The front matter includes the following aids:

- *Key to Pronunciation*, a key to in-text pronunciation, which appears in both volumes.

- *Complete List of Contents*: this alphabetical list of contents appears in both volumes.

- *List of Maps, Tables, and Sidebars*.

- *Maps*: In the front matter to each volume, a section of maps displaying major regions of the world in the period 1454-1600 appear grouped together for easy reference.

The back matter to Volume 2 includes several appendices and indexes:

- *Rulers and Dynasties*, a geographically arranged set of tables listing major rulers and their regnal dates, covering the major regions of the world.

- *Chronological List of Entries*: individuals covered, arranged by birth year.

- *Category Index*: entries by area of achievement, from architecture to warfare.

- *Geographical Index*: entries by country or region.

- *Personages Index*: an index of all persons, both those covered in the essays and those additionally discussed within the text.

- *Subject Index*: a comprehensive index including personages, concepts, books, artworks, terms, battles, civilizations, and other topics of discussion, with full cross-references from alternative spellings and to the Category and Geographical Indexes.

USAGE NOTES

The worldwide scope of *Great Lives from History* resulted in the inclusion of many names and words that must be transliterated from languages that do not use the Roman alphabet, and in some cases, there is more than one transliterated form in use. In many cases, transliterated words in this set follow the American Library Association and Library of Congress (ALA-LC) transliteration format for that language. However, if another form of a name or word was judged to be more familiar to the general audience, it is used instead. The variants for names of essay subjects are listed in ready-reference top matter and are cross-referenced in the subject and personages indexes. The Pinyin transliteration was used for Chinese topics, with Wade-Giles variants provided for major names and dynasties. In a few cases, a common name that is not Pinyin has been used. Sanskrit and other South Asian names generally follow the ALA-LC transliteration rules, although again, the more familiar form of a word is used when deemed appropriate for the general reader.

Titles of books and other literature appear, upon first mention in the essay, with their full publication and trans-lation data as known: an indication of the first date of publication or appearance, followed by the English title in translation and its first date of appearance in English; if no translation has been published in English, and if the context of the discussion does not make the meaning of the title obvious, a "literal translation" appears in roman type.

Throughout, readers will find a limited number of abbreviations used in both top matter and text, including "r." for "reigned," "b." for "born," "d." for "died," and "fl." for flourished. Where a date range appears appended to a name without one of these designators, the reader may assume it signifies birth and death dates.

Finally, in the regnal tables dispersed throughout the text, the reader will find some names appearing in small capital letters. These figures are covered in their own separate essays within these two volumes.

THE EDITORS AND CONTRIBUTORS

Salem Press would like to extend its appreciation to the many fine academicians and scholars who prepared essays for this work. Without their expert contributions, a project of this nature would not be possible. A full list of contributors and their affiliations appears in the front matter of Volume 1.

CONTRIBUTORS

Wayne Ackerson
Salisbury State University, Maryland

Patrick Adcock
Henderson State University, Arkansas

Richard Adler
University of Michigan, Dearborn

James W. Alexander
University of Georgia

Arthur L. Alt
College of Great Falls, Montana

J. Stewart Alverson
*University of Tennessee at
    Chattanooga*

Nancy Fix Anderson
Loyola University, New Orleans

Madeline Cirillo Archer
Duquesne University, Pennsylvania

Stanley Archer
Texas A&M University

Christopher Armitage
*University of North Carolina at
    Chapel Hill*

Sharon Arnoult
Midwestern State University

Dorothy B. Aspinwall
University of Hawaii at Manoa

Bryan Aubrey
Independent Scholar

Theodore P. Aufdemberge
Concordia College

Tom L. Auffenberg
Ouachita Baptist University

Christopher Baker
Armstrong Atlantic State University

Renzo Baldasso
Columbia University

Barbara Ann Barbato
Webster University

John W. Barker
University of Wisconsin, Madison

Frederic J. Baumgartner
*Virginia Polytechnic Institute and
    State University*

Blake Beattie
University of Louisville

Graydon Beeks
Pomona College

S. Carol Berg
College of Saint Benedict, Minnesota

Milton Berman
University of Rochester

Robert L. Berner
University of Wisconsin, Oshkosh

Cynthia A. Bily
Adrian College

Nicholas Birns
New School University

Charlene Villaseñor Black
*University of California at Los
    Angeles*

Jill Elizabeth Blondin
University of Texas at Tyler

Harold Branam
Temple University

Jeff R. Bremer
*California State University,
    Bakersfield*

Jean R. Brink
Huntington Library

William S. Brockington, Jr.
University of South Carolina

Alan Brown
Livingston University

Kendall W. Brown
Hillsdale College

Jeffrey L. Buller
Mary Baldwin College

Elwira Buszewicz
Jagiellonian University

Joseph P. Byrne
Belmont University

Byron Cannon
Independent Scholar

Peter Carravetta
*The Graduate Center, City University
    of New York
    Queens College*

Douglas Clouatre
Mid Plains Community College

Arnold Victor Coonin
Rhodes College

Randolf G. S. Cooper
Florida State University

Christine Cornell
St. Thomas University

Daniel A. Crews
Central Missouri State University

Carol Crowe-Carraco
Western Kentucky University

Victoria Hennessey Cummins
Austin College

Marsha Daigle-Williamson
Spring Arbor University

J. D. Daubs
*University of Illinois at Urbana-
    Champaign*

Ronald W. Davis
Western Michigan University

Thomas Derdak
University of Chicago

M. Casey Diana
University of Illinois at Urbana-Champaign

Reidar Dittmann
Saint Olaf College

Paul M. Dover
Georgian Court College

Steven L. Driever
University of Missouri, Kansas City

Thomas Drucker
University of Wisconsin, Whitewater

Surjit S. Dulai
Michigan State University

Burton L. Dunbar III
University of Missouri at Kansas City

David Allen Duncan
Tennessee Wesleyan College

John P. Dunn
Valdosta State University

Eric R. Dursteler
Brigham Young University

Bruce L. Edwards
Bowling Green State University

David G. Egler
Western Illinois University

Mary Sweeney Ellett
Randolph-Macon Women's College

Robert P. Ellis
Worcester State College

Thomas L. Erskine
Salisbury State University

Clara Estow
University of Massachusetts, Boston

Barbara M. Fahy
Albright College

James J. Farsolas
University of South Carolina
Coastal Carolina Community College

Randall Fegley
Pennsylvania State University

Gary B. Ferngren
Oregon State University

Luminita Florea
University of California at Berkeley

Ronald K. Frank
Pace University

Ronald H. Fritze
Lamar University

C. George Fry
Saint Francis College

Maia Wellington Gahtan
University of Pennsylvania

Michael J. Garcia
Arapahoe Community College

John Gardner
Delaware State College

Gayle Gaskill
College of St. Catherine

Stephannie S. Gearhart
Lehigh University

Leonardas V. Gerulaitis
Oakland University

Paul E. Gill
Shippensburg University

K. Fred Gillum
Colby College

Paul Gleed
State University of New York at Buffalo

Joseph A. Goldenberg
Virginia State University

Lewis L. Gould
University of Texas at Austin

Ronald R. Gray
Beijing Language and Culture University

Johnpeter Horst Grill
Mississippi State University

Michael Wayne Guillory
Georgia State University

Gil L. Gunderson
Monterey Institute of International Studies

Surendra K. Gupta
Pittsburg State University

David B. Haley
University of Minnesota

Gavin R. G. Hambly
University of Texas at Dallas

Sheldon Hanft
Appalachian State University

Fred R. van Hartesveldt
Fort Valley State University

Paul B. Harvey, Jr.
Pennsylvania State University

Peter B. Heller
Manhattan College

Mark C. Herman
Edison Community College

Sally Hickson
Brock University

Sharon Hill
Virginia Commonwealth University

Richard L. Hillard
University of Arkansas, Pine Bluff

John R. Holmes
Franciscan University of Steubenville

Lisa Hopkins
Sheffield Hallam University

Ronald William Howard
Mississippi College

James Carlton Hughes
University of North Carolina at Chapel Hill

CONTRIBUTORS

Edelma Huntley
Appalachian State University

Raymond Pierre Hylton
Virginia Union University

Bruce E. Johansen
University of Nebraska at Omaha

Loretta Turner Johnson
Mankato State University

Lynn M. Johnson
Towson University

Richard W. Kaeuper
University of Rochester

Donald R. Kelm
Northern Kentucky University

Robert W. Kenny
George Washington University

Jean Moore Kiger
University of Mississippi

Leigh Husband Kimmel
Independent Scholar

Ann Klefstad
Sun and Moon Press

James Kline
Independent Scholar

Grove Koger
Boise Public Library

Jane Kristof
Portland State University

Lynn C. Kronzek
Independent Scholar

Paul E. Kuhl
Winston-Salem State University

Eugene Larson
Pierce College

William T. Lawlor
University of Wisconsin, Stevens Point

J. David Lawrence
David Lipscomb University

Harry Lawton
*University of California at Santa
Barbara*

Thomas Tandy Lewis
Anoka-Ramsey Community College

James Livingston
Northern Michigan University

Pietro Lorenzini
St. Xavier University

Javier Lorenzo
East Carolina University

Eric v.d. Luft
*State University of New York Upstate
Medical University*

R. C. Lutz
CII

Garrett L. McAinsh
Hendrix College

C. S. McConnell
University of Calgary

Thomas McGeary
Independent Scholar

James Edward McGoldrick
Cedarville College

Caroline McManus
*University of California at Los
Angeles*

Corinne Noirot Maguire
Rutgers University

E. Deanne Malpass
Stephen F. Austin State University

Patricia W. Manning
University of Kansas

Carl Henry Marcoux
University of California at Riverside

Elaine Mathiasen
Independent Scholar

Rose Ethel Althaus Meza
Queensborough Community College

Joan E. Meznar
Eastern Connecticut State University

Robert E. Morsberger
*California State Polytechnic
University*

Terence R. Murphy
American University

Alice Myers
Simon's Rock of Bard College

John W. Myers
*University of North Carolina at
Wilmington*

Holly Faith Nelson
Trinity Western University

Edwin L. Neville, Jr.
Canisius College

Richard L. Niswonger
John Brown University

Veronika Oberparleiter
Universität Salzburg

Charles H. O'Brien
Western Illinois University

Edward J. Olszewski
Case Western Reserve University

Joseph M. Ortiz
Princeton University

William A. Paquette
Tidewater Community College

Robert J. Paradowski
Rochester Institute of Technology

Martha Moffitt Peacock
Brigham Young University

Jan Pendergrass
University of Georgia

Matthew Penney
Independent Scholar

Susan L. Piepke
Bridgewater College

Monica Piotter
Harvard University

George R. Plitnik
Frostburg State University

Marjorie J. Podolsky
Behrend College of Pennsylvania State University

Ronald L. Pollitt
University of Cincinnati

Dorothy Turner Potter
Lynchburg College

Charles Pullen
Queen's University

P. S. Ramsey
Independent Scholar

John D. Raymer
Indiana University at South Bend Indiana Vocational College

Rosemary M. Canfield Reisman
Charleston Southern University

Bernd Renner
Brooklyn College

Orsolya Réthelyi
Central European University

Ann E. Reynolds
Independent Scholar

Betty Richardson
Southern Illinois University at Edwardsville

Edward A. Riedinger
Ohio State University Libraries

John O. Robison
University of South Florida

Carl Rollyson
Baruch College

Victor Anthony Rudowski
Clemson University

Joyce E. Salisbury
University of Wisconsin, Green Bay

Rosa M. Salzberg
University of Melbourne

Victor A. Santi
University of New Orleans

Richard Sax
Madonna University

Stephen P. Sayles
University of La Verne

Daniel C. Scavone
University of Southern Indiana

Eric Van Schaack
Colgate University

Per Schelde
York College

Randy P. Schiff
University of California at Santa Barbara

William C. Schrader
Tennessee Technological University

R. Baird Shuman
University of Illinois at Urbana-Champaign

Marcello Simonetta
Wesleyan University

Richard L. Smith
Ferrum College

Roger Smith
Independent Scholar

Ronald F. Smith
Massachusetts Maritime Academy

Stefan C. A. Halikowski Smith
Brown University

Julie Robin Solomon
American University

Robert M. Spector
Worcester State College

Joseph L. Spradley
Wheaton College

C. Fitzhugh Spragins
Arkansas College

S. J. Stearns
College of Staten Island

David R. Stevenson
Kearney State College

Paul Stewart
Southern Connecticut State University

Gerald H. Strauss
Bloomsburg University

Taylor Stults
Muskingum College

Donald D. Sullivan
University of New Mexico

James Sullivan
California State University, Los Angeles

Glenn L. Swygart
Tennessee Temple University

Bart L. R. Talbert
Salisbury University

Larissa Juliet Taylor
Colby College

Cassandra Lee Tellier
Capital University

Nicholas C. Thomas
Auburn University

Louis P. Towles
Southern Wesleyan University

M. J. Tucker
State University of New York at Buffalo

William Urban
Monmouth College

Lisa Urkevich
American University of Kuwait

Larry W. Usilton
University of North Carolina at Wilmington

Michiel Verweij
Katholieke Universiteit Leuven

Anne R. Vizzier
University of Arkansas

Eric L. Wake
Cumberland College

William T. Walker
*Philadelphia College of Pharmacy
and Science*

J. Francis Watson
Grace Lutheran Church

Martha Ellen Webb
University of Nebraska at Lincoln

Ann Weikel
Portland State University, Oregon

Allen Wells
Bowdoin College

Richard Whitworth
Ball State University

Michael Witkoski
*South Carolina House of
Representatives*

Shelley Wolbrink
Drury University

Diane Wolfthal
Brooklyn Museum

Amanda Wunder
University of New Hampshire

Clifton K. Yearley
*State University of New York at
Buffalo*

Kristen L. Zacharias
Albright College

Robert Zaller
Drexel University

Lilian H. Zirpolo
Independent Scholar

C. K. Zulkosky
Independent Scholar

KEY TO PRONUNCIATION

Many of the names of personages covered in *Great Lives from History: The Renaissance, 1454-1600* may be unfamiliar to students and general readers. For these unfamiliar names, guides to pronunciation have been provided upon first mention of the names in the text. These guidelines do not purport to achieve the subtleties of the languages in question but will offer readers a rough equivalent of how English speakers may approximate the proper pronunciation.

Vowel Sounds

Symbol	Spelled (Pronounced)
a	answer (AN-suhr), laugh (laf), sample (SAM-puhl), that (that)
ah	father (FAH-thur), hospital (HAHS-pih-tuhl)
aw	awful (AW-fuhl), caught (kawt)
ay	blaze (blayz), fade (fayd), waiter (WAYT-ur), weigh (way)
eh	bed (behd), head (hehd), said (sehd)
ee	believe (bee-LEEV), cedar (SEE-dur), leader (LEED-ur), liter (LEE-tur)
ew	boot (bewt), lose (lewz)
i	buy (bi), height (hit), lie (li), surprise (sur-PRIZ)
ih	bitter (BIH-tur), pill (pihl)
o	cotton (KO-tuhn), hot (hot)
oh	below (bee-LOH), coat (koht), note (noht), wholesome (HOHL-suhm)
oo	good (good), look (look)
ow	couch (kowch), how (how)
oy	boy (boy), coin (koyn)
uh	about (uh-BOWT), butter (BUH-tuhr), enough (ee-NUHF), other (UH-thur)

Consonant Sounds

Symbol	Spelled (Pronounced)
ch	beach (beech), chimp (chihmp)
g	beg (behg), disguise (dihs-GIZ), get (geht)
j	digit (DIH-juht), edge (ehj), jet (jeht)
k	cat (kat), kitten (KIH-tuhn), hex (hehks)
s	cellar (SEHL-ur), save (sayv), scent (sehnt)
sh	champagne (sham-PAYN), issue (IH-shew), shop (shop)
ur	birth (burth), disturb (dihs-TURB), earth (urth), letter (LEH-tur)
y	useful (YEWS-fuhl), young (yuhng)
z	business (BIHZ-nehs), zest (zehst)
zh	vision (VIH-zhuhn)

COMPLETE LIST OF CONTENTS

VOLUME 1

VOLUME 2

List of Maps, Tables, and Sidebars

Volume 1

VOLUME 2

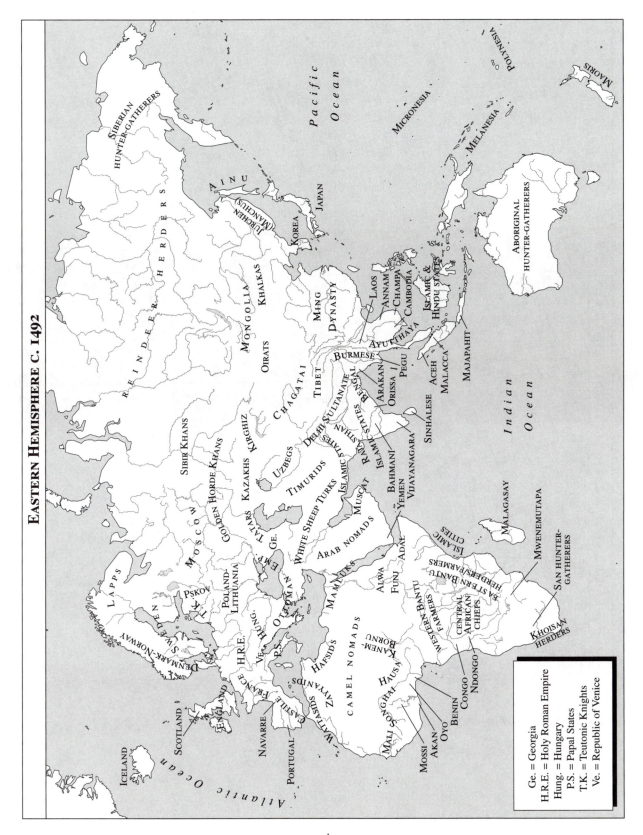

EASTERN HEMISPHERE C. 1492

ATLANTIC OCEAN
PACIFIC OCEAN
INDIAN OCEAN

ICELAND
SCOTLAND
ENGLAND
NAVARRE
PORTUGAL
CASTILE
FRANCE
SWEDEN
DENMARK-NORWAY
LAPPS
PSKOV
T.K.
POLAND-LITHUANIA
MOSCOW
H.R.E.
HUNG.
VEN.
P.S.
WATTASIDS
ZAYYANIDS
HAFSIDS
OTTOMAN EMP.
Ge.

SIBERIAN HUNTER-GATHERERS
REINDEER HERDERS
AINU
JURCHEN (MANCHUS)
KOREA
JAPAN
MONGOLIA
KHALKAS
OIRATS
MING DYNASTY
SIBIR KHANS
GOLDEN HORDE KHANS
TATARS
KAZAKHS
KIRGHIZ
CHAGATAI
TIBET
UZBEGS
DELHI SULTANATE
TIMURIDS
WHITE SHEEP TURKS
ISLAMIC STATES
MUSCAT
ARAB NOMADS
MAMLUKS
CAMEL NOMADS
KANEM-BORNU
HAUSA
SONGHAI
MALI
MOSSI
AKAN
OYO
BENIN
CONGO
NDONGO
WESTERN BANTU FARMERS
CENTRAL AFRICAN CHIEFS
EASTERN BANTU HERDERS/FARMERS
ISLAMIC CITIES
ADAL
FUNJ
ALWA
YEMEN
BAHMANI
VIJAYANAGARA
SINHALESE
RAJASTHAN
BENGAL
ORISSA
ARAKAN
PEGU
BURMESE
AYUTTHAYA
LAOS
ANNAM
CHAMPA
CAMBODIA
ISLAMIC & HINDU STATES
ACEH
MALACCA
MAJAPAHIT
MALAGASAY
MWENEMUTAPA
SAN HUNTER-GATHERERS
KHOISAN HERDERS

MICRONESIA
MELANESIA
POLYNESIA
MAORIS
ABORIGINAL HUNTER-GATHERERS

Ge. = Georgia
H.R.E. = Holy Roman Empire
Hung. = Hungary
P.S. = Papal States
T.K. = Teutonic Knights
Ve. = Republic of Venice

xxix

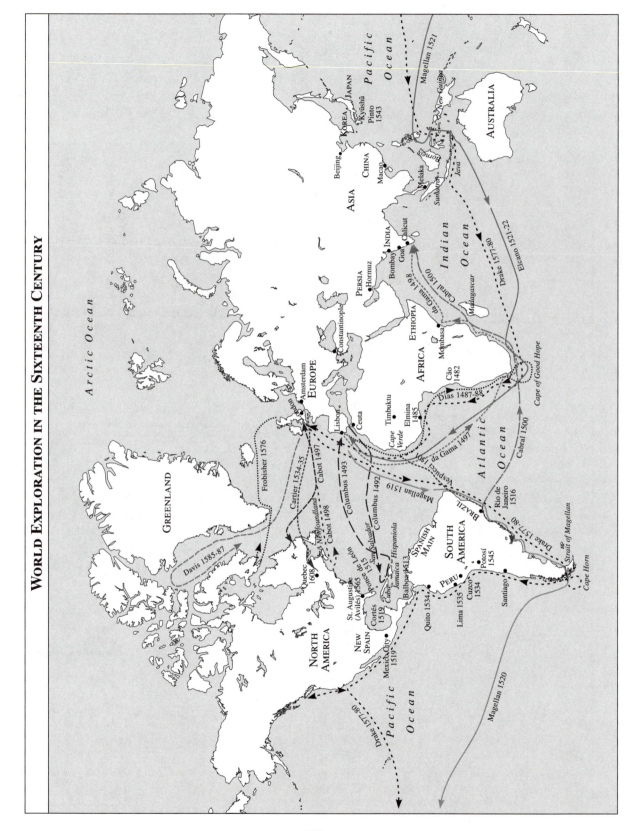

WORLD EXPLORATION IN THE SIXTEENTH CENTURY

Arctic Ocean

GREENLAND

NORTH AMERICA

Davis 1585-87

Frobisher 1576

Cartier 1534-35

Cabot 1497

Cabot 1498

Quebec 1608

Newfoundland

Columbus 1493

Columbus 1492

San Salvador

NEW SPAIN

St. Augustine (Avilés) 1565

de León 1513

Cortés 1519

Mexico City 1519

Ponce 1513

Cuba

Jamaica

Hispaniola

Balboa 1513

SPANISH MAIN

SOUTH AMERICA

Quito 1534

PERU

Lima 1535

Cuzco 1534

Potosí 1545

Santiago

BRAZIL

Rio de Janeiro 1516

Cape Horn

Strait of Magellan

Drake 1577-80

Magellan 1520

Magellan 1519

Vespucci 1501

da Gama 1497

Cabral 1500

Atlantic Ocean

Pacific Ocean

Drake 1577-80

Lisbon

Amsterdam

EUROPE

Constantinople

PERSIA

Hormuz

Ceuta

Cape Verde

Timbuktu

Elmina 1485

AFRICA

ETHIOPIA

Mombasa

Cão 1482

Dias 1487-88

Cape of Good Hope

Cabral 1500

da Gama 1498

Madagascar

Indian Ocean

Bombay

Goa

Calicut

INDIA

ASIA

Beijing

CHINA

Macao

Melaka

Sumatra

Java

Borneo

New Guinea

AUSTRALIA

KOREA

JAPAN

Kyūshū

Pinto 1543

Pacific Ocean

Magellan 1521

Elcano 1521-22

Drake 1577-80

xxx

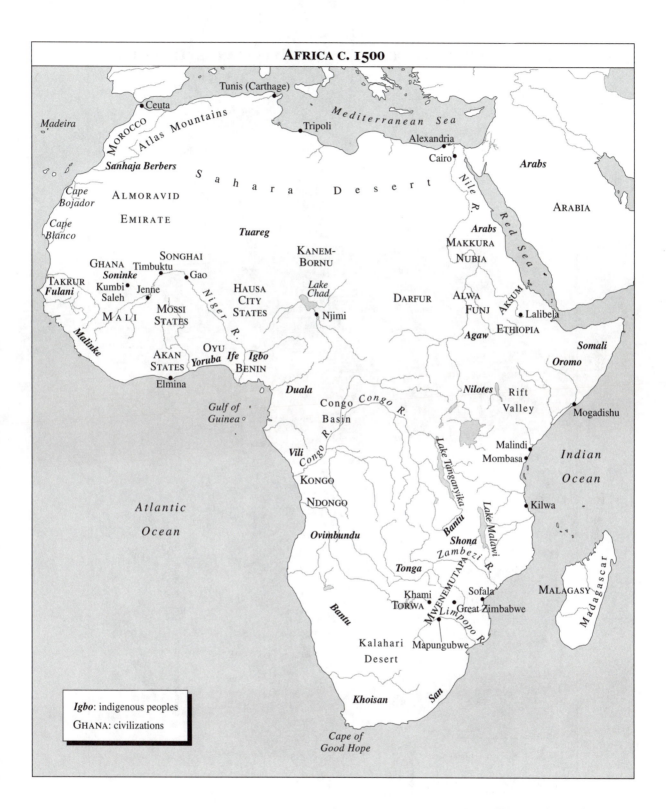

AFRICA C. 1500

Madeira

Ceuta

Tunis (Carthage)

MOROCCO

Atlas Mountains

Tripoli

Mediterranean Sea

Alexandria

Cairo

Arabs

Sanhaja Berbers

Sahara Desert

Nile R.

Red Sea

ARABIA

Cape Bojador

ALMORAVID

Arabs

ARABIA

Cape Blanco

EMIRATE

Tuareg

KANEM-BORNU

MAKKURA

NUBIA

GHANA   Timbuktu

SONGHAI

Lake Chad

ALWA

AKSUM

TAKRUR

Soninke

Gao

DARFUR

FUNJ

Lalibela

Fulani

Kumbi

Jenne

HAUSA

Njimi

Agaw

ETHIOPIA

Saleh

CITY

MALI

MOSSI

STATES

Somali

Malinke

STATES

Niger R.

Oromo

AKAN

OYU

Ife

Igbo

Nilotes

Rift

STATES

Yoruba

BENIN

Valley

Elmina

Duala

Mogadishu

Gulf of

Congo

Congo R.

Guinea

Basin

Congo R.

Vili

Malindi

Mombasa

Indian

KONGO

Ocean

NDONGO

Lake Tanganyika

Kilwa

Atlantic

Bantu

Ocean

Ovimbundu

Shona

Lake Malawi

Tonga

Zambezi R.

Khami

Sofala

MALAGASY

TORWA

Great Zimbabwe

MWENEMUTAPA

Bantu

Limpopo R.

Madagascar

Kalahari

Mapungubwe

Desert

Khoisan

San

Cape of

Good Hope

Igbo: indigenous peoples

GHANA: civilizations

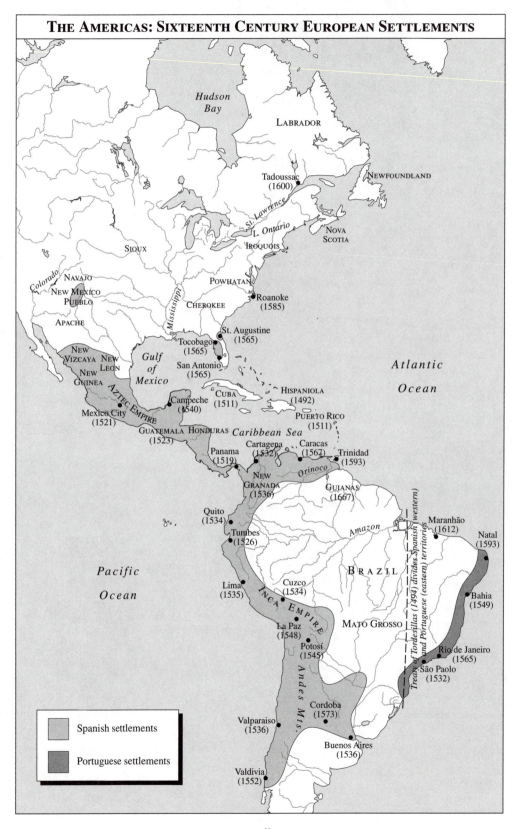

THE AMERICAS: SIXTEENTH CENTURY EUROPEAN SETTLEMENTS

Hudson Bay

LABRADOR

NEWFOUNDLAND

Tadoussac (1600)

St. Lawrence

L. Ontario

NOVA SCOTIA

SIOUX

IROQUOIS

Colorado

NAVAJO

NEW MEXICO

PUEBLO

POWHATAN

CHEROKEE

Mississippi

APACHE

Roanoke (1585)

St. Augustine (1565)

Tocobago (1565)

NEW VIZCAYA

NEW LEON

NEW GUINEA

Gulf of Mexico

San Antonio (1565)

AZTEC EMPIRE

Campeche (1540)

CUBA (1511)

HISPANIOLA (1492)

Mexico City (1521)

GUATEMALA (1523)

HONDURAS

PUERTO RICO (1511)

Caribbean Sea

Atlantic Ocean

Cartagena (1532)

Caracas (1567)

Trinidad (1593)

Panama (1519)

NEW GRANADA (1536)

Orinoco

GUIANAS (1667)

Quito (1534)

Amazon

Maranhão (1612)

Natal (1593)

Tumbes (1526)

B R A Z I L

Pacific Ocean

Lima (1535)

Cuzco (1534)

INCA EMPIRE

Bahia (1549)

La Paz (1548)

MATO GROSSO

Potosí (1545)

Treaty of Tordesillas (1494) divides Spanish (western) and Portuguese (eastern) territories

Rio de Janeiro (1565)

São Paolo (1532)

Andes Mts.

Cordoba (1573)

Valparaiso (1536)

Buenos Aires (1536)

Valdivia (1552)

	Spanish settlements
	Portuguese settlements

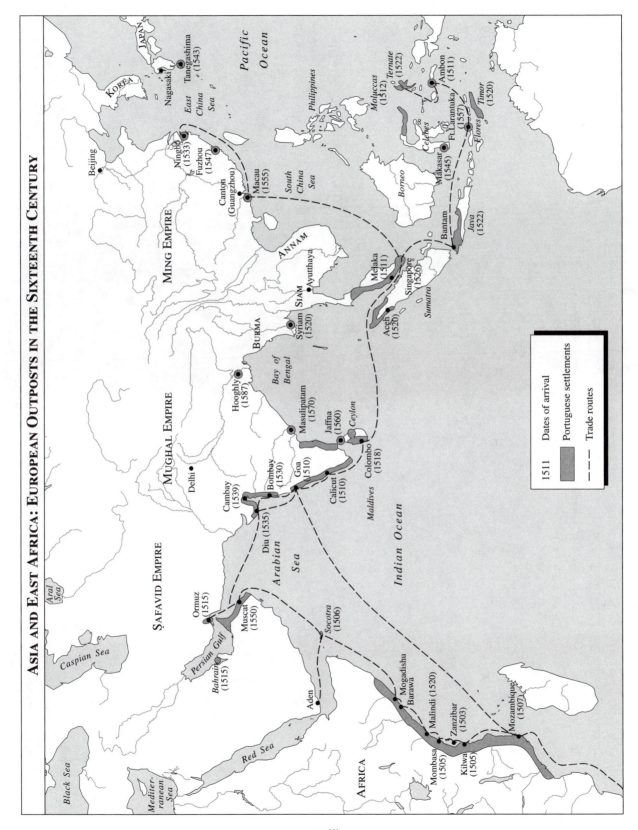

ASIA AND EAST AFRICA: EUROPEAN OUTPOSTS IN THE SIXTEENTH CENTURY

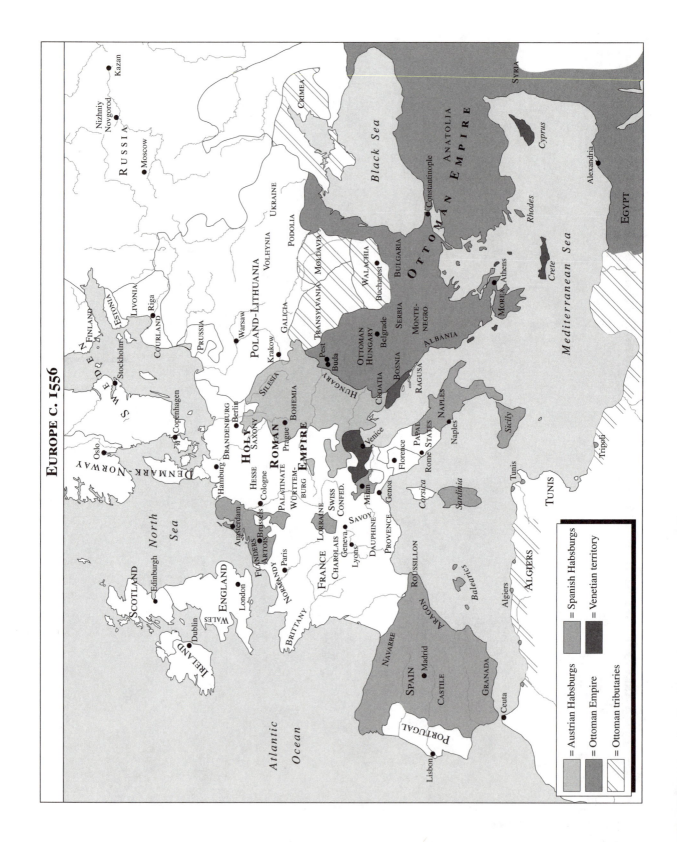

EUROPE C. 1556

= Austrian Habsburgs
= Ottoman Empire
= Ottoman tributaries
= Spanish Habsburgs
= Venetian territory

The Renaissance & Early Modern Era

1454 - 1600

ISAAC BEN JUDAH ABRAVANEL
Spanish theologian and statesman

Abravanel's biblical commentaries addressed religious and philosophical questions in order to strengthen the faith of Spanish Jews, a faith that was especially tried and tested during the crisis of confidence following the expulsion of Jews from Spain, ordered in 1492.

BORN: 1437; Lisbon, Portugal
DIED: November, 1508; Venice, Republic of Venice (now in Italy)
ALSO KNOWN AS: Isaac Abrabanel; Isaac Abarbanel
AREAS OF ACHIEVEMENT: Religion and theology, philosophy, government and politics

EARLY LIFE

The family of Isaac ben Judah Abravanel (ee-sah-AHK behn jew-dah ahb-rah-vah-NEHL) claimed direct descent from Israel's King David and asserted that they had arrived in Spain before the Romans. Isaac Abravanel's grandfather fled Spain for Portugal around 1400 to escape pressures to convert to Christianity.

Young Isaac received an extensive education; he mastered Hebrew, Latin, Portuguese, and Castilian, and he read widely in Latin philosophical literature. Isaac also explored the works of Christian medieval Scholastics and church fathers. He also studied medicine and astrology.

Abravanel married in his early twenties and by the 1470's was active in the family business, which assisted King Afonso V of Portugal and members of the nobility in their monetary affairs. He became especially close to the duke of Bragança. When newly crowned king John II, Afonso V's son, attacked the powerful aristocracy and arrested the duke, Abravanel feared for his life and fled to Spain on May 31, 1483. Two years later, he was sentenced to death in absentia on charges of treasonable conspiracy against the king.

LIFE'S WORK

In Spain, Abravanel began exhibiting a pattern of seclusion following political disappointments, and he indulged himself in cycles of intensive literary activity. During the months between October, 1483, and March, 1484, he wrote four volumes of biblical commentary, totaling some 400,000 words. Commenting on Joshua, Judges, and Samuel—biblical books full of descriptions of the failures and successes of human leaders—Abravanel drew from his experience to present his own ideas on history and politics.

Abravanel started writing religious and philosophical tracts while still active in business in Lisbon. *Ateret Zequenim* (mid-1460's; crown of the ancients) discussed the concept of God and the meaning of prophecy, rejecting rationalist Aristotelian philosophy and insisting on the primacy of faith over reason. Abravanel also began a critical commentary on Moses Maimonides' *Dalālat al-Hā'rīn* (1190; *The Guide of the Perplexed*, 1881-1185), respectfully rejecting Maimonides' rationalistic approach to Judaism. He would work on this project from time to time during the rest of his life, but at his death, it remained unfinished.

Abravanel planned a series of commentaries on the books of the Bible, covering the Pentateuch, the historical books, and the prophets. His exegesis clarified aspects of the Scriptures, reassuring Jews that God's promises to them were still valid. Abravanel insisted on a literal reading of the sacred text, while also using allegorical interpretations. When Genesis said God created heaven and earth, Abravanel maintained that God created the universe out of nothing, and he rejected views accommodating the Greek concept that matter had always existed. Abravanel also asserted that the Bible contained hidden meanings. He accepted the esoteric belief that the six days of creation predicted the world would last six thousand years, and the seventh day of rest forecast that God would finish his work at the seventh millennium, bringing the universe to an end.

Familiar with the writings of Christian commentators, Abravanel considered, and at times accepted, their biblical interpretations. Along with Christian theologians, he viewed the expulsion from Paradise as a truly catastrophic event in the history of humanity. He could not, however, accept the concept of an original sin afflicting all humankind—a sin exculpated only by belief in the sacrifice of Christ.

Abravanel saw history as depicting the degeneration of Israel and humanity. Israel had rebelled against the government established by Moses; by asking for a king instead of remaining loyal to the Lord as king, it suffered in consequence. Jewish political ideas in the Middle Ages favored monarchy—the rule of King David was idealized as the best of historical times. In contrast, Abravanel, who had known royalty firsthand, believed kingship abominable and referred to kings as malignant plagues. He viewed hereditary monarchs, whether absolute or limited rulers, as dangerous; it was best to have neither type of royalty.

Subjects, nevertheless, had no right to rebel, because no one could become king unless God had first willed it. Israel, whose ruler was God, did not need a king. Abravanel cited the Italian republics as evidence that states could be ruled effectively by temporary, nonhereditary leaders. Abravanel did not favor democracies or republics; his ideal was the government he believed Moses had instituted—a theocracy, with a prophet as its head, assisted by a sanhedrin (a supreme council and tribunal) of priests and Levites.

When King Ferdinand and Queen Isabella of Spain appointed Abravanel to the post of tax farmer in 1484, his writing stopped. Successful financially, he also became a leader of Spanish Jewry. Despite his own negative view of monarchical government, Abravanel was shocked when the king and queen ordered the expulsion of Jews from Spain in 1492. He took his family to Italy because only the Kingdom of Naples was willing to accept Jewish refugees. In his first year at Naples, he completed a commentary on the two books of Kings, a record of a period of national disaster and exile from Israel paralleling the Jewish expulsion from Spain.

Abravanel provided financial advice to the king of Naples and accompanied him into exile when the French invaded Naples in 1495. By February, 1496, he was in Monopoli, a town on the Adriatic coast controlled by the Venetian navy, where he remained, writing commentaries and religious treatises for more than seven productive years.

In 1497 and 1498, Abravanel wrote three messianic tracts predicting the imminent coming of the Messiah. He hoped to strengthen the faith of his coreligionists as they reeled under the shock of expulsion from Spain and pressures to convert to Christianity. Abravanel listed twenty-two criteria that the Messiah must fulfill, arguing that Jesus failed to meet that standard. Nevertheless, the present crisis indicated to Abravanel that the age of the Messiah was approaching.

Abravanel found clues to the date of redemption in the symbolic language of the book of Daniel. His interpretation stated that deliverance from exile would begin in 1503, exactly 1,435 years after the destruction of the Second Temple. He found confirmation of his expectation in a rabbinic legend that the soul of Adam was infused in the fourth hour of the sixth day. Following the allegorical interpretation that each day predicted one thousand years, Abravanel calculated that the fourth "hour" would last from 1490 to 1573. If the Messiah did not arrive in 1503,

he would surely make his appearance by 1573. Abravanel foresaw a series of cataclysmic conflicts between Christianity and Islam that would prepare the way for the triumphant return of Israel to Jerusalem.

In 1503, Abravanel moved to Venice to live with his son Joseph, a physician. The Venetian government consulted Abravanel for advice regarding trade negotiations with Portugal. While in Venice, Abravanel completed his commentaries on the prophets and the Pentateuch. In 1505, three of his books, which had previously circulated as manuscripts, appeared in print in Constantinople.

When Abravanel died in 1508, his body was taken to Padua for interment because Venice forbade the burial of Jews within its precincts.

SIGNIFICANCE

The mystical, antirationalist center of Abravanel's writings marked him as being of the Middle Ages rather than of the Renaissance. Yet no Jewish writer was read more widely by both Christians and Jews during the sixteenth and seventeenth centuries. Theologians and Bible critics from various Christian denominations studied his works, translated them into Latin, and discussed his arguments.

Critics found Abravanel's biblical commentary intriguing, in part because, more than any other Jewish religious thinker, he cited and discussed Christian interpretations of the Bible. Christian theologians strove to refute Abravanel's denial that Jesus was the Messiah, an assertion striking at the heart of Christianity.

Abravanel thought the world too rotten to be saved and that it must be destroyed. He assured his coreligionists that soon this destruction would happen.

He was the forerunner of the many messianic movements that agitated Jews during the sixteenth and seventeenth centuries, as one false Messiah after another aroused hope that redemption was finally at hand. During the optimistic eighteenth and nineteenth centuries, Abravanel was ignored and largely forgotten. The disasters of the twentieth century revived interest in his response to an earlier traumatic era and led to significant scholarly attention.

—*Milton Berman*

FURTHER READING

Borodowski, Alfredo Fabio. *Isaac Abravanel on Miracles, Creation, Prophecy, and Evil: The Tension Between Medieval Jewish Philosophy and Biblical Commentary.* New York: Peter Lang, 2003. Asserts that Abravanel read the Bible seeking answers to questions about the meaning of existence and the possibility and purpose of miracles.

Feldman, Seymour. *Philosophy in a Time of Crisis: Don Isaac Abravanel, Defender of the Faith.* New York: RoutledgeCurzon, 2003. A systematic analysis of Abravanel's defense of the main philosophical and theological beliefs of Judaism, examined partly as a response to the expulsion of Jews from Spain.

Lawee, Eric. *Isaac Abarbanel's Stance Toward Tradition: Defense, Dissent, and Dialogue.* Albany: State University of New York Press, 2001. Focuses on Abravanel's biblical commentaries and Messianic works.

Netanyahu, Benzion. *Don Isaac Abravanel: Statesman and Philosopher.* 3d ed. Philadelphia: Jewish Publication Society of America, 1972. This standard scholarly biography recounts Abravanel's life and examines his ideas and influence.

SEE ALSO: Joseph ben Ephraim Karo; Isaac ben Solomon Luria.

RELATED ARTICLE in *Great Events from History: The Renaissance & Early Modern Era, 1454-1600:* 1492: Jews Are Expelled from Spain.

BARBE ACARIE
French church reformer

Barbe Acarie established the Carmelite order of nuns in France. She was the central figure and host of the Acarie Circle, a group of clergy and devout laypersons concerned with the spiritual renewal and reform of Roman Catholicism and its religious orders.

BORN: February 1, 1566; Paris, France
DIED: April 18, 1618; Pontoise, France
ALSO KNOWN AS: Barbe-Jeanne Avrillot (given name); Marie de l'Incarnation; Mary of the Incarnation; Barbara Avrillot; Barbe Aurillot; Barbara Aurillot
AREAS OF ACHIEVEMENT: Religion and theology, church reform

EARLY LIFE

Barbe Acarie (bahrb ahk-ahr-ee) was born Barbe-Jeanne Avrillot Acarie to Nicholas Avrillot, lord of Champlâtreux, and Marie Luillers, who was from a family of French nobles. She was educated just outside Paris at Longchamp, an abbey founded in 1260 by Blessed Isabelle, the sister of King Louis IX. Her instructors were Roman Catholic nuns belonging to the Poor Clares, the religious order of Franciscan nuns. Attracted to their spiritual life and commitment to poverty, simplicity, and prayer, she wanted to join the order, to which one of her aunts already belonged.

Nevertheless, in obedience to her parents, she married her second cousin, Pierre Acarie, the vicomte of Villemor, on August 24, 1582, and moved into her mother-in-law's spacious mansion, the Hôtel Acarie. Within ten years, by the age of twenty-seven, she was the mother of three sons and three daughters.

As her early interest in spirituality, contemplative prayer, and mysticism continued to grow, her reputation for holiness and a devout spiritual life began to draw people to her home. Her younger cousin, Pierre de Bérulle (diplomat, spiritual reformer, and future cardinal), who was equally interested in a renewal of Catholic spirituality, began to introduce other reformers to what became known as the Acarie Circle.

LIFE'S WORK

In the sixteenth century, a wave of spiritual renewal in the Catholic Church was occurring throughout Europe in the wake of the Protestant Reformation. The shape of this renewal—called the Counter-Reformation—included the founding of new religious orders as well as the reformation of preexisting ones, a growing interest in spirituality on the part of both clergy and laypersons, and a desire for a return to traditional spiritual disciplines, asceticism, mysticism, and prayer. In France, the center of that renewal was the home of Barbe Acarie.

Acarie's home became the nexus of revival for all the leading figures of renewal for that country. Her guests included theologians such as André Duval (regius professor of theology at the Sorbonne) and her counselor and future biographer; spiritual directors such as the Jesuit Pierre Coton, the king's spiritual director; wealthy laypersons interested in charitable works, including her cousin, Madame de Sainte-Beuve; and clerics of all kinds, such as Vincent de Paul. Her circle also included international guests who shared an interest in church renewal and a radical commitment to Christian life.

Benet of Canfield, from Essex, England, the Capuchin writer of a manual for mystics, became Acarie's spiritual director. Francis de Sales, the future bishop of Geneva, was almost a daily visitor to her home during the months he visited Paris in 1601 and 1602 and became her confessor for a period of time. All these spiritual leaders shared a common interest in a revival of monastic and contemplative life and a social concern for the poor.

In such an atmosphere, Acarie's group had a keen interest in the reform of the Carmelite order in Spain, spearheaded by Teresa of Ávila and Saint John of the Cross. Teresa's reforms combined practicality and common sense with contemplative prayer and mysticism. Jean de Brétigny's French translations of Teresa's manual for nuns and her biography appeared in 1601. That fall, Acarie reportedly received a vision of Teresa (who had died almost twenty years earlier, in 1582) in which Teresa asked her to establish the Reformed Carmelites in France.

Acarie took the lead in the discussions about setting up Carmelite convents in France. Such an undertaking required a team effort by various members of the circle. Catherine, the duchess of Longueville, obtained King Henry IV's approval in July, 1603; Francis de Sales was the liaison to Rome for this request and received Pope Clement VIII's approval in November, 1603. By October, 1604, de Bérulle had returned from Spain with six Carmelite nuns from Teresa's order, headed by Anne of Jesus, and the first convent, called the monastery of the Incarnation, was established in the suburb of Saint-Jacques. Acarie oversaw the construction of that first house, and by 1618 she had helped establish several other houses in France.

Although the establishment of the Reformed Carmelites was her primary achievement, Acarie was an active participant in other significant renewal activities. She was influential in helping to establish a branch of the new Italian order of nuns, the Ursulines, who were responsible for the education of young women in Paris. She was involved in the reform of the Benedictine abbeys in Paris and was also instrumental in helping de Bérulle in the founding of his Congregation of the Oratory in 1611, a community of priests seeking deeper spiritual life through common prayer and discipline.

Widowed in 1613, she entered the Carmelite convent, joining her three daughters who were already Carmelites. At the convent in Amiens, she became a lay sister, doing menial household chores, and took the name Marie de l'Incarnation. In 1616, she moved to the convent at Pontoise, the second convent she had helped to set up, where she spent the last two years of her life.

Her holiness and devotion to God were recognized not only by the French nation but also by all of Europe. In 1622, her second son, the vicar of Rouen, asked his archbishop to begin the process of inquiry for her canonization, and, on June 5, 1791, she was beatified by Pope Pius VI, receiving the title Blessed Marie de l'Incarnation.

SIGNIFICANCE

Acarie's founding of the Reformed Carmelites in France continued to have an effect far beyond her lifetime: Within fifty years of the original establishment of a convent in Paris, more than sixty other Carmelite convents had been set up in all the major cities and towns of France.

Famous French Carmelite women include Louise of France (Teresa of Saint Augustine), the daughter of King Louis XV; the Martyrs of Compiègne, sixteen Carmelite nuns guillotined in 1794 during the French Revolution; and one of the most famous modern French saints, Theresa of Lisieux.

Acarie was not single-handedly responsible for any of the renewal movements in France, but her facilitation of that renewal in her spiritual salon and her personal influence on the spiritual leaders whose work affected the whole of France and beyond cannot be overestimated. She remains a role model of a dedicated Christian, and, in particular, a role model of a married woman who combined family and business duties with a deep inner spiritual life of contemplation.

—*Marsha Daigle-Williamson*

FURTHER READING

Discalced Carmelites of Boston and Santa Clara. *Carmel: Its History, Spirit, and Saints.* New York: P. J. Kenedy & Sons, 1927. Standard history of the Carmelites, including reform movements. Acarie and the history of the French Carmelites are discussed in chapters 8 and 28.

Dubois, Elfrieda. "The Hôtel Acarie: A Meeting Place for European Currents of Spirituality in Early Seventeenth-Century France." *Durham University Journal* 71 (1970): 187-196. Discusses the effect of Acarie's mentors and their writings on her development. Detailed account of her last years as a Carmelite.

Hsia, R. Po-Chia. *The Catholic World of Renewal, 1564-1770.* New York: Cambridge University Press, 1998. Overview of the Counter-Reformation in Europe, with discussion of French reforms.

Jones, Kathleen. *Women Saints: Lives of Faith and Courage.* Maryknoll, N.Y.: Orbis Books, 1999. Section 4 includes a description of Acarie's life and spirituality.

Sheppard, Lancelot C. *Barbe Acarie: Wife and Mystic.* London: Burns & Oates, 1953. A full-length biography of Acarie. Includes a detailed index.

_____. "Madame Acarie's Spiritual Teaching." *Downside Review* 70, no. 219 (1951): 53-61. A description of the spiritual manuals that shaped Acarie's mysticism.

Stopp, Elisabeth. *A Man to Heal Differences: Essays and Talks on St. Francis de Sales.* Philadephia: Saint Joseph's University Press, 1997. Discusses in the book's introduction and in chapters 5, 6, and 8 Acarie's influence on this contemporary spiritual reformer.

Welsh, John. *The Carmelite Way: An Ancient Path for Today's Pilgrims.* New York: Paulist Press, 1996. Expla-

nation of Carmelite traditions with "Rule of Carmel" in the appendix. Acarie's French reform discussed in chapter 1.

SEE ALSO: Saint Angela Merici; Vittoria Colonna; Henry IV; Saint John of the Cross; Ana de Mendoza y de la Cerda; Saint Philip Neri; Saint Teresa of Ávila.

RELATED ARTICLES in *Great Events from History: The Renaissance & Early Modern Era, 1454-1600:* August 15, 1534: Founding of the Jesuit Order; 1545-1563: Council of Trent.

JOSÉ DE ACOSTA
Spanish Jesuit missionary and writer

José de Acosta is best known for his magisterial work The Natural and Moral History of the Indies, *a pioneering study of the indigenous cultures of the Americas and American geography, climate, flora, and fauna. He also favored the humane treatment of American Indians.*

BORN: 1540; Medina del Campo, Spain
DIED: February 15, 1600; Salamanca, Spain
AREAS OF ACHIEVEMENT: Historiography, religion and theology, scholarship, literature, science and technology, education

EARLY LIFE

José de Acosta (hoh-SAY day ah-KOH-stah) was born the same year that the Jesuit order (the Society of Jesus), founded by fellow Spaniard Ignatius Loyola, won official approval in Rome. The Jesuits would come to play a pivotal role in the colonization and Christianization of Spanish America, and Acosta's life work would make an important contribution to that effort.

José was one of nine children born to the well-to-do Acosta family in Medina del Campo, a key trading town located between Valladolid and Madrid on the central plateau of Spain. Some scholars have speculated that the Acostas were of Portuguese-Jewish ancestry. The paterfamilias, Don Antonio de Acosta, was a successful merchant who patronized the Jesuit order in Medina del Campo. Five of his six sons, including José, would join the Society of Jesus.

Few details are known about José's earliest education, except that he studied some Latin grammar prior to beginning his novitiate in 1552. That year, at the age of twelve, he ran away from home to join the Jesuits in

Salamanca; despite their strong support for the society, José's parents were opposed to his joining the order at such a young age.

Acosta devoted the next fifteen years of his life to his studies. He received an excellent Jesuit education, which included rigorous training not only in theology but also in classical Greek and Roman literature, philosophy, and rhetoric. A gifted writer with a special flair for Latin, Acosta won a reputation for his religious dramas and sermons. Acosta spent eight years at the renowned university of Alcalá de Henares (1559-1567), where he studied philosophy and theology and trained for the ministry.

After completing his studies, Acosta taught and preached in provincial Spain; but what the young Jesuit truly desired was, in his own words, "to go to the Indies, but also to work among the Africans, and to work out of love of the Lord unto death."

LIFE'S WORK

In 1569, Acosta petitioned Francis Borja, the general of the Society of Jesus in Spain, for a transfer to the Americas. It was not until 1571 that Acosta finally heard word that he was to set sail for Peru.

Acosta and two fellow Jesuits arrived in Lima on April 27, 1572, the third party of Jesuits to arrive in Peru (the first five Jesuits had arrived in 1568, the second group in the following year). The Kingdom of Peru (which included almost all of South America, except for Brazil) was a jewel in the Spanish crown, with its rich silver mines at Potosí (now in Bolivia). Acosta would make it his home for almost fifteen years.

Acosta had been in Lima for just more than a year, teaching theology at the Jesuit College of San Pablo, when he was sent to visit the region to reform extant missions and to assess the potential for founding new ones. During his sixteen months of traveling in what is now southern Peru and Bolivia, Acosta encountered many new lands and indigenous cultures and began to gather the ethnographic and scientific data that would ultimately form his *Historia natural y moral de las Indias* (1590; *The Natural and Moral History of the Indies*, 1604). He most likely acquired some skills (though not fluency) in South American Indian languages during these travels.

In 1574, Acosta returned to Lima, where he was appointed professor of theology at the University of San Marcos. Shortly thereafter, he became the provincial of Peru, a three-year appointment to govern a Jesuit province, which was a post he held from 1576 to 1581. During his provincialate, the number of Jesuits in Peru increased from 77 to 113. Acosta opened several Jesuit colleges and residences and established a new *reducción*, or reduction, a South American Indian village at Juli (on Lake Titicaca), which would become a model ministry for the founding of later communities. Acosta stressed the importance of preaching to the indigenous in their own tongue, and his tenure saw an increased effort to train priests in local languages.

Acosta wrote the first of his three important works on the Americas, the *De procuranda Indorum salute* (wr. 1576, pb. 1588; English translation, 1996). The first book written by a Jesuit in the region, *De procuranda Indorum salute* made the case for evangelizing the indigenous of the New World and provided practical guidance for accomplishing that daunting task. Acosta wrote this work in Latin for an audience of fellow clergy. The book reflects Acosta's realistic optimism: He was confident in the ability of the Church to convert the South American Indians, but experience had taught him that this would come neither quickly nor easily.

Following the completion of his term as provincial, Acosta spent another six years in Peru, serving as theological consultant to the reformist Third Provincial Council of Lima, convoked by Archbishop Toribio de Mogrovejo. On behalf of the council, Acosta authored a trilingual book of catechisms and sermons for the indigenous of Peru in Spanish and the local languages Aymara and Quechua. Acosta's *Doctrina Christiana, y catecismo para instrucción de los Indios* (pb. c. 1584; Christian doctrine and catechism for the instruction of the Indians) was the first full-length book printed in Peru. In 1587, Acosta began his return journey to Spain, stopping first in Mexico. He spent almost a year there, where he visited

his brother at the Jesuit college of Oaxaca and gathered materials on Aztec culture for his forthcoming *The Natural and Moral History of the Indies*.

Finally back in Spain, Acosta completed this massive work. It comprises seven books. The first four concern natural history, from general considerations about the shape and size of the earth and the place of the New World, to detailed descriptions of the unique minerals, plants, and animals found in the Americas. Books five through seven comprise Acosta's moral history, that is, the history of human beings, in which Acosta relates the history, culture, and religion of the Incas and Aztecs. Part of *The Natural and Moral History of the Indies* was published in Latin in 1589 with the *De procuranda Indorum salute* under the title *De natura novi orbis libri duo et promulgatione evangelii*. After the complete Spanish-language edition was published at Seville in 1590, Acosta's *Historia natural y moral de las Indias* was quickly translated and printed in many other European languages.

Meanwhile, Acosta found himself much in demand at the court of King Philip II as an expert on the American possessions that the king would never see for himself. Acosta spent two years from 1592 to 1594 in Rome as Philip II's representative to the Fifth General Congregation, an international gathering of the Society of Jesus, where elected representatives were to debate issues of fundamental importance to the order.

Acosta returned to Spain in the spring of 1594, where he served as rector at Valladolid and then at the Jesuit college of Salamanca. Acosta remained in Salamanca, preaching, writing, and ministering to the poor, until his death in 1600.

SIGNIFICANCE

Acosta has been called the Pliny of the New World for *The Natural and Moral History of the Indies*, which provided a compendium of knowledge on the geography, climate, flora, fauna, history, language, and religion of the Aztecs and Incas. The Jesuit scholar attempted to reconcile his classical learning with the staggering newness of what he had encountered firsthand in the New World.

Acosta was also a strong proponent of the humane treatment of the American Indian, denouncing Spanish brutality. Determined to evangelize the Indians of the New World through peaceful means, Acosta argued against the use of force and coercion and stressed the need for flexibility and adaptability, in recognition of the diversity of native cultures.

—Amanda Wunder

FURTHER READING

Acosta, José de. *Natural and Moral History of the Indies.* Translated by Frances López-Morillas and edited by Jane E. Mangan. Durham, N.C.: Duke University Press, 2002. Modern English translation of Acosta's seminal work with explanatory notes. Brief introduction places Acosta's history in its intellectual context.

Burgaleta, Claudio M. *José de Acosta, S.J. (1540-1600): His Life and Thought.* Chicago: Loyola Press, 1999. Part 1 gives a chronological biography of Acosta. Part 2 analyzes Acosta's theology, writing style, and intellectual method. Includes appendices with brief excerpts of Acosta's writing.

Ford, Thayne R. "Stranger in a Foreign Land: José de Acosta's Scientific Realizations in Sixteenth-Century Peru." *Sixteenth Century Journal* 29, no. 1 (Spring, 1998): 19-33. Explores the importance of Acosta's scientific contributions.

O'Malley, John W., et al., eds. *The Jesuits: Cultures, Sciences, and the Arts, 1540-1773.* Toronto, Canada: University of Toronto Press, 1999. Thirty-two essays on various aspects of Jesuit contributions to the arts and sciences, with an introductory essay on the historiography of the Society of Jesus.

SEE ALSO: Atahualpa; Pierre Belon; Hernán Cortés; Cuauhtémoc; Saint Ignatius of Loyola; Doña Marina; Philip II; Francisco Pizarro; Saint Francis Xavier.

RELATED ARTICLES in *Great Events from History: The Renaissance & Early Modern Era, 1454-1600:* 1500-1530's: Portugal Begins to Colonize Brazil; April, 1519-August, 1521: Cortés Conquers Aztecs in Mexico; 1532-1537: Pizarro Conquers the Incas in Peru; 1537: Pope Paul III Declares Rights of New World Peoples; 1552: Las Casas Publishes *The Tears of the Indians.*

ADRIAN VI
Dutch pope (1522-1523)

The last non-Italian pope before John Paul II, Adrian was the most important theologian of Leuven University and governor of Spain for Charles V. He was elected pope when Lutheranism began to have considerable success, and he worked for reforms in response to the Lutheran challenge.

BORN: March 2, 1459; Utrecht, Bishopric of Utrecht (now in the Netherlands)

DIED: September 14, 1523; Rome, Papal States (now in Italy)

ALSO KNOWN AS: Adrian Florensz Boeyens (given name); Adrian Dedel of Utrecht; Adrianus Florisz Boeyens; Adriaan Florisz Boeyens; Hadrian VI

AREAS OF ACHIEVEMENT: Government and politics, religion and theology

EARLY LIFE

Adrian (AY-dree-an) was born the son of a middle class couple, Floris Boeyens, master carpenter, and Geertruyt. Earlier attempts to fabricate a noble descent for him have failed. The pope's later coat of arms has been compared with that of the family Dedel (understood as D'Edel, "the noble"), but without any reason or justification: Adrian's family name was not "Dedel." After his first education in Utrecht itself, he may have gone to one of the more famous Latin schools at Zwolle or Deventer (to the east of

Utrecht), but this speculation is not proven.

If he did attend one of these schools, he went to the best schools in the area. They thoroughly imbibed in the religious climate of the *Devotio moderna,* a teaching that strove after true piety and brotherhood, and that had considerable success in the Low Countries, especially in the valley of the Ijssel River. Whether Adrian visited one of these schools or not, he appeared later, as a pope, to be in line with this *Devotio moderna.*

On June 1, 1476, he matriculated at Leuven University (now in Belgium), the only university of the Low Countries at the time. In 1478, he passed the examinations for *magister artium* as primus, first of his year, after which he continued to study theology. In 1490, he was ordained a priest and, in 1491, promoted to a doctor in theology. Meanwhile, he had started teaching philosophy in one of the Leuven colleges.

LIFE'S WORK

After his promotion, Adrian also started teaching theology as a university professor. In fact, he was to become one of the main theologians at Leuven University. Apart from some sermons, two of his academic works were published in Leuven and republished after his election as pope (*Quaestiones quotlibeticae XII,* Leuven, 1515, 1518; Paris, 1522, 1523, 1527, 1531; and *Quaestiones in*

Adrian VI. (Hulton|Archive by Getty Images)

quartum sententiarum praesertim circa sacramenta, Paris, 1516, 1530; Rome, 1522; Venice, 1522), in which he proved himself to be an adherent of Scholastic methods. Another, perhaps more interesting work by him is a letter to the Leuven divines in reaction to their questions regarding the theological teachings of Martin Luther (*Epistola Reverendissimi Domini Cardinalis Dertusensis ad facultatem theologiae Lovaniensem,* 1520).

Although he persuaded the Leuven city magistrates to offer a chair to the Humanistic philosopher Erasmus at his first visit to Leuven in 1502 (which Erasmus, however, declined), Adrian did not seem to be in close contact with Humanism. Adrian was rector of Leuven University from February 28 to August 31, 1493, and from August 31, 1500, to February 28, 1501. More important was his appointment as dean of St. Peter's church (since 1497), which made him chancellor of the university as well (and responsible for degrees). In 1507, Adrian was appointed as one of two teachers of the young duke Charles of Burgundy, the future Charles V, Holy Roman Emperor.

In 1515, when Charles's grandfather, Ferdinand of Aragon, lay on his deathbed, Adrian was sent to Spain to secure the young prince's inheritance. He fulfilled this mission successfully, and after Ferdinand's death in January, 1516, he was appointed regent of Spain for the time

of Charles's absence. Although Adrian personally made a favorable impression on the Spaniards by his ascetic and honest way of life, the attitude of the other representatives of the new king finally led to the Comunero Revolt, which was subdued in 1522. In the meantime, Adrian was appointed to the See of Tortosa (on the Spanish east coast) on August 18, 1516, and he was made inquisitor general for Aragon, Valencia, and Navarra on November 14, 1516, and for Castilia and Leon on March 4, 1518. This series of high ecclesiastical nominations came to its peak when he was nominated cardinal on July 1, 1517, with SS. Giovanni e Paolo as his primary church.

After the death of Pope Leo X in December, 1521, the conclave could not come to a decision on his successor. In the end, it decided to elect an unknown cardinal without any political ties to the existing Roman factions. In this way, Adrian was elected pope on January 9, 1522. He was still in Spain at the time, and significant time passed before he could be informed. At last, he entered Rome at the end of August, 1522, and was crowned pope on August 31.

The situation in which Adrian found himself was highly complicated. On a worldly level, tensions in Italy ran high between Charles V and the king of France, Francis I, and their respective allies. Charles had supposed that his former tutor would defend his interests without a second thought, but Adrian tried to retain a neutral position in order to establish a coalition of all major Christian princes against the threat of the Ottoman Turks, who were to take Rhodes in December, 1522. When this policy failed, Adrian eventually joined a large coalition of Venice, Charles V, and Henry VIII of England against France.

In religious matters, he was the first pope to understand the importance of Lutheran reforms. He expressed his intention to reform the Roman Curia and thus heal the Church from the top, but his acknowledgment of mistakes at the Diet of Nuremberg in 1523 bewildered Catholics. Lutherans, conversely, seized the opportunity to interpret this acknowledgment as a sign of papal weakness. Although Adrian tried to make a serious start on reform at the top, his early death prevented him from achieving much.

His position in Rome was made more difficult because he had no understanding of contemporary Renaissance art or the love of antiquity that characterized contemporary Italian and Roman culture. On the contrary, his ascetic way of life and his piety made him an easy target for Roman popular caricatures. Major orders for works of art in the Vatican were brought to a standstill.

However, the depleted treasury after the lavish pontificate of Leo X was the main cause for this lack of commissions. Moreover, Adrian appointed mostly fellow countrymen at high places because they were the only people he found trustworthy. Among these appointments were cardinal Willem van Enckenvoirt (who would order Adrian's tomb) and Theodoricus Hezius.

On September 14, 1523, Adrian died after a short illness. His tomb can be found in the Flemish-German church of S. Maria dell'Anima in central Rome.

SIGNIFICANCE

Adrian is a primary example of the clash between the worlds of northern European late medieval culture and the Italian Renaissance at the beginning of the Lutheran reform. He was the first pope to realize the significance of what was happening, but he failed to take any measures to stop it; this failing was partly due to a lack of time. Polarization was running high in Europe, and his pontificate was perhaps the last to avoid a complete breaking up of European Christendom. The fact that this chance was tragically lost eventually led to the wars of religion that devastated large parts of Europe in the late sixteenth and early seventeenth centuries.

—*Michiel Verweij*

FURTHER READING

Coppens, J., and M. E. Houtzager. *Paus Adrianus VI, Herdenkingstentoonstelling: Gedenkboek, Catalogus*. Utrecht, the Netherlands: Central Museum, 1959. Exhibition catalog (with illustrations and some contributions in French) of the fourth centennial of Adrian's birth, held in Utrecht and Leuven.

McNally, R. E. "Pope Adrian VI (1522-1523) and Church Reform." *Archivum Historiae Pontificiae* 7 (1969): 253-285. Discusses the attempts and difficulties of Adrian with regard to the reform of the Catholic Church.

Zimmermann, T. C. Price. *Paolo Giovio: The Historian and the Crisis of Sixteenth Century Italy*. Princeton, N.J.: Princeton University Press, 1995. Explores the writing of history, particularly the writing of the sixteenth century Italian historian Paolo Giovio, with a chapter on Adrian VI.

SEE ALSO: Charles V; Desiderius Erasmus; Leo X; Martin Luther.

RELATED ARTICLES in *Great Events from History: The Renaissance & Early Modern Era, 1454-1600:* January 23, 1516: Charles I Ascends the Throne of Spain; 1520-1522: Comunero Revolt.

AFONSO I

King of Kongo (r. 1506-1543)

Afonso I expanded the economic and political power of the Kingdom of Kongo by forming strategic trade alliances with the Portuguese and by accepting and adopting Christianity, thereby encouraging Portuguese colonization.

BORN: c. late 1450's or early 1460's; probably Mbanza Kongo, Kingdom of Kongo (now M'banza Congo, Angola)

DIED: 1543; São Salvador do Congo, Kingdom of Kongo (now M'banza Congo)

ALSO KNOWN AS: Affonso; Nzinga Mbemba (given name)

AREAS OF ACHIEVEMENT: Government and politics, religion and theology, diplomacy

EARLY LIFE

Afonso (a-FOHN-sew) I was the son of King Nzinga Nkuwa and his principal wife. He was most likely born at the royal compound in Mbanza Kongo, the Kongo capital. His father was the first Christian monarch of the king-dom, which had developed over the previous century from a federation of chiefdoms.

At its peak in the early sixteenth century, the kingdom straddled the delta region of the Congo (or Zaïre) River, extending along the Atlantic coast from what is now called Cabinda in the north to Luanda (now in Angola) in the south. The kingdom ranged inland along a corridor of land between the Congo River and the northern Angola plateau, occupying an area about the size of Austria. It had a population of several million people.

In the fifteenth century, the Portuguese pioneered voyages of discovery down the Atlantic coast. By 1483, they reached the mouth of the Congo River. Their wealth and power impressed King Nzinga Nkuwa, who adopted their religion, Roman Catholicism, for himself and his entourage. He assumed the name and title of John I, king of Kongo, addressed the Portuguese king, John IV, as "brother," and changed the name of the Kongo capital to São Salvador do Congo. During this period, he appointed Nzinga Mbemba, who now bore the Christian name of

Afonso, as governor of the copper-rich, northeastern province of Nsundi.

Nsundi was of great interest to the Portuguese because they believed its mineral wealth might also include gold and that it could be a stepping-stone to a lost Christian kingdom lying farther east. Under pressure from Kongo traditionalists, Afonso's father relaxed his support of Catholicism, and he may even have recanted his support. Afonso continued to support the new religious faith, however, which stabilized his position in Nsundi, where the Portuguese supported him strategically.

LIFE'S WORK

The death of Afonso's father created a crisis in the royal succession. Followers of Kongo tradition supported Prince Mpanzu a Kitima, Afonso's half brother, to become king. Afonso, however, backed by the Portuguese and Catholic clergy, argued that he was the legitimate heir. Moving south to the capital with a small band that included well-armed Portuguese, he confronted his opponents, whom he defeated and slaughtered in a battle outside São Salvador do Congo in 1506. Because his forces had been smaller than those of his enemies, he believed his victory was a divine miracle. The strength of the kingdom he inherited derived from sources considerably older and less spiritual.

Legend relates that a century earlier, Kongo tribesmen had migrated across the Congo River to settle an area south of where they located their capital, Mbanza Kongo. Situated on a plateau, the area would dominate two important trade routes. It commanded trade between the coast and the interior, a trade in salt and seashells valued as currency for goods such as ivory, animal hides, and cloth made of palm tree fiber. The city also intersected another major trade route, which moved high-quality copper mined north of the Congo with lesser quality copper, iron, and metalworking of the south.

Kongo developed into a distinct realm through alliances among the participating regions along these trade routes. A council (the *mwissikongo*), made up of representatives of participating districts, governed the region and chose the *manikongo*, or lord of the Kongo.

Kongo society was divided into a small elite of nobility, many of whom lived in the capital, and a majority of peasants, who lived in rural villages. The lowest class consisted of slaves, who were mostly individuals captured in war. Warfare was not, however, a dominant feature of Kongo society. To defend the realm, the king could depend only on a levy of warriors from district chiefs.

On becoming king in 1506, Afonso I strengthened his political position by allying himself with the economic and religious authority of the Portuguese. The Kongo kingship had grown based on its control of trade routes. The kingship levied taxes on trade goods and received tributes from the territories the trade routes traversed. Also, the king maintained lordship over the *mwissikongo* by distributing luxury goods and trade goods among them, appointing them to district and court offices, and ensuring territorial security over the region's trading network.

Afonso secured a monopoly of trade with the Portuguese. They were especially interested in obtaining high-quality copper, for which they traded luxury European products. This monopoly was further strengthened as he sponsored the foundation and spread of Catholicism in the kingdom. A son that he sent to study in Portugal was consecrated a bishop; he built a cathedral in São Salvador do Congo, dedicated to Our Lady of Victory, rising over the sacred grove of the king's ancestors; and Catholic churches were built in district capitals and villages.

Through Portuguese trade and Catholicism, Afonso I internationalized the power of the Kongo kingship. A threat to this power rose in the 1520's as the Portuguese changed their trading interests from copper to slaves. Because Afonso had only a limited number of captives to sell, the Portuguese sought sources beyond his control, which threatened his monopoly on commerce. Afonso became a vehement opponent of slavery, denouncing to the Papacy the trade's moral repugnance.

By the following decade, however, increasing warfare in the upper Congo River interior produced a growing number of captives, who were sold as slaves at the Kongo frontier, below the Malebo Pool, an expansion of the Congo River, where Afonso had firm control. They were then moved through São Salvador do Congo to the coast for shipment abroad.

Afonso reversed his opposition to slavery, as the trade came to comprise an ever larger portion of his and the nobility's wealth. The kingdom expanded as territories and chiefs paid him homage in order to participate in Kongo wealth and avoid capture and enslavement. Afonso I died in 1543, and his reign is still commemorated for its prosperity and power.

SIGNIFICANCE

The thirty-seven-year reign of Afonso I established the most prosperous and powerful Christian kingdom of its time in sub-Saharan Africa. Based on extensive trade, especially of slaves, through the region of the lower Congo

River, the kingdom's prosperity solidified Afonso's political position.

Moreover, by basing his rule on international trade and a "foreign" religion, he changed the nature of Kongo kingship and society. Succession to the monarchy was now determined by descent from Afonso rather than by selection by the *mwassikongo*.

Furthermore, the hierarchical separation of nobility, peasant, and slave became more marked as new wealth was concentrated in the hands of the ruling class supporting the monarchy. Class and religious tensions would grow in Kongo after Afonso's reign. The wealth of the kingdom attracted invaders who occupied and debilitated it. The reign of Afonso I offered a few decades of glory for an isolated African kingdom that inaugurated centuries of slave-trading from southern Africa, across the Atlantic, and to the Americas.

—*Edward A. Riedinger*

FURTHER READING

Blier, Susanne Preston. *The Royal Arts of Africa: The Majesty of Form*. New York: Harry N. Abrams, 1998. Chapter 5 analyzes the iconography and regalia of Kongo monarchy, presenting a rich array of illustrations that frame Kongo within the context of other African kingdoms.

Hilton, Anne. "Family and Kinship Among the Kongo South of the Zaire River from the Sixteenth to the Nineteenth Centuries." *Journal of African History* 24, no. 2 (1983): 189-206. Discusses the role of family and kinship among the peoples of the Kingdom of Kongo.

_____. *The Kingdom of Kongo*. Oxford, England: Clarendon Press, 1985. Analytical history, supported by maps and tables, of Kongo over a peak period from the fifteenth to seventeenth centuries, with a summary of events to the twentieth century.

Thornton, John. "The Development of an African Catholic Church in the Kingdom of Kongo, 1491-1750." *Journal of African History* 25, no. 2 (1984): 147-167. Reexamines the question of the authenticity of Christianity in Kongo and changing European views of its African Catholicism's orthodoxy.

_____. "The Origins and Early History of the Kingdom of Kongo, c. 1350-1550." *International Journal of African Historical Studies* 34, no. 1 (2001): 89-120. Detailed examination of historical texts to determine a more precise chronology of Kongo origins.

Vansina, J., and T. Obenga. "The Kongo Kingdom and Its Neighbors." In *Africa from the Sixteenth to Eighteenth Century*. Vol. 5 in *UNESCO General History of Africa*, edited by B. A. Ogot. Berkeley: University of California Press, 1992. Details the socioeconomic and geopolitical factors determining Afonso's reign.

SEE ALSO: Bartolomeu Dias; John II.

RELATED ARTICLE in *Great Events from History: The Renaissance & Early Modern Era, 1454-1600:* 1491-1545: Christianity Is Established in the Kingdom of Kongo.

GEORGIUS AGRICOLA
German scientist and physician

Agricola was a forerunner of the new period of scientific investigation involving the study and description of natural phenomena, the preparation of metals from ores, and the development of mechanical procedures. He is regarded as the father of modern mineralogy.

BORN: March 24, 1494; Glauchau, Saxony (now in Germany)

DIED: November 21, 1555; Chemnitz, Saxony

ALSO KNOWN AS: Georg Bauer

AREAS OF ACHIEVEMENT: Science and technology, medicine

EARLY LIFE

Born the son of a draper and named Georg Bauer, he later Latinized his name, in the fashion of the time, to

Georgius Agricola (ah-GRIH-koh-lah). Little is known about his life before 1514, at which point he entered the University of Leipzig. In 1518, he was graduated, then went to Italy to continue his studies at the Universities of Bologna and Padua. His subsequent career began as a philologist, an expert in classical languages and the works of the classical writers. He then turned to medicine, took his degree at the University of Ferrare, and adopted medicine as a profession.

While in Venice, he was employed for two years in the printing and publishing house of Aldus Manutius. At the Aldine Press, Agricola collaborated with John Clement, secretary to Thomas More. During this period, he also met and became friends with Desiderius Erasmus, who encouraged him to write and later published a number of his books. Coming home, Agricola began his medical practice in 1527 in Joachimsthal, in Bohemia, as city physician until 1533. In 1534, he moved to Chemnitz, another mining town, where he stayed for the rest of his life. In 1545, he was appointed Burgermeister.

LIFE'S WORK

Like that of his contemporary Paracelsus, Agricola's interest in mineralogy grew out of its possible connections with medicine and the diseases of the miners he treated. For more than two centuries, this combination of physician-mineralogist was to be prominent in the development of chemistry and geology. Agricola spent much time with the miners, in the mines and smelters, thus gaining an intimate knowledge of mining, mineralogy, and allied sciences. Most of his writings dealt with the geological sciences, although he wrote on many aspects of human endeavor. The beauty of his works lies in his use of illustrations, the woodcuts clear enough to let a modern builder re-create models of the ancient machines. His works were extremely difficult to decipher, particularly as they are written in Latin, a language ill equipped with appropriate terms for the mining trades. Because his ideas were based on German sources, he had to invent a new Latin vocabulary. As a result, some parts

Georgius Agricola. (Library of Congress)

of the texts were difficult to understand even by contemporary readers. Only centuries after his death did Agricola get the credit he so richly deserved.

At Chemnitz, Agricola first became court historian, then city physician. Beginning in 1546, he published six works on mining and geology, a small work on the plague, and works on medical, religious, political, and historical subjects. It was a measure of his liberalism that, as a staunch Catholic, he served two Protestant dukes and worked diligently with other men of the Reformation. He served his dukes on many diplomatic and military missions, and he dedicated his major work, *De re metallica* (1556; English translation, 1912), to them.

Abandoning inductive speculation as he had learned it through his classical studies, Agricola disregarded biblical beliefs about the nature of the world, expressed his impatience with the alchemists, and concentrated on exploring the structure of the world on the basis of scientific observation. Such observation led him to the first adequate description of the part played by erosion in the shaping of mountain ranges, the origin of ores, the filling of rock interstices by circulating solutions, and the classifying of minerals on the basis of special physical characteristics, such as solubility and hardness.

Working with the miners in the two cities in which he had settled, Agricola began accumulating a massive amount of information on mining, smelting, the characteristics of ore deposits, and chemical analysis. *Bermannus sive de re metallica dialogus* (1530) was his first contribution to geology. It covered the rise of the mining industry in Germany and the early development of the great mining centers in the region of the Erzgebirge. Agricola discussed topics in mineralogy and mining, and various ores, such as silver, copper, and other metals. He showed some of the prejudices of his time, however, by dealing with the demons that supposedly haunted many of the mines. This was really an introduction to his greater work.

In 1546, he published *De ortu et causis subterraneorum*, treating the origin of ore deposits. After critically reviewing the opinions of early writers, particularly Aristotle, he rejected them, specifically the notion that metals are formed from watery vapors, and the alchemic view that all metals are composed of mercury and sulfur. He also criticized the astrological belief that the stars influence the earth's interior. Two major ideas came from this work: the origins of mountains and the origins of ore deposits. For mountains, Agricola found five means of formation: the eroding action of water, the heaping of sands by winds, subterranean winds, the actions of earthquakes, and volcanic fires. For ores, he presented the theory of lapidifying juices, solutions carrying dissolved minerals that, when cooled, left the deposits in the cracks of the rocks, thus giving rise to mineral veins. Here he predates two of the modern theories of ore deposits, the theory of ascension and the theory of lateral secretion.

Agricola's next important work, published in 1546, was *De natura fossilium* (English translation, 1955), in which he introduced a new basis for the classification of minerals (called "fossils" at that time). Agricola reviewed and rejected the systems of Aristotle, Avicenna, and others. His system was based on physical properties such as color, weight, transparency, taste, odor, texture, solubility, and combustibility. He carefully defined and explained the terms he developed. He also discussed the medicinal properties of the minerals.

Agricola's problem was understanding what he called "mista," composed of two or more fossils so intermingled as to be inseparable except by fire. His problem was a result of the alchemy of the time, the lack of a microscope, and the lack of real chemical analysis. Even without that knowledge, however, Agricola managed to remove the tales of supernatural forces in minerals and the theories of thunderstones and rocks with crystal power.

Agricola wrote three other works before his great opus: *De natura eorum quae effluent ex terra* (1546), on subsurface waters and gases; *De veteribus et novis metallis* (1546), sketching the history and geographical distribution of the various metals as far as they had been known to the ancients, and *De animantibus subterraneis* (1549), dealing with creatures that lived underground.

De re metallica, his greatest work, concentrated on mining and metallurgy and contained an abundance of information on the conditions of the time, such as mine management, machinery used, and processes employed. The book is still in print, having the unique distinction of being translated and edited (1912) by the former U.S. president Herbert Hoover and his wife, Lou Henry Hoover. Indeed, it was the leading textbook for miners and metallurgists for two centuries. At a time when it was customary to hold industrial processes secret, Agricola published every practice and improvement he could find.

In *De re metallica*, Agricola's interests are all-consuming. Tracing the history of mineralogy and mining, Agricola addressed the earliest Greek and Roman sources, using them as a springboard for a major study in the locating of mines and a classification of the types of liquids emanating from them. In part of his opus, Agricola covered the specific working of metallic veins and ores in mines. Original contributions by him include the idea that rocks containing ores are older than the ores themselves and that the ores are deposited from solutions passing through fissures in the rocks—revolutionary ideas. He also suggested the procedure of using a magnetic compass for exploring and charting underground tunnels and provided the first real assessment of the wealth available for the three richest mines of the area. The work also includes hundreds of informative drawings showing the mechanical aspects of mining.

Agricola benefited greatly from the period of tolerance during which he worked. The religious wars of the period eroded this tolerance. Well regarded by his contemporaries, Agricola died in Chemnitz on November 21, 1555.

SIGNIFICANCE

Agricola has been considered one of the most outstanding figures in the history of geological sciences. Johann Wolfgang von Goethe compared him to Roger Bacon. Alfred Werner called him the "father of mineralogy," and Karl von Vogelsang addressed him as the "forefather of geology." His works became the most comprehensive source on mining and metallurgy, acknowledged as the true beginning of geological sciences. Equally important, however, was that, in publishing that which tradition had retained as family and guild secrets, such as the process of smelting, he brought alert and innovative minds into the field of geology. Among those contemporaries were Conrad Gesner, who classified minerals on the basis of the form of the stone, gem, or fossil, avoiding all references to magic and miraculous properties of minerals, and Lazarus Ercker, who amplified Agricola's descriptions for separating precious metals through smelting. The instructions and descriptions that Agricola, Gesner, and Ercker prepared were so accurate that they would be used as handbooks for the next two centuries.

Agricola's works also helped establish, at Freiberg, a central source of mining and metallurgy knowledge, leading to a formalized, definite curriculum emphasizing observation and information sharing. Agricola's work and his determination to use observation as the basis of science led to the use of scientific theories based on observation and experimentation.

—*Arthur L. Alt*

FURTHER READING

Adams, Frank Dawson. *The Birth and Development of the Geological Sciences*. Reprint. New York: Dover, 1954. Traces the history of ideas and people contributing to the science of geology. Topics covered include the origins of metals, mountains, rivers, and oceans, and the nature of earthquakes.

Dibner, Bern. *Agricola on Metals*. Norwalk, Conn.: Burndy Library, 1958. Concise treatment of Agricola's life, with special emphasis on his major work *De re metallica*. Contains a book-by-book explanation of topics of interest. Excellent reproductions of original woodcuts.

Ellenberger, François. *From Ancient Times to the First Half of the Seventeenth Century*. Vol. 1 in *History of Geology*. Brookfield, Vt.: A. A. Balkema, 1996. Meticulously researched text on the history of geology, discusses not merely the beliefs of early geologists but also the logic informing those beliefs. Offers insight into the nature of scientific inquiry and the evolution of scientific truths. Includes bibliography, illustrations, map, index.

Faul, Henry. *It Began with a Stone*. New York: John Wiley & Sons, 1983. A comprehensive work on the history of geology. Emphasizes people and their ideas, particularly as to how they arrived at their discoveries, and provides some original writings.

Fenton, Carroll Lane, and Mildred Adams Fenton. *Giants of Geology*. New York: Doubleday, 1952. Details the thinking of the pioneers of geology, concentrating on the men who nurtured geological knowledge in exploring new areas of the world. Shows how ideas have altered over time, based on explorations and exquisite observations used to overthrow prejudices. Excellent references.

Geikie, Archibald. *The Founders of Geology*. 2d ed. Reprint. New York: Dover, 1962. Tracing the slow growth of geology from ancient to modern cultures, the book deals with the controversies surrounding such geological ideas as volcanism, fossils, Earth's origin, and geological succession.

Kranzberg, Melvin, and Carroll W. Pursell, Jr., eds. *The Emergence of Modern Industrial Society*. Vol. 1 in *Technology in Western Civilization*. New York: Oxford University Press, 1967. This work portrays technology as one of the major determinants in the overall development of Western civilization. Attempting to integrate technological development with other aspects of society affected by it, the book deals nicely with the people and machines giving rise to modern society.

Oldroyd, David. *Sciences of the Earth: Studies in the History of Mineralogy and Geology*. Brookfield, Vt.: Ashgate, 1998. Collection of essays on the invention and development of mineralogy from the Renaissance to the early nineteenth century. Focuses on the relationship between mineralogy and chemistry, as well as the influence of philosophy of nature and philosophy of science on the new discipline. Includes bibliography, index, illustrations.

Singer, Charles, E. J. Holmyard, A. R. Hell, and Trevor Williams, eds. *From the Renaissance to the Industrial Revolution, c. 1500-c. 1750*. Vol. 3 in *A History of Technology*. New York: Oxford University Press, 1957. A superb overview of the development and emergence of modern science during the Renaissance and later periods. Chronicles the development of technology and the people involved.

SEE ALSO: Desiderius Erasmus; Girolamo Fracastoro; Conrad Gesner; Aldus Manutius; Sir Thomas More; Paracelsus.

RELATED ARTICLES in *Great Events from History: The Renaissance & Early Modern Era, 1454-1600:* 1490's: Aldus Manutius Founds the Aldine Press; 1499-1517: Erasmus Advances Humanism in England; 1517: Fracastoro Develops His Theory of Fossils; 1600: William Gilbert Publishes *De Magnete*.

AKBAR
Mughal emperor of India (r. 1556-1605)

As one of India's greatest Mughal emperors, Akbar conquered and unified northern India under his rule. In addition to military conquest, his most significant achievements include the development of an efficient bureaucratic structure, patronage of the arts, and enlightened policies of religious tolerance.

BORN: October 15, 1542; Umarkot, Sind (now in Pakistan)
DIED: October 16, 1605; Āgra, India
ALSO KNOWN AS: Abū-ul-Fath Jahāl-ud-Dīn Muḥammad Akbar (full name)
AREAS OF ACHIEVEMENT: Government and politics, religion and theology, patronage of the arts, military, warfare and conquest

EARLY LIFE
Akbar (AK-bahr) was born Abū-ul-Fath Jahāl-ud-Dīn Muḥammad Akbar in the kingdom of Sind. Of mixed Turkish, Persian, and Mongol ancestry, Akbar was a descendant of both Tamerlane and Genghis Khan. His grandfather, Bābur the Tiger, a Muslim chieftain of a small state in Turkestan, invaded India in 1526 and within four years conquered Hindustan in northern India and Afghanistan. The Mughal Dynasty, founded by Bābur, ruled northern India until the British took over in the eighteenth and nineteenth centuries.

Bābur was succeeded in 1530 by his son Humāyūn, who was unable to prevent the conquest of the empire by the Afghan chieftain Shēr Shāh Sūr. Driven from his throne at Delhi, Humāyūn fled to Persia to seek support. During this flight, his Persian wife, Hamida, in 1542 gave birth to Akbar while in the kingdom of Sind. In 1555, with the aid of Persian troops, Humāyūn reconquered the area around Delhi and reclaimed his throne. He died the next year, in January, 1556, as a result of an accident caused by the effects of opium.

Akbar was thirteen when he succeeded his father as the third Mughal emperor of India. He had been reared in the wilds of Afghanistan, where he developed a love of hunting and riding. Throughout his life, he sought reckless, dangerous activities, such as riding wild elephants and spearing tigers. Such risk taking was probably the result of his recurrent bouts of depression, which caused him to take extreme chances in order, he said, to see whether he should die. A kindly person, he was also high-strung and had a violent temper.

Of only moderate height, Akbar was muscular and broad-shouldered. He had narrow eyes (reflecting his Mongolian ancestry), a dark complexion, a thin mustache, and long hair. Although his head drooped slightly toward the right and he suffered from epilepsy, he had an impressive, commanding presence. He had a keen intelligence but never learned to read or write, even though he had been provided with a tutor from age five. He had, however, a deep love and knowledge of literature, and he was skilled in mechanical arts.

When he became emperor, Akbar, despite his youth, was already serving as governor of the Punjab and had military experience. His claim to the throne, however, was immediately challenged by ambitious rivals, the most threatening of whom was a Hindu named Hemu. Akbar's rule was secured when his father's loyal and capable general Bairam Khan, on November 5, 1556, defeated Hemu's large army at Panipat, north of Delhi. Bairam Khan then ruled as the young emperor's regent for five years, until Akbar's ambitious nurse, Maham Anaga, had the regent deposed so that she could run the empire herself. In 1562, at age twenty, Akbar took personal control of his empire.

LIFE'S WORK
At the beginning of Akbar's rule, only a portion of the territory originally conquered by Bābur was under Mughal control. Akbar's reign was characterized by successful military conquests, and he regained that territory and much more. With a large, efficient standing army that he himself often led, he extended Mughal authority over Afghanistan and all India except the Deccan, in the south. The greatest resistance to his rule came from the fiercely independent Hindu Rajputs, who controlled the area known as Rājasthān. The Rajputs were eventually subdued through both conciliatory and ruthless policies.

In 1562, Akbar married the daughter of Raja Bihari Mal of Amber, one of the leading Rajput rulers. Although Akbar had a large harem, this Hindu princess was his favorite wife and mother of his heir Salim (later known as Jahāngīr). As a result of the marriage alliance, many Rajputs came to serve in the Mughal administration and army. The princes could continue to rule, but they had to acknowledge Akbar's suzerainty and supply him with money and soldiers. To facilitate Indian acceptance of Mughal rule, Akbar abolished the enslavement of prisoners of war and no longer forced those he conquered to convert to Islam. If rulers nevertheless resisted, they were mercilessly crushed. When the Rajput ruler of Mewar refused to follow his orders, Akbar, in 1568, captured the fortress of Chitor and ordered the massacre of thirty thousand prisoners.

Despite episodes of draconian cruelty, Akbar's reign was generally marked by enlightened reforms promoting social peace. Most notably, he instituted a policy of religious toleration. In addition to his own sense of fairness and interest in unrestricted religious dialogue, Akbar believed that the conquering Mughals, who were Muslim, had to have the support of the native Hindu populace. Akbar therefore removed many of the penalties that had burdened Indian Hindus. In 1563, he abolished a tax, which dated from well before Bābur's invasion, on Hindu pilgrims who traveled to holy places. In 1564, he abolished the *jizya*, a tax on non-Muslims. He ended the destruction of Hindu temples and allowed new ones to be built. He encouraged Muslim acceptance of Hindu traditions, although he did try to eliminate the Hindu practices of child marriage and widow burning (suttee). Schools were founded under government sponsorship for Hindus as well as Muslims. Hindus served and advanced equally with Muslims in the government and the army.

Akbar's economic policies were also fair and effective. Taxation was based on landed property, and one-third of the value of the harvest went to the royal treasury. (This was a lower taxation than before or after Akbar.) In times of poor harvest, taxation was reduced or suspended. Efficient tax collection, coupled with a sound currency and flourishing trade, created great prosperity. Most of the hundred million people under Akbar's rule were still very poor, but historians have suggested that peasants were probably better off then than they were in more modern times.

Akbar maintained centralized control over his empire by instituting an effective bureaucratic hierarchy based on standardized ranks and salaries. The higher administration was divided into thirty-three ranks, classified according to the number of cavalry the officeholder was expected to raise for the emperor. There was no distinction between civil and military ranks, and all were theoretically appointed by and responsible to the emperor. The empire was territorially divided into twelve provinces and further subdivided into systematic administrative units. The civil code was based on Muslim law, but local disputes that took place between Hindus could be decided according to Hindu law.

The prosperity of the empire allowed Akbar to amass a huge fortune, making him the richest king in the world.

Akbar. (Hulton|Archive by Getty Images)

He had an elaborate court, which for many years he held at a magnificent new palace-city, Fatehpur Sikri (city of victory). Despite the grandeur of his public life, in which he assumed an almost godlike persona, Akbar in his personal life had simple, even austere habits. He maintained a very moderate diet, with usually only one main meal a day. Near the end of his life, under Jain influence, he almost entirely gave up eating meat. He did, however, drink liquor excessively and, like his father, was a regular user of opium. He slept very little, no more than about three hours per night.

During Akbar's reign, Mughal culture flowered, characterized by a distinctive, elegant blend of Persian and Hindu styles, with some European influence. Akbar employed more than one hundred painters at court who regularly exhibited their work to him. He himself was a gifted artist. He was also a musician, performing on a kind of kettle drum, and was skilled in Hindu singing. Although illiterate, he collected a large library and encouraged literary production. He created the post of poet laureate for Hindi, the northern Indian vernacular that became India's national language, and had Sanskrit works translated into Persian for his courtiers.

Akbar's primary interest was religion. He built at Fatehpur Sikri a house of worship in which to discuss theological questions. At first limited to Muslims, the debates were soon opened to Hindus and those of other faiths. He invited Jesuits from the Portuguese colony at Goa to come to his court, and he listened so intently to them that they thought he was about to convert to Christianity. He did reject Orthodox Islam, but instead of becoming a Christian, he sponsored his own religion, known as the Divine Faith, a mystical blend of Hinduism and Islam. Akbar claimed that he was God's vice-regent, with authority to rule over spiritual as well as temporal matters. This new religion had little influence and disappeared after his death.

Akbar's last years were marred by his son Salim's attempts to usurp his throne. Salim may have caused his father's death in 1605 by poisoning him. When he succeeded Akbar, Salim took the Persian name Jahāngīr, meaning world seizer. Akbar is buried in a mausoleum at Sicandra, near Āgra.

SIGNIFICANCE

Known as the Great Mughal (Persian for Mongol), Akbar created an imperial government that lasted until the nineteenth century. His administrative system, efficient and open to the promotion of talent, was adopted by the British when they later conquered India. Although there were enormous disparities of income between the Mughal elite and the impoverished peasants during his reign, his reign was characterized by a level of general prosperity unmatched in later years. The contemporary of Elizabeth I of England and Philip II of Spain, Akbar surpassed both of them in wealth, power, and majesty. He enjoyed a semidivine status but nevertheless had a personal concern for the well-being of his subjects. He was humble enough to disguise himself sometimes in order to mix with his subjects and listen to their views.

Akbar succeeded in establishing internal peace within his empire because he combined a realistic assessment of the limits of power with a humanistic concern and just administration. His system of taxation, for example, which brought great wealth into his treasury, was flexible enough to encourage rather than crush those suffering economic hardship. The glory of Akbar's reign included a cultural blending that produced the beautiful, distinc-

tive Mughal style. This creativity was stimulated by the toleration for cultural and religious differences, a toleration that was perhaps Akbar's greatest achievement. With India later to be so torn apart by conflict between Hindu and Muslim, Akbar's policy of religious toleration and mixing makes him a model of enlightened rule.

—*Nancy Fix Anderson*

FURTHER READING

Binyon, Laurence. *Akbar.* New York: D. Appleton, 1932. A brief, readable biography of Akbar with emphasis on his personality rather than on his rule.

Burn, Richard, ed. *The Mughal Period.* Vol. 4 in *The Cambridge History of India.* Reprint. New Delhi: S. Chand, 1987. This history of the Mughal Empire from the conquest of Bābur to the eighteenth century includes a detailed account of Akbar's rule, with emphasis on his military conquests and religious thought. Includes bibliography, illustrations, maps.

Du Jarric, Pierre. *Akbar and the Jesuits: An Account of the Jesuit Missions to the Court of Akbar.* Translated with an introduction and notes by C. H. Payne. New Delhi: Tulsi, 1979. A translation and reprint of an early seventeenth century French account of Akbar and his rule, based on reports and letters by Jesuits in Akbar's court.

Habib, Irfan, ed. *Akbar and His India.* New York: Oxford University Press, 1997. Anthology collects essays on Akbar himself, as well as essays on Indian culture and the general environment in which Akbar ruled. Includes bibliography, illustrations, map.

Husain, Afzal. *The Nobility Under Akbar and Jahāngīr: A Study of Family Groups.* New Delhi: Manohar, 1999. Details the kinship structures of nine noble families and the social structure of Mughal culture in general. Explains the relationship between family, politics, and religion in Akbar's empire. Includes appendices, bibliography, index.

Smith, Vincent A. *Akbar, the Great Mogul, 1542-1605.* 2d rev. ed. Delhi: A. Chand, 1966. Still the most complete biography of Akbar. A balanced account that assesses the strengths and weaknesses of Akbar's personality and rule. Contains a lengthy annotated bibliography, maps, and illustrations.

Wellesz, Emmy. *Akbar's Religious Thought, Reflected in Mogul Painting.* London: Allen & Unwin, 1952. A lucid account of how Akbar's eclectic religious interests and policy of religious toleration influenced the creation of Mughal painting. Includes forty black-and-white art plates.

Wolpert, Stanley. *A New History of India*. 7th ed. New York: Oxford University Press, 2004. The chapter on Akbar in this general history, written by one of the leading historians of India, provides an accessible introduction. Includes bibliography, illustrations, maps, index.

SEE ALSO: Bābur; Elizabeth I; Humāyūn; Ibrāhīm Lodī; Krishnadevaraya; Nānak; Philip II.

RELATED ARTICLES in *Great Events from History: The Renaissance & Early Modern Era, 1454-1600*: December 30, 1530: Humāyūn Inherits the Throne in India; 1540-1545: Shēr Shāh Sūr Becomes Emperor of Delhi; 1556-1605: Reign of Akbar; February 23, 1568: Fall of Chitor; March 3, 1575: Mughal Conquest of Bengal; 1580-1587: Rebellions in Bihar and Bengal; February, 1586: Annexation of Kashmir.

LEON BATTISTA ALBERTI
Italian scholar, writer, and architect

Alberti is identified by Renaissance historians as an archetype of the universal individual. He established a leading reputation as a theorist and practitioner of the visual arts, notably in the field of architecture. As a Humanist, he was the author of numerous moral dialogues.

BORN: February 14, 1404; Genoa (now in Italy)
DIED: April, 1472; Rome, Papal States (now in Italy)
AREAS OF ACHIEVEMENT: Architecture, art, philosophy, scholarship

EARLY LIFE

Leon Battista Alberti (LEE-on bah-TEES-tah ahl-BEHR-tee) was born to the prominent Alberti family, who were textile merchants and bankers. In Florence, they were associated with the Popular Party. Their decline began with the exile of Leon Battista's grandfather Benedetto, who left Florence with his son Lorenzo in 1387. Leon Battista was born in Genoa, the second natural son of Lorenzo and Bianca Fieschi, widow of a prominent Genoese family. On his mother's death from the plague in 1406, Lorenzo moved to Venice, where he joined another brother, Ricciardo, in trade, shortly thereafter marrying a Florentine woman in 1408.

Leon Battista and his brother Carlo received the best Humanist education available. At Gasparino, Barzizza's academy in Padua, he studied with many who were to become major scholars in the world of Renaissance learning, such as Panormita and Francesco Filelfo. In 1421, Alberti went to Bologna, where he deepened his knowledge of Greek and Latin literature and began his studies of mathematics. Following the death of his father in 1421 and his uncle Ricciardo a year later, the brothers were deprived of their legitimate inheritance by the machinations of their cousins, Ricciardo's sons. A combination

of grief and academic pressure led to a serious deterioration of Leon Battista's health, in particular his eyesight. During his recuperation, he turned from the study of ancient texts to that of mathematics, an interest that profoundly affected his future researches.

Alberti's friendship in Bologna with Tommaso Parentucelli da Sarzana—the future Pope Nicholas V—led to an appointment as secretary to a cardinal of Bologna. In 1428, the Florentine ban on the Albertis was lifted. It is most likely that Leon Battista made a brief visit to the city of his father that year, or early in 1429. These years coincide with the climax of the struggle between the Albizzi faction and the Popular Party, resulting in the eventual consolidation in Florence of Medici power under Cosimo I de' Medici: Historically the Albertis had been closely allied to the Medicis.

LIFE'S WORK

As a papal secretary in the service of Eugenius IV, Alberti followed the pope to Florence, where he had been invited on the expulsion of the Papacy from Rome. Here he came into contact with all the major personalities responsible for the explosion of the new art and architecture of the Renaissance. In Florence, he established strong ties of friendship with the sculptor Donatello and the architects Filippo Brunelleschi, who had completed the dome of the cathedral; Michelozzo, who was to design the Palazzo Medici; and Lorenzo Ghiberti, who was working on the doors of the baptistery. The first fruits of this experience are the *De pictura* (1435; *Of Painting*, 1726) and *De statua* (possibly pre-1435; *Of Sculpture*, 1726), in both of which Alberti displays the fundamental principles of Renaissance art, in particular the relationship between mathematics and composition, the consequent rules of perspective, and the use of nature as a model. Alberti wrote both Latin and Italian versions of these treatises.

While the majority of his moral dialogues are in Latin, Alberti also turned to the vernacular in a conscious attempt to reach a wider audience and to restore to Tuscan the literary prestige it had enjoyed in the previous century as the result of the works of Dante, Petrarch, and Giovanni Boccaccio. *Theogenius* (c. 1440) and *Della tranquillità dell' anima* (c. 1442; of peace of mind) mark moments of deep reflection in Alberti's career: an internal debate on the relative merits of the active and contemplative life. The high point of these years came earlier, with the completion of the first three books of Alberti's most popular work, *Della famiglia* (1434; *The Family in Renaissance Florence*, 1969). In dialogue form, he details the moral basis of the family and its role in civic life, offering to the coming generation, in spite of the reverses he himself suffered at the hands of certain relatives, the example of the contributions made by their ancestors to the commercial expansion and intellectual vigor of Renaissance Florence.

Alberti's career as an architect was launched in Ferrara in 1442, when he was asked to judge the designs for an equestrian statue in honor of Nicolò d'Este. Alberti designed the minitriumphal arch for the statue's base.

Leon Battista Alberti. (Library of Congress)

With the elevation of Parentucelli to the Papacy as Nicholas V, Alberti was named the pope's principal architectural adviser: the one he depended on more than any other in an ambitious program of restoration, street widening, and building projects designed to return to Rome the dignity it deserved as the seat of the Catholic Church. The years that followed were to be the most productive of his career, and the achievements recorded between 1450 and 1470 were to give him his greatest satisfaction and ensure Alberti enduring fame. The buildings completed and designed were all the fruit of an experience that had ripened in the light of extensive theoretical meditation. Alberti's principles of architecture are detailed in the ten volumes of *De re aedificatoria* (1452; *The Architecture of Leon Battista Alberti in Ten Books*, 1726), dedicated to his patron Nicholas V. In it, Alberti acknowledges the contribution of the Roman theorist Vetruvius. His intention was to take the principles of harmony and proportion and apply them to the aesthetic and practical requirements of his own age.

Passing from theory to practice, he accepted a commission from Sigismondo Malatesta (1450) to transform the Gothic Church of San Francesco into the Tempio Malatestano, with its bold classical façade; divided into three triumphal arches. Also around 1450, he was called by the merchant Giovanni Rucellai to redesign the facade of his family's palazzo in Florence that, with its elegant pillars and flat beveled masonry, makes the building rather more inviting than the more fortresslike structures such as the Palazzo Medici-Ricciardi.

During the reign of Pius II, one of the foremost Renaissance Humanists, Alberti accepted the invitation of Ludovico Gonzaga of Mantua to build the Church of San Sebastiano in that city. The same princely patron gave Alberti his final commission, to design the Church of Sant' Andrea in Mantua. The latter was only completed in the eighteenth century, following modified Albertian concepts. He did live to see the completion of a major project: the façade of Santa Maria Novella in Florence, again commissioned by his patron Rucellai. Here the addition of classical forms harmonizes with existing Gothic elements of the basilica, and the use of the characteristic black-and-white marble blends Santa Maria Novella with other major Florentine churches, including Santa Maria del Fiore. Alberti, who served popes and princes, also remained in touch with his allies the Medicis; in the tradition of the scholar advising civic leaders, he dedicated a small treatise on rhetoric (*Trivia senatoria*, c. 1460) to Lorenzo de' Medici, who was still in his teens. Alberti died in Rome in April, 1472.

> ## ALBERTI ON PAINTING AND ON KNOWING THE ARCHITECT
>
> *Leon Battista Alberti was a keen observer of the arts of painting and architecture, questioning what makes a work ideal and what makes the ideal artist and architect. Although little known outside circles of the history of art and architecture, his influence on Renaissance geniuses such as Leonardo da Vinci and on Renaissance Humanism cannot be overstated. Two samples of his reflections are excerpted below, the first on painting and the second on architecture.*
>
> An admirable and praiseworthy narrative picture [painting] will present itself so charming and adorned with pleasant features that it will hold anyone who looks at it, taught or untaught, in delight and emotion. The first thing that pleases us in a narrative picture is abundance and variety of objects. As in foods and music, novelty and number please insofar as they differ from old and familiar things. For this reason abundance and variety are pleasing in a painting. I would call that historical picture extremely rich in which there is at the proper places a miscellany of old men, young men, boys, women, girls, children, chickens, cattle, birds, horses, sheep, buildings, views, and all such things. . . . And it happens that the painter's richness gains much good will when the spectator lingers to observe all the things there.
>
> [T]he only obligation we have to the Architect is not for his providing us with safe and pleasant places, where we may shelter ourselves from the Heat of the Sun, and from Cold and Tempest (tho' this is no small Benefit); but for having besides contrived many other things. . . . Daedalus [legendary Greek architect] in his times was greatly esteem'd for having made the Selinuntians a Vault, which gather'd so warm and kindly a Vapour, as provoked a plentiful Sweat, and thereby cured their Distempers with great ease and pleasure. Why need I mention others who have contrived many things of the like sort conducive to Health. . . . [W]hy should I mention the Rocks cut, Mountains bored through, Vallies fill'd up, Lakes confined, Marshes discharged into the Sea, Ships built, Rivers turn'd, their Mouths clear'd.
>
> *Source: The Middle Ages and Renaissance. Vol. 1 in A Documentary History of Art*, edited by Elizabeth Gilmore Holt (New York: Anchor Books, 1957), pp. 213, 219, 220.

SIGNIFICANCE

Alberti's writings in Italian, both on art and on social behavior, explore all the major themes of Renaissance Humanism. Scholars and editors of his works have asserted that he shaped and defined this movement in the history of ideas and that the Renaissance would not have made the intellectual advances it did without his contributions and prodding.

In the introduction to *The Family in Renaissance Florence*, he expounds on the themes of virtue and fortune that so exercised the speculative curiosity of fifteenth century thinkers. In the decline of glory of his own family, he sees a parallel with the rise and fall of states. Against the thesis of inevitability and the stoic acceptance of a fate governing human affairs, Alberti juxtaposes the Renaissance idea of free will that allows individuals to shape an independent life for themselves in defiance of even the direst circumstances. This is what he means by virtue, which must never allow fortune to serve as an alibi for failure or incompetence. Virtue is also dedicated hard work and the determination to cultivate all the seeds of natural talents and curiosity with which one is endowed. The proclamation of these ideals makes Alberti a principal spokesperson of the spirit of the active life that animates the mercantile ethic of civic Humanism in the first half of Quattrocento Florence. Humans were born, he says, to be useful to other humans.

While the impact of Alberti the moralist deserves emphasis, his dominant role as art theorist and architectural mentor is his most enduring achievement. Architecture could be taken as a metaphor for the highest ideals of Renaissance culture, for it involves the most detailed knowledge of an infinite variety of activities, skills, and materials that must ultimately be synthesized into a harmonious whole. Granted his major achievements in so many fields, it is amazing to observe that Alberti's final significance was nearly overlooked. His original insights into art theory had been so integrated into practice and elaborated on by Leonardo da Vinci and others that the originator of the ideas had been largely forgotten.

—*Harry Lawton*

FURTHER READING

Alberti, Leon Battista. *The Family in Renaissance Florence*. Translated by Renee Neu Watkins. Columbia: University of South Carolina Press, 1969. This modern translation includes a good introduction and bibliography of writings on civic Humanism in English.

Gadol, Joan. *Leon Battista Alberti: Universal Man of the Early Renaissance*. Chicago: University of Chicago

Press, 1969. A very useful study detailing Alberti's contributions to the theory and practice of art and the development of architecture in the fifteenth century. Although mostly directed to his work in the visual arts (with reference to optics and perspective), the book places its subject firmly in the context of Humanism. The first chapter is biographical and includes a critical survey of views on Alberti's ultimate significance.

Garin, Eugenio. *Italian Humanism: Philosophy and Civic Life in the Renaissance.* Translated by Peter Munz. New York: Harper & Row, 1965. This extremely lucid intellectual history of Renaissance Humanism includes some indispensable pages on Alberti in chapter 2 on the subject of civic life. Garin presents him as a major representative of the spirit of *negotium* (the active life) and thus a key figure in the intellectual life of the first half of the Quattrocento.

Grafton, Anthony. *Leon Battista Alberti: Master Builder of the Italian Renaissance.* New York: Harvard University Press, 2002. An impressive attempt to do justice to the many facets and multidisciplinary accomplishments of Alberti, including his critical and creative writings, painting, architecture, and even his athletic prowess. Combines cultural history with personal biography and psychological insight. Includes bibliography, illustrations, index.

Grayson, Cecil. "The Humanism of Alberti." *Italian Studies* 12 (1957): 37-56. An essential synopsis of Alberti's thought and moral imperatives by the writer's most distinguished commentator and the major editor of his works. Grayson succinctly relates Alberti's thought to his family's commercial activity and the intellectual atmosphere of fifteenth century Florence.

Harries, Karsten. *Infinity and Perspective.* Cambridge, Mass.: MIT Press, 2001. This controversial philosophical text reviews the history of theories of perspective in an attempt to argue in favor of objective truth. Includes important discussion of Alberti's theory of perspective and the relationship between art, science, and philosophy in the Renaissance. Includes illustrations, index, bibliographic references.

Sparti, Barbara. "Humanism and the Arts: Parallels Between Alberti's *On Painting* and Guglielmo Ebreo's *On Dancing.*" In *Art and Music in the Early Modern Period: Essays in Honor of Franca Trinchieri Camiz,* edited by Katherine A. McIver. Burlington, Vt.: Ashgate, 2003. Essay detailing the importance of Humanism to Alberti's theories of painting, as well as comparing Alberti's brand of Humanism to that of Ebreo. Includes bibliographic references and index.

Tavernor, Robert. *On Alberti and the Art of Building.* New Haven, Conn.: Yale University Press, 1998. In-depth study of each of Alberti's architectural projects, analyzing his intentions and artistry as a master builder. Attempts to resolve many points of dispute resulting from the unfinished nature of many of Alberti's projects, as well as their subsequent modification by others. Includes illustrations, index, references, and a bibliography of Alberti's writings.

SEE ALSO: Donato Bramante; Leonardo da Vinci; Andrea Mantegna; Cosimo I de' Medici; Lorenzo de' Medici; Andrea Palladio; Pius II; Jacopo Sansovino.

RELATED ARTICLES in *Great Events from History: The Renaissance & Early Modern Era, 1454-1600:* c. 1510: Invention of the Watch; 1563-1584: Construction of the Escorial.

AFONSO DE ALBUQUERQUE
Portuguese explorer

Albuquerque's most lasting contribution was the foundation of the Portuguese colonial empire in the East. He conquered Goa in India and Malacca on the Malay Peninsula, ended the Arabian trade monopoly in Asia, made Goa a center of the Portuguese colonial government and commerce, and developed colonial administration using indigenous officials.

BORN: 1453; Alhandra, near Lisbon, Portugal

DIED: December 15, 1515; at sea, near Goa Harbor, India

ALSO KNOWN AS: Albuquerque the Great; the Portuguese Mars

AREAS OF ACHIEVEMENT: Exploration, government and politics, military

EARLY LIFE

Afonso de Albuquerque (uh-FOHN-sew dee ahl-bew-KUR-kuh) was born the second son of Gonzalvo de Albuquerque, lord of Villaverde. Through his father, he was related to the royal house of Portugal (through illegitimate descent), the males in the family having for several generations been confidential secretaries to Portuguese kings. On the maternal side, his grandfather had served as high admiral of Portugal. With these connections, it is not surprising that Afonso's early education was at the court of King Afonso V. He served in the army of Portugal in North Africa, gaining military experience crusading against the Muslims. He fought in the conquest of Arzila and Tangier (1471), participated in the invasion of Spain (1476), and served in the expedition led by King Afonso against the Turks and in the Battle of Otranto (1480-1481).

On the death of King Afonso, Albuquerque returned to Lisbon and the court, where he was appointed chief equerry (master of the horse) under John II. He served again in military expeditions against the Muslims in North Africa (at the defense of Graciosa) and under King Manuel I in Morocco. During this period of Portuguese history, the court was continually concerned at home with the struggle of the king for dominance over the nobles. Albuquerque was little engaged in these affairs but did seemingly arouse jealousy and make enemies among the nobles at court. He later fell victim to court intrigues.

LIFE'S WORK

While his education had been at the Portuguese court and his military service for the most part crusading against the Muslims in Northern Africa and Europe, Albuquer-

que's fame was made in the East during the reign of Manuel. Here, again, he was engaged in battles against the Muslims, this time for trade dominance and empire. In a relatively short period of time (1503-1515), he secured Portuguese hegemony of the Deccan in India, Portuguese control of the spice trade through conquest and fortification of the Malay Peninsula and Sunda Isles, and dominance of the waters through the Malaccan Strait. He governed the eastern empire of Portugal (though he never received the title of viceroy).

After the history-making voyage of Vasco da Gama, who rounded the Cape of Good Hope to India in 1499, the way was opened for the Portuguese to challenge the monopoly held by the Venetians and Muslims of the spice-trade routes between Europe and the East. In 1503, Albuquerque, with his kinsman, Francisco de Albuquerque, sailed under Pedro Álvars Cabral to open relations and trade with India. During this first of his voyages to Asia, Albuquerque assisted the Hindu ruler of Cochin in a bid for power against the provincial ruler at Calicut, who was friendly to the Arabs. In return, the Portuguese were able to build a fortress at Cochin and establish a trading post at Quilon; thus began the Portuguese empire in the East.

In July, 1504, Albuquerque returned to Lisbon, where Manuel received him with honor. For a time, Albuquerque assisted in the formulation of policy at court. When Tristão da Cunha sailed from Portugal in April, 1506, with a fleet of sixteen ships, Albuquerque sailed with him as an officer in command of five of the ships. The object of the voyage was to explore the east coast of Africa and to build a fortress at the mouth of the Red Sea to block Arab trade with India. Admiral da Cunha's fleet successfully attacked several Arab cities on the African east coast, explored the coasts of Madagascar and Mozambique, and built a fortress on Socotra Island, effectively blocking the mouth of the Red Sea. On September 27, 1507, Albuquerque led his squadron in a successful siege of the island of Hormuz, which commands the Strait of Hormuz between the Persian Gulf and Gulf of Oman. Hormuz was one of the trade centers of the Arab monopoly. The captains of his ships wanted to ply their trade on the seas more than to be engaged in fortifying Hormuz, however, and Albuquerque temporarily was forced to abandon the project.

In 1505, Dom Francisco de Almeida was appointed the first governor in India with the rank of viceroy. In

1508, Manuel appointed Albuquerque to succeed Almeida at the end of his term. This commission did not, however, include the rank of viceroy, though the distinction seems never to have been made in the colonies or by Albuquerque.

Albuquerque proceeded to the Malabar Coast and arrived in December, 1508, at Cannanore, India, where Almeida refused to honor the commission and jailed Albuquerque. In previous skirmishes that Almeida had had with Arab forces from Egypt, his son had been killed, and Almeida was determined to remain in command in India until he had avenged his son's death. Almeida defeated the Muslims near Diu in February, 1509, and the Portuguese fleet arrived in November, 1509, confirming Albuquerque's commission. Albuquerque was then released from jail and subsequently assumed his position as governor. Almeida returned to Lisbon.

Albuquerque set out to control all the major sea trade routes to the East and to establish permanent colonial posts with fortresses and settled populations. He destroyed part of Calicut, which he had been unable to seize control of, in January, 1510. He moved next to secure a permanent center for commerce and government on the Indian coast. Rather than moving to displace the Hindu rulers to the south, he attacked and captured Goa from the Muslims in March, 1510, with a fleet of twenty-three ships. He was driven back by the Muslim army two months later but regained the city permanently for the Portuguese in November. He executed the Muslim defenders of the city. This hard-won victory also persuaded Hindu rulers on the eastern coast of India to accept the Portuguese presence.

Albuquerque was able then for a short time to turn his attention to administration. Using the government of Lisbon as a model, he established a senate for Goa, the first such senate in Asia, and gave financial and judicial responsibilities to native officials. He encouraged the intermarriage of his men with the population of Goa. He also developed a network of supply from interior villages for the coastal city.

In 1511, Albuquerque resumed his attempts to break the trade monopoly of the Muslims by journeying to the Spice Islands (Moluccas). He established the Portuguese in Ceylon and the Sunda Isles. He attacked and sacked Malacca in July, 1511. He built a Portuguese fortress there, established control of the straits between the Malay Peninsula and the Island of Sumatra, and by these means guaranteed for Portugal the domination of the maritime route to the Spice Islands. While in Malacca, he established a colonial government with native officials (as in Goa) and developed trade relations with Pegu, Cochin (in what is now South Vietnam), China, Siam (modern Thailand), and Java.

Once more, in February, 1515, Albuquerque undertook a military expedition, this time with twenty-six ships, to the Red Sea. This early commission, from his first coming to the East, to establish Portuguese trade over the Persian Gulf region was yet unaccomplished. He laid siege to Aden (1513) unsuccessfully, led what was probably the first modern European voyage in the Red Sea, and retook Hormuz (1515). The retaking of Hormuz effectively established Portuguese dominance over the Persian Gulf trade. In September, 1515, Albuquerque became ill and set sail for Goa.

Whether his enemies at court succeeded in their jealous intrigues against him or whether Manuel was concerned about the state of Albuquerque's health, a successor to Albuquerque was appointed to govern the Portuguese holdings in the East. Albuquerque met the vessel from Europe carrying news of the appointment and learned, as he approached the harbor of Goa, that the post had been given to his enemy, Lope Soares. Manuel had recommended that Soares pay special deference to Albuquerque; weakened by illness and embittered by

Afonso de Albuquerque. (Library of Congress)

what he considered betrayal, Albuquerque died on December 15, 1515, while still at sea. Before his death, he wrote to the king giving an account of his service in the East and claiming for his natural son, Brás (later called Afonso the Younger), the reward and honor that he claimed as his own.

Albuquerque was buried in Goa in the Church of Our Lady, which he had built. For many years, Muslims and Hindus visited his grave to solicit his intercession against the injustices of their later rulers. A superstition held that the Portuguese dominion would be safe as long as Albuquerque's bones lay in Goa. These were, however, moved to Portugal in 1566. His son was later honored by Manuel as befitted the accomplishments of his father.

SIGNIFICANCE

Albuquerque was one of those men distinguished in leadership, military achievements, and administration of which southern Europe seemed to have a bounteous supply at the end of the fifteenth century and through the mid-sixteenth. Facing long lines of supply and communication around the Cape of Good Hope, facing enemies by sea and by land who were often as accomplished as the Europeans of the time in military organization and technology, Albuquerque was able to establish the basis for a Portuguese empire in the East. He was able to organize in the area colonial administration and trade practices that endured to times past Portuguese domination. He did not amass vast fortunes (that which he did have he lost through shipwreck early in his adventures in the East). He did not obtain enormous land holdings or accrue glorious titles. A loyal son of Portugal, his ambition was tied to its glory, wealth, and position; in Portugal's name, he gained control of all the main sea trade routes of the East and built permanent fortresses that, with their settled populations, were the foundation of Portugal's eastern hegemony.

—*Barbara Ann Barbato*

FURTHER READING

Albuquerque, Afonso de. *The Commentaries of the Great Afonso Dalboquerque, Second Viceroy of India.* Edited and translated by Walter de Gray Birch. 4 vols. New Delhi: Asian Educational Services, 2000. This resource includes Albuquerque's reports and letters compiled originally by his son Brás. It was first published by the Lisbon Academy of Sciences in 1576.

Armstrong, Richard. *Discoverers.* Vol. 2 in *A History of Seafaring.* Westport, Conn.: Praeger, 1969. The work is general in scope, designed for the general reader, and well illustrated with diagrams, maps, and repro-

ductions. The short and vivid sketch of Albuquerque presents the major accomplishments of his career within the context of the history of discovery. Includes a good index and bibliography.

Boxer, C. R. *The Portuguese Seaborne Empire, 1415-1825.* London: Hutchinson, 1969. A social history by one of Great Britain's leading Portuguese scholars. These tales of Portuguese sailing and trading and the transplantation of their social institutions to India are easy to read. Basing his research on original sources, Boxer contradicts the Portuguese myth of "no color bar" as the secret of successful governing of an empire vaster than its base. Good maps are included.

Neilson, J. B. *Great Men of the East.* London: Longmans, Green, 1947. Neilson gives a glowing portrait of Albuquerque and his achievements.

Russell-Wood, A. J. R. *The Portuguese Empire, 1415-1808: A World on the Move.* Reprint. Baltimore: Johns Hopkins University Press, 1998. Organized thematically rather than strictly chronologically, this account of Portuguese colonial expansion includes discussions of Albuquerque as a conqueror, intelligence gatherer, diplomat, reformer, and merchant. Illustrations, maps, bibliographic references, and index.

Sanceau, Elaine. *Indies Adventure.* Hamden, Conn.: Archon Books, 1938. Albuquerque's voyages and achievements in the East are vividly chronicled with emphasis on what made them remarkable.

Shastry, B. S. *Goa-Kanara Portuguese Relations, 1498-1763.* Edited by Charles J. Borges. New Delhi, India: Concept, 2000. History of Portuguese trade and colonization of India beginning with the arrival of the Portuguese in 1498. Focuses particularly on Goa and on Albuquerque's actions and legacy in the area. Includes bibliographic references and index.

Stephens, Henry Morse. *Albuquerque.* Oxford, England: Clarendon Press, 1892. Part of the Rulers of India series. This is a standard biography of Albuquerque and is one of the most complete available in English. It is found in most libraries of the United States and is a scholarly chronicle of and commentary on Albuquerque's achievements.

Subrahmanyam, Sanjay, ed. *Sinners and Saints: The Successors of Vasco da Gama.* New York: Oxford University Press, 1998. Anthology of essays by international scholars detailing the history of Portuguese trade and missionary work in India from the beginning of the sixteenth century. Includes illustrations, map, bibliographic references.

SEE ALSO: Pêro da Covilhã; Bartolomeu Dias; Vasco da Gama; John II; Manuel I; Tomé Pires.
RELATED ARTICLES in *Great Events from History: The Renaissance & Early Modern Era, 1454-1600:* 1505-1515: Portuguese Viceroys Establish Overseas Trade Empire; 1511-c. 1515: Melaka Falls to the Portuguese.

MATEO ALEMÁN
Spanish writer

Mateo Alemán published the two parts of Guzmán de Alfarache, *one of the foundational texts of the picaresque genre. Not only was Alemán's novel one of the most popular works of its era, but it also influenced his contemporaries, such as Miguel de Cervantes and Francisco de Quevedo. Ultimately, the picaresque in general and Alemán's narrative style in particular continue to influence literature.*

BORN: September 28, 1547; Seville, Spain
DIED: c. 1614; Mexico
AREA OF ACHIEVEMENT: Literature

EARLY LIFE

Although the exact birth date of Mateo Alemán (mah-TAY-oh ahl-ay-MAHN) is not known, he was baptized on September 28, 1547. The future author was born to a medical doctor, Hernando Alemán, and his second wife, Juana de Enero. Both of Alemán's parents belonged to the Spanish New Christian population. In 1492, the Spanish Jewish population was given a difficult choice: convert to Catholicism or leave Spain. Those who remained and converted were called New Christians or *conversos*.

The New Christians were objects of a great deal of discrimination. Regulations prohibited New Christians from certain religious orders, excluded them from the most prestigious educational institutions, and prohibited their emigration to the New World. Furthermore, the Spanish Inquisition policed the religious practices of these inhabitants with particular vigor.

As historian Donald McGrady notes in *Mateo Alemán* (1968), the only details concerning Alemán's early education are from Alemán's own comments about it in his *Ortografía castellana* (pb. 1609; Castilian orthography), in which Alemán laments that his education included the detailed study of various styles of penmanship. Although the young Alemán studied to be a doctor at several universities and eventually completed his degree, he never practiced medicine. The years immediately after Alemán's college graduation established a pattern that would continue throughout his life: failed business dealings and incarceration for debt. In 1582, Alemán applied for a permit to emigrate to the Spanish colonies in the New World. Even though the author perjured himself and affirmed that he had no Jewish ancestors, his application was denied, most likely because of his New Christian origin.

LIFE'S WORK

Had Alemán lived in a different era, he might well have been a professional writer. Because he lived before such a profession existed, this was not the case. Throughout Alemán's adult life, he held a variety of government positions, including judge and accountant. Records show that Alemán also engaged in other business dealings, such as real estate ventures, to supplement his income. Yet, because he was imprisoned for debt at several points throughout his life, apparently none of these business transactions proved highly lucrative.

In 1599, Alemán published part 1 of the book that would become his masterpiece: *La vida y hechos del pícaro Guzmán de Alfarache* (best known as *Guzmán de Alfarache* in both Spanish and English; originally translated as *The Rogue: Or, The Life of Guzman de Alfarache*, 1622), the second work in the literary genre that would come to be called the picaresque. The anonymous 1553 *La vida de Lazarillo de Tormes y de sus fortunas y adversidades* (best known as *Lazarillo de Tormes* in both Spanish and English; originally translated as *Lazarillo: Or, The Excellent History of Lazarillo de Tormes, the Witty Spaniard*, 1653) was the first work in the new genre. Like all picaresque novels, *Guzmán de Alfarache*'s main character is a *pícaro*, a rogue, from the lower social strata. Prior to these texts, most literary protagonists were nobles. Also, the protagonist is an older first-person narrator, generally but not always male. Guzmán, in Alemán's novel, recounts the misdeeds of his youth in a fictitious autobiography. During the course of the narrative, the rogue travels to various locales in the company of a series of masters. This life of crime, trickery, and deceit critiques the hypocrisy of society.

At the narrative level, *Guzmán de Alfarache* embellished the standard picaresque plotline with interpolated novels, independent narratives not related to the main plotline, and sermons. In fact, the alternation between Guzmán's life of crime and religious discourse forms one of the most fascinating aspects of the text. As a result, critics frequently debate whether Guzmán's narrative actually preaches doctrine or whether his inclusion of moralizing discourse is another trick.

Despite the fact that the novel was a best-seller, the author apparently received little monetary remuneration. A cousin of Alemán's, Juan Bautista del Rosso, rescued the author from several financial scrapes in the early 1600's. Historian McGrady notes that since popular Renaissance texts were frequently reprinted in unauthorized (pirated) editions, an author's earnings generally did not reflect the commercial success of his or her work. Alemán's literary problems deepened in 1602 when an apocryphal continuation of *Guzmán de Alfarache* appeared under the pseudonym Mateo Luján de Sayavedra; however, Alemán's second part identifies the author of the spurious volume as Juan Martí. In 1604, Alemán continued Guzmán's adventures in his own second part, subtitled *Atalaya de la vida* (watchtower on human life).

As is the case with another renowned Spanish author, Miguel de Cervantes, critics speculate that Alemán's colorful life and travels inspired his literary production. Although life experience most likely motivated literary creativity in both authors, with regard to one of Alemán's works in particular, the 1604 *San Antonio de Padua*, this was certainly the case. During a 1591 trip to the port city of Cartagena, burning shrapnel from a cannon pelted Alemán in the head. Because the author credited Saint Anthony of Padua for his escape from fatal injury, he celebrated the saint's life in a biography.

In 1607, Alemán bribed an official to circumvent the official prohibition against New Christian emigration to the New World; however, concerns over piracy scrapped the fleet's voyage that year. When Alemán departed Spain in 1608, one of companions on the voyage to Mexico was the new archbishop of Mexico, Father García Guerra.

Once in Mexico, Alemán published a number of nonfictional works. As Alemán describes in his preface to the 1609 *Ortografía castellana*, he began the work in Spain but could not publish it on the peninsula because it was not yet finished. In the same year, Alemán wrote the prologue to Luis de Belmonte Bermúdez's *Vida del Padre Maestro Ignacio de Loyola* (life of the reverend fa-

ther Ignatius of Loyola). In 1613, Alemán wrote *Sucesos de D. Frai García Guerra* (*The Sucesos*, 1911), which narrated Alemán's former shipmate's arrival in Mexico, rise to viceroy of Mexico, and subsequent sudden death. The last reference to Alemán placed him in the small town of Chalco in 1614. The precise date of the author's death is not known.

SIGNIFICANCE

Alemán's biography embodies several of the most important historical tendencies of the Spanish Renaissance. Like many Spaniards of his era, Alemán sought to improve his economic position via emigration to the Americas. Furthermore, his status as a New Christian excluded him from the higher echelons of Spanish society.

Alemán's greatest legacy, however, is his novel *Guzmán de Alfarache*. Like the author's life, the text represents paradigmatic concerns of the era. While this picaresque novel harshly critiques social mores, it also moralizes. This combination of social criticism and religious values is called *desengaño* in Spanish, a virtually untranslatable term for disenchantment. This disdain for the world combined with religious motivation characterizes much of the literary production of the Spanish Renaissance. Yet, as Edward H. Friedman suggests, Guzmán's contradictory espousal of thievery and religious virtue forces the reader to decide between the two and interpret the text as either moralizing or entertaining. It is this ambiguity that continued to interest readers of later generations and that influences the course of literary production through the creation of a more complex narrative structure.

—Patricia W. Manning

FURTHER READING

Davis, Nina Cox. *Autobiography as Burla in the "Guzmán de Alfarache."* Lewisburg, Pa.: Bucknell University Press, 1991. Posits trickery as the fundamental meaning of the text. Discusses word choice in the James Mabbe 1622-1623 English translation.

_____. "Confidence and the *Corullero: Guzmán de Alfarache*." In *Conflicts of Discourse: Spanish Literature in the Golden Age*, edited by Peter W. Evans. New York: St. Martin's Press, 1990. Davis analyzes Guzmán's use of repentance to deceive.

Friedman, Edward H. "Insincere Flattery: Imitation and the Growth of the Novel." *Cervantes: Bulletin of the Cervantes Society of America* 20, no. 1 (2000): 99-114. Contextualizes *Guzmán de Alfarache* in the picaresque genre in Spain. Demonstrates that the spurious second part influences Alemán's second part.

Kamen, Henry. *The Spanish Inquisition: A Historical Revision*. 2d ed. New Haven, Conn.: Yale University Press, 1998. Excellent overview of the Spanish Inquisition. Chapter 6 analyzes the impact of the Spanish Inquisition on intellectual endeavors.

Kaplis-Hohwald, Laurie. "The Sermon as Literature in *Guzmán de Alfarache*." *Romance Quarterly* 48, no. 1 (Winter, 2001): 47-53. Supports the authenticity of Guzmán's religious conversion.

Leonard, Irving A. "Mateo Alemán in Mexico: A Document." *Hispanic Review* 17, no. 4 (1947): 316-330. Detailed biography of Alemán in Mexico. Includes transcriptions of archival material.

McGrady, Donald. *Mateo Alemán*. New York: Twayne, 1968. Accessible biography of Alemán that believes Alemán's life is antecedent for Guzmán's adventures. Includes notes, references, and bibliography.

_____. "A Pirated Edition of *Guzmán de Alfarache*: More Light on Mateo Alemán's Life." *Hispanic Review* 34, no. 4 (1966): 326-328. Concerns Alemán's lawsuit regarding a 1601 piracy of *Guzmán de Alfarache*.

Smith, Paul Julian. *Writing in the Margin: Spanish Literature of the Golden Age*. New York: Oxford University Press, 1988. Section three contains a highly informative overview of the picaresque novel.

SEE ALSO: Miguel de Cervantes; Saint Ignatius of Loyola.

RELATED ARTICLES in *Great Events from History: The Renaissance & Early Modern Era, 1454-1600:* 1492: Fall of Granada; 1492: Jews Are Expelled from Spain.

ALEXANDER VI
Italian pope (1492-1503)

Alexander VI's policies contributed to the growth of papal temporal power in the Papal States. A discriminating patron of the arts, he employed a number of noteworthy artists, including Pinturicchio and Michelangelo.

BORN: 1431; Játiva, Valencia (now in Italy)

DIED: August 18, 1503; Rome, Papal States (now in Italy)

ALSO KNOWN AS: Rodrigo de Borja y Doms (Spanish name); Rodrijo Borgia (Italian name)

AREAS OF ACHIEVEMENT: Religion and theology, government and politics, patronage of the arts

EARLY LIFE

Born Rodrigo de Borja y Doms (Borgia), the boy who was to become Pope Alexander VI was the nephew of Pope Calixtus III, who adopted him, showered him with church benefices, and sent him to the University of Bologna to study law. In 1456, Rodrigo was appointed a cardinal-deacon, and the following year he was made the vice chancellor of the Church, a lucrative post that he held until his own elevation to the Papacy in 1492.

Rodrigo's many benefices enabled him to live in great magnificence and to indulge himself in such pastimes as cardplaying and merrymaking. His youthful indiscretions prompted Pope Pius II to send a scathing letter of reproof in 1460 for his alleged scandalous misconduct at Siena sometime earlier. His ordination to the priesthood in 1468 did not cause him to change his immoral behavior. Sometime in the early 1470's, Rodrigo entered into an illicit relationship with the beautiful Vannozza dei Cattanei, who was to be the mother of four of his children, Juan, Cesare, Lucrezia, and Jofré. In spite of these moral failings, Rodrigo was appointed bishop of Porto in 1476 and made dean of the Sacred College in Rome. On August 11, 1492, he was elected pope by a bare two-thirds majority, amid charges, never substantiated, that he had bribed several cardinals to switch their votes in his favor. So worldly had the office of pope become by his time that there was little public criticism of his elevation to the See of Saint Peter, despite his reputation for moral irregularity. In fact, the Roman people held torchlight processions and erected triumphal arches to commemorate his election.

LIFE'S WORK

Described as a handsome and imposing figure, Pope Alexander brought considerable talent to his office. Francesco Guicciardini, a contemporary historian, noted that "in him were combined rare prudence and vigilance, mature reflection, marvelous power of persuasion, skill and capacity for the conduct of the most difficult affairs."

He began his pontificate by restoring order to Rome, which had been the scene of considerable violence, including more than two hundred assassinations, in the several years before Alexander's elevation. He divided the city into four districts, over each of which he placed a magistrate who was given plenary powers to maintain order. In the course of his pontificate, he subjugated the fractious Orsini and Colonna families, who had been troublesome elements in Roman politics for generations. In addition, he designated Tuesday of each week as a time for any man or woman in Rome to come before him personally to present his or her grievances.

As pope, Alexander advanced the interests of his own children, not only for their sakes but also as a means of strengthening papal political power. He betrothed his daughter Lucrezia to Giovanni Sforza in order to link the Borgia family with the powerful Sforza rulers of Milan. When this union ceased to be politically useful, Alexander annulled it and married Lucrezia to the son of the king of Naples. When Lucrezia's second husband was killed in 1501, Alexander arranged her marriage to Duke Alfonso I of Ferrara in the hope that it would further papal schemes in the Romagna. Favorite among his children, however, was his eldest son, Juan, the duke of Gandía, and Alexander provided richly for him until Juan was murdered in 1497, whereupon the pope then placed his fondest hopes in Cesare. Alexander encouraged Cesare to establish a powerful principality in the Romagna, the most troublesome part of the Papal States.

Italy was subjected to two French invasions while Alexander was pope. While the French kings had hereditary claims to both the Duchy of Milan and the Kingdom of Naples, as long as the Triple Alliance powers of Naples, Florence, and Milan had been united, a French effort to make good these claims seemed remote. By January of 1494, however, the Triple Alliance had collapsed.

Ludovico Sforza, the duke of Milan, finding himself politically isolated in Italy, attempted to ingratiate himself with the French king, Charles VIII, by encouraging him to invade Italy and claim the kingdom of Naples. Pope Alexander joined King Alfonso II of Naples, and Neapolitan troops were sent northward to block Charles's advance through the Papal States.

Alexander's position worsened when two of his enemies, Cardinals Giuliano della Rovere (the future Pope Julius II) and Ascanio Sforza secretly went to the advancing Charles and tried to persuade him to call a council that would put Alexander on trial and depose him. Alexander met with King Charles, and an agreement was reached whereby Charles was allowed to enter Rome on December 31. A month later, Charles set out for Naples. In March of 1495, with Charles in possession of Naples, Pope Alexander formed the League of Venice, also known as the Holy League, consisting of the empire, Spain, and all the major Italian states except Florence. Its main purpose was to drive the French from Italian soil, a goal achieved by the end of the year.

When Louis XII succeeded Charles VIII as king of France in 1498, he quickly began planning an invasion of Italy to lay claim to the duchy of Milan. Before executing this invasion, however, he dissolved the League of Venice by negotiating with Alexander, who agreed to remain neutral in return for Louis's assistance to Alexander's son Cesare in his efforts to conquer the Romagna. Louis invaded Milan in August of 1499, and by April of the fol-

Depiction of the poisoning of Alexander VI. (Library of Congress)

lowing year, he was firmly entrenched there. Louis then prepared for the conquest of Naples. King Ferdinand II also had claims to Naples, and Alexander arranged a settlement in November of 1500, whereby Naples would be partitioned between them, with Louis in control of the northern provinces and Ferdinand, the southern.

Meanwhile, Cesare, encouraged by the promise of the French king's friendship and assistance, waged vigorous war against the petty tyrants of the Romagna. His masterful and unscrupulous resourcefulness, coupled with his father's unstinting support, made Cesare remarkably successful. In April of 1501, Alexander made his son duke of the Romagna, and it appeared that a powerful state would soon be his. The death of Alexander in August, 1503, however, ended Cesare's successful course. Cesare was defeated by the forces of Pope Julius II, a bitter enemy of the Borgia family, and his lands were added to those of the Papacy. Julius would eventually make a modern Renaissance state of the papal holdings.

In 1495, Alexander first took official notice of the Dominican friar Girolamo Savonarola when he ordered the latter to cease preaching in Florence. Savonarola's fiery sermons, in which he spared neither prince nor pope, had led to the expulsion of the Medicis from Florence, and he had begun to denounce the political machinations of Alexander. Savonarola had defied the pope, asserting, "You err; you are not the Roman Church, you are a man and a sinner." Pope Alexander excommunicated Savonarola in May of 1497 and again ordered him to cease preaching. While Savonarola had many supporters in Florence, the pope had many enemies. In order to restore public order to the city, the magistrates arrested the monk in April of 1498; after papal commissioners officially pronounced him guilty of heresy, Savonarola was ordered hanged and burned in May of that year.

Among the more positive acts of Pope Alexander were his efforts to preserve peace between Spain and Portugal by proclaiming the Line of Demarcation in 1493, whereby he allocated the New World to Spain, and Africa and India to Portugal for the purposes of exploration. Though he was generally preoccupied with worldly affairs, Alexander did, on occasion, assert religious leadership. He was the first pope to give strong support to missionary activity in the New World. The beginnings of *Index librorum prohibitorum*, or the Index of Prohibited Books, can be traced to his pontificate. The Sapienza was considerably augmented under his direction. He proclaimed the year 1500 a jubilee year, and pilgrims flocked to Rome. That same year, Alexander preached a

crusade against the Turks, and, in a period of remorse and reflection after the death of his favorite son Juan, Alexander appointed a commission of cardinals that was charged with establishing proposals for extensive reform within the Church.

Despite the "moral miseries of the reign of Alexander VI," he was a splendid patron of the arts. Alexander employed architects and painters who beautified the region around the Vatican called the Borgo Nuovo. The artist Pinturicchio decorated many of the rebuilt and new Borgia apartments in the Vatican. His work included a famous portrait of Alexander kneeling in adoration of the miracle of the Resurrection. Churches and buildings were renovated, and new ones, such as the Tempietto, designed by Donato Bramante, were erected. It was under the patronage of Alexander that Michelangelo's *Pietà* was completed in 1499.

Pope Alexander and his son Cesare both became seriously ill at a banquet that they were attending in August of 1503. Although Cesare recovered, the pope died on August 18. While there were rumors that Alexander was the victim of poison that he had intended for certain of his enemies at the banquet, it is generally believed that he died as a result of a plague.

SIGNIFICANCE

Modern scholarship has tended to reject many of the more vicious moral crimes charged to Alexander VI. While few scholars have attempted and none has succeeded in exonerating him of corruption, immorality, and Machiavellian statecraft, it has been noted that many of the Renaissance popes were guilty of similar behavior. Although he did use the power and wealth of his office to advance the interests of his children, he was able to enhance papal power as well. The petty tyrannies in the Romagna that were destroyed by Cesare Borgia were never reestablished, and Julius II would be able to build a strong papal government in the Papal States on the foundation laid by Alexander's son. Although the political machinations practiced by Alexander hardly seem appropriate for the Vicar of Christ, the necessity to protect papal lands in Italy from encroachments by the empire, France, and Spain led many medieval and early modern popes to practice a diplomacy characterized by capriciousness and deceit.

Although some scholars might be willing to acknowledge that Alexander's failure as pope was in a measure counterbalanced by his patronage of the arts or that his encouragement of missions to the Americas more than compensated for his unwholesome example as a spiritual leader, most will not. Catholic scholars generally conclude, however, that "the dignity of Peter suffers no diminution even in an unworthy successor."

—*Paul E. Gill*

FURTHER READING

Chamberlin, Russell. *The Bad Popes*. Stroud, Gloucestershire, England: Sutton, 2003. Alexander is one of seven popes profiled in this study of papal corruption across the six hundred years leading up to the Reformation. Includes photographs, illustrations, genealogical tables, bibliographic references, and index.

De la Bedoyere, Michael. *The Meddlesome Friar: The Story of the Conflict Between Savonarola and Alexander VI*. London: Collins, 1957. A good discussion of the early lives of the two men, with an explanation of the political events that led to the conflict. Dispels many of the legends that have surrounded both men. A well-balanced reassessment of the much-maligned Alexander. This book is based on extensive documentary research, although there are no footnotes and no bibliography.

Ferrara, Orestes. *The Borgia Pope, Alexander the Sixth*. New York: Sheed & Ward, 1940. An attempt by a practicing lawyer to rehabilitate the character of Alexander and to refute the legends of his misdeeds and evil influence on the Church and the secular history of his time. While based on extensive research, the author's interpretation of evidence is often questionable. Must be read in conjunction with other works on Alexander.

Mallett, Michael. *The Borgias: The Rise and Fall of a Renaissance Dynasty*. New York: Barnes & Noble Books, 1969. Hailed as the best treatment of the Borgia family in any language. Presents Alexander as a representative personality of the Renaissance and places his achievements as well as his vices into a sound historical perspective. Discredits many of the legends concerning the Borgias. Includes extensive footnoting, an annotated bibliography, genealogies, and maps.

Pastor, Ludwig. *The History of the Popes from the Close of the Middle Ages*. Vols. 5 and 6. Reprint. Wilmington, N.C.: Consortium, 1978. Much of both of these volumes in this classic, monumental history of the modern Papacy is devoted to the pontificate of Alexander. In part based on archival material not available to earlier scholars, Pastor's account is well balanced and strongly documented. While acknowledging the merits of Alexander's cultural patronage, this account is critical of Alexander's failure as a spiritual leader. Includes an extensive bibliography, much of which is not in English.

Pellegrini, Marco. "A Turning-Point in the History of the Factional System in the Sacred College: The Power of the Pope and Cardinals in the Age of Alexander VI." In *Court and Politics in Papal Rome, 1492-1700*, edited by Gianvittorio Signorotto and Maria Antonietta Visceglia. New York: Cambridge University Press, 2002. Close and detailed study of the institutional mechanisms of power and the ways in which it was exercised within the Sacred College. Analyzes specific shifts in the balance of power and their consequences for Alexander's papacy. Includes bibliographic references and index.

DUKE OF ALVA
Spanish diplomat and military leader

One of the greatest European soldiers and diplomats of the sixteenth century, Alva fought for and represented the Habsburg emperor Charles V and his son King Philip II of Spain.

BORN: October 29, 1507; Piedrahita, Spain
DIED: December 11, 1582; Lisbon, Portugal
ALSO KNOWN AS: Fernando Álvarez de Toledo; third duke of Alba; the Iron Duke
AREAS OF ACHIEVEMENT: Diplomacy, military

EARLY LIFE

Fernando Álvarez de Toledo, the third duke of Alva, was descended from one of the most illustrious Spanish families. Alva's father, Garcia, was killed in 1510 in Tunis in battle with the Moors. Alva's grandfather Fadrique, the second duke of Alva, gave him a Humanistic education and nurtured in him a great fascination with the martial arts. By 1534, Fernando (the "great duke" of Alva, as he has commonly been called), had caught the eye of the Habsburg emperor Charles V of Austria (Charles I of Spain), who had visited him in that year at the ducal palace in Alva de Tormes near Salamanca. The Alva holdings consisted of some three thousand acres, a considerable block of western Castile.

In 1535, the duke was chosen for military service by the emperor and participated with him in battles in Tunis. In the same year, Charles decided that he would have to take action against French invasions in Italy. In the ensuing campaign, in which Alva had his first independent field command, he revealed a mastery of the art of war that left an indelible impression on the emperor. Thus, by the age of twenty-eight, Alva had developed a close working relationship with Charles, who increasingly called on him for his advice and participation in military and diplomatic matters. In 1542, he brilliantly repelled an attempted French invasion of Spain at the Battle of Perpignan, and he was involved in the negotiations that led to the 1544 Treaty of Crépy. Conflicts between the two countries had produced inconclusive results, and among the provisions of the treaty, Charles was to cede either Milan or the Netherlands to French control.

In view of his later experiences in the Low Countries, it is one of the great ironies of history that Alva presented cogent geopolitical arguments for maintaining Milan and ceding the Netherlands. Indeed, Alva advocated the complete abandonment of the Low Countries. Neverthe-less, Charles, preoccupied with Germany, decided in favor of keeping the Netherlands.

LIFE'S WORK

By his late thirties, Alva had developed into a somber and forbidding man. Lean and tall, of sallow complexion and prominent nose, he dressed well but not ostentatiously, ate and drank moderately. Although of a fiery and arrogant disposition, he seems to have kept iron control of himself in dealing with others. Alva's only known sexual escapade occurred in 1527 and resulted in the birth of an illegitimate son, whom the duke acknowledged and had educated as a gentleman. In 1529, Alva married his cousin Maria Enríquez de Gúzman. The couple had four children, three of whom survived to adulthood. Perhaps Alva's most striking characteristic was his fervent devotion to Catholicism and his distinct aversion to "infidels" and "heretics"—Muslims and Protestants.

In 1546, war broke out between Charles and the Protestants in his domains in Germany. He immediately called on Alva to prepare for the coming battles. In 1547, the duke cemented his reputation as a military leader with his victory at the crucial Battle of Mühlberg. There was universal agreement that the triumph there, openly acknowledged by Charles, over forces led by John of Saxony was the result of Alva's brilliant tactical maneuvers. As a consequence, Alva became a powerful courtier at the imperial court, and Charles later counseled his son Philip II to honor and favor him—though circumspectly—and to consult him in matters of war and statecraft. He added that he considered the duke to be the best person available in such matters.

Sometime before his death in 1558, Charles retired and divided his empire between his brother Ferdinand and his son Philip. Ferdinand was awarded the imperial title of emperor and given the Habsburg lands in Austria and Germany. Philip was given all the rest, including Spain, Italy, and the Low Countries. In 1554, French forces again posed a threat to Philip's inherited territories in Italy, and he dispatched an army under the command of Alva to defeat them.

The Italian Wars (1554-1557) began with Alva under severe disadvantages: unpaid and disaffected troops, lack of supplies, and scheming enemies at Philip's court. Alva surmounted all these difficulties. A devout Catholic, he eventually found himself in the position of having to invade the Papal Territories in Italy in order to achieve victory, but he was able to negotiate a face-saving peace for and with the pope. Thus, through a combination of military and diplomatic finesse, he solved a delicate situation with the pope without sacrificing Spanish interests. Alva was most active in negotiating the Treaty of Cateau-Cambrésis, which ended the Italian Wars, delineated the Spanish relationship with the Papacy, and served to settle various issues between Spain and France.

The most troublesome of the Spanish possessions was the Low Countries, particularly the northern part, the Netherlands. An underlying problem in dealing with the Low Countries was that they were not homogenous. They consisted of a patchwork of differing and conflicting religions, languages, and classes. Previous attempts by Charles to create a viable government had largely failed. Taxes were levied, but with poor results. Various Protestant denominations—Lutherans, Anabaptists, and Calvinists—found the busy mercantile cities of the north places of refuge and profit. The stronghold of the Catholic Church was located in the south, but the nomination and investiture of its hierarchy was effectively controlled by the great nobles. To devout Catholics such as Philip and Alva, the reform of both church and state in the Low Countries was an obvious imperative.

By the summer of 1566, overt opposition to Spanish authority constituted a serious rebellion. Alva counseled Philip himself to go to suppress it. At first Philip agreed, but he then reversed himself. He decided that a surrogate should suppress the revolt by harsh measures, directed particularly against Protestants, and that he would then follow, which he did not. A reluctant Alva, therefore, was sent on a fourfold mission: to establish a strong military presence; to punish those responsible for earlier disorders; to set up and enforce an effective system of taxation; and to restore and strengthen religious unity.

In 1567, Alva moved some fifteen thousand troops and auxiliaries—far fewer than he had requested—into the Low Countries. The garrisons in major cities were maintained and strengthened and local militias were disbanded. Several rebel leaders were imprisoned or executed, and a Council of Blood, as it was called by the insurgents, tried and ordered the execution of some one thousand people. Alva's attempt to impose a tax on sales was a complete failure. Quite successful, however, was his reformation of the Catholic clergy in the Low Countries. Thousands, most notably the future leader of the Dutch struggle for independence, Prince William of Orange (William the Silent), fled to neighboring countries, where they proceeded to plot against Alva and his forces. It is against this background from 1567 to 1573 that a vir-

Duke of Alva. (Library of Congress)

tual civil war developed in which cities and towns were taken and retaken by the opposing forces. Meanwhile, back at the royal court, there were allegations that Alva's harsh policies had made the situation worse. In 1573, Philip replaced Alva as commander, and the duke was returned to Madrid.

On his return, Alva was put under virtual house arrest for months as the result of these events and continuing court intrigues against him. It is significant, however, that when the next important emergency in Spanish affairs arose—the conflict over Philip's claim to the Portuguese throne in 1580—he turned to Alva to mount and carry on a war to resolve the crisis. Although the duke is said to have complained at the time that he was being sent in chains to subjugate a kingdom, the seventy-two-year-old took up his last campaign. Profiting from his experience in the Low Countries, where he had not been adequately supported, Alva asked for and was provided with forty thousand troops and ample supplies. More lenient in dealing with the Portuguese insurgents, probably in part because they were all Catholics, Alva by 1582 had reduced the countryside and captured Lisbon, the capital. The erstwhile claimant to the throne fled into exile,

Philip was acknowledged as the Portuguese ruler, and Alva governed in his name. In December of that year, however, the old duke succumbed to an undiagnosed disease and died.

SIGNIFICANCE

At an early age, the duke of Alva became a leading figure at the court of Charles V, and he continued to influence the policies of Philip II at the time when Spain was at the zenith of its power. He was relied on by both monarchs for advice and active conduct of military and diplomatic missions, often of a sensitive nature. For example, the duke played the leading role in the delicate arrangements leading to the marriage of Philip to Queen Mary I of England in 1554 and in 1559 to Elizabeth of Valois, daughter of Henry IV of France. In 1558, he single-handedly negotiated the seemingly impossible settlement whereby the city of Calais was transferred from English to French control.

Had Alva succeeded in resolving the problems facing Spanish rule in the Low Countries, the history of Western Europe would have been quite different. The failure was not completely his, however, as he was undermined by intrigues at the Spanish court, lacked adequate support, and from the outset was permitted and even encouraged by Philip to follow a harsh and repressive policy, particularly against Protestants. Still, at critical junctures he could have exercised more discretion and moderation, and he has been strongly censured over the years for the excesses of his governance of the Low Countries. On balance, though, Alva can truly be said to have been indispensable for more than half a century to two of the most powerful rulers of Renaissance Europe, and, with one exception, to have successfully advanced their causes and that of Roman Catholicism.

—*Jean Moore Kiger*

FURTHER READING

Elliott, John H. *Imperial Spain, 1469-1716*. Reprint. New York: Penguin, 1990. A survey that provides considerable insight into the world in which Alva operated. Pays particular attention to warfare of the time.

Kamen, Henry. *Empire: How Spain Became a World Power, 1492-1763*. New York: HarperCollins, 2003. Wide-ranging portrayal of the Spanish Empire emphasizes the multicultural, heterogeneous nature, not merely of Spain's holdings but also of its colonizing forces. Looks at the crucial roles played by Hungarians, Italians, Netherlanders, and Muslims in the military expansion and maintenance of Spain's global holdings. Includes illustrations, maps, bibliographic references, index.

Maltby, William S. *Alba: A Biography of Fernando Álvarez de Toledo, Third Duke of Alba, 1507-1582*. Berkeley: University of California Press, 1983. The best biography in English on Alva; an entertaining and objective account. Reflects exhaustive research on all aspects of Alva's life and career. Includes a "Notes on Sources" section that provides a fine description and location of all materials used in the work.

Motley, John Lothrop. *The Rise of the Dutch Republic: A History*. 3 vols. Reprint. New York: E. P. Dutton, 1950. A thoroughly researched and well-written history of the revolt in the Netherlands. Distinctly biased against Spain, however, and uncompromisingly harsh in its criticism of Alva's attempts to suppress the revolt.

Pierson, Peter. *Philip II of Spain*. London: Thames and Hudson, 1975. Concentrates on the political aspects of Philip's career and details Alva's diplomatic relationship to the monarch.

Ruiz, Teofilo F. *Spanish Society, 1400-1600*. New York: Longman, 2001. A detailed and diverse look at all aspects of Spanish cultural history in the fifteenth and sixteenth centuries. Includes extensive discussions of the courts of Charles V and Philip II, as well as descriptions of everyday life and the important values and traditions that defined Alba's Spain. Includes map, bibliographic references, index.

Thompson, I. A. A. *War and Government in Hapsburg Spain, 1560-1620*. London: Athlone Press, 1976. Describes the effect of wars on the government in Spain and discusses Alva's role in the interaction of the two.

PEDRO DE ALVARADO
Spanish conquistador

Alvarado was a key subordinate to Hernán Cortés in the sixteenth century Spanish exploration and conquest of Mexico and Central America.

BORN: 1485; Badajoz, Extremadura, Castile (now in Spain)
DIED: 1541; in or near Guadalajara, New Spain (now in Mexico)
AREAS OF ACHIEVEMENT: Exploration, military

EARLY LIFE

Pedro de Alvarado (pay-DROH day ahl-vah-RAHD-oh) was born in the city of Badajoz in the Spanish province of Estremadura, an area that had furnished Spain with many professional soldiers in the country's centuries-long war to oust the Arab invaders from the Iberian Peninsula. He was descended from a family that belonged to the minor nobility, and he played an active role in Spain's battle against the Arabs. Like most of the nobles of his time, he learned little of such skills as reading and writing. Alvarado knew how to use a sword and was an excellent horseman, but he had few other marketable talents. The defeat of the Arab armies therefore left him, like many of his countrymen, unemployed.

The voyages of Christopher Columbus opened the Western Hemisphere to both exploration and exploitation by the Spaniards. Alvarado—in the company of his four brothers, Jorge, Gonzalo, Gómez, and Juan—joined the flood of soldiers who saw this new frontier as an opportunity for both wealth and advancement. In 1510, the brothers emigrated to Cuba.

In 1511, Alvarado enlisted in an expedition headed by Juan de Grijalva; the expedition was sent from Cuba to explore the Yucatán. Although Grijalva had problems controlling his young lieutenant, he regarded him highly enough to send him back to Cuba carrying the spoils of the venture. Alvarado's tendency to go his own way without regard for his orders would prove to be a constant problem throughout his subsequent military career.

LIFE'S WORK

After his initial exposure to the newly explored territories of North America, Alvarado became one of the four chief lieutenants to Hernán Cortés during the conquest of central Mexico in the years 1518 to 1521. Subsequently, Cortés delegated to his subordinate the responsibility for bringing much of Central America into the Spanish colonial empire.

Alvarado joined Cortés's expedition in 1518 at the Cuban port of Trinidad, where Cortés had begun the process of recruiting followers. Cortés also undertook the acquisition of military stores and provisions and the overhaul of the ships that he planned to use in the voyage to the mainland.

The relationship between the two adventurers would remain a mercurial one throughout the many years of their association. Alvarado, headstrong and independent, was nevertheless an outstanding leader and soldier. Although Cortés regarded Alvarado as one of his top lieutenants, he would later have cause to regret giving command of certain undertakings to his undisciplined subordinate.

Alvarado often behaved unpredictably. On one occasion, he interfered with Cortés's scheduled execution of a condemned soldier, cutting the noose from the unfortunate's neck as he stood on the scaffold. He could also be generous; reportedly, he once forgave a debt of 20,000 ducats (equivalent to about $80,000) owed him by a fellow officer. His baser nature, however, led him to commit such heinous acts as burning prisoners alive, turning ferocious dogs on unarmed Mexican Indians, and assaulting the new bride of an indigenous chief. Throughout his career, moreover, he regarded the property of colonized peoples as his for the taking.

Cortés's expedition consisted of 11 vessels, 110 sailors, 553 soldiers, and 16 horses. With that force, Cortés launched a successful campaign that seized control of all Mexico and destroyed the Aztec Empire in the short span of three years. The Spaniards were ruthless in their dealings with Mexican Indians. They slaughtered those who opposed them, and they exploited mercilessly those who sought to placate them. The invaders not only seized all the wealth that they could extract from indigenous peoples but also demanded that they abjure their ancient religions and accept Christianity.

Although the Spanish force was small, their firearms, body armor, horses, and fighting dogs gave them such an overwhelming advantage over the armies of the indigenous peoples that resistance proved futile. Moreover, the guileful Cortés succeeded in allying his troops with powerful indigenous peoples' nations such as the Tlaxcalans, who hated the brutal Aztec regime. The Tlaxcalans feared and admired Alvarado. Because of his imposing physique and flaming red hair, they called him Tonatiuh, or "child of the sun."

Accompanied by his Tlaxcalan allies, Cortés marched on Tenochtitlán (now Mexico City), the Aztec capital, destroying the armies he encountered in the intervening countryside. The Aztec emperor Montezuma II, consumed by doubt about the origin of the Spanish forces and believing that perhaps they were gods, chose to bargain with Cortés, hoping to bribe the latter to leave the country. Once in the capital, however, the Spaniards pursued their usual policy of demanding both riches and the destruction of all the local deities. Moreover, the resourceful Cortés took Montezuma prisoner in order better to control the populace.

Although the Aztec capital was secure, Cortés faced a new problem. His enemy Diego Velázquez, the governor of Cuba, had organized an army three times the size of Cortés's forces to follow Cortés into Mexico and take him prisoner. The governor had become jealous of Cortés's success and planned to take over conquered Mexico himself.

Leaving Alvarado in charge in Tenochtitlán, Cortés

Pedro de Alvarado. (Library of Congress)

not only defeated the superior pursuing force but also persuaded the majority of its soldiers to join his own army. Meanwhile, Alvarado had created a problem for his chief by slaughtering a number of Aztec nobles during a religious festival. The outraged Aztecs began a massive rebellion.

Cortés, his army now strengthened by new recruits, marched quickly west once more, reentering the capital and rescuing the hard-pressed Alvarado and his small contingent. Nevertheless, the Aztecs continued their attacks despite heavy losses. Even Montezuma's appeal to his countrymen to lay down their arms failed and they killed their emperor as he tried to address them. Recognizing his peril and running short of food and ammunition, Cortés decided to retreat to the coast.

What followed proved to be a harrowing adventure for the Spaniards. The night of the retreat came to be known as La Noche Triste (the sad night). Cortés, in a prodigious effort, managed to extricate his forces, although the Aztecs killed and captured many. At one point, Alvarado, commanding the rear guard, found himself alone and surrounded by his enemies on the bank of a canal. He thrust his lance firmly into the water below and vaulted to the canal's opposite side. The jump that he made was so impressive that even today the spot is called Salto de Alvarado (Alvarado's Leap).

Arriving once more at Veracruz, Cortés rested, rearmed, and assembled an even greater force for the recapture of the Aztec capital. He stopped short of the city and built several brigantines to ensure his control of the city's waterways. The Spaniards attacked the Aztec defenders and reconquered the city in the face of suicidal resistance. Estimates of the Aztec casualties from battle, hunger, and disease ranged from 120,000 to 240,000. Some 30,000 to 70,000 survived, and the victorious Spaniards allowed them to leave the ruined capital.

Spain's emperor, Charles V, named Cortés a marquis and granted him extensive holdings throughout New Spain, as central Mexico was known. At the same time, the emperor designated new civil authorities in the colony, and Cortés never again held the political power that he had achieved as a conqueror. Nevertheless, in his continued capacity as captain general, Cortés did authorize Alvarado to move south to subjugate most of Central America. Alvarado began the invasion of Central America in 1523. He adopted the same techniques employed by the Spaniards in the Mexican campaign: the slaughter of any indigenous peoples offering resistance and the exploitation of those who did not. He conquered what today is Guatemala, El Salvador, and northern Nicaragua.

Arriving at the kingdom of Cuzcatlán, now El Salvador, Alvarado emulated the behavior of Cortés at Tenochtitlán. Welcomed by the country's king, Atlacatl, and his nobles, furnished with sumptuous quarters and provisions, the Spanish leader repaid this hospitality by seizing the leaders and holding them hostage. When forced to retrace his steps temporarily, Alvarado had Atlacatl and his contingent slaughtered. Although the Spaniards found some gold, the area offered merely a fraction of the wealth that they had acquired in Mexico. Only the Aztec Empire possessed such fabulous wealth.

Named governor and captain general of the kingdom of Guatemala by Charles V, Alvarado turned to other means to build wealth. Recognizing the value of their labor as a commodity, the new governor sought to stop the wholesale slaughter of the Central American Indians. Charles V granted Alvarado the right to build a fleet and explore the southern seas. The new governor also attempted to enter Peruvian ports with his ships and to share in the wealth of the Inca Empire, but he was denied entry by the Spanish authorities already established there.

His final campaign occurred in northern Mexico, at that time known as New Galicia. Asked by the king's viceroy in Mexico City to come to the aid of beleaguered Spanish forces in that territory, the irrepressible Alvarado moved north and launched an attack against the Native Indians in mountain country during a heavy rain. During the engagement, his horse lost its footing and rolled over Alvarado, killing him. At the time, Alvarado was fifty-six years old.

SIGNIFICANCE

The Spanish conquistadores, soldiers such as Pedro de Alvarado, Hernán Cortés, and Francisco Pizarro, invaded and conquered what is now Mexico, Central America, and Peru, for both wealth and prestige. Seasoned fighting men, they and their followers overcame tremendous odds to achieve their victories. In the process, they killed thousands of the indigenous peoples who opposed them. Thousands more died from the hunger and disease that resulted from the warfare itself. The Spaniards rationalized their behavior on the grounds that they brought Christianity to pagan peoples. Priests accompanied every expedition to convert the indigenous to the Christian faith. In their eagerness to spread the tenets of their religion, they also aided in the destruction of the existing indigenous cultures.

Alvarado, a brave, accomplished, if somewhat erratic military man, personified the Spanish conquistador. His cruelty and rapaciousness helped to create the anti-Spanish "Black Legend," the reputation for brutality that the country earned not only in the eyes of the oppressed peoples of the New World but also among other European nations.

—Carl Henry Marcoux

FURTHER READING

Collis, Maurice. *Cortés and Montezuma*. New York: New Directions, 1999. In-depth description of the meeting between Cortés and Montezuma and the subsequent conquest of Mexico, with significant discussion of Alvarado's role, especially in the massacre of Atlacatl and his nobles. Includes illustrations, map, index.

Díaz, Bernal. *The Conquest of New Spain*. London: Penguin Books, 1963. An autobiography of one of the soldiers who accompanied the Cortés expedition, a brother-in-arms of Pedro de Alvarado.

Holmes, Maurice G. *From New Spain by Sea to the Californias, 1519-1668*. Glendale, Calif.: Arthur H. Clark, 1963. Covers the final years of Alvarado's military economic, and political career, including his attempts to open up new areas for trade overseas.

Kelly, John Eoghan. *Pedro de Alvarado, Conquistador*. Princeton, N.J.: Princeton University Press, 1932. Reprint. Port Washington, N.Y.: Kennikat Press, 1971. One of the few complete biographies of Alvarado available in English.

Prescott, William H. *The Conquest of Mexico*. New York: Bantam Books, 1964. A complete, detailed history of the Cortés expedition and the role that Alvarado played in it.

White, Jon Manchip. *Cortés and the Downfall of the Aztec Empire*. 2d ed. New York: Carroll & Graf, 1996. Discusses Alvarado's role in Cortés's expedition and the effects of his actions on Spanish colonial history. Includes illustrations, maps, bibliography, index.

Woodward, Ralph Lee, Jr. *Central America: A Nation Divided*. New York: Oxford University Press, 1976. Chapter 2, "The Kingdom of Guatemala," provides an overview of Alvarado's efforts to subjugate the inhabitants of Central America and add that area to Spain's empire.

SEE ALSO: Vasco Núñez de Balboa; Álvar Núñez Cabeza de Vaca; Charles V; Christopher Columbus;

Francisco Vásquez de Coronado; Hernán Cortés; Cuauhtémoc; Juan Sebastián de Elcano; Ferdinand II and Isabella I; Doña Marina; Pedro Menéndez de Avilés; Montezuma II; The Pinzón Brothers; Francisco Pizarro; Juan Ponce de León.

RELATED ARTICLES in *Great Events from History: The Renaissance & Early Modern Era, 1454-1600:* Beginning 1519: Smallpox Kills Thousands of Indigenous Americans; April, 1519-August, 1521: Cortés Conquers Aztecs in Mexico.

AMINA SARAUNIYA ZAZZUA
Queen of Hausaland (r. c. 1576-c. 1610)

An able military leader, Amina greatly expanded the territory of Zazzua to its largest size by conquering and seizing neighboring lands, which expanded trade and enabled Zazzua to become one of the most prosperous and well-known states in the western Sudan.

BORN: c. 1532; Zazzua, Hausaland (now Zaria, Nigeria)
DIED: c. 1610; Zazzua
ALSO KNOWN AS: Amina the Great; Queen Amina; Amina of Zaria; Sarauniya Aminatu
AREAS OF ACHIEVEMENT: Government and politics, warfare and conquest, military

EARLY LIFE

Not much is known about the early life of Amina (ah-MEE-nah). The seven Hausa states of what is now Nigeria did not keep written records, but rather maintained their cultural history through a rich oral tradition. Many of the oral histories and king lists (a chronological but not archaeological record of reigns) are quite consistent and supported by modern scholarship, but precise dates and other details are impossible to verify.

Nevertheless, it is clear that Amina was descended from a family of rulers. Her grandfather was Sarkin Zazzua Nohir, king of Zazzua until his death around 1535. He was succeeded by a brother, who died after only a year. The next to rule was Bakwa of Turunku, Amina's mother, who became the first Hausa *sarauniya*, or queen, in many centuries of remembered history. Nothing is known about Amina's father. According to tradition, there was a great affection between Amina and her grandfather the king, and as a toddler, she sat on his lap while he conducted his official business. From a young age, then, Amina began to understand the workings of politics and the logistics of warfare.

At the age of sixteen, Bakwa gave Amina, her oldest child, the title *magajiya*, or heir to the throne. In this position, Amina was drawn closer into the political and military life of the state, as she was responsible for administering it and meeting in daily councils. Though Bakwa was not interested in warfare or conquest, Amina was fascinated by both, and she learned all she could. Bakwa's reign, remembered mostly for the fervor of its ceremonial singing and dancing, ended with her death around 1566. She was succeeded by her younger brother Karama, who immediately turned to war and expansion. One of his best and most eager warriors was his niece Amina.

LIFE'S WORK

According to the oral histories, Amina was brave and skilled in battle. Refusing all suitors, who were eager to marry the *magajiya*, she devoted her energies to warfare. Already wealthy because of her mother's inheritance, she amassed a greater fortune by seizing slaves and booty as the Zazzua conquered new territory. When Karama died around 1576, Amina was chosen to be *sarauniya*, the new queen. Within months of her appointment, Amina led her people to war again, and it is said that her mind was on battle for the rest of her life.

Throughout the sixteenth century, the seven Hausa states had battled each other, expanding and contracting their borders through a series of wars. Shortly after Amina became queen, neighboring states Borno and Kano indicated their intentions to attack Zazzua, while at the same time, another neighbor, Songhai, showed signs of collapse. Amina seized on this complicated situation as an opportunity to undertake a massive campaign to expand Zazzua. Her successes were dazzling and became the stuff of legend. When Amina conquered part of Nupeland, the king of Nupe sent her either a one-time payment or an annual tribute of forty eunuchs and ten thousand kola nuts, making Amina the first Hausa ruler to possess these impressive signs of wealth and power. Gradually, as she conquered more states, she received great amounts of tribute, including slaves, horses, leather, and kola nuts. Amina continued to expand her domain until Zazzua was the largest of the Hausa states and Amina the mightiest ruler.

As Amina's territory increased, she established strategically spaced commercial centers, which operated independently but maintained a feudal relationship to the queen. These commercial cities made it possible to hold land far from the capital of Zaria and also to trade farther afield, increasing the strength and the wealth of Zazzua. As Zazzua people migrated to these distant cities, the culture's influence expanded accordingly. Amina's primary goal was to have more land not for its own sake but to guarantee that her people could travel safely to conduct trade with more distant civilizations. Zazzua became the center of north-south trade across the Sahara Desert, and east-west trade across the Sudan.

Amina herself was constantly on the move during her three-decade reign. Tradition says that she was never at home for more than three months at a time once she became queen. At her insistence, protective walls were built around any town or encampment she stayed at for any length of time. After she departed for the next campaign, the security offered by the walls encouraged more migrants to settle within them, and small encampments became cities. Fragments of many of these walls are still standing, known through the Hausa region as *ganuwar Amina*, or Amina's walls. A Hausa proverb still in use labels venerable people or objects as *wane ya cika takama da tsufa kamar ganuwar Amina* (proud and old as Amina's walls).

Amina inspired loyalty and pride among her subjects, and although she must have had trusted advisers, she invariably traveled herself to witness firsthand any difficulties in her land. Stories about her private life are conflicting: Some say she never married and others that she married many times. When she died around 1610, she left no heirs.

SIGNIFICANCE

Amina is remembered in Nigeria as one of the great queens of old, important because she ruled a generally patriarchal society and was accepted because of her firmness and military strength. Following her mother, Bakwa, Amina was only the second female ruler in recorded history of what is now called Nigeria.

Nigerians speak of her, in the Songhai language, as *Amina, yar Bakwa ta san rana:* Amina, the daughter of Bakwa, a woman as strong as a man. Her accomplishments, however, extend far beyond showing that a woman could rule capably. She increased the size of her state to its greatest size in history and built cities and walls that stand to this day. The earthen walls that she de-

signed were so effective as fortifications that neighboring states also adopted their use.

—Cynthia A. Bily

FURTHER READING

Abubakr, Sa'ad. "Queen Amina of Zaria." In *Nigerian Women in Historical Perspective*, edited by Bolanle Awe. Lagos, Nigeria: Sankore/Bookcraft, 1992. This volume, intended for a Nigerian audience, offers the stories of Nigerian women's contributions to the nation's development. The chapter on Queen Amina, written by a historian, draws on oral traditions for much of its information.

Clay, Denise. "Amina Sarauniya Zazzua." In *Heroines: Remarkable and Inspiring Women: An Illustrated Anthology of Essays by Women Writers*, edited by Sara Hunt. New York: Crescent Books, 1995. The tone of this collection of fifty brief biographies is inspirational, as it seeks to define heroism and show women's capabilities. The illustrated biography of Amina summarizes her accomplishments in clear and compelling language.

Davidson, Basil. *West Africa Before the Colonial Era: A History to 1850*. New York: Addison-Wesley, 1998. Davidson, a leading historian of precolonial Africa, describes several kingdoms and cultures in this accessible volume. His analysis places Amina and the Zazzua in the broad context of a complex region, and the text is illustrated with maps and a time line.

Mernissi, Fatima. *The Forgotten Queens of Islam*. Minneapolis: University of Minnesota Press, 1997. Mernissi, a well-regarded scholar of the Qur'ān, tells the story of Amina and fourteen other Islamic female rulers, placing them within the context of the Muslim world today. She argues that the one-sided view of Muslim women held by many in the West does not take into account the rich history of women such as Amina.

Ogunyemi, Wale. *Queen Amina of Zazzua*. Ibadan, Nigeria: University Press, 1999. A dramatization interpreting the life of Amina, by an award-winning Nigerian playwright. In this version of Amina's life, she is brought down in battle through the forces of sexism and disloyalty; her own success leads to her fall.

SEE ALSO: Leo Africanus; Askia Daud; Muḥammad ibn ʿAbd al-Maghīlī; Mohammed I Askia.

RELATED ARTICLES in *Great Events from History: The Renaissance & Early Modern Era, 1454-1600:* 1460-1600: Rise of the Akan Kingdoms; 1500's: Trans-Saharan Trade Enriches Akan Kingdoms.

ANDREA DEL SARTO
Italian painter

Andrea del Sarto is one of the most important Florentine painters of the early sixteenth century. His work was clearly inspired by the classical ideals of the central Italian High Renaissance, particularly by Raphael and Leonardo da Vinci, but his pupils were to become the creators of the anticlassical style later known as mannerism.

BORN: July 16, 1486; Florence (now in Italy)
DIED: September 28, 1530; Florence
ALSO KNOWN AS: Andrea d'Agnolo (given name)
AREA OF ACHIEVEMENT: Art

EARLY LIFE

Andrea del Sarto (ahn-DRAY-ah dehl-SAHR-to), the son of Agnolo di Francesco Lanfranchi and Constanza, was born Andrea d'Agnolo in Florence, probably one of twins, for the surviving documents indicate that Agnolo di Francesco's two sons, Andrea and Domenico, were both baptized on July 17, 1486, the day after their birth.

Andrea's great-grandfather had been an agricultural laborer, his grandfather a linen weaver, and his father a tailor (*un sarto*), and for that reason Andrea was given the nickname of Andrea del Sarto.

Andrea left school at the age of seven to work for a goldsmith before beginning his training as a painter, first in the studio of the little-known Andrea di Salvi Barile and later with Piero di Cosimo. It has also been persuasively argued by modern critics that Andrea must have studied with the technically accomplished Raffaellino del Garbo, or at least been strongly influenced by his work.

On December 11, 1508, Andrea was matriculated in the guild of Florentine painters. About two years earlier, he had entered into a partnership with Francesco di Cristoforo Bigi, known as Franciabigio. The two artists shared a studio and were later joined by the young sculptor Jacopo Sansovino, who had come from Rome.

LIFE'S WORK

Two fresco cycles in Florence are the major works of the collaboration of Andrea and Franciabigio. In the forecourt of the Church of Santissima Annunziata in Florence, they continued the fresco cycle begun in the fifteenth century that illustrated the life of Saint Filippo Benizzi and scenes from the life of the Virgin. The scenes from the life of Saint Filippo Benizzi, the chief saint of the Servite Order (of which the Santissima Annunziata is the mother church), were Andrea's first fresco commissions and show him experimenting with a variety of compositions. Two of the scenes are loosely organized and recall the pictorial ideals of the preceding century, but in the *Saint Curing the Possessed Woman*, *The Death of the Saint*, and the *Miracles Performed by the Relics of the Saint*, dated 1510, Andrea introduced rigidly organized, symmetrical compositions that reveal his debt to Leonardo da Vinci, while his handling of color, light, and shade shows how much he admired the work of Raphael. The finest work in this cycle is the last one that Andrea painted, the *Birth of the Virgin* (1514). In this remarkable work, which marks the beginning of his artistic maturity, the severity of the earlier scenes has given way to a more flexible and subtly harmonious type of composition. One can see in this work how completely Andrea had absorbed the pictorial ideals of the High Renaissance.

The two artists also collaborated in a commission they received from the Florentine Compagnia dello Scalzo, a secular confraternity. The oratory of the compagnia was located not far from the Church of San Marco, and the frescoes by Andrea del Sarto and Franciabigio, which are still extant, are in what was once the cloister. The subjects are scenes from the life of Saint John the Baptist and the Cardinal Virtues. These frescoes are executed in grisaille, that is, in varying shades of gray. Although they were probably begun as early as 1511, Andrea continued to work on them from time to time until 1526. Ten of the scenes are by Andrea, who also painted *The Cardinal Virtues*, while two are by Franciabigio. The Scalzo frescoes are among the finest examples of the High Renaissance style in Florence. Each scene is elegantly composed, but with a naturalism of attitude and gesture that makes it completely plausible, a reality that is convincing but one that has become a realm of grace and beauty.

While he was working on these commissions, Andrea also had a hand in the preparation of the civic decorations in celebration of the return of the Medici family from their exile (February, 1513) and for the ceremonial entrance of the Medici pope Leo X into Florence in 1515. In 1517, he completed one of his most impressive paintings, the *Madonna of the Harpies*. In this, the characteristic elegance of composition and pose is enriched by startling innovations in color, intermittent passages of light and shadow, and a softness of modeling that create a richly atmospheric effect.

The work at the cloister of the Scalzo was interrupted

Andrea del Sarto. (Library of Congress)

by Andrea's departure from Florence to enter the service of Francis I of France. He accepted the invitation to go to Fontainbleau in the late spring or early summer of 1516 and remained there until 1519. Only a few paintings can be identified as having been painted in France, but one of these, the *Charity* (signed and dated 1518), is a masterpiece, one of his most completely realized works. Like the *Madonna of the Harpies*, it fuses the discipline of classical composition with a richly pictorial palette. The *Charity*, however, is enriched by a beautifully painted landscape background in which the idealistic transformation of nature echoes the visionary grace of the figures.

Andrea probably returned to Florence because he did not want to remain separated from his wife, Lucrezia del Fede, whom he had married shortly after her husband died in 1516. She was about four years younger than Andrea and, at the time of their marriage, was already the mother of a small child. Andrea's biographer Giorgio Vasari states that the French king gave him money to purchase paintings and sculptures for the royal collection after Andrea had solemnly promised that he would come

back to France within a few months. Instead, he remained in Florence. While Vasari's account has been doubted, it is known that Andrea arrived in Florence with a large sum of money and that in October, 1520, he bought a plot of land on which he later built a large house and studio. He visited Rome about 1520 and in 1523 left Florence because of an outbreak of the plague. He went to the Mugello, north of Florence, where he worked for the nuns of San Piero a Luco for about a year before he returned to his native city. In November of 1524, he was back in Florence; very little is known about his activities from this point until his death in 1530 at the age of forty-four.

Andrea continued to work in the Scalzo until 1526 and produced a number of altarpieces for churches in and around Florence. The *Madonna and Child with Saints* of 1525-1526 is typical of his work during this period, with its soft modeling, strong color harmonies, and strong, simple grouping. Paintings such as this one made a great impression on the younger painters in Florence. Two artists who had studied with Andrea earlier, Jacopo Carucci da Pontormo and Giovanni Battista di Jacopo, called Rosso Fiorentino, had by this time evolved their striking anticlassical or early mannerist styles, but between 1520 and 1530 a new generation of painters turned to Andrea for inspiration. He strongly influenced the subsequent development of Florentine painting.

One of the finest of his late works is *The Last Supper* in the refectory of the former convent of San Salvi in Florence (1526-1527), a work of great pictorial interest that comes close to the dramatic intensity of Leonardo da Vinci's rendering of the subject. The *Madonna del Sacco* of 1525 in the Chiostro dei Morti of the Santissima Annunziata is another impressive example of his mature style, which shows the lack of emotional content seen in many of his last works.

SIGNIFICANCE

Andrea was an artist of great virtuosity. His surviving drawings, most of which are studies from life, are superb examples of draftmanship. He is equally skillful as a colorist and as a composer. He was also proficient at fresco painting and panel painting. Modern critics have noted that his work not only directly inspired a number of younger artists but also laid the foundations for some of the most exciting developments of Italian art during the seventeenth century. For Vasari, however, Andrea was an artist whose work was flawed because he lacked the moral strength to make the exertions required to achieve the highest results. There is a certain justice to this criticism, particularly in Andrea's late works, many of which are interesting for the virtuosity of their pictorial effects but are lacking in strong emotional content.

His frescoes in the Scalzo and the Santissima Annunziata, however, are some of the finest achievements of Florentine art. It is to Andrea's credit that while many of his contemporaries were able to imitate certain aspects of the style of Leonardo and Raphael, he was one of the few who were able to assimilate their styles without losing individuality.

—*Eric Van Schaack*

FURTHER READING

Borsook, Eve. *The Mural Painters of Tuscany: From Cimabue to Andrea del Sarto*. 2d ed. Oxford, England: Clarendon Press, 1980. A detailed analysis of Andrea del Sarto's frescoes in the oratory of the Compagnia dello Scalzo in Florence. Includes much information on the relationship of the murals to the site and on the technique.

Cheney, Liana de Girolami, ed. *Readings in Italian Mannerism*. New York: P. Lang, 1997. Anthology of essays by major art historians and Andrea del Sarto scholars, including Sydney J. Freedberg, John Shearman, and Ernst Gombrich. Looks at both the history and the historiography of mannerism in art. Includes illustrations, bibliographic references, index.

Freedberg, Sydney J. *Andrea del Sarto*. 2 vols. Cambridge, Mass.: Harvard University Press, 1963. A comprehensive study of all aspects of the artist's career. This book and one by John Shearman are the standard monographs on the artist. While Freedberg traces Andrea's development within the context of the classical style of the High Renaissance, Shearman shows the importance of Andrea's work, particularly his use of color, for subsequent developments in Italian art of the seventeenth century.

McKillop, Susan Regan. *Franciabigio*. Berkeley: University of California Press, 1974. The author publishes a number of new documents and includes a careful evaluation of the collaboration between Andrea del Sarto and Franciabigio.

Natali, Antonio. *Andrea del Sarto*. Translated by Jeffrey Jennings. New York: Abbeville Press, 1999. An important reinterpretation of Andrea del Sarto by a director of one of Italy's most famous museums, the Uffizi Gallery. Looks closely at both the artist's work and his environment to argue that his career was based on a rigorous commitment to humility in style, reinforced by a circle with similar values. Many color illustrations, bibliographic references, and index.

Neufeld, Gunther. "On the Genesis of the *Madonna del Sacco*." *The Art Bulletin* 47 (1965): 117-118. A study of the preparatory drawings for Andrea del Sarto's *Madonna del Sacco* (1525) in the Cloister of the Santissima Annunziata, Florence, and its derivation from a work by the Venetian artist Titian.

O'Gorman, James F. "An Interpretation of Andrea del Sarto, *Borgherini Holy Family*." *The Art Bulletin* 48 (1965): 502-504. A study of the religious significance of Andrea del Sarto's painting of *Mary, Joseph, the Christ Child, and Young Saint John the Baptist* and its relationship to Florentine religious and political ideals of the late fifteenth and early sixteenth centuries.

Shearman, John. *Andrea del Sarto*. 2 vols. New York: Oxford University Press, 1965. One of the two standard monographs on the artist.

Vasari, Giorgio. *Lives of the Most Eminent Painters, Sculptors, and Architects*. Vol. 3. Translated by Gaston du C. de Vere. Reprint. New York: Abrams, 1979. The standard translation of the second edition (1568) of the only contemporary biography of the artist. Although Vasari was only nineteen when Andrea died, he had access to reliable information about the artist when he was preparing his biography.

SEE ALSO: Sofonisba Anguissola; The Carracci Family; Correggio; Francis I; Leo X; Leonardo da Vinci; Michelangelo; Piero della Francesca; Raphael; Jacopo Sansovino; Tintoretto; Maria Tintoretto; Titian; Giorgio Vasari; Paolo Veronese.

RELATED ARTICLES in *Great Events from History: The Renaissance & Early Modern Era, 1454-1600:* c. 1500: Revival of Classical Themes in Art; 1508-1520: Raphael Paints His Frescoes; December 23, 1534-1540: Parmigianino Paints *Madonna with the Long Neck*.

ISABELLA ANDREINI
Italian actor, poet, and playwright

Isabella Andreini was the leading lady of the Gelosi, the traveling professional troupe of actors renowned for commedia dell'arte, *or improvised comedy. She wrote songs, sonnets, letters, and* La Mirtilla, *the first pastoral drama known to be written by a woman.*

BORN: 1562; Padua, Republic of Venice (now in Italy)
DIED: July 10, 1604; Lyon, France
ALSO KNOWN AS: Isabella Canali (given name);
    Accesa (literary name)
AREAS OF ACHIEVEMENT: Literature, music

EARLY LIFE

Little is known about the childhood of Isabella Andreini (ee-zah-BEHL-lah ahn-dray-EE-nee). The main source about her life is a 1782 biography by Francesco Saverio Bartoli. According to Bartoli's account, Isabella Canali was born to a Venetian family in Padua. Although the Canali family was poor, Isabella received a complete classical education. She was especially interested in literary culture and became fluent in several languages.

In 1576, at the age of fourteen, she joined the traveling theatrical troupe, the Gelosi (Compagnia dei Comici Gelosi) and thus began her stage career. She was invited into the troupe by its director, Flaminio Scala, a nobleman, theatrical manager, and scenario writer. The Gelosi was a well-established theatrical company of professional actors who performed both fully scripted plays and *commedia dell'arte* (comedy marked by a combination of improvisation and prepared scripts). *Commedia dell'arte* was popular for more than three centuries in Italy.

With the Gelosi, Isabella would play the lead female role of *prima donna inamorata* (romantic prima donna) or *inamorata* (woman beloved and in love.) In 1578, at the age of sixteen, Isabella Canali married thirty-year-old Francesco Andreini, a fellow actor in the troupe. They had four daughters and three sons.

LIFE'S WORK

Isabella and Francesco often performed on stage together, with Francesco playing the leading male role of *inamorato* (man in love), and later, the role of the Spanish captain, Capitan Spavento. Eventually, the couple became codirectors of the Gelosi and then toured Italy and France. Isabella would create a new kind of *inamorata*, who was educated, eloquent, and beautiful, and she enjoyed great success acting in the title role in a series of plays: *Lucky Isabella, Isabella's Pranks, Isabella the Astrologer*, and *Jealous Isabella*.

She was also a published writer, whose sonnets were included in Italian anthologies by the mid-1580's. In 1588, Andreini published *La Mirtilla* (English translation, 2002), a pastoral play in verse, modeled after Torquato Tasso's *Aminta* (1573; English translation, 1591), which the Gelosi company had performed in 1573. Tasso was the greatest Italian poet of the late Renaissance and a personal role model for Andreini. Unlike *Aminta*, however, *La Mirtilla* reverses gender roles in favor of the female, often humorously. In act 3, Satiro, for example, a satyr (half man and half goat) is attracted to the nymph Filli and plans to capture and ravish her if she does not accept his attention. Filli, though, flatters Satiro into releasing her and then tricks him into being tied to a tree. He begs to be untied, but she just mocks him and leaves him crying out to her.

> SATIRO: Filli, Filli, where are you going? Stop, listen,
>   at least untie me so that I do not become
>   a joke, a tale, and a game
>   for other pitiless nymphs like you!
>   Oh me, what can't a woman do
>   when she is resolved to deceive?

The play was tremendously successful and it was published in numerous editions.

On May 13, 1589, in Florence, Andreini performed her most famous piece, *La Pazzia d'Isabella* (the madness of Isabella), at the wedding festivities of Ferdinand de' Medicis and the French princess, Christine of Lorraine. In 1599, they performed before Henry IV of France and his new Italian wife, Marie de Médicis.

In 1601, Isabella was accepted as a member of the prestigious Accademia degli Intenti of Pavia. It was unusual for women to be accepted into academies, but her literary work earned her this great honor. Accesa became her pseudonym. Later that year, she published a collection of poems called *Rime* (partial English translation, 1997), which included madrigals, eclogues, sonnets, and other poetic forms. She had also collected 148 fictional epistles or letters to be published under the title of *Lettere* (partial English translation, 1997). A French translation of *Rime* was published and received critical acclaim.

In 1602, the Gelosi traveled in northern Italy. In 1603-1604, the troupe was in France performing for the court of Henry IV and Queen Marie de' Medici, who praised Isabella's acting. On their return trip, Andreini miscarried her eighth child and died in Lyon, France, on July 10, 1604. She was forty-two years old. In Lyon, there was a great public funeral, where she was deeply mourned by the public. A commemorative medallion was created and inscribed with the Latin words *aeterna fama* (eternal fame).

Her grieving husband disbanded the Gelosi, retired from acting, and moved to Mantua, where he worked on editing and publishing Isabella's remaining works. In 1605, he published *Rime . . . Parte seconda* (rime, part two). This book included poetry written by Isabella after 1600, poems written about her, and some pastoral poems, monologues, and dialogues from her comedies. In 1606, one of their sons, Giambattista Andreini, a prolific playwright, dedicated a collection of poems to his mother.

In 1607, Francesco Andreini published Isabella's *Lettere*. These fictional epistles were not dated nor did they indicate the place written or the addressee. They were reflections on various subjects, such as love and moral or social issues. The value of virtue and propriety, which characterized Isabella's public image, was a pervasive theme of the epistles. The most famous is the eloquent defense of women called "Del nascimento della donna" (on the birth of women), addressed to a father who was disappointed that his newborn was a daughter and not a son.

SIGNIFICANCE

Isabella Andreini was the most celebrated *comica* (dramatic actress) of her time. A great beauty who could speak and act in several languages, she was one of the greatest *inamorati* in the history of Italian comedy. She was the only female actor of the time to write and publish her own compositions.

As both a famous actress and paragon of virtue, she showed that it was possible to have a family and to be successful as an actor. Such theatrical families became more common after Isabella's time.

—*Alice Myers*

FURTHER READING

Andreini, Isabella. *La Mirtilla: A Pastoral*. Translated by Julie D. Campbell. Tempe: Arizona Center for Medi-eval and Renaissance Studies, 2002. This is the first English translation of *La Mirtilla*, including complete biographical information and a discussion of the work. Illustrated.

Hunningher, Benjamin. *Essays on Drama and Theatre*. Amsterdam: Baarn Moussault, 1973. Includes Robert Erenstein's essay "Isabella Andreini: A Lady of Virtue and High Renown." Illustrated, with bibliography.

MacNeil, Anne. *Music and Women of the Commedia dell'Arte in the Late Sixteenth Century*. New York: Oxford University Press, 2003. Scholarly analysis of musical settings of Andreini's poems, the original Italian and English translations of twelve poems from *Rime*, and the singing contest from *La Mirtilla*. Illustrated, with music, bibliography, and an index.

Panizza, Letizia, ed. *A History of Women's Writing in Italy*. New York: Cambridge University Press, 2000. The section on the Renaissance, the Counter-Reformation, and the seventeenth century includes discussions of Andreini's letter writing, lyric poetry, and fiction writing. Bibliography.

_____. *Women in Italian Renaissance Culture and Society*. New York: Oxford University Press, 2000. Chapter 18, "Isabella Andreini and Others: Women on Stage in the Late Cinquecento," is a scholarly account of Andreini's life and contributions to the Italian Renaissance. Extensive footnotes.

Russell, Rinaldinia, ed. *Italian Women Writers: A Bio-Bibliographical Sourcebook*. Westport, Conn.: Greenwood Press, 1994. The chapter on Andreini includes biographical information, an analysis of recurring themes in her works, a survey of criticism, and a lengthy bibliography.

Stortoni, Laura Anna, ed. *Women Poets of the Italian Renaissance: Courtly Ladies and Courtesans*. Translated by Laura Anna Stortoni and Mary Prentice Lillie. New York: Italica Press, 1997. A section on Andreini presents a biography and selected pieces from *La Mirtilla*, *Rime*, and *Lettere*, in Italian and in English; with useful footnotes. Map, comprehensive bibliography.

SEE ALSO: Henry IV; Torquato Tasso.

SAINT ANGELA MERICI
Italian religious leader

Angela Merici, noted for her ministry to the poor, the disabled, the sick, and the orphaned, founded the Order of Saint Ursula, the first Catholic teaching order for girls. The Ursuline order, as it came to be called, has been instrumental as an institution devoted to girls' and women's literacy, general education, and well-being.

BORN: March 21, 1470, or 1474; Desenzano, Republic of Venice (now in Italy)

DIED: January 27, 1540; Brescia, Republic of Venice (now in Italy)

ALSO KNOWN AS: Angela of Merici; Angela de Marici; Angela Merici; Suor Angela Terziaria; Sister Angela Tertiary

AREAS OF ACHIEVEMENT: Religion and theology, education, social reform, women's rights

EARLY LIFE

Angela Merici (AHN-jay-lah may-REE-chee) was born to a prosperous and literate farmer, who read to her regularly. Angela later credited her father with inspiring her early devotion to a contemplative way of life. Her mother was from the minor nobility, the Biancosi, a well-connected family important for Angela's later upbringing. Angela also enjoyed the company of several siblings.

When still a young girl, Angela suffered the loss of her parents and a sister and was sent to live with a maternal uncle in Salò, a relatively prosperous town nearby. She did not receive formal schooling but lived in comfort while humbly performing her share of domestic chores. While still an adolescent, Angela had a vision that was to change the course of her life. Merici was praying in the fields at harvest time and looked up to see a group of angels, and among them was her deceased sister. Accounts of the vision vary, but all are consistent in attributing to this event Angela's devotion to a spiritual calling.

It was around the time of this vision that Angela was admitted to the Third Order Franciscans, which afforded her more frequent communion and introduced her to a vocation devoted to caring for the poor, sick, and disadvantaged. Until the end of her life, Angela referred to herself as Suor Angela Terziaria and wore the habit of this Franciscan order.

LIFE'S WORK

In 1516, the Franciscans approved sending Angela Merici to Brescia, an important city in northern Italy that had been suffering the effects of social disruption caused by war and political conflicts. Though assigned originally to comfort a bereaved widow, Angela soon broadened her mission to minister more generally to the suffering and needy in the city. She also became acquainted with a group of individuals active in a charitable organization. Through this charity, Angela helped care for women and young girls who had sexually transmitted diseases, had been abused, or had been orphaned during the political conflicts.

Angela involved herself with these charitable activities in a way that was both self-effacing and completely devoted. Contemporaries describe her during these missions as "on fire with the love of God." She never slept in a bed, using instead a straw mat on the ground with a piece of stone or wood for a pillow. She slept little, in any case, and spent most of each day in charitable work, in prayer, or in reading. She received constant visitors and eventually acquired the appellation Mother Angela.

During this period, Angela traveled regularly for spiritual benefit. Her most eventful trip was a pilgrimage to the Holy Land in 1524, a journey filled with mysterious and miraculous episodes, including her temporary loss of sight and enduring threats from storms, pirates, and hostile Turks. A visit to Rome in 1525 culminated in a meeting with Pope Clement VII, and a trip in 1532 to Varallo, an important pilgrimage site in northern Italy, marked Angela's last major journey.

Thereafter, Angela devoted most of her energy to the formation of a revolutionary new religious company in Brescia to address the needs of young women, the first of its kind anywhere. Angela's following would become the Ursuline order. Key elements in her original vision are that her companions would follow a life of chastity, poverty, and obedience, and that they would live with their families rather than being cloistered. The notion that unmarried girls could lead chaste spiritual lives outside the cloister was a radical idea, and it was symptomatic of the practical and progressive company that Angela began.

In 1535, on November 25, the feast day of Saint Catherine of Alexandria, Angela Merici and twenty-eight companions attended mass in a small oratory and signed their names in the book of the Company of Saint Ursula, thus founding the company and devoting themselves to God. The day was an auspicious one, being the eleventh anniversary of Angela's return from the Holy Land and the feast day of a virgin martyr, Saint Catherine, whose own erudition, chastity, and devotion to Christ would become a model for the Ursulines. The founding of the company is celebrated in a famous early sixteenth century painting by Girolamo Romanino, now in the Memphis Brooks Museum, entitled *The Mystic Marriage of Saint Catherine*. This masterpiece, symbolizing the Ursulines' spiritual betrothal to Christ, includes a portrait of Angela Merici, an image of Saint Ursula, the company's patron saint, and a depiction of Saint Lawrence, which honors Lorenzo Muzio, vicar general of Brescia, who gave the company its initial approbation in 1536.

Under Angela's leadership, the company prospered and held a unique status as an uncloistered religious community of women integrated with families and workplaces. Progressive for its time, the community was hard pressed to follow Angela's original vision after her passing in Brescia on January 27, 1540, by which time the company numbered about 150 members. Pope Paul III formally approved the company in 1544, and shortly thereafter it was recognized as the Ursuline order. Angela Merici was beatified in 1768 by Pope Clement XIII and eventually canonized as a saint on May 24, 1807, by Pope Pius VII.

SIGNIFICANCE

The Ursulines developed into the first female teaching order within the Catholic Church. From the sixteenth century onward, the Ursulines had a major impact on education throughout Europe and later continued their work in North America. The achievements in North America have been particularly profound, and include the first female missionaries, the first Catholic school for girls, and, in many communities, the first schools for girls or colleges for women.

The Ursuline order has seen much change since the death of its founder. In the mid-sixteenth century, a split began over the degree to which Angela's original rule should be followed, especially regarding the issue of enclosure. The original idea of the Company of Saint Ursula spread to several cities in northern Italy before the time of the Council of Trent (1545-1563). The reforms of the Council of Trent included the directive that publicly vowed women should live in cloistered convents as nuns, a directive followed by some Ursulines. Others, particularly in Italy, elected to continue to live with their families or in small groups as women with private vows; these

women became known as Angelines, after Angela Merici.

As new companies were introduced in France in the early seventeenth century, they tended to be founded as monasteries with enclosure. It was monastic enclosure that led to the long tradition of Ursuline education, and it was in seventeenth century France that Ursuline schools flourished. From France, Ursuline convents and their girls' boarding schools spread throughout Europe and to North America between the seventeenth and nineteenth centuries.

Today there are Ursulines throughout the world who, with public vows, live in religious communities, many of whom continue the mission of women's and girl's education. Angelines, a secular institute with private vows, live alone, with their families, or in small groups. Both branches seek to live in close harmony with Angela's original vision.

—Arnold Victor Coonin

FURTHER READING

Caraman, Peter. *Saint Angela: The Life of Angela Merici, Foundress of the Ursulines (1474-1540)*. London: Farrar, Straus, 1963. The most widely available and easily read biography of Merici.

Coonin, Arnold Victor, ed. *Old Masters in Context: Romanino's Mystic Marriage of Saint Catherine*. Memphis, Tenn.: Memphis Brooks Museum of Art, 2003. This exhibition catalog includes useful essays on Angela Merici, Saint Ursula, and Saint Catherine, and discusses Merici in the context of the visual arts.

"Follow the Spirit": Angela Merici and the Ursulines. Rome: Éditions du Signe, 1998. A brief, informative booklet published by the Ursuline community, which covers both historical and modern events.

Ledóchowska, Therese. *Angela Merici and the Company of St. Ursula*. 2 vols. Rome: Ancora, 1967. A definitive monograph on both Angela Merici and the later history of the order. Translated from the French, with original sources and documents.

Waters, Peter Maurice. *The Ursuline Achievement: A Philosophy of Education for Women*. Victoria, Australia: Colonna, 1994. Discussion of the Ursulines in the context of general educational theory. Also includes a translation of important Ursuline documents and a comprehensive bibliography.

SEE ALSO: Barbe Acarie; Saint Catherine of Genoa; Clement VII; Paul III; Saint Teresa of Ávila.

SOFONISBA ANGUISSOLA
Italian painter

Sofonisba Anguissola was one of the first European women to achieve international recognition as a painter. She was renowned for her innovative portraits, which were characterized by their naturalism, psychological intimacy, and emotional expression, and for her family-oriented genre scenes.

BORN: c. 1532; Cremona, duchy of Milan (now in Italy)

DIED: November, 1625; Palermo, Kingdom of Sicily (now in Italy)

ALSO KNOWN AS: Sofonisba Angosciola; Sofonisba Anguisciola; Sofonisba Angussola

AREA OF ACHIEVEMENT: Art

EARLY LIFE

Sofonisba Anguissola (soh-foh-NEEZ-bah ahn-GWEES-soh-lah), the eldest of seven children, was born and reared in the northern Italian city of Cremona to Amilcare Anguissola and Bianca Ponzoni. A member of the nobility, Amilcare educated his six daughters and one son according to Baldassare Castiglione's *Il libro del cortegiano* (1528; *The Book of the Courtier*, 1561), an influential treatise that stressed the importance of a Humanist education in areas such as art, music, literature, and Latin for upper-class children of both genders.

Sofonisba Anguissola studied painting in Cremona with Bernardino Campi from around 1546 and with Bernardino Gatti from 1549. Women and girls sometimes studied with their artist-fathers, but apprenticeships such as Anguissola's were rare.

Despite her educational advantages, Anguissola faced societal constraints that barred her from studying anatomy and undertaking the large-scale, multifigured history and religious paintings that were so popular at the time. Portraiture, however, was an area that was accessible to her as a female painter. Friends and family members served as subjects. She developed a naturalistic style that captured individual personalities. This style is evident in the shy expression and fluid drapery of one of her earliest known works, *Portrait of a Nun* from 1551, which probably depicts her sister Elena.

LIFE'S WORK

Developing her powers of observation, Anguissola pioneered genre painting in Italy and often introduced an element of humor. This is apparent in *A Laughing Girl Teaching an Older Woman to Read* from the 1550's. Be-

lieved to depict her sister Lucia, the drawing was so inventive that it was shown to Michelangelo, who was impressed with Anguissola and challenged her to draw a crying boy. She sent him *Asdrubale Being Bitten by a Crab* (c. 1554), showing a range of emotions, from the distressed boy to the girl who is smiling at his dilemma. Again, the models for the drawing were probably her brother Asdrubale and her sister Minerva.

One of her best-known works is *The Chess Game* from around 1555. This group portrait depicts sisters Lucia, Europa, and Minerva playing chess. Here portraiture merges with genre painting as the work captures the individuals in a moment from daily life. Anguissola carefully observed details: The girls are shown well groomed and dressed in velvets and brocades; the table is covered with a Holbein rug; and the game is taking place outdoors with a vista of the surrounding countryside. There is an unconventional sense of dynamism: Lucia experiences the moment of victory; Minerva signals her defeat; young Europa grins with mischievous glee; the servant quietly observes from the background.

The painting was praised by Giorgio Vasari, one of Anguissola's first biographers. It provides an early example of the conversation piece, a type of group portrait with individuals engaging in an everyday collective activity, which was popularized by Dutch painters a century later.

More than a dozen of Anguissola's self-portraits survive, but, unfortunately, many are not dated. In early examples, she appears serious and unadorned in simple dark dress. Her hair is pulled back and plainly netted. She portrayed herself with the accoutrements of a noblewoman educated in Humanism. In her self-portrait of 1554, she holds an open book. A self-portrait from around 1556 shows her at her easel, working on a painting of the Madonna. In her self-portrait of 1561, she is shown at a spinet with her chaperone. In later portrayals, she appears in more opulent dress, indicating her social position.

Anguissola's father actively promoted her work, and in 1559, she was invited to the court of Spanish king Philip II. There she became a great favorite of the royal family. She served as a painting instructor and lady-in-waiting to the young queen, Isabel of Valois.

There has been some difficulty in identifying Anguissola's work from this time period. She seldom signed her compositions. As a noblewoman, she did not accept monetary payment or public commissions, thus limiting documentation of her paintings. Many of her images were copied. Some were destroyed in subsequent fires or damaged to an extent that identification has proved difficult. Some pieces were mistakenly attributed to male artists. Nevertheless, scholarship has documented many of her works from this period.

There is a marked change in style from the family-oriented themes of her Cremona period to the portraits that she executed in her fourteen-year residence in Spain. The influence of official Spanish court art is evident in her work, but her interest in the subject's personality, fluid contours, greater freedom of pose, and softer treatment of the painted surface contrasts with the severity of traditional royal portraits. Her full-length portrayal of Isabel (c. 1565), an official pose showing the queen holding Philip II's portrait, still reveals the vitality of her subject. The portrait of Philip II (c. 1565), first painted before the deaths of Isabel and Don Carlos in 1568, shows a more relaxed, youthful king. The severe dark cape was added later.

After the unexpected death of the queen, King Philip began the search for a suitable husband for Anguissola.

Sofonisba Anguissola. (Hulton|Archive by Getty Images)

In 1573, she married Don Fabrizio de Moncada, a Sicilian nobleman. King Philip gave her in marriage and bestowed dowry gifts, including a lifelong pension, which provided her with some financial independence. She and her husband resided in Palermo. Sources indicate that she was involved with painting miniatures, but no works from this time are firmly identified. Don Fabrizio met an untimely death by drowning in 1578, leaving Anguissola with financial entanglements. She dissolved the Palermo household and headed back to Cremona.

On this journey, she met the ship's captain, Orazio Lomellino of Genoa, whom she married shortly thereafter in 1579. As she entered this marriage over her brother's objections and without the permission of the king, it is assumed that the contract was based on a strong emotional attachment. A busy hub connecting northern and southern Italy, Genoa was a prime location for the artist. Over the next four decades, Anguissola pursued her painting, established a salon, and was highly respected. Letters suggest that she worked for the duke of Tuscany, Francesco de' Medici. Her small-scale devotional paintings from this time derived from existing works of other artists such as Luca Cambiaso. Inventories show that she painted portraits of family and friends, but none of these have been firmly identified.

Nevertheless, representations of members of the Spanish court have survived from this mature period, dating from around 1580. The only signed portrait is a replica of her first depiction of Isabel (c. 1590). This work reveals some changes in style from her days at the Spanish court: The features are more delicate and the technique is more fluid. Also from this period are portraits of Infanta Catalina Micaela (c. 1585) and Infanta Isabella Clara Eugenia (c. 1599), daughters of Queen Isabel.

Around 1615, Anguissola and her husband moved to Palermo. Anthony van Dyck visited her there in 1624, when he drew a portrait of her in his *Italian Sketchbook*. He noted that she was in her nineties and that her failing eyesight prevented her from painting. She died in 1625.

SIGNIFICANCE

Anguissola was in the vanguard of artists, with a career that spanned seventy years. Because of the constraints put on sixteenth century women, her subjects were limited, and she turned to portraiture.

Her style was natural and insightful, combining miniaturist detail with fluid brushwork. She was internationally recognized in her lifetime, a distinction unusual for female artists. She was honored as an official painter of the Spanish court, was recognized by Michelangelo and

Vasari, and was awarded a lifetime pension by the king of Spain. Other artists such as Peter Paul Rubens copied her work.

Her work inspired others to consider painting as an acceptable profession for women. Precluded from achievement in the field of large-scale historical and religious painting, she learned to observe her subjects more keenly, to capture the essence of their personalities, and to give them life.

—Cassandra Lee Tellier

FURTHER READING

Ferino-Pagden, Sylvia, and Maria Kusche. *Sofonisba Anguissola: A Renaissance Woman*. Washington, D.C.: National Museum of Women in the Arts, 1995. Catalog that accompanied exhibition by same title. Essays with 24 color plates and extensive descriptions of Anguissola's most important works.

Martin, Elizabeth, and Vivian Meyer. *Female Gazes: Seventy-five Women Artists*. Toronto, Canada: Second Story Press, 1997. Essays explore the lives and works of diverse female artists.

Perlingieri, Ilya Sandra. *Sofonisba Anguissola: The First Great Woman Artist of the Renaissance*. New York: Rizzoli, 1992. Pioneering biography accompanied by more than 120 plates, many reproduced in color.

Slatkin, Wendy. *Women Artists in History from Antiquity to the Present*. Upper Saddle River, N.J.: Prentice Hall, 2001. Focuses on women artists and their contributions to visual culture. Incorporates scholarship and detailed analyses of individual works.

Vigué, Jordi. *Great Women Masters of Art*. New York: Watson-Guptill, 2002. Introductory overview followed by short essays on outstanding women painters in the history of Western art.

SEE ALSO: Caravaggio; Baldassare Castiglione; Lavinia Fontana; Catharina van Hemessen; Michelangelo; Philip II; Giorgio Vasari.

RELATED ARTICLES in *Great Events from History: The Renaissance & Early Modern Era, 1454-1600*: c. 1500: Revival of Classical Themes in Art; 1508-1520: Raphael Paints His Frescoes; November 3, 1522-November 17, 1530: Correggio Paints the *Assumption of the Virgin*; December 23, 1534-1540: Parmigianino Paints *Madonna with the Long Neck*; 1563-1584: Construction of the Escorial; June, 1564: Tintoretto Paints for the Scuola di San Rocco.

ANNE OF BRITTANY
Queen of France (r. 1491-1498, 1499-1514)

Duchess of Brittany and twice queen of France, Anne was one of the most educated and powerful women of her time. She devoted her life to preserving Brittany's independence from France and her court was host to poets, musicians, and scholars.

BORN: January, 25, 1477; Nantes, Brittany (now in France)
DIED: January, 9, 1514; Blois, France
ALSO KNOWN AS: Anne de Bretagne
AREAS OF ACHIEVEMENT: Government and politics, patronage of the arts, education

EARLY LIFE

Anne of Brittany was the daughter of Francis II of Brittany and Marguerite de Foix. She was raised in the Nantes castle in her family duchy of Brittany (little Britain), a small but powerful neighbor of France that for the most part remained independent of the larger nation.

Brittany had its own army, minted its own currency, and established its own diplomatic relations. Unlike France, Brittany did not follow Salic Law, which prohibited women from inheriting direct rule. Anne had no brothers, but she did have one sister, Isabeau; being the eldest, Anne was raised from the age of three as the heir. She was taught Breton, which is related to Welsh, French, Latin, Greek, and some Hebrew, and from her father, she learned lessons of statecraft. Consequently, she was one of the most educated girls of her time.

Brittany had been in a long-standing struggle for independence from France. When Anne of Beaujeu became regent of France on behalf of her young brother, King Charles VIII, she saw the lack of a male heir in Brittany as a weakness that could permit France to finally take control of the duchy. Anne of Beaujeu's French troops invaded Brittany in 1488 and defeated the Bretons and their coalition at Saint-Aubin-du-Cormier in July. Duke Francis II was compelled to accept the Treaty of Le Verger, which included a clause stating that Anne could marry only with the consent of the French crown.

LIFE'S WORK

Anne of Brittany's mother died in May, 1488, and her father died in September of the same year, just a few months after he signed the Le Verger treaty. Thus, Anne was left as a young orphan, merely eleven years old. She was a small child with a congenital deformity, one leg being shorter than the other, but she wore heels of unequal height to compensate. She was attractive, pleasant, quite pious, and extremely intelligent—moreover, she was now the ruler of the richest and perhaps most powerful duchy in Europe.

Naturally, there were many claimants for her hand in marriage, including Juan of Spain and Duke Louis d'Orléans (the future King Louis XII), but Anne accepted the proposal of the twenty-nine-year-old Maximilian I, archduke of Austria, German king, and king of the Romans, who appeared to be the best choice for Brittany. The two were wed by proxy in 1490.

Anne of Beaujeu could not tolerate this union between Brittany, a formidable neighbor that had been a thorn in the side of France for years, and her country's enemy, Maximilian I. The shrewd French regent sent troops into the duchy, forcing Anne of Brittany, a beleaguered teenager, to dissolve her union with Maximilian and to agree to marry the regent's brother, the French king Charles VIII.

Anne married Charles in 1491, but she still ruled Brittany. Nevertheless, she was distressed to find herself wed to a foe who for years had devastated her beloved homeland. She eventually warmed to Charles, however, and her superior education and training soon gained her the respect and devotion of the king and the French people. The pair maintained a happy marriage but suffered disappointment, since none of Anne's children survived infancy. Their seven-year union came to an end in 1498, when Charles died following a freak accident in which he bumped his head on a low door beam.

The duke Louis d'Orléans, Charles's cousin and now Louis XII, assumed the throne, while the bereaved Anne returned to Brittany and aggressively worked toward reestablishing her government. The new French monarch, concerned about the powers of neighboring Brittany, an-

Anne of Brittany (left) meets Charles VIII. (F. R. Niglutsch)

nulled his marriage to the deformed and childless Jeanne de France, sister of Anne of Beaujeu and Charles VIII, and set his sights on his charming friend Anne of Brittany, whom he had known for years from the time she was a young child in her duchy. He recalled Anne on the basis of a stipulation in her original marriage contract, which stated that, if Anne and Charles VIII were childless and Charles died, the widow would have to marry the next king of France so that her duchy would not pass beyond the realm. Therefore, as the wife of Louis XII, Anne of Brittany became the queen of France for a second time. As she did when married to Charles, Anne maintained control over Brittany.

Anne and King Louis XII produced no sons, but they did have two daughters, Claude and Renée. Claude was heir to Brittany (which still was not bound by Salic Law), and Anne, who had devoted her life to safeguarding the autonomy of her duchy—particularly keeping it independent from France—made every effort to unite her infant daughter with the house of Austria. In 1501, on their way to Spain, Archduke Philip of Austria (King Philip I of Spain) and his wife Joan of Spain visited Blois to solidify a marriage treaty between Princess Claude and their son Charles (the future Holy Roman Emperor Charles V). King Louis had no choice but to go against Anne's wishes and invalidate the proposed union, since Claude's large inheritance, which included Brittany, Burgundy, and the French claims to Milan, Asti, Genoa, and Naples, was too significant to alienate from the kingdom of France. Louis supported a marriage between Claude and his young cousin Francis, comte d'Angoulême, a libertine youth known for his excesses, who would succeed to the throne in any event should Louis have no sons.

Anne of Brittany died in January of 1514 at the age of thirty-seven, knowing that with her daughter's impending marriage, her family would forever lose Brittany. She had reigned alongside her husband Louis XII for fifteen years, during which time he treated her with the utmost respect. Likewise, he buried her in splendor: Her funeral ceremonies surpassed even those of her first husband, King Charles VIII. Her heart was removed and sent back to Brittany, where it always had been metaphorically, and now literally, enshrined in her hometown of Nantes.

SIGNIFICANCE

Anne of Brittany was one of the most intelligent and powerful women of her time. As queen, she developed a great respect for Brittany and France and concern for its residents, was generous in her dealings with the people, and often provided her husband with wise advice on affairs of state.

She cultivated a brilliant court, frequented by the finest of poets, musicians, and scholars. She founded an order of ladies, the first queen to do so, which she called La Cordelière. She welcomed myriad women and girls into her association and provided them with a noble education and guidance. Aside from her daughters, her deepest love and consideration was toward the people of Brittany,

whom she never forgot. She stayed most active in running her duchy, maintained its court, and brought many of her compatriots to France to work in her service and assist her in preserving contact with Brittany.

—*Lisa Urkevich*

FURTHER READING

Baumgartner, Frederic. *Louis XII.* New York: Palgrave, 1994. Biography of King Louis XII, with information on Anne of Brittany and their court and political environment.

Brantome, Abbé de. *The Book of the Ladies (Illustrious Dames).* Boston: Hardy, Pratt, 1902. Written in the sixteenth century, this work includes an account of Anne of Brittany and personal tales from primary sources.

Hopkins, Lisa. *Women Who Would Be Kings: Female Rulers of the Sixteenth Century.* London: Vision Press, 1991. An accessible, compact history that includes information on several great women of the sixteenth century. A short book that sometimes oversimplifies issues.

Matarasso, Pauline. *Queen's Mate: Three Women of Power in France on the Eve of the Renaissance.* Burlington, Vt.: Ashgate Press, 2001. Focuses on the lives of Anne of Brittany, Anne of Beaujeu, and Louise of Savoy. Well cited, with a notable bibliography.

Neuschel, Kristen B. "Noblewomen and War in Sixteenth Century France." In *Changing Identities in Early Modern France*, edited by Michael Wolfe. Durham, N.C.: Duke University Press, 1997. Chapter on the role of aristocratic women in warfare and their obtaining weapons.

Sanborn, Helen J. *Anne of Brittany.* Boston: Lothrop, Lee & Shepard, 1917. The most comprehensive book in English on Anne of Brittany, her life, and her relationships. Lacks detailed citation.

SEE ALSO: Charles V; Charles VIII; Louis XII; Maximilian I.

RELATED ARTICLES in *Great Events from History: The Renaissance & Early Modern Era, 1454-1600:* 1482-1492: Maximilian I Takes Control of the Low Countries; August 19, 1493-January 12, 1519: Reign of Maximilian I.

ANNE OF CLEVES
Queen consort of England (r. January-July, 1540)

German-born Anne of Cleves helped promote a brief alliance between her husband King Henry VIII of England and her brother, Duke William of Cleves, a Protestant leader in Germany. Also, she displayed great courage in the face of an often unforgiving and ruthless Henry when she first refused his formal request for a divorce.

BORN: September 22, 1515; Cleves, Germany
DIED: July 16, 1557; London, England
AREA OF ACHIEVEMENT: Government and politics

EARLY LIFE

Anne of Cleves was part of a politically influential family. Duke William of Cleves, her brother, embraced the new Protestantism that was spreading through northern Europe during the Reformation. William was seen as politically useful to Henry VII, who broke from Roman Catholicism and established the Church of England following his divorce from his first wife, Catherine of Aragon. A marriage to Anne would ally Henry's Church of England with the German Protestants.

Anne's lineage can be traced to Edward I of England and John I of Burgundy. Like most young noblewomen of that time, Anne lived under the close surveillance of her mother, her chief teacher. Living with her immediate family until she was betrothed, she quickly learned modesty, humility, and passivity. She mastered the gestures expected of a lady: controlling her gaze and using her eyebrows expressively. Her education revolved around religion and needlepoint, in which she became adept. German was the only language she spoke fluently when she married Henry.

LIFE'S WORK

Before King Henry VIII married Anne of Cleves, he had married three other women: Catherine of Aragon, a union whose annulment caused England to break away from the Roman Catholic Church; Anne Boleyn, whom he had beheaded; and Jane Seymour, who died in 1537 shortly after giving birth to Henry's first son, Edward VI. Although Henry appeared shattered by Jane Seymour's death, he realized that he had to remarry to produce additional heirs to the throne. He did not, however, plunge into a quick remarriage.

Henry's minions spent three years seeking a suitable mate for him, finally dismissing the possibility of his marrying any of the English candidates. Henry needed to strengthen his political position by forming an alliance with the nobility of some northern European country, and Duke William of Cleves was finally considered the nobleman who could cement such an alliance. William's sister, Anne of Cleves, was under consideration to become Henry's next wife.

Lord Thomas Cromwell, Henry's chief ambassador to Germany, actively promoted the king's marriage to Anne of Cleves. The king's emissaries lauded Anne's physical attractiveness, intelligence, and purity of body and soul. Late in 1539, Henry, eager for an alliance with Germany, agreed to marry the twenty-four-year-old princess without having met her. He had, however, seen Hans Holbein's portrait of Anne, a flattering rendition of the princess painted hastily in August, 1539.

The prospective bride journeyed to Calais before her voyage to England, arriving there on December 12. Bad weather delayed her departure from Calais until December 27, when she was finally able to cross the English Channel, landing at Downs, where the duke and duchess of Suffolk received her. Inclement weather delayed Anne's progress to London. She paused in Rochester where, on January 1, 1540, a bullfight was arranged for her amusement.

Suddenly, six men, identically dressed in colorful cloaks and hoods, entered her apartment, where she was observing the bullfight from a window. One of the men advanced, kissed her, and presented her with a gift, supposedly from the king. He continued his advances, which Anne rebuffed. Finally, the man left, only to return dressed in the royal purple of his office. Henry, eager to meet his bride, had traveled to Rochester to surprise her.

Henry's initial impression of Anne was highly unfavorable. He barely spoke to her, retreating from her presence as quickly as he could. The reports of her beauty obviously had been exaggerated. The Holbein portrait portrayed someone far more attractive than the person Henry now faced.

Henry was desperate to cancel the marriage contract to which he was committed. There was no way to do this, however, without jeopardizing the political gains he hoped his marriage to Anne would assure. The wedding that was planned for January 4 was postponed while Henry attempted to find a reasonable way out of his dilemma, but none surfaced. On January 6, Henry was forced to marry Anne.

As Henry came to know Anne better, his distress heightened. The language barrier precluded easy communication. Their conversations required the presence of a translator, a situation hardly encouraging to intimacy. Henry considered Anne limited intellectually. She suffered from a pervasive homesickness, adding another complication to an already troubled marriage.

Rumors that the royal marriage was unconsummated generated consternation in Henry's court. Cromwell and his associates knew that something must be done to remedy the situation. No one, however, was willing to intervene on such a delicate matter, largely because of the king's reputation for dealing harshly with those who displeased him. Cromwell shifted much of the responsibility for mending the marriage to the earl of Rutland, who was reluctant to risk royal disfavor by entering into the fray.

Anne's only possible confidante in court was Mrs. Loew, a German woman who had accompanied Anne to England and, in a break from tradition, had remained following the marriage to assume a prominent place in Henry's household as surrogate mother to the German maids. Anne, however, was too diffident about her situation to discuss it with anyone. Indeed, she pretended ignorance when some of the ladies in court questioned why she had not yet become pregnant. She confided to no one the true state of her marriage.

Henry, on the other hand, conferred with his physicians and with Cromwell about the state of his unhappy union with Anne. Word circulated about the crumbling royal marriage. By the beginning of summer, Henry was frequently seen crossing the Thames to visit the dowager duchess of Norfolk's palace, where he had clandestine meetings with Catherine Howard, with whom he had fallen in love and whom he would eventually marry.

On June 24, Henry dispatched Anne from his palace to Richmond Palace, explaining that the climate there was better. On July 6, however, Anne learned that her marriage to Henry was the subject of considerable scrutiny with the obvious aim of termination. On July 9, she was served with a formal request that she sign divorce documents. Fearing that she might suffer the fate of Catherine of Aragon, Anne refused to sign the necessary papers, thereby making divorce unlikely. She demanded that her marriage to Henry be judged by a convocation, which would, predictably, rule in the king's favor, after which she would accept an annulment. She then wrote to the king, signing her letter "Your Majesty's most humble sister and servant, Anne."

Henry, amazed at Anne's conciliatory attitude, wrote, in a letter dated July 12, that he would henceforth regard Anne as his sister rather than his wife. Following the annulment, Anne received an annual stipend of four thousand pounds, a handsome sum for the time. She also received palaces at Richmond and Bletchingley and was still accepted at court. The annulment agreement stipulated that Anne remain in England. This hurdle behind him, Henry married Catherine Howard on August 8, 1540.

SIGNIFICANCE

Anne of Cleves lived for seventeen years following her annulment. She showed deference to Catherine Howard, who had been one of Anne's maids during Anne's brief tenure as queen, and approached her with a becoming humility and courtesy. For the remaining years of her life, Anne visited court occasionally and was remarkably amiable despite being deposed.

Although she had no far-reaching political significance, Anne demonstrated remarkable survival skills, negotiating the volatile realm of Henry's court. Her mere

Anne of Cleves. (Hulton|Archive by Getty Images)

survival was miraculous, brought about by her stubbornness and shrewdness. The very political advantage that Henry hoped to gain by his marriage to a northern European became moot, however, when the alliance between northern Europe's Catholic powers stalled, making the whole matter of his marriage to Anne of Cleves embarrassing politically.

—*R. Baird Shuman*

FURTHER READING

Chamberlain, Arthur B. *Hans Holbein the Younger.* London: G. Allen, 1913. Dated but valuable for its account of Hans Holbein's conscription to paint a hasty portrait of Anne so Henry could see what she looked like.

Crawford, Anne, ed. *The Letters of the Queens of England, 1066-1547.* Stroud, Gloucestershire, England: 1994. Contains letters from Henry's wives, including several from Anne of Cleves.

Starkey, David. *Six Wives: The Queens of Henry VIII.* New York: HarperCollins, 2003. A valuable resource that views Henry's marriage to Anne in the context of his five other marriages.

Warnicke, Retha M. *The Marrying of Anne of Cleves: Royal Protocol in Early Modern England.* New York: Cambridge University Press, 2000. The most comprehensive account of Anne's marriage to Henry and its subsequent annulment.

Weir, Alison. *Henry VIII: The King and His Court.* New York: Ballantine Books, 2001. Weir provides vivid descriptions of Anne's arrival in England and, eventually, in court.

SEE ALSO: Anne Boleyn; Catherine of Aragon; Thomas Cranmer; Thomas Cromwell; Henry VIII; Hans Holbein, the Younger; Catherine Howard; Catherine Parr; Jane Seymour; The Tudor Family.

RELATED ARTICLES in *Great Events from History: The Renaissance & Early Modern Era, 1454-1600:* 1531-1540: Cromwell Reforms British Government; 1532: Holbein Settles in London; May, 1539: Six Articles of Henry VIII.

PIETRO ARETINO
Italian writer

Aretino thrived in the use of the vernacular, wrote biting satire that exposed the corruption of Renaissance Rome, and produced comedies that are among the best in Italian literature. He has often been criticized for the explicit sexual prurience of his works, and his virtuoso exploitation of the press made him perhaps the world's first paparazzo.

BORN: April 19 or 20, 1492; Arezzo, Republic of Florence (now in Italy)
DIED: October 21, 1556; Venice, Republic of Venice (now in Italy)
ALSO KNOWN AS: Pietro of Arezzo; Scourge of Princes
AREA OF ACHIEVEMENT: Literature

EARLY LIFE

Pietro Aretino (PYEH-troh ah-ray-TEE-noh), whose original family name is not known, took his name from his birthplace, Arezzo. The events of his life have often been embellished with slanderous anecdotes, especially in an anonymous biography published in Perugia in 1538. Born the son of Tita, his mother, and Luca, either a cobbler or an artisan, Aretino went to Perugia some time before 1510, possibly to work as a journeyman bookbinder or even to receive an education there.

The title of his first published poetical work, *Opera nova* (1512), might indicate that in his youth he was thinking of a double career as a writer and painter. Opting for a writing career, Aretino left Perugia in 1516, intent on seeking a patron in Rome. There he was admitted to the house of the wealthy banker Agostino Chigi, a generous patron of writers and artists (among them the painter Raphael) and host to cardinals and popes.

Chigi's promotion of unknown writers speaks well for Aretino's talent to please and his genius for witty improvisation in the vernacular. Aretino was also, possibly, autodidactic, and he had a mocking contempt for the Humanistic ideals of education, erudition, and writing. Aretino rejected the Humanists from the outset, and from his early works onward, he sneered at them as *pedanti* (pedants).

LIFE'S WORK

Having gained insight into the public and private affairs of Roman ecclesiastical society while at Chigi's house, Aretino's appetite for gossip was indulged further when Pope Leo X summoned him to the papal court. After the death of the extravagant pope in 1521, Aretino's time as the so-called Pasquino's chancellor had come: By means

ARETINO'S MAJOR WORKS

1512	*Opera nova*
1524	*Sonetti lussuriosi* (*The Sonnets*, 1926)
1525	*La cortigiana* (rev. 1534; *The Courtesan*, 1926)
1527	*Il marescalco* (rev. 1533; *The Marescalco*, 1986)
1532	*Marfisa*
1534	*I sette salmi de la penitenzia di David* (*Paraphrase upon the Seaven Penitentiall Psalmes of the Kingly Prophet*, 1635)
1534	*La passione di Gesù*
1534	*Ragionamento della Nanna et della Antonio* (*The Ragionamenti: Or, Dialogues*, 1889)
1536	*Dialogo nelquale la Nanna il primo giorno insegna a la Pippa*
1537-1557	*Lettere* (*The Letters*, 1926)
1538	*Il Genesi*
1538	*Ragionamento de le Corti*
1538	*I quattro libri de la humanità di Cristo*
1539	*Vita di Caterina Vergine*
1539	*Vita di Maria Vergine*
1540	*Lo ipocrito*
1540	*L'Orlandino*
1542	*La Talanta*
1543	*Le carte parlanti*
1543	*Vita di San Tomaso Signor D'Aquino*
1546	*La Orazia*
1546	*Il filosofo*

of pasquinades (named after the Pasquino, a statue on which people pinned comments on current affairs), Aretino scoffed at the papal conclave. He canvassed support for Giulio de' Medici, from whom he and others expected a continuation of patronage.

After the election of the puritanical Adrian VI to the Papacy, Aretino left Rome. After some months in Mantua, at the court of the marquis Federigo Gonzaga, Aretino moved to the military camp of the general Giovanni de' Medici (also known as Giovanni delle Bande Nere), a condottiere (mercenary leader) who became a good friend. The early death of Adrian VI and the election of Giulio de' Medici, who became Pope Clement VII, induced Aretino to return to Rome. There he found himself in the midst of a political controversy, which had arisen between the faction supporting King Francis I of France (led by the datary Gian Matteo Giberti), and those on the side of Charles V of Habsburg. Both Francis and Charles would later become Aretino's benefactors.

Aretino broke with Giberti by lending support to the engraver Marcantonio Raimondi, who had worked on a series of drawings (depictions of sexual positions) by Giulio Romano. After having published the scandalous *Sonetti lussuriosi* (1524; *The Sonnets*, 1926), a set of poems that accompanied the engravings, Aretino had the good fortune of being received by Giovanni de' Medici, and it was through him that he met Francis I. When the pope formed an alliance with Francis, Aretino returned to Rome, where in 1525 he narrowly escaped an assassination attempt, carried out, in all probability, on the orders of Giberti. Disillusioned by the inactivity of the pope, Aretino announced his departure in the first version of the comedy *La cortigiana* (wr. 1525, pr. 1534, pb. 1537; *The Courtesan*, 1926) and duly returned to Giovanni. Meanwhile, Francis I was defeated and imperial troops invaded Italy.

Following the fatal wounding of Giovanni, Aretino predicted a dark future for Rome. He then moved to Mantua, where he wrote the comedy *Il marescalco* (wr. 1527, rev. 1533; *The Marescalco*, 1986) and, in the second version of *The Courtesan*, announced his intention to go to Venice. On his arrival there, Aretino was already a celebrity, and the doge, Andrea Gritti, received Aretino's announcement (by letter) of his intention to stay. Aretino came to regard his beloved Venice as his home.

Soon he made friends with Titian, who painted six portraits of him—the first already completed in 1527. Another friend was the sculptor and architect Jacopo Sansovino, who moved to Venice after the sack of Rome (1527), an event that contributed strongly to Aretino's prophetic repute. It was in 1532 that Aretino coined for himself the agnomen (or additional name) Il Flagello dei Principi, il divin Pietro Aretino (the Scourge of Princes, the divine Pietro Aretino).

In 1534, Aretino published not only a revised version of *The Courtesan* but also his earliest religious writings, *La passione di Gesù* (the passion of Jesus) and *I sette salmi de la penitenzia di David* (*Paraphrase upon the Seaven Penitentiall Psalmes of the Kingly Prophet*, 1635). None of his religious works, however, is of major literary merit. The notable *Ragionamento della Nanna et della Antonio* (*The Ragionamenti: Or, Dialogues*, 1889), which looks at the lives of nuns and married women, was published in 1534. The second part to this work, *Dialogo nelquale la Nanna il primo giorno insegna a la Pippa*, which dealt with prostitution, was published in 1536. Certainly, it was the publication of *Lettere* (1537-1557; *The Letters*, 1926) that guaranteed his reputation and his income.

Apart from the dialogues, he published other comedies, *Lo ipocrito* (pb. 1540), *La Talanta* (pr., pb. 1542), and *Il filosofo* (pb. 1546), and a tragedy, *La Orazia* (pb. 1546). Aretino, although never married, had two daughters whom he cherished greatly. He revisited Rome in 1553, hoping in vain to obtain a cardinal's hat from Julius III. Anecdote also surrounds the circumstances of his death: Anselm Feuerbach (1829-1880), in a painting of 1854, depicts Aretino falling back and breaking his neck after a fit of laughter.

SIGNIFICANCE

Though Aretino was condemned to *damnatio memoriae* shortly after his death, his writings have been read not so much for the author's interest in sexuality as for his inci-

Pietro Aretino. (Library of Congress)

sive satirical commentary on the corruption pervading official life in Renaissance Rome. The pasquinades are of interest in regard to ecclesiastical and cultural history. His letters have proven to be a valuable source for contemporary history.

The unremittingly satirical dialogues, intended to expose Roman demoralization, impress with their rich linguistic color. His dramas, which abandoned existing plot-structural norms, and may have influenced writers such as François Rabelais and William Shakespeare, consolidated Aretino's position in Italian literary history.

Aretino's rejection of Humanistic education was as open as his pride in being a spontaneous writer with little education. Nevertheless, his works reveal that he was a careful thinker and writer, and that he had a capacity (paradoxically) to mask, beneath a satirical surface, a clarity of expression and indeed a warmth of feeling.

Aretino, an expert in using the press for purposes of scandalmongering and favor with the powerful—and to disseminate his own works—may be regarded as the pioneer of modern yellow, or sensational, journalism.

—*Veronika Oberparleiter*

FURTHER READING

Andrews, Richard. "Rhetoric and Drama: Monologues and Set Speeches in Aretino's Comedies." In *The Languages of Literature in Renaissance Italy*, edited by Peter Hainsworth et al. New York: Oxford University Press, 1988. A study of Aretino's plays.

Cairns, Christopher. "Aretino's Comedies and the Italian 'Erasmian' Connection in Shakespeare and Jonson." In *Theatre of the English and Italian Renaissance*, edited by J. R. Mulryne and Margaret Shewring. New York: St. Martin's Press, 1991. A study of Aretino's plays by one of the modern authorities on Aretino.

_____. *Pietro Aretino and the Republic of Venice: Researches on Aretino and His Circle in Venice, 1527-1556*. Florence, Italy: Olschki, 1985. Research on the most important phase of Aretino's life.

Cottino-Jones, Marga. "Rome and the Theatre in the Renaissance." In *Rome in the Renaissance: The City and the Myth*, edited by P. A. Ramsey. Binghamton, N.Y.: Center for Medieval and Renaissance Studies, 1982. Another study of Aretino's plays.

Richardson, Brian. *Printing, Writers, and Readers in Renaissance Italy*. New York: New York University Press, 1999. Observations on Aretino's formidable ability to make use of the press.

Ruggiero, Guido. "Marriage, Love, Sex, and Renaissance Civic Morality." In *Sexuality and Gender in*

Early Modern Europe: Institutions, Texts, Images, edited by James Grantham Turner. New York: Cambridge University Press, 1993. An ethical study of sexuality and gender during Aretino's time. Includes bibliography and index.

SEE ALSO: Adrian VI; Baldassare Castiglione; Charles V; Clement VII; Francis I; Leo X; François Rabelais;

Raphael; Jacopo Sansovino; William Shakespeare; Tintoretto; Titian.

RELATED ARTICLES in *Great Events from History: The Renaissance & Early Modern Era, 1454-1600:* June 28, 1519: Charles V Is Elected Holy Roman Emperor; 1521-1559: Valois-Habsburg Wars; May 6, 1527-February, 1528: Sack of Rome.

LUDOVICO ARIOSTO
Italian poet and playwright

Ariosto, although an accomplished Latin poet, made vernacular Italian the established language for serious poetry from lyrics and satires to drama and the epic.

BORN: September 8, 1474; Reggio Emilia, duchy of Modena (now in Italy)
DIED: July 6, 1533; Ferrara (now in Italy)
AREA OF ACHIEVEMENT: Literature

EARLY LIFE

The life and works of Ludovico Ariosto (lewd-oh-VEE-coh ahr-ee-OH-stoh), like those of his administrator-soldier father, are closely bound to the house of Este, the dukes of Ferrara. In spite of the instability created by the almost-constant struggles between this city-kingdom and other rival city-states, the Estensi court in Ferrara was one of the finest in Renaissance Europe. It supported an army, a university, jousts and hunts, and many artists.

Architects, painters, sculptors, musicians, and poets were an everyday presence in the life of this court, which was located on the main pilgrimage and trade routes of Spain, France, and Italian city-states such as Venice and Bologna. The young Ariosto was introduced to this center of gracious living in 1485, when his father, Niccolò, after commanding citadels surrounding Ferrara for twelve years, was recalled. Ariosto had been born in Reggio, one such vast citadel, the first of ten children.

Ariosto's love of literature became a problem only when Count Niccolò, his father, enrolled him in the five-year law curriculum at the university about 1489. He completed slightly more than two uncongenial years toward his doctorate of law, while working with the court theater in his spare time, before his father relented and allowed him to study classical poetry in about 1494. Gregorio da Spoleto, who also taught the sons of the Strozzi and Este families, was a gifted and devoted teacher. Within one and a half years, Ludovico was the

prize student, giving recitations at court and composing humorous poems about student life as well as lyrics and eclogues in Latin. It was not until 1503-1505, under Pietro Bembo, that Ariosto started composing serious poetry in the vernacular.

Ariosto's devotion to such work, however, was interrupted by family financial problems in 1498. That year, to help his family after his father's fall from ducal grace, Ariosto entered the service of Ercole I d'Este. Two years later, Niccolò died, leaving Ariosto head of the family, with four younger brothers to educate and five sisters to support until their marriages, with only meager income from properties surrounding Ferrara. Duke Ercole appointed him to a more lucrative position as captain of a garrison in 1502. The next year, however, the last of his uncles died, and Ariosto was forced to return to Ferrara to look after his family. He was then given a position in the household of Ercole's son, Cardinal Ippolito d'Este, which he kept until 1517. Ippolito's household, rather than being churchly, rivaled his father's and his brother Alfonso's in all aspects—art, women, hunting, feasting, and battling. Services demanded by a courtier might range from overseeing feasts to accompanying Ippolito on diplomatic or military missions. Ariosto's health declined, and stomach disorders, which would plague him all his life, began.

LIFE'S WORK

The first written evidence of an inner conflict between Ariosto's art and his courtier occupation is found in two poems written at about the same time. One was in praise of Ippolito's purity and chastity, and the second was an epithalamium for Lucrezia Borgia, already twice married. These poems helped establish his position as the court poet and are, perhaps, the first evidence of what was to become his dominant tone as a poet—irony.

Ludovico Ariosto. (Library of Congress)

His burdens were not lightened by the birth of his first illegitimate son, Giambattista, after a brief liaison, probably with a servant. It is also possible that during this time, in order to increase his income, he took minor Holy Orders, but he steadfastly refused the hypocrisy of the lucrative benefices of full priesthood. By 1507, his growing reputation as a poet relieved him from some of the least congenial aspects of his service. That year, he was sent to Ippolito's sister's court in Mantua to convey a poem celebrating the birth of Princess Isabella's first son. Isabella and her court welcomed him and especially admired a work in progress he read to them, a work all scholars agree must have been the first draft of the *Orlando furioso* (1516, 1521, 1532; English translation, 1591).

During the time between this visit and the poem's publication, Ariosto's time was doubly occupied. At court, he was in charge of many theatrical productions. In 1508, his own comedy, *La cassaria* (*The Coffer*, 1975), was elaborately produced and popularly received for Carnivale. He followed with another success, *I suppositi* (*The Pretenders*, 1566), in 1509, and prepared *Il negromante* (*The Necromancer*, 1975) for Carnivale in 1510, although its production was stopped because of the precarious political and military concerns of the city. Violence plagued Ferrara. In 1508, Ariosto's best friend, Ercole Strozzi, was assassinated, supposedly by Alfonso's

men. Ariosto himself was mediating between Ferrara and the Papacy in Rome and France, with whom Ferrara had allied itself between 1507 and 1509, attempting to reassure each faction. He was on such a mission when Pope Julius II's troops attacked Ferrara, and Alfonso was excommunicated. He rejoined Ippolito the next year, in time to witness the sacking of Ravenna in 1512. Later that year, when an attempted reconciliation between Alfonso and the pope suddenly failed, he accompanied Alfonso in a dangerous escape from Rome to Florence. In between, he worked on *Orlando furioso*. Probably in Florence, in 1513, he fell in love with a married woman, Alessandra Strozzi-Benucci.

Ariosto continued to travel on diplomatic missions for Ippolito and Alfonso, finding time to write between the assignments. Somehow, the first forty cantos of *Orlando furioso* were completed in 1515, the same year that Alessandra's husband died. Still, the couple did not marry. *Orlando furioso* was published in 1516, and all two thousand copies of the first edition sold within five years, making it the first best-seller of the Renaissance. Ariosto became famous throughout Europe.

His means of support still came primarily from his service at court. When Ippolito, who was also primate of Hungary and bishop of Buda, decided to move his court to Hungary in 1517, Ariosto chose to stay in Ferrara. Ippolito agreed but dismissed Ariosto from his services. Yet Alfonso almost immediately took Ariosto into service at his court in Ferrara at a better salary.

For the next three years, Ariosto's life was quite pleasant. He had time to finish and rewrite one of his earlier dramas, *The Necromancer*. He wrote his first three satires and started revising *Orlando furioso*. Its second edition was published in 1521, to be followed by multiple editions in the next seven years. By 1519, however, Ferrara was again rumored to be the target of a papal invasion.

Renewal of warfare drained Ferrara's resources and forced Alfonso to suspend pay to the professors and to many artists, including Ariosto. By 1522, Ariosto was forced to accept a post as commissioner of the Garfagnana district, which was controlled by Alfonso. He found himself temperamentally unsuited to deliver the severe punishment perhaps needed to establish peace and law in the area. Ariosto found the post beyond his powers and felt exiled rather than rewarded. When offered an ambassadorship to the court of Clement VII, he refused it and returned to his beloved Ferrara and Alessandra in June, 1525.

Finally, Ariosto had the leisure and enough money to live as he wished. Between 1526 and 1528, he composed

ARIOSTO'S MAJOR WORKS	
1508	*La cassaria* (rev. 1530; *The Coffer*, 1975)
1509	*I suppositi* (*The Pretenders*, 1566)
1516	*Orlando furioso* (rev. 1521, 1532; English translation, 1591)
1517-1525	*Satire* (pb. 1534; *Ariosto's Satyres*, 1608)
1519	*I studenti* (*The Students*, 1975)
1520	*Il negromante* (rev. 1529; *The Necromancer*, 1975)
1528	*La Lena* (*Lena*, 1975)
1545	*Cinque canti*, 1545

Cinque canti, which was published posthumously in 1545. In 1528, the people of Ferrara elected him to be Judge of the Twelve Sages. Also in 1528, he was appointed director of the court theater, which Alfonso wanted restored to its former glory after the disruptions of the wars. Not only did Ariosto supervise construction of sets and productions but also he had a chance to revise his own dramatic works to fit his newer ideas of dramatic style. *La Lena* (1528; *Lena*, 1975) and *The Coffer* (rev. 1530) were both performed. His prestige as a diplomat was the highest, and he was asked to make a few visits to Florence, Venice, and Mantua for Alfonso. Meanwhile, he worked on his final version of *Orlando furioso*, which was published in October, 1532. Weeks later, he was in Mantua with Alfonso to welcome Charles V, the Holy Roman Emperor, and give him a presentation copy. Most biographers also believe that Ariosto and Alessandra were secretly married between 1526 and 1530, but that they continued to live separately, perhaps to keep income from minor benefices conferred by Ippolito. By December, 1532, his lifelong stomach problems and later chest pains had taken their toll. Ariosto fell severely ill and died on July 6, 1533.

Alessandra and his second son, Virginio, were by his bedside. He was buried by the monks of San Benedetto at their church, quietly, as he desired. His body was later entombed in the Biblioteca Ariostea of Ferrara beneath a marble tomb supplied by Napoleon.

SIGNIFICANCE

Ariosto is a prime example of the Renaissance man. An outstanding poet in all forms—lyrical, satirical, dramatic, and epic—he also was always involved in the active life of the courts of Ferrara as administrator and diplomat. He was always conscientious and loyal to family, friends, and patrons. He never sought great riches or titles but only enough to support himself and his family comfortably while he pursued his writing.

Ariosto became the poet for whom Dante had called, one who would embody the greatest of Italian culture in a new form fit for the greatest of Italian vernacular poetry. *Orlando furioso* was a best-seller not only in Italy but also in France and in England, where Elizabeth I ordered an English translation. The almost picaresque structure of simultaneous multiple plots, the mixture of comic and tragic material, and the persona of a semidetached narrator were inventive strokes that allowed Ariosto to examine the form and values of the dying chivalric romance tradition while deeply investigating the problems of society in general and those of human nature. *Orlando furioso* is great poetry, great fun for the reader, and full of great wisdom about humanity and the world.

—*Ann E. Reynolds*

FURTHER READING

Beecher, Donald, Massimo Ciavolella, and Roberto Fedi, eds. *Ariosto Today: Contemporary Perspectives.* Buffalo, N.Y.: University of Toronto Press, 2003. Anthology of essays by American, Canadian, and Italian scholars on contemporary Ariosto criticism. Addresses topics ranging from traditional criticism of Ariosto's lyric poetry to cinematic adaptations of *Orlando furioso*. Includes bibliographic references.

Brand, C. P. *Ludovico Ariosto: A Preface to the "Orlando Furioso."* Edinburgh, Scotland: Edinburgh University Press, 1974. An excellent overview of Ariosto's life and works. Contains full chapters on life, lyrics, satires, and dramas while concentrating on a thematic study of the *Orlando furioso*. Emphasizes the opposition of love and war. Contains brief bibliographies for each chapter and two indexes.

Croce, Benedetto. *Ariosto, Shakespeare, and Corneille.* Translated by Douglas Ainslie. New York: Holt, Rinehart and Winston, 1920. Reprint. New York: Russell & Russell, 1966. An extremely influential early modern essay on *Orlando furioso*. Rebutting the traditional criticism, Croce argues that the work achieves unity through the artist's control of point of view and style, a unity that ultimately reflects the rhythm and harmony of God's creation.

Gardner, Edmund G. *The King of Court Poets: Ariosto.* New York: E. P. Dutton, 1906. Reprint. New York: Haskell House, 1968. Gardner's full-length biography contains a wealth of material and is easy to read. He includes a social, cultural, and political background of Ariosto's life and work. Contains a dated bibliography, a useful index, and three foldout genealogies of the houses of Ariosto, Este, and Pio.

Griffin, Robert. *Ludovico Ariosto.* Boston: Twayne, 1974. Good introductory work on Ariosto, beginning with a chapter on his life and ending with a survey of criticism. Also contains chapters on lyrics, satires, dramas, and a thematic analysis of *Orlando furioso.* Argues that the unity of the poem rests on man's inability to accept the will of fortune in a world beyond his limited comprehension. Contains chronology, notes, selected bibliography with brief annotations, and two indexes.

Kisacky, Julia M. *Magic in Boiardo and Ariosto.* New York: Peter Lang, 2000. Monograph comparing *Orlando furioso* to Matteo Maria Boiardo's *Orlando inamorato.* Looks at the representation of magical artifacts, supernatural creatures, and magic practitioners in each work. Includes bibliographic references and index.

Rodini, Robert J., and Salvatore Di Maria. *Ludovico Ariosto: An Annotated Bibliography of Criticism, 1956-1980.* Columbia: University of Missouri Press, 1984. Contains 930 entries from journals, monographs, essays in books, North American dissertations, and books. Although meant primarily for scholars, the entry synopses are excellent and can easily be skimmed. Arranged by author, the book also contains a detailed subject index and an index by works treated.

Wiggins, Peter De Sa. *Figures in Ariosto's Tapestry: Character and Design in the "Orlando Furioso."* Baltimore: Johns Hopkins University Press, 1986. Agreeing with Galileo's early comments on the psychological consistency of Ariosto's characters and his exact knowledge of human nature, Wiggins suggests that their complex inner lives are universal human types. This invisible interior world, at odds with an exterior world of folly and depravity, is a major theme of the work. Excellent index and notes for each chapter.

_____. *The Satires of Ludovico Ariosto: A Renaissance Autobiography.* Athens: Ohio University Press, 1976. A bilingual text, using the Italian original edited by Cesare Segre with Wiggins's clear prose translations on the facing page. Each satire is placed in biographical and historical context with its own separate preface and notes. Argues that the narrator of the satires is an idealized poet courtier in typical situations rather than a factual mirror of Ariosto himself. Suggests that the satires share similarities with *Orlando furioso:* the theme of illusion and reality, the ironic humor, and the use of a dramatic persona as narrator.

SEE ALSO: Lucrezia Borgia; Luís de Camões; Charles V; Clement VII; Julius II; Marguerite de Navarre; Pierre de Ronsard; Edmund Spenser; Torquato Tasso.

RELATED ARTICLES in *Great Events from History: The Renaissance & Early Modern Era, 1454-1600:* 1481-1499: Ludovico Sforza Rules Milan; September, 1494-October, 1495: Charles VIII of France Invades Italy.

JACOBUS ARMINIUS
Dutch theologian and minister

Arminius was a Dutch Reformed minister and professor of theology whose views on free will, sin, grace, and predestination made his name synonymous with the larger movement against Calvinism.

BORN: October 10, 1560; Oudewater, Holland (now in the Netherlands)

DIED: October 19, 1609; Leiden, Holland (now in the Netherlands)

ALSO KNOWN AS: Jacob Harmensen (given name); Jacob Hermans; Jacob Hermansz; Jacob Harmans; James Arminius; Jakob Hermann; Jacob Harmenszoon; Jacob Hermannsoon; Jacob Hermansen

AREA OF ACHIEVEMENT: Religion and theology

EARLY LIFE

Jacobus Arminius (ahr-MIHN-ee-uhs) was born in Oudewater, Holland, a town near Utrecht. Many biographical details of his early boyhood are obscure at best and possibly misreported at worst. It seems, however, that his parents were of middling rank.

It is certain that he experienced several losses during his youth: His father died shortly before Arminius was born, and, in 1575, his mother and siblings died in the general massacre in Oudewater at the hands of Spanish troops. Indeed, the struggle of many of the Dutch cities against Spanish domination, the success of the northern provinces in this endeavor, and the subsequent political and religious divisions in the newly independent state of the United Provinces served as a backdrop to Arminius's entire life.

After his father's death, the young Arminius's education was to be sponsored by charitable individuals and, eventually, the magistrates of Amsterdam. His first benefactor was Theodore Aemilius, a Catholic priest who accepted many Protestant ideas, especially about the Mass. He took the boy into his household, where Arminius received an excellent education. Even while Oudewater and nearby Utrecht remained officially Catholic, the movements of many Protestants and Protestant sympathizers in the area can be detected. Arminius himself moved in Protestant circles, and his first choice for university studies was at Marburg, which had been established in 1527 as a Protestant alternative to the Catholic universities in the north and was Europe's first Protestant university.

Arminius, however, was among the first students to enroll in the newly founded University of Leiden. There, he began serious theological studies and observed firsthand the lines of fissure between Protestants. In the 1570's and 1580's, Leiden the town and the university became the scene of controversy between rival Protestant views on various matters. Those under Geneva's influence criticized the Dutch Reformed Church mostly on the matter of rituals, which they described as Catholic vestiges, and on the matter of church governance, which allowed the involvement of civic magistrates.

In the moderate tradition that had produced Desiderius Erasmus, Caspar Coolhaes wrote the justification for the Dutch church's practices. In this document, Coolhaes outlined a model of toleration for diverse Protestant views. Coolhaes was condemned by a national synod, a fate posthumously shared by Arminius. Later in life, Arminius recognized Coolhaes as one of his early influences.

In 1582, Arminius left Leiden to study in Geneva, then under the influence of Theodore Beza. At Geneva, Arminius encountered Beza's belief that before creation God had foreordained which individuals would be saved and which would be damned. Human striving, which could be interpreted as the exercise of free will, while a sign of election, can make no difference in the outcome. This position would later be known as supralapsarianism. Also present in Geneva, however, were others who argued for a less drastic view and for a toleration of diverse viewpoints on this issue. Scholars disagree about Arminius's own views at this time. One can only note that he was in a position to hear these issues aired at an early stage in his own career.

In 1587, Arminius began his pastoral duties in Am-

sterdam, and he would continue there for fifteen years. He also began a family around this time, marrying Lijsbet Raeal in 1590. The marriage connected him with merchants and government figures in the city.

LIFE'S WORK

Arminius began to air his own doubts about Calvinist interpretations during his ministry in Amsterdam. He did so in a sermon in which he suggested that sinners can strive to do good. Calvinists argued that the unregenerate sinner is characterized by a lack of striving. From this period until his death in 1609, Arminius would frequently be forced to defend his position before various church governing bodies: classis, consistory, and synod. He had on occasion demanded that a public inquiry be made into his opinions. The reason for this was that his accusers resorted to circulating rumors that were difficult to refute as they were not put into a formal accusation. In 1603, Arminius accepted a position teaching theology at the University of Leiden. Some of his bitterest enemies would emerge from that setting.

Among Arminius's major works are the "Examination of Perkins's Pamphlet on the Order and Mode of Predestination," the "Examination of Gomarus's Theses on Predestination," and "A Declaration of the Sentiments of Arminius." (William Perkins was an English theologian whose writings supported an extreme Calvinist viewpoint; Franciscus Gomarus was a Dutch theologian and Arminius's fiercest critic during the last years of his life at the University of Leiden.) In these works, in his public statements under examination, and in correspondence, Arminius expresses the basic ideas that have become associated with his name.

At the foundation of all else is Arminius's claim that individuals have a right to doubt points unclear to their individual conscience. The exact nature of God's choice of the elect and the damned was a point that Arminius wanted to explore further. From the right to doubt there followed his willingness to accept a diversity of confessions within the Reformed Church. In this case, he had a long, liberal tradition in the Dutch Reformed Church to support him.

Arminius also held views on church government. In this he was consistently Erastian, always insisting that civic magistrates should be involved. Arminius and others feared that the Calvinist insistence on autonomy for the consistory would lead to the same problems that they believed clerical, especially papal, control of the Catholic church faced.

Most important historically, however, were Arminius's views on predestination. Arminius argued that God's condemnation of nonbelievers, or the unregenerate, was not a condemnation of particular, predetermined individuals to eternal damnation. Arminius saw Christ's intervening grace as significant and capable of working to create a believer from a nonbeliever who could then be saved.

SIGNIFICANCE

The criticisms Arminius voiced against Calvinist views did not originate with him, nor was he the sole theologian who felt uneasy with the role that Calvinism had assigned to both God and the sinner. As the body of criticism grew and became widespread in Protestant Europe, Calvinist ministers and theologians—those who accepted the idea that predestined election or damnation for each individual had occurred before creation and no recourse lay open to the individual to change that destiny—began to see the critics of this point of view as a coherent group. In response, the critics began as well so to identify themselves as a group. The examination of these dissenting ideas in various conferences promoted the sense of a coherent movement. The movement became known as Arminianism in 1619, a decade after Arminius's death, when the international Calvinist Synod of Dort condemned his ideas.

Condemnation did not, however, destroy the movement. In England, it remained a force, at times dominant during the seventeenth century, against Puritans. John Wesley, the founder of Methodism, cited Arminius as an influence. In the Netherlands, the Remonstrants maintained the Arminian position. The issues opened in the sixteenth and seventeenth centuries by those who doubted strict Calvinism continued to stir passions and to be debated along much the same lines as they were in Arminius's time.

—*Lynn M. Johnson*

FURTHER READING

Arminius, Jacobus. *The Works of James Arminius*. Translated by James Nichols and William Nichols. 3 vols. Grand Rapids, Mich.: Baker Book House, 1986. One of the standard translations of Arminius's works used by scholars.

Bangs, Carl. *Arminius: A Study in the Dutch Reformation*. 2d ed. Grand Rapids, Mich.: Francis Asbury Press, 1985. Bangs attempts to provide a thorough examination of the development of Arminius's theological positions in the political, religious, and commercial context of late sixteenth century Holland. He also carefully critiques a number of reports about Arminius's life and work that he believes to be erroneous.

Harrison, Archibald Harold Walter. *The Beginnings of Arminianism to the Synod of Dort*. 1926. Reprint. Springfield, Ill.: Scholarly Reprints, 2000. A useful account of the theological points and of the development of a coherent critique of Calvinism.

Tyacke, Nicholas. *Anti-Calvinists: The Rise of English Arminianism, c. 1590-1640*. New York: Oxford University Press, 1990. This book provides an analysis of the development of an anti-Calvinist position outside Holland, thus demonstrating the international nature of the movement. England is especially important because the movement there is labeled Arminian. The chapter on the Synod of Dort will help the reader carry the story beyond Bangs's study.

SEE ALSO: John Calvin; Desiderius Erasmus.

RELATED ARTICLES in *Great Events from History: The Renaissance & Early Modern Era, 1454-1600:* October 31, 1517: Luther Posts His Ninety-five Theses; April-May, 1521: Luther Appears Before the Diet of Worms; March, 1536: Calvin Publishes *Institutes of the Christian Religion*; May, 1559-August, 1561: Scottish Reformation; April or May, 1560: Publication of the Geneva Bible; August 24-25, 1572: St. Bartholomew's Day Massacre.

ANNE ASKEW
English writer and martyr

Askew documented her experiences as a Protestant accused of heresy in England, writing about the court proceedings, interrogations, and torture that led to her execution. Her Examinations *are singular, for no other female martyr of the Henrician or Marian periods in Tudor England recorded her own trial and torture.*

BORN: c. 1521; Lincolnshire, England
DIED: July 16, 1546; Smithfield, England
ALSO KNOWN AS: Anne Ayscough; Anne Kyme; Anne Ascue
AREAS OF ACHIEVEMENT: Literature, religion and theology, church reform

EARLY LIFE

Anne Askew, born into a wealthy Lincolnshire family, was the daughter of Elizabeth Wrottesley and Sir William Askew. Her father, knighted by Henry VIII in 1513, served as a courtier, the high sheriff of Lincolnshire and a member of Parliament. Though the breadth of her education is unknown, Askew's extensive knowledge of Scripture and striking aptitude for oratory suggest she received some academic instruction.

Askew was compelled by her father to marry Thomas Kyme of Friskney, the fiancé of her late sister Martha, by whom she had two children. Askew's Protestantism, however, troubled her Catholic husband, who forced her from their home after she slighted local priests. Askew sought to divorce her unreformed spouse. Unable to persuade John Longland, the bishop of Lincoln, to grant her a divorce, Askew probably appealed to the Court of Chancery in London, where her petition was apparently denied.

LIFE'S WORK

On her arrival in London, Askew became involved with Protestant reformers associated with Catherine Parr, the sixth wife of Henry VIII. Though Henry VIII had broken with the Roman Catholic Church and formed the Church of England in 1534 to secure a divorce from his first wife, he remained a practicing Catholic until his death. During his reign, reformers were viewed with suspicion and sanctioned for violating the Act of Six Articles (1539), which encoded Catholic doctrine. Suspected of denying Christ's real presence in the bread and wine of the Eucharist, Askew was repeatedly arrested for heresy under the first of the six articles.

While imprisoned at Newgate and the Tower of London in March, 1545, and June, 1546, Askew found herself re-

lentlessly interrogated about her beliefs. During her final imprisonment, she was illegally tortured on the rack when she refused to implicate others who shared her faith, particularly those noblewomen in Catherine Parr's circle. Angered at her silence, Thomas Wriothesley, the lord chancellor, and Sir Richard Rich, a chancery officer and future lord chancellor, racked Askew with their bare hands. Askew was condemned to death on June 28, 1546. On July 16, 1546, she was brought to Smithfield for her execution, carried because her tortured, broken body prevented her from walking. Askew refused a final opportunity to recant and to receive the king's pardon, and was burned at the stake in the company of three fellow reformers.

Askew composed a detailed account of her two interrogations, *The First Examinacyon of Anne Askewe* (1546) and *The Lattre Examinacyon of Anne Askewe* (1547), better known collectively as *Examinations*. Protestant reformers often recorded the substance of their interrogations to reveal their ability to challenge, with divine aid, the orthodox doctrine of their Catholic inquisitors. Askew, unlike male reformers subjected to questioning, had to defend herself not only as an accused heretic but also as a woman. Her interrogators asserted that she, as a woman, should neither defy ecclesiastical authority nor openly discuss Scripture, an activity prohibited by the Act for Advancement of True Religion (1543).

Despite the restrictions placed on Renaissance women, Askew found within herself a source of authority. Her *Examinations* reveal her confidence in her ability to read, interpret, and expound Scriptur7es without the assistance of church officials. She thereby dodged the authority of the priests whom she rejected as mediators between herself and God. Throughout her *Examinations*, Askew confidently cites Scripture to support her doctrinal claims and to condemn the beliefs and conduct of her accusers. When she wishes to remain silent on a subject, however, she reminds her questioners, with understated irony, that "it was against St. Paul's learning, that . . . a woman, should interpret the scriptures, specially where so many wise learned men were."

Askew's confidence in her being an agent of spiritual truth is transparent in the lines of a ballad she wrote during her imprisonment, the last words in *Examinations*: "The Ballad Which Anne Askew Made and Sang When She Was in Newgate." In this ballad, Askew assumed, through simile, a masculine military identity. She was an "armed knight appointed to the field" and as such, was

> ## A SUMMARY OF THE CONDEMNATION AND TORTURE OF ANNE ASKEW
>
> They said to me there, that I was a heretic and condemned by the law, if I would stand in my opinion. I answered that I was no heretic, neither yet deserved I any death by the law of God. . . . Then would they need to know, if I would deny the sacrament to by Christ's body and blood: I said, yes. . . . And as for that you call your God, is but a piece of bread. For a more proof thereof let it lie in the box but 3 months, and it will be moldy, and so turn to nothing that is good. Whereupon I am persuaded, that it cannot be God. . . . Then they said [after more interrogation], there were of the counsel that did maintain me. And I said, no. Then they did put me on the rack, because I confessed no ladies nor gentlewomen to be of my opinion, and thereon they kept me a long time. And because I lay still and did not cry, my lord Chancelor and master [Sir Richard] Rich, took pains to rack me with their own hands, till I was nigh [nearly] dead.
>
> *Source:* Excerpted from Askew's account of her trial and torture, published posthumously by John Bale as *The Examinations of Anne Askew* (1546, 1547), in *The Renaissance in Europe: An Anthology*, edited by Peter Elmer, Nick Webb, and Roberta Wood (New Haven, Conn.: Yale University Press, 2000), pp. 257, 260. (Rendered into modern English by Desiree Dreeuws.)

mony to the significant role played by women in the transition from Catholicism to Protestantism in Renaissance England. Traditionally called to silence and obedience, women during this time period were granted a degree of spiritual agency and authority by the reformed religion, which championed the priesthood of all believers, regardless of gender.

Askew's writings are one of the earliest extant examples of an Englishwoman's vocal opposition to ecclesiastical and civic authority. The *Examinations*, as edited by John Bale and John Foxe, endorse the female adoption of the traditionally masculine role of scriptural interpreter and guide and also reestablish women as active agents in religious history.

—*Holly Faith Nelson*

free to offer a critique of the unjust power structure that imprisons innocent followers of Christ. Askew self-assuredly engaged in a battle with the world, shielded only by her reformed faith, and concluded with a prayer of forgiveness for her enemies.

Askew's *Examinations* and Newgate ballad were published in 1546 and 1547 by the playwright and Protestant propagandist John Bale, later bishop of Ossory. Bale claimed to have access to Askew's handwritten account of her examinations, although no original manuscript is extant. Bale has been criticized for his copious, invasive commentary, which reshapes and disrupts Askew's narrative to advance his religious ideals. Nevertheless, by locating Askew within the broader narrative of Protestant history, he also helps present a Renaissance woman's authoritative public voice. The historian John Foxe later included Askew's *Examinations*, without Bale's commentary, in his martyrology *Actes and Monuments of These Latter and Perillous Dayes* (1563; better known as *Foxe's Book of Martyrs*). Though his subtler editorial intervention has been seen as less troubling, Foxe also manipulated her text to produce an unblemished Protestant martyr. Therefore, Askew's autobiographical voice—her textual identity—has been shaped by her male editors, and it remains, as she wished, partially hidden from view.

SIGNIFICANCE

The *Examinations* and ballad of Askew stand as a testi-

FURTHER READING

Beilin, Elaine V. *Redeeming Eve: Women Writers of the English Renaissance*. Princeton, N.J.: Princeton University Press, 1987. A seminal work on Askew as a figure of female political resistance in Renaissance England

_____, ed. *The Examinations of Anne Askew*. New York: Oxford University Press, 1996. The introduction to this critical edition offers another review of Askew's biography.

Betteridge, Thomas. "Anne Askew, John Bale, and Protestant History." *Journal of Medieval and Early Modern Studies* 27, no. 2 (Spring, 1997): 265-284. An examination of the expression of modern subjectivity in Askew's writings, partially undermined by the attempt of Renaissance editors to reduce Askew to a martyr in Protestant history.

Coles, Kimberly Anne. "The Death of the Author (And the Appropriation of Her Text): The Case of Anne Askew's *Examinations*." *Modern Philology* 99, no. 4 (2002): 515-539. A comparison of the editorial practices of John Bale and John Foxe.

_____. "Reproductive Rites: Anne Askew and the Female Body as Witness in the *Acts and Monuments*." In *Consuming Narratives: Gender and Monstrous Appetite in the Middle Ages and the Renaissance*, edited by Liz Herbert McAvoy and Teresa Walters. Cardiff: University of Wales Press, 2002. An analysis of

Askew's interior self-fashioning and denial of bodily experience, and her "re-embodiment" in *Foxe's Book of Martyrs* (*Actes and Monuments of These Latter and Perillous Dayes*).

Kemp, Theresa D. "Translating (Anne) Askew: The Textual Remains of a Sixteenth-Century Heretic and Saint." *Renaissance Quarterly* 50, no. 4 (Winter, 1999): 1021-1045. An examination of Askew's textual body as a site on which Henrician conservatives and Protestant reformists dispute religion and politics.

Kesselring, Krista. "Representations of Women in Tudor Historiography: John Bale and the Rhetoric of Exemplarity." *Renaissance and Reformation* 22, no. 2 (1998): 41-61. A defense of Bale's editions of the *Examinations*, which render Askew a public exemplary agent worthy of imitation.

Mazzola, Elizabeth. "Expert Witnesses and Secret Subjects: Anne Askew's *Examinations* and Renaissance Self-Incrimination." In *Political Rhetoric, Power, and Renaissance Women*, edited by Carol Levin and Patricia A. Sullivan. Albany: State University of New York Press, 1995. A psychoanalytic (Freudian) reading of Askew's *Examinations*, which explores Askew's identity as a subject of secret knowledge.

Travitsky, Betty, ed. *The Paradise of Women: Writings by Englishwomen of the Renaissance.* Westport, Conn.: Greenwood Press, 1981. A collection of noteworthy excerpts from Askew's works, accompanied by a detailed analysis of Askew's strategies of resistance.

SEE ALSO: Thomas Cromwell; Henry VIII; Balthasar Hubmaier; Mary I; Catherine Parr; Nicholas Ridley.

RELATED ARTICLES in *Great Events from History: The Renaissance & Early Modern Era, 1454-1600:* 1473-1600: Witch-Hunts and Witch Trials; May, 1539: Six Articles of Henry VIII.

ASKIA DAUD
Emperor of the Songhai Empire (r. 1549-1582)

Under Askia Daud, the Songhai Empire realized its golden age, its most prosperous and stable period. In land area, the empire in its day made up one of the largest states anywhere in the world.

BORN: Early sixteenth century; Songhai Empire (now in Mali)

DIED: July or August, 1582; Tondibi, Songhai Empire

ALSO KNOWN AS: Daud; Dāwūd; Daoud

AREAS OF ACHIEVEMENT: Government and politics, warfare and conquest

EARLY LIFE

Askia Daud (AS-kyah dowd) was the sixth of his line to rule the Songhai Empire in central West Africa. His dynasty was founded in 1492 by his father, Muhammad Ture (Mohammed I Askia), under whom the term "askia" became both a title signifying "emperor" and a dynastic name. The system of royal succession was patrilineal, but the rule of primogeniture was not strong, resulting in considerable instability.

Trouble began in 1529 when a group of royal brothers, which included Askia Daud, overthrew their father. Following this, three half brothers and a cousin preceded Askia Daud, the totality of their reigns amounting to twenty years. Members of the royal family were both the foundation of the Askia Dynasty's power and the major threat to it. The first act of any new askia was to determine which of his brothers and cousins he could trust. The loyal ones would be appointed to high posts; those who posed a threat would be eliminated.

Askia Daud's immediate predecessor was Askia Ishaq I, said to be pious and intelligent but also cruel and authoritarian, a ruler who kept himself in power through terrorizing others. Ishaq's reign, which spanned a decade, degenerated into plots, counterplots, murder, and extortion.

LIFE'S WORK

Askia Daud had attained the rank of *kurmina-fari*, viceroy of the western half of the empire, by 1545. The preceding two *kurmina-fari* had been purged by Ishaq. Askia Daud's major achievement in this position was to attack the capital city of the declining Malian Empire to the southwest. On his approach he was so successful in ravaging the countryside that the Malian ruler and most of the inhabitants abandoned their city. Askia Daud remained there for a week, remembered only for being a vandal. He ordered his soldiers to pack the royal palace full of filth so that when the Malians returned, they would find it unusable.

Ishaq died in March of 1549. He had named a son as heir, but the ruling circles in the capital of Gao promptly ignored this. They had been impressed by Askia Daud's ability to survive in a government ruled by a paranoid like Ishaq, a feat requiring considerable political skill, even though Askia Daud had not been a favorite of his father.

Askia Daud was in the right place at the right time. As the Timbuktu chronicler Mahmud Kati put it,

> His father the Askia Muhammad and his brothers had labored and sowed for him, and, when he came, he had only to harvest; they had prepared the ground and, when his turn came, he had only to stretch out in order to go to sleep.

By the time Askia Daud came to sit under the royal dais, a large number of his brothers and cousins had killed one another, and more had died on the battlefield serving Songhai. This depletion of the royal brood kept Askia Daud's reign relatively free from internal strife.

Askia Daud had considerable abilities and likable personal traits. He was small, smart, tenacious, and brave. He was an eloquent speaker and a wit who loved to joke, somehow escaping the dour strain characteristic of his family. He also was experienced as a politician, having been involved in affairs of state since the overthrow of his father. Once in power, he proved to be a statesman of moderation and wisdom. He knew that the might of the empire rested on economic strength, so he encouraged agriculture and commerce. He was the only ruler of his era in the Western Sudan who is reported to have had a treasury of coined money. He supported intellectual pursuits, becoming the all-time most generous benefactor of the scholars at the university at Timbuktu, and he created an imperial library where he employed scribes to copy manuscripts.

Askia Daud also was an able military strategist. While his brothers had been focusing their energies on internal foes of the empire, provinces on the periphery had quietly slipped back into independence and external foes had recouped their power. Askia Daud took the empire to where it had been under his father. His most notable success was in the west against the Malians, where campaigns in 1550 and 1558-1559 added new lands in the upper Niger Valley to his empire. He was also successful in raiding the Mossi, who lived to the south (in what is now called Burkina Faso), although his objective here was to capture slaves rather than to conquer new territory.

He had less success to the east, where his effort to bring Kebbi (northwestern Nigeria) into the empire was unsuccessful, and his attempt to quell a revolt in the city of Katsina, an eastern outpost of the Songhai Empire, failed also.

Near the end of his reign, imperial borders remained stable. In 1570-1571, Askia Daud led an expedition of twenty-four thousand Tuareg allies against Arab tribesmen who were revolting in the western Sahel (southeastern Mauritania). A revolt by the Fulbe of Macina (the inland delta region of Mali) was put down with such ferocity by one of Askia Daud's sons, the askia announced his official disapproval.

During the last few years of his life, Askia Daud spent much of his time on his farm at Tondibi, thirty miles upstream from Gao. He died there of natural causes in the summer of 1582.

SIGNIFICANCE

Askia Daud's reign marked the golden age of the Songhai Empire. Its borders were secure, internal peace brought prosperity, commerce and agriculture flourished, and trans-Saharan trade boomed. Unfortunately, Askia Daud's reign proved to be an aberration. Eight askias succeeded Muhammad Ture, together ruling more than sixty-three years. Seven of those askias reigned for a total of thirty years; Askia Daud alone reigned for thirty-three years.

Askia Daud had at least sixty-one children, ten of whom ascended to royal power. Within a decade of Askia Daud's death, a major civil war known as the Revolt of the Balama, fought between rival half brothers in 1588, weakened the empire in the face of external enemies. In 1591, one of these, the sultan of Morocco, who had been kept in check by Askia Daud's judicious diplomacy and a timely subsidy in gold, sent an army across the Sahara Desert that eventually destroyed the Songhai Empire.

—Richard L. Smith

FURTHER READING

Bovill, E. W. *The Golden Trade of the Moors*. 1958. Reprint. Princeton, N.J.: Markus Wiener, 1995. A still-useful, seminal study that provides an overview of the rise and fall of the Songhai Empire.

Cissoko, Sekene Mody. "The Songhay from the Twelfth to the Sixteenth Century." In *Africa from the Twelfth to the Sixteenth Century*. Vol. 4 in *General History of Africa*, edited by D. T. Niane. Berkeley: University of California Press, 1984. Cissoko is an African scholar recognized as an authority on the Songhai Empire and the Askias who ruled it.

Hunwick, John. "Secular Power and Religious Authority in Muslim Society: The Case of Songhay." *Journal of African History* 37 (1996): 175-194. A look into the internal workings of the Songhai government, particularly the relationship between church and state.

_____. *Timbuktu and the Songhay Empire: Al-Sadi's Ta'rikh al-Sudan Down to 1613 and Other Contemporary Documents*. Leiden, the Netherlands: Brill, 1999. The only full English translation of al-Sadi's classic seventeenth century work about the Songhai Empire. Includes a lengthy section on Askia Daud's reign and should be used as the starting point for any serious research on this subject.

Levtzion, Nehemia. "The Western Maghrib and Sudan." In *The Cambridge History of Africa*, edited by Roland Oliver. Vol. 3. Cambridge, England: Cambridge University Press, 1977. Written by the doyen of medieval West African studies, this volume provides the standard interpretation of the Songhai Empire and Askia Daud's place in it.

Saad, Elias N. *Social History of Timbuktu: The Role of Muslim Scholars and Notables, 1400-1900*. New York: Cambridge University Press, 1983. Saad explores how Askia Daud was famous as a patron of the Timbuktu intelligentsia, and looks deeper into this relationship, revealing curious insight.

SEE ALSO: Amina Sarauniya Zazzua; Leo Africanus; Mohammed I Askia; Sonni ʿAlī; Zara Yaqob.
RELATED ARTICLES in *Great Events from History: The Renaissance & Early Modern Era, 1454-1600:* 1460-1600: Rise of the Akan Kingdoms; 1493-1528: Reign of Mohammed I Askia; 1500's: Trans-Saharan Trade Enriches Akan Kingdoms; 1591: Fall of the Songhai Empire.

ATAHUALPA
King of the Inca Empire (r. 1525-1533)

Atahualpa won a civil war against his half brother Huáscar and took control of the Inca Empire, but Atahualpa also fatally weakened the empire, which ultimately fell to the Spanish conquistadores.

BORN: c. 1502; Cuzco, Inca Empire (now in Peru)
DIED: August 29, 1533; Cajamarca, Inca Empire (now in Peru)
ALSO KNOWN AS: Atabalipa; Atahuallpa
AREAS OF ACHIEVEMENT: Government and politics, warfare and conquest

EARLY LIFE

Atahualpa (ah-tah-WAHL-pah) was the favorite son of Huayna Capac, the Inca (ruler) of the Inca Empire. His name is said to mean "virile-sweet," apparently reflecting a desire that he show a balance between manly and gentle characteristics. He is described as an illegitimate son. Because his mother, Palloca, has been identified as a descendant of Pachacuti, an earlier Inca, it is more likely that she was simply a concubine rather than the legal queen, or *qoya*. Inca nobles were expected to have numerous concubines, but because of frequent succession struggles, the inheritance of the Inca throne had become restricted to the sons of the legal queen.

Little is known of Atahualpa's childhood, but it may be safely assumed that he received the typical upbringing and education of an Inca noble. He would have learned the arts of war and of administration in a tradition-bound empire in which every aspect of each subject's life was prescribed and managed. At the appointed age, he would have had his ears ceremonially pierced and stretched with large ear ornaments, a visible sign of the upper classes of Inca society. He appears to have served in his father's army during campaigns in Quito, although not always to his father's credit.

LIFE'S WORK

Although Atahualpa was barred by Inca law from succeeding to the throne, Huayna Capac wanted his beloved son to be assured a position of honor and authority. As a result, Huayna Capac gave Atahualpa the governorship of Quito, making it a sort of northern capital, but subordinate to Cuzco, the traditional capital of the empire.

Huayna Capac originally named one of his sons by his *qoya*, Ninan Cuyochi, to be his heir. He agreed to name a second son, Huáscar, as heir, however, if the omens were not favorable for Ninan Cuyochi. The high priest of the sun slaughtered two llamas and studied the entrails to determine that the sun god favored Huáscar as heir. Ninan Cuyochi died shortly afterward of smallpox, a disease introduced to the Americas by the Spaniards and brought to the high Andes along the extensive messenger system maintained by the Incas to control their empire.

Shortly after Huayna Capac's death in 1525, Huáscar began to suspect certain members of his retinue of supporting Atahualpa, since they were from the same faction as the latter. Huáscar ordered them executed as traitors. Because Atahualpa had made no formal claim to his father's throne, he sent conciliatory messages to Huáscar, assuring him of his loyalty and asking only to be confirmed in the governorship of Quito. Huáscar had the majority of the messengers killed and their skins made into drumheads, but he sent a few back to Atahualpa with insulting messages and gifts of women's clothing, implying that Atahualpa was effeminate.

The accounts of subsequent events are muddled, but all agree that Huáscar attacked first, taking Atahualpa's palace at Tumebamba and imprisoning Atahualpa. Nevertheless, Atahualpa was subsequently able to escape, supposedly by means of a silver bar given to him by a noble lady. Atahualpa then assembled a large force that defeated Huáscar's foremost commander at Ambato, south of Quito, inflicting massive casualties on Huáscar's army. Atahualpa then marched on Cuzco and met Huáscar in battle. After a brief setback at Cotampampa, Atahualpa captured Huáscar.

The civil war was marked by atrocities on both sides. Huáscar is said to have preferred drunkenness and debauchery to sober command, and to have taken delight in torturing his half brother's emissaries even when peace might still have been possible. He also treated the descendants of previous Incas badly, seizing the lands that were supposed to support them while they tended the cults of their royal ancestors' memories. On the other hand, Atahualpa tortured and murdered many of Huáscar's supporters and exterminated the entire clan of

Tupac Inca, even burning Tupac's mummy, an act of sacrilege horrifying to a society in which religion and law were one and the same. On capturing Huáscar, Atahualpa ordered that his deposed half brother be fed offal (animal by-products) and excrement, and he forced Huáscar to witness such abominations as the execution of eighty of his children and the pillage of shrines throughout Cuzco.

Even as Atahualpa was celebrating his victory, messengers brought him news of the arrival of a strange force of white men bearing arms and armor of alien design. These were Spanish conquistadores led by Francisco Pizarro, a fortune hunter of impoverished noble background who wished to follow the example of earlier Spanish victories in Mexico and Central America. After two abortive expeditions in Ecuador, Pizarro had determined to find the wealthy empire in the highlands, of which he had heard rumors among the coastal tribes.

Atahualpa sent envoys to invite Pizarro and his men to visit him at Cajamarca. Pizarro gladly accepted the invitation, sending two Venetian goblets and a fine shirt from Holland as gifts to the Inca. Atahualpa turned Pizarro's arrival into a grand ceremonial pageant intended to impress the visitors with his might and majesty, but the display of wealth only inflamed Pizarro's greed. By a ruse, he captured Atahualpa, and the subsequent battle left several thousand Inca warriors dead on the plains beyond Cajamarca's walls.

Not understanding the people with whom he was dealing, Atahualpa tried to negotiate his own ransom in exchange for a room full of gold and silver. Pizarro made a mark on the wall of the room, and the Incas filled the room to that height. The Spaniards then took the priceless work of countless Inca goldsmiths and melted it down into bars for shipping back to Spain.

Pizarro, however, had no intention of keeping his side of the bargain. He soon found a pretext in Atahualpa's orders to kill his half brother, the deposed Huáscar, as a potential rival around whom his enemies might rally. In a parody of justice, Pizarro tried Atahualpa for murder and sentenced him to death by burning, the fate of infidels. He agreed, though, to spare Atahualpa's life under the condition that Atahualpa embrace Christianity. Atahualpa solemnly renounced his people's traditional religious practices and submitted to baptism, only to have Pizarro renege on his sworn word once again. Atahualpa was garotted (strangled) with a silken cord, although his body was given Christian burial. By executing Atahualpa, Pizarro won the support of the faction that had followed Huáscar.

Atahualpa. (Hulton|Archive by Getty Images)

ATAHUALPA'S CIVIL WAR BATTLEFIELD

After Atahualpa defeated Huáscar's troops in battle, he instructed his own troops to leave the dead bodies of their enemies on the battlefield, marking Atahualpa's victory both through story and through the bones of his victims. Susan Niles examines how the Inca civil war has been remembered, in part, because the shrewd Atahualpa ordered that the remains of his enemies be left as evidence of his victory.

The civil war battlefields might be thought of as a combination of keen military strategy and history in the making. There is no doubt that the frightful prospect of bodies heaped up at an important pass through the mountains would be daunting to enemies marching up from either direction, and that a field planted with their native lords may have discouraged disgruntled Cañari subjects from further subversive acts. But the commemoration of the victories is also a way to impose history on a landscape that the young Inca [Atahualpa] was just beginning to claim. The gruesome monuments would be evidence of the glorious victories that surely would have been part of the *cantares* sung in his praise had his own defeat by the Spaniards not come so soon.

Source: The Shape of Inca History: Narrative and Architecture in an Andean Empire, by Susan A. Niles (Iowa City: Iowa University Press, 1999), p. 65.

just how critical the civil war was in the catastrophic collapse of the Inca armies in the face of a much smaller force. Many writers have emphasized the differences of culture and technology that would have ultimately made a Spanish victory inevitable, although perhaps at a much greater cost.

The magical-ritual worldview of the Inca, in which great effort was expended on propitiating the gods before, during, and after each battle, could not compete with the Spaniards' drive for total victory and long-term conquest. Atahualpa's naïve trust of Pizarro's promises and his unwillingness to see the Spaniards' motivations for what they were only made the process easier for the Spanish.

—*Leigh Husband Kimmel*

Subsequent to Atahualpa's judicial murder, many of his followers continued to resist, particularly in the area of Quito. Pizarro fought four fierce battles against Atahualpa's foremost surviving general, Quizquiz. After the final decisive victory in the mountains above Cuzco, the Quitan faction's resolve was broken and the army deserted. Pizarro then installed Huáscar's younger brother, Tupac Huallpa, as a puppet Inca, but he survived only a few months. Blaming his death on poison, Pizarro replaced him with another son of Huáscar, Manco Capac II, and permitted some of the traditional observances to continue so long as suitable tribute flowed into Spanish coffers. Manco Capac, however, subsequently rebelled and raised an army that briefly troubled the Spaniards before being destroyed. The last puppet Inca, Tupac Amaru, was executed, and henceforth, the Spaniards ruled directly.

SIGNIFICANCE

Atahualpa's civil war with Huáscar weakened the Inca Empire at a time when it needed all its resources to repel an external invader. Later historians have hotly debated

FURTHER READING

Davies, Nigel. *The Incas.* Niwot: University of Colorado Press, 1995. A readable and rigorous study of the Inca Empire from its legend-shrouded origins to its catastrophic collapse.

Gabai, Rafael Varon. *Francisco Pizarro and His Brothers: The Illusion of Power in Sixteenth Century Peru.* Norman: University of Oklahoma Press, 1997. A study of the relationship of Pizarro and his three brothers, who cooperated in the conquest of Peru.

Hemming, John. *The Conquest of the Incas.* San Diego, Calif.: Harvest Books, 2003. A sympathetic account, giving equal time to the Inca resistance and Pizarro's conquest.

SEE ALSO: José de Acosta; Hernán Cortés; Huáscar; Pachacuti; Francisco Pizarro.

RELATED ARTICLES in *Great Events from History: The Renaissance & Early Modern Era, 1454-1600:* 1493-1525: Reign of Huayna Capac; 1525-1532: Huáscar and Atahualpa Share Inca Rule; 1532-1537: Pizarro Conquers the Incas in Peru.

BĀBUR
Mughal emperor of India (r. 1526-1530)

Bābur, the first of the Mughal rulers in India, spread the Mughal Empire over most of northern India. He was a wise king whose memoirs have revealed much about his life.

BORN: February 14, 1483; principality of Fergana (now in Uzbekistan)

DIED: December 26, 1530; Āgra, India

ALSO KNOWN AS: Ẓahīr-ud-Dīn Muḥammad; Bābar; Bāber

AREAS OF ACHIEVEMENT: Military, government and politics, literature

EARLY LIFE

Bābur (BAH-bewr), whose name means lion, tiger, or panther, was born in Fergana (modern Afghanistan), on February 14, 1483. A descendant of Genghis Khan and Tamerlane, Bābur became king of Fergana in 1494 at the age of eleven, when his father, ʿUmar Shaykh Mīrzā, died. Along with the kingdom, Bābur inherited his father's struggles with his cousins for the kingdom of Transoxiana and its capital, Samarqand.

LIFE'S WORK

Bābur spent the first three years of his reign fighting his cousin Faisunqur, from whom he captured Samarqand in 1497 after a siege of seven months; yet he was soon forced to relinquish the city.

Between 1498 and 1499, Bābur married, and he divided Fergana with his brother. In 1501, Bābur once again attempted to conquer Samarqand. Between April and May of 1501, Bābur suffered a defeat at Sar-i-Pul and retreated to Samarqand. After taking the city by surprise, Bābur and the inhabitants of Samarqand tried to repel the forces of Muḥammad Shaybānī Khān, chief of the Uzbeks, who had agreed to help Baisunqur Mīrzā fight his cousin, Bābur. Bābur was able to hold off Shaybānī Khān's men for four months but was finally forced to surrender the city. Bābur was released from his captivity, but only after he had agreed to give his sister's hand in marriage to the Uzbek khan.

Once free, Bābur spent the next three years in hiding at Tashkent, which had been given to him by his uncle, Sultan Mahmud Khan. Even though Bābur's uncle furnished him with a command of one thousand men, Bābur was defeated in 1503 at Arciyan by Tanbal, who had appealed to Shaybānī Khān for assistance. Having lost Fergana, Bābur spent the next year as a nomad in the re-

mote territories of Sukh and Hushyar. In June, 1504, Bābur and his brother formed another army, composed of refugees from the Uzbeks, and secured Kabul, from which he would maintain himself until 1525. While at Kabul, Bābur was influenced by Persian culture, traces of which can be found in his poetry.

From Kabul, Bābur conducted unsuccessful raids in central Asia and northwestern India. In January, 1505, Bābur made his expedition to Hindustan in search of badly needed supplies. Bābur, at the invitation of Husain Baiqara, who died soon afterward, marched on Herāt against Shaybānī Khān but returned to Kabul, because he was not prepared for the fierce winter. In June, 1507, Herāt surrendered to Shaybānī Khān. Meanwhile, Bābur's uncle, Muḥammad Ḥussayn, had proclaimed Bābur's cousin Khan Mīrzā lord of Kabul in Bābur's absence.

After suppressing this rebellion by attacking the rebels without warning in the streets of Kabul, Bābur decided to gain possession of Qandahār, which was strategically important. Thus, when the Arghun princes in Qandahār asked Bābur for military assistance, he rushed to their aid. He had not traveled very far, though, before the Arghun princes changed their minds and decided to oppose Bābur. After defeating them in combat, Bābur learned that Shaybānī Khān was preparing to attack Qandahār. Instead of meeting Shaybānī Khān in combat, Bābur took a more prudent though admittedly less courageous course: He undertook his second invasion of India in 1507. During his return to Kabul, Bābur decided to change his title from *mīrzā* (prince) to *padishah* (emperor).

Three years later, Bābur conquered Samarqand for the third time by taking advantage of the political situation at the time. Shaybānī Khān's dispute with the Ṣafavid shah Ismāʿīl erupted into warfare. In 1510, Ismāʿīl lured Shaybānī Khān from his refuge at Merv and slew him. As a result, the Uzbeks withdrew to Transoxiana. Elated by Ismāʿīl's victory, Bābur sent Khan Mīrzā to thank him. Ismāʿīl responded by returning Bābur's sister whom Bābur had given in marriage to Shaybānī Khān years before.

As a client of Ismāʿīl, Bābur lost much of his popular support among the Mughals. Because Ismāʿīl would not allow Bābur to break his pact, Bābur believed that the most expedient thing to do was to give lip service to the Shīʿite creed while remaining faithful to the Sunni doctrine. Years later, he was to prove the sincerity of his beliefs by writing a lengthy religious poem.

In 1511, Bābur once again invaded Samarqand and was pronounced king in 1511. Yet Bābur's reign as ruler of Samarqand proved to be short-lived. The Uzbeks, who were determined to remain in Transoxiana, encountered and defeated Bābur's forces at Kul-i-Malik. Bābur retreated to Hisar. He managed to solidify his hold on Badakhshān by placing his cousin, Khan Mīrzā, on the throne, but he relinquished all hope of again ascending the throne of Samarqand. Instead, he occupied himself between 1515 and 1518 by waging wars in every direction in order to force the mountain dwellers of Kabul and Ghazni to fear and respect him.

The second phase of Bābur's career—his invasion and conquest of Hindustan—began only after he had finally relinquished his boyhood dream of conquering Samarqand. In a sense, Bābur decided to assimilate into his empire people who were not of Indo-Aryan stock because he considered the Hindu Kush to be his lawful heritage, passed down to him from his ancestor Tamerlane, who had established his rule in all the country between the Oxus and the Indus on his passage to India. One could also say that Bābur compensated for his failure to conquer Samarqand by turning his attention toward India. While it is true that Bābur prepared the way for the Mughal Empire in India, his forays into India were really nothing more than a military preparation for the more permanent rule that would be established years later by his grandson.

Before Bābur could become lord of India, he had to dethrone the five Muslim and two pagan rulers who governed Hindustan. Bābur initiated this campaign in 1519, when he cemented an alliance with the Yusufzais by marrying the daughter of one of their chiefs. He concluded what he considered to be his first expedition into Hindustan by conquering Bhera but winning the hearts of its occupants by sparing their lives.

Owing to the dearth of details in Bābur's memoirs concerning the second, third, and fourth expeditions, it is with his fifth expedition that the history of Bābur's Hindustani campaigns continues. Bābur agreed to assist Dawlat Khān Lodī in deposing Lodī's kinsman, who ruled most of northern Hindustan. In return for Dawlat Khān Lodī's promise to regard Bābur as his sovereign, Bābur utterly defeated the army of Ibrāhīm Lodī near Lahore, which Bābur claimed for his own. This impetuous decision on Bābur's part brought his alliance with Dawlat Khān Lodī to an abrupt end.

Bābur quickly formed another alliance with ʿĀlam Khān, the uncle of Ibrāhīm Lodī, who offered to cede Lahore to Bābur if Bābur helped him conquer Delhi. Bābur

Bābur. (Hulton|Archive by Getty Images)

hoped that by substituting ʿĀlam Khān for Ibrāhīm Lodī, he would not only be given the legitimate right to Lahore but also have control over ʿĀlam Khān, who was old and feeble. Thus, Bābur ordered his soldiers to assist ʿĀlam Khān in the assault on Delhi, but he decided that his presence was more sorely needed at Balkh, which Ismāʿīl was defending against the Uzbeks. Dawlat Khān Lodī then seized the opportunity to recover Lahore by offering to help ʿĀlam Khān conquer Delhi. After failing to take Delhi, Dawlat Khān Lodī's army scattered in disorder, so he and his son retreated to the fortress of Milwat, where they surrendered. Dawlat Khān Lodī died while being taken to the prison at Bhera.

Having secured Lahore, Bābur began his campaign to conquer Delhi. Aware of the political advantages of having the loyalty of an Afghan prince, Bābur gave ʿĀlam Khān a command at Panipat and Khanua. Bābur then marched on Delhi with his eighteen-year-old son, Humāyūn, who led the forces that defeated the armies of one of Ibrāhīm Lodī's emirs. Taking a defensive position at Panipat, Bābur's Mughals utterly defeated the vastly superior numbers of Afghan forces by flanking them with arrows and bombarding them with gunfire from the front. At the battle's end, Ibrāhīm Lodī was dead, and Bābur had reached his greatest goal: the conquest of northern India. As soon as he made his grand entrance into Delhi, he won the favor of the people by preventing his soldiers from looting and by protecting the wives and children of the raja of Gwalior. On April 27, 1526, a week after his arrival at Delhi, Bābur was proclaimed emperor of Hindustan in the Grand Mosque.

The founding of Bābur's vast empire in Hindustan, which began with the capture of Lahore in 1524, was completed in six years. With his victory at Panipat in 1526, most of the Afghan chiefs united under Bābur's rule. Bābur most likely restricted his conquests to northern India because of his reluctance to offend Ismāʿīl by attacking Persian territory.

Bābur's death cannot be attributed to only one cause. From boyhood, he had suffered from a troublesome lesion, and throughout his adult life he was stricken with bouts of marsh fever. His body was further weakened by his intemperate ways, particularly his fondness for wine. He also became seriously ill as the result of an attempted poisoning by the mother of Ibrāhīm Lodī. His eventual death is enshrouded in mystery and legend. In 1530, when Bābur's son Humāyūn was attacked with fever, Bābur prayed that God would accept his life in exchange for that of his son. Coincidentally, Bābur was taken ill as his son slowly recovered, and he died three months later in Āgra on December 26, 1530. Several years later, his body was moved to its present location at Kabul.

SIGNIFICANCE

Bābur is a prime example of a class of political entrepreneurs who vied with other seminomadic rulers from Central Asia for revenues from the herdsmen and territory. Like those of his rivals and enemies, Bābur's kingdom was linked and sometimes divided by the loyalties of clan and family, not by treaties of national states. He was also typical of the rulers of that time in the savagery he displayed during battle.

Even though Bābur was born to the ruling class, he maintained and increased his kingdom as a result of his own adaptability and courage. He was a resourceful general who learned about musketry and artillery from the Uzbeks; he then applied these methods with great success against the lords of Hindustan. Thus, he became one of the first military commanders in Asia to realize the full potential of artillery.

Bābur was a skillful diplomat, who prepared Hindustan for conquest by playing the emirs of Ibrāhīm Lodī against one other. He also performed the seemingly im-

possible task of molding an array of fiercely independent and competitive bands of Mughals into a nation by employing a prudent blend of force and kindness. In addition, he displayed moral courage as he risked the disapproval of other Sunni Muslims in his decision to appease Ismāʿīl by adopting the Qizilbash headdress for himself and his soldiers. In addition, Bābur's custom of showing mercy to his defeated enemies endeared him to the people he conquered.

While Bābur inherited some of the barbaric ways of the descendants of Tamerlane, he differed from most of the Mughal rulers of the sixteenth century in his love of beauty. An accomplished poet and diarist, Bābur composed works that rank with the best literature written at that time.

—Alan Brown

FURTHER READING

Bābur. *The Bāburnāma*. Edited and translated by Wheeler M. Thackston. Introduction by Salman Rushdie. New York: Modern Library, 2002. An exciting and revealing firsthand history of Bābur's life and times in his own words. This is the primary source for most of the biographies that have followed. Includes illustrations, maps, bibliographic references, and indexes.

Brown, F. Yeats. *Pageant of India*. Philadelphia: Macrae Smith, 1942. A brief biographical sketch of Bābur's life, heavily laced with quotations from Bābur's memoirs. Provides interesting anecdotes, especially regarding the assassination attempt by the mother of Ibrāhām Lodī.

Burn, Richard, ed. *The Mughal Period*. Vol. 4 in *The Cambridge History of India*. Reprint. New Delhi: S. Chand, 1987. Chapter 1 is an excellent summation of Bābur's life. Although the chapter emphasizes his military campaigns, it also provides historical background, sketching the personalities who had an important influence on Bābur's life.

Foltz, Richard C. *Mughal India and Central Asia*. New York: Oxford University Press, 2001. A study of the legacy of Bābur's conquests for his people, this book argues that the background of the Mughals and their origins in Central Asia are crucial to understanding their culture in India. Discusses the nostalgia of Indian Mughal rulers for their Central Asian homeland. Includes bibliographic references and index.

Grenard, Fernand. *Baber: First of the Moguls*. New York: Robert McBride, 1930. Based entirely on Bābur's memoirs, this is a biased but highly readable account of his life. The fanciful story line is enhanced by the reproduction of sixteenth century paintings.

Lewis, B. "Bābur." In *Encyclopaedia of Islam*, edited by B. Lewis, Ch. Pellat, and J. Schacht. Leiden, the Netherlands: Brill, 1959. This concise treatment of Bābur's life concentrates almost exclusively on his military conquests, paying little attention to his personal life.

Williams, L. F. Rushbrook. *An Empire Builder of the Sixteenth Century*. London: Longmans, Green, 1918. A standard biography covering Bābur's entire life. Beautifully illustrated with paintings from the period. The book refrains from romanticizing Bābur's life, opting for the objective approach instead. Recommended for the serious student of Bābur's life and of this period of Mughal history.

Ziad, Zeenut, ed. *The Magnificent Mughals*. New York: Oxford University Press, 2002. Authoritative anthology of essays by top scholars, each summarizing the history of a different aspect of Mughal culture. Provides accounts of Mughal economics, religion, and the arts, as well as the contributions of women to Mughal society. Includes illustrations, maps, bibliographic references, index.

SEE ALSO: Akbar; Humāyūn; Ibrāhīm Lodī; Krishnadevaraya.

RELATED ARTICLES in *Great Events from History: The Renaissance & Early Modern Era, 1454-1600:* 1451-1526: Lodī Kings Dominate Northern India; 1507: End of the Timurid Dynasty; December 2, 1510: Battle of Merv Establishes the Shaybānīd Dynasty; April 21, 1526: First Battle of Panipat; March 17, 1527: Battle of Khānua; December 30, 1530: Humāyūn Inherits the Throne in India.

FRANCIS BACON
English philosopher

The first to use the English language instead of Latin for a philosophical treatise with his Advancement of Learning, *Bacon is credited with the formulation of modern scientific thought. His essays are widely admired for their worldly witticism and have become classics of the form.*

BORN: January 22, 1561; London, England
DIED: April 9, 1626; London
ALSO KNOWN AS: Baron of Verulam; Viscount Saint Alban (or Albans)
AREAS OF ACHIEVEMENT: Philosophy, literature, science and technology, government and politics

EARLY LIFE

Francis Bacon was born at York House in London to Sir Nicholas Bacon, lord keeper of the Seal of England, and his second wife, née Ann Cooke, who was related to nobility through her sister, the wife of William Cecil, the later Lord Burghley. In 1573, at the age of twelve, Bacon entered Trinity College, Cambridge, which he left in 1576 for Gray's Inn, thus following in his father's steps and beginning a legal career.

After a brief visit to the French court in the entourage of Sir Amias Paulet from 1576 until his father's death in 1579, Francis Bacon stayed with the Inn and was called to the bar in 1582, two years before he began to complement his legal work with an ambitiously undertaken political career that commenced with his membership in Parliament.

After advancement to the position of queen's counsel in 1589, his career stalled under Elizabeth I, whom he seemed to have offended in a parliamentary debate regarding the implementation of regal subsidiaries in 1593; his enemies at court used the opportunity to bar his way to promotion, seeing in Bacon (not wholly unjustly) not only an ambitious, prolific writer of political advice but also an unscrupulous seeker of preferment. Again, on the personal level, his friendship with the young earl of Essex did not bring him hoped-for political gain; in 1601, after Essex's ill-considered rebellion against the queen, Bacon's position required him to partake in the prosecution of his former friend.

Whereas *An Advertisement Touching the Controversies of the Church of England* (1589) had brought Bacon political advancement, his later work of political advice did not benefit him professionally. During a long period of arrested political development until Elizabeth I's death, Bacon showed himself stubborn and inclined to use the common practice of patronage and favoritism to lobby for a higher position. In his own office, he became a rather successful mediator of conflicts and tried hard but finally inefficiently to smooth the waves after Essex's insubordination preceding his open revolt against the queen.

A later painting shows Bacon as a tall, bearded officer wearing his regalia and insignia proudly; the picture suggests the reserved, somewhat unemotional yet nevertheless personally sensitive character that his later biographers have asserted on the basis of accounts from Bacon's chaplain and secretary William Rawley. At forty-five, he married Alice Barnham, daughter of a London alderman, who survived him; they had no children.

LIFE'S WORK

Bacon's long period of relative political inactivity under Elizabeth I gave him time to write the first ten of his *Essayes*, which saw publication in 1597, and again, because of their popularity, in 1612 and in 1625, both times with significant enlargements that brought the total number to fifty-eight. A master of the essay form, which he helped to forge, Bacon here looks at people and their government realistically, free of passionate idealism and zeal for the betterment of humanity. What his critics have called his Machiavellian and emotionless coldness nevertheless facilitated a witty discourse on the world as it really is, and not as it should be in the eyes of reformers. With this was coupled political advice, as in "On Dissimulation" or "On Plantations," against the shortsightedness, greed, and abuses of his time.

The Twoo Bookes of Francis Bacon of the Proficience and Advancement of Learning Divine and Humane (1605), which he later enlarged into the Latin version *De augmentis scientiarum* (1623; best known as *Advancement of Learning*), represents his first step toward the formulation of a new method for looking at the natural world through the eyes of the experimenting and hypothesizing scientist who has purged his vision of religious allegory or Platonic metaphysics or Aristotelian dialectics.

Bacon's political fortunes changed in the reign of James I, which saw his ascension from his knighthood in 1603 through the office of attorney general (1613) to the high position of lord keeper in 1617, before he was made lord chancellor and baron verulam and ultimately created Viscount Saint Albans in 1621, at the age of sixty.

During these years of success, Bacon wrote the *Instauratio magna* (1620; *The Great Instauration*, 1653), the planned preface, never completed, for six different works intended to describe a restoration of human knowledge; as is, it is a powerful model for radical change in the pattern of Western scientific thought, characterized by Bacon's clear sense of ordering and classification. *Novum organum* (1620; English translation, 1802), published in the same year, contains Bacon's

---

BACON ON THE ILLUSIONS OF HUMAN UNDERSTANDING

Francis Bacon's philosophy was nothing less than a new understanding of scientific thought and logic. His method was to observe through experience, then to collect and organize the results of his experience to arrive at some sort of truth. A key component to Bacon's philosophy, however, was recognizing the "idols," or illusions, that color or impinge upon reason and imagination. In more modern terms, one could call this bias or preconception. Below, Bacon discusses the illusions of human nature, what he called the Idols of the Tribe.

The human understanding is no dry light, but receives an infusion from the will and affections; whence proceed sciences which may be called "sciences as one would." For what a man had rather were true he more readily believes. Therefore he rejects the difficult things from impatience of research; sober things, because they narrow hope; the deeper things of nature, from superstition; the light of experience, from arrogance and pride, lest his mind should seem to be occupied with things mean and transitory; things not commonly believed, out of deference to the opinion of the vulgar [the common]. Numberless in short are the ways, sometimes imperceptible, in which the affections color and infect the understanding.

But by far the greatest hindrance and aberration of the human understanding proceeds from the dullness, incompetency, and deceptions of the senses; in that things which strike the sense outweigh things which do not immediately strike it, though they may be more important. Hence it is that speculation ceases where sight ceases; insomuch that of things invisible there is little or no observation. . . .

Such then are the idols which I call *Idols of the Tribe;* and which take their rise either from the homogeneity of the substance of the human spirit [human nature], or from its preoccupation, or from its narrowness, or from its restless motion, or from an infusion of the affections, or from the incompetency of the senses, of from the mode of impression.

Source: A World of Ideas: Essential Readings for College Writers, 3d ed., edited by Lee A. Jacobus (Boston: Bedford Books, 1990), p. 406.

argument for a "new logic," the discovery of a finite number of "natures" or "forms" lying at the base of the natural world, and an exhaustive description of natural history.

After he had reached the zenith of his power, Bacon's fall came when old enemies charged him with bribery; he admitted to the charges since he indeed not only had taken gifts from suitors, which was more generally acceptable, but also had accepted donations from individuals whose cases were pending with him as their judge (and in which he often decided against them despite the offerings given). Bacon resigned from his office, was fined forty thousand pounds, was briefly imprisoned in the Tower of London, and was banished from the court. He made slow progress at rehabilitation, but at the time of his death in the house of Sir Arundel in 1626, he had not yet received full royal pardon from the new king, Charles II.

SIGNIFICANCE

Although his public fall from grace as a result of misconduct in office linked Bacon to his literary model Seneca, who showed similar excellence in thought and corruption in public life, the British naturalist and states-

man must be remembered for his new, practical approach toward the natural environment; his proposed outlook at science bears the seeds of modern scientific thought.

In his last, unfinished work, *New Atlantis*, posthumously published in 1627, Bacon argues that there is no conflict between the free pursuit of scientific exploration and the dogmas of the Christian religion. He sums up the ancient Hebrew view of the natural world as there to use and explore rather than as the manifestation of sundry natural deities, and he connects this thought to the idea that scientific research is ultimately undertaken so that God (the final spiritual authority) "might have the more glory" in the "workmanship" of the scientists and men "the more fruit" in the "use" of their discoveries.

On a final note, Bacon's idea, in the utopian *New Atlantis*, for an organization dedicated to the free pursuit of all natural sciences that would collect and display its findings in central "houses," has been realized in the British Royal Society and the British Museum, two institutions that, founded in the spirit of Bacon, are thriving today.

—*R. C. Lutz*

Francis Bacon. (Library of Congress)

FURTHER READING

Anderson, Fulton H. *Francis Bacon: His Career and His Thought.* Los Angeles: University of Southern California Press, 1962. Based on a series of lectures, this work attempts to link Bacon's philosophy with his politics and to relate his thought to contemporary problems.

_____. *The Philosophy of Francis Bacon.* Reprint. Chicago: University of Chicago Press, 1971. Influential book revealing Bacon's thoughts primarily through his own words. Somewhat dry and over-inclusive, it makes up for the lack of critical discussion with its useful compilation of primary texts.

Bacon, Francis. *The Works, the Letters, and the Life of Francis Bacon.* Edited by James Spedding, R. L. Ellis, and D. D. Heath, 14 vols. London: Longmans, 1857-1874. Includes William Rawley's *The Life of the Right Honourable Francis Bacon* (1657). Still the authoritative, standard edition of Bacon's complete work. Detailed biography with an impressive collection of primary sources such as Bacon's letters and notes. The standard against which all later works have to be judged.

Bowen, Catherine Drinker. *Francis Bacon: The Temper of a Man.* Boston: Little, Brown, 1963. Enjoyable bi-

BACON'S MAJOR WORKS

1597	*Essayes* (rev. 1612, 1625)
1601	*A Declaration of the Practices and Treasons Attempted and Committed by Robert, Late Earle of Essex*
1605	*The Twoo Bookes of Francis Bacon of the Proficience and Advancement of Learning, Divine and Humane* (rev. 1623; best known as *Advancement of Learning*)
1609	*De Sapientia Veterum* (*The Wisdom of the Ancients*, 1619)
1620	*Novum Organum* (English translation, 1802)
1620	*Instauratio Magna* (*The Great Instauration*, 1653)
1622	*Historia Ventorum* (*History of Winds*, 1653)
1622	*The Historie of the Raigne of King Henry the Seventh*
1623	*Historia Vitae et Mortis* (*History of Life and Death*, 1638)
1625	*The Translation of Certaine Psalmes into English Verse*
1627	*Sylva Sylvarum*
1627	*New Atlantis*
1653	*Valerius Terminus* (*View of Form*, 1734)

ography that brings Bacon alive while not neglecting scholarly accuracy. Careful and perceptive; Bowen's favorable portrait forgives Bacon almost everything but his coldness toward women.

Bozeman, Theodore Dwight. *Protestants in an Age of Science: The Baconian Ideal and Antebellum American Religious Thought*. Chapel Hill: University of North Carolina Press, 1977. Traces the roots of modern fundamentalism to the antebellum Presbyterians, who used Bacon's idea to prove themselves right and all their pre-Darwinian opponents wrong. An interesting contribution to the history of ideas.

Eiseley, Loren. *Francis Bacon and the Modern Dilemma*. Lincoln: University of Nebraska Press, 1963. Slim booklet emphasizing Bacon's achievements as a scientist; does not account for his deficient understanding of mathematics. Eiseley stresses Bacon's view of an integrated, responsible science.

Farrington, Benjamin. *The Philosophy of Francis Bacon*. Liverpool, England: Liverpool University Press, 1964. Valuable discussion of Bacon's philosophical ideas; Farrington includes a fine translation of Bacon's minor Latin works and thus makes them accessible to a broader audience.

Fuller, Jean Overton. *Sir Francis Bacon*. London: East-West Press, 1981. Ingeniously relates events in Bacon's life to contemporaneous passages from Shakespeare's work. Lavishly produced reiteration of the generally discredited theory that Bacon was the true author of Shakespeare's oeuvre.

Gaukroger, Stephen. *Francis Bacon and the Transformation of Early-Modern Philosophy*. New York: Cambridge University Press, 2001. Important study of Bacon's attempt to turn the private, esoteric practice of philosophy into a publically performed and evaluated discipline, thereby changing the history of ideas. Includes bibliographic references and index.

Henry, John. *Knowledge Is Power: How Magic, the Government, and an Apocalyptic Vision Inspired Francis Bacon to Create Modern Science*. Cambridge, England: Icon, 2004. Explores Bacon's role in the development of scientific methodology, his legacy, and the events and forces influencing his accomplishments.

Rossi, Paolo. *Francis Bacon: From Magic to Science*. Translated by Sacha Rabinovitch. Chicago: University of Chicago Press, 1968. Examines the European magical and alchemical tradition of science that Bacon rejected. Important bibliography.

SEE ALSO: Elizabeth I; Conrad Gesner; William Gilbert; William Shakespeare.

RELATED ARTICLE in *Great Events from History: The Renaissance & Early Modern Era, 1454-1600:* 1600: William Gilbert Publishes *De Magnete*.

VASCO NÚÑEZ DE BALBOA
Spanish conquistador

Balboa explored the Caribbean and the Central American mainland during the early sixteenth century. In 1513, he was the first European to discover the eastern limits of the Pacific Ocean.

BORN: 1475; Jeres de los Caballeros, Extremadura, Castile (now in Spain)
DIED: January, 1519; Acla, Castillo de Oro, Panama
AREAS OF ACHIEVEMENT: Exploration, military

EARLY LIFE

Vasco Núñez de Balboa (VAHS-koh NEWN-yayz day bahl-BOH-uh) was born in 1475 in Jeres de los Caballeros in the Spanish province of Estremadura. Although part of the Hidalgo class of nobles, Balboa's family was very poor. Thrilled by the reports of Christopher Columbus's voyages to the New World in 1492 and 1493, he was drawn toward the vibrant atmosphere of Spain's port cities. He served eight years under Don Pedro Puertocarrero, lord of Moguer, and acquired a reputation as an excellent fighter. In 1501, Balboa sailed to the New World under Don Pedro de Bastides, who discovered Barbados and sailed along the north coast of Tierra Firme (northern South America). The Bastides expedition terminated disastrously when his ships became infested with shipworms and eventually sank off the coast of Hispaniola (Haiti).

Balboa remained on Hispaniola to farm near Salvatierra, to mine for gold, and to fight Caribbeans. He fell deeply into debt, and his creditors constantly harassed him for payments. As a fighter, however, Balboa acquired great renown for his spirit and skill. Equally famous was Balboa's dog, the great "Leoncico" (little lion), who was noted for his ferocity in combat. Indeed, Leoncico was said to have been paid the equivalent of a captain's pay for his services.

LIFE'S WORK

At the age of thirty-five, Balboa was tall and well built, with red hair and blue eyes. He was charming and blessed with great energy and stamina. His presence on Hispaniola, however, had become untenable because of his creditors. Thus, in September, 1510, learning of an expedition bound for Tierra Firme under Martín Fernández de Enciso, Balboa arranged to have both himself and Leoncico smuggled on board in a large barrel. Once safely beyond Hispaniola, Balboa presented himself to an astonished and angry Enciso, who reluctantly allowed him to remain with the expedition.

Balboa became the key member of an extraordinary adventure in Latin American colonial history. In 1507, King Ferdinand II of Spain had given grants and powers to Diego de Nicuesa and Alonzo de Ojeda to explore and settle areas of Tierra Firme. Enciso was a lawyer and Ojeda's second-in-command, and he was expected to meet Ojeda at San Sebastian with supplies and reinforcements. At San Sebastian, Enciso learned that Ojeda, mortally wounded, had returned to Hispaniola, leaving behind forty-one near-starved survivors under Franciso Pizarro, later of Peruvian fame. San Sebastian was too difficult to hold in the face of Indian hostility, and Balboa suggested that they move to a more defensible site across the Bay of Urabá. Here, on the bank of the Darién River, Enciso established Santa María la Antigua del Darién, the first permanent settlement on the mainland.

Thereafter, Balboa's life was mired in political intrigue at Darién and the royal court. Enciso proved to be an arbitrary and unpopular leader, and settlers rallied behind the charismatic Balboa, who overthrew the petty tyrant. By spring, 1511, a three-way power struggle was under way. The Balboa-Enciso fight was complicated by the claims of Nicuesa, in whose grant Darién was mistakenly located. Nicuesa, however, was stranded and starving at Nombre de Dios. When supplies and news of the Darién colony arrived, he recovered and sought to impose his authority over the trespassers. Balboa led the resistance and sent Nicuesa away on a worm-infested vessel. Nicuesa was never seen alive again.

Balboa now moved aggressively on many fronts. He consolidated his authority over Darién and banished Enciso. He rescued the remaining survivors at Nombre de Dios, compelled settlers to grow crops and build homes, and pushed Spanish power into the interior. During these *entradas*, Balboa heard rumors of a great ocean to the south and of a great civilization in Peru. He also brought Franciscan priests to convert and baptize the Indians and to make them loyal subjects of the king.

Balboa discussed these events and other matters in an extraordinary letter to Ferdinand in January, 1513. He provided a detailed description of the land and climate, and he defended himself against charges of usurpation of power and mistreatment of Central American Indians. He noted the discoveries that he made, particularly gold mines, and rumors that a vast sea existed to the south. If he had only one thousand men, he wrote, he would bring the South Sea and all the gold mines under the dominion of the king.

In June, 1513, Balboa received contradictory news from Spain. He was made captain and interim governor of Tierra Firme, but he received stunning news that a new governor would soon replace him and that he would face arrest and trial for Nicuesa's death. Also, unknown to Balboa, Ferdinand sent a secret agent, Don Pedro de Arbolancha, to investigate affairs in Darién. Balboa's successor proved to be Don Pedro Arias Dávila (Pedrarias), an elderly, but iron-willed and cruel, military man. He left Apin in April, 1514, carrying *el requerimiento* (the requirement), a document designed to justify war with—and hegemony over—the Central American Indians.

To save himself, Balboa decided to find the South Sea. He left Darién on September 1, 1513, with 190 men, beginning a grueling and arduous ordeal. On September 25 or 27, 1513, however, 4Balboa reached the crest of a mountain and sighted the South Sea. He promptly made a formal act of possession in the name of Ferdinand V. On September 29, 1513, he reached the ocean's shore at the Gulf of San Miguel. The party remained in the area for several weeks, found pearl beds, and learned more about the Inca civilization to the south. On November 3, 1513, they began their return trip to Darién, which concluded without major incident on January 19, 1514. Among the cheering throng was the secret agent, Arbolancha, who determined that he would endorse Balboa's continued rule over the settlement.

Events occurred too rapidly, however, for Balboa to rescue himself from his enemies. Pedrarias arrived at Darién with the crushing news that he was governor of the province, now called Castillo de Oro (golden castle). Balboa, bitterly disappointed, nevertheless sought to make the transition in leadership successful. Matters, however, soured almost immediately. Pedrarias quickly implemented his instructions to hold a two-month-long *residencia* (investigation) of Balboa's conduct. Then Darién was hit with a devastating plague, and Pedrarias's men made savage and bloody forays among nearby Indian tribes, killing, enslaving, and stealing gold, silver,

Nineteenth century engraved depiction of Vasco Núñez de Balboa's arrival on the shore of California in 1513. (Library of Congress)

and food. Pedrarias allowed these activities to continue well into 1515, undoing Balboa's earlier work to secure these tribes' friendship and loyalty.

Meanwhile, Arbolancha's report induced Ferdinand to appoint Balboa adelantado, or governor, of the coast of the South Sea and of Panama and Coiba. Although Balboa remained under Pedrarias's authority, the latter became embittered and alarmed over the former's restored reputation. Accordingly, Balboa was arrested on a charge of conspiracy to rebel against Pedrarias and was kept in a cage in the latter's home. Finally, Balboa was released on the condition that he marry Pedrarias's daughter in Spain by proxy; once Pedrarias had consolidated his position with the marriage, he allowed Balboa to go to the Pacific coast and erect a shipbuilding yard.

SIGNIFICANCE

During subsequent years, Vasco Núñez de Balboa and Pedrarias were wary of each other. Balboa was the more popular of the two leaders. He took the nearby Pearl Islands and seemed intent in moving south against Peru. By late 1518, Pedrarias had had enough of Balboa and ordered him to Acla, where he arrested Balboa on a charge of treason. In January, 1519, Balboa and several of his associates were beheaded, and Balboa's head was placed on a pike and put on display in Acla's plaza.

Thus died Balboa, one of the greatest conquistadores for *los reyes católicos*, a person of humble origins who possessed attributes of greatness: bravery, valor, humility, and a sense of fairness. He provided the inspired leadership that placed Spain on the mainland of Central America, setting the stage for the great conquests to the north and south. His greatest achievement was the discovery of the Pacific Ocean, which reinforced the growing realization that Columbus had discovered a great barrier to the Asian market. The temporal and spiritual power of the Spanish crown was rarely served better in the New World.

—*Stephen P. Sayles*

FURTHER READING

Fritz, Jean. "Vasco Núñez de Balboa." In *Around the World in a Hundred Years: From Henry the Navigator to Magellan*. New York: Putnam, 1994. Account of Balboa's contributions to exploration, geography, and cartography, and the discovery of the Pacific Ocean. Includes illustrations, map, bibliographic references, index.

Méndez Pereira, Octavio. *El Tesoro del Dabaibe*. Panama City, Panama: Talleres Gráficos "Benedetti," 1934. Argues Balboa was fair in his treatment of the Indians. Méndez Pereira was a Panamanian diplomat and educator.

Ober, Frederick A. *Vasco Núñez de Balboa*. New York: Hayes & Brothers, 1906. A volume of the Heroes of American History series; a popular account of Balboa's life.

Romoli, Kathleen. *Balboa of Darién: Discoverer of the Pacific*. Garden City, N.Y.: Doubleday, 1953. The best account of the life and career of Balboa. Very readable and scholarly. Sympathetic toward Balboa while giving an objective analysis of the men who served with and under him.

Strawn, Arthur. *The Golden Adventures of Balboa, Discoverer of the Pacific*. London: John Lane, 1929. Another useful though dated account of Balboa. Like Romoli, Strawn was a great admirer of Balboa as a warrior and as a diplomat.

Todorov, Tzvetan. *The Conquest of America: The Question of the Other*. Translated by Richard Howard. Reprint. Norman: University of Oklahoma, 1999. Examines the encounter between Spanish conquistadores and indigenous Americans from the point of view of conflicting worldviews and misinterpretation of each by the other. Includes illustrations, map, bibliographic references, index.

SEE ALSO: Pedro de Alvarado; Álvar Núñez Cabeza de Vaca; Charles V; Christopher Columbus; Francisco Vásquez de Coronado; Hernán Cortés; Juan Sebastián de Elcano; Ferdinand II and Isabella I; Guacanagarí; Pedro Menéndez de Avilés; The Pinzón Brothers; Francisco Pizarro; Juan Ponce de León.

RELATED ARTICLE in *Great Events from History: The Renaissance & Early Modern Era, 1454-1600:* September 29, 1513: Balboa Reaches the Pacific Ocean.

BARBAROSSA
Ottoman military leader

Barbarossa, a corsair, was instrumental in commanding and advancing the Ottoman Empire's most powerful naval fleet, which dominated the eastern Mediterranean region for more than a century after his death. Barbarossa's exploits helped extend Ottoman control to North Africa.

BORN: Date unknown; Mytilene, Greece
DIED: 1546; Constantinople, Ottoman Empire (now Istanbul, Turkey)
ALSO KNOWN AS: Khiḍr (original name); Khayr al-Dīn; Khair al-Dīn; Redbeard
AREAS OF ACHIEVEMENT: Government and politics, military

EARLY LIFE

The early lives of Barbarossa (bahr-bah-RAW-sah)—whose original name was Khiḍr—and his older brother, Arūj (d. 1518), were passed on the island of Mytilene in Greece. Apparently, their father was a Muslim convert and possibly a member of the Ottoman military establishment. Nothing is known about the educational background of either brother, but their careers suggest that they had practical training as sailors.

By the time Khiḍr was an adult, around 1500, both he and his brother had left their Greek homeland as privateers, roaming the eastern Mediterranean Sea in search of prey, either Christian or Muslim. The main focus of their activities, however, was along the southern coast of the Mediterranean, where a number of Spanish enclaves had been established alongside small non-Ottoman Muslim states between Egypt's borders and Morocco to the west. Spanish presence along the coast had grown after the final victory at Granada and expulsion of the Moors from Spain in 1492. Wherever they could, the Spaniards exploited weaknesses in Muslim rule along the coast eastward, to what is now Tripoli in Libya. Such outposts challenged Muslim military response.

No Islamic state, however, even the by-then-powerful Ottoman sultanate in Constantinople, appeared ready to do battle to remove Christian enclaves from North Africa. In such a setting, the arrival of only partially organized Turkish corsair formations could work either to the disadvantage or to the advantage of Christian interests in the area. If independent corsairs fought for the Spaniards in exchange for safe harbor rights, they became informal allies. In the case of Arūj and Khiḍr, such dealings appeared treasonous, and they committed themselves to fighting in support of menaced Muslim rulers from Tripoli to the western borders of what later became the Ottoman province of Algeria.

LIFE'S WORK

Barbarossa and his elder brother were not the only renegade Muslim corsairs who were active in mid-Mediterranean and North African coastal waters in the first decades of the sixteenth century. The Spanish and Muslim populations employed a general word derived from the Arabic term for "head men," *ru'asa*, to describe leaders (in this case naval leaders, or captains) of individual ships or small groups of ships engaged in sporadic attacks on Mediterranean maritime movements. These attacks did not seem to pit Muslims against Christians or vice versa, but were instead motivated by booty from any source.

Barbarossa and Arūj, however, developed fairly systematic arrangements to carry out sea raids in the name of a specific Muslim sponsor: al-Ḥasan, the then-reigning sultan of the Ḥafṣid Dynasty located in Tunis. The Ḥafṣids offered the adjacent port of Halq al-Wadi as a safe haven for the Barbarossa brothers. Initially, around 1510 to 1513, the Ḥafṣids might have done this to obtain protective services on the sea against threats of Spanish attacks from their small enclave in Bejaïa on what eventually became the Algerian coast. Soon, however, it was apparent that the Barbarossa brothers wanted more independence in making their own decisions.

After Arūj seized another small town on the western side of Ḥafṣid territory, the port of Djidjelli, the Barbarossas not only undertook sea raids in their own name but also established contacts with the hinterland Berber tribal populations. These tribes, known as Kabyles (from the Arabic *qabilah*), may even have agreed to form armed units to serve the Barbarossas on land. Ḥafṣid reaction to this upstart small state in Djidjelli involved one of the major contradictory moves in the last decades of their rule from Tunis: They concluded a treaty with the Spanish Christians to protect them against possible threats from their former but unpredictable Muslim protégés.

These tense developments led the brothers to take a major step that would determine the future status of Barbarossa, in particular. In 1516, the corsairs landed in the area near three Spanish-held islets in what would become the Bay of Algiers. The weak Muslim ruler there was lit-

Prisoners of Barbarossa. (F. R. Niglutsch)

erally under the guns of the Spanish and was forced to pay them tribute. The Barbarossas not only forced the ruler out of power but also used this new base of operations to move even farther inland than they had been able to do in Djidjelli. Attacks on the territory of the sultan of Tlemcen (an inland town with an important Islamic regional role) proved to be a turning point. The new sultan of the Zayyanid Dynasty had just renewed Tlemcen's long-standing tributary status to the strong Spanish garrison at Oran, but he was challenged by a rival to the succession, who called on Arūj and Barbarossa to help him free the region from Spanish influence.

Although this goal was in the process of being achieved, the protracted inland struggle and the expansion of fortifications against Spanish attacks against Algiers were not yet completed when Arūj met his death in 1518. Almost immediately Barbarossa called on the Ottoman sultan Selim I for military assistance. Ottoman forces arrived too late to save Barbarossa from having to evacuate Algiers. The threat came not from the Spanish, however, but from an alliance between the Ḥafṣid sultan

of Tunis and disgruntled Berbers from the Djidjelli area, who refused to recognize Barbarossa. It took Barbarossa nearly five years to retake Algiers, but this time he made certain that his authority to rule would be recognized without hesitation by Sultan Süleyman the Magnificent, the strongest Muslim ruler in the entire Mediterranean area.

Süleyman not only granted the formal title of Ottoman commander and *bey* (governor) to Barbarossa in Algiers but also sent troops to help expand territory under his control. Much of Barbarossa's final success, however, was gained by allowing local leaders substantial autonomy if they would agree to recognize his governorate in Algiers. In 1534, he was called to Constantinople to serve as the general commander of the Ottoman fleet. Despite a full-scale Ottoman naval effort under Barbarossa to dislodge the Ḥafṣids from Tunis, capture of the city was temporary (1534-1535). Barbarossa carried out one more major, successful service for the Ottomans (at the naval Battle of Preveza in 1538 against the fleet of Holy Roman Emperor Charles V) before he retired in 1544. He died in Constantinople in 1546.

SIGNIFICANCE

Because the Ottoman Empire had not undertaken formal military campaigns in North Africa prior to Sultan Selim I's 1517 conquest of Syria, Egypt, and the Hijaz region's Muslim holy cities, Barbarossa's establishment of outposts along the coast offered attractive possibilities to Sultan Süleyman. In fact, the Ottomans did not have to send land forces to North Africa; it was enough to announce Barbarossa's status as main deputy of imperial authority and to send more or less token forces to formalize imperial presence in the area. Such methods seem to have worked in general terms for Barbarossa's governorship in the then ill-defined zone that became Algeria. In more traditionally autonomous Muslim areas, however, especially Ḥafṣid Tunis, his claim of ascendancy would not be imposed as easily.

Many historians believe that, by the time Barbarossa was called back to Constantinople to serve at the highest level of Ottoman administration, the North African zones he conquered and over which he had been appointed were already changing into very loosely organized Ottoman provinces. Many of the local elements supporting what the Ottomans still called their beylicates would not, in the generations following Barbarossa's appointment as *beylerbey* (provincial governor),

have been recognizable as part of the temporary system established so quickly in the first half of the sixteenth century.

—*Byron Cannon*

FURTHER READING

Heers, Jacques. *The Barbary Corsairs, 1400-1580*. London: Stockpile, 2003. A history of corsair activity in North Africa before and after Barbarrosa's career.

Hess, Andrew. *The Forgotten Frontier.* Chicago: University of Chicago Press, 1978. Still the most detailed study of the early interaction between Ottoman and European politics in North Africa.

Perkins, Ken. *Historical Dictionary of Tunisia*. Lanham, Md.: Scarecrow Press, 1997. Covers the personal careers of corsairs who played similar roles in Tunisia's history before and during the Ottoman period.

SEE ALSO: Bayezid II; Charles V; İbrahim Paşa; Qāytbāy; Süleyman the Magnificent.

RELATED ARTICLES in *Great Events from History: The Renaissance & Early Modern Era, 1454-1600:* Beginning 1504: Decline of the Ḥafṣid Dynasty; 1520-1566: Reign of Süleyman; 1529-1574: North Africa Recognizes Ottoman Suzerainty; September 27-28, 1538: Battle of Préveza; October 20-27, 1541: Holy Roman Empire Attacks Ottomans in Algiers.

ELIZABETH BÁTHORY
Hungarian countess and murderer

Elizabeth Báthory, according to legend the most notorious female mass-murderer in European history, reportedly tortured and then killed more than six hundred girls and young women for their blood. Báthory's life, along with that of Walachian prince Vlad III the Impaler, partly inspired Bram Stoker's story of Dracula. For many centuries in Hungary, it was forbidden to speak Báthory's name.

BORN: August 7, 1560; Ecsed Castle, Transylvania (now in Romania)

DIED: August 21, 1614; Cséjthe, Hungary (now Čachtice Castle, Slovakia)

ALSO KNOWN AS: The Blood Countess; Erzsébet Báthory; Elizabeth Nadasdy

KNOWN FOR: Crime

EARLY LIFE

Elizabeth Báthory (ih-LIHZ-ah-behht ba-TOHR-ee) was born into the powerful and eccentric Báthory family, which played a leading role in late medieval and early modern Hungary. In 1571, she was betrothed to sixteen-year-old count Ferenc Nadasdy and then lived at his familial castle at Sarvar. Around this time, she was influenced by a sadistic aunt, Karla Báthory, who initiated her into the torture of servant-girls.

The disorderly world in which Báthory lived could lead to criminal psychosis. Since the Ottoman Turkish triumph at Mohács in 1526, the sprawling medieval kingdom of Hungary had been partitioned, and Elizabeth lived almost her entire life in Royal Hungary, the western and northern districts ruled from Pozsony (Bratislava, Slovakia) by the Habsburgs. Border raiding across the

Ottoman/Habsburg frontier was endemic. None suffered more from the prevailing instability than the peasants, whom the landowners reduced to total serfdom, exercising powers of life and death over them. It was in this environment that Báthory inflicted brutalities on the daughters of her serfs.

Hungary was also racked by religious strife, and where religious dissent and spiritual deviancy flourished, witchcraft and pre-Christian cults were widespread. Elizabeth seems to have become obsessed by the black arts, and she surrounded herself with witches, who served as her familiars in her sadistic sexual games.

LIFE'S WORK

Elizabeth Báthory and Ferenc Nadasdy were married in May of 1575. The Hungarian ruler at the time was King Rudolf II, an eccentric recluse obsessed with alchemy and magic, who established himself in Prague and left his brother, the archduke Matthias, to rule from Vienna and to attend to Hungarian affairs. The Ottoman threat across the border remained a reality, eventually developing into what became known as the Fifteen Years' War (1591-1606). Nadasdy, a born warrior with an insatiable thirst for glory, was almost on campaign permanently. Meanwhile, Elizabeth stayed at Sarvar, torturing her female servants.

For ten years, Báthory and Nadasdy were childless, but they had a daughter, Anna, around 1585, followed by Ursula and Katharina; in 1598, they had a son, Pal. Elizabeth informed her husband that all the births had been induced by witchcraft. During these years, the Fifteen Years' War was going at full throttle, but sheer exhaustion and a devastated countryside eventually forced both sides to seek peace. Nadasdy did not live to see peace because he died at Sarvar on January 4, 1604.

With her husband's death, Báthory became more reckless. By Nadasdy's will, Sarvar and his other estates, and the education of her son, were entrusted to Imre Megyery, a mysterious figure, perhaps an illegitimate son or a close kinsmen. With good reason, Báthory hated and feared Megyery.

Báthory first moved to the Nadasdy palace in Vienna, where the monks in the monastery across the street complained of inhuman shrieks issuing from the opposite building at night and of blood running from its drains into the street. The monastery's abbot was told that the countess needed fresh meat for her health.

Báthory spent much time at her various castles, one in western Hungary and others in western Slovakia. Sur-

rounded by trusted female confidants, she was especially intimate with a witch from Sarvar named Anna Darvulia, possibly her lover. Anna may have initiated the practice for which the countess later became so notorious. One day, when one of the countess's maids was combing her mistress's hair, the countess struck the girl so hard for her clumsiness that some of the girl's blood fell on the countess's arm. When another servant rushed to wipe off the blood, the skin seemed whiter than before. Anna later assured Báthory that she would retain her extraordinary beauty if she bathed in the blood of young virgins. Peasant girls were systematically rounded up, tortured, and then bled to death so that Báthory could bathe in their blood. In her castles were iron cages: A girl placed inside was slashed to ribbons by moveable steel blades, while the countess, standing underneath, was showered in warm blood.

As with many psychopaths, Báthory sought evermore violent stimulation, and as the tortures became more grotesque and the victims more numerous, rumors spread. At some unknown date, Anna Darvulia died, and Báthory replaced her with a new confidant, a witch named Erzsi Marjorova, a local farmer's widow from nearby Csejthe. Báthory was beginning to have doubts about the efficacy of her blood baths—age was catching up to her—and it was Marjorova who suggested that the remedy was to replace the local Slovak peasant-girls with virgins from a higher social class, which Báthory proceeded to do with reckless abandon.

Few questions had been asked regarding the disappearance of peasant girls, but missing higher-class victims provoked inquiry. The Lutheran pastor at Csejthe clashed with the countess over the burial of so many young girls, and he left his successor a report of his suspicions. The second pastor, too, questioned the number of burials, and he uncovered putrefying bodies of young girls in a vault beneath his church. Because of the pastor's suspicions, Báthory, ostensibly pious, abandoned giving her victims Christian burials. Disposing of the bodies now became an acute problem, and her servants grew careless. Once, when the husband of her eldest daughter, Anna, was visiting Csejthe, his hounds dug up some human remains in the garden.

Times were changing, however. The archduke Matthias yearned for the throne. In January, 1608, the Hungarian diet, headed by prominent Protestant notables such as Báthory's kinsman, György Thurzo, elected Matthias king of Hungary in exchange for a promise of religious tolerance. On January 25, 1608, Rudolf abdicated the Hungarian throne in favor of his younger brother, and on November 16, 1608, Matthias was crowned in St. Martin's Cathedral, Pozsony. Báthory probably attended the ceremony, after which Thurzo was appointed palatine (royal deputy) of Hungary. Matthias's eyes were now fixed on Bohemia and the imperial crown. Although a Catholic, he was much beholden to his Protestant subjects for his recent coronation. Elizabeth Báthory's behavior presented a dilemma: She was a Protestant and a Báthory, and her kinsman, Gabor Báthory, was prince of Transylvania, but Matthias favored a public inquiry.

Thurzo was more circumspect than the king. He did not doubt the accusations—the evidence was overwhelming—but a Báthory was a Báthory, and the family had served the state well for generations. His solution was to remove Elizabeth Báthory by force from Csejthe and to incarcerate her in a nunnery; thus, her estates could pass to her legal heirs. Before this plan could be carried through, however, Báthory's nemesis, Imre Megyery, late in 1610, presented a deposition against her before the Hungarian diet. Events were moving fast, and Thurzo was compelled to act. On December 29, 1610, accompanied by Báthory's sons-in-law, Miklos Zrinyi and György Drugeth, and Imre Megyery, Thurzo took a company of armed retainers to Csejthe. There was no lack of horrors to uncover; they merely confirmed known facts. Outraged, Báthory protested her innocence, but she was placed under house arrest in the castle. Her servants were transported to Thurzo's residence at Bytca for questioning.

Two trials ensued, one on January 2, 1611, the other on January 7, 1611. At the first, thirteen witnesses testified; in addition, four of Báthory's servants testified, providing lurid details of how the countess tortured. At the second trial, conducted in secret at Thurzo's insistence, a servant girl produced a list of 650 victims' names, written in the countess's handwriting.

Two female servants were condemned to have their fingers torn off by the executioner, before being burnt alive. A male servant was beheaded and his body burnt. The fourth escaped a capital sentence. A few days later, the witch, Erzsi Majorova, was apprehended, condemned, and burnt. Elizabeth Báthory was never tried for her crimes, but she was condemned to perpetual confinement in her chamber, where the door and the windows were sealed, leaving only a food hatch for communication. She died, still a prisoner, on August 21, 1614, and her body was eventually removed to Ecsed for interment. Her vast properties were divided between her son and her sons-in-law.

Matthias was not pleased with these secret proceedings; he would have preferred a public trial with confiscation of the countess's property, but Thurzo was unyielding, supported by petitions from Pal Nadasdy and Miklos Zrinyi, pleading for no further disgrace. Matthias deferred to their pleas: He had other priorities. On May 23, 1611, the Bohemian diet elected him king of Bohemia. In December, 1611, the fifty-five-year-old ruler married his twenty-six-year-old cousin. Finally, on June 13, 1612, he was elected Holy Roman Emperor. The horrors of Csejthe could be forgotten.

SIGNIFICANCE

Belief in witchcraft and the occult was widespread in early Renaissance Central Europe. Elizabeth Báthory's crimes mirror the sadistic mutilations, serial murders, and even cannibalism recorded by the twenty-first century press, as well as those crimes from the distant past.

What is unique about Báthory is the sheer number of her reported victims and the length of her grisly career, which was tolerated in the unjust social order of contemporary Hungary. There were surely criminal psychopaths in Jacobean England, but the social system most likely would have made it nearly impossible for a mass-murderer to kill more than six hundred people.

—*Gavin R. G. Hambly*

FURTHER READING

Elsberg, R. A. von. *Die Blutgrafin (Elisabeth Báthory).* 2d ed. Breslau, Poland: Schlesiche Verlags-Anstalt v. S. Schottländer, 1904. This is the standard, still-useful biography.

Evans, R. J. W. *Rudolf II and His World.* Oxford, England: Oxford University Press, 1973. A brilliant account of the occultism embedded in contemporary intellectual life.

McNally, Raymond T. *Dracula Was a Woman: In Search of the Blood Countess of Transylvania.* New York: McGraw-Hill, 1984. A popular account for a nonspecialist readership.

Pocs, Eva. *Between the Living and the Dead.* Budapest, Hungary: Central European University Press, 1999. An authoritative study of witchcraft in early modern Hungary.

Turoczy, Laszlo. *Erzébet Báthory.* Budapest, Hungary: 1744. Turoczy discovered the transcripts of the Bytca trials, which Thurzo had suppressed, and published the Latin texts in this rare book, which forms the foundation for all later studies.

CHEVALIER DE BAYARD
French military leader

The ideal of chivalry, exemplified in Bayard's actions, became a significant element in the education of young men of the upper classes in the Renaissance period.

BORN: c. 1473; Château de Bayard, Pontcharra, France
DIED: April 30, 1524; near Roasio (now in Italy)
ALSO KNOWN AS: Pierre Terrail
AREA OF ACHIEVEMENT: Military

EARLY LIFE

Chevalier de Bayard (sheh-vawl-yay bay-ahrd), born Pierre Terrail, lord of Bayard, was the son of Aymon Terrail and Hélène Alleman. He received a rudimentary education under the eye of his uncle, Laurent Alleman, bishop of Grenoble. In 1486, he left home to serve as page at the court of Charles I, duke of Savoy, where he was expected to acquire the experience and skills of a young nobleman. That same year, he followed his master on a trip to Italy, where he observed the flowering of Renaissance culture without noticeable effect on his medieval chivalric mind. On returning to Savoy in 1489, Bayard traveled with the duke to the court of Charles VIII of France, where he served the French king first as a page and then as a soldier. He took part in the king's expedition to Naples and, in 1495, was knighted for his valor in the Battle of Fornovo.

In 1501, as Louis XII reasserted his claim to the kingdom of Naples, Bayard became one of the most celebrated knights in the French army, widely known for his horsemanship and swordplay. By July, 1502, the French were clashing with the Spanish, who also claimed Naples. Lack of supplies and adverse conditions made for small-scale operations that offered opportunities for Bayard to display courage and skill in individual combat. Encased in steel armor and wielding an enormous two-handed sword, Bayard led the charge of the French into the breach of the Spanish fortress at Canossa.

In the winter of 1503, Bayard joined ten other French knights in a duel with eleven Spaniards. Bayard saved the French cause from disaster, and the match ended in a draw. In another incident, the capture of a Spanish paymaster's hoard, Bayard distributed the treasure with characteristic magnanimity, half to a fellow captain and the rest to his men, keeping nothing for himself.

Bayard gained honor even as the campaign turned against the French. He killed the Spaniard Alonzo de Soto-Mayor in a famous duel. Despite fighting at a disadvantage—he was weakened by fever and on foot rather than mounted—Bayard dispatched his much larger opponent, then honored him by preventing a trumpeting of the victory. During the retreat from Naples, without armor and wielding a pike, he held the bridge over the Garigliano against hundreds of Spanish.

LIFE'S WORK

At his prime, about twenty-five years old, tall and slender, his eyes black, his nose aquiline, his beard shaved close, Bayard exuded energy and good humor. His loyal service to his king was rewarded with greater responsibility in the Italian campaign that began in 1509. Having earlier received the title of captain, he was given command of 500 infantry and 180 horsemen in the War of the League of Cambrai, which pitted France, the Holy Roman Empire, and the Papacy against the Republic of Venice. Under his discipline, the infantry, little more than rabble, became an effective fighting force, distinguishing itself in the Battle of Agnadello on May 14, 1509. Subsequently, he fought in several skirmishes, leading his men in the thick of battle.

In September, 1510, as second in command, he defended the duchy of Ferrara against Pope Julius II, now a Venetian ally, and nearly captured the aged, warlike prelate. To the astonishment of his Ferrarese allies, however, he rejected with horror a plot to have the pope poisoned.

The following summer, Bayard was given command of the duke of Lorraine's company of six hundred horses; he had risen to approximately the rank of brigadier general in a modern army, and he had a significant voice in councils of war. After campaigning in the Friuli during the summer and fall against the Venetians, he hastened to support French garrisons in the duchy of Milan, which was threatened by the Swiss from the north, papal and Spanish armies from the south, and Venetians from the east. He was severely wounded in the thigh in the French capture of Brescia. Although the French brutally sacked the rest of the city, Bayard took nothing from the family with whom he convalesced, and he left large dowries for each of the family's two daughters.

He recovered well enough to participate in the French victory over the Spaniards at Ravenna in April, 1512. Deprived of their leader, Gaston de Foix, who died in the battle, and pressed by the Swiss and the Venetians, the French largely abandoned the duchy of Milan. Covering the retreat, Bayard was wounded in the shoulder.

Back in France, he recovered from a bout of typhoid fever in time to participate in a failed campaign in Spanish Navarre against the duke of Alva. Bayard again commanded the rearguard in the retreat under winter conditions over the Pyrenees back to France. By the midsummer of 1513, he was in Picardy with French troops awaiting an invasion by Henry VIII and Emperor Maximilian I. In the ensuing rout of the French, Bayard was captured by Burgundians during rearguard action at the bridge of Guinegatte. He spent several weeks in imperial Flanders and is said to have met the English king and the emperor. After a ransom was paid for him, Bayard returned to France in October.

Following the death of Louis XII on January 1, 1515, his successor, Francis I, appointed Bayard lieutenant-governor of Dauphiné, his home province, where he was beloved and esteemed. He assembled a force of four hundred cavalry and five thousand infantry; his troops were to pave the way for the main body of the king's army in a confrontation with a new coalition of enemies—the Swiss, the new pope Leo X, and the Spaniards. Francis would once more reconquer Lombardy. After a daring passage over the Alps, Bayard's men captured the papal commander, Prospero Colonna, and his supplies.

On September 13, 1515, Bayard shared in the French victory over the Swiss pikemen at Marignano, delivering Milan to the young French king. Exalted by the occasion and his own worthy contribution to it, Francis chose to be knighted by Bayard, the most highly reputed knight of the age.

By the summer of 1516, Bayard was back in Grenoble, tending to his duties as the king's representative in Dauphiné; his military skills were employed in running down marauding bands of former soldiers who ventured into his province. There were also opportunities for his legendary kindness and generosity. Urged by strong religious faith, he aided needy widows and comrades and helped others in distress, always with tact. By reason of this charity, and because he refused to profit by war, he remained throughout his life a relatively poor man.

In 1521, he left the peace of Dauphiné to assume command of the eastern frontier fortification of Mézières, which was threatened by an imperial army of thirty thousand. Beginning in August, Bayard, with fifteen hundred men, most of them peasants, held out for several weeks until Francis raised an army strong enough to relieve them. Having saved the country's eastern provinces, Bayard received the gratitude of his king, who made him captain-in-chief, a rank for the command of an army corps. His reputation among his country folk, borne with characteristic modesty, reached its zenith.

Chevalier de Bayard. (Library of Congress)

By year's end, he was en route to Genoa to shore up French control of that city. He could do little, however, to prevent first the duchy of Milan, then Genoa from being overrun by imperial and papal forces. At the end of 1522, France was threatened by enemies on all its frontiers. In the spring of 1524, Bayard, at the head of a company of fifteen hundred men, marched again with the French army toward Lombardy. It was an ill-fated expedition under an incompetent commander, the royal favorite Admiral Bonnivet. Though Bayard's force grew to make up a third of the French army, it accomplished little in the face of a qualitatively superior and better-led enemy. Bayard retreated with the rest of the army to the west of Milan. Sick, his energy diminished, he was surprised in camp at Robecco, and his division was routed.

In the crossing of the Sesia River, April 29, Bonnivet was injured, and he turned his command over to a reluctant Bayard. Ill, entrusted with the wreckage of an army, the great captain resumed the retreat toward France, himself leading the rearguard. Near Roasio, April 30, in a skirmish with the enemy's vanguard, he was struck by a bullet that pierced his armor and broke his spine. Realizing the wound was fatal, he had himself laid against a tree, facing the enemy. The Spanish captain, Pescara, approached him with awe, placed him on a camp bed, raised a tent above him, and stationed a guard of honor around him. He lived eight hours while his enemies paid him respect. His body was carried to Grenoble, where he was buried.

SIGNIFICANCE

Bayard lived out the knightly ideal of medieval Christianity, *sans peur et sans reproche* (without fear or reproach), a motto conferred on him by contemporaries. Like Joan of Arc, he became a great mythic figure, a national hero. Other less famous soldiers achieved as much or more, but Bayard's reputation was rooted in the personal qualities that he demonstrated so remarkably under adverse circumstances, often in defeat, fighting rearguard actions.

In a pragmatic world of decaying chivalric ideals and amoral statecraft, he remained brave, loyal, sincere, and generous. His piety, sustained by regular prayer and devotion, informed his knightly ethos. Neither defeat nor the agnosticism or hypocrisy prevalent among his peers ever shook his simple belief in his calling by God to be a Christian knight. Neither a saint nor a prude, he enjoyed the pleasures of the flesh. A liaison with an Italian woman produced a daughter, Jeanne Terrail, to whom he

gave his name and whom he lovingly supported. He never married.

The measure of Bayard's influence is evident in a vast body of writing that has grown around him, beginning in his lifetime and extending unbroken to the present, especially in France. His valor and sense of duty also can be detected in the lives of admirers such as the French president and military leader Charles de Gaulle (1890-1970), American military leader Robert E. Lee (1807-1870), and many less well-known military men.

—*Charles H. O'Brien*

FURTHER READING

Arnold, Thomas F. *The Renaissance at War*. London: Cassell, 2001. Detailed examination of the developing technologies and conventions of war in Bayard's time, including the impact of chivalry on military tactics, and of military tactics on chivalry.

Baumgartner, Frederic J. *Louis XII*. New York: St. Martin's Press, 1994. Treats Bayard briefly in the context of Louis XII's Italian campaigns.

Garrisson, Janine. *A History of Sixteenth-Century France, 1483-1598: Renaissance, Reformation, and Rebellion*. Translated by Richard Rex. New York: St. Martin's Press, 1995. Provides political, social, and cultural background for an understanding of Bayard's life.

Grummitt, David, ed. *The English Experience in France, c. 1450-1558: War, Diplomacy, and Cultural Exchange*. Burlington, Vt.: Ashgate, 2002. Explores the role of chivalry in influencing the personal relationships of key French and English figures of the period, and the influence of those relationships in turn on the development of both France and England into early modern states. Includes illustrations, bibliographic references, index.

Guyard de Berville, Guillaume François. *The Story of the Chevalier Bayard*. Translated by Edith Walford. Edited, with notes and introduction by James H. Friswell. London: S. Low and Marston, 1868. De Berville in 1760 amplified the memoirs of the Loyal Servant, most likely Bayard's steward, Jacques Jeoffre of Millieu.

Hale, John Rigby. *War and Society in Renaissance Europe 1450-1620*. New York: St. Martin's Press, 1985. Treats Bayard in terms of the transition from medieval to early modern systems of warfare.

Knecht, Robert Jean. *Renaissance Warrior and Patron: The Reign of Francis I*. 2d ed. London: Cambridge

University Press, 1994. The most detailed study of French history for the last decade of Bayard's life.

Shellabarger, Samuel. *The Chevalier Bayard: A Study in Fading Chivalry.* 1928. Reprint. New York: Biblio and Tannen, 1971. The best study of Bayard in English separates facts from myths about the great captain.

Simms, William Gilmore. *The Life of the Chevalier Bayard.* New York: Harper & Brothers, 1847. Reflects the attractiveness of Bayard's chivalric ethos to the planter aristocracy of the antebellum South.

Wiley, W. L. *The Gentleman of Renaissance France.* Cambridge, Mass.: Harvard University Press, 1954. This analysis of social attitudes uses Bayard to illustrate the qualities of a complete gentleman.

SEE ALSO: Duke of Alva; Charles VIII; Francis I; Henry VIII; Julius II; Leo X; Louis XII; Maximilian I; Sir Philip Sidney.

RELATED ARTICLE in *Great Events from History: The Renaissance & Early Modern Era, 1454-1600:* August 19, 1493-January 12, 1519: Reign of Maximilian I.

BAYEZID II
Sultan of the Ottoman Empire (r. 1481-1512)

Although not among the great sultans of the Ottoman Empire, Bayezid II filled an important transitional role, in which much of his time was spent trying to unsuccessfully respond to conflicts with the East. The fame of his father as well as the symbolic memory of his namesake would have made it difficult for Bayezid to earn a reputation for strong rule or aggressive foreign policy.

BORN: December, 1447, or January, 1448; Demotika, Ottoman Empire (now in Turkey)
DIED: May 26, 1512; en route to Demotika
ALSO KNOWN AS: Bayezid the Just
AREAS OF ACHIEVEMENT: Government and politics, military

EARLY LIFE

Little or nothing is known about the early life or education of Bayezid (bi-eh-ZEED) II prior to his first official appointment to a key government training post. This appointment occurred a few years before the death of his father, Mehmed II, the more famous sultan who conquered Constantinople (now Istanbul, Turkey) in 1453, a few years after Bayezid's birth.

As governor of Amasya Province (between Ankara and the Black Sea), Bayezid received important military experience, particularly at the distant Battle of Otluk Beli in 1473. This encounter marked a turning point in the long Ottoman struggle to subdue the Turkmen populations in the zone spanning western Iran and eastern Anatolia that had rallied around the famous tribal chief Uzun Hasan.

The most significant chapter of Bayezid's early life came when his father died in 1481. His younger brother Cem (or Jem), governor of Karaman, with its influential religious capital Konya, challenged Bayezid's right to succeed. This succession struggle would go on, in various forms, for some fourteen years. Bayezid's claims were apparently supported by the main imperial military forces and high officials of the "new" capital at Istanbul. Cem's challenge depended on a number of different sources of resistance, and it even included attempts to establish alliances with influences far from the Ottoman imperial homeland. Thus, Cem first tried, but failed, to defeat Bayezid with the support of Egyptian Mamlūk forces provided by Sultan Qāytbāy of Cairo. He then sought refuge with the Knights of Saint John on their island fortress at Rhodes. The knights decided not to join in the succession fray but turned Bayezid's brother over to the French kingdom. Several Christian states' use of the Ottoman pretender as their possible preferred ally over the next ten years forced Bayezid to keep close surveillance over his army to avoid possible betrayals. This limitation on the sultan's power in the early years of his reign (at least until Cem's death in 1495) held the Ottomans back from carrying out the major yearly military campaigns that had characterized most reigns to and including that of Mehmed II.

LIFE'S WORK

Bayezid scored some early successes in maintaining and even expanding Ottoman control over key Balkan zones (capture of Herzegovina in 1483, seizure of the lower Danubian fortress of Kilia in 1484, and increased control over the Dniester River approaches to Crimea on the north coast of the Black Sea). The new sultan did not possess for some years, however, sufficient strength to fortify his southeastern provinces against the threat of Mamlūk forays into agriculturally rich Cilicia. By 1491, an inconclusive peace was signed that would leave this southeastern zone in an indecisive position until Bayezid's son and successor Selim I marched into the area with force.

Bayezid's main attentions prior to the rise of Ṣafavid Iranian threats to his eastern imperial flank would remain tied to Balkan Europe and the Krim Tatar zone of the north Black Sea coast, where Poland's kings aimed at making Moldavia (now part of Romania) a Slavic dependency. This was a claim that Bayezid would only reverse militarily in 1499. During the same period, he became seriously engaged in the Aegean Sea itself, where the Ottomans faced a formidable trade and military rival in the powerful city-state of Venice.

Perhaps to divert attention from rising heterodox religious discontent and sedition in the eastern provinces, Bayezid pursued an openly aggressive policy toward his closest Christian rival, Venice. The break began in 1491, when the Venetian *balyos* (the diplomatic representative recognized by his father after the 1453 conquest) was expelled from Istanbul. Political tensions turned to material frustrations when, in 1496 (one year after the death of his rebellious brother Cem), Bayezid closed Ottoman ports to Venetian trade. For the next four years, clashes with the ships of Venice occurred throughout the eastern Mediterranean and the Aegean zones.

This protracted war of maritime encounters, which Pope Alexander VI would have liked to expand into a full-scale crusade, had an important effect on Bayezid's priorities as ruler. First, it made it necessary for the Ottomans to spend money on the development of seaports in western Turkey. Also, a new supreme naval commander, Kemal Reis (a former pirate captain whose ships had raided as far west as France and Spain), was named head of a largely rebuilt and heavily armed Ottoman navy.

The peace that was finally signed in 1502 restored most of Venice's trading privileges but limited its physical control of key ports considerably: Only Albania on the Adriatic and the Morea (southern Greece) could be called Venetian preserves in Ottoman territory by the first years of the sixteenth century. A second major repercussion of these years of Ottoman emphasis on naval development was a gradual assimilation of Mediterranean renegade captains into Turkish service. In addition to Kemal Reis, Bayezid encouraged a number of other important raiders (*gazis*) to pledge loyalty to his sultanate. Among these would be some of the great captains of the next generation, whose home ports were in North Africa.

These would, by the end of Bayezid's son's reign, play a major role in attaching the provinces of Algiers, Tripolitania, and, eventually, Tunisia to the Ottoman realm.

Bayezid himself, however, did not live to see the rebirth of expansive Ottoman military power under his son Selim or, especially, Selim's successor Süleyman the Magnificent. Many historians note that, after the Venetian peace of 1502, Bayezid tended to withdraw more and more from direct management of imperial matters. This decision to retreat from direct responsibilities of rule offered the possibility for Bayezid to live a contemplative life. He was himself interested in music and poetry, and invited a number of recognized scholars of history, science, and religion to frequent his court in Istanbul. One of these, Kemal Pasha Zade, wrote a commissioned history of the Ottoman Empire under Bayezid's auspices.

There were, however, negative factors that stemmed from Bayezid's decision to let others take responsibility for key affairs of state. On the one hand, apparently the influence of certain less tolerant religious leaders who were protégés of the court rose. This even went to the point of allowing zealots to denounce violently their rivals with the tacit and sometimes direct support of the sultan. On the other hand, increasing social and religious ferment in the Ottoman eastern Anatolian provinces, spurred on by unorthodox proponents of Shia Islam under the banner of Ṣafavid shah Ismāʿīl I, had spread considerably by the early 1500's. The sultan's lack of a determined policy of reaction nearly assured that a party of political opposition to him would emerge.

Bayezid's approach to the problem of Shia heterodoxy and its willingness to sponsor anti-Ottoman rebellions in far-flung provinces was to try to convince Ismāʿīl to respect the integrity of a single unified community of Islam. By 1508-1509, the futility of expecting Ismāʿīl to reason with the Ottoman sultan was apparent: Ismāʿīl invaded Iraq and added it to Ṣafavid domains. Concerned Turkish military leaders feared that Syria and perhaps Ottoman Cilicia would be next. When an Ottoman army led by Grand Vizier ʿAlī Pasha and Prince Ahmed only barely succeeded in expelling Ismāʿīl's supporters from the southeast province around Kayseri (August, 1511), a party of militant opposition to Bayezid's rule began to plan his overthrow.

Although, as Bayezid's eldest son, Ahmed should have been considered the legal successor, military professionals most anxious to see a strong force dispatched to the East preferred the candidacy of Selim. Bayezid's appointment (in 1507) of Ahmed to the same Amasya provincial governorate that he had held prior to defending his claim to the succession in 1481 seemed to be a sign that the sultan was unaware of such preferences. Thus, Selim and his supporters decided not to await Bayezid's demise before claiming the throne. They revolted against Bayezid and divided the army against itself. Several incidents of open clashes occurred before Bayezid was formally deposed (April, 1512). Only a month later, while attempting to return to forced exile at his birthplace in Demotika, Bayezid died, presumably of natural causes.

Within a year after Bayezid's demise, his son Selim (the Grim) had begun to mount a major military reconquest of threatened Ottoman provinces in the East. In only two years, Ismā'īl would be defeated and a military route opened for Selim's conquest of the core countries of Arabistan: Syria and Egypt.

SIGNIFICANCE

The reign of Bayezid II demonstrates that, despite the obvious imperial determination and military capacities of the Ottoman Empire, certain signs of internal dissension that would paralyze the political apparatuses of state in later centuries were already present in 1500. One of these is represented by the divisive influence of Cem's fourteen-year-long challenge to his brother's succession. Intrigues involving supporters of different scions of the Ottoman family as claimants to the throne had not been unknown before this date but had never affected so many different interest groups, both domestic and foreign.

Another negative characteristic of Bayezid's reign that would be repeated again and again in later centuries was his tendency to delegate active authority to govern. The sultan's retirement to the intellectually and aesthetically rarefied atmosphere of the imperial court left the field open for self-seeking politicians, military authorities, and religious zealots to play a larger role in high Ottoman affairs than had been possible under his predecessors. Although Selim's overthrow of his father in 1512 prepared the way for a reversal of these trends during the next two great reigns, the elements operating in Bayezid's period of rule would return to weaken many of the original bases of Ottoman imperial authority in the seventeenth century.

—*Byron Cannon*

FURTHER READING

Brummett, Palmira. *Ottoman Seapower and Levantine Diplomacy in the Age of Discovery.* Albany: State University of New York Press, 1994. Seeks to integrate Ottoman history into European, Asian, and world history by demonstrating the importance of inherited Euro-Asian trade networks to the development and expansion of the Ottoman Empire, as well as the effects of continual commercial struggles between the empire and other world trading powers on all aspects of imperial and mercantile history. Includes illustrations, maps, bibliography, glossary, and index.

Creasy, Edward S. *History of the Ottoman Turks.* London: R. Bentley, 1878. Reprint. Karachi, Pakistan: S. M. Mir, 1980. A detailed historical work based on the massive mid-nineteenth century German classic by Von Hammer-Purgstall. The author states that he not only abridged Von Hammer but also incorporated a wide range of other sources, including memoirs of Europeans who witnessed the events described. Includes illustrations, fold-out maps, bibliographic references.

Fisher, Sidney N. *The Foreign Relations of Turkey, 1481-1512.* Urbana: University of Illinois Press, 1948. One of the most complete and detailed studies of Bayezid, emphasizing relations with foreign powers, both European and Muslim.

Har-el, Shai. *Struggle for Domination in the Middle East: The Ottoman-Mamluk War, 1485-1491.* New York: E. J. Brill, 1995. An in-depth account of Bayezid's war with the Mamlūk Empire, detailing the foundations of the conflict in the fourteenth century, a step-by-step account of the war itself, and some discussion of the second and conclusive war that occurred less than a decade after Bayezid's reign. Includes illustrations, maps, bibliographic references, index.

Inalcik, Halil. "The Rise of the Ottoman Empire." In *The Cambridge History of Islam,* edited by P. M. Holt, Ann K. S. Lambton, and Bernard Lewis. Vol. 1. Cambridge, England: Cambridge University Press, 1970. The most concise survey of the entire early period of Ottoman expansion, with a specific section on Bayezid. The material on Bayezid is useful both for its cultural foci and for its discussion of social subgroupings, especially that of the Turcomans.

Itzkowitz, Norman. *Ottoman Empire and Islamic Tradition.* New York: Alfred A. Knopf, 1972. Contains a short but complete subchapter on Bayezid and chronological coverage of sultanic reigns. Three other sections deal with various Ottoman institutions such as bureaucracy and provincial structure, which shed light on conditions, practical and legal, faced by Bayezid.

Shaw, Stanford J. *Empire of the Gazis: The Rise and Decline of the Ottoman Empire, 1280-1808.* Vol. 1 in *History of the Ottoman Empire and Modern Turkey.* New York: Cambridge University Press, 1976. Of several general works on Ottoman history, this volume is a good resource on Bayezid's reign. Provides useful information on key cultural questions, including undercurrents of religious discontent and some elements of courtly literature from the late fifteenth and early sixteenth centuries.

Turnbull, Stephen. *The Ottoman Empire, 1326-1699.* New York: Routledge, 2004. This history of Ottoman rule, imperial expansion, and military tactics focuses especially on the struggle for the Balkans and battles against European powers. Includes illustrations, maps, index.

SEE ALSO: Alexander VI; Barbarossa; Mehmed II; Mehmed III; Pius II; Qāytbāy; Süleyman the Magnificent; Vladislav II.

RELATED ARTICLES in *Great Events from History: The Renaissance & Early Modern Era, 1454-1600:* April 14, 1457-July 2, 1504: Reign of Stephen the Great; 1481-1512: Reign of Bayezid II and Ottoman Civil Wars; May, 1485-April 13, 1517: Mamlūk-Ottoman Wars; 1501-1524: Reign of Ismāʿīl I; 1512-1520: Reign of Selim I; 1520-1566: Reign of Süleyman.

LADY MARGARET BEAUFORT
English noblewoman

Lady Margaret Beaufort was closely involved in the political life of her day, playing a significant role in her son Henry's return to England from exile and his battle for the English crown in 1485. Contemporaries saw in Margaret a particularly religious woman, and her charity gave rise to two colleges at Cambridge University: Christ's and St. Johns.

BORN: May 31, 1443; Bletsoe Castle, Bedfordshire, England
DIED: June 29, 1509; London, England
ALSO KNOWN AS: Countess of Richmond and Derby
AREAS OF ACHIEVEMENT: Government and politics, education

EARLY LIFE

The family of Margaret of Beaufort (MAHR-greht uhv BOH-fuhrt) first formed through an adulterous relationship between John of Gaunt and Katherine Swynford in the late 1300's. Margaret's father was John Beaufort, the first duke of Somerset, who fell sharply from royal favor and died, perhaps committing suicide, in the year of Margaret's birth. This sad event overshadowed her early years, and she was placed in an arranged marriage to John de la Pole while still a very young child. The marriage was disbanded when she was six.

If she came to marriage young, she also was a mother at a very tender age. Her second marriage, to Edmund Tudor, was brief, but one that would have historic consequences. Edmund died of the plague in 1456, but the twelve-year-old Margaret was already pregnant with

Henry Tudor, the future Henry VII. Historians have suggested that the birth was a very difficult one and that the young mother experienced severe problems—she would have no more children in her lifetime.

LIFE'S WORK

It is an often-told episode from the life of Lady Margaret Beaufort that she wept when her son was crowned King Henry VII of England. The tears were not of joy but of anxiety and concern for the future. Her fears were founded on the belief that even in current moments of happiness and triumph, an unstoppable change in fortune was looming. As many have suggested, Lady Margaret's foreboding sense existed with good reason, no doubt shaped by the events of her own life and times. After all, she lived through a period remarkable for its instability and political strife, and her own life seems to have reflected the ebbs and flows of fate no less dramatically.

Not long after the death of Edmund Tudor, her second husband, Margaret married Henry Stafford in 1458. It was the beginning of what is widely understood to have been a very long and contented marriage. Even if Margaret found stability, events in England during the following years were far from peaceful. During more than three decades of what is known as the Wars of the Roses, the years between 1469 and 1471 saw especially significant and violent upheaval. Edward IV seized the Crown from Henry VI in the name of the Yorkist camp, but a rebellion by the Lancastrian side restored Henry to the throne and forced Edward into exile. The wheel of fortune would turn once more, however, as Edward returned from exile and won a famous victory at the Battle of Tewkesbury (1471). Henry died soon after in the Tower of London. The aftermath of the battle was significant for Margaret: Stafford, who had fought on Edward's side, died soon after, and her son Henry was sent to France for his safety. By 1472, moreover, Margaret had married her fourth and last husband, Thomas Lord Stanley.

In 1483 Edward IV died, and his brother usurped the Crown to become Richard III. Richard's reign was filled with drama (William Shakespeare, a century later, would see enough material in Richard to create one of his most memorable villains). Margaret, with typical caution, had not been hostile to the new king, but she soon joined others in actively resisting his monarchy. Many have said she played a key role in the return of her son, Henry, bidding to defeat Richard for the Crown. Margaret's husband, Thomas Lord Stanley, who had been loyal to Richard, was also active in aiding Henry's triumphant return. Henry would defeat Richard at the Battle of Bosworth in August, 1485, to become Henry VII, marking the start of the Tudor Dynasty, one of England's most successful royal lines.

Henry VII was a broadly successful king, and Margaret was a close and influential aid to her son. She was active in, among many other affairs of court, the marriage of Henry to Elizabeth of York, thereby uniting the houses of York and Lancaster. Her biographers show Margaret as a woman who played a very important role in the reign of Henry VII, who enjoyed her authority, worked to exert and maintain it, and became very wealthy indeed. She was a first-rate businesswoman. Still, with all her skill with policy and finance, Margaret was an exceptionally devout woman, committing herself to sober and intensive worship. She spent large portions of the day taking Mass and offering prayer.

The first decade of the sixteenth century, however, would see many changes in, and indeed the loss of, Margaret's life. Before Margaret's own death in 1509, however, she experienced the death of her husband in 1504. There has been speculation about the closeness of Margaret and Thomas Lord Stanley. Some have made the case that they were a distant couple, existing in a marriage that was founded on political expediency rather than love. Those who have taken this point of view have pointed to Margaret's increased independence during the marriage, particularly the establishment of her own household and a vow of chastity before her husband's death. There has been an effort to reconsider this picture, suggesting that Margaret's move away from Stanley

Lady Margaret Beaufort. (Hulton|Archive by Getty Images)

could be explained in political terms rather than as a result of any hostility between the couple. The biographers who make this claim highlight Stanley's frequent and seemingly welcome visits to Margaret's estate, as well as the very proper period of mourning that Margaret faithfully observed after Stanley's death.

The young Prince Arthur, Henry's oldest son, had passed away in the same decade, as had Henry's mother, Queen Elizabeth I. Finally, in 1509, Henry VII himself passed on. Margaret had outlived her husbands, her daughter-in-law, her son, and her oldest grandchild. With the coronation of her grandson, Henry VIII, however, she did not outlive the dynasty to which she had given birth.

In the last years of her life, Margaret had been busy securing a legacy visible still today. She had for some years been developing a deep and profound tie to higher education. Her interest turned into direct and groundbreaking levels of support for Oxford University, but especially Cambridge University. Her first gift was to both, providing for each university endowments for lectureships in theology. Soon her abundant resources and energies were directed almost singularly toward Cambridge, however, as she diligently lobbied and funded the transformation of the smaller God's House at Cambridge into Christ's College. The founding of the college was significant, and Margaret had not been simply a figurehead sanctioning the work. She had been involved at every level, and the immense success of the project was largely because of her support.

She seems to have enjoyed the labor, or at least found it very rewarding. At the close of her life, she had begun plans to establish a second college at Cambridge. This late design involved the transformation of an old Cambridge hospital into St. John's College. She died before the project was much more than a concept, but her wishes for St. John's were realized in the years after her death.

SIGNIFICANCE

Margaret was the fountainhead of the Tudor Dynasty, a royal line that continued into the seventeenth century. Her contribution to one of the world's finest seats of learning, moreover, was meaningful and lasting. On an individual level, however, Margaret was a complex, often admirable, though frequently calculating woman. Her life is worthy of study for the significance of her actions, for her important place in the lineage of a royal family, and for her example of how one woman operated with intelligence and sharp skill within the limits of a strict patriarchal culture.

—*Paul Gleed*

FURTHER READING

Jones, Michael K., and Malcom G. Underwood. *The King's Mother.* New York: Cambridge University Press, 1992. This biography of Margaret is admirably balanced, avoiding the different extremes that have traditionally been part of Margaret's legend.

Seward, Desmond. *Wars of the Roses.* New York: Viking Press, 1995. This volume uses a small number of key figures (one of which is Margaret) through which to tell the wider tale of the Wars of the Roses. It is useful especially for students who wish to understand the vast complexity of Margaret's time. A number of chapters focus specifically on Margaret.

Simon, Linda. *Of Virtue Rare.* Boston: Houghton Mifflin, 1982. Thinner, and perhaps less substantial than Jones and Underwood, this biography is nonetheless very enjoyable and a wonderful read.

Stanton, Graham, et al. *Lady Margaret Beaufort and Her Professors of Divinity at Cambridge.* New York: Cambridge University Press, 2003. A scholarly investigation of the legacy Margaret left at Cambridge through her endowed lectureships.

SEE ALSO: Edward IV; Elizabeth I; Saint John Fisher; Henry VI; Henry VII; Henry VIII; Richard III; William Shakespeare; The Tudor Family.

RELATED ARTICLE in *Great Events from History: The Renaissance & Early Modern Era, 1454-1600:* 1455-1485: Wars of the Roses.

FRANCIS BEAUMONT AND JOHN FLETCHER
English dramatists

With their light, witty comedy and melodramatic tragicomedy, Beaumont and Fletcher introduced a new style and aristocratic outlook into Renaissance English drama.

FRANCIS BEAUMONT

BORN: c. 1584; Grace-Dieu, Leicestershire, England
DIED: March 6, 1616; London, England

JOHN FLETCHER

BORN: December, 1579; Rye, Sussex, England
DIED: August, 1625; London, England
AREAS OF ACHIEVEMENT: Theater, literature

EARLY LIVES

Both Francis Beaumont (BOH-mont) and John Fletcher were products of the English upper class. Fletcher was the second son (the fourth of nine children) of Richard Fletcher, a leading Anglican clergyman. His father served as president of Bene't College (Corpus Christi), Cambridge; was dean of Peterborough, officiating at the execution of Mary, Queen of Scots; and was successively bishop of Bristol, Worcester, and London, this last position making him Queen Elizabeth's chaplain.

The background of Beaumont was even more aristocratic. As a member of an old Anglo-Norman family, Beaumont was related by either blood or marriage to a large portion of the English aristocracy. Many of these

MAJOR COLLABORATIVE PLAYS OF BEAUMONT AND FLETCHER	
c. 1606	*The Woman Hater*
1608-1610	*The Coxcomb*
c. 1609	*Philaster: Or, Love Lies A-Bleeding*
c. 1609-1612	*The Captain*
1610-1611	*The Maid's Tragedy*
1611	*A King and No King*
1612	*Cupid's Revenge*
c. 1612	*Four Plays, or Moral Representations, in One* (commonly known as *Four Plays in One*)
1615-1616	*The Scornful Lady*
1617?	*The Tragedy of Thierry, King of France, and His Brother Theodoret* (commonly known as *Thierry and Theodoret*)

aristocratic connections came through his mother, Anne Pierrepoint. His father, a Court of Common Pleas judge and owner of Grace-Dieu Manor, was also named Francis. Francis the playwright was the third son among four children. The families of both Beaumont and Fletcher had a number of poets, including Beaumont's older brother John and Fletcher's younger first cousins, the Spenserian poets Phineas and Giles Fletcher.

Thus, the social circle—educated, urbane, and artistic—in which they were reared gave Beaumont and Fletcher a running start as Renaissance playwrights. They grew up with clever, informed talk and, unlike fellow playwright William Shakespeare, did not have to imagine how the upper classes who populated Renaissance drama lived. Their educations were rounded off at Cambridge and Oxford and at the London Inns of Court, England's law school but also a center of literary and dramatic activity. Fletcher entered Bene't College, Cambridge, in 1591 and probably moved on to the Inns of Court in 1594 or 1595, after his father became bishop of London. It is uncertain whether he received a Cambridge degree. Beaumont entered Broadgates Hall (now Pembroke College), Oxford, in 1597, left without receiving a degree, and enrolled at the Inns of Court in 1600.

Neither Beaumont nor Fletcher completed his legal studies. In Fletcher's case, there were financial reasons. His father lost Queen Elizabeth's favor in 1595 and died in 1596, leaving the family in debt. Fletcher was forced to drop out, and there is no record of his activities for the next ten years. In Beaumont's case, the record is even more uncertain. Possibly he was not interested in law and gradually drifted into literary and dramatic endeavors. *Salmacis and Hermaphroditus*, an Ovidian narrative

poem published anonymously in 1602 and in 1639 attributed to Beaumont, offers some evidence for this possibility. The next sure record, however, is in 1606, when Beaumont and Fletcher were practicing playwrights.

LIVES' WORK

At first, each of the two playwrights apparently practiced on his own, experiencing the kind of uneven success typical of apprentices. Both wrote for the private theaters, indoor playhouses that drew a more exclusive audience than the outdoor public theaters, and their first plays were acted by boys' companies, then-popular offshoots of choir schools. Of the early plays attributed solely or mostly to Beaumont, *The Woman Hater* (pr. c. 1606, pb. 1607), a comedy, was fairly successful, but the masterful satire-burlesque *The Knight of the Burning Pestle* (pr. 1607, pb. 1613) was a flop when it was first performed. An early tragicomedy attributed solely or mostly to Fletcher, *The Faithful Shepherdess* (pr. c. 1608-1609), was similarly unsuccessful. The two young playwrights might have overestimated the sophistication of their audiences or the child actors.

When and why Beaumont and Fletcher began collaborating are not exactly known, but the two were probably drawn together by similar backgrounds and common ties. As their commendatory verses to Ben Jonson's *Volpone: Or, The Fox* (pr. 1606, pb. 1607) make clear, both were "Sons of Ben." Johnson's satirical and critical inclinations undoubtedly influenced the two younger men; both socialized with Johnson's famous circle at the Mermaid Tavern. In the poem "Mr. Francis Beaumont's Letter to Ben Jonson," Beaumont described the circle's sparkling conversation.

What things have we seen
Done at the Mermaid! Heard words that have been
So nimble and so full of subtill flame,
As if that every one from whence they came,
Had meant to put his whole wit in a jest,
And had resolv'd to live a foole the rest
Of his dull life. . . .
We left an aire behind us, which alone,
Was able to make the two next companies
Right witty; though but downright fools, more wise.

In this situation, the idea for collaboration was not far off.

Beaumont and Fletcher not only became collaborators but also lived with each other, according to seventeenth century biographer John Aubrey in *Brief Lives* (1898): "They lived together on the Banke-side, not far from the Play-house, both batchelors; lay together (from Sir James Hales, etc.); had one wench in the house between them, which they did so admire, the same cloaths and cloake, etc., between them." It is uncertain how much

of this colorful bohemian picture can be attributed generally to the Renaissance cult of friendship and specifically to the Castor and Pollux myth that grew up around the "twins of poetry." As a matter of fact, however, Beaumont and Fletcher do look somewhat like twins in the extant portraits (which might have been created with the myth in mind or might reflect typical idealization); both are depicted as Van Dyck cavalier types with wide poetic eyes, large, slightly aquiline noses, and reddish or light brown hair (curly in some portraits), mustaches, and beards (Beaumont's trimmed square, Fletcher's pointed).

Some of the performances of their collaborative plays were by the Children of the Queen's Revels, but most were by the King's Men, Shakespeare's company, with which Beaumont and Fletcher became associated when the company took over the private Blackfriars Theater in 1608. Their best collaborations are two tragicomedies, *Philaster: Or, Love Lies A-Bleeding* (pr. c. 1609, pb. 1920) and *A King and No King* (pr. 1611, pb. 1619), and *The Maid's Tragedy* (pr. 1610-1611, pb. 1619), in all of which Beaumont's hand predominates. Collaborative works in which Fletcher's hand predominates include the uneven tragedy *Cupid's Revenge* (pr. 1612, pb. 1615) and three comedies, *The Coxcomb* (pr. 1608-1610, pb. 1647), *The Captain* (pr. c. 1609-1612, pb. 1647), and *The Scornful Lady* (pr. 1615-1616, pb. 1616). Other plays, such as *The Tragedy of Thierry, King of France, and His Brother Theodoret* (pr. 1617?), involved a third collaborator (or later, reviser), usually Philip Massinger.

Beaumont and Fletcher's collaboration tapered off or ended around 1612 or 1613, when Beaumont married an heiress, Ursula Isley. By himself, Beaumont wrote a final dramatic work, *The Masque of the Inner Temple and Grayes Inn* (pr. 1613, pb. 1613), for a royal wedding. Apparently, Beaumont retired to his wife's estate in Sundridge, Kent. They had

FLETCHER'S OTHER MAJOR WORKS	
c. 1604	*The Woman's Prize: Or, The Tamer Tamed*
c. 1608-1609	*The Faithful Shepherdess*
1609-1614	*Bonduca*
1610-1614	*Valentinian*
1610-1616	*Monsieur Thomas*
c. 1611	*The Night Walker: Or, The Little Thief*
c. 1612-1613	*The Two Noble Kinsmen* (with William Shakespeare)
1613	*Henry VIII* (with Shakespeare)
c. 1614	*Wit Without Money*
1616?	*The Nice Valour: Or, The Passionate Madman*
1616?	*Love's Pilgrimage*
c. 1616	*The Mad Lover*
1616-1617	*The Queen of Corinth* (with Philip Massinger and Nathan Field)
1616-1618	*The Knight of Malta* (with Massinger and Field)
c. 1617	*The Chances*
1618	*The Loyal Subject*
1619	*The Humourous Lieutenant*
1619	*Sir John van Olden Barnavelt* (with Massinger)
c. 1619-1620	*The Custom of the Country* (with Massinger)
1619-1621	*The Island Princess: Or, The Generous Portugal*
1619-1623	*The Little French Lawyer* (with Massinger)
1619-1623	*Women Pleased* (pb. 1647)
c. 1620	*The False One* (with Massinger)
1621	*The Wild-Goose Chase* (with Massinger)
1621	*The Pilgrim*
c. 1621	*The Double Marriage* (with Massinger)
1622	*The Prophetess* (with Massinger)
1622	*The Sea Voyage* (with Massinger)
1622	*The Spanish Curate* (with Massinger)
c. 1622	*The Beggars' Bush* (with Massinger)
1623	*The Lover's Progress* (revised by Massinger, 1634)
1623	*The Maid in the Mill* (with William Rowley)
1624	*Rule a Wife and Have a Wife*
1624	*A Wife for a Month*
1625	*The Elder Brother* (with Massinger)
1626	*The Fair Maid of the Inn* (with Massinger?)
1647	*Wit at Several Weapons* (possibly with Beaumont)

Francis Beaumont; John Fletcher (Library of Congress)

two daughters, Elizabeth and Frances, the latter born a few months after Beaumont died on March 6, 1616. He was buried in the Poets' Corner of Westminster Abbey in London.

After Beaumont's retirement, Fletcher continued to write plays for another dozen or so years, succeeding Shakespeare as the chief writer for the King's Men. Sometimes he wrote alone, but for the most part he worked in collaboration with other playwrights. His most notable collaborator was Shakespeare, with whom he and possibly other contributors wrote a play called *Cardenio*, which was lost; *The Two Noble Kinsmen* (c. 1612-1613); and *Henry VIII* (1613). Other collaborators included Nathan Field and William Rowley. Fletcher's primary collaborator during this period, however, was Massinger, with whom he formed a friendship and working association similar to that with Beaumont, except that Massinger was the junior partner. They collaborated on about fifteen plays, including the tragedies *Sir John van Olden Barnavelt* (1619) and *The Double Marriage* (c. 1621), the tragicomedies *The Queen of Corinth* (1616-1617) and *The Knight of Malta* (1616-1618), both also involving Field, and the comedies *The Little French Lawyer* (1619-1623), *The Custom of the Country* (c. 1619-1620), *The Sea Voyage* (1622), and *The Spanish Curate* (1622). Plays written by Fletcher alone include the tragedies *Valentinian* (1610-1614) and *Bonduca* (1609-1614); the tragicomedies *The Mad Lover* (c. 1616), *The Humorous Lieutenant* (1619), *The Island Princess: Or, The Generous Portugal* (1619-1621), and *A Wife for a Month* (1624); and the comedies *Monsieur Thomas* (1610-1616), *Wit Without Money* (c. 1614), *The Chances* (c. 1617), *The Pilgrim* (1621), *The Wild-Goose Chase* (1621), and *Rule a Wife and Have a Wife* (1624). Fletcher died in August, 1625, a victim of the plague, and was buried at Saint Savior's Church in London.

SIGNIFICANCE

Beaumont and Fletcher are considered the greatest collaborators in English literature, but the extent of their collaboration is something of a myth. Of the fifty or so plays attributed to the Beaumont and Fletcher canon, most are by the two playwrights working alone or in collaboration with other people. Fletcher's collaboration with Massinger, who typically receives little credit for his share in the canon, was actually more extensive than his collaboration with Beaumont, which lasted only six or seven years

BEAUMONT'S OTHER MAJOR WORKS	
1602	*Salmacis and Hermaphroditus*
1607	*The Knight of the Burning Pestle*
1613	*The Masque of the Inner Temple and Grayes Inn*
1640	*Poems*

and involved a dozen or fewer plays. In these plays, one or the other's hand usually predominates; the plays best known today are those attributed solely or mostly to Beaumont, who is considered the better writer of the two. Still, Beaumont and Fletcher made the practice of collaboration fashionable among the playwrights of their time; even Shakespeare ended his career as a collaborator.

Of far more importance, Beaumont and Fletcher crystallized the turn of Renaissance English drama toward the tastes of the upper class, a trend already started by the private theaters and the satirical, classical bias of Jonson. They embodied this turn in their own social backgrounds. With their satire of bourgeois citizens, their light repartee, and their absolutist cavalier values, they gave the upper-class turn a definite form. The entertaining drama they created was highly regarded at the time—even ranked above that of Shakespeare's—but is virtually no longer produced. To modern audiences and readers, most of their work may seem somewhat juvenile; in fact, Beaumont was no more than a young-man-about-town—the writer as young gallant—when he penned his work, and Fletcher, repeating what had been successful, hardly advanced beyond Beaumont's attitudes.

Besides turning the drama away from the development of more serious themes, Beaumont and Fletcher helped split the Renaissance English audience, which in the public theaters had represented all social classes. Indeed, the English drama had begun in the Middle Ages with performances of religious mystery cycles by the town burghers, the very kind of people whom Jonson and then Beaumont and Fletcher satirized. From a negative standpoint, the damage Beaumont and Fletcher wrought on English drama is outweighed only by that of the Puritans, who on the other side opposed the theaters and finally closed them down in 1642. When the theaters reopened in the Restoration period, the elite classes had absorbed the English drama, and its typical fare—the heroic play and the comedy of manners—clearly reflected the influence of Beaumont and Fletcher.

—*Harold Branam*

FURTHER READING

Appleton, William W. *Beaumont and Fletcher: A Critical Study.* London: Allen and Unwin, 1956. This brief study of Beaumont and Fletcher's work also treats their influence in the Restoration and their later reputation; includes a useful checklist of plays with dates and collaborators.

Beaumont, Francis, and John Fletcher. *The Dramatic Works in the Beaumont and Fletcher Canon.* Edited by Fredson Bowers. 10 vols. Cambridge, England: Cambridge University Press, 1966-1996. Definitive edition of Beaumont and Fletcher's entire dramatic corpus.

Danby, John F. *Poets on Fortune's Hill: Studies in Sidney, Shakespeare, Beaumont, and Fletcher.* London: Faber and Faber, 1952. Reprint, as *Elizabethan and Jacobean Poets*, 1964. An excellent critical study that places these writers in their social and historical contexts. Sees Beaumont and Fletcher as the final, decadent stage of a great Elizabethan tradition.

Gayley, Charles Mills. *Beaumont, the Dramatist.* 1914. Reprint. New York: Russell and Russell, 1969. Somewhat dated but contains the fullest biography of Beaumont as well as considerable information on Fletcher and numerous miscellaneous topics. Digressive style with some fascinating trivia.

Hirschfeld, Heather Anne. "Beaumont, Fletcher, and Shakespeare: Collaborative Drama, the Stuart Masque, and the Politics of Identification." In *Joint Enterprises: Collaborative Drama and the Institutionalization of the English Renaissance Theater.* Amherst: University of Massachusetts Press, 2004. Study of the mutual influence of Beaumont and Fletcher on each other, as well as the influence of Shakespeare on both, placed against the background of the evolution of English theater from low cultural spectacle to high cultural institution. Includes bibliographic references and index.

Hoy, Cyrus. "The Shares of Fletcher and His Collaborators in the Beaumont and Fletcher Canon." *Studies in Bibliography* 8-12 (1956-1962). The authoritative study on this subject but many details remain open to dispute and may never be settled.

Kinney, Arthur F., ed. *A Companion to Renaissance Drama.* Malden, Mass.: Blackwell, 2002. Anthology of essays by leading scholars. In addition to a chapter on Beaumont and Fletcher by Lee Bliss, the volume contains many chapters on the aspects of Renaissance culture that shaped their plays, including politics, religion, the family, playhouses, theatrical conventions, popular culture, censorship, witchcraft, and science, among others. Includes illustrations, bibliographic references, and index.

Leech, Clifford. *The John Fletcher Plays*. London: Chatto and Windus, 1962. Perceptive analyses of Fletcher's main plays, with *The Humorous Lieutenant* seen as his masterpiece.

Squire, Charles. *John Fletcher*. Boston: Twayne, 1986. Concentrates on Fletcher but includes brief biographies of both Beaumont and Fletcher and introductions to all the plays in the canon. Contains useful notes and annotated bibliography.

Wallis, Lawrence B. *Fletcher, Beaumont, and Company: Entertainers to the Jacobean Gentry*. New York:

King's Crown Press, 1947. Surveys critical opinions of Beaumont and Fletcher's work from their time to the modern period, then defends them as successful entertainers of their particular audience.

SEE ALSO: Elizabeth I; William Shakespeare.

RELATED ARTICLES in *Great Events from History: The Renaissance & Early Modern Era, 1454-1600:* 1558-1603: Reign of Elizabeth I; 1576: James Burbage Builds The Theatre; c. 1589-1613: Shakespeare Writes His Dramas; October 31, 1597: John Dowland Publishes *Ayres*; December, 1598-May, 1599: The Globe Theatre Is Built.

GIOVANNI BELLINI
Italian painter

As the leading painter of the Republic of Venice through more than two generations, Bellini achieved a synthesis of major currents in art deriving from Italian centers such as Tuscany and Padua as well as from Northern Europe. His work on the poetry of light and color was the foundation of the greatness of Venetian painting in the sixteenth century.

BORN: c. 1430; Venice, Republic of Venice (now in Italy)

DIED: 1516; Venice

AREA OF ACHIEVEMENT: Art

EARLY LIFE

Giovanni Bellini (jyoh-VAHN-nee bay-LEE-nee) was possibly the second of two sons born to Jacopo Bellini and his wife, Anna Rinversi. Giovanni's brother, Gentile, was born probably about two or three years earlier, and a sister, Nicolosia, two or three years later. The proximity of the children's ages is significant for Venetian art, as the brothers were frequently to work in close association, and a major artistic influence on Giovanni was his sister's husband, the painter Andrea Mantegna, whom she married in 1453.

There is little information about Giovanni's early life, but a few biographical facts do offer some insight. For example, it is known that Giovanni's mother was a native of the region of Pesaro, south of Venice on the Adriatic coast; Giovanni may have found it convenient to reside there while creating one of his early masterpieces, *Coronation of the Virgin* (c. 1473). The family connection

with Pesaro suggests Giovanni's receptiveness to the world outside the city-state of Venice. Similarly, Jacopo Bellini's important early contact with the vibrant art of Tuscany is shown by his apprenticeship to Gentile da Fabriano.

During the early Renaissance, it became increasingly possible for a talented individual to transcend the status of craftsperson to become an artist, a person endowed with intellectual as well as manual skills. Jacopo is this sort of transitional figure in the art of early fifteenth century Italy, and his sons—more particularly Giovanni—were to enjoy an even higher social position than their father. To Jacopo, however, goes the credit both for the technical education of his sons and for their introduction to Renaissance ideals, including the enthusiasm for antiquity and the respect for learning embodied in the concept of Humanism.

At an unrecorded date, Giovanni married a woman named Ginevra Bocheta, and they later had a son, Alvise. His departure from his parents' household around 1459 may not indicate his artistic independence but only his move to new quarters. Gentile was the first of the brothers to win large public commissions, and it was in this field that he specialized, producing throughout his career many monumental decorations for the Venetian fraternal groups called *scuole*—literally, but not actually, "schools." While it is acknowledged that Giovanni was a more adventurous and accomplished artist than Gentile, the brothers' achievement has often been regarded collectively because of their joint dominance of Venetian art during their lifetimes and because they seemed to have esteemed each other very highly.

Giovanni's likeness is known from an anonymous and mediocre woodcut in the 1568 edition of Giorgio Vasari's famous work on the lives of painters as well as from a drawing (now in the Condé Museum of Chantilly, France) by one of Giovanni's students. This profile portrait shows the middle-aged Bellini as handsome, with a well-proportioned face and a prominent but straight nose. Adjusting for the slightly different treatment of the face in the later woodcut, one might accept the argument of a prominent scholar that Giovanni pictured himself in a late work, *Feast of the Gods* (c. 1514), as the mythological figure Silvanus.

LIFE'S WORK

Bellini's independent career can be regarded as beginning around 1460. It is often impossible to determine the contributions of assistants to the collective work of a studio, and in the case of the Bellini family this is especially true in the production of the 1450's. There is also little basis for distinguishing some of the work of this period by Giovanni from that of his brother-in-law Mantegna, who may have studied with Jacopo and worked in his studio on the same basis as his sons. Thus, Bellini's earliest work can be conceived only in the general terms of a range of stylistic qualities and types of objects.

Aside from preparatory drawings, Bellini's earlier work consists of small paintings of religious character, some executed on vellum and others on wooden panels of modest dimensions. The paintings on vellum have a delicacy befitting both their size and their derivation from the traditions of manuscript illustration, but the panels show added concern with the treatment of the human figure as a sculptural volume and with the placement of the figure in a natural landscape.

In Giovanni's early panels, the influence of Mantegna is believed to be manifest. A native of the region of Padua, Mantegna was an extremely precocious artist whose style is characterized by somewhat schematized and muscular linear forms rendered with tone to achieve an incisive sculptural effect. Bellini's debt to Mantegna may be seen in his firm contours and crisp detail as well as in his pictorial construction, but Bellini's adaptations are more sensitively observant of nature, as in his *Agony in the Garden*, dating from the early 1460's. The same subject as treated by Mantegna is more tautly composed, favoring drama over poetry; Bellini's landscape is almost pastoral, while Mantegna's represents, in one scholar's words, an almost "lunar ideal of natural landscape."

Giovanni Bellini. (Library of Congress)

From Giovanni's studio in the 1460's came a remarkable outpouring of paintings of Christ, of the Madonna and Child, and of various saints. These show a mastery of form and a depth of feeling that place Giovanni, still only in his thirties, at the forefront of Venetian art. The works are freshly approached on both the technical and the emotional levels and show that, even at a considerable distance from sources of innovation in Tuscany and central Italy, Bellini was receptive to the more advanced artistic tendencies of his time. His *Pietà with Virgin and Saint John*, in the Brera gallery in Milan, is representative of the artist's fully developed early manner in the way it combines assurance of form with a powerful yet restrained rendering of its subject, the sorrow at Christ's death. Notwithstanding its relatively early date in Bellini's career, it is one of the great achievements of European art.

The next phase in Bellini's career is notable for the increasing use of the medium of oil paint and a growing affinity for Flemish art, within which oil techniques had been ascendant since the 1420's. Neither the oil medium nor the influence of Northern art were entirely novel in Venice in the early 1470's, but both were given prominence in Venice by the brief presence there of the Sicilian-born artist Antonello da Messina around 1475. It is evident that Antonello learned much of his technique from someone with close ties to the Flemish painter Jan van Eyck (c. 1390-1441) or one of his contemporaries, because his style was formed far less by Italian art than by the Northern tradition of rendering exact detail and effects of light. The influence of Antonello's Flemish orientation on Bellini's work, and thus on later Venetian painting, was lasting; the oil medium allowed for more fluid and colorful rendering of surfaces than did the traditional, fast-drying tempera paints, and provided Bellini and his successors with a material that was well suited to the Venetian artistic temperament, which was by nature more spontaneous and emotional than that of their central Italian counterparts.

During the 1470's, Bellini's appreciation of monumental form seems to have been enhanced by contact with the work of great Italian predecessors such as the sculptor Donatello (c. 1386-1466) and the painter Masaccio (1401-1428), though there is only indirect evidence of this. The influence of the frescoes of Piero della Francesca seems likely; Giovanni could have seen his work at Rimini, on the road between Venice and Pesaro. There is something of Piero's austere integration of form, light, and color in the large panel of Bellini's *Coronation of the Virgin*, part of the Pesaro altarpiece of the early 1470's. A small panel of the *Adoration of the Child*, part of the *predella*, or frame, of this altarpiece, shows Bellini's ability to create a convincing landscape environment for his solidly painted figures, but more particularly it reveals a poetic mastery of effects of light and atmosphere that was unmatched by his Italian contemporaries.

Another panel (of disputed date, but perhaps painted as early as 1475), the *Saint Francis in Ecstasy* in the Frick Collection in New York, is considered one of Bellini's masterpieces. Conceived as an independent picture, this painting has a design that recalls the art of Mantegna, but its underlying character is more reflective. Bellini's art, increasingly receptive to the beauty of landscape, is in perfect harmony with the spirit of Francis of Assisi, of all the saints the one most devoted to nature.

In the following decade, Bellini continued with much the same range of subject matter as before, but he painted with increasing assurance. An *Enthroned Madonna and Child* of the late 1480's, also know as the San Giobbe altarpiece, is monumental both in size and in conception: It is more than fifteen feet high and eight feet wide and was originally installed in a Venetian church, where its pictorial space could be viewed as an extension of the actual interior space of the church. Another dimension of Bellini's work in this period was to meet the continuing

needs of the *scuole* for large commemorative paintings, a task he often shared with his brother, but none of these has survived.

A continuous sequence of portraits by Bellini's hand—as distinct from works of his studio—cannot be established, but there are several portrait masterpieces that are unquestionably his own. His *Portrait of Doge Leonardo Loredan*, an exquisitely detailed rendering of Venice's leader, was probably painted following Loredan's election in October, 1501. In this work, Bellini gives a sense of the whole person in two senses: physically, by choosing a composition that shows more of the subject's attire, and psychologically, by means of rare human insight. Bellini's approach to portraiture soon became the norm with the new generation of painters, and his ability to keep abreast of the innovations of his younger contemporaries made him a sought-after artist into his final years.

Among Bellini's most important paintings is a work of his last years, the *Feast of the Gods*. Loosely based on a subject taken from Ovid's *Fasti* (c. 8 C.E.; English translation, 1859), the painting was commissioned by a knowledgeable patron, possibly Isabella d'Este of the court of Ferrara. Isabella, a woman of decided tastes as well as strong intellect, had begun a project of decorating some study rooms in her private apartment with paintings of pagan subjects, and she may have engaged Bellini to paint a companion piece to a work by Mantegna. *Feast of the Gods* is a painting that celebrates classical mythology while paying respects to the lively world of Italian Renaissance culture. One of Bellini's few paintings on classical subjects, its humor, lyricism, and mildly erotic content show that he could be moved by antique as well as Christian themes.

SIGNIFICANCE

Bellini's exceptionally long and productive career spanned more than six decades. The larger part of his work belongs to the 1400's, when Italian art evolved a unity of approach to pictorial organization and content within which local and individual styles are still strongly manifest. Bellini was Venice's foremost painter of this period, providing one of many regional inflections to the technical and expressive development of Italian art.

Like his great contemporaries, Bellini sought with success to enhance the sense of reality in his paintings through the study of space, volume, light, and color, but, among his varied achievements, art historians have credited him with a particularly astute understanding of atmosphere. Bellini learned to give his landscape-based compositions the reality of specific times of day and conditions of atmosphere, and he applied his discoveries to reinforcing the mood of his chosen subject.

Though Bellini developed his sense of light and color within the medium of tempera paint, his use of oil paint was particularly consequential for Venetian art, which increasingly exploited the brilliance and versatility of the oil medium. Bellini's mastery of oil was accomplished well before 1500, but his continuing conquest of its capabilities late in his career serves as a reminder that he not only survived into the new century but also was an active participant in it. Bellini remained extraordinarily vital in old age, perhaps spurred by friendly rivalry with a younger generation of painters that included Giorgione and Titian. It is likely that Giorgione was in some fashion Bellini's pupil, but the influence of pupil on teacher is also suggested by scholars. Not long after Bellini's death, when the *Feast of the Gods* came into the hands of Alfonso d'Este in Mantua, the young Titian was engaged to revise it. Titian's kinship with Bellini—to an extent one of taste as well as of technical practice—is virtually the only explanation for the fact that Titian's alterations, though regrettable from the perspective of art history, are nevertheless quite successful in their own terms.

After a half century of work, Bellini achieved a style as unified and expressive as that of his greatest contemporaries. The German artist Albrecht Dürer, visiting Bellini in Venice in 1506, had found him *optimo pytor* (a great painter) and *pest in Gemoll* (the very best). After hundreds of years, Bellini's achievement still places him in the highest rank of European artists.

—*C. S. McConnell*

FURTHER READING

Freedberg, S. J. *Painting in Italy, 1500-1600.* Baltimore: Penguin Books, 1970. This discerning guide to Italian painting of the fourteenth through the seventeenth centuries deals in proportion with the Bellini family, but it has a particular virtue in giving a sense of the proportion of one artist's achievement to another, when many belong in the category "great." A minor irritant is that illustrations are separated from the text.

Hartt, Frederick, and David G. Wilkins. *History of Italian Renaissance Art: Painting, Sculpture, Architecture.* 5th ed. New York: H. N. Abrams, 2003. This standard survey of the field discusses the Bellini family very extensively. An excellent prelude to specialized reading, it retains its value for convenient reference to artists and works referred to in scholarly works. The illustrations are integrated with the text.

Hendy, Philip, and Ludwig Goldscheider. *Giovanni Bellini.* New York: Oxford University Press, 1945. This volume consists of more than one hundred illustrations of Bellini's works with an introductory essay by Hendy. The text is aimed at a general audience and contains comparative information useful to the student without an extensive background in Renaissance art. Color reproductions are given of five key works.

Humphrey, Peter, ed. *The Cambridge Companion to Giovanni Bellini.* New York: Cambridge University Press, 2004. Collection of essays presented at a Scottish Bellini conference in 2000. Discusses Bellini's status in Venetian society, his contributions to sculpture and architecture, and the relationship of his painterly style to general trends in both Flemish and Italian painting, among other topics. Includes illustrations, bibliographic references, index.

Meiss, Millard. *Giovanni Bellini's "St. Francis."* Princeton, N.J.: Princeton University Press, 1964. This short monograph on one of Bellini's most beautiful and celebrated paintings shows that scholarship in art history can be graceful as well as illuminating. The excellent illustrations (only the title painting is shown in color) include many works by Bellini and others that help place the Saint Francis work in context.

Pächt, Otto. *Venetian Painting in the Fifteenth Century: Jacopo, Gentile, and Giovanni Bellini and Andrea Mantegna.* Edited by Margareta Vyoral-Tschapka and Michael Pächt. Translated by Fiona Elliott. London: Harvey Miller, 2003. Extended study of Giovanni Bellini, his father, his brother, and his brother-in-law. Pays close attention to the father's artistic influence on the sons, and the entire family's impact on the use of color, light, and perspective in Venetian painting. Includes illustrations, bibliographic references, index.

Robertson, Giles. *Giovanni Bellini.* Oxford, England: Clarendon Press, 1968. Robertson's full-length study has the advantage of later scholarly research to differentiate it from Hendy and Goldscheider's monograph. The author negotiates a quantity of detailed information with surprising clarity. The absence of color plates may be accounted for by the extent of the black-and-white illustrations, of which there are 120.

Wind, Edgar. *Bellini's "Feast of the Gods": A Study in Venetian Humanism.* Cambridge, Mass.: Harvard University Press, 1948. Despite its many erudite references to issues in ancient literature and Renaissance

Humanism—many of which appear only in Latin or Italian—this excellent small monograph is directed to nonspecialists as much as to scholars. Both the text and the plates give a broad sense of Bellini's later career and his cultural environment, and, though Wind's conclusions are questioned by later scholars, his observations are unfailingly interesting.

SEE ALSO: Albrecht Dürer; Giorgione; Isabella d'Este; Andrea Mantegna; Piero della Francesca; Sesshū; Titian; Giorgio Vasari.

RELATED ARTICLE in *Great Events from History: The Renaissance & Early Modern Era, 1454-1600:* c. 1500: Revival of Classical Themes in Art.

PIERRE BELON
French historian

Pierre Belon wrote monographs on birds, trees, and marine life, contributing to the advancement of botany and zoology. His studies of dolphin embryos and bird skeletons signal the founding of modern embryology and comparative anatomy. His descriptions of eastern lands introduced Europeans to Ottoman culture and fueled a contemporary interest in exotic travel literature.

BORN: c. 1517; La Soultière, near Le Mans, France
DIED: April, 1564 or 1565; Paris, France
ALSO KNOWN AS: Petrus Bellonius
AREAS OF ACHIEVEMENT: Science and technology, geography, historiography, literature

EARLY LIFE

Pierre Belon (pyehr beh-lohn) was born in La Soultière, a former hamlet in northwestern France. His date of birth is based on early published portraits depicting him at age thirty-six. Little is known for certain about his family origin or his early education. According to autobiographical comments contained in his work *Cronique de Pierre Belon, médecin* (wr. 1562-1565, pb. 2001; chronicle of Pierre Belon, physician), he spent much of his youth in lower Brittany, where he became familiar with the regional flora and fauna. As a young man, probably around 1535, he entered the household of René du Bellay, bishop of Le Mans, who provided him the opportunity to follow his curiosity.

In 1540, Belon visited Germany, studied botany under Valerius Cordus at the University of Wittenberg, and explored with Cordus mines and forests in Germany and Bohemia. On his return to France in 1542, Belon went to Paris to study medicine and soon obtained a position as an apothecary in the service of Cardinal François de Tournon, one of the chief artisans of French foreign policy. Belon's knowledge of several languages, including Latin, some German, and his native French, and his de-

sire to travel and study nature directly, made him an obvious choice for some of the cardinal's diplomatic missions abroad.

During trips to Germany, Switzerland, Luxembourg, and Italy (1543-1544), he collected information on plants, trees, and animal life, which contributed to his expertise in natural history. In 1546, he was a cultural attaché on an expedition to Constantinople organized by Monsieur d'Aramon. Over the course of three years, Belon explored various regions in the Middle East and Asia Minor, including the island of Crete, all the while recording his observations for future publication.

LIFE'S WORK

Shortly after his return from the Levant in 1549, Belon accompanied Tournon on a trip to Rome, then returned the following year to Paris to resume his study of medicine and prepare his works for publication. From 1551 to 1558, he published in rapid succession a series of books that established his reputation as one of Europe's leading natural historians. Accusations that Belon published under his own name work that belonged to Pierre Gilles, a contemporary naturalist and fellow traveler in d'Aramon's expedition to the Middle East, appear unfounded.

Belon's first published work, *L'Histoire naturelle des éstranges poissons marins* (pb. 1551; natural history of unusual marine animals), is a noteworthy contribution to ichthyology—the study of fish. Along with descriptions of several major species of marine life, ranging from sturgeons and breams to tuna and hammerhead sharks, the work contained lifelike woodcut illustrations prepared by the Parisian artist François Pérrier. It also included an in-depth study of dolphin and porpoise anatomies. Historians of science call attention to the work's detailed study of the cetacean embryo, which preceded the foundation of modern embryology. Equally noteworthy is the author's comparison of a dolphin's cerebrum with that of a human.

Two years later Belon published a similar work called *De aquatilibus* (pb. 1553; on aquatic animals), another illustrated work that greatly expanded his catalog of aquatic mammals, amphibians, and fish. It was later translated into French under the title *De la nature et diversité des poissons* (pb. 1555; on the nature and diversity of fishes).

Belon was interested in herbs, plants, and trees as well. In *De arboribus coniferis, resiniferis, aliis quoque nonnullis sempiterna fronde virentibus* (pb. 1553; on coniferous, resinous, and other evergreen trees), Belon described eight major categories of resin-bearing conifers, each category preceded by an accurate illustration. In *Remonstrances sur le default du labour et culture des plantes* (pb. 1589; remonstrance on the neglect of horticulture), addressed to the royal councilor, he asserted the necessity of collecting and acclimating nonnative plants and trees in France. In *De admirabili operum antiquorum . . . praestantia* (pb. 1553; on the wondrous pre-eminence of antique works), he delved into the majesty of the Egyptian pyramids and the ancient art of embalming corpses.

Belon was also a dedicated ornithologist. His *L'Histoire de la nature des oyseaux* (pb. 1555; natural history of birds) provides descriptions and illustrations of more than 150 different birds classified into six major groups based on habitat or behavior. The book's first section discusses the general nature of birds and concludes with a comparative study of human and avian skeletons founded on valid homologies. The work's illustrative woodcuts attributed to the artistry of Pierre Goudet are remarkable for their accuracy and realism. That another version of Belon's natural history of birds soon appeared along with a host of exotic images in *Portraits d'oyseaux, animaux, serpens, herbes, arbres, hommes et femmes d'Arabie et Egypte* (pb. 1557; portraits of birds, animals, snakes, plants, trees, men and women of Arabia and Egypt) attests to the avid curiosity of contemporary readers.

The author's most enduring work, *Observations de plusieurs singularitez et choses memorables trouvées en Grèce, Asie, Judée, Egypte, Arabie, et autres pays étranges* (pb. 1553; observations of several curiosities and memorable things found in Greece, Asia, Judæa, Egypt, Arabia, and other foreign countries), contains eyewitness descriptions of antique ruins, exotic customs, and animals and plants encountered during his travels in the Ottoman Empire and neighboring regions. The author's curiosity touched on subjects as diverse

as the ruins of legendary ancient Troy, women's attire in Cairo, giraffes, chameleons, winged reptiles, and local myth.

Having noted that in Egyptian lore there are wide variations in the artistic representation of the Sphinx, Belon denied that such an animal could have ever existed. If the Sphinx had existed, he argued, its numerous portraits would reveal greater uniformity. Bookbinder and printer Christophe Plantin of Antwerp published a Latin version of the work in 1579. Excerpts appeared in English translation in John Ray's *A Collection of Curious Travels and Voyages* (1693).

Belon lived in troubled times. France's opposition to the Habsburg Dynasty and to England produced numerous wars during the reigns of Francis I and Henry II, making just about any form of travel inherently dangerous. Sometime between 1554 and 1555, Belon was captured by Spanish soldiers on his way to Metz. He was, however, released unharmed. Between 1561 and 1562, as the first signs of the impending French Wars of Religion (1562-1598) became evident, he undertook trips to Poissy, Lyon, Moulins, and Bourges without incident. It appears likely that he served as a messenger for the royal family and its ministers, conducting official business under the cloak of scientific research. One April night of 1564 or 1565, as he was returning to his Paris lodgings through Bois de Boulogne, he was attacked, robbed, and killed by unknown individuals.

SIGNIFICANCE

Belon was a foundational figure in Renaissance natural history. His detailed descriptions, classifications, and graphic representations of birds, marine life, and coniferous trees rate among the period's many outstanding achievements. Historians of science cite, in particular, his illustrated comparison of human and avian skeletons, his study of porpoise embryos, classification attempts, and discoveries of new species as important contributions to the progress of natural history, but they are quick to note that his finest intuitions predate the foundations of modern science.

As a cultural historian, Belon provided firsthand observation of foreign cultures, describing social and religious practices, local industry, art, architecture, geography, climate, and historical artifacts. His naturalistic approach to the singularities he encountered helped dispel many common superstitions of his day, among them the belief that distant lands were full of monstrosities beyond the purview of nature's laws.

—Jan Pendergrass

FURTHER READING

Barsi, Monica. *L'Enigme de la chronique de Pierre Belon: Avec édition critique du manuscrit Arsenal 4651*. Milan, Italy: LED, 2001. Offers current information on Belon's life and work, the first complete edition of his *Cronique de Pierre Belon, médecin*, and a good bibliography. Written entirely in French, this work is intended for specialists.

Cole, Francis Joseph. *A History of Comparative Anatomy: From Aristotle to the Eighteenth Century*. 1944. Reprint. New York: Dover, 1975. Discusses Belon's contributions to science and, in particular, to zoology, and considers him a pioneer in comparative anatomy.

Hellyer, Marcus, ed. *The Scientific Revolution: The Essential Readings*. Malden, Mass.: Blackwell, 2003. The section titled "Natural History and the Emblematic World View," by William B. Ashworth, Jr., discusses Belon's place in the history of Renaissance science, before the advent of modern scientific discourse.

Huppert, George. "Antiquity Observed: A French Naturalist in the Aegean Sea in 1547." *International Journal of the Classical Tradition* 2 (1995): 275-283. Discusses how Belon exposed common superstitions through careful observation and rational thought.

_____. *The Style of Paris: Renaissance Origins of the French Enlightenment*. Bloomington: Indiana University Press, 1999. Section one, titled "Portrait of a Discreet *Philosophe*," describes how Belon resisted cultural prejudice in writing his major work.

SEE ALSO: José de Acosta; Andrea Cesalpino; Leonhard Fuchs; Conrad Gesner; İbrahim Paşa; Joseph Justus Scaliger.

RELATED ARTICLE in *Great Events from History: The Renaissance & Early Modern Era, 1454-1600:* 1517: Fracastoro Develops His Theory of Fossils.

BESS OF HARDWICK
Countess of Shrewsbury

Born into relative obscurity, Bess of Hardwick is remembered principally for building the mansions Hardwick Hall, Chatsworth, and Oldcotes. She rose through four increasingly grand marriages to become countess of Shrewsbury, wife of the guardian of Mary, Queen of Scots, and grandmother of a potential claimant to both the Scottish and English thrones.

BORN: c. 1527; Derbyshire, England
DIED: February 13, 1608; Hardwick Hall
ALSO KNOWN AS: Elizabeth Hardwick (given name); Elizabeth Talbot; Elizabeth Shrewsbury
AREAS OF ACHIEVEMENT: Government and politics, architecture, patronage of the arts

EARLY LIFE

Bess of Hardwick was born Elizabeth Hardwick, a member of an obscure Derbyshire gentry family of one boy and four girls, of whom Bess was the third. Her father, John Hardwick, died probably when Bess was about one year old. At the age of twelve, she is believed to have entered the service of her distant relatives, Lord and Lady Zouche, after the remarriage of her mother.

It was at the Zouche residence that she seems to have met her first husband, Robert Barlow. They married when both were in their early teens (the precise date is not known), but Barlow, never strong, soon died, leaving Bess the first of the three jointures, or widow's portions, from which she was ultimately to make her fortune. Her great leap in status came with her second marriage, to the much older, wealthier, and already twice-widowed Sir William Cavendish, whom she married in 1547 and who died in 1557. This was the only one of her four marriages to be fruitful, producing eight children. Three sons and three daughters survived to maturity.

Her marriage to Cavendish also brought her contacts with the court and with circles of influence, since Cavendish had been one of Henry VIII's commissioners for the dissolution of the monasteries (it was through this connection that he was able to acquire the land on which Chatsworth was later built).

LIFE'S WORK

Bess of Hardwick's principal efforts were directed toward two interrelated areas: the advancement of her children and the building of houses that would not only serve as homes for them but also give visible expression to the grandeur and status she hoped to achieve for them. For all her children, Bess sought to engineer suitably splendid marriages.

She pulled off a brilliant coup when, three years after the death of her third husband—Sir William Saint Loe, whom she had married in 1559 and who died in 1564—she arranged for the marriages of her daughter Mary and her son Henry to the son and daughter of George Talbot, sixth earl of Shrewsbury, at the same time that she herself married their father.

This last and most splendid of her marriages brought her enormous wealth and also great responsibility, for two years after it took place Shrewsbury was appointed guardian of Mary, Queen of Scots, who had fled to England hoping that Elizabeth would help restore her to the Scottish throne but instead found herself imprisoned until her execution nineteen years later.

Talbot was chosen because he was considered trustworthy and because he had a considerable number of properties relatively close to each other, and the queen and her servants needed to be moved frequently for cleaning and security purposes. At first Bess and the queen got along well; they sewed together, and they also plotted together, as was evident in 1574 when Bess and her daughter Elizabeth Cavendish entertained Margaret, countess of Lennox, and her son Charles, at Rufford Abbey in Nottinghamshire. Margaret Lennox was the niece of Henry VIII and the mother of the second husband of Mary, Queen of Scots, Lord Darnley; Charles, her only surviving child, thus had a potential claim to the thrones of both England and Scotland.

Between them, and with the encouragement of Mary, Queen of Scots, Bess and the equally formidable Margaret encouraged a romance and ultimately a wedding between their children, which delighted them but enraged Elizabeth I, who imprisoned the countess of Lennox and made her displeasure with Bess very clear. The next year the marriage produced a child, Lady Arbella Stuart, but both Elizabeth Cavendish and her husband died shortly after, leaving Bess as the guardian of the child she called "my jewel Arbella." From that point on, Arbella was the center of her plans, particularly as jealousy of Mary, Queen of Scots, led to an increasingly bitter estrangement from her husband.

Bess also began to pour her energies into architecture. She had already done so much work on the original Elizabethan Chatsworth that Sir William Cavendish actually referred to her as "my sweet Chatsworth"; she bought Hardwick Old Hall from her heavily indebted brother in 1583 and began the new hall in 1585, pressing on apace after the death of Shrewsbury in 1590.

Nominally, the grandeur of the decorative scheme was ascribed to Bess's hope of a visit by the queen, but Elizabeth I, who had never ventured so far north even in her youth, was hardly likely to do so in old age, and it seems clear that Bess's real hope was that her granddaughter Arbella would be the queen's successor, a hope that received a tremendous boost when the queen sent for the young girl to attend to her at court and reportedly told the assembled courtiers that one day Arbella "will be even as I am." Arbella, however, was mentally unstable—she, like her aunt Mary, Queen of Scots, may well have suffered from porphyria, the disease that caused the madness of King George III—and her behavior became increasingly erratic, alienating the queen and ultimately Bess as well, who virtually imprisoned her at Hardwick.

Not until after Bess's death did Arbella ultimately succeed in arranging the marriage which, because of her royal blood, had always been denied her, but her attempt to escape to the Continent with her new husband failed, and she died insane in the Tower of London. Bess also suffered other family problems in her old age, principally from "my bad son Henry"; she died lonely in 1608, the richest woman in England.

SIGNIFICANCE

Three great ducal families, the dukes of Devonshire, the dukes of Portland, and the dukes of Kingston, claimed descent from Bess of Hardwick, and though the Chatsworth that Bess built has now disappeared entirely beneath the later alterations to the house and Oldcotes mansion is forgotten almost entirely, her great house, Hardwick Hall, still stands much as she left it, towering above England's major highway, with the initials "E. S." for "Elizabeth Shrewsbury," clearly visible. Farther along the ridge, the splendid Renaissance palace of Bolsover Castle, built by her son and grandson, also testifies to her influence.

Much of her embroidery also survives, as well as her splendid tomb in Derby Cathedral, and the decorative scheme she designed for Hardwick, with its rich program of allegorical meanings, can still be seen and understood in its entirety, giving a unique insight into the life and mind of an extraordinary woman, who was a longstanding and formative presence in the life of Mary, Queen of Scots, and who, but for the accidents of history, might also have been responsible for the crowning of another queen.

—*Lisa Hopkins*

FURTHER READING

Durant, David. *Bess of Hardwick: Portrait of an Elizabethan Dynast*. Newark, England: Cromwell Press, 1988. The standard scholarly biography, clearly and accessibly written.

Girouard, Mark. *Robert Smythson and the Elizabethan Country House*. New Haven, Conn.: Yale University Press, 1985. This evocative and scholarly book offers the fullest and clearest account of the original significance of Bess's vision for Hardwick Hall.

Gristwood, Sarah. *Arbella: England's Lost Queen*. London: Bantam Press, 2003. Although focused primarily on Arbella, this work nevertheless offers considerable insight into Bess's life and her hopes for her granddaughter.

Kettle, Pamela. *Oldcotes: The Last Mansion Built by Bess of Hardwick*. Cardiff, Wales: Merton Priory Press, 2000. An account of the least-known of Bess's houses.

Levey, Santina, and Peter K. Thornton, eds. *Of Household Stuff: The 1601 Inventories of Bess of Hardwick*. London: National Trust, 2001. Provides a glimpse into the full scale of Bess's wealth and into daily life at Hardwick Hall.

Steen, Sara Jayne, ed. *The Letters of Arbella Stuart*. New York: Oxford University Press, 1995. This carefully edited volume reprints Arbella's numerous surviving letters and traces the course of her mental instability.

SEE ALSO: Elizabeth I; Henry VIII; Mary, Queen of Scots.

RELATED ARTICLE in *Great Events from History: The Renaissance & Early Modern Era, 1454-1600:* August 22, 1513-July 6, 1560: Anglo-Scottish Wars.

BOABDIL
Emir of Granada (r. 1482-1492)

Boabdil lost Moorish territory in Spain after challenging his father's rule and aligning with Spain's King Ferdinand II and Queen Isabella I. His actions led to the eventual end of several centuries of Muslim rule in Spain.

BORN: c. 1464; Granada, Kingdom of Granada (now in Spain)
DIED: 1527 or 1538; possibly Morocco
ALSO KNOWN AS: Abū ʿAbd Allāh Muḥammad XI (full name); Muḥammad XI; Muḥammad XII
AREAS OF ACHIEVEMENT: Warfare and conquest, government and politics

EARLY LIFE

Boabdil (boh-ahb-DEEL) was the first-born son of Abū al-Ḥasan ʿAlī (r. 1464-1485), the Naṣrid emir of Granada and the last vestige of the Muslim state of al-Andalus (Andalusia) on the Iberian Peninsula. Boabdil's mother, Fāṭimah, was al-Ḥasan's first wife and a daughter of a previous emir, Muḥammad X. Although better known as Boabdil, he would rule as Emir Muḥammad XI.

Virtually nothing is known of Boabdil's early life, but he would have been raised at the Granadan court. During his youth, the major Spanish Christian states of Castile, ruled by Queen Isabella I, and of Aragon, ruled by King Ferdinand II, were united by the couple's marriage. Pope Alexander VI called them the Christian monarchs. Isabella and Ferdinand sought the conquest of Islamic (Moorish) Granada to form a Spanish-Christian nation-state. Granada's emirs had stopped paying tribute to Castile in the late fourteenth century, and Spain's new rulers wanted it reinstated. Islamic armies had taken Constantinople in 1453 and were moving through the Balkans, fueling Crusader fervor.

The time seemed ripe, since large-scale Muslim aid from North Africa was unlikely, and Ferdinand was not distracted by other Mediterranean affairs. To participants in this venture, the pope provided the usual spiritual benefits offered to Crusaders. Granada's Muslims sought to coexist in peace amid their rich fields and strong fortresses, but they would defend them against Christian encroachment. Granada and the Christian monarchs signed a formal truce in 1478.

Raiding and other forms of violence were common along the Muslim-Christian frontier, but al-Ḥasan's capture of the Castilian castle of Zahara in 1481 ended a period of *convivencia* (coexistence) and set off the last war of the Reconquista (reconquest). In February of 1482, Ferdinand's troops seized a fortress town that was a mere twenty-five miles from the city of Granada. Al-Ḥasan tried to retake the city in the spring, but only managed to isolate it. In July, Ferdinand attempted to connect with the town, but even as he blocked the Spanish move, al-Ḥasan heard of Boabdil's seizure of power in Granada.

LIFE'S WORK

Boabdil's coup against his father was supported by their native clan, who apparently looked favorably on the heir. The Muslims were now split, with some supporting the bellicose emir and others his son, who was said to favor accommodation and peace with the Christians.

Boabdil's reign as Muḥammad XI dates from the summer of 1482. The victory of al-Ḥasan and his brother Muḥammad al-Zaghall over Christian troops at Málaga in March of 1483 prompted Boabdil to seek a victory of his own to solidify his pretensions to leadership in Andalusia. In mid-April, he led ten thousand men against Lucena and initiated a siege of the Christian town. A warning about a relief force broke the siege, and Boabdil's men returned east into Granada. Bogged down by booty and captives, and blocked by the raging Genil River, the Muslims were beaten badly. Boabdil was captured by a common foot soldier, Martin Hurtado, who proved immune to the emir's attempted bribe. He remained a guest of the Christian monarchs at Córdoba for five months and signed a treaty of peace. In October, Muslim clerics declared a fatwa, a condemnation, against Boabdil for his accommodative stance and actions. This weakened his moral authority.

Ferdinand's army attacked southern Granada in the spring of 1484. Shortly thereafter, al-Ḥasan suffered a stroke, and his brother and field commander, al-Zaghall (the Valorous), claimed the title of emir as Muḥammad XIII. The following February, al-Zaghall came close to trapping his rebellious nephew at Almería. Boabdil narrowly escaped and ran to the Spanish camp, earning himself the nickname al-Zuguybī, the Unfortunate. Al-Zaghall took control of the city of Granada.

It was only after several Christian victories in 1485 that Ferdinand released Boabdil. Al-Zaghall and Boabdil made peace between them, and the latter was entrusted with the defense of the strategic city of Loja. In late May, 1486, Ferdinand captured the city, perhaps with Boabdil's collusion. Boabdil was once again in Christian custody, during which time he and Ferdinand signed a treaty of peace.

Boabdil was promised unfettered control of the towns of Guadix and Baza and other territories in the northeast, provided he would take them from al-Zaghall's followers. Boabdil essentially became Ferdinand's puppet: On September 15, 1486, Boabdil led his own and Christian troops into the city of Granada, beginning a seven-month siege of the Alhambra, the emir's palace. After this cita-

Boabdil surrenders the keys of Granada to King Ferdinand II and Queen Isabella I of Spain. (P. F. Collier and Son)

del fell, Boabdil offered the city to Isabella, should she make yet another treaty with him. The summer saw more Castilian victories, which left Boabdil with only Granada and a few towns, and his uncle in control of the region's richest areas, around Baza, Almería, and Guadix.

Christian campaigns in the summer of 1487 picked off all Boabdil's towns except Granada. This angered the young leader, who refused to hand over the capital as agreed. During the even more successful campaigns of 1488, al-Zaghall lost well-protected Baza and Almería. The emir surrendered, agreeing to peace in return for a tiny kingdom of his own in the Alhaurin Valley. This left the suddenly defiant Boabdil the last standing Muslim leader in Andalusia. He desperately sought the aid of other Muslim leaders but none saw fit to support him. By skillful raids, he pushed out the boundaries of his foothold. Ferdinand responded by carrying out *tala*, or environmental destruction, in the region. In April, 1491, Boabdil mustered his forces for the last campaign of the Reconquista.

Within Granada, opinion split on whether to surrender. Fighting was the honorable and noble thing to do; surrendering was viewed as a betrayal of Islam, a move at least tacitly condemned by the earlier fatwa. Supplies and food were growing scarce, however. Ferdinand and Isabella ringed the city and constructed a small siege city from which to conduct operations and in which to house the troops over the winter. Christian artillery threatened the city's walls, but the monarchs seemed content to let time take its toll. Small skirmishes and single combats broke the tedium for both sides, but the Muslims proved so deadly that these were halted and forbidden. When stone buildings replaced the siege city's huts in the fall, Boabdil decided to treat with the monarchs.

Negotiations were carried out in secret and led to both private agreements and public capitulations. The stipulations were generous: The Christians would not interfere in the religious lives of the inhabitants or the processes of Muslim law. Those who wished to leave would be given safe passage to North Africa. Boabdil was to remain in Granada to oversee the change in government. The Alhambra was handed over to the Christians on January 1, 1492, secretly, at which time Boabdil received a receipt for the property. He publicly surrendered the citadel the next day.

On January 6, he presented the keys to the city gates to the monarchs of Spain as they made their royal entrance into the city. Boabdil received three villages in the rich Alpujarres Hills, and he handed over five hundred hostages whose safety was guaranteed by Muslim good behavior.

Boabdil remained in his new fiefdom until his wife's death in late 1492 or 1493. This led to his sale of the villages to Ferdinand and to self-exile in North Africa. His departure abrogated the terms of the capitulations, giving the Christians any excuse they needed to mistreat the Granadans. From Tlemcen in Algeria, Boabdil eventually moved to Fez, Morocco. Undoubtedly living in infamy, his last years are lost to history, including the year of his death.

SIGNIFICANCE

Boabdil's life, however long, was dominated by the decade he spent alternately serving and battling the Spanish-Christian monarchs. Whether led by mere pragmatism or by an accommodationist ideology, Boabdil walked a fine line to the end. His personal intentions or motivations can only be inferred, since Muslim records are silent.

In the end the Christians needed a brilliant victory, rather than a short siege and surrender, to crown the half-millennium Reconquista; Boabdil's honor, and that of Andalusia, demanded a stalwart defense and honorable terms of surrender. Ultimately, both parties were satisfied. In light of the era's realpolitik, Boabdil's abandonment of Granada was little more than a legal technicality that lent legitimacy to the anti-Muslim persecutions later that decade.

—*Joseph P. Byrne*

FURTHER READING

Harvey, L. P. *Islamic Spain: 1250 to 1500*. Chicago: University of Chicago Press, 1990. Concludes with detailed narrative of Boabdil's reign and his relations with his father, uncle, and the rulers of Christian Spain.

Nicolle, David. *Granada 1492: The Twilight of Moorish Spain*. London: Osprey, 1998. Well-illustrated study of the military campaigns from 1481 to 1491 that led to the conquest of Granada. Includes sketches of leaders and descriptions of opposing armies.

Prescott, W. H. *The Art of War in Spain: The Conquest of Granada, 1481-1492*. Edited by Albert D. McJoynt. London: Greenhill Press, 1995. Classic account of the campaigns that led to Boabdil's defeat.

SEE ALSO: Ferdinand II and Isabella I; Henry IV of Castile.

RELATED ARTICLE in *Great Events from History: The Renaissance & Early Modern Era, 1454-1600:* 1492: Fall of Granada.

SIR THOMAS BODLEY
English scholar

Bodley founded the Bodleian Library at Oxford University in England, which quickly became and remains one of the world's great research libraries.

BORN: March 2, 1545; Exeter, Devon, England
DIED: January 28, 1613; London, England
AREAS OF ACHIEVEMENT: Education, diplomacy

EARLY LIFE

Thomas Bodley (BAHD-lee) was born in Devon. His father was John Bodley, a successful merchant of that city, and his mother was Joan, the daughter of Robert Hone of Ottery Saint Mary, Devon. The family was staunchly Protestant and went into exile during the reign of the Catholic queen, Mary I. In May, 1557, the Bodleys moved from Frankfurt to Geneva. There, the twelve-year-old Thomas Bodley studied divinity from John Calvin and Theodore Beza while he learned Greek from Philip Beroaldus and Hebrew from Antoine Chevallier, later a professor of Hebrew at Cambridge.

The death of Queen Mary on November 17, 1558, brought the Protestant Elizabeth to the English throne and ended the Bodley family's exile. They returned to London, and in 1559 the fifteen-year-old Thomas began his studies at Magdalen College, Oxford, under Lawrence Humphrey, a friend of his father and a fellow Marian exile. Bodley received his bachelor of arts in 1563 and in the same year became a probationary fellow of Merton College. The next year, Merton granted him a full fellowship.

During his time as a senior member of the university, Bodley was moderately successful. He began lecturing without fee on Greek at Merton in 1565 with such success that the college voted him a stipend and made the lectures a permanent institution. After receiving his master of arts degree in 1566, he began giving university lectures on natural philosophy, was elected a university proctor in 1569, and served as deputy public orator. It was during these years that he matured into a square-built, distinguished person with close-cropped dark hair and beard. Then, in 1576, Merton granted him a leave of absence to go abroad and study modern foreign languages. Four years of travel in Italy, France, and Germany allowed him to achieve proficiency in a number of foreign languages, particularly Italian, French, and Spanish.

LIFE'S WORK

When Bodley left Oxford in 1576, he had little intention of returning. Instead, he hoped ultimately to enter the service of the English government. By the early 1580's, he appeared to have secured the patronage of Sir Francis Walsingham and Robert Dudley, the earl of Leicester. One of them probably obtained for him a seat as a member of Parliament for Portsmouth in 1584. His first diplomatic mission came in the next year, when he traveled to Denmark to obtain support for Henry of Navarre and the French Protestants.

After his return from Denmark, Bodley scored the greatest triumph of his life when he married Ann, the daughter of Richard Carey (or Carew) of Bristol and the widow of the wealthy merchant Nicholas Ball of Totnes, Devon, on July 19, 1586. It was Ball's fortune that allowed Bodley to refound and endow the library that bears his name. Ball had died in March, so his wife had remained a widow for a mere four months. Yet even then, Bodley was not Ann's first suitor. Another man was on the verge of "winning" her when Bodley arrived. Examining the situation, he persuaded the hapless man to play his hand in a card game. With his rival thus occupied, Bodley sought out the widow Ann in the garden, wooed her, and won her promise of marriage. In this way, he acquired a wife, a fortune, and seven stepchildren who would later receive little benefit from their natural father's wealth as a result of its philanthropic diversion by their stepfather. Bodley and Ann had no children of their own.

Bodley's marriage quickly proved its value. Ann's contacts in Devon and Cornwall gained for Bodley a place in the session of Parliament called on September 15, 1586, for the borough of Saint Germans, Cornwall. During 1588, the Elizabethan government sent him on a confidential mission to the fugitive King Henry III of France. Almost as soon as he returned home, he found himself appointed to replace Henry Killigrew as the resident English envoy on the Netherlands Council of State. Bodley served in that difficult post from 1589 to 1596. Queen Elizabeth complicated relations with the Dutch by insisting that they pay for the full cost of English military assistance in the war with Spain. Again and again, Bodley found himself thwarted by the uncooperative Dutch or placed in an impossible position by his own government. By 1592, he was hoping for recall, and in

1594, he quarreled with William Cecil (Lord Burghley), the queen's chief minister, and asked to be relieved. That did not occur, but the incident was probably a big step in Bodley's progress toward deciding to abandon government service altogether.

Still unable to accomplish Queen Elizabeth's diplomatic bidding by 1596, Bodley returned home to discover that in his irascible queen's opinion he deserved hanging. Furthermore, the mutual animosities of Robert Devereux, the earl of Essex, and Lord Burghley had cost him a promotion to be secretary of state. At that point, he decided to retire. Never again would he resume his career of government service and diplomacy. A mission was offered but refused in 1598, and James I's government tried one last time to coax him out of retirement during 1604 and 1605. This effort gained for him a knighthood but it did not change his mind.

The weary and disillusioned Bodley desired a project for his labor and talents that would bring him peace and satisfaction. After some thought, he settled on the refounding of a university library for Oxford. The original had disappeared in the middle of the sixteenth century during the turmoil of the Edwardian Reformation. Thus, on February 23, 1598, Bodley wrote to the vice chancellor of Oxford University offering to refurbish the library, to secure books for it, to hire a staff, to attract other benefactors, and, above all, to establish a perma-

nent endowment he believed was essential to the library's long-term survival.

Work and planning for the new library proceeded quickly. From the first, Bodley persuaded the university to appoint six delegates to oversee the library. These included his trusted friends Thomas Allen and William Gent, fellows of Gloucester Hall, and John Hawley, the principal of the same college. By the end of 1599 at the latest, a librarian had been found, although the university did not officially confirm his appointment until April, 1602. Thomas James of New College practiced scholarship with a deeply antipapal thrust and proved to be an able head for the new library.

Meanwhile, the work of refurbishing the library approached completion in June, 1600. It was a source of great relief to Bodley, since he could now begin to solicit in earnest the books and money needed to build up the library's collection.

Bodley took great interest in collecting books for his library. His house at Fulham, in London, continued to be his principal residence, and it was there that he collected the books he sought or solicited until they were dispatched in yearly batches to Oxford. Even the most casual offers of gifts were followed up. Potential donors were never allowed to forget exactly what they had offered. Thomas Allen, the library delegate, and Thomas James, the librarian, both significantly assisted Bodley in his efforts to attract donations of books, manuscripts, and money. In fact, James made the suggestion that resulted in the Stationers' Company agreeing in 1610 to deposit one free copy of every book that they printed in the Bodleian. Thanks to these efforts, between 1600 and 1605, seventeen hundred pounds were raised to buy books. By 1605, the collection contained fifty-six hundred volumes, for which James had compiled an up-to-date printed catalog. Growth continued so that by Bodley's death in early 1613 the library housed about seven thousand volumes or about fifteen thousand titles along with eight hundred manuscripts. The Bodleian Library had quickly grown to be one of the significant research collections of its day.

Bodley believed that it was his library's purpose to preserve the entire range of human knowledge. This attitude is reflected in his continuing efforts systematically to acquire Hebrew and Arabic books. As early as 1603, the Bodleian purchased its first Chinese books, although there was no one who could read them. Policies concerning admission to the library also reflected a broad-minded philosophy. Almost any member of the university could use the library if he fulfilled certain conditions. Further-

Sir Thomas Bodley. (Library of Congress)

more, students from foreign universities were also admitted if their subject of research met the approval of university authorities.

The library's rapid growth caused it to overflow quickly its original quarters. Bodley's last years and large amounts of his treasure were spent getting the Arts End extension built during 1610-1612. This building was the first to use wall shelving in a public library in England. Bodley's other final worry was to secure the permanent endowment to the Bodleian from challenge by any of his disgruntled heirs. He therefore produced a will on January 2, 1613, which gave his endowment firm protection with powerful overseers such as William Abbot, the archbishop of Canterbury, and Edward Coke, then chief justice of Common Pleas. Although Bodley remembered most members of his family and his servants in his will, their portions were much reduced by the immense endowment of seven thousand pounds that he gave to his library. Many criticized his lack of generosity to his family and stepchildren (Ann had died in 1611). After his death, his brother Lawrence Bodley and a niece, Elizabeth Willis, unsuccessfully contested the will. In the meantime, Bodley died on January 28, 1613, at his home in London after a lingering illness. He was buried with great pomp in the Merton College chapel.

SIGNIFICANCE

Sir Thomas Bodley had great ability, immense pride, and a sensitive ego. If he had not possessed those traits, his energies would probably not have been redirected from a reasonably successful diplomatic career into the role of library benefactor. His premier achievement of refounding Oxford's university library has overshadowed his state service. Although battered and frustrated, Bodley survived the rigors of diplomatic service in the Netherlands. A close association with the ill-fated earl of Essex did not permanently taint him in the eyes of the English government, which continued to seek his valuable skills long after he had lost any desire to offer them. Voluntarily forgoing the disconcerting world of diplomatic service, Bodley secured his place in history by benefiting scholarship. The Bodleian Library became the best academic library in England during his lifetime and remained in a class by itself until the British Museum and the Cambridge University Library began to catch up in the nineteenth century.

—*Ronald H. Fritze*

FURTHER READING

Bodleian Library. *Wonderful Things from Four Hundred Years of Collecting: The Bodleian Library, 1602-* *2002—An Exhibition to Mark the Quatercentenary of the Bodleian, July to December, 2002.* Oxford, England: The Library, 2002. Exhibition catalog from an exhibition of the Bodleian's most famous and important holdings. Includes illustrations, photographs, facsimiles, maps, and music.

Bodley, Thomas. *Letters of Sir Thomas Bodley to the University of Oxford, 1598-1611.* Edited by G. W. Wheeler. Oxford, England: Oxford University Press, 1927. An edition of fifteen letters from Bodley to the various vice chancellors of the university concerning his library. These letters are also available in the *Bodleian Quarterly Record*, volume 5. Wheeler has also edited the correspondence between Bodley and his librarian Thomas James.

Chamberlain, John. *The Chamberlain Letters: A Selection of the Letters of John Chamberlain Concerning Life in England from 1597 to 1626.* Edited by Elizabeth McClure Thomson. New York: Capricorn Books, 1966. A selection of extracts from Norman Egbert McClure's two-volume *The Letters of John Chamberlain* (Philadelphia: American Philosophical Society, 1939). Includes Chamberlain's description of the Bodleian's buildings and his critical comments concerning Bodley's vanity in leaving a fortune for a library named after himself while neglecting his legitimate heirs and family.

Doran, Susan. *Elizabeth I and Foreign Policy, 1558-1603.* New York: Routledge, 2000. Short monograph on Elizabeth's foreign policy. Discusses her personal abilities as a stateswoman, as well as the general diplomatic objectives Bodley was expected to fulfill. Includes genealogical tables, maps, bibliographic references.

Mallet, Charles Edward. *A History of the University of Oxford.* 3 vols. London: Methuen, 1924-1927. Reprint. New York: Barnes and Noble Books, 1968. Mallet's work is to be superseded by the projected multivolume "Oxford History of Oxford University." Ian Philip's account of the foundation of the Bodleian is superior, but Mallet has some unique information.

Morris, Jan, ed. *The Oxford Book of Oxford.* New York: Oxford University Press, 1978. An anthology of extracts of documents and anecdotes relating to Oxford. Includes several items relating to Bodley and the early years of his library. Bodley's letter of February 23, 1598, offering to refurbish and restore the university library, is in this collection.

Philip, Ian. *The Bodleian Library in the Seventeenth and Eighteenth Centuries.* New York: Oxford University

Press, 1983. A scrupulously researched and well-written account of the Bodleian Library from 1598 to 1800 by a retired member of its staff who is also a recognized library historian. The best work available on the subject.

Wernham, R. B. *After the Armada: Elizabethan England and the Struggle for Western Europe, 1588-1595.* New York: Oxford University Press, 1984. An excellent account of English foreign policy and military relations during a time of great international turmoil. Provides a context for Bodley's diplomatic efforts in the Netherlands and gives a good indication of why he found his service there to be so frustrating.

Wood, Anthony. *Athenae Oxonienses: An Exact History of All the Writers and Bishops Who Have Had Their Education in the University of Oxford.* 2 vols. London: Thomas Bennet, 1691-1692. Reprint. New York: Burt Franklin, 1968. A collection of biographical sketches of famous Oxford men starting with 1500 and including most of the seventeenth century. Originally published in 1691 and 1692 by one of Oxford's most famous antiquarians. Bodley's entry is located in volume 2 and its eulogistic tone shows the deep gratitude that his library benefaction inspired in the scholarly community by the late seventeenth century.

SEE ALSO: John Calvin; William Cecil; Elizabeth I; Henry III; Mary I; First Earl of Salisbury.

RELATED ARTICLE in *Great Events from History: The Renaissance & Early Modern Era, 1454-1600:* April or May, 1560: Publication of the Geneva Bible.

ANNE BOLEYN
Queen of England (r. 1533-1536)

The desire of England's King Henry VIII to marry Anne Boleyn, his second wife and the mother of Queen Elizabeth I, led to the establishment of the Church of England.

BORN: c. 1500-1501; probably at Blickling Hall, Norfolk, England
DIED: May 19, 1536; London, England
ALSO KNOWN AS: Anne Bullen
AREAS OF ACHIEVEMENT: Church reform, government and politics

EARLY LIFE

Future queen of England Anne Boleyn (boh-LIHN) was born into an ambitious family at a time when ambitions were realized through interactions with the court and marriage into the nobility. Young women from such families were expected to marry as their families dictated. Anne's great-grandfather, Geoffrey Boleyn, a tradesman lacking in social status, rose to become lord mayor of London in 1457 but improved his position even more through marriage; Sir William Boleyn, her grandfather, made an even more impressive marriage to Margaret Butler, daughter of an Irish earl. Thomas Boleyn, Anne's father, was the eldest of their four sons. A highly successful courtier and diplomat, he married Elizabeth Howard, daughter of Thomas Howard, earl of Surrey; Elizabeth Howard was descended from King Edward I, thus bestowing a touch of royal blood on her children.

While Elizabeth Howard was frequently pregnant, only Mary, Anne, and George survived to adulthood. To prepare Anne for an advantageous marriage, she was sent abroad, first, in 1513, to the court of Margaret of Austria, regent of the Netherlands. When Mary Tudor (Mary I), sister of Henry VIII, married King Louis XII of France in 1514, Anne was moved to their court, where she joined her sister Mary. When Louis died, the sisters remained at court serving Claude of Valois, wife of the new king, Francis I, whose court was conspicuously vice-ridden. Mary Boleyn's reputation became tarnished; Anne remained aloof, although she developed the charm, wit, and love of French manners and fashions expected of her in that sophisticated environment.

She returned to England in 1521 or 1522, gaining a place in the household of Henry VIII's queen Catherine of Aragon, where her social skills brought her immediate attention. Her sister Mary was then mistress of the king, which may have facilitated Sir Thomas Boleyn's ennoblement as Viscount Rochford. During this period, Anne attempted to marry Henry Percy, heir to the earldom of Northumberland. Her desire to arrange her own marriage was itself shocking; her plans were thwarted by Cardinal Thomas Wolsey, archbishop of York and lord chancellor of England. Anne temporarily left court.

LIFE'S WORK

Anne returned to court in 1524 or 1525. King Henry VIII's affair with Anne's sister ended, and he was attracted to Anne. She resisted his approaches, either because she was genuinely repelled or because she was unwilling to settle for a role as a mistress. Since 1509, Henry had been married to Catherine, daughter of Isabella of Castile and Ferdinand of Aragon, rulers of Spain, but the king was increasingly frustrated by Catherine's inability to bear a male heir. A series of pregnancies had resulted in only one child, Mary, who survived infancy. While miscarriages and high infant mortality rates were common, Henry was concerned that he have a legitimate successor to protect England against a recurrence of the previous century's civil wars. Moreover, the birth of his illegitimate son to Elizabeth Blount had proved to his satisfaction that he could sire sons.

In 1527, Henry sought a "divorce"—essentially a modern annulment, since rather than dissolving the marriage, it would show that a legitimate marriage had never taken place. The king's argument was that despite the papal dispensation for his marriage to Catherine, his marriage was forbidden by the Bible, specifically by Leviticus 20:21, which forbids marriage with a brother's wife. In November, 1501, Catherine had married Henry's elder brother Arthur, who died in April, 1502, probably without consummating the marriage. Catherine's failure to bear a son was proof, Henry believed, of divine displeasure with the marriage.

Such divorces were frequent. The duke of Suffolk, who had married Henry's sister Mary in 1515, had secured two; Henry's older sister, Queen Margaret of Scotland, similarly secured one and remarried in 1527. Henry expected the process to be rapid, entrusting Cardinal Wolsey with what came to be called the King's Great Matter. In 1527, however, the troops of the Holy Roman Emperor Charles V had invaded Rome; the emperor was Queen Catherine's nephew. Pope Clement VII was now his prisoner and was unwilling to take steps against the emperor's aunt. He began a series of delaying actions.

Anne's role as rival with Catherine for Henry's affection was known by early 1526. Flirtatious, volatile, outspoken, arrogant, and sophisticated where the queen was grave, mild-mannered, modest, and restrained, Anne was intelligent in an age that rarely acknowledged the value of female intelligence. Anne gained few friends. Many could not understand Henry's attraction to her. She was no beauty. She was dark-haired; the ideal of the day was blond. She was thin, and her skin was sallow. She was said to have a rudimentary extra nail on one hand. To much of the court and the public, she became a stereotypical image of the temptress, although her frequent absences from court may have been serious attempts to

Anne Boleyn. (Library of Congress)

avoid the king's attentions. Anne was blamed for Wolsey's fall from power. Henry, accustomed to having his way, replaced Wolsey with Thomas Cromwell, who was more in sympathy with Anne. Anne was accused of avenging herself for Wolsey's earlier interference in her romance with Henry Percy. By 1529, however, she could not have saved herself from the king's plans had she chosen to do so.

Henry was not in sympathy with the Protestant movement, which had swept through northern Europe since Martin Luther had posted his designs for church reform on a church door at Wittenberg in 1517. Henry considered himself a good Catholic and had been given the title "Defender of the Faith" for his opposition to Luther. Nevertheless, in 1529, determined to impose his will and gain a male heir, Henry convened a parliament that was to bring about a religious revolution, as Pope Clement continued to thwart Henry's plans. In 1530, Clement told Henry to dismiss Anne from the court; in 1531, he banned the king's remarriage while the divorce case was being heard, apparently indefinitely, in Rome.

Anne, however, had allowed Henry increasing intimacy, and by the end of 1532 they had become lovers. By December, 1532, she was pregnant, and, probably sometime in January, 1533, Anne and Henry were secretly married. Henry's logic, apparently, was that he had a right to this second marriage because the marriage to Catherine had never been valid. On June 1, 1533, Anne Boleyn, visibly pregnant, was crowned queen of England in an elaborate ceremony that was to be the high point of her life. Despite the public pageantry, crowds were quiet and occasionally hostile as the new queen passed. Queen Catherine's many charities and conventional domesticity won for her friends that the new queen could never possess.

In July, Pope Clement VII ordered Henry to renounce Anne and declared any child of the new marriage illegitimate. That child, the future Elizabeth I, was born on September 7, 1533. She was the wrong gender for an heir, but Henry and Anne assumed that Anne would continue to bear healthy children, although Anne by then was about thirty-three years of age, well into middle age at a time of low life expectancy. In 1534, Anne gave birth to two stillborn infants. Understanding the importance to her wellbeing of a healthy son, she continued to become pregnant. The increasing insecurity of her position did not improve her disposition.

Bent on having his way, Henry, via the Act of Supremacy, made himself, not the pope, the spiritual father of the English people, thus separating England from the Roman Catholic Church. From February, 1535, it would be high treason to deny Henry's supremacy. He had already begun the series of executions that would taint his reputation for the remainder of his reign. He purged those who defied him, including his old friend the Humanist scholar Sir Thomas More, who was beheaded in 1535, and the aged John Fisher, bishop of Rochester. They and many others could not accept the Act of Supremacy. Unwilling to accept any challenge to his will, he was also tiring of Anne's quick tongue and her apparent unwillingness to accept his unfaithfulness as had Catherine; like Catherine, Anne also failed to provide him with a son.

In January, 1536, Catherine of Aragon died. Henry was unlikely to marry for a third time while Catherine and Anne both lived, but he was pursuing Jane Seymour by November, 1535. Catherine's death freed him to rid himself of Anne and start anew. He maintained that Anne had bewitched him into marriage; he claimed she was a sorceress and was guilty of adultery. He also claimed that she had discussed what would happen when the king died, and such discussions constituted high treason. On May 2, Anne was arrested and taken to the Tower of London. There, where she had been received on the eve of her coronation three years before, she was made a prisoner.

Despite public hatred of Anne, few believed she was guilty. According to the case prepared by Thomas Cromwell, she had committed incest with her brother, George Boleyn (Lord Rochford). Three prominent courtiers, Sir Henry Norris, Sir Francis Weston, and William Brereton, as well as her musician, Mark Smeaton, were arrested as her partners in adultery. Smeaton was not a nobleman; as a commoner, he could be and apparently was tortured into a confession. Charges included conspiracy to murder the king.

The duke of Norfolk, Anne's uncle Thomas Howard, presided over the trials of Norris, Weston, Brereton, and Smeaton on May 12; all were condemned to death. Anne and her brother were tried separately on May 14; again, Anne's uncle presided. Actual evidence against them was lacking, and the case was poorly prepared, but the results were foreordained. Both were condemned. On May 17, Archbishop Thomas Cranmer convened a court at Lambeth to annul Henry's marriage to Anne, thus preparing the way for Henry's marriage to Jane Seymour on May 30 as, essentially, his first valid marriage. Anne Boleyn was beheaded on May 19 at the Tower of London; her remains were buried in the Royal Chapel of St. Peter ad Vincula of the Tower.

SIGNIFICANCE

Scholars have argued over the degree to which Anne Boleyn was a Protestant rebel against the Church of Rome. She encouraged individual reading of the Bible and the reading of works banned by the church, but there is little other evidence that she was a conscious Protestant. Nevertheless, because she was, willingly or otherwise, a pawn in the King's Great Matter, she was at the heart of the separation of England from the Roman Catholic Church and of the despoliation of convents and monasteries that was to follow. Her independence of spirit and attempts at autonomy, despite the great powers that controlled her destiny, seem to ally her with the Protestant movement, whatever her intent, and cause modern feminist historians to view her with sympathetic eyes.

—*Betty Richardson*

FURTHER READING

Bernard, G. W. "The Fall of Anne Boleyn." In *Power and Politics in Tudor England: Essays*. Burlington, Vt.: Ashgate, 2000. Examines Boleyn's function, as monarch, pawn, and victim, in the power struggles of her time. Includes bibliographic references and index.

Chapman, Hester. *The Challenge of Anne Boleyn*. New York: Coward, McCann & Geoghegan, 1974. Places Boleyn in the context of a politically ambitious family in an age of melodramatic excess; pays particular attention to the courts in which Boleyn was trained.

Erickson, Carolly. *Mistress Anne: The Life and Times of Anne Boleyn*. New York: Summit Books, 1984. Reprint. New York: St. Martin's Griffin, 1998. In one of a series of Tudor biographies that include *Bloody Mary* (1978) and *Great Harry* (1980), Erickson vividly recreates the world in which these people lived; her work is scholarly, but her style is popular. Her portrait of Anne is not generally sympathetic.

Fraser, Antonia. *The Wives of Henry VIII*. New York: Alfred A. Knopf, 1993. Originally published in London as *The Six Wives of Henry VIII* (1992). Fraser balances anti-Boleyn propaganda with information from other sources to achieve a convincing portrayal, in part sympathetic.

Lindsey, Karen. *Divorced, Beheaded, Survived*. Reading, Mass.: Addison-Wesley, 1995. A feminist interpretation of Boleyn's life, this work emphasizes Boleyn as a victim of an all-powerful monarch determined to conquer her. Cites as evidence a poem by Sir Thomas Wyatt, who knew Anne well.

Shagan, Ethan H. *Popular Politics and the English Reformation*. New York: Cambridge University Press, 2003. Study of the way in which ordinary English subjects interpreted and reacted to Henry's split from the Catholic Church. Argues that religious history cannot be understood independently of political history, because commoners no less than royals understood religion and politics as utterly intertwined. Includes bibliographic references and index.

Warnike, Retha M. *The Rise and Fall of Anne Boleyn: Family Politics at the Court of Henry VIII*. Cambridge, England: Cambridge University Press, 1989. Focusing on Anne's society and its conventions, Warnike argues that Anne's failure to produce a male heir doomed her.

Weir, Alison. *The Six Wives of Henry VIII*. London: The Bodley Head, 1991. Depending heavily on the virulently anti-Boleyn commentary of Spanish ambassador Eustace (or Eustache) Chapuys, Weir presents an almost totally unsympathetic portrait of Boleyn as manipulative seducer.

Zahl, Paul F. M. *Five Women of the English Reformation*. Grand Rapids, Mich.: William B. Eerdmans, 2001. Discusses Boleyn's role as an advocate of Protestantism in general and of the "justification by faith" doctrine in particular. Includes bibliographic references.

SEE ALSO: Anne of Cleves; Catherine of Aragon; Charles V; Clement VII; Thomas Cromwell; Elizabeth I; Ferdinand II and Isabella I; Saint John Fisher; Francis I; Henry VIII; Catherine Howard; Louis XII; Martin Luther; Margaret of Austria; Mary I; Sir Thomas More; Catherine Parr; Jane Seymour; The Tudor Family; Cardinal Thomas Wolsey.

RELATED ARTICLES in *Great Events from History: The Renaissance & Early Modern Era, 1454-1600:* 1515-1529: Wolsey Serves as Lord Chancellor and Cardinal; 1531-1540: Cromwell Reforms British Government; December 18, 1534: Act of Supremacy; May, 1539: Six Articles of Henry VIII.

CESARE BORGIA
Italian military leader and politician

Cesare Borgia was one of the most formidable of Renaissance dynasts, a skillful campaigner and ruthless politician who helped establish his family among the premier houses of Renaissance Italy. He was later immortalized as the hero and archetype of Niccolò Machiavelli's The Prince.

BORN: 1475 or 1476; probably Rome, Papal States (now in Italy)
DIED: March 12, 1507; Viana, Navarre (now in Spain)
ALSO KNOWN AS: Duke of Valentinois; duke of Valencia
AREAS OF ACHIEVEMENT: Government and politics, military, warfare and conquest

EARLY LIFE

The family of Cesare Borgia (CHAY-zahr-ay BAWR-jah) originated near Valencia, on the Mediterranean coast of Spain, rising to prominence in the time of Cardinal Alfonso de Borja, who became Pope Calixtus III in 1455. In 1456, Calixtus elevated one of his nephews, Rodrigo Borja, Cesare's father, to the rank of cardinal.

Rodrigo (who Italianized his name to "Borgia") devoted himself to the continued advancement of his family. Even by the lax moral standards of the Renaissance Papacy, Rodrigo lived scandalously; he fathered at least ten illegitimate children, showering special favor on the four (including Cesare) born to him by his favorite mistress, Vannozza Cattanei.

An engraved depiction of the expulsion of Cesare Borgia from the Vatican. (F. R. Niglutsch)

Private vices notwithstanding, Rodrigo was a shrewd and effective administrator who served as vice-chancellor (chief administrative officer) of the papal curia for thirty-five years. His election as Pope Alexander VI in 1492—achieved in no small part by massive bribes—marked the culmination of a brilliant, if morally dubious, ecclesiastical career.

Alexander VI worked tirelessly to establish the Borgia family as preeminent in the Papacy's Italian territories. In and of itself, this was hardly remarkable; for medieval and Renaissance popes, nepotism and family patronage were essential tools of effective pontifical government. The scope of Alexander's ambitions, however, and his family's Iberian origins were exceptional and quickly aroused considerable opposition from the leading Italian houses, particularly the royal house of Naples.

At first, the pope pinned his hopes to his favorite son, Juan, for whom he acquired the Spanish duchy of Gandia. Cesare, by contrast, was marked for ecclesiastical preferment; he studied law at Pisa before successive appointments to the Spanish sees of Pamplona and Valencia. In 1493, he was named cardinal-deacon of Santa Maria Nuova, but the restless and martial Cesare was ill-suited to a career with the Church. When Juan died under mysterious circumstances in the spring of 1497, it was widely believed that Cesare had had him murdered. The disconsolate pope, himself convinced of Cesare's guilt, had little choice but to release Cesare from his vows and to place Juan's temporal holdings at Cesare's disposal.

LIFE'S WORK

Cesare showed himself a far more capable and energetic agent of his family's interests than the feckless Juan had been; his personal motto, *aut Caesar aut nihil* (either Caesar or nothing), speaks to his single-minded and boundless ambition. In May, 1499, he secured an important alliance with the French king, Louis XII, from whom he received the French duchy of Valentinois. Soon afterward, also in 1499, he married Charlotte d'Albret, a sister of the king of Navarre. Cesare then turned his attention to the reconquest of the Papal States, substantial portions of which had become effectively independent of papal control in the course of the previous generation.

As captain-general of the Church, Cesare built up a formidable army, including substantial numbers of

French and Swiss mercenaries. From his headquarters at Cesena, he moved against the petty tyrants of the cities of Romagna and Marches. In 1499, he captured Imola; the following year he took Forlì, Rimini, and Pesaro in quick succession. After the fall of Faenza in 1501, Alexander VI named Cesare duke of Romagna. Clearly, the pope sought to create a great Borgia patrimony in central and northern Italy, with Cesare as its dynastic founder.

In the face of Cesare's astonishing victories, his enemies set their differences aside and made common cause against him. Even some of his allies, fearing for their own possessions, began to conspire against him. Rebellions broke out in the eastern Papal States, and Cesare suffered several major setbacks over the course of 1502. His alliance with Louis XII soon proved its value, however: The mere suggestion of a French invasion put an end to the uprisings, and by the end of 1502 Cesare was once again in firm control of his territories. Before he could press on to further conquests, however, both he and his father fell gravely ill in the summer of 1503. It was long believed that they accidentally took poison intended for an enemy, but the malaria that thrived in the miasmal Roman summer is a more likely culprit. In any event, the seventy-two-year-old pope died on August 18.

During Cesare's long and difficult convalescence, his enemies, led by the powerful Roman Orsini family, exploited his incapacity and rose up against the Borgia hegemony. On September 22, the cardinals elected a new pope, Pius III, but when the frail Pius died less than one month later, the cardinals elected Cardinal Giuliano della Rovere as Pope Julius II. The able and bellicose Giuliano had long been among the most implacable opponents of the Borgias. Cesare fled to Spain, where he was arrested and imprisoned on the orders of King Ferdinand II. He escaped in 1506 and took refuge at the court of his brother-in-law, King John of Navarre.

Cesare doubtless hoped to make an eventual return to the Italian theater. On March 12, 1507, however, Cesare was killed at the castle of Viana while fighting a rebellious vassal of King John. Any hopes of a Borgia restoration in Italy died with him. In less than one decade, the remarkable Borgia achievement in Italy had vanished without a trace.

SIGNIFICANCE

Cesare remains a controversial and intriguing figure. Tales of his extravagance were doubtless exaggerated by his enemies, and rumors of an incestuous relationship with his sister, Lucrezia, are without merit. He was handsome and athletic, but he lacked the breadth of accomplishment of the greatest Renaissance princes. Cesare defined success entirely in political and military terms. Despite an excellent private education, Cesare was indifferent to scholarship and the arts (though he did briefly employ Leonardo da Vinci as a military engineer).

There is no denying the remorseless cruelty with which he struck at his enemies, however, and his condottiere, Michelotto Coreglia, was an assassin and enforcer of unparalleled brutality. Suspicious of all, trusted by none, Cesare commanded fear and admiration but could not inspire loyalty or affection.

Still, at least some of Cesare's contemporaries viewed his legacy in a more positive light. Niccolò Machiavelli argued in *Il principe* (wr. 1513, pb. 1532; *The Prince*, 1640) that Cesare's conquests rendered an invaluable service to the public good. While acknowledging the amoral character of Cesare's political activities, Machiavelli held that Cesare's firm hand brought stability and peace to lands that had too long been rent by lawlessness and civil strife. Even more significant, Machiavelli saw Cesare as a potential bulwark against the competing ambitions of the French and Spanish crowns, though whether even a commander of Cesare's ability could have preserved Italian independence before the imminent tide of foreign conquest seems doubtful.

Cesare's career was most significant in marking the apogee of papal patronage and the politics of nepotism. Alexander VI came closer than any other pope to transforming papal patronage into the basis of a new type of regional, dynastic state building in Renaissance Italy. In the end, the Borgia experiment could not survive the death of its papal architect, but it could not have enjoyed its spectacular, if short-lived, success without the considerable talent and determination of Cesare.

—*Blake Beattie*

FURTHER READING

Bradford, Sarah. *Cesare Borgia.* New York: Macmillan, 1976. Though hardly groundbreaking in its presentation, this polished and readable biography does an excellent job of capturing the character and ambition of this most feared of Renaissance princes.

Burchard, Johann. *At the Court of the Borgia.* Edited and translated by Geoffrey Parker. London: Folio Society, 1963. An excellent edition and translation, with scholarly commentary, of Johannes Burchard's fascinating (if sometimes deliberately misleading) contemporary account of life at the court of Alexander VI.

Corvo, Frederick Baron. *A History of the Borgias.* New York: Modern Library, 1931. Written by an author every bit as colorful as his subjects, this elegant, over-wrought, and hugely entertaining book revels in the more lurid aspects of the Borgia legacy. Despite its erudition and thorough research, this one should probably be read more as entertainment than as a work of scholarship.

Johnson, Marion, and Georgina Masson. *The Borgias.* New York: Penguin Books, 2002. Originally published in 1981, this lively, readable, and relatively brief work is an important contribution to the ongoing rehabilitation of the Borgia reputation.

Machiavelli, Niccolò. *The Prince.* Translated by George Bull, with an introduction by Anthony Grafton. New York: Penguin Books, 2002. This masterpiece of Western political thought portrays Cesare Borgia as the perfect exemplar of the late medieval and early modern ruler: intelligent, unsentimental, and wholly willing to subordinate moral concerns to *raison d'état* (reason of state).

Mallett, Michael E. *The Borgias: The Rise and Fall of a Renaissance Dynasty.* New York: Barnes & Noble Books, 1969. One of the best English-language studies of the dynasty, Mallett's work examines the Borgia family fortunes in the context of the ever-shifting political circumstances of Renaissance Italy.

Sabatini, Rafael. *The Life of Cesare Borgia.* New York: Brentano's, 1912. This classic biography was written by a celebrated novelist with a flair for swashbuckling adventures. Still, it was one of the earliest works to attempt a more balanced portrait of Cesare Borgia.

SEE ALSO: Alexander VI; Charles VIII; Julius II; Leonardo da Vinci; Louis XII; Niccolò Machiavelli.

RELATED ARTICLES in *Great Events from History: The Renaissance & Early Modern Era, 1454-1600:* 1500: Roman Jubilee; July-December, 1513: Machiavelli Writes *The Prince.*

LUCREZIA BORGIA
Italian noblewoman

Lucrezia Borgia, a patron of scholars and artists but also a pawn in her family's dynastic ambitions, was celebrated for her beauty and wit, immortalized in opera and melodrama, and reviled as the epitome of Renaissance immorality. She might best be seen as embodying the straitened circumstances of aristocratic women in Italian Renaissance society.

BORN: April 18, 1480; Subiaco, Papal States (now in Italy)
DIED: June 24, 1519; Ferrara, Papal States (now in Italy)
ALSO KNOWN AS: Lucretia Borgia
AREAS OF ACHIEVEMENT: Patronage of the arts, government and politics

EARLY LIFE

Lucrezia Borgia (lew-KREHT-syah BAWR-jah) was the daughter of the powerful Cardinal Rodrigo Borja (later Borgia), who became Pope Alexander VI in 1492. Her mother, the Roman noblewoman Vannozza Cattanei, was Rodrigo's favorite mistress, and Vannozza's children always enjoyed special favor with their father.

Lucrezia was raised in the house of a kinswoman, Adriana de Mila. Adriana provided young Lucrezia with the education her social station demanded, with a heavy emphasis on courtly manners and etiquette. By the time she reached her early teens, Lucrezia was fluent in Spanish, Italian, and French, with a refinement and sophistication suited to any of the great Renaissance courts. Soon after her father's election as Pope Alexander VI, she began to spend more and more time at the papal court, where her beauty and elegance established her as a leading figure on the Roman social scene.

Enemies of the Borgias later portrayed Lucrezia's youth as a time of exceptional depravity; some went so far as to accuse her of incest with her father and her brothers, Juan and Cesare. One of the most damning accounts of Lucrezia's early life is found in the *Diarium sive rerum urbanarum commentarii* (1503) of Pope Alexander's master of ceremonies, Johannes Burchard, who placed Lucrezia at the very heart of an often scandalously extravagant court. Even so well placed a source as Burchard, however, must be regarded with some skepticism; he was hardly sympathetic to Alexander's papacy, and he seems to have gone to considerable lengths to discredit the Borgias.

LIFE'S WORK

Lucrezia Borgia was a woman of exceptional ability. When she was still in her teens, her father had no qualms about leaving her in charge of his affairs in Rome while he was away from the city. In her later years, she often governed Ferrara during the absences of her husband, Duke Alfonso I d'Este.

Nevertheless, throughout her life, her considerable talents were valued less than her usefulness in securing strategic marriages for the continued advancement of her family. First as cardinal and later as pope, her father worked to establish the Borgias in the front ranks of the great Italian dynasties. To this end, Lucrezia was intended from earliest childhood for an important and diplomatically beneficial marriage.

Before her eleventh birthday, she was already twice betrothed (though both engagements were subsequently terminated). At just thirteen, she married Giovanni Sforza, a nephew of the wily duke of Milan, Ludovico Sforza. The union, negotiated chiefly through the offices of Ludovico's brother, Cardinal Ascanio Sforza, aimed at providing the pope with a powerful ally in the face of potential threats from both King Ferdinand II of Naples

Detail of a painting, The Disputation of St. Catherine *by Florentine artist Bernardino Pinturicchio, depicting Lucrezia Borgia in the guise of Saint Catherine.* (Hulton|Archive by Getty Images)

and Charles VIII of France. The marriage was in every respect a failure. The Milanese alliance proved less valuable than the pope had hoped. Moreover, Lucrezia found little to her liking in Giovanni, a dull and rather stupid man nearly fifteen years her senior. The pope had the marriage annulled in 1497, claiming (in the face of vehement denials from Giovanni) that it had never been consummated.

With her divorce pending and amid rumors of an illicit pregnancy (the existence of which remains an object of debate), Lucrezia sought to flee from unwanted scrutiny by retiring to the Roman convent of San Sisto. It is possible that she contemplated a monastic vocation at the time, though her father and brother had other plans for her. In 1498, Lucrezia was called out of the convent to marry Duke Alfonso of Bisceglie, a nephew of King Federico of Naples. It was hoped that the marriage might accelerate a thaw in relations between Naples and the Papacy. It was by all accounts a far happier union than Lucrezia's first, but when it failed to pave the way to a marriage between Cesare and one of Federico's daughters, Cesare forged an alliance with King Louis XII of France and Lucrezia's marriage to Alfonso became a political liability.

In July of 1500, Alfonso barely survived an assassination attempt, only to perish in a second attack a month later. There was no doubt as to the identity of the conspirators: Alfonso's assassin, Michelotto Coreglia, was one of Cesare's most feared henchmen. Barely twenty years of age and pregnant, Lucrezia found herself a widow.

Alfonso's murder devastated Lucrezia. She remained true, however, to the family cause—indeed, she christened Alfonso's posthumous son Rodrigo, after her father—and, in 1501, she entered into her third (and final) marriage, this time to Alfonso I d'Este from the ruling house of Ferrara. Alfonso's father, Duke Ercole I d'Este, was at first apprehensive of a union with Lucrezia but soon discovered that her evil reputation was wholly unwarranted. In fact, d'Este remained devoted to Lucrezia even after her father's death and Cesare's ruin deprived her of all political value in 1503.

Unlike her brother Cesare, who demonstrated little interest in the arts or scholarship, Lucrezia became a great patron of Renaissance culture, presiding at Ferrara over a court of exceptional brilliance. Among her friends and protégés she numbered the writer Ludovico Ariosto and Pietro Bembo, a Humanist poet and cardinal with whom she formed a powerful friendship and entered into a remarkable correspondence. She distinguished herself as an especially generous patron of charities and ecclesiastical foundations; her death in childbirth at the age of thirty-nine occasioned great grief in Ferrara.

SIGNIFICANCE

Lucrezia remains one of those unfortunate historical figures for whom a fair-minded historical assessment is rendered almost impossible by the weight of a persistently and overwhelmingly hostile tradition. The scandals and sexual license ascribed to her youth seem to have little basis in fact. The piety of her later years need not derive, as is often asserted, from some radical break with a grossly immoral past. Even the most intimate and suggestive of her letters to Bembo reveal a woman with a delicately, almost naively romantic, sensibility, wholly unlike the lascivious siren denounced by her critics.

Lucrezia was exceptionally close to her father and brothers, but accusations of incest are entirely without merit. Indeed, that charge seems to have originated with her embittered first husband, Giovanni Sforza. Her depiction as a murderous seductress, poisoning one unfortunate husband after another, is absurd; not a single murder can be laid in her lap.

In the final judgment, Lucrezia's life provides a window into the lives of wealthy, high-born women during the Renaissance. Even with her great abilities, Lucrezia had few options beyond the politics of the bridal bed. Her retreat to San Sisto in 1497—to the considerable consternation of her father—was a momentary assertion of independence, and the murder of Alfonso of Bisceglie in 1500 placed serious strains on her relationship with her father and Cesare.

In the end, though, she had little choice but to continue in the service of her family's dynastic interests. Indeed, only after she ceased to have any real value as a dynastic bargaining chip could she mature into the great Renaissance patron of scholars and charities that she became at Ferrara, where she was long and fondly remembered as *la buona duchessa* (the good duchess).

—*Blake Beattie*

FURTHER READING

Bellonci, Maria. *The Life and Times of Lucrezia Borgia.* Translated by Bernard and Barbara Wall. New York: Harcourt Brace, 1953. This classic Italian biography was among the first major studies to reject the conventional portrait of Lucrezia as a murderous seductress.

Burchard, Johann. *At the Court of the Borgia.* Edited and translated by Geoffrey Parker. London: Folio Society, 1963. An excellent edition and translation, with scholarly commentary, of Johannes Burchard's fascinating (if sometimes deliberately misleading) contemporary account of life at the court of Alexander VI.

Corvo, Frederick Baron. *A History of the Borgias.* New York: Modern Library, 1931. Written by an author every bit as colorful as his subjects, this elegant, overwrought, and hugely entertaining book revels in the more lurid aspects of the Borgia legacy. Despite its erudition and thorough research, this one should probably be read more as entertainment than as a work of scholarship.

Erlanger, Rachel. *Lucrezia Borgia: A Biography.* New York: Hawthorn Books, 1978. Though less impressive than Bellonci's treatment, this is an eminently readable biography treating Lucrezia as a hapless pawn in the dynastic program of her father and brother.

Gregorovius, Ferdinand. *Lucrezia Borgia: A Chapter from the Morals of the Italian Renaissance.* Translated by John Leslie Garner. New York: Phaidon, 1948. Written by the great nineteenth century German historian of medieval and Renaissance Rome, this meticulous and detailed study embodies the moralizing tone that has so long characterized treatments of Lucrezia's life and significance.

Johnson, Marion, and Georgina Masson. *The Borgias.* New York: Penguin Books, 2002. Originally published in 1981, this lively, readable, and relatively brief work is an important contribution to the ongoing rehabilitation of the Borgia reputation.

Mallett, Michael E. *The Borgias: The Rise and Fall of a Renaissance Dynasty.* New York: Barnes & Noble Books, 1969. One of the best English-language studies of the dynasty, Mallett's work examines the Borgia family fortunes in the context of the ever-shifting political circumstances of Renaissance Italy.

SEE ALSO: Alexander VI; Ludovico Ariosto; Cesare Borgia; Charles VIII; Vittoria Colonna; Louis XII; Niccolò Machiavelli; Ludovico Sforza.

RELATED ARTICLE in *Great Events from History: The Renaissance & Early Modern Era, 1454-1600:* 1500: Roman Jubilee.

HIERONYMUS BOSCH
Dutch painter

Bosch produced strikingly original paintings, whose brilliant style, flickering brushstrokes, and fantastic, nightmarish visions influenced twentieth century Surrealists. Bosch's message, however, is rooted in the preoccupations of the early sixteenth century. His obsessions—sin, death, and damnation—reflect orthodox Christian concerns.

BORN: c. 1450; 's-Hertogenbosch, North Brabant (now in the Netherlands)
DIED: August 9, 1516; 's-Hertogenbosch
ALSO KNOWN AS: Jeroen van Aeken
AREA OF ACHIEVEMENT: Art

EARLY LIFE

Hieronymus Bosch (hihr-AHN-uh-muhs BAHSH) was a fascinating early Netherlandish painter, in part because he was most puzzling. Little is known about his life. Like most northern Renaissance artists, he left no self-portraits, letters, diaries, or theoretical writings. Contemporary sources mention several works by him, but none of these survives. Conversely, the paintings that are attributed to him are all undocumented. Hundreds of works bear his name, but few of these signatures are authentic.

The two principal archival sources for Bosch are the city records of his hometown, 's-Hertogenbosch, and the account books of one of the town's confraternities, the Brotherhood of the Blessed Virgin. These documents reveal that Bosch's family had settled in 's-Hertogenbosch by the year 1426 and that Bosch entered the family business: His grandfather, three uncles, his father, and his brother were all painters, and Bosch was probably trained by a family member, most likely his father. Since Bosch's name does appear with regularity in the 's-Hertogenbosch archives, he must have lived there throughout his life. His family name was van Aeken (possibly a reference to the city of Aechen), but by 1504 he adopted Bosch as his surname, to refer to the town where he lived and worked.

Bosch, like his grandfather, uncles, and father, was a member of the Brotherhood of the Blessed Virgin, a large and wealthy confraternity devoted to the worship of the Virgin Mary. Much of Bosch's work for the brotherhood was created for their new chapel in the cathedral of 's-Hertogenbosch. He painted a panel of living and dead members, offered advice on gilding and polychroming a sculpted altarpiece, and designed a crucifix, a chandelier, and a stained glass window. None of this work survives.

Sometime between the years 1479 and 1481, Bosch was married to a wealthy woman, Aleyt Goyaerts van den Meervenne, the daughter of pharmacists. It has often been noted that alchemical equipment appears to underlie many of the forms in Bosch's most important work. Bosch could have become acquainted with such apparatuses through his in-laws.

There was no active court life in 's-Hertogenbosch, but documents show that the nobility elsewhere were patrons of Bosch. In 1504, Philip the Handsome, duke of Burgundy, commissioned an altarpiece of *The Last Judgment*, now lost, and Henry III of Nassau owned Bosch's most famous work, *The Garden of Earthly Delights*, by 1517. Margaret of Austria's inventory of 1516 includes paintings by Bosch, and in the middle of the sixteenth century Philip II, king of Spain, favored his works.

LIFE'S WORK

Bosch's art stands outside the mainstream of early Netherlandish painting. While Bosch's holy figures are plain and at times awkward, most Netherlandish artists, such as Jan van Eyck, Rogier van der Weyden, and Hans Memling, idealize and dignify the Holy Family and saints. While Bosch tended to paint thinly and rapidly, most Netherlandish painters used a painstaking technique of multilayered glazes and meticulous brushwork. Whereas Bosch showed little interest in the individual, portraiture is a hallmark of the early Netherlandish school. In addition, Bosch depicted themes that were new to large-scale painting, such as the *Haywain* and *The Ship of Fools*, and he interpreted traditional themes, such as *Hell* or *Christ Carrying the Cross*, in a strikingly original way. More fundamentally, evil and corruption dominate Bosch's world. Hermit saints, such as Saint Anthony, strive to resist temptation through the contemplative life, but, as scholar Max J. Friedländer observed, with Bosch, "innocence was pale." God is small and passive, humankind weak and sinful, and the Devil powerfully seductive. The disturbing quality of Bosch's works is far from the grace, beauty, and serenity that typify early Netherlandish painting.

Bosch's obsession with sin, death, and corruption expresses an undercurrent that is easily detected in northern Europe. Some in the North accepted new ideas, such as the Humanistic belief in the dignity of humanity; however, for others, the time around 1500 produced only fear, conflict, and uncertainty. Millennial fears were widespread; the *Malleus maleficarum* (1486; English translation, 1928), a handbook on witchcraft, was a best-seller. The disturbing quality sensed in Bosch's paintings can also be found, for example, in the contemporary work of German artists such as Matthias Grünewald, Hans Baldung Grien, and Hans Burgkmair and in sculptures of Death, alone or with a lover.

Dating early Netherlandish paintings is notoriously hazardous. None of Bosch's works can be dated with certainty. Scholars generally agree that the early works, generally dated before 1485, such as the *Adoration* in Philadelphia, are characterized by an uncertain sense of foreshortening and perspective, timid brushwork, and simple, traditional compositions. As Bosch matured, his brushwork became freer, more painterly; his perspective and foreshortening improved; and his paintings achieved a power, an immediacy not seen earlier. The *Landloper* in Rotterdam, the *Adoration* triptych in Madrid, and *The Crowning with Thorns* in London are generally viewed as late works, dating after 1500.

Scholars have suggested varying theories to explain Bosch's art. Some explanations, such as one that holds that Bosch was a member of a heretical sect, must be rejected as totally lacking in evidence. Others are more convincing. Astrology, alchemy, and Netherlandish folklore have been shown to be among the sources to which Bosch turned for his imagery. The widespread use of Netherlandish proverbs in Bosch's oeuvre has also been noted.

Bosch used a pictorial language that is largely lost to modern viewers. For example, his *Saint John the Baptist* shows an upright bear beneath a tree, a well-known symbol of the desert, used, for example, by Andrea Pisano on the Campanile and by the Limburg brothers (Pol, Hermann, and Jehanequin) in the *Belles Heures*. The saint's pose seems at first glance inappropriate; he seems to lounge on the ground. Yet his recumbent position, head in hand, refers to his dreamlike state, favorable for visions.

Modern scholarship has tried to place Bosch's art in its historical context. His images of Saint Anthony should, in part, be seen against the large numbers of victims suffering from Saint Anthony's Fire, a disease that produced hallucinations. Scholar Walter S. Gibson suggested that Bosch's works may have appealed to members of the societies of rhetoric and to the rich intellectual community of 's-Hertogenbosch.

Most scholars agree that Bosch held traditional, orthodox Christian views. For example, some of his works, such as the Philadelphia *Adoration* and the Madrid *Adoration* triptych, show Eucharistic symbolism. In the interior of the latter work, Bosch uses Old Testament prototypes and alludes to the Virgin as altar; on the exterior, he depicts *The Mass of Saint Gregory*. Many of his works moralize against sin, specifically lust (*The Ship of Fools* and *The Garden of Earthly Delights*) or avarice (*The Death of the Miser* and *Haywain*). Others point the way to a devout life. The numerous images of *Christ Carrying the Cross* suggest that one should imitate Christ, as the writings of the fifteenth century Dutch theologian Thomas à Kempis had advised. Bosch recommends the contemplative life through his depictions of hermit saints such as Saint Anthony.

Bosch's work remains, to a great extent, a puzzle. No literary or visual precedents are known. There is also considerable disagreement as to the interpretation of individual motifs. For example, the letter "M" that appears on the knives in Bosch's *The Garden of Earthly Delights* has been explained alternately as referring to the painters Jan Mandyn or Jan Mostaert; to Malignus, the Antichrist; to the word "mundus," meaning "the world"; to the male sex organ; and to a cutler of 's-Hertogenbosch.

The Garden of Earthly Delights reveals the artist's variety of sources, fertile imagination, brilliant style, and

Hieronymus Bosch. (Hulton|Archive by Getty Images)

moralizing message. The title dates from a later time; the contemporary title is unknown. The interior left wing shows Adam and Eve in the Garden of Eden. Bosch makes their identity clear by their nudity, the apple orchard behind, the serpent coiled around the palm tree in the left middle ground, and the animal-filled garden. The moment depicted is rare in large-scale painting: the introduction of Adam to Eve. Adam's position, seated on the ground, seems inappropriate, but it refers to an earlier incident, his creation from the earth. Adam gazes eagerly at Eve, who modestly casts down her eyes. The rabbit to her right refers to her fertility.

This is clearly not the typical Garden of Eden. Creepy, slimy animals crawl out of the pool in the foreground. Animals fight, kill, and devour one another. Monstrous animals and bizarre rock formations further indicate that this is a corrupt Earth. The central panel shows hordes of naked young men and women frolicking in an outdoor setting. Both blacks and whites are included to suggest all humankind. Bosch indicates their lust in several ways; directly, by depicting embracing couples; metaphorically, through oversize strawberries and fish; and by association, through references to fruits, animals, gardens, dancing, and bathing.

Bosch condemns these amorous activities. Genesis I:28 had advised: "Be fruitful and multiply and replenish the earth and subdue it and have dominion over the fish of the sea and over the fowl of the air and over every living thing that moveth upon the earth." Clearly, humankind has disobeyed God. No children are shown, and the oversize fish and birds overwhelm the people. The mouse about to enter the bubble that holds an embracing couple suggests that their act is unclean. The owl, which was thought to be evil in contemporary Dutch folklore because it attacked day birds, is embraced by a lustful youth. The hollowness and fragility of earthly things are indicated by the numerous egg shapes, glass tubes, shells, and bubbles, as well as by such motifs as the figures standing on their heads, precariously balanced on a narrow ledge encircling a cracked globe that bobs in the water.

The right interior wing depicts Hell, a nightmarish vision with fire and ice, monstrous devils, and countless tormented souls. A literary source for this wing is known. The anonymous *Vision of Tundale*, which was published in 's-Hertogenbosch in 1484, describes a monster who ingests and excretes damned sinners. Bosch also illustrates traditional punishments for specific vices. The glutton vomits; the avaricious excrete coins; the proud woman admires her reflection in the polished rear end of a demon.

Another traditional motif is the world upside down: The rabbit, dressed in a hunting jacket, blows a hunter's bugle as he carries, hanging by the feet from a pole, his booty: a man. Bosch reflects a popular Dutch saying with the woman whose arm is burned by a candle (the modern equivalent is "burning the candle at both ends"). The man who coasts on an oversized skate into a hole in the ice suggests the saying "to skate on thin ice."

SIGNIFICANCE

Although much of the content is traditional, Bosch's work stands apart, to some extent because of his wide variety of sources. Yet, more important, Bosch was able through his technical skill to translate his strikingly imaginative visions into visual form. His ability, for example, to express textures convincingly, whether ice or fire, metallic sheen or watery bubble, the strings of a lute or the smoke of Hell, made his visions believable. Bosch convinces one of the impossible. One accepts as reality, for example, the Tree-Man with barren trunks for legs, a broken eggshell body, and a face that wistfully directs its gaze at the viewer. Irrational visions haunt and frighten because they seem so real.

Bosch's message is moral: Beware the consequences of sin. His worldview is pessimistic: Humankind goes straight from a corrupt Eden to a world full of sinners, to a nightmarish Hell. No alternative is offered; the power of his art is overwhelming.

Bosch had a tremendous impact on his age. Hundreds of works dating from 1500 to 1530 show the imprint of his style. His nightmarish visions continue to haunt later generations. The Surrealists were his children; indeed, even in the 1980's a play based on *The Garden of Earthly Delights* was performed in New York.

—*Diane Wolfthal*

FURTHER READING

Belting, Hans. *Hieronymus Bosch, Garden of Earthly Delights*. New York: Prestel, 2002. Book-length study of one of Bosch's most famous and enigmatic works. Includes foldout illustration of the complete triptych, as well as many detail photographs. Also included are reproductions of related works.

Bosch, Hieronymus, et al. *Hieronymus Bosch: The Complete Paintings and Drawings*. Translated by Ted Alkins. New York: Harry N. Abrams, 2001. Definitive catalog of all paintings and drawings attributed to Bosch and his workshop, as well as reproductions of works by his contemporaries and by later artists who were influenced by him. Includes detail insets of every painting, as well as three essays by European scholars on Bosch's culture and the meaning of his work. Bibliographic references and index.

Dixon, Laurinda. *Bosch*. New York: Phaidon, 2003. Detailed interpretation of Bosch's works based on various aspects of his contemporary culture, including religion, science, medicine, alchemy, and new developments in the technology of painting. Includes color illustrations, map, bibliographic references, index.

Friedländer, Max J. *Geertgen tot Sint Jans and Jerome Bosch*. Vol. 5 in *Early Netherlandish Painting*. Edited by G. Lemmens. Translated by Heinz Norden. Leiden, the Netherlands: Sijthoff, 1969. The English translation of the 1927 edition. This is the fundamental discussion of Bosch's style and character. Includes a section on Bosch's drawings and engravings. Contains high-quality photographs of many works by Bosch and his school. Extremely well written.

Gibson, Walter S. *Hieronymus Bosch*. Reprint. New York: Thames and Hudson, 2001. A thoughtful, balanced survey of Bosch's life and art.

Koldeweij, Jos, Bernard Vermet, and Barbera van Kooij, eds. *Hieronymus Bosch: New Insights into His Life and Work*. Translated by Beth O'Brien et al. Rotterdam, the Netherlands: Museum Boijmans van Beuningen, 2001. Anthology of original essays by leading Bosch scholars, designed to be read by both laypeople and art historians. Includes illustrations, bibliographic references.

Snyder, James. *Northern Renaissance Art*. New York: Abrams, 1985. Includes one chapter on Bosch. Less cautious than Gibson. Good introductory text, meant for college undergraduates.

SEE ALSO: Pieter Bruegel, the Elder; Lucas Cranach, the Elder; Matthias Grünewald; Catharina van Hemessen; Margaret of Austria; Philip II.

RELATED ARTICLE in *Great Events from History: The Renaissance & Early Modern Era, 1454-1600:* c. 1500: Netherlandish School of Painting.

SANDRO BOTTICELLI
Italian painter

Botticelli has been celebrated for the linear flow of his paintings and for the graceful and thoughtful cast of so much of his work. One of the greatest colorists of Renaissance painting, Botticelli created idealized figures that suggest great spirituality and somewhat less interest in humanity than was depicted in the works of many of his contemporaries.

BORN: c. 1444; Florence (now in Italy)
DIED: May 17, 1510; Florence
ALSO KNOWN AS: Alessandro di Mariano dei Filipepi (given name)
AREA OF ACHIEVEMENT: Art

EARLY LIFE

Sandro Botticelli (bawt-tee-CHEHL-ee) was born Alessandro di Mariano Filipepi. Not much is known about his childhood or family life, except that, like many Florentine painters, he came from the artisan class. He grew up in an international city, already renowned for its art and commerce, for its wool and silk products, and for its bankers and princes—the Medicis, who determined much of the city's politics and art and who would become his patrons.

Around 1460, Botticelli was apprenticed to Fra Filippo Lippi, one of the greatest Florentine painters of the early Renaissance. Known especially for his coloring and draftsmanship, he was to exert a lifelong influence on Botticelli's work. Lippi conveyed enormous human interest in his religious paintings, a characteristic Botticelli emulated while expressing a much more exquisite sensitivity to the devotional aspects of his subjects.

Botticelli's earliest commissioned paintings date from about 1470. The figure of *Fortitude*, now in the Uffizi in Florence, reveals many of his mature qualities and interests, as well as details he learned to apply in Lippi's workshop. *Fortitude* is portrayed as a full-figured woman with a characteristically swelling midsection and delicately featured face. The small head, angled toward her left shoulder, and her eyes, following the line of her left arm, suggest a contemplative, even melancholy, figure, whose thoughts are drawn together as tightly as her tiny closed mouth. The only expansive part of her face is her forehead, which is high and wide, and decorated with a pearl-studded crown (a touch borrowed from Lippi). This is a monumental work, which suggests both great volume and extraordinary finesse.

A companion piece from this period, *Judith and Her Maid*, depicts the characters walking through a beautiful landscape, returning to the Israelite camp after Judith has severed the head of Holofernes with a sword. Sword in one hand, and olive branch in the other, the picture of Judith with her head inclined toward her right shoulder resembles the figure of *Fortitude*. Although the sword is bloody, her expression is contemplative and in marked contrast to the maid, whose head juts forward under the strain of carrying Holofernes' head. Judith, in the foreground of the painting, seems to inhabit a space of her own, a spirituality to which the maid and the background landscape must be subordinated. Judith's face resembles Lippi's Madonnas, and the utterly composed quality of her expression is starkly contrasted with the battling troops, just visible on a plain below the path of Judith's progress. In this painting, Botticelli first seems to grasp the division between the realms of the mystical and the natural that is characteristic of his later work.

LIFE'S WORK

Botticelli is renowned for painting several versions of *Adoration of the Magi*, which can be studied as evidence of his artistic development. There is, for example, a painting (1482) in the National Gallery of Art in Washington, D.C., that is remarkable for its vivid color and for its striking portrayal of individual figures—all arranged in highly distinctive reverential positions. At the apex of the painting are the Madonna and Child, framed by a monumental yet open-ended and airy architectural structure; its triangular roof (through which the blue sky can be seen) is paralleled by the human triangle of the Magi presenting their gifts to the Christ child. This is a beautiful painting that reads like a moment of suspended time. It also has a subtlety and suggestiveness to it that is less apparent in a version at the Uffizi (c. 1475), in which the portraits of figures at the Adoration are more individualized and realistic but also somehow less important, because they contribute less to the meaning of the whole composition.

In a modern restoration of *Adoration of the Magi*, however, it was discovered that the painting had been cropped, so that earlier comments by art historians on the painting's restrictiveness have had to be revised. As in the earlier painting of Judith, the restored Uffizi *Adoration of the Magi* shows Botticelli employing an open landscape in the background to give perspective to the spiritualized content of his enclosed space.

The power of spirit over space is evident in Botticelli's painting *Saint Augustine in His Cell* (c. 1495). Augustine

Sandro Botticelli. (Hulton|Archive by Getty Images)

is presented as a massive, robed figure, holding a book in his powerful left hand while his right hand, with open tensile fingers, is stretched diagonally across his upper body. That he is in the grip of intense thought is also indicated by the lines of concentration on his forehead and his strongly focused eyes. While he is surrounded by the implements of the scholar and the churchman, his gaze is clearly heavenward, for he transcends all earthly instruments, which are merely the means to a spiritual end.

In such paintings, Botticelli retains enough objects and pays enough attention to the human body to create a sense of realism, but in comparison with his contemporaries it is evident that he is more concerned with the spiritual presence of his subjects. Thus, they are less individualized in terms of their clothing or bodily structure. For all his massiveness, Augustine has none of the muscularity associated with Renaissance painting. Similarly, the details of a scholar's study are kept to a minimum and the sense of a domestic scene is not emphasized, especially when compared with the paintings of Saint Jerome by Ghirlandajo, Jan van Eyck, and Petrus Christus, which served as models for Botticelli's Augustine.

As significant as his religious painting is Botticelli's treatment of classical subjects. Two of his most famous paintings, *Primavera* (c. 1478) and *The Birth of Venus* (c. 1480's), reflect his concern for line and form rather than for story or for close copying of his Greek models. The central figure of *Primavera* has been taken to be Venus, surrounded by the dancing Graces of spring. The figure's expression suggests much of the same pensiveness of his Madonnas, as does her oval-shaped, tilted head and rounded body. Although an allegorical scene is being illustrated, which includes Flora (the figure of spring), Mercury, Zephyr, and Cupid in order to suggest the arousal of passion in the new season, most commentators have been struck by the elegant choreography of the setting, in which the Graces appear to be dancing while lightly touching one another and entwining their hands. There is a dreaminess, a magical lightness to this locale that evokes the feeling of spring.

For sheer elegance, Botticelli never surpassed *The Birth of Venus*. She stands in the nude on a seashell, blown to shore by the entwined allegorical figures of the winds at her left. Like so many of his female figures, Venus has soft lines—narrow, rounded shoulders and breasts and an upper body that swells out gracefully to wide hips and a rounded stomach. It is the continuity and fullness of his figures that constitutes beauty, not muscle tone or bone. Venus's attendant, at her left, moves toward her with billowing clothes, while the serene goddess stands perfectly poised with knees slightly bent, her hair flowing in the wind. Botticelli had classical sources for this rendering of Venus, but as in *Primavera*, the overwhelming impression of the painting is of the arrival of beauty and perfection, of an aesthetic ideal that is meant to be treasured in and for itself and not particularly for what it represents in myth.

SIGNIFICANCE

Ethereal feminine beauty is so much a part of Botticelli's classical and religious paintings that it has been speculated that he was deeply influenced by the Neoplatonists, who equated the concept of Beauty with Truth. Botticelli's Venus and his Madonnas could have the same expression, these critics argue, because their perfection was emblematic of the divine. Clearly the unity of his paintings and the way they minimize narrative in favor of tableaux suggests a Platonic bias. The softness of his colors, the vagueness of his landscapes, and his lack of interest in the structure of the human form are reflective of a sensibility that yearns toward some deep, inner mystical sense of the origins of things.

Although Botticelli was viewed as a technically resourceful painter in his time, he was eventually eclipsed by Leonardo da Vinci, whose range of human gestures, dynamic compositions, and use of light and shade made Botticelli seem old-fashioned. Not until the late nineteenth century, when he was taken up by the English Pre-Raphaelites, was Botticelli reinstated. To them, he represented the simplicity and sincerity of early Italian art. Similarly, the nineteenth century English art critic John Ruskin used Botticelli as an example of an artist who presented nature and human figures as expressions of a divinely created world. Art historians still marvel at the refinement, purity, and poignancy of Botticelli's painting. His figures have an otherworldly aura that is attributed to the artist's own faith. His paintings are not so much illustrations of his subjects as they are the subjects themselves—as though the apprehension of eternal beauty and perfection were itself a matter composed of his rhythmical lines, soothing colors, and elongated shapes.

—*Carl Rollyson*

FURTHER READING

Baldini, Umberto, ed. *Primavera: The Restoration of Botticelli's Masterpiece*. Translated by Mary Fitton. New York: Harry N. Abrams, 1986. Although this book concentrates on one painting (it includes several essays by different art critics), it also provides important criticism of Botticelli's other works and a helpful description of his period in history. A useful bibliography, an index, and handsome color plates make this an indispensable volume on the artist.

Ettlinger, Leopold D., and Helen S. Ettlinger. *Botticelli*. New York: Oxford University Press, 1977. An excellent introduction to Botticelli's oeuvre, including 138 illustrations, eighteen in color. An annotated bibliography and an index make this a particularly useful resource.

Hatfield, Rab. *Botticelli's Uffizi "Adoration": A Study in Pictorial Content*. Princeton, N.J.: Princeton University Press, 1976. As the subtitle indicates, this is a specialized study, aimed at developing a vocabulary to describe the pictorial content of Botticelli's paintings. All plates are in black and white. Essentially a book for advanced scholars, this might prove useful to students concentrating on one aspect of the artist's career.

Kanter, Laurence B., Hilliard T. Goldfarb, and James Hankins. *Botticelli's Witness: Changing Style in a Changing Florence*. Boston: Isabella Stewart Gardner Museum, 1997. Exhibition catalog contains forty illustrations as well as three essays detailing the relationship of Botticelli's work to Florentine culture and surveying the history of Botticelli criticism.

Lightbrown, Ronald. *Complete Catalogue.* Vol. 2 in *Sandro Botticelli.* Berkeley: University of California Press, 1978. This is an enormous work of scholarship, identifying paintings attributed to the young Botticelli, autograph paintings, workshop paintings, drawings, works wrongly attributed to Botticelli, and lost works. This book will help to correct errors made in earlier volumes of art criticism and history. Each catalog entry includes a description of the work, its condition, location, history, and background. Also notes whether a given work exists in other versions.

_____. *Life and Work.* Vol. 1 in *Sandro Botticelli.* Berkeley: University of California Press, 1978. Reprint. New York: Abbeville Press, 1989. This is a superb study, with individual chapters on the artist's early life, his early works, his relationship with the Medicis, his period in Rome, his religious and secular paintings, and his drawings. An appendix of documents, notes, an annotated bibliography, and an index make this an essential and accessible scholarly work.

Venturi, Lionello. *Botticelli.* 2d ed. London: Phaidon Press, 1971. A competent introduction to Botticelli's life and work, with helpful references to his place in the history of art criticism. Forty-eight large color plates make this an especially good volume for studying the paintings.

Zöllner, Frank. *Botticelli: Images of Love and Spring.* Translated by Fiona Elliott. New York: Prestel, 1998. Interpretation of several famous Botticelli paintings, focusing on the artist's intent that they be hung in bridal chambers, as well as the influence of classical and Renaissance iconography on the works. Includes illustrations and bibliographic references.

SEE ALSO: Leonardo da Vinci; Cosimi I de' Medici; Lorenzo de' Medici; Piero della Francesca; Raphael; Sixtus IV.

RELATED ARTICLES in *Great Events from History: The Renaissance & Early Modern Era, 1454-1600:* 1462: Founding of the Platonic Academy; 1477-1482: Work Begins on the Sistine Chapel; c. 1500: Revival of Classical Themes in Art.

SOPHIE BRAHE
Danish astronomer and alchemist

Sophie Brahe assisted her brother, noted astronomer Tycho Brahe, in making and recording sky observations, including the lunar eclipse of 1573. Most historians consider that her greater lifetime contributions were in the fields of genealogy and horticulture. Sophie produced a substantial manuscript recording the genealogy of sixty Danish noble families and was well known for the magnificent gardens she designed and the rare plants she grew.

BORN: September 22, 1556, or August 24, 1559; Knutstorp Castle, Scandia, Denmark (now in Sweden)

DIED: 1643; Elsinore, Denmark

ALSO KNOWN AS: Sophie Brahe Thott; Sophie Brahe Lange

AREAS OF ACHIEVEMENT: Astronomy, science and technology

EARLY LIFE

The Brahe (BRAH-hee) family at the time of Sophie's birth had a long and noble history both in Denmark and in Sweden. Beate Bille and Otto Brahe were Sophie's parents. Otto was governor of Helsingborg Castle in Denmark and considered to be a generous and kind ruler who was fond of studies and learning. As the youngest of ten children, Sophie was born when her oldest brother, Tycho Brahe, was a teenager.

In the later half of the sixteenth century, Scandinavia was in the midst of a cultural renaissance. Denmark as a country placed great store in education and often cosseted men of learning, providing them with income and property holdings, which supported continued studies. Yet even in a renaissance, the right to an education was reserved for wealthy men. Brahe was unique among her female contemporaries in that Otto paid to have her schooled at home. Brahe's desire for knowledge was strong enough that she continued to educate herself once the formal education provided by her father ended. She was superbly fluent in German and confident also in Latin. Tycho, recognizing his sister's great intellect, also undertook to teach her, specifically subjects of interest to him such as chemistry, alchemy, and astronomy.

Brahe was reared at Helsingborg Castle and at Knutstorp Castle, the family seat in Scandia in the most southern province of the Scandinavian Peninsula, which was then still a part of Denmark. Following her father's illness and death in 1571, the family withdrew to Knutstorp, where young Brahe was able to spend time with Tycho. Sophie's older brother was building a chemistry lab in the nearby Abbey and pursuing his astronomy dreams. Brahe was a teenager when she assisted Tycho in his observations of the December 8, 1573, lunar eclipse.

LIFE'S WORK

Over the next thirty years, Sophie Brahe often assisted Tycho in his work while continuing to educate herself. How much work Brahe did with Tycho cannot be fully appreciated since few records exist that credit Brahe directly. It is known that Tycho trusted her absolutely and that she not only helped but also actually participated in his astronomy work.

Brahe was a woman of noble birth who, despite being brilliant and learned, also had social responsibilities other than her passionate pursuit of knowledge. In her early twenties, Brahe married the rich nobleman Otte Thott. The marriage of convenience was apparently a happy one resulting in the birth of a son, Tage Thott, on May 27, 1580. The Thott family lived in luxury at Eriksholm Castle (now Trolleholm) in Scandia.

Even as a married woman, however, Brahe found time to assist Tycho. Records indicate that she was a frequent visitor to Tycho's island observatory, Uraniborg. On one auspicious occasion in August, 1586, Queen Sophie of Denmark and Norway visited Uraniborg. Sophie Brahe arrived two days before the queen, most likely to help her brother in his hosting of the royal guests.

Brahe was widowed in 1588 and found respite from grief by throwing herself into a variety of pursuits. She created a superb Renaissance garden at the Eriksholm estate. Her unique horticultural design included a chemical laboratory within the garden, which she used to create alchemic medications.

Brahe also taught herself the basics of astrology and horoscopes. In the sixteenth century, astrology was fashionable. Star charts and heavenly based predictions were believed true and prophetic. Tycho did not want to teach astrology to Sophie, having lost faith in the art and believing that the subject was too abstract for a woman. He relented after she determined to master the field with or without his help. Brahe's skills were respected and in demand. She is said to have carried a book that contained friends' horoscopes. Tycho came to think enough of her

skill to publish her astrology work, even though publication of learned letters written by women was rare.

Brahe's knowledge of chemistry and alchemy is believed to have rivaled that of her gifted and famous brother. Her potions, elixirs, and medicines were in demand by noble and commoner alike. As was true of many alchemists in the sixteenth century, at some point she fell prey to the lure of riches promised for the transmutation of base metals into gold. In this futile pursuit, she also found a soul mate in Erik Lange, brother-in-law to her brother Knud Brahe. Sadly, their transmutation quest would bring financial ruin first to Lange and eventually to Sophie.

Early in 1590, Brahe and Lange were betrothed. Every member of Brahe's family except Tycho was against the match, primarily because of Lange's obsession with alchemy. Lange eventually became so mired in debt that he fled Denmark to escape debtors. For most of twelve years, the lovers were separated. Lange was in exile and Brahe would not leave Denmark until her son was old enough to assume his inheritance.

Though in favor of the match, Tycho felt compelled to attempt to warn Sophie and Erik against the folly of their scientific pursuits. Around 1594, Tycho wrote *Urania Titani*, a 700-verse Latin poem in the form of a letter from Sophie to Erik. In it, Tycho blended a biography of his sister with a discussion of the validity of alchemy and astronomy as sciences. Tycho painted a picture of Sophie as a confident and talented woman, focusing on her successes in horticulture, chemistry, and astronomy. It also looked at her as a young widow in a time of grief. The poem is considered masterful. Tycho denounced alchemy as a science by masking the discussion in the format of a love letter between Sophie and Erik.

Due to the practice of recording only the accomplishments of men, history has largely overlooked Brahe's contributions to astronomy and chemistry. History has been no kinder to her accomplishments in astrology and alchemy and has barely acknowledged her gifts for horticulture. History has, however, fully acknowledged her role in recording the genealogy of the noble houses of Denmark. In 1600, Brahe completed the first edition of a huge genealogical manuscript that detailed the heritage of Scandinavian noble families.

In 1602, with her manuscript completed and her son grown and in control of his estates, she finally was free to marry Lange. It was not to be a pleasant life for the couple. Lange remained deeply in debt and obsessed with transmutation. Their great debt forced them to live abroad in poverty. On Lange's death in 1613, Brahe returned to Denmark and Elsinore.

Brahe remained active, even near the end of her life in her eighties. She grew rare plants, corresponded with friends and family, and pursued her scientific interests. In 1626, she completed the second edition of her nine-hundred-page genealogical manuscript detailing and charting some sixty noble families. The manuscript resides in the library of Stockholm's Lund University.

SIGNIFICANCE

Brahe was a cultured and learned woman who would be outstanding in any age and was especially unusual for her time. In *Urania Titani*, Tycho said that Sophie "has a strong mind and so much self-confidence that she is equal to any man in spiritual matters. . . ." Her brilliant and questing mind drove her to excel in chemistry, alchemy, astronomy, horticulture, and genealogy, fields of endeavor all but closed to women of the sixteenth century.

—*C. K. Zulkosky*

FURTHER READING

Christianson, John Robert. *On Tycho's Island: Tycho Brahe and His Assistants, 1570-1601.* New York: Cambridge University Press, 2000. Includes the most comprehensive English-language resource about Sophie Brahe and also detailed information about her contemporaries.

Dreyer, J. L. E. *Tycho Brahe: A Picture of Scientific Life and Work in the Sixteenth Century.* New York: Dover, 1963. Unabridged and corrected reprint of an 1890 publication. Less than a dozen pages refer to Sophie Brahe and are spread throughout the book, but the pages are indexed.

Zeeberg, Peter. *Tycho Brahes "Urania Titani": Et digt om Sophie Brahe.* Copenhagen: Museum Tusculanums Forlag, 1994. Biography of Sophie Brahe written by her brother Tycho in seven hundred Latin verses. Includes a Dutch translation of the poem and a summary in English.

SEE ALSO: Tycho Brahe.

RELATED ARTICLES in *Great Events from History: The Renaissance & Early Modern Era, 1454-1600:* 1572-1574: Tycho Brahe Observes a Supernova; 1576-1612: Reign of Rudolf II; 1580's-1590's: Galileo Conducts His Early Experiments.

TYCHO BRAHE
Danish astronomer

Brahe realized early that the existing means for observing and measuring celestial bodies and their motions were inaccurate. His great achievements led to significant improvements in existing instruments, the invention of new instruments, and amazingly accurate observations.

BORN: December 14, 1546; Knudstrup Castle, Scandia, Denmark (now in Sweden)
DIED: October 24, 1601; Prague, Bohemia (now in the Czech Republic)
ALSO KNOWN AS: Tyge Brahe Ottosøn
AREAS OF ACHIEVEMENT: Astronomy, mathematics, science and technology

EARLY LIFE

Tycho Brahe (TI-koh BRAH-hee), born Tyge Brahe Ottosøn, was the eldest of ten children born to Otto Brahe. The Brahes were an old and noble family with both Danish and Swedish branches. Tyge's father was privy councillor to the king of Denmark at the time of Tyge's birth and ended as governor of Helsingborg Castle in Scandia—then part of Denmark. Tycho was not reared with his parents and younger siblings. His father's brother Jørgen, who was childless, stole him while he was still a baby. Initial turmoil in the family was stilled when Otto's second son was born. It was therefore in the home of his uncle that Tyge was reared, showing so much early scholarly promise that, in addition to the requisite training for a young nobleman in horseback riding and swordsmanship, he was allowed to learn Latin in the hope that he would become a statesman and counselor to the king.

At thirteen, Tyge entered the University of Copenhagen, head held high above a piped collar and small rapiers by his side. Thirteen was not an unusual age for university entry at the time. He studied, as did most of his colleagues, philosophy, rhetoric, and law. The curriculum was in Latin. His academic career was planned for him: After finishing his studies in Denmark, he would go to one of the more famous German universities and study law, still in preparation for a career in government. The problem was that young Tyge (he took the name Tycho on graduation) was not interested in law. An event that took place on August 21, 1560, when he was nearly fourteen, came to fascinate him so deeply that it, in effect, determined his choice of career. He heard that an eclipse of the sun had been predicted for that day. That the prediction proved to be correct and that the sun was indeed eclipsed seemed to him divine.

It was not considered good form for one of Brahe's social station to become a mere scientist, and his fascination with astronomy was greeted with far less than enthusiasm by his uncle and father. His astronomical studies were performed in secrecy and at night. When he went to Germany, a tutor accompanied him to ensure that he did not stray from his legal studies. The two arrived in Leipzig in 1562, when Brahe was not quite sixteen. Anders Sørensen Vedel, the tutor, kept a rapt eye on his charge, and Brahe studied law by day and reserved his nights for gazing at the stars. He also managed to study mathematics, which would be necessary for him in his astronomical studies, and he met two of the more famous astronomers of his day, who happened to reside in Leipzig—Bartholomaeus Scultetus and Valentin Thau. The instruments he used for his observations were quite crude: a globe, a compass, and a radius.

LIFE'S WORK

The tutor eventually became aware of his charge's illicit nightly activities, and the two of them were called home to be under Jørgen Brahe's intense scrutiny. Yet Jørgen died not long afterward, leaving the nineteen-year-old Brahe wealthy and independent. Brahe could embark on his life's work. For a while, out of a sense of duty, he performed his responsibilities as a nobleman and oversaw the Tostrup estate in Scandia that was part of his inheritance. In 1566, however, he decided to make his scientific studies the center of his life and activities.

To the accompaniment of his family's scorn, Brahe moved to Wittenberg and worked with Kaspar Peucer, a then-famous astronomer, until an outbreak of the plague forced his return to Denmark. Later, he went to Augsburg because of its famous instrument makers; he wanted new, more precise, better designed instruments made for his observations. He had a new globe, sextant, and radius made. His fame in the scientific community began to grow.

Brahe concentrated his early studies on the apparent movements of the planets and the fixed stars. His father's death and an appointment as cantor of the Roskilde Cathedral devoured much of his time, but he steadfastly

Tycho Brahe. (Frederick Ungar Publishing Co.)

continued his work. His growing fame changed the attitudes of his family and peers toward his work: His uncle Steen Brahe had a lab outfitted for him. His first major breakthrough was the observation of a new star, first seen on November 11, 1572. The star, which he appropriately called Stella Nova in a book entitled *De nova et nullius aevi memoria prius visa stella* (1573; about the new star), appeared in the Cassiopeia constellation. Large and bright, the new star remained visible until 1574. The accuracy of the observations, down to the minute details, caused a sensation in the scientific community, and Brahe was established as a great scholar.

Brahe, at this time a grown man, cut quite a striking figure. Bejeweled and flamboyantly dressed, he was stocky, with reddish-yellow hair combed forward to hide incipient baldness, and he sported a pointed beard and a flowing mustache. When he was young and while in Germany, Brahe had been in a duel, and his opponent sliced off a large piece of his nose, for which Brahe had a substitute made of gold and silver and painted to look natural. He always carried a box with glue and salve.

Brahe's plan was to settle abroad and continue his studies, but the king changed his plans by donating to him the small island of Ven, in the channel between Denmark and Sweden. The position of the island was perfect for his purposes, and Brahe accepted the generous offer. On Ven, he built his famous observatory: the architecturally beautiful Uraniborg (after the muse of astronomy Urania), which contained a chemistry lab, his famous mural quadrant, and observatories in the attic. He also built the smaller, but equally famous, Stellaburg, which, except for a cupola, was built underground. This building contained many observational instruments, including his renowned revolving quadrant. It also had portraits, in the round, of the greats of astronomy: Timocharis, Hipparchus, Ptolemy, Nicolaus Copernicus, and himself.

On the official front, Brahe became royal mathematician and lecturer at the University of Copenhagen. Little is known about his private life. He married a bondwoman, Kirstine, by whom he had eight children, five girls and three boys. Brahe did not reveal this part of his life in his own writings, and his contemporaries restricted themselves to expressing disapproval of this alliance. In his observatories, he continued his work, making surprisingly accurate observations of celestial bodies. He always had a number of students living with him, who helped him in his observations.

By 1582, Brahe had reached a point at which he could propose his own astronomical system. He rejected both the static Ptolemaic system with the sun and planets moving around Earth in individual orbits and the Copernican system, which has Earth and the other planets moving around the sun. Brahe's system is an amalgam. For reasons involving both the laws of physics and the Bible, he could not accept a system that makes Earth simply one of the planets that revolve around the sun. In Brahe's system, Earth is static and the moon and the sun revolve around it, with the other planets revolving around the sun. It remained for Brahe's student Johannes Kepler to reinstate the correct Copernican system reinforced by Brahe's minutely correct measurements and observations.

On Ven, Brahe had his own printing press and published, besides his own works, calendars and horoscopes for the king and other high dignitaries. Like many of his contemporaries, Brahe did not distinguish sharply between astronomy and astrology, but he apparently did not think highly of horoscopes and made them only under duress. Many kings and dignitaries from around Europe visited the island to see the famous observatories.

On the island, Brahe did the bulk of his scientific work. He made accurate observations of the sun, moon, and planets. Many scholars find that his greatest achievement, besides his introduction of the use of transversals on the graduated arcs of astronomical instruments and his improvements of existing instruments (such as the equatorial armillae, which are spheres used to establish differences in longitude and latitude), was his catalog of fixed stars, which stood until such improved instruments as telescopes and clocks of precision came into use.

Unfortunately, Brahe did not adhere to his scientific studies. As he grew older, his idiosyncrasies became more obvious and he became involved in some petty suits that alienated the king, who had been one of his staunchest supporters. Brahe's intransigence finally caused the king to confiscate land that had been bequeathed to him, leaving Brahe without an adequate source of income.

Finally, in July, 1597, Brahe left native shores and moved to Rostock, Germany. He sent a submissive letter to King Christian IV, in which he asked the king to take him back into his good graces. The letter elicited a direct and angry response from the king, who said that until Brahe came to his senses, admitted his faults, and promised to do as he was told, he should not return.

Brahe, determined not to give in, decided to find a new mentor. He approached Emperor Rudolf II in Prague. Rudolf had a reputation as a patron of the sciences and indeed took Brahe and his collaborator Kepler under his wing. The two famous astronomers had, at times, a stormy relationship, and, after several years, Kepler had a nervous breakdown and left Prague. Brahe died on October 24, 1601, in Prague.

SIGNIFICANCE

Tycho Brahe was a transitional figure in the history of astronomy. His theoretical work was flawed and actually a step back from the work of Copernicus. His great achievements were in the areas of practical and spherical astronomy. He devised new and more sophisticated instruments for observations and recorded an astounding body of observations that represented a quantum leap forward in knowledge about the movements and relative positions of celestial bodies.

Brahe's observatories represented the state of the art in sixteenth century astronomy. Here he gazed at and recorded the stars, made mathematical computations, and had his most famous instruments built and installed: three equatorial armillae; a mural quadrant, which he used to determine time; and sextants with transversals on the graduated arc and improved sights that allowed for pointing the instrument with great precision to measure distances and angles.

Brahe's legacy, which has made him, in one biographer's somewhat hyperbolic phrase, "a king among astronomers," is his large body of accurate observations and measurements performed by means of instruments and methods devised by him.

—Per Schelde

FURTHER READING

Christianson, John Robert. *On Tycho's Island: Tycho Brahe and His Assistants, 1570-1601.* New York: Cambridge University Press, 2000. Extensive study of Brahe's life and accomplishments in many fields, including philosophy, chemistry, poetry, and reform. The book focuses especially on the vital intellectual community he created, and it provides short biographies of more than twenty members of that community. Includes illustrations, maps, bibliographic references, and index.

_____. *Tycho Brahe: A Picture of Scientific Life and Work in the Sixteenth Century.* Reprint. New York: Dover, 1963. The most detailed work on Brahe in terms of his work and studies. Early in the book, Dreyer sets the general scientific and astronomical stage Brahe was to enter. While somewhat technical, the book gives a thorough and minute description of Brahe's instruments and observations.

Ferguson, Kitty. *Tycho and Kepler: The Unlikely Partnership That Forever Changed Our Understanding of the Heavens.* New York: Walker, 2002. Tells the story of the relationship between Brahe's work and Kepler's, as well as the relationship between the two men.

Argues that neither would have achieved fame or lasting effects on science without each other's aid. Includes eight pages of photographic plates, illustrations, maps, bibliographic references, and index.

Gade, John Allyne. *The Life and Times of Tycho Brahe.* Princeton, N.J.: Princeton University Press, 1947. Reprint. New York: Greenwood Press, 1969. Gade gives the social and political backdrop to Brahe's life and work. His emphasis is not so much on technical descriptions as on Brahe the person and the community member. Gade writes amusingly of Brahe's childhood and youth and gives a fairly complex psychological profile of the adult scientist and nobleman. The most personal portrait of Brahe extant.

Gray, R. A. "Life and Work of Tycho Brahe." *Royal Astronomical Society of Canada Journal* 17 (1923). Starts with a careful statement of the Ptolemaic and other theories current before the advent of Brahe. Lists among Brahe's achievements his statement that comets are not, as previously believed, within Earth's atmosphere. Also mentions Brahe's improvements on existing instruments.

Thoren, Victor E., with John R. Christianson. *The Lord of Uraniborg: A Biography of Tycho Brahe.* New York: Cambridge University Press, 1990. Massive and comprehensive biography that attempts to reevaluate and reinterpret nearly every aspect of Brahe's career and contribution to science. Includes illustrations, bibliographic references, index.

SEE ALSO: Sophie Brahe; Giordano Bruno; Nicolaus Copernicus; William Gilbert; John Napier; Georg von Peuerbach; Rheticus.

RELATED ARTICLES in *Great Events from History: The Renaissance & Early Modern Era, 1454-1600:* 1572-1574: Tycho Brahe Observes a Supernova; 1576-1612: Reign of Rudolf II.

DONATO BRAMANTE
Italian architect

One of the greatest architects of the Italian Renaissance, Bramante stands out for the pure classicism of his buildings. His influence and work extended throughout Europe, including his design for St. Peter's Cathedral in Rome.

BORN: 1444; Monte Asdruvaldo, near Urbino, Papal States (now in Italy)
DIED: April 11, 1514; Rome, Papal States (now in Italy)
ALSO KNOWN AS: Donato d'Agnolo; Donato d'Angelo; Donato di Pascuccio d'Antonio; Bramante Lazzari
AREA OF ACHIEVEMENT: Architecture

EARLY LIFE

Donato Bramante (doh-NAH-to brah-MAHN-tay) took his father's nickname, Il Bramante (the dreamer), as his cognomen. At first a painter, he may have studied at Mantua with Andrea Mantegna and with Piero della Francesca at Urbino. Their influence is visible in Bramante's interest in the science of perspective. At Mantua, he may have met the architect Leon Battista Alberti, designing there his noted church of S. Andrea.

LIFE'S WORK

In the 1470's, Bramante primarily designed architectural decorations for interiors and facades. In the new ducal palace at Urbino in about 1476, he helped decorate the *studiolo* of the duke of Urbino. In this small office, the walls are covered with pictures formed by inlaid wood of different tones so as to create an atmosphere both of intimacy and of illusionary space. Bramante also made illustrations of illusionistic perspective in the duke's chapel and library.

At Urbino, Bramante had access to the graceful architectural plans of Luciano Laurana, patronized by the duke of Urbino along with Piero della Francesca. Alberti may have contributed to the design of the new palace, influencing Bramante, who would soon become an architect. Alberti's classically inspired treatise on architecture, as well as those of Filarete and Francesco di Giorgio, were certainly available as manuals for Bramante. In the Palazzo del Podestà in Bergamo in 1477, Bramante created the illusion of "opening" a wall by painting on it a loggia or corridor, with philosophers seated between the columns.

From about 1479 to 1499, Bramante was in Milan. His first project there was to construct the three-aisled, barrel-vaulted, domed church of S. Maria presso (near)

S. Satiro, a diminutive ninth century Carolingian church. About this same time (1481) can be dated the large print prepared by Prevedari. It contains fanciful classical architectural themes and is signed by Bramante.

Commissioned by Cardinal Ascanio Sforza, Bramante's plan for the cathedral of Pavia in 1488 foreshadowed in boldness his future conception for St. Peter's. A high dome was to rest on eight massive piers, creating a large central space. The choir was to be cruciform, its three arms ending in apses, the whole arranged in a harmonious hierarchy of proportions. In 1492, Bramante left the project, which was completed after his death and much altered by later architects.

Bramante designed the loggia (or *ponticella*) of Ludovico Sforza and decorated some rooms in Castello Sforzesco, of which all that remains is his painting of mythical Argus. The Brera Pinacoteca contains paintings certainly by Bramante: *Christ at the Pillar* and eight frescoes of artists and warriors that, with his *Heraclitus* and *Democritus*, once decorated a room in Milan's Palazzo Panigarola. In these, Bramante painted shadows that reflected the actual light source and give the figures an impression of three-dimensionality.

Leonardo da Vinci came to Milan in 1482, and his writings manifest a respect for Bramante. The latter may have learned to appreciate the "central space" concept from Leonardo's sketches of Greek-cross type churches. Both worked for the monks of Santa Maria delle Grazie, where Leonardo painted *The Last Supper* and where, from 1492 to 1497, Bramante constructed a choir and transepts. The crossing of nave and transepts here is a spacious open square surmounted by a dome-on-pendentives spanning sixty-five feet. Outside, this interior dome appears as a sixteen-windowed cylinder or drum with sloping roof and a lantern. The crossing was planned as a crypt area for the ducal Sforza family of Milan, Bramante's employers.

During these same years, Bramante designed, for Cardinal Sforza, Duke Ludovico's brother, several cloisters for the Abbey of S. Ambrogio (1492-1497); some additions to the ducal palace at Vigevano, where he resided while in Milan at least until 1495; and a west facade for the abbey church at Abbiategrasso (1497). He also designed a partial city plan, whose main feature was a large square like that of S. Marco in Venice, but here serving as a court area between palace and cathedral. The work was interrupted by the French invasion of Milan in 1499, which relieved Bramante of several unfinished projects.

Also in 1499, Bramante arrived in a Rome electric with building activity in preparation for the coming jubilee year. The popes had even authorized the use of the Colosseum and other ancient monuments as stone quarries. Bramante received immediate employment to design a cloister for S. Maria della Pace, a two-storied arcade or loggia that on the ground level appears as a wall in which round arches have been cut. Its Ionic pilasters continue above, supporting a horizontal architrave. Between these, slender columns ride directly above the centers of the arches below, creating twice as many openings above as below.

Bramante's famous *Tempietto* absorbed him in 1501-1502. As a sort of monumental reliquary built on the spot where Saint Peter was reputedly crucified, it had the round design and central plan customary for churches commemorating martyrdom. It is a two-storied drum of only fifteen feet in diameter, with a dome and a lantern. Around it is a Doric colonnade supporting a classical triglyph-metope architrave. Above, the drum is pierced by alternating windows and shell-topped niches. It achieves perfectly the avowed Renaissance aim to imitate the dignity of classical antiquity.

Donato Bramante. (Library of Congress)

Appalled by the wholesale destruction of ancient Rome in the interests of Holy Year, Bramante campaigned for preservation of the past, or at least of an exact plan of imperial Rome. His first years there saw him devoted to drawings and three-dimensional projections of ancient monuments (his own new technique). His study of antiquity taught him much about Roman building secrets, most notably that of inserting brick ribs into walls before filling them with concrete. The new St. Peter's, built on a scale many times greater than normal, would depend on this knowledge.

Bramante's career in Rome (1500-1514) is closely tied to the regime of Pope Julius II (1503-1513). The architect rearranged the streets of Rome for this pope, receiving the nickname "Ruinante" because of his destruction of old streets and of so much of old St. Peter's. Julius invited the congenial, well-read architect to accompany him on military campaigns so that they could enjoy evenings of Dante together. In 1504, Bramante designed the courtyard of St. Damasus with three levels of columned arcades, to ensure papal privacy.

In 1505, he won the competition to design and supervise the construction of the new St. Peter's, to be the crowning glory of Christendom. Fund-raising for the project would destroy Christian unity. The fourth century Constantinian edifice was falling apart, and under Pope Nicholas V (1447-1455) a major restoration was begun. Julius decided on a complete reconstruction, the domed choir of which would contain his own massive tomb carved by Michelangelo with forty figures (the *Moses* is the masterpiece of a much-reduced monument in the church of St. Peter in Chains).

Bramante's concept was a Greek-cross design with a gigantic central hemispheric dome flanked by four equal naves ending in apses. Each corner would have a chapel surmounted by smaller cupolas, and, farther out, four towers would give the building the form of a perfect square with the four apsidal projections. This original design can be seen in the Uffizi Gallery, Florence, and in Caradosso's official souvenir medal. Though finally altered into a Latin cross, the present basilica retains Bramante's spirit and his entirely new massive scale. At his death, only the central piers for supporting the dome were in place. Significant but largely unnoticed is Bramante's bedrock substructure for this colossal edifice. Remarkable, too, is his sculptural modeling of walls. This awareness of the "plastic potentiality" of a wall, also used by Filippo Brunelleschi, was late Roman in origin and important in subsequent Baroque development.

Nicholas V also began the refurbishment of the papal residence into the imposing Vatican palace. Bramante's last important design (1514) was the Palazzo Caprini, planned as his own private residence. It is better known as the House of Raphael, since it was bought in 1517 by the painter.

SIGNIFICANCE

Otto H. Förster, a Bramante scholar, has urged the theory that Bramante, and not Raphael, was the author of a 1510 treatise on the architecture of imperial Rome addressed to Julius II. It is full of confidence that the dome of St. Peter's could rival that of the Pantheon, the scale of which Raphael and others found impossible to contemplate. In it the author is critical of the Palazzo della Cancellaria, a building often attributed incorrectly to Bramante. It is, in fact, difficult to verify Bramante's part in many structures because of the damage and reconstructions of the centuries.

Despite his reputation for magnanimity, Bramante did not get on well with Michelangelo, who in a letter of 1542 voiced the suspicion that the older artist had enviously persuaded Julius to pull him away from the precious sculptural project for the great tomb in order to paint in the Sistine. Still, in a letter of 1555 the sculptor remarked, "Bramante was as gifted an architect as anyone from antiquity until now. . . . His plan for St. Peter's was clear and pure, full of light. . . . Whoever departs from Bramante's plan departs from the truth." Thus, one may assert Bramante's influence over Michelangelo the architect. Sebastiano Serlio imitated Bramante's use of columns; Andrea Palladio's S. Giorgio Maggiore in Venice manifests Bramantean influence.

In 1517, Bramante was satirized as arriving at the Gates of Heaven and immediately proposing improvements. He would replace the difficult road to paradise by a spiral ramp so that Heaven could be attained on horseback, "and I would tear down this Paradise and build a new one with finer accommodations for the blessed. If you agree, I'll stay; if not, I'll head for Inferno." Thus were perceived the confident assertiveness and integrity of Bramante at about the time of his death in 1514.

—*Daniel C. Scavone*

FURTHER READING

Baroni, Constantino, ed. *Bramante.* Bergamo: Istituto Italiano d'Arti Grafiche, 1944. In Italian, a fifty-page biography. Useful for its 134 excellent black-and-white photographs.

Burckhardt, Jacob. *The Architecture of the Italian Renaissance.* Translated by James Palmes. Chicago: University of Chicago Press, 1985. Offers a useful or-

ganization into genres, but the book's style is difficult. Excellent illustrations and bibliography.

Clarke, Georgia. *Roman House—Renaissance Palaces: Inventing Antiquity in Fifteenth-Century Italy.* New York: Cambridge University Press, 2003. Examines the appropriation and reinterpretation of ancient Roman architecture by fifteenth century Italian architects and Humanists. Includes illustrations, bibliographic references, index.

Durant, Will. *The Renaissance.* New York: Simon & Schuster, 1953. Views Bramante in the context of Renaissance Italy. A very readable appreciation.

Förster, Otto H. *Bramante.* Vienna: A. Schroll, 1956. The best book on Bramante, in German. Useful for its numerous illustrations.

Hersey, George L. *High Renaissance Art in St. Peter's and the Vatican: An Interpretive Guide.* Chicago: University of Chicago Press, 1993. Detailed study of the contributions of Bramante, Michelangelo, and Raphael to the art and architecture of the Vatican. Discusses the influence of political and religious intrigue on the development of the Vatican, as well as providing specific histories and interpretations of the artists' works. Includes illustrations, bibliographic references, index.

Mayernik, David. *Timeless Cities: An Architect's Reflections on Renaissance Italy.* Boulder, Colo.: Westview Press, 2003. Written by an accomplished modern architect, this study of five Italian Renaissance cities discusses the philosophical importance of architecture and its role in realizing the ideals of Humanism. Includes illustrations, map, bibliographic references, index.

Pevsner, Nikolaus. *An Outline of European Architecture.* Baltimore: Penguin Books, 1963. A good survey of major architectural achievements and theory. Bramante is seen in a wider European perspective.

Rossiter, Stuart, ed. *Rome and Environs.* Chicago: Rand McNally, 1971. Thorough description of art and architecture in Rome for the scholarly traveler. Bramante's buildings receive generous and detailed coverage. Identifies all buildings in which Bramante may have had some role.

SEE ALSO: Leon Battista Alberti; Alexander VI; Julius II; Leo X; Leonardo da Vinci; Pierre Lescot; Michelangelo; Andrea Palladio; Piero della Francesca; Jacopo Sansovino; Ludovico Sforza; Diego de Siloé.

RELATED ARTICLE in *Great Events from History: The Renaissance & Early Modern Era, 1454-1600:* 1508-1520: Raphael Paints His Frescoes.

PIETER BRUEGEL, THE ELDER
Dutch-Flemish painter

In an era dominated by portraiture, Bruegel teamed his subjects with their larger environment, greatly elevating landscape art. Bruegel's miniaturist style also chronicled everyday life in sixteenth century Flanders.

BORN: c. 1525; in or near Breda, Brabant (now in the Netherlands)
DIED: September 5, 1569; Brussels (now in Belgium)
ALSO KNOWN AS: Peeter Brueghels
AREA OF ACHIEVEMENT: Art

EARLY LIFE

Pieter Bruegel (PAY-tur BROY-gehl), called the Elder, hailed from the Brabant region, the Dutch-Flemish countryside that straddles the southern part of the Netherlands and northern Belgium. Little can be ascertained about his early life, or when and where it exactly began. Although 1525 is often cited as the year of Bruegel's birth, scholars have hypothesized various dates ranging from 1520 to 1530.

When the artist arrived in Antwerp to commence his career, he was listed as Peeter Brueghels. Since country-born Flemings often lacked surnames, one near-contemporary, the early seventeenth century biographer Carel van Mander, states that the artist adopted "Bruegel" or "Brueghels" from his place of birth. Other scholars speculate that it was a family name, although such a nomenclature often was preceded by "van." The artist's origin also remains unclear. Three Flemish towns bore some form of the name Bruegel, and at least the same number of families shared the appellation. Since two of the towns are close together, near the city of Brée in modern Belgium, this area frequently has been cited as Bruegel's birthplace.

Excepting the folktales that come from each of the artist's alleged hometowns, his biography begins in 1545, when he first apprenticed with Pieter Coecke van Aelst, a successful painter, architect, and ornamental/tapestry designer. Bruegel's master maintained operations in both Brussels and Antwerp, and he subscribed to the Italian Renaissance style then dominating art. It remains difficult to trace Bruegel's creative evolution during his apprenticeship because guild rules dictated that students could not sign or sell any of their work; they were totally under the direction of the masters. Yet some very tangible benefits resulted from Bruegel's association with Coecke. The master's wife, Mayken Verhulst, was a talented miniaturist who may have imparted some of her skills to Bruegel. The apprentice also married the Coeckes' daughter, Mayken, some years later, in 1563. After the death of both Bruegels, Mayken Verhulst instructed the couple's young, artistic sons, Pieter and Jan.

LIFE'S WORK

Coecke's sudden demise in December, 1550, led his apprentice Bruegel to Hieronymus Cock, a copper-plate engraver who became less known for his personal artistry than for a rare ability to capitalize on the spirit of the day. Antwerp at mid-century was Europe's most active commercial center, attracting traders from all over the Continent and spawning a cosmopolitan, consumer-oriented existence. Art proved to be a major beneficiary of the economic climate. Realizing the public's increasing desire for affordable creations, Cock opened the Four Winds publishing house. The owner/entrepreneur successfully marketed prints of popular artists, such as Hieronymus Bosch, and used a broader approach to fulfill the demand for art: Cock engaged young, local talents to execute new works.

Bruegel thus arrived at Four Winds. Within several months, he became a master in the Antwerp chapter of the Guild of St. Luke, a brotherhood including painters, graphic artists, ornamental and interior designers, glassworkers, and others. Most craftspersons of the era proved to be extremely versatile. Bruegel himself was to draw and paint in oils; he also skillfully engraved at least one of his own works, though print-related processes usually were reserved for other craftspersons.

One advantage of Bruegel's association with the publisher Cock was that his employer dispatched him to Italy in 1552, possibly in search of new subject matter or because the trip might yield popular Italian-style art. During the journey, Bruegel witnessed the burning of the Calabrian seaport, Reggio, by Süleyman's Turks. The scene is later documented in *Sea Battle in the Straits of Messina*, Bruegel's only real historic painting.

Besides the exposure to Italy—which inspired several seascapes—the artist gained much from his trip across the Alps. Mountain vistas often appear in his work, with results that never could have been attained had he not ventured forth from the Flemish flatlands. It also is said that Bruegel acquired a new perspective: His paintings frequently seem to be executed from a higher ground, looking down. This approach, perhaps a manifestation of his Alpine travels, was rather uncommon during the mid-1500's.

Returning to Antwerp in 1553, Bruegel continued his employment with Four Winds, creating drawings largely for public consumption. Some of his earlier works, such as the *Seven Deadly Sins* series (1556-1557), show elements of fantasy. Scholars thus debate whether Bruegel was creatively motivated by Bosch or whether he imitated the established artist to satisfy public demand. Many factors may explain Bruegel's attraction to fantasy: a possible escape from politics, particularly Catholic Spain's harsh rule over the Reformist-leaning Low Countries; the superstition and magical beliefs that sometimes dominated daily life; or the artist's inclination toward social commentary and satire. Yet, as one expert notes, Bruegel rendered *The Temptation of Saint Anthony* without signing it. A previous Bosch engraving bore the same title and a similar style. Commercial factors therefore could have prevailed in some of Bruegel's earlier drawings.

Although association with the publishing firm perhaps muted the artist's powers of self-expression (at least through 1557), the connection served him well in other ways. Four Winds, complete with coffeehouse, became an intellectual center and mecca for art dealers. The atmosphere netted Bruegel excellent contacts, including a string of patrons who supported his best-known work—the oil paintings created from 1557 until the end of his life.

The biographer van Mander describes Bruegel's steadfast friendship with one patron, Hans Franckert: With Franckert, Bruegel often went out into the country to see the peasants at their fairs and weddings.

> Disguised as peasants they brought gifts like the other guests, claiming relationship or kinship with the bride or groom. Here Bruegel delighted in observing the droll behavior of the peasants, how they ate, danced, drank, capered or made love.

Perhaps the artist derives his greatest renown from these so-called rustic scenes. Combining peasant life with miniaturist technique, he produced his acclaimed *The Blue Cloak* in 1559. The painting illustrates anywhere from seventy-five to one hundred sayings common during the sixteenth century. Some, such as a variation on the "he speaks from both sides of his mouth" theme, continue to be used. *The Battle Between Carnival and Lent* (1559) and *Children's Games* (1560) give further substance to this Bruegelian genre. The two paint-

ings reveal literally hundreds of adults and youths, respectively, having fun. Given the abundant activity and immense cast of characters illustrated, it is interesting to note that each of the three works measures only about four feet by five feet.

Later paintings concentrate more on smaller-scale activities. *Peasant Wedding* (1568) and *Peasant Dance* (1568) are well-known examples of Bruegel's ability to make the everyday, bucolic lifestyle of sixteenth century Flanders accessible to modern viewers. *Parable of the Blind* (1568) and *The Cripples* (1568) hold additional virtues. With its theme of "the blind leading the blind," the former painting depicts six men, each suffering from a different form of eye disease. Similarly, *The Cripples* shows various implements used by the era's disabled. These subjects also sport foxtails, a sign of the Beggars, a political order seeking independence from Spain.

Indeed, scholars debate the level of sociopolitical commentary found in Bruegel's work. Some say that he moved from Antwerp to Brussels in 1563 partly to escape the volatile atmosphere pervading the port city. The primary reason for the relocation, however, remains simple: marriage. According to van Mander, Bruegel was permitted to marry Mayken Coecke only on the condition that he move to Brussels. The artist had previously been living with a servant girl, and apparently his new family wanted him to forget the relationship.

Subsequent to his marriage and move, Bruegel became a more prolific painter, perhaps because of his distance from the commercial lure of Four Winds. His work included landscapes populated by lively peasants, as well as biblical scenes. Some of the religious themes, however, may have masked political intentions. Soldiers garbed in sixteenth century regalia, marching through Alpine paths and snowy fields far from the Holy Land, dominate *The Road to Calvary* (1564) and *The Massacre of the Innocents* (1566). Artists of the era sometimes placed historical figures in contemporary surroundings, but Bruegel's inspiration remains subject to speculation. With orders from King Philip II of Spain, the duke of Alva raised about fifteen thousand soldiers to invade the Low Countries during the mid-1560's, just as Bruegel executed his somber themes.

Arguments about Bruegel's politics notwithstanding, the last years of his short life proved to be the most successful. A wealthy patron, Niclaes Jonghelinck, offered the artist his first commission: a series of six "seasons" paintings to be used for the decoration of a mansion. Out of this endeavor came *Hunters in the Snow* (1565), perhaps Bruegel's finest work. Public recognition soon followed. Shortly after 1569 commenced, the Brussels city council advanced the artist money for a series of paintings commemorating the opening of a new canal. The paintings remained unfinished: Bruegel died on September 5, 1569.

SIGNIFICANCE

Bruegel left behind approximately 150 drawings, 50 oil paintings, various prints, and a legacy: his two sons, Pieter, the Younger (1564-1638) and Jan (1568-1625). His namesake largely became known as an imitator of his father's work; Jan, however, helped to usher in a new creative era with his elaborate, Baroque nature subjects. Nicknamed velvet Brueghel (both sons reinstated the "h" in their family nomenclature), he also developed a lifelong friendship and collaborated with one of the era's most outstanding painters, Peter Paul Rubens. The Bruegel art dynasty, in fact, survived for about two hundred years.

The reputation of Pieter, the Elder, outlived him, too, but not by more than a few decades. Changing trends—some spawned by the heated political events occurring during the mid-1500's—rendered his work unfashionable. Interest in Bruegel resurfaced only at the dawn of the twentieth century, with the very first exhibit of the artist's work in 1902. Perhaps nostalgia for a diminishing peasant lifestyle fostered this revival. Surely one of Bruegel's major contributions was in replacing elite faces with those of the rural lower classes. Yet, while Bruegel painted people, he refused to confine himself to the then-dominant portraiture. His crowded street scenes depict not so much individuals as they do the social landscape. Bruegel also forced his vibrant peasants to share attention with the wheat-covered fields and steep Alpine paths that offered the essence of human activity.

—*Lynn C. Kronzek*

FURTHER READING

Delevoy, Robert L. *Bruegel.* Translated by Stuart Gilbert. Lausanne, Switzerland: Éditions d'Art Albert Skira, 1959. Using an advanced approach, this book explores Bruegel's artistic techniques as well as the content of his work. A biographical chapter debates various theories about the artist's life. Also included are an extensive bibliography, a list of major Bruegel exhibitions, translated documents, and color plates.

Denis, Valentin, ed. *All the Paintings of Pieter Bruegel.* Translated by Paul Colacicchi. New York: Hawthorn Books, 1961. A catalog of Bruegel's works containing 160 plates, this volume cites lost paintings and those which may not have been created by the artist. An introductory chapter presents Bruegel as one who withstood prevalent artistic influences and only gradually introduced his concepts into the mainstream. Also featured are selected criticism, biographical notes (timeline), and a brief bibliography.

Foote, Timothy. *The World of Bruegel c. 1525-1569.* New York: Time-Life Books, 1968. Portrays the artist as an innovator who, nevertheless, reflected—rather than attempted to comment on—social conditions. Also explores Bruegel's predecessors, peers, and successors; contemporary artistic trends; and the politics and religious attitudes of the sixteenth century. Contains a bibliography, a listing of other European masters, and both color and black-and-white plates.

Glück, Gustav. *Peter Brueghel, the Elder.* New York: George Braziller, 1936. Reprint. London: Thomas and Hudson, 1958. Depicts Bruegel as having been a nonjudgmental, realistic painter of a chaotic world. Emphasizes the master's artistic progression and increasing ability to convey nature accurately. Glück also argues that Bruegel defined later genres of Dutch painting. This oversize book features forty-nine superb color plates and a bibliography.

Kavaler, Ethan Matt. *Pieter Bruegel: Parables of Order and Enterprise.* New York: Cambridge University Press, 1999. Argues that Bruegel used images taken from popular fables to advocate traditional values and cultural stability and to resist the destabilization of a growing commodity culture. Includes illustrations, bibliographic references, index.

Klein, H. Arthur, and Mina C. Klein. *Peter Bruegel, the Elder: Artist of Abundance.* New York: Macmillan, 1968. Bruegel appears as a social critic in this general biography. Details of the artist's environment and contemporary lifestyle are explored. Heavily illustrated in black and white, the book uses both Bruegel's works and those of his peers. Also contains a short color section and list of American museums housing Bruegel paintings.

Roberts-Jones, Philippe, and Françoise Roberts-Jones. *Pieter Bruegel.* New York: Harry N. Abrams, 2002. Co-written by an art historian and an art restorer, this study of Bruegel includes detailed practical discussions of the physical materials and techniques that went into his paintings, as well as broad cultural interpretations of the meaning and influence of his works. Includes illustrations, maps, bibliographic references, index.

Sullivan, Margaret A. *Bruegel's Peasants: Art and Audience in the Northern Renaissance.* New York: Cambridge University Press, 1994. Examination of the cultural and philosophical import of Bruegel's work focusing on the common background and assumptions of the artist's intended audience, and the meanings that audience would most likely find in his work. Includes eight pages of photographic plates, illustrations, bibliographic references, index.

See also: Duke of Alva; Hieronymus Bosch; Lucas Cranach, the Elder; Matthias Grünewald; Catharina van Hemessen; Margaret of Austria; Sesshū; Süleyman the Magnificent.

Related articles in *Great Events from History: The Renaissance & Early Modern Era, 1454-1600:* c. 1500: Netherlandish School of Painting; 1531-1585: Antwerp Becomes the Commericial Capital of Europe.

Giordano Bruno
Italian philosopher and cosmologist

With his daring and speculative theories in cosmology and philosophy, Bruno anticipated many of the achievements of modern science, but his stubborn personality and arcane interests brought him into inevitable conflict with the authorities of his time.

Born: 1548; Nola, near Naples (now in Italy)
Died: February 17, 1600; Rome, Papal States (now in Italy)
Also known as: Filippo Bruno (given name); Il Nolano
Areas of achievement: Philosophy, astronomy

Early Life

Giordano Bruno (johr-dah-noh BREW-noh) was the son of Juano Bruno, a professional soldier, and his wife, Fraulissa Savolino. As a child, Bruno was named Filippo; he took the name Giordano when he entered the Dominican Order. He was sometimes known as "the Nolan," after the town of his birth, and he often referred to himself in this fashion in his works.

From contemporary records and his own writings, Bruno seems to have been a particularly intelligent and impressionable child. He left several accounts of odd, almost visionary experiences in his youth, including an extended, quasi-mystical dialogue with the mountain Vesuvius that first revealed to him the deceptiveness of appearances and the relativity of all material things. These were to become two dominant themes in his philosophy.

As a youth, Bruno was sent to Naples, where he attended the Studium Generale, concentrating in the humanities, logic, and dialectic. It is clear that Bruno had a thorough grounding in Aristotle and his philosophy and also was well acquainted with the works of Plato and the writings of the Neoplatonists, who were then creating considerable intellectual activity and controversy, especially in Italy.

In 1565, when Bruno was seventeen, he entered the Dominican Order, moving within the walls of the monastery of San Domenico in Naples. There he took the name Giordano. Bruno's decision to enter the Dominican Order is puzzling, for in retrospect it clearly stands as the major mistake in his often-turbulent life. Although he was well suited for the intellectual studies of the Dominicans, he was quite unfit for the accompanying intellectual discipline and submission required for the monastic and clerical life. His thoughts were too wide-ranging and innovative to be restrained within traditional confines, a situation that eventually placed him in mortal conflict with the Church.

Bruno spent eleven years in the monastery of San Domenico. He studied Saint Thomas Aquinas, Aristotle, and other traditional figures, but at the same time was reading in the mystical doctrines of the Neoplatonists, the new works of Desiderius Erasmus, and other reformers and seems to have become suspiciously well acquainted with the works of heretics such as Arius. These unorthodox diversions brought him into conflict with the Dominican authorities, and reports were made that Bruno was defending the Arian heresy. Arius had taught that God the Father and God the Son were not the same in essence. When the Dominicans learned that Bruno was suspected of defending Arianism, charges were prepared against him. Learning of this, he fled the monastery in 1576. He was twenty-eight, and he would spend the rest of his life in exile or in prison.

Life's Work

When Bruno fled the monastery, he embarked on twenty-one years of wandering throughout Europe. Many of his stops lasted merely a matter of months, and the most productive, for only three years. Controversy and conflict dogged him on his travels—much of it a result of not only his daring and speculative thought but also his unrestrained attacks on those who opposed him in any degree and his innate lack of common sense or practical judgment. Employment was difficult, and income was insufficient and insecure. Yet, during this period, Bruno wrote and published an enormous body of work whose content far outpaced even the most advanced thinkers of his time.

Bruno's first extended sojourn was in Geneva. There, safe from the power of the Church, he soon plunged into local intellectual conflicts. In 1579, he published a scathing attack on Antoine de la Faye, a noted professor of philosophy at the University of Geneva. Bruno's assault was more than an academic exercise, for he seemed to undermine de la Faye's theories, which were the basis for the quasi-theological government of Geneva. Bruno, the renegade Dominican on the run, had put himself in disfavor with the Calvinists of Switzerland. He was arrested, then released; he soon left Geneva, moving first to Lyons, then to Toulouse, France. In 1581, Bruno went to Paris, where he found his first real success. He lectured on his own techniques of memory, and the results were so impressive that King Henry III summoned Bruno to court to explain his methods. As a result, the king appointed Bruno to the College de France. Bruno held the post for two years, lecturing on philosophy and natural science and publishing a number of books, many of them on his art of memory.

Still, he managed to alienate many fellow professors and intellectuals in Paris. Some were outraged by his arrogant and self-proclaimed superiority, while the more conventional were troubled by his unorthodox views and desertion of his monastic vows. In 1583, Bruno left for London, with a letter of recommendation to the French ambassador Michel de Castelnau.

The London period, from 1583 through 1585, was the most productive of Bruno's career. Perhaps he was stimulated by the intellectual climate of England, for not only did he deliver a series of lectures at Oxford, explaining the Copernican theory, but also he had among his acquaintances men such as Sir Philip Sidney, Sir Walter Ralegh, and Sir Fulke Greville, noted figures of the English Renaissance. In 1584, Bruno produced a series of six dialogues expounding his philosophy; three of these dealt with cosmological issues and three with moral topics.

In *La Cena de le Ceneri* (1584; *The Ash Wednesday Supper*, 1975), Bruno laid the foundation for his scien-

Giordano Bruno. (Library of Congress)

tific theories. He began with the view of Nicolaus Copernicus that the Sun, rather than the Earth, was the center of the solar system. Bruno recognized that the Sun was itself a star, and he concluded that other stars must have their attendant planets circling them. He came to the conclusion that the universe was infinite, and that it therefore contained an infinite number of worlds, each world capable of having intelligent life on it. Such a theory ran counter to the traditions of both the Catholic Church and the newer Protestant faiths.

Bruno continued the development of his theories in *De l'infinito universo e mondi* (1584; *On the Infinite Universe and Worlds*, 1950). He systematically criticized the prevailing Aristotelian cosmology, and in its place put forth a precursor of the modern theory of relativity later developed by Albert Einstein. Bruno maintained that sensory knowledge could never be absolute, but only relative, and it is this relativity that misleads humans in their attempts to understand the universe. Human perceptions are incapable of truly and completely comprehending the universe, and that universe itself can be accurately comprehended only as a total unity, rather than in isolated parts. Therefore, neither senses nor imagination can be fully trusted, but only reason, which allows humans to penetrate to the divine essence of creation.

Bruno also developed a theory that the universe was composed of "minima," extremely small particles much like the atoms proposed by the ancient Roman philosopher Lucretius. Like Lucretius, Bruno thought that certain motions and events were inevitable and that the universe develops inexorably out of inherent necessity. In order to resolve the conflict between this deterministic view and free will, Bruno postulated that the universe itself was divine; he projected a universal pantheism in which the Creator manifests himself through and within creation.

Finally, Bruno resolved the difficulty of the relationship of human beings to God, of the finite to the infinite, of ignorance to knowledge. These were long-standing puzzles to theologians and philosophers, for it seemed impossible that the limited human mind could comprehend or understand the perfect and infinite attributes of divinity. Bruno believed that there was an identity of opposites at work in which the essential elements of creation and divinity are found in all parts of the universe. Opposition is only relative and illusory; on the most fun-

damental level, everything is the same, and everything is therefore divine.

In 1585, Castelnau was recalled to Paris, and Bruno, left without a patron, was forced to leave England. For the next six years, he wandered through Europe, accepting and losing posts at a number of universities in Germany and the Holy Roman Empire. He continued to write and publish prolifically, including his special area of memory, and, in the fall of 1591, he received an invitation from a Venetian nobleman, Zuane Mocenigo, to come to Venice and teach him the art of memory.

Bruno accepted, believing that he would be safe in Venice, which was at that time a fairly liberal and independent state that carefully guarded its freedom from the Papacy. There was a dispute between Bruno and his patron, however—apparently the nobleman believed that he was being cheated and that Bruno planned to flee to Germany—and on May 23, 1592, Bruno was arrested by the Venetian Inquisition. He was questioned through September, but no decision was made.

On February 27, 1593, Bruno was delivered into the hands of the Roman Inquisition, and for the next seven years he was held in prison, repeatedly questioned and examined, and urged to recant his heresies and confess his sins. Bruno tried to play a crafty game, willing to admit minor infractions but pretending not to comprehend how his cosmological and philosophical writings could run counter to the teachings of the Church. Finally, in February, 1600, the Inquisition found him guilty and delivered him to the secular authorities for punishment. When Bruno heard the decision, he replied, "Perhaps you who pronounce my sentence are in greater fear than I who receive it." On Saturday, February 17, 1600, Bruno was burned in the Square of Flowers in Rome.

SIGNIFICANCE

Giordano Bruno was a philosopher of great insight and imagination, yet a thinker who could link science to magic and yoke philosophical understanding to mnemonic tricks. He was poised amid the thought and traditions of the Church, the mystical teachings of the Neoplatonists, and the rapid advances of the sciences, especially astronomy.

BRUNO ON EARTH'S RECURRENT CYCLE OF DIVISION, EXPANSION, AND RE-FORMATION

Giordano Bruno advanced the heliocentric theory of Nicolaus Copernicus, believing in an infinite universe with an infinite number of worlds, and thus theorized the expansive and everlasting nature of everything that exists. To expand and re-form, all things, including Earth, "move" so that they may renew themselves.

It (the earth) moves that it may renew itself and be born again, for it cannot endure for ever in the same form. For those things which cannot be eternal as individuals . . . are eternal as a species; and substances which cannot be everlasting under the same aspect, change themselves into other appearances. For the material and substance of things is incorruptible and must in all its parts pass through all forms. . . . Therefore, since death and dissolution are unfitted to the whole mass of which this globe, this star, consists, and complete annihilation is impossible to all nature, the earth changes all its parts from time to time and in a certain order and so renews itself. . . . And we ourselves and the things pertaining to us come and go, pass and repass. . . . And nothing is of itself eternal, save the substance and material of which it is made, and this is in constant mutation.

Source: From the 1584 work *La Cena de le Ceneri*, translated as *The Ash Wednesday Supper* (1975), Giordano Bruno, quoted in *Giordano Bruno and the Hermetic Tradition*, by Frances A. Yates (Chicago: University of Chicago Press, 1979), p. 242.

From the combination of these three traditions, he forged a new and highly individual vision of the cosmos and humankind's place in it.

Bruno's influence was recognized by scientists and Humanists in the years following his death. Scientists, even to modern times, admire the startling insights that he drew concerning the infinite number of worlds in an infinite universe. Bruno's early recognition of the concept of relativity and the place it must play in humanity's conception and understanding of the universe is also a prime legacy that Bruno left to science. Humanists of the period were profoundly influenced by his insistence on the need for tolerance in matters of religion and belief. Perhaps because Bruno himself was so often a victim of the intolerance of the age, he was especially eloquent in his plea for patience and understanding.

Finally, Bruno combined the sense of infinite expansion and relativity of all things with a new approach to human knowledge and culture. He refused to divide the world into the sacred and the profane, the Christian and the heathen, the orthodox and the heretic. Instead, he saw human life and culture as a single strand and the universe as a divine manifestation that carried with it all knowledge and truth. To Bruno, the cosmos was God's creation and therefore all good, and humanity's role was not to judge but to understand.

—*Michael Witkoski*

FURTHER READING

Boulting, William. *Giordano Bruno, His Life, Thought, and Martyrdom*. New York: E. P. Dutton, 1916. Reprint. Freeport, N.Y.: Books for Libraries Press, 1972. As indicated by its title, this biography is a highly favorable account of Bruno's life and thought. On the whole, it presents his philosophical and scientific views in a fair and unbiased light.

De Santillana, Giorgia. *The Age of Adventure: The Renaissance Philosophers*. Boston: Houghton Mifflin, 1957. An introductory survey of Bruno and his work, with particular attention paid to his influence on later scientists and writers.

Feingold, Mordechai. "The Occult Tradition in the English Universities of the Renaissance: A Reassessment." In *Occult and Scientific Mentalities in the Renaissance*, edited by Brian Vickers. Cambridge, England: Cambridge University Press, 1984. An enlightening study of Bruno's 1584 visit to Oxford and the state of learning at that time, with special emphasis on which areas of knowledge were believed to be beyond the boundary of conventions.

Gatti, Hilary. *Giordano Bruno and Renaissance Science*. Ithaca, N.Y.: Cornell University Press, 1999. An explicit attempt to rescue Bruno's reputation as an important contributor to the development of modern science by arguing against seeing him solely as a hermetic philosopher. Compares Bruno's cosmology to those of Copernicus and Kepler; analyzes the scientific import of his overall methodology and worldview. Includes illustrations, bibliographic references, index.

_____, ed. *Giordano Bruno: Philosopher of the Renaissance*. Aldershot, Hampshire, England: Ashgate, 2002. Anthology of eighteen essays about Bruno's life, philosophy, and legacy, organized into sections on his relationship to Italian culture, his experiences and work in England, major philosophical themes in his work, and his historical function as both a receiver of earlier traditions and a source of influence on later thinkers. Includes illustrations and index.

Kristeller, Paul Oskar. *Renaissance Thought and Its Sources*. New York: Columbia University Press, 1979. Does not provide an extended treatment of Bruno as an individual but is an excellent source for understanding the intellectual climate of his time and how it developed.

Singer, Dorothea. *Giordano Bruno: His Life and Thought*. New York: Henry Schuman, 1950. A sympathetic but generally unbiased biography of Bruno, with emphasis on his thought and theory. The volume contains several helpful appendices and an excellent annotated translation of the dialogue *On the Infinite Universe and Worlds*.

White, Michael. *The Pope and the Heretic: The True Story of Giordano Bruno, the Man Who Dared to Defy the Roman Inquisition*. New York: William Morrow, 2002. One of the few Bruno biographies targeted at general readers. Details the social setting in which Bruno lived and the political and religious structures that condemned him to death. Provides a useful account of his influence on later thinkers. Includes bibliographic references and index.

Yates, Frances. *Giordano Bruno and the Hermetic Tradition*. Chicago: University of Chicago Press, 1964. By one of the most distinguished scholars of Renaissance thought. Yates's account of Bruno's place is invaluable. Particularly good in situating him within the confines of a broad philosophical stream.

_____. *Lull and Bruno*. Boston: Routledge & Kegan Paul, 1982. The section "Essays on Giordano Bruno in England" is particularly valuable for its studies of

Bruno's lectures on Copernicus at Oxford and his views of religion and the established church.

SEE ALSO: Tycho Brahe; Nicolaus Copernicus; Desiderius Erasmus; Marsilio Ficino; Henry III; Georg

von Peuerbach; Sir Walter Ralegh; Peter Ramus; Rheticus; Sir Philip Sidney.

RELATED ARTICLE in *Great Events from History: The Renaissance & Early Modern Era, 1454-1600:* 1583-1600: Bruno's Theory of the Infinite Universe.

MARTIN BUCER
German theologian and religious scholar

During the Reformation, Bucer served as mediator between Protestant Reformers Huldrych Zwingli and Martin Luther and attempted to reconcile the Roman Catholic Church and the Protestants. He made lasting contributions to the liturgy of Protestant sects, particularly in England.

BORN: November 11, 1491; Schlettstadt, Alsace (now in Germany)
DIED: February 28, 1551; Cambridge, England
ALSO KNOWN AS: Martin Butzer; Martin Kuhhorn
AREAS OF ACHIEVEMENT: Church reform, religion and theology

EARLY LIFE

Born to Nicholas Butzer, a shoemaker, and his wife, an occasional midwife, Martin Bucer (BEWT-sur) lived in Schlettstadt, in the Alsace region, until he was ten years old. By the time he had moved to Strasbourg and was put under the care of his grandfather, also a shoemaker, Bucer had already acquired the religious and scholarly zeal that characterized his entire life. At fifteen, however, he had to decide whether to follow family tradition and become an apprentice shoemaker or to continue his education by the only means available to poor young men, service in the Church. Although he did not really want to become a monk, he joined the Dominican Order and spent the next ten years in the monastery at Schlettstadt. There he was subjected to medieval Scholasticism, embodied in the works of Thomas Aquinas, and deprived of the new learning of the Humanists, notably the reformer Desiderius Erasmus.

The turning point in Bucer's life occurred ten years later, when he was transferred to the Dominican monastery at Heidelberg, a university town. There he was caught in the conflict between the medieval Scholasticism advocated by the Dominicans and the Humanism taught by the university professors. Bucer, a voracious reader, soon became a devoted follower of Erasmus, and his liberal leanings were strengthened by his meeting

with Martin Luther, who came to Heidelberg in April of 1518 to defend his views. When he received his bachelor of theology degree and was made master of students in 1519, Bucer also received permission to read the Bible; he subsequently wrote biblical commentaries and grounded his own religious beliefs in Scriptures, not in the writings of the church fathers.

After joining the local literary society and meeting other religious insurgents, Bucer, whose models were Luther and Erasmus, became convinced that his views were incompatible with his life as a Dominican and attempted to win his release from his monastic vows. That first step in his break from the Catholic Church occurred in 1521; after brief stints as a court chaplain to Count Frederick of the palatinate and as a parish priest, he married Elizabeth Silbereisen. While his marriage did not result in his immediate excommunication, Bucer's fervid defense of Luther's teachings, particularly the primacy of the Bible and the emphasis on faith rather than good works, eventually and inevitably brought him to the attention of his church superiors. Bucer was regarded as a threat because he used his preaching ability and debating skill to challenge conservative theologians who were reluctant to engage him in religious disputations. When, in 1523, he refused to go to Speier to meet with his bishop, Bucer was excommunicated. He was left virtually homeless when he lost his religious and political supporters and the Council of Wissembourg requested that he leave the city in May of 1523.

LIFE'S WORK

When he arrived, uninvited, in Strasbourg in 1523, Bucer found a city congenial to his views on the Reformation and strategically located between the warring strongholds of the Swiss Reformer Huldrych Zwingli and Martin Luther. In the eight years between his first sermon and his appointment in 1531 as official head of the Strasbourg clergy, Bucer brought his adopted city to prominence as a theological center. Under his unofficial leadership, ties were established between the church and the state; a public school system, with a religious emphasis, was inaugurated; and religious tolerance of a sort was established, though that tolerance was repeatedly tested by the Separatists and Anabaptists.

For the most part, Bucer's biblical commentaries were written during this period—a commentary on Romans, written in 1536, was the exception. Rather than using the traditional grammatical approach, he relied on close readings of the passages, which were placed in their historical context and compared to similar passages from elsewhere in the Bible. This comparative approach was especially helpful in his commentaries on the Gospels, but some critics believe that his best exegesis is contained in his work on the Psalms. (Unfortunately, this work was published under a pseudonym, Aretius Felinus, in order to gain for it an objective reading in Catholic France, but the stratagem left him open to charges of duplicity and earned for him the ire of both Luther and Erasmus.)

Shortly after Bucer arrived in Strasbourg, the Supper Controversy, the conflict over the meaning of the Eucharistic phrase "This is my body," between Zwingli and Luther threatened Reformation unity. Zwingli's followers—and Bucer must be included among them—maintained that the bread and wine were merely symbols of Christ's body and blood, not his actual body and blood, as Luther's followers, and the Roman Catholic Church, believed. Although he sided with Zwingli, Bucer attempted to reconcile the two factions, who became engaged in pamphlet wars, by glossing over the real doctrinal differences and by attempting, through ambiguous language, to effect an apparent compromise where none was, in fact, possible. Bucer's conciliatory efforts were, unfortunately, hampered by his own writings, which revealed his own theological beliefs and which were attacked by Lutherans, Zwinglians, and Catholics: The middle ground was treacherous territory.

From 1524 until 1548, when he was exiled to England, there was hardly a religious conference in Germany or Switzerland that Bucer did not attend in his role of theological conciliator. The first significant conference, the Marburg Colloquy of 1529, established a tenuous peace between Luther and Zwingli on all religious doctrine except for the Supper Controversy, but the real differences between the two opponents kept surfacing. Working with Wolfgang Capito, another Strasbourg Reformer, Bucer drafted in 1530 at the Diet of Augsburg the Tetrapolitana, or Confession of the Four Cities—Strasbourg, Zurich (Zwingli's stronghold), Basel, and Bern—but the ambiguous language concerning the Eucharist resulted in its rejection by Luther and Zwingli, both of whom wanted changes of a more specific kind. After Zwingli died in 1531, Bucer renewed his efforts at establishing concord, and the resulting Wittenberg Concord of 1536 did effect a consensus, if not a lasting peace, primarily because of Bucer's gift of obscuring meaning through ambiguous wording. While Philipp Melanchthon secured Luther's approval of the compromise, Bucer's efforts with the Zwinglians, already suspicious because of Luther's endorsement, effectively brought the moderate Zwinglians into the Lutheran fold while permanently alienating the ultra-Zwinglians.

The Protestant cause, already adversely affected by the Luther/Zwingli hostilities, suffered another setback when Philip the Magnanimous, a supporter of the Reformers, sought their religious sanction for his bigamy. Appealing to Scripture, the authority for the Reformers, Philip approached Bucer through an intermediary. Although he had not sanctioned Henry VIII's earlier divorce from Catherine of Aragon and although his initial response to Philip's request was negative, Bucer weighed the religious and political factors and reluctantly acquiesced to Philip. In fact, Bucer wrote a defense of bigamy, but his ultimate response was typically equivocal:

Martin Bucer. (Library of Congress)

He sanctioned Philip's secret bigamy. Unfortunately, Bucer's attempts to keep the marriage a secret were thwarted by Philip, who made it public and who also sought approval from the Catholic Church.

Although the Reformation was an accomplished fact, the Catholic Church was intent on returning the Reformers to the fold, and Bucer himself participated in several councils whose ostensible purpose was to unite all Christians. In 1540, the year of Philip's bigamous marriage, the Colloquy of Worms was convened, but no real progress was made, despite Bucer's efforts, which included secret meetings with liberal Catholic reformers. The following year, Bucer attended the Diet of Regensburg, which was called by Emperor Charles V, who had two aims: religious unity and military assistance against an impending Turkish invasion of the Holy Roman Empire.

The authorship of the Regensburg Book, which served as the basis for the ensuing discussions, was unknown; the material, however, was drawn from the secret meetings conducted at the earlier Colloquy of Worms. At these secret meetings, Bucer had made compromises that, when they were made public, brought criticism from the Protestants, especially the Lutherans. When both sides rejected the Regensburg Book, Bucer apparently despaired of effecting a Protestant/Catholic reconciliation, and he became very anti-Catholic. Subsequent meetings, which were also futile, were held, but they were conducted, as Bucer suspected, more for political than for religious reasons. Charles V, who had been conducting secret negotiations with the pope, the French, and the Turks, finally attacked the Protestant German princes in 1546 and quickly defeated them. After the defeat of the Schmalkaldic League, Charles V instituted the Augsburg Interim, which reflected not only his ideas but also some of the articles of the Regensburg Interim, which had been drafted in part by Bucer. Despite the similarities between the two documents, Bucer adamantly opposed the Augsburg Interim because it was the product of force, not negotiation, and because he had become more intolerant of the Catholics. Bucer resisted Charles V until 1549, when he was officially requested to leave Strasbourg.

Although he had various options, Bucer chose to accept Archbishop Thomas Cranmer's invitation to aid the Reformation effort in England. After all, his Cologne Ordinances had been included in the first Book of Common Prayer, and he had many friends and supporters in that country. Soon after his arrival at Cambridge, where he taught, he was again embroiled in the Supper Controversy, this time, however, with Catholic opposition.

In his service to Edward VI, he refuted the Catholic elevation of good works over faith, resisted the radical views of the Scottish Reformers, wrote *De regno Christi* (1557), a design for converting England into the Kingdom of Christ, and aided in the development of the English Books of Prayer. For his efforts he received the doctor of theology degree from Cambridge before he died on February 28, 1551. Even in death he was involved in controversy: English Catholics under Mary tried and condemned him posthumously for heresy, then exhumed and burned his body in 1555; Elizabeth, the Protestant queen, atoned for the Catholic desecration in 1560.

SIGNIFICANCE

Unlike his more famous Reformation contemporaries—Luther, Zwingli, and John Calvin—Bucer was a mediator occupying the middle ground in most of the religious controversy of the sixteenth century. Rather than establishing his own sect, he sought to reconcile the intransigent extremes within the Reformation movement. His ecumenical efforts with such divergent groups as the Anabaptists and Catholics led him to make concessions, although for the goal of church unity, which undermined his credibility with his colleagues. Though he never abandoned the essential tenets of his faith, he did appear occasionally too willing to compromise, even to surrender, on the details that preoccupied other Reformers. Though he was inevitably unsuccessful in mediating what were irreconcilable differences, he did succeed in negotiating the reform of several German cities that were attempting to resolve questions about the disposition of church property and the use of images in worship services. Under his leadership, Strasbourg became an influential Reformation city that attracted young Reformers, most notably Calvin, who incorporated some of Bucer's ideas in his *Christianae religionis institutio* (1536; *Institutes of the Christian Religion*, 1561).

Because he occupied the middle ground on theological disputes, Bucer is not a theologian whose influence is readily traced. His theology, because of his wide reading, was eclectic and drawn from many sources, some of them—Anabaptist and Catholic—inherently contradictory. Bucer's contribution was in his synthesis of theology, not in his creation of it. Centuries later, his ecumenical approach to theology seems more appropriate to the times than the dogmatic intransigence of his more famous contemporaries.

—Thomas L. Erskine

FURTHER READING

Burnett, Amy Nelson. *The Yoke of Christ: Martin Bucer and the Christian Discipline*. Kirksville: Northeast Missouri State University, 1994. Awarded a prize by the American Society of Church History, this monograph details the Bucer's interpretation of the "discipline of Christ." Includes bibliographic references and index.

Eells, Hastings. *Martin Bucer*. New Haven, Conn.: Yale University Press, 1931. Reprint. New York: Russell & Russell, 1971. The definitive biography of Bucer, this lengthy book contains valuable information about the historical context, theological differences between the Reformers, and the personalities of the major figures. The book is well organized, well indexed, and very readable. Though his sympathies are clearly with Bucer, Eells is fairly objective in his discussion of Luther, Zwingli, and the Roman Catholic Church.

Höpf, Constantin. *Martin Bucer and the English Reformation*. Oxford, England: Basil Blackwell, 1946. A thorough review of Bucer's influence on the English Reformation. Höpf, who includes copious illustrations, original correspondence, and a comprehensive bibliography, extends Bucer's influence beyond his *Censura* (wr. 1550) of the First Edwardian Prayer Book and details how Bucer's psalms were printed in the English primers. Bucer, for Höpf, was more influential in England than either Zwingli or Luther.

Pauck, Wilhelm, ed. *Melanchthon and Bucer*. Philadelphia: Westminster Press, 1969. Pauck includes his translation of Bucer's *De regno Christi*, which he introduces by discussing Bucer's substantial contribution to the Reformation and explaining how Bucer's Strasbourg experiences affected his recommendations for England in *De regno Christi*. Of particular interest are Pauck's comments about the relationship of church and state.

Selderhuis, Herman J. *Marriage and Divorce in the Thought of Martin Bucer*. Translated by John Vriend and Lyle D. Bierma. Kirksville, Mo.: Thomas Jefferson University Press at Truman State University, 1999. Voluminous attempt to clarify Bucer's position on divorce. Provides extensive background on pre-Reformation marital laws, as well as detailed analysis both of Bucer's treatises on marriage, celibacy, and divorce and of the biographical details of his own marriages. Includes bibliographic references and index.

Stephens, W. P. *The Holy Spirit in the Theology of Martin Bucer*. Cambridge, England: Cambridge University Press, 1970. A close examination of the Holy Spirit in Bucer's theology. Stephens provides an introduction establishing Bucer's theology in the context of his times and summarizes the various influences that affected the development of his religious thought. Excellent bibliography.

Wendel, François. *Calvin: The Origins and Development of His Religious Thought*. Translated by Philip Mairet. New York: Harper & Row, 1963. Although the book concerns the many sources of Calvin's theology, Wendel establishes Bucer as being particularly influential. Bucer's influence is especially prominent in the predestination material found in Calvin's *Institutes of the Christian Religion*, and Calvin's theology is regarded as being aligned with the theology of the Tetrapolitan Confession of 1530.

Wright, D. F., ed. *Martin Bucer: Reforming Church and Community*. New York: Cambridge University Press, 2002. Anthology of essays examining Bucer's lasting contributions to theology and church history. Includes essays on subjects ranging from specific sacraments to general cultural history. Bibliographic references and index.

SEE ALSO: John Calvin; Charles V; Miles Coverdale; Thomas Cranmer; Edward VI; Elizabeth I; Desiderius Erasmus; Stephen Gardiner; Martin Luther; Mary I; Philipp Melanchthon; Menno Simons; Philip the Magnanimous; Huldrych Zwingli.

RELATED ARTICLE in *Great Events from History: The Renaissance & Early Modern Era, 1454-1600:* March, 1536: Calvin Publishes *Institutes of the Christian Religion*.

GEORGE BUCHANAN
Scottish historian and poet

George Buchanan's political thought and historical scholarship influenced ideas about limited monarchy and constitutional theory. In his work De juri regni apud Scotos, *he argued that monarchs rule by the will of the people.*

BORN: February, 1506; Killearn, Stirlingshire, Scotland
DIED: September 29, 1582; Edinburgh, Scotland
AREAS OF ACHIEVEMENT: Scholarship, historiography, government and politics, literature, religion and theology, church reform

EARLY LIFE
George Buchanan was the third son of Thomas Buchanan and Agnes Heriot, farmers in Stirlingshire. Thomas Buchanan died around 1513, and George's uncle, James Heriot, sent him to study Latin in Paris when George was fourteen. After the death of his uncle less than two years later, George returned home.

At seventeen he enlisted in the Scottish army and served at the Siege of Werk in 1523. In 1524, Buchanan attended the lectures of John Major, an important theorist of conciliar church government at St. Andrews University in Edinburgh. Buchanan received his bachelor of arts degree from the university in 1527. Buchanan followed Major to Paris and took his master of arts degree there in 1528.

He set off on his career as a Humanist and educator in the same year by taking up a position teaching grammar at the college of Saint Barbe. Leaving his college post in 1531, he became private tutor to the Scottish earl of Cassilis. While tutoring, Buchanan found the time to publish *Rudimenta*, his 1533 Latin version of Thomas Linacre's *Rudiments of Latin Grammar*. In 1535, Buchanan and Kennedy together returned to Edinburgh. In the same year, Buchanan penned his satire on the Franciscan community, *Somnium*. From 1536 to 1538, he served King James V as a tutor to one of the king's illegitimate sons. Also, at the behest of the king, Buchanan wrote *Franciscanus et fratres* (1537), another satire against the Franciscans, whom the king suspected of plotting against him.

Although Buchanan acted on the king's commission, his reformist attack on the morals of the Franciscans angered the Scottish cardinal David Beaton. In 1539, Beaton had Buchanan arrested and would have had him prosecuted if the poet had not escaped and fled, first to London, then to Paris, and finally to settle for a time in Bordeaux.

LIFE'S WORK
After fleeing Scotland in 1539 and until his return home in 1561, Buchanan assumed the role of an itinerant Humanist, teacher, and poet, with politically progressive sympathies and unorthodox religious views. He taught at the College of Guienne in Bordeaux, from 1539 to 1543. Around 1544-1545, he taught briefly in Paris, then returned to Bordeaux for a stay of two years. At Bordeaux, he translated Euripides' *Medea* and *Alcestis* into Latin and wrote two dramas of his own, *Baptistes* (1534; *Tyrannical-Government Anatomized: Or, A Discourse Concerning Evil-Councellors*, 1642) and *Jepthes* (1578; *Tragedies*, 1983). The former drama displayed his sympathy with protorepublican and antityrannical views.

Buchanan taught in a new Portuguese university in Coimbra in 1547. He was, however, apprehended and tried by the Portuguese Inquisition on charges of eating flesh during Lent, writing against the Franciscans, and other matters. He was sequestered in a monastery for re-education in Catholic orthodoxy. Fortunately, he was allowed to leave Portugal in 1552. He sailed to England and then returned to Paris in 1553, where he taught for a brief time at the College of Boncourt and then worked as a tutor to the son of the governor of French territory on the Italian coast. While serving in this capacity, he lived alternately between Italy and France. During this time he worked on *De sphaera* (1555; *The Sphera of George Buchanan*, 1952), an astronomical poem in five books, and wrote *Epithalamium* (1558) to commemorate the marriage of Mary, Queen of Scots, to the French dauphin, Francis.

The exact date of his return to Scotland is in doubt, but certainly Buchanan was in Edinburgh by 1561. Safe in Scotland from the reaches of the Inquisition on the Continent, Buchanan now participated in efforts to establish a reformed Scottish church and a university system, and to reform governmental affairs. During this period, he became a member of a commission to revise the Book of Discipline, headed a commission to examine the foundations of St. Andrews and other universities, and served in the Scottish general assembly from 1563 to 1567.

At court, Buchanan wrote celebratory verses to commemorate the marriage of Queen Mary and Lord Darnley (Henry Stewart). After Darnley's murder in 1567 and the

George Buchanan. (Hulton|Archive by Getty Images)

queen's precipitous remarriage to James Hepburn, earl of Bothwell, however, Buchanan and his patron, the earl of Moray, opposed the queen. They then prepared a legal case against her. Buchanan was sent to England to confer with Queen Elizabeth I about the matter. He also published the *De Maria Scotorum regina* (*Detection of the Actions of Mary Queen of Scots, Concerning the Murder of Her Husband, and Her Conspiracy, Adultery, and Pretended Marriage with the Earl Bothwel*, 1689), his history of Queen Mary's reputed involvement in Darnley's murder and in other crimes.

In 1569, Buchanan, in the midst of this political turmoil, was appointed tutor to the young James VI, a post in which he remained until the young king reached the age of emancipation. In the course of his educational and governmental duties in the 1560's and 1570's, Buchanan still found time for significant literary activity. He wrote new verses, completed the poem *De sphaera*, compiled his history of Scotland–*De rerum Scoticarum historia* (1582; *The History of Scotland*, 1690)—and, perhaps most important, wrote *De jure regni apud Scotos* (1579; *De jure regni apud Scotos: Or, A Dialogue, Concerning*

the *Due Priviledge of Government in the Kingdom of Scotland*, 1680).

De jure regni apud Scotos contains his principal political ideas, and it attained such popularity that there were six new editions of it within two years. The work was written in part to defend those who had deprived Queen Mary of her authority on the grounds that she had violated the natural law that valued the maintenance of the common good above all else. For Buchanan, the good monarchy was a limited monarchy, constrained by law. The king or queen held office through the people's mandate. Tyrannicide was permissible in extreme cases. Buchanan's views were presumably shaped by the conciliarist theory of his old teacher, John Major, as well as the political writings of his contemporary, John Ponet.

Many political historians continue to view Buchanan's work as preliminary to the later formulation of English constitutional theory in the works of John Milton, Algernon Sidney, and John Locke. It was thus after a long, active, and productive life, that Buchanan died on September 29, 1582.

SIGNIFICANCE

Buchanan's political writings and dramas helped to validate the notions of limited monarchy, of subjects holding their kings accountable under the law, and of expelling tyrannous rulers. His work helped pave the way for later seventeenth proponents of constitutional theory.

—*Julie Robin Solomon*

FURTHER READING

Clarke, M. L. "The Education of a Prince in the Sixteenth Century: Edward VI and James VI and I." *History of Education* 7, no. 1 (1978): 7-19. Considers Buchanan as pedagogue to James VI and I.

Macfarlane, Ian Dalrymple. *Buchanan.* London: Duckworth, 1981. Most comprehensive biography of Buchanan available with careful attention paid to the literary works.

Oakley, Francis. "On the Road from Constance to 1688: The Political Thought of John Major and George Buchanan." *Journal of British Studies* 1 (May, 1962): 1-31. Analyzes the role of conciliarism in the political thought of Major and Buchanan.

Skinner, Quentin. "The Origins of the Calvinist Theory of Revolution." In *After the Reformation: Essays in Honor of J. H. Hexter*, edited by Barbara C. Malament. Philadelphia: University of Pennsylvania Press, 1980. Examines the thinking of Buchanan, John Know, Christopher Goodman, and John Ponet on the question of political revolution.

Walters, Barrie. "Pierre Bayles' Article on George Buchanan." *Seventeenth-Century French Studies* 20 (1998): 163-173. Examines Bayles' view of Buchanan.

Williamson, Arthur H. "George Buchanan, Civic Virtue and Commerce: European Imperialism and Its Sixteenth-Century Critics." *Scottish Historical Review* 75, no. 1 (1996): 20-37. Argues that Buchanan opposed imperialism while advocating conditional monarchy and republicanism.

_____. "Scots, Indians, and Empire: The Scottish Politics of Civilization: 1519-1609." *Past and Present* 150 (1996): 46-83. Explores Buchanan's defense of Scottish civilization against English and continental imperialist ideology.

SEE ALSO: Elizabeth I; James V; Mary, Queen of Scots.
RELATED ARTICLE in *Great Events from History: The Renaissance & Early Modern Era, 1454-1600:* July 29, 1567: James VI Becomes King of Scotland.

WILLIAM BYRD
English composer

Byrd was the outstanding English composer of the Renaissance, notable both for the variety of forms and styles in which he composed and for the outstanding quality of the individual pieces within each genre. He was apparently the first English composer to understand fully the new technique of imitative polyphony as developed in the Netherlands, and he passed this understanding on to his students.

BORN: 1543; possibly Lincoln, Lincolnshire, England
DIED: July 4, 1623; Stondon Massey, Essex, England
AREAS OF ACHIEVEMENT: Music, education

EARLY LIFE

Nothing definite is known of the early life of William Byrd (burdh). The year of his birth is assumed to have been 1543, since he described himself in his will of November 15, 1622, as being in his eightieth year. He may have come from Lincoln, but he must have been reared in London because he was reliably reported to have been a student of Thomas Tallis, composer and organist of the Chapel Royal. He may have been a Child of the Chapel Royal, but the records from this period are incomplete and the names of many of the boys are lost. Thomas Byrd, gentleman of the Chapel Royal in the 1540's and 1550's, may have been his father.

Byrd probably began composing music while still in his teens, and several compositions attributed to him are, if genuine, likely to have been student works. The motets "Alleluia, Confitemini Domino" and "Christus resurgens," the latter published in 1605, are two texts from the Sarum liturgy and could possibly have been written before the death of Queen Mary in 1558, when Byrd was fifteen or sixteen. Both are cantus firmus motets with extensive use of canon in the older style of Tallis and his contemporaries. Several works for viol consort and for organ may also come from this period, although the exact dating of most of his compositions has not been established.

LIFE'S WORK

The only portrait of Byrd comes from the early eighteenth century and is not reliable. He seems to have had strong convictions and a tenacious character. He was a staunch Roman Catholic at a time when this was strongly discouraged, and he repeatedly paid fines for his own and his family's recusancy. That he retained his Chapel Royal position to the end of his life is a tribute to his skill both as an organist and as a composer. He was somewhat courageous, willing to publish settings of the forbidden Mass Ordinary carrying his own name on each page. He was also a diligent and not altogether sympathetic litigant in numerous cases involving property during his later years. From his own compositions one derives the impression that he had great energy and organizational skills and was imbued with both a sense of artistic purpose and deep personal convictions.

In March, 1563, Byrd was appointed organist and master of the choristers at Lincoln Cathedral, a post that involved teaching the boys as well as composing and directing music. In 1568, he married Juliana Birley, who died around 1586, and the first of his five children from two marriages was baptized in 1569. Byrd was given an unusually large salary, and the cathedral continued to pay him at least a portion of it until 1581, when he had been in London for more than a decade, in return for his continuing to send occasional compositions to Lincoln.

During his time at Lincoln, Byrd seems to have set out to master a variety of musical styles and forms. He looked principally to Tallis, Christopher Tye, John

Redford, Robert White, and Alfonso Ferrabosco, the Elder, for models, sometimes borrowing specific musical ideas from their works. He composed settings for organ based largely on Latin hymns and began his lifelong interest in writing music for the virginals (an early smaller form of the harpsichord). He wrote a number of "In nomine" settings for instrumental consort, presumably intended for viols, and these seem to have been widely circulated in manuscript copies. He also wrote the first of his so-called consort songs for solo voice and viol consort, of which some are settings of metrical psalms and others of the sort of alliterative poetry popular at the time. Some of these pieces have simple choruses at the ends of stanzas and prefigure the development of the verse anthem, a form developed fully by Byrd's students Orlando Gibbons and Thomas Tomkins, in which music for solo voice or voices alternates with that for chorus, to an accompaniment of organ or viol consort.

Most of Byrd's music for the new Anglican liturgy seems to have been written at Lincoln and includes anthems, litanies, preces, suffrages, two Evening Services, and the so-called Short Service, based on a similar work by Tallis. Ironically, this music, which formed only a small portion of Byrd's output, survived in the repertoire after his death and carried his fame into the eighteenth century.

His Latin motets from this period appear to have been attempts to master both the older style of cantus firmus writing and the newer style of pure, imitative polyphony as developed in the Netherlands by such composers as Josquin des Prez in the early sixteenth century and only just being imported into England. Cantus firmus motets such as "Libera me, Domine, de morte aeterna" and purely imitative ones such as "Attollite portas" are unlikely to have been sung at Lincoln in the 1560's, but they probably served as good advertisements for the young composer by demonstrating his grasp both of various styles and of large-scale formal planning.

Byrd was sworn in as a gentleman of the Chapel Royal in February, 1570, and as joint organist with Tallis in December, 1572. This necessitated a move to London, where he occupied himself both with his Chapel Royal duties and with acquiring influential patrons. In 1575, Queen Elizabeth granted Byrd and Tallis a monopoly on the printing and selling of both part-music and lined music paper. In the same year, they published their *Cantiones, quae ab argumento sacrae vocantur*, a collection of Latin motets—seventeen by each composer—for from five to eight voices. The volume was dedicated to the queen, and it is possible, but by no means certain,

that some of or all the contents had been sung in her Chapel Royal, where the singing of Latin texts was still permitted.

The 1575 collection gives the impression of being an anthology of what Byrd considered to be his best work to that date, together with several newly composed pieces. The newer works, primarily penitential in character, demonstrate Byrd's mastery of the Netherlands style and his debt to Ferrabosco. The most famous of these works is the motet "Emendemus in melius." At this time, Byrd also continued writing instrumental music, his most famous works being his Browning variations for five-part consort, the Walsingham variations for keyboard, and a series of dances (pavans and galliards), also for keyboard.

Beginning in 1581, with the discovery of a Jesuit plot to kill the queen and the subsequent brutal executions of Father Edmund Campion and other Jesuits, life for English Catholics became more difficult. Byrd maintained his Chapel Royal position and even composed works for official celebrations, including *Look and Bow Down* to words by the queen herself, written to celebrate the defeat of the Spanish Armada in 1588. He seems to have reacted to the persecution of his Catholic brethren by composing a series of deeply personal penitential motets, some lamenting the Babylonian captivity of Jerusalem, others petitioning for the coming of God and the deliverance of the faithful. The most famous of these works is the motet *Ne irascaris*, printed in the first of his two retrospective collections of Latin motets titled *Cantiones sacrae*, published in 1589 and 1591, respectively. Whether these motets were meant to be sung in a liturgical context or merely circulated in support of Roman Catholicism is not clear. The penitential texts seldom have a specific liturgical function and seem to have been chosen, by Byrd or his patrons, to make a religious and political point—one, however, which was not so obvious as to warrant their suppression.

In 1588, Byrd published his first collection of settings of English texts, titled *Psalmes, Sonets, and Songs of Sadness and Pietie* for five voices. This work contained mostly earlier consort songs, slightly reworked and with words added to the original accompanying parts in an attempt to capitalize on the new vogue for the Italian madrigal. The most famous piece from this collection was "Lullaby," while the most striking was perhaps "Why Do I Use My Paper, Ink, and Pen?," a setting of the innocuous first verse of a well-known seditious text concerning the execution of Father Campion.

In 1589, Byrd published *Songs of Sundrie Natures* for from three to six voices. This contained, in addition to material similar to that in the 1588 volume, a consort song in its original form ("And Think Ye, Nymphs"), two carols, and the verse anthem "Christ Rising Again." Byrd then contributed two madrigals to Thomas Watson's *First Sett of Italian Madrigalls Englished* (1590), but he was in general not much influenced by the newer Italian style that so permeated the music of his student Thomas Morley and that of the other composers of the younger generation, especially John Wilbye and Thomas Weelkes.

Byrd's second collection of 1591 was the manuscript of keyboard music entitled *My Ladye Nevells Booke*, which preserved the best of his virginal music to that date. It included pavans and galliards, two new settings on a ground bass, some newly composed fantasias, and a number of earlier works, some of them extensively revised. Byrd's so-called Great Service, his largest and most outstanding contribution to the Anglican liturgy, may also date from around 1590.

Beginning at about this time, Byrd's attitude toward English Catholicism and the role in it of his own music seems to have changed. In 1593, he moved to Stondon Massey, Essex, near the seat of his patrons, the staunchly Catholic Petre family, at Ingatestone. After this date, he seems to have spent progressively less time in London and instead to have immersed himself in the life of the recusant Catholic community that surrounded the Petres. Instead of highly personal nonliturgical and penitential texts, Byrd began to set purely liturgical texts in a more emotionally restrained and less grandiose style. This music was apparently designed to be sung at clandestine Catholic services at Ingatestone Hall and elsewhere.

Byrd eventually gathered together this body of liturgical settings and published it in two collections, each entitled *Gradualia*, in 1605 and 1607; they were reissued together in 1610. The more than one hundred items included in these two volumes can be recombined in a variety of ways to provide the Mass propers for all the major feasts of the Catholic liturgy, including Marian feasts and votive masses. To provide the Mass ordinary texts, Byrd created settings for three, four, and five voices, of which the one for four voices is the most remarkable and that for five voices the most immediately accessible. These settings he had printed in the early 1590's, without title pages but with his own name clearly printed on each page.

Byrd's last published collection, the *Psalmes, Songs, and Sonnets of Sadness and Pietie* of 1611, was a miscellany, including both full and verse anthems to English texts, consort songs, madrigal-like songs for three to five voices, and instrumental fantasias. He subsequently included a number of his keyboard pavans and galliards in *Parthenia: Or, The Maydenhead of the First Musicke That Ever Was Printed for the Virginalls* (1613), a joint publication with the composers John Bull and Orlando Gibbons, both of whom were probably his students. His last published works were four sacred songs included in Sir William Leighton's *Teares or Lamentacions of a Sorrowfull Soule* (1614). His works continued to circulate in manuscript, the most famous collections being those of the Catholic Paston family of Appleton Hall, Norfolk, and the three volumes compiled between 1609 and 1619 by Francis Tregian, the first popularly known as *The Fitzwilliam Virginal Book*.

Byrd continued to live at Stondon Massey, his last years increasingly troubled by lawsuits over his various property holdings. His second wife, Ellen, died sometime around 1606 and he, himself, died there on July 4, 1623, and is presumably buried in the churchyard, according to his own wishes. The *Old Cheque-Book: Or, Book of Remembrance of the Chapel Royal, from 1561-1744* (1872), noting his passing, called him "a Father of Musick." His son Thomas, also a musician, survived until about 1652.

SIGNIFICANCE

William Byrd was one of the four greatest composers of the High Renaissance, the others being Orlando di Lasso, Tomás Luis de Victoria, and Giovanni Pierluigi da Palestrina. Byrd surpassed all except Victoria in the emotional fervor of his music and all but Lasso in his variety of forms and styles. If Byrd was less able than Lasso and Palestrina to come to terms with the new style of the Italian madrigal, he surpassed them both in his command of instrumental forms.

Byrd is that rare example of a composer who was at once the consolidator of older traditions and the instigator of new ones. If Byrd's initial efforts in various genres are based more directly on earlier models than had previously been thought, his achievements are not lessened thereby. He appears to have been the first English composer to understand and successfully employ Netherlands imitative polyphony, and he thereby established the dominant style for his successors. Although he wrote comparatively little Anglican church music, his Great Service was the crowning achievement of the Elizabethan period; many of his smaller works survived the Commonwealth and, together with English *contrafacta* of some of his Latin works, formed the basis of the Tudor style as copied by such Restoration composers as Henry Purcell and William Croft and eulogized by eighteenth century writers on music.

Byrd made only a few fleeting efforts at writing in the new and popular style of the Italian madrigal. Instead, he developed the older, more sober form of the secular consort song to its full maturity and created from it the form of the verse anthem, initially either secular or sacred, which was to dominate English church music for nearly two hundred years. He essentially created a genre and repertoire of keyboard music from the slimmest of beginnings, polished it over a period of some fifty years, and bequeathed it to his successors Bull and Gibbons. His compositions for viol consort are more conservative in character and were overshadowed by the newer Italian fantasias at the turn of the seventeenth century, but they were still influencing native composers some twenty years later.

Byrd was the most influential musical composition teacher of his time, producing such disparate pupils as the forward-looking Morley, the brilliant émigré composer Peter Philips, the keyboard virtuoso John Bull, and the conservative and essentially serious Tomkins and Gibbons. The teaching style employed in Morley's *A Plaine and Easie Introduction to Practicall Musicke* (1597) can probably be taken as Byrd's own. He appears as quite a modern figure, both in his attitude toward composition and in his tendency to revise his own works, collect them into anthologies, and then carefully supervise their publication.

Throughout his life, Byrd's consuming passion was his faith, and it is in his Latin church music that his greatest works are found. His early works are notable for their size and scope, his works of the 1580's for their penitential intensity, and his later works for their formal sweep and inner confidence. Although Byrd was capable of writing pedestrian music, his best works are unsurpassed, displaying a sense of technical command and personal conviction which set him apart as a great composer.

—*Graydon Beeks*

FURTHER READING

Andrews, H. K. *The Technique of Byrd's Polyphony.* London: Oxford University Press, 1966. An extremely detailed technical discussion of Byrd's musical style and compositional techniques.

Brown, Alan, and Richard Turbet, eds. *Byrd Studies.* New York: Cambridge University Press, 1992. Anthology of essays written for a symposium marking Byrd's 450th birthday. Includes music, discography, bibliographic references, and index.

Brown, Howard Mayer, and Louise K. Stein. *Music in the Renaissance.* 2d ed. Upper Saddle River, N.J.: Prentice Hall, 1999. Places Byrd in the context of his precursors and contemporaries, especially Giovanni Pierluigi da Palestrina, Orlando di Lasso, and Tomás Luis de Victoria. Includes illustrations, bibliographic references, and index.

Fellowes, Edmund H. *William Byrd.* 2d ed. London: Oxford University Press, 1948. A pathbreaking biography by the editor of the twenty-volume *The Collected Works of William Byrd* (1937-1950). Especially strong on biographical details, including many documents not printed elsewhere; it is somewhat dated.

Harley, John. *William Byrd: Gentleman of the Chapel Royal.* Brookfield, Vt.: Ashgate, 1997. Study of Byrd's life and works provides insight into the precariousness of his simultaneous relationships with the court of Queen Elizabeth I and with the Catholic Church. Includes photographs, illustrations, bibliographic references, a list of Byrd's compositions, and an index.

Holst, Imogen. *Byrd.* New York: Praeger, 1972. A charming, short introduction, intended primarily for children, with extensive illustrations and musical examples.

Howes, Frank. *William Byrd.* Edited by Landon Ronald. London: J. Curwen and Sons, 1928. Reprint. Westport, Conn.: Greenwood Press, 1978. Pioneering biography, useful but outdated, with a brief but solid discussion of the music. Includes photographs, bibliographic references, index.

Kerman, Joseph, and Oliver Neighbour. *The Music of William Byrd.* Vols. 1 and 3. Berkeley: University of California Press, 1978-1981. The most detailed discussions of Byrd's music, with special attention to sources, style, and compositional techniques.

Le Huray, Peter. *Music and the Reformation in England, 1549-1660.* Rev. ed. Cambridge, England: Cambridge University Press, 1978. An excellent survey of the entire period. Chapter 8 is especially relevant.

SEE ALSO: Elizabeth I; Andrea Gabrieli; Giovanni Gabrieli; Josquin des Prez; Orlando di Lasso; Luca Marenzio; Mary I; Thomas Morley; Giovanni Pierluigi da Palestrina.

RELATED ARTICLES in *Great Events from History: The Renaissance & Early Modern Era, 1454-1600:* 1567: Palestrina Publishes the *Pope Marcellus Mass*; 1575: Tallis and Byrd Publish *Cantiones Sacrae*; 1588-1602: Rise of the English Madrigal; 1590's: Birth of Opera; October 31, 1597: John Dowland Publishes *Ayres*; 1599: Castrati Sing in the Sistine Chapel Choir.

ÁLVAR NÚÑEZ CABEZA DE VACA
Spanish geographer and explorer

Cabeza de Vaca's capture by Native Americans in Texas unwittingly gave him the chance to explore the region in detail and write an invaluable account of the people and topography of Texas and northern Mexico, which stimulated further Spanish exploration.

BORN: c. 1490; Jerez de la Frontera, Castile (now in Spain)
DIED: c. 1560; Spain
AREAS OF ACHIEVEMENT: Geography, cartography, exploration

EARLY LIFE

Álvar Núñez Cabeza de Vaca (AHL-vahr NEWN-yayz kah-BAY-zah day VAH-kah) was the oldest of the four children of Francisco de Vera and Teresa Cabeza de Vaca. Cabeza de Vaca used his mother's surname (which means "cow's head") because of its honored association in Spain with the struggle against the Islamic Moors. At a battle in 1212, an ancestor had used a cow's head to designate an unmarked pass for Christian soldiers against the Moors. As a result of this action, which helped to win the victory, the ruler at the time had given the name "cow's head" to the ancestors of Cabeza de Vaca's mother.

Cabeza de Vaca's parents died when he was young, and he lived with an aunt and uncle until he launched his career as a soldier. He began as a page while still in his teens and was involved in fighting in Italy. He received serious wounds at a battle near the Italian town of Ravenna in 1512. During the next fifteen years, Cabeza de Vaca fought in battles with the armies of the Spanish king against rebels and also in struggles with the French in Navarre.

LIFE'S WORK

In 1527, Cabeza de Vaca joined the expedition of Pánfilo de Narváez that had been established to conquer Florida for Spain. The Spanish king, Charles I, designated Cabeza de Vaca as the treasurer and what was called the chief constable of the expedition. Five ships carrying six hundred people left for the Americas in June, 1527. The expedition soon encountered obstacles. More than one hundred of its members elected to remain at Santo Domingo. A significant number then perished in a hurricane in Cuba. By the time Narváez and his men had sailed from Cuba in April of 1528, there were only four hundred men left in his command. A few days later, the expedition made landfall in Florida and claimed the territory for Spain.

Then the expedition began to fall apart. Narváez decided to explore the interior and left his ships and supplies. Eventually he and his men found themselves running low on food. Attacks from North American Indians put the Spaniards in even greater danger. Narváez had his men build some crude barges, and he decided to head for Mexico, which he believed was not far away. In fact, it was hundreds of miles distant.

The flotilla of five barges made good progress for a month and passed by the mouth of the Mississippi River. Then a violent storm scattered the vessels, two of which came to rest on an island near the Texas coast on November 6, 1528. Eighty men survived, including Cabeza de Vaca. They were alone in a wilderness, however, at a great distance from any settlement of their European comrades.

Cabeza de Vaca's primary concern now was his own survival and eventual journey to Mexico to rejoin his countrymen. He later recalled that "the cold was severe, and our bodies were so emaciated the bones might be counted with little difficulty, having become the perfect figures of death." He had no way of knowing that it would be seven years before he found his way back to Mexico and his own civilization.

For four years until 1532, Cabeza de Vaca lived among the American Indians of the Texas coast and ventured inland to trade goods with other tribes. He became a kind of medicine man to the American Indians in the area. Since he had no real medical skill, all he could do was pray over the sick and sometimes blow on their injuries. Cabeza de Vaca saw a great deal of the land because the American Indians ranged widely to find the prickly pear fruits and pecan nuts that formed the major part of their diet.

Throughout this part of his adventure, Cabeza de Vaca thought constantly of escape, and he often considered his chances of making a break for freedom. Finally, he persuaded three other Spanish captives to go with him, though he would have made his expedition alone if necessary. By the autumn of 1534, he and his companions, Andrés Dorantes, a black slave named Estevanico (Estevan), and Alonso del Castillo Maldonaldo, fled southward in the direction of Mexico.

The exact route that they traversed has been the object of controversy. Because he was the first European to cross many Texas landmarks, Cabeza de Vaca has become a part of Texas nationalism or state identity. Modern efforts to trace Cabeza de Vaca's steps through Texas and Mexico have indicated that "the four ragged castaways," as Cabeza de Vaca's party became known, spent twenty-two months on their route to Mexico. The final thirteen months saw the most sustained and purposeful travel. Their trek began in what is now known as southeast Texas near the Guadalupe River. They then moved southward toward the Rio Grande. They crossed that waterway near the location of what is now the International Falcon Reservoir.

At the Rio Grande, they turned northwest and went in the direction of the present-day city of El Paso. Thinking that they could reach Spanish settlements on the Pacific coast and eager to discover new lands, Cabeza de Vaca and his colleagues moved through northern Mexico and then headed south and east down the Pacific coast of Mexico. This detour added two thousand miles to their journey.

During this phase of Cabeza de Vaca's trip, he once again practiced the medical skills he had used among the American Indians. He came on a man who had an arrow lodged near his heart. With a cauterized knife, Cabeza de Vaca removed the arrow and closed the incision that he had made. The success of this rough operation added to the four Spaniards' fame among the American Indians. Cabeza de Vaca has become known as the "patron saint" of the Texas Surgical Society for having performed the first such operation within Texas.

Cabeza de Vaca and his associates encountered a band of Spanish slave hunters on April 11, 1536, marking the end of their ordeal in the wilderness. They then went on to Mexico City, arriving in July, 1536. Cabeza de Vaca wanted to leave for Spain immediately, but circumstances delayed his departure until the spring of 1537.

After he returned to Spain, Cabeza de Vaca prepared a detailed account of his years in the wilds of Texas and Mexico. His narrative, written during the three years after he came home and published in 1542, became known

This painting depicts Álvar Núñez Cabeza de Vaca and three companions in the desert southwest, the sole survivors of Pánfilo de Narváez's expedition to Florida in 1528. (Hulton|Archive by Getty Images)

FROM CABEZA DE VACA'S *LA RELACIÓN* (1542)

Spanish explorer Álvar Núñez Cabeza de Vaca wrote an account of his journey on foot with three companions through the arid lands of the southwestern United States and Mexico after a failed voyage to explore and conquer Florida for Spain. Cabeza de Vaca's chronicle is the first known written description of the region.

With these people [the North American Indians] we suffered greater hunger than with the others, because the only thing we ate all day was two handfuls of that fruit. It was so green and had so much milky juice that it burned our mouths. There was little water and it made anyone who ate it very thirsty....

I've already mentioned that we went naked all this time. Since we were not used to this, we shed our skins twice a year like serpents. The sun and the air caused very large sores on our chests and backs, which caused much pain because of the great loads we had to carry, the weight of which caused the ropes to cut our arms. The country is very rugged and overgrown. We often gathered firewood in the woods, and by the time we carried it out, we were scratched and bleeding in many places, since the thorns and thickets we brushed against cut any skin they touched. Many times the gathering of firewood cost me a great deal of blood and then I could not carry it or drag it out. When I was afflicted in this way, my only comfort and consolation was to think about the suffering of our redeemer Jesus Christ and the blood he shed for me, and to consider how much greater was the torment he suffered from the thorns than what I was suffering at that time.

Source: La Relación, by Álvar Núñez Cabeza de Vaca. Electronic translation of the 1555 edition, part of the Cabeza de Vaca Relación Digitization and Access Project, Southwestern Writer's Collection at Texas State University, San Marcos. http://www.library.txstate.edu/swwc/cdv/la_relacion/. Accessed September 22, 2004.

as *La Relación*. It later appeared in subsequent editions under the title *Los Naufragios* (the shipwrecks). Another source, written by Cabeza de Vaca and two of his companions on the trek, was prepared in Mexico in 1536. These two versions became classics of the period of Spanish colonization and are the basic sources for any understanding of Cabeza de Vaca as an explorer and historical figure.

Once back in Spain, Cabeza de Vaca was given the post of governor of the province of Rio de la Plata (what is now Paraguay) in 1540. There he tried without success to apply some of the lessons he had learned with the American Indians in Texas. His humane treatment of the indigenous people there aroused political opposition among the Spanish settlers and he was returned to Spain in chains to face charges of misrule. The legal proceedings against him resulted in his banishment for a time to North Africa. Eventually, he was cleared of the charges and returned to Spain, where he died in poverty, probably around 1560.

SIGNIFICANCE

Cabeza de Vaca's experience is one of the great sagas of the period of Spanish colonialism, and it won for him an enduring historical fame. His work was also important to the future course of Spanish activity in North America. Because of the clarity of Cabeza de Vaca's account of his journeys, the Spanish in Mexico obtained a better sense of the geographical extent of Texas and northern Mexico. The information that Cabeza de Vaca provided also served to stimulate interest in the area north of where Cabeza de Vaca had traveled. Perhaps that region might contain the gold that animated so much of the Spanish impulse to conquer territory and subdue the Indians in the Americas.

To verify what Cabeza de Vaca had discovered, the Spanish authorities sent a priest, Friar Marcos de Niza, northward, along with Cabeza de Vaca's companion, Estevanico, the black slave. During this expedition, Marcos de Niza viewed a Pueblo Indian settlement and saw what he believed to be the glitter of silver and gold. He interpreted his findings as specific evidence of the legendary Seven Cities of Cíbola that would contain the gold that the Spaniards had long sought. From this report stemmed the expedition of Francisco Vásquez de Coronado that led to Spanish penetration of the interior of North America. In that sense, Cabeza de Vaca's wanderings and subsequent reports of his adventures proved a significant turning point in the history of the Spanish presence in what would become Texas and the United States.

—Lewis L. Gould

FURTHER READING

Adorno, Rolena, and Patrick Charles Pautz. *Alvar Núñez Cabeza de Vaca: His Account, His Life, and the Expedition of Pánfilo de Narváez*. Lincoln: University of Nebraska Press, 1999. Volume 1 of this three-volume set contains Cabeza de Vaca's own narrative of his adventures. Volumes two and three provide close readings and interpretations of the narrative together with analyses of the place of the work in literary history and the general history of Spanish exploration in the Americas.

Cabeza de Vaca, Álvar Núñez. *The Narrative of Cabeza de Vaca*. Edited and translated by Rolena Adorno and Patrick Charles Pautz. Lincoln: University of Nebraska Press, 2003. A stand-alone edition of Adorno and Pautz's critically praised translation of Cabeza de Vaca's narrative.

Campbell, T. N., and T. J. Campbell. *Historic Indian Groups of the Choke Canyon Reservoir and Surrounding Area, Southern Texas*. San Antonio: Center for Archaeological Research, University of Texas at San Antonio, 1981. Despite its title, this work is a valuable interpretation of Cabeza de Vaca's route in Texas and the information that his account offers about Indian life and customs during the sixteenth century.

Chipman, Donald E. "Álvar Núñez Cabeza de Vaca." In *The New Handbook of Texas*, edited by Ron Tyler et al. Vol. 4. Austin: Texas State Historical Association, 1996. The best brief biography of Cabeza de Vaca, with a good review of the issue of his route to Mexico and his historical significance.

_____. "In Search of Cabeza de Vaca's Route Across Texas: An Historiographical Survey." *Southwestern Historical Quarterly* 91 (October, 1987): 127-148. An excellent survey of the long-standing controversy about the route that Cabeza de Vaca took to return to Mexico during the mid-1530's.

González-Casanovas, Roberto J. *Imperial Histories from Alfonso X to Inca Garcilaso: Revisionist Myths of Reconquest and Conquest*. Potomac, Md.: Scripta Humanistica, 1997. Examines the political and ideological functions of official historiographies of Spanish conquest in the Americas and reconquest in Iberia. Includes a reading of Cabeza de Vaca's narrative and the ways it authorizes Spanish colonialism. Includes bibliographic references and index.

Hedrick, Basil C., and Carroll Riley. *The Journey of the Vaca Party: The Account of the Narvaez Expedition 1528-1536, as Related by Gonzalo de Oviedo y Valdes*. Carbondale: Southern Illinois University Press, 1974. A good translation of the so-called Joint Report of the expedition of which Cabeza de Vaca was a part.

Howard, David A. *Conquistador in Chains: Cabeza de Vaca and the Indians of the Americas*. Tuscaloosa: University of Alabama Press, 1997. A biography of Cabeza de Vaca that sees his Texas experience as a key influence in his change from exploiter to protector of the Native Americans in the Rio de la Plata province.

SEE ALSO: Vasco Núñez de Balboa; Juan Rodríguez Cabrillo; Charles V; Francisco Vásquez de Coronado; Hernando de Soto.

RELATED ARTICLES in *Great Events from History: The Renaissance & Early Modern Era, 1454-1600:* 1528-1536: Narváez's and Cabeza de Vaca's Expeditions; February 23, 1540-October, 1542: Coronado's Southwest Expedition.

JOHN CABOT
Italian explorer

Cabot, the first of a long and continuous line of European explorers of North America, persuaded the English to explore new lands beyond the western horizon and laid the foundations of England's claim to and eventual control of the North American continent.

BORN: c. 1450; Genoa?, Italy
DIED: c. 1498; place unknown
ALSO KNOWN AS: Giovanni Caboto; Juan Caboto
AREAS OF ACHIEVEMENT: Exploration, cartography

EARLY LIFE

John Cabot (KAB-eht) was born probably in Genoa and was given the name Juan Caboto. By the early 1460's, he

had moved to Venice, and in the late 1470's he became a citizen and married a Venetian named Mattea. Venice was then the center for Asian goods, especially spices, entering the European market. Thus Caboto became a merchant in the spice trade. He learned what he could about the trade by reading the works of Marco Polo. A desire for direct knowledge and a willingness to venture his life prompted the young merchant to disguise himself as a Muslim and make the pilgrimage to Mecca. It is doubtful the knowledge he gained through reading or travel helped him. He was the only person in a city of wealthy merchants engaged in a trade that was already beginning to diminish, thanks to the Turkish control of the eastern Mediterranean.

Seeking broader economic opportunity, Caboto and his family settled in Valencia in 1490. Juan Caboto, the Venetian, as he became known, developed a reputation as a cartographer and navigator. In 1492, Caboto presented local officials with a proposal for harbor improvements. The project material was forwarded to King Ferdinand, then residing in Barcelona—two hundred miles along the coast above Valencia. Caboto had several audiences with the ruler to discuss the harbor proposal. That royal approval followed suggests how persuasive the arguments and the plans of the foreign expert could be. Unfortunately, the project was later abandoned. What is important about this incident is that it brought Juan Caboto to Barcelona at the time when Christopher Columbus entered to announce that he had reached the land of the great khan.

Caboto was skeptical. There was no evidence that Columbus had reached the densely populated and highly cultivated lands described by Marco Polo. Caboto tried to persuade potential backers in Seville that Columbus had reached only an island partway to his destination. Thus the wealth of the Indies could yet be attained by organizing an expedition under Caboto. While some Spaniards shared the doubts of Caboto, King Ferdinand and Queen Isabella did not. Besides, given the choice between two men from Genoa, it made sense to support the one who had already crossed the Atlantic Ocean and had returned with gold. Like Columbus, Caboto decided to move to where support for his project might be found.

In the late fifteenth century, Bristol was, after London, England's most active port, and its venturesome spirit was unmatched anywhere. Its ships carried local wool to Iceland and returned with dried codfish. Bristol merchants dominated the wine trade with Spain and Portugal. Always ready to try new trades, the merchants had sent ships to the eastern Mediterranean and to the islands of the Atlantic—especially Madeira. From the 1480's, Bristol ships made voyages of discovery seeking the legendary Isle of Brasil in the western Atlantic. The men of Bristol, both merchants and mariners, had more experience in the waters of the Atlantic than any men in any country. Naturally, John Cabot, as he was known thenceforth, selected Bristol as his new home and base of exploration.

LIFE'S WORK

Soon after his arrival in 1495, Cabot persuaded several Bristol merchants to try the westward route to Asia. A westward course in the high latitudes would bring a ship to the northeast part of Asia, which, Cabot argued, was much closer to Europe than the tropical region reached by Columbus. Cabot constructed a globe to demonstrate the advantages of his route. Like Columbus, Cabot reduced the size of the earth and increased the eastward limits of Asia to shorten the western route. The Cabot proposal was sent to King Henry VII.

King Henry was famous for persuading reluctant subjects to make large contributions to the royal treasury. To such a ruler, Cabot's proposal was quite attractive. It was a second chance for the ruler who had rejected, in 1489, a

An engraved depiction of John and Sebastian Cabot's discovery of North America. (Library of Congress)

similar scheme by Bartholomeo Columbus on behalf of his brother Christopher. Still, Henry VII was not about to risk his own money in a doubtful venture. He granted a patent to Cabot in March, 1496, to discover islands in the world unknown to Christians. Cabot would govern and receive the revenue (minus one-fifth for Henry VII) of the towns and islands he could "conquer, occupy and possess."

With the royal patent and the financial backing of some Bristol merchants, Cabot put to sea, only to return a short time later. Officially he returned because of a shortage of provisions. Unofficially, the crew probably lacked confidence in the foreign expert and decided to end the voyage. Masters of ships at this time had limited powers and generally acceded to the wishes of their crew. On his next voyage, for example, Cabot followed the wrong course and made his landfall on the French coast because his crew did not trust the more northerly (and correct) heading proposed by Cabot.

In May, 1497, Cabot tried again. His small ship was named *Matthew*—probably an Anglicized version of his wife's name, Mattea. Cabot and his crew of eighteen men sailed toward the southwest tip of Ireland and then headed directly west. The passage was swift, thanks to smooth seas and fair winds. Land was sighted on June 24, only thirty-three days after leaving Ireland. As late as the eighteenth century, ships might take three or four months to make the same passage. Some scholars believe that Cabot's speed is attributable to the fact that he timed his departure and course to coincide with favorable weather patterns learned by earlier voyagers from Bristol. Cabot probably made landfall at the northern tip of Newfoundland. That particular site had been settled briefly by Vikings nearly five hundred years earlier. The crew of the *Matthew* went ashore and raised the standards of Henry VII, the pope, and Venice. Cabot claimed possession of the land but wisely kept his men near the water's edge; they had found evidence of local inhabitants. This brief ceremony was the only time that the men ventured ashore.

For the next month Cabot coasted along the foreign shore. Circumstances suggest that the *Matthew* sailed along the eastern coast of Newfoundland and then headed southwest past Nova Scotia to Maine. The southwest heading of the land mass matched the one Cabot had predicted for the easternmost area of Asia. The ship then turned home, crossed the Atlantic in fifteen days, and arrived at Bristol on August 6, 1497.

Cabot wasted no time. He left Bristol within hours of his arrival, bound for London and Henry VII. Four days later the king received Cabot and presented him with honors and a pension (the latter to be paid by the Bristol Customs House). There was general agreement that Cabot had reached the northwest corner of Asia and that the next voyage would reach the Indies and the much-desired spice trade. Bristol merchants were also excited over the vast quantities of fish reported off the "new found land." Whatever became of the western passage, Bristol now possessed a new source of fish to replace the declining trade with Iceland. Thus Cabot's brief voyage of 1497 promised rich returns to merchants prepared to risk the trade with Asia and fish to men of more modest means and ambitions.

There was no shortage of backers for the follow-up voyage. Henry VII outfitted a large ship, and London and Bristol furnished four more vessels. This was not a voyage of exploration. Cabot expected to establish an island base to service British ships making the long passage to the Indies. If Cabot failed to build and hold such a base, then he possessed nothing and lacked a claim to any revenue from the Asian trade. Discovery entailed more than simply finding a site: One had to inhabit the site. (Columbus met this requirement when his flagship was wrecked and its crew built a camp ashore to await their leader's return from Spain.) Cabot's fleet departed in May, 1498. A storm struck the fleet, and one damaged ship entered an Irish port. There was no more news of the fleet.

There have been many guesses about the fate of Cabot's fleet. The discovery by Portuguese explorers in 1501 of Newfoundland Indians with several items of Italian origin provides a possible clue. Perhaps Cabot did establish his base during the mild Newfoundland summer. If so, then no one would have been prepared for the Arctic winter conditions common to the northern part of the island.

SIGNIFICANCE

Cabot, whose activities gave Great Britain its claim to North America, remains almost unknown to this day. There are few references to him. Unlike Columbus, Cabot left no journals to detail his work. Whereas Columbus had sons who preserved and enlarged their father's claim to fame, Cabot had Sebastian, a scoundrel who claimed his father's work as his own.

Cabot was not the first European to set on the North American continent. The Vikings certainly came earlier, and in turn they may have been preceded by Romans and Greeks a thousand years before. Cabot's arrival, however, was different. He was the first of a constant stream of European explorers. Cabot ended the ancient isolation of the North American continent. The charts he made during the voyage of 1497 have long since disappeared. His contemporaries, however, made use of the charts. Juan de La Cosa's famous world map of 1500 shows a series of Tudor banners along the coast visited by Cabot.

It is customary to note the similarities in the lives and careers of Cabot and Columbus. Both were born in the same Italian city at about the same time (although in Cabot's case, place of birth is not certain), and both convinced foreign monarchs to back a search for a westward route to Asia. While Columbus achieved greater fame and fortune, he lived long enough to suffer greater disgrace. Cabot the explorer simply disappeared and left all controversy behind. He died an explorer's death

—*Joseph A. Goldenberg*

FURTHER READING

Davis, Ralph. *The Rise of the Atlantic Economies*. Ithaca, N.Y.: Cornell University Press, 1973. Although only the first chapter of this book deals with fifteenth century exploration, the author's description and analysis of the maritime trades that used the Atlantic Ocean is unequaled.

Firstbrook, Peter. *The Voyage of the Matthew: John Cabot and the Discovery of North America*. London: BBC Books, 1997. Book chronicling the re-creation of Cabot's 1497 voyage by a modern crew sailing in an exact replica of the *Matthew*. Combines narrative of the first journey with a narrative of the journey commemorating it. Includes bibliographic references and index.

Morison, Samuel Eliot. *The European Discovery of America: The Northern Voyages, A.D. 500-1600*. New York: Oxford University Press, 1971. The most famous maritime scholar and the leading authority on Columbus presents detailed chapters on all known explorers. The book is distinguished by excellent charts and photographs of the possible landfalls of the various explorers.

Parry, J. H. *Discovery of the Sea*. New York: Dial Press, 1974. The preeminent maritime historian discusses the development of skills and technologies that opened up maritime exploration in the fifteenth and sixteenth centuries.

Parsons, John. *On the Way to Cipango: John Cabot's Voyage of 1498*. St. John's, Nfld: Creative, 1998. A meticulously researched attempt to reconstruct Cabot's final voyage and determine what really happened to the explorer and his crew. Includes illustrations, maps, and bibliographic resources.

Penrose, Boles. *Travel and Discovery in the Renaissance*. Cambridge, Mass.: Harvard University Press, 1952. A fascinating study of how scholars and navigators, from the time of ancient Greece to fifteenth century Europe, viewed the world.

Pope, Peter Edward. *The Many Landfalls of John Cabot*. Toronto, Canada: University of Toronto Press, 1997. In-depth study of the historical disputes over the exact location of Cabot's landfall in North America. Looks at the various plausible candidates for Cabot's landing point, as well as the competing national traditions that attempt to appropriate Cabot for their own purposes. Includes illustrations, maps, bibliographic references, index.

Quinn, David Beers. *England and the Discovery of America: 1481-1620*. New York: Alfred A. Knopf, 1974. Though working with very limited sources, the author presents a strong case for the discovery of North America by English seamen before Columbus.

Skelton, R. A. *Explorers' Maps: Chapters in the Cartographic Record of Geographical Discovery*. London: Routledge and Kegan Paul, 1958. An outstanding description of how the discoveries of explorers were incorporated into the rapidly changing world maps of sixteenth century cartographers.

Williamson, James A. *The Cabot Voyages and Bristol Discovery Under Henry VII*. Cambridge, Mass.: Harvard University Press, 1962. In addition to presenting the best balanced account of Cabot's work, the author has assembled all known documents about the explorer so that readers may draw their own conclusions.

SEE ALSO: Jacques Cartier; Christopher Columbus; John Davis; Ferdinand II and Isabella I; Sir Humphrey Gilbert; Henry VII; Gerardus Mercator; Juan Ponce de León.

RELATED ARTICLES in *Great Events from History: The Renaissance & Early Modern Era, 1454-1600:* June 24, 1497-May, 1498: Cabot's Voyages; Early 16th century: Rise of the Fur Trade.

SEBASTIAN CABOT
English cartographer, explorer, and navigator

Sebastian Cabot's journeys to North and South America provided detailed knowledge of the east coasts of the two continents. His status as an expert cartographer was ensured by his highly praised 1544 map of the world.

BORN: c. 1474; Venice, Republic of Venice (now in Italy), or Bristol, Gloucestershire, England

DIED: 1557; London, England

ALSO KNOWN AS: Sebastiano Caboto

AREAS OF ACHIEVEMENT: Geography, exploration, warfare and conquest, government and politics

EARLY LIFE

Sebstian Cabot was born the second son of explorer John Cabot, either in Venice or in England. Sebastian's life was inextricably tied to his father's legend. Much of what is known about father and son is speculative because early accounts disagree.

It is known that John Cabot, most likely born in Genoa, became a citizen of the Republic of Venice. He had sailed Mediterranean waters and traveled the Middle East. Some suggest that John, independent of Christopher Columbus, concluded that Asia could be reached by crossing the Atlantic Ocean.

In search of a sponsor, John moved to England. On March 5, 1496, Tudor king Henry VII granted John and his three sons (Ludovico, Sebastiano, and Sancto) the right to sail on voyages of discovery. With charter in hand, John Cabot sailed westward. Though there is no definitive proof that Sebastian accompanied his father, some argue that he did because the grant expressly named John and his sons. The excursion, though, was unsuccessful.

The following year another attempt was made. On May 20, 1497, John set sail on the *Matthew*. Some contend that Sebastian accompanied him yet again. The ship crossed the Atlantic, making this the first recorded crossing of this body of water by an English vessel. On June 24, 1497, the expedition reached land, most likely Cape Breton Island, Labrador, or Newfoundland. Interestingly, once ashore, both English and Venetian flags were planted. After sailing the coastline and making navigational notations, the ship left for home.

On arrival in Bristol, another voyage was approved. John sailed in May, 1498, but Sebastian did not leave with him. After departing, John Cabot was never heard from again. Whether Sebastian accompanied his father on the earliest expeditions or not, John's dreams and exploits continued to be Sebastian's driving inspirations long after John's last voyage.

LIFE'S WORK

The facts concerning Sebastian Cabot's life in the immediate years after his father's disappearance on the 1498 voyage remain murky. There is some evidence that Sebastian led an expedition in 1508 to discover a northwest passage to the Orient. Sailing toward Labrador, Sebastian traveled along a passage leading westward, then turned in a southerly direction. Though Sebastian was certain he had found a sea passage west toward Asia, his men mutinied. Eventually, he was forced to sail back to England, but not before exploring the coastline as far south as New England.

Reviewing Sebastian's description of seas thick with floating ice, some modern scholars believe he may have discovered what is now called Hudson Strait and that he sailed part of what is now called Hudson Bay before his crew made him abandon this northerly route. Other writers fully refute this assertion, claiming that the entire voyage is unsubstantiated.

Back in England, however, it is certain that in 1512, Sebastian accompanied the English army of Henry VIII to the European continent in the king's attempt to aid the Spanish against the French.

King Ferdinand II of Spain, impressed by Sebastian's skills as a cartographer and his knowledge of the North American coastline, awarded Cabot a commission in the Spanish navy in order that he might head an exploratory expedition. Sebastian's plans for a new voyage across the Atlantic, however, came to an early end with the death of Ferdinand. Fortune then took Sebastian to the court of the Holy Roman Emperor Charles V, where he was appointed to the Spanish Council of the New Indies. Later, Sebastian also was appointed pilot-major, and he was given the authority to examine ships' pilots sailing under the emperor's banners.

For the next few years, Cabot's activities in Spain remain obscure. There is some evidence that Sebastian returned to England by 1520 when it was proposed that he be given a command in the small navy of Henry VIII. In the end, that command did not materialize. By 1525, Sebastian was back in the services of the Spanish crown. Never having abandoned his ambitions as an explorer, Sebastian was only too glad to accept a mission to navigate South American waters for Spain.

The expedition of 1526 to 1530 was a voyage fraught with mystery and intrigue. Spanish financiers sponsored this voyage to discover a passage to the Orient through the waters of South America. Unfortunately, what little information is available about this trip comes from those who later brought Sebastian up on charges for misdeeds and incompetence. What is certain is that, after Sebastian's expedition reached the southern shores of what is now called Brazil, he allowed himself to be enticed by tales of treasure.

For the next three years, Sebastian and his men sailed along the coast of eastern South America looking for gold and silver. Making his way up the La Plata River, some of Cabot's men mutinied and he responded by forcing them to disembark. Sailing up and down the La Plata River and its varied tributaries, Sebastian and his crew stopped to replenish supplies and build small fortifications. A good number of his men would be killed by indigenous peoples. In 1528, Cabot sent a ship back to Spain for provisions and reinforcements. The original promoters of the expedition, however, loudly criticized Sebastian. Nevertheless, the king's faith in the navigator remained strong, but no royal expedition was sent back to relieve Cabot and his men.

Meanwhile, indigenous peoples continued to attack the beleaguered Spanish adventurers, killing and wounding many. In 1529, the survivors decided to abandon their quest for riches and to sail back to Spain. On Cabot's return, he faced formal judicial proceedings. Two years into the dispute, Cabot was pronounced guilty of failure to carry out his formal mission. Though he was sentenced to banishment to Morocco, the expulsion was never enforced and he was eventually pardoned. As a testament to Sebastian's continued prestige, he remained in the service of the Spanish crown for some years to come.

Cabot continued to pursue his skills as a mapmaker and, in 1544, produced a greatly prized map of the world. With the succession of Edward VI to the English throne, Sebastian was invited back to the British Isles. After his return to England, Cabot was pensioned by the Crown and appointed governor of the Merchant Adventurers. He thereafter organized plans to search for a northeastern passage from which English ships could sail to the northernmost reaches of Russia and then to distant Asia. While such a route was never found, English trade with Russia was promoted by expeditions sent to the northern seas.

SIGNIFICANCE

Sebastian Cabot was a skilled navigator, an admired cartographer, and a determined explorer who, sailing for the English and later for the Spanish, visited both the North American and South American continents, lands that were unknown to Europeans of his day. While Cabot's adventurous spirit led him to make dangerous yet thrilling voyages, his intellectual interests encouraged him to chart those expeditions.

Cabot's journeys and detailed maps would later serve to further the colonial interests and claims of two of the most successful empires to emerge from Renaissance Europe, Spain and England. In addition, even though Cabot's explorations did not discover quicker sea passages from Europe to the Orient, his journeys to North America and South America, and his plans for a new trade route through Russian waters, offer lessons in the power of a person's vision and determination.

—*Pietro Lorenzini*

FURTHER READING

Firstbrook, Peter L. *The Voyage of the Matthew: John Cabot and the Discovery of North America*. San Francisco, Calif.: Publishers Group West, 1997. This work addresses the voyage of the *Matthew* with a decidedly favorable bias describing the subsequent English claim to lands in North America.

Mattern, Joanne. *The Travels of John and Sebastian Cabot*. Austin, Texas: Raintree Steck-Vaughn, 2001. This short work, primarily intended for middle-school readers interested in the travels of John and Sebastian Cabot, succeeds in providing basic information in a concise, complete fashion.

Quinn, David B. *Sebastian Cabot and Bristol Exploration*. Bristol, England: Bristol Historical Association, 1993. A brief, well-written account of Cabot's exploratory quest and his connection with the English port of Bristol, an area of study not often covered by other works on the Cabots.

Roberts, David. *Great Exploration Hoaxes*. New York: Modern Library, 2001. Attempting to tackle various legends concerning great explorations, the author fully analyzes the writings of a good number of Cabot scholars and comes to some controversial conclusions concerning Cabot's varied expeditions.

SEE ALSO: John Cabot; Charles V; Christopher Columbus; John Davis; Edward VI; Ferdinand II and Isabella I; Sir Humphrey Gilbert; Henry VIII; Gerardus Mercator; Sir Walter Ralegh.

RELATED ARTICLE in *Great Events from History: The Renaissance & Early Modern Era, 1454-1600:* June 24, 1497-May, 1498: Cabot's Voyages.

JUAN RODRÍGUEZ CABRILLO
Portuguese explorer

After taking part in the Spanish conquest and settlement of Central America, Cabrillo led an expedition north to explore Alta California and claim that area for Spain. He provided valuable information on the indigenous peoples and on the geography, flora, and fauna of what is now the west coast of the United States.

BORN: c. 1500; probably Portugal
DIED: January 3, 1543; at sea off San Miguel Island (now in California)
ALSO KNOWN AS: João Rodrigues Cabrilho
AREAS OF ACHIEVEMENT: Exploration, cartography, military

EARLY LIFE

Very little is known about the early life of Juan Rodríguez Cabrillo (wawn rawd-REE-ghahz kah-BREE-yoh). Most historians believe that he was born in Portugal but lived most of his early years in Spain. As a young man in about 1520, he very likely sailed from Spain to Cuba with Spanish soldier Pánfilo de Narváez. When Narváez was sent to Veracruz, Mexico, to arrest Hernán Cortés, Cabrillo was imprisoned by Narváez for disloyalty but was freed by Cortés at Veracruz.

The first historical record of Cabrillo, from 1519, documents his release from his incarceration by Cortés. He is listed as a captain of crossbowmen in the army of Cortés during the conquest of the Aztecs in Mexico. He was part of the later expeditions that conquered southern Mexico, Guatemala, and San Salvador (now in El Salvador). Cabrillo then made his home in Guatemala, becoming a leading and wealthy citizen in the town of Santiago. Most of his wealth came from gold mining and from trade with the Central American Indians, with whom he had a reputation of fair treatment.

In 1532, Cabrillo returned to Spain. While there he met and married Beatriz Sanchez de Ortega. The couple returned to Guatemala, where their two sons were born. When an earthquake destroyed Santiago in 1540, Cabrillo wrote a report to the Spanish government about the disaster, the first known piece of secular journalism from the Americas.

LIFE'S WORK

In 1541, Cabrillo was serving under Pedro de Alvarado, who had been a trusted lieutenant of Cortés but was now independent as the *adelantado* (frontier governor) of Guatemala. Alvarado's nephew, Juan de Alvarado, led an expedition up the west coast of Mexico, with Cabrillo as a captain. Juan de Alvarado was killed when a warhorse fell on him during a skirmish with Indians. Cabrillo assumed command of the expedition, but it was delayed for several months, partly to settle the estate of Alvarado. Cabrillo's own finances were in disarray because of the disaster at Santiago, and he may have considered abandoning the expedition.

In the spring of 1542, Antonio de Mendoza, the viceroy of New Spain, summoned Cabrillo to Navidad and confirmed his appointment to continue the expedition, giving Cabrillo the assurance that he would have the financial backing required for such an expedition. Navidad was on the west coast of Mexico, near what is now Manzanillo. In addition to his flagship, the *San Salvador*, which Cabrillo built himself, he was given the *Victoria* and the *San Miguel* to complete his flotilla. A planned companion expedition west to the Philippines failed when its leader was killed in a mutiny after reaching the Philippines. The plan had been for a reunion of the two expeditions at a nonexistent strait that the Spanish believed connected the north Pacific and the north Atlantic Oceans.

Cabrillo was now ready for his major undertaking, which spanned a period of only six months. In June of 1542, his flotilla sailed north up the west coast of Mexico. Cabrillo's chief pilot was Bartolome Ferrelo. Like similar expeditions, the primary goal of Cabrillo's expedition was wealth, particularly gold, but also the spoils from Indian trade. After exploring the coast of Baja California, on September 28, Cabrillo reached a beautiful bay that he named San Miguel, marking the European discovery of Alta, or upper, California. A later explorer, the Spaniard Sebastián Vizcaíno, renamed the bay San Diego in 1602-1603.

After six days at San Miguel, on an island that still bears that name, Cabrillo sailed north and reached what is now Santa Monica, California, on October 9, Santa Barbara on October 13, and Point Conception on October 17. At various points along the coast and on islands such as Santa Cruz, Catalina, and San Clemente, Cabrillo carried out the established ritual for claiming land in the name of the king of Spain.

North American Indians, such as the Chumash of the Santa Barbara Channel, watched the Spanish with much curiosity. They often came out in their canoes to greet the visitors and to trade with them. At one point Cabrillo was so impressed by the numbers of fine canoes that he named the place Pueblo de las Canoas (town of canoes). Cabrillo's trade with the Chumash seems to have continued his earlier reputation for fairness.

Adverse winds delayed the flotilla, and not until November 11 did they advance north of Santa Maria. They reached Monterey Bay and continued north, but they missed San Francisco Bay because they were likely blown out to sea at that point along the coast. Near Point Reyes, just north of San Francisco Bay, storms again forced the expedition south to San Miguel, in the Channel Islands near Santa Rosa Island, where they planned to winter.

On January 3, 1543, six months and six days after leaving Navidad, Cabrillo died on board the *San Salvador*, anchored off San Miguel. He had lost his footing during a skirmish with Indians on the island and broke bones in his leg. He was taken to the ship and, realizing he was dying, tried to update the log of the expedition. He turned command over to his pilot, Ferrelo, urging him to continue the expedition. The log was completed and later published by Ferrelo.

On January 19, the discouraged crew, led by Ferrelo, again sailed north, perhaps reaching the Rogue River in Oregon. On their return trip, they again missed San Francisco Bay, which was not discovered until 1769. With the ships in need of serious repair and short on supplies, Ferrelo arrived back in Navidad on April 14, 1543.

The exact burial spot of Cabrillo is unknown. Most historians believe it is on San Miguel Island, where a monument was built in 1937. Other possibilities include Santa Rosa Island, where a stone was found in 1901 that could have been Cabrillo's grave marker, or Santa Cruz Island, or even as far south as Catalina Island, off the coast of what is now Los Angeles.

SIGNIFICANCE

Some believe the Cabrillo expedition was a failure because the explorers did not find gold-laden cities or a connecting route to the Atlantic Ocean, though given the crew's courage of sailing into the unknown and given the magnitude of what was discovered in terms of geography, the expedition was successful to some degree. Later explorers had much to gain from Cabrillo's and, later, Ferrelo's journeys along the California coastline to Oregon, even though Cabrillo missed places such as the San Francisco Bay.

Also, contact with the American Indian tribes of the western coastal region paved the way for the establishment of Roman Catholic missions, beginning in 1769,

from San Diego to San Francisco. The missions marked the beginning of European colonization of California.

—*Glenn L. Swygart*

FURTHER READING
Bancroft, Hubert. *History of California*. Vol. 1. New York: Arno Press, 1967. Offers the most detailed coverage of Cabrillo's and other early explorations of California.
Cabrillo National Monument Foundation. *An Account of the Voyage of Juan Rodríguez Cabrillo*. San Diego, Calif.: Cabrillo Historical Association, 1999. An excellent account of the voyage of Cabrillo, including a foldout map of the expedition.
Kelsey, Harry. *Juan Rodríguez Cabrillo*. San Marino, Calif.: Huntington Library, 1986. An illustrated biography with the best account of Cabrillo's life before his journey. A good discussion of the voyage and the attempt to continue it after Cabrillo's death. Speculates about Cabrillo's death and burial in a way that is different from most accounts.
Lavender, David. *De Soto, Coronado, Cabrillo: Explorers of Northern Mystery*. Washington, D.C.: National Park Service, 1992. Includes a brief account of Cabrillo's journey, a full-color map of the route, a color drawing of Cabrillo's flagship, and an illustrated description of the American Indians encountered by Cabrillo.
Lemske, Nancy. *First European Explorer of the California Coast*. San Luis Obispo, Calif.: 1991. A detailed examination of Cabrillo's expedition. Includes several maps and illustrations of ship travel and American Indian life during Cabrillo's time.
Lowrey, Woodbury. *The Spanish Settlements Within the Present Limits of the United States*. New York: Russell and Russell, 1959. Provides a chapter on the discovery of Alta California based on the expedition of Cabrillo as recorded in his log.
Wagner, Henry R. *Juan Rodríguez Cabrillo*. San Francisco: California Historical Society, 1941. A good account of Cabrillo's journey, including Wagner's translation of Cabrillo's log, which was first published in 1543 and is attributed to Cabrillo's chief pilot, Bartolome Ferrelo. A 1929 publication by Wagner includes a facsimile of the original log in Spanish.

SEE ALSO: José de Acosta; Pedro de Alvarado; Vasco Núñez de Balboa; Hernán Cortés; Doña Marina; Montezuma II.

RELATED ARTICLE in *Great Events from History: The Renaissance & Early Modern Era, 1454-1600:* June 27, 1542-c. 1600: Spain Explores Alta California.

John Calvin
French theologian and church reformer

Calvin was one of the most significant theologians of the Protestant Reformation of the sixteenth century. The Reformed Church that he established in Geneva became a model for Calvinist churches throughout Europe. Calvinism itself became the most dynamic Protestant religion of the seventeenth century.

Born: July 10, 1509; Noyon, Picardy, France
Died: May 27, 1564; Geneva (now in Switzerland)
Areas of achievement: Religion and theology, church reform

Early Life

John Calvin was born the second son of Gérard Cauvin and Jeanne le Franc Cauvin. His father was the secretary to the bishop of Noyon and fiscal procurator for the province, and his mother was the daughter of a well-to-do innkeeper. The young Calvin was tutored for a career in the Church, and in 1523 he entered the Collège de la Marche at the University of Paris. It was there that he Latinized his name to Calvinus for scholarly purposes. Next, he attended the Collège de Montaigne, an institution of great importance in the Christian Humanistic tradition of the day. After having received his master of arts degree, he studied law at the University of Orléans. He returned to Paris in 1531, where he furthered his studies with some of the greatest Humanists of the period.

Sixteenth century Europe was in ecclesiastical ferment. The Roman Catholic Church had long been under attack because of its weaknesses and abuses. Religious reformers had, for more than a century, called for a thorough cleansing of the Church. In 1517, Martin Luther had initiated the action that ultimately became the Protestant Reformation. Given this environment, Calvin was soon affected by these ideas of protest and of reform. During this period of transition, Calvin published his first book, a study of Seneca's *De clementia* (c. 55-56; *On Clemency*), which revealed him to be a forceful and precise writer.

Soon after the publication of this work, Calvin was converted to Protestantism. Fearing for his safety, he fled Paris and went first to Angoulême and later to Basel. He devoted himself to a study of theology, concentrating on the Bible, as Luther had done. In 1536, he published the results of his study in the first edition of his most important work, *Christianae religionis institutio* (*Institutes of the Christian Religion*, 1561). This work was to be refined, expanded (quadrupled in size from this edition to the final, 1559 edition), and developed over the course of his life. It quickly won for him a reputation as a Protestant authority. Indeed, most scholars agree that it is the single most important work produced during the Reformation.

The *Institutes of the Christian Religion* provided the foundation for a different form of Protestantism. Calvin's training as a lawyer helped him to produce a work that was well organized, clear, and logical. There were two primary themes within the work: the absolute majesty of God and the absolute depravity of humans. God is omnipotent and omniscient, and therefore he knows all that was, is, and will be. Humans, because of their corrupt nature, cannot determine their salvation; only God can do so. Indeed, because of God's omniscience, he has predetermined who is to be saved and who is to be damned.

The doctrine of predestination, while it did not originate with Calvin, made good works useless. While this may seem fatalistic, to Calvin it was not. A member of the elect would most assuredly perform good works as a sign that God was working through him. Hence, one of the elect would work hard and strive for earthly success in order to prove himself as having received God's grace. Calvin also stated that Christ is present in spirit when believers gather prayerfully; priests are not necessary, for they have no special powers. He also rejected all sacraments except for baptism and the Eucharist.

Life's Work

Shortly before the *Institutes of the Christian Religion* was published, Calvin left Basel for Ferrara, Italy. There, he visited the duchess of Ferrara, a sympathizer who had protected a number of reformers. Calvin made a strong appeal to her for more financial support of the Reformation. This was the first of many of his efforts to acquire aristocratic support, which was essential in an age when aristocrats still controlled much power and wealth. Calvin returned to Basel, traveled to France, and, in 1536, stopped in Geneva, a city-state that had just become Protestant.

In this time period, everyone in a given place had to be of the same religion. Geneva had revolted against its bishop, but the city had not determined which Protestant ritual it would follow. Calvin, thus, stepped into a religious vacuum. He held public lectures on the Bible, and he printed a tract to prepare the Genevese for his concept of the Reformed faith. His dour version of Christianity,

John Calvin. (Library of Congress)

come the cornerstone of Reformed Church (Calvinist/Presbyterian) polity throughout Europe. The ministry was divided into four categories: doctors, pastors, lay elders, and deacons. The doctors were to study the Bible and to develop theology; Calvin was the only doctor at that time. Pastors were to proclaim the word of God; elders were to oversee the carrying out of the Reformed Church's dicta, that is, they were to be moral police officers; and deacons were to help those who could not help themselves, that is, to perform benevolent works. The Company of Pastors was the official governing body of the Reformed Church. Under the leadership of Calvin, the Company of Pastors determined religious assignments, worked with Protestants in other countries, and determined theology. The Company of Pastors also worked with the elders to control Geneva.

There were occasional sharp conflicts with the city council, but Calvin won absolute control of the city by 1555. All Genevese were forced to accept the moral laws of the Reformed faith or to suffer the consequences. From 1555 until his death in 1564, 58 people were executed and 786 were banished in order to preserve the morals of the community. The most celebrated case was that of Michael Servetus, a somewhat eccentric Spanish theologian, who wished to debate Calvin on the doctrine of the Trinity. Calvin warned him not to come to Geneva. Servetus ignored the warning, came to Geneva in 1553, was arrested and convicted of heresy, and was burned. Calvin was not a believer in religious toleration.

With Geneva under his absolute control, Calvin devoted more time to the spread of his Reformed Church to other areas. He created in 1559 a religious academy, which ultimately became the University of Geneva. Protestants from all over Europe were encouraged to come to Geneva to study. As his native land was his particular area of interest, hundreds of refugees were trained in the new theology and then were assisted in their return to France. Calvin also established an underground network throughout France to bind these French Reformed, or Huguenot, parishes together. Representative assemblies of pastors and elders were also encouraged. Drawing on his earlier experiences in France and elsewhere, Calvin appealed to sympathetic French nobles for protection for the Huguenots. His most notable convert was the king of Navarre, although this ultimately resulted in the French Wars of Religion.

The last years of Calvin's life were spent in dominating Genevese theological issues, in working with Calvinists everywhere, and in developing the *Institutes of the Christian Religion* further. In the 1560's, he had serious

however, was met with antipathy by many less austere Genevese. In 1538, Calvin and his associate, Guillaume Farel, were ordered to leave Geneva.

Calvin went to Strasbourg for the next three years. There he developed a liturgy in French, created an organization for running a parish, and attended many religious debates on the Holy Roman Empire. He debated with Lutheran theologians, especially Philipp Melanchthon, and with Catholic theologians as well. During the debates, he became convinced that Roman Catholics could never be negotiated with and that there would never be a reunion with the Roman church. He also became convinced that Lutheranism had not resulted in enough reforms within its church. In 1540, he married Idelette de Bure. They had one child, who died in infancy. Idelette died in 1549, and Calvin never remarried. A naturally reticent man, Calvin rarely permitted outsiders a glimpse of his personal life.

In 1541, Calvin was asked by the Genevese council to return. He was promised total cooperation in building the religious state that he wanted. His first activity was to propose a series of ecclesiastical ordinances, which were ratified on January 2, 1541. The ordinances were to be-health problems, and he permitted his heir apparent, Theodore Beza, to take over most of the responsibilities of managing the affairs of the Reformed Church. On May 27, 1564, Calvin died. Throughout his life he had devoutly believed that he had been called by God to reform his church; this Calvin had done. His powerful intellect and his unswerving devotion to his theology do much to explain Calvin's enormous impact on Western theology and on Western religion.

SIGNIFICANCE

Calvin's intellectual talents, quick mind, forceful writing style, and precise teaching skills enabled him to become one of the most important figures in Western religious history. While in Geneva, he created a religious dictatorship that became a model for Reformed Church/Calvinist churches throughout Europe. His *Institutes of the*

Christian Religion became one of the most important documents in Western theology. Even during his lifetime, his significance was well recognized, and Geneva itself was called a Protestant Rome.

Calvinism, as this second-generation Protestantism came to be called, quickly became the most dynamic theology in a Europe wracked by religious debate. Although Calvinism was austere in the extreme, its success may be explained. First, the Roman Catholic Church was so corrupt and so filled with abuses that a thorough purging was viewed as absolutely necessary by most religious reformers of the day. To many, Luther had simply not gone far enough; Calvin, on the other hand, created an absolutely cleansed church. Second, Calvin's rules for a godly life were clear and succinct in comparison with those of the Roman church, and this clarity was appealing to those who hoped for salvation. Third, Calvin's tenet of predestination, while on the surface appearing to be fatalistic, came to be a rationale for the behavior of the middle class. While Calvin had stated that no one could know whether one was a member of the elect, it was believed that God's grace could be measured by one's success. Although this conclusion is much debated by historians, it is nevertheless true that the Calvinist areas of Europe were to be the most economically successful over the next several centuries.

Following Calvin's death, Calvinism became the dominant Protestant theology in the religious wars that occurred over the next century. Calvinist leaders played major roles in a number of European wars. Calvinism became the dominant religion of the Low Countries, southwestern France, Scotland, central Germany, and southeastern England. In each of these areas, strong economic growth took place, an educated middle class emerged, and demands for political power developed. Indeed, the period from 1550 to 1700 and afterward cannot be understood without an awareness of the impact of the theology of John Calvin.

—*William S. Brockington, Jr.*

CALVIN ON ARROGANCE AND PRESUMPTION IN THE CURIOUS

Protestant Reformer John Calvin, a contemporary of Martin Luther, outlined his reformist theology in his highly influential work Institutes of the Christian Religion. *His ideas on the limits of curiosity in the face of predestination, on the ultimate power of God's grace and all-knowingness, are excerpted here.*

The discussion of predestination, a subject of itself rather intricate, is made very perplexed, and therefore dangerous, by human curiosity, which no barriers can restrain from wandering into forbidden labyrinths and soaring beyond its sphere, as if determined to leave none of the divine secrets unscrutinized or unexplored. As we see multitudes everywhere guilty of this arrogance and presumption, and among them some who are not censurable in other respects, it is proper to admonish them of the bounds of their duty on this subject. First, then: let them remember that when they inquire into predestination they penetrate the inmost recesses of divine wisdom, where the careless and confident intruder will obtain no satisfaction to his curiosity, but will enter a labyrinth from which he will find no way to depart. For it is unreasonable that man should scrutinize with impunity those things which the Lord hath determined to be hidden in Himself; and investigate, even from eternity, that sublimity of wisdom which God would have us to adore and not comprehend, to promote our admiration of His glory. The secrets of His will which He determined to reveal to us He discovers in His Word; and these are all that He foresaw would concern us, or conduce to our advantage. . . .

Predestination we call the eternal decree of God, by which He hath determined in Himself what He would have to become of every individual of mankind.

Source: Excerpted in *The Portable Renaissance Reader,* edited by James Bruce Ross and Mary Martin McLaughlin (New York: Viking Press, 1968), pp. 710-711.

FURTHER READING

Bouwsma, William J. *John Calvin: A Sixteenth-Century Portrait*. New York: Oxford University Press, 1988. This work by a distinguished historian has been acclaimed as the best modern biography of Calvin. At the same time, as the subtitle indicates, Bouwsma uses Calvin's experience "to illuminate the momentous cultural crisis central to his century." Includes sixty pages of notes, a bibliography, and an index.

Calvin, John. *Institutes of the Christian Religion*. Edited by John T. McNeill. 2 vols. Philadelphia: Westminster Press, 1960. These volumes provide an annotated edition of Calvin's work and include a lengthy introduction and an extensive bibliography.

Cottret, Bernard. *Calvin: A Biography*. Translated by M. Wallace McDonald. Grand Rapids, Mich.: W. B. Eerdmans, 2000. This biography seeks to recount the history of Calvin's hopes and ideas, as well as of his actions. Less focused on Calvin himself than most biographies, this account is more interested in the institutions he created and the effects he has had on the world. Includes bibliographic references and index.

Haller, William. *The Rise of Puritanism: Or, The Way to the New Jerusalem—As Set Forth in Pulpit and Press from Thomas Cartwright to John Lilburne and John Milton, 1570-1643*. New York: Columbia University Press, 1938. Reprint. Philadelphia: University of Pennsylvania Press, 1972. While his prose is at times turgid, Haller offers insight into the spread of Calvinism into England. His study is useful for understanding why Calvinism spread so rapidly.

Kingdon, Robert M. *Geneva and the Coming of the Wars of Religion in France, 1555-1563*. Geneva: Librairie E. Droz, 1956. Important for understanding Calvin's methods of exporting his theology to other areas of Europe.

McNeill, John T. *The History and Character of Calvinism*. New York: Oxford University Press, 1954. A carefully balanced source that offers an excellent interpretive discussion of the theory and practice of Calvinism. Includes a lengthy biography of Calvin, followed by a series of chapters on the spread of Calvinism throughout Europe and to the United States.

Naphy, William G. *Calvin and the Consolidation of the Genevan Reformation*. 1994. Reprint. Louisville, Ky.: Westminster John Knox Press, 2003. This meticulously researched study of the Genevan Reformation includes twenty-seven statistical tables and eleven appendices of information on Calvin's Geneva. Focuses on the challenges posed to the Reformation by the large number of refugees flooding into Geneva. Illustrations, bibliographic references, index.

Oberman, Heiko A. *The Two Reformations: The Journey from the Last Days to the New World*. Edited by Donald Weinstein. New Haven, Conn.: Yale University Press, 2003. Posthumous collection of essays by one of the foremost Reformation scholars of the twentieth century. Attempts to recover an adequate picture of Calvin the man, as opposed to the figure historians have created. Argues that medieval religious thought was essential to both Calvin's and Luther's understandings of Christianity. Includes bibliographic references and index.

O'Connell, Marvin R. *The Counter Reformation, 1559-1610*. New York: Harper & Row, 1974. Places Calvin and the spread of Calvinism in perspective. Includes an excellent bibliography.

Parker, Thomas H. L. *John Calvin: A Biography*. Philadelphia: Westminster Press, 1975. Parker's work is a concise, single volume on the life of John Calvin. Particularly useful for a study of the impact of university life on Calvin and on Calvin's scholarship. Well written and easily understood. Useful bibliography.

Wendel, François. *Calvin: The Origins and Development of His Religious Thought*. New York: Harper & Row, 1963. First published in French in 1950, Wendel's work is essential for an understanding of the evolution of Calvin's theology.

SEE ALSO: Martin Bucer; Miles Coverdale; Henry IV; François Hotman; John Knox; Hugh Latimer; Martin Luther; Marguerite de Navarre; Philipp Melanchthon; Philippe de Mornay; Saint Philip Neri; Michael Servetus; Huldrych Zwingli.

RELATED ARTICLES in *Great Events from History: The Renaissance & Early Modern Era, 1454-1600*: March, 1536: Calvin Publishes *Institutes of the Christian Religion*; 1553: Servetus Describes the Circulatory System; May, 1559-August, 1561: Scottish Reformation; April or May, 1560: Publication of the Geneva Bible.

LUÍS DE CAMÕES
Portuguese poet

Camões is the author of The Lusiads, *the national epic of Portugal. Celebrating the voyage of explorer Vasco da Gama, the poem recites the heroic history of the Portuguese nation.*

BORN: c. 1524; Lisbon, Portugal
DIED: June 10, 1580; Lisbon
ALSO KNOWN AS: Luís de Camoëns; Luís Vaz de Camões (full name)
AREA OF ACHIEVEMENT: Literature

EARLY LIFE

Luís de Camões (lew-EESH duh kah-MOYNSH) was born around 1524. By 1527 his family was living with Luís's grandparents in Coimbra; most likely they fled from Lisbon to escape the plague, which reached the capital in that year.

Luís's father was Simão Vas de Camões, a gentleman of no great power or wealth. Little is known of Anna de Sá e Macedo, Luís's mother, beyond her name. When his father returned to Lisbon to take a position in the king's warehouse, Luís remained in Coimbra with his mother in the home of her family, who were influential people there.

As Luís grew into adulthood, Coimbra was undergoing its own development into the educational center of Portugal. Under the guidance of John III, a great university was permanently established. In or near 1539, Luis entered the university and must have read Vergil, Ovid, Lucan, and Cicero in the original Latin. He learned to speak Spanish fluently and was also exposed to Italian, Greek, geography, history, music, and many other subjects. During this period, he developed many friendships with young aristocrats, from whom he learned courtly tastes and manners. He also suffered his first taste of love, leading to some of his earliest, most tragic lyrics. After the conclusion of his studies, he left Coimbra for Lisbon, never to return.

LIFE'S WORK

When Camões traveled to Lisbon to make his fortune, in or near 1543, he began a life of adventure and accomplishment as exciting as any legendary hero's. He started quietly enough: Camões took a position as a tutor to the young son of a count. During these years, he learned all he could of his country's history and culture. Camões was considered charming and attractive. Surviving portraits from this time show he was handsome, with reddish-gold hair and blue eyes. In 1544, in church, he saw a young girl, Catarina de Ataíde, and fell immediately and passionately in love with her. For the rest of his life, Camões would consider Catarina the great spiritual love of his life; many of his most beautiful lyrics are dedicated to her.

While still in Lisbon, Camões also wrote three well-received comedies: *El-Rei Seleuco*, performed in 1542, *Enfatriões*, performed in 1540, and *Filodemo*, performed in 1555. As he became more widely known as a writer, Camões was drawn deeper into the inner circles of the court, where he found many who admired his talents and charms, and many who despised his smugness and sharp tongue. Never one to feign modesty, he dedicated impassioned poetry to a series of lovers, in spite of his devotion to Catarina. Finally, his brashness led to his disgrace at court, though the actual sins committed are uncertain. Because of the scandal, he enlisted, under duress, in the army in 1547, served two years in northern Africa, and lost the use of his right eye in a battle at Ceuta in Morocco.

Camões returned to Lisbon no wiser than he had left; his wild living soon earned for him the nickname Trinca Fortes, or Swashbuckler. His absence had done nothing to restore his favor with the court, but he found himself equally capable of carousing with a lower class of companion. For the next two years, the poet earned a meager living as a ghostwriter of poetry and did all he could to enhance his reputation as a scalawag. On June 16, 1552, the intoxicated poet was involved in a street fight with a member of the royal staff, whom he stabbed. Camões was promptly arrested and sent to prison, where he languished for eight months.

When the stabbed official recovered, Camões's friends obtained the poet's release, but under two conditions: He was to pay a large fine, and he was to leave immediately on an expedition to India. On March 26, 1553, he set sail on the *São Bento*, playing out the dangerous existence of the warrior-adventurer described in his epic. The voyage to India took six months, and the seafaring life was not an easy one. Boredom, hunger, scurvy, cold, seasickness, and storms—Camões and his companions had suffered it all before the ship rounded the Cape of Good Hope.

In September, 1553, the ship reached the Indian city of Goa, the Portuguese seat of power and wealth. During his residence there, Camões observed the local people and their exotic costumes, manners, and traditions, and began writing *Os Lusíadas* (1572; *The Lusiads*, 1655). He took part in several expeditions up the Malabar Coast, along the shores of the Red Sea, and through the Persian Gulf.

Camões continued to write poetry and satire, and to work on his epic; his play *Filodemo* was performed for the governor. The play's success nearly brought him advancement and a return home, but it was not to be. A satire mocking local officials was wrongfully attributed to him, and the officials concerned goaded him into an intemperate display of public indignation. To restore order, he was sent to a new position as trustee for the dead and absent in Macao, China.

In Macao, Camões was happy for a time. He enjoyed the company of a woman he loved, and he continued to write new poems and to polish his epic. The silks, jades, porcelains, and teas of China provided him with new material, and he spent much time alone dreaming and writing. After three years in Macao, he was accused, apparently falsely, of misappropriating funds. Camões was forced to sail again for Goa to stand trial.

Luís de Camões. (Library of Congress)

On the voyage to Goa, fate intervened. A typhoon struck the ship off southern Indochina, and the ship was wrecked. Camões grabbed the box containing his manuscripts before he was swept off the ship; when he recovered his wits, he was floating on a scrap of wood, and the manuscripts were still in his hand. He struggled to shore and was taken to a fishing village on the Mekong River. In 1561, he somehow was able to return to Goa. Yet his troubles did not end there. He learned that Catarina, his great inspiration, had died, and a few days later he was again cast into prison to face the misappropriation charges. No evidence was produced against him, and he was released. Camões remained in India for several more years, again living a life of poverty.

In the spring of 1567, he arranged passage to Mozambique, and in 1569, after an absence of seventeen years, he set sail for home, arriving in Lisbon in 1570 with the completed manuscript of *The Lusiads* his only possession. He dedicated his time to finding a publisher for his greatest work. Finally, in 1572, the poem was published, and he was granted a small royal pension. Of the next several years of the poet's life little is known, but he appears to have written almost nothing after his return to Lisbon. In 1580, he died of the plague, and his body was placed in an unmarked mass grave.

SIGNIFICANCE

Had he written only the three comedies and his large variety of *Rimas* (1595; *The Lyrides*, 1803, 1884), Camões might be acknowledged merely as one of the finest European poets of the sixteenth century. With *The Lusiads*, however, Camões was able to capture the passion and nobility of a nation, and it is as the creator of the national epic of Portugal that he will always be remembered.

The Lusiads tells the dramatic story of Vasco da Gama's discovery of a sea route to India, but in the process, da Gama as narrator relates virtually the entire history of "the sons of Lusus," or the Portuguese. *The Lusiads* relies heavily on Camões's classical learning, especially his reading of Vergil (for its structure and tone) and Ludovico Ariosto (for its ottava rima). Yet Camões brought much that was new to the epic. Of the epics written before his, none is grounded so heavily in actual events; Camões demonstrated how actual historical figures could be given the stature of mythical heroes. Unlike Homer, Dante, and others, Camões described countries, peoples, and storms at sea that he had witnessed firsthand.

The Lusiads was immensely popular when it was published and has never been out of print since. School-

CAMÕES'S MAJOR WORKS

1540	*Enfatriões*
c. 1542	*El-Rei Seleuco*
1555	*Filodemo*
1572	*Os Lusíadas* (*The Lusiads*, 1655)
1580	*Cancioneiro*
1595	*Rimas* (*The Lyrides*, 1803, 1884)

children throughout the Portuguese-speaking world still memorize its opening stanzas, and the poem has been translated into English many times. English poets such as John Milton, Lord Byron, William Wordsworth, and Elizabeth Barrett Browning have treasured and praised *The Lusiads*, which has been called "the first epic poem which in its grandeur and universality speaks for the modern world."

—*Cynthia A. Bily*

FURTHER READING

Bell, Aubrey F. G. *Luis de Camões*. London: Oxford University Press, 1923. This is a brief treatment that includes a biography of the poet, a description of his moral character as revealed by the poetry, an analysis of *The Lusiads*, and a chapter entitled "Camões as Lyric and Dramatic Poet." A difficult book, its approach assumes that the reader is familiar with previous biographies and with the major Romance languages.

Bowra, C. M. "Camões and the Epic of Portugal." In *From Virgil to Milton*. New York: St. Martin's Press, 1945. Reprint. New York: Humanities Press, 1963. An explication of *The Lusiads* as an epic poem, a poem of the ideal in manhood, demonstrating Camões's indebtedness to classical tradition and especially to Homer, Vergil, and Ariosto. The discussion of how the poet reconciles his use of pagan divinities with his Christian message is particularly illuminating.

Burton, Richard Francis. *Camoens: His Life and His Lusiads*. 2 vols. London: Bernard Quaritch, 1881. This is a commentary on *The Lusiads* in five sections: biography, bibliography emphasizing English translations, history and chronology of Portugal through the death of the poet, geographical study of the world as it was understood by da Gama and Camões, and annotations of specific passages in the poem. Appendix includes a table of important episodes in the poem and a glossary.

Camões, Luis de, et al. *Epic and Lyric*. Edited by L. C. Taylor. Translated by Keith Bosley. Manchester, England: Carcanet, 1990. Translations of Camões's works, accompanied by interpretive essays, illustrations, and engravings. Includes bibliographic references.

Freitas, William. *Camoens and His Epic: A Historic, Geographic, and Cultural Survey*. Stanford, Calif.: Institute of Hispanic American and Luso-Brazilian Studies, Stanford University, 1963. A historic and geographical study using *The Lusiads* as a source for information on Portugal's clashes with other nations. The final chapter traces the poem's roots of nationalism through the next four centuries of Portuguese history. Includes a bibliography of biographical, critical, and historical works in several languages as well as twenty illustrations, including portraits and maps.

Hart, Henry H. *Luis de Camoëns and the Epic of the Lusiads*. Norman: University of Oklahoma Press, 1962. A comprehensive, readable biography, filled with colorful detail of the scenery, culture, and history through which the poet walked. Appendices provide several examples of Camões's poems and a listing of books on the Orient which he may have read. Includes a generous bibliography and eight illustrations.

Monteiro, George. *The Presence of Camoes: Influences on the Literature of England, America, and Southern Africa*. Lexington: University Press of Kentucky, 1996. Study of Camões's influence on such later writers as Poe, Melville, Longfellow, Dickinson, Elizabeth Barrett, and Elizabeth Bishop. Includes illustrations, bibliographic references, and index.

Nicolopulos, James. *The Poetics of Empire in the Indies: Prophecy and Imitation in "La Araucana" and "Os Lusíadas."* University Park: Pennsylvania State University Press, 2000. In-depth study of colonial ideology in *The Lusiads* and in Alonso de Ercilla y Zauaniga's poem about the Spanish colonization of Chile. Examines the attitudes of the poets toward the colonial projects of their respective nations, as well as evidence within the poems of Spanish-Portuguese rivalries. Includes bibliographic references and index.

O'Halloran, Colin M. *History and Heroes in the "Lusiads": A Commemorative Essay on Camoëns*. Lisbon: Commissão Executiva do IV Centenário da Publicação de "Os Lusíadas," 1974. A short book examining Camões's use of the history of Portugal in the creation of the heroes and kings in his poem. Discusses the poem as a record of and tribute to Portugal's national drive to conquer new lands and convert the people there. It is interesting and accessible, but all quotations from the poem are in Portuguese.

SEE ALSO: Ludovico Ariosto; Vasco da Gama; John III.
RELATED ARTICLES in *Great Events from History: The*

Renaissance & Early Modern Era, 1454-1600:
c. 1485: Portuguese Establish a Foothold in Africa; January, 1498: Portuguese Reach the Swahili Coast; 1500-1530's: Portugal Begins to Colonize Brazil; 1505-1515: Portuguese Viceroys Establish Overseas Trade Empire.

CARAVAGGIO
Italian painter

Caravaggio's bold use of chiaroscuro, provocative reinterpretations of canonical subjects, and revolutionary commitment to realism established a new painting style that made a significant contribution to the definition of Baroque painting. He was a prolific and influential painter whose style became popular quickly, producing an international movement known as Caravaggism.

BORN: Autumn, 1571; Milan or Caravaggio, Spanish Lombardy (now in Italy)
DIED: July 18, 1610; Porto Ercole, Tuscany (now in Italy)
ALSO KNOWN AS: Michelangelo Merisi (given name)
AREA OF ACHIEVEMENT: Art

EARLY LIFE
Caravaggio (kahr-ah-VAHD-joh) was born Michelangelo Merisi in the northern Italian region of Lombardy. Little is known about his infancy and early artistic training. In 1584 he became an apprentice to Simone Peterzano, a renowned painter from Bergamo who was active in Milan, where Caravaggio remained through 1588.

Legal documents concerning the sale of his family estate place him in the town of Caravaggio from September, 1589, to April, 1591. It is known that he arrived in Rome on May 11, 1592, but there is no information on his whereabouts or his activities. Later seventeenth century historians who favored Caravaggio's main rival in Rome, Annibale Carracci, asserted that he spent time in jail, but their bias places these assertions in question. Although there are no known autograph works from this period, the consensus is that Caravaggio was exposed to and mastered the achievements of the three manners of painting styles prevalent in the region: the Lombard, Leonardesque, and Venetian.

LIFE'S WORK
Information about the four years of Caravaggio's stay in Rome is vague. Presumably he collaborated with several painters, producing cheap portraits and other paintings sold on the general market. More certain is his collaboration with the painter Giuseppe Cesari, also known as Cavaliere d'Arpino, a leading mannerist painter in Rome, for whom Caravaggio probably painted naturalistic details of plants.

Although no signed examples survive, *Boy Peeling Fruit* and two paintings in the Galleria Borghese (Rome), *Boy with a Basket of Fruit* and *Self-Portrait as Bacchus*, are probably representative of this interlude of Caravaggio's career. These works introduce two essential themes of the artist's style: a striking realism and an interest in endowing the pictures with multiple meanings and allusions.

After leaving Cavaliere d'Arpino, Caravaggio continued engaging these very issues, producing several provocative paintings such as *The Cardsharps* and *The Penitent Magdalen* (generally dated to 1594-1598). The latter presents a young woman dressed in contemporary clothes, identified as the saint only by her jewels and a small flask of perfume on the floor. Isolating the figure, the background was left unqualified save for the shaft of light across the upper right, which quickly became a hallmark of the painter's style.

In *The Cardsharps* and similar paintings depicting musicians and fortune-tellers, Caravaggio explores the compositional solutions that inject the scene with drama and immediacy; he crops the figures at half length and places them close to the picture plane, often adding illusionistic details that intentionally break the separation between the space of the painted scene and that of the beholder. These works indicate that Caravaggio formed a mature painting style.

In 1596, Caravaggio entered Cardinal Francesco del Monte's household as a paid retainer, remaining there through 1600. While working for del Monte, the artist met the marchese Vincenzo Giustiniani, who became the artist's major supporter and an avid collector of his works, as confirmed by the thirteen paintings listed in his possession in a 1637 inventory. Giustiniani helped Caravaggio gain an important commission, showcasing his new style by decorating the Contarelli Chapel in the church of Saint Luigi dei Francesi.

Between July 23, 1599, and July 4, 1600, Caravaggio produced two large canvases, representing *The Calling of Saint Matthew* and *The Martyrdom of Saint Matthew*. Capitalizing on the darkness of the chapel, Caravaggio created two scenes dominated by a previously unseen contrast of light, leaving most of the painting black and highlighting parts of realistically rendered figures. This extreme chiaroscuro endowed the paintings with an emotional charge while also identifying and freezing the instance of depicted time. The success of these two paintings was immediate and long lasting, procuring to Caravaggio a steady stream of commissions and winning him the election to the Academy of St. Luke, Rome's prestigious painting academy.

The next major commission, the Cerasi Chapel, was an occasion for a direct comparison with Annibale Carracci, Italy's leading painter, who was to paint the chapel's altarpiece. In 1601, Caravaggio painted *The Crucifixion of Saint Peter* and *The Conversion of Saint Paul* for the chapel's side walls. On seeing Annibale's *Assumption of the Virgin*, Caravaggio repainted his works, pursuing an even more striking chiaroscuro and theatrical composition. Despite the success of his works at these two chapels, the boldness of his revolutionary solutions were cause for the criticism of important altarpieces he delivered between 1600 and 1605; charged with a lack of decorum and a stagelike quality, three out of five pieces were rejected. His militant realism was both praised and criticized in the many religious paintings privately commissioned, two of which, *Supper at Emmaus* (London, National Gallery) and *The Incredulity of St. Thomas* (Potsdam), epitomize Caravaggio's mature style.

Charged with murder, Caravaggio fled from Rome in May, 1606, first to southern Latium and Naples, where he stayed through the summer of 1607, then to Malta. Despite the troubling circumstances, he continued to receive notable commissions. No longer competing with Annibale's classicism, Caravaggio altered his style, and his works from the Neapolitan period are more evenly lit and display a certain idealization of forms.

He remained in Malta until October, 1608, when he became a knight of the Order of Saint John. Following a violent dispute, he was imprisoned, but he managed to escape to Sicily. His Sicilian paintings reflect that he had to work quickly because the Order of the Knights of Saint John tried to force him to relocate on a continuous basis. Some of the paintings, like *The Adoration of the Shepherds* in Messina, also document a change concerning the size and placement of the figures that become smaller and are set farther away from the picture plane; similarly, the emotional directness is replaced by more contrived and calculated gestures and facial expressions.

Having been promised a pardon by the pope, Caravaggio traveled to Rome in the summer of 1610. Unfortunately, he died of a sudden fever in Porto Ercole.

SIGNIFICANCE

Caravaggio's untimely death prevented his style from becoming a viable alternative to the classicism of the Carracci school—whose art influenced Italian painting for the next two centuries. Nevertheless, Caravaggio's lessons and achievements, represented first and foremost by his new realism and bold use of chiaroscuro, were not lost or forgotten. If his Italian followers did not become famous painters, elsewhere in Europe Caravag-

The Cardsharps *(c. 1596) by Caravaggio.* (Harry N. Abrams, Inc.)

gism was a major force. The art of Rembrandt (1606-1669) in the Netherlands, Jusepe de Ribera (1588-1652) in Spain, and Georges de La Tour (1593-1652) in France is inconceivable without Caravaggio's examples. That Annibale Carracci's classicism came to dominate Baroque painting influenced early modern art critics; they passed a negative judgment on Caravaggio, virtually burying his name for centuries. Early in the twentieth century, however, art historians—Roberto Longhi among them—recognized the artist's revolutionary genius. Since the 1950's, Caravaggio has been the subject of hundreds of scholarly studies, reflecting his significance as an influential and unique painter and his renewed popularity.

—Renzo Baldasso

FURTHER READING

Christiansen, Keith, et al., eds. *The Age of Caravaggio.* New York: Metropolitan Museum of Art, 1985. The last important comprehensive exhibition of Caravaggio's works together with comparative material and examples of the works of his followers. The essays and the catalog entries are particularly informative.

Hibbard, Howard. *Caravaggio.* New York: Harper & Row, 1983. A standard introduction to Caravaggio. Also contains useful translations of pertinent primary sources.

Langdon, Helen. *Caravaggio: A Life.* Denver, Colo.: Westview Press, 2000. A best-seller, this is an in-formed, reliable, and very readable biography of the artist that offers many insights on his art.

Longhi, Roberto. "Caravaggio and His Forerunners." In *Three Studies.* New York: Sheep Meadow Press, 1995. This long essay on the Lombard origins of Caravaggio is both thought-provoking and the canonical starting point on the issue.

Puglisi, Catherine. *Caravaggio.* London: Phaidon, 1998. The most complete monograph on the artist, especially useful to navigate the vast historical scholarship on his work. The author carefully reviews many of the interpretations extant in the literature.

Spike, John T. *Caravaggio.* New York: Abbeville, 2001. Lavishly illustrated, this large volume contains good reproductions of most of the paintings and many details. It offers interesting insights and interpretations, includes a CD-ROM containing a catalog of the paintings.

SEE ALSO: Andrea del Sarto; Sofonisba Anguissola; The Carracci Family; Correggio; Lavinia Fontana; Michelangelo; Raphael; Tintoretto; Titian; Paolo Veronese.

RELATED ARTICLES in *Great Events from History: The Renaissance & Early Modern Era, 1454-1600:* c. 1500: Netherlandish School of Painting; 1508-1520: Raphael Paints His Frescoes; December 23, 1534-1540: Parmigianino Paints *Madonna with the Long Neck.*

GEROLAMO CARDANO
Italian mathematician

Cardano, best known for a quarrel over intellectual property with fellow mathematician Niccolò Fontana Tartaglia, also helped to transmit the results of a flurry of sixteenth century work in algebra. Cardano also initiated studies in the field of probability theory, which evolved into games of chance in the seventeenth century.

BORN: September 24, 1501; Pavia, duchy of Milan (now in Italy)
DIED: September 21, 1576; Rome, Papal States (now in Italy)
ALSO KNOWN AS: Jerome Cardan; Girolamo Cardano
AREAS OF ACHIEVEMENT: Mathematics, medicine

EARLY LIFE

Gerolamo Cardano (jay-RAW-lah-moh kahr-DAH-noh) wrote an autobiography describing the activities of his early life, but much subsequent scholarship has clarified his recollections. Cardano denied having been born illegitimately, but his parents, Fazio Cardano and Chiara Michena, apparently were not married at the time of his birth. They did marry, however, in 1524.

Cardano's father was a distinguished scholar as well as a lawyer, and he encouraged Cardano in his intellectual pursuits. At the time of his death, he left his son a small inheritance to help support him in his studies. In general, Cardano seems not to have enjoyed his childhood, and he accused those who were looking after him of neglect, even with regard to food.

Cardano began his university studies at Pavia in 1520 but proceeded to a medical degree in Padua in 1526. While his medical degree may have been intended to provide a livelihood for Cardano, his attention was not restricted to medical issues. He was perhaps fated to be known more for his mathematical work (which he presented to the public) than for his medicine.

It was his medical income, though, that enabled him to marry in 1531, and he had two sons and a daughter. It can be said that his family life was not a happy one, as one of his sons poisoned his wife and was executed. By 1534, Cardano had become an instructor of mathematics in Milan, where he also practiced medicine, earning a reputation in the process.

LIFE'S WORK

Algebra—from the Arabic word *al-jabr*—and Hindu-Arabic numerals were introduced to the West through the work of the Arabic mathematician and astronomer al-Khwārizmī (c. 780-c. 850). His work *Kitāb al-jabr wa al-muqābalah* (c. 820), which gave the word *al-jabr*, "algebra," to the West, means "the book of integration and equation." In the Western world, even into the last years of the Middle Ages, the influence of Euclid's *Elements* guaranteed that mathematics would be approached as a branch of geometry. While this was not much of a handicap when it came to solving algebraic equations in which the highest power of the variable is a second power (called a quadratic equation), it was not helpful in tackling equations in which there was a third power of the variable (called a cubic equation). With al-Khwārizmī's work, there had been progress in dealing with cubic equations, but this was not immediately known to Western Europe. The end of the Eastern Roman Empire with the fall of Constantinople in 1453 helped to direct a flow of scholarly material from the Middle East to Europe.

Another source of difficulty among Europeans in solving the cubic equation was the lack of a suitable notation. The Roman numeration system was scarcely designed for mathematical work, but it was still in common use in the sixteenth century. Also, the description of mathematical problems and their solutions was usually carried out with words rather than with the symbols later used to put together algebraic equations. The more complicated the problem, the more the lack of a helpful notation was felt, and the leap in level of difficulty between quadratic and cubic equations was substantial.

The first large step toward solving the cubic equation was taken by Scipione del Ferro. While he developed a

Gerolamo Cardano. (National Library of Medicine)

method for solving a whole class of cubic equations, he did not reveal the method publicly because the method's secrecy was worth something as a weapon in public disputations. Such disputations helped one build a reputation in the intellectual circles of Italy at that time. Del Ferro passed along the secret to his student Antonio Fiore, who tried using it as a tactic in a public disputation with the mathematician Niccolò Fontana Tartaglia. Tartaglia, however, more so than del Ferro, had managed to solve an even broader class of cubic equations and was able to emerge triumphant from his dispute with Fiore.

Cardano learned of Tartaglia's success and wanted to profit from his discovery. Tartaglia followed del Ferro in refusing to bring his technique before the public, but he did disclose the technique to Cardano under condition of confidentiality. Cardano's subsequent actions have been the subject of detailed scrutiny, but he seems to have felt absolved from his vow to Tartaglia for two reasons.

First, he discovered that del Ferro had a version of the formula for solving cubic equations before Tartaglia, even if it was not so general. Then Cardano worked with his own son-in-law, Ludovico Ferrari, who pushed the ideas of Tartaglia even further. Once Ferrari came up with a method for solving an equation with a fourth power of the variable (called a quartic equation),

Cardano felt that he owed it to the world to reveal these discoveries.

As a result, Cardano published a volume called *Artis magnae, sive de regulis algebraicis* (1545; *The Great Art: Or, The Rules of Algebra*, 1968). In it he detailed the various contributions of his predecessors and the work of Ferrari. Since the solution of the quartic equation depended in part on the solution of the cubic equation, he discussed the cubic equation and gave credit to Tartaglia, but he assumed credit for the quartic equation. Tartaglia was outraged, and his subsequent denunciations of Cardano's infidelity did a great deal to blacken Cardano's reputation in the scholarly world. A scholarly community that regards publication as an important part of the process of scientific discovery views Cardano with less distrust than does a community that believes discoveries are the property of their initial discoverer.

The other branch of mathematics to which Cardano made his most notable contributions was the field of probability. There had been a certain amount of discussion of counting cases (the number of possible outcomes for experiments) through the Middle Ages, but there was no basic mathematical formula connecting the ideas of probability from philosophy and religion with the calculation of possible outcomes, as in the work of Raymond Lull (c. 1235-1316). Cardano was the first to offer a definition of the probability of an event: the number of outcomes where that event occurs to the total number of possible outcomes. From this definition he went on to state a form of the law of large numbers. Cardano's important contributions, however, remained unpublished until after his death and the start of the work of the French mathematicians Pierre de Fermat (1601-1665) and Blaise Pascal (1623-1662) in the seventeenth century, to which are traced most subsequent developments in the field of probability.

Cardano obtained the chair of medicine at the University of Pavia in 1542 and remained there for almost twenty years. His autobiography bears witness to the envy of his contemporaries and also the extent to which his life was embittered by their comments. He proceeded to the chair of medicine at Bologna in 1562 and was involved in public disputations on Galen (the Greek physician) as part of the intellectual life of the city and the university.

In 1570, however, Cardano was arrested by the Inquisition and imprisoned for casting the horoscope of Jesus. Theological objections to Cardano's act suggested that the events of the life of Jesus were the result of the influence of the stars rather than direct divine intention. That

Cardano had worked on various ways of concealing texts of messages probably helped make him an object of suspicion.

After a time in prison, Cardano was forced to recant and abandon teaching. Cardano managed to outwait the ban and proceed to Rome by the time that a new pope had been elected. In this new environment Cardano was able to secure an annuity. Perhaps more important to Cardano was that he was able to use the more tolerant reception for his writings to write his autobiography *De propria vita liber* (1576; *The Book of My Life*, 1930).

SIGNIFICANCE

Cardano contributed to many areas of scholarship, such as geology, hydrodynamics, and mechanics, and he argued against the continued influence of Aristotle in the physical sciences. His most enduring legacy, however, remains the creation of a discipline of algebra based on the researches of the Italian school to which he belonged. After generations of secrecy, Cardano brought recent advances in mathematics to the scholarly community at large.

Cardano introduced variations on the methods he had learned from others and took seriously the possibility of solutions that involved imaginary numbers. Even though he may have suffered abuse from contemporaries, posterity benefited as much from his arrangement of solution methods as from his own particular discoveries.

—Thomas Drucker

FURTHER READING

Cardan, Jerome. *The Book of My Life*. Translated by Jean Stoner. New York: E. P. Dutton, 1930. An English translation of Cardano's autobiography. Includes a brief bibliography.

Cardano, Girolamo. *The Great Art: Or, The Rules of Algebra*. Translated and edited by T. Richard Witmer. Cambridge, Mass.: M.I.T. Press, 1968. A translation of Cardano's *Artis magnae*. Illustrations, bibliographical footnotes.

Eckman, James. *Jerome Cardan*. Baltimore: Johns Hopkins University Press, 1946. A supplement to a bulletin of the history of medicine, but giving an overall view of Cardano's life written in English, with Latin chapter titles.

Mankiewicz, Richard. *The Story of Mathematics*. Princeton, N.J.: Princeton University Press, 2000. Captures the difficulty of trying to do algebra in the absence of suitable notation and vocabulary.

Ore, Oystein. *Cardano: The Gambling Scholar*. Princeton, N.J.: Princeton University Press, 1953. By a distinguished mathematician, especially devoted to

Cardano's work on probability. Includes a translation of Cardano's book on games of chance.

Wrixon, Fred B. *Codes, Ciphers, and Other Cryptic and Clandestine Communication.* New York: Black Dog and Leventhal, 1998. Description of some of Cardano's contributions to the field that may have led to his facing the Inquisition.

SEE ALSO: John Napier; Georg von Peuerbach; Rheticus; Simon Stevin; Niccolò Fontana Tartaglia.

RELATED ARTICLES in *Great Events from History: The Renaissance & Early Modern Era, 1454-1600:* Beginning 1490: Development of the Camera Obscura; 1550's: Tartaglia Publishes *The New Science.*

THE CARRACCI FAMILY
Italian painters

From the mid-1580's onward, the paintings and frescoes of the Carracci family of Bologna made their city one of the major centers of reaction against the mannerist style, an elegant and often overrefined style that had dominated Italian art for sixty or seventy years. When Annibale Carracci went to Rome in the early 1590's, his work laid the foundation for the magnificent pictorial accomplishments of the Baroque period.

LUDOVICO CARRACCI

BORN: April 21, 1555 (baptized); Bologna, Papal States (now in Italy)
DIED: November 13, 1619; Bologna

AGOSTINO CARRACCI

BORN: August 16, 1557; Bologna
DIED: February 23, 1602; Parma (now in Italy)

ANNIBALE CARRACCI

BORN: November 3, 1560; Bologna
DIED: July 15, 1609; Rome, Papal States
AREA OF ACHIEVEMENT: Art

EARLY LIVES

The Carracci (cah-RAHT-chee) family came to Bologna from Cremona, and Ludovico's father was a butcher named Vincenzo. Agostino and Annibale were his second cousins, the sons of Antonio Carracci, who was a well-known tailor. Ludovico began his artistic studies with Prospero Fontana, the father of painter Lavinia Fontana. According to the Carracci family's seventeenth century biographer, Carlo Cesare Malvasia, Ludovico's work was so laborious that Fontana nicknamed him the ox and advised him to not continue with his studies.

Ludovico then went to Florence. For a time he worked with Domenico Passignano and later traveled through northern Italy, where he saw at first hand the works that were to be so important in his artistic development: works by Correggio and Parmigianino, the great sixteenth century masters of Parma and of the region known as Emilia, and by Titian and Paolo Veronese in Venice. By 1578, Ludovico was back in Bologna and was a member of the local painters' guild.

Agostino initially received some training as a goldsmith and also studied with Fontana. His real master, though, was Domenico Tibaldi, from whom he learned the art of engraving. His engravings, after works by Michelangelo and Baldassare Peruzzi, brought him some success, and he later went to Venice, where he produced engraved copies of works by Veronese and Tintoretto.

Annibale's training was much less formal, and it is possible that his cousin Ludovico was his only teacher in painting and that he learned engraving from his brother Agostino. In the spring of 1580, Annibale went to Parma in order to see and to paint copies of the works that had made such a deep impression on Ludovico a few years earlier. By late 1580 or early 1581, he was in Venice with Agostino; by about 1582, the brothers had returned to Bologna.

LIVES' WORK

In the early 1580's, all three Carraccis were involved in the development of a unique combination of artistic workshop and art academy, which they called the academy of the eager ones or the academy of the progressives. Considerable emphasis was put on drawing from life, but there were also lessons in anatomy and perspective as well as in architecture. What the Carraccis developed at their "academy" was a program of practical and theoretical instruction aimed at reforming the art of painting, which, as they saw it, had deteriorated into a vapid and boringly repetitive set of formulas, devoid of life and energy.

In the early 1580's, the Carraccis began to emerge as individual artists, but they also often worked together. By 1584, they had completed their first major joint commission, which was the series of frescoes illustrating the *History of Jason* in the Palazzo Fava, Bologna (now called the Società Majestic Baglioni). Unfortunately, the frescoes are not in good condition, but their strong illusionism and richness of color can still be appreciated, and there is a remarkable lack of artifice in the easy and naturalistic poses of the figures. This was the first major public manifestation of their doctrine of artistic reform. The fresco cycle in the former Palazzo Magnani was also a joint production, and, when asked to tell which parts each of them had painted, they are said to have replied: "It's by the Carracci. All of us made it."

For the next ten years, the Carraccis were actively engaged in creating altarpieces for Bolognese churches, many of which can now be seen in the Pinacoteca Nazionale, Bologna. While Agostino devoted much of his time to engraving and to teaching, he was also a painter of note, and *The Last Communion of Saint Jerome* (1591-1593) is his masterpiece of the period, admired by artists as diverse as Nicolas Poussin and Peter Paul Rubens. Ludovico's painting of the *Madonna of the*

Bargellini Family (1588) is one of his strongest early paintings, and critics have recognized the qualities of his work. Yet it is clear that by the end of the 1580's, Annibale had emerged as the most important artist of the three, a painter of great power whose richness of color is matched by his masterful drawing. His *Madonna with Saint John Evangelist and Saint Catherine* (1593) reveals his brilliant synthesis of the formal order of the High Renaissance with the colorism of Venice and Parma. Annibale also had a lighter side. He was one of the first artists to produce caricatures in the modern sense of the art of caricature, and in his early twenties he painted a number of genre paintings. *The Bean Eater* (c. 1585) in the Colonna Gallery, Rome, is one of the best—a small-scale scene of everyday life rendered with an astonishing boldness and naturalism.

In the mid-1590's, the Carraccis were invited to go to Rome to work for Cardinal Odoardo Farnese, the brother of the duke of Parma and Piacenza. Annibale accepted the cardinal's invitation, and Agostino later joined him; Ludovico chose to remain in Bologna, where he continued to direct the Carraccis' academy, and, in order to ensure that the academy would continue, he tried to have it officially incorporated into the professional association of Bolognese artists. Ludovico's own late work is uneven, and it is unfortunate that the fresco cycle that he and his pupils executed in San Michele in Bosco (about 1605) is lost and is known only from engravings. Two of the finest works from Ludovico's later period are the enormous paintings *Funeral of the Virgin* (1606-1607) and *Apostles at the Tomb of the Virgin* (c. 1612). He died in Bologna in 1619.

After Annibale's arrival in Rome in 1595, he developed into an artist of great historical importance. In the Palazzo Farnese, he was first asked to decorate the ceiling and upper walls of a room, now known as Camerino Farnese (Farnese's little room), with scenes illustrating the adventures of Hercules and Ulysses. In 1597, he began work on a fresco cycle in one of the principal rooms of the palace, the so-called Farnese Gallery.

The Farnese Gallery is Annibale's masterpiece, and subsequent generations considered it worthy of comparison with Raphael's frescoes in the Vatican Palace and Michelangelo's Sistine Chapel ceiling. A fictive architecture provides the framework for what appears to be framed easel pictures moved up the ceiling. There are bronze medallions, simulated marble statues, and naturalistic figures of youths sitting on pedestals—all painted with such convincing illusionism that distinctions between the real and the painted worlds seem to vanish. The

Annibale Carracci. (Library of Congress)

theme is the power of love, and incidents illustrating the loves of the gods and goddesses of antiquity fill the ceiling and the upper walls. Many of the frescoes' stories are drawn from *Metamorphoses* (c. 8 C.E.; English translation, 1567) by the Roman poet Ovid; yet behind this joyous and lighthearted exuberance, Annibale's contemporaries discerned a serious moral allegory.

In the execution of the Farnese Gallery, Annibale had been helped by Agostino, but about 1600 Agostino left Rome and went to Parma, where he remained until his death in 1602. His principal work there was a fresco cycle for the Palazzo del Giardino, but it was not finished when he died and was completed much later by other artists. Annibale continued to work on the gallery, whose lower walls were probably not finished until about 1604. Among his surviving easel paintings from the Roman period are some religious works of great power, such as the *Mourning of Christ*. His late landscapes were also of great importance for the subsequent history of painting. The finest of these landscapes are the ones that he and his pupils painted for the chapel in the Aldobrandini Palace (modern Galleria Doria-Pamphili, Rome).

In the early part of 1605, Annibale suffered a breakdown, at least partially caused by his bitterness over the small sum of money he was paid for the Farnese Gallery. For the next four years, he was unable to work, and in the summer of 1609, he died in Rome. He was buried in the Pantheon, an unusual honor and one that had also been accorded to Raphael.

SIGNIFICANCE

The three Carraccis had a major role in the reformation of the mannerist style, and, while they often worked together, they were distinct and highly individual artists. Ludovico was a gifted teacher, and several of the younger men who were trained by him in the Carraccis' academy after Annibale left for Rome went on to become important artists. Two of these students, Guido Reni and Domenichino, later became major figures of the Baroque era; yet there were many others of lesser-known distinction but considerable talent whose work provided the basis for the flourishing seventeenth century schools of painting in Bologna and Emilia.

Agostino was more interested in art theory than were the other Carraccis, and, according to one of his biographers, he was a student of mathematics and philosophy. He also composed verses and was a musician. To some extent, his posthumous fame has been dependent on his reputation as a theorist and an intellectual, but his qualities as an artist should not be discounted. He was a fine engraver, and his engravings after Venetian masters such as Veronese helped to spread the fame of their art. Yet he was also an excellent painter, although not as productive as his brother or his cousin.

Annibale's work gave new life to the tradition of monumental art in the grand manner. In Rome, under the influence of the work of Michelangelo, Raphael, and the sculpture of antiquity, his art matured and his combination of idealism and illusionism provided the greatest inspiration for the younger generation of painters. The Farnese Gallery was the first great fresco cycle of the Baroque era and set a precedent for the fresco cycles of the next two centuries.

—*Eric Van Schaack*

FURTHER READING

Bellori, Giovanni Pietro. *The Lives of Annibale and Agostino Carracci*. Translated by Catherine Enggass. University Park: Pennsylvania State University Press, 1967. Giovanni Pietro Bellori's book was first published in Rome in 1672. This translation of the portion devoted to the Carraccis is the only contemporary biography available in English. Most of the work is devoted to a description of the Farnese Gallery and an explanation of its symbolic meaning.

Boschloo, Anton Willem Adriaan. *Annibale Carracci in Bologna: Visible Reality in Art After the Council of Trent*. Translated by R. R. Symonds. 2 vols. New York: A. Schram, 1974. A detailed study of Annibale's work in Bologna and its relationship to the art of his contemporaries and predecessors.

Dempsey, Charles. *Annibale Carracci and the Beginnings of the Baroque Style*. 2d ed. Fiesole, Italy: Cadmo, 2000. An extensive review of the critical evaluations of Annibale's work and a discussion of the Carracci academy and its role in the reform of painting. Includes illustrations, six leaves of photographic plates, and bibliographic references.

_____. *Annibale Carracci: The Farnese Palace, Rome*. New York: G. Braziller, 1995. Monograph on one of Carracci's most important frescoes. Includes illustrations, glossary, bibliographic references.

Freedberg, Sydney J. *Circa 1600: A Revolution of Style in Italian Painting*. Cambridge, Mass.: Harvard University Press, 1983. Three lectures given at Cornell University in 1980 and dealing with Annibale and Ludovico Carracci and Caravaggio. Excellent exposition of the nature of the artistic accomplishments of the Carraccis. The final lecture, dealing with Ludovico, is particularly illuminating.

Malvasia, Carlo Cesare, and Anne Summerscale. *Malvasia's "Life of the Carracci": Commentary and Translation.* University Park: Pennsylvania State University Press, 2000. The first translation in any language of one of the most widely referenced biographies of the Carraccis, first published in 1678. The biography is accompanied by a study of the biographer and the place of his work in literary and art history. Includes illustrations, thirty-eight pages of plates, bibliographic references, and index.

Martin, John Rupert. *The Farnese Gallery.* Princeton, N.J.: Princeton University Press, 1965. The basic study of Annibale's work in the Palazzo Farnese. Richly illustrated and fully documented.

Posner, Donald. *Annibale Carracci: A Study in the Reform of Italian Painting Around 1590.* 2 vols. New York: Phaidon Press, 1971. The standard monograph on Annibale. Contains excellent plates and detailed catalog entries of extant works.

Wittkower, Rudolf, Joseph Connors, and Jennifer Montagu. *Art and Architecture in Italy, 1600-1750.* 6th ed. New Haven, Conn.: Yale University Press, 1999. Still the basic study of the period. The chapter on the Carraccis is an admirable summary, and there are excellent bibliographies for all the major artists of the period.

SEE ALSO: Andrea del Sarto; Sofonisba Anguissola; Caravaggio; Correggio; Lavinia Fontana; Michelangelo; Raphael; Tintoretto; Titian; Paolo Veronese.

RELATED ARTICLES in *Great Events from History: The Renaissance & Early Modern Era, 1454-1600:* November 3, 1522-November 17, 1530: Correggio Paints the *Assumption of the Virgin*; December 23, 1534-1540: Parmigianino Paints *Madonna with the Long Neck*; June, 1564: Tintoretto Paints for the Scuola di San Rocco.

JACQUES CARTIER
French explorer

Cartier explored the St. Lawrence River and the Gulf of St. Lawrence in what is now Canada, claiming the area for France, and wrote a detailed account of his travels.

BORN: c. 1491; Saint-Malo, Brittany, France
DIED: September 1, 1557; Saint-Malo
AREAS OF ACHIEVEMENT: Exploration, cartography

EARLY LIFE

Nothing is known about the early years of Jacques Cartier (zhahk kahr-tyay), although it is likely that he sailed to the waters near Newfoundland on fishing trips. His only known early voyage was in a Portuguese ship that crossed the South Atlantic to Brazil.

In 1519, Cartier married Marie Catherine, the daughter of Messire Honoré des Granches, chevalier and constable of Saint-Malo. Stocky, with a sharp profile and high, wide brow, Cartier dressed as a worker in an unpretentious cloak and tunic. He was religious but strong-spirited and showed himself to be capable, courageous, and fair to his crew. His methodical nature was shown by the detailed journals he kept daily on his voyages.

LIFE'S WORK

Intrigued by the stories of earlier explorers, King Francis I commissioned Cartier to sail to Newfoundland to look for gold and to search for a waterway through the New World to India. On April 20, 1534, Cartier left Saint-Malo with two small caravels, weighing not more than sixty tons each.

The ships sighted Newfoundland within twenty days but, because of the bad weather, took shelter in a harbor south of Bonavista Bay. Choosing to investigate the Gulf of St. Lawrence, Cartier sailed through the straits of Belle Isle, entered the Gulf of Chaleurs, and landed on the Gaspé Peninsula. There he erected a cross, claiming the area for France. At Gaspé he met the Iroquois and their chief, Donnacona. When Cartier left, he took with him Donnacona's two sons. It may be that Cartier persuaded the chief to allow him to take the young men, but more likely Cartier tricked the chief and kidnapped the two brothers. As the autumn storms were beginning, the two ships headed back toward Saint-Malo.

Although Cartier had not found a northwest passage or riches, he convinced the king of the possibilities of the new land. One of these was the opportunity to convert the heathen North American Indians to the Catholic faith, thereby recouping the Church's losses to Calvinism and Lutheranism. Because of this and the potential for riches, King Francis sent Cartier on a second voyage in 1535 to explore further.

Leaving Saint-Malo with three ships and 110 men, Cartier entered and named the Gulf of St. Lawrence. The ships passed Anticosti, and then, with Donnacona's sons as guides, they sailed up the St. Lawrence River to Saguenay and on to the village of Stadacona, near the site of what is now called Quebec. There, Donnacona welcomed back his sons and received the gifts the French had brought.

The North American Indians used trickery and false warnings to prevent Cartier from going to the next village, as they did not want their rivals to receive any of the French trinkets. Despite Indian protestations, Cartier and about thirty of his men traveled farther up the river to the village of Hochelaga, where Montreal was later established. The Indians there indicated that up another river were great stores of silver and copper, a story that would impress the king of France.

The men returned to Stadacona, where hostility between the Indians and the explorers had grown. For protection, a stockade had been built and fortified with cannons. Cartier had not expected the severity of the winter, and for five months the fort and ships were buried under snow. In addition to enduring subzero temperatures, the men were stricken with scurvy because no fresh foods were available. At least twenty-five had died before the Iroquois showed the French their remedy—the bark and needles of white spruce boiled in water.

Eventually, the weather warmed, and Cartier prepared to return to France. Since he thought that only the North American Indians could convince King Francis of the riches in the land, Cartier took Donnacona and several of his tribesmen prisoner. Promising to return them in a year, he sailed downriver and back to Saint-Malo, reaching it on July 16, 1536. Despite Cartier's words, he did not return in a year, and the Indians never again saw their homeland; all died in France.

Cartier's and Donnacona's stories intrigued the king, but war with Spain prevented Francis from sending out another expedition until 1541. This expedition was not only to explore the land and find the precious metals but also to establish a permanent colony in Canada.

The commander would be a Protestant nobleman, Jean-François de La Rocque de Roberval, and Cartier would serve on the ship as his subordinate, his captain-general and master navigator. The king provided funds for ten ships, four hundred sailors, three hundred sol-

diers, skilled tradesmen, and all kinds of supplies and livestock. It was difficult to recruit artisans and laborers, however, so criminals were taken from prison to become Canada's first settlers.

Cartier sailed with five ships in May, 1541, but Roberval was delayed until the following year. Cartier reached Stadacona on August 23, four years after he had promised to return with the kidnapped North American Indians. When the Iroquois asked about them, Cartier admitted that Donnacona was dead but then lied and said that the others had been well and that they enjoyed France so much they did not want to leave. The truth was that only one young girl had been alive; the others had already died.

Since the Indians did not seem especially friendly, Cartier proceeded up the St. Lawrence to Cap Rouge. There, the men built two forts, planted a garden, and named the settlement Charlesbourg. While these preparations were being made, samples were found of what appeared to be gold and diamonds. Two of the ships were sent back to France to report on these discoveries and Roberval's nonappearance. The rest of the explorers wintered in Charlesbourg, and while scurvy was not a problem this time, the Iroquois were. In June, 1542, after enduring months of severe weather and threats from the Indians, Cartier set sail for France.

On the way, Cartier met Roberval at St. John's in Newfoundland and was ordered to turn back. For reasons known only to himself, Cartier disobeyed and slipped

Jacques Cartier. (Library of Congress)

away in the night to continue his voyage to France. Once there, he discovered that his gold chips were iron pyrites and the diamonds worthless quartz.

Inexperienced and with little leadership ability, Roberval spent a tragic and unsuccessful winter at Charlesbourg. Disease, lack of food, and probably violence killed many before the winter was over. In 1543, Roberval returned to France, and the first effort to found a French colony in Canada ended.

Little is known of Cartier's remaining years except that he spent them on his estate near Saint-Malo. He wrote an account of his travels in 1545, which was translated into English by Richard Hakluyt in 1600. Mapmakers and geographers occasionally consulted him, and he sometimes served as a Portuguese interpreter. Cartier died at Saint-Malo on September 1, 1557.

SIGNIFICANCE

Although Cartier is known as the European discoverer of the St. Lawrence River and the Gulf of St. Lawrence, historians differ as to the importance of his explorations, and most believe that Cartier's travels primarily covered areas that other Europeans had already discovered. He left the first detailed account of voyages up the St. Lawrence, however, and this was valued by later explorers and historians. Although he explored that waterway as far as anyone had gone, he did not proceed farther when he had the opportunity. He did discover that the river was not a passage to India and claimed the gulf and valley of the St. Lawrence for France.

One significant discovery, which no one appreciated at the time, was that furs could be obtained from the North American Indians at bargain prices. When beaver hats became popular, traders went to the tribes near the St. Lawrence.

Cartier's fame as an explorer is marred by his dishonest and treacherous dealings with the North American Indians. When he first met with them, the Iroquois were friendly and helpful; after they experienced French betrayal, they became hostile and uninviting to the French.

Cartier's vision and first voyage awakened a spirit of discovery among the French, and this produced maps and information not known before. Although colonization would not occur for years after his death, Cartier did establish the future center of the French effort in North America.

—*Elaine Mathiasen*

FURTHER READING

Cartier, Jacques. *The Voyages of Jacques Cartier*. Translated and edited by H. P. Biggar. Introduction by Ramsay Cook. Toronto, Canada: University of Toronto Press, 1993. Modern edition of Cartier's narrative of his travels includes an introductory analysis of the voyages, as well as appendices reproducing letters, charters, and other historical documents. Bibliographic references; no index.

Costain, Thomas B. *The White and the Gold: The French Regime in Canada*. Garden City, N.Y.: Doubleday, 1954. This history of early Canada, written by a popular historical novelist, re-creates the lives of the people who helped to shape the nation. Detailed yet easy to read, it begins in 1490 and continues to the end of the seventeenth century.

Coulter, Tony. *Jacques Cartier, Samuel de Champlain, and the Explorers of Canada*. New York: Chelsea House, 1993. Brief monograph, geared toward younger readers but still informative, detailing the exploration of Canada by the French. Includes illustrations, maps, bibliographic references, index.

Creighton, Donald. *Canada: The Heroic Beginnings*. Toronto, Canada: Macmillan, 1974. Readable history of Canada's settlement and development to the middle of the twentieth century. Written in cooperation with two government agencies, it contains many pictures of individuals and scenes in Canadian history.

Eccles, William J. *The Canadian Frontier, 1534-1760*. New York: Holt, Rinehart and Winston, 1969. In this history of the Canadian frontier, Eccles captures the spirit of the times as he describes the hardships, adventures, and rewards experienced by the early explorers and pioneers. He also gives background to the explorations and discusses the reasons for them.

Francis, R. Douglas, Richard Jones, and Donald B. Smith. *Origins: Canadian History to Confederation*. 5th ed. Scarborough, Ont.: Nelson Canada, 2004. Textbook on early Canadian history; discusses the cultures and lifestyles of Canadian Indians and Cartier's encounters with them. Publisher Web site contains many links to online resources for further study of early Canadian exploration, including a Cartier Web site.

Lower, Arthur R. M. *Colony to Nation: A History of Canada*. Don Mills, Ont.: Longmans, Green, 1964. Lower examines topics such as Indian-French cultures, exploitation of peoples, and imperialism and colonialism. He also includes material on the governments of Canada and how the wars affected those governments.

McInnis, Edgar, with Michael Horn. *Canada: A Political and Social History*. 4th ed. Toronto, Canada: Holt, Rinehart, and Winston of Canada, 1982. Comprehensive history of Canada written in terms of politics and government. McInnis discusses Canada's periods of economic and social difficulties and how these difficulties have been overcome and followed by progress in independence, unity, and economic growth.

Parkman, Francis. *France and England in North America*. Vol. 1. New York: Literary Classics of the United States, 1983. Depicts the struggle between France and England for possession of the North American continent. Includes some Spanish history and covers in detail the years between 1512 and 1635.

Pendergast, James F., and Bruce G. Trigger. *Cartier's Hochelaga and the Dawson Site*. Montreal: McGill-Queen's University Press, 1972. Scholarly examination of the possible locations of Hochelaga, an Iroquoian village Cartier visited and described. Much of the research used in this study is based on Cartier's data and account of his travels.

Winsor, Justin. *Cartier to Frontenac*. Boston: Houghton Mifflin, 1894. Describes the explorations of North America from 1492 to 1698. Maps and charts of the voyages are included to expand the geographical descriptions of the area. Includes a brief history of Cartier and discusses the results of his explorations.

SEE ALSO: John Cabot; Sebastian Cabot; Thomas Cavendish; John Davis; Deganawida; Francis I; Sir Martin Frobisher; Sir Humphrey Gilbert; Richard Hakluyt; Hiawatha.

RELATED ARTICLES in *Great Events from History: The Renaissance & Early Modern Era, 1454-1600:* Early 16th century: Rise of the Fur Trade; April 20, 1534-July, 1543: Cartier and Roberval Search for a Northwest Passage.

BALDASSARE CASTIGLIONE
Italian writer and diplomat

One of the most noted writers on Renaissance court life, Castiglione helped influence what contemporary and succeeding generations in the West have regarded as good manners, taste, elegance, and the idea of the cultured.

BORN: December 6, 1478; Casatico, duchy of Mantua (now in Italy)
DIED: February 2, 1529; Toledo, Spain
AREAS OF ACHIEVEMENT: Literature, diplomacy, government and politics

EARLY LIFE

Baldassare Castiglione (bahl-dahs-SAHR-ay kahs-teel-YOH-nay) was born in the Lombard (north Italian) town of Casatico, not far from the city of Mantua. His parents were both members of distinguished local families, with his father, Cristoforo Castiglione, holding the title of count. Because of his high social position, the young Baldassare received what his parents regarded as the best education of his day: a reading knowledge of the Latin and Greek classics, athletics, music, and art.

Studying under Humanist scholars Giorgio Merula and Demetrio Calcondila, Castiglione was exposed to some of the most enlightened examples of Humanistic and classical thought of his period. When he was eighteen, Castiglione was sent by his parents to the court of the Milanese prince Ludovico Sforza, where he be-

gan to learn the rudiments of chivalry. When Castiglione's father died in 1499, the twenty-one-year-old Castiglione left Sforza and accepted a commission from Francesco II Gonzaga, the marquis of Mantua, who was expanding his army because of his ongoing conflict with Spain.

Castiglione returned to Italy in 1505, traveling to Rome where he met Guidobaldo da Montefeltro, the duke of Urbino. Montefeltro gave Castiglione a commission as his envoy to King Henry VII of England, where Castiglione remained for about a year. In 1507, he returned to Urbino, where he lived until 1513 as a knight and member of Montefeltro's court. During the six years that he spent in Urbino, Castiglione met the city's most famous painter, Raphael, who became a close friend and who created a famous portrait of the author, now in the Louvre.

LIFE'S WORK

While he was still in his twenties, Castiglione began establishing a reputation as an accomplished author. In 1506, he published the pastoral drama *Tirsi*, drawing his inspiration from both ancient works, including the *Eclogues* of Vergil (43-37 B.C.E.; also known as *Bucolics*; English translation, 1575), and the Renaissance bucolic poems of Angelo Poliziano and Jacopo Sannazaro. In addition, Castiglione wrote sonnets in imitation of Petrarch

(1304-1374), numerous letters, and a series of courtly poems in both Latin and Italian.

In 1516, Castiglione returned to Mantua, where he married Ippolita Torelli. What then followed was a period of both stunning accomplishments and great personal disappointments. Castiglione served as envoy to Pope Leo X and was sent as ambassador to Spain in 1524 by Leo X's cousin, Pope Clement VII. Nevertheless, during these same years, both Castiglione's wife and his friend Raphael died (prompting him to write two elegies in their memory), many of his diplomatic commissions proved to be unsuccessful, and he eventually lost the trust of those with whom he had been building his diplomatic career. On May 6, 1527, the Holy Roman Emperor Charles V (Charles I of Spain) of the House of Habsburg invaded Rome with twelve thousand mercenaries, forcing Clement VII to take refuge in the Castel Sant'Angelo. Charles's troops pillaged Rome for eight days, destroying or looting many of the city's most important works of art and killing thousands of its residents.

Clement VII suspected that Castiglione knew in advance of Charles's intentions but did not inform him. His reputation and health jeopardized, Castiglione wrote a letter defending himself to the pope and then left Italy for Toledo, where he would spend the final years of his life.

In 1528, Castiglione published his most influential work, *Il libro del cortegiano* (*The Book of the Courtier*, 1561), a four-volume treatise that he had drafted between 1513 and 1518 and been polishing ever since. *The Book of the Courtier* is a fictionalized version of the elegant discussions that Castiglione remembered from his years at the court of Urbino. The characters in the book were based on real people whom Castiglione met during his service to Guidobaldo da Montefeltro. The interlocutors in the book include Francesco Maria della Rovere, Guidobaldo's nephew whom Castiglione served after the duke's death; the duchess Elisabetta Gonzaga; Ludovico da Canossa, a bishop who had become one of the author's close friends; Giuliano de' Médici, who knew both Leonardo da Vinci and Niccolò Macchiavelli; Pietro Bembo, Leo X's papal secretary and an author who wrote several works on platonic love; Bernardo Accolti, a poet; and many others.

In the course of what Castiglione presents as an extended series of conversations, the interlocutors in *The Book of the Courtier* describe their concept of the ideal courtier: He should be an individual of noble birth who is well educated in both classical and modern languages, has an appreciation for music and painting, is accomplished in military matters and athletics (most notably

An engraving of Baldassare Castiglione, modeled on a portrait by Raphael. (Hulton|Archive by Getty Images)

tennis, running, and swimming), dances gracefully, is well read in literature as well as in science, and, most important, is well mannered and affable in conversation.

The courtier should never be haughty or conceited in his many accomplishments but should always do everything in his power to put others at ease. He should have a good sense of humor and should freely use charm, even wit, in the most trying of situations. One of the courtier's most important qualities, according to Castiglione, is *sprezzatura*, the ability to do difficult things with the appearance of ease. This nonchalance, a sense of effortless dignity, composure, and self-control under even the most difficult of circumstances, is the supreme refinement of courtly civilization and helps to add immeasurably to the grace and style of courtly life.

Castiglione's classical education is apparent throughout *The Book of the Courtier*, where brief allusions are frequently made to fairly obscure events from ancient history and mythology. In other ways, however, Castiglione's book was quite progressive for its time. Although not all speakers in the book agreed with the idea, Castiglione's treatise supported a more modern view of women's intellectual abilities than had been accepted in the Middle Ages and early Renaissance. Several of the most interesting speakers in the work are women, and Castiglione himself took for granted the idea that women were intellectually equal to men if they were given the same benefits of education.

SIGNIFICANCE

Castiglione's *The Book of the Courtier* had an immediate impact on views of elegance and good manners throughout Italy. Moreover, the book was quickly translated into Latin (1538), Spanish (1540), German (1560), and English (1561), making it influential in many parts of western Europe.

Castiglione's account of the ideal courtier, originally intended to be a descriptive account of what he had witnessed, soon came to be seen as prescriptive by those wishing to emulate the high standards of courtly behavior in Renaissance Italy. As such, Castiglione's *The Book of the Courtier* came to influence the Western world's understanding of etiquette, manners, and elegant sophistication in many periods since its publication. Nearly every guide to manners and courtly behavior written in Europe since the sixteenth century owes at least some of its perspective either directly or indirectly to Castiglione.

Ernest Hemingway's concept of "grace under pressure" and even such popular heroes as James Bond and the characters portrayed by Cary Grant in numerous films could all trace their origins to Castiglione's treatise. Moreover, the concept of the Renaissance man, which became popular in Europe after Castiglione's death, largely was inspired by the figure of the ideal courtier presented by the interlocutors in *The Book of the Courtier*.

—*Jeffrey L. Buller*

FURTHER READING

Ady, Julia Cartwright. *Baldassare Castiglione, the Perfect Courtier.* 2 vols. New York: E. P. Dutton, 1908. The still-useful, standard biography of Castiglione.

Berger, Harry, Jr. *The Absence of Grace: Sprezzatura and Suspicion in Two Renaissance Courtesy Books.* Stanford, Calif.: Stanford University Press, 2000. The most authoritative book on the quintessential virtue discussed in *The Book of the Courtier: sprezzatura,* or the art of making the difficult look easy. Also examines this concept in Giovanni della Casa's *Il Galateo ovvero de' costumi* (1558), another Renaissance guide to courtly manners and polite conduct.

Burke, Peter. *The Fortunes of the Courtier: The European Reception of Castiglione's "Cortegiano."* University Park: Pennsylvania State University Press, 1996. Through an examination of admirers of Castiglione's book outside Italy, Burke provides insight into a broader pattern of changing social and intellectual attitudes in Renaissance Europe. Bibliography, index.

Finucci, Valeria. *The Lady Vanishes: Subjectivity and Representation in Castiglione and Ariosto.* Stanford, Calif.: Stanford University Press, 1992. Examines the role of women in Ludovico Ariosto's *Orlando furioso* (1516, 1521, 1532) and Castiglione's *The Book of the Courtier.*

Raffini, Christine. *Marsilio Ficino, Pietro Bembo, Baldassare Castiglione: Philosophical, Aesthetic, and Political Approaches in Renaissance Platonism.* New York: Peter Lang, 1998. Interprets Castiglione's views as heavily influenced by the Platonic theories of Marsilio Ficino and his efforts to reconcile Christian authority with Renaissance individualism. Bibliography, index.

Wiggins, Peter DeSa. *Donne, Castiglione, and the Poetry of Courtliness.* Bloomington: Indiana University Press, 2000. While focusing primarily on the poetry of John Donne, Wiggins provides a useful case study in the reception of Castiglione throughout Europe after his death and helps explain the author's important role in the history of Western ideas.

SEE ALSO: Sofonisba Anguissola; Pietro Aretino; Charles V; Clement VII; Vittoria Colonna; Marsilio Ficino; Giorgione; Henry VII; Leo X; Leonardo da Vinci; Niccolò Machiavelli; Raphael; Ludovico Sforza.

RELATED ARTICLE in *Great Events from History: The Renaissance & Early Modern Era, 1454-1600:* 1528: Castiglione's *Book of the Courtier* Is Published.

CATHERINE DE MÉDICIS
Queen of France (r. 1547-1559)

Catherine de Médicis contributed to maintaining a strong centralized monarchy in spite of challenges from noble and religious factions. Her attempts to balance Roman Catholic and Calvinist interests in France also encouraged at least a minimum of toleration in the seventeenth century.

BORN: April 13, 1519; Florence (now in Italy)
DIED: January 5, 1589; Blois, France
AREA OF ACHIEVEMENT: Government and politics

EARLY LIFE

The father of Catherine de Médicis (MEHD-eh-chee), Lorenzo de' Medici, was *capo dello stato* in Florence, *gonfalonier* of the Church, and, after a victorious expedition, duke of Urbino. His uncle, Pope Leo X, hoping to restore the Medicis to their earlier status, arranged a marriage between Lorenzo and Madeleine de la Tour d'Auvergne, a distant relation of Francis I, king of France. The young couple was married at Amboise in 1518, and within a year their daughter was born. Two weeks later, Madeleine was dead of puerperal fever, and five days later Lorenzo also died.

The baby Catherine was the last legitimate heir of the family. Immediately, she became a tool in the hands of her guardian, Pope Leo X, and of his half brother Giulio, later Pope Clement VII, to recoup the Medici fortune. Catherine's childhood was spent in Rome and Florence, where she was at times ignored and at other times the center of attention. In 1527, during a Florentine revolution, she was the hostage of anti-Medici forces and handled her desperate situation with great diplomacy. At the age of ten, she returned to Rome, where Pope Clement VII negotiated a marriage between Catherine and Henry, the second son of Francis I.

On October 26, 1533, Catherine and Henry, both fourteen years of age, were married at Avignon. Small and thin, with strong rather than beautiful features and the bulging eyes of the Medicis, Catherine was vivacious, self-assured, witty, bright, and eager to learn. As a new wife, she traveled everywhere with the French court and joined a group of young women, protégées of her father-in-law, to study Latin, Greek, French, mathematics, science, astronomy, and astrology. She hunted, danced, and rode using a sidesaddle she invented. Still a child when she married Henry, she had to call on all her habits of diplomacy to handle two major crises. The first was her husband's attachment to his mistress, Diane de Poitiers.

Catherine handled this problem by being a patient wife and by making an ally of her rival. The second difficulty was more critical and became especially important in 1536, when Henry's older brother died and Henry became the heir to the French throne. That difficulty was her inability to bear children and the possibility that Henry would obtain a divorce to marry a fertile bride and leave Catherine without resources. Catherine's charm and vivacity saved her from this fate, and, after ten years of marriage, she presented Henry with an heir.

During the next thirteen years, Catherine bore ten children, including four sons, and settled into a mutually respectful relationship with Henry and Diane de Poitiers. When Francis died in 1547, Henry arranged a coronation ceremony for Catherine, an unusual innovation for sixteenth century French kings. In 1551, when Henry went to war in Burgundy, he left Catherine as his regent, and, although Diane was his chief adviser, he also consulted with Catherine. In 1559, Catherine was one of the architects of the Treaty of Cateau-Cambrésis, which temporarily calmed the Franco-Spanish rivalry. The new amity was sealed with the marriage of Philip II of Spain and Catherine's daughter Elizabeth. A tournament was held to celebrate this alliance, and, during one event, a splinter from a broken lance pierced the French king's eye and he died.

LIFE'S WORK

Although she did not know it at the time, Catherine's life's work began with the death of her husband. Francis became king at the age of fifteen. A year earlier, he had married Mary Stuart (Mary, Queen of Scots), a niece of the Guises, a prominent French noble family. Mary's relatives assumed responsibility for advising the young king. If Francis had lived, Catherine would not have become an important political figure in France. When Francis died, Charles IX, aged ten, assumed the throne. After observing the arrogant despotism of the Guises, Catherine determined to become regent to her son.

During her years as regent, Catherine responded to two major crises in the face of four significant enemies. One struggle was to preserve royal authority against two noble families—the Guises and the Bourbons—who were determined to dominate the king and the royal family. The Bourbons were the hereditary kings of Navarre and the next in line to inherit the throne after Catherine's sons. The other major crisis for Catherine was the religious conflict between Roman Catholics and Protestant Calvinists, called Huguenots, in France. To complicate her task, the Guises became associated with the Roman Catholic position and often looked to the Spanish for assistance, while the Bourbons—at least the queen of Navarre and her brother-in-law the fiery prince of Condé—openly adhered to the Protestant faith. Even before Francis II's death, the prince of Condé had mobilized Huguenot support against the Guises in a conspiracy aimed at kidnapping the king and executing his Guise advisers. His efforts failed, but the lines of conflict were drawn. Catherine also faced a powerful Spanish king, Philip II, who would act in his own dynastic interest even though he was Catherine's son-in-law. Finally, she had to deal with an inadequate treasury and the imminent bankruptcy of the Crown. As a woman and a foreigner, Catherine's task was doubly difficult.

The queen mother's response to the religious difficulties was to organize a national religious council to mediate between French Protestants and Catholics. The Colloquy of Poissy, which met in 1561, succeeded in getting the French religious parties to talk together, but it also polarized them. The Guises and other staunch Roman Catholics united and sought help from the Spanish king to challenge royal efforts at mediation. Religious passions intensified. In January, 1562, when Catherine issued the Edict of Toleration granting government protection to the Huguenots, the Catholics left

Catherine de Médicis. (Library of Congress)

the royal court, and the first of the French religious wars began.

During the next ten years, France was torn by three major civil wars motivated by religious and noble rivalry. Catherine tried desperately to maintain a balance among all these forces, but she failed. The third and most savage of the first set of religious wars ended in August, 1570, with the Peace of Saint-Germain and a backlash against the Guises and their Spanish allies. A new party, the Politique Party, grew out of this disgust with foreign influence. Composed of Roman Catholic and Huguenot moderates who believed that the integrity of the state was more important than religion, this party reflected Catherine's own position.

Catherine's diplomatic expertise became especially important in 1572, in negotiating defense treaties with the English and the Ottoman Turks against Philip II and in gaining the throne of Poland for her third son, Henry. As Henry departed for Poland, Europe was rocked by news of the St. Bartholomew's Day Massacre. The occasion was the wedding of Catherine's daughter Marguerite to Henry, king of Navarre, heir to the French throne after Catherine's sons. All the important nobles of France were gathered in the capital, including the Huguenot leaders. Whether Catherine and Charles IX intended to kill all the Protestants in Paris on August 23, 1572, or whether Catherine only meant to kill one or two of the Protestant leaders, the result was a massacre of Protestants by Catholics in the capital city and in other cities throughout the nation. War broke out again and, in spite of their losses, the Huguenots managed to retain several key fortresses. After Charles IX died in 1574 and Henry III returned from Poland, the new king was also unable to seize the Protestant strongholds and to subdue the opposition. In 1576, peace was negotiated on the basis of the status quo. Henry III, Catherine's favorite son, was an adult when he came to the throne, and Catherine no longer played an important policy-making role. Since the king was unmarried and preoccupied with war, his mother continued to direct the ambassadors and to send and receive letters from agents and diplomats throughout Europe.

In June of 1584, Catherine's youngest son died of influenza. Thus, the Protestant Henry of Navarre would inherit the throne if Henry III were to die. War raged, and, fearing the Spanish king would send in troops, Henry III was forced to put himself at the head of the Catholic League in order to control its excesses. The Estates General refused to grant the government more money to fight the wars they did not want. On December 23, 1588,

Henry III summoned the cardinal of Guise to the royal chamber, where armed guards killed him. Shortly thereafter, Henry had the duke of Guise assassinated as well. Catherine was in the castle at Blois that evening, on her deathbed, when Henry carried news to her of the death of the Guises. She was not pleased; by destroying one faction, Henry had put himself in the hands of the other, and he no longer had a weapon against the Bourbon and Protestant nobles. The collapse of Spain would give Geneva and the Calvinists the victory.

Catherine died less than two weeks later, on January 5, 1589, and her son was assassinated before the end of the year. Henry IV, the Protestant king of Navarre, officially inherited the throne, but the war continued until 1595, when he had reconquered the north and converted to Catholicism. Henry was able, however, to protect his Huguenot friends and relatives by issuing the Edict of Nantes that granted the Huguenots several armed cities and freedom to worship.

SIGNIFICANCE

Catherine de Médicis set out to destroy the resistance to royal power, to secure for her sons the French throne, to build a government with a centralized power in the hands of the French monarchy, and to limit the authority of the nobles. She succeeded in gaining those ends but failed to achieve them peacefully and permanently. Accused by contemporaries and historians of being a Machiavellian, Catherine must at least plead guilty to being a realist in her exercise of power. She changed sides, made secret agreements, and even sent ambassadors to the Turks to negotiate a treaty against the Spanish in 1570. She met with all parties and used every means available to achieve her ends. She condoned war and murder in the interest of her duty as the regent of France.

It may have been her failure to balance the dynastic and religious conflicts that brought on the civil wars, but it was her success at identifying the factions in the conflict and her attempts to balance them that allowed Henry IV to obtain his throne intact with Huguenots alive to tolerate. The religious civil wars were horrible, but some of the changes resulting from the wars moved France closer to the centralized, bureaucratic state that was more nearly modern than was the sixteenth century dynastic structure. The wars served to redistribute the land from the hands of a few large noble families to those of a number of smaller families who were loyal to the monarchy. The most significant result of the civil wars, however, was the creation of the Politique Party, a party that recognized the need for a strong monarchy regardless of religious affiliation and regardless of noble demands for power. Catherine's contribution to French government in the sixteenth century was the principle of centralized power in the hands of the monarchy.

—*Loretta Turner Johnson*

FURTHER READING

Frieda, Leonie. *Catherine de Medici*. London: Weidenfeld & Nicolson, 2003. Extensively researched, well-written attempt to rejuvenate Catherine's reputation and produce a balanced evaluation of her place in history. Includes illustrations, bibliographic references, index.

Héritier, Jean. *Catherine de Medici*. Translated by Charlotte Haldane. New York: St. Martin's Press, 1963. Long biography of Catherine as a great national and moderate leader who preserved for Henry IV a kingdom which was battered but intact.

Knecht, R. J. *Catherine de' Medici*. New York: Longman, 1998. Biography of Catherine produced more as a work of historical documentation than a literary narrative. Contains many useful details and facts. Includes maps, genealogical tables, bibliographic references, index.

Kruse, Elaine. "The Woman in Black: The Image of Catherine de Medici from Marlowe to Queen Margot." In *"High and Mighty Queens" of Early Modern England: Realities and Representations*, edited by Carole Levin, Jo Eldridge Carney, and Debra Barrett-Graves. New York: Palgrave Macmillan, 2003. Survey of representations of Catherine from the Renaissance to the present, investigating the uses to which she has been put as a literary character.

Neale, J. E. *The Age of Catherine de Medici*. New York: Harper & Row, 1943. Reprint. London: J. Cape, 1971. Short and colorful presentation of Catherine's rule as foolish, misguided, and middle class.

Roeder, Ralph. *Catherine de Medici and the Lost Revolution*. 2d ed. New York: Vintage Books, 1964. Presents the problem of sixteenth century France as the inability of Catherine to balance the dynastic and religious conflicts of the age.

Sichel, Edith. *Catherine de' Medici and the French Reformation*. London: Constable, 1905. Reprint. London: Dawsons, 1969. Presents Catherine as the evil nemesis of the rightful rulers of France, never quite in control of her plans. Sichel also relates the art and literature of the period of the French Reformation to Catherine's reign.

Strage, Mark. *Women of Power: The Life and Times of Catherine de' Medici*. New York: Harcourt Brace Jovanovich, 1976. A conventional rehash of the story focusing on Catherine's relationship with Diane de Poitiers and Margaret of Valois.

Sutherland, N. M. "Catherine de Medici: The Legend of the Wicked Italian Queen." *Sixteenth Century Journal* 9 (1978): 45-56. An analysis of the attitudes of historians about Catherine de Médicis and her role in history from her contemporaries to the present day.

Van Dyke, Paul. *Catherine de Médicis*. 2 vols. New York: Charles Scribner's Sons, 1923. General study of Catherine within the context of her time. Catherine is held responsible for not solving the religious and political problems but not through inherent malice.

SEE ALSO: Clement VII; Diane de Poitiers; Francis I; Henry II; Henry III; Henry IV; Leo X; Mary, Queen of Scots; Lorenzo de' Medici; Philip II.

RELATED ARTICLES in *Great Events from History: The Renaissance & Early Modern Era, 1454-1600:* January 1-8, 1558: France Regains Calais from England; March, 1562-May 2, 1598: French Wars of Religion; January 20, 1564: Peace of Troyes; August 24-25, 1572: St. Bartholomew's Day Massacre; July 7, 1585-December 23, 1588: War of the Three Henrys.

CATHERINE OF ARAGON
Queen consort of England (r. 1509-1533)

Twice married to English princes, Spanish-born Catherine, the first wife of Henry VIII, refused to accept a royal divorce, which led to Henry's expulsion of the Roman Catholic Church and the establishment of the Protestant Church in England.

BORN: December 16, 1485; Alcalá de Henares, Spain

DIED: January 7, 1536; Kimbolton, Huntingdonshire, England

ALSO KNOWN AS: Catalina of Aragon

AREAS OF ACHIEVEMENT: Church reform, patronage of the arts, education, women's rights, religion and theology

EARLY LIFE

Born Catalina (Catherine), an infanta of Spain, to Queen Isabella of Castile and King Ferdinand of Aragon, Catherine of Aragon was the fifth surviving child and youngest daughter, named for her maternal English great-grandmother, Catherine of Lancaster. The young Catherine was twice descended from English kings: maternally from Edward III and paternally from Henry II.

For the first fifteen years of her life, she remained under the tutelage of her mother, Queen Isabella, who considered her own education so deficient that she had Catherine tutored by scholars Peter Martyr and Antonio and Alessandro Geraldini. Catherine was instructed in the Bible, Latin histories, and Roman and Christian writers. She spoke fluent classical Latin, in addition to Spanish; studied heraldry, genealogy, and civil and canon law; and gained proficiency in music, dancing, drawing, and the domestic arts of spinning, weaving, and embroidery.

Contemporary accounts describe the young Catherine as having naturally pink cheeks, white skin, a fair complexion, and fairly thick hair with a reddish-gold tint. Catherine's features were neat and regular in an oval face. Lacking in height and usually described as short, tiny, and plump, with a low voice, Catherine appeared to be a young infanta who would be a healthy producer of children.

The unification of Spain led Ferdinand and Isabella to use their children as marital pawns on the chessboard of European diplomacy. Their first- and third-born daughters wed Portuguese kings. The second daughter and the only son wed Austrian Habsburgs. Marriage negotiations between Madrid and London for Catherine to wed Prince Arthur of Wales, the eldest son of Henry VII, were opened in 1487 and formalized by the Treaty of Medina del Campo in 1489. A dowry settlement committing Spain to a payment of 200,000 crowns, plus plate and jewels valued at 35,000 crowns, formalized the Spanish-English alliance. Catherine (by proxy) and Arthur were first engaged in 1497 and then married in 1499.

Catherine's London arrival on November 12, 1501, and her official marriage to Prince Arthur two days later were greatly acclaimed by the English people. The usually parsimonious Henry VII gave Catherine and Arthur a lavish wedding at St. Paul's Cathedral. For Henry VII, the Spanish marriage publicly legitimized the Tudor Dynasty in England; contributed to the encirclement of

Catherine of Aragon. (Library of Congress)

England's enemy, France; and provided King Henry with a substantial dowry to use for his own political purposes.

Unfortunately, at Ludlow Castle in the Marches of Wales, the physically frail Arthur succumbed to illness on April 2, 1502. The cause of death remains unknown, but speculation has centered on tuberculosis or an undetermined plague. Catherine herself was too ill to attend her husband's funeral and burial at Worcester Cathedral. In widowhood, the young Catherine, now princess dowager of Wales, confessed to the bishop of Salisbury, Cardinal Lorenzo Campeggio, that her marriage had never been consummated. The couple had shared the marital bed only seven times.

LIFE'S WORK

During her years of her widowhood, 1502 to 1509, Catherine found herself a political pawn used by both her father and her father-in-law. Catherine was first pledged in marriage to and then repudiated by both her widower father-in-law, Henry VII, and Henry VII's second son, Prince Henry. At issue was whether or not Catherine was still a virgin. If Catherine's marriage to Arthur had been

consummated, an impediment of affinity prevented her from marrying another member of Prince Arthur's family. In 1506, Pope Julius II granted a dispensation and waived the issue of affinity, even if the marriage had been consummated.

Catherine's status remained unclear, however, because 100,000 crowns of her dowry remained unpaid by her father, who continuously pleaded poverty, and because her father-in-law repeatedly reevaluated Catherine's value as a future English royal bride in comparison with royal princesses in France and Austria. Increasing poverty forced Catherine to live more frugally at Durham House, where she supported her household from her partial dowry and the sale of her plate and jewelry and suffered from frequent fevers.

Catherine's ambiguous status ended within two months of Henry VII's life when she wed her former brother-in-law, now Henry VIII, on June 11, 1509. Later, witnesses claimed that Henry VIII boasted his wife was a virgin. Henry VIII's change of attitude toward Catherine was probably caused by his desire to retain her dowry and to keep Spain allied against France, as well as his need for an adult wife to found a dynasty. The possibility that Henry VIII actually loved Catherine should also not be discounted.

As queen, Catherine encouraged the arts, established her own library open to scholars, and befriended English writers. Queen Catherine contributed money to lectureships, supported poor scholars, and endowed the colleges of Ipswich and Oxford. She actively corresponded with leading Humanists Thomas More, Desiderius Erasmus, and Juan Vives. Catherine's greatest contribution to learning was as a pioneer of women's education. Catherine sponsored the publication of five handbooks on Humanist instruction for women, including Vives's *De institutione feminae Christianae* (1523; *The Instruction of a Christian Woman*, 1557).

Henry VIII appointed Catherine regent of England during his absences fighting the French on their territory. This action certainly demonstrates his appreciation and trust of Catherine's intelligence and diplomatic ability. While Henry was in France, Catherine gave the military orders, launching an English army that defeated the invading Scots and killed their king, James IV (Henry's brother-in-law), at Flodden Field in 1513. Yet Catherine's promotion of a Spanish alliance and her continued involvement in policy making led her into conflict with Henry's lord chancellor, Cardinal Thomas Wolsey. Catherine would later blame Wolsey for Henry's desertion of her and his demands for a divorce.

The more important issue facing Catherine was her failure to produce a living male heir. The number of pregnancies and miscarriages suffered by Catherine has been the subject of much debate. Sir John Dewhurst, who has provided the best analysis of the existing period documents, concluded that there could have been only six pregnancies between the years 1509 and 1525: four stillbirths; a son, Henry, born January 1, 1511, who died seven weeks later; and their only surviving child, Mary I, born February 18, 1516.

Exactly what caused Henry to announce his intention to divorce Catherine remains a topic of considerable debate. It seems that Henry's attitude toward Catherine changed abruptly after 1525, when the intended betrothal of their daughter Mary to Catherine's nephew, Charles V, king of Spain and Holy Roman Emperor, was broken by Charles so that he could marry an older Portuguese cousin. The termination of this marriage plan ended Henry's dreams of an Anglo-Spanish alliance dominating Europe. It is also true that Henry was involved with Anne Boleyn by 1526.

Henry's May, 1527, decision to challenge the validity of his marriage to Catherine is known as the King's Great Matter. Using the biblical passages Leviticus 20:21 and Deuteronomy 25:5-7, Henry claimed that a man marrying his brother's wife did so against God's will. Henry further argued that the papal dispensations granted by Julius II to remove the issue of affinity and allow the marriage were invalid.

Henry's actions divided the Roman church in England. He failed to anticipate Catherine's refusal to go quietly and Charles V's seizure of Rome and imprisonment of Pope Clement VII. On March 6, 1529, Catherine appealed to Rome, asking the pope to take her case. Her only appearance before the Blackfriars Court on May 31, 1529, witnessed a queen defending the legality of her marriage and intent on saving it.

Both Clement VII and his English representative, Cardinal Campeggio, delayed clerical action, hoping for reconciliation. After 1530, Catherine's health began to decline. Henry last saw Catherine at Windsor on July 11, 1531, whereupon she was removed to increasingly remote locations and finally to Kimbolton. Pressure from the Boleyn supporters, Henry's increasing desire for a legitimate male heir, and clerical resistance to an annulment forced the king to begin the process of disestablishing the English Roman church.

Attempts to encourage Catherine to lead a rebellion against her increasingly unpopular husband and the Boleyn party were rebuffed by the queen. Wars in north-ern Italy, Germany, and France prevented military intervention in support of Catherine by Charles V and the pope. Finally, almost five years after Catherine's initial appeal to Rome, on March 24, 1534, the pope declared the marriage valid in the eyes of God and the Church. By that time, however, Henry had taken matters into his own hands. The English Roman church was disestablished (1532), Parliament annulled Henry's marriage to Catherine (1533) so that he could legalize his marriage to an already pregnant Anne Boleyn, and the king was enthroned as the head of the English church (1534).

Increasing ill health led to Catherine's death on January 7, 1536. Henry celebrated with a ball at Greenwich. Although rumors circulated of Catherine's having been poisoned, she probably died from either cancer or a coronary thrombosis. In violation of Catherine's instructions, she was buried at Peterborough Cathedral with the honors of princess dowager.

SIGNIFICANCE

First as an infanta of Spain, then as princess of Wales, and lastly as queen of England, Catherine of Aragon was sacrificed to diplomacy and statecraft by her parents, Ferdinand and Isabella of Spain; her father-in-law, Henry VII; and her husband, Henry VIII. In all her titled positions, Catherine represented the emerging Renaissance woman who was educated, spoke several languages, and was lauded by contemporary scholars for her support of Humanism and culture.

Although contemporary and later historians have praised Catherine's virtue, trust, and high-mindedness, they have faulted her for her inability to use her popularity with the English people, the nobles, and the Church to maintain Catholicism in England or to lead an army into battle against Henry VIII in order to make their daughter, Mary I, queen of England. Catherine's obedience to her husband, her willingness to accede to all Henry's royal commands during the King's Great Matter, and her absolute faith and devotion to the institutions of marriage and the Church enabled her to defend her marriage and keep her daughter in the Roman faith and in the line of succession, but those characteristics ultimately contributed to England's Protestant Reformation.

—*William A. Paquette*

FURTHER READING

Albert, Marvin. *The Divorce*. New York: Simon & Schuster, 1965. A detailed study of the events leading to the divorce of Catherine of Aragon by Henry VIII. The reader becomes a participant in one of history's most celebrated divorce trials.

Dewhurst, John. "The Alleged Miscarriages of Catherine of Aragon and Anne Boleyn." *Medical History* 28 (1984): 49-56. The best medical analysis of historical documents to determine the number and outcomes of Catherine's pregnancies.

Dowling, Maria. "A Woman's Place? Learning and the Wives of Henry VIII." *History Today* 41 (June, 1991): 38-42. Dowling reintroduces the reader to the wives of Henry VIII as promoters of education, religion, and scholarship.

Fraser, Antonia. *The Wives of Henry VIII*. New York: Alfred A. Knopf, 1992. Fraser's careful analysis and re-evaluation of archival and published works produce a thoughtful reinterpretation of Catherine's role in shaping England's entrance into the modern age.

Kipling, Gordon. *The Receyt of the Ladie Katheryne*. Oxford, England: Oxford University Press, 1990. A scholarly analysis of sixteenth century documents describing Catherine of Aragon's arrival in England, her entry into London, her marriage to Prince Arthur, and her subsequent widowhood.

Levin, Carole, Jo Eldridge Carney, and Debra Barrett-Graves, eds. *"High and Mighty Queens" of Early Modern England: Realities and Representations*. New York: Palgrave Macmillan, 2003. Anthology of essays on queens in the English Renaissance includes three articles on Catherine, discussing her education, the contemporary representation of her Englishness, and her later representation in the Victorian period. Includes illustrations, bibliographic references, and index.

Mattingly, Garrett. *Catherine of Aragon*. Boston: Little, Brown, 1941. Reprint. New York: Vintage Books, 1960. Mattingly's access to extensive archival material provides a detailed analysis of Catherine's character; the dynasties of Spain, England, Scotland, and France; and the politics of the Papacy in the turbulent sixteenth century. Still the definitive biography of Catherine.

Roll, Winifred. *The Pomegranate and the Rose: The Story of Katherine of Aragon*. Englewood Cliffs, N.J.: Prentice-Hall, 1970. A highly readable study of a young woman whose fate was determined by the statecraft of Spanish and English kings and the Roman Church.

Scarisbrick, J. J. *Henry VIII*. Berkeley: University of California Press, 1968. British historian Scarisbrick's extensive access to French, German, Latin, Spanish, and English primary sources and his careful analysis of Henry's character and relationship with his wives, ministers, and church officials reveals a king whose achievement fell below his potential greatness.

Witte, John, Jr. *From Sacrament to Contract: Marriage, Religion, and Law in the Western Tradition*. Louisville, Ky.: Westminster John Knox Press, 1997. Survey of Christian theory and practice of marriage through history. Section 4 discusses Catherine of Aragon and the Anglican tradition. Includes bibliographic references and indexes.

SEE ALSO: Anne of Cleves; Anne Boleyn; Charles V; Clement VII; Desiderius Erasmus; Ferdinand II and Isabella I; Henry VII; Henry VIII; Catherine Howard; James IV; Julius II; Mary, Queen of Scots; Mary I; Sir Thomas More; Catherine Parr; Jane Seymour; The Tudor Family; Cardinal Thomas Wolsey.

RELATED ARTICLES in *Great Events from History: The Renaissance & Early Modern Era, 1454-1600:* Beginning 1485: The Tudors Rule England; 1515-1529: Wolsey Serves as Lord Chancellor and Cardinal; 1531-1540: Cromwell Reforms British Government; December 18, 1534: Act of Supremacy; May, 1539: Six Articles of Henry VIII.

THE RENAISSANCE & EARLY MODERN ERA

SAINT CATHERINE OF GENOA
Italian noblewoman, mystic, and saint

Catherine of Genoa was admired for her humanitarian work caring for the sick and the destitute. Her teachings and writings, as recorded by disciples, continue to inspire and influence religious leaders.

BORN: 1447; Genoa (now in Italy)
DIED: September 15, 1510; Genoa
ALSO KNOWN AS: Caterina Fieschi; Caterinetta Fieschi Adorno
AREA OF ACHIEVEMENT: Religion and theology

EARLY LIFE

Catherine of Genoa was born into the distinguished, aristocratic Fieschi family in the northern Italian city of Genoa. She was the youngest of five children born to Giacopo Fieschi and Francesca di Negro, both of noble birth. Her father was viceroy of Naples and a descendant of Roberto Fieschi, the brother of Pope Innocent IV. An older sister, Limbania, was an Augustinian nun, and there were at least two cardinals from the family during that time.

At the age of eight, Catherine already was inspired to do penance, and she disdained social status and wealth. At thirteen, she was pious and gifted in the way of prayer, but her request to enter the Augustinian convent, Santa Maria delle Grazie, was denied because she was too young. After her father died in 1461, her oldest brother decided, for financial and political reasons, to marry her into the powerful, aristocratic Adorno family. On January 14, 1463, at age sixteen, she married Giuliano Adorno.

For the next five years, Catherine was isolated, lonely, and depressed. She did not participate in the active social life expected of a noblewoman. Her marriage to Giuliano was unhappy and childless. Her husband was frequently unfaithful, and he fathered illegitimate children. He also had a violent temper and squandered both his and Catherine's fortunes. During the next five years, she attempted to join in the social life of Genoa but again became depressed.

LIFE'S WORK

After years of misery, there was a turning point in Catherine's life. On March 22, 1473, as she was about to make her Lenten confession, she had a life-changing and mystical experience. She suddenly felt deeply the overwhelming love of God for her, in spite of her sinfulness. As a result of this revelation and conversion, she determined to live a life of devotion, contemplation, and service to the

sick and the poor. A few days later, she felt even greater remorse for her sins when she had a vision of the Passion, of Christ carrying the cross, dripping with blood.

Consequently, she entered into years of intense personal penance, prayer, and mortification. She cared for the impoverished in the slums of Genoa. She also helped her ill husband, who had gone into bankruptcy. With her support, he became a sincere, religious convert and dedicated his life to helping the sick and the indigent. He became a Franciscan tertiary and agreed to live in a celibate marriage with Catherine.

From 1473 to 1496, Catherine and Giuliano Adorno worked together at Genoa's Pammatone Hospital, which was a place of last resort for the chronically ill, the aged, and incurables. Catherine also cleaned the homes of poor people and washed their vermin-filled clothing. In 1479, Catherine and Giuliano had moved into two small rooms at the Pammatone and worked without pay. From 1490 to 1496, Catherine served as director of the hospital. During this time, she had mystical visions and frequently fasted and prayed for long periods of time. In 1493, a plague struck Genoa and killed four-fifths of the population. Catherine established an outdoor infirmary in the space behind the Pammatone to care for the dying. She herself caught the plague from kissing a dying woman, but recovered.

In 1496, when Giuliano became seriously ill, Catherine resigned from her hospital position in order to care for him. In 1497, her husband died. In 1499, Catherine became the spiritual student of Don Cattaneo Marabotto, a secular priest and her successor as director of the Pammatone. She accepted him as her confessor and spiritual guide. Ending her spiritual isolation, she shared the experiences of her inner life with him and other disciples. Marabotto, along with a disciple and wealthy notary named Ettore Vernazza, would record her sayings, teachings, and experiences.

Catherine began suffering poor health in December of 1509, and on September 15, 1510, she died, surrounded by friends and disciples.

In 1551, Marabotto and Vernazza's collection of Catherine's sayings and teachings was published as *Libro de la vita mirabile e dottrina santa de la beta Caterinetta da Genoa* (*The Spiritual Doctrine of Saint Catherine of Genoa*, 1874). In 1683, Pope Innocent XI approved this collection, on which all later biographies and translations are based.

Catherine never actually wrote any books or developed a body of doctrine, but her teachings and revelations, recorded by Marabotto and Vernazza, have been compiled into two works, *Purgatorio* and *Dialogo* (*Purgation and Purgatory* and *The Spiritual Dialogue*, 1979). *Purgation and Purgatory* argues that there is continuity between life on Earth and life after death and that human beings are given the chance to atone for their sins as early as during their life on Earth. In *The Spiritual Dialogue*, two characters, Body and Soul, travel around the world and are joined by Self-Love, Human Frailty, and the Spirit in a debate about the conflicts among them.

Catherine was beatified by Pope Clement X in 1675. The Catholic Church determined that her writings alone were sufficient justification for sanctification or sainthood, and she was canonized by Pope Clement XII in 1737.

SIGNIFICANCE

Saint Catherine of Genoa was a great Christian mystic and visionary, whose life and teachings have inspired many theologians and religious leaders. Although she was a married layperson who never joined a religious order, her life of poverty and service to the poor and the sick became an example of the perfect Christian life.

Catherine's life and work inspired spiritual leaders such as Saint Francis de Sales (1567-1622), the bishop of Geneva; Saint Robert Bellarmine (1542-1621), the Jesuit theologian, writer, and cardinal; and Saint John of the Cross (1542-1591), the great mystic and theologian. Others who were inspired include Friedrich von Schlegel (1772-1829), philosopher, critic, writer, and the leader of the German Romantic school, who translated *The Spiritual Dialogue*; Cardinal Henry Edward Manning (1808-1892), who acknowledged learning from her teachings; and Cardinal John Henry Newman (1801-1890), who based his great visionary poem *The Dream of Gerontius* (1866) on Catherine's writings about the soul's journey to God.

Catherine also was a popular example of the perfect Christian for nineteenth century Protestants in the United States, including Thomas C. Upham (1799-1872), the prolific author and professor, who published *Life of Madame Catherine Adorna* in 1845. He presented her as an example of Christian perfectionism, which was popular in the Congregationalist and Methodist tradition. The monumental classic on mysticism, *The Mystical Element of Religion as Studied in Saint Catherine of Genoa and Her Friends* (1908), by Baron Friedrich von Hügel (1852-1925), revolves around Catherine's spirituality.

The Catholic Church named Saint Catherine of Genoa an Apostle of Purgatory. She was also named the patron saint (special protector or guardian) of brides, childless people, people ridiculed for their piety, victims of adultery, victims of unfaithfulness, and widows, and protector over temptations and difficult marriages.

—*Alice Myers*

FURTHER READING

Garvin, Paul, trans. and ed. *The Life and Sayings of Saint Catherine of Genoa*. New York: Alba House, 1964. Garvin has sorted through and selected content from the massive materials in Catherine's vita (1551). He has organized the biographical information in chronological order (the first third of the book) and categorized the doctrines by subject matter.

Hughes, Serge, trans. *Catherine of Genoa: Purgation and Purgatory, The Spiritual Dialogue*. New York: Paulist Press, 1979. Translations of *Purgatorio* and *Dialogo*, with a lengthy examination of her life, mysticism, teachings, and influence. Bibliography, notes on translations, index.

Jones, Kathleen. *Women Saints*. Maryknoll, N.Y.: Orbis Books, 1999. The chapter about Catherine of Genoa is a detailed discussion of her life, spirituality, and writings. Illustrated with the earliest known portrait of Catherine, by her cousin Tommasina Fieschi, from 1510. Bibliography.

Marabotto, Don Cattaneo, and Catherine of Genoa. *The Spiritual Doctrine of Saint Catherine of Genoa*. Rockford, Ill.: Tan Books, 1989. Originally compiled by her confessor, translated from Italian, and first published in English in 1874, this book offers useful insight into Catherine's religious experiences beginning in childhood. It is a comprehensive, illustrated collection of her sayings and teachings.

Oden, Amy. *In Words: Women's Writings in the History of Christian Thought*. Nashville, Tenn.: Abingdon Press, 1994. A modern English translation of excerpts from Catherine's dialogues of the soul and the body, with an explanation of the theological and historical context. Bibliography.

Reichardt, Mary. *Catholic Women Writers: A Bio-Bibliographical Sourcebook*. Westport, Conn.: Greenwood Press, 2001. The chapter on Catherine consists of biographical information, an analysis of recurring themes in her works, a survey of criticism, and an extensive bibliography.

SEE ALSO: Saint Angela Merici; Saint John of the Cross; Saint Teresa of Avila.

THOMAS CAVENDISH
English explorer

A boldly enterprising voyager, Cavendish was the second Englishman to circumnavigate the globe. In the course of his expedition, he captured one of the richest prizes in the history of English privateering against Spain.

BORN: September 19, 1560 (baptized); Grimston Hall, Trimley St. Martin, Suffolk, England
DIED: c. May, 1592; at sea, near Ascension Island
ALSO KNOWN AS: Thomas Candish
AREA OF ACHIEVEMENT: Exploration

EARLY LIFE

Thomas Cavendish (KAV-ehn-dihsh) was born at his family's estate of Grimston Hall, near the town of Harwich, in Suffolk, and he was baptized on September 19, 1560. He was the heir of William Cavendish and his wife, Mary Wentworth, sister of Lord William Wentworth. William Cavendish died when his son was only twelve, leaving a reduced estate. Thomas and his mother went to live with Lord Wentworth at Nettleshead, Suffolk.

At the age of fifteen, he entered Cambridge University, attending Corpus Christi College; he left in 1577 without taking a degree. In the next years he may have spent some time at the Inns of Court in London, studying law. In 1580, he went to the court of Queen Elizabeth I, where his sister Anne became one of the queen's ladies-in-waiting. Through his family, he had easy access to important figures at court; he became a friend of Sir George Carey, son of Lord Hunsdon; of Lord Chamberlain; and of George Clifford, earl of Cumberland, who became the most active aristocratic privateer in the country. Through the patronage of the earl of Pembroke, he was elected to Parliament from Shaftesbury, Dorset, in 1584 and for Wilton, Dorset, in 1586.

LIFE'S WORK

As part of an ambitious and venturesome court circle, Cavendish was soon drawn into naval enterprises. When Sir Walter Ralegh organized a fleet of seven ships to send his first colony to Virginia in 1585, Cavendish contributed a ship of his own, the *Elizabeth*, and was high marshal for the expedition. The fleet under Sir Richard Grenville left from Plymouth in early April and sailed first to Puerto Rico, where, under the cover of building a pinnace to enlarge their fleet, they planned to attack Spanish shipping. Two well-laden Spanish vessels were captured and their crews held for ransom, an action that whetted Cavendish's appetite for more privateering.

The fleet sailed on to Haiti, the Bahamas, and Florida before arriving on the Virginia coast near the end of June, 1585. In the next weeks, Cavendish became one of the party, including also Grenville and the artist John White, who conducted an exploring foray into what is now North Carolina. They came on three Native American villages, one of which they burned after a Native American stole a silver cup. Their reprisal may have generated some of the hostilities suffered by the ill-fated colony. In August, Cavendish was one of those who accompanied Grenville back to England, leaving 108 men behind under the governorship of Ralph Lane. En route, they were able to capture another rich Spanish prize.

The privateering success of the voyage, apart from the misfortunes of the colony, stimulated Cavendish to organize a much more ambitious enterprise. The example he chose to follow was that of Sir Francis Drake, who, eight years earlier, had won wealth, reputation, and honor in a plundering voyage around the world. Many English believed that the Spanish claims to monopoly on the territories of Latin America and the East Indies were invalid and that the riches being drained away from overseas possessions were legitimate targets for sailors bold enough to take them. The Spanish considered what they did to be piracy, but their own government favored them unofficially. Queen Elizabeth and her officers often took shares in the major voyages and always absorbed much of the profits.

His preparations must have begun almost immediately after he returned to England, since he was ready to sail the following summer. He had one major ship, the *Desire*, at 140 tons, and two small ones, the *Content* and the *Hugh Gallant*, with a crew of 123 men. A joint expedition with the earl of Cumberland may have been planned, since Cumberland was preparing a fleet at the same time, but Cavendish finished his preparations and sailed nearly a month before Cumberland was ready. He went first to Sierra Leone, then crossed to Brazil, where he paused to replenish his supplies and to build a small pinnace. Continuing southward, he stopped to slaughter thousands of penguins and take them on as food for the passage through the difficult and dangerous Strait of Magellan. Cumberland had followed him as far as Brazil but then turned back because of inadequate supplies.

Entering the strait, Cavendish came on a party of

Thomas Cavendish. (Library of Congress)

Spanish survivors from a failed colony; he took one of them with him and left the others to try to make their way to the Rio de Plata. Later, he found the remains of their settlement and took the cannon they had abandoned. After waiting a month for favorable weather, he was able to proceed through the straits without incident. The next eight months he spent cruising up the Pacific coast as far as Baja California, raiding Spanish ports and pillaging and burning some twenty ships.

On the coast of Ecuador, Cavendish learned from a captive of the expected arrival of a great ship from Manila; the capture of that ship became Cavendish's principal aim and most striking achievement. The ship was the *Santa Ana*, which was bringing to Mexico the yield of gold mines in the Philippines. He waited off the tip of Baja California, his men occupying themselves by pearl fishing, until November 4, when the *Santa Ana* appeared, its crew ready for the end of their long trans-Pacific voyage and its cannon put away in the hold. The first two English attacks were repulsed, but the third forced a surrender. The Spanish aboard were put ashore at San Lucas, and then the English spent two weeks sorting out their winnings. The ship carried gold worth seventy thousand pounds and great quantities of pearls, silks, and other goods.

Loss of the *Santa Ana* was a serious blow to the Spanish—it represented much of the year's profits from the

East Indies. Now, however, it presented Cavendish with a problem of surfeit. He did not have a crew big enough to staff the ship and take it home, and he could not even unload its cargo into his own vessels. He had been forced to abandon the *Hugh Gallant* on the South American coast, and he already had much of the cargo space in the remaining ships filled. In the end, he took what was most valuable and most easily portable and burned the rest, probably 90 percent of the cargo, along with the ship itself (it burned to the water line, but the Spanish were later able to salvage and rebuild it).

After the capture of the *Santa Ana*, the rest of the long voyage was anticlimactic. With the aid of a captured Spanish pilot, he crossed to the Philippines, arriving in January, 1588, but having lost the *Content* on the way. The pilot was hanged after trying to warn Spanish authorities, but without him Cavendish proceeded to the Sulu Sea, along the western shore of Mindanao, through the Banda and Flores Seas to Java. At every opportunity, he collected information about Spanish fortifications and apparently encouraged the Filipinos to resist the Spanish; conspirators arrested in Luzon the next year said that he had promised English support for their resistance. In March, he left again for England, arriving finally at Plymouth in September. The goods he brought back were officially valued at nearly ninety thousand pounds, a tremendous fortune for the time, but it is not known how much Cavendish kept after the queen and other officials took their shares. Cavendish made a great show of bringing his ship into the Thames, his crew in silk and golden chains, the ship itself rigged with sails of blue damask.

Cavendish was only twenty-eight years old when he returned to the acclaim of England. He was, for the moment, rich and famous, but his good fortune did not last. He expected to be knighted by the queen but was not, and the two-thousand-pound bond he had posted before the voyage was forfeited, possibly because of a skirmish with some Newfoundland ships or because he tried to conceal part of his prize. In the next years, he spent most of his new wealth, and by 1590 he was ready to try the exploit again. This time, however, he was plagued with misfortune. He left Plymouth in August, 1591, with five vessels and sailed for the Straits of Magellan, his fleet including John Davis in command of the *Desire*. The fleet was separated in heavy storms in the straits, however, and Cavendish turned back toward Brazil. He made unsuccessful attempts to land at Santos and Espírito Santo, then tried to reach Ascension Island. He died en route, believing that he had been deserted by his other ships.

SIGNIFICANCE

Cavendish's great voyage was one of the most daring exploits of Elizabethan seamanship. It inflicted a heavy economic blow and a more damaging psychological blow in demonstrating the vulnerability of Spanish trade even in the Pacific. Even more bitterly than the loss of the *Santa Ana* itself, the king of Spain is said to have mourned that it was taken by "an English youth . . . with forty or fifty companions." On the remainder of the voyage, Cavendish collected useful information to supplement what Drake had learned about not only the Straits of Magellan and the Pacific coast of America but also the Philippines and the Indonesian islands.

—Robert W. Kenny

FURTHER READING

Andrews, Kenneth R. *Elizabethan Privateering*. Cambridge, England: Cambridge University Press, 1964. The most complete and careful study of how privateering worked, who took part, and who shared in the proceeds. Cavendish can be traced in the context of Cumberland, Drake, and the other privateers.

Dudley, Wade G. *Drake: For God, Queen, and Plunder*. Washington, D.C.: Brassey's, 2003. Monograph on Sir Francis Drake's naval exploits paints a picture of Elizabethan privateering and the naval battles between England and Spain in Cavendish's time.

Hakluyt, Richard. *The Principall Navigations, Voiages, and Discoveries of the English Nation*. London, 1589. Reprint. Cambridge, England: Hakluyt Society/Cambridge University Press, 1965. One of the most important early achievements of English scholarship, a massive and exhaustive compilation of narratives of English voyages. Includes a lengthy account of the 1586-1588 voyage around the world based on the description of Francis Pretty, one of the members of the expedition.

Loades, David. *England's Maritime Empire: Seapower, Commerce, and Policy, 1490-1690*. New York: Longman, 2000. Exploration of the role of men like Cavendish in England's development into a colonial power, and especially a maritime empire. Includes maps, bibliographic references, index.

McDermott, James. *Martin Frobisher: Elizabethan Privateer*. New Haven, Conn.: Yale University Press, 2001. History of Elizabethan privateering focusing on Frobisher's naval campaigns. Includes illustrations, eight pages of plates, bibliographic references, and index.

Quinn, David Beers. *The Last Voyage of Thomas Cavendish, 1591-1592*. Chicago: University of Chicago Press, 1975. A contemporary account, believed to be Cavendish's own, of the voyage on which he died. Includes an excellent biographical and textual introduction.

_____. *The Roanoke Voyages*. Vol. 1. London: Hakluyt Society, 1955. A narrative of the 1585 expedition that incorporates all the major documentary sources. With careful and scholarly explanatory notes.

Sinclair, Andrew. *Sir Walter Raleigh and the Age of Discovery*. New York: Penguin Books, 1984. An attractive and highly readable description of the world that Cavendish shared with Ralegh at court, at sea, and in the colonies.

SEE ALSO: Sir Francis Drake; Elizabeth I; Sir Martin Frobisher; Sir Richard Grenville; Miguel López de Legazpi; Pemisapan; Sir Walter Ralegh.

RELATED ARTICLE in *Great Events from History: The Renaissance & Early Modern Era, 1454-1600:* June 27, 1542-c. 1600: Spain Explores Alta California.

WILLIAM CAXTON
English inventor and translator

In 1476, Caxton set up the first printing press in England, and before he died, he had published some one hundred items, many of them his own translations, at the same time helping to determine a standard for English usage and the establishment of an English literary canon.

BORN: c. 1422; the weald of Kent, England, possibly in the village of Hadlow
DIED: c. 1491; London, England
AREAS OF ACHIEVEMENT: Science and technology, scholarship

EARLY LIFE
Little is known of the early life of William Caxton (KAKS-tuhn), and both the date and place of his birth (somewhere in Kent) remain uncertain. He was apprenticed in 1438 to Robert Large, a successful mercer. This suggests a birth date between 1422 and 1424, because apprentices usually began their work between ages fourteen and sixteen.

Presumably Caxton's father was the William Caxton buried in Saint Margaret's churchyard at Westminster in 1478. Whether Oliver Cawston, buried at Saint Margaret's in 1474; Richard Caxston or Caston, a monk there from 1473 until his death in 1504; or John Caxston, known to have belonged to the church from 1474 to 1477, are related to the William Caxton who became a printer in Westminster remains uncertain.

When Robert Large, who became lord mayor of London in 1439, died in 1441, Caxton went to Bruges (now in Belgium), the hub of the brisk European wool trade, settling into the comfortable life of an English tradesman in the Lowlands. He remained there about thirty years, in the course of which he became wealthy, influential, and highly respected.

By 1453, Caxton was a member of the livery of the Mercer's company. Ten years later, he held the enormously influential position of Governor of the English Nation of Merchant Adventurers. During this time, the British government often called on him to transact delicate trade negotiations for the Crown.

Indirect evidence suggests that Caxton married a woman named Mawde around 1461 and that she died in England in 1490. In that year, the vestry accounts of Saint Margaret's Church record the cost of torches and tapers for the burial of a Mawde Caxston. In the same year,

Caxton left off the printing of *Fayts of Arms* (1489) to turn his attention to completing *The Arte and Crafte to Know Well to Die* (1490), a piece of circumstantial evidence that suggests that the Mawde Caxston who was buried in 1490 was his wife and that as a result of her death he was preoccupied with death.

Caxton apparently had one child, a daughter. The Public Records Office has a copy of a document recording the separation of Elizabeth Croppe from her husband in Westminster on May 11, 1496. This document identifies Elizabeth as William Caxton's daughter and refers to her late father's will.

Resigning his governorship around 1470, Caxton entered the service of Margaret, duchess of Burgundy, who was the sister of King Edward IV of Britain. Although Caxton continued in governmental service until 1475, around 1469, Caxton became extremely interested in literature.

LIFE'S WORK
Caxton did not begin his life's most significant work until he was nearly fifty. Already distinguished as a mercer and as a royal servant, Caxton, around 1469, turned his energies to translating compiler Raoul Le Fèvre's *Recueil des histoires de Troye* (1464; *The Recuyell of the Historyes of Troye*, 1475), which he finally completed at the behest of Margaret of Burgundy, on September 19, 1471, in Cologne, where he lived from 1470 until 1472.

Caxton, complaining that his pen had become worn from copying, bought a printing press and two fonts of type. Colard Mansion of Bruges helped Caxton set up his press, and, in 1475, Caxton printed in Bruges his translation of *Recueil des histoires de Troye*, the first book ever printed in English. He followed this book with his translation of a French allegory, *The Game and Playe of the Chesse*, in 1476, the same year in which he printed two or three books in French. (The original work, which Caxton translated, was itself a translation of 1360 by Jean de Vignay of Jacobus de Cessolis's *De ludo scaccorum*, c. 1300.)

In 1476, Caxton returned to England, where he spent the rest of his life. At an age when many people of his position would have retired, Caxton embarked on the demanding new career that assured him his place in history. In the city of Westminster, in an area behind and to the right of the transept of Westminster Abbey, Caxton set up the first printing press in England. From it was to issue the first document known to have been printed in England, an indulgence from Abbot Sant dated December 13, 1476.

The first book from Caxton's press, *Dicteis or Sayenges of the Phylosophers* (1477), was translated from the French by the Earl Rivers, who commissioned Caxton to print it. The only extant copy of this book, which exists in two later printings, has been dependably dated as being issued before November 18, 1477.

Scholars have questioned Caxton's reasons for setting up his press across the Thames in Westminster rather than in London, the hub of cultural and mercantile activity of his day. Church records indicate that numerous Caxtons (Caxstons, Cawstons, Caustons, Castons) were associated with Saint Margaret's Church in Westminster during the fifteenth century, suggesting that Caxton had family connections there. Also, Westminster was then inhabited by people of means who had the leisure to read, so that Caxton could sell his output more easily there than he might have elsewhere.

Caxton was probably also attracted by the royal court of Westminster, to which he had easy entrée because of the favor in which he was held by the royal family, whom he had served well. Certainly Caxton realized that being

William Caxton. (Library of Congress)

close to the Abbey would assure him regular printing jobs because of the volume of written material that issued from the Abbey regularly in manuscript form. That Caxton was in the good graces of John Esteney, the abbot of Westminster, is indicated by the fact that the abbot provided choice space near the Abbey for Caxton to set up his press, today marked by a commemorative plaque. Members of the Commons, who met in the Abbey, passed Caxton's printery when they left to go to the Chapter House, as did members of the royal family, who usually entered the Abbey through the south door. Caxton was assured that those in the best position to use his services would be reminded frequently of his availability.

The Humanism that had earlier ignited in Italy now spread through much of Europe and began to be felt in England. The demand for writing in Latin and Greek was substantial, but continental printers, who exported their books to England, met this need. Caxton realized that his best market was in original works or translations in the vernacular. It was in this field, as a precursor of Martin Luther and other Humanists who called for works in the vernacular that common people could read, which Caxton made his most significant contributions.

In 1481, the first illustrated book in English, *The Myrrour of the Worlde* (1481), came from Caxton's press. Caxton's books found a ready market among the nobility and the rich merchants who flocked to London during Caxton's later life. Because his books were printed in the vernacular, however, and because many of them were illustrated, it is clear that Caxton reached a broader audience than merely the nobility and rich merchants.

Caxton's press ran at capacity most of the time. When it was not in use printing books, it was fully engaged printing shorter documents for the Church or the Crown. Printing was a profitable commercial enterprise, but Caxton's motives were not strictly financial. He felt keenly his responsibility to provide useful reading material to a public hungry to read.

Caxton was meticulous in his editing. He issued Geoffrey Chaucer's *The Canterbury Tales* (1387-1400) around 1478, but, in 1484, when deficiencies in the earlier edition were pointed out to him, he printed an improved version of the work from a more reliable manuscript. From Caxton's press came editions of most of the important literature of England—in 1485 Thomas Malory's *Le Morte d'Arthur*, in 1483 John Gower's *Confessio Amantis* (1386-1390), and most of the writings of John Lydgate.

Caxton translated twenty-four books and was actively engaged in translating from French, Dutch, and Latin until the very day of his death. He was a careful editor of the books his press printed, often writing prologues or epilogues for them. Modern critics regarded his editing of Malory's Arthurian legends as remarkably sensitive. Caxton's prologue to Malory's *Le Morte d'Arthur* is knowledgeable and intelligent.

In his fifteen years as a printer at Westminster, Caxton published more than one hundred titles. In so doing, he helped to preserve and promote the canon of early English literature. Although the exact date of his death has not been established, Caxton probably died in 1491, a year after the death of the Mawde Caxston who, supposedly, was his wife. Church records at Saint Margaret's similar to those mentioning Mawde Caxston's burial expenses contain a bill for torches and tapers for the burial of William Caxton in 1491. Although some books with his imprint are dated as late as 1493, presumably those are editions he left behind that his faithful assistant, Wynken de Worde, printed and published after Caxton's death.

On Caxton's death, his printing shop, which had been expanded in 1483-1484 to the almonry adjacent to Westminster, did not pass to his heirs, suggesting that no son survived him. The press was instead taken over by Wynken de Worde, who continued to run the operation.

SIGNIFICANCE

Caxton's greatest contribution to later generations is twofold. By printing most of the notable English literature that existed in his day, he established and preserved the canon that constitutes early English literary studies. As important as that achievement was, however, there was perhaps even greater significance in Caxton's conscious determination of the level of English usage to be employed in printed books.

A year before his death, in the prologue to *Eneydos* (1490), a paraphrase of Vergil's *Aeneid* (first century B.C.E.) that Caxton had translated from the French, Caxton commented on the problems that face translators and printers. Acknowledging that he could not please everyone, Caxton explained that he would employ in his books an English between the "rude and curious." In doing so, he helped to establish a standard for English and to fix that standard so that the broad regional variations in the language that he observed during his lifetime would eventually be minimized.

Caxton tells of a merchant who, when he was traveling, "came into a house and asked for food; and asked especially for egges. The good wife answered that she could speak no French, and the merchant was angry, because he also could speak no French. And then another said that he would have eyren. The good wife said that she understood him well." Caxton asks, "What should a man in these days now write, egges or eyren?"

By grappling with such problems, Caxton determined for all time the level of usage that would predominate in printed works. For this contribution he will be longest remembered.

—*R. Baird Shuman*

FURTHER READING

Baugh, Albert C., and Thomas Cable. *A History of the English Language*. 5th ed. Upper Saddle River, N.J.: Prentice Hall, 2002. The portions on Caxton are excellent. They help define his contributions to English literature and language. A good starting point for those unfamiliar with Caxton.

Blades, William. *The Biography and Typography of William Caxton, England's First Printer*. London: Trübner, 1877. Reprint. Totowa, N.J.: Rowman & Littlefield, 1971. Updates Blades's *The Life and Typography of William Caxton* (1861, 1863); was the standard work on Caxton until Blake's biography (below).

Blake, N. F. *William Caxton and English Literary Culture*. Reprint. London: Hambledon & London, 2003. Study of the impact of Caxton's press on the literary history of England, and its role in shaping Renaissance literary culture. Includes illustrations, bibliographic references, index.

Caxton, William. "Translation of Christine de Pizan's Book of Fayttes of Armes and of Chyvalrye: Prologue" and "Translation of Geoffroy de la Tour-Landry, Book of the Knight of the Tower: Prologue." In *The Idea of the Vernacular: An Anthology of Middle English Literary Theory, 1280-1520*, edited by Jocelyn Wogan-Browne et al. University Park: Pennsylvania State University Press, 1999. These prologues by Caxton provide insights into his theory and practice of translation and his contributions to the development of formal written English.

De Ricci, Seymour. *A Census of Caxtons*. London: Oxford University Press, 1909. An indispensable book for serious Caxton scholars. Lists all extant copies of works known to have been printed by Caxton, including fragments.

Katō, Takato. *Caxton's "Morte d'Arthur": The Printing Process and the Authenticity of the Text*. Oxford, England: Society for the Study of Medieval Languages and Literature, 2002. Monograph on Caxton's printing process focuses on a single work, Sir Thomas Mallory's *Morte d'Arthur.* Details the effects of the printing process on textual claims to authenticity. Includes illustrations and bibliographic references.

SEE ALSO: Edward IV; Charlotte Guillard; Martin Luther; Sir Thomas Malory; Aldus Manutius; William Tyndale.

RELATED ARTICLES in *Great Events from History: The Renaissance & Early Modern Era, 1454-1600:* August 29, 1475: Peace of Picquigny; 1490's: Aldus Manutius Founds the Aldine Press.

WILLIAM CECIL
English administrator and statesman

Combining his enormous capacity for work with his dedication to Queen Elizabeth I, Cecil effectively managed the affairs of the English government for forty years, from 1558 to 1598.

BORN: September 13, 1520; Bourne, Lincolnshire, England
DIED: August 4, 1598; London, England
ALSO KNOWN AS: Lord Burghley; Lord Burleigh; First Baron Burghley
AREA OF ACHIEVEMENT: Government and politics

EARLY LIFE
William Cecil (SEE-sihl) was born in Lincolnshire. His father, Richard, was a minor officeholder (groom of the wardrobe) in the court of Henry VIII. William's grandfather, David Cecil, was a Welshman who assisted Henry Tudor (Henry VII) in his defeat of Richard III at Bosworth Field in 1485. Through his rewards from Henry VII, which included Stamford, and his marriage alliance with a wealthy family, David Cecil initiated his family's ascendancy in English society.

William Cecil attended schools in Grantham and Stamford and served as a page at court. At fifteen, Cecil entered St. John's College, Cambridge, to study the classics. At Cambridge, he came under the influence of the renowned Humanist John Cheke. Cecil fell in love with Cheke's sister, Mary. Despite family opposition, William married Mary in 1541. Before her untimely death in 1543, Mary bore William a son, Thomas. It was also during the early 1540's that Cecil studied law at Gray's Inn, London.

While at Cambridge, Cecil became a Protestant and, in 1542, was rewarded for his advocacy of Henrician policies by being granted a position within the Court of Common Pleas. In 1543, Cecil entered Parliament. During the last years of Henry VIII's reign, Cecil associated with Protestants both politically and socially; he married Mildred Cooke, a devout Protestant, in 1545.

On the succession of Edward VI in January, 1547, Cecil served as an assistant in the regency government to Edward Seymour (known also as Lord Hertford and duke of Somerset). After Seymour's fall from power in 1551, Cecil aligned himself with the duke of Northumberland (John Dudley). His allegiance to Northumberland, however, was short-lived; when Cecil learned of Northumberland's plans to change the line of succession as prescribed by Henry VIII's will, Cecil abandoned Northumberland in 1553 on the death of Edward VI. The Protestant Cecil served Catholic Mary Tudor's (Mary I) government in a variety of minor posts and gained considerable knowledge of and experience with the workings of the English government, and both Mary and Cardinal Reginald Pole, the papal legate, recognized his contributions and integrity. Cecil's commitment to his Protestant faith did not prove to be a barrier to his continuing service to the government. During the Marian period (1553-1558), Cecil maintained his contact with Princess Elizabeth, and it was on her accession to the throne in 1558 that Cecil began his four decades of power in English politics.

LIFE'S WORK
On her accession to the throne in 1558, Elizabeth named Cecil as her secretary. During the next several years, Cecil assisted his queen in resolving a long-standing conflict with the Scots (in the Treaty of Edinburgh, 1560), in implementing the Protestant Elizabethan religious settlement (1559), and in administering the recoinage scheme (1561) developed by the marquess of Winchester. The recoinage program curbed inflation and provided a sound financial basis for the government.

Throughout the early decades of Elizabeth's reign, Cecil supported the movement to have her marry and produce an heir, although he did not support the candidacy of Robert Dudley. (Dudley was Elizabeth's primary romantic interest during the 1560's.) Indeed, Cecil's position was threatened by Dudley's popularity. In 1564, Dudley was named earl of Leicester and became a royal councillor. In response, Cecil brought Thomas Howard, the duke of Norfolk, into the council. The principal issue that dominated political concerns during the late 1560's was the problem of Mary Stuart, the Catholic former queen of France and queen of Scotland who fled to England for protection in 1568. It was in this atmosphere that Leicester and Norfolk joined in an effort to remove Cecil, but a rebellion of northern Catholic earls (1569) resulted in a situation that strengthened Cecil's position at court. In 1571, Elizabeth named him the first Baron Burghley and in the following year, he was named lord treasurer.

During the 1570's and 1580's, the primary problems confronting the queen were the tenacity of the English Catholics (the Recusants), the rebellion in the Netherlands against Spain, and the rather chaotic relations with Valois France. The English Recusant cause gained momentum and focus after the establishment of the English College at Douai (1568) by William Allen, the papal bull (*Excelsis Regnans*) on the excommunication of Elizabeth in 1570, and the creation of the Jesuit Mission to England in 1575. The issue was complicated further by the continuing presence of Mary Stuart: She provided a Catholic alternative to Elizabeth. Conspiracies were fre-

William Cecil. (Library of Congress)

quent, and Cecil responded to the threat by escalating the measured response of the government. During the early 1580's, the Jesuit Edmund Campion was executed, and later, in 1587, Mary Stuart was beheaded as a traitor. Throughout this experience, Cecil did not seek to produce Catholic martyrs; rather, he sought to maintain the unity of church and state. In *The Execution of Justice in England* (1583), Cecil advanced his contention that both law and theology demanded the enforcement of the Elizabethan Settlement. A violation of the religious code was comparable to a violation of the civil code, and if serious, it constituted a treasonable offense.

In the 1570's, Protestants in the Netherlands under William the Silent mounted a rebellion against Catholic Spain. After some initial reluctance, Cecil joined Leicester in convincing Elizabeth to support the rebels in 1576. For a decade, the issue would place an increasing strain on Anglo-Spanish relations, and ultimately it led to the Spanish Armada. By 1588, Cecil had prepared England militarily, financially, and diplomatically to defeat the Spaniards.

Political instability was the primary characteristic of French society during the 1570's and 1580's. From the St. Bartholomew's Day Massacre (1572) through the War of the Three Henrys (1587-1588), France was in the grip of a dynastic, political, and religious crisis, which would be resolved with the victory of the Protestant king Henry IV in 1589. When possible, Cecil manipulated the French situation to benefit England at Spain's expense. At best, the French were unpredictable, and arrangements with them were short-lived.

Cecil's principal rival, Leicester, died in 1589, but he was replaced soon by the earl of Essex. Cecil prevented the ambitious Essex from gaining substantive power during the mid-1590's. Cecil's son, Robert, became secretary to Elizabeth in 1596 as a result of his father's efforts.

Cecil's domestic accomplishments as secretary and lord treasurer were based on his conservatism, honesty, and dedication to his duty. He exposed and eliminated corruption, required public officeholders to work, and opposed increased taxation. When the long war against Spain threatened the solvency of the treasury, Cecil only considered the curtailment of expenditures rather than seeking innovative measures to increase income. Cecil maintained that enhanced efficiency would result in cost reductions.

Privately, Cecil led a quiet life. He possessed an extensive library and was interested especially in cartography and genealogy. From 1557, he served as chancellor of Cambridge University, but his tenure in that position did not result in any significant contributions. Cecil involved himself in the detailed design and construction of his three houses: Burghley House at Stamford, Cecil House in the Strand, and Theobalds in Hertfordshire. Cecil died on August 4, 1598, at Cecil House; he was still in office and at work on negotiations to end the war with Spain.

SIGNIFICANCE

During an extremely volatile period in English political history, Cecil contributed competent political management and continuity of policy. Cecil's management skills, combined with his political wisdom, enabled him to retain his position of prominence though challenged by Leicester and Essex. Cecil did not possess the charm, boldness, or personal attractiveness of these two ambitious men, but he did pursue consistent, well-formulated policies that were based on elementary tenets of English national interest. In doing so, Cecil not only retained the support of Elizabeth I but also established a model for subsequent advisers and ministers of state.

Cecil refined and manipulated the centralizing procedures that were established earlier by Thomas Cromwell, who served as Henry VIII's principal adviser during the 1530's. His administration of the Elizabethan Settlement and the later problems associated with the English Recusants and the Puritans serve to document his effective and, at times, restrained use of power in the interests of the state. During the turbulent days of the Rebellion of the Northern Earls (1569), the Ridolfi plot (1571), the Throckmorton plot (1583), the Babington plot (1586), and the Spanish Armada (1587-1588), Cecil's management of the Elizabethan regime was firm, and his responses to these crises were within the law. In each of these instances, England prevailed and English interests were enhanced as a result of Cecil's actions.

Cecil's contributions to English politics went beyond these specific achievements. Along with Cromwell, Cecil provided a historic base for early modern political management. Cecil and Cromwell influenced the evolution of the English constitution through their use of power at the ministerial level. Cecil was a Royalist who served his monarchs and worked with, and not for, Parliament. Nevertheless, much of his substantive contribution survived not only his tenure but also the crises that dominated English political history during the seventeenth century. During the 1590's, Cecil's administration came under increasing criticism for not being in touch with the problems which confronted the country. Essex, among others, accused Cecil of providing uninspired and often inadequate advice to Elizabeth. Yet Cecil, not Essex, has been vindicated by later generations of national leaders and scholars.

—William T. Walker

FURTHER READING

Alford, Stephen. *The Early Elizabethan Polity: William Cecil and the British Succession Crisis, 1558-1569.* New York: Cambridge University Press, 1998. In-depth study of the crisis caused by Elizabeth's refusal to marry or to name a successor, using Cecil's personal papers as a lens to understand Elizabeth's court, the national and international scene, and the long-term consequences of the crisis. Includes bibliographic references and index.

Croft, Pauline, ed. *Patronage, Culture, and Power: The Early Cecils.* New Haven, Conn.: Yale University Press, 2002. Interdisciplinary anthology of essays about the patronage activities of William Cecil and his son. Discusses their effects on painting, music, architecture, and other arts, as well as the relationship between their patronage and their political goals. Includes illustrations, maps, bibliographic references, index.

Dickens, A. G. *The English Reformation.* 2d ed. University Park: Pennsylvania State University Press, 1991. In this general review of the Anglican Reformation, Cecil emerges as an able and dedicated Protestant who provided Elizabeth with significant assistance in the establishment and maintenance of the Elizabethan Settlement. While sympathetic to Cecil, Dickens does not consider Cecil as an individual primarily motivated by religious considerations.

Erickson, Carolly. *The First Elizabeth.* New York: Summit Books, 1983. This biography of Elizabeth portrays Cecil as a tireless, knowledgeable, and astute public servant who conducted the bulk of governmental business personally. Cecil is also interpreted as one motivated by principles, faith, and a strong sense of duty.

Haigh, Christopher, ed. *The Reign of Elizabeth I.* Athens: University of Georgia Press, 1985. A scholarly collection of essays by such notable historians as G. R. Elton, Penry Williams, Patrick Collinson, J. D. Alsop, Norman Jones, and others. The interpretations of the impact of William Cecil on the reign and on English government are sympathetic.

Levine, Joseph M., ed. *Elizabeth I.* Englewood Cliffs, N.J.: Prentice-Hall, 1969. This book consists of excerpts from both primary and secondary sources.

Cecil's personal relationship with Elizabeth is highlighted, and her growing dependence on Cecil is documented.

Lockyer, Roger. *Tudor and Stuart Britain, 1471-1714.* 2d ed. New York: St. Martin's Press, 1985. In this authoritative study of the period, Cecil's substantive contributions as Elizabeth's adviser and as bureaucrat are applauded and documented.

MacCaffrey, Wallace. *The Shaping of the Elizabethan Regime.* Princeton, N.J.: Princeton University Press, 1968. Cecil's impact on English political history during the second half of the sixteenth century is considered throughout this important study. Cecil emerges as an efficient and durable administrator who was a master of court intrigue and factional politics.

Read, Conyers. *Mr. Secretary Cecil and Queen Elizabeth.* New York: Alfred A. Knopf, 1955.

_____. *Lord Burghley and Queen Elizabeth.* New York: Alfred A. Knopf, 1960. This two-volume biography on Cecil constitutes the most scholarly and detailed study of Elizabeth's chief adviser. Cecil is viewed as the force of continuity within the regime—an able, intelligent, and loyal servant of his queen.

Rowse, A. L. *The England of Elizabeth.* New York: Collier, 1966. In this volume, Cecil is interpreted as Elizabeth's partner in running the government. While differences between them emerged on occasion, their mutual respect for each other prohibited such differences from escalating into major conflicts.

Usher, Brett. *William Cecil and Episcopacy, 1559-1577.* Burlington, Vt.: Ashgate, 2003. Examines Cecil's role in the reform and restructuring of the Church of England. Details his attempts to do away with a bishopric defined by temporal wealth and power and replace it with properly humble superintendents supported by their church, but not lavished with its wealth. Includes bibliographic references and index.

SEE ALSO: Thomas Cromwell; Edward VI; Elizabeth I; Henry IV; Henry VII; Henry VIII; Mary, Queen of Scots; Mary I; William the Silent.

RELATED ARTICLES in *Great Events from History: The Renaissance & Early Modern Era, 1454-1600:* 1558-1603: Reign of Elizabeth I; January 20, 1564: Peace of Troyes; November 9, 1569: Rebellion of the Northern Earls.

BENVENUTO CELLINI
Italian sculptor and writer

Cellini is acknowledged as perhaps the finest goldsmith in Renaissance Italy. His sculpture, represented by his bronze Perseus, was also superb. He is also known for his lively and spirited autobiography, which transmits the spirit of the Italian Renaissance to modern readers.

BORN: November 3, 1500; Florence (now in Italy)
DIED: February 13, 1571; Florence
AREAS OF ACHIEVEMENT: Literature, art

EARLY LIFE

Benvenuto Cellini (behn-veh-NEW-toh chayl-LEE-nee) was born in Florence at the beginning of the Cinquecento. He was the son of Giovanni Cellini, an architect and engineer, who was also a passionate amateur musician, and of Elisabetta Granacci, the daughter of a neighbor. Cellini describes his parents' marriage as a love match: Elisabetta married without a dowry. Benvenuto was born to them after some twenty years of marriage, during which time they had one daughter. Cellini's father

dearly wished him to become a musician, a flutist, while Benvenuto himself wished to study art. This struggle, a friendly one, continued between the two for many years.

When Benvenuto reached the age of fifteen, he apprenticed himself, against his father's will, as a goldsmith in the studio of Andrea di Sandro Marcone. He was not paid wages and so was not compelled to do much of the menial labor that fell to paid apprentices. He used his extra time to study drawing, a study he continued all his life and one of the things that made him much more than a mere craftsperson.

About a year into this apprenticeship, he became involved in a duel in support of his younger brother; the duel rapidly developed into a brawl. In this year, 1516, Benvenuto was banished from Florence for six months. He went to Siena and worked for a goldsmith there, until he was recalled to Florence by the Cardinal de' Medici at the elder Cellini's request (the Cellinis were Medici adherents through all the changes in Florentine government; Benvenuto continued this tradition, although his vigorous sense of *amour propre* meant that his relations

Benvenuto Cellini. (Library of Congress)

with the great were always rather testy). Benvenuto was then sent by his father to study music in Bologna, but the youth also worked with a goldsmith there. He returned to Florence after several months and eventually made peace with his father on the art or music question.

Leaving for Rome at about age sixteen, Benvenuto ended up in Pisa for a year. While in Pisa, he worked as a goldsmith and studied the local antiquities. Returning to Florence, he studied the work of Michelangelo, whom he regarded as the greatest modern sculptor. Finally, in 1519, he did travel to Rome, he but returned, after two years, to Florence, from where in 1523 he had to flee under sentence of death for fighting.

Benvenuto fled to Rome and soon began to receive important commissions from the bishop of Salamanca, Sigismondo Chigi, from his wife, Porzia, and from Pope Clement VII. At this time, he was artistically mature; he began to work for himself and not for other goldsmiths and established a shop of his own in Rome. What would be the pattern of his life had taken shape: a peripatetic habit, often set in motion of necessity, because of his terrible temper and tendency to violence; many important

commissions; a great reputation for his work coupled with frequent disputes with his patrons; and much trouble with the law.

LIFE'S WORK

In Rome, Cellini's fine work in drawing, jewelry, and larger pieces such as serving plates and candelabras very soon caught the notice of rich and influential patrons. He was a musician, briefly, in Clement's orchestra. He produced many drawings in the style of Michelangelo and Raphael, made jewelry and set and estimated the value of jewels, made cast and carved plate and ornamental silver, and designed and struck medals and coinage.

He was also drawn to military life during this period and participated in the defense of Rome in 1527, during the invasion of Italy by the Holy Roman Empire. He claimed to have shot the constable of Bourbon and the prince of Orange during the defense, and there is some evidence that his claims could be true. At this time, his sculptor's knowledge of structure and spatiality, translated into engineering, was useful in ordering the pope's artillery. Later he would design fortifications in Florence. (It was common for sculptors in this period to be called on to use their engineering skills to design weapons, fortifications, and buildings for their cities of residence.)

While in Rome, Cellini was often distracted from his art by his music and also by romantic dalliance. His ambition to excel in all branches of goldsmithing, coinage, and sculpture also served to distract him from the relatively single-minded pursuit of one medium that was the norm then and now, for craftspeople. Most artists specialized in certain aspects of their art. Cellini was an endlessly ambitious and curious student of many arts and always was a leader in technical innovations in sculpture and goldsmithing.

After the invasion of Rome, Cellini left for Florence, intending to raise a company and become a captain under the famous condottiere Orazio Baglioni. On hearing this, Cellini's father sent him to Mantua so that he would not be called on to fulfill his obligation to Baglioni. Cellini went to Mantua, executed some small works for the duke there, quarreled with him, and returned to Florence, where he discovered that his father and sister Cosa had died of the plague. His brother and another sister remaining, he stayed in Florence until Clement declared war on the city and requested Cellini's presence in Rome.

In danger of being arrested as a traitor or spy because of these communications from Clement, Cellini traveled to Rome in 1529. He received at this time the commission from Clement for the famous morse (a clasp or button for a cope), now lost. Its design is recorded in three eighteenth century drawings in the British Museum: God the Father, in half relief, is over a large diamond in the center of the morse, and the diamond is supported by three children. At this time also, Cellini began to make the steel dies for the pope's coinage and was appointed *maestro della stampe* at the papal mint.

After Clement's death in 1534, Cellini seized the opportunity of the resultant civic disorder to kill a rival goldsmith, Pompeo; he was absolved of this murder by the new pope Paul III, partly because of the support of influential friends such as Cardinal Francesco Cornaro and Cardinal Ippolito de' Medici, and partly because the new pope wished to retain him as master of the mint.

In 1536, Holy Roman Emperor Charles V arrived in Rome for his triumphal entry as conqueror of the city. Cellini had been commissioned by Paul to make the gifts for the emperor and empress: a crucifix in gold and a jeweled golden case for a richly illuminated Book of Hours. The works were not finished at the time of the arrival of the emperor (April 6, 1536), and the pope told Cellini to offer himself along with the gifts in order to see the work to its conclusion. By the time this was done, an enemy of Cellini (of which he always seemed to have a good supply) had slandered him to the pope, who became angry at Cellini, underpaid him for his work, and refused to send him with the book to the emperor, who had requested his presence.

At this point, Cellini decided to travel to France (he left April 1, 1537). He met at this time Ippolito I, cardinal d'Este of Ferrara, who commissioned a basin and a jug from him; this friendship later proved to be his entrée with the king of France, Francis I. Becoming ill, Cellini returned to Rome. He was soon recalled to France by Francis through the cardinal d'Este but, before he could leave, he was arrested by the pope and imprisoned in the Castle Sant' Angelo for allegedly stealing the papal jewels, entrusted to him at the time of the invasion of Rome in 1527. Pier' Luigi, the pope's natural son, was apparently behind this plot; Cellini writes that Pier' Luigi wanted to obtain Cellini's property. Francis requested Cellini of the pope but was refused.

During Cellini's long prison stay, which severely impaired his health, he survived poisoning attempts and political maneuvering; he was finally extracted from the papal clutches in 1539 by means of the deft diplomacy of the cardinal d'Este, at the behest of Francis. Cellini brought out of prison a long poem he had composed there, which he reproduced in his autobiography, *La vita*

di Benvenuto Cellini (*The Life of Benvenuto Cellini*, 1771), which was not published until 1728. The cardinal d'Este brought Cellini back to France, where he arrived in 1540. Soon after his arrival, Cellini became dissatisfied with his treatment by the cardinal and tried to leave France on a pilgrimage to the Holy Sepulchre. This near loss made the cardinal more attentive and drew the attention of the king, who gave Cellini a large salary and a small castle in Paris in which to work. In 1542, Cellini was granted letters of naturalization by the king, and in 1543 he completed for the king the great saltcellar.

This saltcellar, one of Cellini's most famous works, has two figures in gold: a male representing the sea who holds a small ship (which holds the salt) and a facing female figure representing the land. Her hand rests on a small temple (which holds the pepper). The legs of the figures are intertwined as they halfway recline on an oval base. The piece is beautifully ornamented and enameled, and it can be seen in any illustrated collection of Cellini's works. Cellini created many other works for Francis. Among these was a silver candlestick: a life-size figure of Jupiter, mounted on rollers, holding a (functioning) torch in one hand. Several pieces he did in France do survive: the *Nymph of Fontainebleau* (1545) and an accompanying satyr are among them. He began to make models for a monumental figure of Mars and accompanying smaller allegorical figures for a fountain at Fontainebleau, but this work never reached completion. Cellini had incurred the ire of the king's mistress, Madame d'Étampes; he apparently did not realize the extent of her power, especially in the realm of art commissions. She resented Cellini's obliviousness to her power and bitterly opposed his projects; her opposition was sufficient to prevent any new projects of his from coming to fruition.

Frustrated in his work, in 1545 Cellini asked leave to travel to Florence. The king denied him permission while the cardinal d'Este told him he could leave; he left on what was meant to be a brief trip, but he never returned. In his autobiography, he often regrets his departure from France. In Florence, he visited Cosimo I de' Medici and described for him all that he had done for Francis. Cosimo asked Cellini to make, for the piazza of Florence, a statue of Perseus, symbolizing Cosimo's own victory over the Gorgon of republicanism. The *Perseus* would be in grand company—Michelangelo's *David* (1501-1504) and Donatello's *Judith and Holofernes* (1456-1457) already stood in the piazza. This was Cellini's chance to make his name as a sculptor in his home city, a city renowned for sculpture. He regarded the commission as an honor but received only about a third of the money he requested for the piece. The piece was finally finished and revealed fully to the public on April 27, 1554. It was greeted with great public acclaim; art criticism was a democratic activity in the Florence of those days. Cosimo, standing half-hidden at a window of the palace, heard the praise of the crowds. He apparently wanted to know the sentiments of the crowd before he expressed his own. The acclaim of the public allowed him to be equally pleased with the piece.

During his stay in Florence, Cellini had begun to work in marble. He restored an antique Ganymede for Cosimo and did a life-size Christ in white marble on a cross in black marble; this was to be for his own tomb (the piece is now in the Escorial). At this time, he induced Cosimo to have a competition among the Florentine sculptors for a beautiful block of marble, meant for a statue of Neptune, which had been quarried for Bandinelli (a hated rival of Cellini who had since died). Cellini did not get this commission, he thought, because of the opposition of Cosimo's wife, who thought him too haughty. At the end of his autobiography, he portrays himself as involved in rather acrimonious negotiations with Cosimo for making the *Neptune* from a different block of marble. This task was never accomplished.

Soon afterward, Cellini left Cosimo's service and established his own shop again, doing goldsmith's work for many clients. His life is poorly documented after this time, because it is not included in his autobiography and because he had fewer dealings with influential people. The writing of his autobiography is his most important work of this period, during which he also wrote his treatises on sculpture and on goldsmithing, *Trattati dell'oreficeria e della scultura* (1568; *The Treatises of Benvenuto Cellini on Goldsmithing and Sculpture*, 1898), which he published himself much later.

In 1557, in Florence, Cellini was condemned to four years in prison for sodomy, though this sentence was reduced to four years of confinement in his own house. During this time, he dictated his autobiography to a fourteen-year-old boy, while working at projects in his studio. In 1559, a version of his autobiography was completed, and Cellini gave it to the famed Benedetto Varchi, a Florentine writer and scholar, for criticism. Varchi liked the colloquial style and told Cellini to retain it. Cellini continued work on his autobiography until 1562. He died in Florence in 1571.

SIGNIFICANCE

Cellini's life represents what is meant by the phrase Renaissance man. He was an immensely able, curious, and active practitioner of many civilized arts: drawing, music, sculpture, goldsmithing, swordplay, military strategy and architecture, conversation, and literature. His appearance was apparently pleasing, though no contemporary likenesses exist. He was social, well connected, and confident, and felt himself the equal of any by virtue of his skill. His directness and enthusiasm in *The Life of Benvenuto Cellini* seem to represent the spirit of his age.

As an artist, Cellini was both an excellent craftsperson and a technically innovative and formally inventive sculptor. He could combine the Renaissance virtues of beautiful form and new technologies into works that can stand with the best of his day. It is unfortunate that, because of his temperament, the circumstances of his life, and the occasional uncooperativeness of patrons, his skill was not generally allowed the scope it needed. It is also unfortunate that, because many of his works were executed in precious metals, few of them survive, many having been melted down. His greatest work, however, is not so much a work of art, perhaps, as of personality. His autobiography provides a most vivid picture of life in the Renaissance; it is undoubtedly tainted by exaggeration and boasting, but even these characteristics reveal aspects of an age of great energy. Cellini was an extremely subtle observer; through his description, figures that would otherwise be little more than names are revealed in detail. His own personality is revealed without caution and a thoroughly charming self-portrait of a fascinating person appears.

—*Ann Klefstad*

FURTHER READING

Avery, C. "Benvenuto Cellini's Bust of Bindo Altoviti." *The Connoisseur* 198 (May, 1978): 62-72. An unusual look at one of Cellini's portrait bronzes. Not very penetrating, but it does give some account of a mode of work in which the sculptor excelled and for which he is little remembered.

Cellini, Benvenuto. *My Life*. Translated with an introduction by Julia Conaway Bondanella and Peter Bondanella. New York: Oxford University Press, 2002. An authoritative translation of Benvenuto's autobiography. Includes explanatory notes, bibliographic references, and index.

_____. *The Treatises of Benvenuto Cellini on Goldsmithing and Sculpture*. Translated by C. R. Ashby. London: E. Arnold, 1898. Reprint. New York: Dover, 1967. This work by Cellini describes his beliefs about the trades to which he devoted his life.

Gallucci, Margaret A. *Benvenuto Cellini: Sexuality, Masculinity, and Artistic Identity in Renaissance Italy*. New York: Palgrave Macmillan, 2003. This work places Cellini in the context of contemporary Renaissance—or early modern—studies, by examining his life and work from the point of view of interdisciplinary academic approaches to culture. Looks at Cellini's relationship to Renaissance understandings of law, sexuality, masculinity, honor, and magic. Includes illustrations, bibliographic references, and index.

Parker, Derek. *Cellini: Artist, Genius, Fugitive*. Stroud, Gloucestershire, England: Sutton, 2003. This biography emphasizes the flamboyant nature of Cellini's adventures and portrays him as a quintessentially romantic figure from a tempestuous historical era. Includes illustrations, photographic plates, bibliographic references, and index.

Pope-Hennessy, John. *Cellini*. New York: Abbeville Press, 1985. This magnificent work contains full photo documentation of Cellini's surviving works and drawings, as well as the casts of some that have been lost. Pope-Hennessy has written an absorbing and readable essay on Cellini's life and works for the book. Contains much information not in Cellini's autobiography. His descriptions of Cellini as an accountant, record-keeper, and litigant are especially fascinating, revealing Cellini's nonswashbuckling side. The book is probably the best source on Cellini next to the autobiography and makes good use of many contemporary sources. Includes a good index, notes, and a bibliography.

Vasari, Giorgio. *Lives of the Painters, Sculptors, and Architects*. Translated with an introduction by William Gaunt. London: Dent, 1963. This four-volume work is a trove of biographical information on Renaissance artists, compiled and written by a fellow artist and contemporary. Although there is no separate entry on Cellini, he is mentioned in many of the other artists' biographies. Includes an index.

SEE ALSO: Charles V; Clement VII; Francis I; Cosimo I de' Medici; Michelangelo; Raphael; Jacopo Sansovino; Giorgio Vasari; Andrea del Verrocchio.

RELATED ARTICLE in *Great Events from History: The Renaissance & Early Modern Era, 1454-1600*: c. 1500: Revival of Classical Themes in Art.

MIGUEL DE CERVANTES
Spanish writer

Poet, playwright, and novelist, Cervantes was Spain's greatest writer, chiefly because of his Don Quixote de la Mancha, *the first European novel and one of the supreme works of world literature.*

BORN: September 29, 1547; Alcalá de Henares, Spain
DIED: April 23, 1616; Madrid, Spain
ALSO KNOWN AS: Miguel de Cervantes Saavedra
AREA OF ACHIEVEMENT: Literature

EARLY LIFE

In 1547, the year that Miguel de Cervantes (mee-GEEHL day sehr-VAHN-teez) was born, Henry VIII of England and Francis I of France died, leaving Charles I of Spain (Holy Roman Emperor Charles V) the dominant ruler in Europe and the Spanish dominions, the most powerful empire on earth.

The sixteenth century is known in Spanish history as the Siglo del Oro (the golden century, or Spanish Golden Age), partly because of Cervantes, who perhaps was the greatest of all Spanish writers. His parents were impoverished members of the gentry, and Miguel, the fourth of their seven children, was born some twenty miles from Madrid. His father, Rodrigo, was an apothecary surgeon who was usually in debt and was even sent to debtors' prison. In 1551, he moved the family to Valladolid, and in 1553 to Córdoba, once the greatest city of Moorish Spain. There Miguel probably studied under Father Alonso de Vieras and later at the Jesuit College of Santa Catarina, where he is likely to have seen his first plays.

For six years after 1558, the family's whereabouts cannot be determined, but in 1564, they appeared in Seville, the major city of Andalusia. There Miguel attended the new Jesuit college and saw the great actor Lope de Rueda and his company perform. The residence in Seville was brief, however, for in 1566, the family moved to Madrid, the new seat of the royal court under Philip II. There, Cervantes became a student in the city school. When Queen Elizabeth de Valois died, Cervantes' teacher composed a commemorative book in 1569 that included four poems by young Cervantes on the death of the queen.

That same year, however, a warrant was issued for Cervantes' arrest for wounding a man in a duel, apparently in the royal court, because the penalty was for Cervantes to have his right hand amputated and to be exiled for ten years. Not waiting for the sentence to be carried out, Cervantes escaped to Rome, then proceeded to Naples, where he enlisted in the Spanish army; his brother Rodrigo joined him. In 1571, the brothers were among the troops aboard the immense fleet of two hundred galleys and one hundred additional ships that engaged the equally formidable Turkish armada at Lepanto in the Gulf of Corinth. On the eve of the battle, Cervantes was ill with malaria and was ordered to stay below, but he insisted that he be posted "where the danger is greatest and there I shall remain and fight to the death."

During the Battle of Lepanto, one of the greatest naval combats in history, Cervantes held his post on the deck of the *Marquesa*, and at the end of the day, when the Spanish were victorious, he was found there covered with blood, his sword in his right hand, his left hand shattered, and his chest bleeding from two severe wounds. The victorious admiral, Don Juan of Austria, must have been aware of Cervantes' valor, for that day he ordered an increase in his pay. It was three weeks before Cervantes had his wounds properly treated at the hospital in Messina. It is not clear whether his left hand had been amputated or if it had been so injured that is remained useless for the rest of his life. Nevertheless, Cervantes considered that day in battle as one of the greatest of his life and said that he would rather have been in the battle than have missed it and the wounds he suffered.

After six months of hospitalization, Cervantes recovered, rejoined the fleet, and was present when Don Juan captured the Turkish flagship on which the galley slaves rebelled and killed their captain, the grandson of the pirate Barbarossa. He was also present when Don Juan captured Tunis without a battle in 1573. Garrisoned in Naples for a year, he fell in love with a woman who became the model for Silena in his first novel, *La Galatea* (1585; *Galatea: A Pastoral Romance*, 1833).

On a voyage home in 1575, his ship was attacked by Algerian galleys, and after a sharp fight the ship was captured and the survivors, including Miguel and Rodrigo de Cervantes, were taken as slaves to Algiers. Cervantes later described the event in a verse epistle to the king's secretary, Matteo Vásquez. Because Cervantes was bearing letters of praise from Don Juan of Austria and the duke of Sessa, his ransom was made impossibly high. During five years of brutal captivity, though usually

Miguel de Cervantes. (Library of Congress)

loaded down with chains, Cervantes masterminded four escape attempts. Each was thwarted, yet, despite the strong danger of being mutilated, impaled, hooked, or burned alive, as some of his confederates had been, he kept trying. Each time he was caught, he claimed sole responsibility for the plot. Each time, he was chained and imprisoned more severely, yet his courage, resourcefulness, and lust for freedom were irrepressible.

At one time, he may have planned to organize a massive slave insurrection. According to one account of Algerian captivity, the pasha lived in perpetual fear of "the scheming of Miguel de Cervantes." Apparently only greed for his ransom kept his master from putting him to a horrible death. Such ransom as was provided was inadequate for both Cervantes brothers, so Miguel relinquished his share so that Rodrigo could go free. Not until three years later was Miguel finally ransomed, in October, 1580. His captivity provided the basis for the captive's tale in part 1 of *El ingenioso hidalgo don Quixote de la Mancha* (1605, 1615; *The History of the Valorous and Wittie Knight-Errant, Don Quixote of the Mancha*, 1612-1620; better known as *Don Quixote de la Mancha*).

LIFE'S WORK

Back in Spain, after a twelve-year absence, Cervantes sought preferment and was sent on a confidential mission to Spanish territory in North Africa. Thereafter, he spent seven months in Lisbon seeking employment and even requesting a post in the New World. When his money ran out, he began to devote himself to literature, turning to the theater, for which he wrote, in his own words, "twenty or thirty plays," of which all but two have been lost.

One of the surviving plays is *El trato de Argel* (1585; *The Commerce of Algiers: A Comedy*, 1870), about Christian lovers imprisoned in Algiers. Artistically, it is not impressive, but it is valuable as a realistic picture of Algerian life and the lot of prisoners, one of whom, a soldier named Saavedra who assists his fellow captives, is a self-portrait. The other play, *El cerco de Numancia* (wr. 1585, pb. 1784; *The Siege of Numantia*, 1870), dramatizes the tragic siege of a city in Spain by Scipio the Younger. Rather than yield to the Romans, every citizen chooses death. The play became symbolic of Spanish courage and was performed during Napoleon I's siege of Saragossa in 1809, to strengthen the resistance of the defenders.

During his years with the theater, Cervantes had an affair with Ana de Villafranca, who in 1584 bore him a daughter, Isabel. Shortly thereafter, Cervantes was married to Catalina de Salazar y Palacios. Though she was eighteen years younger than he, though his business often kept them apart for the next thirteen years, and though they had no children, the marriage endured for the rest of his life.

The next year, Cervantes published his first novel, *Galatea*, in the then-popular genre of pastoral romance. His income from literature was not enough to support his family, however, for with his father's death in 1585, Cervantes had to care for his wife, mother, two sisters, daughter, and niece. Accordingly, he took a position to procure grain in Andalusia for the Spanish Armada. Outraged at his confiscating some wheat from powerful churchmen, the vicar general of Seville had Cervantes excommunicated, but Cervantes managed to get the ban removed.

Further commissions sent him through many Andalusian towns and cities in search of grain and olive oil. Having difficulty collecting his salary, Cervantes applied for

	CERVANTES' MAJOR WORKS
1585	*El cerco de Numancia* (pb. 1784; *The Siege of Numantia*, 1870)
1585	*El trato de Argel* (*The Commerce of Algiers*, 1870)
1585	*La Galatea* (*Galatea: A Pastoral Romance*, 1833)
1605	*El ingenioso hidalgo don Quixote de la Mancha* (rev. 1615; *The History of the Valorous and Wittie Knight-Errant, Don Quixote of the Mancha*, 1612-1620; better known as *Don Quixote de la Mancha*)
1613	*Novelas ejemplares* (*Exemplary Novels*, 1846)
1614	*El Viaje del Parnaso* (*The Voyage of Parnassus*, 1870)
1615	*Ocho comedias y ocho entremeses nuevos*
1617	*Los trabajos de Persiles y Sigismunda* (*The Travels of Persiles and Sigismunda: A Northern History*, 1619)

one of four positions vacant in America, but the Council of the Indies rejected him. Instead, he returned to work as a royal commissioner, traveling extensively through Andalusia and between Seville and Madrid. His intimate knowledge for nearly thirteen years of roads, inns, folklore, and travelers and their speech provided him with a rich background for his exemplary novels and for *Don Quixote de la Mancha*. Finally, in 1594, Philip II abolished the royal commissions, and Cervantes, then forty-six years old, had to look for new employment.

His first job was to collect back taxes in the provinces of Málaga and Grenada. In 1595, he won first prize (three silver spoons) in a poetry competition at Saragossa, and the next year he wrote a celebrated sonnet satirizing the English sack of Cádiz. In 1597, he was still collecting taxes, and when an accountant made an error that showed Cervantes' accounts to be short, he was imprisoned for seven months in Seville. There he may have begun *Don Quixote de la Mancha*.

In 1598, Philip II decreed that the theaters be permanently closed, thus interrupting Cervantes' career as a playwright. When the king died later that year, Cervantes wrote a poem in his honor and then wrote and read in the cathedral of Seville a far better sonnet satirizing the monarch's exceedingly grand catafalque. In the final years of the century, Cervantes probably wrote some of his exemplary novels and continued work on *Don Quixote de la Mancha*. He associated with most of the leading writers of the day, such as Lope de Vega, Francisco de Quevedo, and Luis de Góngora y Argote. When the new king, Philip III, moved the court to Valladolid, all the writers followed him there, including Cervantes in 1604.

At the beginning of 1605, part 1 of *Don Quixote de la Mancha* was published. Probably parts of it had already circulated in manuscript, for there is evidence that it was already known in literary circles. The first edition quickly sold out, and Cervantes soon found himself famous internationally, though still in financial difficulties, for he had sold the work outright and got no royalties. His new fame did not prevent him and most of his household, though innocent, from being imprisoned briefly in the summer of 1605 after testifying about a fatal duel fought in front of their home.

There is no record of Cervantes for the next three years, but in 1608, he appeared in Madrid, which was to be his main residence for the rest of his life. These final years were those of his most intense literary activity, for he was working on part 2 of *Don Quixote de la Mancha* as well as on more plays, a long poem, and a series entitled *Novelas ejemplares* (1613; *Exemplary Novels*, 1846). These are actually long short stories or short novellas, intended to instruct as well as to entertain. Cervantes prided himself on being the first person to write novels in the Castilian tongue. In the prologue, he presents a vivid description of himself as being of average height with stooping shoulders and a somewhat heavy build, with an aquiline countenance, chestnut hair, a smooth brow, a hooked nose, a once golden beard turned silver, a large mustache, and a small mouth with only half a dozen teeth remaining.

One of the works he mentions in the prologue is *El Viaje del Parnaso* (1614; *The Voyage of Parnassus*, 1870), a narrative poem that in eight chapters tells of a journey to Mount Parnassus, home of the Muses, where a battle is fought between good and bad poets. The poem is of considerable autobiographical importance, for in it Cervantes discusses the other poets of his day, his relationship with them, and his evaluation of his own work. In 1615, he published *Ocho comedias y ocho entremeses nuevos* (English translation, 1807). His full-length plays have not made a lasting mark, but the interludes made him the greatest Spanish creator of one-act comedies.

Meanwhile, *Don Quixote de la Mancha* went through innumerable editions in Spain and abroad. In 1614, a spurious sequel attributed to Alonso Fernández de Avellaneda appeared—a meretricious work lacking any literary distinction and full of obscenities and vulgar details, together with insulting comments on Cervantes' poverty, advanced age, and crippled hand. Incensed, Cervantes turned back to his own work in progress and completed part 2 of *Don Quixote de la Mancha*, which was published in the fall of 1615, about half a year before the author's death.

In the remaining months of his life he completed *Los trabajos de Persiles y Sigismunda* (1617; *The Travels of Persiles and Sigismunda: A Northern History*, 1619), the dedication and prologue to which he wrote after he had received extreme unction, only four days before he died of dropsy on April 23, 1616, the same day and year that William Shakespeare died. A few years before his death, Cervantes had joined the Tertiary Order of the Franciscans, and they buried him in an unknown grave.

Cervantes' poems, plays, and exemplary novels are minor works, but *Don Quixote de la Mancha* is generally regarded as one of the world's supreme works of literature, ranking with the masterpieces of Homer, Dante, and Shakespeare. Cervantes conceived of it as a satire on books of chivalry. Having read chivalric romances until his wits are scrambled, Alonso Quejana decides to become a knight errant, renames himself Don Quixote de la Mancha, dons a suit of battered armor, proclaims his skinny nag to be the war horse Rosinante, and, accompanied by a peasant, Sancho Panza, as his squire, goes forth to set the world right. At first, he is a figure of satire, as he confuses illusion with reality, mistakes windmills for giants, inns for castles, and flocks of sheep for armies, wears a barber's basin for a helmet, and generally causes chaos and confusion by meddling in matters that do not need mending.

Gradually, Don Quixote evolves into a heroic figure, even a Christlike one. An aged man, lean as a rake, with no help but his lance, sword, and the often-reluctant help of the commonsensical Sancho, he tries single-handedly to right wrongs, help the oppressed, succor widows and orphans, and bring about justice, only to be mocked, reviled, ridiculed, beaten, and almost crucified for his efforts.

In a famous essay, the Russian novelist Ivan Turgenev contrasts Don Quixote with Shakespeare's Hamlet, finding the latter to be obsessed with himself, whereas Don Quixote is quite selfless in his desire to help others. The novel develops and deepens from comedy into tragicomedy. The nineteenth century French critic Charles Sainte-Beuve called it the "Bible of humanity." Far from being opposed to chivalry, Cervantes was chivalric to a fault, and in his life he showed many of the traits of Don Quixote himself. It is Quixote's gallantry, his idealism, and his panache that has made him, rather than the historic El Cid, the symbolic national hero of Spain.

SIGNIFICANCE

In the *Exemplary Novels* and in *Don Quixote de la Mancha*, Cervantes wrote a model of clear Castilian prose and portrayed a realistic panorama of Spain, particularly of the lives of ordinary people, even while he created a hero whose idealism makes him confuse reality with his illusions. His idealism and illusions have made Don Quixote a legend.

Edmond Rostand's Cyrano de Bergerac takes him as a model. From the beginning, *Don Quixote de la Mancha* was immensely popular and profoundly influential. In England, it inspired Francis Beaumont's play *The Knight of the Burning Pestle* (pr. 1607, pb. 1613), the picaresque novels of Henry Fielding and Tobias Smollett in the eighteenth century, such novels as *The Spiritual Quixote* (1773) and *The Female Quixote: Or, The Adventures of Arabella* (1752), and Charles Dickens's *The Pickwick Papers* (1836-1837).

Don Quixote and Sancho Panza are surely in the background of Tom Sawyer and Huckleberry Finn. W. Somerset Maugham has Don Quixote reappear as a character in his novel *Catalina* (1948), and Graham Greene's *Monsignor Quixote* (1982) has a twentieth century priest who claims to be a descendant of the don go on a similar pilgrimage around Spain.

Innumerable artists have illustrated *Don Quixote de la Mancha* or done paintings inspired by it, including Francisco Goya, Honoré Daumier, Gustave Doré, and Pablo Picasso. There also are dozens of operas, operettas, ballets, and songs based on *Don Quixote de la Mancha*. There are several film and television versions of *Don Quixote de la Mancha*, as well as a popular musical. Don Quixote is one of the best-known and best-loved literary characters in the world, and the term "quixotic" has come to mean gallantly chivalrous, romantically idealistic, and courageously visionary.

—Robert E. Morsberger

FURTHER READING

Bell, Aubrey F. G. *Cervantes.* Norman: University of Oklahoma Press, 1947. Studies Cervantes' work in the context of the Renaissance and of his life and times. Argues that *Don Quixote de la Mancha* must be read in relationship to all Cervantes' writings.

Bloom, Harold, ed. *Cervantes's "Don Quixote."* Philadelphia: Chelsea House, 2001. A volume in the series Modern Critical Interpretations, with an introduction by Bloom. Bibliographical references, index.

Byron, William. *Cervantes: A Biography.* Garden City, N.Y.: Doubleday, 1978. A complete life and times, providing graphic detail on Cervantes' activities, the Battle of Lepanto, Cervantes' captivity, the theater, and the like. Analyzes the writings both for their intrinsic artistry and as part of the literary scene of the golden age.

Canavaggio, Jean. *Cervantes.* Translated by J. R. Jones. New York: Norton, 1990. A well-informed biography. See especially the preface, in which Canavaggio details the problems of separating myth and fact in Cervantes' life.

Clamurro, William H. *Beneath the Fiction: The Contrary Worlds of Cervantes's "Novelas ejemplares."* New York: Peter Lang, 1997. Examines the settings of the stories. Includes bibliographical references and an index.

Durán, Manuel. *Cervantes.* Boston: Twayne, 1974. Part of the Twayne World Authors series, Durán's study examines the universality of Cervantes' work, the clarity of his style, his relationship with his public, the humor and realism of his fiction, his compassion for the humble, and his democratic spirit.

Flores, Angel, and M. J. Benardete, eds. *Cervantes Across the Centuries.* New York: Gordian Press, 1969. A collection of critical essays dealing with the genesis, composition, style, realism, and social and historical background of *Don Quixote de la Mancha*.

Fuentes, Carlos. Introduction to *The Adventures of Don Quixote de la Mancha.* New York: Farrar, Straus & Giroux, 1986. This introduction by Mexico's leading novelist discusses the influence of Desiderius Erasmus on Cervantes and the duality of realism and imagination in *Don Quixote de la Mancha*. Argues that this work can be considered the beginning of a modern way of looking at the world.

Hart, Thomas R. *Cervantes' Exemplary Fictions: A Study of the "Novelas Ejemplares."* Lexington: University Press of Kentucky, 1994. A reading of Cervantes' stories in the context of the knowledge of everyday life and literary conventions shared by Cervantes' contemporaries. Concludes that speculations of how old books were read when they were new cannot tell us how they should be read today.

McCrory, Donald P. *No Ordinary Man: The Life and Times of Miguel de Cervantes.* Chester Springs, Pa.: Peter Owen, 2002. A thorough biography. Includes bibliographical references and an index.

Nabokov, Vladimir. *Lectures on Don Quixote.* Edited by Fredson Bowers. New York: Harcourt Brace Jovanovich, 1983. College lectures by a great twentieth century novelist. Divided into portraits of Don Quixote and Sancho Panza, the structure of the novel, the use of cruelty and mystification, the treatment of Dulcinea and death, and commentaries on Cervantes' narrative methods. An appendix contains sample passages from romances of chivalry.

Predmore, Richard L. *Cervantes.* New York: Dodd, Mead, 1973. A clear and concise biography by a leading Cervantes scholar, lavishly illustrated with 170 pictures from Cervantes' time and by later artists.

Riley, E. C. *Cervantes's Theory of the Novel.* 1962. Reprint. Newark, Del.: Juan de la Cuesta, 1992. A detailed examination of Cervantes' views on questions of literary practice in terms of traditional issues in poetics, such as art and nature, unity, and purpose and function of literature. Includes a bibliography and indexes of names and topics.

Russell, P. E. *Cervantes.* New York: Oxford University Press, 1985. A slim volume (117 pages) in the Past Masters series. Deals with Cervantes as poet and dramatist, examines his parodies of chivalric romance, analyzes Don Quixote as a Romantic hero, investigates his madness, and gives a close reading of both parts of the novel.

Williamson, Edwin, ed. *Cervantes and the Modernists: The Question of Influence.* London: Tamesis, 1994. Explores the novelist's impact on such twentieth century writers as Marcel Proust, Thomas Mann, Primo Levi, Carlos Fuentes, and Gabriel García Márquez. No index or bibliography.

Ziolkowski, Eric. *The Sanctification of Don Quixote: From Hidalgo to Priest.* University Park: Pennsylvania State University Press, 1991. A detailed exploration of how *Don Quixote* became a classic, tracing its influence from the eighteenth to the twentieth century. Ziolkowski discusses how the novel presents the idea of living a religious life.

See also: Mateo Alemán; Barbarossa; Charles V; Desiderius Erasmus; Philip II; William Shakespeare.

Related articles in *Great Events from History: The Renaissance & Early Modern Era, 1454-1600:* October 7, 1571: Battle of Lepanto; 1580-1581: Spain Annexes Portugal.

Andrea Cesalpino
Italian botanist and physician

Cesalpino systematized botanical classification, wrote the first true textbook in botany, and founded the taxonomical movement, which reached its apex in the work of Linnaeus. Cesalpino's speculation into the anatomy and physiology of the heart anticipated William Harvey's conclusions about the circulation of the blood.

Born: Probably June 5, 1525; Arezzo, Tuscany (now in Italy)

Died: February 23 or March 15, 1603; Rome, Papal States (now in Italy)

Also known as: Andreas Cesalpinus; Andreas Caesalpinus

Areas of achievement: Science and technology, medicine, philosophy

Early Life

Andrea Cesalpino (ahn-DREH-ah chay-zahl-PEE-noh) was the son of a successful artisan, Giovanni de Andrea Cesalpino. As a medical student at the University of Pisa, Cesalpino benefited from some of the world's best professors of medicine, botany, and Aristotelian philosophy.

His botany professor was Luca Ghini, who founded in 1543 the Orto Botanico di Pisa (the Botanical Garden of

Pisa), one of the earliest major botanical gardens dedicated to academic purposes. He learned anatomy from Realdo Colombo, author of *De re anatomica* (anatomical matters), which in 1559 included the earliest description of pulmonary circulation. Guido Guidi, an expert on fractures and dislocations and the discoverer of several anatomical features, taught him surgery and medicine.

Cesalpino received a medical degree and a doctorate in 1551, practiced medicine in Pisa until 1555, became professor of materia medica (medical substances) at the university, and succeeded Ghini as director of the botanical garden. Among his patients and patrons was Cosimo I de' Medici, grand duke of Tuscany. In the 1560's, Cesalpino helped secure for his friend and former student, Michele Mercati, the directorship of the Vatican botanical garden under Pope Pius V.

Life's Work

In 1571, in Venice, seven years before the birth of William Harvey, Cesalpino published *Peripateticarum quæstionum libri quinque* (five books of peripatetic questions), in which he announced that the blood circulates, entering the heart from the vena cava and exiting through the aorta, rather than ebbing and flowing from the heart as Galen had believed. Cesalpino did not support his discovery with scientific evidence, so it remained just a theory. So Harvey rightfully received credit for establishing the theory with his landmark empirical study, *Exercitatio anatomica de motu cordis et sanguinis in animalibus* (1628; anatomical exercise on the motion of the heart and blood in animals).

Cesalpino's second work on the philosophy of medicine, *Daemonum investigatio peripatetica* (peripatetic investigation of demons), appeared in 1580 in Florence and in 1593 in Venice. He analyzed the spiritual dimension of medicine from Hippocrates to his own day, with frequent sympathetic reference to magic, alchemy, and witchcraft. In the first edition, he tended to accept traditional superstitions about demonic possession, even though he urged that it be treated as a medical disorder. In the second edition, he relied more systematically on Aristotelian philosophical method and Hippocratic medicine to suggest a synthesis of these approaches with Roman Catholic teaching about the effects of demons on the human body and spirit.

Cesalpino published his multivolume masterpiece, *De plantis* (books about plants), in Florence in 1583. The first of sixteen "books" derives from Aristotle and Aristotle's student, Theophrastus, expounding Cesalpino's principles for grouping plants. The other fifteen books describe and classify about fifteen hundred species within four main groups: trees, shrubs, undergrowth, and herbs. He departed from contemporary tendencies by grouping plants according to their structure rather than their medicinal properties or other practical uses.

As professor of medicine at Pisa starting in 1569, Cesalpino's naturalism, heterodoxy, and Aristotelianism came under the increasing scrutiny of conservative Roman Catholic officials. Although Duke Cosimo's successor sons, grand dukes Francesco I de' Medici and Ferdinand I de' Medici, were also Cesalpino's patients, they grew more suspicious of his philosophy. Cesalpino was never charged with heresy, but gradually he became less welcome in Pisa. In 1589, Ferdinand appointed a junior member of the medical faculty at a salary substantially higher than Cesalpino's. From that point Cesalpino was determined to leave Tuscany. Michele Mercati interceded with Pope Sixtus V on his teacher's behalf. In 1592, Cesalpino became professor of medicine at the University of Rome, Sapienza, and the next year succeeded Mercati as personal physician to Pope Clement VIII. He remained in both posts until his death in 1603.

His *De metallicis libri tres* (three books on metals), published in Rome in 1596 and in Nuremberg in 1602,

dealt with metallurgy, chemistry, and geology. It contains still-valuable information about Italian ores, rocks, and soils, as well as observations about fossils, crystals, minerals, and magnets.

Cesalpino's last works concerned the clinical practice of medicine. In 1597, some of his philosophical and medical advice was collected with that of six other authors in *Risposta di Hieronimo Veneroso nobile Genovese alla querela sotto nome di Difesa intorno allo sputo di Sangue* (the answer of Genoese nobleman Girolamo Veneroso Lomellino to the complaint, called a defense, about the bloody sputum). In 1602, Cesalpino published the first volume of a projected multivolume treatise, *Artis medicae pars prima: De morbis universalibus* (the art of medicine, part one: on diseases in general), which covered mostly fevers, gynecological ailments, and sexually transmitted diseases. The next installment, *Artis medicae liber VII: De morbis ventris* (the art of medicine, book seven, on diseases of the stomach), appeared in 1603 and addressed many disorders of the abdomen, including gynecological concerns. A revision of the 1602 work, *Katoptron sive speculum artis medicae Hippocraticum* (a mirror on the Hippocratic medical arts) appeared posthumously in Frankfurt in 1605. Also posthumously, and with much overlapping of his previous works, *Praxis universae artis medicae* (practice of the general art of medicine) was published in 1606.

SIGNIFICANCE

Cesalpino's greatest importance is for botany, not medicine, since Harvey deserves most of the credit for revolutionizing physiology by discovering, through empirical study and not just through theory, the circulation of the blood. A few historians of medicine, notably Giovanni Arcieri and Mark Clark, value Cesalpino's contributions to medicine more highly, but historians of science who appreciate the pedigree of Linnaean taxonomy esteem Cesalpino as the progenitor of that mode of thought. All interpreters agree that Cesalpino's work in botany was more empirical than his work in medicine or physiology and that he was the first to devise useful generalizations about plants according to the Aristotelian concepts of genus and species.

Benjamin Smith Barton, a professor of medical botany at the University of Pennsylvania, disciple of Linnaeus, and author of the first American botanical textbook, *Elements of Botany* (1803), explicitly praised Cesalpino as the founder of botanic classification. Barton classified the classifiers according to their method. Cesalpino was a fructist; that is, he classified plants by the qualities of their fruit. By contrast, Barton and Linnaeus were sexualists, classifying plants by their means and structures of reproduction.

French botanist Charles Plumier (1646-1704) honored Cesalpino by naming a New World tropical shrub genus *Caesalpinia*. In the modern Linnaean system, this genus of useful and ornamental plants is in the subfamily *Caesalpinioideae* of the family *Caesalpiniaceae* and contains more than 160 species and cultivars of evergreen and deciduous shrubs, trees, and vines.

—*Eric v.d. Luft*

FURTHER READING

Arcieri, Giovanni P. *The Circulation of the Blood and Andrea Cesalpino of Arezzo.* New York: S. F. Vanni, 1945. Standard but controversial source for information about Cesalpino's work in physiology. Argues that Cesalpino deserves more credit than Harvey for discovering the circulation of the blood.

Clark, Mark Edward, Stephen A. Nimis, and George R. Rochefort. "Andreas Cesalpino, *Quæstionum peripateticarum, libri V, liber v, quaestio iv,* With Translation." *Journal of the History of Medicine and Allied Sciences* 33 (1978): 185-213. Presentation of Cesalpino's work on the circulation of the blood.

Clark, Mark Edward, and Kirk M. Summers. "Hippocratic Medicine and Aristotelian Science in the *Daemonum investigatio peripatetica* of Andrea Cesalpino." *Bulletin of the History of Medicine* 69, no. 4 (Winter, 1995): 527-541. A comparison of the two editions of Cesalpino's book about demonic possession.

Considerations About Cesalpinus' and Harvey's Works on the Blood Circulation Discovery. New York: Alcmaeon, 1964. Illustrated collection of reviews and critiques of Arcieri's research.

Fye, W. Bruce. "Andrea Cesalpino." *Clinical Cardiology* 19 (1996): 969-970. Brief appreciation of Cesalpino's significance in the history of heart physiology. Includes portrait.

Griffiths, Mark. *Language of Life.* London: Harper-Collins, 2003. General history of the development of botanic classification.

Isely, Duane. *One Hundred and One Botanists.* Ames: Iowa State University, 1994. Good scholarly biographical introduction to the leading figures in botany.

SEE ALSO: Georgius Agricola; Pierre Belon; Leonhard Fuchs; Conrad Gesner; William Gilbert; Cosimo I de' Medici; Paracelsus; Pius V; Michael Servetus; Andreas Vesalius.

RELATED ARTICLE in *Great Events from History: The Renaissance & Early Modern Era, 1454-1600:* c. 1560's: Invention of the "Lead" Pencil.

GEORGE CHAPMAN
English poet and dramatist

Best remembered because his translations of Homer's Iliad *and* Odyssey *inspired John Keats to write a well-known sonnet, George Chapman also was a poet and dramatist in his own right whose tragedies reflected his classical background.*

BORN: c. 1559; near Hitchin, Hertfordshire, England
DIED: May 12, 1634; London, England
AREAS OF ACHIEVEMENT: Literature, theater

EARLY LIFE

George Chapman was born near Hitchin, Hertfordshire, England, where his well-connected family had lived for decades. His father, Thomas Chapman, was a local landowner; his mother, Joan, was the daughter of George Nodes, sergeant of the buckhounds to King Henry VIII and later monarchs. On his mother's side, Chapman was related to Edward Grimeston, whose family served the English government in France and who wrote *A General Inventory of the History of France* (1607). The Grimeston relationship probably nurtured Chapman's interest in France and may explain why most of his tragedies are based on French history.

Little is known of his formal education. There is some evidence that he attended both Oxford and Cambridge Universities, but without taking a degree at either. A late seventeenth century account says that at Oxford, Chapman "was observed to be most excellent in the Latin and Greek tongues," but his contemporaries did not consider him much of a classicist. They claimed he accomplished his translations of Homer only with considerable dependence on the works of continental Hellenists, and indeed his work is closer in style to the Elizabethan manner than to the Greek.

In about 1583, Chapman entered service in the household of Sir Ralph Sadler, a member of the Privy Council and chancellor of the duchy of Lancaster, who had an estate in Hitchin. In the late 1580's or early 1590's, Chapman volunteered to fight in the Netherlands, and during this period he may have visited France. On his return to England in 1600, he was arrested and imprisoned for alleged nonpayment of an old debt, the first of his occasional financial problems. Prince Henry, whom he tutored and who became an early patron, promised Chapman a pension for the Homer translations, but the prince died in 1612, four years before the works were completed, so no money was forthcoming. Probably to escape debtors' prison, Chapman left London and his successful career as a prolific playwright. Retiring to Hitchin, he lived there in obscurity from 1614 to 1619, working on his translations.

LIFE'S WORK

Chapman's first published work was the long 1594 poem *The Shadow of Night*, followed the next year by *Ovid's Banquet of Sense*. Aside from these pieces, his translations of Homer's epics, and the completion of Christopher Marlowe's unfinished poem *Hero and Leander* (1598), Chapman's major work was for the London stage. He became a dramatist at about the age of forty, at first writing for Philip Henslowe, the leading theater owner and producer of the time, but he soon left Henslowe's Admiral's Men and became an independent playwright. He wrote comedies and tragedies for other companies such as the Children of the Chapel (later called the Children of the Revels).

Many of his early plays for Henslowe are not extant, but what may have been his first work for stage does survive: *The Blind Beggar of Alexandria* (pr. 1596, pb. 1598), a comedy featuring a cynical quick-change artist who, living by his wits, assumes different identities and attains money, power, and sex through a complexity of intrigues. The comic hero may be a burlesque of Marlowe's Tamburlaine and other larger-than-life tragic figures. Chapman's second play, *An Humourous Day's Mirth* (pr. 1597, pb. 1599), done by Henslowe the following year, foreshadows Ben Jonson's comedies of humors in its focus on universal human foibles. The 1599 *All Fools* (pr. 1604, pb. 1605; also known as *The World Runs on Wheels*), which balances romance and intrigue, was based on two plays by the ancient Roman playwright Terence; it has as its main character a young man who aims to make his fortune by tricking others but who in the end is gulled by one of his victims. The jealous-husband subplot of *All Fools* would become a commonplace in Jacobean comedy. In his early years as playwright, Chapman must have written other comedies as well as tragedies that have not survived, because Francis Meres in *Palladis Tamia* (1598) labels him among the leading dramatists in both genres.

CHAPMAN'S MAJOR WORKS	
1594	*The Shadow of Night*
1595	*Ovid's Banquet of Sense*
1596	*The Blind Beggar of Alexandria* (fragment)
1597	*An Humourous Day's Mirth*
1598	*Hero and Leander* (completion of Christopher Marlowe's poem)
1598	*Iliad* (rev. 1609, 1611; translation of Homer)
1599	*All Fools* (pr. 1604; also known as *The World Runs on Wheels*)
c. 1601/1603	*Sir Giles Goosecap*
c. 1602	*The Gentleman Usher*
1604	*Bussy d'Ambois*
1604	*Monsieur d'Olive*
c. 1605	*The Widow's Tears*
1605	*Eastward Ho!* (with John Marston and Ben Jonson)
1608	*The Conspiracy and Tragedy of Charles, Duke of Byron*
1609	*May Day*
1609	*Euthymiae Raptus: Or, The Tears of Peace*
c. 1610	*The Revenge of Bussy d'Ambois*
1612	*An Epicede or Funerall Song on the Death of Henry Prince of Wales*
1612	*Petrarch's Seven Penitential Psalms*
1613	*The Masque of the Middle Temple and Lincoln's Inn*
c. 1613	*Caesar and Pompey*
1614	*Odyssey* (translation of Homer)
1614	*Andromeda Liberata: Or, The Nuptials of Perseus and Andromeda*
1618	*Georgics* (translation of Hesiod)
1622	*Pro Vere Autumni Lachrymae*
1624	*The Crown of All Homer's Works* (translation of Homer)
1632	*The Ball* (with James Shirley)
1635	*The Tragedy of Chabot, Admiral of France* (with Shirley)

Though he wrote mainly tragedies after the turn of the century, Chapman continued to write comedies, including *The Gentleman Usher* (pr. c. 1602, pb. 1606), *Monsieur d'Olive* (pr. 1604, pb. 1606), *May Day* (pr. c. 1609, pb. 1611), and *The Widow's Tears* (pr. c. 1605, pb. 1612). The first of these is notable for its blending of serious and comic elements in the manner of Francis Beaumont and John Fletcher's tragicomedies, and it portends Chapman's increasingly sardonic attitude toward people's flaws. The last is the most serious of his comedies, presenting a society beset by chaos and corruption, quite the antithesis of the Homeric virtues Chapman celebrates in his translations, but similar to the world he presents in the tragedies. One other comedy warrants mention: *Eastward Ho!* (pr., pb. 1605), a far-ranging portrait of London citizenry, on which Chapman collaborated with Ben Jonson and John Marston. Because King James I was offended by some incidental anti-Scottish satire in it, Chapman, Jonson, and Marston were imprisoned for a while.

The satire in his comedies foreshadows Chapman's didacticism in the tragedies, and he correctly has been described as the most deliberately didactic tragic playwright of his time. In the dedication to *The Revenge of Bussy d'Ambois* (pr. c. 1610, pb. 1613), Chapman wrote that "material instruction, elegant and sententious excitation to virtue, and deflection from her contrary [are] the soul, limbs, and limits of an authentic tragedy." Some critics believe that a key aspect of his development as a tragedian is the progressive exclusion from his plays of elements that did not advance his ethical goals.

His first tragedy, *Bussy d'Ambois* (pr. 1604, pb. 1607), is a melodrama of the Elizabethan Senecan type and probably was written about 1604, perhaps for the Children of the Chapel soon after Queen Elizabeth I died. One of at least four tragedies he wrote based on French history, it was often revived during Chapman's lifetime and later in the century, and he revised it at least once. Like his other tragic plays, it dramatizes the interaction between its hero and society, primarily his morality in conflict with social corruption.

The play is set in Paris in the late sixteenth century after a war has ended. Bussy d'Ambois, a soldier at loose ends, is introduced to the court by the king's brother, a Machiavellian opportunist who aims to usurp the Crown. Bussy is an anomaly at court, an apparently honorable man who eschews political intrigue and sexual hypocrisy, but while striving to remain an outsider, he gains the king's admiration and thus the disfavor of his sponsor, who sees his protégé as a threat. In spite of himself, Bussy becomes entangled in the political and romantic rivalries, kills rival courtiers, engages in adultery, and finally is murdered by assassins engaged by his rivals. Dying, he compares himself to a thunderbolt that "Look'd to have stuck and shook the firmament." These last words suggest the complexity of his character: courageous, self-reliant, unspoiled at the start, but also a braggart who, in a world without order and justice, cannot control his passions and falls victim to them. This first of Chapman's tragedies anticipates the pessimism that prevails in subsequent Jacobean drama, partly because of the difficulty the playwrights had in resolving the moral conflicts they confronted in their society.

The Revenge of Bussy d'Ambois, while not a sequel to the earlier play, represents a continuum. Its main character is Clermont, Bussy's brother, a stoical, virtuous, and self-sufficient individual who believes he has a mandate to avenge his brother's death; instead of restoring natural law to the corrupt society, however, he ends up committing suicide when a friend and admirer dies. The static play is often labeled a "revenge tragedy" in the manner of Thomas Kyd's *The Spanish Tragedy* (pr. c. 1585-1589, pb. 1594?). It is mostly composed of moralizing, and the standard revenge-tragedy machinery appears only in the fifth act.

Chapman's other tragedies deserve only passing mention. *Caesar and Pompey* (pr. c. 1613, pb. 1631) is an undramatic collection of introspective homiletic speeches and has three main characters who are either too static or too inconsistently developed to be credible. *The Conspiracy and Tragedy of Charles, Duke of Byron* (pr., pb. 1608), a play in two parts, is nothing more, according to one critic, than Chapman's rewriting of the Achilles story "in terms of Christian ethics and the Elizabethan stage" and shows the tragic danger of unbridled egotism. Chapman's last play, *The Tragedy of Chabot, Admiral of France* (pr. 1635, pb. 1639), is of interest because its main character resembles William Shakespeare's *Coriolanus*; both are military men who suffer from pride and try to deny their common humanity. Any merits the play has as a stage piece probably derive from James Shirley's revisions, done after Chapman's death.

Little is known about Chapman's later years. He no longer was active as a playwright and may have been too preoccupied by financial and legal difficulties to engage in literary work. He died in London in 1634 and was buried in St. Giles-in-the-Fields. Inigo Jones (1593-1652), the English architect who designed masques (court entertainments) by Chapman, designed a Roman-style monument.

SIGNIFICANCE

Chapman's translations of the classics were his primary literary foci through much of his career, but they have been superseded by later versions and remain useful only because of his infusion of Elizabethan style and sensibility into the ancient works. His comic drama, respected though it was by contemporaries, is understandably forgotten, of interest only because the plays foreshadow humors comedy and other Jacobean stage motifs. Of his tragedies, only *Bussy d'Ambois* retains a place among the major non-Shakespearean plays of the period, primarily because of its hero. The tragedies as a whole merit attention, however, because they differ strikingly from others of the period, with the exception of the Roman plays of Samuel Daniel and Ben Jonson, which also examine the effect of greatness on the political order, how a person's inner and outer selves often are at war, and how ethical and moral individuals sometimes betray their beliefs. Heroic ideals are central forces in Chapman's plots and characters, leading occasionally to major dramatic conflicts, but also slowing the pace of a play to that of a moral interlude or Senecan closet drama. Regrettably, Chapman the philosopher, classicist, and intellectual often got in the way of Chapman the playwright.

—*Gerald H. Strauss*

FURTHER READING

Beach, Vincent W., Jr. *George Chapman: An Annotated Bibliography of Commentary and Criticism.* New York: G. K. Hall, 1995. Complete and extensively annotated bibliography of work on Chapman, his translations, and his drama.

Chapman, George. "Against Mr. Ben Jonson." In *Critical Essays on Ben Jonson,* edited by Robert N. Watson. New York: G. K. Hall, 1997. Chapman's critique of Jonson provides important insights into his own dramatic theory and practice and his place in the Renaissance dramatic scene.

Ide, Richard S. *Possessed with Greatness: The Heroic Tragedies of Shakespeare and Chapman.* Chapel Hill: University of North Carolina Press, 1980. Shakespeare and Chapman, who shared an interest in the epic tradition and military heroism, individually wrote a number of tragedies with soldiers as protagonists: *Othello, Bussy d'Ambois, Antony and Cleopatra, The Conspiracy and Tragedy of Byron,* and *Coriolanus.* In each, the soldier's self-conception and aspirations lead him into fatal conflict with society.

MacLure, Millar. *George Chapman: A Critical Study.* Toronto, Canada: University of Toronto Press, 1966. Valuable for MacLure's discussion of Chapman's intellectual development, this book has a useful biographical section and offers balanced assessments of the poetry and plays. MacLure shows how Chapman's preoccupation with integrity affected his works, particularly the plays.

Rees, Ennis. *The Tragedies of George Chapman: Renaissance Ethics in Action.* Cambridge, Mass.: Harvard University Press, 1954. Rees suggests that Chapman's pattern in his heroic tragedies was to "juxtapose a reprehensible tragic hero . . . against the ethical code of Christian humanism" and to develop his plots and conflicts from that starting point.

Ribner, Irving. *Jacobean Tragedy: The Quest for Moral Order.* London: Methuen, 1962. Chapman is one of six playwrights Ribner considers in this examination of how playwrights in an irreligious age strove to find a moral order. The analyses of the tragedies are enlightening and useful for placing Chapman and his works in their moral and religious milieu.

Spivack, Charlotte. *George Chapman.* New York: Twayne, 1967. An admiring study accessible to the nonspecialist, the book begins with a biographical section and then reviews Chapman's literary work. Spivack considers him an important poet, a great playwright, and a consistent philosopher—a more favorable assessment than that of other critics.

Taunton, Nina. *1590's Drama and Militarism: Portrayals of War in Marlowe, Chapman, and Shakespeare's "Henry V."* Burlington, Vt.: Ashgate, 2001. Reading of Chapman alongside Marlowe, Shakespeare, and nonliterary Renaissance texts such as war manuals and military correspondence. Argues that the playwrights use their plays to respond to and criticize general Renaissance discussions and conceptions of warfare. Includes illustrations, bibliographic references, index.

Waddington, Raymond B. *The Mind's Empire: Myth and Form in George Chapman's Narrative Poems.* Baltimore: Johns Hopkins University Press, 1974. Distinguishing Chapman's verse from metaphysical poetry, to which it often is compared, Waddington sets forth what he sees as Chapman's poetic identity, grounded in classical philosophy and myth. He examines both the nondramatic verse and *Bussy d'Ambois,* which "exhibits a close thematic and mythic bond to the early poetry."

SEE ALSO: Francis Beaumont and John Fletcher; Elizabeth I; Christopher Marlowe; William Shakespeare.
RELATED ARTICLES in *Great Events from History: The Renaissance & Early Modern Era, 1454-1600:* 1576: James Burbage Builds The Theatre; c. 1589-1613: Shakespeare Writes His Dramas; December, 1598-May, 1599: The Globe Theatre Is Built.

CHARLES THE BOLD
Duke of Burgundy (r. 1467-1477)

Charles the Bold attempted to build the duchy of Burgundy into a unified kingdom. He was considered a serious threat to the stability and centralization of the French state.

BORN: November 10, 1433; Dijon, Burgundy (now in France)
DIED: January 5, 1477; near Nancy, Lorraine (now in France)
ALSO KNOWN AS: Charles de Valois (full name)
AREA OF ACHIEVEMENT: Government and politics

EARLY LIFE

Charles was the son of the immensely popular duke of Burgundy, Philip the Good, and his third wife, Isabella of Portugal. Perhaps because Charles was the only son of three to survive, Isabella zealously protected the infant. She tended to his needs personally, refusing to relinquish him to wet nurses, as was the normal custom of the age. As a youth, Charles received the education properly fitting for a future military leader and political ruler. Charles became a skilled horseman, having received his first lessons at the age of two on a specially constructed wooden horse. Charles avidly pursued knowledge of military affairs as well during his early years.

The future duke was familiar with Latin, although he was by no means a Humanist. He read Sallust, Julius Caesar, and the deeds of Alexander the Great, although he was more interested in their martial activities than their literary style. Charles had an aptitude for languages and could conduct himself in Italian and Flemish as well as in his native French. He had limited knowledge of English as well. In appearance, he was tall, fleshy, and well proportioned. His hair, eyes, and coloring were dark, favoring his mother over his father.

Charles was most revealing in his character traits. Like his mother, he was always suspicious, was slow to embrace friends, and seldom had confidantes. He possessed an enormous ego and reveled in excessive flattery. Above all, as his name, Charles the Bold, indicates, he was an impulsive and rash man who followed courses unrelentingly without accepting or listening to prudent advice.

LIFE'S WORK

Charles became the duke of Burgundy on the death of his father in June, 1467. He inherited a large network of territories that consisted of Franche-Comté, Nevers, Bar, Luxembourg, the Netherlands, Artois, and Picardy. His domain lacked cultural, linguistic, and geographic unity. Charles governed his regional conglomeration through a complex feudal system of political, ecclesiastical, and military appointees. Much depended on personal loyalty to the duke on the part of his underlords and his subjects. Charles was a product of his age and his culture. He believed in the feudal concepts of chivalry. Chivalric virtues emphasized military prowess, personal loyalty to one's overlord, courtesy to one's peers, generosity, and intellectual gentility. Charles and his court at Dijon reflected a chivalric society. Burgundian dukes patronized the outstanding artists of the fifteenth century, including Claus Sluter, Jan van Eyck, and Rogier van der Weyden. Their generosity as patrons was well known. Tapestries depicting heroic feats of Alexander the Great, Caesar, and Charlemagne lined the walls of Dijon. Charles continued this benevolent tradition by supporting the historians Georges Chastellain, Olivier de La Marche, and Philippe de Commynes.

Unfortunately, early in his reign, he learned that reality was less pleasant than the courtly activities at Dijon. Urban centers, in particular, had little time for chivalry. Their citizens preferred practicality, and they resented excessive taxation and deprivation of privileges. With an eye toward independence, the cities Ghent and Liège rebelled in 1468. Charles responded quickly and forcefully with an army that brought both cities to heel. Because he suspected that the citizens of Liège had conspired against him with the French king Louis XI, Charles planned ruthless punishment for the city. Louis, in the meantime, had come to Peronne, which was within the duke's lands, in October, 1468. The king hoped to negotiate with

Charles the Bold. (Library of Congress)

Charles. The French monarch found himself a virtual prisoner at the castle of Peronne after Charles had received what he regarded as evidence of the king's treacherous complicity with Liège. Louis was forced to watch the systematic pillage, carnage, and burning at Liège at the hands of the fully enraged duke. Louis witnessed Charles's impetuosity, a lesson he learned to put to good use in his future dealings with the duke.

Events at Peronne and Liège merely provided the necessary impetus for descent into formalized warfare between the ambitious duke of Burgundy and his natural rival, the equally acquisitive Louis, correctly called the universal spider. In order to outwit the monarch, his legal overlord, Charles activated his political design. In 1468, Charles was married to Margaret of York, the sister of Edward IV, the king of England. Through his marriage, Charles hoped to keep the English alienated from any potential alliance with the French. With the English federation under his control, the duke actively pursued his grander plan. Charles embarked on his dream of creating an independent Burgundian kingdom as a buffer state between France and Germany. This conceptualized kingdom would extend from the North Sea to Switzerland.

Alsace and Lorraine, the heart of the old Carolingian Lotharingia, were to become the nucleus of the future Burgundian realm. In 1469, under the conditions of the Treaty of Omer, Charles happily received the mortgage of Upper Alsace from the impoverished and improvident Duke Sigismund of Austria-Tirol. The fifty thousand Rhenish florins loaned to Sigismund permitted Charles to take a firmer step toward further aggrandizement.

At his next juncture, he negotiated with Frederick III, the Holy Roman Emperor. These transactions were seriously conducted from 1469 to 1471. His goal was to secure the emperor's promise that Charles would receive the imperial coronation on the abdication or the death of the old emperor. Part of the diplomatic arrangements ensured the hand of Mary of Burgundy, Charles's only child, to Frederick's son, Maximilian I. A planned meeting between the emperor and the duke in November, 1473, at Trier was intended to seal the negotiations as far as Charles was concerned. Charles may have expected the coronation on November 18, 1473. The emperor delayed and then slipped away from Trier, almost secretly, on November 24, without crowning Charles and without finalizing the marital arrangements between Mary of Burgundy and Maximilian.

Charles was disappointed, and gravely so, but did not sulk for long. He proceeded to expand his territory in Alsace and then to secure Lorraine by force toward the end of 1475. His aggressive movements alarmed the Swiss, who were neighbors of Alsace and Lorraine. The spider king, Louis, managed to spin a web of intrigue around the oblivious Charles. Louis fed the fears of the Swiss and, simultaneously, managed to ally them with Sigismund of Austria-Tirol in 1474, after the transactions with the emperor and Charles had failed and before Charles's final aggression against Lorraine. Then Louis added René II of Lorraine to the federation. René was a willing cohort since his territory had been snatched by the duke in 1475. Open warfare erupted between the German and Swiss league on one side and Charles the Bold on the other. Charles was soundly defeated at Grandson, Morat, and, finally, Nancy. The Battle of Nancy, fought in freezing cold on January 5, 1477, claimed Charles's life.

Charles's page later reported that the duke's horse had come to the edge of a ditch, stumbled, and unseated his rider. The duke died during the carnage of battle. His body was found several days later. It was an ironic and cruel trick of fate that the last of the proud and glorious house of Burgundy should come to an ignoble end, lying nude, stripped of clothing, weapons, and jewels, mutilated, and partly eaten by animals in a land that he coveted.

SIGNIFICANCE

The political situation in Europe during the last half of the fifteenth century was in a process of rapid change. The balance of power between the monarchs and their magnates teetered in a precarious manner. Both sides battled furiously for control within and outside geographical boundaries. Louis and Charles the Bold were locked in such a conflict. Charles, in some ways, was a Janus-like figure. He idealized the chivalric virtues of military prowess and personal obligations. Yet he combined these with the Renaissance characteristics of fame and glory. He looked back to the Carolingian middle kingdom of Lotharingia with nostalgia as he tried to remold it into a new state. Yet he hoped that this new kingdom would balance the power between Germany and France. At the beginning of his reign, it seemed quite possible to political observers (including Louis) that Charles might very well succeed.

He reached his peak with the submission of Ghent and Liège. The acquisition of Alsace and Lorraine represented an anticlimax since rapid defeats in Switzerland and Lorraine caused the death of the duke and the collapse of the Burgundian state in 1477. Charles was to blame, in part. He often acted rashly and consistently refused to follow the advice of his seasoned advisers, a fact that writers such as Niccolò Machiavelli and even Desiderius Erasmus would find troubling.

Fortune turned against him as well. He had no sons. The male line, consequently, ended with Charles. His daughter, Mary, was married to Maximilian I, the German emperor's son, in 1477. While this seemed a prudent move at the time, Mary died five years later, and the entire Burgundian inheritance disappeared into the domain of either Germany or France.

Two significant historical developments resulted from Charles's career and his ambitions, neither of which was intentional. First, Charles provided the setting for the last stage of the Franco-Burgundian struggle, with the monarch winning over the magnate. Centralization of France was completed with the fall of Burgundy. Second, a more remote result was the eventual independence of the Low Countries from German and French competition. The seeds of discontent were originally sown during Charles's era but did not fully blossom until the seventeenth century, when the Netherlands attained the formal status of independence.

—*Barbara M. Fahy*

FURTHER READING

Bennett, Adelaide Louise. *Medieval Mastery: Book Illumination from Charlemagne to Charles the Bold, 800-1475*. Turnhout, Belgium: Brepols, 2002. Catalog from an exhibition charting the evolution of illuminated manuscripts and the cultural contexts within which they were produced. Discusses Charles the Bold's society and the function of the book within it. Includes illustrations, bibliographic references, and indexes.

Calmette, Joseph. *The Golden Age of Burgundy: The Magnificent Dukes and Their Courts*. Translated by Doreen Weightman. New York: W. W. Norton, 1963. Places Charles in the environment of the age of Burgundian power. Calmette is the only historian to treat the Burgundian court within the context of its intellectual and artistic milieu.

Kirk, John Foster. *History of Charles the Bold, Duke of Burgundy*. 3 vols. Philadelphia: J. B. Lippincott, 1864-1868. A detailed and straightforward account of the life of Charles. Generous quotes from letters, reports, and treaties. Strictly conforms to the nineteenth century historiographical emphasis on factual information. Would be most useful as a source for an in-depth study of the duke, even though its interpretation is dated.

Putnam, Ruth. *Charles the Bold, Last Duke of Burgundy, 1433-1477*. New York: G. P. Putnam's Sons, 1908. Standard biography that is part of a larger series dealing with heroic individuals. A lively account of the duke's life and an equally vivid portrayal of the mores of the fifteenth century. The author stresses the role of the individual as hero in history.

Small, Graeme. *George Chastelain and the Shaping of Valois Burgundy: Political and Historical Culture at Court in the Fifteenth Century*. Rochester, N.Y.: Boydell Press, 1997. Study of Charles the Bold's official chronicler, who was also the official chronicler of Philip the Good. Begins with a biography of Chastelain, then reads his chronicle to gain insight into the courts of Philip and Charles and their impact on the history of France and Burgundy. Includes bibliographic references and index.

Vaughan, Richard. *Charles the Bold: The Last Valois Duke of Burgundy*. New ed. Rochester, N.Y.: Boydell & Brewer, 2004. An excellent interpretation of Charles and his complicated relationship with his lands. The author penetrates the political motives of Charles, Louis, and other major figures. Ample quotes from diaries, dispatches, histories, and letters. Contains a full and detailed bibliography.

Velden, Hugo van der. *The Donor's Image: Gerard Loyet*

and the Votive Portraits of Charles the Bold. Translated by Beverley Jackson. Turnhout, Belgium: Brepols, 2000. Close study of the portraits of Charles commissioned as votive gifts for various churches. Includes analysis of Charles's representation in the portraits, as well as his motives for commissioning and donating them. Illustrated, with bibliographic references and index.

SEE ALSO: Edward IV; Desiderius Erasmus; Frederick III; Louis XI; Niccolò Machiavelli; Maximilian I.
RELATED ARTICLES in *Great Events from History: The Renaissance & Early Modern Era, 1454-1600:* July 16, 1465-April, 1559: French-Burgundian and French-Austrian Wars; August 29, 1475: Peace of Picquigny.

CHARLES V
Holy Roman Emperor (r. 1519-1556)

Charles V initiated one hundred fifty years of Habsburg dynastic hegemony in Europe, stopped the Turkish advance in Europe, promoted reform, and expanded Spanish colonization in the Americas.

BORN: February 24, 1500; Ghent, Burgundy (now in France)
DIED: September 21, 1558; monastery of San Jerónimo de Yuste, Extremadura, Spain
ALSO KNOWN AS: Charles I
AREAS OF ACHIEVEMENT: Government and politics, religion and theology

EARLY LIFE

Charles V was born in Ghent, the ancient capital of Flanders and the heart of the duchy of Burgundy. In 1477, Burgundy escheated to Holy Roman Emperor Maximilian I, of the house of Habsburg. Maximilian's rivalry with the French over the Burgundian lands led to an alliance with Spain that resulted in the marriage of his son, Philip, to Joan, daughter of Ferdinand II and Isabella I. Charles, as the eldest son of the couple, became duke of Burgundy in 1506, king of Spain in 1516, and Holy Roman Emperor in 1519.

When Charles entered Spain in 1517, he could not speak the native language and was surrounded by a Flemish court that sought to monopolize high offices in the Spanish church and state. Physically, Charles appeared rather awkward, a lanky teenager with the jutting Habsburg jaw. After two years of ineffective kingship in Spain, Charles was elected Holy Roman Emperor to the dismay of many Spaniards, who believed that Charles would relegate their country to a peripheral province to be drained of wealth for imperial ambitions. Thus, almost immediately after Charles left Spain for his coronation, the Castilian cities initiated the Comunero Revolt (1520-1522) to force Charles's return and a reform of political administration.

The imperial election brought Charles problems outside Spain as well. Since the Investiture Conflict of the twelfth century, the powerful German princes, especially the seven imperial electors, had limited the emperor's power through the Germanic Diet, the major representative and administrative institution of the Holy Roman Empire. In addition, Germany's political weakness meant that its church was more directly under the control of the Papacy and, therefore, paid a disproportionate amount to the papal treasury. The desire of some of the princes to end papal taxation, obtain vast church lands, and maintain a decentralized political administration quickly merged with Martin Luther's call for a doctrinal reform of the Church following his attack on the sale of indulgences in Germany in 1517.

Charles held a diet of the Holy Roman Empire at Worms in 1521 to determine the fate of Martin Luther and his princely supporters. After listening to Luther speak, the emperor had the diet condemn the reformer with an imperial ban, though by that point most Protestant princes had left the meeting and, therefore, considered the ban nonbinding on them. Charles could not take action against the Protestants because of the Comunero Revolt and a simultaneous French attack in Italy that aimed to regain Naples from Spain.

LIFE'S WORK

In 1522, Charles returned to Spain and began his life's work, the forging of Habsburg hegemony in Europe based on Spanish wealth and power. At Worms, he had received reports from Hernán Cortés about his conquest of Mexico. From that point, Charles's new empire in the Americas contributed its silver to the protection of his European inheritance. Cortés would be followed by Francisco Pizarro, conqueror of the Incas, and a host of lesser-known conquistadores. Charles reformed his court and from then on Spaniards predominated in high offices throughout his empire. His residence in Spain led Charles to appoint his brother Ferdinand as regent in Germany. Charles's decision to make Spain the center of his empire contributed to a resounding victory in Italy over the French king, Francis I, at the Battle of Pavia in 1525.

Charles could not enjoy his victory long, as a new and more dangerous enemy appeared to threaten his empire, Süleyman the Magnificent, sultan of the Ottoman Empire. The Ottoman Turks mounted the greatest Muslim attack on Christendom since the eighth century. In 1529, Süleyman led a huge army into Austria (personal lands of the Habsburgs) and laid siege to Vienna; only inclement weather prevented the fall of the great city. Sensing an advantage, Francis renewed his attacks, forcing Charles to fight in Italy and Burgundy as well as southern Germany. The French and Turkish cooperation led to their formal alliance in 1535.

The Franco-Turkish War forced Charles to adopt a more conciliatory policy in regard to the religious conflict in Germany. (He was influenced as well by his own reform inclinations, which were similar to those of Desiderius Erasmus, the famous Humanist and counselor to the emperor.) Charles sanctioned a series of diets in Germany to reach a settlement on the religious conflict in order to meet the Turkish threat. The diets of Speyer (1526) and Augsburg (1530) failed to achieve agreement, but they recognized the legal existence of the Lutheran religion pending the convocation of a general church council that Charles pledged to convene. In return, the German princes, Protestant and Catholic, rallied to Charles's war against the French and the Turks. As a result, the Turkish advance into Central Europe was finally halted during a decisive campaign in 1532.

Pope Clement VII sided with France during the war in order to avoid the emperor's pressure for a general council that might reduce the pope's authority. This proved disastrous as a combined German-Spanish army marched on Rome and sacked it in 1527. Clement agreed to call a general council, though it failed to materialize because of the renewal of war between Charles and Francis over Milan in 1535.

As the Franco-Turkish Alliance became operative during the war, Charles decided to deliver another blow against the Turks. In 1535, he organized a massive armada and captured Tunis, the base of Turkish power in the western Mediterranean. Following his victory, Charles triumphantly marched through Italy and appeared at the papal court, where he spoke in Spanish condemning the French for their alliance with the Turks and preventing the convocation of a general council. Charles finally secured a favorable peace with the Franco-Turkish Alliance in 1544 and gained the support of Francis for a general council. Charles then turned his attention toward resolving the religious conflict in Germany.

Pope Paul III recognized the urgent need to reform the Church but wanted to avoid any diminution of papal authority and any doctrinal compromise with Protestantism that might result from a general council. He sanctioned

An engraved depiction of Charles V accompanied in a procession by the pope.
(F. R. Niglutsch)

the Jesuit Order (founded by Saint Ignatius of Loyola), whose schools cleansed Humanistic studies of paganism and used them to reinforce Catholic doctrine and improve the quality of the clergy. Having earned the reputation of a reformer, Paul agreed to call a general council in the city of Trent on terms that ensured papal domination of the council.

Charles tried to create a sympathetic atmosphere for a religious compromise at the pending council by convening the German Diet in Regensburg in 1541. Papal and Lutheran representatives agreed on several points, including a compromise position on faith and justification (double justification), but failed to settle issues surrounding the role of the Sacraments. In the end, even the agreement on double justification met with condemnation by the pope and Luther.

Charles abandoned his policy of peaceful negotiation in 1545 for three reasons: The Lutherans refused to participate in the Council of Trent because they correctly believed that it would be dominated by the pope, the French and Turks were no longer threatening, and Charles feared that the spread of Lutheranism among imperial electors would lead to the election of a Protestant emperor. Charles believed that with a victory over the Schmalkaldic League, the alliance of Protestant princes, he could force the Lutheran princes to cooperate with the Council of Trent and reunite the Church.

The Schmalkaldic War (1546-1547) ended with a dramatic victory for Charles at the Battle of Mühlberg. Yet the fruits of victory were spoiled at the Council of Trent, where the pope, fearing an overly powerful emperor, rejected Charles's demands to move slowly, saving doctrinal issues for later discussion with Lutheran representatives. Instead, Paul enumerated and condemned Protestant doctrines and clarified traditional Catholic orthodoxy. The initial decrees of Trent meant that Charles would have to pacify the religious conflict in Germany himself.

The result was the Augsburg Interim of 1548, which provided for clerical marriage, communion in two kinds, and the half-Protestant doctrine of double justification. Otherwise, the interim reimposed the rites of the old religion. The interim applied only to German Protestants and was almost universally hated: The pope believed that it was a usurpation of his authority, the Lutherans viewed it as the reimposition of a foreign (Roman) church, and it failed to bring about the religious reunification of Germany sought by moderates. The breach was irreconcilable.

Even princes who were neutral during the Schmalkaldic War grew impatient with Charles's German policies.

Political concerns loomed as large as religious ones. Charles had humiliated great princes with arrest and imprisonment. Following the war, his attempts to create an Imperial League and to make the imperial office hereditary threatened the princes' traditional predominance in the Holy Roman Empire. In order to regain their religious and political liberties, Protestant princes struck an alliance with the young French king Henry II in 1552. In return for helping to secure Protestant liberty, France gained the strategic fortress cities of Metz, Toul, and Verdun in the Rhineland; thus, the gates into Germany were opened to French influence. In order to defend his lands from French attack, Charles quickly made peace with the Protestant princes. The final religious settlement for Germany was the Peace of Augsburg of 1555, which stated that each prince in the Holy Roman Empire would determine whether his state would be Catholic or Lutheran. The settlement also ended Charles's attempts to create strong monarchical power in the Holy Roman Empire.

Charles did not sign the Peace of Augsburg, as he began divesting his authority in Germany to Ferdinand. He divided his lands between Ferdinand and his son Philip: Ferdinand was given Germany and the imperial title, while Philip received Spain, Naples, the American colonies, Burgundy, and Milan. Following the territorial division, Charles abdicated the Spanish throne in 1556 and retired into a Spanish monastery, San Jerónimo de Yuste, where he studied religious works and contemplated his failure to maintain the religious unity of Christendom. He died two years later.

SIGNIFICANCE

At Yuste, Charles V considered his reign a failure. Yet his moderate policy toward the Protestants prior to 1545 was essential for the defeat of the Turks and the reform of the Catholic Church. He led Spain into its Golden Age (1500-1650), when it became, for the first time in its history, the dominating political and cultural power in Europe.

Philip II became the sword of the Counter-Reformation, while Spanish spirituality, exemplified by the Jesuits, was its soul. The Council of Trent represented a crucial turning point for Catholicism, as internal reform was essential for the reversal of Protestant gains in France, Poland, Hungary, and southern Germany.

If Charles was depressed for having lost part of Europe to Protestantism, he could take comfort in his opening of two new continents to Western influence. The colonial enterprise represented more a drain than a boon to

Spain's resources prior to the 1530's. Given Charles's European commitments, he might have stalled the conquests rather than encouraged them. Mexico, Central America, and most of South America were all conquered during Charles's reign. He began the institutionalization of the colonial empire by creating the Council of the Indies and formulating the New Laws of 1542 and 1543, which aimed to make the assimilation of native South, Central, and North Americans more humane.

Charles was both the end of one chapter in European history and the beginning of another. He was the last Holy Roman Emperor to dominate Europe and the last monarch to adhere to medieval ideals of chivalry. On the other hand, the division of his empire and development of Spain encouraged the emergence of the European state system and began a process of global Westernization that has continued into the twenty-first century.

—*Daniel A. Crews*

FURTHER READING

Blockmans, Wim. *Emperor Charles V, 1500-1558*. Translated by Isola van den Hoven-Vardon. London: Arnold, 2002. Blockmans attempts to survey the scope of the vast territory and diverse culture of the Holy Roman Empire by analyzing the relationship between Charles as an individual and the complex, rigid, yet unstable power structures within which he governed. Includes illustrations, maps, bibliographic references, index.

Brandi, Karl. *The Emperor Charles V: The Growth and Destiny of a Man and a World Empire*. Translated by C. V. Wedgwood. 1939. Reprint. London: J. Cape, 1963. This is a standard biography though somewhat slanted toward Charles's German concerns. Contains a detailed account of Charles as a classic Renaissance monarch who ruled each realm through traditional institutions but integrated them through dynastic policy. The thesis that Charles desired a world empire has long been contested.

Fernández-Santamaría, J. A. *The State, War, and Peace: Spanish Political Thought in the Renaissance, 1516-1559*. Cambridge, England: Cambridge University Press, 1977. An excellent analysis of the impact Charles V's imperial policies had on the evolution of Spanish political thought. Argues that Charles's elevation of Spain led to a modern theory of state and empire. Also provides a detailed analysis of debates arising from American conquests over the legitimacy and extent of Spanish authority in the New World.

Fischer-Galati, Stephen A. *Ottoman Imperialism and German Protestantism, 1521-1555*. Cambridge, Mass.: Harvard University Press, 1959. A survey of Charles's relations with the Turks and how they influenced his policies toward the Lutheran princes. Argues that early Protestant success was dependent on Turkish advances. Temporary guarantees of security granted in 1526 and 1532 could not be revoked because of the continued pressure of the Franco-Turkish alliance.

Koenigsberger, Helmut B. "The Empire of Charles V in Europe." In *The Reformation, 1520-1559*. Vol. 2 in *The New Cambridge Modern History*, edited by G. R. Elton. 2d ed. New York: Cambridge University Press, 1990. A good, short survey of political administration in Charles's heterogenous empire. This is the best place to begin a study of how Charles governed his empire: the type of institutions he had to work through in each area and the amount of revenue they contributed. This is also a good insight into Charles as the model Renaissance monarch, neither an absolutist nor a feudal monarch.

Lynch, John. *Spain, 1516-1598: From Nation State to World Empire*. Cambridge, Mass.: B. Blackwell, 1991. This revised edition of the first volume of *Spain Under the Habsburgs* provides a topical survey of Spain during the reigns of Charles and Philip. Particularly good on economic and social developments that contributed to the decline of Spain in the seventeenth century. Also demonstrates the impact of the American colonies on the Spanish economy and Habsburg military campaigns. Good synthesis of a vast amount of secondary scholarship.

Maltby, William. *The Reign of Charles V*. New York: Palgrave, 2002. Monograph balances biography of Charles with broad analysis of his foreign and domestic policies and their historical consequences. Includes maps, bibliographic references, index.

Tracy, James D. *Emperor Charles V, Impresario of War: Campaign Strategy, International Finance, and Domestic Politics*. New York: Cambridge University Press, 2002. Examination of the financial and political consequences of Charles V's military campaigns. Discusses Charles as a field commander of his armies, as well as the international financial community that loaned Charles the money to pay for battles and thereby gained control over parts of his lands. Also discusses the local governments within the empire that learned to exploit Charles's need for money. Includes illustrations, maps, bibliographic references, index.

Wallenstein, Immanuel. *The Modern World-System: Capitalist Agriculture and the Origins of the European World-Economy in the Sixteenth Century.* New York: Academic Press, 1974. This book argues that Charles's empire and the impact of American silver contributed to the shift of Europe's economic axis from the Mediterranean to a northwestern European core, which fostered the development of capitalist nation-states and an international division of labor based on peripheral reaction to core demands. An intriguing argument but difficult reading for the novice in history and economics.

SEE ALSO: Duke of Alva; Catherine of Aragon; Clement VII; Hernán Cortés; Desiderius Erasmus; Ferdinand II and Isabella sI; Francis I; Henry II; Saint

Ignatius of Loyola; Martin Luther; Margaret of Austria; Margaret of Parma; Mary of Hungary; Mary I; Maximilian I; Mehmed II; Mehmed III; Paul III; Philip II; Francisco Pizarro; Süleyman the Magnificent; Andreas Vesalius; William the Silent.

RELATED ARTICLES in *Great Events from History: The Renaissance & Early Modern Era, 1454-1600:* July 16, 1465-April, 1559: French-Burgundian and French-Austrian Wars; June 28, 1519: Charles V Is Elected Holy Roman Emperor; 1520-1566: Reign of Süleyman; 1521-1559: Valois-Habsburg Wars; May 6, 1527-February, 1528: Sack of Rome; February 27, 1531: Formation of the Schmalkaldic League; 1536: Turkish Capitulations Begin; October 20-27, 1541: Holy Roman Empire Attacks Ottomans in Algiers; 1555-1556: Charles V Abdicates.

CHARLES VII
King of France (r. 1422-1461)

Charles VII successfully created a strong standing army, unified most of the French nation under one king, greatly improved government administration, and established a permanent tax. He was a ruler who left a country much more powerful than it was when he assumed kingship.

BORN: February 22, 1403; Paris, France
DIED: July 22, 1461; Mehun-sur-Yèvre, France
ALSO KNOWN AS: Charles the Well-Served; Charles the Victorious
AREAS OF ACHIEVEMENT: Government and politics, military

EARLY LIFE

Historians agree that Charles VII was an enigmatic character. A member of the Valois Dynasty, he was the fifth son of King Charles VI and Isabella of Bavaria. In 1413, he was betrothed to Marie of Anjou, daughter of Louis II, duke of Anjou, and Yolande of Aragon. In 1417, the death of the last of his older brothers made him the dauphin (heir to the throne). The next year, when his enemies occupied Paris, he fled to Anjou, where his future mother-in-law supervised his education. He was considered a slow learner as a child.

Throughout his youth, France was in great turmoil. The duke of Burgundy and the count of Armagnac were engaged in a bitter civil war. In 1415, the king of England, Henry V, who claimed the French throne, entered

into an alliance with the Burgundians and launched an invasion of the country. The Armagnacs gave their support to the French king, who was suffering increasingly from mental illness.

After Henry won the famous battle at Agincourt, he waged successful campaigns in other regions of northern France. In 1418, his Burgundian allies massacred most of the leaders of the Armagnacs.

These English victories enabled Henry to coerce Charles VI into signing the Treaty of Troyes of 1420, which disinherited the dauphin, declared Henry heir to the French throne, and announced a marriage between him and the dauphin's sister, Catherine. The dauphin repudiated the treaty. His widowed mother-in-law, Yolande, who was now duchess of Anjou, gave him economic and military support, which allowed Charles to prevail in the battle at Baugé in 1421. About this time, his mother, Isabella, likely to gain the favor of the English, began to refer to the "so-called dauphin," raising questions about Charles's legitimacy.

LIFE'S WORK

After Henry V and Charles VI died in 1422, most of northern France, which was then controlled by English and Burgundian troops, recognized the kingship of the infant son of Henry and Catherine, Henry VI. The duchy of Artois and a few regions in the east and south of the Loire River supported Charles VII as rightful king. His opponents derisively called him the king of Bourges (af-

The coronation of King Charles VII of France in Reims cathedral. (F. R. Niglutsch)

glish to leave Orleans, Joan achieved several more military victories and successfully led a march through enemy territory to Reims, the place of Charles VII's coronation on July 17, 1429.

With Joan's victories, an increasing number of French regions were acknowledging Charles as legitimate king. Yet, when Joan was captured by the Burgundians in 1430, Charles did not ransom her release, although he did try to overturn the verdict later. At this time, Charles's court had been beset by many competing factions, including a rivalry between the Armagnacs and his in-laws from the House of Anjou. A bitter feud between Richemont and Georges de La Trémoille, who had tried to block Joan's efforts, was especially harmful. Richemont's triumph in 1433 brought a degree of stability to the regime.

In 1435, Charles's government negotiated with Burgundy the Treaty of Arras, which was a major turning point in the war. The new alliance shifted the balance of power fundamentally in favor of Charles VII. The next year, Richemont's army marched triumphantly into Paris. Having consolidated his power, Charles was strong enough to challenge the Papacy, and, in 1438, he issued the pragmatic sanction of Bourges, which asserted the authority of the French king over the income and personnel of the Church in France.

ter his temporary residence). In this difficult period, Charles looked to the advice and support of Yolande. In 1427, she used her influence to enlist the dynamic Arthur de Richemont, the brother of the duke of Brittany, as constable of Charles's government.

Despite Richemont's leadership, Charles's forces appeared unable to stop the English advance led by the duke of Bedford. In February, 1429, however, the situation changed dramatically when a peasant girl, Joan of Arc, met with Charles at Chinon and solemnly informed him that Christian saints had called her to break the English siege at Orleans. According to legend, she impressed Charles with her knowledge of some secret. Duchess Yolande strongly supported Joan and provided the finances for her battle campaign. After forcing the En-

One of the French government's long-standing problems had been its inability to meet its financial obligations. When soldiers were not paid, the countryside suffered from brigandage (plundering). In 1439, the estates-general (France's representative assembly) agreed to an apportioned direct tax, called the taille, which provided an effective, if unfair, system of taxation. In 1440, Charles's allies defeated the Praguerie, a revolt led by the powerful nobles of the realm. Five years later, to prevent another such rebellion, Charles established France's first standing army, called the *compagnies d'ordonnance*, which consisted of nine thousand mounted police on regular salary.

Charles VII's reign saw a significant growth of commercial activity, growth that is credited usually to the work of Jacques Coeur, a banker and merchant who became the wealthiest man in France. After serving as master of the mint and steward of royal expenditures, Coeur became a member of the king's council and supervised diplomatic missions to Rome, Italy, and Spain. In 1447, he oversaw the reform of the country's coinage. He also loaned to Charles the money needed to defeat the English on the battlefield.

From 1444 to 1450, the young, vivacious, and beautiful Agnès Sorel (also known as Dame de Beauté) was the acknowledged mistress of the king, the first woman to hold this semiofficial position that became common among French monarchs. It was considered scandalous by many that the king had a mistress, and the relationship promoted intrigue at court. Charles provided her with wealth, lands, and castles. After giving birth to her fourth child, Sorel died of dysentery, and the enemies of Coeur spread the rumor that he had poisoned her. In 1453, a court found Coeur guilty, despite weak evidence. Although he escaped to Rome, the government confiscated much of his wealth.

For good reason, Charles VII acquired the nicknames Charles the Victorious and Charles the Well-Served. In 1450, the Battle of Formigny helped him regain control over Normandy. In 1453, the victories at Castillon and Bordeaux marked the end of the Hundred Years' War. The only remaining territory controlled by the English was Calais. Although often a ruthless and self-serving ruler, Charles had the good sense to follow a conciliatory policy toward towns and regions that had collaborated with the English, which helped to restore peace and harmony to the country.

During the last two decades of his reign, Charles VII and his ambitious and stubborn heir, the future Louis XI, were bitterly estranged from one another. The dauphin participated in the Praguerie, and, in 1446, he conspired against Agnès Sorel. After yet another revolt, Louis was living in exile at the court of Philip the Good of Burgundy in 1461, when he was overjoyed to learn of his father's death.

SIGNIFICANCE

Charles VII has often been criticized as a lazy and lethargic monarch who tolerated harmful rivalries at court, especially in the early years. Some modern historians, however, have argued that Charles was an intuitive leader who skillfully neutralized competing interests. Even those who question his intelligence admit that he usually surrounded himself with competent advisers, military leaders, and administrators.

Charles VII's reign was highly important in the history of France. Before his ascendancy, France was bitterly divided and doing poorly in the Hundred Years' War, but by the end of his reign, the country was well on its way to becoming a unified nation with an efficient system of taxation and administration. Some historians classify Charles as a new monarch, whose reign laid the foundations for a modern national state.

—*Thomas Tandy Lewis*

FURTHER READING

DeVries, Kelly. *Joan of Arc: A Military Leader.* Stroud, England: Sutton, 1999. An interesting account of Joan's military exploits, giving considerable information about her relationship to Charles VII.

Kerr, Albert B. *Jacques Coeur: Prince of the Middle Ages.* New York: Books for Libraries Press, 1971. This work includes material about Coeur's relationship to Charles VII and discusses the death of Agnès Sorel, which ended Coeur's career in France.

Major, J. Russell. *From Renaissance Monarchy to Absolute Monarchy: French Kings, Nobles, and Estates.* Baltimore: Johns Hopkins University Press, 1994. A scholarly survey of how the French political system changed from the influences of the reign of Charles VII to that of Louis XIV. The author emphasizes the importance of alliances between king and nobility.

Miskimin, Harry. *Money and Power in Fifteenth Century France.* New Haven, Conn.: Yale University Press, 1984. A scholarly study of how banking and economics had an influence on French political development during the fifteenth century.

Seward, Desmond. *The Hundred Years' War: The English in France, 1337-1453.* New York: Penguin Books, 1999. An interesting and dramatic summary of the century-long conflict, focusing on major personalities such as Charles VII.

Vale, Malcolm. *Charles VII.* Berkeley: University of California Press, 1974. The standard biography in English, written by an outstanding scholar of the Middle Ages. Vale emphasizes Charles's challenges and presents a positive interpretation of his reign.

CHARLES VIII
King of France (r. 1483-1498)

Charles VIII continued Louis XI's policy of increasing the power of the French monarchy over the nobility and continued the improvement and professionalization of the French army. He also launched the Italian Wars, the struggle between France and Spain for dominance in Renaissance Italy.

BORN: June 30, 1470; Royal Chateau Amboise, France
DIED: April 7, 1498; Amboise, France
AREAS OF ACHIEVEMENT: Government and politics, military, warfare and conquest

EARLY LIFE

Charles VIII of the House of Valois was the only son of King Louis XI, and Charlotte of Savoy. Though legally of age to rule after his father's death in 1483, the thirteen-year-old Charles was weak and lacked intelligence. On his deathbed, Louis charged his eldest daughter, the twenty-two-year-old Anne and her husband Pierre de Bourbon, seigneur de Beaujeu, as unofficial regents for Charles.

The Beaujeus did an admirable job of dealing with the noble backlash that followed the authoritarian reign of Louis. They made concessions, which included reducing taxes and restoring rights to hostile nobles, especially to the twenty-one-year-old Louis, the duke of Orleans who was also Charles's cousin and the new heir to the throne. The Beaujeus also agreed to a calling of the estates-general at Tours for 1484. When the estates sided with the Beaujeus in a dispute over control of the regency, however, the disaffected nobles led by Orleans eventually revolted and were supported by Duke Francis II of Brittany, the archduke Maximilian I of Austria (later Holy Roman Emperor), King Ferdinand II of Aragon, and Henry VII of England.

The "mad war" that followed was won by the royal party at the decisive Battle of Saint-Aubin-du-Cormier that same year, though skirmishing continued until 1491. Duke Francis died in 1488, Brittany passed to his daughter Anne, and immediately there began a competition for her hand in marriage and thus control of the last major fief in France that was independent of the Crown. Duchess Anne, in an attempt to protect her birthright from French domination, married Maximilian by proxy on December 19, 1490, but her new husband was unable to come to her aid militarily, and besieged at Rennes in 1491, she was forced to annul her marriage and accept betrothal to Charles VIII.

LIFE'S WORK

Charles's marriage to the fifteen-year-old Anne seemed to give him a new independence, as he broke free from Beaujeus control. Filled with chivalric dreams, tempted by disaffected Italian nobles, and drawn, as many French monarchs before and after, to the riches of Italy, Charles proceeded to launch a "war of magnificence." The first step in this great crusade against the Turks would be to seize Naples from Ferdinand as a staging area to take Constantinople or Jerusalem and win his place as emperor of the east. Many Italian leaders favored a French invasion, thinking that it would help them dominate parts of or all the peninsula, which included more than a dozen jealous states in the late fifteenth century.

To free himself for this great venture to the southeast, Charles proceeded to make a series of unwise treaties designed to secure France's frontiers. He bought off Henry VII with the enormous sum of 750,000 gold crowns in the Treaty of Étaples (1492). To gain Brittany, Charles had to break his engagement to Margaret of Austria, daughter of Maximilian I, and forfeit Artois and Franche-Comté. He had attempted originally to hold these provinces, but he returned them by the Treaty of Senlis (1493) to stabilize his eastern border. Charles also pacified his frontier with Spain in 1493 by signing the Treaty of Barcelona; this foolish agreement gave 200,000 gold crowns and Roussillon and Cerdagne to Ferdinand of Aragon, thereby forfeiting the hard-won gains of his father's reign.

Charles, with an army of more than twenty-five thousand, which included eight thousand Swiss mercenaries, the best infantry in Europe, crossed the Alps into Italy in September of 1494. Except for a bloody battle fought at Rapallo in September, the French moved through Lombardy easily. They were welcomed at Milan and Ferrara, forced their way into Florence, and then proceeded through Sienna to Rome. The new pope, Alexander VI, was forced to deal with Charles, quickly making concessions to facilitate his departure from papal lands. Charles entered Naples, which he called his kingdom, on February 22, 1495, and was crowned there on May 12.

The ruthlessness and efficiency of the French army had come as a shock to the Italians. The formalized warfare of late fifteenth century Italy revolved around captains known as condottieri, who raised large armies of mercenaries and sold their services to the highest bidder. Battles between these mercenary forces, who had little loyalty to anyone save themselves, were like great blood-less chess matches. Tens of thousands of men would fight all day and casualties might scarcely number in the hundreds. The French system spawned by the Hundred Years' War and honed during the Franco-Austrian War of 1477 to 1493 was infused with a national spirit and was designed to kill. The French men-at-arms and Swiss infantry that formed the core of Charles's army were vicious and unmerciful. The most devastating aspect of the French onslaught, however, was the new-style artillery arm. French guns were operated by disciplined professionals and were superior in quantity, quality, mobility, and caliber to any artillery in Europe. The proficiency of French guns dominated battlefields and reduced walled places within hours instead of weeks.

Charles was cheered by the people of Naples initially, but his policies soon alienated the Neapolitan nobility. Furthermore, his soldiers' obvious contempt for the Italians, who they saw as decadent and inferior, made the French unpopular. The terrified leaders of Italy quickly put aside their quarrels and banded together to oust him. Pope Alexander VI organized the first Holy League, or League of Venice, which included the Papacy, Venice, England, the Holy Roman Empire, Ferdinand, and Charles's former ally, Ludovico Sforza of Milan. In an attempt to dupe the French, the league was announced as a defensive alliance to protect Italy against the Turks.

Charles and his advisers, however, quickly recognized the threat that the Holy League's army posed to his line of communications through Italy. Leaving a garrison in Naples, he marched north with forty-one hundred cavalry and seventy-five hundred infantry in May of 1495. The French encountered the condottiere Francesco II Gonzaga's twenty thousand Italian mercenaries on July 6 at Fornovo. Gonzaga took up a strong defensive position in one of the defiles (narrow gorges) of the Appenines. As Charles's army marched through the pass, Gonzaga launched a flank attack. The French artillery unlimbered and tore into the mercenaries, while their infantry launched a violent assault that cut down the Italians by the thousands.

Afterward, Charles marched leisurely back into France, vowing to return to Italy to seek more glory. He never got the chance because he hit his head on a doorpost at Amboise in April of 1498, went into a coma, and died soon thereafter. He had been in the process of raising new forces. The French hold on southern Italy also did not survive 1498. A Spanish army under Gonzalo Fernández de Córdoba was sent to Naples in 1495, slowly pushed out the French, and reinstalled a member of the House of Aragon on the throne.

SIGNIFICANCE

Charles's reign marked the end of the Middle Ages and the dawn of the Renaissance era. The incursion of his new-style army south of the Alps is considered by many to be the climax of the Italian Renaissance and the catalyst for spreading Renaissance ideas into northern Europe. Medieval forms and ideas, however, would die hard.

Charles, like many of his contemporaries, exhibited the style of a new monarch when he continued his father's policy of breaking the power of the great nobles; yet, he neglected the real French national interests: the consolidation of recent gains in Burgundy and Brittany. Instead, he embarked on an adventure into exotic Italy and beyond that aroused the jealousies of his enemies. Crusades to acquire Jerusalem in search of glory were the dreams of a medieval monarch.

Charles's successors continued to pursue control of Italy at great cost. The Italian Wars saw the Europeans selfishly fight over small pieces of Italy while the Turks pushed the banners of Islam up the Danube and into the Mediterranean. For all the men and treasure expended, France was finally forced to sign the humiliating Treaty of Cateau-Cambrésis on April 3, 1559, which, after a sixty-five-year struggle, left Spain firmly in control of Italy.

—*Bart L. R. Talbert*

FURTHER READING

Abulafia, David. *The French Descent into Renaissance Italy, 1494-95: Antecedents and Effects.* Brookfield, Vt.: Ashgate, 1995. Questions whether the French invasion upset a relatively calm Italy and looks into political, military, diplomatic, and technological aspects of the occupation.

Bridge, John S. C. *A History of France from the Death of Louis XI.* Vol. 2. Oxford, England: Clarendon Press, 1922-1924. A detailed account of Charles's reign, the economic prosperity and political degeneracy of Italy, and the diplomatic and military history of the first phase of the Italian Wars.

Commines, Philippe de. *Memoires.* 2 vols. Translated by I. Cazeaux, edited by S. Kinser. Columbia: University of South Carolina Press, 1973. Contains autobiographical portraits of Louis XI and Charles VIII and analyzes leaders, purposes, and institutions.

Johnson, Arthur Henry. *Europe in the Sixteenth Century, 1494-1598.* London: Rivington's, 1964. The first chapter offers a thorough description of the diplomacy and politics of the Italian Wars.

Nicolle, David, and Richard Hook. *Fornovo, 1495*. Oxford, England: Osprey, 1996. An excellent volume that provides an in-depth look into the background of the campaign, the fighting, and its consequences.

Taylor, Frederick Lewis. *The Art of War in Italy, 1494 to 1529*. Cambridge, England: Cambridge University Press, 1921. An examination of the changes in warfare caused by the French invasion during the first half of the Italian Wars.

SEE ALSO: Alexander VI; Anne of Brittany; Chevalier de Bayard; Cesare Borgia; Lucrezia Borgia; Ferdinand II and Isabella I; Francis I; Henry VII; James IV; Julius II; Louis XI; Louis XII; Margaret of Austria; Maximilian I; Ludovico Sforza.

RELATED ARTICLES in *Great Events from History: The Renaissance & Early Modern Era, 1454-1600:* 1481-1499: Ludovico Sforza Rules Milan; September, 1494-October, 1495: Charles VIII of France Invades Italy; 1500: Roman Jubilee; 1504: Treaty of Blois.

CLEMENT VII
Italian pope (1523-1534)

While Clement's pontificate was marred with failures, especially with regard to halting the spread of the Protestant Reformation and witnessing the sack of Rome, he did manage to encourage reforms within the Catholic Church through newly established religious orders and did much to enrich the art treasures of the Vatican.

BORN: May 26, 1478; Florence (now in Italy)
DIED: September 25, 1534; Rome, Papal States (now in Italy)
ALSO KNOWN AS: Giulio de' Medici
AREAS OF ACHIEVEMENT: Religion and theology, church reform

EARLY LIFE

Giulio de' Medici, who would become Pope Clement VII, was born the illegitimate son of Giuliano de' Medici. Giuliano was the brother of Lorenzo de' Medici, ruler of the powerful city-state of Florence. Within a year of Giulio's birth, his father was killed by an assassin, and the boy was left in the care of his uncle Lorenzo. Lorenzo died when Giulio was only fourteen, and guardianship of the boy was then assumed by Lorenzo's second son, Giovanni, himself only three years older than his cousin Giulio.

Giovanni became Pope Leo X in 1513. As pope, he quickly promoted his cousin Giulio to the rank of cardinal and also made him his personal vice-chancellor. Giulio proved an able administrator, serving his cousin Leo until the pope's death in 1521. He continued in this same capacity during the short reign of Leo's successor, Pope Adrian VI, who became pope in 1522 but died in 1523.

Adrian's short papacy left the church facing another papal election in 1523. After nearly six weeks of deliberations among the cardinals, Giulio de' Medici emerged from the Vatican's Sistine Chapel as Pope Clement VII on November 17, 1523. The election had been marred by deceit and trickery on the part of factions among the cardinals, including Clement himself. Subsequently, as Clement VII, Giulio de' Medici was to face some of the most serious challenges yet to befall the Papacy—challenges that would end in the destruction of Rome and a weakening of papal influence.

LIFE'S WORK

Pope Clement VII began his papacy caught between the political ambitions of King Charles V of Spain (who was also emperor of the Holy Roman Empire) and King Francis I of France. Both kings wanted control of the duchy of Milan as well as other parts of northern Italy. Fearing he might end up under the complete domination of Charles, since the Spanish already ruled the entire southern part of Italy, Clement threw his support to Francis and entered into an alliance with the French in December, 1524. Siding with Francis meant a greater possibility of papal independence and the likelihood that France would leave Clement's home city of Florence under Medici rule. On hearing of Clement's alliance with Francis, Charles became furious and sought revenge.

On February 25, 1525, Charles's troops met the French army at Pavia. After a tremendous battle, the Spanish army emerged victorious, taking Francis I as prisoner. On receiving news of the victory, Clement, now fearing for the future of the Papacy, sought an alliance with Charles, which when finalized essentially placed all Italy under Spanish protection.

In time, dissatisfied with the imperial rule, the duke of Milan, Francesco Sforza, conspired to overthrow his Spanish conquerors by bribing the commander of Charles's imperial troops, the marquis of Pescara. The plot called for offering Pescara the kingdom of Naples, already under Spain's control, in exchange for leading a revolt against Spanish forces in Italy. Clement was told of the plan and agreed to endorse it despite his previous alliance with Charles, but Pescara, loyal to the Spanish king, informed his sovereign of the plot and arrested Sforza. In the meantime, Charles, who knew of Clement's subversion, was content to leave the pope wondering what the future held for the Papacy.

After nearly a year, Charles agreed to release Francis on condition that the French king, under oath, renounce all claims to the Burgundy region of France as well as all northern Italian territories. Francis agreed and was released. Hoping to reunite in an alliance with the freed French king and thus regain more autonomy for the Papacy, Clement pursued Francis, offering to absolve him from breaking his oath to Charles on condition that Francis ally himself with the Papacy, Venice, and Milan against the Spanish. This alliance, the League of Cognac, was formed May 22, 1526.

The league, though, proved ineffective. Francis had neither the money to support the military needs of his allies nor the funds to ensure an adequate defense of Rome. Likewise, Clement's Italian allies, Milan and Venice, never delivered the support necessary to mount a strong opposition force. With little to stop the advancing forces under the command of Pompeo Colonna, a pro-Spanish cardinal, from attacking the Vatican, Clement, fearing for his life, fled the city to the safety of the papal Castle of Sant' Angelo.

Colonna's attack was followed by another attack by a united force of German mercenaries, known as *landsknechts*, and Spanish soldiers. The attackers made their way to the gates of Rome determined to take the city. In a panic, Clement attempted a hastened treaty with the Spanish ambassador to the Vatican, but it was too late. Angry because they had not been paid sufficiently for their services, the German mercenaries saw the spoils of war as a much more enticing reward than soldiers' pay and advanced on Rome, scaling its walls the morning of May 6, 1527. The sack of Rome had begun.

The siege and subsequent five-month occupation of Rome were chronicled in vivid detail. Captives were held for ransom, and those who could not pay were executed.

Drunkenness and debauchery abounded. The German mercenaries, primarily Protestants, rejoiced in the open desecration of Catholic churches and religious objects. Nuns were raped, tortured, and killed. The Tiber River, which ran through the heart of Rome, was filled with the dead bodies of so many murdered victims that by midsummer a plague had overrun what was left of the city. The inhabitants of Rome blamed the destruction of the city on Clement's clandestine treaties and broken promises.

With Rome in ruins and the papal treasury empty, Clement had no choice but to sign yet another treaty that subjugated the pope to the Spanish king's dominion. In return, Charles agreed to remove his troops from Rome on the conditions that the Vatican refrain from future political entanglements and plots against the Spanish sovereign and that Clement call for a Vatican council to discuss reforms within the Church. Clement agreed, but in doing so, he relinquished much of the Vatican's political and religious influence to Charles.

The final crisis to face Clement was the matter of English king Henry VIII's divorce from Catherine of Aragon. Catherine, the aunt of Charles V, had previously been married to Henry's elder brother, Arthur, who had

Clement VII. (Library of Congress)

died shortly after their marriage. According to Catherine, her marriage to Arthur had never been consummated. Henry argued that it had and asked for an annulment on that basis, although his real motive in seeking the annulment involved Catherine's inability to provide the king a male heir. The annulment controversy put Clement, once again, in the middle. If the pope granted Henry a divorce, he would certainly incur the wrath of Charles. On the other hand, Clement's uncle, as Pope Leo X, had previously praised Henry as defender of the faith for Henry's defense of the Church against the attacks of Martin Luther. The pope was thus faced with a difficult choice.

At first, Clement agreed to support Henry if the king could prove that Catherine's marriage to Henry's brother had been consummated. Then, within months, Clement reversed his offer before the king could substantiate his case. The pope's propensity for indecision and vacillation soured Henry's view of the Papacy, and he decisively put away Catherine to pursue his own resolution of the matter. In 1533, Henry installed Thomas Cranmer as archbishop of Canterbury. Cranmer subsequently proclaimed Henry's marriage to Catherine invalid, allowing Henry to marry his second wife, Anne Boleyn. The next year, Henry established himself as head of the Church of England. Henry's break with Rome further strengthened the progress of Protestantism and represented yet another loss for the Catholic Church.

Despite the criticism leveled against Clement VII's papacy, he might be better viewed as a victim of his times. Bred in an environment that was focused on the maintenance of political power, he knew that people and institutions could survive only by pursuing the advantages of power. As a Medici, Clement knew this particularly well; his family excelled in the art of political deal making. While his indecisive character may have benefited Protestantism to the detriment of the Catholic Church, the religious reforms that were to follow Clement's reign may well have come about only at the point at which the Catholic Church reached the crisis of the Protestant Reformation.

SIGNIFICANCE

Despite its many failures, the papacy of Clement VII did produce some achievements. Clement's deep appreciation for the arts inspired him to devote considerable attention to enriching the interior of the Vatican. He commissioned Michelangelo to paint the famous *Last Judgment* in the Sistine Chapel, and he enabled the talented goldsmith and sculptor Benvenuto Cellini to begin his career in the papal court. Clement also encouraged

church reforms, particularly by endorsing the establishment of reform-minded religious orders such as the Jesuits, the Capuchin Franciscans, the Theatine Fathers, and the Ursuline order of nuns.

On the other hand, Clement's propensity for indecision gave strength to the progress of the Protestant Reformation. Had Clement agreed, for example, in 1526 to call a reformation council to address the growing protests of the German states about conditions in the Catholic Church, he may have been able to halt the total loss of Germany and Scandinavia to Lutheranism. Likewise, his indecisiveness on the matter of Henry VIII's divorce from Catherine of Aragon left Henry enough time to deliberate his own decision to marry Anne Boleyn and subsequently to part with the Catholic Church.

—*Michael J. Garcia*

FURTHER READING

Berni, Francesco, and Anne Reynolds. *Renaissance Humanism at the Court of Clement VII: Francesco Berni's "Dialogue Against Poets" in Context*. New York: Garland, 1997. Translation of Berni's 1526 dialogue, accompanied by extensive background and critical commentary. Discusses Clement VII's court and the general political and religious culture of 1520's Rome. Includes illustrations, photographic plates, bibliographic references, and index.

Chamberlin, E. R. *The Bad Popes*. Stroud, Gloucestershire, England: Sutton, 2003. An informative discussion of seven medieval popes who reigned between 955 and 1534 and whose papacies were marred by elements of political intrigue and corruption. Includes photographs, illustrations, genealogical tables, bibliographic references, and index.

Flemer, Paul. "Clement VII and the Crisis of the Sack of Rome." In *Society and Individual in Renaissance Florence*, edited by William J. Connell. Berkeley: University of California Press, 2002. Detailed account of the 1527 sack of Rome and Clement's response to it.

John, Eric, ed. *The Popes: A Concise Biographical History*. Vol. 2. New York: Hawthorn Books, 1964. Briefly chronicles the lives of the popes. Volume 2 covers the Papacy from Boniface VIII (1294) through Paul VI (1963).

Knecht, R. J. *Renaissance Warrior and Patron: The Reign of Francis I*. Rev. ed. New York: Cambridge University Press, 1994. The most comprehensive coverage of Francis I and his times. Contains an excellent account of Francis's interactions with Pope Clement

VII as well as the king's response to the Protestant Reformation.

McBrien, Richard P. *Lives of the Popes*. San Francisco, Calif.: HarperCollins, 1997. Provides a complete listing of brief papal biographies. The appendices contain informative articles explaining how popes are elected and how they can be removed from office.

Maxwell-Stuart, P. G. *Chronicles of the Popes*. London: Thames and Hudson, 1997. A good reference source on the Papacy. Includes time lines, data files, and illustrations, many with sidebars that provide anecdotal information on the personalities and times of the popes.

Spitz, Lewis W. *The Protestant Reformation, 1517-1559*. New York: Harper & Row, 1985. A comprehensive narrative by a noted historian about the causes and impacts of the Protestant Reformation. Provides a good discussion of the dynamics of the Reformation in England and Henry VIII's break from Rome.

SEE ALSO: Adrian VI; Saint Angela Merici; Ludovico Ariosto; Anne Boleyn; Baldassare Castiglione; Catherine de Médicis; Catherine of Aragon; Benvenuto Cellini; Charles V; Francis I; Francesco Guicciardini; Henry VIII; John III; Leo X; Martin Luther; Niccolò Machiavelli; Cosimo I de' Medici; Lorenzo de' Medici; Michelangelo; Paul III.

RELATED ARTICLES in *Great Events from History: The Renaissance & Early Modern Era, 1454-1600:* Early 1460's: Labor Shortages Alter Europe's Social Structure; July 16, 1465-April, 1559: French-Burgundian and French-Austrian Wars; 1508-1512 and 1534-1541: Michelangelo Paints the Sistine Chapel; 1515-1529: Wolsey Serves as Lord Chancellor and Cardinal; 1521-1559: Valois-Habsburg Wars; November 3, 1522-November 17, 1530: Correggio Paints the *Assumption of the Virgin*; May 6, 1527-February, 1528: Sack of Rome; December 18, 1534: Act of Supremacy.

JOHN COLET
English religious scholar

As the founder of St. Paul's school and dean of St. Paul's Cathedral, Colet wrote, preached, and led other Humanists in educational, social, and religious reform.

BORN: Probably 1466; London, England
DIED: September 16, 1519; Sheen, Surrey, England
AREAS OF ACHIEVEMENT: Education, religion and theology, church reform

EARLY LIFE

Little is known of the early life of John Colet. That he was born in London to a privileged position, probably in 1466, is clear. His father, Sir Henry Colet, a respected member of the Mercers' Company (an ancient guild of textile merchants of considerable prestige), was twice lord mayor of London. His mother, Christian Knevet, had important connections through marriage to some of the greatest families of England. John was the oldest of twenty-two children born of this union and the only one who reached maturity. No explanation of this astounding mortality exists. Contemporaries believed that the tragic family history may have accounted for the serious, almost austere, cast of Colet's personality and his frequent statements of preference for the celibate life.

Colet probably attended St. Anthony's Hospital, Threadneedle Street, for his early schooling. It was supported by the Mercers' Guild and would have been a likely choice for a boy of his social class. It is thought that he went to Oxford in 1483 and enrolled in Magdalen College. His work there would have been shaped by the tradition of the liberal arts. The *trivium*—grammar, rhetoric, and logic—required two and a half years of effort. The *quadrivium*—arithmetic, astronomy, geometry, and music, later broadened to include natural and moral philosophy, and metaphysics—required another five and a quarter years. The curriculum led to a master of arts degree.

In 1493, Colet left England for an extended period of study on the Continent, a sojourn in France, and a longer period in Italy. The Italian Renaissance, with its emphasis on the arts and the revival of the classical languages and literature, was at its height. In Florence, the young Colet met and studied with Marsilio Ficino, who directed the Platonic Academy in Florence. Greek, Platonic, and Neoplatonic studies filled these years. Colet returned to England in the spring of 1496. In the fall of that year, Colet gained international prominence among the coterie of Humanists by a series of lectures on the Pauline epistles. Although he was not yet a deacon and had no credentials from theological courses, his use of Humanist scholarship established his reputation and began his distinguished career. At the same time, he determined on his vocation, becoming deacon in December of 1497 and ordained a priest on March 25, 1498.

LIFE'S WORK

Colet remained at Oxford until 1504, where he completed his theological training. His theological and scriptural lectures were well attended and widely discussed. Yet no stipend was paid him. He received no academic honors or titles. He lived on the income from several ecclesiastical preferments he had held since his youth. A long-standing custom of support for young men to pursue educational goals, benefices, and church offices were sometimes heaped together to bring in considerable revenue. The practice led to widespread abuse, and Colet came to be highly critical of the practice. He resigned all his preferments but one (it was supported by family) when he was appointed dean of St. Paul's Cathedral. The revenue he had saved was expended for charitable enterprises.

The Oxford years were also important to Colet for the study of patristic literature, his continued work in Greek, and the many important contacts made with other Humanists. Desiderius Erasmus, whom he met in 1498, may have been his most important friend. The relationship continued to Colet's death, and Erasmus became Colet's first biographer and publicist.

In 1504, Colet's appointment as dean of St. Paul's Cathedral began the most public and the most productive part of his life. His first effort was reform at St. Paul's. He reviewed the discipline of the Chapter and Canons, those forty or so appointed to serve in various capacities at the cathedral. He cleared the nave of sleeping beggars and the ambulatories of businessmen plying their trade within the sacred precincts. He set the tone of dedication by the simplicity and the abstinence of his own life and household.

Colet also became a powerful and effective preacher, attacking abuses in the Church and speaking out on issues he considered immoral or menacing to the human condition. He preached against war before the young king Henry VIII on Good Friday in 1513, as that monarch was about to embark on an expedition to France. Yet Colet retained the king's favor.

It was education, however, which was Colet's greatest concern. In 1509, he founded a new St. Paul's School, supported by his private fortune, which was to teach 153 boys in the tradition of the "new learning." The curriculum was liberal and centered in sound training in the

A portrait of John Colet, from a painting at Magdalen College, Oxford. (Hulton|Archive by Getty Images)

Latin and Greek languages. The hours were long and the demands many on the young scholars, their lives shaped by the dean's love of neatness, order, and simplicity. Taught by the best masters available, they were to fill the professions and the Church with a new leadership.

Colet authored a new Latin grammar with William Lily, his first headmaster and a notable grammarian. Generations of English schoolboys used it. Nothing was overlooked in Colet's plans for the school. While Colet knew many moments of satisfaction, his tenure as dean also brought problems. His denunciation of abuses in the Church incurred suspicion, and charges of heresy were brought against him. Exonerated, he continued as dean of the cathedral, admired by the circle of friends who shared his interests.

Late in his life, Colet seriously entertained the notion of retirement from the world to take up residence in a cloister. What caused him to change his plans is unknown. His last two years were also troubled by illness. In August of 1519, he made his will, disposing of his worldly goods by endowing boys who showed academic promise but were too poor to attend St. Paul's without assistance. Helpless, shortly after these efforts, he lingered on until September 16, 1519. At his death, he was buried in a simple sepulcher on the south side of the choir. William Lily wrote his equally simple epitaph.

In the seventeenth century, old St. Paul's was destroyed in the Great Fire of London, and the final resting place of Colet's remains is unknown. A bust and several portraits have survived. Each of these depicts a serious, dignified face, sensitive and thoughtful, befitting one of the sixteenth century's most important Christian Humanists.

SIGNIFICANCE

Colet, perhaps the most neglected member of a distinguished group of English Humanists, became the subject of considerable scholarship in the nineteenth century. If one reads the correspondence of Erasmus, Thomas More, or the Flemish jurist Franciscus Cranevelt, the influence of Colet on his contemporaries is evident.

Part of a group, laypeople and clerics, who sought the improvement of society, Colet believed that good education informed by Christian principles could lead to a better world. Characteristic of his circle, he recognized that the world was changing. The Church, he believed, must provide leadership in such a world. It must offer help to the poor and advice and admonition to monarchs, help to outlaw and curtail war, and enhance moral values in every class. It should provide assistance in material ways so that rehabilitation of the disadvantaged could be achieved.

Colet's sermons, tracts, and commentaries all manifest this optimistic view that with God's help, human beings can promote these lofty goods. A grammarian and linguist, he sought the purest interpretation of Scripture, although he did not believe in literal interpretation. His criticism of popular religious practices has led to a modern debate as to his loyalty to the Church of Rome that he served. His death in 1519 precludes an answer as to what might have been his role had he lived into the period of the Reformation. A moderate, his works did not manifest viewpoints at odds with historic doctrines but called for reform within the Church. His service to his peers and endless search for improved conditions of life place him high in that distinguished group known as the Christian Humanists of the Northern Renaissance.

—Anne R. Vizzier

FURTHER READING

Adams, Robert P. *The Better Part of Valor*. Seattle: University of Washington Press, 1962. The author's stated purpose is to present the reader with a study of the men and ideas of the Renaissance period. Specifically deals with the thoughts and writings of Colet, More, Erasmus, and Juan Luis Viven on war and peace. Excellent source.

Colet, John. *Letters to Radulphus on the Mosaic Account of Creation, Together with Other Treatises*. Translated by J. H. Lupton. Reprint. Ridgewood, N.J.: Gregg Press, 1966. A short treatise on the Mosaic account of the Creation. Students or general readers will gain a sense of Colet's explanation of biblical texts.

Harper-Bill, Christopher. "Dean Colet's Convocation Sermon and the Pre-Reformation Church in England." In *The Impact of the English Reformation, 1500-1640*, edited by Peter Marshall. New York: St. Martin's Press, 1997. Rereading of Colet's 1512 reformist sermon in light of recent scholarship. Seeks to achieve a more accurate understanding of the popular English attitude toward the Church in the early sixteenth century, and to reexamine the nature of Colet's criticisms. Includes bibliographic references and index.

Jayne, Sears. *John Colet and Marsilio Ficino*. Oxford, England: Clarendon Press, 1961. A specialized study that ambitiously attempts to analyze the influence of the Italian scholar and philosopher on Colet's work. It is useful to the general reader in establishing the general background of Colet's work and lists a full bibliography of his works.

Lupton, Joseph Hirst. *A Life of John Colet*. London: George Bell and Sons, 1887. Reprint. New York: Burt Franklin, 1974. A sympathetic and searching biography by a nineteenth century headmaster of St. Paul's School, one of Colet's greatest admirers and scholars. Lupton discovered twenty-eight of Colet's writings. The fullest and most satisfactory biography despite its date.

Marshall, Peter. *Reformation England, 1480-1642*. New York: Oxford University Press, 2003. Study of English religious history from Colet's time through the mid-seventeenth century. Includes bibliographic references and index.

Miles, Leland. *John Colet and the Platonic Tradition*. LaSalle, Ill.: Open Court, 1961. Examines the relationship of the Platonic tradition and the work of Colet, More, and Erasmus; a somewhat easier work on an intellectual problem.

Seebohm, Frederick. *The Oxford Reformers: John Colet, Erasmus, and Thomas More*. Reprint. New York: AMS Press, 1971. A work first written in 1867 and updated as a result of Lupton's work and discoveries, it retains much that is useful by describing the "fellow-work" of Colet, Erasmus, and More. Especially good in placing the writers in the framework of their times.

Trapp, J. B. *Erasmus, Colet, and More: The Early Tudor Humanists and Their Books*. London: British Library, 1991. Detailed catalog and analysis of all books known to be written by, owned, read, printed, or referenced by Colet, More, and Erasmus. Shows not only the specific influences of the Humanists but also their general literary milieu as well. Includes illustrations and bibliographic references.

See also: Desiderius Erasmus; Marsilio Ficino; Henry VIII; Sir Thomas More.

Related article in *Great Events from History: The Renaissance & Early Modern Era, 1454-1600:* 1499-1517: Erasmus Advances Humanism in England.

Vittoria Colonna
Italian noblewoman, church reformer, and poet

Colonna was a proponent of the early Reform movement within the Catholic Church. As an acquaintance of many of the leading ecclesiastical, artistic, and Humanist figures of her time, she was able to contribute significantly to the call for reform from various quarters. She was also a poet who wrote a number of secular sonnets in the style of Petrarch.

Born: 1492; Marino, near Rome, Papal States (now in Italy)
Died: February 25, 1547; Rome
Also known as: Victoria Colonna
Areas of achievement: Literature, religion and theology, patronage of the arts

Early Life

Vittoria Colonna (veet-TAWR-yah koh-LOHN-nah) was part of the famous Colonna family of Rome, the daughter of Fabrizio Colonna (who would become grand constable of Naples) and Agnese di Montefeltro of Urbino. Born at Marino, Vittoria was raised primarily at the family's Neapolitan residence.

Little is known about her early education, but her career as a successful poet and intellectual attests to a Humanist formation. She was betrothed at the age of four to Fernando Francesco de Ávalos, marquis of Pescara, a key Neapolitan military captain of the imperial forces of Charles V. The two were married in 1509 at Ischia, in Naples, but were frequently separated by his military campaigns. In 1525, he was wounded at the Battle of Pavia and died soon afterward. The two had no children.

Life's Work

Following her husband's death, Colonna divided her time between Ischia and Rome and traveled extensively throughout Italy. Her independence was facilitated by her position as a prominent and financially secure aristocratic widow.

Choosing to devote herself to the memory of her dead husband, she wrote a number of love sonnets mourning his death. These seem to have been widely circulated among a circle of literary acquaintances and admirers, among them Pietro Bembo and Baldassare Castiglione. Castiglione stated in the preface to his own major work, *Il libro del cortegiano* (1528; *The Book of the Courtier*, 1561), that it was Colonna's wide circulation of the work in its initial manuscript form that prompted him to publish it as quickly as possible. Colonna was one of the initial recipients of the first printed edition of *The Book of the Courtier.*

Colonna assumed a kind of secular religious life, devoting herself to the evolving Reform movement within the Catholic Church. Catholic reform was prompted by Lutheran and particularly Calvinist currents in central Europe. The early Reform preoccupation with the Pauline doctrine of justification by faith called into question the ritual and performative aspects of orthodox Catholicism, focusing instead on the spiritual concerns of individual prayer and the formation of a personal relationship with God. Some beliefs within what came to be called the *spirituali* movement, beliefs that aligned too well with Protestantism, prompted accusations of Calvinism, and while there is no evidence that Colonna would have converted to Protestantism, her association with the Capuchin evangelical Bernardino Ochino of Naples could have prompted the interest of the Inquisition. She seems to have broken with Ochino after he fled to Geneva in 1542, and, although she did not modify her religious stance, she assumed a less public profile, retiring to a convent at Viterbo. Her personal confessor, the En-

Colonna, Vittoria

THE RENAISSANCE & EARLY MODERN ERA

glish cardinal Reginald Pole, was also instrumental in preventing a rupture with the Church.

Colonna wrote her love poems in the 1520's and the early 1530's, and then turned her attention completely to her spiritual poems, the most famous of which is "The Triumph of Christ's Cross," a meditation on the body of Christ as an offering for the salvation of humankind, the precise subject that preoccupied Michelangelo in his late depictions of the *Pietà* (1499). A complete edition of Colonna's poems, *Rime della divina Vettoria Colonna, marchesana di Pescara*, was published for the first time in around 1539.

There is some evidence that Colonna was a patron of the arts, and her interest in particular religious subjects mirrored her devotional sympathies. In the early 1530's, through the agency of her brother-in-law, Alfonso de Ávalos, marquis of Vasto, and Federigo II Gonzaga of Mantua, she obtained a painting of Mary Magdalene from Titian (now lost, but a painting of the same iconographic type is now in the Pitti collection in Florence). The Magdalene painting was the epitome of female religious devotion; her close personal relationship with Christ was embraced as an exemplar of salvation through individual spiritual devotion by women of Colonna's sympathies.

In the late 1530's, in Rome, Colonna's religious sympathies brought her into contact with Michelangelo, with whom she exchanged a series of letters on religious themes. The letters can also be related to Michelangelo's execution of two drawings for Colonna, *Pietà* and *Crucifixion*. A third drawing, *Christ and the Woman of Samaria*, was also inspired by this relationship. Colonna's sonnets addressed these subjects as well. In his turn, Michelangelo also wrote sonnets dedicated to his spiritual love for Colonna. Their friendship was also documented by the Portuguese artist Francisco de Holanda, who recorded his memories of Colonna and Michelangelo in his *Dialogo da pintura* (1548; *Four Dialogues on Painting*, 1928).

After Ochino's definitive departure from Rome in 1542, Colonna succumbed to a series of debilitating illnesses that confined her largely to various convents at Viterbo. She died February 25, 1547, with Michelangelo at her side.

SIGNIFICANCE

Colonna was able to persuade and encourage reform-minded individuals to support changes within the Catholic faith, as she made contact with many through her friendships and through sharing her religious sonnets.

Scholars, however, are just beginning to understand Colonna's significance also as an exemplar to aristocratic widows of the Catholic reform period. The aristocratic women who shared Colonna's interest in religious reform followed her example by using their social and financial status to contribute to the building of monasteries and to the support of reformed religious orders, particularly in Rome.

—*Sally Hickson*

FURTHER READING
Gibaldi, Joseph. "Vittoria Colonna: Child, Woman, and Poet." In *Women Writers of the Renaissance and Reformation*, edited by Katherina M. Wilson. Athens: University of Georgia Press, 1987. Provides a brief biographical sketch and an analysis of both secular and sacred sonnets in the broader context of other female poets of the period.
Jerrold, Maud. *Vittoria Colonna: With Some Account of Her Friends and Her Times*. New York: E. P. Dutton, 1906. Still the only complete biography in English, based on documentary evidence. Slightly out of date with respect to the interpretation of Colonna's reform activities.
Och, Marjorie. "Vittoria Colonna and the Commission for a Mary Magdalene by Titian." In *Beyond Isabella: Secular Women Patrons of Art in Renaissance Italy*, edited by Sheryl E. Reiss and David G. Wilkins. Kirksville, Mo.: Truman State University Press, 2001. A complete overview of the commission to Titian for a Mary Magdalene, with specific reference to the contextual interpretation of Magdalene images in artistic and religious circles of the period. Includes the complete file of documents on this commission.
Wood, Jeryldene M. "Vittoria Colonna's Mary Magdalen." In *Visions of Holiness: Art and Devotion in Renaissance Italy*, edited by Andrew Ladis and Shelley E. Zuraw. Athens: Georgia Museum of Art, University of Georgia, 2001. Examines Colonna's interest in the image of Mary Magdalene as an expression of her Reform beliefs, and traces the specifics of her commission to Titian in light of the iconographical canons detectable in her poetry on the Magdalene. Also considers Colonna's development of a personal iconography in her commissions and portrait medals.

SEE ALSO: Barbe Acarie; Lucrezia Borgia; Baldassare Castiglione; Charles V; Gregory XIII; Isabella d'Este;

236

Marguerite de Navarre; Michelangelo; Saint Philip Neri; Saint Teresa of Ávila; Titian.

RELATED ARTICLES in *Great Events from History: The Renaissance & Early Modern Era, 1454-1600:* 1469-1492: Rule of Lorenzo de' Medici; 1477-1482: Work Begins on the Sistine Chapel; c. 1500: Revival of Classical Themes in Art; 1500: Roman Jubilee; 1508-1512 and 1534-1541: Michelangelo Paints the Sistine Chapel; 1528: Castiglione's *Book of the Courtier* Is Published.

CHRISTOPHER COLUMBUS
Italian explorer

Columbus's expedition to the Americas was the first recorded transatlantic voyage. It led directly to Europe's colonial settlement and exploitation of the New World, and it altered the course of Western history.

BORN: Between August 25 and October 31, 1451; Genoa (now in Italy)
DIED: May 20, 1506; Valladolid, Spain
ALSO KNOWN AS: Cristóbal Colón; Colombo Cristoforo
AREA OF ACHIEVEMENT: Exploration

EARLY LIFE

Christopher Columbus's father, Domenico, was a wool weaver and gatekeeper in Genoa. In 1470, he moved his family to nearby Savona, where he worked as an innkeeper. Christopher Columbus was the eldest of five children, of whom Bartolomé and Diego played a large part in his life. Christopher had little formal education, having become an apprentice at sea at about age ten, not entirely surprising in the great port city of Genoa. His knowledge of mathematics, astronomy, and Latin came with experience.

Columbus's early days at sea brought him as far as Tunis and Chios, a Greek island that was then a Genoese possession. He next traveled to Ireland, Iceland, and Madeira, where, in 1478, he married Felipa Perestrello e Moniz of a noble Portuguese family with a hereditary title to govern Porto Santo, one of the Madeira islands. They had a son, Diego, and Columbus resided in Porto Santo for perhaps three years and worked as a seaman or merchant.

In the early 1480's, having sailed in either capacity to São Jorge da Mina on Africa's Gold Coast, then the southernmost point in the known world, Columbus gained experience of the south Atlantic. By 1484, his hair prematurely white, he had conceived the plan for a great *empresa de las Indias* (enterprise of the Indies). In that year, the Portuguese king John II rejected Columbus's idea of reaching Cathay, the islands of Japan, and India by sailing westward. Portugal was deeply committed to its search for an African route to India.

The concept of sailing westward was not new; indeed, it did not even originate with Columbus. A mathematician from Florence, Paolo Toscanelli dal Pozzo, had articulated this idea in a letter with a map sent to Prince Henry the Navigator in 1474. It was, moreover, widely accepted that the world was round. Columbus had researched his plan well. Perhaps he had seen Toscanelli's letter in the archives. Certainly he had read Marco Polo and Ptolemy. These books and Pierre d'Ailly's *Imago mundi* (c. 1483; English translation, 1927), which Columbus had studied—he made hundreds of marginal notes in his copy—were authoritative at that time, though filled with errors tending to understate the size of the earth. The miscalculation of the journey's length by about two-thirds nearly destroyed Columbus's project.

By 1486, Portugal's repeated failure to cut through the Congo (Kongo) or to attain the southern tip of Africa allowed Columbus's plan a second hearing. In 1488, however, Bartolomeu Dias rounded the Cape of Good Hope, and Columbus was again disappointed in Portugal. Henry VII of England entertained the offer of Columbus's agent, brother Bartolomé. Yet it was Ferdinand II and Isabella of Spain who, after shunting his proposals into committee for four years, finally, in the flush of victory over Muslim Granada early in 1492, awarded him his chance. The Franciscan friar and astronomer Antonio de Merchena had helped him gain an interview with Isabella in about 1490, and court treasurer Luis de Santangel finally gained for Columbus Isabella's support by pledges of Jewish investment in the project.

During his pursuit of the Spanish royal court, Columbus had acquired in Córdoba a mistress, Beatriz Enríquez de Harana. She bore him a son, Fernando, who wrote an affectionate and thorough biography that is a chief source for modern knowledge about Columbus.

LIFE'S WORK

Fernando relates the exorbitant terms by which the Spanish monarchs agreed to grant Columbus 10 percent of all the gold or other goods acquired in the lands he might discover; he and his heirs were to hold the titles of Admiral of the Ocean Sea and viceroy of such lands. He was provided with two ships of the caravel type, the *Niña* and the *Pinta*, procured by Martín Alonso Pinzón of the port city of Palos; the round-bellied neotype *Santa Maria* was chartered from its owner by Columbus. For his efforts in raising money and crews numbering ninety men in all, mostly from Palos, and for his skill in commanding the *Pinta*, Pinzón would later claim a share in the credit and glory of Columbus's discoveries. The two smaller vessels were about fifty feet long, and the *Santa Maria* was about eighty-two feet long. They were equipped for any contingency with weapons, a translator of Hebrew and Arabic to deal with the Mongol ruler Kublai Khan if found, and goods to sell for gold.

The first voyage of Columbus left Palos on August 3, 1492. After a stopover at Spain's Canary Islands, the tiny fleet began its ocean trek on September 6. Constantly favorable trade winds caused the sailors to despair at ever gaining a wind to aid their return home. The southwesterly flights of birds persuaded Columbus to accept Pinzón's advice to change his course to the southwest. A *Niña* lookout was the first to sight land. Columbus named the land San Salvador, landed, and, thinking he had reached an outlying island of Japan, claimed it for Spain.

Japan, and Cathay itself, he thought, must be only ten days distant. The search brought him to what are modern Haiti and the Dominican Republic, which together he named Hispaniola (little Spain). The Arawaks were simple hunter-fishers who wore almost no clothes. Columbus was charmed by their courtesy. The Cubans were equally friendly. Arawak references to the *caniba* people (cannibals) and Cuban allusions to gold in the interior at Cubanacam further conjured images of Marco Polo's khan in Columbus's mind. Establishing the Hispaniola

Nineteenth century engraving from Harper's New Monthly Magazine *depicting Christopher Columbus's arrival in Hispaniola (Haiti).* (The Institute of Texan Cultures)

settlement of Navidad, the first in the New World, to organize gold-mining operations, Columbus departed for Spain before a favorable west wind, carrying six Arawak captives and news of the discovery of tobacco.

Having lost Pinzón with the *Pinta*, which departed on November 21, and the *Santa Maria*, on a reef on Christmas Day, 1492, Columbus had only the *Niña* for his return. He suspected Pinzón of trying to precede him to the khan, or to the sources of the gold, or back to Spain to claim the honor for his own discoveries. Therefore, their meeting at sea on January 6, 1493, precipitated a quarrel between the two captains. It was not until January 16 that the transatlantic return voyage commenced. Storms blew the *Niña* first into the Portuguese Azores on February 18 and then into Lisbon on March 9, causing King John II to charge Spain with illegal explorations of the African coast and to claim Columbus's discoveries for Portugal. This litigation was later settled in Spain's favor by the pope. Columbus's arrival in Palos on March 14 and subsequent reception by Ferdinand and Isabella at Barcelona at the end of April, accompanied by American Indians in full ceremonial dress, was the admiral's greatest moment.

The royal announcement of a second voyage was met with numerous volunteers. A fleet of seventeen ships and fifteen hundred men departed Cádiz on September 25, 1493. On board were animals, seeds, plants, and tools for the establishment of a colony. Among Columbus's discoveries were Dominica Island (spied on Sunday), the Virgin Islands, and Puerto Rico. He found Navidad, however, destroyed by the indigenous and its settlers slain. Farther east on the north coast of what is now the Dominican Republic, he built the first European city in the New World, which he named Isabella. Leaving his brother Diego in charge there, he himself led the exploration of Cibao, the inland mountainous region of Hispaniola. There he founded the fortress settlement of Santo Tomás. He had still not seen the khan, but Columbus did discover Jamaica on May 5, 1494.

Convinced that Cuba was indeed the Asiatic mainland, Columbus forced his crew to sign an agreement to that effect. Back in Isabella, Columbus found the settlers angry and the indigenous in rebellion. Diego had been inadequate to the task of governing. Columbus's response

---

FROM COLUMBUS'S LOG

Christopher Columbus first encountered indigenous Americans in October of 1492. This passage from his personal log details his initial plans and interactions with these inhabitants of the Bahamas.

I want the natives to develop a friendly attitude toward us because I know that they are a people who can be made free and converted to our Holy Faith more by love than by force. I therefore gave red caps to some and glass beads to others. They hung the beads around their necks, along with some other things of slight value that I gave them. And they took great pleasure in this and became so friendly that it was a marvel.

Source: From *The Log of Christopher Columbus*, translated by Robert H. Fuson (Camden, Maine: International Marine, 1987), p. 76.

---

was to ship five hundred indigenous people to the slave market at Seville. Those who survived the journey, however, were returned to Hispaniola by the monarchs, who may have had in mind a more humane program of Christianization and agricultural exploitation for the colonies.

Columbus left Hispaniola again on March 10, 1496, leaving his brother Bartolomé to build a settlement at Santo Domingo. In the short space of four years since the coming of the Europeans, a flourishing indigenous population had been decimated by exploitation, massacre, disease, and famine. Charges of misgovernment and cruelty greeted his arrival in Cádiz on June 11.

For Columbus's third voyage in six ships, there were no volunteers. Indeed, the two-hundred-man crew had to be shanghaied or bribed by release from prison. Departure was from Sanlúcar, near Cádiz, on May 30, 1498. Sailing a more southerly route, the fleet was becalmed eight days in unbearable heat. On July 31, Columbus named three-peaked Trinidad, and the next day, the fleet first spied the South American mainland. The first Europeans landed in the Paria Peninsula of Venezuela on August 5. Noting the fresh water flowing from the Orinoco River and the pearls worn by the women, Columbus believed that this was one of the four rivers of the Garden of Eden.

Arriving to find violence and syphilis in Hispaniola, Columbus was returned to reality. He came to terms with his rebellious governor, Francisco Roldán, only by means of the infamous *repartimiento*, or distribution of indigenous serfs among the settlers as laborers and miners. On August 23, 1500, Francisco de Bobadilla arrived, sent by Ferdinand to replace Columbus as viceroy. In response to the admiral's resistance, Bobadilla sent Columbus and Diego back to Spain in chains.

Yet Columbus won the sympathy of the royal couple. On May 9, 1502, with brother Bartolomé and son Fernando, age thirteen, Columbus left on his "high voyage" (*alto viaje*) to find a way through Hispaniola to the Indian Ocean and restore his reputation. He was specifically prohibited, however, from landing at Hispaniola, where Nicolás de Ovando now governed with twenty-five hundred men.

Fernando records Ovando's flotilla making for Spain after ignoring Columbus's warnings of a storm at sea; twenty of twenty-four ships were lost. Fernando also relates the discovery of Martinique in the Lesser Antilles, the exploration of the coasts of Nicaragua and Costa Rica, and the acquisition of gold from the indigenous of Honduras. The Isthmus of Panama blocked all access to an "Indian Ocean." Ovando could not have known that he was only forty miles from the Pacific Ocean.

Columbus ultimately fared little better. His entry into the unexplored western Caribbean Sea cost him more than a year at sea and the loss of his ships to storm and sea worms. Ovando waited another year before extricating the marooned men from Saint Ann's Bay in June, 1504. Sick in body and mind but rich with gold and new maps, Columbus reached Sanlúcar on November 7, 1504. The queen would die on November 26. He saw only a disinterested Ferdinand the following spring at Segovia.

SIGNIFICANCE

Columbus spent his last years in vain demands for his rights and titles under the original royal charter and back pay for his men. Nevertheless, his share of the wealth of what came to be called the West Indies allowed him to live comfortably. His son Diego did retain the titles of admiral and viceroy after a long litigation. Columbus's library fell to Fernando, who bequeathed it, as the Biblioteca Colombina, to the Cathedral of Seville, where it remains. Columbus's body was eventually buried in the Cathedral of Santo Domingo (Hispaniola), but its specific site is uncertain.

Columbus believed himself guided by Providence and biblical prophecy in all his undertakings, a faith that made him intolerant of opposition and capable of great brutality in the name of God. His instincts at sea were regarded by his sailors as divine. He found winds and currents and reckoned directions as if inspired. His achievements were immense. European economic and political power would leave the Mediterranean lands and focus forever on the Americas.

—*Daniel C. Scavone*

FURTHER READING

Colón, Fernando. *The Life of Admiral Christopher Columbus by His Son, Ferdinand.* Translated by Benjamin Keen. New Brunswick, N.J.: Rutgers University Press, 1959. An intimate and affectionate biography by Columbus's son. Fernando's book is the basis of all the extremely favorable accounts of Columbus's career.

Davidson, Miles H. *Columbus Then and Now: A Life Reexamined.* Norman: University of Oklahoma Press, 1997. Rigorous reconsideration of Columbus's life surveys and criticizes decades of Columbus biographers for their unreflective and outright errors. Davidson is especially critical of Morison's biography, and of those later biographers who follow it. Includes maps, bibliographic references, index.

Fuson, Robert H., trans. *The Log of Christopher Columbus.* Camden, Maine: International Marine, 1987. This translation is based on the abstract of Columbus's log made by Bartolomé de Las Casas, with additions from his *Historia de las Indias* (1875-1876) and from Fernando Columbus's history of the Columbus family.

Heat-Moon, William Least. *Columbus in the Americas.* Hoboken, N.J.: John Wiley, 2002. Careful reappraisal of Columbus as explorer, colonizer, and man, by a best-selling Native American author. Heat-Moon uses many quotations from Columbus's journals to provide insight into the thoughts and motives of the explorer. Includes maps.

Landström, Björn. *Columbus.* London: Allen & Unwin, 1967. Ample illustrations, especially maps and ship designs, are extremely useful for illuminating the background, life, and voyages of Columbus. This is an interestingly written biography.

Madariaga, Salvador de. *Christopher Columbus: Being the Life of the Very Magnificent Lord Don Cristóbal Colón.* New York: Macmillan, 1940. An engrossing biography of immense scholarship. Its extensive notes support a thorough discussion of debated Columbian issues. This book must be read by anyone serious about Columbus.

Morison, Samuel Eliot. *Admiral of the Ocean Sea.* Rev. ed. New York: Book-of-the-Month Club, 1992. This is an eminently readable biography. Emphasizes Columbus as a seaman more than as an administrator. Does not stop at the "water's edge," as Morison claims other biographies do.

_____. *The European Discovery of America: The Southern Voyages, A.D. 1492-1616*. New York: Oxford University Press, 1974. Devotes eight chapters to Columbus, viewing him in the larger context of his southern voyages. This volume, by a lifelong student of Columbus, features photographs of coastlines as Columbus might have seen them. Includes forty-two pages of maps.

Summerhill, Stephen J., and John Alexander Williams. *Sinking Columbus: Contested History, Cultural Politics, and Mythmaking During the Quincentenary*. Gainesville: University Press of Florida, 2000. Thorough examination of the contemporary legacy of Columbus as seen through the lens of the failure of the planned five hundredth anniversary celebration of his voyage. Includes illustrations, bibliographic references, index.

SEE ALSO: Pedro de Alvarado; Vasco Núñez de Balboa; John Cabot; Hernán Cortés; Pêro da Covilhã; Bartolomeu Dias; Juan Sebastián de Elcano; Ferdinand II and Isabella I; Guacanagarí; Henry VII; John II; Bartolomé de Las Casas; The Pinzón Brothers; Juan Ponce de León; Amerigo Vespucci.

RELATED ARTICLES in *Great Events from History: The Renaissance & Early Modern Era, 1454-1600:* 1462: Regiomontanus Completes the *Epitome* of Ptolemy's *Almagest*; October 12, 1492: Columbus Lands in the Americas; June 7, 1494: Treaty of Tordesillas; 1495-1510: West Indian Uprisings; Beginning c. 1500: Coffee, Cacao, Tobacco, and Sugar Are Sold Worldwide; 16th century: Worldwide Inflation; 1516: Sir Thomas More Publishes *Utopia*; 1552: Las Casas Publishes *The Tears of the Indians*.

NICOLAUS COPERNICUS
Polish astronomer

Copernicus dismissed the Ptolemaic system and introduced the theory that the planets, including Earth, revolve around the sun. He defended the rights of the educated to discuss scientific theories, even when those theories differ from currently accepted beliefs and contradict religious dogma.

BORN: February 19, 1473; Thorn, Prussia (now Toruń, Poland)
DIED: May 24, 1543; Frauenburg, East Prussia (now Frombork, Poland)
ALSO KNOWN AS: Mikołaj Kopernik
AREAS OF ACHIEVEMENT: Astronomy, church reform

EARLY LIFE

The family origins of Nicolaus Copernicus (nihk-uh-LAY-uhs kuh-PUHR-nih-kuhs) and the commercial interests of his hometown, Thorn, reflect the dual claim that Germans and Poles alike have on him. His father, also named Mikołaj (Nicolaus) Kopernik, was an immigrant from Kraków who married a daughter of a prominent burgher family, Barbara Watzenrode, and like other Thorn merchants, prospered from the exchange of Hanseatic goods for the wheat, cattle, and other produce of Poland. Thorn burghers were subjects of the Polish king, but Polish tradition allowed associated lands such as

Prussia to govern themselves autonomously. Consequently, they made their political wishes felt through their representatives in the Prussian diet rather than directly to the king.

Had Mikołaj not died in 1483, his sons, Andreas and Nicolaus, would probably have entered into careers in commerce. Their guardianship, however, fell to their uncle, Bishop Lucas Watzenrode of Ermland (Warmia), who was best able to provide for them a future in church administration. A university education being indispensable to holding church offices, Bishop Lucas sent the boys to study first in Kraków, then in Italy. Nicolaus not only became a master of mathematics and astronomy but also acquired knowledge of medicine, painting, and Greek.

On his return to Prussia in 1503, Nicolaus followed the contemporary practice of Latinizing his name, Copernicus, and became one of the canons in the Ermland cathedral chapter. As his uncle's physician, assistant, and heir apparent, Copernicus was present during inspection tours, provincial diets, and royal audiences. For several years, he managed the diocese efficiently but without enthusiasm—his uncle was a hard taskmaster who lacked a sense of humor. Eventually, Copernicus announced that his interests in astronomy were greater than his ambition to become a bishop. From that time on, like most of the other canons, he lived according to clerical rules but remained a simple administrator who had no thought of becoming a priest.

LIFE'S WORK

The first of several portraits made during his lifetime show Copernicus to have been handsome and dressed in simple but elegant clothing, with nothing of either the cleric or the dandy about him. He was so utterly unremarkable in other respects that few anecdotes about him exist, leaving relatively little information about his personal life and intellectual development. Yet two facts stand out. First, Copernicus was a Humanist whose closest friends and associates were poets and polemicists. His translation of an ancient author, Theophilactus Symocatta, from Greek into Latin was the first such publication in the Kingdom of Poland, and he dedicated the work to his Humanistically trained uncle, Bishop Lucas. Copernicus later used Humanist arguments to defend his astronomical theories.

Second, Copernicus must be seen as a bureaucrat whose busy life made it difficult for him to make the observations of the heavens on which his mathematical calculations were based. At one time or another, he was a medical doctor, an astrologer, a cartographer, an administrator of episcopal lands, a diplomat, a garrison commander in wartime, an economic theorist, an adviser to the Prussian diet, and a guardian to numerous nieces and nephews.

About 1507, Copernicus seems to have become persuaded that the Ptolemaic system (which asserted that Earth was the center of the universe) was incorrect. From that point on, he spent every spare moment trying to demonstrate the correctness of his insight that the sun was the center of the planetary movements (the solar system).

His first description of his theory, the *Commentariolus* (1514; English translation, 1939), circulated among his friends for many years. Eventually, it came to the ears of Cardinal Schönberg, who wrote a letter asking Copernicus to publish a fuller account. This letter was ultimately published in *De revolutionibus orbium coelestium* (1543; *On the Revolutions of the Heavenly Spheres,* 1952; better known as *De revolutionibus*) as a proof that high officials in the papal curia approved of scholars discussing the existence of a solar system. Copernicus made no answer. Instead, he asked his bishop to assign him light duties at some parish center, where he could make his observations and concentrate on mathematical calculations. This request was difficult to grant because Co-

Nicolaus Copernicus. (Library of Congress)

pernicus was known to be one of the more capable diocesan administrators.

For several years, his work was interrupted by war. In 1520, the last grandmaster of the Teutonic Order, Albrecht of Brandenburg, made a final effort to reestablish his religious order as ruler of all Prussia. Copernicus led the defense of Allenstein (Olsztyn) and participated in the peace negotiations. In 1525, Albrecht, defeated at every turn, secularized the Teutonic Order in Prussia and became a Protestant vassal of the king of Poland. This brought about an immediate improvement of Albrecht's relationship to the rest of Prussia. Albrecht later called on Copernicus's services as physician, and in 1551, he published a volume of Copernicus's astrological observations.

Copernicus labored for several years to restore order to the war-ravaged Ermland finances. He advised the Prussian diet to reform the monetary system, explaining that since everyone was hoarding good coins and paying taxes with debased coins, the income of the diet was being reduced significantly. Having expounded this early version of English financier Sir Thomas Gresham's law, he recommended that all coins be called in and new ones issued. The diet, aware that it did not have the bullion to mint a sufficient number of full-weight coins, took no action. There were other, more pressing problems: politics and religion.

The spread of Lutheran reforms through Poland was halted by royal action, but not before many cities and some prominent nobles had become Protestant. The ensuing era was filled with strident debate as fanatics on both sides denounced their opponents and demanded that all parties commit themselves to what they perceived as a struggle against ultimate evil. Copernicus sought to avoid this controversy but could not. When Ermland bishop Johann Dantiscus sought to rid himself of all canons who gave any appearance of Protestant leanings, his eye fell on Copernicus, whose friends were corresponding with prominent Protestants and who, moreover, had as his housekeeper a young woman with children. Copernicus responded that his housekeeper was a widowed relative who could have no interest in a man as aged as he, but he argued in vain. He dismissed his housekeeper and watched as his friends went into exile. His health failing, Copernicus was indeed isolated from friends and family.

In 1539, a Lutheran mathematician at Wittenberg, Rheticus, made a special journey to Frauenburg to visit Copernicus. Finding him ill and without prospect of publishing the manuscript he had completed at great labor, Rheticus extended his stay to three months so that he could personally copy the manuscript. He then arranged for the publication of *Narratio prima de libris revolutionum* (1540; *The First Account*, 1939) in Danzig and for the publication of the mathematical section in Nuremberg in 1542. Unable to supervise the printing of the theoretical section personally, Rheticus gave that task to another Protestant scholar, Andreas Osiander of Wittenberg.

Osiander was at a loss as to how to proceed. He saw that Copernicus had not been able to prove his case mathematically. Indeed, it would have been difficult for him to do so without inventing calculus (which was later created by Gottfried Wilhelm Leibniz and Sir Isaac Newton independently of each other for the very purpose of calculating the elliptical orbits of the planets). Consequently, Copernicus had defended his ideas by demonstrating that Ptolemy's was not the only ancient theory describ-

ing the universe; indeed, there were ancient philosophers who believed that the sun was the center of the solar system. Moreover, he had argued that free inquiry into science was as necessary as freedom to write literature or produce fine art. In this respect, Copernicus was presenting his case to Renaissance Humanists, especially to the well-educated pope to whom he dedicated his book, as a test of free thought.

Osiander, who perceived that the Catholic world was hostile to all innovations and was equally well aware of the debates raging in the Protestant world over biblical inerrancy, saw that Copernicus was treading on dangerous ground by suggesting an alternate view of the universe than the one presented in Scripture. Consequently, there was a real danger that the theory would be rejected entirely without having been read. To minimize that possibility, he wrote an unauthorized introduction that readers assumed was by Copernicus. This stated that the solar system was merely a hypothesis, a way of seeing the universe that avoided some of the problems of the Ptolemaic system. This led to much confusion and angered Copernicus considerably when he saw the page proofs. Copernicus, however, was too weak and ill to do anything about it. With a justice that is all too rare in this world, a copy of

---

COPERNICUS'S HELIOCENTRIC SOLAR SYSTEM

Nicolaus Copernicus moved against the tide of his time by proposing in his De revolutionibus, *known in English as* On the Revolutions of the Heavenly Spheres, *that the sun was at the center of the known universe, a theory that countered the longstanding geocentric theory of Ptolemy and of Scripture.*

Why should we hesitate to grant it [Earth] a motion, natural and corresponding to its form, rather than assume that the whole world [the universe], whose boundary is not known and cannot be known, moves? And why are we not willing to acknowledge that the appearance of a daily revolution belongs to the heavens, its actuality to the earth. . . .

In the middle of all dwells the Sun. Who indeed in this most beautiful temple would place the torch in any other or better place than one whence it can illuminate the whole at the same time? Not ineptly, some call it the lamp of the universe, others its mind, others again its ruler—Trismegistus, the visible God, Sophocles' Electra the contemplation of all things. And thus rightly inasmuch as the Sun, sitting on a royal throne, governs the circumambient family of stars. . . . We find, therefore, under this orderly arrangement, a wonderful symmetry in the universe, and a definite relation of harmony in the motion and magnitude of the orbs, of a kind it is not possible to obtain in any other way.

Source: The Portable Renaissance Reader, edited by James Bruce Ross and Mary Martin McLaughlin (New York: Viking Press, 1968), pp. 592-593.

De revolutionibus arrived in time for him to know that his life's work was to survive.

SIGNIFICANCE

Copernicus's theory was not immediately accepted, and not because of the controversies of the Reformation alone—although they made it dangerous for any scientist to suggest that the biblical descriptions of the heavens were incorrect. Copernicus's idealistic belief that God would create only perfectly circular planetary orbits made it impossible for him to prove his assertions mathematically. Nevertheless, Copernicus's theory was the only one to offer astronomers a way out of a Ptolemaic system of interlocking rings, which was becoming impossibly complex. His insights undermined the intellectual pretensions of astrology and set astronomy on a firm foundation of observation and mathematics.

Although Copernicus's defense of the freedom of inquiry was less important in the struggle against religious dogmatism than later demonstrations of the existence of the solar system, Copernicus became a symbol of the isolated and despised scientist who triumphs over all efforts by religious fundamentalists to silence him.

—*William Urban*

FURTHER READING

Armitage, Angus. *Sun, Stand Thou Still: The Life and Works of Copernicus, the Astronomer.* New York: Henry Schuman, 1947. The best-known of many biographies, its explanation of the conceptual problems facing Copernicus is easily followed by any good reader.

Barrett, Peter. *Science and Theology Since Copernicus: The Search for Understanding.* Reprint. Poole, Dorset, England: T&T Clark, 2003. Traces the legacy of Copernicus over four hundred years. Examines the history of the debate between science and Christianity, attempting to fashion a philosophical basis for the simultaneous embrace of scientific method and religious faith in the modern world.

Beer, Arthur. *Copernicus Yesterday and Today.* Elmsford, N.Y.: Pergamon Press, 1975. A collection of useful essays that were delivered during the Copernicus celebration.

Copernicus, Nicolaus. *Three Copernican Treatises: The Commentariolus of Copernicus, The Letter Against Werner, The Narratio Prima of Rheticus.* Edited and translated by Edward Rosen. 3d ed., rev. New York: Octagon Books, 1971. This timeless translation of basic documents relating to Copernicus's achievement is accompanied by an extensive learned commentary. Rosen demonstrates that Copernicus put forward a "hypothesis" rather than a "theory" out of a fear of arousing opposition from religious fundamentalists rather than from any doubt that he was right. The third edition includes a biography of Copernicus and bibliographies of works written about Copernicus between 1939 and 1970.

Gingerich, Owen. *The Book Nobody Read: Chasing the Revolutions of Nicolaus Copernicus.* New York: Walker, 2004. A fascinating and original work of scholarship. Gingerich spent years tracking down and examining every extant copy of the original printing of Copernicus's *De revolutionibus.* Using this bibliographic analysis, he demonstrates who read the work, what they thought of it, and how exactly Copernicus's ideas spread throughout Europe. Includes illustrations, photographic plates, maps, bibliographic references, and index.

Henry, John. *Moving Heaven and Earth: Copernicus and the Solar System.* Cambridge, England: Icon, 2001. Argues that Copernicus's discovery had revolutionary effects for the cultural status afforded to theoretical science and mathematics in Western culture. He asserts that before Copernicus, pure knowledge was believed to come only from the traditions of ancient scholars, whose work was preserved only in fragments. Copernicus demonstrated that abstract mathematics and formal scientific inquiry could produce pure knowledge on their own, thereby transforming the nature of thought and truth in the West. Includes illustrations and bibliographic index.

Kesten, Hermann. *Copernicus and His World.* New York: Roy, 1945. This biography deals with Copernicus's contemporaries as much as with the astronomer himself. Kesten presents Copernicus as a warrior in the contest between science and religion. He concludes with chapters on Giordano Bruno, Tycho Brahe, Johannes Kepler, and Galileo.

Rusinek, Michat. *The Land of Nicholas Copernicus.* Translated by A. T. Jordan. New York: Twayne, 1973. The text is relatively sparse, but the pictures are unequaled in quality. The author traces the life of the astronomer through photographs of cities, castles, and personal possessions.

Stachiewicz, Wanda M. *Copernicus and the Changing World.* New York: Polish Institute, 1973. The four hundredth anniversary of Copernicus's birth brought forth many publications. This one is unique.

SEE ALSO: Tycho Brahe; Giordano Bruno; Girolamo Fracastoro; William Gilbert; John Napier; Georg von Peuerbach; Rheticus.
RELATED ARTICLES in *Great Events from History: The Renaissance & Early Modern Era, 1454-1600:* 1462: Regiomontanus Completes the *Epitome* of Ptolemy's *Almagest*; 1500: Roman Jubilee; 1543: Copernicus Publishes *De Revolutionibus*; 1582: Gregory XIII Reforms the Calendar.

FRANCISCO VÁSQUEZ DE CORONADO
Spanish conquistador

As the leader of the 1540-1542 expedition to the Seven Cities of Cíbola and Quivira, Coronado explored what became Arizona, Texas, New Mexico, Oklahoma, and Kansas and opened what is now the southwestern United States to Spanish colonization and settlement.

BORN: 1510; Salamanca, Spain
DIED: September 22, 1554; Tenochtitlán, Aztec Empire (now Mexico City, Mexico)
AREA OF ACHIEVEMENT: Exploration

EARLY LIFE

Francisco Vásquez de Coronado (frahn-SEES-koh VAHS-kayz day kaw-ruh-NAHD-oh) was the second son of noble parents, Juan Vásquez de Coronado and Isabel de Luján (his proper family name was Vásquez, but Americans mistakenly call him Coronado). Only a few details abut his childhood are known. His father became governor (*corregidor*) of Burgos in 1512, an important royal appointment. In 1520, his father created an entailed estate, whereby the family property passed to Francisco's older brother Gonzalo. Although the other children received onetime settlements, with provision made for their education, they had to make their own way in life.

Coronado decided to seek his fortune in the New World. Handsome (perhaps fair complexioned, if a portrait of his brother Juan is any indication), generous, modest, and loyal, Coronado was a favorite at court and won the friendship and patronage of Antonio de Mendoza, the first viceroy of New Spain. Coronado sailed with Mendoza, arriving in Mexico City in November, 1535.

LIFE'S WORK

Mendoza's patronage was invaluable. In 1537, he chose Coronado to put down a rebellion of black miners. The following year, the viceroy named his young friend to a seat on the Mexico City council without even seeking royal approval for his appointment. Meanwhile, Coronado helped found the Brotherhood of the Blessed Sacrament for Charity, which provided alms for the needy and educated orphan girls. He was also married, to Beatriz de Estrada, whose father, Alonso de Estrada, had been New Spain's royal treasurer and was rumored to have been the illegitimate son of King Ferdinand. His wife's dowry included half of a large country estate. Coronado, the fortune seeker, had become a landed country gentleman. The marriage produced five children.

Again the viceroy called on Coronado. A serious Mexican Indian rebellion had convulsed the mining towns of New Galicia (northwestern Mexico), and Mendoza sent Coronado to suppress it and act as governor of the region. Coronado surmised that the Mexican Indians had risen because of horrible abuse and exploitation at the hands of the Spaniards.

News had begun to filter into Mexico about rich Indian cities lying far to the north. First had come Álvar Núñez Cabeza de Vaca, who had survived Panfilo de Narváez's disastrous expedition to Florida. He staggered into Mexico in 1536, with tantalizing but enigmatic stories about seven great and wealthy cities to the north. Mendoza sent Fray Marcos de Niza to verify Cabeza de Vaca's stories in early 1539. Coronado accompanied the friar on his way through New Galicia to the Seven Cities but then returned to his duties as governor. Fray Marcos returned in the fall, claiming to have actually visited Cíbola, the land of the Seven Cities. His report was more wondrous than Cabeza de Vaca's. Mendoza and Coronado began to plan an expedition to explore and conquer Cíbola. Speed was important. Charles V had commissioned Hernando de Soto, the new governor of Cuba and Florida, to explore north from Florida, and Hernán Cortés himself had returned from Spain, anxious to claim Cíbola as his own.

While men gathered in New Galicia for the expedition, Mendoza and Coronado dispatched another scouting party to Cíbola under Melchior Díaz, who was more knowledgeable about the northern frontier than any Spaniard. Before Díaz returned, a force of more than three hundred Spaniards was ready at Compostela, along with several priests, perhaps a thousand Mexican Indian allies, and about fifteen hundred horses and pack animals. Although subject to the viceregal government, the expedition was privately financed. Mendoza invested sixty thousand ducats in it, and Coronado, fifty thousand ducats from his wife's estate. Mendoza initially hoped to lead the foray himself but eventually named Coronado to head it on January 6, 1540. Meanwhile, a small squadron under Hernando de Alarcón was to sail up the Gulf of California and support Coronado by sea, although Alarcón never did find Coronado.

The Coronado party set out from Compostela on February 23, 1540, without waiting for Díaz's report, but met the scout at Chiametla. He secretly told Coronado that he had been to Cíbola and had found no gold, silver, or great cities. Rumors about the report upset the men, who were young adventurers and soldiers of fortune looking for gold, glory, and empire. Yet Fray Marcos reassured them

that great riches awaited those with the courage to persevere.

After the force reached Culiacán, Coronado decided to push ahead quickly to Cíbola with a small party of eighty Spaniards, along with some Mexican Indian allies. The main group would follow later. During the long trek through Sonora and eastern Arizona, supplies dwindled and horses died. When Coronado reached Cíbola (Hawikuh) in July, 1540, his men were starving. Mendoza had ordered Coronado neither to abuse the Indians nor to make slaves of them. He thus tried to negotiate with the Zuni at Cíbola (there and elsewhere, most communication with the Indians was probably by sign language), but they ambushed his scouts and then attacked the whole party. After repelling the initial assault, Coronado besieged the fortified pueblo but was nearly killed in battle. García López de Cárdenas, second in command, captured Cíbola but found none of the promised riches.

Recovered from his wounds, Coronado again assumed command. On July 15, 1540, he sent a small party under Pedro de Tovar to explore Tusayán to the northwest, home of the Hopi. It returned with reports of a great

Nineteenth century painter Frederic Remington's depiction of Coronado's march through Colorado in 1541. (Library of Congress)

river and a land of giants somewhere beyond. In late August, Coronado dispatched López de Cárdenas with twenty-five horsemen to investigate: They discovered the Grand Canyon. For several days, three men tried to reach the Colorado River far below but managed to climb down only a third of the way. Disappointed but determined to press on, Coronado sent messengers, including a disgraced Fray Marcos, back to Mendoza.

Several Pueblo Indians arrived in Cíbola and invited the Spaniards to visit Cicúique (Pecos) and Tiguex, two hundred miles to the east near the headwaters of the Rio Grande. Coronado sent Hernando de Alvarado and twenty men to reconnoiter. They found pueblos of multistoried houses and friendly Indians but no riches. In late November of 1540, Coronado decided to move his force there for the winter, including the main expedition which had just arrived at Cíbola.

The Spaniards and Mexican Indians were not equipped for the harsh winter. Despite Coronado's attempts to treat the American Indians humanely, the Spaniards forced one village of Indians to vacate their pueblo so that the intruders could live there. They took large amounts of food and winter clothing, and when a Spaniard molested an Indian woman and received no punishment, resentment smoldered.

Meanwhile, Alvarado found two Indian slaves, whom the Spaniards called Turk and Sopete. They told Alvarado about Quivira, a fabulously rich land farther to the east. Turk, whose fertile imagination concocted the type of reports the Spaniards wanted to hear, claimed that he had owned a gold bracelet from Quivira, which a Pueblo chieftain had stolen from him. This was the closest the expedition had come to gold, and Alvarado immediately imprisoned the chief.

Torture of the chief to locate the imaginary bracelet, together with the other abuses, transformed the previously friendly Indians into sullen and finally hostile hosts. The Tiguex War erupted. Coronado sent Cárdenas to deal with the rebellion, and he brutally suppressed it by March, 1541, mistakenly burning at the stake thirty or forty warriors who had surrendered during a truce at Arenal.

Coronado then decided to push on to Quivira, even though Sopete said that Turk's stories were lies. The expedition left for Quivira on April 23, 1541. The men found no gold, but their trek revealed huge buffalo herds and the plains Indians, including the Tejas tribe, which gave its name to Texas. With no topographical features to orient them on the flat plains, they piled buffalo chips to mark their trail. In the Texas panhandle, Coronado finally realized that Turk had deceived him. He placed Turk in chains, chose thirty-six men to continue on with Sopete as guide, and sent the remainder of the expedition back to Tiguex to wait. Sopete led them into central Kansas. There they found Quivira, land of the Wichita Indians, and final disappointment, for there was no gold or silver. In revenge, the Spaniards strangled Turk but left Sopete in his homeland as a reward for his service. Coronado then turned back toward Tiguex, arriving there in September.

A discouraged Coronado dispatched a report to the viceroy and spent the winter at Tiguex. On December 27, 1541, during a horse race, Coronado fell, and a horse stepped on his head, nearly killing him. Coronado never fully recovered. More somber and less vigorous, he consulted with his men and decided to return to Mexico. Three friars stayed to work among the Indians, however, and a few soldiers criticized him for not allowing them to remain and settle in the region. The expedition left Tiguex in April and straggled into Culiacán in June, 1542, where it disbanded.

Coronado's later years added nothing to the great explorer's fame. Despite Mendoza's disappointment over the expedition's failure, he sent Coronado back to New Galicia as governor. In 1543, Charles V ordered an inquiry into the conduct of the expedition, particularly its treatment of the Indians, and the following year, Coronado's performance as governor came under royal scrutiny. Absolved of the most serious charges, Coronado was nevertheless removed as governor by Mendoza, as much because of his poor health as for his misdeeds. Coronado thereafter lived in Mexico City, serving on the city council and administering his estates. He died on September 22, 1554.

SIGNIFICANCE

As a leader, Coronado pales in comparison with someone such as Cortés. He owed his appointment to head the expedition to Mendoza; others, such as Melchior Díaz, were better qualified and more experienced. Perhaps his greatest weakness was his naïve acceptance of Fray Marcos's and Turk's lies. Still, Coronado endured the same hardships as his men, fought in the front ranks, and lost only about twenty men over the course of the entire expedition. Although a strict disciplinarian, he was not a tyrant but usually consulted with his men before making important decisions. Despite the Arenal atrocities, for which he was at least indirectly responsible, Coronado was remarkably humane in comparison with other Spaniards of his day.

Coronado's expedition was a major step in the exploration of North America. Although the Spaniards considered his mission a huge disappointment because it produced no gold, Coronado made important contributions by other standards. The trails he blazed, following the old Mexican Indian paths, served later Spanish parties as they moved north to settle and colonize the Southwest. He proved that the continent was much wider than previously thought and discovered the continental divide. His expedition brought back valuable information about the Indian tribes, wildlife, and geography of the region and added vast territories to the Spanish crown.

—*Kendall W. Brown*

FURTHER READING

Aiton, Arthur S. *Antonio de Mendoza: First Viceroy of New Spain*. Durham, N.C.: Duke University Press, 1927. Reprint. New York: Russell & Russell, 1967. A scholarly biography of Coronado's patron. Discusses Coronado's expedition and provides valuable information on contemporary New Spain.

_____. "The Later Career of Coronado." *American Historical Review* 30 (January, 1925): 298-304. By Mendoza's biographer, this article analyzes the period after the great expedition. Probably too critical of Coronado.

Bolton, Herbert Eugene. *Coronado on the Turquoise Trail: Knight of the Pueblos and Plains*. 1949. Reprint. Albuquerque: University of New Mexico Press, 1964. A masterpiece based on a thorough use of archival records and the accounts left by its members. Bolton traveled the entire Coronado trail.

Flint, Richard, and Shirley Cushing Flint, eds. *The Coronado Expedition: From the Distance of 460 Years*. Albuquerque: University of New Mexico Press, 2003. Anthology studying all aspects of Coronado's expedition, from the names of its members to the technical design of their horseshoes to the interactions with Native Americans.

_____. *The Coronado Expedition to Tierra Nueva: The 1540-1542 Route Across the Southwest*. 1997. Reprint. Niwot, Colo.: University Press of Colorado, 2004. A companion to the anthology above, this multidisciplinary study provides archaeological, ethnographic, historical, and geographic research into the specific route followed by Coronado's expedition. Explains the evidence, details the most likely route, and discusses the importance of these findings.

Hammond, George Peter, and Agapito Rey, eds. *Narratives of the Coronado Expedition, 1540-1542*. Albuquerque: University of New Mexico Press, 1940. Reprint. New York: AMS Press, 1977. Extremely useful collection of English translations of reports, dispatches, and correspondence by Coronado, Mendoza, Alarcón, and others relating to Coronado's expedition and trail.

Correggio, Frederick W., ed. *Spanish Explorers in the Southern United States, 1528-1543*. New York: Charles Scribner's Sons, 1907. Reprint. Austin: Texas State Historical Association and the Center for Studies in Texas History, University of Texas at Austin, 1984. Contains a translation of the account of Coronado's expedition written by Pedro de Castañeda, a participant, although he was not present at all the important events. Also contains a translation of Cabeza de Vaca's narrative.

Ortiz, Alfonso, ed. *Handbook of North American Indians*. Vol. 9. Washington, D.C.: Smithsonian Institution, 1979. Deals specifically with the Zuni, Pueblo, and Hopi Indians and contains historical, anthropological, and archaeological studies by experts in the various fields. Also contains an extensive bibliography.

Sauer, Carl O. *Sixteenth-Century North America: The Land and the People as Seen by the Europeans*. Berkeley: University of California Press, 1971. The leading historical geographer of sixteenth century North America includes a chapter on the Coronado expedition, focusing on the environment rather than the man.

Udall, Stewart L. *Majestic Journey: Coronado's Inland Empire*. Rev. ed. Sante Fe: Museum of New Mexico Press, 1995. The former Secretary of the Interior leads the reader through a retracing of Coronado's route in order the demonstrate the historical importance of his expedition. Includes photographs by Jerry Jacka, maps, and index.

SEE ALSO: Pedro de Alvarado; Vasco Núñez de Balboa; Álvar Núñez Cabeza de Vaca; Charles V; Christopher Columbus; Hernán Cortés; Juan Sebastián de Elcano; Pedro Menéndez de Avilés; Montezuma II; The Pinzón Brothers; Francisco Pizarro; Juan Ponce de León.

RELATED ARTICLES in *Great Events from History: The Renaissance & Early Modern Era, 1454-1600:* 1528-1536: Narváez's and Cabeza de Vaca's Expeditions; February 23, 1540-October, 1542: Coronado's Southwest Expedition.

Correggio
Italian painter

Correggio produced frescoes and paintings of religious and mythological subjects that demonstrate his skills as one of the greatest masters of the High Renaissance. His innovations in composition, expressiveness, and particularly in the illusionistic foreshortening of figures seen from below were to have a tremendous influence on later Baroque painters.

Born: c. 1489; Correggio, duchy of Modena (now in Italy)
Died: c. March 5, 1534; Correggio
Also known as: Antonio Allegri
Area of achievement: Art

Early Life

Correggio (kohr-RAYD-joh) was born Antonio Allegri in the town from which his name is taken. The date of his birth to Pellegrino Allegri and Bernardina Ormani has been debated. The year was once thought to have been 1494 because artist-biographer Giorgio Vasari stated that Correggio died at the age of forty; however, most scholars now place his birth nearer to the year 1489.

Correggio's uncle, Lorenzo Allegri, was a painter, under whom he may have studied. The apprenticeship is unclear, however, as are many details of his life because of the absence of documents. While the story that he was Bianchi Ferrari's pupil in Modena is plausible, Mantua is a more important place for Correggio's formative career. Some work there has been attributed to him, and the strong influence of both Andrea Mantegna and Lorenzo Costa on Correggio's work between 1510 and 1518 argues strongly for his presence in nearby Mantua around that time. Influences from Dosso Dossi in nearby Ferrara are also likely.

Yet by far the greatest formative influence on Correggio was Rome. The evidence is stylistic, based especially on paintings in the cupola of S. Giovanni Evangelista. There is a blend of antique classicism; Raphael's *Stanza della Segnatura* (1508-1511) and the Sistine Chapel ceiling by Michelangelo are evident. Generous borrowings from Leonardo da Vinci suggest that he may also have traveled to Milan.

While no known description of the artist exists, it has been proposed that the Saint Anthony of Padua in the *Madonna and Child with Saint Francis* in Dresden is a self-portrait. Half smiling, he appears there as having been graceful and decidedly shy or withdrawn, as Vasari described him.

Life's Work

With the varied impressions made on Correggio, including Florentine cultural stimuli, one might assume Correggio to have been merely eclectic. Yet the opposite is true. His handling of figure, space, and color was accomplished with fluid, sensual harmony. Even the classical references are never dry or academic and appear with the graceful casualness that suggests intimate familiarity.

The earliest documentary evidence for a painting, the *Madonna of Saint Francis*, is the contract made on August 30, 1514. References to Leonardo da Vinci and Raphael may indicate that the Rome visit had already been made. Earlier than this, but firmly attributed to Correggio, are *Christ Taking Leave of His Mother* (1514-1517) and two pictures of the *Marriage of Saint Catherine* (1510-1514), which show the strong influence of Costa and Mantegna. Other works attributed to Correggio from the period prior to 1518 include *The Holy Family with the Infant Saint John the Baptist*, *Adoration of the Magi*, *Judith*, and *Nativity*. The atmospheric effects in landscape from the *Nativity* and the *Adoration of the Magi* suggest a Venetian origin by way of Ferrara; the latter also indicates familiarity with the protomannerism of Emilia such as is seen in the works of Dosso Dossi.

In 1518, Correggio was summoned to Parma to decorate the suite of Giovanna da Piacenza, abbess of the convent of S. Paolo. As no sightseers were admitted to the room for two centuries, the first detailed account of the work was not published until 1794. It is the artist's first major work in fresco. The largely decorative treatment of the vault, with a network of reeds carrying festoons of fruit pierced by ovals through which putti glance downward, is largely Mantegnesque. The bands of reeds terminate in illusionistic, monochromatic lunettes that reflect extensive familiarity with the antique. A figure of Diana moves across the great hood of the chimney, glowing with soft flesh tones. The total effect is rich, harmonious, and enchanting.

By 1520, Correggio was at work on the decoration of the church of S. Giovanni Evangelista in Parma. The dome frescoes came first, then the half-dome of the apse, followed by frescoes on the underarches of the dome. He provided drawings for the nave frieze, executing a small portion of it that was finished by Francesco Mario Rondani and others. While he was in Parma, on November 3, 1522, Correggio signed a contract for the decoration of the choir and dome of the Cathedral of Parma.

Correggio. (Library of Congress)

This year was the turning point in his career. Commissions for work began pouring in from various places. It is speculated that enough of the frescoes in S. Giovanni Evangelista were completed to have astonished Italy and created his fame.

The subject of the fresco in the dome of S. Giovanni Evangelista is the Vision of Saint John on Patmos, showing the risen Christ in the center surrounded by the glow of rich, luminous light. Cherubim surround this light, with the other apostles lining the base of the dome. There is a soaring effect, and illusionism, which was to impress later Baroque artists. It is evident that an audacious imagination was at work. The sculptural effect of the figures against the neutral background recall Raphael and Michelangelo. The atmospheric effect is the result of contact with Leonardo, the latest Venetians, and the swirling, last scenes by Michelangelo in the Sistine Chapel. The coloration and the sinuous soft form of Raphael's *Triumph of Galatea* (1511-1513) are present, but the overall effect is uniquely Correggio's, with his harmonious, fluid forms.

The ceiling painting in the Cathedral of Parma is a logical consequence of the preceding dome and can be seen as the culmination of Correggio's artistry and as his most imaginative and creative effort. The *Assumption of the Virgin* (1526-1530) is an exciting celestial vision with great illusionistic depth of space. It is filled with the fluid, energetic movements of frolicking angels on soft masses of clouds amid a golden, mysterious glow of light. Throughout there is a festive gladness and a sensual exaltation. The virtuosity of illusionism plus the intertwining and piling up of figures is a tour de force unequaled before the seventeenth century.

During the period of his work at Parma, Correggio executed many other single paintings, plus altarpieces and mythological scenes. He did two paintings for the private chapel of the Del Bono family around 1524. The new elements are to be present in the remainder of the artist's works. The two paintings, now in Parma's Galleria Nazionale, *The Deposition* and *The Martyrdom of Four Saints*, are both very emotional, exhibiting a bolder color, a stronger, more direct source of light, and the use of relative clarity to give attention to the focal points. In addition, there is a decided mannerism, shown in the flattening of space, choice of color, and prominent use of hands for expression. Among the notable paintings executed during the early to mid-1520's are the *Madonna of Saint Jerome*, "La Notte," or *Adoration of the Shepherds*, with its brilliant illumination amid the darkness, and the *Holy Family with Saint Francis*.

Correggio executed several mythological and allegorical paintings for Federigo II Gonzaga, the duke of Mantua, which are among the most delightful and popular of his works. These include the *School of Love* and its pendant, *Venus, Cupid, and Satyr*, both of which may have been executed in the 1520's. The four great *Loves of Jupiter* were done in the 1530's and a second series of *Loves of Jupiter* were under way when Correggio died. The *Danae, Leda, Io*, and *Ganymede* were given by Federigo to Holy Roman Emperor Charles V. All contain nudes executed with great subtlety and grace. The figures are monumental but softened by atmospheric shadows, sensual poses, and rich flesh tones.

SIGNIFICANCE

The works attributed to Correggio constitute a prodigious oeuvre. Had he lived past his forty odd years, Correggio probably would have revolutionized art. As it is, his stature is only now coming to be appreciated. The illusionistic space of Correggio's domes, with its antecedents in Mantegna's ceiling in Mantua, masterfully anticipated the artists of Baroque decoration from the Carracci family and Guercino to Giovanni Lanfranco and Baciccia.

The lessons of strength and drawing that Correggio learned from Raphael and Michelangelo were softened by the Venetian atmosphere and the shadows and smiles of Leonardo. In his own time, Parmigianino was profoundly influenced by Correggio when he worked by his side in Parma. Correggio in turn absorbed the lessons of the mannerists to a certain degree. The final outcome is a confusion about the exact position of Correggio's place in history. His art escapes easy labeling.

Correggio's abilities were to be greatly admired in the eighteenth century, the period of the discovery of his frescoes in San Paolo and the publication of documents by Girolamo Tiraboschi such as *Notizie de'pittori, scultori, incisori, e architetti natii degli stati del serenissimo duca di Modena* (1786), as well as a history by Correggio's greatest admirer, Anton Raphael Mengs. Correggio's importance was eclipsed in the nineteenth century, and some scholars see his tremendous impact on artists from the later sixteenth and seventeenth centuries, from Baroccio, even Gian Lorenzo Bernini and the Carracci family, to a host of other lesser-known artists. Correggio evoked the true grandeur of Renaissance classicism but indicated a new direction that was profoundly to affect art for centuries.

—Sharon Hill

FURTHER READING

The Age of Correggio and the Carracci: Emilian Painting of the Sixteenth and Seventeenth Centuries. Washington, D.C.: National Gallery of Art, 1986. A beautifully produced catalog of more than two hundred Emilian paintings of the sixteenth and seventeenth centuries, organized and written by dozens of scholars for the exhibition appearing at the National Gallery of Art in Washington, the Metropolitan Museum of Art in New York, and the Pinacoteca Nazionale, Bologna. With beautiful illustrations, many in color, this is the most extensive treatment of the effects of Correggio on later sixteenth and seventeeth century art.

Brown, David Alan. *Una Pietà del Correggio a Correggio/A Pietà by Correggio in Correggio.* Milan, Italy: Silvana Editoriale, 2003. Bilingual English and Italian monograph on Correggio's *Pietà.* Includes illustrations, bibliographic references, index.

Ekserdjian, David. *Correggio.* New Haven, Conn.: Yale University Press, 1997. This study of Correggio focuses especially on his altarpieces, but it covers the entirety of his output and attempts to trace the influence of his predecessors and contemporaries in his work. Includes almost three hundred illustrations, bibliographic references, bibliography, appendices, and index.

Fornari Schianchi, Lucia. *Correggio.* Translated by Christopher Evans. New York: Riverside, 1994. Part of the Library of the Great Masters series, this book is meant as an introduction to and general survey of Correggio's life and career. Includes illustrations, some bibliographic references, and an index.

Gould, Cecil. *The Paintings of Correggio.* Ithaca, N.Y.: Cornell University Press, 1976. The most comprehensive, definitive, and up-to-date assessment of Correggio's paintings. It is well illustrated and includes documents and a helpful catalog of all surviving pictures including a discussion of attributions.

Popham, Arthur E. *Correggio's Drawings.* London: Oxford University Press, 1957. A valuable and well-illustrated treatment of the known drawings. Includes a discussion of drawings of questionable attribution.

Smyth, Carolyn. *Correggio's Frescoes in Parma Cathedral.* Princeton, N.J.: Princeton University Press, 1997. Book-length study of the frescoes portraying the Assumption of the Virgin Mary, focused on the physical relationship between the frescoes and the viewer and on Correggio's use of perspective and space within the cathedral. Includes seventy-eight pages of plates, bibliographic references, and index.

Wind, Geraldine Dunphy. *Correggio: L'eroe della cupola/Hero of the Dome.* Milan, Italy: Silvana Editoriale, 2002. Bilingual English and Italian study of Correggio's frescoes in the Parma Cathedral and in the Church of San Giovanni Evangelista in Parma. Includes illustrations, bibliographic references, index.

SEE ALSO: Andrea del Sarto; The Carracci Family; Lavinia Fontana; Giorgione; Isabella d'Este; Leonardo da Vinci; Andrea Mantegna; Michelangelo; Raphael; Tintoretto; Giorgio Vasari.

RELATED ARTICLE in *Great Events from History: The Renaissance & Early Modern Era, 1454-1600:* November 3, 1522-November 17, 1530: Correggio Paints the *Assumption of the Virgin.*

HERNÁN CORTÉS
Spanish conquistador

Cortés skillfully led a small band of Spaniards and numerous Mexican Indian allies to the heart of the Aztec capital of Tenochtitlán (later Mexico City), and within two years he conquered the powerful Aztec Empire. His most lasting contribution has been the exploration and settlement of the New World.

BORN: 1485; Medellín, Extremadura, Castile (now in Spain)

DIED: December 2, 1547; Castilleja de la Cuesta, near Seville, Spain

ALSO KNOWN AS: Hernán Cortéz; Fernando Cortés; Hernando Cortés

AREAS OF ACHIEVEMENT: Exploration, warfare and conquest, military

EARLY LIFE

Hernán Cortés (ehr-NAHN kawr-TEHZ) came from a Spanish region, Extremadura, where so many of the New World conquistadores originated. Although Cortés was born into a Spanish noble (Hidalgo) family, his parents—Martín Cortés de Monroy, an infantry captain, and Catalina Pizarro Altamirano—were of limited means. At the age of fourteen, Hernán was sent to school in Salamanca to prepare for a career in law. Cortés soon abandoned his studies and decided to follow in his father's footsteps and join the Spanish army, serving in Naples. In 1504, at the age of nineteen, hamstrung by what he perceived as limited possibilities in the Old World, the restless youth, like so many of his class, decided to board a ship bound for the Spanish Indies.

In many ways, the impressionable Cortés was a product of his times. Renaissance Spain was undergoing tremendous ferment during the last decades of the fifteenth century. For more than seven centuries, Spanish Catholics had fought an epic struggle against Islamic Moors called the Reconquista (reconquest), and in 1492, under the unified leadership of King Ferdinand II of Aragon and Queen Isabella I of Castile, the Moors' final stronghold, Granada, fell. The Reconquista markedly influenced succeeding generations of Iberians: It united Spain's divided kingdoms and regions into a strong nation-state with a powerful army; it rallied the country together under the banner of Catholicism—the young nation would embrace the faith with such religious fervor that it would take on the responsibility of defender of the Church throughout Europe and the New World; and it opened up economic possibilities for those Hidalgos

who fought for the Crown and were rewarded for their efforts. Militarism, the rise of a Spanish national identity, the Catholic faith, and the seemingly unlimited potential for personal aggrandizement imbued succeeding generations of Hidalgos with a sense of commitment, purpose, and service to their Crown.

In the same year that Granada fell, Christopher Columbus made the first European discovery of the New World, opening new military, religious, and economic possibilities for the expansion-minded Spanish state and for ambitious Hidalgos such as Cortés. Cortés secured a position as a notary on the island of Santo Domingo in the Caribbean and was given a small grant of Mexican Indians who provided labor and commodity tribute (*encomienda*). For six years, Cortés profited from Indian labor, but once again he grew restless. In 1511, he joined Diego Velázquez's military conquest of Cuba, serving as a clerk to the treasurer. Rewarded by the conquistador Velázquez, who subsequently became governor of the island, Cortés was rewarded with another *encomienda* in Cuba and a government position. In Santiago de Baracoa, Cuba, Cortés attended to his bureaucratic duties, became a prominent local merchant, raised cattle, and had his *encomienda* Indians mine gold.

LIFE'S WORK

Just when it appeared that Cortés would settle down and tend to his thriving business concerns, reports began filtering back to Cuba from advance scouting expeditions of a fabulous Aztec Empire on the Caribbean mainland. In 1519, Governor Velázquez commissioned the thirty-four-year-old Cortés to lead an expedition to the Mexican mainland. As Cortés outfitted his expedition with men, ships, and provisions, Velázquez had second thoughts about Cortés's arrogant, pretentious manner. Fearing that he could not control his ambitious commander, Velázquez ordered the commission revoked. When Cortés learned that the governor planned to rescind his orders, he quickly set sail from Cuba on February 18, 1519, with 550 Spaniards, several Cuban Indians and black slaves, a few small cannons, sixteen horses, several mastiff dogs, and eleven small ships.

Cortés's two-year assault on the heavily populated Aztec Empire, against almost insurmountable odds, was one of the most formidable challenges of the age of exploration and conquest. Driven by the traits shared by all Reconquista Hidalgos—religious zeal, dedication to the

Crown, and a lust for glory and gold—Cortés, both in his personal correspondence and in his riveting speeches to his men, evinced a single-minded obsession: to conquer the Aztecs or die trying. Chroniclers describe the conquistador as being of average height with a pale complexion and a muscular frame. The standard that he carried into battle was particularly appropriate; fashioned of black velvet, embroidered with gold, with a red cross laced with blue-and-white flames, its motto was emblazoned in Latin: "Friends, let us follow the Cross; and under this sign, if we have faith, we shall conquer." From the moment the expedition landed off the coast of Yucatán until the final assault on the Aztec capital of Tenochtitlán in 1521, Cortés stayed true to that motto and never considered retreating or compromising.

Although the enemy enjoyed an overwhelming numerical superiority—the population of Tenochtitlán has been estimated at three hundred thousand in 1519—Cortés was able to take advantage of a number of favorable factors. First, Cortés shrewdly perceived that many

of the Indian subject provinces chafed under and bitterly resented Aztec rule. The Spanish invasion signified—to Indians such as the Tlaxcalans and later the Tarascans—a fortuitous opportunity to ally themselves with the foreign invaders, to overturn onerous Aztec tribute, and to regain their independence. These subject populations provided Cortés with literally thousands of warriors and also complicated matters politically for the Aztec emperor Montezuma II. The emperor, who was coronated in 1503, had squelched serious rebellions throughout his reign. Yet, after more than a century of Aztec imperial rule, subject provinces who had provided commodity tribute and human sacrifice victims to the Aztecs on an unprecedented scale saw hope in an alliance with the Spaniards.

Cortés also benefited from the Aztecs' fatalistic religious vision. The Aztecs believed that the world had been destroyed and reborn by the gods on four separate occasions. Every fifty-two years, the cycle of destruction was at risk and the world might be destroyed. Cortés arrived in Mexico in the fateful fifty-second year (*ce atl*). Moreover, the Spanish at first were believed by the Indians to be gods, or at least, messengers of the gods. Native myth told of a light-skinned, bearded god, Quetzalcóatl, who believed in love, compassion, and mercy, and who forbade human sacrifice, practiced oral confession, baptism, and ascetic denial. This god, according to myth, had left the Valley of Mexico centuries before, vowing one day to return to reclaim his kingdom. The Christianity espoused by the Europeans almost surreally approximated the Quetzalcóatl cult. Montezuma, a devout philosophical and religious thinker in his own right, at times appeared almost mesmerized by the religious implications of the Spanish expedition.

Cortés did little to discourage the religious uncertainties of the indigenous population. The Spanish possessed the technological advantages of Spanish steel, muskets, crossbows, and armor. In addition, Cortés used psychological ploys to startle unsuspecting Aztec emissaries at propitious moments. From the deafening noise of the Spaniards' small cannons to the judicious use of the horses and menacing dogs—two animals that the Indians had never seen before—Cortés created an aura of invincibility around his troops that fortified his Indian allies, created indecision in the minds of the Aztec leadership, and bolstered the confidence of his soldiers.

Yet Cortés faced daunting odds. His expedition had lost its legal sanction from Velázquez, and he was perilously close to becoming an outlaw in the eyes of the Crown. Cortés, however, feigned ignorance of the revoked commission and founded a settlement on the coast

Hernán Cortés. (Library of Congress)

of Mexico, La Villa Rica de la Vera Cruz (later Veracruz), claiming all the lands that he conquered for the king of Spain, Charles V. He shrewdly dispatched a ship to Spain with a letter to the king professing his loyalty to the Crown. Still, Cortés faced serious problems from Velázquez supporters in his midst.

Time and again on his climb to Tenochtitlán, the Spanish commander demonstrated his uncanny ability to act decisively before the Aztecs and their allies could react. For example, at Cholula, the last major city on Cortés's route to the Aztec capital, the Spanish learned that they were about to be ambushed by an Aztec army. Cortés ordered a preemptive strike and massacred more than six thousand Indian warriors. An Indian version of the conquest denies the ambush and characterizes Cortés's massacre as premeditated. From that point on, no serious attempts were made by the Aztecs to stop Cortés's advance on Tenochtitlán.

Another bold move was the decision to put Montezuma under house arrest while the Spanish stayed in the capital. As "guests" of the emperor, Cortés and his troops could ensure that Montezuma was not organizing an uprising. The decision to rule through the emperor bought the Spanish valuable time.

When the Aztecs revolted on July 1, 1520 (called La Noche Triste, "the sad night," by the Spanish), Cortés was forced to abandon Tenochtitlán. Bernal Díaz relates that 860 Spaniards died during the battle. Despite this overwhelming defeat, Cortés rallied his armed forces, convinced more than one hundred thousand indigenous allies to join his cause, and launched a tactically brilliant land and naval invasion of Tenochtitlán less than a year later. Cortés's devotion to this cause was too much for the Indians, who by this time had been decimated by smallpox infection and were dying by the thousands in Tenochtitlán. On August 13, 1521, after fierce hand-to-hand combat in the capital, the last Aztec emperor, Cuauhtémoc, surrendered.

Cortés proved to be an able administrator of the colony, which he renamed New Spain. Charles V, facing troubles from nobles in Spain, was understandably reluctant to let conquistadores such as Cortés become too powerful. Royal officials replaced Cortés soon after the conquest, and Cortés returned to Spain to argue his case before the king. Although Cortés never became governor of New Spain, he was allowed to choose twenty-two towns of *encomienda* Indians (approximately twenty-three thousand Indians). Cortés chose the richest settlements in the colony. Moreover, he was named captain-general and awarded the title of Marqués del Valle de Oaxaca.

While at the royal court, Cortés married the daughter of a count, further ingratiating himself with the Spanish aristocracy. He returned to New Spain in 1530 and lived there for ten years, where he introduced new European crops and products, looked for silver and gold mines, and encouraged exploration. Cortés's wealth and status made him a target of Crown officials who distrusted his independent demeanor and feared his political contacts with the nobility in Spain. His last few years were spent in frustration in Spain. In 1547, he fell ill and died at his estate, Castilleja de la Cuesta, just outside Seville. According to his wishes, his bones were moved to Mexico in 1556.

SIGNIFICANCE

More than any other conquistador, Cortés embodied the characteristics of the group of fearless men who, imbued with the heady ideals of the Reconquista, forged a massive Spanish Empire in the New World. Committed to service to the Crown, convinced that their cause was noble and just, comforted by the belief that they brought Christianity and civilization to barbarian peoples, and clearly motivated by material gain and glory, Cortés and his fellow conquistadores, at times ruthlessly and at times diplomatically, conquered the numerically superior Indians during the early sixteenth century. Unlike other conquistadores, however, Cortés had a strong commitment to the religious conversion of the indigenous. Moreover, he demonstrated himself to be an able and fair administrator in the first years after the conquest; again, a trait not shared by many conquerors. Although Cortés was denied the political post that he thought he deserved, he became one of the wealthiest men in the empire.

—Allen Wells

FURTHER READING

Collis, Maurice. *Cortés and Montezuma*. New York: New Directions, 1999. Extensively researched, and highly accessible account of the meeting between Cortés and Montezuma provides many details to make the points of view of both men, and their followers, come to life. Includes illustrations, map, and index.

Cortés, Hernán. *Letters from Mexico*. Edited and translated by Anthony Pagden. Rev. ed. New Haven, Conn.: Yale Nota Bene, 2001. Self-serving letters written in the heat of battle by the conquistador, which detail conditions in Mexico during the conquest and give insight into the character of Cortés. Includes illustrations, maps, bibliographic references, index.

Díaz del Castillo, Bernal. *The Discovery and Conquest of Mexico, 1517-1521*. Edited by Genaro García. Translated by A. P. Maudslay. Reprint. Introduction by Hugh Thomas. New York: Da Capo Press, 1996. A classic, riveting, first-person narrative of the conquest recollected by Díaz in his old age. Although Díaz believed that he was never given his just due—he was rewarded with a paltry *encomienda* in the hostile backlands of Guatemala—his account is relatively balanced. His descriptions of the Spanish entry to Tenochtitlán and the great Aztec market at Tlateloco are stunning.

León-Portilla, Miguel, ed. *The Broken Spears: The Aztec Account of the Conquest of Mexico*. Translated by Lysander Kemp. Expanded and updated ed. Boston: Beacon Press, 1992. A compilation of Aztec and early missionary sources that offers a much-needed corrective to the Spanish versions of the conquest. Although these sympathetic "native" sources are as biased as the Spanish accounts they reject, this is an evocative portrayal of the Indian defeat. Some of the Aztec poetry included is powerful and moving and gives readers a sense of the psychological loss felt by the Aztecs.

Padden, R. C. *The Hummingbird and the Hawk: Conquest and Sovereignty in the Valley of Mexico, 1503-1541*. Columbus: Ohio State University Press, 1967. A provocative account of the conquest that emphasizes Cortés's religious zeal and the fundamental importance of human sacrifice to the Aztec faith. Nowhere else in the literature are Cortés's religious motivations portrayed so prominently. Good bibliography of the secondary literature included.

Prescott, William H. *History of the Conquest of Mexico*. Reprint. New York: Modern Library, 2001. A standard mid-nineteenth century, secondary narrative of the conquest that relies heavily on Spanish chroniclers. Extraordinarily detailed account of the background, motivations, and battles of the conquest.

White, Jon Manchip. *Cortés and the Downfall of the Aztec Empire*. 2d ed. New York: Carroll & Graf, 1996. A psychological and analytical portrait of Cortés and Montezuma that places both leaders in their religious and cultural milieus.

SEE ALSO: Pedro de Alvarado; Vasco Núñez de Balboa; Álvar Núñez Cabeza de Vaca; Juan Rodríguez Cabrillo; Charles V; Christopher Columbus; Francisco Vásquez de Coronado; Cuauhtémoc; Juan Sebastián de Elcano; Ferdinand II and Isabella I; Doña Marina; Pedro Menéndez de Avilés; Montezuma II; Nezahualcóyotl; The Pinzón Brothers; Francisco Pizarro; Juan Ponce de León.

RELATED ARTICLES in *Great Events from History: The Renaissance & Early Modern Era, 1454-1600:* 16th century: Worldwide Inflation; 1502-1520: Reign of Montezuma II; Beginning 1519: Smallpox Kills Thousands of Indigenous Americans; April, 1519-August, 1521: Cortés Conquers Aztecs in Mexico; August, 1523: Franciscan Missionaries Arrive in Mexico; 1527-1547: Maya Resist Spanish Incursions in Yucatán; 1542-1543: The New Laws of Spain.

MILES COVERDALE
English translator and scholar

The first translator of the complete and official Bible into a readable, accessible English, Coverdale in the late Elizabethan era provided a link between the English Reformation and the first English Puritans.

BORN: c. 1488; York, Yorkshire, England
DIED: January 20, 1568; London, England
AREAS OF ACHIEVEMENT: Religion and theology, literature, scholarship

EARLY LIFE
Miles Coverdale was born in Yorkshire, England, probably in the city of York. Little is known about his family or about his early childhood years. He studied philosophy and theology at Cambridge, became a priest at Norwich in 1514 when he was twenty-six, and entered the convent of Augustinian friars at Cambridge. His friend John Bale said that he drank in good learning with a burning thirst.

No authentic portrait of Coverdale exists. One that has traditionally been accepted as a copy of an early sketch of Coverdale shows him as a grim-faced, austere, middle-aged Puritan with anxious brow and a sharply downturned mouth. His friends, however, described him as friendly and upright with a very gentle spirit. These friends were from all areas of society and opinion. Among them were a number of young men who met at the White Horse Inn in Cambridge to discuss the new Lutheran religious reform ideas. Many of England's earliest Protestants—Robert Barnes, Thomas Bilney, William Roy, George Joye, and John Frith—were in this group.

Coverdale's friends also included Sir Thomas More, a reformer who later died as a martyr because he could not give up his allegiance to the Roman Catholic religion, and Thomas Cromwell, a royal minister who became a powerful supporter of Coverdale.

In 1528, when Robert Barnes was arrested for preaching against the luxurious lifestyle of Cardinal Thomas Wolsey, the king's chief minister, Coverdale went to London to help Barnes prepare his defense. The charge was serious and Barnes was forced to recant his Protestant opinions in order to save his life. This experience affected Coverdale deeply. Shortly thereafter, he left the monastery to preach in the English countryside against the Mass, image worship, and confession to a priest. Forced to flee from England to avoid royal persecution, he joined William Tyndale in Hamburg in 1529 to help him translate the Old Testament. At the home of Margaret von Emersen, a well-to-do Lutheran widow, Coverdale and Tyndale spent six or seven months translating the first five books of the Bible. This edition of the Pentateuch was published in 1530 in Antwerp, where Coverdale, preparing for his life's work, then spent several years working as a proofreader for the printer Martin de Keyser.

LIFE'S WORK

In 1534, Coverdale published his first book, an English translation of a Latin paraphrase of the Psalms written by John van Kempen (Campensis). This book was followed in October, 1535, by Coverdale's English translation of the complete Bible—the first to appear anywhere. The merchant-printer Jacob van Meteren financed and printed this translation, which he had asked Coverdale to undertake.

The fate of this English Bible hung on political events of the time. As an orthodox Roman Catholic, King Henry VIII believed that ordinary people needed the help of the clergy to understand the Bible. By 1534, however, he had separated the English church from the Roman Catholic Church, divorced his first wife, Catherine of Aragon, and married Anne Boleyn, whose family was Protestant. Henry promised Anne to have the Bible translated into English and available in the churches. Because the English bishops declared Tyndale's and Coverdale's versions to be inaccurate and inadequate, the king asked Archbishop Thomas Cranmer to oversee a new translation.

Cranmer's first attempt to have the bishops translate the Bible themselves failed, and in 1538, Cromwell asked Coverdale to prepare a new official English Bible.

Cromwell chose Coverdale as the most experienced translator of the time and the best scholar available. Coverdale used his own Bible published in Antwerp in 1535, Tyndale's New Testament and Pentateuch, and the new Matthew Bible translated by John Rogers as the basis for the new edition. He added a flattering dedication to King Henry VIII and omitted prologues and annotations. Cromwell ordered all bishops to have an English Bible conveniently located in each of their churches and to discourage no one from reading it.

King Henry licensed Coverdale and the printer Richard Grafton to provide this official Bible to be published in Paris, where better paper and type and more skilled workers were to be found. Henry requested and received for the project a Royal License from the French king. Even so, the printers in Paris were harassed, and in December, 1538, the French inquisitor general halted the printing. Coverdale fled to England, and twenty-five completed Bibles were seized by French church officials. Coverdale and the English printers then exported the necessary type, printers, and paper to London, and in April,

Miles Coverdale. (Library of Congress)

1539, the Great Bible was finally distributed as the official edition to be used in all English churches.

Once again, English politics intervened. Anne Boleyn fell from favor, and Henry's Protestant wife Jane Seymour died in childbirth. The conservative bishops and Parliament issued the Six Articles in June, 1539, inaugurating a new wave of Protestant persecution. On July 28, 1540, Barnes was burned for his religious beliefs; on July 30, Cromwell himself was beheaded. Coverdale for the second time fled to Strasbourg in Germany with other English Protestants. Nevertheless, churches continued to be required to provide Bibles, and by 1541, seven editions had been printed.

Shortly after leaving England, Coverdale married Elizabeth Macheson, whose sister had married Joannes Macchabaeus MacAlpinus, another religious exile, who was a cleric in the service of the king of Denmark and assisted with the translation of the Bible into Danish. In 1541 or 1542, Coverdale received his own doctor of divinity degree at Tübingen, and on the recommendation of Conrad Hubert, secretary of the great Protestant reformer Martin Bucer, he was named assistant minister and headmaster of the school at Bergzabern in the Rhineland. His assistance was a godsend to the head pastor, who wrote letters full of appreciation for Coverdale's piety, hard work, and scrupulous performance of his religious duties. Although Coverdale was shocked by the frivolous public dances of the townspeople and their irreverent behavior during divine services, he enjoyed his work. He begged money from friends to pay school fees for poor children and arranged for jobs in nearby churches and schools for fellow English exiles. Coverdale preferred exile with the people of God to living a life of compromise and hypocrisy in his native land. Meanwhile, in England in 1543, King Henry ordered all Bibles to be burned, and in 1546, Bishop Bonner burned Coverdale's books.

On March 26, 1548, several months after King Henry VIII had died and Edward VI had become king of England, Coverdale returned from exile. Edward's advisers revived Henry's early efforts toward reform and began to incorporate more of the ideas of Martin Luther and John Calvin. They recognized that Coverdale's goals were the same as theirs and named him to a post as royal chaplain. Serving also as almoner to the dowager queen, Catherine Parr, Henry's last wife, Coverdale wrote a dedication to a new English translation of Desiderius Erasmus's Latin paraphrases of the Bible. When Queen Catherine died in September, 1548, Coverdale preached her funeral sermon.

In the early summer of 1549, Coverdale served as preacher to Lord John Russell on a military expedition to Devon and Cornwall to quell a rebellion against the new prayer book. When Russell had completed his task, Coverdale remained to pacify the people and return Protestant practice to the churches. Coverdale's loyalty and competence were rewarded by Northumberland in August, 1551, when Bishop John Veysey, whose sympathies were not with the Reformation, was ejected from office and Coverdale was appointed as the new bishop of Exeter. As bishop, Coverdale was charged with restoring property to Exeter, with enforcing Protestant practices in his churches, and with serving in the House of Lords. Coverdale and his wife were without question good and holy Christians, but Protestant supporters noted that the common people, still Roman Catholic at heart, would not accept him because he was a married man preaching the gospel. Despite this stubborn opposition, Coverdale continued to preach and carry out the duties of his office until Mary Tudor (Mary I) became queen in July, 1553, after Edward's death. Within a month after her accession to the throne, Coverdale was under house arrest, and in September, Veysey—now eighty-eight—was reinstated as bishop of Exeter.

Mary Tudor, eldest daughter of Henry VIII and his first wife, Catherine of Aragon, did not make substantial changes in religion immediately. She did not ban the English Bible nor order public burnings of it until 1556. Nevertheless, Coverdale had no doubts about her power or her intentions. Prepared to die for his faith, he was determined not to recant, go into exile again, or consent to do anything contrary to his beliefs in order to stay alive. He even added his name to a Protestant statement of belief written by twelve of his imprisoned brethren.

For more than a year, Coverdale remained under house arrest although not in the Tower of London. His wife's brother-in-law, MacAlpinus, enlisted the help of the king of Denmark, who wrote a series of letters to Queen Mary demanding Coverdale's release. Finally, in 1555, Mary issued Coverdale a passport. For the third time, Coverdale and his wife left England, this time for Denmark en route to the village of Bergzabern, where Coverdale spent the next two years teaching. His last years in exile were spent in Switzerland, first at Aarau and then in Geneva, where he stood as godfather to John Knox's son.

Queen Mary died in December, 1558, unable to restore her people's allegiance to the pope and unable to secure the throne with an heir. The following year, Coverdale, by this time seventy-one years old, returned once again with his family to England.

In exile, Coverdale had become more puritanical in the practice of his religion. At the consecration of Archbishop Matthew Parker in 1559, when other returned Protestant clergy wore Anglican vestments, Coverdale insisted on wearing a plain black suit and hat. He refused to resume his place as bishop of Exeter. It was not inability or timidity that kept him from the ministry, it was his age and his reluctance to participate in the rituals that were part of Queen Elizabeth's religious compromise. Finally, in 1565, his friend the bishop of London succeeded in getting him to accept a living at St. Magnus Church near London Bridge.

Coverdale preached at St. Magnus until Elizabeth ordered uniformity of practice among pastors—uniformity that included the dress they wore in the pulpit. Coverdale and several Puritan colleagues asked the queen to excuse them from wearing vestments. When the request was denied, Coverdale resigned his church. He continued to preach and to attract a following of Elizabethan Puritans who wanted less ritual and more Calvinism in their worship.

Coverdale died on January 20, 1568. His last sermon was preached in early January at the Church of the Holy Trinity in the Minories, a church that before the Reformation had been associated with the Augustinian friars—Coverdale's earliest religious home.

SIGNIFICANCE

Coverdale died protesting the royal religious policy, not violently but quietly, as he had lived most of his life. In contrast to other reformers of the period, Coverdale was moderate and accommodating. Because he was not shrill or dogmatic, he succeeded in getting royal approval for his Bible where Tyndale and others had failed. Coverdale's patient hard work, his modesty and overriding concern that all English people have immediate access to the Scriptures, disarmed even his most conservative critics. The omission of commentary, prologues, and annotations illustrates his faith in each person's ability to interpret the Bible.

Although Coverdale was less learned than Tyndale, he was more adept at writing smooth prose and poetry with an ear for the musical qualities of a sentence. Indeed, the Church of England had continued to use Coverdale's translations of the Psalms in the Psalter. Coverdale's English Bible was written for all people. Clear, graceful, free of Latinisms and learned jargon, it is a valuable heirloom of the English Reformation.

—Loretta Turner Johnson

FURTHER READING

Arblaster, Paul, Gergely Juhász, and Guido Latré, eds. *Tyndale's Testament*. Turnhout, Belgium: Brepols, 2002. Written to accompany an exhibition of William Tyndale's manuscripts, this study of Tyndale's translations of the Bible into English follows the influence and even direct transmission of those translations through Coverdale's 1535 Bible.

Bruce, F. F. *The English Bible: A History of Translations from the Earliest English Versions to the New English Bible*. New York: Oxford University Press, 1970. One of the most recent histories of Bible translations, it is easier to read than Westcott's study but less rich in stories and not as well documented. The focus is on literary comparison.

Clebsch, William A. *England's Earliest Protestants, 1520-1535*. New Haven, Conn.: Yale University Press, 1964. An excellent description of intellectual life in England as new Renaissance ideas about scholarship and religion seeped in before Henry VIII began to reform the church. Although Coverdale is seldom mentioned, this book is about people with whom he lived and worked.

Dickens, A. G. *The English Reformation*. 2d ed. University Park: Pennsylvania State University Press, 1991. A general survey of the English Reformation concentrating on its effect on ordinary men and women. Well written and documented, this work emphasizes religion, not politics.

_____. *Thomas Cromwell and the English Revolution*. London: English Universities Press, 1959. One of several excellent short general works about the English Reformation and Cromwell's role in it. Discusses the relationship between Cromwell and Coverdale, and Cromwell's support for the Great Bible.

Lupton, Lewis. *Towards King James, 1535-1568: Introductory Volume to the Authorized Version*. History of the Geneva Bible 22. London: Olive Tree, 1990.

_____. *Up to Hampton Court, 1508-1604: More Steps Towards King James's Bible*. History of the Geneva Bible 23. London: Olive Tree, 1992. These two volumes in the author's twenty-five volume opus detail Coverdale's contributions to the development of the Bible in English.

McGrath, Alister E. *In the Beginning: The Story of the King James Bible and How It Changed a Nation, a Language, and a Culture*. New York: Anchor Books, 2002. Detailed history of the King James Bible includes significant discussion of Coverdale's contributions to the history of the English Bible.

Mozley, James Frederick. *Coverdale and His Bibles.* London: Lutterworth Press, 1953. The standard biography. Although the focus is on Coverdale's writings, this book includes the most recent information about Coverdale's personal life. Presents Coverdale's best side.

Westcott, Brooke Foss. *A General View of the History of the English Bible.* 3d ed. Revised by William Aldis Wright. Reprint. New York: Lemma, 1972. Although old, this well-documented and carefully annotated study is a valuable standard work. Based on letters and contemporary observations, it includes many stories about the early writers of the English Bible.

SEE ALSO: Martin Bucer; John Calvin; Catherine of Aragon; Thomas Cranmer; Thomas Cromwell; Charlotte Guillard; Henry VIII; John Knox; Martin Luther; Aldus Manutius; Mary I; Philipp Melanchthon; Sir Thomas More; Matthew Parker; Catherine Parr; William Tyndale; Cardinal Thomas Wolsey.

RELATED ARTICLE in *Great Events from History: The Renaissance & Early Modern Era, 1454-1600:* April or May, 1560: Publication of the Geneva Bible.

PÊRO DA COVILHÃ
Portuguese explorer

Covilhã was the first Portuguese explorer to visit many lands new to Europeans, including India and southern Mozambique. His report on his travels in India, Arabia, and East Africa may have influenced the course of Portuguese exploration of those regions, and his extended albeit unwilling residence in Abyssinia was critical in the opening of diplomatic relations between its emperor and Portugal.

BORN: c. 1447; Covilhã, Beira, Portugal
DIED: After 1526; Abyssinia (now in Ethiopia)
ALSO KNOWN AS: Pedro de Covilham; Pedro de Covilhão
AREAS OF ACHIEVEMENT: Exploration, geography, diplomacy

EARLY LIFE

Pêro da Covilhã (PAY-rew duh kew-veel-YO) was born of humble parents in a town about thirty miles from the Spanish border. In his teens, Covilhã served the duke of Medina-Sidonia in Spain, the head of the greatest of Castilian grandee families, the Guzmans. Their entourage was later to include both Christopher Columbus and Juan Ponce de León. While he was in Spain, Covilhã learned to fight and, more importantly, to rely on his wits; he also learned to speak both Spanish and Arabic fluently.

Covilhã returned to Portugal in 1474 and entered the service of Afonso V. In his years with Afonso, he gained distinction as a soldier in Afonso's campaign to enforce the claim of his wife, Princess Joan (Juana La Beltraneja), daughter of Henry IV of Castile, to its throne against her aunt, Isabella the Catholic. Covilhã also visited France and Burgundy with the king in an unsuccessful attempt to gain aid from Louis XI and Charles the Bold.

When Afonso died in 1481, Covilhã continued in royal service under his successor, John II, holding the official position of squire of the royal guard. King John used Covilhã as a spy and diplomatic agent both in Spain, where there was a dangerous colony of rebellious Portuguese nobles living in exile, and in Morocco, where the Portuguese had captured Ceuta in 1415 and had been active ever since. On one of his trips to Morocco, Covilhã apparently used the purchase of horses as a cover for espionage and secret diplomacy.

Covilhã's proven resourcefulness, willingness to travel, courage, loyalty to the Crown, experience as a spy, and knowledge of Arabic were almost certainly the reasons why John and his successor, Manuel I, chose him for a mission that would take the rest of his life and secure for him a shadowy but significant place in the history of the Age of Exploration.

LIFE'S WORK

In May of 1487, John ordered Covilhã, about forty years old and married, and an Arabic-speaking Canarian, Afonso de Paiva, to carry out two exceedingly difficult missions: to gather information on India and the navigation and ports of the Indian Ocean, and to visit and establish contact with Prester John, the legendary emperor of Abyssinia. Traveling by way of Valencia, Barcelona, Naples, and Rhodes, Covilhã and Paiva began their Eastern travels disguised as merchants buying honey in Alexandria to sell farther east.

Since neither was ever challenged, it may be assumed that both Paiva and Covilhã had dark hair and complexions and spoke perfect Arabic. Both contracted fever in Alexandria and nearly died. The local authorities confiscated their cargo, anticipating their deaths, but indemnified them when they recovered, which allowed them to buy new trade goods. After this illness at the beginning of his travels, Covilhã was to remain healthy for the remainder of his life.

From Alexandria, they first went to Cairo and from there to Tor, on the Sinai Peninsula at the northern end of the Red Sea. From Tor they sailed down the Red Sea to Aden, where they parted company, agreeing to meet in Cairo in 1490. Paiva left for Abyssinia, but it is uncertain whether he ever reached the court of the emperor. The only fact known about his travels is that he died in Cairo, before Covilhã returned for their rendezvous.

Covilhã sailed from Aden to Cannanore on the west coast of India, disguised as an Arab merchant. From Cannanore, he went to Calicut, the major port for ships embarking westward with cinnamon, pepper, cloves, silk, pearls, gems, and other valuable Asian products. From Calicut, he sailed, probably in early 1489, to Goa, then primarily a port for shipping horses. Impressed with the site, Covilhã apparently suggested it as a very promising center for Portuguese trade and occupation in his lost report to the Crown.

Leaving India, Covilhã sailed to Hormuz, then the richest city on the Indian Ocean. From Hormuz, he continued his travels in the Indian Ocean, sailing down the west coast of Africa, and arriving at Sofala in Mozambique at about the time that Bartolomeu Dias reached the Great Fish River on the east coast of South Africa. While on the African coast, Covilhã heard of the Isle of the Moon (Madagascar), which he also recommended as a potential Portuguese port of call or base. From Sofala, Covilhã returned to Cairo for his rendezvous with Paiva, stopping at Mozambique, Kilwa, Mombasa, and Malindi on the way.

In his travels, Covilhã had gathered priceless information, not only about trade, bases, and ports of call, but also about the monsoons and their use by Arab and Chinese ships in the Indian Ocean. He had sailed from Aden to India on the summer monsoon of 1488 and had left for Hormuz and Arabia on the fall monsoon, shipping in both voyages as a passenger on merchant ships, which took advantage of the prevailing winds. This Arab practice of sailing with the monsoons was to become equally standard for Europeans sailing to India, starting with Vasco da Gama.

Arriving in Cairo in late 1490, Covilhã learned that Paiva had died and had left no account of his travels after

they had parted company in Aden more than two years before. In Cairo, he met two Jewish agents sent by John II to find him, Rabbi Abraham of Beja and Joseph of Lamego, a shoemaker. They brought him new instructions from the Crown—that the mission to Abyssinia was essential and that Covilhã should finish it. Joseph of Lamego would take Covilhã's letters back to Portugal, but Covilhã and Rabbi Abraham would visit Hormuz; from Hormuz, Covilhã would go to Abyssinia alone.

There is some doubt as to whether the Crown ever received the reports from Covilhã, which have never been found, although the majority of authorities believe that Lamego did return with them to Portugal and that copies were furnished to da Gama. Since many Portuguese records were destroyed in the Lisbon earthquake of 1755, it seems unlikely that they ever will be found. It is also possible that the reports carried by Lamego were lost in transit or even that Lamego never returned to Portugal. Even if the king never received any reports from Lamego, his successor, Manuel I, doubtless received some kind of oral report on Covilhã's eastern travels from Rabbi Abraham after his return from Hormuz.

Rabbi Abraham and Covilhã sailed together to Hormuz, where they parted company. Before he left for Abyssinia, Covilhã made a daring side trip; he visited Jidda, Mecca, and Medina. From Medina, he journeyed by caravan to Syria, hearing mass at the Convent of Saint Catherine on Mount Sinai. From Syria, he continued his travels, finally arriving at the court of the emperor of Abyssinia in early 1494. There his travels ended.

Three successive neguses would not allow Covilhã to return to Portugal, although they sent an Abyssinian priest to Portugal as an envoy in 1510. Covilhã was granted lands and made an adviser and confidant of the royal family. He married an Abyssinian, by whom he had several children. He was not the only long-term honored captive. Other Europeans detained in Abyssinia included another Portuguese, two Catalans, a Basque, a German, a Greek, a Venetian, and eleven Genoese, mostly captives who had escaped from the Turks.

In 1520, Covilhã emerged from obscurity to play a crucial role in opening diplomatic relations between Portugal and Abyssinia. After many vicissitudes, a diplomatic expedition sent by the Portuguese from India led by Rodrigo de Lima arrived at the court of the reigning emperor, Lebna Dengel Dawit (David). Covilhã was able to assist the embassy through his knowledge of the language, country, and court. After a long stay in Abyssinia, the embassy was successful, finally returning to Portugal by way of Massawa and Goa in 1527. Covilhã did not return with the party but sent in his place a son, who died on the journey. Father Francisco Alvares, the chaplain of the embassy, published a memoir of the Lima mission, *Verdadeira informação das terras do Preste João das Indias* (1540; *The Prester John of the Indies: A True Relation of the Lands of the Prester John, Being the Narrative of the Portuguese Embassy to Ethiopia in 1520,* 1961), which is the principal source of both the mission and the career of Covilhã.

Nothing is known of the last years of Covilhã's life. He was still living when the Lima mission left Abyssinia in 1526, but he had died before the military expedition led by Estevão da Gama to assist the Abyssinians against an invasion by Islamic Somalis arrived in late 1541.

SIGNIFICANCE

The effect of Covilhã is extremely difficult to assess. No writings by him are known to exist, although the authenticity of his travels has never been questioned. If his accounts reached Lisbon in time to be of use to Vasco da Gama, then he is one of the most significant travelers in history; if not, then he is of secondary importance. His assistance to the Lima expedition is unquestionable, so it can safely be said that his place in history in helping to open diplomatic relations with the empire of Abyssinia is secure.

By any standard, Covilhã ranks with Marco Polo, Álvar Núñez Cabeza de Vaca, and Sir Richard Burton as one of history's great wanderers. Traveling alone in hostile country—the Muslim world—he ran far greater risks than did Burton or Polo. Moreover, as a secret agent, Covilhã could anticipate only a pension and a title if he succeeded. These were ample rewards but hardly those that a successful sixteenth century conquistador or a nineteenth century explorer and travel writer might have received. Covilhã's travels seem an expression of a personal sense of duty to the Crown and of the spirit of adventure that was characteristic of the Renaissance.

—*John Gardner*

FURTHER READING

Alvares, Francisco. *The Prester John of the Indies: A True Relation of the Lands of the Prester John, Being the Narrative of the Portuguese Embassy to Ethiopia in 1520.* Edited and revised by C. F. Beckingham and G. W. B. Huntingford. Translated by Lord Stanley of Alderley. Cambridge, England: Cambridge University Press, 1961. This is the fullest account of Covilhã and the source for most writings on him. Alvares, generally considered a very reliable source, came to know Covilhã well, and liked and admired him. Internal evidence indicates that the manuscript for *The Prester John of the Indies* was begun while Alvares was still in Abyssinia.

Diffie, Bailey W., and George D. Winius. *Foundations of the Portuguese Empire, 1415-1580.* Minneapolis: University of Minnesota Press, 1977. Diffie and Winius give an adequate description of Covilhã's travels, although they do not mention his trip to Mecca, Jidda, and Medina. They believe that news of Covilhã's travels did not reach Portugal before da Gama sailed, basing their judgment on errors that da Gama made in India, which a knowledge of Covilhã's travels would have prevented.

Hale, John R. *Age of Exploration.* New York: Time, 1966. Like Diffie and Winius, Hale omits Covilhã's side trip to Mecca but believes that Covilhã's message to the king did arrive before da Gama left.

Hanson, Carl. *Atlantic Emporium Portugal and the Wider World, 1147-1497.* New Orleans, La.: University Press of the South, 2001. Survey of the Portuguese sphere of influence from the twelfth to fifteenth centuries, covering political, economic, and cultural history. Places Covilhã's journeys in the larger context of his nation's history, goals, and effects on the world stage. Includes illustrations, bibliographic references, and index.

Landström, Björn. *The Quest for India.* Garden City, N.Y.: Doubleday, 1964. Translated by Michael Phillips and Hugh Stubbs. Contains one of the fullest accounts of Covilhã's eastern travels but very little about his stay in Abyssinia and its significance.

Parry, J. H. *The Age of Reconnaissance.* Cleveland, Ohio: World, 1963. Parry gives a complete and sympathetic sketch of Covilhã's Asian travels but says virtually nothing about his stay in Abyssinia.

Penrose, Boies. *Travel and Discovery in the Renaissance, 1420-1620.* 1955. Reprint. Cambridge, Mass.: Harvard University Press, 1967. Penrose writes an account much like Landstrom's—full on Covilhã's Asian travels, weaker on his Abyssinian years.

Prestage, Edgar. *The Portuguese Pioneers.* London: A. & C. Black, 1933. Reprint. New York: Barnes & Noble Books, 1967. Prestage's work is the fullest of all on Covilhã's African years and very good on his Asian travels. He also devotes more space to showing his significance than any other author except Beckingham.

Sanceau, Elaine. *The Land of Prester John: A Chronicle of Portuguese Exploration.* New York: Alfred A. Knopf, 1944. Sanceau provides what is both the fullest and most readable of all accounts of Covilhã's career. Writing for a popular audience, Sanceau says little on the significance of Covilhã's travels but compensates her readers with a very complete view of his life in Abyssinia.

Winius, George D. *Studies on Portuguese Asia, 1495-1689.* Burlington, Vt.: Ashgate, 2001. Anthology of essays by Winius about the exploration and exploitation of India by Portugal. Includes illustrations, maps, bibliographic references, index.

SEE ALSO: Álvar Núñez Cabeza de Vaca; Charles the Bold; Christopher Columbus; Bartolomeu Dias; Vasco da Gama; John II; Louis XI; Manuel I; Juan Ponce de León; Zara Yaqob.

RELATED ARTICLES in *Great Events from History: The Renaissance & Early Modern Era, 1454-1600:* August, 1487-December, 1488: Dias Rounds the Cape of Good Hope; 1505-1515: Portuguese Viceroys Establish Overseas Trade Empire; 1509-1565: Vijayanagar Wars; 1552: Struggle for the Strait of Hormuz.

LUCAS CRANACH, THE ELDER
German artist

A friend of Martin Luther, Cranach was one of the first German artists to incorporate elements of early Reformation theology into his work. His numerous examples of mythological subjects and portraits can be related to Humanist scholars and to erudite tastes of the Saxon court.

BORN: 1472; Kronach, Upper Franconia (now in Germany)
DIED: October 16, 1553; Weimar, Saxony (now in Germany)
ALSO KNOWN AS: Lucas Müller; Lucas Sunder; Lucas Maler
AREA OF ACHIEVEMENT: Art

EARLY LIFE

Lucas Cranach (LEW-kahs KRAHN-ahk), the Elder, probably received his first training as an artist from his father, Hans Müller, in Kronach. Cranach later changed his name to reflect the town of his birth. Older accounts of Lucas's life suggest that he might have accompanied Frederick III, elector of Saxony, on a trip to the Holy Land in 1493. He is mentioned in Kronach documents between 1495 and 1498 and in Coburg in 1501.

Between this time and 1504, Cranach settled in Vienna, where he produced a series of distinctively dramatic paintings and woodcuts. The most notable of the Vienna paintings include the double betrothal portraits of the university rector Johannes Cuspinian and his wife, Anna (1502-1503), a *Saint Jerome in Penitence* (1502), and an asymmetrically composed *Crucifixion* (1503). Along with woodcuts, such as the *Agony in the Garden* (1502), these works show Cranach's flair for exaggerated gestures, emotive facial expressions, and bold draftsmanship. His interest in placing his figures in the ambient

space of primordial Alpine landscape settings credits him with being an early founder of the Danube style of landscape painting.

Some compositional elements in these early works show that Cranach was familiar with the art of his famous Nürnberg contemporary, Albrecht Dürer. Cranach's works to 1504, however, show a conscious decision on his part to reject the studied geometry and classic proportions of Dürer's figures. Instead, Cranach's pictures seem more spontaneous and free, rendered in an almost nervous drawing style.

LIFE'S WORK

Cranach may have joined the court at Wittenberg as early as 1504, but he was definitely in Frederick's employ in April, 1505, at which time he was paid for making decorations at the elector's castle in Lochau. Cranach worked, uninterruptedly, for the court until his death in 1553, serving three successive heads of the Saxon court: Frederick III, John the Steadfast, and John Frederick the Magnanimous. In 1508, Frederick held him in high enough regard to grant him a coat of arms of a winged serpent, a device Cranach used to sign his pictures throughout his life.

In the same year, Frederick entrusted him with a diplomatic mission to the Lowlands. Cranach's biographer and friend, Christoph Scheurl, related the attention Cranach received from Netherlandish artists with his lifelike portrait of the youthful Charles V (which he supposedly painted on an Antwerp tavern wall). Cranach's familiarity with Netherlandish art is documented in his monumental *Holy Kinship Altarpiece* of 1509, which is clearly derived from Quenten Massys's triptych, now in Brussels.

Lucas Cranach, the Elder. (Library of Congress)

After his return from the Lowlands, Cranach settled into a prominent and extremely comfortable life in Wittenberg. His wife, Barbara Brengbier, bore him two sons, Hans and Lucas the Younger, and three daughters. He was so successful in his business affairs that in 1528 he was listed as the second wealthiest burgher in Wittenberg. He owned an apothecary (which has functioned to modern times in the town), a winery, several houses, and a publishing house. He served on the city council between 1519 and 1549, and he was elected to three consecutive terms as burgomaster, 1537-1543.

Cranach's busy life and the vast number of pictures he produced have led most historians to believe that he was aided by a large and well-ordered shop of assistants. Certainly his two sons were central to his production. Little is known of Hans, but two dated paintings of 1534 and 1537 by him survive, along with an interesting sketchbook in Hannover; he died in Italy in 1537. It seems clear that Lucas the Younger was the inheritor of his father's workshop, and he no doubt played an increasingly important part in the workshop, especially in Lucas the Elder's later years. The role of the Cranach shop makes definite attributions of individual works to Cranach himself difficult to establish, even when they are signed and dated.

The terms of his court appointment were apparently never written down, but his position did entitle him to a yearly stipend and to a rather pampered life; moreover, there were seemingly no restrictions on commissions he could accept from outside the court. Court documents show that his clothing and that of his assistants, feed for his horse, kitchen provisions, and various household services were all provided to him on request. Except for the trip to the Lowlands in 1508 and local visits to the elector's castle in Lochau and his hunting lodge in Torgau to supervise decorations, Cranach rarely traveled. He was extremely reluctant late in his career to follow the court of John Frederick and consequently was dismissed from service temporarily between 1547 and 1550. He ultimately did obey John Frederick's request to move to Augsburg in 1550 and subsequently to Weimar in 1552, where he died the following year.

Between 1505 and 1510, Cranach's style manifests an interest in solid, three-dimensional figures, including a series of drawings on tinted paper, two-color chiaroscuro woodcuts, and large-scale altarpieces, particularly the Saint Anne Altar. By 1515, however, Cranach's style shifted to emphasize silhouetted shapes, strongly patterned compositions, and images with flatter, less insistent volume. Excellent examples of this stylistic change are two nearly life-size, full-length marriage portraits of Duke Henry the Pious and his wife, Duchess Catherine, of 1514. Accompanied by their pet dogs, the figures are spotlighted against plain dark backgrounds and dressed in rich, colorful costumes. The jaunty attitude of the two and the decorous surfaces of the panels communicate a statement of class rank that is unmistakably present in any number of other court portraits, including that of John Frederick of 1532-1535. The finery and aloofness of his court portraits contrast with another class of portraits of wealthy burghers of Wittenberg (such as *Dr. Johannes Scheyring*, 1529), in which Lucas presents a more straightforward and even plain characterization of his sitters.

There is a clear change in Cranach's art from his Vienna days. The boldness and expressiveness of his early works give way to works designed to cater to the effete tastes of a court hungry for decorative surfaces, erotic subjects, rich colors, and elaborately designed brocades. As a component of his "court style," Cranach developed a distinctive type of female figure, more Gothic than Renaissance. In his early engravings of *The Judgment of Paris* of 1508 or his *Venus and Cupid* woodcut of 1509, his nudes followed the Vitruvian proportions of Jacopo de' Barbari and Dürer. Barbari had preceded Cranach at the Wittenberg court, and the two may have known each other. In these early works, Cranach's figures are full-bodied, with insistent three-dimensional modeling; they are faithful in spirit to the classical sources of Italian art. From the 1520's on, Cranach's nudes change dramatically from the geometric proportions and the volume influenced by Italian art. He preferred instead female nudes who are adolescentlike, with large abdomens, small buttocks, and tiny breasts. They are willowy and lithe but ungainly and self-conscious. They assume choreographed poses that conform totally to the decorative surface rhythms of his later pictures.

Among the many mythological subjects produced by his shop, three themes recur frequently: the judgment of Paris, the sleeping water nymph, and the Venus with Cupid. These subjects are preserved in a number of versions dating in the 1520's and 1530's. In the 1530 version of *The Judgment of Paris* in Karlsruhe, Cranach transforms the mythological narrative into a courtly event with Mercury and Paris dressed in contemporary armor. Similarly, Minerva, Venus, and Juno wear jewelry of the period and sport the latest coiffures. Their awkward poses and the coy expression of one of the graces, who brazenly looks out at the spectator, serve to heighten the eroticism of the scene.

Cranach's interest in mythological subjects was no doubt reinforced by Humanist scholars at the University of Wittenberg. Founded in 1502, the university had a distinguished faculty of Humanists teaching the classics and rhetoric, including Nikolaus Marschalk and Christoph Scheurl. Such works as the *Reclining River Nymph at the Fountain* (1518) and *Venus with Cupid the Honey-Thief* (1530) were inspired by specific classical inscriptions. Cranach must have had help with these classical literary sources from his Humanist friends.

In 1508, Martin Luther was appointed professor of theology at the University of Wittenberg. Cranach knew him intimately. Cranach was a witness at Luther's wedding in 1525 and a godfather to his son Johannes. He also published some of Luther's writings and provided the designs for the title pages for two books by Luther published in 1518 and 1519. Cranach made several painted and printed portraits of Luther that serve to document Luther's life under the protection of Frederick III. Two of the most interesting of these are a painted panel and a woodcut, both of about 1521, which depict Luther in his disguise as Junker Georg after Luther's condemnation at the Diet of Worms.

The Lutheran message of direct redemption and the importance of faith alone in attaining salvation are themes that occur in several of Cranach's pictures and of those by Lucas the Younger. A late panel, often entitled the *Allegory of Redemption*, portrays the aging Cranach standing next to Luther beneath Christ on the Cross. Luther points to a passage in his translation of the Bible that promises direct salvation from Christ, while an arc of blood streams directly from the side of Christ onto Cranach's head. Begun by Cranach the Elder before his death, the work was completed by Cranach the Younger in 1555. A picture dating earlier in Cranach's career, the *Allegory of the Law and the Gospel* (1529), documents Luther's position that the Old Testament is incomplete without the New Testament. Such works by Cranach are clearly didactic, serving as a visual form to Luther's teachings.

SIGNIFICANCE

The lasting contribution of Lucas Cranach, the Elder, to sixteenth century German art lies primarily in the quality of his works themselves. A prolific artist, no doubt aided by a well-supervised shop, Cranach produced a varied array of subjects in various media. They range in their scope from the naturalism of his portraits of real people to the impossible anatomy of his mythological nudes.

Lacking the intellect of Albrecht Dürer's art or the sheer emotional power of Matthias Grünewald's paintings, Cranach's images seem more comfortable and less challenging. Yet Cranach was one of the first German artists to give visual form to early Reformation religious thought in his paintings, prints, and book illustrations. He developed conventions for illustrating classical mythology in an artistic tradition that had none. His art is a visual chronicle of the tastes and personalities of half a century of the Wittenberg court, a society that had a profound impact on the intellectual, religious, and political formation of sixteenth century Germany.

—*Burton L. Dunbar III*

FURTHER READING

Bax, D. *Hieronymus Bosch and Lucas Cranach: Two Last Judgment Triptychs*. Translated by M. A. Bax-Botha. New York: North-Holland, 1983. A detailed discussion of the subject matter of a painting attributed to Hieronymus Bosch in Vienna and a work related to it ascribed to Cranach in East Berlin. A focused study, the book concludes that Cranach copied the front of a now lost altarpiece by Bosch.

Christensen, Carl C. *Art and the Reformation in Germany*. Athens: Ohio University Press, 1979. Discusses more than a dozen paintings by Cranach and his shop that demonstrate subjects directly influenced by Protestant thought. There is also an excellent summary of Luther's theology and its relation to sixteenth century German art.

Cuttler, Charles D. *Northern Painting from Pucelle to Bruegel*. New York: Holt, Rinehart and Winston, 1968. A general survey of painting outside Italy during the Renaissance, the book devotes a separate chapter to Cranach's art. A short biography of Cranach is combined with a thorough stylistic survey of specific paintings and prints by the artist.

Dillenberger, John. *Images and Relics: Theological Perceptions and Visual Images in Sixteenth-Century Europe*. New York: Oxford University Press, 1999. Study of the relationship between theology and the visual arts in the first half of the sixteenth century. Divided into seven chapters, each focusing on a specific artist, including one chapter on Cranach. Includes illustrations, bibliographic references, and index.

Falk, Tilman, ed. *Sixteenth Century German Artists, Hans Burgkmair the Elder, Hans Schäufelein, Lucas Cranach the Elder*. Vol. 11 in *The Illustrated Bartsch*, edited by Walter L. Strauss. New York: Abaris Books, 1980. Contains large illustrations of 155 engravings and woodcuts attributed to the artist. There is no commentary, but the illustrations provide an excellent resource of the prints by Cranach and his shop.

Friedländer, Max J., and Jakob Rosenberg. *The Paintings of Lucas Cranach*. Translated by Heinz Norden and Ronald Taylor. Ithaca, N.Y.: Cornell University Press, 1978. The new English translation, along with the original German publication, is largely a detailed catalog of nearly four hundred works ascribed to Cranach and to his sons. Many details of the 1932 catalog have been updated with a new introduction by Rosenberg.

Grossmann, Maria. *Humanism in Wittenberg, 1485-1517*. Nieuwkoop: B. de Fraaf, 1975. The author surveys the impact of German Humanism on the Reformation. Her chapter on the visual arts discusses Cranach's pictures in this context.

Hollstein, F. W. H. *Cranach-Drusse*. Vol. 6 in *German Engravings, Etchings, and Woodcuts, ca. 1400-1700*, edited by D. G. Boon and R. W. Scheller. Amsterdam: Menno Hertzberger, 1959. Provides lists of 140 prints and their locations by Cranach, the Elder, Cranach, the Younger, and impressions attributed to the Cranach workshop. Most entries are illustrated.

Schade, Werner. *Cranach: A Family of Master Painters*. Translated by Helen Sebba. New York: G. P. Putnam's Sons, 1980. The most comprehensive treatment of the subject to date. Schade's work discusses Cranach's life and art within the context of the contributions of his two sons. Profusely illustrated with many plates in color, the book also reprints in translation all documents relevant to the Cranach family with an extensive bibliography.

Snyder, James. *Northern Renaissance Art*. Englewood Cliffs, N.J.: Prentice Hall, 1985. Intended as a general survey of Netherlandish, French, and German art, the book contains a separate chapter on Cranach. The author stresses Cranach's ties to Wittenberg Humanism and the Reformation aspects of his paintings.

Stepanov, Alexander. *Lucas Cranach the Elder, 1472-1553*. Translated by Paul Williams. Bournemouth, England: Parkstone, 1997. Stepanov's analysis is clumsily translated, but the book contains some of the best reproductions of Cranach's work available, most full-page and in color. Includes bibliographic references.

SEE ALSO: Hieronymus Bosch; Pieter Bruegel, the Elder; Charles V; Albrecht Dürer; Matthias Grünewald; Martin Luther.

RELATED ARTICLES in *Great Events from History: The Renaissance & Early Modern Era, 1454-1600:* 1499-1517: Erasmus Advances Humanism in England; October 31, 1517: Luther Posts His Ninety-five Theses; April-May, 1521: Luther Appears Before the Diet of Worms.

THOMAS CRANMER
English church reformer and scholar

Cranmer presided over the creation of the Anglican Church in England and its separation from the Catholic Church along with Henry VIII and Thomas Cromwell. Cranmer was responsible for giving an English Bible to the English people, drafting a new English service through the Book of Common Prayer, and sealing England's commitment to a Protestant form of worship.

BORN: July 2, 1489; Aslacton, Nottinghamshire, England
DIED: March 21, 1556; Oxford, England
AREA OF ACHIEVEMENT: Religion and theology

EARLY LIFE

Thomas Cranmer (KRAN-muhr), the son of a country squire, was born at Aslacton, Nottinghamshire. As a child he learned to hunt, shoot, and ride. He suffered under a cruel schoolmaster before going to Cambridge University, where he studied the classics, philosophy, logic, and Desiderius Erasmus's works. He received the bachelor of arts degree in 1511-1512 and the master of arts degree in 1515.

He held a fellowship from Jesus College but lost it on marrying "Black Joan" of the Dolphin Inn. Both Joan and a child died within a year, and Cranmer returned as a fellow at Jesus College. He took Holy Orders as a priest prior to 1520 but did not take an oath of celibacy, since that was not required at the time. He received the bachelor of divinity degree in 1521 and the doctor of divinity degree in 1526, whereupon he became a public examiner in theology at Cambridge.

Cranmer's idea of enlisting European universities' opinions on the validity of Henry VIII's marriage to his first wife, Catherine of Aragon, brought him to Henry's attention in the summer of 1529. The marriage cause had been returned to Rome for final determination. At Henry's behest, Cranmer wrote a treatise on the subject and convinced learned men at Cambridge to side with the king. Eventually, Oxford and the University of Paris took Henry's part, but no other universities did. Cranmer became chaplain to Anne Boleyn and a member of the household of her father, Thomas Boleyn, accompanying him on a mission in 1530 to Charles V, the Holy Roman Emperor. Two years later, Henry sent Cranmer as ambassador to Charles at Ratisborn and Nuremberg. While there, the forty-three-year-old Cranmer married Margaret, the twenty-year-old niece of Andreas Osiander, the Lutheran reformer. On the death of Thomas Warham,

archbishop of Canterbury, Henry determined to replace him with Cranmer and succeeded in securing Rome's approval of the appointment. Before returning to England, Cranmer secretly sent his wife there.

Reluctantly, Cranmer accepted the post as archbishop, being appointed March 30, 1533. Before taking his oath, however, he made a protest that the new oath did not bind him to do anything contrary to Henry's will. His first business was to pronounce in an ecclesiastical court on May 23 the invalidity of Henry's marriage to Catherine. Next, on May 28, he declared Henry's marriage of January 25 to Anne Boleyn lawful. On September 10, he became godfather to Henry and Anne's daughter Elizabeth, the future Elizabeth I, born on September 7.

Cranmer was short. The July, 1545, painting done by Fliccius shows him with a somewhat stern, forbidding countenance, but that may have been a pose for the painter, since Cranmer was gentle in his dealings with all. Clean-shaven in the portrait, with the suggestion of a fast-growing beard, he did grow a long beard during his imprisonment under Mary, Henry and Catherine's daughter, a devout Catholic.

LIFE'S WORK

As archbishop, Cranmer deferred to Henry, who was made supreme head of the Church by parliamentary statute in 1534, and to his friend Thomas Cromwell, who was appointed vicar general in spirituals in 1535. Cranmer saw that the pope's name was eliminated from all service books. Personally sympathetic to Thomas More, the former lord chancellor, and John Fisher, bishop of Rochester, he saw them executed in 1535 for refusing to accept Henry's new succession to Anne's heirs and to Henry's new authority. The following year, in May, he visited Anne in the Tower of London, where she had been placed on charges of having had sexual relations with several men, including her brother Thomas. On May 17, Cranmer declared Anne's union with Henry as invalid from its inception, thus bastardizing Elizabeth, and gave Henry a dispensation to marry Jane Seymour, who, like Henry, was descended from Edward III. Anne was executed on May 19. Jane died twelve days after giving Henry a male heir, Edward, on October 12, 1537. Cranmer became Edward's godfather—evidence, again, of Henry's intimate affection.

Early in 1536, Cranmer had directed the religious convocation to approve the Ten Articles of Religion, the first formula of faith made by the Church of England. The articles, as their revision the next year in the Bishop's Book reveals, had been set by Henry and edited by Cranmer. Collectively they denoted a drift toward reformation. Four of the seven Sacraments—matrimony, confirmation, religious orders, and extreme unction—were not mentioned; only baptism, the Lord's Supper, and penance were discussed.

Cranmer's longtime wish to make the English Bible available to the English people was successful when he secured, in August of 1537, Cromwell's permission to sell copies of Matthew's Bible, based on the work of the reformers William Tyndale and Miles Coverdale, to the public. This Bible, subsequently revised, became the Great Bible, known for its size, and was placed in each parish church from 1541 on. Parliament, however, in 1543 forbade the reading of the Bible at home by women and common folk.

The Reformation in England had seen the abolition of holy days in 1536, including the celebration of Saint Thomas Becket's feast. Cranmer scandalized conservatives by eating meat on the feast's eve. Moreover, worship of images and veneration of relics were forbidden. Becket's shrine at Canterbury was destroyed. Nevertheless, Cranmer had little to do with the suppression of the monasteries that had led, in 1536-1537, to the uprising known as the Pilgrimage of Grace in the north of England. Even Henry had second thoughts about how far reform had gone, and he introduced into Parliament the Six Articles of religious belief that reaffirmed transubstantiation in the Mass and clerical celibacy. Immediately Cranmer sent his wife to Germany. A common rumor was that she was carried from place to place in a large trunk, ventilated by air holes, to preserve the secrecy of his marriage.

Obediently, Cranmer married Henry to Anne of Cleves, then dissolved that marriage in 1540. Other council members asked Cranmer in the fall of 1541 to inform Henry of his fifth wife Catherine Howard's infidelity and loose morality. Like Anne, Catherine was executed. Even Cranmer did not escape the threat of the Tower. In 1543, the king's council secured Henry's consent to send Cranmer to the Tower, where he would be examined concerning his unorthodox religious views. Rather than let events take their course, Henry told Cranmer in advance and gave him his ring, by which he might appeal to the king for justice. Thus, the tables were turned on Cranmer's enemies, and no one said anything against him as long as Henry lived. That same year, Cranmer made known to Henry his secret marriage, and Margaret returned to England. At the king's request, dur-

ing the following year, he issued prayers in English and an English litany. Cranmer was with Henry the night he died, January 28, 1547.

The new king was Henry's nine-year-old son, Edward VI, who, along with Lord Protector Edward Seymour, duke of Somerset, favored Protestantism. Thus it was possible for Cranmer in 1547 to prescribe new English homilies for preachers, the use of Erasmus's paraphrases of the New Testament to assist in reading the English Bible, and in the following year to secure Communion in both kinds for the laity and the legality of clerical marriage. Furthermore, candles on Candlemas Day, ashes on Ash Wednesday, and palms on Palm Sunday were abolished. A new English catechism, based on a Lutheran one, was issued. In 1549 came the new order for the service in English in the Book of Common Prayer, mostly written by Cranmer. This occasioned revolt in the counties of Devon and Cornwall. Cranmer also invited distinguished European Protestants to England. He was unsuccessful in his attempts to secure a European synod of leading Protestants, and he was unable to secure a new revision of ecclesiastical law.

On Somerset's fall from power, Cranmer began to absent himself from the court of Somerset's successor, John Dudley, duke of Northumberland. The Reformation proceeded nevertheless, and a revised prayer book was issued in 1552 and, in the following year, the Forty-two Ar-

Thomas Cranmer. (Library of Congress)

ticles of Religion. On Edward's death, July 6, 1553, Cranmer reluctantly agreed to Northumberland's plan to make Lady Jane Grey (the granddaughter of Henry's favorite sister, Mary) queen. When this plan failed and Mary, Henry's daughter by Catherine of Aragon, became queen, Cranmer was sent to the Tower, deprived of his rank, and ultimately executed, on March 21, 1556, despite seven recantations of his Protestant views. In fairness to Mary, one must note that Cranmer was sent to the Tower for writing a tract against the Catholic Mass. Cranmer had fortuitously sent his wife to Germany in 1555. After his death, she married twice.

The spectacle of Cranmer's death at Oxford is one of the famous moments in Protestant history. Fear for his life brought him to recant. When he learned that Mary would not spare him, he courageously declared his true views. Before he was burned at the stake, he spoke of his great regret at recanting his true faith and then almost ran to the place of burning. He bravely held the hand that had written the recantations in the flame and neither stirred nor cried out. He died quickly.

SIGNIFICANCE

Henry VIII's need for a male heir and his decision to dissolve his union with Catherine of Aragon so that he could marry Anne Boleyn provided Cranmer with an opportunity to serve his king as archbishop of Canterbury and his country as a facilitator of Reformation doctrines. As archbishop under Henry, Cranmer brought the English people the English Bible, the English Our Father and Creed, English prayers in the Litany of 1544, the abolition of holy days and images, and a subtle movement away from the Mass to a Communion service. Under Henry's son Edward, Cranmer's reformist tendencies flowered in the new English worship service as prescribed in the Book of Common Prayer, issued in 1549 and again, in altered form, in 1552. The Forty-two Articles of Religion approved by Parliament in 1552 ultimately became the basis of the Thirty-nine Articles, the basic tenets of Anglicanism today.

Though Cranmer's language was ambiguous, most scholars agree that he personally believed in a symbolic rather than a real presence in the Lord's Supper. By emphasizing Scripture as the determinant of religious belief and practice, Cranmer helped Bible-oriented Christians appropriate Scripture as a guide to life. By his own example, he showed the world that clergy should marry. His stress on general confession (in which the whole congregation makes a general confession together) and his invitation to take Communion in both bread and wine were

attempts to stimulate more frequent Communion by laypeople. Finally, Cranmer's death for his faith became an important link in the building of the Anglican faith—that is, the faith of communicants in the Church of England—under his goddaughter, Elizabeth I, who chose to incorporate most of Cranmer's reforms in her religious settlement on succeeding her sister Mary as queen. Thus, Cranmer, along with Henry VIII, Edward VI, Elizabeth I, and Thomas Cromwell, became founders of the Church of England and the Anglican faith.

—M. J. Tucker

FURTHER READING

Ayris, Paul, and David Selwyn, eds. *Thomas Cranmer: Churchman and Scholar.* Rochester, N.Y.: Boydell Press, 1999. Anthology of essays on all aspects of Cranmer's thought and career, including his facility with the English language, his stint as ambassador, his revisions of ecclesiastical canon law, and the relationship of his ideas to those of Erasmus and Luther. Includes illustrations, bibliographic references, index.

Bromiley, G. W. *Thomas Cranmer, Theologian.* New York: Oxford University Press, 1956. Assesses Cranmer's theological contributions, noting that he came only slowly to his views and that for the most part they were derivative, influenced in his view of the Eucharist by his friend Nicholas Ridley, bishop of Rochester.

Cranmer, Thomas. *Cranmer's Selected Writings.* Edited by Carl S. Meyer. London: S.P.C.K., 1961. Contains the Litany of 1544, assorted prayers and collects, the preface to the English Bible, sample homilies, and Cranmer's writings on baptism and the Lord's Supper. Gives the flavor of Cranmer's language and thought, as do the various editions of the Book of Common Prayer throughout history.

Dickens, A. G. *The English Reformation.* 2d ed. University Park: Pennsylvania State University Press, 1991. Thoughtful, perceptive, and informed by vast learning. The best short explanation of Cranmer's view of the Eucharist.

Elton, G. R. *Reform and Reformation: England, 1509-1558.* Cambridge, Mass.: Harvard University Press, 1979. A detailed text for the period. Stresses the role of Thomas Cromwell rather than Cranmer in bringing the English Bible to the English people.

Hutchinson, F. E. *Cranmer and the English Reformation.* New York: Macmillan, 1951. A brilliant book and a good place to start one's search for an understanding of how the Reformation came to England and Cranmer's role.

MacCulloch, Diarmaid. *Thomas Cranmer: A Life*. New Haven, Conn.: Yale University Press, 1996. Influential and award-winning biography of Cranmer incorporates newfound sources. Includes several appendices, illustrations, bibliographic references, and index.

Maynard, Theodore. *The Life of Thomas Cranmer*. London: Staples Press, 1956. Brief, readable account that stresses Cranmer's contributions to the Protestant tradition and emphasizes the drama of his life.

Null, Ashley. *Thomas Cranmer's Doctrine of Repentance: Renewing the Power to Love*. New York: Oxford University Press, 2000. Detailed study of Cranmer's doctrine of repentance examines the medieval notions of repentance Cranmer inherited, then engages in a close analysis of the evolution of his doctrine from 1520 to 1537 to 1544. Includes illustrations, bibliographic references, index.

Ridley, Jasper. *Thomas Cranmer*. Oxford, England: Clarendon Press, 1962. Solid, scholarly, yet readable study of Cranmer and his times. Sets Cranmer in the context of the Protestant-Catholic historiographical debate in an introductory section. Puts Cranmer's Reformation contributions in the frame of his loyalty to the Crown. Definitive account.

Smith, Lacey Baldwin. *Henry VIII: The Mask of Royalty*. London: Jonathan Cape, 1971. Brilliant study of the aging Henry VIII at the time of the English Reformation.

Wilson, Derek. *In the Lion's Court: Power, Ambition, and Sudden Death in the Reign of Henry VIII*. New York: St. Martin's Press, 2002. Vivid study of the perils of Henry VIII's court details the fates of six members of the court, including Cranmer and five other men named Thomas. Provides Cranmer's background and education, as well as a thorough survey of his activities in the court, and the way he avoided the fate of the other five. Includes illustrations, maps, sixteen pages of plates, bibliographic references, and index.

SEE ALSO: Anne of Cleves; Anne Boleyn; Catherine of Aragon; Charles V; Miles Coverdale; Thomas Cromwell; Edward VI; Elizabeth I; Desiderius Erasmus; Saint John Fisher; Lady Jane Grey; Henry VIII; Mary I; Sir Thomas More; Nicholas Ridley; Jane Seymour; William Tyndale.

RELATED ARTICLES in *Great Events from History: The Renaissance & Early Modern Era, 1454-1600:* 1531-1540: Cromwell Reforms British Government; December 18, 1534: Act of Supremacy; May, 1539: Six Articles of Henry VIII; July, 1553: Coronation of Mary Tudor; January, 1563: Thirty-nine Articles of the Church of England.

THOMAS CROMWELL
English administrator and statesman

During the 1530's, one of the most crucial and turbulent decades in English history, the chief minister of Henry VIII was Thomas Cromwell, who helped bring about the king's marriage to Anne Boleyn, the separation of the Church of England from Rome, the dissolution of the monasteries, and the establishment of Protestantism in England.

BORN: 1485?; Putney, near London, England
DIED: July 28, 1540; London
ALSO KNOWN AS: Baron Cromwell of Okeham; Earl of Essex
AREAS OF ACHIEVEMENT: Government and politics, religion and theology

EARLY LIFE

Thomas Cromwell was born to Walter Cromwell, a blacksmith, brewer, armorer, and cloth merchant. Records of Thomas Cromwell's youth are scanty, based mostly on gossip or on Cromwell's own possibly unreliable accounts of his life. According to them, he fled from home in his teens and went to Italy, where he served as a soldier under the Italians and French. Leaving the army, he set himself up as a wool merchant in Florence and in the Netherlands. Some accounts say that while in Italy, he met Niccolò Machiavelli; what is certain is that he had read Machiavelli's work in manuscript and became a disciple of it. Largely self-educated, Cromwell became a book lover and taught himself Greek and Latin, Italian, and French.

By 1512 or 1513, he was back in England, where he married Elizabeth Wykys or Wykeys, a wealthy widow, and began to practice law, while continuing to operate as a wool merchant. Between 1514 and 1520, he made several trips to Rome. Around 1520, he began to perform legal and administrative jobs for Cardinal Thomas Wolsey, archbishop of York and lord chancellor of England. In 1523, Cromwell became a member of the House of Commons, and the next year, a member of Gray's Inn.

LIFE'S WORK

Cromwell became increasingly useful to Cardinal Wolsey, who in 1525 employed him to dissolve several monasteries so that their confiscated wealth could be used to endow Wolsey's colleges at Oxford and Ipswich. Cromwell did this so satisfactorily that he became Wolsey's confidential secretary and thus the power behind the power behind the throne. No scruples deterred Cromwell from doing whatever was required to gain and keep power; in 1527, he advised cardinal-to-be Reginal Pole to forget about ethics and practice the cynical power politics of Machiavelli's *Il principe* (wr. 1513, pb. 1532; *The Prince*, 1640).

In 1527, Elizabeth Cromwell died, leaving her husband with a son and two daughters. He never remarried. Henry VIII, however, was eager to divorce his wife, Catherine of Aragon, and to marry his mistress Anne Boleyn. When Wolsey failed to obtain for the king either an annulment or a divorce, Henry removed him from his offices and brought a bill of attainder against him. Despite his Machiavellian views, Cromwell defended Wolsey so ably that he earned the appreciation of the king, who took him into the service of the Crown and in 1531 made him privy councillor.

The following April, he became master of the king's jewels and shortly thereafter clerk of the hanaper. In September, 1532, he became acting secretary of state and in April, 1534, succeeded in ousting Secretary of State Stephen Gardiner and taking the post himself. A year earlier, he had already become chancellor of the exchequer. As Cromwell worked his way deeper into the king's confidence, he was rewarded by being made master of the rolls and in July, 1536, lord privy seal and Lord Cromwell of Wimbledon.

To win the royal confidence and favor, Cromwell worked out a plan to obtain for Henry his divorce, his marriage to Anne Boleyn, supremacy over the Church in England, and the remaining wealth of the monasteries. To begin with, he proclaimed that all the nation's clergy had violated the Statute of Praemunire in recognizing the Legatine authority of Cardinal Wolsey, even though the king had sanctioned that authority. In consequence, the clergy had to pay an immense fine and acknowledge the king as the "Only Supreme Head" of the Church. In 1533, Cromwell wrote and forced through Parliament the Act in Restraint of Appeals, canceling appeals to the Papacy in

Thomas Cromwell. (Library of Congress)

marriage and testamentary cases. In January of 1533, Henry married the pregnant Anne Boleyn, and in May, the new archbishop of Canterbury, Thomas Cranmer, pronounced Henry's first marriage invalid and his new one legitimate.

Continuing to gratify the king, Cromwell engineered through Parliament more legislation that led to the Act of Supremacy, which in defiance of Pope Clement VII, who had declared in favor of Queen Catherine, made the king Supreme Head of the Church in England, effectively severing England from Rome and placing it in the Protestant camp. Cromwell also had passed a new Act of Succession, in favor of Anne Boleyn and her children, and a new Treason Act making it treasonable to challenge either the king or the new queen. Thus, Cromwell forged an absolute despotism for King Henry and used it to execute any who obstructed his policies, chiefly Chancellor Thomas More and John Fisher, bishop of Rochester. Cromwell harbored no hatred for his opponents; they were simply like chess pieces that must be removed.

When Henry became Supreme Head of the Church, he appointed Cromwell its vicar-general. In that capacity,

Cromwell ordered an investigation of the monasteries and between 1536 and 1540 dissolved the monastic houses and confiscated their wealth for the Crown. Cromwell's harsh attacks on the clergy and monasticism led to several Catholic rebellions, most notably the Pilgrimage of Grace in Yorkshire, which was brutally suppressed. In 1538, Cromwell claimed to have discovered a conspiracy in Salisbury and Exeter, and though the evidence was questionable at best, he had the abbot of Glastonbury and other monastic leaders hanged and the king's cousin the marquess of Exeter and the leaders of the Pole family executed as traitors. Systematically, Cromwell consolidated absolute power in the monarchy and enjoyed his share as the virtual ruler of England.

Meanwhile, Henry's matrimonial problems increased. When he wearied of Anne Boleyn, who had borne him a daughter, Elizabeth, rather than the son he craved for the royal succession, he wished to marry Jane Seymour, accused Anne of adultery and incest, and had Cromwell serve as prosecutor in the rigged trial that resulted in the execution of the queen and four of her alleged lovers, including her own brother, Lord Rochford. Jane Seymour bore Henry the male heir for which he so longed but died in childbirth. After a brief period of mourning, Henry began to look for a fourth wife.

Undertaking the role of marriage broker, Cromwell looked for a favorable foreign alliance. Though he had no strong religious principles and had engineered the break with Rome for reasons of expediency rather than belief, Cromwell had been maneuvering for an alliance with the German Lutherans to maintain a balance of power against a possible alliance between Spain and France in opposition to England. King Henry, who had earned the title "Defender of the Faith" by an early attack on Martin Luther, still considered himself a Catholic of sorts, despite his break with Rome, and balked at such an alliance. Cromwell, however, was persuasive, and the king reluctantly allowed him to proceed. Accordingly, Cromwell negotiated a marriage with Anne, the niece of the duke of Cleves.

Henry had not met her but was persuaded of her charms by a flattering portrait of her by Hans Holbein, the Younger. Yet when she arrived in England at the end of December, 1539, Henry was disenchanted, emphatically disliked her looks, and complained that Cromwell had deceived him. From that moment, Cromwell's days were numbered. The duke of Norfolk introduced his attractive niece Catherine Howard to allure the king, who had already ordered Cromwell to extricate him from his latest marriage. Trying to keep the royal favor, Cromwell

in April had Parliament confiscate the wealth of the Knights Hospitalers of St. John, and on April 17, the king named him earl of Essex and on the next day made him lord great chamberlain.

Cromwell, however, reached this height only to fall. Led by Norfolk, his enemies plotted against him and persuaded Henry that the man who had made the king the Supreme Head of the Church of England was a heretic and hence a traitor. Cromwell's fate was that he had succeeded too well; he had done everything necessary to give the king absolute power, he had subdued the Church and seized its wealth, and he had killed off anyone who might be inclined to further rebellion. Only in foreign policy might he still be necessary, but it turned out that the French-Spanish alliance did not materialize and that the marriage to thwart it was a disaster. Not noted for gratitude, Henry attacked Cromwell with his own weapons and with no warning had him arrested on June 10, under a bill of attainder for treason. Imprisoned for a month and a half in the Tower of London, Cromwell was beheaded on July 28, at Tyburn.

SIGNIFICANCE

As Henry VIII's chief minister during the 1530's, Cromwell brought about the separation of the Church of England from Roman Catholicism, and though he seems to have been utterly indifferent to religion himself, he was the person chiefly instrumental in making England officially Protestant. By making it possible for Henry to marry Anne Boleyn, Cromwell was in part responsible for her daughter Elizabeth's eventually becoming the legitimate heir and queen. Cromwell did more than anyone else to consolidate royal power and to create a national administration. A descendant of his sister was Oliver Cromwell.

He appears as a minor character in William Shakespeare's *Henry VIII* (pr. 1613, pb. 1623; with John Fletcher) and is the title character in the apocryphal Shakespearean play *History of Thomas, Lord Cromwell* by "W. S." (1592). The latter play, written from a Protestant perspective shortly after the defeat of the Spanish Armada, makes Cromwell a martyr to the Protestant cause and portrays him as a paragon of Puritan virtues. Subsequent playwrights and novelists have all seen Cromwell as a cold, ruthless, unscrupulous person, the embodiment of Machiavellian ideology, who would not hesitate to dispose of any person or any institution that got in his way. He appears as a treacherous and self-serving antagonist in H. F. M. Prescott's novel *The Man on a Donkey* (1952), in Robert Bolt's play *A Man for All Seasons* (pr. 1954), in the 1969 film version of *Anne of the Thousand Days* (pr., pb. 1948), and in the British Broadcasting Company television series *Henry VIII and His Six Wives* (1972).

Historians are divided in their judgment of Cromwell, some seeing him as an efficient administrator, others deploring his ruthless methods. Yet he was loyal to Wolsey and to the king, and he changed the course of English history profoundly and irrevocably.

—*Robert E. Morsberger*

FURTHER READING

Beckingsale, B. W. *Thomas Cromwell, Tudor Minister.* Totowa, N.J.: Rowman and Littlefield, 1978. Sees Cromwell as a dynamic visionary but also as a ruthless opportunist for whom the end justifies the means: "Amidst the sordid struggles of court politics he did retain a vision of a great monarchy, a prosperous commonwealth and a religion, purged of superstition."

Bernard, G. W. "Elton's Cromwell." In *Power and Politics in Tudor England: Essays.* Burlington, Vt.: Ashgate, 2000. Reexamination and critique of G. R. Elton's biography of Cromwell. Includes bibliographic references and index.

Dickens, A. G. *Thomas Cromwell and the English Reformation.* New York: Macmillan, 1959. A brief study in the Teach Yourself History Library. Admires Cromwell's energy and abundance of new ideas; considers that "all the great constructive and destructive achievements of his [Henry VIII's] long reign were crowded into the eight brief years of Thomas Cromwell's ministry."

Elton, Geoffrey Rudolf. *Reform and Renewal, Thomas Cromwell and the Common Weal.* Cambridge, England: Cambridge University Press, 1973. One of the few studies that presents Cromwell approvingly. Sees Cromwell operating on "firm principles of a spiritual renewal resting on the truths of the past" and accordingly "less determinedly secular and less ruthlessly radical" than formerly portrayed.

Innes, Arthur D. *Ten Tudor Statesmen.* 1934. Reprint. Port Washington, N.Y.: Kennikat Press, 1971. Devotes one chapter to Cromwell, stresses the influence of Machiavelli on Cromwell's evolution into a relentless practitioner of political expediency. Sees Cromwell as the heartless forger of absolute despotism for Henry VIII.

Loades, David. *Politics and Nation: England, 1450-1660.* 5th ed. Malden, Mass.: Blackwell, 1999. Examination of Cromwell's life and career against the backdrop of the extended power struggle between the Tudors and the aristocracy and Henry VIII's consolidation of power. Includes bibliographic references and index.

Marius, Richard. *Thomas More, a Biography.* New York: Alfred A. Knopf, 1984. Examines Cromwell's role in the persecution of More for his refusal to approve the dissolution of the marriage between Henry VIII and Catherine of Aragon and Henry's marriage to Anne Boleyn. Shows Cromwell manipulating the law to cause More's downfall and death. Illustrated.

Maynard, Theodore. *The Crown and the Cross: A Biography of Thomas Cromwell.* New York: McGraw-Hill, 1950. The standard biography. Admires Cromwell's administrative, legal, financial, and diplomatic abilities but expresses disgust at his cold-blooded and sinister lack of compassion. Illustrated.

Scarisbrick, J. J. *Henry VIII.* Berkeley: University of California Press, 1968. The standard biography of Henry VIII, this volume considers Cromwell in his role of formulating and carrying out royal policy. Makes no judgment of Cromwell and sees him as a competent administrator who gave England "good governance." Illustrated.

Williams, Neville. *The Cardinal and the Secretary: Thomas Wolsey and Thomas Cromwell.* New York: Macmillan, 1975. Studies Cromwell as Wolsey's subordinate and successor. Sees Cromwell as a "real innovator, directing the complicated moves in the break with Rome to establish a national state." Considers Cromwell stronger in domestic concerns than in diplomacy.

Wilson, Derek. *In the Lion's Court: Power, Ambition, and Sudden Death in the Reign of Henry VIII.* New York: St. Martin's Press, 2002. Vivid study of the perils of Henry VIII's court details the fates of six members of the court, including Cromwell and five other men named Thomas. Provides Cromwell's background and education, as well as a thorough survey of his activities in the court, and the events leading up to his beheading. Includes illustrations, maps, sixteen pages of plates, bibliographic references, and index.

SEE ALSO: Anne of Cleves; Anne Askew; Anne Boleyn; Catherine of Aragon; Clement VII; Thomas Cranmer; Elizabeth I; Henry VIII; Hans Holbein, the Younger; Niccolò Machiavelli; Sir Thomas More; Jane Seymour; William Shakespeare; Cardinal Thomas Wolsey.

RELATED ARTICLES in *Great Events from History: The Renaissance & Early Modern Era, 1454-1600*: Beginning 1485: The Tudors Rule England; 1531-1540: Cromwell Reforms British Government; 1532: Holbein Settles in London; December 18, 1534: Act of Supremacy; July, 1535-March, 1540: Henry VIII Dissolves the Monasteries; 1536 and 1543: Acts of Union Between England and Wales; October, 1536-June, 1537: Pilgrimage of Grace; May, 1539: Six Articles of Henry VIII.

CUAUHTÉMOC
King of the Aztec Empire (r. 1520-1521)

Cuauhtémoc, the last Aztec king and the nephew and son-in-law of Montezuma II, resisted incursions of the Spaniards and their Mexican Indian allies into the Aztec Empire. Despite ultimately losing the empire and being hanged by Hernán Cortés, he remains a symbol of national pride in Mexico because of his courage, fierce resistance, tenacity, and leadership.

BORN: c. 1495; Tenochtitlán, Aztec Empire (now Mexico City, Mexico)
DIED: February 28, 1525; Honduras
ALSO KNOWN AS: Guatémoc; Guatemozín; Quauhtémoc; Cuauhtemoctzín
AREAS OF ACHIEVEMENT: Government and politics, warfare and conquest

EARLY LIFE

Born into the family of Aztec kings, Cuauhtémoc (kwow-TEHM-ohk) lived an early life of privilege. He was reared to become a warrior and devoted to the cult of the war god Huitzilopochtli. Cuauhtémoc's childhood coincided with early Spanish expeditions into the Caribbean basin, when unsettling rumors drifted into Mexico.

His uncle, Montezuma II, who ruled during this time of growing uncertainty, continued Aztec expansion into the south, spreading toward Maya territory. As a warrior, Cuauhtémoc undoubtedly participated in the campaigns of expansion, taking prisoners whose hearts were offered in sacrifice to Huitzilopochtli, high atop the central pyramid of Tenochtitlán.

When Hernán Cortés and a small group of Spanish soldiers arrived on the coast of Mexico in 1519, Cuauhtémoc witnessed Montezuma's concern about who they were and what they wanted. The arrival of the Spaniards transformed local politics. While Montezuma tried to convince the Europeans to return to the islands without coming to his capital city, enemies of the Aztecs joined with the invaders, hoping to remove the Aztecs from power. Cuauhtémoc was privy to the events that eventually brought the foreigners into Tenochtitlán, where they took Montezuma hostage.

LIFE'S WORK

Cuauhtémoc was among those Aztec nobles who believed Montezuma was too cautious in dealing with the Spaniards. Although he respected his uncle's authority, and his role as Huitzilopochtli's high priest, Cuauhtémoc would have preferred more drastic measures to rid the Aztecs of the interlopers. He watched in dismay as the coarse Spanish soldiers moved into one of the palaces on the temple square. Montezuma, however, continued to insist that they be provided with food and gifts.

Another of Montezuma's nephews, Cuitláhuac, also was determined to get rid of the Spaniards. The opportunity to attack the invaders came when, on the absence of Cortés from the capital city, one of his lieutenants ordered Spanish soldiers to attack unarmed Aztec warriors dancing at a festival to Huitzilopochtli. This act brought on the Spaniards the rage of the Aztecs, who could no longer be restrained by Montezuma's orders. When Cortés returned to Tenochtitlán and found his men under siege, he prepared to evacuate them from the city under cover of darkness. In this tense situation, Montezuma attempted to address his people from a palace rampart; there he was struck by a rock and died.

With Montezuma's death, the Aztecs elected Cuitláhuac to fill his position. Under the leadership of Cuitláhuac, armed opposition to the Spaniards intensified. As the Aztecs attacked the fleeing Spaniards and inflicted many casualties, their spirits rose. Their new leader, Cuitláhuac, however, came down with smallpox (brought into Mexico by the Spaniards) and died shortly after coming to power. To rule in his place, the Aztecs chose Cuauhtémoc. Still a young man, Cuauhtémoc faced an ominous situation. Cortés and his men, having found shelter among their Indian allies, were resting and regrouping, preparing for an assault on Tenochtitlán.

This time they would lay siege to the city with ships that they planned to build in the heart of Mexico.

Unlike Montezuma, Cuauhtémoc had few doubts or illusions about who the Europeans might be and what they hoped to accomplish in Mexico. He was convinced that they were dangerous enemies who had duped his uncle and who were bent on seizing the empire. He brooked no compromise with them and prepared to fight them to the death. Cuauhtémoc was determined to feed the war god Huitzilopochtli with the hearts of Spanish soldiers. Thus began the battles for the city of Tenochtitlán and ultimate control of the Aztec Empire.

The Spaniards continued to count on the support of those Indian allies who had chafed under Aztec rule. Despite valiant attempts by Cuauhtémoc to convince his Indian enemies that the Spaniards posed the greatest danger, he could not win back the support of those who felt their day of liberation from Aztec rule had finally come.

Yet Cuauhtémoc was fully convinced that Huitzilopochtli would lead him to victory. When his armies inflicted casualties on the enemy forces, he took great pleasure in marching the captured Spanish soldiers up the steps of the great temple of Huitzilopochtli, where their hearts were ripped out and offered to the god as Aztec warriors feasted on their limbs. The Spaniards often watched in horror, praying to the Christian God and the Virgin Mary that they might be spared death at the hands of what they believed were heathens.

As the siege of Tenochtitlán tightened, the Aztecs stubbornly fought on, refusing to surrender even when the food and fresh water supplies to their island city were cut off. When the victorious Spaniards entered Tenochtitlán, they found a decimated population. Survivors had resorted to eating rats and grass in order to survive. Many had died from dehydration because the brackish water of the lake was unfit for human consumption.

Even with the horrible circumstances of the devastated city, Cuauhtémoc refused to surrender. Instead, he and his advisers decided that he would attempt to flee with his family across the lake to a safer spot where he might continue to lead the resistance against the invaders. When Spanish soldiers captured the vessel in which he was leaving Tenochtitlán, however, he was finally turned over to Cortés.

Many of the Spaniards hoped that Cuauhtémoc would reveal the location of the gold and other treasure they had lost when they were forced to flee Tenochtitlán. Because he steadfastly refused to reveal the location, he was tortured. His captors burned his feet with hot oil; he finally relented and told them that the treasure they had taken from Montezuma had been thrown into the lake. Even taking into account the sacrificial religion of the Aztecs, the barbarous torture of Cuauhtémoc and the Spanish greed for gold became enduring symbols of the crass violence of the invaders.

Cortés had assured Cuauhtémoc that he would allow him to continue as ruler of his people, but only if

---

THE SURRENDER AND CAPTURE OF CUAUHTÉMOC

Spanish conquistador and chronicler Bernal Díaz del Castillo tells of the siege and fall of Mexico City in 1521, namely the surrender of the fiercely resistant and courageous Aztec king Cuauhtémoc. In the following account, Díaz includes the words of Cuauhtémoc as he faces capture and as he is brought before the conquest's leader, Hernán Cortés.

It pleased our Lord God that [Spanish soldier] García Holguin should overtake the canoes and piraguas in which Guatémoc was travelling. . . . [Holguin] made signals for them to stop, but they would not stop, so he made as though he were going to discharge muskets and crossbows. When Guatémoc saw that, he was afraid, and said: "Do not shoot—I am the king of this City and they call me Guatémoc, and what I ask of you is not to disturb my things that I am taking with me nor my wife nor my relations, but carry me at once to Malinche."

. . . Cortés embraced Guatémoc with delight, and was very affectionate to him and his captains. Then Guatémoc said to Cortés: "Señor Malinche, I have surely done my duty in defence of my City, and I can do no more and I come by force and a prisoner into your presence and into your power, take that dagger that you have in your belt and kill me at once with it." . . . Cortés answered him through Doña Marina and [interpreter Jerónimo] Aguilar very affectionately, that he esteemed him all the more for having been so brave as to defend the City, and he was deserving of no blame.

. . . Guatémoc and his captains were captured on the thirteenth day of August at the time of the vespers on the day of Señor San Hipólito in the year one thousand five hundred and twenty-one, thanks to our Lord Jesus Christ and our Lady the Virgin Santa Maria, His Blessed Mother. Amen.

Source: The Discovery and Conquest of Mexico, 1517-1521, by Bernal Díaz del Castillo, edited by Genaro García, translated by A. P. Maudslay (New York: Farrar, Straus and Cudahy, 1956), pp. 452-453, 454.

Cuauhtémoc did the bidding of the Spaniards. In 1524, however, when Cortés realized he had to take a group of men to Honduras to put down Spanish soldier Cristóbal de Olid's challenge to his authority, he took with him the Aztec nobles he suspected would lead a rebellion in his absence. Cuauhtémoc and several other Indian leaders were forced to march south with the Spaniards. For reasons that remain unclear, some Spaniards became convinced that these men posed a danger to them even while traveling south. Consequently, in February of 1525, Cuauhtémoc and two other Mexican Indian rulers were found guilty of treason and were hanged in Honduras, marking the end of Aztec rule.

SIGNIFICANCE

Cuauhtémoc's life serves as a reminder that even in defeat, heroes are made. Cuauhtémoc was the last ruler of the great Aztec Empire. The Spanish siege of Tenochtitlán and Cuauhtémoc's valiant death marked the end of Aztec rule and the beginning of colonial rule over Mexico by the Spanish. Into the twenty-first century, Cuauhtémoc is revered as a true symbol of Mexican pride for his perseverance and his refusal to be subjugated at the hands of the Spaniards.

—*Joan E. Meznar*

FURTHER READING

Díaz del Castillo, Bernal. *The Conquest of New Spain.* Translated by J. M. Cohen. New York: Penguin Putnam, 1963. This firsthand account of the conquest of Mexico provides a Spanish soldier's view of Cuauhtémoc's strategy, fierce resistance, and bravery.

Leon-Portilla, Miguel, ed. *The Broken Spears: The Aztec Account of the Conquest of Mexico.* Boston: Beacon Press, 1992. An excellent counterpoint to Bernal Díaz del Castillo's account, this compilation of indigenous responses to the conquest contrasts Montezuma's vacillation with Cuauhtémoc's steadfast opposition to the Spanish presence in Mexico.

Meyer, Michael C., William L. Sherman, and Susan M. Deeds. *The Course of Mexican History.* 7th ed. New York: Oxford University Press, 2003. This engagingly written and beautifully illustrated textbook gives an authoritative account of the rise of the Aztecs and their precipitous fall to the Spaniards.

Padden, R. C. *The Hummingbird and the Hawk: Conquest and Sovereignty in the Valley of Mexico, 1503-1541.* New York: Harper & Row, 1970. An account of the conquest of Mexico, steeped in adventure and drama, which provides a thorough description of the encounter between Cortés and Cuauhtémoc.

West, Rebecca. *Survivors in Mexico.* Edited by Bernard Schweizer. New Haven, Conn.: Yale University Press, 2003. Provides a short account of the enduring influence of Cuauhtémoc on Mexican culture, focusing on the 250-foot monument erected in his honor on one of the principal thoroughfares of downtown Mexico City.

SEE ALSO: José de Acosta; Pedro de Alvarado; Juan Rodríguez Cabrillo; Hernán Cortés; Doña Marina; Montezuma II; Nezahualcóyotl.

RELATED ARTICLES in *Great Events from History: The Renaissance & Early Modern Era, 1454-1600:* Beginning 1519: Smallpox Kills Thousands of Indigenous Americans; April, 1519-August, 1521: Cortés Conquers Aztecs in Mexico.

JOHN DAVIS
English explorer

The most diligent and successful of the English explorers who attempted to find a northwest passage to the Far East, Davis greatly enlarged knowledge of the islands, waters, and coastline of the northern edge of North America.

BORN: c. 1550; Sandridge Barton, Devonshire, England
DIED: December 29 or 30, 1605; near Singapore
ALSO KNOWN AS: John Davys
AREA OF ACHIEVEMENT: Exploration

EARLY LIFE

John Davis was born at Sandridge Barton, a farm in Devonshire, England. His father was a yeoman farmer of some substance, enough that Davis was later able to describe himself as a "gentleman." He grew up not far from the family of Humphrey Gilbert, and in adult life, the Gilbert family would help to sponsor his voyages. He went to sea while probably still an adolescent and became a privateer and shipmaster. On September 29, 1582, he married Faith Fulford, daughter of an important local landowner. By that time, he had become the close friend of Adrian Gilbert, younger brother of Humphrey; it was Gilbert who interested him in voyages to Canada in search of a new route to the Pacific.

LIFE'S WORK

After the early voyages of the Cabots, the English had been slow in developing their interest in exploring and colonizing outside Europe. When that interest became active in the late sixteenth century, they found themselves closed off by the Spanish and Portuguese from the rich trade with China and South Asia, coveted by all European nations. Several Englishmen became convinced that they could gain access to Asia by sailing around the northern coast of Canada to the Pacific; they included Martin Frobisher (who made voyages to Greenland and Canada, with the aid of the Gilberts and others in 1576, 1577, and 1578) and John Dee, the resident philosopher, physician, and mathematician at the court of Elizabeth I, who argued that it was possible to get to Asia either by going west around Canada or north across the Pole. After the failure of Frobisher's third voyage, Davis and Adrian Gilbert met with Dee in 1579 to discuss possibilities for a new attempt. Another meeting in January, 1583, included the queen's secretary, Sir Francis Walsingham, and conferred the queen's approval of their undertaking.

In February, 1585, Gilbert and Davis received a patent from the queen to explore either to the north or northwest, giving them the right to create colonies and to hold trading monopolies with any regions they discovered. There was at that time no realistic possibility of exploring the North Pole—the technological and logistical difficulties would not be overcome before the twentieth century—but they found backers among London merchants for a northwestern voyage and within five months Davis was ready to set out, with two ships and forty-two men, including four musicians.

Davis left from Dartmouth on June 7, 1585, and crossed first to Greenland, which he called "Land of Desolation." He had his first encounter with indigenous populations on the western coast of Greenland, near what is now Godthaab; in an effort to please the possibly hostile Inuit, he had his orchestra play while he and the crew danced on a rocky island. The tactic worked, and he was able to trade with the Inuit for sealskin clothes and boots. The first voyage explored the waters between Greenland and Baffin Island; he believed that he had found a northwest passage in Cumberland Sound, a large bay of Baffin Island. After sailing up the bay for 180 miles, he began to fear that he would be trapped by winter weather and returned to England, arriving near the end of August.

Davis was absolutely convinced that he had found the entrance to the northwest passage; he wrote to Sir Francis Walsingham that it "is a matter nothing doubtful, but at any time almost to be passed, the sea navigable, void of ice, the air tolerable, and the waters very deep." On the strength of his belief, he organized a new expedition the next year, funded by merchants of Exeter and Totnes as well as London. He took four vessels, plus a spare that had been dismantled and stored inside the largest ship. His plan was to test two possibilities simultaneously: He would take two ships back to Cumberland Sound while shipmaster Richard Pope would take the other two north to look for John Dee's polar route. Both efforts were fruitless.

Davis substantially repeated his 1585 voyage, again skirting the coast of Greenland, where his men visited an Inuit village and challenged the men to jumping and wrestling contests, then crossing to Baffin Island and Cumberland Sound. The weather, however, did not favor him; icebergs and contrary winds prevented him from exploring the sound; the Hudson Strait, which he passed after turning south; or Hamilton Inlet in Labrador, all of which he hoped would be the coveted passage to the Pacific. He returned to England in October after catching a good haul of codfish on the Newfoundland Banks. Meanwhile, his other two ships were inevitably thwarted by pack ice as they tried to sail north; they ended by following Davis to Greenland, where they had a football match with one village of indigenous and a fight with another in which three Inuit were killed, and returned home. Davis remained optimistic; he believed that the entrance to the Northwest was one of four places he had found "or else not at all," and he was ready to sell his family estate, if necessary, for funds to try again.

The third voyage came closer to his goal. He took three small vessels from Dartmouth on May 19, 1587, a full month earlier than his previous tries, and proceeded much farther north up Davis Strait, now called Baffin Bay. At the end of June, he reached a point he named Sanderson's Hope, after his principal London backer. If he had turned northwest, he would have approached Lancaster Sound, the actual entrance to a northwest passage, but he was turned back by ice. A month later, he again passed the Hudson Strait, leading to Hudson Bay, but could not explore it and returned to England, stopping on the way in Labrador to fish—and to try deer hunting with some hounds he had brought. His haul of fish apparently paid for his voyage, but Davis never realized any personal wealth from his travels.

Davis remained convinced that a northwest passage would be found; he wrote after his return, "The passage is most probable, the execution easy." He was, however, diverted to other enterprises. He may have taken part in the fight against the Armada in 1588, and he later privateered in the Atlantic. When Thomas Cavendish attempted his second voyage around the world in 1591, Davis accompanied him to South America, trying three times to pass the Straits of Magellan in a lone ship, but was finally turned back by bad weather. He did become the first European discoverer of the Falkland Islands before he returned to England in 1593. In 1594 and 1595, during an enforced stay in England because of legal problems, he wrote two books, *Seaman's Secrets* (1594) and *World's Hydrographical Description* (1595). The former, a guide to practical navigation, became very widely used, with eight editions before 1660. His most ambitious voyage, across the Pacific to Southeast Asia, led to his death: He was killed in a fight with Japanese pirates on an island near Singapore at the end of 1605.

SIGNIFICANCE

A careful navigator, a courageous and skilled captain, and a humane explorer, John Davis added much to knowledge of the waters and the land masses of the most inhospitable parts of North America, and he sailed farther to the north than anyone before his time. Although he remained convinced that a practical northwest passage would be found, his voyages demonstrated that the route would be difficult and dangerous at best.

Davis's later voyages in the South Atlantic helped to show that routes around Cape Horn could be used, and, meanwhile, English and Dutch seamen were able to reach the East by the long but less treacherous route around Africa. So interest in a northwest passage faded, and there was no successful navigation around the Canadian coast until modern times.

By the standards of the time, Davis was a considerate and even compassionate commander. He never sent his men where he would not go himself; he allowed a shipload of men who fell ill on the second voyage to return home; he maintained a careful eye on his supplies and did not allow his men to run short of food. He also treated North American Indians with greater courtesy and respect than most European explorers, recognizing that in the long run the outcome of his voyages might depend on their goodwill. He gained less contemporary recognition than some of his more flamboyant peers, and he never profited from his expeditions, but he was one of the most persevering and courageous of the North American explorers.

—Robert W. Kenny

FURTHER READING

Dodge, Ernest S. *Northwest by Sea*. New York: Oxford University Press, 1961. The best overall narrative of efforts by English and Dutch explorers to establish a northwest passage. Davis receives careful and sympathetic attention.

McDermott, James. *Martin Frobisher: Elizabethan Privateer*. New Haven, Conn.: Yale University Press, 2001. Biography of Davis's contemporary discusses his previous attempts to find the Northwest Passage. Includes illustrations, photographic plates, bibliographic references, index.

Manhart, George B. *The English Search for the Northwest Passage in the Time of Queen Elizabeth*. Vol. 2 in *Studies in English Commerce and Exploration in the Reign of Elizabeth*, by Albert Lindsay Rowland and George Born Manhart. Reprint. New York: B. Franklin, 1968. A meticulous scholarly work that traces the

Davis voyages with greater detail than most readers will need. Originally a Ph.D. thesis.

Markham, Sir Albert, ed. *The Voyages and Works of John Davis the Navigator.* London: Hakluyt Society, 1878. Reprint. New York: Burt Franklin, 1970. Difficult reading, but the most important source on Davis's life. It includes his two treatises on seamanship, otherwise unavailable to modern readers.

Markham, Sir Clements. *Life of John Davis.* London: G. Philip and Son, 1889. The closest approach to a full biography, now dated. Full of admiration for the subject but lacking in historical analysis.

Morison, Samuel Eliot. *The Great Explorers.* New York: Oxford University Press, 1978. A lively and readable narrative of European voyages to the Americas between 1490 and 1600. Probably the most accessible and attractive introduction to the subject. Includes an excellent chapter on Davis.

Savours, Ann. *The Search for the North West Passage.* New York: St. Martin's Press, 1999. Extensive survey of centuries of attempts to find the Northwest Passage, from the Elizabethans to the Victorians. Includes illustrations, maps, photographic plates, bibliographic references, and index.

Wright, Louis B. *West and by North: North America Seen Through the Eyes of Its Seafaring Discoverers.* New York: Delacorte Press, 1971. A compilation of selections from the accounts written by explorers and their contemporaries, skillfully arranged to present a coherent view of North America as it was seen by sixteenth century Europeans.

SEE ALSO: John Cabot; Sebastian Cabot; Jacques Cartier; Thomas Cavendish; John Dee; Elizabeth I; Sir Martin Frobisher; Sir Humphrey Gilbert.

RELATED ARTICLE in *Great Events from History: The Renaissance & Early Modern Era, 1454-1600:* Early 16th century: Rise of the Fur Trade.

JOHN DEE
English scientist, mathematician, and scholar

Arguably the most influential astrologer in Renaissance England, Dee had an extensive education in continental Europe that enabled him to bring to England developments in cartography, navigation, mathematics, astronomy, and cryptography. His practice with alchemy and astrology made him a regular consultant to Queen Elizabeth I, even as these same interests exposed him to charges of necromancy.

BORN: July 13, 1527; London, England
DIED: December, 1608; Mortlake, Surrey, England
AREAS OF ACHIEVEMENT: Mathematics, astronomy, government and politics, philosophy

EARLY LIFE

John Dee was the son of Roland Dee, a successful merchant of fabrics and textiles during the reign of Henry VIII, under whom Roland was employed. In 1542, Dee entered St. John's College at Cambridge University and devoted himself wholeheartedly to the traditional curriculum, which included the *trivium* (grammar, rhetoric, logic) and the *quadrivium*, or scientific arts (astronomy, geography, music, mathematics). He was a distinguished student, receiving the bachelor of arts degree and a readership at Trinity College in 1546. Dee studied mathematics and navigation intensively, and in 1548, he received the master of arts degree, also from Cambridge.

With the ascension of the Catholic Queen Mary I in 1553, Roland Dee was indicted by the Privy Council and briefly imprisoned in the Tower of London, presumably because of his close ties to Protestant reformists and to sympathizers of the late king Edward. John Dee was also arrested by Mary's examiners in 1555, on charges ranging from necromancy (conjuring, magic, sorcery) to conspiracy with Elizabeth (Mary's rival). Dee was ultimately acquitted of all charges, and one biographer has even suggested that Dee subsequently worked closely with Bishop Bonner, Mary's most ardent and lethal persecutor of Protestant sympathizers.

LIFE'S WORK

In 1547, Dee took his first of several trips to continental Europe, where he regularly sought the acquaintance of cutting-edge authorities on mathematics, navigation, astronomy, and natural magic. At the University of Louvain (now in Belgium), Dee became acquainted with Flemish cartographer and geographer Gerardus Mercator, maker of terrestrial globes and navigational maps.

England was the regular beneficiary of Dee's travels, since he often shared his intellectual findings in the Low Countries with his associates, some of whom were em-

John Dee. (Hulton|Archive by Getty Images)

ployed (after 1558) by Queen Elizabeth. Dee's discovery of the works of Trithemius in 1562, for example, effectively introduced to England the study of modern cryptography, a subject in which the queen took personal interest. Dee himself developed a reputation on the Continent as one of the leading scientific figures of the day. His lectures on Euclid, for example, were wildly popular and earned him an offer to join the faculty at the prestigious Sorbonne University in Paris.

Despite his popularity abroad, however, Dee's accomplishments in mathematics and astrology were less warmly received in his homeland. Mathematics was sometimes regarded as a "magical" subject in England by persons who were suspicious of its grandiose claims, and Dee's serious involvement in mathematics and astrology made him vulnerable to charges of necromancy. Dee himself regarded natural magic as a legitimate course of scientific study, and his own *The Mathematicall Praeface to the Elements of Geometrie of Euclid of Megara*, published in 1570 in one of the earliest English translations of Euclid, lists several of the magical arts as derivative subjects of mathematics. Nonetheless, Dee's reputation made him an ambivalently popular figure at court, and he was visited on more than one occasion by Queen Elizabeth herself, for whom he periodically cast horoscopes.

Dee's role in England's burgeoning campaign for North American colonization was considerable. Throughout the sixteenth century, exploration of the New World was dominated by Spain and Portugal. When England belatedly entered the scene, Dee's previous experience with continental navigational theory, as well as his knowledge of cartography and mathematical modeling, was particularly useful. In the early 1550's, Dee advised Richard Chancellor on his expedition through the North Sea, an undertaking financed by the Muscovy Company that resulted in a trade route stretching from England to Moscow. More important, Dee had personally instructed Martin Frobisher and Christopher Hall on their expedition to discover a northwest passage to China in 1576, an expedition that was fruitless in terms of its stated aim but which led the way for later English settlements in Canadian North America.

Throughout his lifetime, Dee ardently encouraged Queen Elizabeth to challenge Spanish predominance in the colonial sphere, and his *Brytanici imperii limites* (English translation, 1995), presented to the queen in 1577, went so far as to suggest that the Americas had been discovered centuries before by King Arthur.

In 1583, Dee relocated his entire family to Kraków, Poland. Many reasons have been suggested for Dee's sudden move, such as the idea that Dee was acting as a foreign spy for the queen. On August 1, 1584, Dee left Kraków for Prague, where he incurred the suspicions of Rudolf II, the Holy Roman Emperor. Rudolf ultimately banished Dee from the empire, whereupon Dee took his family to Trebon, a small town in southern Bohemia. During this period in his life, Dee carried on an intense and somewhat inscrutable relationship with Edward Kelley, his personal scryer, that is, a person who acts as a medium between the spiritual and physical worlds. Dee's diary recounts at length a series of angelic conversations carried out through Kelley as medium, many of them centered on Dee's attempt to recover the original language spoken by Adam before the confusion at Babel.

Dee returned to England in 1589 to find his home ransacked and his library pillaged. After several unsuccessful petitions to the queen for a bishopric in Winchester, Dee accepted a wardenship in Manchester, a position that effectively removed Dee from his former position of influence in the court. Dee faced periodic charges of necromancy and illegal conjuring until his death in 1608.

SIGNIFICANCE

Although Dee's reputation as an astrologer and natural magician has endured, it is important to realize that he was also an extremely accomplished mathematician, and Dee himself (like most of his contemporaries) would not have considered astrology and mathematics to be discrete subjects. In 1558, for example, he published *Propaedeumata aphoristica* (*John Dee on Astronomy*, 1978), a work that explicitly connects the study of astrology and mathematics by arguing that the universe is structured mathematically and harmonically. In this work, as in several of his others, Dee followed the theories of previous natural magicians, such as Proclus (c. 410-485) and Roger Bacon (c. 1220-c. 1292), who also considered magic, astrology, and mathematics inextricably linked parts of a unified natural philosophy.

In effect, then, Dee greatly contributed to the propagation and dissemination of Neoplatonic theories about the universe in Renaissance England. The influence of his numerous writings on astrology and mathematics extended to subjects as wide-ranging as physics, music, philosophy, optical theory, and mechanical engineering. His published work reveals the Renaissance's theoretical basis for connecting these different areas of scholarship, an interdisciplinary endeavor that stands in sharp contrast to the modern academic preference for disciplinary specialization.

—*Joseph M. Ortiz*

FURTHER READING

Clulee, Nicholas H. *John Dee's Natural Philosophy.* New York: Routledge, 1988. Analyzes Dee's theories on mathematics, metaphysics, and natural magic in the context of Renaissance intellectual history. Several chapters devoted to *The Mathematicall Praeface to the Elements of Geometrie of Euclid of Megara.* Includes several plates of Dee's notes and sketches.

Deacon, Richard. *John Dee: Scientist, Geographer, Astrologer, and Secret Agent to Elizabeth I.* London: Garden City Press, 1968. Well-documented, chronological account of Dee's life. Includes bibliography and plates of early modern illustrations of Dee's contemporaries.

Gouk, Penelope. *Music, Science, and Natural Magic in Seventeenth-Century England.* New Haven, Conn.: Yale University Press, 1999. Discusses the theoretical relationship in the Renaissance between science and natural magic as it was propagated by Dee and his contemporaries.

Harkness, Deborah E. *John Dee's Conversations with Angels: Cabala, Alchemy, and the End of Nature.* New York: Cambridge University Press, 1999. Analyzes Dee's transcripts of his angelic conversations and argues that they represent a coherent development of his natural philosophy.

Woolley, Benjamin. *The Queen's Conjurer: The Science and Magic of Dr. John Dee, Adviser to Queen Elizabeth.* New York: Henry Holt, 2001. An engaging account of Dee's life, more novelistic than academic, with particular attention given to Dee's relationship with Edward Kelley. Includes plates of Dee's writings and illustrations of Dee's contemporaries.

SEE ALSO: John Davis; Elizabeth I; Martin Frobisher; Henry VIII; Mary I; Gerardus Mercator; John Napier; Nostradamus; Georg von Peuerbach; Rudolf II.

RELATED ARTICLES in *Great Events from History: The Renaissance & Early Modern Era, 1454-1600:* 1462: Founding of the Platonic Academy; 1462: Regiomontanus Completes the *Epitome* of Ptolemy's *Almagest*; 1486-1487: Pico della Mirandola Writes *Oration on the Dignity of Man*; 1576-1612: Reign of Rudolf II; 1583-1600: Bruno's Theory of the Infinite Universe.

Deganawida

Iroquois founder and prophet

Deganawida enlisted the aid of an orator and diplomat, Hiawatha, to spread his vision of a united and peaceful Iroquois Confederacy of separate nations, which had suffered from internal wars and feuds that nearly destroyed Iroquois civilization.

Born: c. 1550; place unknown
Died: c. 1600; place unknown
Also known as: Deganawidah; The Peacemaker
Areas of achievement: Government and politics, law

Early Life

Little is known of the early life of Deganawida (deh-gahn-ah-WEE-dah), whose name means, roughly, "two rivers flowing together." Oral accounts maintain that he was the product of a virgin birth that surprised his mother and grandmother, both poor women who lived alone in the forest. They feared that the virgin birth might portend evil, so they tried to drown him three times in an icy river, only to find Deganawida safe at home after each attempt. His mother then came to realize that he was meant to live.

As a young man, Deganawida is said to have possessed *orenda*, a force or energy that enabled him to unite all things. He had dreamed of a mighty white pine tree, whose reaching roots united warring tribes as an eagle soared overhead. Deganawida had proposed that the weapons of war be buried under the roots of this white pine. He was a stutterer who could hardly speak, a manifestation that Iroquois oral history attributes to a double row of teeth.

Deganawida mourned the waste of war and the pain of torture. He asked the Huron, the tribe to which he was a part, to cease warfare, but they did not listen, so he set off to visit the Iroquois nations to the south and to the east. Oral tradition relates that Deganawida arrived in Iroquois country in a stone canoe.

Life's Work

Deganawida traveled for many years through Iroquois land, presenting his vision of peace, but no one seemed ready to listen to a stuttering prophet. As he despaired, Deganawida met Hiawatha, who supported Deganawida's vision, and they joined forces. With Hiawatha advancing their vision of peace, both men won agreement from each of the five Iroquois nations, one by one, over several years.

The toughest to convert from the ways of war were the Onondagas, who were led by an evil, twisted leader, the wizard Atotarho, who used magic to make birds fall dead from the sky and to kill members of Hiawatha's family. After an epic battle, Atotarho agreed to follow the path of peace. Eventually, he became the chief executive of the grand council. The last of the five nations to agree to follow Deganawida's law of peace was the Senecas, who came into the fold after a "sign on the sky," probably a total eclipse of the sun, in what is now western New York State.

Deganawida sought to replace blood feuds that had devastated the Iroquois with peaceful modes of decision making. The result was the Great Peace and Power and Law (sometimes called the Great Binding Law, or Kaianerekowa) of the Iroquois, which endures to this day as one of the oldest forms of participatory democracy. The confederacy originally included the Mohawks, Oneidas, Onondagas, Cayugas, and Senecas. Deganawida's confederacy was founded before first European contact in the area, possibly as early as 900, or as late as 1550; debate has continued for many years about the confederacy's age.

The Great Peace has been passed from generation to generation by use of wampum, a form of written communication using strings of shell beads, which outlines a complex system of checks and balances between the confederacy's nations. A complete oral recitation of the Great Peace can take several days; encapsulated versions have been translated into English for more than one hundred years, but a close-to-complete version was not developed until the 1990's.

Each of the five Iroquois nations in Deganawida's confederacy maintained its own council, whose sachems, or loved ones, were nominated by the clan mothers of families holding hereditary rights to office titles. The grand council at Onondaga was drawn from the individual national councils. The rights, duties, and qualifications of the sachem were outlined explicitly, and the women could remove (or impeach) a sachem who was found guilty of any of a number of abuses of office, from missing meetings to murder. A sachem was given three warnings, then removed from the council if he did not mend his ways, and a sachem guilty of murder lost not only his title but also deprived his entire family of its right to representation. The female relatives holding the rights to the office lost those rights, and the title transferred to a sister family.

FROM THE IROQUOIS CONSTITUTION

Deganawida developed, with Hiawatha, the Iroquois constitution, considered by some to have influenced the framing of the constitution of the United States. The Iroquois constitution, called the Great Peace and Power and Law, is an oral law, so no primary documentation exists. There are a number of versions, however, on the Web, including three paraphrased principles outlined here.

RIGHTEOUSNESS

In order to keep violence from interfering in the stability of the community, the people, clans, chiefs, clan mothers, and the entire nation must treat each other fairly. Such conduct will assure that political and social justice is maintained.

HEALTH

Health means that the soundness of mind, body, and spirit will create a strong individual. Health is also the peacefulness that results when a strong mind uses its rational power to promote well-being between peoples, between nations.

POWER

The laws of the Great Law provide authority, tradition, and stability if properly respected in thought and action. Power comes from the united actions of the people operating under one law, with one mind, one heart, and one body.

Source: Excerpted from the Web site of the Native American Haudenosaunee (traditional leadership of the Seneca, Cayuga, Onondaga, Oneida, Mohawk, and Tuscarora Nations). http://sixnations.buffnet.net. Accessed September 22, 2004.

The circumstances of Deganawida's death are not known. After his work of unification, he is said to have dressed in shining white buckskin and paddled away in a luminous, white canoe.

SIGNIFICANCE

The Iroquois Great Peace and Power and Law has been cited frequently, along with European precedents, as a forerunner of modern democratic traditions. Deganawida, for example, said that leaders' skins must be seven spans thick to withstand the criticism of their constituents. The law pointed out that the sachem should take pains not to become angry when people scrutinized their conduct in governmental affairs. Such a point of view pervades the writings of Thomas Jefferson and Benjamin Franklin.

Under Deganawida's law, the sachem was not allowed to name its own successors, nor could it carry its title to the grave. The Great Peace provided a ceremony to remove the "antlers" of authority from a dying chief. The Great Peace also provided for the removal from office of a sachem who could no longer function in office adequately, a measure remarkably similar to the twenty-fifth amendment to the U.S. Constitution (1967), which provides for the removal of an incapacitated president or a president who dies while in office.

In some ways, the grand council operates like the U.S. House of Representatives and the U.S. Senate, which have conference committees. As it was designed by Deganawida, debating protocol in the grand council calls for debate to begin with the elder brothers. After debate by the older brothers, the younger brothers debate in much the same manner. Once consensus is achieved by the younger brothers, the discussion is then given back to the elders for confirmation. Next, the question is laid before a "judicial" council for its review and decision.

At this stage, the judicial reviewer can raise objections to the proposed measure if it is believed inconsistent with the Great Peace. Essentially, the "legislature" can rewrite the proposed law on the spot so that it accords with established law. When the reviewers reach consensus, a sachem who presides over debates between the delegations, is asked to confirm the decision.

Deganawida's Great Peace also included provisions guaranteeing freedom of religion and the right of redress before the grand council. It also forbade unauthorized entry of homes—all measures that sound familiar to United States citizens through the Bill of Rights. Public opinion is of great importance within the League of the Iroquois. Iroquois people can have a direct say in the formulation of government policy, even if a sachem chooses to ignore the will of the people. The Great Peace stipulates that the people can propose their own laws even when leaders fail to do so, adding them to the rafters of the metaphorical longhouse. This provision resembles provisions for popular initiatives in several states of the United States, as well as the mechanism by which the federal and many state constitutions may be amended.

—Bruce E. Johansen

FURTHER READING

Colden, Cadwallader. *The History of the Five Nations.* Ithaca, N.Y.: Great Seal Books, 1958. Colden's work is an early (1727) Anglo-American account of the Iroquois Confederacy and its political system.

Mann, Barbara A., and Jerry L. Fields. "A Sign in the Sky: Dating the League of the Haudenosaunee." *American Indian Culture and Research Journal* 21, no. 2 (1997): 105-163. This article makes a case that the Iroquois Confederacy was founded about 1142, not between 1450 and 1550, as most European-American scholars believe.

Wallace, Paul A. W. *The White Roots of Peace.* Santa Fe, New Mex.: Clear Light, 1994. This book provides an encapsulated account of the Great Peace's founding epic.

Wilson, Edmund. *Apologies to the Iroquois.* 1959. Reprint. Syracuse, N.Y.: Syracuse University Press, 1992. Wilson provides a modern-day account of the Great Peace's workings in a historical context.

Woodbury, Hanni, Reg Henry, and Harry Webster, comps. *Concerning the League: The Iroquois League Tradition as Dictated in Onondaga.* Algonquian and Iroquoian Linguistics Memoir 9. Winnipeg, Canada: University of Manitoba Press, 1992. This is the first (and, to date, only) partial account of the Great Peace's provisions. Earlier accounts have been only summaries.

SEE ALSO: Jacques Cartier; Hiawatha.

RELATED ARTICLE in *Great Events from History: The Renaissance & Early Modern Era, 1454-1600:* 16th century: Iroquois Confederacy Is Established.

DIANE DE POITIERS
French noblewoman

Although primarily known as the mistress of King Henry II and rival of Queen Catherine de Médicis, Diane de Poitiers wielded great influence at court in religion, politics, and arts patronage. She used her power to advance Catholicism and to patronize great artists and writers of the French Renaissance.

BORN: September 3, 1499; Saint-Vallier, France
DIED: April 25, 1566; Anet, France
ALSO KNOWN AS: Dianne de Poitiers; duchess of Valentinois
AREAS OF ACHIEVEMENT: Patronage of the arts, religion and theology, government and politics

EARLY LIFE

Daughter of Jean de Poitiers and from one of the oldest noble families in the Dauphiné region of what is now southeast France, Diane de Poitiers (dee-ahn duh pwa-tyay) had the advantage of growing up in aristocratic surroundings on the road followed by travelers to and from Italy. Exposed at an early age to prominent visitors acquainted with the literary and artistic achievements of the Italian Renaissance, Diane's father had her trained in some of the talents necessary for a Renaissance noblewoman.

As a child, Diane displayed the talents for horsemanship and hunting that would later earn her comparisons to the mythical goddess of the hunt, Diana. She continued her education in the court of Princess Anne de Beaujeu (Anne of France), where she studied the classics, church history, and the personal qualities needed for a lady at court. At the age of fifteen, Diane was married to Louis de Brezé, the fifty-six-year-old seneschal of Normandy.

In 1524, her father was sentenced to death after being implicated in a noble conspiracy. Acceding to Diane's pleas, King Francis I freed her father at the scaffold. Diane's court life continued as lady in waiting to the queen mother, Louise of Savoy, and Queen Eleanor of Austria. When her husband died in 1531, Diane chose to remain a widow. The revenues from his Norman estates, which she managed with great skill, gave her considerable freedom to live at court and raise her daughters.

LIFE'S WORK

At the time of her husband's death in 1531, Diane, now the marquise de Brezé and seneschal of Normandy, had spent many years at royal courts. Yet her influence, based on a finely honed sense of courtly politics and diplomacy, would grow in the three decades that followed.

Diane's education included several protofeminist works, including the writings of Christine de Pizan (c. 1365-c. 1430), Martin le Franc (1410-1461), and Guillaume Postel (1510-1581), manuscripts and books that later were part of her library at the château of Anet. Diane also acquired works on philosophy and medicine, in which she was considered a court expert. A contemporary text on gynecology was dedicated to Diane, who was called on regularly to exercise such skills as a matron of honor and governess.

The future Henry II, son of Francis I, was married to Catherine de Médicis in 1533, when both were fourteen years old. Yet Diane, Catherine's cousin and almost twenty years her senior, would become the love of Henry's life and the power behind the throne beginning in 1535. When Henry became king in 1547, Pope Paul III sent the new queen a gift, but he also sent a pearl necklace to Diane in recognition of her power. In the royal entry to Lyon in 1548, of which Diane was a part, one of the allegorical plays depicted the hunter Diana holding a lion on a leash.

The following year, Henry bestowed the title of duchess of Valentinois on his mistress. Despite Catherine's jealousy, Diane's influence over Henry and events at court grew. The king entrusted her with the crown jewels, asked her to write official letters (signed "HenriDiane"), and asked her to meet with visiting ambassadors. The initials "H" and "D" were everywhere interlaced and her official colors of black and white appeared in all public festivities. Although Diane gave birth to a third daughter by the king, most believe Diane was responsible for ensuring that the king did his royal duty by begetting legitimate heirs to the throne by Catherine.

In addition to her role at court and as governess to the royal children, Diane's influence extended into two other areas: religion and artistic patronage. Diane was a staunch Catholic during a time of tremendous turmoil, when Protestant reformers were trying to spread their message in France. During the reign of Francis I, she had opposed the reforming tendencies of the king's mistress, Anne de Pisseleu, duchess of Étampes. Diane's opposition marked the beginning of a series of alliances based on religion.

While Anne de Pisseleu allied with the king's reform-minded sister, Marguerite de Navarre, a Catholic party dominated by the Guise and Montmorency families formed around Diane. By Henry's reign, the intimate circle of Catholic supporters had supplanted those with reforming tendencies. In years of tension with the Papacy, Diane met with papal envoys, had leading Catholics ap-

Diane de Poitiers. (Hulton|Archive by Getty Images)

pointed to military positions, and pushed for the extirpation of heresy in France.

Diane's patronage of the arts is reflected in the château of Anet that was commissioned for her in 1552 by the king, built on property she had inherited from her husband. Chosen for the project was the leading architect of the French Renaissance, Philibert Delorme, the royal architect to Henry. Sculptor Jean Goujon assisted with the decoration, creating the fountain of Diana and several of the tapestries. Anet was not simply a castle but also a symbolic celebration of the love between Henry and Diane. Delorme created a perfect blend of Renaissance style with a design intended for private pleasure.

During her stays at the château of Chenonceau given to her by Henry, Diane patronized some of the greatest artists and architects of the time. One of her projects involved extending the castle by building a bridge over the River Cher. In addition to nearly one hundred letters, Diane composed numerous lyrics and songs that were intended primarily for Henry but which were unfortunately destroyed by the king. She was honored in dedications and poems by the poets of La Pléiade, including Pierre de Ronsard and Joachim du Bellay. The courtier, soldier, and chronicler, Pierre de Bourdeille, who saw her just before her death, referred to her as "the most beautiful of beautiful women."

For all her power, Diane's life was bound with that of the king. After his freak death from a jousting accident in 1559, Catherine, by then a powerful regent, forced Diane to exchange the château of Chenonceau for the inferior one at Chaumont. Diane lived there a short time only before retiring to Anet and spending the rest of her life managing her estates, acting as a midwife, and founding a home for unwed mothers. She died on April 25, 1566, and was buried in the chapel at Anet. Diane's will exhibits the strength of her character in her carefully worded bequests to her children and her insistence that they and their children keep to the Catholic faith.

SIGNIFICANCE

An educated and powerful woman, Diane de Poitiers's influence at court to control and determine political and religious events came at a critical juncture in French history. Her championship of the Catholic faith in the period immediately before the beginning of the French Wars of Religion (1562-1598) cemented alliances between the leading families in the realm.

Recognized for her artistic taste, Diane consulted with and patronized the leading figures of the French Renaissance in both arts and literature. Although sometimes dismissed in her own time and later as simply "the king's mistress," Diane skillfully exploited the role to become one of the most powerful figures in sixteenth century France.

—*Larissa Juliet Taylor*

FURTHER READING

Baumgartner, Frederic. *Henri II, King of France 1547-1559*. Durham, N.C.: Duke University Press, 1988. An excellent biography of Henry by one of the leading sixteenth century specialists in North America. Although the focus is on Henry, this is one of the only books in English in which one can gain an understanding of the court life and politics in which Henry, Diane, and Catherine lived.

Cloulas, Ivan. *Diane de Poitiers*. Paris: Éditions Fayard, 1997. This is one of the few biographies of Diane de Poitiers in either French or English. While Cloulas often embellishes the life and events to appeal to a popular audience, most of the available information in print on Diane can be found in this volume.

McHenry, Bannon. "Gift from a King: From Henry II to Diane de Poitiers, the Superb Chateau d'Anet." *Connoisseur* 214 (1984): 81-89. An illustrated and detailed description of the chateau where Diane spent much of her life, with details about the work of Philibert Delorme and Jean Goujon.

Sider, Sandra. "The Woman Behind the Legend: Dianne de Poitiers." In *Women Writers of the Renaissance and Reformation*, edited by Katharina M. Wilson. Athens: University of Georgia Press, 1987. A succinct account of Diane's life, writing, and artistic patronage, with excerpts from some of her letters.

SEE ALSO: Catherine de Médicis; Joachim du Bellay; Francis I; Henry II; Marguerite de Navarre; Paul III; Pierre de Ronsard.

RELATED ARTICLES in *Great Events from History: The Renaissance & Early Modern Era, 1454-1600:* July 16, 1465-April, 1559: French-Burgundian and French-Austrian Wars; 1549-1570's: La Pléiade Promotes French Poetry.

BARTOLOMEU DIAS
Portuguese explorer

Dias was the first to command a sea expedition around South Africa's Cape of Good Hope, a feat that had been attempted for more than fifty years before his success and one that led to the opening of sea trade between Portugal and Asia.

BORN: c. 1450; probably near Lisbon, Portugal
DIED: May 29, 1500; at sea in the South Atlantic, near the Cape of Good Hope
ALSO KNOWN AS: Bartolomeu Diaz
AREA OF ACHIEVEMENT: Exploration

EARLY LIFE

Bartolomeu Dias (bor-tew-lew-MAYOO DEE-uhsh), like many Portuguese explorers of his time, remains an enigma. Nothing is known about his life except for an incomplete account of his voyage around the Cape of Good Hope in 1488 and two other references regarding one previous and one subsequent voyage. He may have been related to Dinis Dias, another Portuguese captain, who also explored the African coast in search of a sea route to Asia in 1445. Dias had at least one brother, Pedro, who accompanied him on the historic voyage around the cape. Dias was undoubtedly from a poor social class, since most seamen and explorers shared a similar humble upbringing, some of them even having criminal records.

The major reason for the lack of any solid information about Dias is that virtually all the early Portuguese explorations were conducted under strict secrecy. Portugal and Spain were in fierce competition at the time, both attempting to discover the most profitable trade route to Asia. Since land routes from Europe through the Middle East to Asia were nearly impossible to traverse because of the Muslim empire's hostile monopoly of the area, a sea route around the uncharted seas of Africa seemed to be the only alternative.

More than fifty years before Dias's historic voyage, the idea of sailing past Cape Bojador (the bulging cape) located off the coast of the Sahara Desert in southern Morocco, was unheard of. There was a great fear that just south of this barren cape was the end of the world, where the sea boiled and monsters thrived. The person most responsible for stimulating interest in exploring the African coast in the hope of finding a trade route to Asia was Prince Henry, third son of King John I and Queen Philippa of Portugal, later to be known as Prince Henry the Navigator.

Henry's motivation for so fervently supporting sea exploration around Africa to Asia stemmed from his fierce hatred of the Muslims. He was a devout Christian and grand master of the militant Order of Christ, who believed that if he could locate the whereabouts of a legendary African empire ruled by a powerful Christian king called Prester John, Portugal could join forces with this influential king and overpower the Muslims, thus liberating the Holy Land and opening trade with Asia. By sending ships along the African coast, Henry planned to seek Prester John while simultaneously seeking a sea route to Asia.

In 1433, Henry sent his first captain, Gil Eanes, with the explicit order to sail past the desolate and feared Cape Bojador. This was at a time when no reliable maps existed of the African coast, navigational equipment was primitive, and sailing ships were experimental, still evolving from a traditional small Mediterranean sailing vessel to a larger and more rugged European caravel specifically designed for long voyages. Eanes failed to conquer Cape Bojador on his initial voyage, but the following year he tried again and this time sailed one hundred miles past the intimidating cape. What followed over the next five decades was a painfully gradual exploration of the African coast by dozens of Portuguese captains. Key outposts and fortresses were established along the coast and a lucrative though cruel slave trade began.

The earliest known reference to Dias is connected with the establishment of a major new fortress along the Guinea coast near Mina in 1481, twenty-one years after the death of Henry. Dias was one of the captains who sailed with the chief engineer of the project and who helped construct this key outpost. The principal explorer of this time, however, was Diogo Cão, who, in two long voyages, sailed as far south as Cape Cross, fifty miles north of Walvis Bay in Namibia. Along the way, and under direction of King John II, Cão erected huge seven-foot limestone markers called *padrões*, which he mounted on prominent points where they could be seen by passing ships. When Cão died during his final voyage back to Portugal in 1485, preparations were made for the most ambitious voyage yet attempted by Portugal.

LIFE'S WORK

In August, 1487, John commissioned Dias to command another voyage, one of major importance. Secrecy surrounding the expedition was so intense that no official report exists of the voyage. The most up-to-date maps and navigational instruments of the time, as well as the best-equipped and most carefully prepared ships, were used. For the first time, a cargo ship, stocked with food and provisions, accompanied the two sailing ships.

Dias's principal crew members were all distinguished sailors; Pedro de Alenquer, one of the best-known mariners of the period, was chief pilot of Dias's ship, the *São Cristovão*. John Infante, a knight, captained the second ship, the *São Pantaleão*. Dias's brother, Pedro, captained the supply ship with the pilot John de Santiago, who had sailed previously with Cão. Also on board, as a junior pilot, was Bartolomé Columbus, younger brother of Christopher Columbus. Along with the sixty crew members of the ships were six African captives, who carried precious metals and spices and were to be put ashore at various places along the coast to trade with the indigenous people and to try everything possible to locate the elusive Prester John. Dias also carried three *padrões* to mark his progress along the coast.

Dias sailed without serious problems to Mina, the port he had helped establish six years earlier. He restocked his ships and then sailed as far as Port Alexander in Southern Angola, where he landed two of the African captives. Farther south near Cape Cross, Dias anchored the supply ship, and the two remaining ships sailed on, passing Cão's southernmost *padrõe* on December 1. One week later, the ships anchored in Walvis Bay, where they found protection from huge South Atlantic swells. Villages could be seen nearby with the inhabitants herding cattle and sheep.

Two weeks later, they had sailed as far as Luderitz in southern Namibia, three hundred miles farther than any previous expedition. Because of continued foul weather, they anchored there for five days, while Dias put ashore another African emissary. When the winds became more favorable, they embarked again, only to encounter even more fierce weather. On January 6, 1488, Dias decided to sail into deeper waters, hoping to escape from the horrendous winds that had been battering them for a month. Dias and his crew had not been prepared for such harsh conditions, and they suffered horribly as the icy swells bashed their ships for thirteen days.

Finally, Dias gave the command to sail east in search of land. Yet no land was sighted on the eastern horizon. Dias swung from east to north in search of land, his crew becoming more and more frightened that they would never see land again. Finally, on February 3, land was sighted. Now, however, by their calculations, they were sailing east along the coast instead of south. Stunned and hardly believing the truth, Dias realized that during the thirteen days at sea fighting the storms, he and his crew had accomplished what so many before had attempted but failed to do. He had rounded the southernmost cape of Africa.

The weary mariners landed near Mossel Bay in South Africa and attempted to find provisions but were beaten back by hostile Africans. They sailed to Algoa Bay and at last found refuge. Dias was elated with his achievement and erected his first *padrõe*. He was eager to continue on even farther and determined now to sail all the way to India. His crew, however, objected strongly. Many had died during the wicked storms and many more were sick. Provisions were nearly gone, and the ships were tattered and badly leaking. Still, Dias wanted to continue, but the crew threatened to mutiny. Dias pleaded with his men, promising them great wealth if they would continue the great expedition. Second-in-command Infante, a knight with an aristocratic heritage and jealous of the low-born Dias, led the opposition.

In the end, Dias was able only to persuade his men to proceed for three more days before turning back. To avoid dishonor, Dias made his officers and principal seamen sign a document that explained what had occurred. As the two ships turned back and passed the *padrõe* at Algoa Bay, Dias, according to a historian writing twenty years after the voyage, sadly bade farewell to the historic marker, "with as much pain and sentiment as if he were leaving a beloved son in eternal exile."

Six weeks later in April, they encountered the worst weather of the expedition and were forced to anchor for three weeks in South Africa's Cape Agulhas, where they overhauled their battered vessels. By the end of May, they were crawling once again along the coast. On June 6, they sighted the southernmost cape, the one they had passed in the terrible February storm. Because of the difficulties they had encountered in reaching this elusive location, Dias named it the Cape of Storms. Later, King John renamed it the Cape of Good Hope because of the promise it offered in the discovery of a sea route to India. Dias erected his second *padrõe* there and then retraced his course to Luderitz, where he placed the third and last *padrõe*.

After recovering and then burning his supply ship, Dias crawled up the African coast. He made several stops along the way and at one point rescued the shipwrecked crew of a previous Portuguese expedition. Finally, in December, 1488, after fifteen months and sixteen thousand miles, Dias and his crew sailed into Lisbon.

John was ecstatic. He was also determined to keep the success of the voyage a secret, however, and for the next eight years was able to suppress any information about the voyage as well as all other Portuguese voyages. One witness to Dias's historic return, the brother of one of the junior pilots, did make a notation in the margin of one of his books.

> Note: that in December of this year 1488, Bartolomeu Dias, commandant of three caravels which the king of Portugal had sent out to Guinea to seek out the land, landed in Lisbon. He reported that he had reached a promontory which he called Cape of Good Hope. . . . He had described his voyage and plotted it league by league on a marine chart in order to place it under the eyes of the said king. I was present in all of this.

The chronicler was Christopher Columbus, one of many who benefited from Dias's monumental achievement.

SIGNIFICANCE

In addition to Columbus's note, only two other contemporary references to Bartolomeu Dias exist. First, he was influential in designing the ships that in July, 1497, carried Vasco da Gama around the Cape of Good Hope to India. Second, in March, 1500, less than a year after da Gama's historic return from India, Dias captained one of thirteen ships under the command of Pedro Álvars Cabral and sailed in search of an alternate route to Asia. The result of this voyage was the exploration of the Brazilian coast of South America. On setting sail from Brazil to Africa, once again in search of the Cape of Good Hope and India, the expedition encountered a ghastly storm in late May, 1500. Four ships were lost with all crewmen. Dias was one of the casualties.

There is no underestimating the importance of Dias's greatest triumph. He had boldly attained the goal set by Prince Henry the Navigator in the early 1430's, to prove that there was a route around Africa to India that could be used to skirt the land routes monopolized by the Muslims. During his voyage, he accumulated valuable data that were used by John to plan the voyage that would ultimately result in Vasco da Gama's reaching India. He not only paved the way to Asia but also inspired Christopher Columbus and later Ferdinand Magellan to seek their own routes to the Indies.

Dias, however, never reached Asia himself. Another chronicler, writing sixty years after Dias's death, summarized Dias's achievement: "It may be said that he saw the land of India, but, like Moses and the Promised Land, he did not enter in." Ultimately, it was Dias, more than anyone before him, who made it possible for Portugal to dominate the Indian Ocean and secure the vast treasures of Asia.

—*James Kline*

FURTHER READING

Axelson, Eric, ed. *Dias and His Successors*. Cape Town, South Africa: Saayman & Weber, 1988. Compendium of primary sources written by Portuguese explorers together with secondary commentaries by three noted scholars. Includes João de Barros's narrative of Dias's 1487-1488 voyage, as well as illustrations, maps, a bibliography and an index.

Buehr, Walter. *The Portuguese Explorers*. New York: G. P. Putnam's Sons, 1966. This book for young readers gives a detailed history of Prince Henry the Navigator, who was instrumental in igniting interest and financing the first voyages along the African coast. There is also a chapter on the development of the ships used by the Portuguese explorers and a chronicle of the most influential Portuguese captains with an account of Dias's voyage.

Hanson, Carl. *Atlantic Emporium Portugal and the Wider World, 1147-1497*. New Orleans, La.: University Press of the South, 2001. Survey of the Portuguese sphere of influence from the twelfth to fifteenth centuries, covering political, economic, and cultural history. Emphasizes Portugal's contribution to the creation, for the first time, of a global economy, and Dias's role in making that possible. Includes illustrations, bibliographic references, and index.

Hart, Henry H. *Sea Road to the Indies*. New York: Macmillan, 1950. Although the majority of the book chronicles the life and achievement of Vasco da Gama, the first part of the book is a detailed account of the Portuguese explorers who preceded him. Chapter 5 is dedicated to Dias and quotes from early Portuguese historians who later pieced together the long-suppressed details of Dias's voyage. Extensive bibliography of both English and foreign references.

Humble, Richard. *The Explorers*. Alexandria, Va.: Time-Life Books, 1978. Good overview of the most influential early explorers: Dias, Columbus, da Gama, and Magellan, the latter three all inspired by and benefiting from Dias's achievement. Excellent early maps, plus illustrations and text on the development of the ships and navigational equipment used for all the major voyages. Dias's voyage is described in chapter 1, "The First Giant Stride on the Route to India." Profusely illustrated; contains a selected bibliography.

Parr, Charles McKew. *So Noble a Captain*. New York: Thomas Y. Crowell, 1953. This biography on the life of Magellan contains a detailed description of Dias's voyage in chapter 1, plus information on Dias's influence on John and the building of the ships that da Gama used to sail to India. Extensive bibliography includes books on the history of Portuguese exploration, navigation, and sailing-ship construction.

Prestage, Edgar. *The Portuguese Pioneers*. New York: Macmillan, 1933. Reprint. New York: Barnes & Noble Books, 1967. Covers in detail the history of Portuguese exploration from the late fourteenth century to the major expeditions of Dias, da Gama, and Cabral through the early sixteenth century.

Russell, P. E., ed. *Portugal, Spain, and the African Atlantic, 1343-1490: Chivalry and Crusade from John of Gaunt to Henry the Navigator*. Brookfield, Vt.: Variorum, 1995. Anthology of essays detailing the expansion of Portugal's exploration and influence across the African Atlantic in search of a route to India. Includes illustrations, maps, bibliographic references, and index.

Winius, George D., ed. *Portugal, the Pathfinder: Journeys from the Medieval Toward the Modern World, 1300-ca. 1600*. Madison, Wis.: Hispanic Seminary of Medieval Studies, 1995. Anthology of essays in Portuguese exploration, including several on the discovery of the sea route to India and Portugal's subsequent activities in South Asia. Includes a bibliographic essay by the editor surveying all major sources pertaining to the fifteenth and sixteenth centuries.

SEE ALSO: Afonso de Albuquerque; Christopher Columbus; Pêro da Covilhã; Vasco da Gama; John II; Ferdinand Magellan; Manuel I; Amerigo Vespucci.

RELATED ARTICLES in *Great Events from History: The Renaissance & Early Modern Era, 1454-1600:* August, 1487-December, 1488: Dias Rounds the Cape of Good Hope; 1490's: Decline of the Silk Road; January, 1498: Portuguese Reach the Swahili Coast; 1505-1515: Portuguese Viceroys Establish Overseas Trade Empire.

JOHN DOWLAND
English composer and musician

Dowland composed some of the most influential and most often performed lute and voice pieces of the English Renaissance, which remain widely studied, performed, and recorded. Dowland also published a number of lesson manuals and several collections of lute and consort songs.

BORN: 1562 or 1563; possibly London, England, or Dublin, Ireland
DIED: Probably February 20, 1626, London
AREAS OF ACHIEVEMENT: Music, scholarship, education

EARLY LIFE

Although there is some dispute over whether his birth and early years took place in England or Ireland, the fact that John Dowland identified as a Protestant in his early life suggests that his family was based in England (individuals born in Ireland were almost always Catholic).

Dowland's family most likely consisted of middle-class artisans, yet he spent a good part of his early years (1579-1583 and possibly earlier) in an aristocratic household in the service of Sir Henry Cobham. It is likely that Dowland received at least some of his musical training and education while in Cobham's service.

Dowland's association with Cobham brought him to France in the early 1580's, and it was during this time that Dowland converted to Catholicism. (France at that time was predominantly a Catholic country.) The precise details surrounding Dowland's decision to become a Catholic are not clear, although in a letter written several years later, Dowland attributed his conversion to the impressionability of youth. At any rate, Dowland's newfound Catholicism does not appear to have affected his academic prospects; in 1588, Dowland earned a bachelor of music degree from Oxford University.

LIFE'S WORK

For most of his adult life, Dowland had as his chief ambition a position at court, his sights set on the role of a court lutenist in particular. Dowland did not realize this ambition until fairly late in his career, despite being well-connected with members of the royal court throughout most of his professional life and despite being a reputed lutenist and song composer.

Consequently, Dowland's lack of success in gaining a court appointment encouraged him to travel frequently and extensively throughout Europe. In 1594, after being passed over for a vacant royal lutenist position, Dowland traveled to Wolfenbüttel and Hesse (in Germany), where he served in the courts of Heinrich Julius, duke of Brunswick-Lüneburg, and Moritz Landgraf von Hessen-Kassel, respectively. Dowland also traveled through parts of Italy after his stay in Germany, although his plans to study at Rome with the composer Luca Marenzio were abandoned when he became involved unintentionally with a group of English Catholics bent on undermining the English monarchy.

After a second professional disappointment in 1597 (partly due to the death of his most influential champion in Queen Elizabeth I's court, Henry Noel), Dowland went to Denmark in 1588 and entered the service of Christian IV, king of Denmark and Norway (r. 1588-1648).

Dowland's musical reputation became well-established in Europe during his travels, and the generous salaries he received (often higher than what was typical for an ordinary court musician) while in service at the various courts testify to the high regard given to his compositional and performative abilities. Indeed, Dowland noted on more than one occasion and with considerable irony the ease with which he was able to attain court positions abroad rather than in his own country.

In part an attempt to bolster his professional reputation at home, Dowland began to publish collections of his own music, most made of songs for voice and lute. In 1597, Dowland published *The First Booke of Songs or Ayres*, a work that enjoyed nearly unprecedented success and went through several editions. Dowland followed this work with several more collections of songs and consort music, all of which were well-received and often reprinted: *The Second Booke of Songs or Ayres* (1600), *The Third and Last Booke of Songs or Ayres* (1603), *A Pilgrimes Solace* (1612), and his most famous work, *Lachrimae: Or, Seaven Teares* (1604), a collection of consort music Dowland dedicated to Anne of Denmark, queen of England who was married to King James I.

Dowland's early publications of lute-song music were original in their presentation of musical notation and print layout. In *The First Booke of Songs or Ayres*, for example, all of the music parts were printed on the same set of open pages (as opposed to the usual habit of having separate song books for the individual parts). He added a considerable number of compositions to the English tradition of pavans and galliards (musical forms based on dances of the same names). His most popular piece, "Lachrimae" (as distinct from the collection of pieces by the same name) helped to establish Dowland as a melancholic musician, during a time when melancholy was beginning to be associated fashionably with artistic expression.

"Lachrimae" (tears) contains Dowland's creation of the so-called tear motif, a musical motive that was adopted or alluded to by legions of subsequent composers. Dowland's reputation in his later life as a writer of complaints—against musical innovations, against court politics, against criticism of music—also undoubtedly helped to solidify the image of his melancholic persona. Although the precise date is uncertain, Dowland died in London, probably on February 20, 1626.

SIGNIFICANCE

Because Dowland was able to travel throughout continental Europe extensively, he was able to introduce to England many of the most prominent developments in Western musical composition. Conversely, Dowland's music appeared frequently in European collections of printed music, and his musical themes were used occasionally (often without permission or acknowledgment) by Continental composers.

England generally lagged behind Europe in terms of musical trends and innovations, and therefore Dowland's ardent attempts to associate with leading European innovators (particularly those in France, Italy, Germany, and Denmark) made him an important channel for the transmission of musical influence between England and the Continent.

Dowland's impact on the history of music publishing in England is substantial. His numerous collections of printed music (mostly songs for lute and voice) went through several editions, all during a period in which music publishing was a relatively new phenomenon in England. Thus, in addition to aiding the growth of a relatively new industry, Dowland's unusual attention to publication has meant that a large body of English Renaissance music is readily available for performance in the twenty-first century.

His "Lachrimae," in addition to being the first printed English work written for five violins and lute, stands as one of the most important musical achievements of the English Renaissance.

—*Joseph M. Ortiz*

FURTHER READING

Holman, Peter. *Dowland: Lachrimae (1604)*. New York: Cambridge University Press, 1999. A short monograph that offers a comprehensive overview of Dowland's well-known collection of songs. Although biographical information is scarce, Holman gives ample attention to the historical details of the work's publication, including its early reception. Most of the monograph is devoted to the contents of "Lachrimae" itself. Includes some musical examples and a select bibliography.

Poulton, Diana. *John Dowland*. Berkeley: University of California Press, 1972. The only book-length study of Dowland's life and works. Includes a substantial biographical chapter on Dowland, while the other chapters are devoted to historical and musicological analyses of his compositions and publications. Illustrations, several musical examples, bibliography.

Spink, Ian. *English Song: Dowland to Purcell*. New York: Scribner, 1974. A critical and stylistic study of the song tradition in seventeenth century England. Includes a long chapter on Dowland's development of the lutesong, situating his compositions in the context of the innovative "new music" that was being developed at the beginning of the seventeenth century. Illustrations, musical examples, bibliography of seventeenth century song books, list of principal songbooks, select bibliography.

Toft, Robert. *Tune Thy Musicke to Thy Hart: The Art of Eloquent Singing in England, 1597-1622*. Toronto, Canada: University of Toronto Press, 1993. Excellent historical study of the principles and practice of seventeenth century song composition and performance, with particular attention paid to modern performance approaches to seventeenth century English songs. Musical examples, glossary.

Wells, Robin Headlam. "John Dowland and Elizabethan Melancholy." *Early Music* 13 (November, 1985): 514-528. Discusses Dowland's place in the Renaissance tradition of melancholy, giving particular attention to the association between artistic inspiration and chronic "morbidity" that was becoming a commonplace in seventeenth century England.

SEE ALSO: William Byrd; Elizabeth I; Andrea Gabrieli; Giovanni Gabrieli; Orlando di Lasso; Luca Marenzio; Thomas Morley; Giovanni Pierluigi da Palestrina.

RELATED ARTICLES in *Great Events from History: The Renaissance & Early Modern Era, 1454-1600:* 1567: Palestrina Publishes the *Pope Marcellus Mass*; 1575: Tallis and Byrd Publish *Cantiones Sacrae*; 1588-1602: Rise of the English Madrigal; 1590's: Birth of Opera; October 31, 1597: John Dowland Publishes *Ayres*; 1599: Castrati Sing in the Sistine Chapel Choir.

SIR FRANCIS DRAKE
English explorer

Drake was the first explorer to circumnavigate the globe. A flair for leadership, combined with fearlessness and a powerful spirit of adventure, afforded Drake the most prominent place among those Elizabethan explorers and naval commanders who pioneered England's overseas expansion.

BORN: c. 1540; Crowndale, near Tavistock, Devonshire, England

DIED: January 28, 1596; at sea off Porto Bello, Panama

ALSO KNOWN AS: El Draque; the Dragon

AREAS OF ACHIEVEMENT: Exploration, military

EARLY LIFE

Francis Drake was born in Crowndale, a village near Tavistock, in Devonshire, England. Nothing is known of his mother. His father, Robert Drake, was the third son of

John Drake of Otterton. Unsuccessful in business and committed to advancing the reformed religion, the father bore responsibility for his family living in humble circumstances. Many of Francis Drake's twelve siblings reputedly were born in the hull of a ship moored in the River Thames in Kent, where the family had been forced to relocate as a result of the father's vocal Protestantism. There is a certain fitness in this connection with the sea, where most of the Drake offspring made their marks and ultimately died.

As a boy, Francis Drake was apprenticed to the master of a coasting vessel and acquired both a love for the sea and the skills that served him well during his career. On the death of the master, Drake assumed command of his ship and continued trading for a brief period. His spirit of adventure and his ambition proved, however, to be too strong, and by 1565, he joined expeditions that were mounted first to Africa and then to the Spanish Main.

These voyages whetted his appetite for exploration and further stirred his ambition, so in 1567, he decided to join the third expedition organized by his cousin, John Hawkins, to capture black slaves in Africa and sell them to the Spanish colonists in the New World.

Drake's decision to join Hawkins's third slaving voyage proved to be the turning point in his career, for Hawkins's fleet, including the ship *Judith*, commanded by Francis Drake, was attacked at San Juan de Ulúa, a small island off Veracruz, by a powerful Spanish force commanded by the viceroy of New Spain. In the ensuing battle, only two of Hawkins's ships, the *Jesus of Lubeck*, commanded by Hawkins, and the *Judith*, captained by Drake, escaped and made their way back to England. Both Hawkins and Drake vowed to be avenged for what they viewed as the "treachery" of the Spaniards, and while both men made good on their vow, Francis Drake not only struck numerous and devastating blows against King Philip II of Spain, but also laid the foundation for the maritime traditions that spread England's power

Sir Francis Drake. (Library of Congress)

and influence around in the world in subsequent centuries.

LIFE'S WORK

In the years following the attack in Mexico, Drake embarked on a series of maritime adventures that established his reputation as the quintessentially daring English sea captain. Determined to strike a blow at Spain, Drake used his knowledge of the flow of Spanish treasure from the Americas to Europe with dramatic effect.

First, in 1570 and 1571, he mounted small reconnoitering voyages to the Gulf of Mexico to collect detailed information. Then, in 1572, he executed his masterstroke by sailing from Plymouth to attack the Spanish at their most vulnerable point, the area of the production of precious metals in the New World. Knowing that the produce of the silver mines of Peru was transported by mule train overland through Panama, Drake determined to attack the unescorted treasure trains and seize their booty. On landing in Panama, Drake made contact with the Cimaroons and developed a plan to waylay the Spanish treasure train that regularly crossed the Isthmus of Panama. Providentially, Drake was taken by his guides to a high point in Panama where he could see both the Gulf of Mexico and the Pacific Ocean, which made him the first Englishman to see the Pacific.

Vowing someday to sail an English ship on the Pacific, Drake and his force pressed on and soon enjoyed spectacular success by capturing an entire treasure train that yielded so much silver that they took what they could carry back to their ships and buried the rest. Drake arrived back in England on August 9, 1573. His expedition made him a wealthy man, endowed him with a reputation for courage and daring, and gave him what proved to be a brilliant idea for his next enterprise against the Spanish.

Knowing that the Spanish treasure route was from Peru to Panama by ship, then across the Isthmus by mule train, and finally on to Spain by ship, Drake plotted to lead a fleet to the western coast of South America. Once there, he intended to attack the unprotected Spanish ships that carried the bullion to Panama, take as much treasure as his ships could carry, and return to England. From the seed of this plan, Drake became the first person to circumnavigate the globe. Leaving Plymouth on December 13, 1577, Drake and his fleet sailed southward. By the time he entered the Pacific through the Strait of Magellan, only his ship the *Golden Hind* remained of the fleet that had left Plymouth. From the autumn of 1578 through the spring of 1579, Drake sailed northward, capturing treasure all along the way. He continued on a northerly course until he reached the area that is now San Francisco, then turned westward, crossing the Pacific and Indian oceans, rounding the Cape of Good Hope, and proceeding northward along the African coast to England. Drake arrived home on September 26, 1580, after nearly three years at sea. A few months later, he was knighted and assumed the premier position among English mariners of his era.

As Anglo-Spanish relations deteriorated during the 1580's, Drake was called on by the Crown to lead the English naval forces against the Spanish. In 1585, Drake led a fleet against Spanish possessions in the New World, where the colonial cities of San Domingo and Cartagena were captured. Shortly after his return home in July, 1586, Drake was placed in command of an English fleet at Plymouth, and in the spring of 1587, he led an expedition against Spain to disrupt the formation of an armada then assembling to invade England. By attacking the Spanish fleet in Cádiz and destroying more than thirty ships and tons of supplies, Drake delayed the formation of Philip's armada for more than a year and also ensured that when it sailed it would be critically weakened.

The effect of Drake's assault in 1587 was demonstrated in July, 1588, when the Spanish Armada approached England. Drake was the first English commander to intercept the Spanish, and throughout the course of the subsequent battle, his ship the *Revenge* was always in the forefront of the action. His leadership was largely responsible for the English victory over the Armada, and the triumph provided the capstone for his reputation. Ironically, his unbroken success against the Spanish indirectly led to his death, for in 1595, Queen Elizabeth appointed Drake and Sir John Hawkins co-commanders of a fleet directed to attack Spanish possessions in the New World. During the campaign, both Hawkins and Drake contracted diseases that led to their deaths. A victim of dysentery, Drake died aboard his flagship the *Defiance* off Porto Bello, Panama, on January 28, 1596, and appropriately was buried at sea.

SIGNIFICANCE

At first glance, Drake's career appears to have been characterized primarily by military exploits at sea. Virtually every action that he took, including even the magnificent feat of exploration and seamanship of the circumnavigation, was warlike, directed against the Spanish empire, and had significant overtones of greed and personal ambition. Yet Drake was far more than one of a long line of successful English warriors, for he personified the spirit of adventure and expressed the indomitable courage and insatiable curiosity that typified the Elizabethan era. Because of Drake and those he inspired, England's knowledge of the world was vastly expanded, the nation's economy was stimulated, a national confidence in the ability to overcome the most daunting obstacles was inspired, and a sense of England's place among the leading powers of Europe was firmly established.

Yet the most important of Drake's accomplishments came in the area of maritime affairs, for he demonstrated to his countrymen that their destiny lay on the oceans of the world, regardless of whether they defended their island against foreign invaders or sought to explore the unknown lands of the Pacific. The ultimate English adventurer, Drake was more responsible than any of his contemporaries for establishing an international presence for England that endures to the present day.

—*Ronald L. Pollitt*

FURTHER READING

Bawlf, Samuel. *The Secret Voyage of Sir Francis Drake, 1577-1580*. Vancouver, B.C., Canada: Douglas & McIntyre, 2003. This book reveals evidence that Drake's secret mission on his circumnavigation of the globe was to explore the Pacific Northwest in an attempt to seek out the Northwest Passage. Beyond this new information, the book provides a multifaceted portrayal of Drake, reconciling his religious convictions with his ruthless acts of piracy. Includes illustrations, maps, bibliographic references, index.

Bradford, Ernle Dusgate Selby. *The Wind Commands Me: A Life of Sir Francis Drake*. New York: Harcourt, Brace and World, 1965. This work tries to portray Drake as a whole person rather than a naval legend, and manages to delineate his compassion as well as his courage. Altogether a respectable biography.

Coote, Stephen. *Drake: The Life and Legend of an Elizabethan Hero*. New York: Simon & Schuster, 2003. Biography combines novelistic dramatization of Drake's life with important analysis of the way his legend became a national symbol through which England understood itself and its global actions. Includes illustrations, maps, bibliographic references, and index.

Corbett, Sir Julian. *Drake and the Tudor Navy: With a History of the Rise of England as a Maritime Power*. 2 vols. London: Longmans, Green, 1898. Reprint. Brookfield, Vt.: Gower, 1988. Despite its overwhelmingly favorable view of Drake, this work remains the standard biographical account. A meticulously scholarly work that includes material gleaned from both English and Spanish manuscript sources, this study also details the rise of England as a maritime power while it relates Drake's career to that development.

Dudley, Wade G. *Drake: For God, Queen, and Plunder.* Washington, D.C.: Brassey's, 2003. This entry in Brassey's Military Profiles series examines Drake's naval career and his role in the defeat of the Spanish Armada. Includes photographic plates, illustrations, maps, bibliographic references, and index.

Hampden, John, ed. *Francis Drake: Privateer.* Tuscaloosa: University of Alabama Press, 1972. A collection of documents relevant to Drake's exploits that provides a unique view of the range and significance of his achievements. Glossary is particularly helpful.

Kelleher, Brian T. *Drake's Bay: Unraveling California's Great Maritime Mystery.* Cupertino, Calif.: Kelleher & Associates, 1997. Extremely technical and detailed discussion of where Drake claimed to have landed in California, where he most likely landed, and the reasons for the discrepancy. Includes illustrations, maps, bibliographic references, index.

Roche, T. W. E. *The Golden Hind.* New York: Praeger, 1973. Fascinating study that concentrates on Drake's ship used in the circumnavigation, life at sea in the sixteenth century, and the role of Sir Christopher Hatton in sponsoring the expedition. The photographs and maps are especially well done.

SEE ALSO: John Cabot; Sebastian Cabot; Thomas Cavendish; John Davis; Elizabeth I; Sir Martin Frobisher; Philip II.

RELATED ARTICLES in *Great Events from History: The Renaissance & Early Modern Era, 1454-1600:* September 14, 1585-July 27, 1586: Drake's Expedition to the West Indies; April, 1587-c. 1600: Anglo-Spanish War; July 31-August 8, 1588: Defeat of the Spanish Armada.

JOACHIM DU BELLAY
French poet

Du Bellay is best known for his work The Defence and Illustration of the French Language, *the theoretical manifesto of an ambitious group of poets known as La Pléiade. Despite his short career, du Bellay's poetic production ranks among the richest and most diverse of La Pléiade's approach, marking the beginnings of a modern, aesthetic conception of poetry.*

BORN: 1522; Château de la Turmelière, Liré, Anjou, France
DIED: January 1, 1560; Paris, France
AREA OF ACHIEVEMENT: Literature

EARLY LIFE

Joachim du Bellay (zhoh-ah-keem dew bay-leh) was part of one of the most influential French families of the period. He lost his parents at a rather early age, by 1533, and was put in the care of his brother, René du Bellay, bishop of Le Mans.

His poetry relates that his literary education was quite neglected in his early years, despite his profound love of letters. He did learn Latin, however, as he left for Poitiers in 1545 to study law. It was in Poitiers that du Bellay entered the literary circles that would determine his career.

First, he encountered the neo-Latin poets Marc-Antoine Muret and Salmon Macrin, and in 1546, he met Jacques Peletier du Mans, who would introduce him in 1547 to Pierre de Ronsard and Jean-Antoine de Baïf, students of the Hellenist Jean Dorat. In fact, du Bellay and Ronsard published their respective first poems in Peletier's *Œuvres poétiques* (1547). Having found his calling, du Bellay abandoned his study of law and followed Dorat to Paris, where he and Ronsard and Baïf would study Greco-Latin and Italian culture under Dorat at the Collège de Coqueret. The Brigade, predecessor of the La Pléiade, was born.

LIFE'S WORK

The publication of Thomas Sébillet's *Art poétique français* (1548; the art of French poetry), the first original treatise in French that defined poetry as a genre independent from rhetoric, stirred the future La Pléiade into action. Du Bellay became the fledgling movement's official theoretician and published in 1549 his *La Défense et illustration de la langue française* (*The Defence and Illustration of the French Language*, 1939). Whereas both treatises stressed the central importance of the imitation of literary models for the project of ennobling the French language and letters, the main discrepancy consisted in determining which models were worthy of such attention.

Sébillet, an advocate of Clément Marot, the foremost early modern French poet prior to La Pléiade, and his followers, exalted the *marotiques* (named after Marot) and the French medieval heritage. Du Bellay, on the other hand, dismissed what he considered an inferior French literary heritage and recommended an exclusive concentration on Greek, Latin, and Italian models. Large parts of his text imitate Sperone Speroni's *Dialogo delle lingue* (1542).

Du Bellay's treatise thus sets the tone for the ambitious group's main objective: to establish themselves as the first true French poets in a direct line from the venerated classical and Italian predecessors. This objective was somewhat paradoxical, however, as it advocated the creation of new and original poetry by means of imitation. It must be stressed that *The Defence and Illustration of the French Language* was actually conceived as a mere introduction to three collections of poems that were originally published with it in 1549, including *L'Olive*, the first French collection of Neoplatonic sonnets in the tradition of Petrarch, the invective *L'Antérotique*, and the *Vers lyriques* (thirteen odes, also a first in French), demonstrating the highly prized Renaissance concept of *varietas* (diversity) by dealing with a wide array of subjects and poetic genres. In general, du Bellay's poetic œuvre has long been underestimated, overshadowed by his groundbreaking treatise as well as by Ronsard's imposing work.

On a larger scale, it is not difficult to discern in this promotion of a great national literature in the vernacular an effort to establish France's cultural supremacy by means of the common concept of the transfer of learning and power from nation to nation (*translatio studii et imperii*). The close link between La Pléiade's cultural, ideological, and political ambitions became even clearer in the summer of 1549. Their great rival, Thomas Sébillet, had been chosen to compose the official poems celebrating the entry of King Henry II into Paris on June 16, a highly prestigious appointment. Du Bellay (as well as Ronsard) was quick to offer his own composition for the occasion, the "Prosphonématique au roy treschrestien Henry II" (English translation, 2000). The campaign for such essential political recognition and, even more important, royal sponsorship seemed to progress well, as du Bellay and Ronsard were introduced to Marguerite de France, Francis I's daughter and King Henry II's sister, who agreed to take them under her wing in November.

DU BELLAY'S MAJOR WORKS	
1549	*Vers lyriques*
1549	*Recueil de poésies*
1549	*L'Olive*
1549	*L'Antérotique*
1549	*La défense et illustration de la langue française* (*The Defence and Illustration of the French Language*, 1939)
1550	*La musagnoeomachie*
1552	*XIII Sonnets de l'honnête amour*
1558	*Poemata*
1558	*Les regrets* (*The Regrets*, 1984)
1558	*Les antiquités de Rome* (partial translation as *Ruines of Rome*, 1591)
1559	*Le poète courtisan*

Du Bellay immediately dedicated a collection of sixteen new odes, the *Recueil de poésie* (1549), to her and the expanded second edition of *L'Olive* (1549).

Du Bellay's health had been fragile since his childhood and was deteriorating dramatically in 1551 and 1552. Severe tuberculosis resulted in near-deafness and confined him to his bed almost for the entire period. Consequently, his literary production slowed down considerably. His main accomplishment during that period was a curious collection that consisted of two parts. The first part was a version of the fourth book of Vergil's *Aeneid* (1552), a translation that showcased one of du Bellay's trademark radical changes of heart. In reacting against Sébillet's praise of translations, he had severely criticized that exercise in *The Defence and Illustration of the French Language* as an inappropriate way to help French culture to advance. In 1552, however, a more mature du Bellay reconciled with Sébillet, published his translation of Vergil, and justified his new attitude in the book's preface.

The second part of the collection featured more translations and a number of solemn religious poems that underlined du Bellay's transformation—accelerated by his health problems—from a young, ambitious, and arrogant upstart in 1549 into someone more patient and pessimistic. He even announced the end of his literary career in those pages but, as was so often the case, changed his mind.

In April of 1553, du Bellay accompanied his cousin, Cardinal Jean du Bellay, to Rome, where the latter acted as ambassador to the Vatican. The trip to Rome was virtually a rite of passage for every Humanist of the time. Passing through Lyons, he met the eminent literary figures Maurice Scève, Pontus de Tyard, and Guillaume des Autels. He would spend four years in the eternal city, from June of 1553 until August of 1557. It was there that he decided to become a bilingual poet, composing in Latin and French, despite his prior condemnation of neo-Latin poets. One of the four main collections that grew out of his Roman experience was entirely in Latin: the *Poemata* (1558). The other three were the *Divers jeux rustiques* (1558), and his two most famous collections: *Les Regrets* (1558; *The Regrets*, 1984) and *Les Antiquités de Rome* (1558; partial translation as *Ruines of Rome*, 1591), followed by *Songe: Ou, Vision sur le mesme suject* (1558; *Visions of Bellay*, 1994).

The *Divers jeux rustiques* contained his famous satire "Contre les Pétrarquistes," in which he criticized the abundance of mediocre poets, or "versifiers," who tried to profit from the popularity of the form. As if to provide a model to follow, many of the collection's poems were actually in the Petrarchist vein. *Les Antiquités de Rome*, dedicated to Henry II, meant to furnish a "general description of Rome's grandeur and a lamentation of its ruins." This highly ambiguous text seems to waver between a pessimistic and an optimistic vision of the possibility of achieving national grandeur, a nuanced approach that illustrates the extent to which du Bellay's thinking had matured in less than ten years. *The Regrets* also proposes a diverse mixture, as Robert Melançon has observed: *The Regrets* is a travel journal, a satire of Roman manners and customs, an Ovidian elegiac meditation, and a panegyric of the French court, thus capping du Bellay's profound transformation as an individual and an artist, first visible in 1552 and strongly influenced by his pivotal time in Rome. This prolific and diverse output showed him at the summit of his art, which made his premature death, striking him in the evening of January 1, 1560, at his desk, all the more deplorable.

SIGNIFICANCE

Du Bellay was one of the most authentic poets of La Pléiade, as his career was limited to the group's most dynamic period, the 1550's. Six editions of his complete works by 1597 underline his status. His poetry, particularly the *The Regrets* and the *Les Antiquités de Rome*, re-

main canonical and have influenced countless poets, the nineteenth century Romantics being the most obvious example.

The Defence and Illustration of the French Language remains his most influential work, as it laid the groundwork not only for future poetic treatises but also for a modern perception of poetry and the poet, based on the notion of divine inspiration.

—Bernd Renner

FURTHER READING

Castor, Grahame. *Pléiade Poetics: A Study of Sixteenth Century Thought and Terminology*. Cambridge, England: Cambridge University Press, 1964. Still the authoritative study in English on La Pléiade's innovative approach to poetry.

Coleman, Dorothy G. *The Chaste Muse: A Study of Joachim du Bellay's Poetry*. Leiden, the Netherlands: Brill, 1980. One of the most solid studies of du Bellay's poetry as a whole.

Shapiro, Norman R. *Lyrics of the French Renaissance: Marot, du Bellay, Ronsard*. New Haven, Conn.: Yale University Press, 2002. The preface and notes provide a critical background to the three poets; puts du Bellay's achievements in a larger context. Good complement to Willett's edition. In French with parallel English translation.

Willett, Laura, trans. *Poetry and Language in Sixteenth Century France: Du Bellay, Ronsard, Sébillet*. Toronto, Canada: Centre for Reformation and Renaissance Studies, 2004. Useful introduction and notes complement the translations of three theoretical texts at the heart of the quarrel between *marotiques* and the La Pléiade.

SEE ALSO: Ludovico Ariosto; Diane de Poitiers; Marguerite de Navarre; Pierre de Ronsard; Torquatto Tasso; François Villon.

RELATED ARTICLE in *Great Events from History: The Renaissance & Early Modern Era, 1454-1600:* 1549-1570's: La Pléiade Promotes French Poetry.

ALBRECHT DÜRER
German artist and scholar

Dürer has often been called the Leonardo of the North because of his diverse talents. Painter, graphic artist, and theorist, he moved in elite intellectual circles that included some of the most famous men of his time. As a graphic artist, Dürer has never been surpassed. He helped bring Italian Renaissance ideas to the art of northern Europe.

BORN: May 21, 1471; Nuremberg, Bavaria (now in Germany)
DIED: April 6, 1528; Nuremberg
AREA OF ACHIEVEMENT: Art

EARLY LIFE

Albrecht Dürer (AHL-brehkt DEWR-ur) was born in Nuremberg at a time when that city was moving from its Gothic past to a more progressive style of Renaissance Humanism, exemplified by Vienna and Basel in northern Europe. His father, a goldsmith, had come from Hungary to Nuremberg, where he met and married Dürer's mother. The third of eighteen children, Dürer showed unusual artistic inclinations at an early age. After working with his father during his younger years, Dürer, at age fifteen, was apprenticed to Michel Wohlgemuth, head of a large local workshop that produced woodcuts for printers as well as painted altarpieces.

It was the custom for apprentices to complete their training period with a Wanderjahre, or wandering journey, in order to seek new ideas from outside sources before submitting their own Meisterstück, or masterpiece, to the guild so as to obtain a license as an artist within the city. Dürer, after completing three years with Wohlgemuth and becoming familiar with both painting and graphic technique, began his own journey. Little is known about the first year or so, but it is known that the young artist traveled to Colmar with the intention of working with the famed engraver and printer Martin Schongauer. Unfortunately, the older artist had already died before Dürer's arrival, so he journeyed to Basel to work with Schongauer's brother, Georg.

Dürer's intellectual curiosity and winning personality, affirmed by references in letters by his contemporaries, soon won for him valuable contacts in Basel. Designs in many of the illustrated books published there have been attributed to him, including those in the 1494 edition of Sebastian Brant's famous *Das Narrenschiff* (*This Present Boke Named Shyp of Folys of the Worlde*, 1509). Scholars agree that he did the frontispiece, *Saint Jerome Curing the Lion*, for *Epistolare beati Hieronymi* (letters of Saint Jerome), published in 1492 by Nikolaus Kessler.

In July of 1494, after a brief stay in Strasbourg, Dürer returned to Nuremberg to marry Agnes Frey, the daughter of a wealthy local burgher. Even considering that the marriage was an arranged one, as was the custom, the young couple seem to have been totally unsuited for each other. They had no children, and a few months after his wedding day Dürer went with friends to Italy, where he stayed for about a year.

Through his friendship with the Nuremberg Humanist Willibald Pirkheimer, a confirmed lover of classical objects, and through his own copying of prints by Italian masters, Dürer took full advantage of his stay in Italy. Drawings and watercolors of Venice, sketches of nudes and statuary, and especially his outdoor paintings of the Alps of the southern Tirol attest Dürer's fascination with the south and its artistic climate. A self-portrait done in 1498 shows the artist's conception of himself as a well-dressed, confident, and dignified young gentleman. Dürer early enjoyed an enviable reputation as a gifted artist and knowledgeable companion, and on returning to Nuremberg, he moved easily in the upper social and intellectual circles of that city. He was a good businessman and took advantage of the psychological impact of the projected year 1500, when the Last Judgment was supposed to occur, by completing German and Latin editions of the illustrated *Apocalypse* in 1498.

LIFE'S WORK

The awakening Renaissance and Humanistic tendencies in the previously Gothic north, along with the popularity of illustrated printed books, created a growing need for graphic artists. Dürer's graphic talents continued to deepen and become more refined. His mature works display a greater luminosity as well as a wider range of dark, light, and middle tonalities. By financing, illustrating, and printing *Apocalypse*, Dürer enhanced his reputation as a master artist. An unusual *Self-Portrait* of 1500 reveals his mature self-esteem, as he shows himself remarkably like images of Christ. On the question of the role of artists—as craftsperson or as creative genius—Dürer clearly assumed the latter designation.

Dürer took a second trip to Italy in the fall of 1505. By then, his reputation was widely established. *The Feast of the Rose Garlands*, made for the altar of the fraternity of German merchants in the Fondaco dei Tedeschi in 1506, is a large panel celebrating Christian brotherhood in the Feast of the Rosary. Perhaps this painting is an attempt to demonstrate the supremacy of northern art. During his time in Italy, Dürer was especially fascinated by Italian theories of perspective and by studies of human proportions.

Two engravings by Dürer, *Adam and Eve* (1504) and *Melencolia I* (1514), illustrate the artist's complex personality and goals. Done very shortly before his second trip to Italy, *Adam and Eve* relied on Italian artists such as Andrea Mantegna and Antonio Pollaiuolo for a canon of the body's ideal beauty. Familiar with the writings of the classical writer Vitruvius on human proportions, Dürer chose two popular statues of antiquity, the Apollo Belvedere and the Medici Venus, as his models. Thus, the models of Italian classicism, only slightly altered in form, find themselves in Dürer's engraving, in a dark, Gothic northern forest. The Tree of Life with the parrot holds a plaque with the Latin inscription "Albertus Dürer Noricus faciebat 1504," demonstrating the artist's pride in his home city of Nuremberg. Dürer's usual signature is inconspicuously added. Eve receives the forbidden fruit from the center Tree of Knowledge. The Fall of Man results in the characters' loss of ideal form as well as loss of paradisiacal innocence; the animals at the first couple's feet symbolize the various human temperaments. The inevitable control these temperaments held on humankind after the Fall displays pessimism regarding the human condition as well as the northern taste for disguised symbolism. An uneasy tension exists between the Italianate classical figures and their northern environment.

Melencolia I was done seven years after Dürer's return from his second Italian trip. He was fully aware of the Italian Renaissance notion of the artist as a divinely inspired creature, but here Dürer shows in the large winged figure the personification of melancholic despair. The objects at her feet are tools for creating art, especially architecture, but they are useless in this context, as the seated figure suffers from the debilitating inactivity caused by the divine frenzy, or *furor melancholicus*. The idea is intensified by the bat, a symbol of the diabolical temperament, which carries the title banner across the sky. Thus, the message is clear that the artist, "born under Saturn" and endowed with potentially special gifts, is frustrated and unproductive in the search for an absolute beauty that only God knows. Both the *Adam and Eve* and *Melencolia I* engravings demonstrate Dürer's astonishing mastery of the medium in their complexity and luminosity.

Dürer's equal expertise with the woodcut medium is shown in *The Four Horsemen of the Apocalypse* (c. 1497-

Albrecht Dürer. (Library of Congress)

1498) from the *Apocalypse* series, which illustrates scenes from Revelation in the Bible. Dürer's rapid development of technique can be traced by comparing one of his earliest engravings, *Holy Family with the Butterfly* of about 1495, with a late work, the *Erasmus of Rotterdam* of 1526. In the former, some hesitancy can be seen in the cross-hatching of drapery folds and unconvincing variations of light and shade. In the mature work, one finds precise and sensitive modeling of forms, a broad range of light-and-shade tonalities, and a luminosity that bathes the figures in reflected light.

Among Dürer's many important patrons was Frederick the Wise, who commissioned a portrait and also asked Dürer to paint the altarpieces *Madonna and Child* (c. 1497) and his *Adoration of the Magi* (1504). In these paintings, Dürer demonstrates that he is primarily a graphic artist, as the paintings are more dependent on linear design than on color. Two paintings of Adam and Eve, done after Dürer's return to Nuremberg in 1507, indicate that he was influenced by premannerist tendencies found in Italian and German art of the early 1500's. The influence of Italian theory is also evident in his four-book study on human proportions, published shortly after his death. In 1511, Dürer published three picture books, *The Life of the Virgin*, *Great Passion*, and

Small Passion. Some of the prints were issued as independent woodcuts.

During 1513 and 1514, Dürer issued three famous prints: *Knight, Death, and Devil, Saint Jerome in His Study,* and the *Melencolia I.* Had these been his only works, his fame would have been assured. In 1512, he was appointed court artist for Emperor Maximilian I, for whom he did a series of large woodcuts. In 1520, Dürer journeyed to western Germany and the Netherlands, and at this time did a portrait of King Christian II of Denmark, who was traveling through Antwerp.

Dürer's last major painting, *Four Apostles* (1526), is in many ways a memorial to the Reformation. He gave it to the city of Nuremberg, which had adopted Lutheranism as the official creed. The text below the figures issues a warning to the city to heed the words of the figures depicted: Peter, John, Paul, and Mark.

SIGNIFICANCE

Dürer was an artist of exceptional talents who lived through a particularly crucial time in Germany, the age of the Reformation. Dürer was very much of his own time. A scholar and theorist as well as a gifted artist, he was cognizant of and contributed to the great accomplishments and ideas in art in the period between the late fifteenth and early sixteenth centuries in Europe. A careful scrutiny of his self-portraits alone suggests his growing self-awareness of the artist as no longer a mere anonymous craftsperson but as an individual of extraordinary ability and special importance. Like one with whom he has often been compared, Leonardo da Vinci, Dürer approached art (that is, painting and the graphic arts) as one of the seven liberal arts rather than as a purely mechanical exercise. With his keen interest in Italian ideas of proportion of the human figure and of perspective, Dürer could be said to have almost single-handedly wedded Italian Renaissance to northern Gothic art.

Dürer was famous in his own time. On his late journeys to Antwerp and elsewhere, he was sought by the highest social and intellectual groups of the area. His diary and his theoretical writings show him to have been a person of broad knowledge and diverse interests. His treatise on proportions, together with that of Leonardo, constitutes a most important contribution to Renaissance art theory. Unlike Leonardo's works, Dürer's contributions became accessible to a large public through printed publication. Through his own use of Italianate classical models, Dürer increased public appreciation for classical art. In turn, Dürer influenced later Italian artists by his integrated style.

Dürer's late works, although fewer in number than his earlier output, do not diminish in power or originality. His great talents are particularly remarkable in the engravings and woodcuts, which he favored since they, unlike commissioned paintings, allowed him independence from patrons and served as a source of income through popular prints. Dürer is one of the central figures of European art.

—*Mary Sweeney Ellett*

FURTHER READING

Anzelewsky, Fedja. *Dürer: His Art and Life.* London: Chartwell Books, 1980. A straightforward account of Dürer's life within the context of Renaissance and Reformation Europe. Special attention is paid to Dürer's writings, especially the treatises on art theory. Emphasizes Dürer's religious and Humanistic beliefs. Good reproductions, many in full color. Useful bibliography.

Dürer, Albrecht. *The Intaglio Prints of Albrecht Dürer: Engravings, Etchings, and Drypaints.* Edited by Walter L. Strauss. New York: Kennedy Galleries, 1977. The most complete catalog of the intaglio prints in English. Illustrations after each catalog entry. Includes introduction, full catalog entries to all previous literature, and an annotated bibliography. Especially useful in that prints are reproduced in actual size. Important to an understanding of Dürer's graphics. Recommended for the general reader.

Eichberger, Dagmar, and Charles Zika, eds. *Dürer and His Culture.* New York: Cambridge University Press, 1998. Anthology of cultural studies essays on various aspects of Dürer, ranging from general surveys of German patriotism and the German cultural scene to specific analyses of Dürer's representations of witchcraft and nature. Includes illustrations, bibliographic references, and index.

Kantor, Jordan. *Dürer's Passions.* 2 vols. Cambridge, Mass.: Harvard University Art Museums, 2000. Catalog and accompanying analytic volume for an exhibition of Dürer's representations of the Passion, analyzes Dürer's approach to Christianity in art. Includes bibliographic references.

Panofsky, Erwin. *The Life and Art of Albrecht Dürer.* 4th ed. Princeton, N.J.: Princeton University Press, 1971. A paperback reprint of a classic, unmatched for sensitivity to and comprehensive analysis of Dürer's life and work. Omits list of Dürer's works but retains excellent interpretive essays. Good illustrations. Very useful for student and general reader.

Price, David Hotchkiss. *Albrecht Dürer's Renaissance: Humanism, Reformation, and the Art of Faith*. Ann Arbor: University of Michigan Press, 2003. Argues that Humanism provided the basis for Dürer's understanding of the relationship between religion and art. Analyzes the relationship between image and text in Dürer's work. Includes illustrations, bibliographic references, index.

Rowlands, John. *The Age of Dürer and Holbein*. New York: Cambridge University Press, 1988. This book contains high-quality reproductions of Dürer prints and drawings as well as several watercolor studies. Surveys, through works in the British Museum and private and public British collections, art development from late Gothic style to Northern Renaissance naturalism. In addition to Dürer and Holbein, offers valuable coverage of their predecessors and contemporaries.

Russell, Francis. *The World of Dürer, 1471-1528*. New York: Time Books, 1967. An excellent text, introductory level, with many good reproductions, some full page and full color, as well as explanatory maps and graphics. Traces Dürer's development and life within the social, religious, and political context of his time. Chronology chart shows artists of Dürer's era. Limited but useful bibliography.

Salley, Victoria. *Nature's Artist: Plants and Animals by Albrecht Dürer*. Translated by Michael Robinson. Edited by Christopher Wynne. New York: Prestel, 2003. Study of Dürer's portraits of nature, revealing both his technical skill as a draftsman and his emotional and intellectual attitudes toward plant and animal life. Includes reproductions of thirty-four sketches and watercolors.

Scheller, Robert W., and Karel G. Boon, comps. *The Graphic Art of Albrecht Dürer, Hans Dürer, and the Dürer School*. Amsterdam: Van Gendt, 1971. This catalog is based on Joseph Meder's classic *Dürer—Katalog* (Vienna, 1932) and is notable for making available in English the pioneering Dürer works by Meder and Hollstein. Excellent introductory section on Dürer as a graphic artist. Many prints, some of uneven quality. Valuable book for all levels.

Snyder, James. *Northern Renaissance Art: Painting, Sculpture, the Graphic Arts from 1350 to 1575*. New York: Harry N. Abrams, 1985. Full coverage of the Northern Renaissance, with an excellent chapter entitled "Albrecht Dürer and the Renaissance in Germany." Discusses in detail, with good reproductions, many examples of Dürer's graphic works and paintings. Text includes recent interpretations and theories. Includes a timetable of the arts, history, and science from 1300 to 1575. Valuable for the general reader.

SEE ALSO: Giovanni Bellini; Lucas Cranach, the Elder; Desiderius Erasmus; Matthias Grünewald; Hans Holbein, the Younger; Leonardo da Vinci; Andrea Mantegna.

RELATED ARTICLE in *Great Events from History: The Renaissance & Early Modern Era, 1454-1600:* 1494: Sebastian Brant Publishes *The Ship of Fools*.

EDWARD IV
King of England (r. 1461-1470, 1471-1483)

Utilizing instruments of government inherited from the Lancastrian kings, as well as molding pragmatic methods that anticipated those of the Tudors, Edward of York restored both the authority and prestige of the English monarchy following the dangers and drift of the reigns of the Lancastrian kings. He was aided in this success by the end of the Hundred Years' War, which had become both a distraction and a financial and military disaster for the English monarchy.

BORN: April 28, 1442; Rouen, Normandy, France
DIED: April 9, 1483; Westminster Palace, England
AREA OF ACHIEVEMENT: Government and politics

EARLY LIFE

Nothing is known of the childhood of Edward IV. He was the son of Richard, duke of York, and of Cecily Neville, daughter of Ralph, earl of Westmoreland. Edward was not born to kingship; he won it at the battles of Mortimer's Cross and Towton Field (both fought in 1461). Although he was proclaimed king between the fighting of the two battles, domestic conflict with the deposed Henry VI and his supporters, foreign complications with France and Burgundy, and the whirling allegiance of Richard Neville, earl of Warwick (the "kingmaker") prevented the full and unchallenged exercise of Edward's royal power until 1471, by which time Henry VI and his son as well as Warwick lay dead.

England, exhausted by 116 years of intermittent and ultimately unsuccessful war in France in the Hundred Years' War, and by the Wars of the Roses, which kept parts of England in turmoil from 1455 until 1471, was ready for a period of tranquillity guaranteed by abundant governance and wise foreign policy. Edward IV provided both.

The young king was handsome, magnificently dressed and groomed, affable, open in his relations with all but those who posed a threat to his rule (such as his brother George, duke of Clarence, who was executed in 1478, allegedly drowned in a barrel of that sweet Mediterranean wine now known as Madeira). Sir Thomas More in his work *History of King Richard III* (1543) described Edward as

> a goodly parsonage, and very Princely to behold, of hearte couragious, politique in counsaille, in aduersitie nothynge abashed, in prosperitie, rather ioyfulle than prowde, in peace iuste and mercifull, in warre, sharpe and fyerce, in the fields, bolde and hardye, and natheless no farther than wysedom woulde, aduenturous.

More also noted Edward's inclination to "fleshlye wantonnesse" and to overindulgence in the pleasures of the table, which led to corpulence in his early middle age.

LIFE'S WORK

Edward's rule did not really begin until after the bootless attempt by Warwick to restore Henry VI to his lost crown ended at the Battle of Barnet in 1471; Warwick died in the battle, and the captured Henry VI died shortly thereafter—Edward IV could hardly tolerate the continued existence of his predecessor. The last Lancastrian king could not be permitted to live; he, alive, would have been a threat to the rule of Edward IV, a focus for the loyalties of those elements of the polity who opposed the policies and rule of the first Yorkist king. Thus, Henry paid the ultimate price for royal failure in fifteenth century England in 1472. Barnet marked the last attempt of overmighty nobles to control or to replace the king; the Wars of the Roses were now over.

From 1471 to 1483, Edward ruled England with vigor and efficiency, providing the businesslike government usually associated with the rule of the Tudors. This period of his reign was facilitated not only by the death of old rivals, but by the eclipse of the Nevilles and of the Woodvilles, the family of his queen, and also by the settlement of the lingering diplomatic problems with France in 1475. As of 1471, then, Edward was unencumbered by extraneous considerations: Domestic conflict was ended and foreign peace achieved, Parliament and council no longer enjoyed public approbation, and attainder (often more important as a threat than as actuality) had undermined the position of the greater nobility. For the first time since the death of Edward III in 1377, the king could concentrate on being king.

Edward IV relied heavily on his administrative officials in the conduct of his government, since council and Parliament had declined in public esteem, although the precedent for the council acting as the Tudor Court of Star Chamber falls to this reign. The Lancastrian parliaments had not inspired general confidence; owing to the lack of effective rule by kings who were successively moribund, absent, or sickly, parliaments had fallen under the control of magnates and their affinities; lacking any real counterbalance to his authority, Edward governed his country with little need to regard institutional opposition as a reality.

Like the Tudors who were to succeed his brother Richard III in 1485, Edward was astute in favoring, and

Edward IV. (Library of Congress)

in winning the support of, the middle classes. This is why monarchy is regarded as a progressive force in the English Middle Ages; the first Yorkist king allied himself and his policies with the new class rising to a political influence that, under the Tudors, was to be commensurate with their economic importance. Edward and his immediate successors knew where money was to be found, and he cultivated the people who had it. The commoners were worth cultivating: They were the source of funds and of attainders against those viewed by the king as dangerous. Yet there were few parliaments convened in Edward's reign, a reflection of the fact that his own personal financial resources were sufficient to maintain a large portion of his needs and of the ending of the French wars. Parliament was not an independent body in the fifteenth century; it was controlled by either the king or the magnates, and so it was to remain until the turbulent seventeenth century. As well, Edward utilized fiscal means derived from sources not granted from Parliament, especially the "benevolences," which were a form of compulsory loan. Edward was not the first English king to find extraparliamentary sources of funding the expenses of government; the precedents go at least as far back as the reign of King Edward I (r. 1272-1307).

Edward was a king who pursued pragmatic policies; there is evidence neither of system nor of theory in his rule. He did much to tidy up the disorder of the Lancastrian period (1399-1461), both in foreign and in domestic policies. The continental involvements of England were ended, and the internal disruption so characteristic of the earlier fifteenth century—livery and maintenance, private war, brigandage beyond the power of the government to control—was effectively stifled by the end of Edward IV's reign. Edward's tools of suppression came to be known as courts of high commission (in this reign, the precursor of the Court of Star Chamber) and special judicial commissions sent out into the shires to hear and determine (*oyer* and *terminer*) cases of criminal conduct. In addition, the reign of Edward IV witnessed yet another innovation usually attributed to the Tudors: Although not yet so called, the Council of Wales and that of the North were in being before the end of Edward's custody of his office. These local councils acted with the king's power in areas distant from London, where endemic local strife made prompt official response necessary.

The cause of Edward's death is not precisely known. Whatever the precise etiology, it is likely that he died of some complication—probably left undefined lest the delicate be offended—of what More, quoted above, called an excess of "fleshly wantonness."

SIGNIFICANCE

While to place kings and reigns into semantic boxes is poor history, Edward IV may be described both as the last medieval and the first modern king of England. He did much to centralize royal authority, to place his rule on a sound financial basis, and to restore its standing both in domestic and in foreign eyes. By the end of his reign, there was no effective domestic challenge remaining to his rule in England. He also brought the culture of his court into conformity with contemporaneous developments in the courts of the Continent, patronizing Humanists, and William Caxton.

—*James W. Alexander*

FURTHER READING

Chrimes, S. B. *Lancastrians, Yorkists, and Henry VII.* New York: St. Martin's Press, 1964. A standard history of late fifteenth century England, stressing dynastic politics.

_____. "The Reign of Edward IV." In *Fifteenth-Century England, 1399-1509: Studies in Politics and Society,* edited by S. B. Chrimes, C. D. Ross, and R. A. Griffiths. New York: Harper and Row, 1972. An excellent brief introduction to the reign.

Clive, Mary. *This Sun of York: A Biography of Edward IV.* London: Macmillan, 1973. This engaging text represents popular history at its best. Includes illustrations, genealogical table, maps, bibliographic references, and index.

Dockray, Keith, ed. *Edward IV: A Sourcebook.* Stroud, Gloucestershire, England: Sutton, 1999. Useful compendium of primary historical sources relating to Edward's life and reign. Includes bibliographic references and index.

Falkus, Gila. *The Life and Times of Edward IV.* London: Weidenfeld and Nicolson, 1981. Another popular and well-written work of popular history. Well illustrated.

Hughes, Jonathan. *Arthurian Myths and Alchemy: The Kingship of Edward IV.* Stroud, Gloucestershire, England: Sutton, 2002. Study of Edward's reigns and the rhetoric and propaganda that facilitated his acquisition and exercise of power. Looks at the portrayal of Edward as the second Arthur who would reunify and heal England and at the influence of alchemy on his propaganda and chosen symbols. Also analyzes the brief embrace of Roman imperial culture when Arthurian myth seemed ineffective. Includes illustrations, bibliographic references, and index.

Kendall, Paul Murray. *Warwick the Kingmaker.* New York: W. W. Norton, 1957. The best biography of Richard Neville, who dominated both the person and the policy of Edward IV in the first nine years of his reign.

Lander, J. R. *Crown and Nobility, 1450-1509.* Montreal: McGill-Queen's University Press, 1976.

_____. *Government and Community: England, 1450-1509.* Cambridge, Mass.: Harvard University Press, 1980. These two books constitute the best narrative and analytical portrayal of English politics and society in the Yorkist period.

Ross, Charles. *Edward IV.* Rev. ed. New Haven, Conn.: Yale University Press, 1997. The major biography, although not definitive. Ross finds Edward culpable for the evils that followed his reign in that of his youngest brother, Richard III. Ross's evaluation of the positive policies of Edward are more critical than is that of the present article.

Scofield, Cora. *The Life and Times of Edward the Fourth.* 2 vols. London: Frank Cass, 1923. Reprint. New York: Octagon Books, 1967. A thorough work that remains a standard narrative history of the reign of Edward IV.

Storey, R. L. *The End of the House of Lancaster.* London: Barrie and Rockliffe, 1966. The dynastic politics of the fifteenth century are presented in a social context.

SEE ALSO: Lady Margaret Beaufort; William Caxton; Henry VI; Sir Thomas More; Richard III; Earl of Warwick.

RELATED ARTICLE in *Great Events from History: The Renaissance & Early Modern Era, 1454-1600:* August 29, 1475: Peace of Picquigny.

EDWARD VI
King of England (r. 1547-1553)

Edward's reign definitively established the strong Tudor monarchy and English Protestantism. Despite his youth, the king played a significant role in both.

BORN: October 12, 1537; Hampton Court Palace, near London, Surrey, England
DIED: July 6, 1553; London
AREAS OF ACHIEVEMENT: Government and politics, religion and theology

EARLY LIFE

Edward VI's birth to Henry VIII and his wife, Jane Seymour, secured the Tudor male succession. Up to this point, Henry had had two wives and had separated the English church from the Papacy. With both of Henry's previous wives now dead, illegitimacy did not shadow Edward as it did his two sisters, Mary and Elizabeth. Jane Seymour died twelve days after Edward's birth; within the next six years, his father took three more wives, but he had no more children. The last marriage, to Catherine Parr in 1543, provided Edward with a stepmother who brought the king's children together in a harmonious household and made the court a center of the New Learning (Protestantism).

Henry VIII was already forty-six at Edward's birth and, though a fond parent, had little association with his son; the boy patterned himself on his tutors and grew up serious and scholarly. He found in the classroom separation from women, among whom he had spent his first six years. His first tutors, Richard Cox and John

Cheke, were Cambridge scholars and staunch Protestants, friends of Archbishop Thomas Cranmer. For schoolmates, they selected sons of noblemen; one of them, Barnaby Fitzpatrick, Edward's whipping boy, remained a lifelong friend. In the Renaissance style, the boys learned classical and modern languages as well as music, astronomy, and athletics. Tutors of Princess Elizabeth, four years older, came from the same background; she and Edward wrote letters to each other as school exercises. Princess Mary, twenty-one years older than her brother and a devoted Roman Catholic, had completed her education, but with Queen Catherine's encouragement, she translated from Desiderius Erasmus's Latin.

Edward's education continued for three years after he became king; he turned from analyzing classical texts to writing position papers on a variety of subjects that he presented to his council. Similarly, the chronicle he wrote in 1552 about his life and times (published as his *Journal* in 1857, and republished, with his political papers, in 1966) developed from early concentration on battles and tournaments to concern about various problems of government. From vicious political struggles in the Council, Edward early learned discretion; he took boyish delight in having his own locked desk. Being his father's son, he showed interest in his own marriage; the characteristic restraint of the *Journal* gives way when he writes about his engagement to Princess Elizabeth, daughter of Henry II of France. Once, he jokingly suggested that he might marry Anne of Cleves, his father's divorced fifth wife.

Portraits of Edward by Hans Holbein, the Younger, William Strates, and others show the young king as a fat baby growing into fragile adolescence: thin, shorter than average, with gray eyes, reddish hair, and a pale complexion. Gerolamo Cardano, the famous Milanese physician, praised Edward's intellectual attainments in the last year of his life, but he also told of what portraits do not show: one shoulder blade higher than the other, nearsightedness, and slight deafness.

LIFE'S WORK

Foreign diplomats remarked on the reverence shown to a mere boy and on his participation in government. Yet, though crowned king of England, Ireland, and France, at first he served as little more than a pawn, and he never stood against whatever faction controlled the Council.

His reign began, as it ended, with a challenge to the will of Henry VIII, which had prescribed government by a council made up of his executors. Instead, Edward's uncle, Edward Seymour, earl of Hertford (soon to be the duke of Somerset), influenced the Council to turn authority over to him as governor of the king's person and protector of the kingdom. Almost immediately, a contest for control developed between Somerset and his brother, Thomas Seymour, Lord Sudley, Lord Admiral, who shared booty with pirates he was supposed to pursue.

Edward VI. (Library of Congress)

Sudley supplied the young king with money and married Dowager Queen Catherine. More ominously, he flirted with Princess Elizabeth, who lived with Catherine, and paid her suit after Catherine's death. Against Somerset's plans, he intrigued for Edward's marriage to Lady Jane Grey, granddaughter of Henry VIII's sister. Arrested and condemned to death, Sudley wrote secretly urging Mary and Elizabeth to conspire against Somerset, charging him with profiteering.

Historians have championed one or another of the politicians around Edward as comparatively high-minded or as victims of circumstances, but all struggled for power in order to despoil the Church in the name of their Protestantism. The exclusion of Catholics, such as Stephen Gardiner, bishop of Winchester, from the Council, and Edward's youth gave them a free hand. By the time Sudley died, John Dudley, earl of Warwick (later the duke of Northumberland), was challenging Somerset's control. Archbishop Cranmer, who shepherded the establishment of English Protestantism, remained financially disinterested. He had already shown himself a trimmer, however, and his basic Erastianism remained suspect from a strictly Protestant viewpoint. Parliament enacted religious changes, and the courts enforced them, in the king's name, emphasizing the question of loyalty rather than theology.

At first, religious changes from Henry VIII's church attracted limited resistance. Few complained about the repeal of heresy laws, and chantries disappeared gradually. A crisis came with the implementation of the Act of Uniformity on Whitsunday, 1549, requiring a new order of worship, Cranmer's Book of Common Prayer, with the obvious change from Latin to English. The rising in Cornwall and Devon (the Western Rebellion) represented a protest in favor of a return to the "old" ways of Henry VIII. A contemporaneous rising in Norfolk (Robert Kett's Rebellion) came mainly from secular problems. Somerset had already attacked enclosure of common lands by the gentry as causing the dislocation of peasants, whose hardship was aggravated by bad harvests and debasement of the coinage. Causes for rebellion varied greatly, however, within the larger pattern.

Somerset's failure to control the uprisings brought his fall from power. Northumberland took control, ended the Protectorate, and imprisoned him. The Council's new leaders put down the rebellions ruthlessly, using German and Italian troops brought over the channel to fight in Scotland. Somerset had proved as inept in foreign affairs as at home. He went to war in 1547 with the intention of aiding Scottish Protestants and undermining French influence by a marriage, discussed almost from Edward's birth, with the child queen Mary Stuart (Mary, Queen of Scots). His armies harried the country and thus drove the Scots into a firm alliance with France, including the queen's marriage to the dauphin. War between England and France followed in 1549.

Even more than Somerset, Northumberland controlled through Edward. From fall, 1551, the young king presided over the Council and signed official documents without a countersignature. He did nothing to save his uncle from execution in January, 1552; Somerset, released from prison, had tried to rally support against Northumberland. Before 1552, Edward had lived close to London; his progress from July to September of that year, taking him as far as Salisbury, showed growing maturity. Without Edward's strong backing, Cranmer would not have pushed the church reform called for by Bishops Hugh Latimer and Nicholas Ridley. A second Prayer Book and Act of Uniformity (1552) mandated attendance at the reformed service, and the Forty-two Articles of Religion defined Englishmen's creed. Northumberland's regime remains controversial. The loss of religious freedom and the destruction of Catholic books and artifacts were balanced by ideals of a Puritan Commonwealth.

Northumberland sacrificed Boulogne to gain peace with France, but Somerset had begun that war. If that peace, including Edward's engagement to the princess, endangered relations with the empire, Charles V had threatened to intervene in England in Princess Mary's interest.

Northumberland's partnership with the king became very clear from the late winter of 1553. Edward's health, deteriorating rapidly from tuberculosis, caused both to feel concern about the provision in Henry VIII's will for Mary's succession. Northumberland bolstered his own position for any eventuality by arranging marriages between his son Guildford Dudley and Lady Jane Grey and their siblings with sons of other counselors, the earls of Pembroke and Huntingdon. Edward, characteristically, had written up a plan for his succession: Before he died, he turned it into a will leaving the throne to Lady Jane Grey. As Edward lay dying, the Council summoned Mary to London, but she retreated to Norfolk, and after Edward's death, on July 6, she proclaimed her succession. In London, the Northumberland faction proclaimed Lady Jane Grey's succession.

Few resisted Mary's triumphant progress to London. Men deserted from the army Northumberland led against her, and the Council did not send reinforcements. When London's populace boisterously welcomed Mary on July

19, the Council proclaimed her queen and ordered Northumberland to disband his army.

Edward was buried in Westminster Abbey on August 8 with little ceremony; no marker was ever raised to his memory. After a futile effort to appease Mary by converting to Catholicism, Northumberland died for his treason against her. Lady Jane Grey and her husband survived until the Thomas Wyatt rebellion in 1554 proved them dangerous. Many Edwardian church reformers died as Marian martyrs.

SIGNIFICANCE

Mary's triumph came neither from lack of parliamentary ratification of Edward VI's will nor from a reaction against his religious reforms. It did not even depend on Northumberland's unpopularity. She triumphed as the generally recognized embodiment of the hereditary English national monarchy. Confirmation and continuation of that tradition proved Edward's principal achievement. His youth, like Mary's womanhood, emphasized the monarchical principle, in clear contrast to the situation of Edward V sixty-five years before.

For a brief moment, European attention focused on Edward's England in a new way. Cranmer failed in his effort to organize a general Protestant equivalent of the Council of Trent, but Edward's church became the great experiment in national Protestantism. Though refugees such as Martin Bucer and Pietro Martire Vermigli (Peter Martyr) contributed to it, it remained a clearly English phenomenon that found its great spokesman in the Elizabethan theologian Richard Hooker.

In other ways, too, Edwardian beginnings found Elizabethan fulfillment. This shows in the careers of men such as William Cecil, Henry Sidney, and Thomas Gresham. Despite upheavals in the Council, government and business continued to cooperate in commercial exploration overseas. A government pension tempted Sebastian Cabot to return from Spain, forging a link between the first exploratory voyages under King Henry VII and the great trading companies of the seventeenth century.

—*Paul Stewart*

FURTHER READING

Alford, Stephen. *Kingship and Politics in the Reign of Edward VI*. New York: Cambridge University Press, 2002. Study of Edward VI's brief reign, emphasizing its stability and the lasting legacy of Edward's conception of the nature of monarchy, which decisively influenced the much longer reign of his sister Elizabeth. Includes illustrations, bibliographic references, index.

Beer, Barrett Lynn. *Northumberland: The Political Career of John Dudley, Earl of Warwick and Duke of Northumberland*. Kent, Ohio: Kent State University Press, 1973. Frankly revisionist, this biography searches beyond Jordan's monumental history of the reign. It sees Northumberland in context, not worse than other members of the council.

_____. *Rebellion and Riot: Popular Disorder in England in the Reign of Edward VI*. Kent, Ohio: Kent State University Press, 1982. A useful, scholarly effort to focus away from court politics. Evident are imperfectly developed classifications and methodology, inevitable in a pioneering work.

Bush, Michael Laccohee. *The Government of Protector Somerset*. Montreal: McGill-Queen's University Press, 1975. Like Beer, Bush demythologizes his subject. Somerset was an ordinary man, a pragmatist governed by consequences of his Scottish war.

Edward VI. *The Chronicle and Political Papers of King Edward VI*. Edited by Wilbur Kitchener Jordan. Ithaca, N.Y.: Cornell University Press, 1966. The indispensable journal kept by Edward between the ages of ten and fifteen. Careful editing and copious notes make this the best edition.

Hoak, Dale Eugene. *The King's Council in the Reign of Edward VI*. Cambridge, England: Cambridge University Press, 1976. Traditional constitutional history and interpretation, blaming Somerset and Northumberland as opportunists. A study of the working of the Council, which Somerset tended to ignore, Northumberland to dominate.

Jordan, Wilbur Kitchener. *Edward VI: The Young King, the Protectorship of the Duke of Somerset*. Cambridge, Mass.: Harvard University Press, 1968.

_____. *Edward VI: The Threshold of Power, the Dominance of the Duke of Northumberland*. Cambridge, Mass.: Harvard University Press, 1970. A long-needed, exhaustively scholarly study of Edward's reign. Carefully revisionist, sees Somerset as being beyond his depths, and the usurpation of Lady Jane Grey as Edward's scheme more than that of Northumberland.

Loach, Jennifer. *Edward VI*. Edited by George Bernard and Penry Williams. New Haven, Conn.: Yale University Press, 1999. This entry in the Yale English Monarchs series contests the accepted notion of Edward as a fragile child, portraying him instead as enjoying a bodily vigor that matched his intellectual prowess. Includes photographic plates, illustrations, bibliographic references, and index.

McConica, James Kelsey. *English Humanists and Reformation Politics Under Henry VIII and Edward VI.* New York: Oxford University Press, 1965. Continuity of the Henrician Renaissance beyond the death of Thomas More, misses its Edwardian Protestant culmination.

MacCulloch, Diarmaid. *The Boy King: Edward VI and the Protestant Reformation.* New York: Palgrave, 2001. In addition to making sense of the complexities of the Renaissance theological and political allegiances that shaped Edward's court, Diarmaid provides a striking account of Edward's lasting legacy. He draws connections between Edward's reign and the English Civil War and examines the impact of Edward on contemporary British culture.

SEE ALSO: Anne of Cleves; Martin Bucer; Sebastian Cabot; Gerolamo Cardano; William Cecil; Charles V; Thomas Cranmer; Desiderius Erasmus; Lady Jane Grey; Henry VIII; Hans Holbein, the Younger; Richard Hooker; Hugh Latimer; Mary, Queen of Scots; Catherine Parr; Nicholas Ridley; Jane Seymour; First Duke of Somerset; The Tudor Family.

RELATED ARTICLES in *Great Events from History: The Renaissance & Early Modern Era, 1454-1600:* August 22, 1513-July 6, 1560: Anglo-Scottish Wars; May, 1539: Six Articles of Henry VIII; 1544-1628: Anglo-French Wars; January 28, 1547-July 6, 1553: Reign of Edward VI; April or May, 1560: Publication of the Geneva Bible; January, 1563: Thirty-nine Articles of the Church of England.

JUAN SEBASTIÁN DE ELCANO
Spanish explorer

After the death of Ferdinand Magellan, Elcano took command of the Vittoria *and completed the first circumnavigation of the globe. The voyage proved that Earth was round and brought forth the question of time changes in world travel.*

BORN: c. 1487; Guetaria, Guipúzcoa, Castile (now in Spain)
DIED: August 4, 1526; at sea, Pacific Ocean
ALSO KNOWN AS: Juan Sebastián del Cano; Juan Sebastián de El Cano
AREAS OF ACHIEVEMENT: Exploration, geography

EARLY LIFE

Juan Sebastián de Elcano (kwawn say-BAWS-tyahn day ehl-KAWN-oh) grew up in the Basque seafaring province of Guipúzcoa. Four of his brothers became mariners; one sister married a pilot. Elcano went to sea at an early age; by age twenty-three, he was captain and owner of a ship chartered to the king of Castile. While in a North African port, Elcano borrowed to pay his crew's wages. When the Crown failed to send money promised for the voyage, he sold his ship to settle the debt, even though it was illegal to transfer an armed Spanish vessel to foreigners. Elcano then attended the school of navigation in Seville, completing a three-year course in piloting.

LIFE'S WORK

Using his new credentials, Elcano applied for a position in Ferdinand Magellan's exploring expedition. Magellan had convinced the king of Spain to sponsor a voyage to the East Indies by sailing westward. In the Treaty of Tordesillas (1494), Spain and Portugal had divided the world, reserving everything east of a line drawn in the Atlantic Ocean to Portugal, while Spain claimed everything to the west. Magellan expected to find a passageway across South America and then sail west to the Moluccas, or Spice Islands (now in Indonesia). Proving they lay on the Spanish side of the line of demarcation would justify Spain's participation in the lucrative spice trade dominated by Portugal.

Magellan appointed Elcano master of the *Concepción.* Master was the third-ranking ship's officer, following captain and pilot. The fleet of five vessels, carrying a crew of 270, left Spain on September 20, 1519, and proceeded along the coast of South America without finding a passage. On March 31, 1520, the flotilla reached the Bay of San Julián in Argentina's Patagonia region, where Magellan intended to spend the winter. Magellan's arrogant behavior and unwillingness to discuss his decisions angered three of his aristocratic Spanish captains. They demanded that Magellan take the fleet back to Spain. When Magellan refused, the captains organized a mutiny.

Elcano joined the mutineers who, after capturing the *San Antonio,* placed him in charge of the vessel. Magellan successfully repressed the revolt and savagely punished the mutineers. Two of the mutinous captains were executed, their remains quartered and displayed on shore; the third was marooned when the flotilla left San Julián. Forty others, including Elcano, were convicted of treason and sentenced to death. Magellan could not spare the manpower and commuted the death sentences to hard labor, placing the mutineers in chains while they cleaned the fetid holds and worked the ships' pumps.

The fleet departed San Julián on August 24, 1520, with Elcano returned to his post of master on the *Concepción*. On October 21, Magellan reached the passageway that would thereafter be named the Strait of Magellan. It took thirty-eight days of cautious navigation to transit the strait. One boat was shipwrecked; a second vessel was deserted and its crew returned to Spain. Three ships–*Trinidad*, *Concepción*, and *Vittoria*—exited the strait on November 28. Magellan and his crew enjoyed the calmer waters of the new ocean and named it the Pacific.

No one in the early sixteenth century realized the extent of the Pacific Ocean. Even the latest maps showing the newly discovered American continents located Japan and the East Indies near America's western shore. Magellan's fleet took ninety-eight days to sail more than seven thousand miles before making landfall on Guam on March 6, 1521. Food ran low during the long voyage,

A detail of Juan Sebastián de Elcano, from an engraving of the Victoria, *the ship he co-captained with Ferdinand Magellan on its successful journey around the globe.* (Hulton|Archive by Getty Images)

and the crews suffered terribly from scurvy and starvation. After taking on supplies, Magellan's expedition continued to the Philippines, becoming the first Europeans to visit those islands. Magellan befriended a local ruler and volunteered to fight his enemies, but his invasion of Mactan Island ran into fierce resistance. Magellan was killed on April 27, 1521.

Immediately after Magellan's death, crew members selected new expedition leaders. Elcano had little respect for the men chosen, believing them deficient in navigational skills. He considered himself far better qualified, but the crewmen had not forgiven his role in the mutiny and preferred Magellan loyalists. On May 2 the *Concepción* (whose hull was being devoured by shipworms) was burned to prevent it from falling into unfriendly hands. Elcano then transferred to the *Vittoria*.

On September 21, 1521, Gonzalo Gómez de Espinosa became captain of the *Trinidad*, still flagship of the fleet, and Elcano received command of the *Vittoria*. Espinosa had no practical navigational experience, and Elcano effectively became leader of the expedition. The flotilla headed more directly toward the Moluccas, arriving at the harbor of the island of Tidore on November 8.

The two ships filled their holds with the precious spices they had acquired. When they prepared to depart, the *Trinidad* began to leak. The men decided that *Vittoria* would return to Spain around the Cape of Good Hope, while *Trinidad* would stay for repairs and head back across the Pacific to Spanish-controlled Mexico. Restoration of the *Trinidad* took three months. Espinosa then justified Elcano's low opinion of his navigational abilities by spending five months trying unsuccessfully to find the way back to the Pacific before returning to Tidore in October, 1522, where the ship was captured by the Portuguese. Of the sixty men who chose to return on the *Trinidad*, only four made it back to Spain.

On December 21, 1521, Elcano left Tidore with forty-seven Europeans and thirteen Indonesians aboard the *Vittoria*. Battling contrary currents and monstrous storms, it took Elcano six months to round the Cape of Good Hope. On July 9 the *Vittoria* reached the Cape Verde Islands. Although this was Portuguese territory, Elcano, desperate for food, risked entering Santiago harbor. At first things went smoothly—Elcano claimed to have been blown off course on the way to Spain from the Caribbean—and the *Vittoria* was allowed to replenish its food supplies. On shore, the men learned it was Thursday, not Wednesday as their records showed; pious men were horrified, realizing they had mistakenly fasted on Saturdays and celebrated Easter on Monday. (When they returned to Spain, they learned they had gained a day by sailing westward around the globe.)

When Elcano sent another boat to seek more food, authorities became suspicious. They seized the longboat and its thirteen men and ordered Elcano to surrender the *Vittoria*. Instead, on July 15, he fled the harbor with a skeleton crew, arriving in Spain on September 6, 1522. Of the sixty men who had left Timor nearly nine months earlier, only eighteen Europeans and four Indonesians reached Seville.

King Charles I of Spain (later Holy Roman Emperor Charles V) welcomed Elcano, rewarding him with a coat of arms and a pension. He pardoned Elcano for his role in the mutiny and for selling a Spanish armed ship on a previous voyage. The king honored the entire crew, including the thirteen men later rescued from the Cape Verde Islands. At a formal hearing on the expedition, Elcano—who had never forgiven Magellan for his treatment during the mutiny—testified that Magellan's arrogant behavior had made the mutiny by proud Castilian gentlemen inevitable. By burning their village, Magellan had goaded the Mactan Islanders into taking revenge, thus bringing about his own death.

In the summer of 1525, Spain sent a second expedition to the Spice Islands, consisting of seven ships and 450 men, commanded by García Jofre de Loaisa, with Elcano as second-in-command and chief pilot. Elcano had trouble finding the Strait of Magellan; storms reduced the fleet to two vessels and scurvy decimated the crews on the long Pacific trek. On July 30, 1526, Loaisa died and Elcano succeeded him, only to succumb to disease himself and be buried at sea after his death on August 4, 1526.

SIGNIFICANCE

The circumnavigation of the globe was the greatest voyage of the Age of Exploration. The arrival of Europeans in the Americas produced more profound consequences, but Christopher Columbus's voyage could be called a pleasure cruise compared with the difficulties faced by Magellan and Elcano.

The Moluccan expedition added to European geographical knowledge considerably. It offered practical proof that the earth was globular. The voyage posed, for the first time, the problem of how to adjust for time gained when traveling westward across the Pacific—a difficulty not solved until the establishment of the International Date Line in 1884. The huge expanse of the Pacific Ocean, revealed by the voyage, changed geographers' conceptions of the globe's size and suggested that Earth was misnamed, since the planet consisted mostly of water, not land.

Historians have tended to praise each explorer at the expense of the other. Denigrating either Magellan or Elcano is unwarranted. Without Magellan's ruthless determination, the voyage would not have taken place, and without Elcano's skillful seamanship, the circumnavigation could not have been completed.

—Milton Berman

FURTHER READING

Bergreen, Laurence. *Over the Edge: Magellan's Terrifying Circumnavigation of the World*. New York: William Morrow, 2003. Sets the voyage, and Elcano's role, into historical perspective.

Levinson, Nancy. *Magellan and the First Voyage Around the World*. New York: Clarion Books, 2001. Well-written account intended for younger readers.

Mitchell, Mairin. *Elcano: The First Circumnavigator*. London: Herder, 1958. The only biography of Elcano.

Morison, Samuel Eliot. *The European Discovery of America: The Southern Voyages, A.D. 1492-1616*. New York: Oxford University Press, 1974. Contains an excellent, carefully documented account of the first voyage around the world.

SEE ALSO: Charles V; Christopher Columbus; John II; Miguel López de Legazpi; Ferdinand Magellan.

RELATED ARTICLE in *Great Events from History: The Renaissance & Early Modern Era, 1454-1600:* 1519-1522: Magellan Expedition Circumnavigates the Globe.

ELIZABETH I
Queen of England (r. 1558-1603)

The last of the five Tudor monarchs, Queen Elizabeth I earned the respect of her associates and the love of her subjects while ruling England longer and more capably than most kings of her time.

BORN: September 7, 1533; Greenwich, England
DIED: March 24, 1603; Richmond, Surrey, England
ALSO KNOWN AS: The Virgin Queen; Good Queen Bess
AREAS OF ACHIEVEMENT: Government and politics, patronage of the arts

EARLY LIFE

The second child of King Henry VIII, Elizabeth was born in Greenwich. Before she was three years old, her father nullified his marriage to her mother, Anne Boleyn, whom he then had tried for adultery and conspiracy, convicted, and beheaded. Like her older half sister Mary before her, Elizabeth was declared to be illegitimate, and Henry immediately married Jane Seymour. A statute of 1544, while not reversing the earlier decree, nevertheless placed Elizabeth third in line to the throne after Edward, born to Henry and Jane in 1537, and Mary, daughter of Henry's first wife, Catherine of Aragon.

Elizabeth's education commenced under several eminent Cambridge scholars, one of whom, Roger Ascham, wrote a distinguished educational treatise called *The Schoolmaster* (1570). She proved an apt student, studying Greek and Latin and attaining fluency in French and Italian. Languages were the key to familiarity not only with literature but also with the New Testament and the scholarship of Europe. Because of her linguistic aptitude, Elizabeth would not later have to rely on translators, as did many sovereigns, when dealing with foreign ambassadors.

Elizabeth learned other practical lessons during the years from 1547, when her father died, until 1558, when she succeeded. While she lived with Catherine Parr, Henry's last wife and the closest approach to a mother she would ever know, Catherine's marriage to the promiscuous Thomas Seymour taught her the importance of being on her guard, for Seymour made advances to the now attractive teenager. Her subsequent determination not to allow men to manipulate her became an important factor in her forty-five-year reign. Political events tested her mettle early. Seymour fell under suspicion of treason against his brother Edward, lord protector of Edward, the boy king, and Elizabeth was sharply questioned about possible complicity. The fifteen-year-old princess responded shrewdly and prudently, and though Seymour was executed, she was permitted to live quietly until Edward's death in 1553.

Those who saw Elizabeth take part in her sister's coronation ceremony saw a young woman somewhat taller than average, with reddish-gold hair and light skin. Although her portrait was often painted, the stylized likenesses of Renaissance royalty often prove unreliable, and even eyewitnesses disagreed considerably about the details of her physical appearance, but everyone credited her with beautiful hands. While not a particularly religious person, Elizabeth deplored Mary's Roman Catholicism and, like many English patriots, was apprehensive about Mary's decision to marry the Catholic prince Philip (Philip II) of Spain. Again, in Mary's reign, Elizabeth was suspected of treason, this time in connection with Sir Thomas Wyatt the Younger's plan to depose Mary in favor of her, for presumably Elizabeth would marry an Englishman and a Protestant and thus avert the danger of the crown passing to an offspring of Philip and Mary. Though imprisoned in the Tower of London for a time, Elizabeth again dodged the extreme penalty; she emerged understanding thoroughly, however, the danger of even the appearance of treason.

Eventually, Philip, seeing his wife childless and ill and viewing Elizabeth as preferable to such a claimant as Mary Stuart (Mary, Queen of Scots), wife of the French dauphin, became the protector of the future queen. This precarious period in the princess's life ended on November 17, 1558, when the unpopular Mary died and Elizabeth, at the age of twenty-five, became the third of Henry VIII's children to wear the English crown.

LIFE'S WORK

Elizabeth understood the presumably modern art of public relations, and from her coronation onward she worked to gain the admiration of her subjects. She also surrounded herself with able advisers, the most faithful of whom was William Cecil (from 1571, known as Lord Burghley), and he served her well for forty years. The domestic question—whom would she marry?—early became a question of foreign relations also, for the most ambitious bachelors of Western Europe recognized her as the greatest available "prize." The archduke Charles of Austria offered a politically advantageous match, but both Elizabeth and her subjects shied away from his Roman Catholicism. Elizabeth appeared to prefer one of her own subjects, Robert Dudley, earl of Leicester, eligible in 1560 after the death of his wife Amy Robsart, but the mystery surrounding her fatal fall down a flight of stairs cast a shadow over his name. There was no lack of other suitors, and all England expected Elizabeth to avert the disorder likely at the death of an unmarried and childless queen, but the strong-willed sovereign did not intend to yield an iota of her sovereignty to any man, and the sort of person who would content himself with being a mere consort probably appealed little to her imagination. Throughout the early years of her reign, she kept everyone guessing about her marriage plans, but she made no commitments.

Mary, Queen of Scots, whose grandmother—Henry VIII's sister—had married the Scottish king James IV, posed one threat to England's security, particularly after her first husband became King Francis II of France in 1559, for France was England's traditional enemy. To neutralize the French threat, Elizabeth encouraged Scot-

tish fears of foreign authority, even suggesting the possibility of her own marriage to the earl of Arran, whose family ranked high in the Scottish succession. When Francis died in 1560, however, Mary's influence declined, and her subsequent marriage to her kinsman, the unstable Lord Darnley (Henry Stewart), led to her undoing. Eventually, she was deposed, Darnley died, and for many years Mary languished, a virtual prisoner of Elizabeth in England. For nearly two decades, Elizabeth allowed no harm to come to her Scottish cousin, but neither did she intend to allow conspirators to build on Mary's claim to the English throne.

For the first decade of her reign, with much of the European continent in turmoil, Elizabeth kept England at peace, but in 1569 she was forced to put down a rebellion in the north fomented by Thomas Howard, duke of Norfolk, whose ambitions spurred him to seek marriage to the deposed Mary, Queen of Scots. The rebellion was speedily checked, and Elizabeth merely placed Norfolk under house arrest until she learned that he was plotting with foreign agents to overthrow her directly. Meanwhile, Pope Pius V excommunicated Elizabeth, who had never considered herself a Roman Catholic anyway, but this action, focusing Catholic enmity on her, created a dangerous atmosphere at a time when English cordiality toward Catholic Spain was steadily lessening. Therefore, Elizabeth, while continuing to spare Mary, allowed Norfolk, the only duke in her kingdom, to be tried, convicted, and executed early in 1572.

At this time, another problem was developing in the Netherlands in the form of a provincial rebellion against Spanish authority. An increased Spanish presence just across the English Channel or the possible alternative of a French buildup in response to Dutch pleas for assistance could spell trouble for England. Remaining officially neutral, Elizabeth encouraged support by volunteers and through private subscriptions; eventually, she made large loans to the rebels out of her treasury, though not in amounts sufficient to turn the tide against Spain decisively. She hoped that the Netherlands could unite under the Protestant William the Silent, but in vain. When, finally, in 1585 she committed troops to the struggle, she chose her old favorite Leicester as commander. He also shared political authority with a provincial council, but his blunders led to serious divisions among the provinces on the eve of the Spanish Armada's attack on England, a crisis brought on in large measure by Sir Francis Drake's harassment of Spain's American colonies.

While England's lighter, more maneuverable fleet took advantage of westerly winds that helped drive the

Elizabeth I. (Library of Congress)

Armada away from England's southern coast toward France, Elizabeth visited her army at Tilbury near the mouth of the Thames and showered encouragement and eloquence on her soldiers. Skillfully, she braced them for the land battle that fortunately never erupted. Instead, what was left of the badly battered Spanish fleet limped back to Spain, and the greatest external threat of her reign ended in increased prestige for the nautical and military skill of England.

During the earlier years of the Netherlands venture, Elizabeth still gave the appearance of considering marriage offers. As late as 1581, Francis of Valois, duke of Alençon, was pursuing her, but Elizabeth, while willing to use him to preserve a truce with the French ruler, Henry III, firmly rejected his offer. By this time, it appeared that the queen, now in her late forties, would probably never marry and almost certainly never bear children, but events of the next few years clarified the succession. James VI, son of the deposed Mary, was demonstrating ability on the Scottish throne, and though he flirted with Roman Catholicism as Elizabeth did with her suitors—for diplomatic leverage—his religious views and sense of the place of religion did not differ greatly from Elizabeth's own. She drew closer to James, and when yet another conspiracy, led by Anthony Babington, implicated James's mother and caused Elizabeth to execute her in 1587, James merely protested formally. Not until she lay on her deathbed did the cautious Elizabeth confirm the fact, but England now understood that the crown would pass peacefully to James.

The foreign operations had imposed a heavy financial burden on Elizabeth. Meanwhile, poor harvests and adverse trade conditions impoverished the realm, and the surge of euphoria occasioned by the repulsion of the Spanish naval threat faded as the century waned. By the final years of Elizabeth's long rule, many agreed with Hamlet: "the time is out of joint." Another of the queen's onetime favorites, Robert Devereux, earl of Essex, mounted a rebellion in 1601, and again she felt obliged to respond with the death penalty. Until her seventieth year, Elizabeth enjoyed robust health; only at the beginning of 1603 did she succumb to what may have been a severe bronchial illness. She continued her duties until her worried councillors persuaded her to take to her bed on March 21. Early in the morning of the third day following, she died quietly.

SIGNIFICANCE

Many students of Queen Elizabeth I's reign have found her to have been shrewd and resourceful, able to keep op-

ponents guessing and off balance while she guided her ship of state through perilous seas. To others, she has seemed procrastinating and indecisive, unable to carry out her policies efficiently. Her subjects expected her to rule firmly and to provide for her successor, but in the case of a queen, one of these goals would easily preclude the other.

If she married to produce an heir or designated a successor, her authority would diminish. If she named an ambitious person without the patience to await her death, she might well endanger both her life and domestic tranquillity. She did well to allow James to emerge gradually as her candidate without officially nominating him. By playing off her suitors against one another, she kept England free from the very real possibility of foreign political and religious domination. Throughout her reign, she bargained adroitly with foreign powers without committing herself to unmanageable situations.

No doubt, Elizabeth sometimes relied too heavily on her favorite strategies, but most often they were well adapted to the needs of the relatively small and poor nation she ruled. Her prudent management kept the cost of government within the capacities and tolerance of her subjects. Under her, England became what it would remain for centuries: a recognized naval power. At a time of serious religious conflict, she pursued a policy remarkably tolerant and unprovocative. A nation that had endured the last unreasoning years of Henry VIII, internecine power struggles under the Edwardian regency, and a few bloody years under the erratic Mary and her Spanish husband, had gained confidence and security.

While not generally extravagant, Elizabeth understood the social and psychological value of magnificent progresses and dignified receptions. She captured the imagination of poets such as Edmund Spenser and Sir Walter Ralegh, who helped spread her fame beyond the range of those who actually saw her. She was Spenser's Faerie Queene in one of that character's guises, the Gloriana who summed up the glory of England. Indeed, Elizabeth appreciated poetry and the arts generally and wrote competent poetry herself. During the second half of her reign, English literature reached an unprecedented peak. Her subjects responded enthusiastically to her preference for the arts—including the art of peace—and to her genuine love for them. The affection of the English for their monarch still alive in the time of the second Elizabeth owes much to the precedent of the first.

She was the first of only two English queens to give her name to a considerable wedge of history, but whereas Victoria merely symbolized an age created by others,

Elizabeth stands as both symbol and substance of hers. The policies of England in the latter half of the sixteenth century, when the nation rose to prominence in Europe, were her policies. The wisdom of most of those policies was her wisdom and that of councillors she appointed. Altogether she is one of history's most remarkable women.

—*Robert P. Ellis*

FURTHER READING

Camden, William. *The Historie of the Most Renowned and Victorious Princesse Elizabeth Late Queene of England*. London: B. Fisher, 1630. Rev. ed. Edited by Wallace T. MacCaffrey. Chicago: University of Chicago Press, 1970. These selections from the annals of a scholar from Elizabethan times represent the earliest authoritative study of her reign. Camden wrote in Latin; this version, the work of an anonymous seventeenth century translator, conveys Camden's commitment to a plain, factual record. Though lacking in color and narrative skill, Camden gives the modern reader a sense of the way Elizabeth's reign looked to a learned contemporary.

Doran, Susan. *Queen Elizabeth I*. New York: New York University Press, 2003. Portrays Elizabeth as a flawed but brilliant manipulator who used this ability to protect her country and to steer it safely through a host of dangers. Includes illustrations, map, bibliographic references, index.

Doran, Susan, and Thomas S. Freeman, eds. *The Myth of Elizabeth*. New York: Palgrave Macmillan, 2003. Anthology of essays examining the body of myth surrounding Elizabeth, including her contemporary portrayal as the "Virgin Queen," her importance in the Jacobean imagination, and film portrayals of Elizabeth. Includes illustrations, bibliographic references, and index.

Dunn, Jane. *Elizabeth and Mary: Cousins, Rivals, Queens*. New York: Alfred A. Knopf, 2004. Study of the rivalry and political intrigue between Elizabeth I and Mary, Queen of Scots, attempting to portray the private emotions behind their public acts. Includes photographic plates, illustrations, bibliographic references, index.

Erickson, Carolly. *The First Elizabeth*. New York: Summit Books, 1983. Erickson counters the traditional emphasis on the "Virgin Queen" by stressing her use of her sexual power to attain her ends. This biography presents a heavily psychological interpretation of its subject.

Jenkins, Elizabeth. *Elizabeth the Great*. New York: Coward-McCann, 1959. Relying on previously published sources, this popular and critical biography continues to deserve praise as a perceptive and readable interpretation of Elizabeth's character. As her title suggests, Jenkins emphasizes the positive elements contributing to Elizabeth's eminence.

Johnson, Paul. *Elizabeth I*. New York: Holt, Rinehart and Winston, 1974. Johnson depicts court life clearly but is less convincing on some aspects of the background of the age, particularly Puritanism. The informing theme of his study is the relationship between Elizabeth's exercise of her secular power and the political implications of the religious authority that she inherited from her predecessors.

Levin, Carole, Jo Eldridge Carney, and Debra Barrett-Graves, eds. *Elizabeth I: Always Her Own Free Woman*. Burlington, Vt.: Ashgate, 2003. Anthology of essays by scholars of literature, history, and culture, examining the relationship of Elizabeth with her court, her advisers, and the wider English culture. Includes illustrations, bibliographic references, and an index.

MacCaffrey, Wallace T. *The Shaping of the Elizabethan Regime*. Princeton, N.J.: Princeton University Press, 1968. This specialized study should interest readers seeking a detailed understanding of the first fifteen years of Elizabeth's rule, or what the author calls its "testing time." This work makes extensive use of state papers and documents from the Public Record Office in London.

Neale, J. E. *Queen Elizabeth I: A Biography*. London: Jonathan Cape, 1934. Reprint. New York: Doubleday, 1957. The great pioneer among modern biographers of Elizabeth, Neale is a master of unpretentious narrative history. Though undocumented, this classic biography has earned the respect of all Elizabethan researchers. Time has not dimmed its appeal.

Read, Conyers. *Lord Burghley and Queen Elizabeth*. New York: Alfred A. Knopf, 1960. The second volume of a life mostly of Elizabeth's ablest adviser, this book, covering the years 1570 to 1598, explores in meticulous detail the working relationship between the two. Read is one of the greatest of modern Elizabethan scholars.

Williams, Neville. *Elizabeth the First: Queen of England*. New York: E.P. Dutton, 1968. A senior official of the Public Record Office, Williams predictably draws extensively on the documents thereof. He presents a particularly good picture of Elizabeth's domestic life. An objective, competently written, but sometimes stodgy biography.

SEE ALSO: Bess of Hardwick; Anne Boleyn; Catherine of Aragon; William Cecil; John Dee; Sir Francis Drake; Edward VI; William Gilbert; Henry III; Henry VIII; James IV; Margaret of Parma; Mary, Queen of Scots; Mary I; Bernardino de Mendoza; Catherine Parr; Philip II; Pius V; Sir Walter Ralegh; First Earl of Salisbury; Jane Seymour; Edmund Spenser; William the Silent.

RELATED ARTICLES in *Great Events from History: The Renaissance & Early Modern Era, 1454-1600:* Janu-

ary 25-February 7, 1554: Wyatt's Rebellion; 1558-1603: Reign of Elizabeth I; January 1-8, 1558: France Regains Calais from England; April 3, 1559: Treaty of Cateau-Cambrésis; January, 1563: Thirty-nine Articles of the Church of England; January 20, 1564: Peace of Troyes; July 29, 1567: James VI Becomes King of Scotland; November 9, 1569: Rebellion of the Northern Earls; February 25, 1570: Pius V Excommunicates Elizabeth I; April, 1587-c. 1600: Anglo-Spanish War; July 31-August 8, 1588: Defeat of the Spanish Armada; May 2, 1598: Treaty of Vervins; December 31, 1600: Elizabeth I Charters the East India Company.

DESIDERIUS ERASMUS
Dutch scholar

Of the intellectuals who transmitted and adapted the Renaissance spirit to northern Europe, Erasmus was the greatest. Taken together, his writings reflect a rare combination of practical Christian piety, biblical and patristic scholarship, and broad Humanistic learning.

BORN: October 28, 1466?; Rotterdam, Holland (now in the Netherlands)
DIED: July 12, 1536; Basel, Switzerland
AREAS OF ACHIEVEMENT: Education, religion and theology, philosophy, literature

EARLY LIFE
Desiderius Erasmus (dehz-ih-DEHR-ee-uhs eh-RAS-muhs) was born in Rotterdam to Margaret, a physician's daughter, and a priest probably named Gerard, for whom she served as housekeeper. As one of two illegitimate sons born to this couple, the sensitive Erasmus (he took the additional name Desiderius later in life) would endure shame and legal problems, but his parents lived together for many years and appear to have been devoted parents. Erasmus's childhood coincided with the ongoing war between the duchy of Burgundy, which controlled Holland, and France. He grew to despise the Burgundian knights, whose cruelty belied the chivalric ideal expressed by Charles the Bold. He also developed an aversion to the provinciality and social rigidity of his homeland.

Around 1478, Erasmus's mother enrolled the two boys at a school in Deventer, about seventy-five miles inland, conducted by the Brethren of the Common Life, a lay society dedicated to the imitation of primitive Chris-

tianity. Although Erasmus later expressed contempt for the Brethren's teaching methods, both their piety and a Humanistic strain that entered the school at this time helped shape the young student. His schooling at Deventer ended in 1483 or 1484, when the plague claimed the lives of both his parents. Three guardians appointed by his father sent Erasmus to another more conservative and even less congenial of the Brethren's schools for three additional years.

Erasmus entered the Augustinian priory at Steyn about 1487. There, the critical young man learned to dislike the ascetic routine and prevailing mysticism, but he enlarged his grasp of classical literature and wrote the first two of his many books, a conventional treatise on monastic life and a book of Latin verse. His years at Steyn climaxed with his ordination as priest on April 25, 1492.

LIFE'S WORK
About a year after his ordination, Erasmus accepted a post as Latin secretary to the ambitious Henri, bishop of Cambray. While in his service, Erasmus wrote, in the form of a Platonic dialogue, an attack on Scholasticism, the dominant philosophy of the Church, although the book remained unpublished for nearly thirty years. In 1495, Bishop Henri assisted Erasmus in gaining entrance to the University of Paris, a hotbed of Scholasticism, presumably to study for his doctorate in theology. At the College of Montaigu in Paris, he made Humanist friends, including an elderly man named Robert Gaguin, who had been a pupil of the noted Florentine Platonist Marsilio Ficino, and who now encouraged Erasmus to

study the Neoplatonists. Constantly seeking the independence that would enable him to spend his life studying in reasonable comfort, he accepted in 1499 the patronage of the Englishman William Blount, Lord Mountjoy, and thus visited England for the first time. There he established friendships with leading scholars such as William Grocyn, Thomas Linacre, John Colet, and—preeminently—Sir Thomas More.

Already the wandering pattern of the person who later called himself a citizen of the world was being established. He returned to France the next year and began a routine of scholarly activity that included the study of Greek, the compilation of a book of proverbial wisdom, *Adagia* (1500; *Proverbs or Adages*, 1622), and a manual of Christianity written for the laity from the point of view of a monk who, at this point, was living in the manner of a principled Christian layperson. *Enchiridion militis Christiani* (1503; *The Manual of the Christian Knight*, 1533) became the best known of his works in this genre. His study of Lorenzo Valla's exegesis of the New Testament, a work he edited and published in 1506, quickened his determination to master the original Greek. After another sojourn in England with his Humanist friends there, he accepted a tutoring appointment that took him to Italy.

His work took him on a tour that included Turin, at whose university he received a doctorate in divinity in 1506, and Florence, Bologna, and Venice, where he met the distinguished printer Aldus Manutius, with whom he worked to produce a handsome revision of *Proverbs or Adages*. In Rome, he witnessed the growing corruption of the papal court, after which Mountjoy persuaded him to return to England. It has been argued that had the influential Erasmus remained in Rome during the next crucial decade, he might have furthered the cause of reform, prevented the excommunication of Martin Luther, with whom he corresponded, and thus changed the course of religious history.

After reaching London, while awaiting the arrival of his books, he lived in Thomas More's house and wrote there a book, which he certainly did not consider among his most important but which, more than any other, has immortalized him: *Moriae encomium* (1511; *The Praise of Folly*, 1549). By a species of pun congenial to him and to his host, the title also signifies "the praise of More," though without any suggestion that More was foolish. While the book is, like Sebastian Brant's *Das Narrenschiff* (1494; *The Ship of Fools*, 1509), a satire on human folly, Erasmus's characterization of Folly is a rich and original conception depicting not only gradations of conventional foolishness but also ultimately figuring the Christian fool, whose folly is in reality wisdom.

Later, he became the first to teach Greek at Cambridge. During his two and a half years on the faculty of the English university, he wrote *De duplici copia verborum ac rerum* (1512; *On the Twofold Abundance of Words and Things*, 1978, better known as *De copia*), which would hold its place as a standard textbook on literary style for two centuries. Nevertheless, Erasmus was not happy at Cambridge, blaming the cold, damp climate for undermining his always frail health and finding Cam-

---

ERASMUS'S CALL FOR FOLLY

In The Praise of Folly, *Erasmus presents folly as a middle ground or compromise between knowledge and ignorance, between a total acceptance of what is presented as true and real and a complete denunciation of that knowledge. Accepting folly is accepting that life is a balance between the serious and the foolish. Individuals go on performing their roles in life whether they are steered by rationality and reason or by imagination and pleasure, hence, the play of life.*

Would life without pleasure be life at all? . . . As a matter of fact, even the Stoics do not really dislike pleasure; they carefully pretend to and they loudly denounce it in public, but only in order to deter others and thus have it all to themselves. Just let them explain to me what part of life is not sad, troublesome, graceless, flat, and distressing without a dash of pleasure, or in order words, folly. This is very adequately proved by Sophocles . . . who has left this pretty eulogy of me: "Ignorance is bliss." . . . Just as nothing is more foolish than unseasonable wisdom, so nothing is more imprudent than bull-headed prudence. And he is indeed perverse who does not accommodate himself to the way of the world, who will not follow the crowd, who does not at least remember the rule of good fellowship, drink or begone, and who demands that the play shall no longer be a play. True prudence, on the contrary, consists in not desiring more wisdom than is proper to mortals, and in being willing to wink at the doings of the crowd or to go along with it sociably. But that, they say, is folly itself. I shall certainly not deny it; yet they must in turn admit that it is also to act the play of life.

Source: The Norton Anthology of World Masterpieces, vol. 1, edited by Maynard Mack (New York: W. W. Norton, 1980), pp. 1189, 1190.

bridge intellectually mediocre and provincial. His more enlightened Humanist English friends resided, for the most part, in London.

He was even less pleased with the prospect of returning to monastic life at Steyn, to which he was recalled in 1514, more than two decades after gaining permission to leave: Erasmus relayed his firm intention to return; it required, however, dispensation from Pope Leo X, which took him three years to acquire, to free himself from all possibility of further obligation to his order. While this appeal was pending, he completed his own Latin version of the New Testament, based on Greek manuscripts and more accurate in many (though not all) details than the standard Latin Vulgate. His translation reflected his conviction that Christ's teachings are easily understandable and not meant to be encrusted by the commentary of theologians. Strategically, he dedicated his work to Leo and also recommended that the Bible be translated into the vernacular tongues so that it might be accessible to all readers.

Among his other works in this busy period were a nine-volume edition of the works of Saint Jerome and a manual, *Institutio principis Christiani* (1516; *The Education of a Christian Prince*, 1936). Sharply contrasting with Niccolò Machiavelli's *Il principe* (wr. 1513, pb. 1532; *The Prince*, 1640), Erasmus's advice to the prince

Desiderius Erasmus. (Library of Congress)

included pleas for restraint in taxation and in the waging of war. Unlike Machiavelli, Erasmus regarded politics as a branch of ethics in the classical manner. Unenthusiastic about the tyranny of princes, Erasmus could see no other acceptable alternative to anarchy. In this work and in two other treatises of this period, Erasmus's thought tended toward pacifism, a shocking philosophy in an age that looked on the willingness to wage war as a certification of one's conviction.

During a stay at Antwerp in 1516-1517, Erasmus was painted by Quentin Massys, the first of three famous artists for whom he sat. In this portrait, Erasmus, then middle-aged, is at his writing desk, intently serious. Portraits by Albrecht Dürer and Hans Holbein, the Younger, a few years later interpret the Dutch scholar quite differently, but all three artists agree that Erasmus had a very long, somewhat aquiline nose, a wide mouth with thin lips, and a strong chin. Both Dürer and Holbein (in a late portrait of about 1532) endow the writer with a faint, enigmatic smile, which many viewers have seen as mocking human weakness as does his character Folly. All these portraits show Erasmus wearing a flat cap.

From 1517 to 1521, Erasmus lived at Louvain. He published one of his most enduring works, *Colloquia familiaria* (1518; *The Colloquies of Erasmus*, 1671), and also continued his task of editing the early fathers of the Church, spending all day and much of the night at his writing desk and turning out a stupendous volume of work for publication and hundreds—probably thousands—of gracefully written letters to correspondents all over Europe. Having made a number of severe criticisms of the Church, Erasmus received overtures from his fellow Augustinian Martin Luther, but while refusing for years to denounce Luther—many of whose famous Ninety-five Theses he anticipated—he did not support him either. In the interests of Christian unity, more important to Erasmus than most of the theological points on which Luther challenged the Church, he attempted to mediate the quarrel, but observing the intransigence of both Church and reformers, he refused an invitation to the Diet of Worms, where, in 1521, Luther's doctrines were condemned. Solicited by both sides but widely viewed as cowardly for his unwillingness to back either unequivocally, Erasmus made many enemies. Although he had little reason to fear the Protestant majority in Basel, where he lived during most of the 1520's, he refused to endorse even tacitly the city's denial of religious liberty to Catholic citizens and left for Freiburg in 1529.

Erasmus unsuccessfully urged the warring Christians to compromise and focus on the Turkish threat in the Bal-

ERASMUS'S MAJOR WORKS

1500	*Adagia* (*Proverbs or Adages*, 1622)
1503	*Enchiridion militis Christiani* (*The Manual of the Christian Knight*, 1533)
1511	*Moriæ encomium* (*The Praise of Folly*, 1549)
1512	*De rationae studii* (*A Method of Study*, 1978)
1512	*De duplici copia verborum ac rerum* (*On the Twofold Abundance of Words and Things*, 1978; better known as *De copia*)
1516	*Institutio principis Christiani* (*The Education of a Christian Prince*, 1936)
1516	*Novum instrumentum* (Latin translation of the New Testament with an edited Greek edition)
1517	*Querela pacis* (*The Complaint of Peace*, 1559)
1518	*Colloquia familiaria* (*The Colloquies of Erasmus*, 1671)
1520	*Antibarbarum* (*The Book Against the Barbarians*, 1930)
1524	*De libero arbitrio* (*On the Freedom of the Will*, 1961)
1528	*Dialogus, cui Titulus Ciceronianus sive, de optimo dicendi genere* (*The Ciceronian*, 1900)
1529	*Opus epistolarum* (partial translation *The Epistles*, 1901)

kans and continued to prepare editions of early Christian thinkers. In 1535, his own health failing, he learned of King Henry VIII's execution of his good friends More and Bishop John Fisher. In the final months of his life, he returned to Basel. In 1540, a wooden statue of Erasmus was erected in Rotterdam, the city he claimed as his birthplace, and Johann Froben published an edition of his collected works in Basel. The statue did not survive the Spanish occupation of the Netherlands and many of his books were burned, but the centuries that followed have proved Erasmus ineradicable.

SIGNIFICANCE

Before the heyday of the Protestant reformers, Desiderius Erasmus articulated his dismay at the excesses of an increasingly worldly and corrupt Church and urged a return to Christian essentials. His numerous editions of early Christian theologians and his Latin version of the New Testament signaled his contempt for the decadent but still-prevailing Scholasticism, while his manuals of practical piety reflected his conviction that what he called the philosophy of Christ was a simple and achievable attainment.

Erasmus's tolerance and pacifism, which owed something to his physical timidity but more to his capacity for rational analysis and insight into the futility of religious confrontation, turned both the Catholics and Protestants against him. In an ecumenically minded world, however, what appeared to his contemporaries as cowardice or indecisiveness looks more like wisdom.

As the greatest of the northern Humanists, he communicated not only the learning of the ancients but also their spirit of inquiry and independence to educated people of his time. He saw harmony in the best of classical and Christian thought. He also understood the potentialities of mass-produced books—a new development in his lifetime—and thus devoted his life to incessant writing. A bibliographical analysis by an Erasmian scholar in 1927 produced an estimate that two million copies of Erasmus's books had been printed, one million of them textbooks. Erasmus never understood, however, why more people did not submit to the logic of his arguments. Paradoxically, his books enjoyed more popularity in the later sixteenth and seventeenth centuries, when his personal reputation was ebbing; today a torrent of scholarly works interpret his character much more favorably, but he is much less read. Only *The Praise of Folly* is still widely admired for its wit, subtlety, and the universality of its analysis of human folly. Readers who find their way to *The Colloquies of Erasmus*, however, discover that no writer since Plato has used dialogue so well to express his thought in a persuasive and readable form.

Taken as a whole, Erasmus's writings cast more light on the great European movements of his time—the Renaissance and the Reformation—than does the work of any other eyewitness. This wandering Augustinian monk was an intellectual seismograph who registered the brightest hopes and most profound disappointments of Western civilization in the stormy period of his life.

—*Robert P. Ellis*

FURTHER READING

Bainton, Roland H. *Erasmus of Christendom*. New York: Charles Scribner's Sons, 1969. Probably the closest thing to a standard biography, Bainton's study has relatively little to say about Erasmus's more imaginative works but is particularly good on those less well known. Scholarly, thoroughly documented, yet never ponderous, this book ably interprets Erasmus's complex relationships with Luther and other reformers.

Bejczy, István. *Erasmus and the Middle Ages: The Historical Consciousness of a Christian Humanist.* Boston: Brill, 2001. Like Herwaardeen's book, this study emphasizes the importance of medieval theology for Erasmus and examines his historical research and philosophy of history. Includes bibliographic references and index.

Bentley-Taylor, David. *My Dear Erasmus: The Forgotten Reformer.* Fearn, Scotland: Christian Focus, 2002. Study emphasizing Erasmus's almost legendary reputation among his contemporaries, as evidenced by the deference afforded his knowledge and opinions by myriad European intellectuals and by his voluminous correspondence with those intellectuals. Includes maps and indexes.

Faludy, George. *Erasmus of Rotterdam.* London: Eyre & Spottiswoode, 1970. An excellent general reader's biography. Faludy explains the historical and intellectual contexts of Erasmus's work clearly and tactfully. He uses few footnotes but displays a thorough grasp of Erasmian scholarship.

Herwaardeen, Jan van. *Between Saint James and Erasmus: Studies in Late-Medieval Religious Life: Devotions and Pilgrimages in the Netherlands.* Translated by Wendie Shaffer and Donald Gardner. Boston: Brill, 2003. Study of the influence of the medieval cult of Saint James on Erasmus's thought and beliefs. Explores Erasmus's understanding of the tension between outwardly religious acts and inner beliefs. Includes illustrations, bibliographic references, and indexes.

Huizinga, Johan. *Erasmus and the Age of Reformation.* Translated by F. Hopman. New York: Harper & Row, 1957. Originally published as *Erasmus of Rotterdam* in 1924, Huizinga's biography has worn well. Not only was this Dutch scholar a recognized expert on Erasmus's era, but also he grasped the psychology of his subject as have few other biographers.

Mangan, John Joseph. *Life, Character, and Influence of Desiderius Erasmus of Rotterdam.* 2 vols. New York: Macmillan, 1927. Reprint. New York: AMS Press, 1971. Though dated in some of its interpretations, this lengthy biography prints many translations of Erasmus's writings, especially letters. Its last chapter contains extensive information on Erasmus's later influence as measured by editions and translations of his many works.

Phillips, Margaret Mann. *Erasmus and the Northern Renaissance.* Rev. and illustrated ed. Totowa, N.J.: Rowman & Littlefield, 1981. A somewhat elementary introduction to Erasmus and his age. Contains two recommended chapters: "Portrait" and "The World Through Erasmus's Eye." Useful for beginning students of the Renaissance.

Smith, Preserved. *Erasmus: A Study of His Life, Ideals, and Place in History.* New York: Frederick Ungar, 1962. This reprint of a study published in 1923 views Erasmus as champion of "undogmatic Christianity" and thus emphasizes his subjects' relations with, and differences from, the Protestant reformers. Less useful on the Humanist aspect. A patient, scholarly biography with an extensive bibliography of nineteenth and earlier twentieth century studies, chiefly by European scholars.

Zweig, Stefan. *Erasmus of Rotterdam.* Translated by Eden Paul and Cedar Paul. Reprint. New York: Viking Press, 1956. A lively popular life by a master of general readers' biographies. Although not always accurate in details or judicious interpretations, Zweig's biography may well stimulate the beginning student of Erasmus to delve into more detailed and critical accounts of his life and achievements.

SEE ALSO: Giordano Bruno; John Colet; Thomas Cranmer; Albrecht Dürer; Marsilio Ficino; Saint John Fisher; Henry VIII; Hans Holbein, the Younger; Jacques Lefèvre d'Etaples; Leo X; Martin Luther; Niccolò Machiavelli; Aldus Manutius; Marguerite de Navarre; Philipp Melanchthon; Sir Thomas More; Giovanni Pico della Mirandola.

RELATED ARTICLES in *Great Events from History: The Renaissance & Early Modern Era, 1454-1600:* 1499-1517: Erasmus Advances Humanism in England; 1516: Sir Thomas More Publishes *Utopia*; June 5-24, 1520: Field of Cloth of Gold; 1550's-c. 1600: Educational Reforms in Europe.

Hieronymus Fabricius ab Aquapendente
Italian physician

Fabricius is most famous for his discovery of valves in veins and for teaching William Harvey, who used Fabricius's findings in his proof of blood circulation. Fabricius also made numerous contributions to anatomy, physiology, embryology, and surgery.

Born: May 20, 1537; Aquapendente, near Orvieto (now in Italy)

Died: May 21, 1619; Padua, Republic of Venice (now in Italy)

Also known as: Girolamo Fabrici (given name); Geronimo Fabrizio; Girolamo Fabricius; Girolamo Fabrizzi; Hieronymus Fabricius

Area of achievement: Medicine

Early Life

Girolamo Fabrici, later known in Latin as Hieronymus Fabricius (hi-ur-AWN-ih-muhs fah-BRIHSH-ee-uhs) was born in Aquapendente, a village near Orvieto in Umbria, about sixty miles north of Rome. Named after his paternal grandfather, he received the classical education common for the eldest sons of noble families. The adolescent Fabrici was sent north to Padua to continue his studies in Latin, Greek, logic, and philosophy. While living with a patrician family, he successfully pursued Humanistic studies while also becoming interested in medicine.

The University of Padua's medical school was one of the finest in Europe and was particularly strong in human and comparative anatomy. This tradition began with Alessandro Benedetti—who published a book on human anatomy in 1502—and continued with Andreas Vesalius—who graduated from Padua in 1537 and wrote *De humani corporis fabrica libri septem* (1543; *On the Fabric of the Human Body*, books I-IV, 1998; better known as *De fabrica*). Vesalius's pupil and successor was Gabriel Fallopius, another excellent Paduan anatomist, who then taught Fabricius surgery and anatomy.

After receiving his degree in medicine in 1559, Fabricius taught and did research in anatomy and surgery until he achieved sufficient recognition to take over as professor in these fields at Padua. Fabricius would remain at Padua for the rest of his long and distinguished career.

Life's Work

Fabricius lived and worked during the scientific revolution, a time when foundational ideas about the universe and human beings were being revised from what they had been in ancient and medieval times. Vesalius, like Fabricius after him, was a scientist who straddled the medieval and modern worlds. Though Vesalius challenged many of great ancient physician Galen's ideas on anatomy, he accepted most of Galen's ideas on physiology. Similarly, Fabricius began a revolution in medicine by his accurate and detailed description of the valves in the veins, but he continued to accept Galen's ideas of the blood's creation in the liver and its fundamentally unidirectional flow in the human body.

As a young professor of surgery, Fabricius exhibited the conservative tendencies that had characterized most of the history of medicine. In both his writings and practices, he heavily depended on the works of his predecessors. In describing and diagnosing such ills as fractures and dislocations, tumors and fistulas, and in the surgical techniques and therapies he used to remedy them, he followed such classical authorities as Hippocrates and Galen. He wrote popular books on surgery and made many of his own instruments; his fame as a surgeon became so great that nobles from all over Italy came to him for their operations.

Concurrently with his work in surgery, Fabricius continued the Paduan tradition in anatomy but with some important differences. Vesalius had been interested in the structure of the human body, but Fabricius went beyond descriptive anatomy to study the actions and functions of bones, muscles, nerves, and other body parts. Furthermore, he studied the anatomies and physiologies of many different species. According to some scholars, he was the first to establish the field of comparative anatomy, since he dissected many animals—not just because of their relevance to humans but because this knowledge was valuable in itself.

He also designed and used his own funds to build an anatomical theater at the university, where, for more than 275 years, first Fabricius and then many other professors instructed thousands of students in the art of surgery and dissection.

Fabricius's greatest anatomical work was his precise descriptions of the structure and action of the valves in the veins. Although others had previously observed them, Fabricius studied valves in great detail and published a seminal work about his researches. He first noticed the valves in the 1570's in the course of his dissections. In one of his famous experiments, he wrapped a tourniquet around a subject's arm, causing the valves to appear as periodically spaced protuberances. He could then illustrate the one-way direction of blood flow by using the pressure of one of his fingers to force the blood out of the vessel between the valves, which would refill when his finger was lifted.

In this way, Fabricius recognized that the venous valves blocked blood flow away from the heart and directed blood flow back toward the heart. Influenced by Galen's physiological ideas, however, he erroneously interpreted the valves functions as regulating blood flow into the arms and legs for the purpose of nourishing tissues and vital organs.

When the English student William Harvey arrived at Padua in 1599, Fabricius had already done most of his research on the venous valves and was preparing a book on his findings. Harvey became his devoted pupil and resided for a time in his teacher's house. After spending three years at Padua, Harvey received his medical degree in 1602 and then returned to England, where he became a successful and famous physician and medical researcher in his own right. He once claimed that Fabricius's discovery of the one-way function of the venous valves was the most important factor that led to his own great discovery of blood circulation. A short time after Harvey left Padua, Fabricius published *De venarum ostiolis* (1603; *De venarum ostiolis, 1603, of Hieronymus Fabricius of Aquapendente*, 1933), in which he summarized his nearly thirty years of research on this subject.

Harvey was also impressed by Fabricius's work in embryology, and in the early seventeenth century, Fabricius began to publish the results of his studies. As with his other medical contributions, his embryological work looked both backward and forward. He was familiar with Aristotle's studies of the development of the chick embryo and with his ideas about how creatures such as insects can be spontaneously generated from decomposing materials. Unlike Aristotle, Fabricius believed that most insects, as well as many other animals, are born from eggs. Since the mammalian egg could not be seen with the unaided eye, Fabricius did not think that mammals originated from eggs. He also had a deficient understanding of the structure and function of eggs and sperm. He believed that the yolk and albumen in the egg simply nourished the embryo and that the spiral threads that held the yolk in position were responsible for the chick's origin. Furthermore, Fabricius thought that semen never entered the egg but stimulated the generative process from a distance. Despite the faultiness of these views, his studies of the morphological details of the developing fetuses of a variety of animals, including humans, greatly advanced the knowledge of how these creatures originate, mature, and are nourished in the early stages of development.

Because of his accomplishments as a teacher and researcher, the university kept increasing his salary, thus enabling him to purchase an estate at Bugazzi. Early in the seventeenth century, he was honored with the title of Professor Supraordinarius and given tenure for the rest of his life. Failing health caused him to retire from the university in 1613. His wife died in 1618, and he did not long survive her. He fell ill on May 13, 1619, and died about a week later at his house in Padua. Though he had had an illegitimate son, he left his fortune of more than 200,000 ducats to a niece.

SIGNIFICANCE

Some consider Fabricius's greatest significance to be his teaching rather than his originating new ideas. Fabricius was the product of excellent teaching, and he in turn trained outstanding medical researchers such as William Harvey. Although his insensitivity alienated some of his German students early in his academic career, he matured into Padua's most popular professor. Padua had an excellent reputation when Fabricius arrived, and his more than sixty years of service further enhanced its preeminence. Fabricius was part of a distinguished and innovative faculty that attracted students from all over Europe. Just as Galileo enhanced Padua's prestige in physics, astronomy, and mathematics, so Fabricius made its medical program matchless in comparative anatomy and embryology.

Though he remained faithful to many traditional medical ideas, Fabricius was an excellent researcher whose empirical results led him to criticize both ancient authorities and his immediate predecessors. His skill as a physician and surgeon brought him many patients, including such knowledgeable individuals as Galileo. They obviously shared the view of most of his students and fellow professors that Fabricius was the most talented and erudite physician of his time.

—Robert J. Paradowski

FURTHER READING

Adelman, Howard B. *The Embryological Treatises of Hieronymus Fabricius of Aquapendente.* Ithaca, N.Y.: Cornell University Press, 1942. In addition to translating some of Fabricius's most important works into English, Adelman also provides useful information on his subject's life and work.

Doby, T. *Discoverers of Blood Circulation: From Aristotle to the Times of Da Vinci and Harvey.* New York: Abelard-Schumann, 1963. This work, written for the general reader, contains accounts of the forerunners and contemporaries of William Harvey, including Fabricius. Nine-page bibliography and name and subject indexes.

Kemp, Martin, "Medicine in View: Art and Visual Representation." In *Western Medicine: An Illustrated History,* edited by Irvine Loudon. New York: Oxford University Press, 1997. Written by a team of twenty distinguished medical historians, this book's material spans medicine in Europe and America from its beginnings to the end of the twentieth century. The article by Kemp contains an analysis of Fabricius's work on surgery, which was superbly illustrated. Glossary, chronology, and an extensive index.

Porter, Roy. *The Greatest Benefit to Mankind: A Medical History of Humanity.* New York: Norton, 1997. Porter, a social historian of medicine, emphasizes medical theory and practice in this book that blends "erudition and entertainment." He discusses Fabricius as a great comparative anatomist and an important precursor of William Harvey. Forty-five-page section on further readings and a comprehensive index.

SEE ALSO: Andreas Vesalius.

RELATED ARTICLES in *Great Events from History: The Renaissance & Early Modern Era, 1454-1600:* 1530's-1540's: Paracelsus Presents His Theory of Disease; 1543: Vesalius Publishes *On the Fabric of the Human Body;* 1546: Fracastoro Discovers That Contagion Spreads Disease; 1553: Servetus Describes the Circulatory System.

ALESSANDRO FARNESE
Spanish military leader and duke of Parma (r. 1586-1592)

Combining prodigious military ability and political talent, Farnese came close to retaking the Netherlands for Spain before imperial distractions and drains on King Philip's finances elsewhere combined to undermine his achievements.

BORN: August 27, 1545; Rome, Papal States (now in Italy)

DIED: December 2-3, 1592; Arras, France

AREAS OF ACHIEVEMENT: Military, government and politics

EARLY LIFE

Alessandro Farnese (ahl-ehs-SAHN-droh fahr-NAY-say) had illustrious ancestry. His great-grandfather on his father's side, for whom he was named, was Pope Paul III. His mother, Margaret of Austria, was the natural daughter of Holy Roman Emperor Charles V. Two years after his birth, his father, Ottavio Farnese, inherited the duchy of Parma. Alessandro and his twin, Carlo (named for his maternal grandfather), were the only children of his parents' marriage. Carlo died within a few months of birth, making Alessandro the only legitimate heir to Ottavio and a treasured only child to Margaret.

In 1556, to cement the alliance between his father and Philip, the regent of Spain, Alessandro was sent to Brussels to reside at the Spanish court. For the next nine years, until his marriage and subsequent return to Parma, Alessandro would serve as a hostage to his family's good faith and would complete his education in the Low Countries and Spain. He studied for a time in the great university town of Alcalá de Henares, where his course of study, shared with his contemporaries the crown prince Don Carlos and his uncle Don Juan of Austria, was designed by his uncle Philip II. Although Alessandro and Don Carlos found a common interest in military science, it was his young uncle Don Juan who became his closest friend. The young Italian nobleman was well received at the Spanish court in Madrid and admired for his manners, linguistic ability, and skill in the military arts.

After the number of plans to ally the house of Farnese with other prominent families fell through, at length a suitable match was approved by his father and Philip II. In November, 1565, Alessandro married Princess Maria of Portugal. The bride was considerably older than the groom, and she was considerably more enamored of him than he was of her, but it proved a fruitful marriage, producing two sons and a daughter before Maria died. After the marriage, the young couple settled in Parma, where Alessandro found that the combination of matrimony and the quiet life made him restless. After much pleading and many frustrations, he received the opportunity to join in the Crusade against the Turks in 1571, serving under Don Juan.

LIFE'S WORK

The campaign against the Turks gave Farnese a chance to demonstrate his military prowess and personal courage. He joined the expedition with three hundred soldiers and eighty-two knights from the duchies of Parma and Piacenza. Don Juan gave him charge of several Genoese galleys in the international fleet. Farnese acquitted himself well at the Battle of Lepanto, personally leading the boarding party that captured the treasure ship of the Turkish fleet.

After this great victory, which made Don Juan a national hero, life quieted down again for Farnese until 1577, when he was given command of the relief forces sent to assist Don Juan, now governor of the rebellious Low Countries. In the Netherlands campaigns of the next fifteen years, Farnese would establish a reputation for military genius and political astuteness that would outstrip that of his illustrious uncle. Farnese's army reached the scene of the fighting in time to tip the balance in the Battle of Gembloux in December, 1577. Using a brilliantly conceived strategy, Farnese surprised the rebel army and triggered a rout that completely destroyed it. Farnese quickly became Don Juan's best and most trusted commander, and when this revered leader lay dying in October, 1578, he appointed Farnese as his interim successor. Philip II made the appointment as governor of the Low Countries permanent.

Now in his early thirties, Farnese was revered by his men and respected by his enemies for his intelligence, personal bravery, and skill. As governor of the Low Countries, Farnese combined military genius with an effective diplomacy. Through organizational skill and the sheer force of his personality, he molded an army of disparate elements into an efficient fighting machine that struck fear into the hearts of the enemy. In particular, he was effective in his utilization of mercenary troops.

As a negotiator, he utilized the knowledge of the tensions and jealousies within the Netherlands nobility, gained both from his youthful experiences there and from intelligence from an extensive network of spies. He won defections to the Spanish side using a combination of persuasion and bribery, offered with the utmost delicacy and graciousness. That not only conserved men and money but also allowed Farnese to concentrate his forces on those towns still resisting. By these methods, Farnese became the most successful of Philip's governors of the Spanish Netherlands.

Between 1579 and 1585, Farnese systematically reconquered most of the southern provinces, earning a

Alessandro Farnese. (Library of Congress)

place in history as the creator of modern Belgium. He reached the high point of his military success in the summer of 1585, with the successful culmination of the Siege of Antwerp. He seemed poised to complete his task of subjugating all the rebellious provinces until international politics, in the form of English aid, intervened in 1586. This aid stiffened Dutch resistance and turned Philip's attention toward invading England, which he believed would secure England for Catholicism, perhaps gain for him the throne, and solve the thorny problem of the Netherlands once and for all.

Farnese played a major role in the preparation of the invincible Armada. Philip requested plans for an invasion of England from his greatest sailor, the marquis of Santa Cruz, and his greatest soldier, Farnese. Farnese's original plan was for a secret operation ferrying some thirty thousand crack troops across the Channel in barges to link with an uprising of English Catholics. The marquis of Santa Cruz recommended a large fleet of five hundred vessels carrying sixty thousand soldiers, capable of defeating the English fleet. Philip's plan combined parts of both. Spain would assemble a large fleet with Spanish infantry on board to escort an invasion force from the Netherlands to England.

Farnese recommended October, 1586, for the invasion, but delays in the assembly of the fleet in Lisbon made this impossible. By the time the Armada sailed in the summer of 1588, Farnese's reinforcements were greatly depleted by illness and desertion after months of inactivity. Logistical problems and communication breakdowns between Farnese and the duke of Medina Sedonia, the Armada commander, doomed the invasion even before the defeat of the Armada at Gravelines and its destruction by storms as it attempted the circuitous voyage home.

After the Armada disaster in 1588, Farnese's position in the Netherlands became progressively weaker. Spanish finances, stretched to pay for the Armada, were chronically inadequate to meet Farnese's needs. His unpaid troops began to be hard to control. Worse, perhaps, Dutch resistance was bolstered by this clear sign that the Spanish were not invincible. Events in France, also triggered partly by the Armada, distracted Philip, with consequences harmful to the Spanish Netherlands.

The civil war in France had worsened, and with the assassinations of the duke of Guise and the cardinal of Lorraine at the hands of Henry III, and Henry's subsequent assassination in August, 1589, Philip saw not only a chance to defeat the Protestant forces of Henry of Navarre but also an opportunity to put himself or his heirs on the throne of France. To these ends, he put the Netherlands on the back burner and ordered Farnese to take an army into France in 1590 to relieve the Siege of Paris by Henry and the Protestants.

Farnese relieved Paris, but at the cost of a serious deterioration in his position in the Netherlands. While still struggling to regain control of the situation in the Low Countries, Farnese was again ordered into France in 1591, over his strenuous objections, to help the forces of the Catholic League. He succeeded in that, but the campaign cost him dearly, both personally and as a commander, as he returned sick to Flanders in 1592. He was ordered back to France in 1592 and died at Arras in December. At his death, he was unaware that Philip had sent an envoy with orders to replace Farnese and send him back to Madrid to face charges of defrauding Philip of the money sent to finance military operations in the Low Countries.

SIGNIFICANCE

In spite of Philip's ultimate distrust and rejection of him, Farnese served his monarch well, often at personal sacri-

fice. The demands of his governorship separated him from his home and family. He was unable to return to Italy when his wife died in 1577 or when his only daughter married. He became duke of Parma and Piacenza at his father's death in 1586, but, unable to leave his post in the Netherlands, had to appoint his seventeen-year-old heir, Ranuccio, to serve in his place.

An extensive correspondence between father and son indicates a high degree of interest in the affairs of Parma despite Farnese's major responsibilities in the Low Countries. Despite a growing weariness with the incessant war in the Netherlands, Farnese would not live to retire in peace to rule his inheritance. He died while obediently making one more march into France at the order of his monarch.

—Victoria Hennessey Cummins

FURTHER READING

Bertini, Giuseppe. "The Marriage of Alessandro Farnese and D. Maria of Portugal in 1565: Court Life in Lisbon and Parma." In *Cultural Links Between Portugal and Italy in the Renaissance*, edited by K. J. P. Lowe. New York: Oxford University Press, 2000. Examination of the ties forged between the courts of Lisbon and Parma by Farnese's marriage, as well as the differences between them. Includes illustrations, maps, bibliographic references, index.

Kuyper, W. *The Triumphant Entry of Renaissance Architecture into the Netherlands: The Joyeuse Entrée of Philip of Spain into Antwerp in 1549—Renaissance and Mannerist Architecture in the Low Countries from 1530 to 1630.* 2 vols. Alphen aan den Rijn, the Netherlands: Canaletto, 1994. Extensive study of the architectural and cultural influence of Philip's empire on the Netherlands. Includes an entire volume of photographic plates, as well as maps, bibliographic references, and index.

Lynch, John. *Spain, 1516-1598: From Nation State to World Empire.* Cambridge, Mass.: B. Blackwell, 1991. Addresses Farnese's career in the service of Spain. Lynch takes a very positive view of Farnese's character and abilities and is sympathetic to the constraints and frustrations under which he had to operate in dealing with Philip II. Extensive notes provide citations of mostly foreign-language sources.

Mattingly, Garrett. *The Armada.* Reprint. Boston: Houghton Mifflin, 1987. The most readable account of the invincible Armada. Mattingly highlights Farnese's important role in the planning and implementation of the attempted invasion of England. Defends Farnese's actions in preparing his army to invade England, seeing his lack of preparedness to embark his men in August, 1588, as a sign of his military acumen.

Merriman, Roger Bigelow. *Philip the Prudent.* Vol. 4 in *The Rise of the Spanish Empire in the Old World and in the New.* Reprint. New York: Cooper Square, 1962. Addresses the reign of Philip. Contains a significant amount of material about Farnese in all aspects of his service to the Crown. Merriman's coverage of Farnese is less extensive and his writing is less colorful than that of John Motley, but his treatment of Spain and Farnese is far more objective.

Motley, John Lathrop. *The Rise of the Dutch Republic: A History.* 3 vols. New York: Harper & Brothers, 1852. Reprint. New York: E. P. Dutton, 1950. Volume 3 contains extensive references to Farnese during his involvement in the Netherlands campaigns from 1577 to 1584. Motley has a strong anti-Spanish bias, but the work is useful because it is based on published narratives and documents from the period. Motley admires Farnese's military and political genius, even though it worked against what Motley considers to be the forces of modernism and progress.

_____. *The United Netherlands: A History from the Death of William the Silent to the Twelve Years' Truce, 1609.* 4 vols. London: John Murray, 1904. A continuation of the history of the Netherlands, picking up in 1584 where *The Rise of the Dutch Republic* ends. Volumes 1, 2, and 3 contain extensive discussions of Farnese's service as governor of the Low Countries from 1584 to his death in 1592. This work has the same drawbacks and strengths as Motley's other volumes.

Parker, Geoffrey. *The Dutch Revolt.* Ithaca, N.Y.: Cornell University Press, 1977. A good summary of Farnese's successes and failures in the Netherlands campaigns, based heavily on archival sources. Parker admires Farnese and ascribes much of the blame for his failures to lack of consistent financial support and leadership from Philip.

Schepper, Hugo de. "The Burgundian-Habsburg Netherlands." In *Handbook of European History, 1400-1600: Late Middle Ages, Renaissance, and Reformation,* edited by Thomas A. Brady, Jr., Heiko A. Oberman, and James D. Tracy. Vol. 1. Grand Rapids, Mich.: W. B. Eerdmans, 1996. Essay discusses the political control of the Netherlands by the Habsburg Dynasty.

SEE ALSO: Duke of Alva; Charles V; Kenau Hasselaer; Margaret of Austria; Johan van Oldenbarnevelt; Paul III; Philip II; William the Silent.

RELATED ARTICLES in *Great Events from History: The Renaissance & Early Modern Era, 1454-1600:* 1531-1585: Antwerp Becomes the Commercial Capital of Europe; 1568-1648: Dutch Wars of Independence; July 26, 1581: The United Provinces Declare Independence from Spain; April, 1587-c. 1600: Anglo-Spanish War; July 31-August 8, 1588: Defeat of the Spanish Armada.

GUY FAWKES
English conspirator

Guy Fawkes was a key conspirator in the Gunpowder Plot, a secret attempt to destroy the English king and Parliament. Discovery of the plot intensified Protestant suspicions of Catholics and led to a period of reduced tolerance of Catholicism in England.

BORN: April 13, 1570; Stonegate, York, England
DIED: January 31, 1606; Westminster, England
AREAS OF ACHIEVEMENT: Government and politics, church reform

EARLY LIFE

The parents of Guy Fawkes (fawks), Edward Fawkes and the former Edith Jackson, came from different religious backgrounds. The Fawkeses were conventional Protes-

tants, many of whom held public-service positions. The Jacksons, however, were classified as recusants, or Catholics who refused to join the Church of England. During the reign of Elizabeth I, recusancy was a punishable crime. During Guy's early childhood, the Fawkeses were not openly Catholic. After the death of his father, when Guy was eight, his mother married Dennis Bainbridge, who was also a recusant.

Guy was soon sent to St. Peters Catholic School in York, an experience that reinforced the Catholic influence he now received at home. His friends at school included John and Christopher Wright, who were also destined to become involved in the Gunpowder Plot. These friends, other classmates, and teachers undoubtedly influenced the boy throughout his years at school, and he eventually became a devout Catholic and highly critical of the government persecution of Catholics. For a mere youth such as Fawkes to renounce the official Protestantism of England required considerable moral and physical courage, qualities that he displayed throughout his life.

After he left school, Fawkes assisted his stepfather for several years with the management of his estate in the Yorkshire countryside. There, Fawkes probably first met Thomas Percy, the future instigator of the Gunpowder Plot. During the 1590's, Fawkes embarked on a military career. He became a soldier of fortune in the Spanish army of the Netherlands, not an uncommon practice for English Catholics of the period. By all accounts, he was an exemplary soldier, displaying not only courage and loyalty but also great piety. These qualities, in addition to his experience with explosives, led to Fawkes's involvement in the conspiracy. During several military campaigns, Fawkes had become acquainted with the use of gunpowder and its effectiveness for destroying defensive walls and buildings. The leaders of the Gunpowder Plot knew that the participation of someone with this practical knowledge was crucial if the plot was to be successful.

While abroad, Fawkes grew more and more discontented with the English persecution of Catholics, a view that was fostered by many of his military comrades and leaders. By early 1600, Fawkes left his regiment to work as a steward for Sir William Stanley, a former regiment commander who shared Fawkes's hatred of Elizabethan attitudes toward Catholics. Stanley worked hard to improve conditions for the Catholics and sent Fawkes to Spain in 1601 and again in 1603 to seek miliary aid from King Philip II. These missions proved to be unsuccessful, leaving only civil anarchy as a means to redress the grievances of the disheartened English Catholics.

A seventeenth century engraved depiction of Guy Fawkes (center) preventing Sir William Radcliffe from joining the conspiracy. (Library of Congress)

LIFE'S WORK

Fawkes is best remembered for his role in the Gunpowder Plot, a conspiracy by a small group of English Roman Catholics who were discontented with the policies of King James I. Their plan was to blow up the king, his ministers and family, and the entire executive government during the opening of Parliament on November 5, 1605. After the destruction of the monarchy and the government, the conspirators hoped, an uprising by English Catholics would follow and enable them to take over the country.

Under Elizabeth I, persecution of Catholics was widespread. Executions and imprisonments were not uncommon in extreme cases. The introduction of recusancy laws, which fined people for failure to attend Anglican church services, was also extremely unpopular among English Catholics. Some individuals were forced to pay thousands of pounds in recusancy fines over the years.

The accession of James I to the throne in 1603 brought hopes of greater tolerance for Catholics. Two years earlier, Thomas Percy, who was to become one of the plot's leaders, had even persuaded James, then king of Scotland, to put in writing his intentions to relax Elizabeth's persecution of the Catholics. Once seated on the English throne, however, James broke his promise, to the disappointment and anger of most Catholics.

The broken promise and a general dislike of the accession of the Scottish king to the English throne were important reasons that the Gunpowder Plot conspiracy was initiated. The leader of the plot was Robert Catesby, who, having seen his family persecuted under Elizabeth, was quite willing to seek violent revenge on the Protestant government. In March, 1604, Percy and Thomas Winter were told of the plot to blow up Parliament. At first, they were shocked by the plan; eventually, though, they came to the conclusion that violence was the only way to bring about government concessions for Catholics.

Returning to England from the Netherlands in May, Winter brought with him Fawkes, who he believed would be an asset to the plans because of his military experience. Later that month, the conspirators rented rooms near Parliament House. The conspiracy had grown to include John and Christopher Wright, Robert Winter, and John Grant; in the following year, Ambrose Rokewood, Francis Tresham, and Sir Everard Digby were added to help finance the operation.

The conspirators' plan—to dig a tunnel to the House of Lords and place a large quantity of gunpowder near the government's meeting site, where it could be detonated when Parliament was in session—was fraught with problems from the start. With the exception of Fawkes, who had some experience in mining operations, the conspirators were members of the gentry with no experience of digging. Consequently, they found their task to be very physically challenging. Money was also a problem; the addition of Rokewood, Digby, and Tresham improved the conspiracy's finances, but the full details of the plot were not revealed to all of them.

Although the opening of Parliament was delayed many times, the workers began to despair of the tunnel. In February, 1605, however, they learned of a cellar for rent under the House of Lords. They abandoned the tunnel and rented the cellar, supposedly for the storage of coal and wood. By April, they had succeeded in storing some twenty barrels of gunpowder in the cellar. The conspirators disbanded and arranged to meet later in the year to discuss the final steps of the plot.

While the conspirators waited for Parliament to commence, several began to have second thoughts. Catesby, however, managed to convince most of the conspirators to continue with the plot as planned. He also acquired horses and weapons, which he stationed in small groups throughout the West Midlands. These were to be used in the uprising he believed would follow once the plot had been executed.

When Tresham learned the full implications of the plot and discovered that his brother-in-law, Lord Monteagle, would be a victim of the explosion, he was shocked. Unable to convince Catesby to seek a less violent means of achieving their political goals, Tresham decided to reveal the plot by warning his brother-in-law not to attend the opening of Parliament. On October 26, Monteagle held a dinner party at his home. During the evening, a messenger delivered an anonymous letter to him, which he instructed to be read allowed. The letter warned of a plot to blow up Parliament, although no names of conspirators were mentioned.

It has been suggested that both Tresham and Monteagle conceived the idea of the "anonymous" letter and believed that by having it read in public, it would alert the government to the plot without involving Tresham as a conspirator. It was Tresham's hope that once alerted to the plot, the government would intercede and prevent the tragedy from occurring. In addition, Tresham believed, news that the plot had been discovered would reach his fellow conspirators, and they would abandon their plans and have time to flee to safety abroad.

Between October 26 and November 4, little action was taken by the authorities. It was only during the few days prior to November 5 that most of the conspirators decided to abandon the plot and flee. When the authorities eventually searched the cellar containing the concealed gunpowder, they met a man named Johnson, who claimed to be Thomas Percy's servant. According to Johnson, his master was using the area for coal storage. Moments before midnight on November 4, the cellar was visited again by authorities. This time, the concealed gunpowder casks were discovered, and Johnson was arrested. Johnson was interrogated over several days. He was subjected to torture, and he eventually revealed his true name: Guy Fawkes.

Shortly after Fawkes was discovered, the king appointed a commission to investigate the Gunpowder Plot. The commission was composed of the attorney general, Sir Edward Coke, and seven privy councillors. Over a period of about two weeks, Fawkes eventually provided most of the details of the plot, including the names of the conspirators. By this time, many days of torture had reduced the strong and willful Fawkes both physically and emotionally. Even without Fawkes's early cooperation, the identity of many of the conspirators was probably suspected. Many of them, including Catesby, Percy, Grant, Thomas Winter, and Christopher Wright, were well-known as Catholic sympathizers, and warrants were issued for their arrest.

Around the time of Fawkes's arrest, the remaining conspirators had participated in what they hoped would be the outbreak of rebellion in other parts of the country. The fighting was short-lived, however, and many of the conspirators were killed, including Catesby, Percy, and both the Wrights. Thomas Winter was wounded and arrested with the others shortly thereafter. Those who survived, including Fawkes, were tried, convicted, sentenced to death, and executed at the end of January, 1606.

SIGNIFICANCE

Studies of the Gunpowder Plot have been hindered by a 1619 fire that destroyed many of the Privy Council's records. It has been suggested that the plot was instigated by members of the government in an attempt to discredit the Catholics and that Fawkes may have been simply a "fall guy" for the government. While the existence of a real plot is generally not disputed, the extent of government involvement has long been debated.

Doubt has also been cast on the reliability of Fawkes's testimony under torture. Historically, tortured prisoners have often confessed guilt even for crimes of which they have been innocent. Despite such doubts, the Gunpowder Plot's revelation caused English Protestants to become yet more suspicious of Catholics and reinforced resentment toward them. The unpopular recusancy law was also enforced more rigorously. Since 1606, November 5 has been a day of public thanksgiving in Great Britain; commonly known as Guy Fawkes Day, it is celebrated with fireworks and bonfires.

—*Nicholas C. Thomas*

FURTHER READING

Carswell, Donald, ed. *The Trial of Guy Fawkes and Others: The Gunpowder Plot*. Reprint. Holmes Beach, Fla.: Gaunt, 1995. Reproduces the transcript of the trial of Fawkes and other conspirators for treason. Includes illustrations.

Edwards, Frances. *Guy Fawkes: The Real Story of the Gunpowder Plot?* London: Rupert Hart-Davis, 1969. An easy-to-read account of the plot, with emphasis on the role played by Fawkes.

Fraser, Antonia. *Faith and Treason: The Story of the Gunpowder Plot*. New York: Doubleday, 1996. Draws a parallel between the Gunpowder Plot and instances of modern terrorism.

Gardiner, Samuel R. *What Gunpowder Plot Was*. New York: AMS Press, 1969. Examines the historical evidence for the plot and discounts the possibility of high-level government involvement.

Garnett, Henry. *Portrait of Guy Fawkes*. London: Robert Hale, 1962. Deals with Fawkes's life before, during, and after the plot. Contains an interesting collection of reproduced historical documents related to the incident.

Haynes, Alan. *The Gunpowder Plot: Faith in Rebellion*. Stroud, Gloucestershire, England: Sutton, 1997. Portrays Fawkes as more of a fall guy than an equal conspirator. Includes illustrations, maps, bibliographic references, index.

Nicholls, Mark. *Investigating Gunpowder Plot*. New York: St. Martin's Press, 1991. Examines how King James and his Privy Council approached the investigation of the plot. Contains a useful bibliography.

Toyne, S. M. "Guy Fawkes and the Powder Plot." *History Today* 1 (1951): 16-24. A delightful summary of the events leading to the plot and the reasons behind the conspiracy.

Wormald, Jenny. "Gunpowder, Treason, and Scots." *Journal of British Studies* 24 (1985): 141-168. Attempts to explain why the conspirators resorted to violence to address their grievances.

SEE ALSO: Elizabeth I; Philip II.

RELATED ARTICLES in *Great Events from History: The Renaissance & Early Modern Era, 1454-1600:* January 25-February 7, 1554: Wyatt's Rebellion; Nov. 9, 1569: Rebellion of the Northern Earls.

FERDINAND II AND ISABELLA I

King of Sicily (r. 1468-1516), Castile (r. 1474-1504), Aragon (r. 1479-1516), and Naples (r. 1504-1516); and Queen of Spain (r. 1474-1504)

The Catholic monarchs Ferdinand and Isabella directed Spain's transition from medieval diversity to national unity. They achieved governmental and ecclesiastical reform and established a continuing Spanish presence in Italy, the Americas, and northern Africa.

FERDINAND II

BORN: March 10, 1452; Sos, Aragon (now in Spain)
DIED: January 23, 1516; Madrigalejo, Spain
ALSO KNOWN AS: Ferdinand the Catholic; Ferdinand el Catolicó; Ferdinand III; Ferdinand V

ISABELLA I

BORN: April 22, 1451; Madrigal de las Altas Torres, Castile (now in Spain)
DIED: November 26, 1504; Medina del Campo, Spain
ALSO KNOWN AS: Isabella la Católica; Isabella the Catholic
AREAS OF ACHIEVEMENT: Government and politics, military

EARLY LIVES

Ferdinand (FEHRD-ehn-and) and Isabella (ihz-ah-BEHL-ah) were each born to the second, much younger wives of kings. A much older half brother of Isabella, King Henry IV, stood between each of them and the throne, and their siblings both died with considerable suspicion of poisoning. Thus the young prince and princess grew up the focus of intrigue. Their marriage represented an alliance between Ferdinand's father, John II of Navarre (from 1458 of Aragon), and a faction of Castilian nobles, including his mother's kinsmen, the Enríquez family, and Isabella's protector, archbishop of Toledo, Alfonso Carrillo.

John II of Castile, Isabella's father, died when she was three and her brother Alfonso less than a year old. Their mother, Isabella of Portugal, withdrew to her cities of Arevalo and Madrigal to maintain her independence. This dowager queen, a woman of exemplary piety, became increasingly unstable, and Henry IV, young Isabella's half brother, brought the children to his court in 1461. In 1462, young Isabella stood sponsor at the baptism of the king's daughter Joan. Henry had married Joan of Portugal, mother of Princess Joan, within a year after his divorce from his first, childless wife, Blanche of Navarre, on the grounds of his own impotence. Princess Isabella and her younger brother Alfonso, who died in 1465, became involved in several political plots, including plans to challenge the legitimacy of Princess Joan, depose Henry, and find the most advantageous marriage for Isabella. The latter plot ultimately led to Isabella's union with Ferdinand of Aragon in 1469.

Isabella's isolated childhood and her preferred semi-isolation at Henry's court caused her to grow up pious and rather bookish. Gonzalo Chacón, chosen by their mother to supervise Isabella and Alfonso, proved a guiding influence in both her early and adult life. He had been a confidant of Álvaro de Luna, John II's great Constable of Castile. A description of the princess at the time of her marriage tells of golden red hair, gray eyes with long lashes and arched brows, and a red-and-white complexion. A long neck and slim, erect posture set off her face and gave an effect of dignity and majesty.

Ferdinand early became the focus of a quarrel between his father and his own half brother, Prince Charles of Viana, who was supported by the city of Barcelona. Almost from birth, the boy participated in Barcelona's elaborate ceremonies, and at the age of ten, he and his mother, Queen Juana Enríquez, were besieged in Gerona by the Barcelona army and rescued by his father. Though Ferdinand had tutors and attendants to teach him to read and ride, his father was his great teacher. John II of Aragon involved his son in war and government as much as the boy's years allowed. Aragonese politics involved the same kind of intrigue as Castile's but were complicated by the complex nature of the Crown, which included Aragon, Catalonia, Valencia, Mallorca, Sardinia, and Sicily. In 1468, John II entitled Ferdinand king of Sicily, a position that gave him superior rank to his bride and that gave them both status in their struggle against Princess Joan and her uncle-fiancé, King Afonso V of Portugal, to win Castile.

Ferdinand's portraits show a red-and-white complexion with dark eyes and a full mouth. He wore his dark brown hair rather long, in the style of the day; his hairline began early to recede noticeably. In riding, warfare, athletics, and dancing, he performed with perfect skill and ease.

LIVES' WORK

During the first decade of their marriage, Ferdinand and Isabella struggled to establish themselves in Castile, first to gain the good graces of Henry IV and, after his death, to dominate the barons. Men like Carrillo changed sides as it suited their interests: Having supported Isabella, Carrillo turned to Princess Joan when it became clear that the newlyweds would not take direction from him. An incident in the early stages of the war against Portugal shows the characters of the young couple. When cautious, shrewd, self-confident Ferdinand withdrew, avoiding a confrontation at Toro in July, 1475, rather than risk defeat, his insecure, impetuous, chivalric wife gave him a very chilly homecoming. His subsequent victory on March 1, 1476, near Toro (at Peleagonzalo) was more a

victory of maneuver than a battle, and historians dispute the question of who actually won.

In this period, Isabella played a role of great importance. For example, when the master of the Crusading Order of Santiago died in 1475, she pressured its members into accepting her husband as their leader. That same year, the monarchs put under royal control the militia and treasury of the Holy Brotherhood, the medieval alliance of Castilian cities. With these forces and loyal barons, they subdued the others. Nobles who would not accept royal authority had their castles destroyed. By 1481, Ferdinand and Isabella stood masters of Castile. The longevity of Ferdinand's father, who died in 1479, preserved control in Aragon, while Ferdinand and Isabella won Castile.

The next decade brought the glorious conquest of the Kingdom of Granada. In the medieval tradition, King Abū al-Ḥasan ʿAlī had adopted an aggressive attitude during the Castilian disorders; now his son Muḥammad

Ferdinand II and Isabella I (center) welcome home a kneeling Christopher Columbus after his return from the Americas. (Library of Congress)

XI (or Boabdil to the Spanish) faced a united Aragon and Castile. In the period 1482-1492, the Catholic monarchs, as Pope Alexander VI called Ferdinand and Isabella, waged continuing warfare against the Muslims. Ferdinand headed Castilian forces in this great adventure and so consolidated his personal leadership. Isabella's role in providing funds, men, and supplies confirmed the essential importance of their partnership.

Muḥammad's surrender ended the 780-year Christian reconquest of Iberia and brought Spain's Middle Ages to an end. That same year, sponsorship of the first Christopher Columbus voyage and a decree expelling Jews from Castile signaled the beginning of Spain's modern age.

The years from the victory in Granada to Isabella's death brought signal triumph and personal disappointment. In 1495, Ferdinand and Isabella launched a war commanded by a Castilian nobleman, Gonzalo Fernández de Córdoba, against Aragon's traditional enemy, France, for control of the Kingdom of Naples. Continued by their successors, this struggle brought Spain's domination of Italy. A series of marriage alliances further strengthened them against France.

The Portuguese alliance always remained paramount. Their eldest daughter, Isabella, first married Prince John, son of John II of Portugal, and, after his death, King Manuel I. When this Isabella died, Manuel married her sister Maria. Typical of the new era of peaceful relations with Portugal, the 1494 Treaty of Tordesillas amicably adjusted the 1493 papal line of demarcation that, consequent to the Columbus voyage, had divided the non-European world into Spanish and Portuguese hemispheres. Ferdinand and Isabella's only son, John (d. 1497), married a Habsburg, and their second daughter, Joan, married Philip of Burgundy, who was also a Habsburg. Ferdinand and Isabella's daughter Catherine of Aragon embarked on a tragic career in Tudor England as wife of Prince Arthur and later of King Henry VIII.

After Isabella's death, her husband continued their life's work, his course shaped by a series of accidents. Castile passed to the control of Joan and her Habsburg husband, and Ferdinand married a second wife, Germaine de Foix. Ferdinand and Germaine's son died soon after his birth. Joan's mental instability and her husband's death in 1506 restored Ferdinand's position as regent, now for Joan's son Charles (later King Charles I of Spain and Emperor Charles V). Yet only Ferdinand's military defeat of the Andalusian nobles made the regency effective. A series of ventures in North Africa culminated in the 1509 conquest of Oran, financed by archbishop of Toledo Francisco Jiménez de Cisneros. A final

triumph came in the conquest of Spanish Navarre in 1512, realizing the claim of Queen Germaine to that region. This conquest rounded out Spain's national boundaries; for the rest of his life, Ferdinand devoted himself to aligning Spanish policy with that of the Habsburgs.

SIGNIFICANCE

In many ways, Ferdinand II and Isabella I superintended a transition to the national and cultural unity that provided the base for Spain's modern world influence. Though they left local affairs largely in the hands of barons and city oligarchies, the Royal Council provided a protobureaucratic center. This council took charge of the Holy Brotherhood, and one of its members became president of the *Mesta*, Castile's great shepherds' guild. Through meetings of the Cortes and the junta of the Holy Brotherhood, the monarchs maintained contact with representatives of the cities, and *corregidores* acted as their agents in the cities. If Spain's laws remained as diverse as the multiplicity of its political units, Ferdinand and Isabella compiled Castile's medieval laws together with their own proclamations to serve as a guiding framework. They themselves traveled constantly through their kingdoms, providing personal justice.

Their strengthening of the Catholic culture and fostering of a Spanish national type made Spain a leader in the Catholic Reformation in Europe and the world. A papal decree in 1478 established the Spanish Inquisition under royal control to ferret out crypto-Jews. Combined with edicts in 1492 and 1502 obliging Jews and Muslims respectively either to convert or to leave Castile, the Inquisition largely established a Christian norm in place of medieval cultural diversity. Later it repressed Protestantism in Spain.

In Aragon, Ferdinand reactivated the older Papal Inquisition, but the appointment of Tomás de Torquemada as grand inquisitor for both kingdoms and the establishment of a Council of the Inquisition made it a national institution. Appointment in 1495 of Isabella's confessor, the ascetic, selfless Jiménez de Cisneros, as archbishop of Toledo, in contrast to the lusty and ambitious Carrillo, acted to reform and control the Church. (Jiménez became grand inquisitor in 1507.) Jiménez de Cisneros's reform of the Spanish Franciscans and his founding of the University of Alcalá de Henares show a more positive dimension. The university adopted the Erasmian approach of using Renaissance scholarship for religious purposes.

Certainly no act of the reign had greater long-range impact than sponsorship of Columbus. Though Castile had engaged in conquest of the Canary Islands since 1479, the American voyages looked beyond Africa to world empire. Hampered by very limited revenues, Ferdinand and Isabella continued their sponsorship of this enterprise when significant monetary returns seemed problematical. The new American empire posed unprecedented problems of distance and dimension involving treatment of the American Indians and control of Columbus's enormous claims as discoverer. Their development of viceregal authority went beyond anything in the tradition of Aragon, the conquest of the Canaries, or the feudalism of the Reconquest.

—*Paul Stewart*

FURTHER READING

Boruchoff, David A., ed. *Isabel la Católica, Queen of Castile: Critical Essays*. New York: Palgrave Macmillan, 2003. Anthology of essays that seek to penetrate the carefully crafted public self-image of Isabella to gain insight into the actual woman. Includes photographic plates, illustrations, maps, bibliographic references, and index.

Hillgarth, J. N. *1410-1516, Castilian Hegemony*. Vol. 2 in *The Spanish Kingdoms, 1250-1516*. Oxford, England: Clarendon Press, 1978. A work of solid scholarship, with special emphasis on the reign of Ferdinand and Isabella. The great advantage of the book lies in its consideration of events in Aragon and the other Spanish kingdoms.

Kamen, Henry. *Empire: How Spain Became a World Power, 1492-1763*. New York: HarperCollins, 2003. Surveys the roles played by Ferdinand and Isabella in the fashioning of Spain's global empire. Includes photographic plates, illustrations, maps, bibliographic references, index.

Lunenfeld, Marvin. *Keepers of the City: The Corregidores of Isabella I of Castile*. Cambridge, England: Cambridge University Press, 1987. Based on archival research, this book is the sort of institutional history that has made possible newer interpretations of the subject. Lunenfeld has also written a similar book on the Council of the Holy Brotherhood.

Merriman, R. B. *The Catholic Kings*. Vol. 2 in *The Rise of the Spanish Empire in the Old World and the New*. New York: Macmillan, 1918. Reprint. New York: Cooper Square, 1962. A monumental work with narrative detail not found elsewhere in English, but for this reign, the book is otherwise superseded by the books of Hillgarth and the others cited earlier. Its interpretations are outmoded, and its facts not always reliable. Its long reign as the standard English work on Ferdinand and Isabella partly explains the even longer reign of William H. Prescott's biography.

Miller, Townsend. *The Castles and the Crown: Spain, 1451-1555*. New York: Coward & McCann, 1963. Although written with a lively style and based on chronicles, this book does not take account of modern scholarship. Its interpretations are of the Prescott school.

Nader, Helen. *The Mendoza Family in the Spanish Renaissance, 1350-1550*. New Brunswick, N.J.: Rutgers University Press, 1979. A work of solid scholarship with a very important focus on a great baronial family. The Mendozas were as important in this reign as the kingdoms of Castile and Aragon.

Prescott, William H. *History of the Reign of Ferdinand and Isabella, the Catholic*. 3d ed. 3 vols. New York: Hooper, Clark, 1841. Reprint. Abridged by C. Harvey Gardiner. Carbondale: Southern Illinois University Press, 1962. The pioneering work in English that is also the longest. Many of Prescott's interpretations and his scholarship are completely outdated. The book, for example, overemphasizes Isabella's importance by denigrating Ferdinand. Like Miller's book, it can still be read for pleasure.

Thomas, Hugh. *Rivers of Gold: The Rise of the Spanish Empire*. London: Weidenfeld & Nicolson, 2003. Decidedly conservative and Eurocentric history of Spanish colonialism during Ferdinand and Isabella's rule. Includes photographic plates, illustrations, maps, bibliographic references, and index.

Walsh, William Thomas. *Isabella of Spain, the Last Crusader*. New York: Robert M. McBride, 1930. Deserves attention as a long, detailed work that is a biography of the queen, not a history of the reign or a study of Spain in her times.

Woodward, Geoffrey. *Spain in the Reigns of Isabella and Ferdinand, 1474-1516*. London: Hodder & Stoughton, 1997. Comprehensive analysis of the social, political, religious, and economic aspects of Ferdinand and Isabella's reign, as well as their foreign policies and relations. Includes illustrations, map, genealogical table, bibliographic references, and index.

SEE ALSO: Alexander VI; Vasco Núñez de Balboa; Boabdil; Catherine of Aragon; Charles V; Charles VIII; Christopher Columbus; Henry IV; Henry VIII; Francisco Jiménez de Cisneros; John II; Manuel I; Juan Ponce de León; Tomás de Torquemada; Tudor Family.

MARSILIO FICINO
Italian philosopher and theologian

The foremost Platonic philosopher of the Renaissance, Ficino translated the writings of Plato and the Neoplatonists, headed the Platonic Academy in Florence, attempted to reconcile Plato's thought with Christianity, and wrote voluminously about a variety of philosophical issues.

BORN: October 19, 1433; Figline, Republic of Florence (now in Italy)
DIED: October 1, 1499; Careggi, near Florence, Republic of Florence
AREAS OF ACHIEVEMENT: Philosophy, scholarship, religion and theology

EARLY LIFE

Marsilio Ficino (mahr-SEEL-yoh fee-CHEE-noh) was the eldest son of Diotifeci Ficino, a respected doctor to the ruler of Florence, Cosimo I de' Medici. Little is known about Ficino's mother, Alessandra, except that she lived to an advanced age and was greatly admired by her son. With his upper-class background, he had the advantage of a good education in religion and philosophy. In Pisa, he studied under an Aristotelian scholar, Niccolo Tignosi, and he also was a student at Florence University. Despite his brilliance, Ficino apparently never completed an advanced degree.

By 1452, Ficino had become fascinated by Plato's writings, which were being avidly discussed by Humanists in Italy. About 1456, before learning to read classical Greek, Ficino wrote a long essay entitled "Platonic Institutions" (now lost). Cosimo, who had long admired Plato, convinced Ficino to perfect his Greek before trying to publish in the field. The archbishop of Florence, Saint Antoninus, concerned about the dangers of heresy, cautioned Ficino that he should study less of Plato and more of Saint Thomas Aquinas—advice that he followed partially.

By 1460, Ficino was widely recognized as an outstanding scholar of classical works. His surviving essays of the period are devoted to a large variety of ancient thinkers, including the materialist Lucretius and the legendary occultist Hermes Trismegistus. Because of Ficino's seriousness as a scholar, Cosimo chose him as tutor to the young Lorenzo de' Medici, who would later rule Florence. In 1462, Cosimo provided Ficino with many Greek texts and a rural home a few miles outside Florence at the Medici's villa in Careggi, thus establishing the Platonic Academy. It was at about this time that Ficino decided also to prepare for the priesthood.

LIFE'S WORK

Ficino was called a "translating machine" because of his many translations of classical Greek writings into Latin. By about 1464, he had completed his first major translation, which attained wide circulation, of *Corpus Hermeticum*, a collection of works attributed to Hermes Trismegistus but most likely a compilation by various Alexandrian scholars from the second and third centuries.

Ficino then began to translate all the known works of Plato. By about 1469, he had finished the first complete translation of Plato's dialogues, which was finally published in 1484. Ficino also published a commentary on Plato's *Symposion* (399-390 B.C.E.; *Symposium*, 1701). His translation and commentary of Neoplatonic philosopher Plotinus (205-270) was begun in 1484 and published in 1492. His translations of Porphyry (c. 234-c. 305), Proclus (c. 410-485), and other classical writers appeared in the late 1490's.

In 1473, Ficino was ordained a Dominican priest, and he later became a canon at the Florence cathedral. He wrote frequently that priests performed God's work among humans. Large numbers of people flocked to hear his sermons at the cathedral. Ficino spent most of his time as the leader and guiding spirit of the Platonic Academy, which developed into one of the intellectual centers of the Italian Renaissance. Rather than being a structured institution with a formal curriculum, the academy was a loosely organized community of friends who held conversations and delivered public lectures about Platonic and Neoplatonic topics. Several distinguished scholars, such as Giovanni Pico della Mirandola, spent considerable time at the academy.

Ficino's most important work, *Theologia platonica* (1482; *Platonic Theology*, 2001-2003), was primarily a series of Platonic arguments in favor of the soul's immortality. His treatise, *De Christiana religione* (1474; the Christian religion), presented a rather abstract interpretation of Christianity. His controversial book about medicine and astrology, *De vita libri tres* (1489; *The Three Books of Life*, 1980), led to many charges of heresy. He also published his personal correspondence, *Epistolae* (1495; *The Letters of Marsilio Ficino*, 1975), which is now recognized as a rich source of Renaissance thought.

One of Ficino's major goals was to reconcile Christianity and Platonic philosophy. As a Catholic priest, he acknowledged the truthfulness of the Christian religion, and he asserted that Christianity and Platonic philosophy believed in the same universal truth. While endeavoring to be orthodox, he expressed a tolerant attitude toward other religions, and his approach to Catholic dogma tended to be metaphorical rather than literal. He considered Plato and Plotinus to have been divinely inspired, usually quoting them in preference to Christian theologians. He simply ignored topics such as the Inquisition, and he implicitly defended a syncretistic concept of natural religion, anticipating the perspective of Edward Herbert of Cherbury (1583-1648) and the eighteenth century deists.

Ficino emphasized the doctrine of the soul's immortality, which he considered a natural desire implanted in all people. Without this hope, in his view, human existence could have no ultimate meaning. He argued that the nonexistence of an afterlife was inconsistent with the perfection of natural order and the goodness of God. Skeptical critics responded that such arguments were circular. Ficino tended to minimize and spiritualize the Church's teachings on future punishment, interpreting hell as an absence of the divine presence rather than a place of physical torment.

Ficino emphasized the concept of love, which he approached from a mystical than an ethical perspective. He believed that love among human beings was preparation for the love of God—the ultimate goal of human existence. True love among persons was a product of love for God more than a practical outgrowth of social conditions. Although coining the term "Platonic love" to describe to Plato's teachings about the topic, he preferred to speak of "divine love," which he described as the force holding the universe together.

With his Neoplatonic way of looking at the universe, Ficino declared that the source of all existence was God, from which all things originate and to which all things aspire to return. The elements of nature, including the human soul and physical matter, were part of a chain of being that proceeded, by emanation, from the divine mind. The idea that the human soul was midway between the divine and the carnal provided Ficino with a metaphysical foundation for an optimistic view of human dignity. He therefore downplayed the Christian doctrines of human sinfulness and Christ's atonement. Based on a Neoplatonic idea of a world soul, he emphasized the value of spiritual meditation as a means for attaining a direct understanding and enjoyment of divine love. Perceiving the stars and planets to be a part of this unified cosmos, moreover, he often applied principles of astrology to predict future events.

The personal life of Ficino was relatively uneventful. He devoted most of his energy to studying, discussing, and writing about philosophical matters. Following the expulsion of the Medici regime from Florence in 1494, he retired to his villa in Careggi. Although initially admiring some of Girolamo Savonarola's reforms, he was soon shocked by their fanatical excesses. He was bitter and depressed about political conditions at the time of his death in 1499.

Significance

Ficino's writings, translations, and correspondence had tremendous influence during his own lifetime and in subsequent centuries. Because of the particular time that the printing press was brought to Italy, he became the first important philosopher to have his writings published for widespread circulation. Ficino did more than any other person to expand knowledge about Platonic and Neoplatonic philosophy.

Several of his associates and pupils, such as Pico della Mirandola and John Colet, became outstanding Humanist writers of the period. Ficino's doctrine of Platonic love inspired poets, while his philosophical speculations about immortality and other issues elicited debate among philosophers. Even Aristotelians such as Pietro Pomponazzi were indirectly influenced by some of his ideas.

During the sixteenth century, Ficino's writings were reprinted, discussed, and quoted throughout Europe. His influence was especially strong on Giordano Bruno and other speculative thinkers. During the seventeenth and eighteenth centuries, philosophers tended to neglect Ficino's original writings, even though his translations of Plato and Plotinus continued to exercise a powerful influence. In the nineteenth century, historians of the Renaissance became fascinated by Ficino, and they recognized the critical distinction between his own ideas and those of Plato. As Ficino's work is increasingly translated into English and other languages, many find Ficino's ideas relevant to their own concerns today.

—Thomas Tandy Lewis

FURTHER READING

Allen, Michael J. B., and Valery Rees, eds. *Marsilio Ficino: His Theology, His Philosophy, His Legacy.* Boston: Brill, 2001. Essays about various aspects of Ficino's thought and influence. Allen is recognized as the greatest Ficino scholar of his generation.

Collins, Ardis. *The Secular Is Sacred: Platonism and Thomism in Marsilio Ficino's Platonic Theology.* The Hague, The Netherlands: Martinus Nijhof, 1974. Arguing that Ficino relied on Thomas Aquinas, Collins unfortunately does not address adequately the differences between Ficino's tolerance and Saint Thomas's condemnation of unorthodox doctrines.

Copenhaven, Brian, and Charles Schmitt. *Renaissance Philosophy.* New York: Oxford University Press, 1992. Chapter 3 of this useful synthesis has an excellent and readable summary of Ficino's ideas.

Kristeller, Paul Oscar. *The Philosophy of Marsilio Ficino.* 1943. Reprint. Gloucester, England: Peter Smith, 1987. A classic work, often reprinted, written by an outstanding specialist on the intellectual history of the Italian Renaissance. During more than half a century, Kristeller published many valuable books and specialized articles devoted to Ficino.

Raffini, Christine. *Marsilio Ficino, Pietro Bembo, and Baldassare Castiglione.* New York: Peter Lang, 1998. A good summary of the life and thought of three major Platonists of the Renaissance.

School of Economic Science, London, trans. *The Letters of Marsilio Ficino.* 7 vols. London: Shepheard-Walwyn, 1975. A translation of *Epistolae.* The first volume contains an excellent introduction to Ficino's life and ideas. Many of Ficino's letters summarize his large books.

Shepherd, Michael, ed. *Friend to Mankind: Marsilio Ficino, 1433-1499.* London: Shepheard-Walwyn, 2000. A sympathetic analysis of Ficino's vision of creation as a loving unity, with interesting selections from his writings.

SEE ALSO: Giordano Bruno; Baldassare Castiglione; John Colet; Desiderius Erasmus; Francesco Guicciardini; Leo X; Lorenzo de' Medici; Nicholas of Cusa; Giovanni Pico della Mirandola; Girolamo Savonarola; Edmund Spenser.

RELATED ARTICLES in *Great Events from History: The Renaissance & Early Modern Era, 1454-1600:* 1462: Founding of the Platonic Academy; 1486-1487: Pico della Mirandola Writes *Oration on the Dignity of Man*; c. 1500: Revival of Classical Themes in Art.

Saint John Fisher
English church reformer

Fisher strongly contested the views of Martin Luther through his writings, supporting the Catholic faith, the Catholic Church, and the idea of the real presence in the Eucharist. He was canonized as a saint by the Roman Catholic Church in 1935.

Born: 1469; Beverley, Yorkshire, England
Died: June 22, 1535; London, England
Also known as: John of Rochester
Areas of achievement: Education, religion and theology

Early Life

John Fisher, the eldest son of Robert and Agnes Fisher, was born at Beverley, Yorkshire. His father was a well-to-do mercer who died when Fisher was seven or eight. Fisher was educated at the cathedral school attached to Rochester Cathedral, then went to Michaelhouse, Cambridge. He took his bachelor of arts in 1487 and his master of arts in 1491. He became fellow, then proctor, and finally master of the college in 1497. As a proctor, he went to the royal court on college business and met Lady Margaret Beaufort, Henry VII's mother. In 1497, she made him her confessor. Later, she founded a chair of divinity at Cambridge and appointed him its first incumbent in 1503. Fisher also helped her found Christ's College there in 1505.

In 1504, he had been elected chancellor of all Cambridge University, a post to which he was reelected at ten-year intervals and then for life. In the same year, he became bishop of Rochester, a post that he held until deprived shortly before death, declining to accept other, richer bishoprics. He preached the funeral sermons of both Henry VII, who died on April 21, 1509, and of Margaret Beaufort, who died three months later, and he brought Lady Margaret's works of charity and ascetic practices to the attention of the world.

Fisher was six feet tall, unusually tall for the times, and only two or three inches shorter than his sovereign, Henry VIII. Hans Holbein, the Younger, Henry's court painter, painted Fisher, probably in 1527; the portrait depicts an ascetic face, high cheekbones, and sharp eyes. He was fifty-eight at the time and was plagued by ill health in the last years of his life.

Life's Work

With the death of his patron, Lady Margaret, Fisher was comfortably ensconced in his posts as chancellor of Cambridge University and bishop of Rochester. Like his contemporaries Thomas More, John Colet, and Desiderius Erasmus, he favored the new learning and also a reforming within the Church of lax Christian practice. He demonstrated his commitment to the new education by carrying out Lady Margaret's bequest to found St. John's College at Cambridge (1511). He also facilitated Erasmus's teaching Greek at Cambridge (1511) and set up lectureships at St. John's in Greek and Hebrew. He started learning Greek in his forties. He came afoul of Cardinal Thomas Wolsey, Henry's chancellor, in 1517, when he preached at Westminster against clerical high living and greed. Moreover, in 1523 in the religious convocation, he resisted Wolsey's demand for money to wage a war with Flanders.

Fisher hated Martin Luther and his doctrine. On May 12, 1521, at Paul's Cross, London, he preached against Luther's writings. After the sermon, Luther's books were burned. Fisher wrote several tracts against Luther: *Assertionis Lutheranae confutatio* (1523), *Sacri sacerdotii defensio* (1525), and *Defensio Regie assertionis contra Babylonicam captiuitatem* (1525), a defense of the work that had earned for Henry the papal title defender of the faith. Fisher became more conservative as he aged. At the opening of the Reformation Parliament in the fall of 1529, he spoke out against Henry's plan of church reform. To Henry's demand in the same parliament in 1531 for a submission of the clergy, Fisher convinced the assembly to add the clause "as far as the law of God allows" to give the clergy room to save their individual consciences and to attest their primary allegiance to God.

The Reformation Parliament had been called as a consequence of the king's "Great Matter," Henry's desire to nullify his marriage to Catherine of Aragon in order to marry Anne Boleyn. Before Parliament had been called, a special legatine court had been convened in May, 1529, under the direction of Cardinals Wolsey and Campeggio, specially sent from Rome to hear the case. In June, Fisher stoutly defended the legality of Henry's marriage to Catherine, thus incurring Henry's deep hatred. The marriage case was revoked to Rome in July, 1529, and it was not until May, 1533, that a court convened by the new archbishop of Canterbury, Thomas Cranmer, found for Henry, formally declaring null his first marriage and attesting the legality of his second secret marriage of January, 1533, to Anne Boleyn.

Saint John Fisher. (Library of Congress)

Events then moved quickly as Henry pushed Parliament to legalize his heirs by Anne and disinherit his daughter Mary by Catherine via the Act of Succession of March, 1534. Henry continued his attack on the Church by the Act of Supremacy of November, 1534, by which he became Supreme Head of the Church, denying papal power over the English church. Fisher had been in trouble before the passage of these acts as a consequence of his defiance of Wolsey and Henry and also for his support of Elizabeth Barton, the nun of Kent, who prophesied against Henry's marriage to Anne. Barton was executed. Fisher was implicated in the proceedings against her, but eventually was let off with a fine of three hundred pounds.

After refusing to take the oath required by the Act of Succession, Fisher was sent to the Tower of London on April 16, 1534. On the passage of the Act of Supremacy, he was deprived of his bishopric. His refusal in May, 1535, to swear to Henry being Supreme Head of the Church and Pope Paul III's decision to make Fisher a cardinal sealed his fate. He was tried on June 17, found guilty, and sentenced to death by hanging, drawing, and quartering, which later was commuted to beheading on

Tower Green. Fisher was executed on June 22, 1535; he met his death with calmness and dignity. His head was impaled on a pike on London Bridge and reputedly did not decay, demonstrating to the superstitious Fisher's sanctity. His body, at first sent to the Church of Allhallows Barking, was later taken to the Church of St. Peter ad Vincula in the Tower, where it lies near that of More, who had been executed two weeks after Fisher.

SIGNIFICANCE

Saint John Fisher was both of his age and in some ways for all ages. While he looked forward to the new Humanistic biblical scholarship and fostered the study of Greek and Hebrew, even learning Greek in his forties, he looked backward to the glories of the Roman Catholic Church and defended them with his life. As a scholar and university statesman, Fisher helped Lady Margaret found Christ's and St. John's colleges at Cambridge. At St. John's, he founded lectureships in Greek and Hebrew. He also sponsored the celebrated Humanist scholar Erasmus and his teaching at Cambridge. Moreover, Fisher held the office of chancellor of Cambridge University for life.

In his writings, Fisher defended church doctrine and tradition against Luther and other reformers. When the time came to defend the sanctity of Catherine's marriage to Henry, he alone of the bishops spoke for her with vigor and conviction. He wrote books as well defending her right, nor did he ever desert the woman for whom he served as confessor. Fisher also showed courage in suggesting the saving clause to the clergy's submission in 1531, when he suggested that they protect their consciences by swearing "as far as the law of God allows."

When he could not accept the Act of Succession, which denied Catherine's marital right and her daughter Mary's right to inherit, Fisher was sent to the Tower. He could neither swear to the oath required by the Act of Succession nor the oath required by the Act of Supremacy saying that Henry was Supreme Head of the Church. By supporting Catherine even to the point of writing to Emperor Charles V asking him to invade England and save English Catholicism, Fisher was unquestionably guilty of treason. The evidence that convicted him was his confidential conversation with Richard Rich, solicitor general, when Fisher had denied Henry's supremacy. As Fisher faced the crowd that had come to see him die, he proclaimed to them, "Christian people, I come hither to die for the faith of Christ's holy Catholic Church."

Fisher's death shocked Europe; Henry's decision to have his way with the Church had become clear to all.

Soon, More joined Fisher, being executed July 6, 1535. Both men were canonized as saints by the Roman Catholic Church in May, 1935. In a way, both men, Fisher and More, demonstrated a belief in a higher law, an authority superior to that of the prince and the state. They died for that principle and became examples to others.

—*M. J. Tucker*

FURTHER READING

Dickens, A. G. *The English Reformation.* 2d ed. University Park: Pennsylvania State University Press, 1991. A bit of an intellectual challenge, but still the best one-volume survey of the English Reformation. Puts Fisher in his context.

Dowling, Maria. *Fisher of Men: A Life of John Fisher, 1469-1535.* New York: St. Martin's Press, 1999. Biography focusing on Fisher's scholarly endeavors, his literary and pastoral work, and his political activities. Includes bibliographic references and index.

Elton, G. R. *Reform and Reformation: England, 1509-1558.* Cambridge, Mass.: Harvard University Press, 1977. Massively detailed account of the coming of the Reformation to England, stressing its constitutional and legal ramifications. Utilizes much unpublished doctoral work. Good explanation of the process of oath taking that put Fisher on the spot.

Erickson, Carolly. *Great Harry: The Extravagant Life of Henry VIII.* New York: Summit Books, 1980. Interesting insights into Fisher, especially at death, and a wonderful reading experience. Erickson has the knack of re-creating people from the past by making one see life through their eyes.

Fisher, John. *English Works of John Fisher, Bishop of Rochester (1469-1535): Sermons and Other Writings, 1520 to 1535.* Edited by Cecilia A. Hatt. New York: Oxford University Press, 2002. Anthology of Fisher's writings, including those composed during his imprisonment in the Tower of London and some previously unpublished material. Includes illustrations, bibliographic references, and index.

Macklem, Michael. *God Have Mercy: The Life of John Fisher of Rochester.* Ottawa, Canada: Oberon Press, 1967. A good place to start reading about Fisher. Readable, sympathetic. Based on the sources.

Mueller, Janel. "Complications of Intertextuality: John Fisher, Katherine Parr, and 'the Book of the Crucifix.'" In *Texts and Cultural Change in Early Modern England,* edited by Cedric C. Brown and Arthur F. Marotti. New York: St. Martin's Press, 1997. Reading of a passage in Parr's *Lamentation* describing her attendance of one of Fisher's sermons. Argues that religion and religious identity are as important as gender to understanding the nature of identity in the Renaissance. Includes illustrations, bibliographic references, and index.

Parker, T. M. *The English Reformation to 1558.* New York: Oxford University Press, 1960. Short, crisp account of the Henrician religious reformation that carries it through changes under his son Edward and reaction under his daughter Mary. Easy reading.

Reynolds, E. E. *Saint John Fisher.* Rev. ed. Wheathampstead: Anthony Clarke Books, 1972. Detailed, absorbing, reverent treatment of Fisher's life.

Smith, Lacey Baldwin. *Henry VIII: The Mask of Royalty.* London: Jonathan Cape, 1971. Wonderful insights into the aging Henry as he pushed through his second marriage at the cost of Fisher's and More's lives.

Surtz, Edward. *The Works and Days of John Fisher: An Introduction to the Position of Saint John Fisher, 1469-1535, Bishop of Rochester, in the English Renaissance and Reformation.* Cambridge, Mass.: Harvard University Press, 1967. For the more ambitious student. Defines Fisher's intellectual and theological positions on sixteenth century issues of education, faith, and politics.

SEE ALSO: Lady Margaret Beaufort; Anne Boleyn; Catherine of Aragon; Charles V; John Colet; Thomas Cranmer; Desiderius Erasmus; Henry VII; Henry VIII; Hans Holbein, the Younger; Saint Ignatius of Loyola; Saint John of the Cross; Martin Luther; Sir Thomas More; Saint Philip Neri; Paul III; Saint Teresa of Ávila; William Tyndale; Cardinal Thomas Wolsey.

RELATED ARTICLES in *Great Events from History: The Renaissance & Early Modern Era, 1454-1600:* June 5-24, 1520: Field of Cloth of Gold; December 18, 1534: Act of Supremacy.

LAVINIA FONTANA
Italian painter

Lavinia Fontana was the first professional female artist to have a career outside the realm of the court and the convent. Lavinia is best known for her portraiture, which skillfully depicts the personalities of the sitters and the details and textures of clothing, jewelry, and other objects.

BORN: 1552; Bologna, Papal States (now in Italy)
DIED: August 11, 1614; Rome, Papal States (now in Italy)
AREA OF ACHIEVEMENT: Art

EARLY LIFE

Lavinia Fontana was born in Bologna, a major artistic center at the time. She was trained by her father, Prospero Fontana, one of the leading mannerist painters in Bologna, and teacher to the famed Ludovico Carracci.

In her formative years, Lavinia was able to study the earlier masters, whose works hung in Bologna's private and public spaces. Her godfather owned Raphael's *Vision of Ezekiel* (1514-1518) and Correggio's *Noli me tangere* (c. 1525). In the nearby convent church of Santa Margherita, Parmigianino's *Holy Family with Saints Jerome, Augustine, and Margaret* (c. 1529) was also available for viewing, as was Raphael's *Ecstasy of St. Cecilia* (c. 1513), in the church of San Giovanni in Monti.

Lavinia's paintings show clearly how she was influenced by the works of the masters. Her rich colorism and brushwork evoke Correggio, the elegance of her figures and their costumes comes from Parmigianino, and the delicacy of gestures and facial expressions are from Raphael. Lavinia's *Noli me tangere* (1581) shows the influence of Correggio and his painting of the same subject, except that her Christ is dressed while Correggio's work features a nude torso. For reasons of modesty, women artists of the era were not allowed to draw forms from the nude. The lack of anatomical training because of this restriction shows in some of Lavinia's works, where proportions are sometimes skewed.

LIFE'S WORK

In 1577, Lavinia married Gian Paolo Zappi, a student of Prospero Fontana and a member of a family that held senatorial and judicial posts in Imola since the thirteenth century. The marriage contract specified that Zappi, like Lavinia, was a painter. Carlo Cesare Malvasia, in the *Felsina pittrice* (1678), a biography of Bolognese artists, wrote that Zappi painted the draperies in Lavinia's works.

Lavinia's father-in-law, Severo Zappi, helped her obtain her first documented commission, *Assumption of the Virgin* (1584), an altarpiece for the chapel in the palace of the consiglio communale, Imola's governing body, where Severo held a seat. This painting follows the prescriptions of Cardinal Gabriele Paleotti, archbishop of Bologna, on the appropriate depiction of religious subjects outlined in his *Discorso intorno alle imagini sacre et profane* (1582). Paleotti, who was following Counter-Reformation demands, called for images that related Catholic doctrine unambiguously and inspired piety and devotion in viewers. The kneeling saints in gestures of prayer in Lavinia's painting invite the viewer to assume the same posture and emotional state. This work won Lavinia Paleotti's endorsement and established her reputation as an artist worthy of note. Soon commissions began to flow.

In 1580, Lavinia received a doctorate from the University of Bologna. Her circle of friends included some well-known figures, such as the naturalist and physician Ulisse Aldrovandi. Her *Stigmatization of St. Francis* (1579) shows an accurate rendition of ferns based on Aldrovandi's exotic plant collection. Some of Lavinia's scholar friends were among her clients and sitters. In the 1570's, the philosopher Alessandro Aquilino and the historian Carlo Sigonio had their portraits painted by Lavinia, and in the late 1580's, the scientist Girolamo Mercuriale also sat for her. In 1579, Lavinia painted herself in the same light as these men. Her *Self-Portrait in the Studiolo* (1579) shows the artist as her subjects' equal. She sits at a desk, stylus in hand, preparing to execute a drawing. Ancient statuettes and fragments surround her, presumably to provide intellectual and artistic inspiration.

Among Lavinia's many sitters included prominent women from the Bolognese nobility. Laudomia Gozzadini, daughter of Senator Ulisse Gozzadini, commissioned a family portrait. Lavinia developed a close relationship with her client, naming one of her daughters Laudomia. The portrait of Ginevra Aldrovandi Hercolani, daughter of Senator Ercole Aldrovandi, with a lap dog (1590's) is one of Lavinia's most admired works. Noble children were also part of her repertoire, which included *Ippolita Savignani at Twelve Months* (1583) and *Antonia Ghini* (1583).

Lavinia's output was not limited to portraiture. She also painted several mythologies and a large number of religious works. Among her mythologies is *Venus and Cupid* (1585), which shows figures set against a twilight sky, a light treatment she borrowed from Correggio. Of her religious paintings, many were meant for public spaces, and one commission in particular enhanced her reputation—an altarpiece for the Bernerio chapel in the church of San Sabina in Rome, the *Vision of St. Hyacinth* (1599). She received this commission from Girolamo Bernerio. The work was a great success, and it encouraged Lavinia and her husband to move to Rome. They arrived in 1604, and Bernerio arranged for their accommodations at the Palazzo Monte Giordano.

Bernerio also arranged for Lavinia's next commission, the *Martyrdom of St. Stephen* for the church of San Paolo Fuori le Mura, one of the principal pilgrimage churches of Rome. This work was destroyed by fire in 1823 and is known only through a 1611 engraving. Biographer Giovanni Baglione reported in his *Le vite de' pittori, scultori et architetti dal pontificato di Gregorio XIII* (1642) that this painting was not as well received as the *Vision of St. Hyacinth*, so Lavinia returned to portraiture.

Lavinia's reputation grew in Rome. Camillo Borghese, former papal legate in Bologna and godfather to her son Severo, was elected Pope Paul V. Paul appointed Lavinia official portraitist at the Vatican Palace. In 1609, the rules of the Academy of St. Luke were amended to admit female artists, and Lavinia was allowed to become a member. This meant that she was now free to take on pupils. As a result, prices for her works soared.

In 1611, Lavinia was honored with a bronze portrait medallion cast by the Bolognese sculptor and architect Felice Antonio Casoni. On its face, the medallion shows a portrait of Lavinia, and its inscription identifies her as an artist. The medallion's reverse shows her at her easel, surrounded by compasses and a square, the instruments of her profession. Her hair is disheveled to indicate that she is caught in the frenzy of creation.

Lavinia died in Rome in 1614, leaving the largest body of extant works by any woman artist active before the eighteenth century. Approximately 150 paintings by her are known and many others are recorded but lost.

SIGNIFICANCE

Lavinia Fontana lived in an era when female artists were limited to painting only portraits and still lifes, categories ranked low on the academic scale. Women had no access to membership in academies nor to instruction in anatomy.

Lavinia broke all the rules: Though portraiture was her main subject, she still executed a number of mythological and biblical scenes in both small and large scale. While women rarely received commissions to paint altarpieces, Lavinia did obtain a number of these types of commissions.

By becoming the first female member of the Academy of St. Luke in Rome, she widened the range of possibilities for future women artists, like Artemisia Gentileschi, who, rather than settling for lesser-valued subjects, painted biblical and mythic stories showcasing female heroes.

—*Lilian H. Zirpolo*

FURTHER READING

Chadwick, Whitney. *Women, Art, and Society.* New York: Thames and Hudson, 1994. Places the life and career of Lavinia Fontana within the context of the artistic patronage of female artists in Bologna and the civic and ecclesiastic support they received.

Cheney, Liana de Girolami. "Lavinia Fontana: A Woman Collector of Antiquity." *Aurora: The Journal of the History of Art* 2 (2001): 22-42. Focuses on Lavinia's "Self-Portrait in Her Studiolo," providing an iconographic interpretation of the work. Also presents useful biographical information on the artist.

Fortunati, Vera, ed. *Lavinia Fontana of Bologna, 1552-1614.* Milan, Italy: Electa, 1998. An abridged version of Fortunati's 1994 exhibition catalog published in Italian. The present publication was produced to accompany an exhibition of Fontana's works at the National Museum of Women in the Arts in Washington, D.C.

Murphy, Caroline P. *Lavinia Fontana: A Painter and Her Patrons in Sixteenth-Century Bologna.* New Haven, Conn.: Yale University Press, 2003. The most comprehensive text on Fontana's life and career in Bologna. Includes discussion on the milieu in which Fontana developed her artistic career.

SEE ALSO: Sofonisba Anguissola; The Carracci Family; Correggio; Catharina van Hemessen; Raphael; Giorgio Vasari.

RELATED ARTICLES in *Great Events from History: The Renaissance & Early Modern Era, 1454-1600:* November 3, 1522-November 17, 1530: Correggio Paints the *Assumption of the Virgin*; December 23, 1534-1540: Parmigianino Paints *Madonna with the Long Neck*.

Sir John Fortescue
English politician and author

The first English thinker to recognize that Parliament's power over legislation and taxation had made England a limited rather than an absolute monarchy, Fortescue played a major role in shaping English constitutional concepts. He also is the author of the first substantial discussion of the English government and its legal foundations to be written in the English language.

Born: c. 1385; Norris, Somerset, England
Died: c. 1479; Ebrington, Gloucestershire, England
Areas of achievement: Government and politics, law

Early Life

Lamentably little is known of the early life of Sir John Fortescue (FOHRT-eh-skew). His father, a knight, had much land in Devon, providing for his son's lengthy legal education at the Inns of Court. No man, John Fortescue later asserted, could become a sergeant-at-law—as he did in 1430—without having studied the law for sixteen years. Becoming a sergeant not only marked the culmination of Fortescue's study of and apprenticeship in England's common law but also admitted him to the lucrative practice of law before the Court of Common Pleas. After this, the records indicate, he began to acquire wealth and responsibilities, both from the flourishing of his legal career and from his marriage to an heiress in 1435 or 1436. In 1442, he was appointed chief justice of the Court of King's Bench and was made a knight a few months later.

Fortescue left no private letters or memoirs, and no contemporary penned a description that would permit one to gain personal knowledge of him. Virtually all that can be grasped of his character and personality must be deduced from his books and from the scant facts about his life that have survived. Even a glance at his writings, though, shows us an agile and energetic mind. While other thinkers of his time based their conclusions on the ideal of what should be or on the received wisdom of the past, Fortescue had the strikingly modern habit of observing and analyzing the way things really worked. He would then take this knowledge, gained from long experience in wrestling with problems of law and politics, and use it to suggest changes that could make institutions work better. He had a buoyant, optimistic faith that truth and justice would ultimately prevail, which stands out vividly against the grim fabric of his age. An underlying human decency is also revealed in the abhorrence with which he regarded torture and in the satisfaction he de-

rived from the fact that in England even the peasants lived reasonably well, not crushed by taxes and the exactions of the nobles, as in France.

Life's Work

Fortescue served as chief justice of the Court of King's Bench for nearly two decades, absorbed in his judicial duties and his growing political role as a firm supporter of the ruling Lancastrian dynasty. Meanwhile, the restlessness of a number of powerful barons, led by the duke of York, was creating an increasingly turbulent political situation in England. In 1455, the Wars of the Roses began as these aristocratic opponents of Henry VI, the feckless Lancastrian monarch, turned to violence. By 1461, the Yorkists had triumphed; their leader sat on the throne of England as King Edward IV. Fortescue fled into exile with Henry VI and his family. For the next decade, he would share their troubles; his intelligence, experience, and energy made him one of the most prominent figures in their train. Year after weary year, in Scotland, Burgundy, and France, he participated in an endless round of negotiations and intrigues designed to restore Henry VI to the throne. In 1470, he helped secure French help and an alliance with England's powerful earl of Warwick. This shaky combination was able to force the Yorkists to flee, and for a few heady months, Henry VI was once again England's king. Edward IV quickly rallied his supporters, though, and on April 14, 1471, he again overthrew Henry.

Fortescue had landed in England full of hope that very day, ending his long exile. The bitter news of Henry's defeat was followed a few weeks later by the final crushing of the Lancastrian forces at the Battle of Tewkesbury. The Yorkists permitted neither Henry VI nor his son to live to threaten their power again. With the Lancastrian cause thus irretrievably shattered by their deaths, Fortescue, who had been captured at Tewkesbury, soon made his peace with the triumphant Yorkists. His reputation for wisdom and honor made his support valuable to them. He recognized reality and let himself be persuaded to write a defense of the legitimacy of Edward IV's title to the throne, disavowing his earlier works to the contrary. In return, he was pardoned and his estates were restored to him. He retired to private life and to a death, in Ebrington, Gloucestershire, as obscure as his birth. The last documentary evidence of Fortescue being alive dates from May, 1479.

Fortescue's life spanned some of the most violent decades in English history. He saw ruthless and powerful men subvert the laws, intimidate and corrupt officials, and reduce the royal government to impotence. The bloodshed and disorder of his age had a powerful effect on him, shaping the ideas about royal government that he put into his last important book, apparently written in the years just before his death, *The Governance of England* (1885).

With a keen awareness of the close relationship between wealth and political power, he strongly recommends in *The Governance of England* that the Crown recover its lost riches and keep this wealth under its own control. The king, he argues, should have at least double the disposable income of any of his people, lest an overmighty subject become strong enough to challenge him. Fortescue also advises that a wise king will lessen the power of the nobles and decrease his own dependence on them by choosing men of proven integrity and talent to advise him, rather than let the great barons dominate his council. The king should also regain control of patronage, directly giving offices and commissions to men chosen by and loyal to himself, instead of allowing the barons to distribute these plums. Many of the policies followed by Edward IV and Henry VII, as they rebuilt the crumbling edifice of English monarchy at the end of the fifteenth century, are strikingly in tune with Fortescue's advice, though it is doubtful whether they were consciously using his work as a model.

For all his recognition of the need for a strong king to keep order and secure the property and tranquillity of his subjects, Fortescue was far from recommending absolute monarchy. Indeed, his chief importance in the history of English political thought comes from his insistence on the limited nature of royal authority. His constitutional ideas were spelled out most completely in two Latin tracts: *De natura legis naturæ* (wr. 1461-1463, pb. 1864; English translation, 1980) and the better-known *De laudibus legum Angliæ* (wr. 1470, pb. 1537; *Learned Commendation of the Politique Lawes of Englande*, 1567).

In these works, Fortescue divides monarchies into two types. One, for which France is his model, is characterized as *dominium regale* (absolute monarchy). Here, what pleases the king has the force of law; the bodies and possessions of his subjects are completely at his disposal. England, he states with pride, is not under the heavy hand of such an unlimited ruler. It is an example of the second type of monarchy: *dominium politicum et regale* (limited monarchy). England's kings, he insists, were bound to observe the laws and customs of their kingdom. Indeed, he points out that English judges had to swear not to give judgments that went against existing laws, even if the king himself commanded them to do so. In addition, English kings could neither make laws nor tax their people on their own authority. The consent of Parliament, Fortescue maintains, was necessary for laws or taxes to have validity.

Significance

Fortescue occupies a significant place in the transition from medieval to Renaissance England. His concern for workable solutions to actual problems and his ability to draw on his own direct experience of the institutions and the practices of his day are modern characteristics not often seen in the minds of fifteenth century thinkers. Most important, his demonstration that the kings of England were limited not only by law but by the decisions of Parliament as well is regarded as a milestone in English constitutional thought. His *De laudibus legum Angliæ* was translated into English and published no fewer than seven times in the sixteenth century, with three more editions appearing in the seventeenth. Particularly during the crucial constitutional struggles of the seventeenth century, the opponents of the Stuart kings frequently referred to Fortescue in developing their arguments in fa-

Sir John Fortescue. (Library of Congress)

vor of the prerogatives of Parliament. He stands as one of the fathers of the English concepts of limited monarchy and parliamentary power.

—Garrett L. McAinsh

FURTHER READING

Burns, J. H. "Fortescue and the Political Theory of Dominium." *Historical Journal* 28 (1985): 777-797. A rather complex discussion of the way in which Fortescue used the Latin term *dominium* and its significance in his thought. Some familiarity with Latin is necessary to understand this article.

Chrimes, S. B. *Lancastrians, Yorkists, and Henry VII.* London: Macmillan, 1964. A good, brief introduction to fifteenth century England by a master scholar, particularly strong on government.

Clark, Linda, ed. *Authority and Subversion.* Woodbridge, Suffolk, England: Boydell Press, 2003. Anthology of essays originally presented at a conference on the struggle between the houses of Lancaster and York in fifteenth century England. Includes illustrations, map, bibliographic references, and index.

Fortescue, John. *De laudibus legum Angliæ.* Edited by S. B. Chrimes. Cambridge, England: Cambridge University Press, 1942. Reprint. New York: Garland, 1979. This modern edition of Fortescue's most important work has both the Latin text and an English translation. Chrimes's lengthy introduction is extremely helpful on Fortescue's life and works, including *De natura legis naturæ*, for which as yet no adequate English translation has been published. This book also contains a splendid preface by Harold D. Hazeltine on Fortescue's place in the history of English jurisprudence.

_____. *The Governance of England: Otherwise Called, The Difference Between an Absolute and a Limited Monarchy.* Edited by Charles Plummer. Oxford, England: Clarendon Press, 1885. Reprint. Union, N.J.: Lawbook Exchange, 1999. This is the only acceptable modern edition of the work by Fortescue. Unfortunately, the text has been kept in Middle English rather than modernized, so most readers will find it slow going. Plummer's introduction, though, contains a very fine biographical sketch of Fortescue and a clear discussion of his ideas.

Gross, Anthony. *The Dissolution of the Lancastrian Kingship: Sir John Fortescue and the Crisis of Monarchy in Fifteenth-Century England.* Stamford, Lincolnshire, England: P. Watkins, 1996. Set of three interrelated essays, together with a substantial introductory essay, on Fortescue's life and career. Attempts to understand the political instability and civil wars of the period as a function of genuine philosophical differences between competing theoretical principles of government, and not merely as the Machiavellian maneuverings of self-interested nobles hungry for power. Includes illustrations, bibliographic references, and index.

Hicks, Michael. *The Wars of the Roses, 1455-1485.* New York: Routledge, 2004. Detailed history of the military campaigns of the Wars of the Roses, and the reasons behind them. Includes nine strategic maps, illustrations, bibliography, and index.

Hinton R. W. K. "English Constitutional Theories from Sir John Fortescue to Sir John Eliot." *English Historical Review* 75 (1960): 410-425. Presents Fortescue's ideas in the context of the development of English constitutional thought.

Lander, J. R. *Government and Community: England, 1450-1509.* Cambridge, Mass.: Harvard University Press, 1980. Excellent background on the England of Fortescue and its problems. More detailed than the work by Chrimes cited earlier, particularly strong on social and cultural history.

Shephard, Max Adams. "The Political and Constitutional Theory of Sir John Fortesque." In *Essays in History and Political Theory in Honor of Charles H. McIlwain*, edited by Carl Wittke. Reprint. New York: Russell and Russell, 1967. Once past the debatable claim about Fortescue having been a representative of the rising middle class and its socioeconomic interests, the reader will find a clear and coherent discussion of Fortescue's basic ideas.

Skeel, Caroline A. J. "The Influence of the Writings of Sir John Fortescue." *Transactions of the Royal Historical Society* 10 (1916): 77-114. Though dated, this article has the most-thorough discussion available of the ways in which Fortescue's successors used his concepts. Particularly good discussion of the seventeenth century.

Wilkinson, Bertie. *Constitutional History of England in the Fifteenth Century (1399-1485).* New York: Barnes and Noble Books, 1964. An extremely detailed discussion of the political institutions of fifteenth century England, how they worked, and the theories behind them.

SEE ALSO: Edward IV; Edward VI; Henry VI; Henry VII; Sir Thomas Littleton.

RELATED ARTICLE in *Great Events from History: The Renaissance & Early Modern Era, 1454-1600:* January 28, 1547-July 6, 1553: Reign of Edward VI.

GIROLAMO FRACASTORO
Italian physician, astronomer, and poet

Fracastoro's prophetic hypotheses on the causes of diseases foreshadowed by centuries the modern understanding of microbial infections. He believed infection could be spread through direct or indirect contact by tiny, even insensible, particles. He also believed that poetry was the ideal means to convey knowledge.

BORN: c. 1478; Verona, Republic of Venice (now in Italy)

DIED: August 6, 1553; Incaffi, Republic of Venice

ALSO KNOWN AS: Hieronymus Fracastorius (Latin name); Gerolamo Fracastoro

AREAS OF ACHIEVEMENT: Medicine, philosophy, astronomy, literature

EARLY LIFE

Girolamo Fracastoro (jeer-oh-LAHM-oh frah-cah-STAW-roh) was born into an old and distinguished Veronese family. His grandfather had been a physician to the reigning Scala family of Verona. After training at home, he was sent to the University of Padua, where he was entrusted to an old family friend, Girolamo della Torre, who taught and practiced medicine there.

Before his medical studies began, Fracastoro, following a well-established practice, pursued the liberal arts, which also included mathematics and astronomy, under Nicolo Leonico Tomeo and philosophy under Pietro Pomponazzi. Among his teachers of medicine was Alessandro Benedetti, through whom he could come in contact with the Ferrarese Humanistic medics, as well as with Girolamo della Torre and his son Marcus Antonio della Torre. Among his fellow students were the future cardinals Ercole Gonzaga, Gasparo Contarini, and Pietro Bembo, through whom he might have met members of the Aldine circle at Venice. He also befriended Giovanni Battista Ramusio, who gained fame in later life as a geographer.

Barely finished with his studies at Padua, Fracastoro was there appointed lecturer in logic in 1501 and the next year became an anatomical councillor, thus starting a traditional academic career in medicine. By 1508, wars interrupted his academic career, and the remainder of his life was spent at Verona, practicing medicine or managing his private landed estate at Incaffi. From 1505, when he had been elected to the College of Physicians at Verona, he remained its faithful member. His hour of glory arrived in 1545, when the pope made him physician of the Council of Trent.

LIFE'S WORK

Venice had always maintained close ties with Constantinople, and when Padua came into its hands in 1404, Greek influence became dominant there as well. While in other parts of Italy, Humanists strove to revive Roman glories, Venice was more interested in resurrecting the achievements of the Greeks. At the University of Padua the prevailing form of Aristotelianism, originally developed by the Parisian Averroists, was one in which Aristotle was not perceived as the ultimate "master of those who know," and his theories and methodologies were constructively criticized. Philosophical considerations were subordinated to his scientific work. Theology and metaphysics in general were gradually replaced by a closer study of nature. It was at the University of Padua that Fracastoro's scientific outlook was formed.

The work that brought most fame to Fracastoro was a lengthy narrative poem *Syphilis sive morbus Gallicus* (1530; *Syphilis: Or, A Poetical History of the French Disease*, 1686), written in verses similar to Vergil's *Georgics* (c. 37-29 B.C.E.). Fracastoro started working on this poem as early as 1510, but it was not until 1525 that it was presented in two books to Pietro Bembo, who at the time was considered to be the premier stylist. When it finally appeared in print in 1530 at Verona, it consisted of three books of some thirteen hundred hexameters.

In the first book, Fracastoro describes the horrors of the disease that had appeared in Europe and in a few years after 1495 spread across the whole continent. The disease was supposedly controlled by the sublime influence of the planets, which could be interpreted as the council of gods. The epidemic of syphilis was reminiscent of previous plagues and gave Fracastoro an opportunity to make allusions to pagan science, where the cosmic change is transmitted by the Lucretian seeds (*semina*) through the air.

The second book is devoted to cures. Fracastoro opens by describing his times, an age when disasters have been compensated for by the voyages of discovery. By judicious selection, he lists various cures and preventives for the disease, setting the whole in a bucolic mood. He concludes the book with the myth of Ilceo, a shepherd in Syria, who, like Adonis, kills a stag sacred to Diana. As a punishment, he is stricken with a dreadful malady of the skin for which there is no remedy. Ilceo, through a dream, is directed to the underworld, where he is met by the nymph Lipare, who instructs him to wash himself in the river of flowing silver (mercury), which allows him to shed his skin like a snake and in this way rid himself of the disease. The whole is permeated with the influence of Vergil.

Book 3 contains another extended myth forming a short epos, on Christopher Columbus's voyage to the West Indies and the discovery of the Holy Tree, the guaiacum, which is a specific remedy against syphilis, which was endemic among the Caribbean Indians. The origin of this disease is explained by two stories. In the first, the indigenous are represented as survivors of Atlantis, which was destroyed by earthquakes and floods for its wickedness and afflicted by this dreaded disease. In the second story, Syphilis, another shepherd, blasphemed against Apollo the sun god and encouraged his king, Alcithous, to assume the prerogatives of a god. As a punishment, he was stricken by Apollo with this pestilence. After proper expiatory sacrifices were performed, Juno and later Apollo relented, the healing tree was provided by the gods, and Syphilis was cured.

It has been suggested that the subjects treated in this poem are but a pretext for positing the much deeper problem of the mutations that take place in nature. Nature constantly creates and destroys, distributing misery and happiness, without being influenced in any way by human prayers and supplications. It is only through science that humans can hope to tame nature and make it work for their benefit.

In 1538, Fracastoro published a work on astronomy, *Homocentricorum sive de stellis* (homocentricity on the stars), which he dedicated to Pope Paul III. He tried to represent the motions of the planets without having recourse to the epicycles or eccentrics and relying solely on circular motions about a single center (homocentric spheres). In this work, he was following the notions of two students of Plato, Eudoxus and Callippus, rather than ideas presented by Aristotle and developed by Ptolemy. Fracastoro's theory represents one of the last attempts to solve the planetary riddle before Nicolaus Copernicus.

This same book also contained his tract, this time of medical interest, *De causis criticorum dierum libellus* (1538), in which Fracastoro rejected the astrological explanation of the critical days as being dependent on the quarters of the moon, a notion that had been accepted by Galen. Fracastoro postulated his theory on two grounds: that ascription of critical days to the virtue of number was false, because neither number nor quantity can be the principle of action, and that the days of a disease seldom coincided with the phases of the moon. Fracastoro did not reject critical days as such, but he believed the causes underlying them have to be sought in the nature of the disease itself, that is, qualitative and quantitative alterations of the humors.

Many scholars have praised Fracastoro as a forerunner of the germ theory of infectious diseases, ascribing to him prophetic intuition. Most of his thinking on this subject is found in his *De contagionibus et contagiosis morbis et eorum curatione libri tres* (1546; *De contagione et contagiosis morbis et eorum curatione*, 1930), but one should remember that this tract is preceded in the same volume by his *De sympathia et antipathia rerum* (1546; on the attraction and repulsion of things), in which he stated that without understanding sympathy and antipathy one cannot deal with contagion. It is based on ancient theories of the continuity of nature and avoidance of a vacuum as well as the tendency of the elements toward their own natural places and the attraction of like for like. It is all expounded in terms of Aristotelian philosophy, without any trace of experimental method.

Regarding contagion, Fracastoro postulated three means by which disease can be spread: by simple contact, as in the case of scabies or leprosy; by *fomites*, such as clothing or bedsheets; or at a distance, through the

Girolamo Fracastoro. (Library of Congress)

FRACASTORO ON A HEALTHY BALANCE OF BODY AND MIND

Fracastoro believed the body and mind are interrelated, so the health of the one affects the health of the other. In a letter that veers from the often dry analytical tone of traditional medical texts, he discusses in a more lively way the importance of considering the "particular" and the "insensible" in understanding and treating the poor mental health of the Italian poet and noblewoman Vittoria Colonna.

The error does not arise in general things, which can be clearly seen and known, but in particular things, and there lies all the difficulty: not in things in which one sees a great departure from the right, but in those where the departure is small and insensible, and, because one does not see it, one does not heed it. . . . [W]e go on little by little to our hurt, so difficult it is to find that just mean and balance. . . . I should wish for a physician of the mind to be found, who should minutely calculate and justly balance all the Marchesa's [Colonna's] actions. . . .

Source: Excerpted in *The Portable Renaissance Reader*, edited by James Bruce Ross and Mary Martin McLaughlin (New York: Viking Press, 1968), p. 573.

---

propagation of *seminaria morbi* (seeds of contagion), which propagate either by joining humors that have the greatest affinity or by attraction, penetrating through vessels. These *seminaria* proliferate rapidly in the human body and cause the humor to which they have closest affinity to putrify. He believed, however, that these seeds of contagion perish in a dead body. As far as his explanations are concerned, Fracastoro remains a product of his time, but, when he concerned himself with observed clinical phenomena, he demonstrated an acute ability in differential diagnosis.

Among his philosophical works, one must count three dialogues dealing with poetics, the intellect, and the soul: *Naugerius sive de poetica dialogus* (1549; English translation, 1924), and "Turrius sive de intellectione dialogus" and "Fracastorius sive de anima dialogus," which were published posthumously. The first of these is a panegyric of poetry as the most complete of the arts and the most useful. The second discusses such psychological problems as cognition, mind-object relationships, and the location of memory. It is interesting to note that Fracastoro believed a person to be a microcosm. The last dialogue was claimed to have been written to denounce the teachings of his professor at Padua, Pomponazzi, who promoted the idea that the human soul is perishable; yet not one harsh word can be found against him in this work. Basically, it is an attempt to reconcile Aristotle with Christianity, relying not on dogmatic assertions but on experimental procedure and critical reasoning, which he was forced to abandon when he realized to which conclusions it was leading. In the end, Fracastoro himself was forced to assume a theological position.

Fracastoro produced various other shorter works of literary as well as scientific interest, some of which were printed centuries after his death, on August 6, 1553. He remains an exemplar of Italian Humanism, who, contrary to accepted wisdom, began to show interest in natural sciences.

SIGNIFICANCE

Fracastoro better than anyone else demonstrated the aspirations as well as the limitations of premodern science. To him poetry was the preferred vehicle to transmit information, and he was more concerned with demonstrating to his readers his classical erudition than his medical acumen. He can easily stand for the typical post-Renaissance man, who is clearly exhibiting his intellectual roots.

He is almost an exact replica of Dante, though more than two centuries separate them and no one reading Andreas Vesalius would realize that he and Fracastoro were contemporaries. Yet most people tend to accept the great anatomist as a typical representative of the medical mentality of his age and try to make Fracastoro fit that mold. The fundamental difference between Fracastoro and Dante was their attitudes toward authority. Dante lived in a world of tamed Aristotelianism, where natural philosophy was still the preserve of the theologians, whereas Fracastoro was educated by physicians who believed in the separation of the two realms of theology and science; it was this new attitude that made the scientific revolution possible.

—*Leonardas V. Gerulaitis*

FURTHER READING

Arrizabalaga, Jon, John Henderson, and Roger French. *The Great Pox: The French Disease in Renaissance Europe*. New Haven, Conn.: Yale University Press, 1997. Examination of the responses of various social institutions—including the church, the medical community, royal courts, and local governments—to the emergence of syphilis in Renaissance Italy, France, and Germany. Includes illustrations, bibliographic references, and index.

Fracastoro, Girolamo. *Fracastoro's "Syphilis."* Translated with introduction, text, and notes by Geoffrey Eatough. Liverpool, England: Francis Cairns, 1984. Written mainly from the point of view of a literary scholar who stresses Fracastoro's poetic achievements. Contains a detailed analysis of the poem *Syphilis.* Includes a computer-generated word index.

Greswell, W. Parr, trans. *Memoirs of Angelus Politianus, Joannes Picus of Mirandula, Actius Sincerus Sannazarius, Petrus Bembus, Hieronymus Fracastorius, Marcus Antonius Flaminius, and the Amalthei.* Manchester, England: Cadell and Davies, 1805. An early biography of Fracastoro, based primarily on an even earlier life by F. O. Mencken. It is concerned primarily with Fracastoro as a literary figure. Especially good on reporting on his contemporaries' opinions about him. Contains notes and observations by Greswell.

Haskell, Yasmin. "Between Fact and Fiction: The Renaissance Didactic Poetry of Fracastoro, Palingenio, and Valvasone." In *Poets and Teachers: Latin Didactic Poetry and the Didactic Authority of the Latin Poet from the Renaissance to the Present,* edited by Yasmin Haskell and Philip Hardie. Bari, Italy: Levante, 1999. Examination of the fictitious science or scientific fictions of Fracastoro. Includes bibliographic references.

Rosebury, Theodor. *Microbes and Morals: The Strange Story of Venereal Disease.* New York: Viking Press, 1971. Two chapters are devoted to Fracastoro, dealing specifically with syphilis as a medical problem. This book presents the best semipopular treatment of the origins of syphilis and whether it was brought from the Americas by the crews of Columbus.

Thorndike, Lynn. "Fracastoro, 1478-1553." In *A History of Magic and Experimental Science.* Vol. 5. New York: Columbia University Press, 1941. A short critical treatment of Fracastoro's scientific contributions. Thorndike was one of the first to argue that the Middle Ages were not quite as dark or the Renaissance quite as brilliant as had been commonly accepted. In making this point, Thorndike uses evidence skillfully.

Truffi, Mario. "Fracastor's Life." In *Syphilis,* by Hieronymus Fracastor. St. Louis: Urologic & Cutaneus Press, 1931. A rather laudatory treatment of Fracastoro, written by a physician and slanted toward medical aspects of his life. A good counterbalance for the previous entry.

SEE ALSO: Georgius Agricola; Christopher Columbus; Nicolaus Copernicus; Conrad Gesner; William Gilbert; Paracelsus; Michael Servetus; Andreas Vesalius.

RELATED ARTICLES in *Great Events from History: The Renaissance & Early Modern Era, 1454-1600:* 1517: Fracastoro Develops His Theory of Fossils; 1546: Fracastoro Discovers That Contagion Spreads Disease.

FRANCIS I
King of France (r. 1515-1547)

Francis I, France's Renaissance monarch, increased the power of the Crown within France, led his country in a series of wars against the Habsburgs, created a glittering court, and helped to introduce the Italian Renaissance into France.

BORN: September 12, 1494; Cognac, France
DIED: March 31, 1547; Rambouillet, France
ALSO KNOWN AS: Francis of Angoulême; Francis d'Angoulême
AREAS OF ACHIEVEMENT: Government and politics, patronage of the arts, military

EARLY LIFE

When Francis was born to Charles d'Angoulême and his young wife, Louise of Savoy, he was not expected to be-

come king of France. Only after Charles VIII died childless three years later, making Francis's cousin King Louis XII, did he become next in line to the throne. Indeed, not until Louis died in 1515 without having fathered a son was it absolutely certain that the twenty-year-old Francis would take the throne.

After the somber last years of his aged, weary predecessor, Francis on his accession represented youth, vigor, and enthusiasm to his subjects. He had developed into someone tall and athletic, with a lively and expressive, rather than handsome, face. His education in academics and statecraft had been haphazard at best, and his great passions were for the chase and for seduction, rather than for the sedentary arts of statesmanship. Throughout his reign, Francis maintained a court notorious for its elegance, gaiety, and erotic exuberance. Notwithstanding his sensual self-indulgence, this cheerful, gracious, and dashing young man would become one of France's most respected sovereigns.

LIFE'S WORK

The land to which Francis fell heir in 1515 was growing steadily in prosperity, population, and power. The ravages of the Hundred Years' War were a rapidly fading memory, and the feudal dynasties that had checked the power of France's kings for so long had mostly disappeared. The nobles were clamoring for the adventure, glory, and profits of conquest, and their young king was eager to oblige them. In July, 1515, Francis led an army into northern Italy, continuing Louis XII's policy of seeking to control the wealthy duchy of Milan. In September, he won the greatest victory of his reign at the Battle of Marignano. Charging joyously at the head of his cavalry, Francis shattered the dreaded Swiss pikemen. This left him the master of Milan and the dominant power in northern Italy, a happy situation that would not last long. The deaths of Ferdinand II of Aragon in 1516 and of Emperor Maximilian I in 1519 made their grandson, Charles I of the house of Habsburg, ruler of Spain and its possessions in the New World, of Austria, of the Burgundian lands, and of much of Italy as well. When Charles was elected Holy Roman Emperor Charles V in 1519, France was virtually encircled by his power.

Francis I. (Library of Congress)

Francis spent much of the rest of his reign fighting with Charles, trying to maintain his own power in Italy and to prevent Charles from dominating all Europe. In 1525, Charles's armies routed the French at the Battle of Pavia, and Francis learned the folly of a king trying to lead his troops in the field: He was captured, and Charles replaced him as the dominant power in Italy. Francis was forced to spend the next year as Charles's prisoner in Spain, gaining his release only by agreeing to a humiliating treaty. Once free, Francis swiftly repudiated the treaty and resumed hostilities. In a series of punishing wars over the following two decades, joined at various times by Venice, England, the Papacy, Protestant German princes, and even—to the horror of all Christendom—the Turks, Francis struggled unsuccessfully to regain Milan and to break the Habsburg hold on Italy. This great contest, the rivalry between the house of Habsburg

and the French crown, would continue to dominate European power politics until the eighteenth century.

Francis was able to mobilize his kingdom's human and material resources in the service of his Italian ambitions to an extent that would have dazzled his predecessors. Many scholars, impressed by the obedience and support he commanded, have regarded him as a key figure in the development of France's absolute monarchy. There are strong arguments in favor of this view. Public opinion and the most important French political theorists of the time, reacting against the civil wars and vulnerability to invasion that had bedeviled France in earlier centuries when the Crown was weak, were inclined to stress the absolute nature of the royal prerogative. Tracts such as Guillaume Budé's *De l'institution du prince* (1547, wr. 1518) argued that the king's power was limitless and that he was not bound to respect any rights of his subjects.

Without question, Francis himself subscribed wholly to Budé's views. Throughout his reign, he showed little inclination to let any considerations of customs or rights, no matter how venerable, interfere with the accomplishment of his desires. As he was energetic, charming, intelligent, and determined enough to win the respect and support of most of the politically active population of his kingdom, Francis was generally successful. He was able to absorb into the royal domain the vast holdings of Charles, duke of Bourbon, after Bourbon betrayed him in 1523. Francis also reformed and centralized the fiscal administration of the Crown, and he significantly increased the control of the central government over its provincial officials. He was able repeatedly to bulldoze his way past objections to his policies and edicts voiced by the Parlement de Paris, ignoring its traditional function as a check on the legal absolutism of French kings.

Francis's most important struggles with the Parlement concerned religion. In 1516, fresh from his great victory at Marignano, he negotiated the Concordat of Bologna with the pope. This agreement restored the Papacy's right to tax the French church, in exchange for confirming and extending Francis's power over appointments to high church offices in France. The Parlement's genuine outrage over this double blow to the independence of the French church was contemptuously rejected by Francis, who forced the body to register the Concordat in 1518. The Parlement was equally distressed by Francis's reluctance to persecute religious dissidents, particularly the adherents of the new Protestant ideas that began seeping into France as early as 1519. Again, however, their remonstrances went unheeded by the king. Not until the mid-1530's, when Francis himself became concerned about the increasing radicalism of the reformers, did he inaugurate systematic persecution. By this time, though, the new ideas had become too strong to be dislodged without a protracted, agonizing struggle.

Francis was obviously a far stronger king, more securely in control of his government and his kingdom, than any of his predecessors. That does not, however, mean that his power was absolute. Francis's subjects, particularly the nobles and the wealthy bourgeoisie, continued to possess independent military and political strength that Francis was forced to respect. That can be seen most clearly in the field of finance. Even though Francis's extravagance and his endless wars left him chronically in need of funds, he did not dare to raise taxes enough to meet his needs. He knew too well that his subjects could still rebel against him if he pushed his prerogative too far, infringing on what they considered to be their own traditional rights. That was shown in 1542, when an attempt to impose new taxes in the southwest of France provoked a serious armed rebellion.

For the most part, therefore, Francis had no choice but to raise the money he needed by a series of expedients that inevitably undermined royal power in the long run. He sold public offices and titles of nobility, he sold royal lands, and he borrowed. Thus, he bequeathed to his son and heir, Henry II, a number of officials who could neither be fired nor relied on, shrunken revenues from the royal domain, and a discouraging mound of debts. Clearly Francis's absolutism did not include unlimited power to tap the wealth of his subjects.

In addition, though the Parlement and other institutions had been cowed into obedience by Francis, once his strong hand was removed from the scene, they lost little time in reasserting themselves under his successors. Francis as an individual was popular and respected enough to get most of what he wanted done, but his reign does not appear to have left the monarchy as an ongoing institution significantly stronger than it had been before.

Francis is more admired today for his role as a generous and discriminating patron of culture than for his political or military policies. Throughout his life, Francis maintained a lively interest in intellectual and artistic pursuits, particularly after his early campaigns in Italy exposed him to the Humanism of the Renaissance there. Back in France, he established lectureships in classical Latin and Greek, in Hebrew, and in mathematics, which would ultimately evolve into the Collège de France. He was an avid amasser of both books and manuscripts, and his collections would form the nucleus of the Bibliothèque Nationale, the French national library.

Francis's generosity toward artists attracted Leonardo da Vinci, Benvenuto Cellini, Andrea del Sarto, and other Italian masters to France, helping to establish the Renaissance style there. Many of their works, including Leonardo's *Mona Lisa*, have remained among the treasures of France ever since Francis's reign; indeed, Francis's extensive collection of paintings and other artworks have become the nucleus of the collection of the Louvre.

Francis's interest in the arts can also be seen today in the numerous châteaus that he built or modified, again spreading Renaissance styles into France. Among the most notable are those of Chambord, Blois, and Fontainebleau. At these and similar palaces, Francis did much to introduce a still-coarse and turbulent French nobility to a more elegant, sophisticated, and graceful way of life. His reign significantly improved the manners, if not the morals, of the French elite.

SIGNIFICANCE

Francis I is best remembered for his charm, the refinement and elegance that he brought to the French court, and for his numerous love affairs and gallant dalliances. As a king, he was popular and successful, though not a reformer or innovator of great significance. While it is an exaggeration to regard him as an absolute monarch or even as a major architect of the absolute monarchy of the late seventeenth century, he made the power of the Crown felt in France to an unprecedented extent during his reign. As a statesman, his wars against Charles V, even though unsuccessful, did keep France independent and established it even more firmly as one of the great powers of Europe. As a patron of culture, he is largely responsible for spreading the styles and standards of the Italian Renaissance into France, raising the level of civilization there and endowing his kingdom with many lasting treasures.

—Garrett L. McAinsh

FURTHER READING

Hackett, Francis. *Francis the First*. 1935. Reprint. Garden City, N.Y.: Doubleday, 1968. A highly readable, romantic popular biography, but dated and not always judicious in its conclusions.

Knecht, R. J. *Francis I*. Cambridge, England: Cambridge University Press, 1982. This study will remain the standard English-language biography of Francis for some time to come. Thoroughly researched, elegantly written, and soundly argued, it is a splendid example of modern scholarship. Its 431 pages of text intelligently cover all aspects of Francis's reign and are supplemented by an extensive bibliography. A detailed index increases the usefulness of the work.

_____. *Francis I and Absolute Monarchy*. London: Historical Association, 1969. This brief pamphlet argues cogently in favor of regarding Francis as an absolute monarch. It is basically a response to the work of J. Russell Major.

_____. *French Renaissance Monarchy: Francis I and Henry II*. 2d ed. New York: Longman, 1996. A detailed survey of the first half of the sixteenth century by the leading English language scholar of Francis I. Extends and builds on the two works listed earlier. Includes map, bibliographic references, and index.

McNeil, David O. *Guillaume Budé and Humanism in the Reign of Francis I*. Geneva: Librairie Droz, 1975. Concentrates on religious and intellectual developments during Francis's reign, centering on the life and works of Budé. McNeil also discusses Budé's significant role in the politics of the times. Contains a comprehensive bibliography on the subject.

Major, J. Russell. *Representative Institutions in Renaissance France, 1421-1559*. Madison: University of Wisconsin Press, 1960. Reprint. Westport, Conn.: Greenwood Press, 1983. This controversial, seminal volume by a great scholar argues that the absolutism of Francis and other sixteenth century French kings has been much exaggerated. Should be read in conjunction with the works by Knecht.

Merriman, Marcus. *The Rough Wooings: Mary Queen of Scots, 1542-1551*. East Linton, East Lothian, Scotland: Tuckwell, 2000. Study of Mary's efforts to preserve Scottish autonomy, and of Francis I and Henry II's roles in establishing and exerting French control over the Scots.

Richardson, Glenn. *Renaissance Monarchy: The Reigns of Henry VIII, Francis I, and Charles V*. New York: Oxford University Press, 2002. Comparison of Francis to two other monarchs who helped define Renaissance government and culture. Focuses on their careers as warriors, governors, and patrons. Includes maps, bibliographic references, and index.

Salmon, J. H. M. *Society in Crisis: France in the Sixteenth Century*. New York: St. Martin's Press, 1975. Though the bulk of this book deals with the religious conflicts of the second half of the century, the opening chapters contain a serious analysis of all aspects of the France of Francis. Economic and social structures, the institutions of government, and cultural developments, rather than narrative political history, are emphasized. A detailed index, an extensive bibliography, genealogical charts, and a glossary of French terms.

Seward, Desmond. *Prince of the Renaissance: The Golden Life of François I*. New York: Macmillan, 1973. A beautifully illustrated and lively, though brief and rather superficial, popular biography. Very thorough on Francis's patronage of the arts but tends to exaggerate his role in shaping French culture. The work must also be used with caution on diplomacy and government, as Seward tends to let his flair for the colorful and the dramatic get the best of his judgment. Slim bibliography and few notes.

SEE ALSO: Andrea del Sarto; Chevalier de Bayard; Jacques Cartier; Catherine de Médicis; Benvenuto Cellini; Charles V; Charles VIII; Ferdinand II and Isabella I; Henry II; Leo X; Leonardo da Vinci; Louis XII; Maximilian I; François Rabelais; Süleyman the Magnificent.

FREDERICK III
Holy Roman Emperor (r. 1440-1493)

Frederick III's long rule allowed him to outlive his many rivals, and after his reign the imperial crown remained with the Habsburgs, with one brief interruption, until the end of the empire in 1806. Frederick also united the territories of all branches of the Habsburg family.

BORN: September 21, 1415; Innsbruck, Tirol, Austria
DIED: August 19, 1493; Linz, Austria
ALSO KNOWN AS: Frederick V, archduke of Austria; Frederick IV, king of Germany; Friedrich III; Frederick the Younger
AREA OF ACHIEVEMENT: Government and politics

EARLY LIFE

Frederick was the first son of Ernest and Cimburgis. Ernest was duke of Inner Austria. Innsbruck belonged to Ernest's brother, also called Frederick IV, who had been banned temporarily from Tirol by the emperor for his support of a schismatic pope. To safeguard the Habsburg family's interest in the Tirol, Ernest moved to Innsbruck.

Little is known of Frederick's childhood. To distinguish him from his uncle, Frederick IV, he was called Frederick the Younger. Five of Frederick's siblings died in childhood, but a brother and a sister survived. Like his mother, Frederick had a calm personality and was pious. As a youth he had a tendency to be withdrawn.

Frederick grew up in Wiener Neustadt, his favorite residence later in life, located thirty miles south of Vienna. He received a good education in Latin, legal matters, and writing, and he developed an interest in astrology and secret writing codes. In conversations, he used the local German dialect.

Frederick and his siblings were placed under the guardianship of their uncle, Frederick IV, after their par-

ents died. Frederick reached maturity at age sixteen, but his uncle decided to continue his guardianship. With the help of Duke Albert V of Austria (later King Albert II), Frederick's cousin, he was declared of age on May 25, 1435.

LIFE'S WORK

On August 9, 1436, before turning his attention to issues of state, Frederick went on a pilgrimage to the Holy Land. One month later, he became a knight of the Holy Grave in Jerusalem.

Two deaths in 1439 made Frederick the senior male of the House of Austria. He also became the guardian of his cousin Sigismund, the son of Frederick IV of Tirol, and of Albert II's son, King László V of Germany, Bohemia, and Hungary. The estates in Tirol, Bohemia, and Hungary demanded an early end to the guardianships, but Frederick wanted to exploit them for his own benefit. In 1446, Frederick allowed Sigismund to assume his position in Tirol, and six years later he surrendered his control over László.

On February 2, 1440, the German princes, meeting in Frankfurt, elected Frederick king, and he was crowned in Aachen on June 17, 1442. Frederick's coronation as emperor in Rome occurred ten years later, the last Roman coronation of a German emperor.

The trip to Rome was facilitated by Frederick's agreement with Pope Eugenius IV. In return for Germany's recognition and support of Eugenius, Frederick was offered a coronation in Rome. The German king left for Rome in December, 1451, and was crowned by Eugenius's successor on March 19, 1452. Three days earlier, he had married Eleonore, the daughter of King Edward of Portugal. Eleonore gave Frederick a son and heir, Maximilian I, in 1459, and a daughter, Kunigunde, before she died in 1467. Frederick never married again.

As German king, Frederick attended meetings of the German Reichstag in 1442 and in 1444, where reforms were discussed, restrictions against feuds were issued, and an attempt was made to control coinage. Frederick, however, lacked effective mechanisms to enforce these measures. Not until 1471 did he return to another Reichstag meeting, held in Regensburg, to reconsider reforms and to seek support against the Turks who threatened Austria and Hungary.

During much of his early reign, Frederick faced serious problems in his Habsburg lands. When Frederick met the estates in Vienna in the summer of 1441, he was greeted with shouts of "king of the Jews" and with calls to crucify him. In his diary, the king lamented that the Austrians were more vicious than the Hungarians or the Bohemians.

After returning from Rome in 1452, he faced an uprising of the estates, led by Ulrich von Eytzing and Ulrich von Cilli. His own brother, Albert VI, was a persistent challenge between 1458 and 1463. In the summer of 1461, Vienna sided with Albert's attack on Frederick, and in the following year Frederick was besieged in his residence in Vienna. Only the death of his brother on December 2, 1463, ended this crisis. Still, revolts continued to surface. On April 23, 1471, Frederick executed Andreas Baumkircher, a knight who had led another revolt of the nobles.

Because of Frederick's dynastic interests in Bohemia and Hungary, he had numerous conflicts with the estates and rulers of the two countries. Most serious was his conflict with Matthias I Corvinus, from the House of Hunyadi, who obtained the Hungarian crown in 1458, although Frederick received the title "king of Hungary." Frederick signed the Treaty of Sopron with the Hungarian ruler in 1463, but the conflict resumed in 1480. Matthias I Corvinus occupied Vienna and Wiener Neustadt between 1485 and 1487 and forced the German king to move to Linz, Austria. Again, the death of a rival, Matthias I Corvinus, on April 6, 1490, removed one of Frederick's major problems in his eastern lands. Five Turkish incursions into Carinthia between 1473 and 1483, however, continued the unrest in his eastern Austrian territories.

Frederick also faced major difficulties in the west. The Swiss had absorbed much of the ancestral Habsburg land, and the Bavarian Wittelsbach Dynasty attempted to absorb neighboring territories. The most important challenge and opportunity came from Charles the Bold, duke of Burgundy. In 1473, Frederick traveled to the Rhine area and attempted to negotiate a marriage between his son Maximilian and Charles's daughter, Maria, but negotiations broke down. Frederick then declared an imperial war (Reichskrieg) against Charles after the Burgundian king invaded Cologne.

The Habsburgs also procured an alliance with the Swiss cantons in return for recognizing Swiss territory. Even though Charles was killed at Nancy on January 5, 1477, Maximilian married Maria six months later at Brügge (now in Belgium). In order to help keep the peace and contain the Wittelsbach Dynasty, Frederick created the Imperial League in Swabia in 1488.

Frederick consolidated his dynastic ambitions by having Maximilian elected German king in Frankfurt on February 16, 1486. Frederick also intervened in Tirol and forced the incompetent Sigismund to turn over his office to Maximilian in 1490. Frederick spent the last years of his life in Linz adding to his collections and enjoying his gardens. On August 19, 1493, he died from complications that arose after the amputation of his left leg because of arteriosclerosis.

SIGNIFICANCE

Frederick ruled longer than any other German emperor. He was able to have his son, Maximilian I, crowned as his successor. Moreover, he ruled his Austrian lands for fifty-eight years. Because of this longevity, he was able to unite the lands and titles of the Habsburg lines. After the death of László in 1457, the Albertine line of the Habsburgs ended. Following the death of his brother Albert, Frederick gained control of all of Austria's eastern lands. After the death of Sigismund of Tirol without an heir in 1496, Maximilian acquired Habsburg possessions in Tirol and Swabia. Also, Maximilian's marriage to Maria brought Burgundy and the Netherlands under Habsburg control.

Frederick believed in the special mission of his Habsburg house. In 1453, he recognized a forgery created by Rudolf IV in 1358, which had granted special rights and titles to Austria. He was also keenly aware, however, of his imperial responsibilities. He negotiated the Vienna concordat with Pope Nicholas V in 1448, which gave him control over nominations to Church appointments and eventually enhanced imperial power.

His Burgundian policies added to Habsburg strength, but it also started the long-term Habsburg rivalry with the Valois kings of France. Even though Frederick was not able to overcome the dynastic divisions in Germany, he did prepare the groundwork for the emergence of the

House of Habsburg as a world power in the sixteenth century.

—*Johnpeter Horst Grill*

FURTHER READING

Brady, Thomas A., Jr. *Turning Swiss: Cities and Empires, 1450-1550*. New York: Cambridge University Press, 1985. Evaluates Frederick's policy toward the free cities in southern Germany.

Heer, Friedrich. *The Holy Roman Empire*. Translated by Janet Sondheimer. New York: Frederick A. Praeger, 1968. Highlights Frederick's influence on his son, Maximilian I.

Heinig, Paul-Joachim. "How Large Was the Court of Emperor Frederick III?" In *Princes, Patronage, and the Nobility: The Court at the Beginning of the Modern Age, c. 1450-1650*, edited by R. G. Asch and A. M. Birke. New York: Oxford University Press, 1991. Examines Frederick's administrative policy and strategy, based on a small court of four hundred to five hundred employees.

Press, Victor. "The Habsburg Lands: The Holy Roman Empire, 1400-1555." In *Handbook of European History, 1400-1600: Late Middle Ages, Renaissance, and Reformation*, edited by Thomas A. Brady et al. New York: E. J. Brill, 1994. Places Frederick's reign within the context of dynastic and national rivalries in the empire.

Rees, Valery. "Hungary's Philosopher King Matthias Corvinus, 1458-90." *History Today* 44, no. 3 (March, 1994). Discusses the career of Frederick's most dangerous rival, who occupied Vienna between 1485 and 1490.

Stieber, Joachim W. *Pope Eugenius IV, the Council of Basel, and the Secular and Ecclesiastical Authorities in the Empire: The Conflict Over Supreme Authority and Power in the Church*. Leiden, the Netherlands: Brill, 1978. Discusses Frederick's negotiations with the pope leading to Eugenius's recognition by the German princes.

SEE ALSO: Charles the Bold; Matthias I Corvinus; Maximilian I; Pius II.

RELATED ARTICLES in *Great Events from History: The Renaissance & Early Modern Era, 1454-1600:* 1458-1490: Hungarian Renaissance; October 19, 1466: Second Peace of Thorn; June 12, 1477-August 17, 1487: Hungarian War with the Holy Roman Empire; August 17, 1477: Foundation of the Habsburg Dynasty; 1482-1492: Maximilian I Takes Control of the Low Countries; August 19, 1493-January 12, 1519: Reign of Maximilian I.

SIR MARTIN FROBISHER
English explorer

Frobisher's search for the Northwest Passage failed, but he and his English contemporaries helped establish an English presence in the Atlantic.

BORN: c. 1535; Pontefract, Yorkshire, England
DIED: November 22, 1594; Plymouth, Devon, England
AREAS OF ACHIEVEMENT: Exploration, military

EARLY LIFE

Although Martin Frobisher (FROH-bish-uhr) was born into the country gentry of England, where record keeping usually was more precise than for the lower classes, researchers still do not know the exact date of his birth or even the exact year. What is known is that Frobisher was brought up in Yorkshire until the early death of his father in 1549, when Frobisher had barely reached adolescence. Thereupon, his mother dispatched him to London to be raised by her brother, Sir John York. He early on

showed far more promise as a mariner than he did as a student. Frobisher's personality and talents, indeed, were not typical of his social class, and he was in temperament far more like the common mariners he commanded in later life than he was like the captains who were to be his colleagues.

Frobisher was at sea by the time he entered his teenage years. His first recorded expedition took place at the age of fifteen, on a disastrous pirate voyage to West Africa commanded by Thomas Wyndham, from which he was one of the few to return alive. Frobisher's career could not have prospered, though, without the help Frobisher was given by the powerful Lok family of mariners. John Lok was a merchant whose activities basically amounted to piracy; he spent much of his time at sea while the business affairs were handled by his brother Michael. His approach of aggressive, financially motivated expansionism became Frobisher's own.

In 1562, Frobisher returned to Africa with Lok. Frobisher was taken hostage by the Portuguese and imprisoned for four months. On his release, he became even more dedicated to carrying on the fight against England's enemies.

LIFE'S WORK

Frobisher fought for England in Ireland, where the Catholic population was restive under the control of their newly Protestant overlords. His heart remained with the sea, however, and he participated in raids on the Spanish, Portuguese, and French fleets. As successful as the English were against their opponents in individual raids, Spain and Portugal continued to control the lucrative trade route to Asia. The only alternative was to try to discover the theoretical Northwest Passage to Asia, going to the north of North America in what is now called the Arctic Ocean. Frobisher's relative youth (he was in his early forties in 1576), as well as his energy and experience, led to his appointment to lead the first English expedition in search of the Northwest Passage.

Frobisher embarked on June 7, 1576, with three ships, financed by the Lok brothers and a group of wealthy backers. The ships were stocked with the latest scientific equipment and navigational guides. By July, they had arrived at Greenland. Sailing around the southern tip of that island, they eventually came to Baffin Island in what is now Canada. Here, on August 19, Frobisher and his fleet had their first encounter with the Inuit people of the region. Frobisher was the first English-speaker to encounter the Inuit, many of whom would, centuries later, be subject to the British crown. Though at first Frobisher's relations with the Inuit were friendly, relations deteriorated after the Inuit kidnapped several men of Frobisher's fleet. Soon, Frobisher decided to return home, in the deluded hope that he had found the way to Asia when all he had done was probe deeper into the Arctic ice. His fleet had, however, found some lumps of ore that they determined to be gold, and they brought it home to England. Frobisher became a national hero and was able to marry Isabel Riggatt, a wealthy widow whose money helped finance subsequent voyages.

The gold was not gold at all, and even Michael Lok, who stood to profit substantially if it were gold, did not think it was. Nonetheless, the hunger for gold, more than a pure interest in exploration, allowed for the speedy financing of a second voyage by Frobisher in search of the Northwest Passage and more "gold." This time, Queen Elizabeth I of England contributed to the cost and lent her personal support to the voyage. The expedition had a

Sir Martin Frobisher. (Hulton|Archive by Getty Images)

better crew, including more navigational experts and scientists. It was also better equipped, with the addition of the tall ship *Aid* to the two large ships of the first voyage, the *Gabriel* and *Michael*. Frobisher was generally a popular leader among his men.

Expectations were high that the second voyage would confirm the perceived success of the first. They returned to the inlet of Baffin Island that is now known as Frobisher Bay in commemoration of its first European explorer. It is difficult for readers now to realize how distant in terms of perception the icy, barren landscapes of Baffin Island were from the sailors' home. There was a sense of near-total isolation and remoteness that can only be compared to the feelings of astronauts who explored the Moon, except that the astronauts were in constant communication with Earth. Frobisher and his men not only had no communication with home but also, because of the limitations of the maps and navigational tools available to them, had no sure idea of where they were. Frobisher still believed that Baffin Island was Asia. He laid a cross on a nearby hill, thinking that he was taking possession of Asia in the name of the queen. He thought that the Inuit were some manner of coastal Asian people.

Given the kidnapping on the previous voyage, relations with the Inuit were hostile from the start. Frobisher had to wage a series of skirmishes against them. Defeating the Inuit, he took some more ore as well as two live captives, the first to be taken by the English. Although the captives died a short time after their return to England, they were the subject of a great frenzy in England and, combined with the supposed gold, led to finding a crew easily for a third Frobisher expedition.

Frobisher's final voyage to the Arctic left at the end of May, 1578. Again, the ship approached Greenland, this time landing on the island itself. The voyage then proceeded back to the familiar area of Frobisher Bay. In search of the Northwest Passage, the ships plunged into Hudson Strait, which if explored until the end would have led to the waterways they were seeking, although they were far more icebound and impassable than the Europeans imagined at the time. Once more mining for ore, Frobisher wanted to leave one hundred men on Baffin Island to winter there and set up a permanent gold-mining base. Fearing the harshness of the winter, the crew was not enthusiastic, and Frobisher was persuaded to return to England, losing one of his ships in the process but returning with most of his crew and bounty intact.

Unfortunately, euphoria about this voyage was short-lived, as it was soon proved conclusively that the ore was not gold. From the outset, the English had wanted so badly to believe it was gold that they would not accept the evidence before their own eyes. It was only when all hope had vanished that the reality of its worthlessness was admitted. Frobisher's popularity faded rapidly, even though he was not suspected of using the supposed gold for personal financial gain. Many of the people who had invested in his voyages were ruined financially (as was Frobisher himself) or were furious because they thought they had been defrauded. Adding to his troubles, Frobisher's wife Isabel became disillusioned with him because he lost their wealth; she died not a year after the return of the third voyage.

This financial disaster meant that Frobisher had to return to piracy. As a pirate, he became successful enough to be offered a position of command under Sir Francis Drake. Thereafter, his career would be a more traditionally military one. He would serve under the command of the government rather than as the representative of a privately controlled, mercantile concern. Frobisher redeemed himself by fighting for the English cause in Ireland in 1580. In 1585, he became the major lieutenant to Drake in the West Indies, where his experienced seamanship and empathy with the common sailor proved crucial to Drake's victories in battle after battle against Spain and in the sacking of Cartagena in what is now Colombia. In 1588, the Spanish Armada prepared to invade England itself. Successfully commanding the Channel fleet and then the ship *Triumph,* Frobisher was knighted after the defeat of the Spanish.

His personal relations with Drake, though, were not as positive, as he chafed under the command of the other great captain, whom he suspected of wanting to take all the fleet's profits for himself.

Frobisher, who by this time had married Lady Dorothy Widmerpole, spent his final years in expeditions against the Portuguese-controlled Azores and the French coast. In one of his assaults on the latter, at Brest, he received a wound in his leg that became infected and led to his death at Plymouth in late 1594.

SIGNIFICANCE

Frobisher's lack of learning and the fact that his goals seemed more mercantile than scientific have contributed to his not being one of the more famous European explorers. Still, he deserves fame, not only for being one of the first Englishmen to explore the territory that eventually became Canada but also because his deeds and explorations changed the course of European and North Amer-

---

THE INUIT OF NORTHEASTERN CANADA

In 1578, Frobisher and his crew, on their second voyage to North America, encountered the Baffin Island Inuit, whom Frobisher's second in command, George Best, describes in considerable detail.

They are men of large corporature [stature] and good proportion: their colour is not much unlike the Sunne burnte Countrie man. . . . They weare their haire something long and cut before, either with stone or knife, very disorderly. . . . They eate their meate all rawe, both fleshe, fishe, and foule, or something perboyled with bloud [blood] & a little water, whiche they drinke. For lacke of water, they will eat yce [ice], that is hard frosen, as pleasantly as we doe Sugar Candie.

Source: Quoted in *The Atlas of North American Exploration: From the Norse Voyages to the Race to the Pole,* by William H. Goetzmann and Glyndwr Williams (New York: Prentice Hall General Reference, 1992), p. 28.

ican history. Without his enthusiasm, popularity, and leadership qualities, the three voyages to the Arctic in the late 1570's would never have occurred. Until Frobisher's era, the sea and all world exploration were largely controlled by the Spanish and Portuguese. Frobisher and his English contemporaries helped establish an English presence in the Atlantic. This achievement proved to be a far more enduring one than the search for the Northwest Passage. The Northwest Passage continued to be hunted for another three centuries, by which time it had become of far more scientific than practical interest.

—Nicholas Birns

FURTHER READING

Asimov, Isaac. *The Ends of the Earth: The Polar Regions of the World*. New York: Weybright and Talley, 1975. Skillfully and clearly written history of polar exploration, emphasizing the scientific side of the effort. Also provides some historical background. A good source for students beginning their study of polar discoveries.

Fitzhugh, William W., and Jacqueline S. Olin, eds. *Archeology of the Frobisher Voyages*. Washington, D.C.: Smithsonian Institution Press, 1993. Examines the material remains of Frobisher's three voyages to what is now Canada in search of the Northwest Passage. For supplementary historical or biographical use.

Keating, Bern. *The Northwest Passage: From the Mathew to the Manhattan, 1497 to 1969*. Chicago: Rand McNally, 1970. A convenient source that is indispensable on the geography of Frobisher's voyages. Contains many colorful and detailed maps.

McDermott, James. *Martin Frobisher: Elizabethan Privateer*. New Haven, Conn.: Yale University Press, 2001. Extremely thorough biography, the product of thirty years of research. Provides virtually all known details of Frobisher's life and attempts imaginatively to fill in the undocumented gaps. Includes photographic plates, illustrations, bibliographic references, and index.

McFee, William. *The Life of Sir Martin Frobisher*. New York: Harper & Brothers, 1928. Written by a seaman himself, this is the only reliable, scholarly biography of Frobisher. Out of date and hard to find, it contains much information crucial to the student. It is necessarily sketchy on the early life but provides details on the West Indian years that are not otherwise easily accessible, given that most sources concentrate on the North Atlantic voyages.

McGhee, Robert. *The Arctic Voyages of Martin Frobisher: An Elizabethan Adventure*. Seattle: University of Washington Press, 2001. Study utilizes archaeological evidence and Inuit oral history as well as the written records left behind by Frobisher and his men to develop a complete picture of his three voyages.

Morison, Samuel Eliot. *The European Discovery of America: The Northern Voyages*. New York: Oxford University Press, 1971. The most available and most valuable source on Frobisher. Thorough, insightful, written with wit and flair, and concerned to defend Frobisher against his detractors, particularly those who accuse him of being greedy or unscientific. Also provides an excellent survey of the process of discovery and exploration in the North Atlantic in which Frobisher played such a pivotal role.

Quinn, David Beers. *England and the Discovery of America, 1481-1620*. New York: Alfred A. Knopf, 1974. The best single-volume history of English exploration in the Atlantic, with an excellent bibliography. Occasionally pedantic, this book nonetheless provides a good overview of Frobisher's maritime era.

Symons, Thomas H. B., ed. *Meta Incognita, a Discourse of Discovery: Martin Frobisher's Arctic Expeditions, 1576-1578*. 2 vols. Hull, Que.: Canadian Museum of Civilization, 1999. In-depth report of the findings of the Meta Incognita Project, which excavated, studied, and preserved archaeological sites related to Frobisher's expeditions. Includes illustrations, maps, and bibliographic references.

LEONHARD FUCHS
German botanist and physician

Fuchs wrote the first significant botanical text of the Renaissance era, a massive illustrated work prized for its beauty, accuracy, and originality and considered foundational to the development of natural history. He also wrote or cowrote dozens of texts in the fields of medicine and pharmacology.

BORN: January 17, 1501; Wemding, Bavaria (now in Germany)

DIED: May 10, 1566; Tübingen, Württemberg (now in Germany)

ALSO KNOWN AS: Leonhart Fuchs; Leonhardt Fuchs; Leonhardus Fuchsius

AREAS OF ACHIEVEMENT: Science and technology, medicine

EARLY LIFE

Leonhard Fuchs (LAY-awn-hahrt FYEWKS) was the son and grandson of mayors of the Bavarian town of Wemding. His mother, Anna (Dentener) Fuchs, and grandfather, Johann Fuchs, raised him from the age of four, following the death of his father, Hans Fuchs. His grandfather instilled in him a lifelong love of nature in general and plants in particular. He was educated at home until 1511, then went to Latin school in Heilbronn, and the next year to the Erfurt Marienschule to improve his Latin and to learn Greek.

He matriculated at the University of Erfurt in 1515, received his baccalaureate in 1517, then returned to Wemding to become a schoolmaster. He soon tired of teaching and in 1519 enrolled at the University of Ingolstadt, following the classical curriculum of Latin, Greek, and Hebrew. After earning his master of arts degree in 1521, he switched to medicine, receiving his medical degree at Ingolstadt in 1524.

Fuchs practiced medicine for the rest of his life, the first two years in Munich, where he married Anna Friedberg; they had four sons and six daughters. He taught medicine at Ingolstadt from 1526 to 1528, then, probably because of conflict with the conservative Roman Catholic university administration, left to become court physician to Georg von Brandenburg, margrave of Brandenburg-Ansbach, whom he served until 1535.

The 1520's and 1530's were times of religious unrest throughout Germany. The snowball effect of Martin Luther nailing his Ninety-five Theses to the church door at Wittenberg in 1517 wreaked hostility and ruined careers. Fuchs, always with Humanistic inclinations, was at-tracted to Lutheranism early, but the date of his conversion is unknown. His southern homeland remained mostly Catholic, while northern and western Germany were more receptive to the new faith. Georg, his patron, was Lutheran. In 1533, Ingolstadt, which had stayed Catholic, denied Fuchs a renewal of his old appointment.

LIFE'S WORK

Beginning with *Errata recentiorum medicorum* (errors of recent physicians) in 1530, Fuchs wrote, cowrote, translated, edited, or contributed to at least fifty books, most of which were concerned in some way with medical botany or the pharmacological properties of plants but also a wide field of medical and scientific subjects. His writings were often controversial and even inflammatory, but his polemics sustained themselves by the depth of his arguments. In 1551, he plagiarized Andreas Vesalius on human anatomy, and he is probably guilty of several other charges of plagiarism, but none of that has harmed his reputation as a botanist.

In November, 1534, Ulrich, duke of Württemberg, prompted by Luther's companion, Philipp Melanchthon, asked Fuchs to be professor of medicine at the University of Tübingen. Fuchs eagerly accepted and spent the remainder of his career in that predominantly Protestant environment, seven times serving as rector of the university. One of his first acts after arriving in August, 1535, was to plant the garden that would become the laboratory of his botanical study. About 1543, presumably because of Italy's Catholicism, he turned down the lucrative invitation of Cosimo I de' Medici, grand duke of Tuscany, to teach medical botany at the University of Pisa and to supervise its botanical garden.

At Tübingen, Fuchs removed astrological texts and the works of Persian physician Rhazes (c. 865-between 923 and 935) and Islamic scientist and philosopher Avicenna (980-1037) from the curriculum, but he encouraged careful study of ancient Greek medicine, the new anatomical works of Vesalius, and plants in their natural environments. He was the first professor there to take students on botanical field trips. He translated into Latin and commented on Hippocrates, Galen, and other ancient Greek authors. His approach to medicine was traditionally Hippocratic and Galenic, receptive to modern discoveries, but skeptical of herbal remedies in the hands on those who were not physicians. Even in his work on medical botany, he emphasized the botanical or structural rather than the medical or therapeutic aspects of plants.

Fuchs's masterpiece appeared in 1542 as *De historia stirpium commentarii insignes* (distinguished commentaries on the history of plants; known as *De historia stirpium*), an exquisitely illustrated 39-centimeter (15-inch) folio known best in English as *The Herbal of Leonhart Fuchs* (1928). Its two artists were Heinrich Füllmaurer and Albrecht Meyer, whom Fuchs supervised closely through many drafts of each watercolor. Veyt Rudolff Speckle of Strassbourg executed the woodcuts.

Like his contemporaries Valerius Cordus, Conrad Gesner, and most other systematic botanists until the seventeenth century, Fuchs regarded his work as addenda to the first century treatise of Dioscorides Pedanius of Anazarbos, known as *De materia medica* (*The Greek Herbal of Dioscorides*, 1933), published by the renowned printer Aldus Manutius in 1499. Dioscorides described more than 600 plants. Even though Fuchs added about 100 species not mentioned by Dioscorides, the 512 woodcuts in his *Herbal* represent only 487 plants. He was more concerned with exactitude than thoroughness.

In 1545, Fuchs produced an 18-centimeter (7-inch) octavo, a sort of field guide called *Primi de stirpium historia commentariorum tomi vivae imagines* (living images of the first volumes of commentaries on the history of plants). It consisted of 516 full-page woodcut illustrations of plants, some of which were hand-colored, but no text except for a dedicatory letter and an index.

As was the academic custom until the end of the eighteenth century, Fuchs wrote mostly in Latin. A few of his books appeared in the vernacular, notably *Alle Krankheyt der Augen* (all diseases of the eye) in 1539 and the various popular translations of *De historia stirpium*.

Most of Fuchs's works went through several editions in his lifetime. So great was his reputation throughout Europe that, despite his Protestantism, Holy Roman Emperor Charles V raised him to the nobility about 1555. His wife's death in 1563 hit him like a mighty blow. He married a pastor's widow in 1564, but his health declined rapidly and he died two years later.

SIGNIFICANCE

Germans consider Fuchs the father of botany, but other countries tend to honor their own scholars, such as Nicolao Leoniceno in Italy, Gesner in Switzerland, Theophrastos of Eresos in Greece, or Carolus Linnaeus in Sweden. Even in Germany some disagreement exists about whether Otto Brunfels, Hieronymus Bock, or

---

FUCHS'S MAJOR WORKS

1530	*Errata recentiorum medicorum* (errors of recent physicians)
1531	*Compendiaria ac succincta admodum in medendi artem eisagoge* (a very short and concise guide to the art of healing)
1535	*Paradoxorum medicinae libri tres* (three books on the paradoxes of medicine)
1539	*De medendis singularum humani corporis partium a summo capite ad imos usque pedes passionibus ac febribus libri quatuor* (four books on relieving sufferings and fevers in particular parts of the human body from the top of your head to the tips of your toes)
1539	*Alle Krankheyt der Augen* (all diseases of the eye)
1540	*Libri IIII, difficilium aliquot quaestionum, & hodie passim controversarum explicationes continentes* (four books on some difficult questions, containing random explanations of today's controversial issues)
1541	*Methodus seu ratio compendiaria perveniendi ad veram solidamque medicinam* (a method or a concise reasoning to arrive at a real and true medicine)
1542	*De historia stirpium commentarii insignes* (distinguished commentaries on the history of plants; *The Herbal of Leonhart Fuchs*, 1928)
1542	*De sanandis totius humani corporis* (on cleansing the whole human body)
1545	*Primi de stirpium historia commentariorum tomi uiuae imagines* (living images of the first volumes of commentaries on the history of plants; better known as *Botany*)
1548	*De curandi ratione libri octo* (eight books on the rationale of curing)
1555	*Institutionum medicinae, ad Hippocratis, Galeni, aliorumque veterum scripta recte intelligenda mire utiles libri quinque* (five wonderfully useful books on medical principles, for the purpose of correctly understanding the writings of Hippocrates, Galen, and other ancient physicians)
1555	*De usitata huius temporis componendorum miscendorumque medicamentorum ratione libri quatuor* (four books on the thought of our day on putting together and mixing medicines)

Fuchs deserves the most credit for making botany a respectable science. Brunfels has the edge in implementing empirical method and Bock in discovering new native German species, but Fuchs is renowned for compiling and presenting facts accurately, beautifully, and compellingly. Because of his care and precision, and especially because of the magnificence of its woodcut illustrations, rare book collectors still esteem Fuchs's *Herbal* as the finest of its kind ever published.

The genus *Fuchsia* was named in Fuchs's honor by French botanist Charles Plumier, who, in 1696, discovered a shrub on the Caribbean island of Hispaniola that he labeled *Fuchsia triphylla flora coccinea*.

—*Eric v.d. Luft*

FURTHER READING

Arber, Agnes Robertson. *Herbals, Their Origin and Evolution: A Chapter in the History of Botany, 1470-1670*. New York: Cambridge University Press, 1986. The standard work on the subject, provides extensive discussion of Fuchs.

Kusukawa, Sachiko. "Leonhart Fuchs on the Importance of Pictures." *Journal of the History of Ideas* 58, no. 3 (July, 1997): 403-427. An article by a leading scholar of the history and philosophy of sixteenth century science in Germany.

Meyer, Frederick Gustav, Emily Emmart Trueblood, and John L. Heller. *The Great Herbal of Leonhart Fuchs: De historia stirpium commentarii insignes, 1542 (Notable Commentaries on the History of Plants)*. Stanford, Calif.: Stanford University Press, 1999. A reproduction with scholarly analysis.

Neumann, Felix Jonathan. "Leonhard Fuchs, Physician and Botanist, 1501-1566." In *Annual Report of the Smithsonian Institution for 1917*. Washington, D.C.: 1919. Basic biographical and bibliographical information.

SEE ALSO: Pierre Belon; Andrea Cesalpino; Conrad Gesner; Martin Luther; Aldus Manutius; Cosimo I de' Medici; Philipp Melanchthon; Andreas Vesalius.

RELATED ARTICLES in *Great Events from History: The Renaissance & Early Modern Era, 1454-1600:* 1517: Fracastoro Develops His Theory of Fossils; 1530's-1540's: Paracelsus Presents His Theory of Disease.

ANDREA GABRIELI
Italian musician

Gabrieli was one of the most versatile Venetian musicians of his generation, helping to make Venice an important center of musical activity in Europe. His compositional output includes sacred vocal music, secular vocal music, instrumental ensemble music, and organ music.

BORN: c. 1520; in or near Venice, Republic of Venice (now in Italy)
DIED: 1586; Venice
AREA OF ACHIEVEMENT: Music

EARLY LIFE

Very little is known about the early life of Andrea Gabrieli (ahn-DRAY-ah gah-bree-EHL-ee). He was born probably in the northern (or Canareggio) section of Venice. Although most biographers have stated that he was born around 1510, the lack of available information on Gabrieli until the 1550's suggests a birth date of around 1520. It is possible that he may have received some early training from the organist at San Geremia in Canareggio (Baldassare da Imola), and that he may have been a singer at St. Mark's Cathedral in Venice in 1536, although there is no documentation to prove either of these assumptions. Nor is there evidence to suggest that he was a pupil of Adrian Willaert, the chapel master of St. Mark's at that time.

Since Gabrieli's first published composition appears in a 1554 collection of madrigals by Vincenzo Ruffo, it is possible that he may have been a musician at the Verona cathedral, where Ruffo worked during the 1550's. The first indication of Gabrieli's activities as a church organist dates from 1557-1558, when he was organist at San Geremia. Although he competed unsuccessfully for the position of second organist at St. Mark's Cathedral in 1557, he must have already been an accomplished organist, for he was a member of the Accademia della Fama in Venice by 1558.

Perhaps the most significant event in Gabrieli's musical training is his connection with the court of Munich during the early 1560's. As court organist to Duke Albert V of Bavaria in 1562, he accompanied the duke on several journeys and became friends with the duke's music director, Orlando di Lasso. Before his period at the court of Munich, Gabrieli had published only four compositions, all madrigals that suggest the influence of Cipriano de Rore. This contact with Lasso heavily influenced Gabrieli's many subsequent publications of both sacred and secular compositions and assured his future position as one of the most important musicians in Venice.

LIFE'S WORK

Gabrieli became second organist at St. Mark's in 1564. His growing popularity in Venetian musical life is attested to by the fact that he composed ceremonial music for various state occasions—the visit of Archduke Karl of Graz (1569), the festivities after the Venetian republic's victory against the Turks (1571), and the visit of King Henry III of France (1574). During these mature years, he also attracted a number of talented students, including Hans Leo Hassler, Ludovico Zacconi, and his nephew Giovanni Gabrieli. He became first organist at St. Mark's in 1584, a position that he retained until his death late in 1586.

Unfortunately, much of Gabrieli's music was published late or posthumously, making it difficult to trace the development of his musical style. For this reason, his life's work is best discussed by types of compositions, divided into the following categories: madrigals, villanelle, sacred vocal music, ceremonial music, instrumental ensemble music, and keyboard music. Gabrieli's seven books of mature madrigals were published between 1566 and 1589. With these collections, he established himself as a master of the lighter type of madrigal that became a fashionable reaction to the serious, avant-garde madrigals of many late sixteenth century composers. Petrarch's texts are set in a less serious style, and many madrigals use the lighter pastoral verses of such poets as Battista Guarini and Torquato Tasso. Gabrieli achieves a less contrapuntal, more appealing style in these madrigals through the use of closely spaced imitative entries and through a greater tendency toward homophonic writing with various combinations of voices. Some phrases have two melodic voices and a harmonic bass, a tendency that anticipates the texture of Baroque music. The harmonic style shows a preference for major triads and a feeling for tonal clarity resulting from the use of few altered notes. In these madrigals, Gabrieli is still attentive to the words but avoids the manneristic tendency to disturb the musical flow of a composition by his lighter treatment of the texts.

Gabrieli also contributed to the development of the villanella, a light type of secular vocal composition that was a reaction to the more serious sixteenth century madrigal. He composed two types of local Venetian villanella, greghesche and giustiniane, both influenced by the villanelle of Lasso. Greghesche have verses that characterize *commedia dell'arte* figures and are written in a mixture of Venetian and Greek. Giustiniane have texts that repeat certain syllables to portray the stuttering of a Venetian patrician. In most cases, both types of pieces have three voice parts that move in a simple, homophonic style.

Gabrieli's sacred music also shows the influence of Lasso and suggests that he may have been attentive to the requirements of the Council of Trent. The words are easily understood because of the tendency toward homophonic writing, the syllabic text setting, and the clear-cut phrases. These masses and motets are generally diatonic with a harmonically oriented bass. Like Lasso, Gabrieli was interested in setting the penitential psalms to music. His *Psalmi Davidici* (1583; psalms of David) reflect the Council of Trent's goals by taking a greater interest in sonority, simplifying the texture, and avoiding obvious word painting.

Gabrieli's ceremonial music includes compositions set to both sacred and secular texts. His eight-voiced madrigal "Felici d'Adria" was composed in 1567 for the visit of Archduke Charles of Carinthia to Venice. In the *Concerti*, published posthumously by his nephew Giovanni in 1587, motets for eight or more voices are found that have texts dealing with major festivals of the Venetian year. Some ceremonial works by Gabrieli have separate choirs that alternate unpredictably in phrases of different lengths. At other times, he creates variety by constantly changing the grouping of the voices and by mixing homophonic with contrapuntal writing. His last occasional music may have been written for the opening of the Teatro Olimpico in Vicenza, for which he composed sixty-four choruses to a translated version of Sophocles' *Oidipous Tyrannos* (c. 429 B.C.E.; *Oedipus Tyrannus*, 1715).

Gabrieli's contributions to the development of instrumental music have never been fully appreciated. For four-part instrumental ensembles, Gabrieli composed a number of ricercars that are suitable for many combinations of early string or wind instruments. His interest in thematic unity is clearly seen in these ricercars, which are usually based on one or two melodic ideas that are repeated extensively in all four instrumental parts. He achieves variety by writing duet passages, by alternating overlapping imitative entries with entrances of the thematic material that do not overlap, and by developing one thematic idea sometimes and juxtaposing two thematic ideas at other times.

Gabrieli composed several types of pieces for keyboard instruments: intonazioni, toccate, canzone, and ri-

cercar. His intonazioni and toccate reflect the spirit of sixteenth century improvisation and could have served as preludes to other compositions. Gabrieli composed two types of keyboard canzone, those that are not based on vocal compositions and those that are based on secular chansons of well-known composers. The canzone that are not derived from vocal works are characterized by the imitation of a number of successive thematic ideas and have sections in contrasting meters and tempos. Those that are based on chansons follow their vocal models but add extensive ornamentation.

Some of Gabrieli's keyboard ricercars are freely composed, while others are based on vocal compositions. Those belonging to the latter category do not follow the vocal model as closely as Gabrieli does in his canzone. In these ricercars, each melodic motive is treated at greater length than in the vocal model itself. Thus, instead of imitating each motive once in each of the four polyphonic parts, they show their clearly instrumental character by normally having five to ten imitative entries for a melodic motive.

The freely composed ricercars can be divided into three categories: those that have one thematic idea prevailing throughout, those that employ two complementary thematic ideas, and those that have a number of thematic ideas that are derived from the opening idea. Some of the imitative entries over these thematic ideas overlap in typical Renaissance fashion. At other times, the imitative entries anticipate Baroque fugal procedure by not overlapping. Some ricercars demonstrate Gabrieli's contrapuntal skill by lengthening the thematic idea to two or four times the length of the original note values (augmentation), or by inverting the melodic intervals of the thematic idea. Whatever the special devices, the opening thematic idea or one of the other main thematic ideas is present most of the time.

SIGNIFICANCE

During his lifetime, Gabrieli made significant contributions to many of the genres current in his day—secular vocal music, sacred vocal music, ceremonial music, and keyboard music. His villanelle and madrigals are important to the development of secular vocal music, for they represent a lighter alternative to the more serious, highly expressive avant-garde madrigals that many other composers were writing. Because of their humorous texts, his villanelle are important predecessors of the early seventeenth century madrigal comedies by Adriano Banchieri and Orazio Vecchi.

His sacred vocal music reflects the needs of the Council of Trent; the simpler textures and diatonic style of writing served as a model for other composers wishing to compose in a style acceptable to the Catholic Church. His ceremonial music influenced other composers, particularly because of the changing textures or the alternation of separate choirs. Although the origins of Baroque style lie primarily in the works by those composers who believed in more serious text expression, Gabrieli's vocal works do anticipate certain Baroque traits in their tendency toward homophonic writing, clear-cut phrases, a simpler harmonic style, and an increased vertical orientation.

Gabrieli's greatest impact, however, was in the realm of keyboard music. His intonazioni and toccate reveal much about sixteenth century improvisation. His sectional canzone anticipate the early Baroque canzona and sonata, while his chanson-based canzone are excellent examples of Renaissance ornamentation practices. Gabrieli's ricercars, because of their tendency toward thematic unity, the persistent use of imitation, and the use of special contrapuntal devices, foreshadow the fugal procedures of the seventeenth century. Although the works of Gabrieli are not as well known as those of his nephew Giovanni, Andrea is far more significant, for he contributed to a wider variety of vocal and instrumental genres than did his nephew and had a greater influence on more composers.

—John O. Robison

FURTHER READING

Apel, Willi. *The History of Keyboard Music to 1700.* Translated by Hans Tischler. Bloomington: Indiana University Press, 1972. The most thorough description of Gabrieli's keyboard music. Stresses the importance of Gabrieli's ricercars as predecessors of the Baroque fugue and describes his canzone, intonazione, toccate, and organ masses.

Arnold, Denis. "Ceremonial Music in Venice at the Time of the Gabrielis." *Proceedings of the Musical Association* 82 (1955/1956): 47-59. States that music for separated choirs fulfilled the need for ceremonial music on important festive occasions in Venice. Discusses Gabrieli's role in the history of Venetian ceremonial music and describes the major influences on his music for separated choirs.

_____. *Giovanni Gabrieli and the Music of the Venetian High Renaissance.* New York: Oxford University Press, 1979. Although primarily about Andrea Gabrieli's nephew, this book contains some useful biographical information and general discussions of Gabrieli's motets, masses, instrumental ensemble music, and keyboard music. Emphasizes the influence of Gabrieli on his nephew but clearly distinguishes their musical styles.

Brown, Howard M. "The Madrigalian and the Formulaic in Andrea Gabrieli's Pastoral Madrigals." In *The Pastoral Landscape,* edited by John Dixon Hunt. Hanover, N.H.: University Press of New England, 1992. Examination of the relationship between Gabrieli's pastoral madrigals and the general conventions of the genre. Includes illustrations and bibliographic references.

Einstein, Alfred. *The Italian Madrigal.* Translated by Alexander H. Krappe, Roger H. Sessions, and Oliver Stunk. 2d ed. Princeton, N.J.: Princeton University Press, 1971. A dated but useful discussion of Gabrieli's villanelle and madrigals. Emphasizes Gabrieli's role in the development of the madrigal and suggests that his light madrigals reflect sixteenth century Venetian life. The musical style of several madrigals is described in detail.

Fenlon, Iain. *Music and Culture in Late Renaissance Italy.* New York: Oxford University Press, 2002. Much of this study is devoted to the creation and performance of music in Gabrieli's Venice. Includes illustrations, bibliographic references, and index.

Gabrieli, Andrea. *Andrea Gabrieli: Complete Madrigals.* 12 vols. in 7 books. Edited by A. Tillman Merritt. Madison, Wis.: A-R Editions, 1981-1984. The introduction contains information about Gabrieli's life and musical style. It also lists the major sources of his vocal and instrumental works. All the volumes have detailed discussions of the texts and music edited in each volume.

Whitwell, David. *Aesthetics of Music in Sixteenth Century Italy, France, and Spain.* Northridge, Calif.: Winds, 1996. General study of the aesthetic theories, principles, and conventions shaping Gabrieli's compositions and their reception. Includes bibliographic references.

SEE ALSO: William Byrd; Giovanni Gabrieli; Henry III; Orlando di Lasso; Luca Marenzio; Torquato Tasso.

RELATED ARTICLES in *Great Events from History: The Renaissance & Early Modern Era, 1454-1600:* 1567: Palestrina Publishes the *Pope Marcellus Mass;* 1575: Tallis and Byrd Publish *Cantiones Sacrae;* 1588-1602: Rise of the English Madrigal; 1590's: Birth of Opera; October 31, 1597: John Dowland Publishes *Ayres;* 1599: Castrati Sing in the Sistine Chapel Choir.

GIOVANNI GABRIELI
Italian composer

A gifted Venetian school composer during the Renaissance and Baroque eras, Gabrieli was critical to the development of German music during the Baroque period. Also, Gabrieli was one of the first composers to specify whether music should be played loudly or softly.

BORN: c. 1556; Venice, Republic of Venice (now in Italy)
DIED: August 12, 1612; Venice
AREA OF ACHIEVEMENT: Music

EARLY LIFE

Very little is known of the early life of Giovanni Gabrieli (jyoh-VAHN-nee gah-bree-EHL-ee), as is typical for composers of the Italian Renaissance. Unlike the greatest artists, musicians were usually regarded as servants, not celebrities. Even the exact year of his birth is unknown, since the notice of his death in the records of his parish church lists his age at death as fifty-six, while the Venetian public health records give it as fifty-eight. His parents were Pietro de Fais, a weaver, and Paola, the sister of Andrea Gabrieli, a noted composer. Sadly, many documents relating to Giovanni Gabrieli's life may have been destroyed by Napoleon I's armies in 1797, and others at the end of World War II in 1945.

Giovanni's first teacher was his uncle, with whom he went to Munich, probably in 1575, as a musician at the court of the duke of Bavaria, Albert V. In Munich, Giovanni was associated with a number of other noted composers besides his uncle, notably Orlando di Lasso. Two other gifted composers he came to know in his formative years became lifelong friends, Giuseppe Guami, another musician at the Bavarian court, and Hans Leo Hassler, a student of Andrea. Giovanni's adoption of his uncle's surname and his painstaking editing of his uncle's works after Andrea's death indicate his closeness to his relative and teacher. Giovanni's own pupil Heinrich Schütz was to be another close friend.

It is clear that Gabrieli made friends easily and that many of his friends throughout his life were other musicians, including several Germans. It is quite possible that at least some of Gabrieli's recognized influence on the development of German early Baroque music came about through his friendships as well as his gifts. That would not be unique in musical history. Some of the influence of the Netherlands school may have been as a result of the attractive personalities of its members, particularly Johannes Ockeghem and Lasso. During the classical period, Franz Joseph Haydn's good nature may have contributed to his success. Unfortunately, much more is known about the lives and personalities of Ockeghem, Lasso, and Haydn than is known about the life and personality of Gabrieli.

LIFE'S WORK

Gabrieli was already a respected composer when he returned to Venice, sometime between 1579 and 1584. In 1584, he was hired as a temporary organist at St. Mark's Basilica, and he won the permanent post of second organist the following year. He was to hold it for life. St. Mark's had two organs in lofts at the north and south ends of the building, so there were always two organists. During Gabrieli's tenure, a third (chamber) organ was added. Normally the organists used only one and played on alternate Sundays, but on great feast days all three organs would be used. There was no difference in salary and responsibilities between the first and second organists. When Giovanni was hired, his uncle was the first organist. From 1588 to 1591, the first organist was Giovanni's friend Guami, while for the remainder of Giovanni's life, the other organist was Paolo Giusto. In 1585, Giovanni became organist for a lay religious society, the Scuola Grande di San Rocco. Both posts required the organist to compose as well as to play, which was a general requirement for salaried organists and music directors (Kappelmeisters) until about the beginning of the nineteenth century.

At St. Mark's, Gabrieli had the use of one of the largest and best-trained musical establishments in Europe, partly built by his uncle during the twenty years (1566-1586) Andrea was an organist at the basilica. The paid permanent ensemble included thirty or more singers and four instrumentalists (two cornets and two trombones). Moreover, Gabrieli could draw on far larger resources on special occasions, such as great feasts of the Church and public festivals. Since many of his instrumental pieces called for strings, woodwinds, and additional brasses, it is clear that Gabrieli regularly hired additional musicians. These could have come from many sources and may have included women as well as men.

Venetian *ospedales* (foundling homes and orphanages) included such excellent music instruction that, a century later, Antonio Vivaldi's girls at the Pietà are thought to have been the best ensemble in Europe, providing the orchestra for all his works and the soloists for all his concertos, except those for violin. Other resources that could be drawn on included church choirs, the professional trumpeters who accompanied the doge, and the musicians of the several religious confraternities, among them Gabrieli's own Scuola Grande di San Rocco. Very few other cities had such numerous, varied, and talented bodies of musicians available, and Venetian composers from Adrian Willaert to Vivaldi made full use of them. It was this unmatched abundance of players and singers that helped attract talented composers to Venice and that helped to make the Venetian school distinct from the musicians of other Italian regions.

Venetian music, like Venetian painting, imparts a feeling of opulence. Some of Gabrieli's best works drew on all these resources, stretched them further than had earlier Venetian composers, and achieved a kind of massive grandeur that was opulent even by Venetian standards and entirely appropriate to the richness of St. Mark's.

Associated as he was with St. Mark's and other religious bodies, a great part of Gabrieli's output was of sacred music. He wrote madrigals while in Bavaria, but, apparently, very few after he returned to Venice. There is no evidence of his ever having written dance music. Instead, he devoted himself to the composition of religious works, primarily for St. Mark's, and ceremonial music for both St. Mark's and the religious processions of the Scuola Grande di San Rocco.

Venetian composers, starting with Willaert, who introduced Venice to the advanced ideas of the Netherlands school to which he belonged, had made use of the large size, multiple organs and choir lofts, and long echoes of St. Mark's by separating their choirs and placing choirs or sections in different parts of the cathedral (called *cori spezzati*), often with instrumentalists, chiefly trombones, trumpets, and bassoons. They might play and sing together or antiphonally—choirs answering one another. Listeners hear the music as if it came from different directions, and, if all musicians were playing and singing, from all directions. Ideally suited to St. Mark's, this practice lasted longer in Venice than anywhere else in Italy. Gabrieli was the last major Italian composer to use *cori spezzati* in his church pieces, and he also introduced the practice into his many canzones, short works for instruments, usually brass and organ. The effects were rich and majestic, even by Venetian standards.

Cori spezzati composition and performance endured much longer in Germany than in Italy, for a variety of reasons. The Germans, on the whole, were more religious than the Italians. Gabrieli's successors at St. Mark's,

Claudio Monteverdi and Giacomo Carissimi, were the last significant Italian religious composers before Vivaldi. Even Monteverdi's operas and madrigals are at least as well known as his sacred music. Secular music, not sacred, was what the Italian public wanted. In Germany, on the other hand, the chapel, not the opera house, was where the audience went to hear music. German and Austrian composers continued to write large quantities of church music, Catholic and Protestant, throughout the seventeenth and eighteenth centuries. Many German cathedrals were as suited to separated choirs as St. Mark's. Indeed, many composers who worked in Germany, including Andrea Gabrieli and Lasso, composed for *cori spezzati*.

Another reason for its survival in Germany was that Venetian works were common and appreciated north of the Alps. Many German musicians had studied in Venice because of the excellence of its resources and teaching. Moreover, Venice was then the most important center for music publication. The publication of Gabrieli's own works, begun during his lifetime with madrigals composed while he was in Bavaria, continued with *Sacrae symphoniae* (1597) and the posthumous *Canzoni e sonate* (1615). Many works still remained in manuscript at that time. In 1956, Denis Arnold began publishing Gabrieli's complete works, but some lost ones have been discovered during the 1980's.

As little is known of Gabrieli's later years as is known of his early life. It is probable that he married and had a large family, and it is certain that he spent a good part of his spare time in the German community, where he had many friends. Aside from this, it is known only that he died from kidney stones after a long illness in 1612.

SIGNIFICANCE

Gabrieli's place in history seems secure. Unlike the works of most early Baroque and Renaissance composers, his choral works, in particular, sometimes were performed during the nineteenth and early twentieth centuries. His popularity resulted from one of the earliest important musicological studies, Carl von Winterfeld's *Johannes Gabrieli und sein Zeitalter* (1834), which reintroduced his work at a time when practically no Renaissance and early Baroque music was played or sung, except for that of Giovanni Pierluigi da Palestrina. While Winterfeld's work contained a number of exaggerated claims for Gabrieli that later scholars have rejected, the work did influence continuing research on and performance of the Venetian master. Winterfeld was particularly interested in Gabrieli's choral works, while later studies have concentrated more on his instrumental pieces.

Gabrieli and his younger Roman contemporary, Girolamo Frescobaldi, are usually considered the most important Italian organ composers. In Gabrieli's case, his fame rests on a number of pieces ranging from ricercars, toccatas, and fugues, all exercises in theme and variation, to intonations, short pieces of a few bars that introduce longer works, usually for choir, organ, and instruments. Gabrieli's compositions for instrumental ensembles have especially interested modern musicologists and performers, particularly brass players. Musicologists see them as leading directly to the sonata and concerto. While some are for strings and organ and others for strings, organ, and winds, many are for brass or brass and organ. Since the brass repertory is rather limited, Gabrieli is a favorite of most brass ensembles.

The vocal music of Gabrieli and his German admirers, such as Schütz and Michael Praetorius, has frequently been recorded. Massive works requiring multiple choirs, vocal soloists, organs, and brasses placed in different positions in echoing cathedrals are a perfect subject for stereophonic and quadrophonic recording. A few contemporary musical groups and composers have composed and performed *cori spezzati*.

—John Gardner

FURTHER READING

Arnold, Denis. *Giovanni Gabrieli and the Music of the Venetian High Renaissance*. New York: Oxford University Press, 1979. This is the fullest and most readable biography of Gabrieli in English. Arnold sees Gabrieli as a brilliant conservative, a late sixteenth century Bach.

Charteris, Richard. *Giovanni Gabrieli (ca. 1555-1612): A Thematic Catalogue of His Music with a Guide to the Source Materials and Translations of His Vocal Texts*. Stuyvesant, N.Y.: Pendragon Press, 1996. A companion to the author's twelve-volume edition of Gabrieli's complete works, this text includes thematic, historiographic, and textual analyses of Gabrieli's entire corpus. Includes illustrations, discography, bibliographic references, and indexes.

Fenlon, Iain. *Music and Culture in Late Renaissance Italy*. New York: Oxford University Press, 2002. Much of this study is devoted to the creation and performance of music in Giovanni Gabrieli's Venice. Includes illustrations, bibliographic references, and index.

Grout, Donald Jay. *A History of Western Music*. Rev. ed. New York: W. W. Norton, 1973. This fine general work places Gabrieli and other composers in perspective.

Kenton, Egon. *Life and Works of Giovanni Gabrieli*. Rome: American Institute of Musicology, 1967. A highly technical work for the professional musician, musicologist, or music historian. Kenton's work is of value to the amateur student chiefly as a second opinion to balance that of Arnold.

Robertson, Alec, and Denis Stevens, eds. *Renaissance and Baroque*. Vol. 2 in *A History of Music*. New York: Barnes & Noble Books, 1965. Like that of Grout, this is a general work. Its particular value for the student is in putting Gabrieli and other Renaissance and Baroque composers in perspective in the European musical scenes of their times.

Saunders, Steven. "The Legacy of Giovanni Gabrieli: Priuli's *Missa sine nomine* and Valentini's *Missa Diligam te Domine*." In *Cross, Sword, and Lyre: Sacred Music at the Imperial Court of Ferdinand II of Habsburg (1619-1637)*. New York: Oxford University Press, 1995. Traces Gabrieli's influence on seventeenth century sacred music by looking at two of his Northern successors. Includes sheet music, illustrations, bibliographic references, and index.

Selfridge-Field, Eleanor. *Venetian Instrumental Music from Gabrieli to Vivaldi*. New York: Praeger, 1975. In chapter 4, which is devoted to Gabrieli, Selfridge-Field portrays him as playing a crucial role in the creation of the Baroque era and in anticipating the concerto and the sonata.

SEE ALSO: William Byrd; Andrea Gabrieli; Orlando di Lasso; Luca Marenzio; Giovanni Pierluigi da Palestrina.

RELATED ARTICLES in *Great Events from History: The Renaissance & Early Modern Era, 1454-1600:* 1567: Palestrina Publishes the *Pope Marcellus Mass*; 1575: Tallis and Byrd Publish *Cantiones Sacrae*; 1588-1602: Rise of the English Madrigal; 1590's: Birth of Opera; October 31, 1597: John Dowland Publishes *Ayres*; 1599: Castrati Sing in the Sistine Chapel Choir.

VASCO DA GAMA
Portuguese explorer

Da Gama was the first European during the Age of Discovery to reach India by sailing around Africa. His voyage culminated decades of Portuguese efforts at exploration and began Portugal's era as a spice empire.

BORN: c. 1460; Sines, Portugal
DIED: December 24, 1524; Cochin, India
AREAS OF ACHIEVEMENT: Exploration, military

EARLY LIFE

Vasco da Gama (VAHS-koh dah GAH-muh) was born in a small coastal town in southern Portugal. His parents, Estevano da Gama and Isabel de Sodre, were members of ancient but poor families of the lower nobility. Their marriage produced four children, of whom Vasco was the third son. His two elder brothers were Paulo and Estevano (or Ayres), and there was a sister named Theresa. When he reached the proper age, Vasco was sent to school at the inland town of Evora. What he studied, however, is not known, and little other information survives concerning his early life.

All da Gama men had a reputation for bravery. That reputation was supplemented by a certain notoriety for being quarrelsome and unruly people. According to tradition, Vasco da Gama repelled by sheer force of personality the alcalde and night watch of Setubal during a nocturnal confrontation. His first documentable appearance occurred in 1492, during a diplomatic crisis between King John II of Portugal and Charles VIII, the king of France. As part of the effort to prepare Portugal for the possibility of a war, the king sent da Gama to Setubal to take care of affairs in the Algarve.

The Portuguese king's choice for this important assignment reflected his great confidence in da Gama, which was based on the young man's successful but unspecified service in the fleet, probably against pirates. Some historians also speculate that various undocumented and secret Portuguese voyages of exploration in the southern Atlantic and along the East African coast took place during the last years of the 1480's and the first years of the 1490's. If so, da Gama may have commanded one or more of these expeditions.

LIFE'S WORK

King John II had long planned a follow-up expedition to Bartolomeu Dias's discovery of the Cape of Good Hope in 1488, but various circumstances had delayed it. Originally the king wanted to appoint Estevano da Gama as commander of the expedition, and when he died the post devolved on his son Vasco by at least December, 1495. It may even have been first offered to da Gama's elder brother Paulo, who may have declined because of ill health.

Da Gama's expedition consisted of four ships, which departed from Portugal on July 8, 1497. His objectives were to find a sea route to India, to engage in the Eastern spice trade, and to make contact and treaties with local Christian rulers. The expedition was primarily one of exploration and not trade. Arriving at Santiago in the Cape Verde Islands on July 27, the expedition rested and then took to the high seas on August 3, steering a southwesterly course and ignoring the coastal route used by Diogo Cão and Dias.

The Portuguese were attempting to take advantage of favorable wind patterns that, on this occasion, turned out to be abnormally weak. Turning eastward after a long passage, they did not sight land until November 4, at about the region of Santa Helena Bay. It was an impressive navigational accomplishment for that age. Next, da Gama's fleet rounded the Cape of Good Hope on November 22, after which they broke up their supply ship and distributed its contents. As they sailed up the eastern coast of Africa, scurvy began to appear in the crew, but they soon contacted Arab traders and obtained supplies of fresh fruit.

On March 29, 1498, they arrived at the hospitable city of Malindi, where they took on a skillful pilot, probably the famous Ahmed ibn Madgid. With his aid, they proceeded northward and caught the monsoon, which quickly transported the expedition to the Malabar coast of India on May 18. They arrived at the town of Capocate on May 20, and on May 21 went ashore, where they met two Spanish-speaking Tunisian merchants, who exclaimed, "May the Devil take you! What brought you here?" The Portuguese replied, "Christians and spices." That exchange foreshadowed the type of reception that they would continue to receive in India during their visit.

It was not until May 30, 1498, that da Gama managed to get an audience with the samorin of Calicut, the most powerful local ruler and controller of the spice trade. By that time, the Portuguese had discovered that their trade goods were better suited for the Hottentots of southern Africa, while the sophisticated Hindus held the scruffy Portuguese and their goods in contempt. At the same time, da Gama remained hopeful because of his mistaken belief that the Hindus were Christians of some sort. Mutual suspicions grew, however, and the Portuguese only managed with the greatest of difficulty to trade their shoddy cargo for some spices and precious stones. About August 12, they asked the samorin for permission to depart; he refused and instead took some hostages. The Portuguese retaliated by taking some Indian hostages on August 19. An exchange was negotiated and then made on August 29. Da Gama sailed the next day, although he had to fight a short battle with some of the samorin's navy. Steering north, the expedition stopped at Angediva Island for a rest.

Da Gama and his fleet left Angediva Island on October 5. Unfortunately on this passage, they encountered very unfavorable winds as the monsoons had not yet shifted, and so little progress was made. Scurvy broke out with great intensity, and eventually thirty men died. After the monsoons arrived, the Portuguese finally sighted Africa on January 2, 1499. Losses among the crew forced them to abandon one vessel at Malindi before they went on to Portugal. Da Gama split the expedition at the Cape Verde Islands and rushed his ailing brother Paulo to the Azores in the vain hope of saving his life. Meanwhile, another captain, Nicolau Coelho, sailed for Portugal and arrived on July 10. It was not until late August or early September, 1499, that da Gama reached Lisbon, where he received an enthusiastic reception.

King Manuel rewarded da Gama with the title of Admiral of the Sea of the Indies and made him proprietary owner of his birthplace, Sines. Sometime between 1499 and 1502, da Gama married Catarina d'Atayde. He also prepared detailed sailing instructions for the expedition of his successor, Pedro Álvars Cabral, in 1500. That expedition resulted in even greater hostilities between the Portuguese and the Muslim merchants of Calicut. Apparently dissatisfied with Cabral's performance, Manuel named da Gama commander of the next expedition to India. This expedition's purpose was conquest, not trade, and employed the most powerful fleet yet sent to the Indian Ocean.

The fleet consisted of fifteen ships under the command of da Gama and another five ships under his brother Estevano. They sailed for India in February and March, respectively. Arriving off the Malabar coast, da Gama intercepted a Muslim ship full of pilgrims returning from Mecca; he massacred the passengers and burned the ship. He proceeded to Calicut on October 30, where he demanded the expulsion of the hostile Muslim merchant community. When the samorin refused, the

Portuguese shelled the city. Next, they visited the friendly cities of Cochin and Cananore and picked up a cargo of spices. They then returned to Portugal and arrived home on September 1, 1503. Da Gama left five ships behind under the command of Vincente Sodre to protect Cochin and the Portuguese factory there. These expeditions of Cabral and da Gama forced the Portuguese into a policy of conquest, as the Muslim merchants persuaded the Mamlūks of Egypt and the Gujaratis to form an alliance to drive the intruding Portuguese from the Indian Ocean.

After the expedition of 1502-1503, da Gama returned to private life. His resentment over what he considered inadequate rewards for his great achievements simmered. In 1518, Manuel managed to placate him somewhat by appointing him count of Vidigueira. Meanwhile, the Portuguese empire in the East, which had been estab-

Vasco da Gama. (Library of Congress)

lished by his great successors Francisco de Almeida and Afonso de Albuquerque, began to flounder under a series of incompetent and corrupt governors. In 1524, King John III appointed da Gama viceroy of India. Da Gama left for India on April 9, 1524, and, immediately on his arrival at Goa, began restoring discipline and harassing Portugal's enemies. Traveling to Cochin, he arrested the departing governor Duarte de Menezes, but overexertion and the tropical climate worked their ill effects on the now elderly da Gama. He died on December 24, having barely begun the much-needed reformation of the Portuguese spice empire.

SIGNIFICANCE

The years 1498 to 1945 have been dubbed the "Vasco da Gama Epoch" in Asian history. That era basically consisted of Europe's navies dominating Asian coastlines, which further resulted in European control of the Asian economy and politics. Da Gama began this domination. The goods he brought to Calicut may have been inferior; he and his men may have been almost intolerably dirty and rude by Hindu standards. Yet they possessed decisive superiority in one crucial area: Their ships were more seaworthy and far more heavily armed with cannons than any Asian ships. As a result, da Gama and his successors were able to create a vast spice empire in spite of vigorous Muslim and Hindu resistance. Only similarly and even more heavily armed European rivals, the Dutch, were able to dislodge the Portuguese from their monopoly of the spice trade.

Da Gama served the Portuguese crown as well as any person, exhibiting bravery, cunning, and authority. Yet he was not indispensable; Portugal possessed many individuals like da Gama. It was da Gama's good fortune to be at the right place to obtain the assignment that would make his name live forever. In fact, if he held the same opinions as his descendants, the immediate material rewards of his voyages mattered far more to him than a permanent and respected place in history based on his achievements in Asia.

—Ronald H. Fritze

FURTHER READING

Cortesão, Armando. *The Mystery of Vasco da Gama*. Coimbra, Portugal: Junta de Investigacoes do Ultramar, 1973. The "mystery" is whether any Portuguese voyages of exploration took place between Dias's discovery of the Cape of Good Hope in 1487 and da Gama's voyage to India in 1497. Cortesão contends that such voyages did take place and that da Gama actually commanded at least one of them.

Diffie, Bailey W., and George D. Winius. *Foundations of the Portuguese Empire, 1415-1580*. Minneapolis: University of Minnesota Press, 1977. This detailed and authoritative survey of the early phase of Portuguese trading and colonial enterprise is excellent for obtaining a reasonably detailed introduction to da Gama's career, along with placing it firmly in its historical context. Particularly useful for debunking various misconceptions and myths associated with the Age of Discovery.

Disney, Anthony, and Emily Booth, eds. *Vasco da Gama and the Linking of Europe and Asia*. New York: Oxford University Press, 2000. Anthology of essays originally presented at the Vasco da Gama Quincentenary Conference held in Australia in 1997. The focus of the essays varies greatly, ranging from daily life aboard da Gama's ship to a survey of five hundred years of European relations with Southeast Asia. Includes bibliographic references and index.

Hart, Henry H. *Sea Road to the Indies: An Account of the Voyages and Exploits of the Portuguese Navigators, Together with the Life and Times of Dom Vasco da Gama, Capitão-Mor, Viceroy of India, and Count of Vidigueira*. New York: Macmillan, 1950. Covers both the background to and the substance of da Gama's explorations and the conquests in the Indian Ocean. Detailed and contains many interesting anecdotes. Unfortunately, the author takes an uncritical approach to the sources and should be read with caution.

Jayne, Kingsley Garland. *Vasco da Gama and His Successors, 1460-1580*. Reprint. New York: Barnes & Noble Books, 1970. Originally published in 1910, this well-written study is still worth consulting. The account of da Gama's first voyage is quite detailed. Furthermore, unlike most books dealing with the founding of the Portuguese spice empire, Jayne's narrative supplies information about da Gama's years of retirement between his second voyage to India in 1502-1503 and his viceroyalty in 1524.

Nowell, Charles E. "Vasco da Gama—First Count of Vidigueira." *Hispanic American Historical Review* 20 (August, 1940): 342-358. This useful article discusses why da Gama has been neglected by biographers and blames the situation on the lack of information about his youth and personality. Existing printed primary sources are then described and evaluated. Da Gama is assessed as a product of his time.

Pearson, M. N. *The Portuguese in India*. Cambridge, England: Cambridge University Press, 1988. Largely dealing with the late fifteenth through the mid-seventeenth centuries, this authoritative volume examines Portuguese activity in India. Supplies the Asian context for da Gama's voyages along with a bibliography for further reading on the topic.

Sanceau, Elaine. *Good Hope: The Voyage of Vasco da Gama*. Lisbon: Academia Internacional da Cultura Portuguesa, 1967. This well-written book details da Gama's first heroic voyage to India. Its author has written extensively on the history of Portuguese exploration.

Subrahmanyam, Sanjay. *The Career and Legend of Vasco da Gama*. New York: Cambridge University Press, 1997. Equal parts biography of the actual Vasco da Gama and cultural analysis of the legendary Vasco da Gama. Addresses the relationship between myth and nationalism, as well as the historical accomplishments of da Gama himself for his nation. Includes illustrations, maps, bibliographic references, and index.

Watkins, Ronald. *Unknown Seas: How Vasco da Gama Changed the East*. London: John Murray, 2003. An attempt to bring da Gama's voyage to life by chronicling the experience of his minor crewmen. Highly detailed discussion of every aspect of life aboard ship and the ingenuity of the crew in using then-cutting-edge technology, and even refitting and rebuilding their ship during the voyage. Includes illustrations, map, bibliographic references, index.

SEE ALSO: Afonso de Albuquerque; Luís de Camões; Charles VIII; Pêro da Covilhã; Bartolomeu Dias; John II; John III; Ferdinand Magellan; Manuel I.

RELATED ARTICLES in *Great Events from History: The Renaissance & Early Modern Era, 1454-1600:* Late 15th century: Mombasa, Malindi, and Kilwa Reach Their Height; 1490's: Decline of the Silk Road; January, 1498: Portuguese Reach the Swahili Coast; Beginning c. 1500: Coffee, Cacao, Tobacco, and Sugar Are Sold Worldwide; 1505-1515: Portuguese Viceroys Establish Overseas Trade Empire.

STEPHEN GARDINER
English administrator, religious leader, and statesman

As one of the most talented of the defenders of religious conservatism and traditional doctrine in early Tudor England, Gardiner fought the advance of Protestantism in church and state. Although his personal efforts were largely successful, ultimately his cause suffered defeat.

BORN: c. 1493; Bury St. Edmunds, Suffolk, England
DIED: November 12, 1555; Whitehall Palace, London, England
AREAS OF ACHIEVEMENT: Religion and theology, government and politics, diplomacy

EARLY LIFE
Stephen Gardiner was born at Bury St. Edmunds, England. His parents were the well-to-do clothmaker John Gardiner and his wife, Agnes. Stephen appears to have been the youngest of three sons and as early as 1507 was destined for university study and a clerical career. He duly entered Trinity Hall at Cambridge University in 1511, a college founded to promote the study of civil and canon law. Although he possessed a working knowledge of Humanistic subjects and Greek, his formal degree study was in the law.

In 1518, he earned the degree of bachelor of civil law, followed by the degrees of doctor of civil law in 1521 and doctor of canon law in 1522. Meanwhile, about 1521, he was ordained as a priest. From 1521 to 1524, he lectured on civil and canon law at Cambridge University and attained sufficient respect to be elected master of Trinity Hall in 1525. His old college still possesses two portraits of him that show him as solidly built and clean-shaven, with penetrating eyes and a large straight nose.

During these years, Gardiner also made his initial contacts with the world of the court and government of Henry VIII. His first important post was as a tutor for a son of Thomas Howard, the influential third duke of Norfolk. Possibly through this position or through work representing Cambridge University, Cardinal Thomas Wolsey, the lord chancellor and the king's chief minister, noticed Gardiner's talents and made him his secretary in late 1524. This appointment marked the beginning of Gardiner's career as a clerical statesman.

LIFE'S WORK
Gardiner's first two years in Wolsey's service were quiet and unremarkable, but in 1527 that changed. From that point onward, Wolsey began using Gardiner as a diplo-

mat on three lengthy missions during 1527, 1528, and 1529 to secure Henry VIII's wish for an annulment of his marriage from Catherine of Aragon. When the king's disputed marriage finally came to trial during June and July of 1529, Gardiner served as legal counsel to the king. He performed ably in that capacity and even though the trial ended in failure, a grateful Henry VIII appointed him as his principal secretary on July 28, 1529. This appointment allowed Gardiner to miss the final wreck of his former master Cardinal Wolsey's fortunes in October, 1529.

Initially, Henry VIII's divorce appeared to be a traditional problem in which manipulating the canon law and securing a papal dispensation would secure the desired end. It was a task seemingly well suited to Gardiner's legal training and political skills. As a result, Henry VIII again rewarded his good work in 1531 by making him bishop of Winchester, the second-richest diocese in England. Unfortunately, the diplomatic obstacles that had prevented an annulment persisted. This continuing stalemate left Gardiner powerless to aid the king, since he could envision no solution outside the existing legal and constitutional structures. By the spring of 1532, Gardiner was favoring the abandonment of the quest for an annulment of the royal marriage.

Leadership slipped from Gardiner's hands during 1532 as an activist faction led by Thomas Cromwell came forward. They offered Henry VIII a way out of his marital difficulties by replacing papal control with royal control over the English church. This approach was completely uncongenial to Gardiner, since it involved the reduction of clerical privilege and possessed strong associations with the growing Protestant movement. He defended the clergy's position so vigorously against the Common's Supplication Against the Ordinaries in April, 1532, that Henry VIII was alienated. It was an ill-timed move. Gardiner, previously thought to be next in line for the archbishopric of Canterbury, was passed over. Instead, the vacant office went in 1533 to Thomas Cranmer, a Protestant. Later, in April, 1534, Gardiner lost his principal secretaryship to his archrival Cromwell, also a Protestant.

Gardiner quickly became one of the leaders of the conservative opposition to Protestantism in Henry VIII's court and government. In 1535, he rehabilitated himself with the king by publishing *Episcopi de vera obedientia oratio* (1535; bishop's speech on true obedience), which provided the most convincing intellectual defense of the royal supremacy over the Church of England. Henry VIII rewarded the achievement by making him resident am-

bassador to France, where he stayed from October, 1535, until September, 1538. It was not a particularly satisfying reward, as Gardiner disliked ambassadorial work, and by 1538, Henry VIII and Cromwell were so dissatisfied with his performance that they recalled him.

Returning to England, Gardiner retired to his diocese, where he opposed Cromwell's policies at the local level and his publishing of the Great Bible in English in 1539. Fortunately for him, Henry VIII's basic doctrinal conservatism began to recoil from the increasing Protestant influences over the English church. As a result, Gardiner and the conservatives seized the initiative in Parliament from Cromwell and secured the passage of the doctrinally conservative Act of Six Articles in June. It is highly probable that Gardiner was actually even its author. The conservative offensive continued in the spring of 1540, although at first it appeared that Cromwell might still survive. Yet the incessant and effective sniping of Gardiner and the duke of Norfolk combined with the fiasco of the king's marriage with Anne of Cleves to bring about Cromwell's fall in June, 1540.

Cromwell's fall brought Gardiner little profit except that he replaced his old rival as the chancellor of Cambridge University. Henry VIII quickly sent him off on an embassy to Emperor Charles V at Regensburg from November, 1540, through September, 1541. For the remainder of the reign, Gardiner served the king on various foreign embassies, helped procure supply for the wars against France and Scotland, and aided in the preparation of the conservative doctrinal statement known as the King's Book in 1543. During the spring of 1542, Henry VIII even named him as his chief minister, although he never allowed him to exercise the same authority as Wolsey or Cromwell. It was Gardiner's misfortune that Henry VIII found him to be talented but overly aggressive and therefore contrived to keep him out of the center of power for the remainder of his reign and afterward.

Henry VIII's will barred Gardiner from the regency council of Edward VI. Instead, power rested with Edward Seymour, the young king's uncle and the soon-to-be duke of Somerset. Protestants now controlled the government although Gardiner doggedly resisted their reforms of the Church of England. The problems began when Archbishop Thomas Cranmer issued a set of reformed injunctions for the Church and his *Book of Homilies* in August, 1547. Gardiner protested and quickly found himself either imprisoned in Fleet Prison or under house arrest from September, 1547, through February, 1548. The reformers released him from house arrest for several months in the spring of 1548 when they thought

A drawing by George Cruikshank, which depicts Bishop Gardiner (sitting, center left) in conference with Lady Jane Grey at Beauchamp Tower. (Hulton\Archive by Getty Images)

they had converted him to their cause. Yet they did not trust him. Gardiner publicly proclaimed his adherence to traditional Catholic doctrines during a sermon he delivered at Paul's Cross in London on June 29, 1548. The next day, he was placed under close confinement in the Tower of London, a sentence that lasted until August, 1553, after Edward VI's death.

The Edwardian Protestants had decided to try the stubborn Gardiner in December, 1550, since his continued imprisonment without trial was highly illegal. Although he escaped condemnation for treason, the trial deprived him of the bishopric of Winchester and continued his imprisonment. Sometime earlier he had also lost the mastership of his beloved Trinity Hall. Throughout this ordeal, he retained a sense of optimism, which was repaid when the sickly Edward VI died on July 6, 1553.

With Queen Mary I on the throne, Gardiner soon returned to the center of power. Released from the Tower in August, 1553, he reclaimed his diocese of Winchester,

the mastership of Trinity Hall, and the chancellorship of Cambridge University. Furthermore, Mary appointed him as lord chancellor on August 23, 1553. During the first Parliament of Mary's reign, Gardiner helped to secure the repeal of the Edwardian Protestant statutes but failed to obtain a revival of the medieval heresy laws. More successfully, he began recruiting the faithful bench of Catholic bishops for the Marian church that proved so effective and later fiercely resisted the Elizabethan regime in a way unheard of from their Henrician predecessors.

Gardiner quickly discovered the limits of his new authority. Queen Mary decided to marry Philip II of Spain although her lord chancellor and subjects favored a native English aristocrat. Still, Gardiner swallowed his pride and married the couple at Winchester Cathedral during November, 1554. The next month, Parliament reenacted the old heresy laws, making a systematic persecution of Protestants possible. Gardiner had already vengefully begun arresting available Protestant leaders such as Cranmer, Hugh Latimer, and Nicholas Ridley for treason that autumn. Then, in January, 1555, he tried and condemned to burning five prisoners in the Tower. His hope was that the example of a few burnings would break the Protestants' will to resist. That expectation quickly ended when he discovered that the burnings were instead creating revered martyrs. With that realization, he tried unsuccessfully to persuade Queen Mary and the new archbishop of Canterbury, Reginald Pole, to abandon persecution. Yet time was running out for Gardiner. Overexertion brought on attacks of edema and jaundice in September. Instead of seeking rest, the chancellor continued to labor for his queen. As a result, his condition continued to worsen, and he died on November 12, 1555, at Whitehall Palace in London.

SIGNIFICANCE

Gardiner was the last of a dying breed of English clerical statesmen. He stood as a defender of clerical privilege and attempted to preserve traditional Roman Catholic doctrine just when the course of events was moving the English church into the Protestant camp. Within a mere three years of his passing, the death of Queen Mary would completely undo the restoration of England's obedience to the Papacy that he had helped to bring about. In spite of his great gifts as a scholar, a churchman, an administrator, and a leader of men, he left little legacy except for a somewhat overblown reputation as a reactionary and persecuting Catholic prelate. Few English churchmen would ever again achieve the power and authority in the state that Gardiner exercised.

—Ronald H. Fritze

FURTHER READING

Dickens, A. G. *The English Reformation*. 2d ed. University Park: Pennsylvania State University Press, 1991. The best one-volume survey of the subject, Dickens's work covers the period from late medieval England through the beginning of Elizabeth I's reign and places Gardiner in the context of the religious struggle taking place around him.

Elton, G. R. *Reform and Reformation: England, 1509-1558*. Cambridge, Mass.: Harvard University Press, 1977. The research of this excellent survey places Gardiner firmly in the context of his own times. Interprets events in the light of the author's "Tudor Revolution" thesis, which emphasizes the ideological and religious antagonisms between Gardiner and Cromwell. The author is somewhat hostile to Gardiner.

Gardiner, Stephen. *The Letters of Stephen Gardiner.*

Edited by James A. Muller. Reprint. Westport, Conn.: Greenwood Press, 1970. Reprints 175 letters with annotations and headnotes. An excellent source that includes a biographical sketch, a chronological outline, and a bibliographical essay on the state of Gardiner studies at that time.

_____. *A Machiavellian Treatise*. Edited by Peter Samuel Donaldson. Cambridge, England: Cambridge University Press, 1975. An edition of Gardiner's previously unprinted and unstudied last-known political treatise, which gave his advice to Philip of Spain on the proper way to rule England. Donaldson asserts that Gardiner's opposition to the Spanish match was a negotiating strategy, not a manifestation of a rigid and myopic nationalism. The authenticity and significance of this work remain somewhat controversial.

_____. *Obedience in Church and State: Three Political Tracts by Stephen Gardiner*. Edited by Pierre Janelle. Reprint. New York: Greenwood Press, 1968. A scholarly edition and translation with a lengthy introduction of Gardiner's *Episcopi de vera obedientia oratio* and two unpublished tracts concerning the execution of bishop John Fisher and a view of obedience to the law in contrast to the views of Martin Bucer. Shows Gardiner's development as a supporter of Henry VIII's royal supremacy over the English church but tempered by an increasing firm support of traditional doctrine.

Jelsma, Auke. *Frontiers of the Reformation: Dissidence and Orthodoxy in Sixteenth-Century Europe*. Brookfield, Vt.: Ashgate, 1998. This study of outcasts and outsiders on the fringes of the Reformation includes a chapter on Gardiner and Protestant spirituality. Bibliographic references and index.

Loades, D. M. *The Reign of Mary Tudor: Politics, Governments, and Religion in England, 1553-1558*. New York: St. Martin's Press, 1979. A contemporary study of this troubled period in English history by a leading expert. Loades places Gardiner in his period of greatest triumph and death.

MacCulloch, Diarmaid. *Thomas Cranmer: A Life*. New Haven, Conn.: Yale University Press, 1996. Includes an appendix detailing the household and familial connections between Gardiner and Cranmer.

Muller, James A. *Stephen Gardiner and the Tudor Reaction*. Reprint. New York: Octagon Books, 1970. Dated but still useful biography. It is sympathetic to Gardiner and should always be compared to the relevant account of events presented in Dickens, Elton, or Loades.

Redworth, Glyn. *In Defence of the Church Catholic: The Life of Stephen Gardiner.* Cambridge, Mass.: B. Blackwell, 1990. Biography detailing Gardiner's battle to prevent the spread of Protestantism. Includes bibliographic references and index.

SEE ALSO: Anne of Cleves; Anne Boleyn; Martin Bucer; Catherine of Aragon; Charles V; Thomas Cranmer; Thomas Cromwell; Edward VI; Saint John Fisher; Henry VIII; Hugh Latimer; Mary I; Philip II; Nicholas Ridley; First Duke of Somerset; Cardinal Thomas Wolsey.

RELATED ARTICLES in *Great Events from History: The Renaissance & Early Modern Era, 1454-1600:* May, 1539: Six Articles of Henry VIII; January 25-February 7, 1554: Wyatt's Rebellion.

ALBERICO GENTILI
Italian legal scholar and politician

Gentili brought the study of international law into modern times by arguing that all the states of Europe belonged to one community of law, by applying the principles of morality to international law and particularly to war, and by separating international law from its religious basis and placing it instead on a basis of practicality.

BORN: January 14, 1552; Castello di San Ginesio, Ancona, Papal States (now in Italy)
DIED: June 19, 1608; London, England
ALSO KNOWN AS: Albericus Gentilis
AREAS OF ACHIEVEMENT: Law, government and politics

EARLY LIFE

Alberico Gentili (ahl-BEHR-ee-koh gehn-TEE-lee) was born in an ancient town in the march of Ancona in the Apennines facing the Adriatic Sea. One of seven children born to Matteo, a physician, and Lucretia, Alberico was educated in law at the University of Perugia, where one of the most celebrated teachers was Rinaldo Rodolfini. Shortly after being graduated on September 22, 1572, with a doctor's degree in civil law, Alberico was elected a judge at Ascoli and then in 1575 elected to the office of advocate in San Ginesio.

In 1579, the family was broken up by Matteo's and Alberico's religious tendencies toward Protestantism and their flight in order to escape the Inquisition, with the youngest son, Scipio, to Laibach in Carniola, Austria, where Protestantism was still tolerated. Unwilling to leave, Lucretia stayed behind with the remainder of her children. Thereafter, an additional split in the family occurred when Matteo, remaining for a time in Laibach, sent Alberico to England and Scipio to universities in Germany and the Low Countries. Not long afterward, finding that Austrian policy toward Protestantism was changing, Matteo followed his son to England and died there in 1602. Scipio eventually found fame as a scholar, poet, jurist, and professor of law at Altdorf, where he died in 1616.

LIFE'S WORK

Reaching England in August of 1580, after brief stays in Tübingen and Heidelberg, Alberico Gentili met, through the small congregation of Italian Protestants in London, a number of distinguished people, including Robert Dudley, earl of Leicester, who had been chancellor of the University of Oxford since 1564. From Dudley, Gentili obtained a letter of recommendation to the authorities of the university describing Gentili as one who, "being forced to leave his country for religion, is desirous to be incorporated into your University, and to bestow some time in reading and other exercise of his profession there."

Granted small amounts of money for his support, he took up residence in Oxford, receiving his degree on March 6, 1581, and thereupon devoted himself to teaching and writing. His activities in writing were so extensive as to produce until the end of his life at least one book each year, beginning with *De iuris interpretibus dialogi sex* (1582; six dialogues), which was dedicated to the earl of Leicester.

When the Spanish ambassador to England was found plotting against Queen Elizabeth I in 1584, Gentili and John Hotoman were consulted by the Crown as to the course of action to be followed by the English government. Largely on their advice, the ambassador was treated with civility and permitted to leave the country unharmed. Gentili's research into the field of foreign ministries led to the publication of his *De legationibus libri tres* (1585; *Three Books on Embassies*, 1924).

In the autumn of 1586, through the influence of the queen's close adviser Sir Francis Walsingham,

Gentili accompanied Horatio Pallavicino as ambassador to the elector of Saxony in Wittenberg, but returned to England in 1587 to be appointed regius professor at Oxford, on June 8, 1587. The experience in Germany elevated further his interest in international law and led to the publication of his major work: *De iure belli libri tres* (1588-1589; *The Three Books on the Law of War*, 1931), a work in three volumes that appeared again in a thorough revision in 1599. In 1589, he married Hester de Peigni, and the couple eventually had five children.

In the meantime, Gentili's knowledge was being called more and more into service for actual trial work before the courts in London, where he came to reside. He was admitted in 1600 to Gray's Inn (one of England's Inns of Court), leaving his duties at the University of Oxford more frequently to a deputy. In 1605, Gentili was nominated by the Spanish ambassador to England, Don Petrus de Zunica, with permission of King James I, to be advocate to the Spanish embassy of Philip III of Spain and his successors. England was neutral in the struggle then occurring in the Spanish effort to quell the Dutch Protestant revolt, with the result that many cases involving the British merchant marine came before the English Court of Admiralty. Gentili's notes on these cases were collected and published by his brother Scipio in 1613, five years after Gentili's death, under the title *Hispanicae advocationis libri duo* (*The Two Books of the Pleas of a Spanish Advocate*, 1921).

Gentili suffered obscurity in the light of the work of Dutch legal scholar and Humanist Hugo Grotius (1583-1645) until Gentili's achievement was largely uncovered by Thomas E. Holland of the University of Oxford in 1874; much of what is known of Gentili is the result of Holland's original research. Holland encountered two forces in opposition to the resurrection of Gentili's reputation: the first originating in the Roman Catholic Church, which had centuries before placed Gentili's name in the index of heretics whose writings were not to be read, and the second, among the Dutch, who carefully guarded any diminution in the reputation of their compatriot Hugo Grotius. Not until 1877 was a monument to Gentili placed in St. Helen's Church, Bishopsgate, where he was buried, and a new edition of *The Three Books on the Law of War* was published. In 1908, a statue of Gentili was unveiled in his native town.

Of the many books that Gentili wrote, he is best known for *Three Books on Embassies, The Three Books on the Law of War*, and *The Two Books of the Pleas of a Spanish Advocate*. Although he dealt with the practi-

calities of modern life, divorcing his ideas from the mere dogmas of any specific religion, as the basis for his thought, he infused morality into the foundation of international behavior. In this respect, he departed from the concepts of Niccolò Machiavelli's *Il principe* (wr. 1513, pb. 1532; *The Prince*, 1640) in that he viewed good faith, proper behavior among nations, honesty, and respect as the truly effective qualities, whether in war or peace, among the community of nations. Drawing on his scholarship and experience, Gentili, in the first book of *Three Books on Embassies*, gives his definition of legations and their history. The second book discusses the rights and immunities of ambassadors in foreign lands, and the third book discusses the behavior and conduct of ambassadors and ministers to foreign countries.

In Gentili's opinion, war is *publicorum armorum justa contentio* (the community clothed in arms for a just cause). As to the definition of the term "just," Gentili said that justice expresses not only law but also what is from all perspectives righteous, as exemplified by self-defense, the defense of others, necessity, and the vindication of natural and legal rights. He believed in honest diplomacy, even among warring enemies, and eschewed verbal trickery. He approved strategy but not perfidy, for example. He also analyzed the treatment of prisoners of war, the taking of hostages, the burial of the dead after battle, behavior toward noncombatants, and the rights of noncombatants. In *The Two Books of the Pleas of a Spanish Advocate*, Gentili displays his concern for the neutral rights of nonbelligerents. Acting as counsel for Catholic Spain against the Protestant Netherlands, in determining the claimed right of the Netherlands to capture Spanish prizes in English waters, Gentili presented a strong statement of territorial sovereignty, jurisdiction of sovereignties over adjacent seas, and the rights of both belligerents and neutrals.

In his last will, made in London, Gentili expressed the desire that he be buried as closely as possible to his father and that all his unpublished manuscripts, except those referring to the Spanish advocacy, be destroyed, as he considered the remainder of his manuscripts too unfinished to be preserved. The first request was carried out, and he was buried beside his father in the churchyard of St. Helen's, Bishopsgate. The destruction of the manuscripts apparently did not take place, because twenty-eight volumes came into the possession of a book collector in Amsterdam and were thereafter purchased from his successors in 1804 for the Bodleian Library in Oxford, where they remain.

SIGNIFICANCE

Gentili has been heralded as the first knowledgeable author of modern international law and the first clearly to define its subject matter. Francis Bacon insisted on an empirical or inductive method of achieving a true science, as distinct from the deductive, a method that Gentili maintained is the true method of determining international law: that is, to examine the behavior and situation of states, and the changes of society, and, by a process of induction, to modify, cancel, and adjust international law to suit the specific circumstances as newly discovered facts and situations become available.

He conceived of nations as a community of states; he believed in freedom of the seas and in the freedom of intercourse among nations; he insisted that the monarch or leader of a nation exists for the state, not the state for the monarch; and he opposed war generally but recognized that, if war must take place, it must be conducted with honor insofar as war and honor can coexist

In addition to international law, Gentili gave attention in his writings to other controversies of his time, including the limits of sovereign power, the problem of remarriage, the union of England and Scotland, the respective jurisdictions of canon and civil law, and the use of stage plays for the airing of legal and moral questions.

—*Robert M. Spector*

FURTHER READING

Gentili, Alberico. *De iure belli libri tres*. 2 vols. Oxford, England: Clarendon Press, 1933. Reprint. Buffalo, N.Y.: W. S. Hein, 1995. The first volume is a photocopy of the original edition in Latin; the second volume contains the English translation by John C. Rolfe and a superb introduction by Coleman Phillipson. This introduction deals with the precursors of Gentili; the place, life, and works of Gentili; his position in law; and his method and conception of law.

_____. *De legationibus libri tres*. 2 vols. New York: Oxford University Press, 1924. Reprint. New York: Legal Classics Library, 1997. The first volume is a photocopy of the Latin edition of 1594; the second volume contains the translation by Gordon J. Laing, with an introduction by Ernest Nys dealing with a good concise presentation of the life of Gentili.

Grewe, Wilhelm G. *The Epochs of International Law*. Translated by Michael Byers. Rev. ed. New York: Walter de Gruyter, 2000. Survey of international law, epoch by epoch, from the Middle Ages through the end of the twentieth century. Includes illustrations, bibliographic references, and index.

Holland, Thomas Erskine. *Studies in International Law*. Oxford, England: Clarendon Press, 1898. The article on Gentili was delivered at All Souls College, November 7, 1874, and after some additions by Holland, was translated into Italian by Count Aurelio Saffi, thereby reviving both an interest in and a knowledge of Gentili. The first part of the article gives a substantial chronology of Gentili's life; the second part gives an assessment of his work in international law. Includes an appendix with information on the background of the Gentili family, the controversy over the dates of Gentili's birth and death, his will, his published and unpublished writings, and the revived interest in the subject as a result of the lecture.

Meron, Theodor. *War Crimes Law Comes of Age: Essays*. New York: Oxford University Press, 1998. Survey of international law and the history of the concept of war crimes, beginning with the Middle Ages and the Renaissance. Includes bibliographic references and index.

Phillipson, Coleman. "Albericus Gentilis." In *Great Jurists of the World*, edited by Sir John MacDonnell. Vol. 2. Boston: Little, Brown, 1914. Reprint. South Hackensack, N.J.: Rothman Reprints, 1968. Part of the Continental Legal History series. A brief summary of the facts of Gentili's life, with extensive analysis of his three main works.

Simmonds, K. R. "Some English Precursors of Hugo Grotius." *Transactions of the Grotius Society* 43 (1962): 143-157. This is a paper originally read before the Grotius Society on May 1, 1957, dealing with the English precursors of Hugo Grotius in international law, including Gentili. Contains only a brief presentation of Gentili's life and place in the field of international law.

Walker, Thomas Alfred. *A History of the Law of Nations: From the Earliest Times to the Peace of Westphalia, 1648*. Vol. 1. Cambridge, England: Cambridge University Press, 1899. Reprint. Buffalo, N.Y.: W. S. Hein, 1982. Presents a few facts of Gentili's life but is largely concerned with the content of *The Three Books on the Law of War*.

SEE ALSO: Elizabeth I; Niccolò Machiavelli; Francisco de Vitoria.

RELATED ARTICLE in *Great Events from History: The Renaissance & Early Modern Era, 1454-1600*: July-December, 1513: Machiavelli Writes *The Prince*.

CONRAD GESNER
Swiss scholar and historian

Gesner collected, studied, and published the works of earlier literary, medical, and natural history authorities. He also compiled encyclopedic surveys of earlier scholarship in these fields. Equally important, however, was Gesner's extension of knowledge, particularly in the fields of philology and natural history.

BORN: March 26, 1516; Zurich, Swiss Confederation (now in Switzerland)
DIED: December 13, 1565; Zurich
ALSO KNOWN AS: Konrad Gesner
AREAS OF ACHIEVEMENT: Scholarship, medicine, literature, science and technology, philosophy

EARLY LIFE

Conrad Gesner (GEHS-nuhr) was one of many children of Ursus Gesner, a Zurich furrier, and Agathe Frick. His family formed an undistinguished branch of a Swiss family that would become famous for having produced several acclaimed scholars, physicians, and scientists in the sixteenth through eighteenth centuries. Conrad was the godson and protégé of the Swiss Protestant reformer Huldrych Zwingli, and during his early school years he lived with an uncle, a minister, who engendered in him an interest in theology and botany.

First Gesner attended the Carolinum, then he entered a seminary in Zurich. There, in the Humanist tradition, he studied the Latin classics. After the death of both Zwingli and Gesner's father on the battlefield at Kappel in defense of Zwingli's reformed religion in 1531, Gesner left Zurich for Strasbourg. There he expanded his study of the ancient languages by studying Hebrew with Wolfgang Capito at the Strasbourg Academy.

After his interest in theological studies waned, Gesner began to study medicine alongside his studies of ancient languages. Gesner traveled to Bourges and then to Paris for medical studies. In 1535, he returned to Strasbourg, then to Zurich. In Zurich, Gesner married a young girl from a poor family, whose later ill health placed great strain on his meager financial resources. They lived for some time in Basel before moving to Lausanne.

LIFE'S WORK

From 1537 until 1540, Gesner held the first chair of Greek at the Lausanne Academy, after which he resigned his position in Lausanne and moved to Montpellier to continue medical and botanical studies. He received a doctorate in medicine at Basel in 1541. Later that year, Gesner settled in Zurich, where he became the city's chief physician. In Zurich, Gesner also held the chair of philosophy.

In 1552, a serious illness sapped his strength, and his health suffered during the last years of his life. Gesner lived on the edge of poverty, but about this time he was awarded the position of *canonicus* in an attempt to improve his financial situation. In 1555, the Zurich city magistrates appointed Gesner professor of natural history. He held this professorship until his death during an epidemic of the plague in Zurich in 1565. Gesner's scholarship centered on philology, medicine, and natural history. His work in natural history, which interested him most, was in the fields of botany, zoology, paleontology, and crystallography.

Proficient in many languages, Gesner undertook numerous philological and linguistic studies. His most significant contribution in philology is his four-volume *Bibliotheca universalis* (1545-1555; *Conrad Gesner: A Bio-Bibliography*, 1984), a bio-bibliography of all Greek, Latin, and Hebrew writers, ancient to contemporary, known in Gesner's day. Considered the first great annotated bibliography of printed books, it established Gesner's reputation as a philologist and put him in contact with many contemporary scholars. Gesner also published translations and editions of many classical texts. In linguistics, he produced a Greek-Latin dictionary, one of the first studies ever attempted in comparative grammar, in which he cataloged around 130 ancient to contemporary languages and dialects. Gesner also prepared editions and compilations of classical medical texts, as well as publishing original treatises on medical and pharmaceutical topics.

Gesner's observation of plants, a result of his philological work, led to his interest in their medical uses. He collected and read widely in classical botanical works, from which he extracted information for encyclopedic publications such as his *Historia plantarum et vires ex Dioscoride, Paulo Aegineta, Theophrasto, Plinio, et recētioribus Graecis* (1541; the history of plants and their powers from Dioscorides, Paulo Aegineta, Theophrastus, Pliny, and other Greek authors).

Gesner also developed an interest in plants and animals, and, like most sixteenth century botanists, he focused on collecting, describing, and classifying both known and newly discovered plants. Along with other northern botanists, Gesner increased the number and accuracy of available empirical descriptions of plants in several ways. He recorded many original empirical observations, and he provided numerous descriptions of new and little-known plants. For example, his treatise *De tulipa Turcarum* (1561; on the Turkish tulip) was the first descriptive monograph on that plant. One of the leaders of the trend toward realistic illustrations, this botanist himself drew more than fifteen hundred plates for his *Opera botanica* (1751-1771; botanical works), which contained the bulk of his botanical writings. Gesner also encouraged observation of plants by founding a botanical garden and a natural history collection in Zurich.

Gesner is especially noteworthy in this period for the system of botanical classification he developed. Gesner grouped plants according to whether they were flowering or nonflowering and vascular or nonvascular, among other things. On the suggestion of Valerius Cordus, Gesner also chose a plant's organs of generation, the flower and fruit, as the key characteristics by which to classify it. In addition, Gesner first advanced the idea of natural families, and in so doing he moved biological classification toward natural systems. He distinguished different species of a genus and was the first botanist to utilize seeds to establish kinship between otherwise dissimilar plants.

Conrad Gesner. (Smithsonian Institution)

Among Gesner's contributions to zoology can be listed editions of earlier zoological treatises, but his most important accomplishment in this field was the publication of his monumental, five-volume *Historiae animalium* (1551-1587; history of animals). In *Historiae animalium*, Gesner included all animals described by earlier authorities, generally without questioning the real existence of the animal or the validity of the description. He classified members of the animal kingdom according to the Aristotelian scheme, and within each group he arranged individual animals alphabetically by name. For each animal included, Gesner listed all known names, as well as the animal's range and habitat, habits, diet, morphology and anatomy, diseases, usefulness (including medical uses), and role in literature and history. The work is heavily illustrated, containing a woodcut for every animal. Many of the illustrations, drawn by the author himself, are quite novel and show evidence of careful empirical observation.

In Gesner's only publication in the field of paleontology, *De rerum fossilium, lapidum, et gemmarum maximè, figuris et similitudinibus liber* (1565; on the shapes and resemblances of fossils, stones, and gems), Gesner used the term "fossil" to refer to any object dug from the earth. He included extinct vegetable and animal forms, now rightly called fossils, in this group, but he also included minerals, ores, shells, stone axes, pencils, and other debris and artifacts in the same category. Although Gesner did regard some exceptional fossils as petrified animals, for the most part he accepted the traditional theory that they were figures formed in stone by astral influences, by subterranean vapors, or by internal vegetative forces during the growth of the surrounding stone.

In his classification of these objects, Gesner abandoned the medieval alphabetical system. Instead, Gesner divided his fossils into fifteen categories, using the criteria of their geometric shapes or resemblance to a variety of inanimate and living things. Gesner placed crystals in his first category (fossils whose forms are based on geometric concepts) and described them according to the angles they exhibited. His *De rerum fossilium* was the first work on fossils to contain a significant number of illustrations, as well as one of the earliest works to include illustrations of crystals.

SIGNIFICANCE

As a Renaissance Humanist, Gesner placed great value on studying previous scholarly works; in so doing, he accumulated an encyclopedic knowledge of the arts, the sciences, and medicine. Gesner also collected, edited, and published the works of selected literary, medical, and natural history writers, from the Greek and Latin classics to his own day. He is credited with collecting and surveying a vast amount of previous knowledge in encyclopedic publications in philology and natural history. He was one of the earliest and best postmedieval encyclopedists. In philology, his work initiated modern bibliographical studies and earned for him the title "father of bibliography."

Writing just before European biologists were overwhelmed by the deluge of new plant and animal forms from the New World and the microscopic realm, Gesner sought to collect previous knowledge about the living world, and his massive histories of plants and animals are testaments to his industry. Of the few zoological encyclopedias produced in the sixteenth century, Gesner's *Historiae animalium* ranks as the best, and it immediately earned for him an international reputation. Moreover, Gesner made original contributions to the fields of philology, medicine, botany, zoology, and geology. In philology, his research in comparative linguistics was unprecedented.

In extending knowledge, however, Gesner's most important contribution was to natural history. He was among the first early modern authors to question earlier biological accounts and to present firsthand descriptions and illustrations based on his own observation of nature. In botany, Gesner offered improved illustrations and innovative classification schemes. In presenting a scheme of classification according to structure, particularly according to the reproductive organs, Gesner advanced an idea that would later transform the study of botany. Although Gesner exerted little influence on contemporary natural historians, in the eighteenth century the biologist Linnaeus acknowledged his debt to Gesner's focus on floral structures and the nature of seeds in botanical classification. Today the plant family *Gesneriaceae*, composed of about fifteen hundred species of plants, is named in Gesner's honor.

Gesner also contributed to the sweeping changes under way in the fields of zoology and geology in the sixteenth and seventeenth centuries. His *Historiae animalium*, a landmark in the history of zoology, occasionally displays a critical attitude when presenting collected knowledge. The studies of animal physiology and pathology presented there have led some historians to consider Gesner the founder of veterinary science. The *Historiae animalium* is also significant in the history of zoology because it introduced new and accurate descriptions and illustrations of the animal world. So innovative was that zoological work that Georges Cuvier considered

it to be the founding work of modern zoology. Finally, even in his last treatise on fossils, Gesner broke ancient and medieval bonds. His classification and illustrations of fossils set the stage for the development of modern paleontology and crystallography.

—Martha Ellen Webb

FURTHER READING

Adams, Frank Dawson. *The Birth and Development of the Geological Sciences*. Reprint. New York: Dover, 1954. Adams's excellent history of geology includes the best account in English of Gesner's system of fossil classification, two pages of reprinted illustrations of fossils from *De rerum fossilium*, and a brief biography.

Ashworth, William B., Jr. "Emblematic Natural History of the Renaissance." In *Cultures of Natural History*, edited by N. Jardine, J. A. Second, and E. C. Spary. New York: Cambridge University Press, 1996. Essay devoted by Gesner's contribution to natural history. The anthology also contains several other references to Gesner.

Bay, J. Christian. "Conrad Gesner (1516-1565): The Father of Bibliography." *Papers of the Bibliographical Society of America* 10, no. 2 (1916): 53-86. The best existing biography of Gesner in English. Focuses on Gesner's contribution to bibliographic studies and places it within the context of the Humanistic studies of the Reformation. Contains a helpful bibliography of the early editions of Gesner's *Bibliotheca universalis, Historiae animalium*, and supplements to them where applicable.

Berry, Philippa, and Margaret Tudeau-Clayton, eds. *Textures of Renaissance Knowledge*. New York: Manchester University Press, 2003. An examination of the different sorts of knowledge produced and circulated in Renaissance culture and science. Places Gesner's life and work in the larger context of the transformations in what counted as knowledge that occurred during this period. Includes illustrations, bibliographic references, index.

Crombie, A. C. *Science in the Later Middle Ages and Early Modern Times*. Vol. 2 in *Augustine to Galileo*. 2d rev. and enl. ed. Cambridge, Mass.: Harvard University Press, 1979. Offers a general description of Gesner's work in botany, zoology, and paleontology. Gesner is placed within the broader history of these sciences.

Debus, Allen G. *Man and Nature in the Renaissance*. New York: Cambridge University Press, 1978. Debus presents a very good, brief, and somewhat detailed account of Gesner's *Historiae animalium*. Chapter 3, "The Study of Nature in a Changing World," is especially recommended for placing Gesner's scholarship in natural history within the context of Renaissance science.

French, Roger. *Ancients and Moderns in the Medical Sciences: From Hippocrates to Harvey.* Brookfield, Vt.: Ashgate, 2000. A study of the evolution and nature of medical knowledge in the Middle Ages and the Renaissance. Begins with medieval scholars who believed that all authoritative knowledge was to be derived from ancient texts and concludes with the Renaissance insight that knowledge could be gained through direct investigation of the world, rather than merely reading the ancients. Includes bibliographic references and index.

Reed, Karen M. "Renaissance Humanism and Botany." *Annals of Science* 33 (1976): 519-542. This excellent article describes the translating, collecting, and other work of the Renaissance Humanists in botany in the late fifteenth and sixteenth centuries. Reed gives an account of the milieu in which Gesner's work took place.

Topsell, Edward. *The Historie of Foure-Footed Beastes.* New York: Da Capo Press, 1973.

_____. *The Historie of Serpents.* New York: Da Capo Press, 1973. Both of these works are based heavily on Gesner's work. They are recommended reading as primary documents illustrating Gesner's zoological work.

SEE ALSO: Georgius Agricola; Francis Bacon; Pierre Belon; Andrea Cesalpino; Girolamo Fracastoro; Leonhard Fuchs; Rheticus; Joseph Justus Scaliger; Huldrych Zwingli.

RELATED ARTICLE in *Great Events from History: The Renaissance & Early Modern Era, 1454-1600:* c. 1560's: Invention of the "Lead" Pencil.

SIR HUMPHREY GILBERT
English explorer

One of the great Elizabethan explorers, Gilbert annexed Newfoundland and claimed it for the English crown. His efforts inspired the English to continue to explore and colonize the northeastern coast of North America, which also helped launch the British Empire in the west.

BORN: c. 1539; Greenway, Devonshire, England
DIED: September 9, 1583; at sea, near the Azores
ALSO KNOWN AS: Humfrey Gylberte
AREAS OF ACHIEVEMENT: Exploration, geography, government and politics, military, warfare and conquest

EARLY LIFE

Humphrey Gilbert was the third child and second son of Otho Gilbert, a wealthy landowner, and his wife Katherine, the daughter of a Kentish knight. After Otho died in 1547, Katherine Gilbert married Walter Ralegh, another Devonshire landowner. By him she had three children, one of whom would become the famous English courtier, explorer, and poet Sir Walter Ralegh. Although they have been pictured sharing tales of adventure during their boyhood, the age gap between Humphrey and Walter meant that they probably saw little of each other until their adult years.

Humphrey was educated at Eton and then Oxford University, where it is said he focused on military subjects and on navigation. When he was fifteen, he entered the service of Princess Elizabeth, later Queen Elizabeth I. An appointment as page likely had been obtained for Humphrey by his mother's aunt, at one time Elizabeth's governess and then an important member of her court at Hatfield House, Hertfordshire. Gilbert's devotion to Elizabeth became the ruling force of his life, and she never wavered in her appreciation of his loyalty.

After Elizabeth became queen, Gilbert moved to London and lived in one of the Inns of Court. His military career began when he was twenty-three; he joined the English troops sent to hold Havre-de-Grâce, or New Haven, a French seaport town under siege by the Catholics. In 1567, Gilbert was sent to Ireland, where he was ruthless in helping to suppress an uprising. In 1570, he was knighted for his services. Returning to England, Gilbert married Anne Aucher, a Kentish heiress. They would have six sons and one daughter. The following year, Gilbert was elected a member of Parliament, representing Plymouth. In 1572, he again saw military service, commanding a large force of English volunteers sent to aid the Dutch in their revolt against the Spanish and their occupation of the Netherlands. Though he was an adequate military officer, Gilbert came to realize that his real interests lay elsewhere.

LIFE'S WORK

For some time, Gilbert had been interested in a possible water passage through North America to China, and in 1565, he had petitioned the queen for permission to search for such a route. The following year, he completed *A Discourse of a Discoverie for a New Passage to Cataia* (1576). During his stay in Ireland, Gilbert was involved in a project that sought to establish colonies of English Protestants in Ulster and Munster. When that idea did not bear fruit, he turned his attention once again to North America, this time to England's rivalry with Spain.

In 1577, he approached the queen with a plan for taking Spanish-occupied Santo Domingo and Cuba, seizing the numerous foreign fishing vessels that were based in Newfoundland and converting them into privateers, and then using them to intercept silver-laden Spanish ships headed east across the Atlantic.

After this plan failed to win approval at court, Gilbert came up with a proposal that had more success. On June 11, 1578, the queen granted him the right to find and occupy a site for a colony, so long as the land was not already held by Christians. Though Gilbert now

An imaginative depiction of Sir Humphrey Gilbert (center) asserting England's claim on Newfoundland. (F. R. Niglutsch)

had the queen's permission to pursue his dream, he knew that his time was limited, for the charter would expire at the end of six years. Moreover, he would have to raise the considerable sum of money for the expedition; undoubtedly, he intended to recoup his expenses by seizing Spanish ships. The men with his expedition, however, were undisciplined, and many of them were pirates. Provisions were inadequate, and several of the ships that left England on November 18 had to turn back almost immediately because they were unseaworthy. A second attempt in February, 1579, was no more successful than the first. The venture had cost Gilbert most of his fortune.

Gilbert was able to gather enough financial support, though, so that by June 11, 1583, he could again set sail

from Plymouth. Although the expedition began with five ships, one of them, the *Ralegh*, which was owned and commanded by Gilbert's half brother Walter Ralegh, had to turn back almost immediately. The remaining four included the *Delight*, which was the flagship of the general; the *Golden Hind*, owned and commanded by Edward Haies, or Hayes, who would later write the definitive account of the expedition; the *Swallow*; and a small frigate, the *Squirrel*. On August 2, the ships arrived at St. John's, Newfoundland, and on August 5, Gilbert formally claimed Newfoundland for the Crown and proceeded to explore the area, taking mineral samples, which his expert said included silver ore. Since Gilbert had sent the *Swallow* back to England with the sailors who were sick and those who were incorrigible troublemakers, he had just three ships left when he began to move southward along the coast.

On August 29, the *Delight* ran aground and sank. Only fifteen men were rescued; the ore samples and the mineral expert went down with the ship. After this misfortune, it was evident that the two remaining ships should return to England. Edward Haies urged Gilbert to join him on the larger ship for the journey home; however, Gilbert insisted on remaining on the *Squirrel*, which he had found useful for explorations along the coast. On September 9, after the frigate had survived heavy seas, Haies reports seeing Gilbert near the stern of the ship with a book in his hand. Whenever his friends on the *Golden Hind* were near enough to hear him, he would call out "We are as neare to Heaven by sea as by land," which scholars point out is a paraphrase of a passage in Sir Thomas More's *De optimo reipublicae statu, deque nova insula utopia* (1516; better known as *Utopia*; English translation, 1551). Late that night the lights of the *Squirrel* vanished, and the ship disappeared into the ocean.

SIGNIFICANCE

Although Gilbert failed to find a northwest passage to China and did not establish a settlement in North America, he proved to be one of the most important men of his time. His annexation of Newfoundland did more than provide England with a foothold in North America. His expedition also focused attention on the fishing industry, which the English found would be profitable. This prospect for profit supported Gilbert's arguments for establishing colonies on the eastern seaboard. His possible discovery of valuable minerals, reported by the survivors of his final expedition, also convinced England that North America was worth their attention.

Inspired by Gilbert's *Discourse of a Discoverie for a New Passage to Cataia*, several later explorers went in search of the Northwest Passage he believed existed, and though they, too, were unsuccessful, their accounts of a great, rich, unpopulated wilderness that was just waiting to be claimed further stimulated interest in colonizing North America. Not many years after Gilbert's death, his vision would become a reality, with British colonies in place from Newfoundland and Nova Scotia to Maine, Maryland, and Virginia.

Four hundred years after the annexation, a celebration in Gilbert's honor was held at St. John's, Newfoundland. One of those present, a former premier, named Gilbert's

most important achievement: His vision helped launch the British Empire.

—*Rosemary M. Canfield Reisman*

FURTHER READING

Cell, Gillian T. *English Enterprise in Newfoundland, 1577-1660.* Toronto, Canada: University of Toronto Press, 1969. Explains how the efforts of Gilbert and his associates were motivated by England's political and commercial interests.

Gosling, William Gilbert. *The Life of Sir Humphrey Gilbert, England's First Empire Builder.* 1911. Reprint. Westport, Conn.: Greenwood Press, 1970. The standard biography. Illustrated.

Hart, Jonathan. *Representing the New World: The English and French Uses of the Example of Spain.* New York: Palgrave, 2001. Demonstrates how explorers and colonizers such as Gilbert often imitated Spain even as they sought to expel that nation from North America.

Levin, Carole. *The Reign of Elizabeth I.* New York: Palgrave, 2002. Includes a brief but useful account of Gilbert's participation in Elizabeth's attempts to colonize Ireland.

Miller, Shannon. *Invested with Meaning: The Raleigh Circle in the New World.* Philadelphia: University of Pennsylvania Press, 1998. An analysis of the system of patronage. The author's comments on Gilbert's relationships with the queen and with her other clients are particularly revealing.

Morison, Samuel Eliot. *The Northern Voyages, A.D. 500-1600.* Vol. 1 in *The European Discovery of America.* New York: Oxford University Press, 1971. Contains an excellent account of Gilbert's life, his "glorious failure" in Newfoundland, and his influence. Copiously illustrated.

Quinn, David Beers, ed. *The Voyages and Colonising Enterprises of Sir Humphrey Gilbert.* 2 vols. London: Hakluyt Society, 1940. A collection of the documentary sources often quoted by biographers.

SEE ALSO: John Cabot; Sebastian Cabot; Jacques Cartier; John Davis; Elizabeth I; Sir Martin Frobisher; Sir Richard Grenville; Sir Thomas More; Pemisapan; Sir Walter Ralegh.

RELATED ARTICLE in *Great Events from History: The Renaissance & Early Modern Era, 1454-1600:* June 24, 1497-May, 1498: Cabot's Voyages.

WILLIAM GILBERT
English scientist, physician, and philosopher

Gilbert conducted foundational research in magnetism and electricity and is considered to be the father of electricity studies. He wrote one of the first significant scientific books of the scientific revolution in England and set an early example of experimental methods in science.

BORN: May 24, 1544; Colchester, Essex, England
DIED: December 10, 1603; London or Colchester, England
ALSO KNOWN AS: William Gilberd; William Gylberde
AREAS OF ACHIEVEMENT: Science and technology, medicine, philosophy

EARLY LIFE

William Gilbert was born into a middle-class family of rising status in the town of Colchester, about fifty miles northeast of London. His grandfather, William Gilbert of Clare, County Suffolk, was a weaver who rose to prominence as a sewer of the chamber to Henry VIII. One of his nine children, Jerome Gilbert, moved from Clare to Colchester, where he married Elizabeth Coggeshall. Their oldest of five children was William Gilbert of Colchester. After Elizabeth's death, Jerome married Jane Wingfield.

Following grammar school in Colchester, Gilbert entered St. John's College at Cambridge University in May, 1558, where he received his bachelor of arts degree and became a fellow in 1561. He completed his master of arts degree in 1564, was appointed as a mathematical examiner in 1565-1566, received his doctor of medicine degree in 1569, and was elected senior fellow of St. John's College by 1570. Some less substantiated accounts suggest that he also studied at Oxford during some of this time, and that after 1570 he traveled on the Continent, where a doctoral degree in physics might have been conferred on him.

By the early 1570's Gilbert began to practice medicine in London, where he was elected a fellow of the Royal College of Physicians in 1573. He became a prominent physician in London, serving many clients from the English nobility. In 1577, he was granted a coat of arms by Queen Elizabeth I, evidence of his rising social status. Beginning in 1581, he held several important offices in the Royal College over the next two decades, including censor (editor of journal articles), treasurer, and consiliarium (mediator of disputes).

LIFE'S WORK

Although Gilbert was active in the Royal College of Physicians and conducted important medical and pharmaceutical work, his most important contribution came from nearly twenty years of research on magnetism and electricity. He was one of four physicians in the Royal College requested by the Privy Council in 1588 to provide for the health of the men in the Royal Navy. His early investigations were in chemistry, in which he developed habits of precision that served him well in his pioneering research on magnetism. In 1589 the Royal College assigned him the topic philulae for their publication *Pharmacopoeia* on the use of drugs. In both 1589 and 1594 he was listed among the examiners for this book.

In London, Gilbert lived at Wingfield House on St. Peter's Hill, probably inherited from his stepmother. He never married, and he used the house as a laboratory and perhaps as a center for meetings with other scientists and physicians. His work attracted the attention of Queen Elizabeth I, who is said to have given him an unprecedented annual pension to conduct his philosophical studies.

In 1600 he was appointed royal physician to Elizabeth, and after her death on March 24, 1603, he became physician to King James I. Unfortunately, little is known about the details of Gilbert's life in London because the Great Fire of London of 1666 destroyed records of his past. After Gilbert's death, probably from the plague, he left his books, instruments, and other scientific equipment to the library of the Royal College of Physicians. Wingfield House and the buildings of the Royal College and its library were all destroyed in the Great Fire.

Gilbert's most important work was based on his lifetime interest in magnetism. Central to his approach was his rejection of the Aristotelian concept of a corrupt and immobile Earth at the center of perfect rotating celestial spheres carrying the stars and planets in their daily motions across the heavens. Although he did not espouse the new Copernican system with Earth and the other planets revolving around the sun, he did support the idea of a rotating Earth, which makes it unnecessary to require a daily revolution of all the stars and planets around Earth. In magnetism Gilbert saw the possibility of a mechanical explanation for the daily rotation of Earth on its axis.

Gilbert's study of magnetism was revolutionary in its use of experimental methods and laboratory models in establishing conclusions about the nature of terrestrial

William Gilbert. (Library of Congress)

magnetism. The growing interest in navigation and the use of the magnetic compass motivated his work, and consultations with seamen helped to keep it on a practical and experimental level. He rejected the accepted explanation that the magnetic poles of the compass needle lined up with the poles of the celestial sphere, and he set about to demonstrate that Earth itself is a magnet causing the alignment of the compass.

Gilbert used lathe-turned spherical lodestones (naturally occurring magnetic stones), each called a terrella (little earth), to act as models of the earth. He then moved small compasses (*versoria*) over the terrella's surface to show how they aligned with the poles of the magnetic lodestone. His experiments also revealed the "dip" of the compass needle, with an increasing downward (radial) inclination as it was moved toward a pole of the terrella, and its "declination" from exact polar alignments due to irregularities in the terrella's spherical shape. Navigators had observed both of these effects in practice, and Gilbert recognized that they could be used as aids in navigation. He also floated terrellae (plural for terrella) on cork rafts to show their rotational tendencies in magnetic alignments.

In the course of his studies of magnetism, Gilbert initiated the field of electricity studies and gave it its modern name when he tried to distinguish magnetism from electrical phenomena. Since the time of the ancient Greeks, it was known that amber rubbed with cloth would attract bits of straw and other light materials. Gilbert now demonstrated that about thirty different materials, including solidified sulfur, glass, and several semiprecious stones, could exhibit the amber effect when rubbed. He designated these materials "electrics," after the Greek word for amber (*electron*), and other materials as "non-electrics" if they did not respond in this way when rubbed, such as metals. He invented the first electroscope, or *versorium* as he called it, for measuring electric attraction by pivoting an unmagnetized horizontal needle on a vertical post, which would then deflect when approached by rubbed electrics.

SIGNIFICANCE

Gilbert's significance as a scientist, natural philosopher, and theorist is evident in a work published during his lifetime: *De magnete, magneticisque corporibus, et de magno magnete tellure* (1600; *A New Natural Philosophy of the Magnet, Magnetic Bodies, and the Great Terrestrial Magnet*, 1893; better known as *De magnete*). This groundbreaking book was based on nearly two decades of research on magnetism and was published at the pinnacle of his career, a time in which he was appointed royal physician to Queen Elizabeth I.

The book was unusual for its time in its distrust of earlier natural philosophies—especially ancient ones—and its emphasis on experimental methods, preempting themes later developed by his younger court contemporary Francis Bacon. Ironically, the book was criticized by Bacon for its attempt to develop an entire philosophy based on magnetism.

Whereas Gilbert's main influence was in initiating the study of magnetism and electricity, and in providing a pre-Baconian example of the importance of experimental methods, significantly, he also questioned ancient authorities and encouraged a new view of the world and its place in the cosmos. He was considered an even greater scientist after another work of his was published, nearly fifty years after his death, by his younger half brother, William Gilbert of Melford. In *De mundo nostro sublunari philosophia nova* (1651; *New Philosophy of the Sublunary World*), Gilbert was more explicit but still cautious about an annual orbit for the earth around the sun, with the "motive power" of both the earth and the moon being magnetic. Although the idea of magnetic motive power was eventually rejected, it provided a temporary explanation for the earth's motion until the concept of gravitation could be developed further.

—*Joseph L. Spradley*

FURTHER READING

Gilbert, William. *De magnete.* New York: Dover, 1958. This reprint of P. Fleury Mottelay's 1893 translation of *De magnete* (1600) includes a nineteen-page biographical memoir by the translator, unfortunately with some inaccuracies.

Pumfrey, Stephen. "William Gilbert." In *Cambridge Scientific Minds,* edited by Peter Harman and Simon Mitton. New York: Cambridge University Press, 2002. This is the first chapter in a book about Cambridge scientists that has a good discussion of the context and contributions of Gilbert's work.

Roller, Duane, and Duane H. D. Roller. *The Development of the Concept of Electric Charge.* Cambridge, Mass.: Harvard University Press, 1967. The first chapter of this book in the Harvard Case Histories in Experimental Science series describes Gilbert's electrical studies and theories.

Rossi, Paolo. *The Birth of Modern Science.* Malden, Mass.: Blackwell, 2001. Chapter 9, "Magnetic Philosophy," begins with a discussion of Gilbert's work and the development of Gilbert's ideas by other scientists in the seventeenth century.

SEE ALSO: Francis Bacon; Tycho Brahe; Nicolaus Copernicus; Elizabeth I; Girolamo Fracastoro; Paracelsus; Rheticus.

RELATED ARTICLE in *Great Events from History: The Renaissance & Early Modern Era, 1454-1600:* 1600: William Gilbert Publishes *De Magnete.*

GIORGIONE
Italian painter

The Renaissance celebration of the ordinary human being enjoying the pleasures of natural life, depicted not in the great public paintings but in the intimacy of the small canvas suitable for the simple living room, found its painter in Giorgione, the master of the private moment.

BORN: c. 1477; Castelfranco, Republic of Venice (now in Italy)
DIED: 1510; Venice
ALSO KNOWN AS: Giorgio da Castelfranco; Giorgio Barbarelli; Zorzo de Castelfranco
AREA OF ACHIEVEMENT: Art

EARLY LIFE

Giorgione (jyohr-JYOH-neh) is one of the great mysteries of art history. Little is known of his life, early or middle, and there is no late life since he died so young. Of that death, there is some certainty, since comment is made on it in a letter. He was born probably in the Veneto in the small town of Castelfranco, probably of humble parents. He was probably known originally in Venice as Giorgio da Castelfranco, although Giorgio seems to have given way to the Venetian version of the same name, Zorzo.

Given the extent of his career in Venice, it is likely that Giorgione came into the city sometime around 1500 and joined the workshop of Giovanni Bellini. He seems to have established a reputation for himself quickly, and in the decade left to him he established himself not only as a painter but also as a fresco artist, and several fresco facades on buildings throughout the city are supposed to have been painted by him, none of which is extant.

The source for any knowledge of him lies mainly with the painter and historian Giorgio Vasari, who presents a romantic picture of a handsome, diminutive, gregarious man, socially popular and eagerly sought after for his art. Yet Vasari wrote some thirty years or more after Giorgione's death, and there was a tendency in biography at that time to romanticize subjects. Still in existence, however, is a 1507 document in which Giorgione is commissioned to do a painting for the doge's palace; evidence of a quarrel over a fee for a fresco, which was settled by a panel of adjudicators, including Giovanni Bellini, in Giorgione's favor; and a letter announcing his death.

It is likely that Bellini was Giorgione's teacher as well as employer, since much of what would be seen as Giorgione's style can be traced to certain aspects of Bellini's own work. Whatever the facts, Giorgione was busily at work in the middle of the first decade of the sixteenth century. His was a short career, but he was to be mentioned as one of the great painters by Baldassare Castiglione in *Il libro del cortegiano* (1528; *The Book of* the Courtier, 1561), and Marcantonio Michiel, in *Notizia d'opere di disegno* (wr. 1525-1543, pb. 1800), lists sixteen paintings by Giorgione in Venetian collections and numerous fresco commissions. Hardly a handful of these paintings is extant.

LIFE'S WORK

Vasari speaks confidently of Giorgione as one of the best painters in the "modern style," linking him with Leonardo da Vinci, Raphael, Michelangelo, and Correggio. His modernity, however, is somewhat peculiar to himself, and he is best understood as being at once one of the innovators of the early Renaissance style in painting and an individual stylist of peculiar felicities, which made him so popular with Venetian collectors of paintings. His best work is not public; rather, it is private.

Painting during the Middle Ages was, in general, at the service of the church and state, recording high moments in the histories of those two mainstays of medieval society. In the fifteenth century, particularly in the later years, there was an inclination in the social and religious sensibility to put some emphasis on the life of the individual, to see life as not simply a vale of tears leading to eternal salvation or damnation but as a place of some

Giorgione. (Library of Congress)

pleasure in and of itself. This vague tendency to think about life as worth living began tentatively to reveal itself in the arts thematically, tonally, and technically. Bellini, for example, continued to paint Madonnas, but in his later work the modeling of the figures became less dry and stiff, and tended to dwell on the physical beauty of the human subjects with considerable tenderness. Occasionally, Bellini would explore the beauty of the human form even more. His *Toilet of Venus* (1515) is a quite magnificent painting per se; it is a painting clearly in the full flow of Renaissance enthusiasm for the human body and the richness of life at its best.

Two other aspects of Bellini's work had influence on Giorgione. Tonally, Bellini brought to his Madonnas and to his altarpieces a kind of dreamy hush, a low-keyed softness that is perhaps best exemplified in what are called his *sacra conversazione* paintings, in which the Madonna and Child are adored quietly by a combination of contemplative saints and angels playing musical instruments. This "tonality" was taken out of the sacred realm with great success by Giorgione. Giorgione was also indebted to Bellini in part for his landscapes. Bellini used landscapes in the common tradition of the time as backgrounds for his enthroned Madonnas. These works tend to be somewhat stiffly idealized versions of the local landscapes, but they also tend to become softer and more natural as Bellini's career progressed. Giorgione noticed Bellini's idea of the softened natural scene and created his own version of it.

What is immediately apparent in Giorgione's work is how felicitously he adopted the then-new ideas of allowing human feeling and pleasures onto the face of the work of art and how the use of oils and canvas, both relatively new elements in painting at the time, allowed Giorgione much greater ease in expressing himself. Bellini worked mainly in tempera on wood, and he stayed with the wood in his early oils. Yet younger artists such as Giorgione made the double jump to oils and to canvas, which allowed them to escape the dryness of tempera and the stiffness of modeling, and to achieve great subtlety in the use of color.

Giorgione proved to be the master of the new mode of wedding canvas and oil, and he developed the reputation for modeling through color rather than through line, a technique that was to become the touchstone of Venetian art. In a sense, modern art began with Giorgione. The ideas that art could be used for the simple purpose of enriching life by its very presence without necessarily illustrating some historical or religious act of importance and that the artist might make a living providing

GENRE PAINTING: SIXTEENTH CENTURY SNAPSHOTS

Renowned nineteenth century art historian Walter Pater here describes Giorgione's major legacy, genre painting, which depicts scenes from everyday life. Genre painting, distinct from the tradition of painting objects and scenes of religious devotion or historical scenes, shows people from all walks of life but concentrates mostly on ordinary individuals doing ordinary things.

[Giorgione] is the inventor of genre, of those easily movable pictures which serve neither for uses of devotion, nor of allegorical or historic teaching—little groups of real men and women, amid congruous furniture or landscape—morsels of actual life, conversation or music or play, but refined upon or idealised, till they come to seem like glimpses of life from afar. Those spaces of more cunningly blent colour, obediently filling their places, hitherto, in a mere architectural scheme, Giorgione detaches from the wall. He frames them by the hands of some skilful carver, so that people may move them readily and take with them where they go, as one might a poem in manuscript, or a musical instrument, to be used, at will, as a means of self-education, stimulus or solace, coming like an animated presence, into one's cabinet, to enrich the air as with some choice aroma, and, like persons, live with us, for a day or a lifetime. Of all art such as this, art which has played so large a part in men's culture since that time, Giorgione is the initiator.

Source: The Renaissance: Studies in Art and Poetry, by Walter Pater (London: Macmillan, 1910), p. 141.

Giorgione left, however, a group of quite enchanting paintings, almost all of which have a worldwide reputation and at least two of which, the *Concert Champêtre* (if it is his, or partly his) and *The Tempest* (c. 1505), are among the best-known paintings in the world. These paintings seem to say something about life, which, like poetry, is virtually untranslatable into rational concepts. The tender, soft sweetness of the painting, the colors, the posture of the participants, the opulent dreaminess, the hints of symbolism not quite fully formed, and the elegiac pastoral melancholy come together in surprisingly uncluttered masterpieces of very modest size. These qualities are the signature of Giorgione and can be seen to a slightly lesser extent in his altarpiece at Castelfranco and in *The Three Philosophers* (c. 1510) in Vienna. The paintings seem to say something beyond their content, while drawing the viewer to a kind of hypnotic conclusion that whatever the meaning may be matters little in the face of such glorious modeling, rich coloring, and consummate rendering, particularly of the human body. Giorgione did not live long enough to paint anything of a lesser order.

SIGNIFICANCE

What Giorgione did was to free painting from the institutions that had fostered and dominated it through the Middle Ages. That dominance did not diminish immediately, but painters, and to a lesser extent sculptors, were to discover a new market for their work, a market that was to allow them the opportunity to experiment with new themes. Giorgione also helped to educate the public that art was not only a reminder of social, political, and religious responsibilities but also a medium of pure pleasure.

Giorgione's popularity is an indication of the developing Renaissance sensibility. It was one thing for Giorgione to make paintings of simple, intimate moments of innocent encounter; it is the mark of the great artist to meet instinctively that inchoate appetite of society, vaguely struggling to understand its desire to celebrate and enjoy life rather than simply bear it with religious

canvases of modest size, illustrating modest moments of common life, are obvious aspects of Giorgione's career. He seems only occasionally to have done public commissions, and his patrons, so far as is known, were not the most important members of Venetian society. His patrons tended to be people of property but not of particularly imposing reputation or power, as had usually been the case of patrons prior to this time and would continue to be the case in the career of painters such as Titian.

What might have happened had Giorgione lived is another matter. Titian might have begun as Giorgione's pupil, or both painters might have been with Bellini. What is known is that in the early years of his career, Titian, who was slightly younger than Giorgione, was closely associated with him. They often worked together, and, after Giorgione's death, Titian finished some of Giorgione's work. Indeed, they were so similar stylistically that some paintings, including the famous *Concert Champêtre*, are sometimes credited to Giorgione and sometimes to Titian. Whatever the case, Titian went on to an international career, and it is presumable that, given his early reputation, Giorgione might have taken a similar road to wider reputation had he lived.

stoicism. A Giorgione painting, small enough to be hung in a living room, had nothing to do with religion, or history, or politics, or worldly success; it had to do with the beauty of nature and of human beings, and with the sympathetic connections of humanity with landscape. His paintings provided the example of a metaphysical tenderness, which was later pursued by painters such as Antoine Watteau, Jean-Baptiste-Siméon Chardin, and Paul Cézanne. After Giorgione, paintings no longer had to stand for something but could be something, a center for contemplative pleasure by the individual.

It was more than the discovery of the innocent subject that made Giorgione important. He was one of the first and also one of the finest practitioners of oil on canvas, immediately capable of understanding how that combination made painting more lushly bright and how paint, used tonally, could be used as a medium for supple draftsmanship, which would be one of the distinguishing marks of Venetian painting. Art became part of ordinary life, not simply a record of its more glorious moments. With the intimate Giorgione, art entered the home and made way for the modern idea of the artist as the glory of humanity. The artist was to become as important as the art.

—Charles Pullen

FURTHER READING

Anderson, Jaynie. *Giorgione: The Painter of "Poetic Brevity."* New York: Flammarion, 1997. Reassessment of Giorgione based on original research and scholarship, focused on specific themes in the artist's work. Looks at such issues as Giorgione's representation of women and the effects of sixteenth century Venetian patronage on his art. Includes a complete catalogue raisonné and an index.

Beck, James. *Italian Renaissance Painting.* 2d ed. Cologne, Germany: Könemann, 1999. Places Giorgione's contribution in relation to the evolution of artistic practice as it works its way out of the medieval period and into the early stages of the Renaissance. This sensible survey is easily understood. Includes color illustrations, color map, bibliographic references, and index.

Berenson, Bernhard. *The Italian Painters of the Renaissance.* Rev. ed. Ithaca, N.Y.: Cornell University Press, 1980. Berenson, one of the great critics of Italian art, puts Giorgione in the context of Venetian painting and Venetian social history. Includes illustrations and index.

Carter, Paul. *The Lie of the Land.* London: Faber and Faber, 1996. Fascinating, original, and deeply idiosyncratic reading of Giorgione's *Tempest* as an anti-linear, postcolonial countercultural representation of the world. Focuses on the use of reverse perspective in the work. Includes photographic plates, illustrations, facsimile reproductions, map, bibliographic references, and index.

Phillips, Duncan. *The Leadership of Giorgione.* Washington, D.C.: American Federation of Arts, 1937. A charming book, somewhat heavy on speculation, but wide-ranging in the associations it brings to the contemplation of the mystery of Giorgione's career.

Pignati, Terisio. *Giorgione.* Translated by Clovis Whitfield. New York: Phaidon Press, 1971. A scholar's text, dealing briskly, but with confident economy, with Giorgione's life and the canon.

Pignati, Terisio, and Filippo Pedrocco. *Giorgione.* New York: Rizzoli, 1999. Pignati reconsiders his assessment of Giorgione in the light of new scholarship by Anderson. Pedrocco provides an analysis of every painting in the catalog. Makes a potentially controversial assessment of the relationship between Giorgione and Titian. The reproductions of the artist's work are of extremely high quality.

Vasari, Giorgio. *Lives of the Artists.* Translated by George Bull. Baltimore: Penguin Books, 1965. An inexpensive paperback in which the facts of Giorgione's life and art are presented by a near contemporary. Other artists of the time are also represented and form a valuable frame for considering Giorgione.

SEE ALSO: Giovanni Bellini; Baldassare Castiglione; Correggio; Leonardo da Vinci; Michelangelo; Raphael; Tintoretto; Titian; Giorgio Vasari.

RELATED ARTICLES in *Great Events from History: The Renaissance & Early Modern Era, 1454-1600:* c. 1478-1519: Leonardo da Vinci Compiles His Notebooks; 1495-1497: Leonardo da Vinci Paints *The Last Supper*; November 3, 1522-November 17, 1530: Correggio Paints the *Assumption of the Virgin.*

BORIS GODUNOV
Czar of Russia (r. 1598-1605)

Godunov provided a brief period of stability between the harsh rule of Ivan the Terrible and the unsettled period of the Time of Troubles.

BORN: c. 1551; place unknown
DIED: April 23, 1605; Moscow, Russia
ALSO KNOWN AS: Boris Fyodorovich Godunov (given name)
AREA OF ACHIEVEMENT: Government and politics

EARLY LIFE

Boris Fyodorovich Godunov (buhr-YEES FYAHD-uhr-uhv-yihch guh-dew-NAHF) was born about 1551. His father, Fyodor Ivanovich, was a moderate landowner in Kostroma on the Volga River. Most sources claim that the Godunovs were Tatar in origin and could trace their Muscovite service to approximately 1330. At best, Godunov's education was limited. He was superstitious, which was not unusual for his time. Following his father's death, Godunov became connected with his uncle, Dmitri Ivanovich Godunov. Through the association, the younger Godunov became a member of the Oprichnina, which was organized by Ivan the Terrible to restructure Muscovy (modern Moscow) and provide a secret police.

Godunov's career began to advance rapidly in 1570, when he married Maria, the daughter of Grigori Malyuta, a trusted and loyal supporter of Ivan. Thus entrenched at court, Godunov became a constant companion to the czar's sons and a member of Ivan's personal entourage. Ivan selected Godunov's sister, Irina, to be the wife of Fyodor, his second son. This relationship proved beneficial for Godunov when Ivan's death in 1584 brought the feebleminded Fyodor to the throne. Ivan had previously killed his eldest son in a fit of rage.

There was a drastic difference between the court of Ivan the Terrible and the one ruled by Fyodor and Godunov. Ivan's years had been full of violence and death. The court of Fyodor and Godunov was peaceful and quiet. Ever careful to govern jointly in their names, Godunov was the actual ruler. While many of the princely boyars resented the rise of Godunov to power, the English actually called him "Lord Protector" of Muscovy.

LIFE'S WORK

To many, Godunov was a handsome and striking figure. He was average in height. He was outwardly kind and possessed a captivating charm. To those who were of princely origin, he displayed an appropriate degree of subservience. Many contemporaries commented on his concern for the poor and observed that Godunov did not like to see human suffering.

One of Godunov's major achievements was the establishment of the Moscow Patriarchate. Muscovites considered themselves the "Third Rome." To enhance this claim, they demanded that their church be raised to the position of a patriarchate. This dream became possible when Jeremiah II, the Patriarch of Constantinople, came to Muscovy in 1589 to collect alms for the church. Godunov prevailed on him to approve the establishment of a patriarchate for Muscovy. After much consideration, Jeremiah agreed, even allowing the Russian metropolitan Iov to fill the position. The Council of Eastern Churches officially recognized the decision in the spring of 1590.

Perhaps the most significant event in Godunov's career, however, was the death in May, 1591, of the young Dmitry, the son of Ivan by his seventh wife, Maria Nagoi. While the boy's possible claim to the throne was weak since his mother's marriage was uncanonical, he would have been a serious claimant to the throne when Fyodor died without heirs. Godunov immediately appointed a special commission of inquiry to determine what had happened to Dmitry. The official story that emerged was that, while playing a game with friends, the nine-year-old boy suffered an epileptic fit and killed himself with a knife. Some doubted that story.

Another major crisis began to emerge in the late 1590's because of a decline in population in certain areas of Muscovy. In an attempt to keep people on the lands, Godunov issued in 1597 a decree that ordered all peasants who had deserted the lands since 1592 to be returned to their landlords. This limiting of peasant movement greatly aided the establishment of serfdom.

On January 7, 1598, Fyodor died without heirs, which caused much fear in Muscovy. To Muscovites, the end of a dynasty was similar to the end of the world. The czar was considered a godhead, closer to God than even the patriarch. With the end of the dynasty, many believed that God's favor had been withdrawn.

According to church sources, Fyodor appointed his wife, Irina, to be the ruler. She refused the position, desiring to enter the church instead. Some supporters urged her to reign but to allow Godunov to rule as he had done under Fyodor. She refused. Meanwhile, Godunov had retired to a monk's cell to await the outcome. Undoubtedly, Godunov planned his election. He realized that he had

387

to be careful as there were several other possible claimants to the throne. His most serious opponent was Fyodor Nikitich Romanov, from the powerful Romanov family.

The Patriarch Iov and his party came to Godunov and pleaded with him to take the throne. Godunov knew the boyars would accept him only if they could limit the czar's authority. Since he refused any conditions, he told Iov that he would accept the throne if a *zemsky sobor* (assembly of the land) asked him to do so. Iov immediately called an assembly that, according to custom, contained clergy, boyars, gentry, and merchants, to meet in February, 1598. The assembly offered the crown to Godunov, who accepted. The boyar-dominated duma, however, did not like the election.

Godunov had many plans for his reign. To solidify his dynasty, he tried to arrange a European marriage for his daughter, Kseniya. His first attempt was with the exiled Gustavus of Sweden, but this failed. He then attempted to arrange a marriage with Duke Johann, the brother of Christian IV of Denmark. Johann died, however, before a marriage could take place. Realizing that Muscovy needed Western technology, Godunov hired many European doctors, engineers, and military men. Though not formally educated himself, he wanted to establish a university in Moscow. When this idea failed, he sent eighteen students to study in Europe, but none ever returned.

Religious leaders entreat Boris Godunov (right) to accept his election as czar. (Hulton|Archive by Getty Images)

Heavy rains began to fall during the spring of 1601 and continued for ten weeks; the grain could not ripen. In mid-August, severe frosts killed what few crops there were in the fields. Grain stocks were soon exhausted, and by winter the people were starving. Muscovy had entered the period known as the Time of Troubles. Nothing Godunov did seemed to help. He opened many granaries in Muscovy and distributed their contents to the people, and he launched a massive building program to increase employment. Yet people still died. To Muscovites, a famine signified a visitation of God's displeasure, and they worried.

Godunov became paranoid. He was convinced that plots were being hatched against him. He counteracted

with an elaborate system of spies, who performed effectively. Indeed, they discovered a serious plot concerning the young Dmitry, who had supposedly died in 1591. The false Dmitry, as he is portrayed, appeared in Poland claiming to be the real czar of Moscow. While King Sigismund III of Poland refused to grant the pretender any official support, the monarch allowed the false Dmitry to raise money and men. With this and strong support from the Catholic Church, the false Dmitry invaded Muscovy to claim the throne. Godunov asserted that the false Dmitry was really the monk Grigorii Otrepev, who had at one time been in the employ of the powerful Romanov family, Godunov's major continuing opposition.

Godunov continued to fight the invasion, but on April 23, 1605, he died unexpectedly. His sixteen-year-old son, Fyodor, succeeded him, but the false Dmitry seized control of the throne within six weeks. A popular theory concerning Godunov's death is that he had been poisoned at the dinner table. The more likely story is that he died of heart disease, as he had experienced severe troubles with his heart since suffering a stroke in 1604.

SIGNIFICANCE

Godunov stands as a significant figure in the history of Muscovy. Following the rule of the powerful Ivan, who literally reshaped the state in a brutal fashion, Godunov provided a brief period of peace and governmental reorganization. Fyodor was not able to rule effectively; therefore, Godunov was forced to do so. He reestablished respectable relationships with the West, advocating trade and closer contacts. He wanted European technology and European educational standards for his people. One of his most notable accomplishments was the establishment of the patriarchate. Godunov loved power and proved effective at using it.

Despite his accomplishments, Godunov remains a puzzle to contemporary historians. When the Orthodox Church accepted the false Dmitry as the legitimate czar, Godunov became the incarnation of evil, an attempted murderer. Seventeenth and eighteenth century Russian historians apparently accepted the premise that Godunov attempted to have the young boy killed and thus condemned him. The official Russian version was established by a noted Russian historian, N. M. Karamzin, who painted Boris as nothing more than a power-hungry despot who deserved what happened to him. In the West, Godunov is primarily known through a drama written by Alexander Pushkin, who took his position from Karamzin. Another vehicle of knowledge about Godunov comes from the opera composed by Modest Mussorgsky, who was influenced by Pushkin. A historical consensus on Godunov is unlikely.

—*Eric L. Wake*

FURTHER READING

Dunning, Chester S. L. *Russia's First Civil War: The Time of Troubles and the Founding of the Romanov Dynasty*. University Park: Pennsylvania State University Press, 2001. Massive volume covering the Time of Troubles, beginning with Godunov's czarship. Provides post-Marxist analysis of the civil uprisings, claiming that they were struggles between factions of equal rank, rather than initial attempts by serfs to win their freedom. Includes illustrations, maps, bibliographic references, and index.

Emerson, Caryl. *Boris Godunov: Transpositions of a Russian Theme*. Bloomington: Indiana University Press, 1986. Examines Godunov as he has appeared in the different periods of literature. He explains how Godunov has evolved in literature and how various writers treat him. The notes are valuable in gathering bibliographical information.

Emerson, Caryl, and Robert William Oldani. *Modest Musorgsky and Boris Godunov: Myths, Realities, Reconsiderations*. Cambridge, England: Cambridge University Press, 1994. Study of Mussorgsky's opera about Godunov details the history of its reception, as well as the relationship between the myth constructed in the opera and the reality of the historical Godunov.

Grey, Ian. *Boris Godunov: The Tragic Tsar*. New York: Charles Scribner's Sons, 1973. This book tends to be one of the most apologetic books in English on the subject. Grey depicts Godunov as an able, honest, and even humane ruler, whom historians have slandered. In his attempt to explain Godunov in a good light, Grey often loses sight of his subject. Makes good use of most published biographies. Easy to read and has an adequate bibliography.

Perrie, Maureen. *Pretenders and Popular Monarchism in Early Modern Russia: The False Tsars of the Time of Troubles*. New York: Cambridge University Press, 1995. Study of the claims of the impostors to the throne during the Time of Troubles, and the reactions of the populace to their claims. Begins with discussion of Godunov and the false Dmitry. Includes illustrations, maps, bibliographic references, and index.

Platonov, S. F. *Boris Godunov: Tsar of Russia*. Translated by L. Rex Pyles. Gulf Breeze, Fla.: Academic International Press, 1973. Platonov presents a rather colorful account of his subject's life with the aim of restoring Godunov to his proper place in historical scholarship. Provides a satisfactory overview of the subject. Contains a short bibliography from the translation and one from the author which is in Russian.

_____. *The Time of Troubles: A Historical Study of the Internal Crisis and Social Struggle in Sixteenth and Seventeenth Century Moscow*. Translated by John Alexander. Lawrence: University Press of Kansas, 1970. Platonov offers a picture of the entire period of Russian history known as the Time of Troubles. The work has approximately thirty-seven pages on Godunov and is a good, brief account.

Skrynnikov, Ruslan G. *Boris Godunov.* Edited and translated by Hugh F. Graham. Gulf Breeze, Fla.: Academic International Press, 1982. Skrynnikov published several articles on Godunov during the 1970's, and is generally favorable toward him. He disputes the prevailing view that Godunov's family was descended from Tatar nobility and claims that the story was created to make Godunov appear more in the line of royalty. A straightforward account. The bibliography is short and entirely in Russian, as are most of the notes.

Vernadsky, George. *The Tsardom of Moscow, 1547-1682.* Vol. 5 in *A History of Russia.* New Haven, Conn.: Yale University Press, 1969. Vernadsky is a Russian émigré who has written many books on Russian history. Generally, he presents a balanced but brief view of Godunov. Large bibliography for the entire period.

SEE ALSO: Ivan the Terrible.

RELATED ARTICLES in *Great Events from History: The Renaissance & Early Modern Era, 1454-1600:* 1581-1597: Cossacks Seize Sibir; 1584-1613: Russia's Time of Troubles; 1589: Russian Patriarchate Is Established.

EL GRECO
Spanish painter

Adapting principles he learned in Venice and Rome, El Greco achieved a unique artistic style and became Spain's greatest religious artist and one of the world's foremost portrait painters.

BORN: 1541; Candia, Crete
DIED: April 7, 1614; Toledo, Spain
ALSO KNOWN AS: Doménikos Theotokópoulos; Il Greco
AREAS OF ACHIEVEMENT: Art, religion and theology

EARLY LIFE

Of the family of El Greco (ehl GRAY-koh), little is known, except that his father's name was Jorghi and one brother was named Manoussos. Since his knowledge of languages and his wide intellectual interests suggest a good education, El Greco's biographers have assumed that his Greek family belonged to the middle class. During his boyhood, Crete was a center of Byzantine culture and Greek Orthodox religion. Art on the island was primarily church related, depicting saints in the somber manner of orthodox iconography. Intended to inspire devotion, it often featured stereotypical human forms against a dark and undeveloped background. From a surviving document, it is known that by age twenty-five El Greco was a practicing artist.

For unknown reasons, El Greco left Crete, probably in 1567, for Venice, where he continued his study of painting. There he encountered the warm, rich coloration and carefully balanced perspective of the Venetian school. Biographers have surmised that he became a member of Titian's workshop. In Venice, he adopted the nickname

"Il Greco" (the Greek), later changing the article *Il* to the Spanish *El.*

In 1570, El Greco left Venice for Rome, where he came under the influence of the Florentine-Roman school, dominated by the rich artistic legacy of Raphael and Michelangelo. The mannerist influence of Roman painting, which featured elongated human forms, unusual gestures, convoluted and contorted body positions, foreshortening, and half figures, left a lasting impression on El Greco's work. In 1572, he was admitted to the Roman Academy of St. Luke, the painters' guild, a membership that entitled him to artistic patronage and contracts. Among the paintings that remain from his Roman experience are an extraordinary portrait of his patron Giulio Clovio, *Christ Healing the Blind* (1577-1578), and *Purification of the Temple* (c. 1570-1575), an early work that includes a large group of figures.

According to anecdote, El Greco did not thrive in Rome because he made disparaging remarks about Michelangelo, and, while that cannot be confirmed, his later written comments reveal that he thought Michelangelo's work defective in coloration. Among his circle of acquaintances in Rome were two Spanish theologians who later became his patrons, Luis de Castilla and Pedro Chacón, both from Toledo. Sometime during the middle 1570's, he left Rome for Spain, where he hoped to secure patronage and to establish his reputation.

LIFE'S WORK

In 1577, the year of El Greco's arrival, Toledo reflected the culture of Spain following the Council of Trent, an event that inaugurated the Catholic Counter-Reformation. In art, its canons called for religious themes and events to be related closely to human experience and to embody strong and immediate sensory appeal. The Spanish monarch, Philip II, was intent on preserving Spanish power, prestige, and grandeur, and commissions for artists were readily available. Among El Greco's early Spanish paintings, *The Martyrdom of Saint Maurice* (c. 1580) was commissioned by the king for his palace, El Escorial. The painting did not please the royal patron, for he did not regard it as adequately devotional; thereafter, El Greco acquired most of his patronage from Toledo.

Shortly after his arrival in the city, El Greco settled into domestic life. In 1578, his Spanish mistress, Doña Jerónima de las Cuevas, bore his son Jorge Manuel Theotokópoulos, whom he trained as an artist and collaborator. In the Villena Palace, he acquired spacious apartments (twenty-four rooms) and established a workshop employing several assistants. There is some indication that he lived an affluent if not lavish lifestyle. He accumulated a substantial library, largely of classics and Italian literature, and hired musicians to perform during his dinner. His personality was somewhat haughty and contentious, and he often found himself involved in conflicts over the remuneration for his work, which at times resulted in lawsuits.

The workshop and assistants were necessitated by the exigencies of contracts available at the time. The most profitable were for altarpieces, groups of five or six large paintings arranged above and beside the altars of churches and chapels. These paintings required elaborately sculpted bases and frames, and the artist who was prepared to undertake an entire project held an advantage. Contracts were usually specific as to subject, size, and arrangement. Many of El Greco's best-known paintings resulted from such contracts. His masterpiece *The Burial of the Count of Orgaz* (1586), for example, a painting that measures ten by sixteen feet, has never been removed from the Church of Santo Tomé, Toledo.

El Greco's total output is estimated at 285 paintings, although the number attributed to him has ranged upward to 850. A firm figure is not easily ascertained for several reasons. First, he often produced several versions of the same subject, and these can easily be misclassified as copies or imitations. Second, his workshop produced smaller-scale copies of his better-known works for sale to clients, and these can easily be mistaken for originals. Third, paintings by an obscure contemporary, named Doménikos, have been confused with those of El Greco.

Finally, after his death, his associates continued to paint in his style, and some of their paintings have been misattributed to him.

A number of paintings represent portraits of his contemporaries, usually Spanish clergy, gentry, and nobility. El Greco, however, was primarily a religious painter. His normal subjects are Christ and the Holy Family, New Testament scenes, miracles from the New Testament and from the early Christian era, saints, and significant rites. While some are epic in scale, presenting views of heaven, earth, and hell, and including divine, angelic, and human figures, others portray single saints or clergymen.

El Greco considered himself a learned painter as opposed to an artisan; thus, he sought to formulate a theory of painting and to apply it. Spanish artist Francisco Pacheco mentions his writings on painting, sculpture, and architecture, though none exists today. Yet some evidence of El Greco's aesthetic judgment may be gleaned from extant marginalia in books he owned. In practice, he consciously attempted to combine the rich coloration of the Venetian school with the mannerist style of the Florentine-Roman school. These two cultural influences, combined with the canons of religious art of the Counter-Reformation and his iconographic background, represent the dominant influences on his artistic production. Although nothing in El Greco's art is entirely original, the combination of disparate influences creates a strong impression of originality and even of eccentricity.

In exploring the prominent features of his work, one may consider composition, color, and illumination. Except for the early paintings, incorporating architectural forms and views of Toledo, the paintings usually have a shallow background. Distant perspective is interrupted by a wall or draperies, or by the darkened, cloudy sky so prevalent in his work. In general, dimensions are handled aesthetically, not naturalistically, creating within a single painting a combination of flatness and depth.

The focus of most of El Greco's paintings is the human form, whether in portraits or in the epic paintings featuring numerous individuals. The body is often elongated, perhaps the most characteristic feature of his composition, as if to intimate that the character has striven to surpass human limitations. Often, the heads, with gaunt and angular faces, appear too small for the long bodies. Following the mannerist tradition, El Greco often foreshortens some figures, includes half figures that are cut by the edges, and places human forms in curved positions, contributing to a geometric pattern in the painting as a whole. In addition, arms and legs are sometimes positioned at unusual angles, creating effects of imbalance and distortion.

Viewing El Greco's human forms, one is drawn to their faces and hands, their most expressive elements. The hands are sometimes pointing, sometimes clasped, sometimes at rest, but always refined, graceful, and expressive. The faces—usually angular, unlined, and elongated—reveal a limited range of human expression. El Greco's gaunt faces carry a serious cast, accompanied by the appropriate religious emotions. His subjects are grave, restrained, reserved, devout, and penitent. In some paintings, the eyes peer upward toward heaven with a facial expression mingling devotion, fear, and hope. In others, they look directly at the viewer, but somehow past him or her, as if to perceive a spiritual world that remains invisible to others. It may be that the contrast between the extravagant gestures in the paintings and the taut control of the faces represents El Greco's most compelling technique of composition. The restraint and self-control evident in the faces suggest that the individual will has been conquered, and the gestures denote a spiritual significance that transcends time.

A painter whose early experience was with the dark tones of Orthodox iconography must have found the bright colors of the Venetian school highly pleasing. El Greco sought to use a range of colors to enliven religious art, though the bright reds and blues of his early paintings darken during the course of his career. His preferred colors are blue, red, yellow, yellow green, and slate gray, though his use of neutral tones appears to increase with time.

As critics have observed, El Greco's treatment of illumination, like his handling of dimensions, is aesthetic rather than naturalistic. Typically, light from an undetermined source is directed toward the most significant portions of a painting. In *The Trinity* (1577-1579), for example, God the Father embraces the crucified Christ. Christ's body is illuminated from a source to the left and behind the viewer, while, at the same time, light radiates outward from heaven behind the Father's head. At times, El Greco's illumination has the yellowish-green cast of early morning or of light breaking through a darkened, cloudy, windswept sky, creating heightened tones not of the familiar world.

Despite his success as a painter and his many large commissions, El Greco did not attain wealth, though numerous contemporaries praised his genius. He died in Toledo on April 7, 1614, and was interred in the Church of Santo Domingo el Antiguo, which he had decorated.

SIGNIFICANCE

El Greco's mannered style, his unusual handling of illumination, and his intensely religious subjects proved difficult for succeeding ages to appreciate. Because his paintings were not seen outside Spain and because Spain possessed no critical tradition in art, he became a forgotten artist in the rest of Europe. Although El Greco was capable of finely detailed drawing, he was inclined to leave large portions of his paintings indistinct, producing a blurred effect. This tendency is pervasive in the later paintings, especially those dealing with miracles and mystical events. During the late nineteenth century, he was discovered by the French Impressionist Édouard Manet, who saw in El Greco an earlier practitioner of Impressionist aesthetics. Like the Impressionists, and like the expressionists as well, he freely altered reality in order to enhance aesthetic effect.

Once his artistic power became recognized and widely acclaimed, art critics sought to account for him through a number of highly speculative theories: that he was a mystic, that he elongated figures because of astigmatism, or that he was quintessentially Spanish. More systematic and careful scholarship has demonstrated that El Greco derived from his study and experience, largely of Italian painting, the characteristic elements of his art. To be sure, he combined the influences of Italy in an unusual and highly original way and adapted his painting to the Spanish Counter-Reformation. He is now recognized as among some half dozen of the world's greatest portrait painters and as Spain's greatest religious artist.

—*Stanley Archer*

FURTHER READING

Alvarez Lopera, José. *El Greco: Identity and Transformation—Crete, Italy, Spain.* New York: Abbeville, 1999. Catalog of a major European exhibition of the artist's work includes eight essays by major scholars on various aspects of the artist's evolution and the importance of the various cultures in which he worked and evolved.

Brown, Jonathan, ed. *Figures of Thought: El Greco as Interpreter of History, Tradition, and Ideas.* Washington, D.C.: National Gallery of Art, 1982. An illustrated collection of six essays by El Greco scholars. Centers on individual paintings and portraits. The final essay explores the artist's legal entanglements over the remuneration for his works.

Davies, David, ed. *El Greco.* New Haven, Conn.: Yale University Press, 2003. This catalog of a joint exhibition organized by the Metropolitan Museum of Art in

New York and London's National Gallery includes important interpretive and historical essays as well as reproductions and analysis of the specific paintings in the exhibition.

Guinard, Paul. *El Greco*. Translated by James Emmons. Lausanne, Switzerland: Skira, 1956. In this small book with fifty-three high-quality color reproductions, Guinard presents a biographical and critical study attempting to correlate the painter with his milieu. Back matter includes commentary on the artist by six contemporaries, biographical sketches of twenty-five contemporaries, and an annotated bibliography.

Marías, Fernando. *El Greco in Toledo*. London: Scala, 2001. Detailed analysis of El Greco's Toledo paintings, both landscapes and cityscapes. Emphasizes El Greco's originality, not merely in his art but also in his conception of what it meant to be an artist, within a Spanish culture that still considered painters to be craftsmen rather than creative intellectuals. Includes color illustrations, bibliographic references, and index.

Theotocopuli, Domenico [El Greco, pseud.]. *El Greco*. Edited by Léo Bronstein. New York: Harry N. Abrams, 1950. This work offers reproductions in color of approximately forty of El Greco's better-known paintings, with evaluation and analysis. The comments, written for the nonspecialist, emphasize technique and appreciation.

_____. *El Greco*. Edited by Maurice Legendre. New York: Hyperion Press, 1947. Primarily a volume of re-

productions, most in black and white. Offers a brief, interesting, and highly conjectural assessment of the artist's life, work, and philosophy, plus an extended unannotated bibliography.

_____. *El Greco of Toledo*. Boston: Little, Brown, 1982. A catalog of the 1982-1983 international El Greco exhibit. Includes numerous color and black-and-white reproductions and three valuable scholarly essays concerning the history of Toledo, El Greco's career and life, and the altarpieces that he completed.

Wethey, Harold E. *El Greco and His School*. 2 vols. Princeton, N.J.: Princeton University Press, 1962. Applying sound scholarly research, Wethey explores questions of authenticity in an effort to establish El Greco's canon. He describes each painting and provides a complex classification according to subject matter. His biographical account of El Greco places heavy emphasis on the Venetian period. The work is comprehensive, reliable, and highly detailed—indispensable for serious students.

SEE ALSO: Andrea del Sarto; Michelangelo; Philip II; Raphael; Tintoretto; Titian.

RELATED ARTICLES in *Great Events from History: The Renaissance & Early Modern Era, 1454-1600:* December 23, 1534-1540: Parmigianino Paints *Madonna with the Long Neck*; 1563-1584: Construction of the Escorial.

GREGORY XIII
Italian pope (1572-1585)

Gregory XIII, dedicated to the principles of the Catholic Reformation, implemented the decrees of the Council of Trent, which included a reform of the breviary. This led to the most significant achievement of his papacy: the reform of the Julian calendar. He also founded colleges for training priests and opened up meaningful dialogue with Eastern Orthodox patriarchs and non-Christians beyond Europe.

BORN: January 7, 1502; Bologna, Romagna (now in Italy)
DIED: April 10, 1585; Rome, Papal States (now in Italy)
ALSO KNOWN AS: Ugo Buoncompagni (given name)
AREAS OF ACHIEVEMENT: Religion and theology, science and technology, patronage of the arts

EARLY LIFE

Born to a wealthy Bolognese family as Ugo Buoncompagni, Gregory XIII began his career in the legal profession, earning degrees in both civil and canon law at the University of Bologna in 1530. From 1531 to 1539, he taught these disciplines at the University of Bologna, where he counted among his students Saint Carlo Borromeo and Reginald Pole.

By 1540, he was living in Rome, having been appointed by Pope Paul III to be one of the city's two chief civil judges. Paul III later nominated him to serve as one of the jurists during the first phase of the Council of Trent. His legal training continued to be put to good use by Popes Julius III and Paul IV, the former giving him various legal responsibilities within the curia and the latter charging him to investigate the legitimacy of Charles V's successor to the imperial throne, Ferdinand I. Gregory provided a moderate voice during the final sessions of the Council of Trent (concluded in 1563), and soon after his return to Rome, Pius IV appointed him cardinal of Saint Sisto. Also under Pius IV, he was sent to Spain to help resolve issues of heresy. There he met Philip II, who would later support his own election to the Papacy after the death of Pius V in 1572.

LIFE'S WORK

As pope, Gregory chose his name in honor of Gregory the Great, whose feast day fell on March 12, the calendar day that Gregory XIII had been made a cardinal. Soon after his election, Gregory XIII formally pledged to carry out the decrees of the Council of Trent and to quickly appoint councils and commissions to abolish ecclesiastical abuses, complete the Index of Prohibited Books, and reform the calendar, this latter mandate being implicit in the Council of Trent's demand for a revised breviary.

Responsible for implementing the calendar that today bears his name, Gregory XIII is rightfully admired for finally providing a solution to what had been a thorny scientific and theological issue. Ever since the Council of Nicaea of 325 had established that the date of Easter would depend on a formula involving the lunar calendar and the vernal equinox, which at that time was falling on March 21, the relationship between the Julian calendar then in use and the true tropical year was under scrutiny. The Julian calendar year was more than eleven minutes too long, so that by Gregory XIII's papacy, the vernal equinox was falling on March 11, a full ten days earlier than during the Nicene Council. The solution Gregory XIII adopted eventually was to reduce the number of leap days added (by eliminating those that fell on centuries not divisible by 400) and to suppress ten days from the calendar year of 1582. Although Gregory XIII's reform was inspired by liturgical rather than scientific concerns and made no claim to mirror true planetary motion, the resulting calendar was exceptionally accurate and eventually also adopted by non-Catholic nations.

While the reform of the calendar is Gregory XIII's single most noteworthy achievement, it should be viewed, like his emendation of the Roman martyrology, within the larger context of his desire to place the Catholic Church on a more firm historical foundation and, ultimately, to restore the Catholic Church to a position of preeminence in Europe. Most of his other papal acts were addressed to this latter purpose.

Faced with the increasing threat of Protestantism,

Gregory XIII founded and supported colleges in Rome and in other European cities geared toward the training of priests specifically, the first such institution to benefit being the German College in Rome. Many of these colleges were run by the Jesuits, including the most famous and prestigious of them all: the Collegium Romanum, colloquially referred to as the Gregorian University because of an impressive school building Gregory erected in 1567 to expand it. The university was founded in 1551 by Saint Ignatius of Loyola.

Gregory took a less defensive approach with respect to the Eastern churches, where he sought open dialogue with their patriarchs in the hopes of ultimately reuniting them with the Roman church. Although this larger goal did not succeed, he did achieve amicable relations with both the Greek and Russian Orthodox churches so that Catholics in those areas could practice their religion without fear of persecution.

Further abroad, Gregory's Jesuit missionaries arrived in India, China, Japan, Ethiopia, the Philippines, and South America, and it was at the close of his pontificate in 1585 that the first Japanese Christian delegation arrived on European soil. Considering Gregory's interest in time calculation, it is worthy of note that Matteo Ricci, the Jesuit missionary who introduced Christianity into Chinese cities (and who had studied under the chief

Gregory XIII. (Hulton|Archive by Getty Images)

supporter and defender of Gregory's calendar reform, Bavarian mathematician and astronomer Christoph Clavius), enjoyed particular success by offering a European mechanical clock as gift to the Chinese emperor.

At home in Rome, Gregory's politics were more controversial. He employed his legal expertise to long-forgotten property and tax documents in order to confiscate many noble estates. Convinced that pomp and display were necessary images for a strong Catholic Church, he used these funds, combined with more culled from a dwindling papal treasury, to host lavish events, the most noteworthy being the Holy Year of 1575, the most elaborate jubilee to date. The temporary decorations erected for the occasion emphasized the traditional links between Rome and heavenly Jerusalem while his permanent restructuring of the city focused on providing better access to the principal pilgrimage churches, particularly St. John Lateran.

With an eye to material splendor, he initiated the building of the Quirinal Palace in 1574 and commissioned vast pictorial cycles that commemorated his achievements as pope. The Galleria delle Carte Geografiche (gallery of maps) in the Vatican Palace, for example, boasts frescoed maps of the known world of the sixteenth century, framed by sacred narratives, as if in support of Gregory's global missionary activities. The ceiling of the Sala di Costantino, with its dramatic *di sotto in su* image of the Fall of the Pagan Idols-Triumph of Christianity, represents Constantine's official support of Christianity, a theme with deep resonance in Counter-Reformation Italy.

The Tower of the Winds (1578-1585), a structure that rises out of the Vatican Palace, offers a grand celebration of his calendar reform through the depiction of time and space and the incorporation of a gnomon for measuring the year. Finally, the fresco in the Sala Regia, executed at the beginning of his pontificate, illustrates the achievements of earlier popes who had taken the name of Gregory and illustrates two modern narratives: the Battle of Lepanto (1571), when the Turks were definitively driven from the Mediterranean Sea, and the St. Bartholomew's Day Massacre (1572), in which hundreds of French Huguenots (Protestants) were slaughtered. Although most historians claim that Gregory did not possess prior knowledge of this brutal event, the pope has been criticized heavily for celebrating it in Rome after the fact.

SIGNIFICANCE

Gregory XIII was an extremely vigorous pontiff whose indefatigable defense of the decrees of the Council of Trent earned him a measure of immortality.

Founder of numerous educational institutions still in use today, Gregory's most important and lasting achievement was his expeditious implementation of a long overdue reform of the Julian calendar. Although not the scientific triumph one might expect, Gregory's calendar, along with his other liturgical emendations, permitted the Catholic Church to confront other Christian and non-Christian churches from a position of theological strength. In time this calendar, designed to permit a liturgically sound calculation of Easter, became equally important to civil society. Its swift adoption by Catholic countries is a testament to the continued political power of the Papacy in the Counter-Reformation period and of Pope Gregory XIII in particular, while its early and vehement rejection by non-Catholic nations encapsulates the religious strife that still plagued Europe at the close of the sixteenth century.

—*Maia Wellington Gahtan*

FURTHER READING

Courtright, Nicola. *The Papacy and the Art of Reform in Sixteenth-Century Rome: Gregory XIII's Tower of the Winds in the Vatican.* New York: Cambridge University Press, 2003. An in-depth study of one of Gregory's most important artistic commissions, the Tower of the Winds, in the context of his ecclesiastical goals and the artistic scene of Counter-Reformation Rome.

Coyne, G. V., M. A. Hoskin, and O. Pederson, eds. *Gregorian Reform of the Calendar: Proceedings of the Vatican Conference to Commemorate Its Four-Hundredth Anniversary, 1582-1982.* Vatican City: Specola, 1983. A collection of essays on the scientific, technical, theological, and historical issues and outcomes surrounding Gregory's calendar reform, published by the Vatican in commemoration of the event.

Pastor, Ludwig von. *The History of the Popes from the Close of the Middle Ages.* Translated and edited by Ralph Francis Kerr. 34 vols. 5th ed. St. Louis, Mo.: Herder, 1923-1941. Volume 9 is dedicated to Gregory. Still the most comprehensive discussion of his pontificate in English.

SEE ALSO: Vittoria Colonna; Saint Ignatius of Loyola; Orlando di Lasso; Saint Philip Neri; Paul III; Pius V; Sixtus V; Saint Teresa of Ávila.

RELATED ARTICLES in *Great Events from History: The Renaissance & Early Modern Era, 1454-1600:* 1499-c. 1600: Russo-Polish Wars; 1567: Palestrina Publishes the *Pope Marcellus Mass*; February 25, 1570: Pius V Excommunicates Elizabeth I; 1582: Gregory XIII Reforms the Calendar.

SIR RICHARD GRENVILLE
English military leader

Grenville's heroic death in battle against an overwhelming fleet was an inspiration to Elizabethan Englishmen in their war against a powerful Spanish empire.

BORN: c. June 15, 1542; Buckland Abbey?, Devonshire, England

DIED: c. September 3, 1591; at sea, off Flores, the Azores

ALSO KNOWN AS: Sir Richard Greynville

AREAS OF ACHIEVEMENT: Military, warfare and conquest, government and politics

EARLY LIFE

Sir Richard Grenville (GREHN-vil) was born into an old Cornish family of some distinction. The first record of Grenvilles in the west country can be dated to 1145. Grenville's grandfather was a soldier and trusted official under Henry VIII and became one of the richest men in Cornwall. His father, Sir Roger Grenville, commanded the royal ship *Mary Rose* and was tragically drowned when it sank at Portsmouth in July, 1545. His mother, Thomasina Cole, then married Thomas Arundell of Leigh. On the death of his grandfather in 1550, Grenville inherited his substantial property.

Of Grenville's early life and education little is known, but in 1559 he attended the Inner Temple, one of the Inns of Court, rather than going to one of the universities. Late in 1562, he was involved in a brawl in which he killed a man; he had to be pardoned by the queen. Despite the misadventure, it is possible that he was the same Grenville who was elected to Parliament in 1563 for a Cornish borough. By early 1565, after coming into control of his inheritance, he married Mary St. Leger. Their first son, Roger, died at the end of that year, but in 1567 they had a second son, Bernard, who survived to succeed his father.

Both as a result of his temperament and because of the military tradition in which he had been reared, it was inevitable that, after reaching adulthood, Grenville would join the military. In the summer of 1566, leaving his pregnant wife behind, he went off with some of his cousins to Hungary, where he served for a time in the army of Emperor Maximilian II fighting the Turks. By 1568, after a temporary peace had been negotiated, Grenville returned unscathed to England.

In 1569, still restless, Grenville took his family to Ireland, where, working with Warham St. Leger, the cousin of his father-in-law, he hoped to advance his fortunes. At the time, Ireland was regarded as frontier country, wild and savage as the distant New World and ripe for exploitation and colonization. Grenville found himself involved at once in suppressing a serious revolt by the native Irish. By 1570, disappointed in his hopes, Grenville returned to England.

In 1571, and again in 1572, Grenville was elected to Parliament for Cornwall. Up until that point, there was little remarkable about Grenville's life and career. He had done nothing that might not have been expected from any other wealthy gentleman of the age with a restless temperament and a taste for adventure.

LIFE'S WORK

Although in the 1570's Grenville settled into the prescribed pattern for a leading member of the country gentry—serving in Parliament and taking his place as an important figure in the local government of Cornwall as a justice of the peace and deputy lieutenant and, in 1577, sheriff of Cornwall—his great energies found another outlet. The west country, thrusting out into the Atlantic like a long wedge, was the nursery of many of England's boldest seamen, merchants in foreign trade and explorers. From the area came a stream of brave adventurous captains such as Sir John Hawkins and Sir Francis Drake, ready to take risky voyages for profit anywhere in a widening world. For men of greater wealth and social standing—men such as Grenville and his cousins Sir Humphrey Gilbert and Sir Walter Ralegh—there was a larger role to be played: organizing and securing funds for voyages whose exploration of uncharted waters would add to England's territory as well as enrich its projectors. One great hope was that a passage could be discovered around the New World, a route to the wealth of Asia, one not dominated by a rival power. In the 1570's, Gilbert was promoting a search for a northwest passage. Alternatively, Grenville was trying to drum up interest in a southwesterly route around South America. Going by the southwestern route, Englishmen would be trespassing on Spanish claims, but relations with that great empire were already deteriorating. Eventually, Grenville's own plan for a Pacific expedition came to nothing, and it was Drake who first made the striking voyage of circumnavigation for England on the southerly route from 1577 to 1580, raiding the wealth of the virtually undefended Pacific coast of Spanish South America, coming home ballasted with silver.

After Gilbert died in 1583, Ralegh inherited his role as the leading projector of English schemes to explore, settle, and develop the New World. A colony established there offered the prospects both of cheap land and of a base for privateers to raid Spanish commerce. In this effort, Grenville became one of Ralegh's principal supporters and led the first expedition sent out in 1585 to settle Virginia (the same expedition that established the ill-fated Roanoke settlement). It was his first naval command. Having left a party behind to establish a permanent English settlement in North America, Grenville and his small fleet returned home, capturing a rich Spanish merchant ship en route.

At that point, after a decade and a half of steadily worsening relations, England finally became involved in a full-scale war with Spain. Spain's attempts to close its empire to trade with outsiders and to regard interlopers as pirates had long antagonized English commercial interests and led to an undeclared private war, although neither side was eager for an open conflict. The endless flow of gold and silver from a vast empire, however, transformed Spain into the most powerful state in the Western world. Spain had thus replaced France as the principal threat to English security. In Europe, Spain was committed to the suppression of Protestant heresy. In the nearby Netherlands, Spain had been trying since 1568 to put down a rebellion by Protestants. Many in England feared that if Spain succeeded there, England would be next. Queen Elizabeth, although she detested rebellion, agreed and provided aid to the Dutch.

Once war was declared, England had to be prepared to resist a mighty Spanish invasion fleet. Grenville, returning home from his second Virginia voyage, profitably raided the Spanish Azores on the way home. Then, as an experienced soldier, he was busy organizing the land and sea defenses of the west country, the first line of battle if the country were to be invaded by Spain. When the Armada finally came, it was decisively defeated, though the danger was far from over. Grenville's part in the victory was modest. His own fleet of ships, being outfitted for the resupply of Virginia, had been commandeered to support Drake.

With the most pressing fear of invasion over, the war settled in to a stalemate. Long-standing English naval strategy was to recognize the unequal strength of the two sides. It was impossible for England to defeat preponderant Spanish power directly. Spain could be induced to make peace on favorable terms only if the war could be made too costly for them by cutting the supply of gold and silver from the Americas. The most effective way to carry on such a campaign would be to have a naval base on or close to Spain's gold pipeline, either on the Iberian coast or in the Azores, the principal base from which the Spaniards convoyed the incoming treasure fleets to safety.

Furthering this strategy, in 1591, Lord Thomas Howard commanded a small fleet of some sixteen ships to the Azores. Grenville went out in command of the *Revenge*. At the end of August, the English fleet, after many months cruising off the Azores, was caught by surprise by a large Spanish squadron of fifty-three ships. Howard managed to extricate his ships from the action, but Grenville declined to run. The *Revenge*, alone, stood up to the overwhelming power of the Spanish fleet for some fifteen hours while the ship was pounded to pieces. At last, awash with the blood of her crew, and with Grenville himself mortally wounded, the *Revenge* was forced to strike her colors. The dying Grenville was taken aboard the Spanish flagship, where he died within a few days. Of his crew of 150, only 20 survived. Though the destruction of the *Revenge* was the result of Grenville's foolhardy stubbornness, the episode was quickly taken up by the ballad singers and mythmakers. Grenville's heroism in the face of impossible odds became a watchword for Englishmen, and even the Spaniards acknowledged the raw courage and devotion to honor in a gallant, if useless, death.

SIGNIFICANCE

In the main lines of his career, Grenville was a typical important country gentleman, a member of Parliament and participant in local government. What distinguished him from his fellows and put him in the company of the other gentlemen of late Elizabethan England whose lives acquired legendary stature—Ralegh, Drake, and Hawkins—was that he was one of a small number of bold spirits who were prepared to risk life and fortune for the Virginia project. Though the first Virginia effort, in which he played so large a part, failed, the path had been blazed, and in the next generation, the enduring settlement of British North America began in Virginia. If Grenville's role in the Virginia project entitles him to some special attention, his other claim to fame, and the major reason he is remembered after nearly four hundred years, is one bloody day's fighting at sea. For late sixteenth century Englishmen, the defeat of the *Revenge* was like the Battle of Thermopylae, a moral tale about stout courage and fidelity to duty, the willingness to sacrifice all for the love of queen and country. In the exuberant patriotism of Elizabethan England, this was an episode to be cherished, and so it remained the subject of poems and admiring legend. In a more skeptical age, it might be more readily said of Grenville's death that it was magnificent, but it was not war.

—S. J. Stearns

FURTHER READING

Andrews, Kenneth R. *Elizabethan Privateering, 1583-1603*. Cambridge, England: Cambridge University Press, 1964. An authoritative work on privateering in England during the 1585-1603 war with Spain. Provides background on Grenville's activities, with some specific references to him and to his west country associates. A useful bibliography.

_____. *Trade, Plunder, and Settlement: Maritime Enterprise and the Genesis of the British Empire, 1480-1630*. Cambridge, England: Cambridge University Press, 1984. Provides a careful summary of British voyages of exploration and settlement.

Black, J. B. *The Reign of Elizabeth, 1558-1603*. 2d ed. Reprint. New York: Oxford University Press, 1994. A volume in the standard Oxford History of England series, Black's work is still the best general textbook covering the entire Elizabethan period.

Cheyney, Edward P. *History of England from the Defeat of the Armada to the Death of Elizabeth*. 2 vols. London: Longmans, Green, 1914-1926. Reprint. Gloucester, Mass.: Peter Smith, 1967. Despite its age, this work is still the best detailed history of the period 1588 to 1603 and is very helpful on the general context after the defeat of the Armada.

Loades, David. *England's Maritime Empire: Seapower, Commerce, and Policy, 1490-1690*. New York: Longman, 2000. Study of the development of England into a colonial power. Places the settlement of Virginia within the larger context of England's imperial project. Includes maps, bibliographic references, index.

Miller, Lee. *Roanoke: Solving the Mystery of the Lost Colony*. New York: Penguin Books, 2002. Grenville's role in the establishment of the colony is discussed as Miller attempts to determine the real causes of the colonists' disappearance. Includes illustrations, maps, bibliographic references, and index.

Read, Conyers. *Lord Burghley and Queen Elizabeth*. London: Jonathan Cape, 1960. The second volume of a two-volume work. A detailed study of the queen's principal adviser on domestic and foreign issues and therefore a close account of the policy background for Grenville's public career after 1570.

Rowse, A. L. *Sir Richard Grenville of the Revenge*. Reprint. London: Jonathan Cape, 1977. Rowse provides much critical comment and analysis of the sources as well as a thorough background on the west country itself.

Wernham, R. B. *The Making of Elizabethan Foreign Policy, 1558-1603*. Berkeley: University of California Press, 1980. A brief overview, by a leading scholar, of the foreign policy background for Elizabeth's reign. The best concise introduction, with helpful suggestions for additional reading.

Williams, Patrick. *Armada*. Charleston, S.C.: Tempus, 2000. Monograph on the English defeat of the Spanish Armada. Details the causes of the attempted invasion, the battle itself, and its aftermath. Includes illustrations, maps, bibliographic references, and index.

Williamson, J. A. *The Age of Drake*. 5th ed. London: A. & C. Black, 1965. A study by one of the principal researchers in the field of British maritime history during its great age; a classic in that field. Williamson's other writings also are helpful as background. Includes maps, one foldout in color.

SEE ALSO: Thomas Cavendish; John Davis; Sir Francis Drake; Elizabeth I; Sir Martin Frobisher; Sir Humphrey Gilbert; Henry VIII; Pemisapan; Sir Walter Ralegh.

RELATED ARTICLES in *Great Events from History: The Renaissance & Early Modern Era, 1454-1600:* July 4, 1584-1590: Lost Colony of Roanoke; September 14, 1585-July 27, 1586: Drake's Expedition to the West Indies; April, 1587-c. 1600: Anglo-Spanish War.

LADY JANE GREY
Queen of England (r. 1553)

Lady Jane Grey was queen of England for just nine days, but had her reign been more lengthy, as well as fully legal, she would have been England's first ruling queen and most likely a successful monarch.

BORN: October, 1537; Bradgate, Leicestershire, England
DIED: February 12, 1554; London, England
ALSO KNOWN AS: Lady Jane Dudley
AREA OF ACHIEVEMENT: Government and politics

EARLY LIFE

Lady Jane Grey was born to Henry Grey and Frances Brandon, the duke and duchess of Suffolk. Jane's mother was also a distant heir to the throne as the daughter of Henry VIII's sister Mary. Her parents, being Protestant, saw to it that Jane, the eldest of three daughters, had a proper education in the "new religion," as the Protestant faith was called. Jane was an intelligent, learned, clever, and scholarly girl; by the time of her death, she could read six languages, including Greek and Hebrew. She was well versed in the Greek and Roman classics, philosophy, and contemporary religious doctrine, and she early on developed a reputation as a precocious child nearly obsessed with her studies.

Jane's parents, while neither particularly well educated nor overwhelmingly enthusiastic about their eldest daughter's dedication to learning, did not mind sending Jane off to court to study with her cousins, Princess Elizabeth and the future King Edward. Such connections could potentially benefit Jane's parents, for as provincial nobility, they were constantly struggling for political and social influence. These potential political connections could also benefit them in their pursuit of a suitable husband for their daughter.

LIFE'S WORK

Jane's availability and attractiveness as a marriage prospect, along with her religion, made her a pawn in the political power plays of the day. Henry VIII died in early 1547, and the throne passed to his nine-year-old son, Edward VI. The boy's uncle, Edward Seymour, duke of Somerset, became the protector of the realm and regent to the young king. Somerset suggested several times to Jane's parents that a marriage between Edward and Jane would benefit all involved. There was also talk of Jane marrying Somerset's son. Somerset, though, fell from power, primarily due to political maneuvering by John Dudley, duke of Northumberland, and thereafter the Seymours had little to offer.

The issue of religion was one that plagued all the Tudor family monarchs. Henry VIII had split from the Catholic Church in order to divorce his first wife, unwittingly laying the groundwork for the Church of England. Many of his top advisers during his last years were moderate Protestants, as were virtually all Edward's counselors. As the succession stood, should Edward die before having children, the throne of England would pass to Henry's eldest daughter, Mary. This possibility raised the religious issue again, for Mary was Catholic, and many of Edward's advisers, especially Northumberland, were concerned that Mary's accession would result in England's return to Catholicism. The religious differences between Edward's advisers and Mary also virtually guaranteed for the counselors at best the loss of prestige, and at worst perhaps torture or death for their heretical beliefs.

The ill health of the king also became a major concern. Despite his love of outdoor activities, Edward had never been particularly healthy, and his health worsened as he aged. There was growing alarm that Edward's sicknesses could become life threatening, and Northumberland knew his power rested solely with Edward. In 1553, when the young king was fifteen, a cold developed into a more serious lung ailment. Repeated treatments by doctors proved fruitless, and Edward slowly worsened. It was obvious that the boy-king's days were numbered.

Northumberland, understandably worried about his position should Mary succeed her half brother Edward, and perhaps also concerned about the likely return to Catholicism, agonized over possible courses of action. Edward was getting sicker and sicker, and Northumberland decided that Mary had to be excluded somehow from the succession. According to Henry's will, the next successor after Mary was Elizabeth, his daughter with Anne Boleyn. Elizabeth was a Protestant, but Northumberland had little influence over her. Following Elizabeth was Frances Brandon, followed by Lady Jane. If Northumberland could alter the succession to elevate Frances or Jane to the throne, he could continue to exert his considerable influence over the government.

Lady Jane's dedicated Protestantism and her place in the succession made her an attractive pawn. Jane had engaged in theological debates with numerous religious scholars and had even confronted her cousin Mary re-

An engraved depiction of Lady Jane Grey signing her death warrant. (Library of Congress)

garding the sanctity of the Catholic "host." The details of Jane's accession to the throne, however, are fairly complex.

Northumberland had Edward draft a will of his own that precluded his two sisters, Mary and Elizabeth. (Elizabeth was excluded on the pretext that she might marry a foreigner, which the English did not want.) This left Frances as the heir, but Northumberland had her sign away her claim, essentially "abdicating" in favor of her daughter. Lady Jane was thus left as the primary heir. Yet this new succession was far from secure. While it was entirely a monarch's prerogative to change his or her will, and the duty of the kingdom to follow the will's provisions, any change in the succession had also to be approved by Parliament. Thus, despite the fact that Edward's will was a binding legal document and that anyone who refused to carry out its provisions was guilty of treason, the entire will was not legal until approved by Parliament. Anyone who did follow the will, then, was

breaking the law. There is also some uncertainty as to whether Edward himself wrote the new will or whether Northumberland wrote it and simply had the sick king sign it.

Meanwhile, Northumberland had proposed a marriage between his youngest son, Guildford, and Jane. Such a match was an advantageous one for the Greys, and they approved. Jane protested violently; though noble children rarely had any say in their marriages, she pleaded to not be married. Regardless, Jane and Guildford were hastily married on May 25, 1553. Noble weddings tended to be large affairs, but this ceremony was a small and hasty event, with few guests and little joy. At first, the two newlyweds were allowed to stay with their families rather than to live with each other, but Jane's parents later insisted that they stay together, presumably so that Jane could conceive an heir to the throne. With the potential royal couple waiting in the wings, Edward in June formally changed his will; he also declared his two half sisters illegitimate, which effectively removed them from the succession regardless of the will.

Northumberland took the king's will and had Edward's advisers sign it to acknowledge their support for the plan, though few were eager to do so. Since Parliament was not in session, however, Parliament's approval was not likely to come before Edward's death. In place of a legitimate parliamentary approval, Northumberland had as many parliamentarians as he could locate sign the document, thus providing some semblance of legality. Had it been in session, Parliament as a whole would most likely have debated the new will fiercely, since it skipped the two most rightful heirs. Edward VI died on July 6, 1553, and Northumberland quickly pressured remaining advisers to support his plot. On July 9, at Syon House, north of London, Jane was told that she had been declared queen. She was shocked, and at first she refused the crown. It became clear to her, belatedly, that she was simply a pawn.

News spread of Edward's death, and Jane's accession was announced on July 10, but few greeted either announcement with any enthusiasm. Despite the Catholicism of Mary, she was the rightful ruler, and most preferred a legal Catholic queen over an illegal Protestant one. Most of Edward's counselors fled, many going to Mary personally and begging her forgiveness for their parts in the plotting. For her part, Mary remained in hiding for most of Jane's nine-day reign.

While it is not clear whether Jane might have shed the influence of Northumberland and her parents easily had she remained queen, it seems likely that she would have been a successful ruler. She displayed a fiery spirit and courage, and after ascending the throne, she refused to crown Guildford king, instead making him a duke. As an educated and strong-willed woman, she might have had a long, successful life and reign similar to that enjoyed later by Elizabeth. During her brief occupation of the throne, Jane overruled Northumberland on who would lead troops to capture Mary; Dudley wanted Henry Grey to go, but Jane instead ordered her father-in-law to assume command. What little support Jane enjoyed quickly evaporated, however, and exactly nine days after being crowned, she was placed under house arrest as Mary approached London.

Northumberland and Henry Grey were arrested along with Guildford and Northumberland's other sons. Frances Grey begged Mary for forgiveness for her husband, but it appears that no one pleaded for Jane. Instead, Jane wrote a letter to her cousin asking forgiveness and saying that she had been foolish to have even accepted the crown, since she had never wanted to be queen anyway. Mary, who initially showed great compassion, forgave Henry and Jane, though Jane and Guildford were convicted of treason and confined in the Tower of London. Mary even took Jane's two younger sisters into her employ as attendants. Northumberland, despite a last-minute conversion to Catholicism, was beheaded.

Jane may have lived out a long but lonely life in prison had it not been for a rebellion that started in January, 1554, in southern England. Wyatt's Rebellion was essentially an uprising opposed to Mary's planned marriage to Philip of Spain, but some of the rebels called for Jane to be restored to the throne. Foolishly, Henry Grey also participated in the uprising, which failed when the rebels were prevented from entering London. While Jane was certainly not involved in the rebellion, it was clear that as long as she lived, she could be a catalyst for further unrest. The Spanish ambassadors who were in England making marriage arrangements pressured Mary to rid herself of Guildford and Jane, insinuating that Philip would never marry her if they lived. Much like Jane, then, Mary was a victim of circumstance, and she ordered the execution of Jane and Guildford in early February, 1554.

Jane had been unaware of the rebellion and its aftermath, but she was told of her father's involvement and of her impending execution. Mary sent her priest, Doctor Feckenham, to try to reconvert Jane, and though the two engaged in the religious debate that was so characteristic of the young former queen, she remained dedicated to her Protestant faith.

Guildford was executed outside the Tower on February 12; as his body was brought back into the complex, Jane apparently passed the cart on the way to her own death inside the Tower grounds. On the scaffold, Jane delivered a short speech expressing her faith and asking God to forgive her. After tying a scarf around her eyes, kneeling in the straw, and placing her head on the block, Jane was beheaded.

SIGNIFICANCE

Jane's impact on English history is limited. While potentially an excellent ruler, she did not rule with enough support or long enough to make any lasting contribution. Although Jane displayed the characteristics that made the Tudor family popular, such as courage, a dedication to ideals, and a noble bearing, her story remains primarily a romantic but unfortunate addendum to the Tudor-Stuart period.

—Wayne Ackerson

FURTHER READING

Foxe, John. *Foxe's Book of Martyrs*. Edited by Marie Gentert King. Old Tappan, N.J.: Spire Books, 1987. An account of Protestant martyrs written in the late 1500's. Favorably inclined toward Jane and Edward, but a primary source not to be missed.

Geary, Douglas, ed. *The Letters of Lady Jane Grey*. Ilfracombe, England: Arthur Stockwell, 1951. This work includes virtually all the literary remains of Jane, including letters, notes, and the text of her speech on the scaffold. Invaluable primary material.

Luke, Mary. *The Nine Days Queen*. New York: William Morrow, 1986. A well-written, factually sound account of Jane's life and brief rule. Few footnotes, but the most accessible and accurate modern account.

Mathew, David. *Lady Jane Grey: The Setting of the Reign*. London: Eyre Methuen, 1972. Provides a respectable background to the reign of Jane, though it says little about Jane herself.

Nicholls, Mark. *A History of the Modern British Isles, 1529-1603: The Two Kingdoms*. Malden, Mass.: Blackwell, 1999. Survey of sixteenth century British history includes a chapter on Jane Grey and Guildford. Illustrations, maps, bibliographic references, and index.

Plowden, Alison. *Lady Jane Grey and the House of Suffolk*. New York: Franklin Watts, 1986. Delves into the political workings of Jane's family and Northumberland, and is useful in conjunction with other overall texts on Jane.

_____. *Lady Jane Grey: Nine Days Queen*. Stroud, Gloucestershire, England: Sutton, 2003. Biography of Jane, detailing her home life, her relationship to her parents, and the circumstances leading to her coronation, reign, and execution. Includes photographic plates, illustrations, bibliographic references, and index.

Weir, Alison. *The Children of Henry VIII*. New York: Ballantine Books, 1996. Study of Henry VIII's children; of their cousin, Lady Jane; and of the intrigues for the throne in the years following Henry's death. Includes photographic plates, illustrations, bibliographic references, and index.

Wheeler, Elizabeth Darracott. *Ten Remarkable Women of the Tudor Courts and Their Influence in Founding the New World, 1530-1630*. Lewiston, N.Y.: E. Mellen Press, 2000. Study of Jane's impact on the English colonial project in America. Highly unusual in its treatment of Jane as a ruler with actual effects on her country rather than a mere doomed pawn. Includes illustrations, bibliographic references, and index.

SEE ALSO: Anne Boleyn; Edward VI; Henry VIII; Mary I; Philip II; First Duke of Somerset; The Tudor Family.

RELATED ARTICLES in *Great Events from History: The Renaissance & Early Modern Era, 1454-1600:* July, 1553: Coronation of Mary Tudor; January 25-February 7, 1554: Wyatt's Rebellion.

EDMUND GRINDAL
Archibishop of Canterbury (1576-1583)

An important figure in the establishment of the Elizabethan Church of England, Grindal served successively as bishop of London, archbishop of York, and archbishop of Canterbury.

BORN: 1519?; St. Bees, Cumberland, England
DIED: July 6, 1583; Croyden, Surrey, England
AREA OF ACHIEVEMENT: Religion and theology

EARLY LIFE

Edmund Grindal (GRIHN-dehl) was born the son of a poor tenant farmer, William Grindal, in St. Bees, Cumberland, a rural English parish. His birth date of 1519 remains uncertain. He matriculated to Magdalene College, Cambridge, and appears as a scholar of Christ's College in 1536-1537. Grindal took his bachelor of arts degree in 1538 and his master of arts degree in 1540 from Pembroke Hall. After earning a bachelor's degree in divinity in 1549, he served as a proctor and became vice-master of the college under Bishop Nicholas Ridley.

Through the offices of Ridley, Grindal's role extended beyond Cambridge. After becoming bishop of London, Ridley appointed Grindal as one of his chaplains. By 1551, Ridley arranged a precentorship for Grindal at St. Paul's. In quick succession, Grindal became a royal chaplain, a licensed preacher of Canterbury province, and a prebendary of Westminster.

The death of the Protestant king Edward VI in 1553 and the accession of the Catholic queen Mary I halted Grindal's ecclesiastical advancement. While several of his colleagues, including Bishop Ridley, underwent martyrdom under Mary's administration, Grindal chose exile, primarily in Strasbourg. He returned to London on January 15, 1559, the very day of Queen Elizabeth I's coronation.

During his years on the Continent, Grindal was influenced by the German theologian Martin Bucer's advocacy of church discipline. Grindal played a key role in maintaining the unity of the English exile community. He also helped collect and organize the literary remains of English Protestant martyrs, which John Foxe eventually published as the *Actes and Monuments of These Latter and Perillous Dayes* (1563; better known as *Foxe's Book of Martyrs*). Returning to England in 1559, Grindal was well positioned to take on an important role in Queen Elizabeth's efforts to reinstitute the English church.

LIFE'S WORK

On his return to England in 1559, Grindal was named one of the commissioners to review the liturgy, and he served as a disputant at the Westminster conference, which was held to suppress the Catholic clergy. He also was selected to explain the revised prayer book, was appointed as one of the commissioners for the visitation of the clergy, and was made master of Pembroke Hall. Finally, on July 26, 1559, he was elected to the most populous and cumbersome bishopric in the country—that of London. In addition to overseeing the large and troublesome see of London, Grindal would also serve as the superintendent of the churches of "strangers," Reformist Protestant congregations of French, Dutch, Spanish, and other exiles resident in the city.

Initially, however, doubts about the appointment plagued Grindal, since he, as a moderate Reformist, did not approve of the wearing of episcopal vestments or the exchange of the Church's temporal lands for the impropriations of tithes from parishes previously belonging to monasteries. His friend, the theologian Peter Martyr, advised him to accept the position and to work for reform from within the existing church hierarchy, and this is the path that Grindal chose for himself.

During his tenure as bishop of London, Grindal faced two major challenges owing to natural catastrophes: rebuilding St. Paul's Cathedral after a devastating fire in 1561 and maintaining social order during the London plague in 1563. It was a third challenge, however, that tested his religious conscience: that of how to deal with the growing number of nonconformists who threatened the unity of the Elizabethan church. Grindal, a moderate Reformer, did not always agree with the more conserva-

tive archbishop of Canterbury, Matthew Parker. It was thus that Grindal found himself stuck in the middle of the controversy over vestments, which erupted in 1566.

Parker believed that Grindal's patronage of nonconformist clergy, as well as his sympathy for their views, contributed to disorder in church discipline. The controversy was sparked by the efforts of the queen and Parker to enforce the Act of Uniformity of 1559, which required parish clergy to wear the surplice. A significant number of ministers refused to conform to the mandated attire and were either punished or deprived of their positions. Grindal, who believed in the importance of maintaining church discipline, was nonetheless opposed to the idea of enforcing uniformity in matters that he considered indifferent to religious faith. He preferred to make decisions concerning the enforcement of rules of clerical attire on a case by case basis, depending on the collective leanings of individual parishes and clergy.

At the same time, however, he was suspicious of radical Puritans, Anabaptists, and other separatists or schismatics who refused to obey religious authority and threatened the unity of the newly established Elizabethan church. When forced to decide, Grindal, despite his scruples over conformity, sided with the church hierarchy in the enforcement of the dress code.

In 1570, Grindal was temporarily relieved of the controversies in London through his promotion to the position of archbishop of York, where he took on responsibilities more suited to his theological bent: rooting out the material and ceremonial vestiges of Catholicism from the parishes of this large northern province. He focused his energies on improving the quality of the local clergy; ensuring that rood lofts, crosses, and altars were torn down; and that the Edwardian Book of Common Prayer was followed in church services. He may be credited with realizing the Elizabethan Settlement in the north country in meaningful ways and without undue controversy.

Following the death of Matthew Parker, Grindal was once more called on to face Reformist controversies when he was appointed archbishop of Canterbury in 1576. In the opening months of his tenure as archbishop, Grindal busied himself with the reform of various ecclesiastical and spiritual courts, including the Courts of Faculties, Arches, and Audience, and the Prerogative Court of Canterbury. His normal routine of ecclesiastical duties was soon disrupted.

In June, 1576, reports reached the archbishop of disturbances in Northampton and Warwick caused by a deprived Puritan preacher, Eusebius Paget, and a rector of

Warwickshire, John Oxenbridge, during the performance of academic exercises known as "prophesyings." Belying their name, prophesyings did not involve prognostications. Instead, they constituted meetings of local clergy—open to parishioners—in which two or three ministers offered their interpretations of biblical passages in dignified sermons. The collegial meeting often ended with the clergy retiring for private discussion and dinner. The meetings were thought by many to support the continuing theological education of the clergy and to promote collegiality. Although occasional polemical Puritan abuses of this forum had occurred before 1576, the preponderance of clergymen looked on these exercises with favor.

Grindal favored continuing the practice of prophesyings on the grounds that they were necessary to the continuing education of the clergy, but Queen Elizabeth—ever fearful of Puritan nonconformity—demanded that Grindal suppress them throughout the realm. It was at this point that Grindal took the step for which he is most well known in Anglican history. He wrote a six-thousand-word, somewhat tactless letter to the queen explaining his refusal to obey her direct order to suppress the prophesyings, which he believed were necessary to the edification of the clergy. For Grindal, these exercises were in line with God's will for his ministers and his refusal to suppress them was a matter of religious conscience.

Queen Elizabeth was infuriated by Grindal's disobedience and had him sequestered in 1577, with hopes—never fulfilled—of having him deprived of his position. Despite efforts by various court and church officials to bring the two together, the queen and her archbishop were never reconciled. Although never deprived of his position, Grindal was not allowed to present himself at Court for the remainder of his tenure. His freedom of movement was mostly restricted, and he was limited to performing certain routine administrative duties. Thus, from May, 1577, until his death in July, 1583, the Church of England persevered without a fully functioning archbishop. On Grindal's death, Elizabeth was able to appoint a man to the archbishopric—John Whitgift—who sympathized with her strict views on ecclesiastical conformity and the importance of suppressing Puritan resistance.

SIGNIFICANCE

Although unable to promote his Reformist goals as archbishop of Canterbury, Grindal remained a positive figure

for later Reformers and Puritans. They admired his principled conscience and his Reformist stance against the queen's directive, particularly in the light of such successors as Whitgift, Richard Bancroft, and William Laud, whose repression of Puritan views contributed to the turbulent English Civil Wars of the mid-seventeenth century.

As a moderate ecclesiastic who was well connected to international circles of the Protestant Reformation, Edmund Grindal represented the popular mainstream of English Protestantism. Grindal's opposition to the queen on the basis of religious conscience earned him respect among moderate Puritans and Reformers in subsequent decades.

—*Julie Robin Solomon*

FURTHER READING

Brooks, P. N. "The Principle and Practice of Primitive Protestantism in Tudor England: Cranmer, Parker, and Grindal as Chief Pastors, 1535-1577." In *Reformation Principle and Practice: Essays in Honour of Arthur Geoffrey Dickens*, edited by Peter Newman Brooks. London: Scolar Press, 1980. Compares and contrasts the Reformist policy and styles of three Tudor Protestant archbishops of Canterbury.

Collinson, Patrick. *Archbishop Grindal, 1519-1583: The Struggle for a Reformed Church*. Berkeley: University of California Press, 1979. Full-length comprehensive biography of Grindal and his contributions to the formation of the Elizabethan Protestant church. The first full-length work written on the subject since 1710.

Kaufman, Peter Iver. "Prophesying Again." *Church History* 68 (June, 1999): 337-358. An examination of the Elizabethan controversy over prophesying.

Strype, John. *The History of the Life and Acts of the Most Reverend Father in God, Edmund Grindal, the First Bishop of London, and the Second Archbishop of York and Canterbury Successively, in the Reign of Queen Elizabeth*. Oxford, England: Clarendon Press, 1821. Originally published in 1710, this biography was for centuries the definitive work on Grindal.

SEE ALSO: Martin Bucer; Edward VI; Elizabeth I; Mary I; Matthew Parker; Nicholas Ridley.
RELATED ARTICLE in *Great Events from History: The Renaissance & Early Modern Era, 1454-1600:* January 28, 1547-July 6, 1553: Reign of Edward VI.

MATTHIAS GRÜNEWALD
German painter

Grünewald's work was the culmination of the Gothic tradition in German painting while giving evidence of the primacy of individual artistic expression within the tradition of the Italian Renaissance. He employed Gothic principles of expressiveness and Renaissance pictorial conventions, creating a unique style that transcended the limitations of the traditions out of which he worked.

BORN: c. 1475; Würzburg, bishopric of Würzburg (now in Germany)
DIED: August, 1528; Halle, archbishopric of Magdeburg (now in Germany)
ALSO KNOWN AS: Mathis Gothardt
AREA OF ACHIEVEMENT: Art

EARLY LIFE

Matthias Grünewald (MAHT-tee-ahs GREWN-vahlt), a figure of great stature in his own time, appears to have been quickly forgotten after his death. This neglect may be attributed in part to his preference for Gothic expressiveness in a period given over to the aesthetic concerns of the Italian Renaissance. Grünewald's preoccupation with mystical interpretations and paintings that were largely religious was out of place in an increasingly worldly age for which strong, stark religious themes had less and less impact and significance.

Direct knowledge of Grünewald is scant. Besides his extant works, little was left behind by the artist himself that would give a clear picture. Instead, one must rely on secondary sources and documents and letters of the time. Early knowledge of Grünewald arose from the efforts of Joachim von Sandrart, a seventeenth century German artist and historian. Even Sandrart had difficulty in finding information on Grünewald. In the early twentieth century, another German scholar, Heinrich Schmidt, uncovered some of the facts of Grünewald's life. In the 1920's yet another German scholar, W. K. Zulch, wrote the basic modern work on Grünewald, discovering Grünewald's actual surname in the process. There exists no unchallenged portrait of Grünewald, although the painting of Saint Sebastian in Grünewald's Isenheim altarpiece is thought to be a self-portrait. Grünewald is thought to have been born near Würzburg around 1475. Of his early life little is known. The exact place and source of his training are not known, although it is generally believed that Grünewald's general style and coloring reflect the predisposition of artists who worked in the Franconian region along the Main and Rhine Rivers.

LIFE'S WORK

Grünewald's first known work is the Lindenhart altarpiece, dating from 1503. Between 1504 and 1519, he was a resident in Seligenstadt, outside Würzburg. There he is listed as a master with apprentices; he executed paintings, the Basel *Crucifixion* for one, and was court painter to Archbishop Uriel von Gemmingen from 1508 to 1514. During this same period, Grünewald supervised design and repair of various buildings, notably Schloss Aschaffenburg.

In 1514, during a difficult time between Protestant and Catholic factions in Germany, Grünewald became the court painter for Albrecht von Brandenburg. In 1519, Grünewald is believed to have married, although the marriage may not have been a happy one. His wife brought with her a son, Andreas, whom Grünewald adopted. He apparently used his wife's surname, Niethart, occasionally. In 1525, Grünewald left the service of the archbishop under accusations related to his sympathies with the Peasants' War. He was acquitted by the archbishop but did not return to his service. Books he left behind at his death testify to his Protestant/Lutheran sympathies. These included a New Testament, a number of sermons, and pamphlets, all by Martin Luther. In 1526, Grünewald apprenticed his adopted son, Andreas Niethart, to Arnold Rucker, an organ builder, sculptor, and table maker. Grünewald died in August of 1528, while working on a commission for the cities of Magdeburg and Halle in Saxony.

Grünewald treated exclusively religious subjects when he painted. Only a small number of Grünewald's works have survived, and his total output was probably not extensive. Only two of his works bear autograph dates, and these form the basis for a chronology of all his work. These works include the Bindlach altarpiece (1503) and his greatest work, the Isenheim altarpiece (1515). Two other works are dated on the frames, *The Mocking of Christ* (1503) and the Maria Schell altarpiece (1515). All other dates are conjecture, based on historical clues and stylistic evidence. As did his contemporaries Albrecht Dürer, Hans Burgkmair, and Lucas Cranach, the Elder, Grünewald did not conform to the fashions of the time or concede to the ideals of the Italian Renaissance that dominated in matters of taste and style. In his

Matthias Grünewald. (Library of Congress)

gruesome realism and complex iconography, Grünewald remained German and Gothic in his treatment of his subjects. He restricted himself to illustrating the fundamental themes of Christian faith, rendered with a sense of the mystical and the ecstatic.

Grünewald painted the Madonna and saints, but either by conscious intent or out of religious fervor and fascination with the subject—or both—he specialized in painting the Passion of Christ. From the beginning to the end of his career, Grünewald returned time after time to the subject of the Crucifixion, of which four versions are still preserved in galleries in Switzerland, the Netherlands, and West Germany.

Grünewald's work is subjective, the intuitive product of a personal artist who feels his work deeply. Grünewald's work substitutes force and sincerity in place of the Italian Renaissance preference for beauty and elegance. Instead of the concrete depiction of form through the use of descriptive line and chiaroscuro, Grünewald emphasizes the mystical through expressive line and color. While he understood and made use of the Italian Renaissance conventions of perspective and correct proportion, Grünewald saw them as being of lesser value than the spiritual qualities of his work. For the artists of the Italian Renaissance, the new conventions were at least as important as the old values that arguably might be said to have become means to using the new conventions as much as anything else. All the qualities the Italian Renaissance considered important—dignity, repose, symmetry, balance, serenity, perfection—were for Grünewald merely ornamentation, elements not pertinent to his interest in and interpretation of his subject.

Yet Grünewald's work was not merely emotional display. For one thing, he did not portray superficial emotions. The emotive character of his work came from his use of strong dichotomies—real, temporal, and secular versus ideal, eternal, and spiritual—in his interpretation of his subject. The conditions of his figures are symbolic, with emphasis placed on their devotional and spiritual aspects rather than their merely being descriptive and narrative. His subjects are traditional, but his treatment of them is unique, often overwhelming. An excellent example is Grünewald's interpretation of the risen Christ in the Isenheim altarpiece, which makes use of all the above-mentioned dichotomies. One is prepared by one's initial encounter with the excruciating, visceral vision of the painfully crucified Christ on the outside panel of the altarpiece. Then to behold the risen Christ on the inside is to be moved ecstatically.

Grünewald, moved as he had to have been by his desire to express the spirituality of his subject, transcended the limitations of the medium and conventions he employed. One's admiration is inspired not by the artist's mastery of technique, though clearly Grünewald was a superb craftsperson, but by the spiritual impact of his work, which is as real and felt today as it surely had to have been when it was first viewed in the sixteenth century. His figures appear forced and affected in pose and manner, because they are meant to be larger than life—more than mere representations of a historical event. While understanding line and form in realistic representation, Grünewald gives primacy to expression of qualities rather than to accurate depiction of appearances. He did this through his extreme treatments of the human figure, creating the expressiveness of a psychic condition and presenting a spiritual reality as much as a visual image.

SIGNIFICANCE

Grünewald was a Gothic artist with the sensibility of the spirituality of the Middle Ages. A comparison of Grünewald's work and style with the standards of the Italian Renaissance would be a misplaced attempt to understand and appreciate his work. Judged in terms of the Italian Renaissance, Grünewald's work appears repellent, disdainful of form, contemptuous of moderation, and lacking in grace. Judged in terms of an individual's ability to give form and expression to those images central to Western Christian spirituality, Grünewald's work appears poignant, penetrating, and transcendent.

Grünewald was not so much a Gothic artist as he was an artist who recognized that the Gothic era gave best and fullest expression to spirituality. Grünewald did not imitate the Gothic style, but he adopted fully the principles of the Gothic, realizing their timeless nature. Nor did Grünewald refute the ideals of the Italian Renaissance as much as he ignored them, choosing to use only those formal elements useful to his artistic purpose.

—*Donald R. Kelm*

FURTHER READING

Benesch, Otto. *German Painting from Dürer to Holbein.* Translated by H. S. B. Harrison. Geneva, Switzerland: Éditions d'Art Albert Skira, 1966. Based on a series of lectures given by Benesch in 1959 and 1960 at the University of Vienna. Benesch, an eminent scholar, emphasized the Germanic and Gothic aspects of his subjects' work.

Burkhard, Arthur. *Matthias Grünewald: Personality and Accomplishment.* Cambridge, Mass.: Harvard University Press, 1936. Reprint. New York: Hacker Art Books, 1976. The first comprehensive treatment in English of the life and work of Matthias Grünewald. The author's intent is to suggest the aesthetic and personal underpinnings of Grünewald while connecting him closely with his German Gothic heritage. The extensive bibliography cites only German sources.

Cuttler, Charles D. *Northern Painting from Pucelle to Brueghel: Fourteenth, Fifteenth, and Sixteenth Centuries.* New York: Holt, Rinehart and Winston, 1968. A later study of painting of Northern European artists, attempting not only to place them in context with the Italian Renaissance but also to show their own peculiar characteristics and styles. Suggests the social, philosophical, and aesthetic influences of the time.

Hayum, Andrée. *The Isenheim Altarpiece: God's Medicine and the Painter's Vision.* Princeton, N.J.: Princeton University Press, 1997. Book-length analysis of Grünewald's most famous work, places it first in the context of the hospital chapel for which it was made, then in the broader cultural contexts of contemporary religious sermons and emergent print culture. Includes photographic plates, illustrations, bibliographic references, and index.

Mellinkoff, Ruth. *The Devil at Isenheim: Reflections of Popular Belief in Grünewald's Altarpiece.* Berkeley: University of California Press, 1988. A lavishly illustrated iconographic study of the Isenheim altarpiece. Mellinkoff focuses on the panel depicting the Madonna and Child being honored by a concert of angels; in an original and persuasive interpretation, Mellinkoff argues that among the angels is Lucifer himself, shown in the moment of awareness of the folly of his rebellion.

Richter, Gottfried. *The Isenheim Altar: Suffering and Salvation in the Art of Grünewald.* Translated by Donald Maclean. Edinburgh: Floris Books, 1998. Brief but important study of the meaning of the altarpiece to contemporary viewers, for whom sickness and disease were still inexorably linked to sinfulness. Includes color illustrations.

Scheja, Georg. *The Isenheim Altarpiece.* Translated by Robert Erich Wolf. New York: Harry N. Abrams, 1969. An extensive, authoritative discussion of Grünewald's best-known work. The author cites possible visual and literary sources for the work. The extensive footnotes are an excellent second source of information.

Ziermann, Horst, with Erika Beissel. *Matthias Grünewald.* Translated by Joan Clough-Laub. New York: Prestel, 2001. Survey of what little documentary evidence exists of Grünewald's life to construct both a biography and an analysis of his surviving paintings and drawings. Includes illustrations, bibliographic references, index.

SEE ALSO: Hieronymus Bosch; Lucas Cranach, the Elder; Albrecht Dürer; Martin Luther.

RELATED ARTICLE in *Great Events from History: The Renaissance & Early Modern Era, 1454-1600:* June, 1524-July, 1526: German Peasants' War.

GUACANAGARÍ
Taino tribal leader

Guacanagarí befriended Christopher Columbus during his first voyage to the New World. When Columbus returned to Hispaniola and faced difficulties with the Caribbean Indians, Guacanagarí remained loyal, yet the two eventually lost trust in each other.
Guacanagarí is also remembered for his failure to join an alliance of Indian tribes against the Spanish.

BORN: c. middle fifteenth century; Hispaniola (now Haiti and the Dominican Republic)
DIED: c. early sixteenth century; Hispaniola
AREAS OF ACHIEVEMENT: Government and politics, warfare and conquest

EARLY LIFE

Guacanagarí (gwah-kah-nah-gawr-EE) was a cacique (tribal leader) who ruled a Taino cacigazco (chiefdom) on the northern coast of Hispaniola. Archaeologists believe that the Taino, an indigenous people of Hispaniola in the Caribbean, did not have slaves, but they did have social classes, including classes of caciques (tribal leaders), nitainos (nobles), commoners, and naborias (laborers).

Caciques were treated royally, lived in distinguished houses, often had multiple wives, and sometimes spoke through elder intermediaries only. Caciques directed labor in their communities, and when supplies of food accumulated they were in charge of its distribution. The *batey* (ceremonial ball court) was located outside the home of the cacique, and ball games played between different villages had political significance. *Areytos* (ceremonial dances) were also held in the *batey*. Canoes were important to the Taino, and as a cacique, Guacanagarí traveled in the best and largest canoe.

Guacanagarí led a peaceful community dedicated to agriculture, hunting, and fishing. According to some scholars, the peace in Guacanagarí's community was interrupted by attacks from neighboring Caribs. Nevertheless, in general, the Tainos under the leadership of Guacanagarí led a life of sufficiency and cooperation.

LIFE'S WORK

While the main part of Guacanagarí's life was dedicated to leading his community, he is remembered because of his contacts with Christopher Columbus.

During Columbus's first voyage to the New World, he was greeted by a friendly and generous Guacanagarí. In his journal entry for December 22, 1492, Columbus reported that a large canoe with numerous Tainos approached the ship *Santa Maria*, and a representative of Guacanagarí, the principal chieftain of the region, offered gifts, including an ornamental belt and a mask with inlaid gold to denote facial features. Guacanagarí's representative issued an invitation for Columbus to moor his ship near the cacique's village and make a formal visit, but Columbus first sent several men to evaluate the cacique's town. The Spanish visitors were received as distinguished guests, and the visit revealed that the town was orderly and the largest of any encountered during the voyage. The Tainos offered gifts of cotton garments but expected nothing in return. When Columbus and his crew departed, Guacanagarí sent parrots and gold as gifts to the admiral, and tribal members in canoes escorted the visitors to the *Santa Maria*.

Late on December 24, a fatigued Columbus, seeing that the sea was calm, left control of the *Santa Maria* in the hands of its steersman, who, also tired, in turn left a boy in control. Deceptive sea currents soon lodged the *Santa Maria* on a sandbar, and Columbus was unable to set the ship afloat. Notified of Columbus's plight, Guacanagarí sent his people and all the tribe's canoes to unload the ship. The cargo was brought to shore safely and was protected by Guacanagarí's people. Guacanagarí set aside three houses to store the goods and to house the Spaniards.

On December 26, with Columbus on board the *Niña*, Guacanagarí paid a visit to console the admiral. After dining with Columbus, the cacique invited him to visit the chieftain's town, taste indigenous foods, explore the surrounding groves, and witness ceremonial dances and games. After enjoying these displays, Columbus instructed one of his shipmen to display his archery skills and ordered the firing of several cannon shots. Impressed, the Tainos were reassured to learn that Columbus promised to be their ally against any invasions from troublesome Caribs.

Within ten days, and with the assistance of Guacanagarí's people, Columbus's crew converted the materials from the wreck of the *Santa Maria* into a small fort. Columbus made another display of military power for the Tainos, and confident of their cooperation, he left thirty-eight men at the fort, instructing them to behave harmoniously and to stay within Guacanagarí's territory. Columbus set sail for Spain, promising to return with ample reinforcements to the area he named La Navidad.

On November 27, 1493, Columbus returned with numerous ships to the waters near La Navidad, but signals to the fort received no reply. A canoe approached the Spanish ships, and a person who claimed to be the cousin of Guacanagarí met with Columbus. Communications were limited, but Columbus learned that the fort at La Navidad had been destroyed and all the Spaniards who had stayed behind were dead. Guacanagarí, who had fought to resist an attack led by Caonabo, a cacique from the interior, was wounded and was recuperating in a nearby village.

A subsequent inspection of La Navidad confirmed that the report of destruction was accurate. Testimony revealed that the Spaniards who remained on the island argued amongst themselves, abused local women, and wandered into the territory of Caonabo, instigating revenge. A visit to the wounded Guacanagarí confirmed initial reports of the disaster, but some Spaniards doubted the cacique, believing that he was not truly injured and charging that he himself was guilty of treachery.

Columbus, however, retained faith in Guacanagarí and invited the cacique to board his ship. Impressed by the anchored fleet and stunned by the array of domestic animals the Spaniards had on board, especially horses, the cacique reaffirmed his belief that Columbus came from heaven. Columbus also had on board several indigenous women, however, and Guacanagarí took special notice of one of them. Trust between the cacique and the Spaniards weakened, and Guacanagarí returned to the island.

The next day, Guacanagarí's brother appeared and exchanged gifts with the Spaniards, but he also took time to converse with the captive women before returning to land. At midnight, the women slipped off the ship, swam three miles to shore, and, except for four who were retaken, escaped into the forest. The next day on shore all signs indicated that Guacanagarí and his tribe were gone. Apparently, all had slipped away to the interior.

In September of 1494, Columbus returned from his voyages to Cuba and Jamaica but was seriously ill. Eager to see the admiral, Guacanagarí appeared, reasserted his loyalty, and informed Columbus of an alliance forming among the caciques on the island. He offered to Columbus the services of his warriors. With this intelligence and pledge of allegiance, Columbus sought to establish orderly relations with the Indians, but the future proved to include war and subjugation.

Columbus had been drawn from the territory of Guacanagarí because of duties in other parts of the island and because of problems he had to deal with in Spain, so Gua-

canagarí faced Spaniards who did not recall or did not know of the cacique's kindness and loyalty. His people endured the same subjugation as other Indians. Bullied by the Spaniards, hated by the caciques whose alliance he rejected, and troubled by the misery of his subjects, Guacanagarí retreated to the mountains, where he died.

SIGNIFICANCE

Guacanagarí represents the idyllic sense of the peace and humble prosperity of the pre-Columbian Caribbean world. His kindness, generosity, and sympathy to Columbus show the cacique's noble character. Indeed, the idea of the noble savage might have originated after European contact with the Caribbean Indians.

Because Guacanagarí's cacigazco faced incursions from Carib warriors, his initial connection and loyalty to Columbus may have been a strategy to establish his own security. Guacanagarí's loyalty, however, is not to be written off so easily.

Despite his constancy, he faced the devastating consequences of the arrival of Spaniards other than Columbus, and his failure to join the Caribbean Indian alliance forever stains his reputation.

—William T. Lawlor

FURTHER READING

Columbus, Christopher. *The Journal of Christopher Columbus*. Translated by Cecil Jane and edited by L. A. Vigneras. New York: Clarkson N. Potter, 1960. This translation of Columbus's journal features many illustrations, some in color. Entries in the journal refer to Guacanagarí, and the text includes Columbus's letter, which summarizes the journal and comments on the Tainos. An appendix is titled "The Cartography of the First Voyage."

Columbus, Fernando. *The Life of the Admiral Christopher Columbus by His Son Ferdinand*. Translated by Benjamin Keen. New Brunswick, N.J.: Rutgers University Press, 1959. This life of Columbus draws from the original journal and refers to the meetings of Columbus and Guacanagarí. Includes "The Relation of Fray Ramon Concerning the Antiquities of the Indians, Which He, Knowing Their Language, Carefully Compiled by Order of the Admiral," which gives a firsthand account of the lives and customs of the Tainos.

Las Casas, Bartolomé de. *History of the Indies*. New York: Harper & Row, 1971. An elaborate commentary on the conquest of the Tainos.

Morison, Samuel Eliot. *Admiral of the Ocean Sea: A Life of Christopher Columbus*. Boston: Little, Brown,

1942. This biography reports on the contact between Guacanagarí and Columbus.

Redmond, Elsa M. *Chiefdoms and Chieftaincy in the Americas*. Gainesville: University Press of Florida, 1998. A general view of American Indian leaders.

Wilson, Samuel M. *Hispaniola: Caribbean Chiefdoms in the Age of Columbus*. Tuscaloosa: University of Alabama Press, 1990. This archaeological study analyzes Taino life and customs during the first contact with European culture and reports on Guacanagarí's activities.

_____. *The Indigenous People of the Caribbean*. Gainesville: University Press of Florida, 1999. Offers broader views than Wilson's volume.

SEE ALSO: Vasco Núñez de Balboa; Christopher Columbus; Bartolomé de Las Casas; Doña Marina; The Pinzón Brothers; Juan Ponce de León.

RELATED ARTICLE in *Great Events from History: The Renaissance & Early Modern Era, 1454-1600:* October 12, 1492: Columbus Lands in the Americas.

FRANCESCO GUICCIARDINI
Italian historian

Guicciardini helped revolutionize history writing by breaking with Humanist conventions. He was one of the first historians to present history as a series of interrelated causes and effects and to treat the history of Italy in the larger context of European affairs.

BORN: March 6, 1483; Florence (now in Italy)
DIED: May 22, 1540; Santa Margherita ia Montici, Florence
AREAS OF ACHIEVEMENT: Historiography, government and politics

EARLY LIFE

The family of Francesco Guicciardini (frahn-CHAY-scoh gweeht-chyahr-DEE-nee) was one of the aristocratic supports of the early (c. 1430) Medici regime in Florence. Guicciardini's father had close ties to Lorenzo de' Medici, evidenced by the many positions offered him by Lorenzo and by the fact that Marsilio Ficino, Lorenzo's colleague in the Platonic Academy and a member of the Medici household, was godfather to young Francesco.

At his father's urging, Guicciardini pursued a career in law. He studied at the Universities of Pisa, Ferrara, and Padua. On his return to Florence, he established himself as a lawyer and professor of law and in 1508 married Maria Salviati, whose family was active in the affairs of republican Florence. His earliest writings belong to this period and include his family memoirs and the *Storie fiorentine* (1509; *The History of Florence*, 1970), which covered the years 1378 to 1509. The latter is an important source for historians interested in the Florentine Republic.

LIFE'S WORK

In 1511, the year of Pope Julius II's formation of a Holy League against France—consisting of the Papal States, Venice, Aragon, and the Holy Roman Empire—Guicciardini was elected to his first public post, as ambassador to the court of Ferdinand II of Aragon. When he returned to Florence three years later, he found the Medici family restored to power and Florence a member of the league. He returned to his legal profession, and, though no friend to the younger generation of Medici, he served the new rulers first as a member of the Balìa, or body of eight, in charge of internal security and in 1515 in the Signoria, the governing council of the city.

Guicciardini's career took a new course in 1516, when he was appointed by Pope Leo X to a series of posts. He would serve the Papacy almost continuously until 1534. Until 1521, he was governor of Modena and Reggio and general of papal armies. Temporarily removed from these posts on the death of Leo X, Guicciardini was reappointed by Pope Adrian VI. Under his harsh but efficient rule, these provinces were brought under control. The war in Italy between the Valois French and the Habsburg, Charles V, Holy Roman Emperor and king of Spain, turned Reggio into a military outpost of the Papal States. Guicciardini's major military success was the defense of Parma against the French in December, 1521. He also successfully preserved Modena from the duke of Ferrara, though Reggio capitulated.

Guicciardini's literary output during this time consists of numerous letters and memorandums that manifest his tireless energy in the performance of his duties. From 1521 to 1526 he wrote *Dialogo del reggimento di Firenze* (*Dialogue on the Government of Florence,*

1994). From a historical case study illustrating the defects of one-person rule and of democracy, Guicciardini deduced his ideal Florentine government: a republic in which the aristocratic element has a leading role. In 1521, too, began Guicciardini's correspondence with Niccolò Machiavelli. From 1501 until the restoration of the Medici in 1512, Machiavelli had been a leading actor in Florentine affairs under Piero Soderini, the ensign-bearer of the republic. The Guicciardini and Salviati families had been aristocratic opponents of that regime, and Guicciardini had called Machiavelli the "tool of Soderini." The two found a common bond in their distaste for Medici rule after 1512. Though younger by fourteen years, Guicciardini played the aristocratic patron to Machiavelli the commoner. About 1530, he began *Considerazioni sui "Discorsi" de Machiavelli* (*Considerations on the "Discourses" of Machiavelli*, 1965), which he never finished. He criticized Machiavelli's theories and his interpretation of Roman history as a guide to contemporary political thought.

Guicciardini's star continued to ascend under Pope Clement VII, a Medici family member with whom he was friends. In 1524, he was made president of the Romagna region, and he became a trusted adviser to the pope. The victory of Charles V over Francis I of France at Pavia in 1525 proved a turning point in the life and the historical consciousness of Guicciardini. He was catapulted into the highest echelons of European politics. From then on, he was both enabled and required to comprehend events in Italy as intricately bound up in the larger schemes of the great powers.

In 1526, Guicciardini was in Rome as a papal adviser. His advice was important in the formation of the League of Cognac, the alliance of the Papacy with France and Venice against the Habsburgs; Machiavelli also supported this alliance. Guicciardini became the lieutenant-general of the league's forces. This action by the Medici pope placed Florence in danger of Habsburg reprisal and resulted in another overthrow of Medici rule in 1527, ten days after the sack of Rome by Habsburg troops under the duke of Bourbon. Guicciardini thus found himself out of favor with the pope and unwelcome in Florence, because of his Medici associations. He later commented that he had suddenly been thrown from the height of honor and esteem to the other extreme. He began to comprehend the power of fortune in historical events, a notion that would attain increasing prominence in his thought.

Guicciardini retired to his villa at Finocchietto, where he worked on *Cose fiorentine* (Florentine affairs),

Ricordi (English translation, 1949), and three personal pieces—*Consolatoria*, *Accusatoria*, and the unfinished *Defensoria*. These three personal pieces are written as speeches against himself; they contain indictments of actions that had long bothered him, including his formation of the league, the sack of Rome, and the pope's imprisonment. A major charge by his imaginary accuser was that he had used high position for personal gain. The *Ricordi* is a collection of political maxims culled from his various papers and treatises. Their tone is uniformly cynical, more so, even, than Machiavelli's writings; for example, Guicciardini suggests that one should gain a reputation for sincerity in order to be able to lie successfully on an important matter.

In *Cose fiorentine*, a second history of Florence covering 1375 to 1494, Guicciardini returned to the classical Humanist style of history, but he surpassed the typical Humanist histories by using many sources, including documents. In this and in his conviction that to understand the history of Florence one must also understand events throughout all Italy, Guicciardini was taking the first steps in modern historiography. He never finished his Florentine history; in 1529, the Treaty of Cambrai dictated the return of the Medici to power in Florence, and Guicciardini returned to eminence under Alessandro de' Medici's rule.

Personally opposed to Medici rule, Guicciardini still aspired to a leadership role in Florence, but his political career lacked luster during his later years. Pope Clement appointed him governor of Bologna in 1531, but Pope Paul III removed him in 1534. In Florence, Guicciardini was legal adviser to Alessandro until Alessandro's assassination in 1537. Duke Cosimo I de' Medici allowed Guicciardini to remain in office but with an ever-diminishing influence over affairs.

In 1536 Guicciardini began *Storia d'Italia* (1561-1564; *The History of Italy*, 1579), the only book he wrote not for himself but for public consumption. Retiring in 1537 to his villa, he took with him the entire foreign correspondence of the Florentine republic. *The History of Italy* was written, revised, and polished many times during the last three years of Guicciardini's life. Aside from its value as a source for the years 1494-1532, it is a great milestone in historiography. Guicciardini had come to believe that traditional Humanist history was artificial and prevented history from being useful. He thought that the Humanist view that the moral failures of individual Italian princes were responsible for conflict was inadequate; he believed that not the individual but uncontrollable fortune governed events. Most important, he realized that the wars of foreign powers in Italy had causes from beyond the Alps. Guicciardini viewed *The History of Italy* as a tragedy brought on Italians by themselves. Because of their rivalries, Italian rulers invited foreign powers onto Italian soil.

Guicciardini frequently reiterated that humans act only from self-interest, and the interests of the foreign powers caused the Italian rulers to be initiators of events no longer, so that even their best efforts could not relieve the situation. It was Guicciardini's gift to show how human illusions are an integral part of history and how events, or fortune, and human intentions constantly act and react on one another. Is history still useful if it teaches nothing but the arbitrariness of fortune? Guicciardini believed that the value of history was that it reminded one to consider the effect of every human action on names and dignity. He died on May 22, 1540, while still polishing his book.

SIGNIFICANCE

Guicciardini's achievement was to set the writing of history on a new and intellectually sound path. Before his generation, Humanist historians had slavishly imitated the historians of classical antiquity. If the main subject was a war, then Sallust was to be imitated and attention devoted to the generals' speeches before a battle and to the battle itself. If the focus was the history of a particular city, then Livy was the preferred model. History was regarded as a branch of rhetoric whose purpose was to provide moral instruction by examples. Thus, history did not require completeness but merely those episodes that demonstrated a certain virtue or vice.

Guicciardini accepted the didactic purpose of history (he quoted Cicero's prescription for writing history), but he saw it as teaching the concrete effects of various types of government rather than the general rules of ethics. In the end, he concluded that humans always act from personal interest and that fortune plays its fickle part more frequently than one might think. Throughout a lifetime as an actor at the edge of events, he came to perceive the complex networks of causation between events, so that episodic history was no longer plausible to him. Another contribution was his heightened standard of factual accuracy, possible only by comparing literary sources and documents.

The *Ricordi* and *The History of Italy* were published soon after Guicciardini's death. His other writings, ten volumes of *Opere inedite* (unedited works), did not see print until 1857-1867.

—*Daniel C. Scavone*

FURTHER READING

De Sanctis, Francesco. *History of Italian Literature.* Translated by Joan Redfern. 2 vols. New York: Barnes & Noble Books, 1968. Chapter 15 compares Machiavelli and Guicciardini. Gives an unfavorable view of the career and mind of Guicciardini as advocating self-interest as the motive force of history.

Finlay, Robert. "The Myth of Venice in Guicciardini's *History of Italy:* Senate Orations on Princes and the Republic." In *Medieval and Renaissance Venice,* edited by Ellen E. Kittell and Thomas F. Madden. Urbana: University of Illinois Press, 1999. Contained within a book of interdisciplinary, cutting-edge work on Venetian studies, this reading of Guicciardini's history discusses the republican myth it creates and compares that myth to the rhetoric employed by the Venetian senators of his time.

Gilbert, Felix. *Machiavelli and Guicciardini: Politics and History in Sixteenth Century Florence.* New York: W. W. Norton, 1984. A survey of Guicciardini's career and literary output seen against the tradition of Renaissance historiography prevalent in his day. Contains an excellent annotated bibliography.

Guicciardini, Francesco. *The History of Florence.* Translated by Mario Domandi. New York: Harper & Row, 1970. The complete text in English with an excellent and detailed introductory biography.

_____. *The History of Italy.* Translated by Sidney Alexander. New York: Macmillan, 1969. Contains extensive and well-chosen excerpts in English from his twenty-volume history.

_____. *Maxims and Reflections of a Renaissance Statesman.* Translated by Mario Domandi. New York: Harper & Row, 1965. An English translation of the *Ricordi.*

_____. *Selected Writings.* Edited by Cecil Grayson. Translated by Margaret Grayson. New York: Oxford University Press, 1965. A good sampling of Guicciardini's various writings in English translation.

Luciani, Vincent. *Francesco Guicciardini and His European Reputation.* New York: Karl Otto, 1936. Contains copious scholarly material on Guicciardini; lists editions and translations of his works up to 1936. Discusses *The History of Italy* as a historical source and summarizes the views of it held by Italian, French, Spanish, Catholic, Protestant, and nineteenth century historians.

Moulakis, Athanasios. "Civic Humanism, Realist Constitutionalism, and Francesco Guicciardini's *Discorso de Logrongno*." In *Renaissance Civic Human-*

ism: Reappraisals and Reflections, edited by James Hankins. New York: Cambridge University Press, 2000. Discusses Guicciardini in the context of new scholarship on the historical development of concepts of liberty, law, virtue, and the common good in the late medieval and early modern periods. Includes bibliographic references and index.

Moulakis, Athanasios, and Francesco Guicciardini. *Republican Realism in Renaissance Florence: Francesco Guicciardini's "Discorso de Logrongno."* Lanham, Md.: Rowman & Littlefield, 1998. A translation of Guicciardini's "How to Bring Order to Popular Government," together with Moulakis's analysis of the meaning and importance of the treatise. Includes bibliographic references and index.

Ridolfi, Roberto. *The Life of Francesco Guicciardini.* Translated by Cecil Grayson. New York: Alfred A.

Knopf, 1968. An intimate, thoroughly footnoted, highly favorable biography by a major Guicciardini scholar.

SEE ALSO: Adrian VI; Alexander VI; Charles V; Clement VII; Ferdinand II and Isabella I; Marsilio Ficino; Francis I; Julius II; Leo X; Niccolò Machiavelli; Cosimo I de' Medici; Lorenzo de' Medici; Joseph Justus Scaliger.

RELATED ARTICLES in *Great Events from History: The Renaissance & Early Modern Era, 1454-1600:* April 9, 1454: Peace of Lodi; 1469-1492: Rule of Lorenzo de' Medici; 1486-1487: Pico della Mirandola Writes *Oration on the Dignity of Man*; September, 1494-October, 1495: Charles VIII of France Invades Italy; 1499-1517: Erasmus Advances Humanism in England; May 6, 1527-February, 1528: Sack of Rome.

CHARLOTTE GUILLARD
French printer

One of the first great printers of the Renaissance in France, Charlotte Guillard directed the Soleil d'Or publishing house, which printed or contracted for publication scholarly works in areas such as theology, law, medicine, and natural history. The works of the press were valued especially for their accuracy and beauty.

BORN: c. mid 1480's?; France
DIED: Between April 18 and July 20, 1557; Paris, France
ALSO KNOWN AS: Carola Guillard; Caroline Guillard; C. Guillart; Guillarda; vidua Bertholdi Rembolt; vidua Claudii Chevallonii
AREAS OF ACHIEVEMENT: Literature, science and technology, art, scholarship

EARLY LIFE
Charlotte Guillard (shahr-lawt gee-yahr) was the daughter of Jacques Guillard and Guillemyne Sancy. Archival documents reveal that she had several sisters and a brother and that the family had ties to Paris and the nearby province of Maine.

Historians situate Guillard's marriage to her first husband, Berthold Rembolt, around 1502, or in one unlikely case 1491, but fail to cite evidence for either date. Rembolt had come to Paris from his native Alsace and, from 1494 to 1507, worked in collaboration with Ulrich

Gering, a cofounder of the prestigious Soleil d'Or near the Sorbonne. The Soleil d'Or, or golden sun, was the first printing press in France and the most active print shop in Paris.

When Gering retired in 1508, Rembolt and Guillard set up shop for themselves in a spacious new residence in the nearby rue de Saint-Jacques. There, they worked side by side and specialized in the publication and sale of scholarly works. Rembolt's printer's mark contained his initials "B. R." and two symbols commonly employed by merchants and artists—the number four combined with an orb and cross. When Guillard later began to operate independently, she continued to use Rembolt's mark, but eventually she substituted her own initials, "C. G.," for those of her deceased husband.

LIFE'S WORK
After Rembolt's death in 1518, Guillard took over management of the printery and bookstore, publishing seven books before marrying Parisian book dealer Claude Chevallon around 1520. Although nieces, daughters, and wives would often work alongside husbands and male relatives in the printing industry, only widows were in a position to enter certain contractual agreements, such as hiring correctors (proofreaders). It is therefore not surprising that soon after Guillard's second marriage, books that were sold or printed at the Soleil d'Or carried her

husband's or, on occasion, her former husband's imprint only, as was customary for the time.

For the next seventeen years, her contributions to the history of printing were to a large extent lost in the shadow of her husband's work. Chevallon published the writings of several church fathers, including Saint Jerome (1526), Saint Ambrose (1529), and Saint Augustine (1531). His 1526-1527 edition of Saint Bernard of Clairvaux's complete works contains what is believed a rare family portrait of Guillard and Chevallon and his daughter Gillette genuflecting before the central figures of Saint Bernard, the prophet Malachias, and the Madonna with child. Guillard's likeness is confined to a marginal position at the far right and is barely visible.

It was not until after Chevallon died in 1537 that Guillard again asserted her independence and took charge of the family enterprise. By current estimates, she printed or commissioned and sold under her own name or her widow's name as many as 158 different titles between 1537 and 1557—an average of about eight titles per year. Dealing primarily in works of theology and religion, she also catered to students of law, natural history, and medicine. She sold Bibles and homilies, multiple editions of the works of the church fathers, Justinian I's civil law codes, *Corpus juris civilis* (sixth century; *The Institutes of Justinian*, 1852), Galen's popular *Methodus medendi* (second century; *Galen's Method of Healing*, 1991), and other similar texts. Her boutique, moreover, supported the study of Greek in the French capital, carrying first editions of work by the theologian and saint Justin Martyr (c. 100-c. 165) and Neoplatonic philosopher Proclus of Constantinople (410?-485) and, in 1543, a reprint of Desiderius Erasmus's edition of the New Testament in Greek and Latin. Guillard also offered Parisian readers the first French translation of Erasmus's everpopular *Adagia* (1539).

Continuous operation of the four or five presses under Guillard's control at Soleil d'Or required the coordination of many workers and the investment of substantial sums of money for labor and for paper and other materials, money that often could not be recouped for several years. An inventory prepared in 1556 lists her stock of books at some 13,800 volumes, valued at more than £30,000—figures that suggest the complexities and sums involved in managing one of Paris's major printing houses.

Guillard often shared costs and material with other printers, many of them related through marriage. Her nephew, who began publishing in 1541, produced seventeen editions in association with her, using many of the ornate characters that had belonged to her press previously. Other volumes were published from associations with her in-laws, Guillaume des Boys, Sébastien Nivelle, and Conrad Néobar. Typical in this respect was the monumental ten-volume edition of Saint Augustine's complete works, completed in 1541, a publication that came through collaboration between Guillard, who published the work, Parisian printer Yolande Bonhomme, and Hugues de La Porte, a printer from Lyon who helped finance and then sell it.

Over time, Guillard reprinted many of the first editions she published earlier. A Soleil d'Or edition of Saint Augustine's *De civitate Dei* (413-427; *The City of God*, 1610) made use of an ornate capital "D" that had been discretely refashioned to encompass her initials "C. G.," a sign that she was proud of her work and eager to publicize her accomplishments.

One of Guillard's later ventures led to the first edition of Jacques Toussain's two-volume Greek and Latin lexicon in 1552. Her Latin preface to this work, the only extant sample of her writing in print, tells how the project came to fruition. According to Guillard, publication of the lexicon was already under way when, first, Toussain, then her nephew Jacques Bogard (who had agreed to print the lexicon), unexpectedly died, leaving the work unfinished. At that point Guillard, with the financial support of Parisian book dealer Guillaume Merlin, hired Fédéric Morel as corrector, who then completed the task at hand. As a reference tool for students, Toussain's humble lexicon represented an improvement over existing works on the market and so helped advance the study of ancient Greek literature. It is only fitting that, in the concluding remarks of her preface, Guillard noted with a certain pride her fifty years of dedicated experience in the publishing industry.

Guillard died sometime between April 18 and July 20, 1557. Her nephew-in-law, Guillaume des Boys, then assumed control of the Soleil d'Or, but he died within ten years, leaving his wife Michelle Guillard, Guillard's niece, in charge of the family enterprise.

SIGNIFICANCE

Charlotte Guillard was not the first woman to run a printing and publishing company in Paris, but she was certainly one of the leading printers in the city. Modern book collectors pay substantial sums for books that carry the imprint *Excudebat Carola Guillard* (printed by Charlotte Guillard), attesting to the critical reception of her company's works.

According to Roméo Arbour, a near-contemporary

historian of the sixteenth century, more than one hundred women, either widows or daughters of established printers, took over the management of their family-owned presses in sixteenth century France. Women such as Guillard, once considered an exception to the rule, were major contributors to the renaissance of learning and are only now receiving the attention that past generations of historians have denied them.

—Jan Pendergrass

FURTHER READING

Becker, Beatrice Lamberton. "Charlotte Guillard, Printer of the Renaissance." *Inland Printer* 72 (1923): 438-440. Provides a partial English translation of Guillard's preface to Jacques Toussain's Greek and Latin dictionary, the only text she is known to have written and published herself.

Beech, Beatrice. "Charlotte Guillard: A Sixteenth-Century Business Woman." *Renaissance Quarterly* 36 (1983): 345-367. The standard reference to Guillard's life and work.

Broomhall, Susan. *Women and the Book Trade in Sixteenth-Century France.* Burlington, Vt.: Ashgate, 2002. The chapter titled "Women Working in the Book Trades" discusses the role of women, including Guillard, in the production of manuscripts and books in France from the late thirteenth to the late sixteenth century.

Coppens, Christian. "Une Collaboration inconnue entre Caroline Guillard et Hugues de la Porte en 1544: Le *De civitate Dei* d'Augustin édité par Juan Luis Vives." *Gutenberg-Jahrbuch* 63 (1988): 126-140. This article discusses Guillard's collaboration with a printer from Lyon on publication of Saint Augustine's *De civitate Dei*.

Davies, Hugh William. *Devices of the Early Printers, 1457-1560: Their History and Development, With a Chapter on Portrait Figures of Printers.* London: Grafton, 1935. Identifies a portrait of Guillard and her second husband in the 1526-1527 edition of Saint Bernard's complete works; also explains the origin and significance of her printer's mark.

Driver, Martha W. "Women Printers and the Page, 1477-1541." *Gutenberg-Jahrbuch* 73 (1998): 139-153. Examines women's contributions, including those of Guillard, to the early history of printing.

Masiak, Cory. "On Our Marks: Symbols of Early Printers Adorn Fondren Reference Room." *The Flyleaf: Friends of Fondren Library, Rice University* 40 (1989): 2-7. Discusses Guillard's printer's mark painted on a wall in the reference room of Rice University's Fondren Library.

SEE ALSO: William Caxton; Miles Coverdale; Desiderius Erasmus; Leonhard Fuchs; Hans Holbein, the Younger; Aldus Manutius.

RELATED ARTICLES in *Great Events from History: The Renaissance & Early Modern Era, 1454-1600:* 1490's: Aldus Manutius Founds the Aldine Press; Beginning 1497: Danish-Swedish Wars.

GUSTAV I VASA
King of Sweden (r. 1523-1560)

Gustav created and strengthened the Swedish monarchy, asserting control over both the church and the nobility. He established Sweden as an important secondary power in Europe.

BORN: May 12, 1496; place unknown
DIED: September 29, 1560; Stockholm, Sweden
ALSO KNOWN AS: Gustav Eriksson Vasa; King Bark
AREAS OF ACHIEVEMENT: Government and politics, religion and theology

EARLY LIFE

Gustav Eriksson Vasa (VAH-saw) was the son of a minor Swedish noble, Erik Johansson Vasa, and his wife, Cecilia Mansdotter av Eka. However, as a close relative of Sweden's regent, Sten Sture the Younger (r. 1512-1520), Gustav was reared at the royal court and educated at the University of Uppsala. He participated in the war against Denmark, in 1518, before being sent by his cousin Sten to that nation as a hostage for Sweden's good behavior. Months later, he escaped and made his way to the northern German Hanseatic city of Lübeck, where he was sheltered by friends. In hiding at Lübeck, Gustav missed Sten's death and the Stockholm Bloodbath, the execution by the Danes of nearly ninety nobles, including Gustav's father and many members of his family.

Sweden's situation in 1520 was far from promising. Its nobles and Catholic bishops dominated the country, and neither welcomed the thought of a strong monarchy. Since 1397, both groups had embraced the Union of

Kalmar with Denmark, allowing the Danish king to direct but not to rule Sweden. The death of the last of the Stures and the Stockholm Bloodbath, leaving scores dead and many others imprisoned, transferred the upper hand to Denmark and endangered the position of the nobles and the bishops.

Sweden was further compromised by a weak economy and a lack of allies. Copper, iron, and timber were the primary exports and much in demand, but their sale depended on relations with Lübeck, the Hanseatic League, the Danes, the Dutch, Prussia, and Russia. Lacking an army and navy, Sweden could not hope to defend its independence, its place in the Baltic Sea, or its produce. Furthermore, the Stockholm Bloodbath seemed to undercut the immediate will of the upper classes to resist Denmark.

Gustav, returning from Lübeck to find most of his family either dead or in prison, saw the need to quickly strike back. He raised a rebellion among the peasants and copper miners, an insurrection that rallied most Swedes to his support. The Danes were driven from the country, the Union of Kalmar abrogated, and in 1521 Vasa was selected as regent by the National Assembly, or Riksdag. Two years later, he became Sweden's monarch.

LIFE'S WORK

Sweden's new king was just twenty-seven. Although Gustav I Vasa was known for his common sense, his judgment of character, and his ability to focus on the most important issues in any discussion, he was also known to be cautious. In a reign filled with betrayals, he moved slowly but determinedly and always with an almost single-minded intention of making Sweden into a Baltic power. As a monarch, he was shrewd, wise, and a tough taskmaster, and he continually oversaw his servants either through direct contact or long, detailed correspondence. He diligently sought servants as faithful to the task at hand as himself and rewarded them accordingly. Yet, he had no particular loyalty to those who disagreed with him after his policy was set, and he always vigorously repaid real or imagined insults. His temper was widely known, but it seldom influenced his decisions.

The first twenty years of his reign, from 1523 to 1543, gave little chance for planning. As king, he was expected to live on his own resources, but he was provided with far less than defense and maintenance required. As a result, he lost the island of Gotland to the Danes in 1524 and a defensive alliance with Lübeck, necessitated by the need for other trade outlets and the extensive debts owed to

that city. To defend the realm, the king resorted to higher taxes, forced loans, and the confiscation of estates. He was forced to hire mercenaries and to build two fleets— one for shallow-water fighting and one for battles within the Baltic. He was not safe even at home: peasant revolts, frequently supported by local churches and bishops, followed from 1524 to 1528, 1531 to 1532, and most seriously from 1542 to 1543.

These rebellions identified the weakness of the monarchy and forced Vasa to turn to the Riksdag to either remedy his inadequate income and powers or accept his abdication. In 1527, after a personal appeal by the king, the Assembly granted Gustav virtual control over the church and its considerable revenues. All church fortresses were surrendered to the Crown, and the king was permitted to determine ecclesial salaries, duties, and financial reserves, including whether individual churches or monasteries should continue to exist. While confiscated monies or fines went directly to the royal treasury, the king and his nobles divided discontinued properties. In addition, since the monarch now had power over the bishops and the church, the church began utilizing more pliable and supportive ministers and secretaries, including Lutherans, to gradually displaced Catholic churchmen. While the nobility shared in the largess, its part was much smaller than that of the king, and the reduction of traditional land grants more than compensated for any land that the nobles were given.

At this point, the king slowly started to extend his authority over land and revenues. Churchmen were exiled or displaced, and their support for dissidents and rebellion all but ceased. The addition of properties and revenues to the royal exchequer enabled the Crown to respond more quickly to the crises of 1531 and 1542 and to mount a more aggressive foreign policy against Denmark. It also permitted Gustav to ignore the impending crisis between Protestants and Catholics in Germany.

By 1544, with his greatest challenge in hand, the king was free to enjoy the security, control, and authority that he had sought for twenty-one years. With his opponents at home and abroad either dead or dispersed, Gustav solidified his position and that of his family by a second appeal to the Riksdag. He requested higher taxes to replace unreliable soldiers in the army and the affirmation of an oath of supremacy that effectively guaranteed hereditary succession.

As in 1527, the Riksdag concurred. In the case of the king's death, all fortress commanders and the army were to pledge immediately allegiance to Gustav's eldest son,

Gustav I Vasa of Sweden (at right) presides over a religious debate. (F. R. Niglutsch)

Erik, the defender of the realm. In the meantime, mercenaries and militia, men of questionable trustworthiness, were to be replaced by a national Swedish army. Every twenty peasants were expected to supply a soldier, and even though most of these were allowed to remain at home on call after training, some were to garrison the king's fortresses. The training of these men and its national nature would soon make the Swedish army one of the best on the Continent. With a better army at his back and firm support for his heir, the king now collected the new and heavier taxes necessary to pay for the changes and for suitable increases to his fleet. Having been caught so frequently unprepared in the earlier part of his reign, he now had the money, soldiers, and ships to cope with future emergencies.

Capital improvement, however, was no longer restricted to the military but extended to the economy as a whole. Iron, copper, and timber, long the nation's chief exports, brought limited returns as raw materials. Gustav was advised that these amounts could be increased, almost doubled, if Sweden could refine these products further. Accordingly, in the 1550's Gustav invested in iron foundries that could convert ore, the typical export, into pure bars. By 1560, the king was the chief ironmaster in the country and was using his newfound iron to make his own weapons. Infusions of capital into the copper industry, although not as effective in the short run, would show similar results under Erik XIV. Gustav also invested heavily in his estates, now numbering more than nine thousand farms, and allowed peasants to occupy marginal or waste lands so that they might one day become taxpayers. He further imported craftspeople to supply hard to get goods at a cheaper price and housed them in large workshops throughout the kingdom, where they worked directly for Sweden.

His death in 1560, even though it once again shifted the direction of his policy toward the outside world, did little to stop his ideas and plans. The Succession Pact of 1560 fully recognized the inheritance of his family in the person of Prince Erik, and dukedoms were provided for his younger sons—Johan, Magnus, and Karl. Erik, with his father's permission and encouragement, sought Elizabeth I of England for his bride in order to increase the trade ties between the two nations.

SIGNIFICANCE

Gustav I Vasa forced the Swedish nation to accede to a strong monarchy. The nobility permitted him to rule, and they compromised the church, its land, and its wealth to protect their own. He established an army and a navy, improved the mining of raw materials, encouraged manufacturing, and laid the foundation for the Swedish administrative state.

His improvements were basic and could not elevate Sweden from the status of a secondary power, but the dynasty that he guaranteed would refine his work, conquer most of the Baltic region, and dominate Northern Europe until 1721.

—Louis P. Towles

FURTHER READING

Oakley, Stewart P. *War and Peace in the Baltic, 1560-1790.* New York: Routledge, 1992. Considers the state of the Baltic region from the end of Gustav's reign through 1790.

Roberts, Michael. *The Early Vasas: A History of Sweden, 1523-1611.* London: Cambridge University Press, 1968. Overall, the best and most complete source available on the king. An excellent account of his economic and religious policies.

_____. *Gustavus Adolphus: A History of Sweden, 1611-1631.* 2 vols. London: Longmans, 1953-1957. Focuses on the long-term impact of Gustav's accomplishments.

_____. *On Aristocratic Constitutionalism in Swedish History, 1520-1720.* London: Athlone Press, 1966. Looks at Gustav's relationship with the nobility and defining the monarchy in Sweden.

SEE ALSO: Charles V.

RELATED ARTICLES in *Great Events from History: The Renaissance & Early Modern Era, 1454-1600:* Beginning 1497: Danish-Swedish Wars; 1523: Gustav I Vasa Becomes King of Sweden.

RICHARD HAKLUYT
English geographer and historian

Hakluyt was an Elizabethan chronicler of English exploration and navigation who collected, translated, and published descriptions of early modern sea voyages. His most important work, Principall Navigations, Voiages, and Discoveries of the English Nation, *tells the story of the epic sea adventures of the English.*

BORN: c. 1552; probably London, England
DIED: November 23, 1616; London
ALSO KNOWN AS: Richard Haklyt; Richard Hakluyt, the Younger
AREAS OF ACHIEVEMENT: Geography, historiography

EARLY LIFE

Richard Hakluyt (RIHCH-ahrd HAK-lewt) descended from a family with property in Hereford. His father was a London merchant who died when his family was young, but he was sufficiently prosperous to provide for the education of his four sons.

Hakluyt was educated from 1564 to 1570 as a queen's scholar at Westminster School in London. He and John Beaumont, who also became an author, were selected as outstanding scholars and received bequests in the will of Robert Nowell because of their intellectual promise. During his school years in London, he visited his older cousin and namesake, Richard Hakluyt. His kinsman was a barrister and a member of the Middle Temple, one of the four Inns of Court, which served as intellectual meeting places as well as law schools. The Middle Temple made Sir Francis Drake an honorary member after he returned from his trip around the world. Hakluyt later thanked his cousin for awakening his interest in cosmology and geography.

From Westminster, Hakluyt went on to Christ Church, Oxford University, where he graduated with a bachelor of arts degree on February 19, 1574, and a master of arts degree on January 27, 1575. Nearly 90 percent of those who received the master of arts degree took holy orders, and sometime between 1575 and 1583, Hakluyt took holy orders. His education, particularly in languages, laid the foundation for his later scholarly accounts of discoveries and sea voyages written in classical languages—Greek and Latin—as well as modern languages—Italian, Spanish, Portuguese, and French. After receiving his degrees, he seems to have lectured at Oxford on geography and cosmology, particularly about the use of maps, globes, and spheres.

LIFE'S WORK

In 1582, Hakluyt published his *Divers Voyages Touching the Discouerie of America*, a work that brought him to the attention of the lord admiral, Lord Howard of Effingham. When Sir Edward Stafford, Effingham's brother-in-law, was appointed English ambassador to France in 1583, he took Hakluyt with him as his chaplain. In addition to his official duties, Hakluyt used his time in Paris to collect information on Spanish and French voyages, focusing particularly on European voyages to the Americas. He collected this research into "A Discourse Concerning Western Discoveries." It is known that "A Discourse Concerning Western Discoveries" was written in 1584 because he presented a manuscript copy to the queen, but it did not appear in print until the nineteenth century, when it appeared in *Collections of the Maine Historical Society* (1877). Hakluyt remained in Paris for two more years.

In London in 1586, he translated and had published an account of French exploration by René Goulaine de Laudonnière called *A Notable History Containing Four Voyages Made by Certain French Captains Unto Florida* (1587). In the same year, he published in Paris *De orbe novo* (the new world), translated from the Latin history of travel to the West Indies by Pietro Martire d'Anghiera. Hakluyt's edition was translated into English as *De Orbe Novo* (1612) and reissued in 1625 as *The History of the West-Indies*. The translator, Michael Lok, paid tribute to Hakluyt for his labor and industry.

In 1588, Hakluyt returned to England in company with Lady Sheffield, Lord Howard's sister. In 1589, he published his most important work, *Principall Navigations, Voiages, and Discoveries of the English Nation*. He dedicated his work to Sir Francis Walsingham, Queen Elizabeth I's principal secretary, who was responsible for foreign policy. Attributing to patriotism his motives for publishing these accounts of English voyages, Hakluyt says that while in France he became aware of the burgeoning literature on the discoveries and notable sea enterprises of other nations, but noted that the English were neglected or condemned because no one had compiled their reports. So he took it on himself to become the editor and narrator of the travels and adventures of his countryfolk.

In April, 1590, Hakluyt was appointed rector of Wetheringsett in Suffolk. He was twice married, first around 1594 and a second time in March, 1604, when he is described as fifty-two years old and as having been a widower for about seven years. During the period from 1598 to 1600, he refined his collection of manuscripts and published three volumes on the voyages under roughly the same title, making it difficult to order and describe specific volumes. This difficulty was compounded by contemporary politics.

The first volume celebrated on the title page the defeat of the Spanish Armada in 1588, but it also paid tribute to the exploits of the earl of Essex in Cádiz in 1596. After Essex's disgrace, Hakluyt, or the publisher, might have suppressed this reference to Essex. A new title page bearing the date 1599 was printed with a new dedication mentioning the defeat of the huge Spanish Armada only. Because of the revised date, it was assumed that this was a second edition, but only the title page was revised. More copies of the 1599 edition have survived, but it is substantively the same as that of 1598; only the title page changed. Modern editions of Hakluyt's work appeared in 1809 and 1884.

Hakluyt remained occupied with geographical studies throughout his life and continued to collect and compile manuscripts. In 1601, he stipulated the principal trade places in the East Indies. He was also one of the chief promoters of the petition to King James for patents for the colonization of Virginia. He invested in colonization and was a promotor of and investor in the Virginia Company and the Northwest Passage Company.

In May, 1602, Hakluyt was appointed prebendary (clergyman receiving a stipend) of Westminster; he was made archdeacon the following year. In 1604, he was one of the chaplains of the Savoy.

His last published work was a translation from the Portuguese relating the travels and discoveries of Hernando de Soto, under the title *Virginia Richly Valued* (1609).

Hakluyt died on November 23, 1616, and was buried on November 26 in Westminster Abbey. He left one son, who was reported to have squandered his inheritance and discredited his name. Some of Hakluyt's unpublished manuscripts came to the hands of Samuel Purchas, who incorporated them in an abridged form into his *Purchas His Pilgrimes*. Purchas published four illustrated volumes in 1625, paying tribute to Richard Hakluyt on the title page.

SIGNIFICANCE

Richard Hakluyt's travels throughout England, and his collecting and editing accounts of sea voyages, ensured the survival of the narrative history of English explora-

tion. The Hakluyt Society was later founded in his honor and remains committed to editing and publishing works on the history of exploration and colonization.

—*Jean R. Brink*

FURTHER READING

Bridges, R. C., and P. E. H. Hair, eds. *Compassing the Vaste Globe of the Earth*. London: Hakluyt Society, 1996. Collections of essays on Richard Hakluyt and on the subsequent history of scholarship on navigation and exploration.

Kupperman, Karen Ordahl, ed. *America in European Consciousness, 1493-1750*. Chapel Hill: University of North Carolina Press, 1995. Includes a chapter reevaluating Hakluyt as a historian, titled "The New World and British Historical Thought: From Richard Hakluyt to William Robertson."

Markham, Sir Clements. *Richard Hakluyt: His Life and Work, with a Short Account of the Aims and Achievements of the Hakluyt Society*. London: Bedford Press, 1896. Brief overview of Hakluyt's life, with historical treatment of the society bearing his name.

Parks, George Bruner. *Richard Hakluyt and the English Voyages*. New York: American Geographical Society, 1928. Description of the Hakluyt family and of geography in Tudor England. Includes biographical assessment of Hakluyt and appreciative study of his legacy in the building of empires.

Quinn, David B. *European Approaches to North America, 1450-1640*. London: Ashgate, 1998. Collects essays from Quinn's numerous articles on geography and colonization. Includes a brilliant article analyzing the editing of Hakluyt's 1584 works on the Western discoveries.

Quinn, David B., and Alison M. Quinn, eds. *The First Colonists: Documents on the Planting of the First English Settlements in North America, 1584-1590*. 1973. Reprint. Raleigh: North Carolina Division of Archives, 1995. Collects documents relating to the Virginia voyages, including correspondence between Ralph Lane and Richard Hakluyt. Important source on Hakluyt and North American exploration.

Taylor, Eva, and Germaine Rimington, eds. *The Writings and Correspondence of the Two Richard Hakluyts*. 2 vols. London: Hakluyt Society, 1935. Modern edition of *Divers Voyages*, which includes autobiographical material and correspondence relating to exploration.

Watson, Foster. *Richard Hakluyt*. London: Sheldon Press, 1924. Chapter 2 gives the main facts of Hakluyt's life in a discussion of his influence on British colonization.

SEE ALSO: Jacques Cartier; Thomas Cavendish; Sir Francis Drake; Elizabeth I; Leo Africanus; Gerardus Mercator; Sir Philip Sidney; Hernando de Soto.

RELATED ARTICLES in *Great Events from History: The Renaissance & Early Modern Era, 1454-1600:* 1490-

1492: Martin Behaim Builds the First World Globe; June 24, 1497-May, 1498: Cabot's Voyages; 1569: Mercator Publishes His World Map; June 7, 1576-July, 1578: Frobisher's Voyages; June 17, 1579: Drake Lands in Northern California; July 4, 1584-1590: Lost Colony of Roanoke; September 14, 1585-July 27, 1586: Drake's Expedition to the West Indies; 1596: Ralegh Arrives in Guiana.

CATHARINA VAN HEMESSEN
Flemish painter

Van Hemessen was a renowned portraitist who brought a subdued and naturalistic approach to her subject matter and saw descriptive potential in the painting of details. She was supported by wealthy and powerful patrons, especially Queen Mary of Hungary.

BORN: 1528; Antwerp, Flanders (now in Belgium)
DIED: After 1587; Antwerp?
ALSO KNOWN AS: Catherina van Hemessen; Catarina van Hemessen
AREA OF ACHIEVEMENT: Art

EARLY LIFE

Catharina van Hemessen (kaht-ah-REEN-ah vahn HAY-mehs-sehn) was born in a bustling commercial port and a major center of European banking. A number of important painters established their workshops in Antwerp, including Pieter Aertsen, Frans Floris, and Pieter Bruegel, the Elder, which was home to a vibrant arts scene.

Van Hemessen was the daughter of one of Antwerp's leading mannerist painters, Jan Sanders van Hemessen, known for his moralizing genre scenes and history paintings. Her upbringing was typical of most women artists of the early modern period. Although women had always made art, and famous female artists can be documented from ancient times through the Middle Ages, in the Renaissance it became increasingly difficult for them to pursue professional careers.

As the status of art and artists rose in the Renaissance, professional regulations became stricter, restricting women's and girls' access to apprenticeships. Concurrently, women's lives were increasingly circumscribed by social and political constraints, the demands of family life, and legal restrictions. One could argue that the careers of aspiring female artists fell victim in the Renaissance to the increasingly strict divide between the public and private spheres. As a result, fewer women were able to consider professional careers as artists unless they were noblewomen, such as Italian painter Sofonisba Anguissola, or the daughters of artists, such as van Hemessen and others who received training from their fathers.

LIFE'S WORK

Van Hemessen's work as a painter is especially significant because of the era in which she worked, but her work is especially meaningful because ten known paintings are signed by her: eight portraits and two religious scenes, all of which date from between 1548 and 1552. Because the work of many women artists still remains unknown, waiting to be uncovered in museum storerooms, churches, private collections, and other places, van Hemessen's signature on each of these ten paintings takes on added importance: Her legacy as a painter, and as a painter who was also a woman, can receive its due. That van Hemessen signed these works testifies also to the new awareness of the individual in the Renaissance and to the heightened status of painters and painting during this time.

Even when women in the Renaissance were able to pursue careers as painters, their opportunities for advancement were limited. Most female artists painted miniatures, worked on manuscript illuminations, or worked as copyists. Many pursued careers as portraitists, as did van Hemessen. Very few women worked in the highly regarded genres of historical, biblical, or mythological painting because such compositions required mastery of the male nude. Until the modern era, women were forbidden to draw from the nude male model. Thus, it is noteworthy that van Hemessen executed at least two religious paintings. These are signed depictions of *Christ Carrying the Cross* and *Infant Christ and St. John the Baptist Playing with a Lamb.*

The artist's surviving portraits reveal that although she trained with her father, van Hemessen rejected his complex mannerist style for a more naturalistic approach. This can be seen in her reserved *Self-Portrait*, signed and dated 1548 in a prominent Latin inscription. Van Hemessen presents herself at work at her easel, displaying the tools of her trade and executing a human figure, considered the height of a painter's skill. She appears modestly dressed, with her head covered and wearing a long-sleeved velvet dress with pink trimming. In her right hand she holds a brush, with which she paints a human face, steadying her hand with a tool called a mahlstick. Her left hand grasps a palette and additional brushes. Her strategies of self-presentation are in keeping with the latest in artists' self-portraits and sixteenth century discussions of the status of painting.

Self-Portrait forms a pair with van Hemessen's *Young Woman Playing the Virginal* (1548), which, as suggested by the art historian Eleanor Tufts, most likely depicts her older sister Christina. Viewed together, the paintings give visual form to the importance accorded the liberal arts during the Renaissance by depicting painting, music, and literature, the latter alluded to by the Latin inscription.

Van Hemessen's other portraits hang in world-renowned museums, including *Portrait of a Woman* (1551) and *Portrait of a Man* (1552), both in London's National Gallery. Their style reveals the influence of Netherlandish artist Anthonis Mor. As court painter in Spain, Mor was credited with inventing a more sober approach to portraiture. His influence is revealed in van Hemessen's subdued palette, the two-thirds length view of the sitters, her use of neutral backgrounds, and the overall reserve of her portraits. In keeping with Netherlandish representational strategies, van Hemessen emphasized the descriptive potential of paint, carefully depicting the details of clothing and facial physiognomy.

In 1554, van Hemessen married musician and composer Chrétien de Morien in Antwerp. Two years later, in 1556, the couple left for Spain as part of the entourage of Queen Mary of Hungary, regent of the Netherlands. Queen Mary had resigned her post to retire with her brother Charles V, king of Spain and Holy Roman Emperor, to a secluded monastery in Spain, employing fifty-six ships to transport her entourage and belongings. It has been assumed that while in Spain, van Hemessen painted for the queen, although no paintings have been identified. Queen Mary's female relatives at the Spanish court, including two of the four wives of King Philip II (Charles

V's successor), queens Isabel of Valois and Anne of Austria, both commissioned works from another famous artist, Sofonisba Anguissola, named court painter from 1559 to 1573. It is also possible that, like many other women artists of the time, van Hemessen gave up painting after her marriage.

Van Hemessen and de Morien left Spain in 1558 after Queen Mary's death, the beneficiaries of a lifelong pension provided by the queen. The last years of their life probably were spent in Antwerp, the site of religious and civil wars waged between Catholics and Protestants from 1566 until 1585. Van Hemessen, a Catholic, died sometime after 1587.

SIGNIFICANCE

Van Hemessen was praised by several sixteenth and seventeenth century writers, including the art historian and painter Giorgio Vasari, in his classic work *Le vite de' più eccellenti architetti, pittori, et scultori italiani, da cimabue insino a' tempi nostri* (1550; *Lives of the Most Eminent Painters, Sculptors, and Architects*, 1855-1885). Van Hemessen is also one of the first-documented Flemish woman artists, along with the court painter Levina Teerlinc (d. 1576), and is considered the most important Northern Renaissance woman artist.

Her work has helped fill in the largely empty historical record of women artists. Women have always made art, but their artistic contributions began to "disappear" from official histories in the early twentieth century as art history was institutionalized as a professional discipline. Feminist art historians have argued that many women's artistic contributions were dismissed when a form of quality recognition based solely on the art of men or on men's sensibilities rendered art by women not worthy of study and documentation. Thus, the recovery of women's artworks, like those of van Hemessen, is important not only for correcting the historical record but also for calling into question the canon of art history.

—*Charlene Villaseñor Black*

FURTHER READING

Chadwick, Whitney. *Women, Art, and Society.* 3d ed. London: Thames and Hudson, 2002. An excellent book by one of the most important scholars of women's art, which provides considerable information on the social and political contexts in which women artists worked.

Gaze, Delia, ed. *Dictionary of Women Artists.* 2 vols. London: Fitzroy Dearborn, 1997. An excellent reference work on women artists, this comprehensive dictionary contains a detailed entry for van Hemessen.

Los Angeles County Museum of Art. *Women Artists: 1550-1950*. New York: Alfred A. Knopf, 1976. The catalog of an important exhibition, containing informative essays by two major feminist art historians, Ann Sutherland Harris and Linda Nochlin. Includes reproductions of several of van Hemessen's paintings.

Nochlin, Linda. "Why Have There Been No Great Women Artists?" *Women, Art, and Power and Other Essays*. New York: Harper and Row, 1988. Originally published in 1971, this work is required reading for anyone interested in the history of women artists. It questions the erasure of women from the art-historical record, thus critiquing the underlying biases of the field of art history.

Parker, Rozsika, and Griselda Pollock. *Old Mistresses: Women, Art, and Ideology*. New York: Pantheon, 1981. An important text for the history and politics of writing about women's art, including thought-provoking discussion of the stereotypes associated with women as art makers.

Tufts, Eleanor. *Our Hidden Heritage: Five Centuries of Women Artists*. New York: Paddington, 1975. A book by a pioneer in the "recovery" of women's art. One of the most thorough discussions of van Hemessen's career, including reproductions of her work, with an entire chapter dedicated to the artist.

SEE ALSO: Sofonisba Anguissola; Hieronymus Bosch; Pieter Bruegel, the Elder; Lavinia Fontana; Mary of Hungary; Philip II; Giorgio Vasari.

RELATED ARTICLE in *Great Events from History: The Renaissance & Early Modern Era, 1454-1600:* c. 1500: Netherlandish School of Painting.

HENRY II
King of France (r. 1547-1559)

As king of France, Henry continued the patronage of Renaissance learning and culture begun by Francis I. He also continued the wars against the Habsburgs, resulting in the recovery of Calais from England and the Treaty of Cateau-Cambrésis in 1559. His hostility to the Reformation led to unsuccessful attempts to repress Protestantism in France, and his death while jousting brought chaos to France and led to the French Wars of Religion.

BORN: March 31, 1519; Saint-Germain-en Laye, near Paris, France
DIED: July 10, 1559; Paris
ALSO KNOWN AS: Henri II
AREAS OF ACHIEVEMENT: Government and politics, patronage of the arts

EARLY LIFE
The fourth child and second son of Francis I and Claude of France, Henry was not expected to gain the throne. At age seven, he and his older brother, Francis, were sent to Spain as hostages for their father, who had been captured at the Battle of Pavia near Milan in February, 1525. Henry felt that the Spanish mistreated him and his brother during the four years they spent there, and he bore a permanent grudge against both his father and Charles V, Holy Roman Emperor. After a ransom of 2 million gold crowns had been handed over, the two princes were returned to France in July, 1530.

Among those who welcomed them back to France was Diane de Poitiers. Henry was deeply smitten by her, and several years later, she became his mistress; he loved her until his death, although she was twenty years older than he. In 1534, he married Catherine de Médicis as part of Francis I's attempt to build an alliance with the Médicis pope Clement VII (Giulio de' Médici). The pope soon died, ending the marriage's political value, which also came under strain because of a lack of children during its first ten years. Henry and Catherine, however, eventually had seven offspring who survived to adulthood. Henry's love for Diane further strained the marriage.

LIFE'S WORK
When his older brother died in 1536, Henry became dauphin (the French heir to the throne). As such Henry received nominal command of royal armies and was involved in several campaigns, but with limited success. He ascended the throne at the death of his father on March 31, 1547, his twenty-eighth birthday. He had already formed a cadre of close advisers—Constable Montmorency, the duke of Guise (his younger brother Francis), the cardinal of Lorraine, and Marshal Saint-André—who now dominated the royal council. Diane also wielded broad influence over her royal lover.

In France's government, Henry largely carried on trends begun under his father; his major innovation was creating the offices of the four secretaries of state, each having responsibility for a different area of administration. The selling of royal offices had already become an important source of revenue for the monarchy, and Henry significantly increased the number of venal offices. His major effort in that respect was creating a semester system in the Parlement of Paris, the highest law court, by doubling the number of offices in it and selling them. The Parlement's judges were to serve for six months and then be off for six. The new system soon created problems, however, causing many cases to drag on for years, and bitter complaints from the judges led the king to cancel the semester system, although he did not reduce the number of offices.

A sixteenth century engraved depiction of Henry II sustaining a mortal wound in a jousting tournament in 1559. (Frederick Ungar Publishing Co.)

The war against Charles V continued during Henry's reign, and he allied with the German Lutherans and the Ottoman Turks against him. With the approval of the Lutheran princes, Henry occupied the three bishoprics of Lorraine—Metz, Toul, and Verdun—in April, 1552, and made his famous promenade to the Rhine that same year. Late in 1552, Charles V brought eighty thousand men against Metz to recover it, but the city, well defended by the duke of Guise, withstood the siege, and the three bishoprics remained permanently in French hands. In cooperation with the Ottoman fleet, Henry seized Corsica from Charles V's ally Genoa in 1553, but it remained in French control for only six years.

A devout Catholic, Henry lived at the height of the Protestant Reformation and was aggressively anti-Protestant. His alliance with the German Lutherans prevented him from being excessively severe with the French Protestants, but he took seriously the clause in his coronation oath to protect the Catholic Church. Shortly after becoming king, he created a new chamber in the Parlement of Paris to deal with heresy. Called the *chambre ardente* for its zealous pursuit of Protestants, it condemned thirty-seven persons to death in three years. The Catholic hierarchy's objections to the loss of jurisdiction over heresy persuaded him to close it down in 1550. The rivalry between the Parlement and the Church over heresy prosecution rendered ineffective such harsh edicts against heresy as the Edict of Châteaubriand in 1551. This problem, along with Henry's perception that heresy was lower-class sedition, led him to overlook Protestantism among the French elite and allowed it to flourish despite his pledge to rid his realm of the Protestants. By 1550, Calvinists, directed from the French-speaking Swiss city of Geneva, constituted the overwhelming majority of French Protestants, also known as Huguenots.

Under Henry, the French monarchy continued to be a major patron of Renaissance culture, although he preferred to patronize French talent rather than, as his father had done, Italian talent. He completed several projects begun by Francis I, including the château of Fontainebleau and the reconstruction of the Louvre in Paris, while putting his own stamp on them. Henry assigned the architect Pierre Lescot and the sculptor Jean Goujon to the Louvre, and its Cour Carrée (the central courtyard) is probably the best example of their work. The major building project during Henry's reign was the château of Anet, done for Diane de Poitiers by the royal architect Philibert Delorme. François Clouet painted the best-known portrait of Henry.

In literature, Henry's reign saw something of a reaction against the Humanist emphasis on using classical Latin versus a greater effort to use French. The great literary theoretician Joachim du Bellay argued for using French in *La Défense et illustration de la langue française*

(1549; *The Defence and Illustration of the French Language*, 1939). He was a member of La Pléiade, a group of poets who wrote in French and received patronage from the French court as royal poets. The most famous among them was Pierre de Ronsard. Étienne Jodelle's *Cléopâtre captive*, the first French tragedy, was performed for Henry in 1552.

The end of Henry's reign was shadowed by economic problems, a huge royal debt, an upsurge in religious dissent, and more intense war with the Habsburgs. The severe downturn in climate that would mark the next one hundred years first appeared in 1556, when there was a major crop failure. Inflation caused by the huge influx of American bullion through Spain began to have a negative impact on the finances of most of the French people and the royal budget. Burdened by the huge expenses of the court and war, Henry was forced to resort to heavy borrowing. In 1555, Henry devised a system of amortizing his loans, at 16 percent annually, which is regarded as the first such system to appear in Europe. By the end of his reign, the royal debt amounted to about two and a half times the annual royal revenues.

At the urging of the bitterly anti-Spanish Pope Paul IV, Henry sent an army to Italy to reclaim Naples and Milan, which the pope promised to give to two of the king's younger sons. Philip II, Charles V's successor as king of Spain, responded by invading northern France and defeating Montmorency at Saint-Quentin in 1557, taking the constable captive. Philip failed to push his forces on to Paris, and Henry used the army he had assembled for defending the city to take Calais from the English in January, 1558—since England was allied with Spain in the war. With the fortunes of war balanced, both rulers agreed to the Treaty of Cateau-Cambrésis in 1559. The treaty recognized Philip's sovereignty over Naples and Milan, while leaving Calais and the bishoprics of Lorraine in French hands. It also arranged for a marriage between Philip II and Henry II's eldest daughter, Elisabeth.

Henry, jousting in a tournament in Paris celebrating the peace and the marriage, was mortally wounded when his opponent's shattered lance struck him in the face. He left his fifteen-year-old son, Francis II, a realm beset with problems, the most serious being the religious divisions.

SIGNIFICANCE

Although Henry II was a competent administrator, he was neither the astute politician nor the personally popular king that his father had been. Although he supported the Renaissance arts, he did not champion them as his father had. Where his father had been somewhat tolerant of the Protestant Reformation, Henry II was passionately hostile toward Protestants. This passion would lead to the bloody Wars of Religion. Henry left his son a state deeply divided in religious beliefs and deeply in debt. However, in his children with the powerful Catherine de Médicis, he gave France three future kings (Francis II, Charles IX, and Henry III) and strong allies with the marriages of three daughters (Elisabeth to Phillip II, Marguerite to Henry of Navarre, and Claude to Charles III the Great).

—*Frederic J. Baumgartner*

FURTHER READING

Baumgartner, Frederic J. *Henry II, King of France, 1547-1559*. Durham, N.C.: Duke University Press, 1988. A thorough biography of the king. Includes bibliography and index.

Bonner, Elizabeth. "The Recovery of St. Andrew's Castle in 1547: French Naval Policy and Diplomacy in the British Isles." *English Historical Review* 111 (1996): 578-598. A broad study of France's relationship with Scotland and the Stuart Dynasty.

Frieda, Leonie. *Catherine de Medici*. London: Weidenfeld & Nicolson, 2003. A major study of Henry II's wife that includes significant sections on the king. Includes illustrations, bibliographical references, and an index.

Knecht, R. J. *French Renaissance Monarchy: Francis I and Henry II*. New York: Longman, 1996. Provides a good overview of Henry's reign.

HENRY III
King of Poland (r. 1573-1574) and France (r. 1574-1589)

Henry III, king during the worst years of the French Wars of Religion, lost control over his realm. Intelligent and well-educated, he was also indecisive and erratic. His personal behavior and unbridled spending in the midst of economic depression made him perhaps the most hated French king, and his assassination ended the Valois Dynasty.

BORN: September 19, 1551; Fontainebleau, France
DIED: August 2, 1589; Saint-Cloud, France
ALSO KNOWN AS: Édouard-Alexandre (given name); Henry, duke of Orléans; Henry, duke of Anjou; Henry of Valois; Henri III
AREA OF ACHIEVEMENT: Government and politics

EARLY LIFE

Henry was the fourth son of Henry II and Catherine de Médicis, and the third to survive childhood. He stood behind his brothers Francis and Charles in the line of succession. Baptized Édouard-Alexandre, he became known as Henry at his confirmation. He was regarded as the brightest of the royal sons and received an excellent Renaissance education, learning from the Humanist Jacques Amyot, known for his French translations of Greek works. When his brother Francis became king in July, 1559, Henry received the title duke of Orléans.

LIFE'S WORK

In December, 1560, Francis II died from infection, and the next brother became King Charles IX. Now successor to the throne, Henry began to be trained for rule. He accompanied his brother and mother on their royal progress of 1564-1565 that traversed the entire kingdom, learning at first hand of the economic troubles and the sectarian violence of the religious wars.

At age fifteen, he became duke of Anjou and was named lieutenant-general of the realm. This appointment gave him nominal command of the royal forces sent to pacify the southwest, where a powerful Protestant army was in the field. Although he was expected to defer to the experienced generals in his army, his desire to win glory in war was a major factor in bringing about the Battle of Jarnac in March, 1569. His victory made Henry the hero of Catholic France. Nonetheless, he supported the Peace of Saint-Germain in 1570, which included a marriage contract between his younger sister Marguerite and the Huguenot (Protestant) Henry, prince of Bourbon (later Henry, king of Navarre).

The peace brought Gaspard de Coligny, a Huguenot leader, to the royal court, where his growing influence over Charles led to an assassination attempt on him in August, 1572. Henry's part in the ensuing St. Bartholomew's Day Massacre of the Huguenots in Paris is ambiguous; he is generally assigned a role in persuading Charles that the Huguenot leaders were a threat to the throne. When the massacre led to renewed civil war, Henry served as commander of the royalist forces, and his apparent zeal in defending Catholicism raised his standing among French Catholics to great heights.

Also in 1572, the king of Poland died. The Polish throne was elective, and Catherine, eager to have all her sons wear crowns, secured Henry's election through extensive bribery. In February, 1574, Henry arrived in Poland, where he agreed to the Henrician Articles. They established the principles by which the Polish monarchy functioned until 1791. Barely five months after he reached Poland, word came that his brother had died, and he was king of France, with his mother serving as regent until his return. The Poles refused to allow him to leave, so he slipped away at night. Despite his rush to leave, he always regarded himself as the king of Poland, although the Poles quickly elected a new king, and he signed edicts as king of France and Poland.

His journey home took him through Venice, where he spent several weeks and developed a deep love of Venetian culture. He reached France in September and was crowned on February 13, 1575. At the same time he married Louise of Lorraine, a relative of the Guises, who were the leaders of the ardent Catholics.

Back in France, Henry III found himself in the midst of the religious war that had been festering since 1572. The Catholics were convinced that the victor of Jarnac would lead them to victory over the Huguenots, but Henry badly disappointed them with a policy of reconciliation. Faced with a loose alliance of Huguenots and discontented Catholic nobles, who included his younger brother, the duke of Alençon, Henry issued an edict of pacification in May, 1576. It granted the Huguenots public exercise of their religion, except in Paris, and gave their leaders eight towns to garrison as security places.

The Catholic reaction to these concessions to the Protestants was fierce, and zealous nobles organized the Catholic League to resist the edict. Henry I of Lorraine, duke of Guise, emerged as its head. The king tried to deal with the opposition by calling a meeting of the Estates-

General, which met at Blois in December, 1576. The league dominated the meeting and pressed the king into declaring that there was a "law of Catholicity," which required that the king be Catholic. This law was intended to prevent Henry of Bourbon, who now stood second in the line of succession despite being only a distant cousin, from becoming king. The Estates-General also refused to grant the king new revenues, so the monarchy's disastrous fiscal situation could not be improved. Failing to gain anything from the Estates-General, Henry had to withdraw from his concessions to the Huguenots, designing a new edict in 1577 that limited their right of worship to those places that they controlled.

This change satisfied the Catholic League without drawing the Huguenots back to war, and for the next seven years, France was largely at peace. Henry now had time to indulge his interest in learning and culture. Most notable was his Palace Academy, in which literature, music, philosophy, and science were discussed among the most learned men and women of Europe. The well-known philosopher and lecturer Giordano Bruno participated in it between 1579 and 1581.

In addition to the violent tension between the Catholics and Protestants and the economic shambles of the monarchy, Henry's personal behavior also caused him serious problems. He gathered at the court a cadre of young noblemen whom he called his *mignons* (darlings), on whom he lavished money and titles. The strong hint of homosexuality associated with the mignons was compounded by his enthusiasm for Italian fashion, which most French regarded as effeminate, and his lack of children seemed to confirm the suspicion. His attempts at raising taxes and the royal court's extravagance in the midst of the severe economic problems made him perhaps the most vilified king in French history. Among the charges thrown at Henry were incest with his sister Marguerite and practicing black magic. Because he was very devout in public, he was also accused of being a hypocrite.

Still, Henry probably would have muddled through if his unmarried younger brother had not died in 1584. Since Henry had no son himself, his successor was Henry of Bourbon, the Huguenot leader. The dormant Catholic League reappeared with a vengeance. Now it

Henry III receives a delegation of Dutch ambassadors. (F. R. Niglutsch)

included not only the Catholic nobility but also a great many townspeople, especially in Paris, who largely took over the leadership of the Catholic cause. Supported by Philip II of Spain, the league persuaded Henry III to declare again the law of Catholicity. In response, Henry of Bourbon took up arms, leading to the War of the Three Henrys (the king, Bourbon, and Guise). In late 1587, Guise defeated a Protestant army in eastern France. His victory so elevated his standing among Paris's Catholics that the king, terrified at a Guise-led rebellion, barred him from coming to Paris. He came anyway in March, 1588, and Henry's efforts to keep control of the city led to the Day of the Barricades, in which the leaguers used barricades in the streets to isolate the royal troops and force them to surrender. Henry fled from Paris.

Deeply humiliated but unable to strike back immediately, Henry III agreed to the league's demand that he call a meeting of the Estates-General, whose sole purpose was to bar Bourbon from the throne. When the meeting ended in December, 1588, Henry III ordered the assassination of Guise and his brother, the cardinal of Guise. Catholic rage at the king was enormous. The pope excommunicated him, and leaguer preachers and pamphleteers denounced him as a tyrant whose killing would be a holy deed. A young Dominican brother, Jacques Clément, took them at their word. Gaining entrance on August 2, 1589, to Henry's camp at Saint-Cloud, where the king had joined forces with Bourbon, Clément stabbed him. Before dying, Henry recognized Bourbon as his successor. His death marked the end of the Valois Dynasty and the beginning of the Bourbon.

SIGNIFICANCE

The situation in the realm under Henry III was abysmal. Sectarian violence had destroyed much of its infrastructure, a severe economic downturn had undermined the well-being of almost every economic class, worsening climate was causing frequent crop failures, and the king received only a small portion of the taxes collected in his name. Henry made efforts to deal with the problems. He changed the currency, decreed badly needed reforms of

taxation and the bureaucracy, and saw to the writing of a massive revision of the law code, called the Code Henri. Unfortuantely, he failed to implement these reforms. His popular successor, however, did. Henry IV gained credit that partially belonged to Henry III.

—Frederic J. Baumgartner

FURTHER READING

Bell, David A. "Unmasking a King: The Political Uses of Popular Literature Under the French Catholic League, 1588-1589." *Sixteenth Century Journal* 20 (1998): 371-386. Provides a detailed account of Henry III's erratic behavior and how his enemies used it to undermine his authority and prestige.

Cameron, Keith. *Henri III, a Maligned or Malignant King?* Exeter, England: University of Exeter Press, 1978. Examines Henry's reputation for illicit behavior and largely exonerates him.

Holt, Mack P. *The French Wars of Religion, 1562-1629.* New York: Cambridge University Press, 1995. A well-written account of the civil wars of Henry's era. Includes bibliography and index.

Palm, Franklin. *The Establishment of French Absolutism, 1574-1610.* New York: F. S. Crofts, 1928. Dated but valuable study of the political developments of Henry's reign.

Wood, James B. *The King's Army: Warfare, Soldiers, and Society During the Wars of Religion in France, 1562-1576.* New York: Cambridge University Press, 1996. Offers an in-depth look at the military side of Charles IX and Henry III. Includes bibliographical references and an index.

HENRY IV
King of France (r. 1589-1610)

Henry IV brought peace and national prestige to France after protracted strife, which had included eight civil wars. He settled the long-standing Catholic-Protestant conflict by embracing Catholicism while granting broad toleration to the French Reformed church. He made religious liberty the law of the state.

BORN: December 13, 1553; castle of Pau, Béarn, Navarre (now in France)

DIED: May 14, 1610; Paris, France

ALSO KNOWN AS: Henry of Navarre; Henry III, king of Navarre

AREAS OF ACHIEVEMENT: Government and politics, religion and theology

EARLY LIFE

Henry IV, first of the Bourbon line, was born in the castle of Pau to Antoine de Bourbon, duke of Vendôme, and Jeanne d'Albret, queen of Navarre and daughter of the poet and patron Marguerite de Navarre. Henry was also a direct descendant of Louis IX, one of France's most illustrious rulers. Although he was baptized a Catholic, Henry received instruction in the Calvinist (Reformed) faith at his mother's direction, and he eventually joined the French Protestants, then known as Huguenots.

In 1568, his mother placed Henry in the service of Admiral Gaspard de Coligny, the leader of the Protestant cause. As a soldier in the Huguenot army, he fought bravely and acquired a reputation as a skillful military leader. When Jeanne d'Albret died in 1572, Henry succeeded her as monarch of Navarre. That same year, he married Marguerite of Valois, sister of King Charles IX of France and a grand-niece of Marguerite de Navarre.

LIFE'S WORK

By the time Henry joined Coligny in 1568, France had been wracked by civil war for more than eight years. The death of Henry II in 1559 initiated a power struggle in which political and religious considerations were intertwined. Francis II and Henry II had tried to crush the Protestants, but the Reformed faith had made impressive gains nevertheless, especially among the bourgeoisie and the aristocracy. Calvinism gained adherents who could exert far greater influence than their numbers would seem to indicate.

Because the sons of Henry II were feeble rulers, nobles asserted their authority and rival factions competed for power. Antoine de Bourbon and Louis I de Condé, both princes of the blood, allied with Coligny to promote the Protestant cause. The family of Guise, with Duke Francis at the head, led the Catholic faction. When Francis II succeeded to the throne as a minor in 1559, the Guises obtained control of the government. After they executed some of their opponents, Protestants responded with militant resistance. Francis II died after one year on the throne, and Charles IX became king with his mother, Catherine de Médicis, as regent. She then became the pivotal figure in French politics for the next quarter century. Catherine had no deep religious convictions, so she tried to manipulate both sides and to create a moderate party loyal to the Crown. In 1562, however, the Guises seized power and forced the regent to resume persecuting the Protestants. France became the scene of all-out civil war.

The marriage of Henry of Navarre to Margaret of Valois occurred in 1572, as Catherine de Médicis tried to placate the Huguenots by marrying her daughter to one of their most popular leaders. The nuptial festivities, however, became the occasion for the St. Bartholomew's Day Massacre, in which Coligny and many other Protestants were murdered. Although the assassins may have intended to kill only a few Huguenot leaders, word of the slayings soon led to the slaughter of thousands of Protestants across France. The civil war resumed with renewed fury.

The sickly Henry III of Valois became king in 1574, and soon a militant Catholic faction, now led by Henry I of Lorraine, duke of Guise, organized the Catholic League without royal approval. The civil strife then became the War of the Three Henrys, as Henry III, Henry I, and Henry of Navarre fought for control of the kingdom. The eventual assassination of the king and the duke left the Protestant Henry of Navarre the legal heir to the throne. He declared himself king of France in 1589. Civil war continued, however, until the last remnants of the Catholic League abandoned resistance in 1596. The concurrent war with Spain did not end until 1598.

Although Henry IV had become king legally, he knew that his throne would never be secure so long as he remained a Protestant. His Huguenot supporters, only 10 percent of the population, were unable to cement their leader's authority. Moderate Catholics urged the king to convert, but Henry delayed because he wanted his enemies to recognize his kingship first. When he became convinced that would not happen, he announced his decision to become a Catholic. An old but probably apocryphal account relates that he justified changing religions with the remark "Paris is well worth a Mass." Henry's embrace of Catholicism shows clearly that this king was a *politique*, that is, one without strong religious beliefs who follows the course of action he deems politically advantageous. He had done this before, when he had joined the Catholic Church to marry Margaret of Valois, only to return to the Reformed faith in 1576.

In order to obtain papal approval for his succession, Henry had to seek absolution for his Protestant heresies, something the Vatican was in no hurry to grant. Pope Sixtus V had tried to block his path to the French throne and had declared him deposed as king of Navarre. The reigning pontiff, Clement VIII, chose to defer action on the royal request, even though French prelates had hailed the king's return to the Church.

Henry chose Jacques Davy Duperron as his emissary to Rome. Duperron, who had once been a Huguenot and had adopted Catholicism after reading Thomas Aquinas's *Summa theologiae* (c. 1265-1273; *Summa Theologica*, 1911-1921), supervised the religious instruction of the royal convert. Since Duperron was a learned apologist for Catholicism, he was an effective representative to the pope. As a reward for his services, the king made Duperron a royal chaplain and a councillor of state, and, in 1596, bishop of Evreux. To convince the pope of his sincerity, Henry promised to rebuild monasteries destroyed in the civil wars, and he agreed to support the decrees of the Council of Trent (1563), the Counter-Reformation program to combat Protestantism. At minimum, this meant that the king would maintain the Catholic religion in all areas of France that had supported the Catholic League. He promised similarly to prohibit Protestant worship in Paris, Lyons, Rouen, and other cities.

Moderate Protestants accepted Henry's conversion and his concessions to Rome as necessary for the peace and security of France. Militant Huguenots, however, protested. The king had to deal with them cautiously to prevent them from deserting him. It is a tribute to Henry's diplomacy that he was able to pay the price demanded by the pope without alienating his Protestant supporters completely. By 1598, Henry was convinced that his rule was secure, so he took a bold step to reassure the Huguenots of his goodwill. The king proclaimed the Edict of Nantes, a landmark enactment in the history of religious freedom.

The Edict of Nantes expressed the king's wish for the eventual reunion of all Christians, but its provisions show

that Henry knew that would not occur. This law ratified concessions granted to Protestants earlier, and it recognized full freedom of belief and the right to public worship in two hundred towns and in many castles of Protestant lords. Calvinists could worship in private elsewhere, and they would be eligible for most public offices. The king also granted subsidies for a number of Protestant schools and colleges, and the edict created special sections of the *parlements* (royal courts) to try cases in which Protestant interests were involved. The king allowed the Huguenots to fortify about two hundred towns under their control. The policy of toleration satisfied the Protestants, and it contributed immediately to the achievement of national union. Its provisions, however, created almost a state-within-the-state, a condition that was to cause disruption at a later time, when subsequent monarchs tried to impose their authority on those towns.

Catholic reaction to the Edict of Nantes was predictably hostile. Pope Clement VIII denounced it, and some *parlements* tried to obstruct publication of the royal decree. Militant opponents of toleration tried to reactivate the Catholic League, and the government discovered several plots to assassinate the king. Most of the French, nevertheless, were too weary of strife to support another civil war, and news about the plots against the king caused an upsurge of support for his policy. His opponents could not find a single magnetic leader. Under royal pressure, the Parlement of Paris registered the edict, and the other courts followed suit. Extensive, though not complete, religious freedom became the policy of Western Europe's largest state.

Whatever satisfaction Henry derived from the success of his policy toward religion, it could not obscure the serious problems that confronted him as king. Foreign and domestic wars had brought France to a state of impoverishment approaching bankruptcy. The kingdom was almost impotent in foreign affairs. Henry faced the mammoth task of rebuilding with determination. Although he was an intelligent and energetic ruler, Henry was not a skilled administrator. He entrusted that responsibility to the duke of Sully, a Protestant and a longtime friend. Under Sully's competent direction, the government eliminated much corruption and inefficiency, reformed taxation, and gained solvency. Financial success made it possible to improve the army and to initiate public works for building canals, roads, and harbors to promote economic growth. The government sponsored the expansion of arable lands by draining swamps, and it developed new industries, including the production of silk. Henry founded the French colonial empire by sending the first French explorers and settlers to Canada.

In foreign affairs, Henry sought to protect France from the encircling power of the Habsburgs of Austria and Spain. Because he knew that France was vulnerable to Habsburg attack, he allied with Protestant states in Germany and with the Netherlands. Just when he was ready to strike at his enemies, however, an assassin struck him. He died on May 14, 1610, at the hand of François Ravaillac. The assailant seems to have acted on his own to slay a Catholic monarch who had decided to war against the Catholic Habsburgs, which would have aided the Protestant cause internationally. Although his enemies rejoiced at the death of Henry, the French people mourned the passing of a great, humane king.

SIGNIFICANCE

Henry IV was a popular ruler because he truly cared for the welfare of his subjects. Most of the French people accepted his absolutism as the only alternative to the anarchy that had prevailed for so long. His pragmatic policies brought peace and prosperity with order.

Although Henry was a hero to the Huguenots, despite his defection to Catholicism, his private life must have offended their stern Calvinist moral sensibilities. In 1599, he obtained papal dissolution of his marriage to Margaret of Valois and quickly took Marie de' Medici as his next wife. He was not faithful to either wife and had several mistresses and illegitimate children. He was not above practicing ecclesiastical corruption, as when he made one of his bastard children bishop of Metz at age six. Henry often coerced *parlements* and subjected provincial and local officials to forceful supervision. He controlled the nobles effectively and left his son Louis XIII a kingdom at peace, one where royal authority was supreme and prosperity was in progress.

—*James Edward McGoldrick*

FURTHER READING

Baumgartner, Frederic. "The Catholic Opposition to the Edict of Nantes." *Bibliothèque d'Humanisme et Renaissance* 40 (1970): 525-537. This valuable study relates how Henry shrewdly overcame the criticisms of his opponents. A work of thorough research with a convincing argument. The notes are rich in research data.

Dickerman, Edmund H. "The Conversion of Henry IV." *Catholic Historical Review* 68 (1977): 1-13. While others have concluded on the basis of appearances and superficial research that the king was a *politique*, Dickerman has made a penetrating examination of the

sources to show how and why Henry regarded religion pragmatically.

Finley-Croswhite, S. Annette. *Henry IV and the Towns: The Pursuit of Legitimacy in French Urban Society, 1589-1610*. New York: Cambridge University Press, 1999. Study of Henry's labors to win support from his subjects, focusing on his courtship of the urban population and the consolidation of his claims to legitimate sovereignty. Includes illustrations, maps, bibliographic references, and index.

Gray, Janet Glenn. *The French Huguenots: The Anatomy of Courage*. Grand Rapids, Mich.: Baker Book House, 1981. This decidedly partisan survey of the religious and political climate in France is vivid in descriptions and contains many perceptive interpretations. Places Henry's career in the context of the French and European struggles for religious liberty.

Leathes, Stanley. "Henry IV of France." In *The Cambridge Modern History*, edited by A. W. Ward et al. Vol. 3. Reprint. Cambridge, England: Cambridge University Press, 1969. This substantial essay, despite its age, is indispensable to any serious study of the subject. An excellent introductory source.

Love, Ronald S. *Blood and Religion: The Conscience of Henri IV, 1553-1593*. Ithaca, N.Y.: McGill-Queen's University Press, 2001. An assessment of Henry's reign against the background of civil war and religious strife. Concludes with a discussion of Henry's perception of the conflicting requirements of his crown and his soul, and his 1593 conversion to Catholicism. Includes photographic plates, illustrations, bibliographic references, and index.

Russell, Lord of Liverpool. *Henry of Navarre*. New York: Praeger, 1970. For the general reader, this is probably the most enjoyable biography of the subject. Portrays the king as a humane ruler, licentious in life and a *politique* in religion.

Sutherland, N. M. *Henry IV of France and the Politics of Religion, 1572-1596*. 2 vols. Bristol, Avon, England: Elm Bank, 2002. Extremely detailed account of the role of religion in France's monarchy and political sphere during the late sixteenth century. Each chapter discusses a specific political event or issue from the point of view of the conflict between Protestants and Catholics. Includes illustrations, map, bibliographic references, and index.

_____. *The Huguenot Struggle for Recognition*. New Haven, Conn.: Yale University Press, 1980. This thorough study of the Huguenot movement and the issues it raised for church and state in France is a model of research and writing by a truly erudite scholar. Best for those with some knowledge of the movement.

SEE ALSO: John Calvin; Catherine de Médicis; Henry II; Henry III; François Hotman; Martin Luther; Marguerite de Navarre; Michel Eyquem de Montaigne; Philippe de Mornay; William Shakespeare; Sixtus V.

RELATED ARTICLES in *Great Events from History: The Renaissance & Early Modern Era, 1454-1600:* 1544-1628: Anglo-French Wars; March, 1562-May 2, 1598: French Wars of Religion; August 2, 1589: Henry IV Ascends the Throne of France; April 13, 1598: Edict of Nantes; May 2, 1598: Treaty of Vervins.

HENRY IV OF CASTILE
King of Castile (r. 1454-1474)

Henry IV, although a weak king, was a centralizer, a consistent proponent of an alliance between Castile and Portugal, and an expansionist at the expense of Granada.

BORN: January 6, 1425; Valladolid, Castile (now in Spain)
DIED: December 11, 1474; Madrid (now in Spain)
ALSO KNOWN AS: Henry the Impotent; Henry the Liberal; Enrique el Impotente; Enrique el Liberal; Henry IV the Impotent of Castile; Henry Trastámara (given name)
AREA OF ACHIEVEMENT: Government and politics

EARLY LIFE

Henry was one of three children born to John II, king of Castile (r. 1406-1454). Within days of his birth, the young boy was proclaimed heir-apparent to the throne, or prince of the Asturias. John, who preferred academic pursuits and hunting to the business of the kingdom and raising a family, delegated much of his authority to Álvaro de Luna, a nephew of the powerful archbishop of Toledo.

As the king's chief counselor, de Luna arranged for the care of the young prince and placed him eventually in the hands of three trusted associates. He also introduced Henry to Juan Pacheco, who would soon become the heir's closest friend, and arranged for Pacheco to join the prince's household.

De Luna, the power behind the throne until 1453, kept the nobles under control and maintained the best interests of the monarchy. He negotiated treaties, arranged for the marriage of young Henry to Bianca of Navarre, and oversaw the marriage festivities when John II did not attend. Equally important, he permitted the future monarch to reside in relative obscurity at the fortress of Segovia north of Madrid. Henry preferred to dress simply, often in drab colors, and to dispense with court protocol. He loved the city, its people, and the solitude of its surrounding forests. All that is known about Henry's life in Segovia is that he encountered an earthquake in 1431 that nearly killed him, and he also faced an accident in 1436. He had a good friendship with the Jewish community there, and he was married to Bianca in 1440. De Luna was always careful to have the heir in court in the company of his parents on key ceremonial days.

LIFE'S WORK

The prince's marriage, with the accompanying festivities and gathering of nobles, largely ended his seclusion, and John II's absence from the occasion made it even more notable. When the king, threatened by Aragon and a coalition of his own nobles, found himself forced to fight in 1441, his son ignored the royal summons to assist and instead remained at Segovia. The matter, of course, was more complicated.

Henry favored his mother, Maria, an Aragonese princess, and the war split the royal couple. At this juncture, the king refused to recognize Henry as prince of the Asturias and may have denied his paternity, a not uncommon "weapon." By remaining aloof, Henry and a faction of nobles who supported his position demonstrated that they controlled the balance of power. Yet, it was not until 1443, with John imprisoned by his enemies, that father and son were reconciled briefly. Neither Henry nor his supporters could counsel the imprisonment of his father or a diminishing of the Crown's powers. United, they defeated the forces of Aragon, which had occupied a considerable part of Castile, and drove them from Castile in 1445.

The royal arrangement soon collapsed with Prince Henry negotiating with all factions but siding with none. In 1452, Henry again withdrew from active politics. By doing this, he permitted de Luna to arrange a second marriage for his father with Isabella of Portugal, a position the prince supported, and then allowed his father, John, to turn on de Luna and have him executed.

Unfortunately, Henry's inactivity and lack of policy were unpopular among the nobles, who expected their future king to assume a strong and consistent stance. In addition, it was evident to the nobility that Henry was falling more and more under the influence of his childhood friend, Juan Pacheco. Juan, like Henry, was indifferent to his dress and preferred seclusion to grandeur. Yet, he was also everything that the king was not—a good speaker, a persuasive debater, a master politician, and an excellent judge of people. It was not surprising, then, that Henry turned to Pacheco as a spokesperson, or favorite, and requested his father to bestow Crown lands and titles on Pacheco.

The rule of Henry IV began auspiciously in July of 1454. The young king was twenty-nine, blond, bearded, and blue-eyed. He quietly confirmed most of his father's civil servants in their positions for the purpose of continuity and appointed others to fill vacancies. He preferred people with experience and education, and if the position required a noble, he made it a point to elevate lower nobles rather than greater ones, people who would be dependent on him.

As an absolutist he expanded the use of royal agents (*corregidores*) and sales taxes (*alcabala*) and supported the wool trade through the Mesta, a sheep-owner's guild. According to tradition, he released most of those that John II had imprisoned and rewarded his own supporters with land and money. The bulk of his promotions were to the rank of count and were applauded, but two promotions, that of Juan Pacheco to marquis of Villena and of Pedro Giron, Juan's brother, to master of Calatrava, were met with distrust and resistance. Juan and Pedro were able and astute, but their meteoric rise from obscurity and their insatiable search for wealth and lands brought them few friends. While being Portuguese by birth made them even less desirable, Castile's nobles would use Juan, in particular, to advance their goals and agendas because they understood that he usually got what he sought.

Henry IV, however, could not focus on the job and preferred, like his father, to allow others—the constable of Castile, the duke of Albuquerque, and Pacheco—to rule in his stead. With his friends working at cross-purposes and without adequate direction from the king, the early reforms were soon neglected. More significantly, Henry allowed the war against Moorish Granada to wind down because he could not resolve conflicting goals. The king understood that his nobles desired the conquest of the region to enhance their properties, but as monarch he knew that he needed to preserve the Islamic Moors and their industries. It was, thus, not surprising or popular when he opted for limited war against key fortresses, such as Gibralter. In return, his nobles, including Pacheco, accused him of "loving" Arabs and of cowardice. Many turned, as they did under his father, to Aragon, and the crises of the previous regime returned. Since Henry was no better than his father in defusing these threats to his authority, he failed to notice or could not believe that his favorites were destroying his authority.

The king's control was so weakened by 1457 that talk began about his younger half brother, Alfonso, being named prince of the Asturias. While the king was able to sidestep this obvious reduction of his power, he was forced to accept the arrangement in 1462. The birth of a daughter, Joan, only postponed the plan, with Alfonso being declared prince and then king by Pacheco and the rebels in 1465. The young Alfonso's unexpected death in 1468 allowed Henry's half sister, Isabella, to take his position as heir in 1470. She became Queen Isabella I of Castile in 1474 and joint ruler with her husband, King Ferdinand II of Aragon, in 1479.

Ignoring the less important question of inheritance, Henry IV concentrated his last years on maintaining the realm and passing it on intact. He allied with Portugal, Granada, and France in 1464 in anticipation of civil war and resumed conflict with Aragon. He offered land and money to key supporters and pardoned his enemies. Yet, his failure to act decisively repeatedly opened the way for his opponents to block his designs. As a result, he would die quietly in 1474 without achieving his long-term goal of reunifying Castile. Although unintended, Queen Isabella I and King Ferdinand II would accomplish what Henry IV failed to do by using many of the centralist instruments that Henry so ineffectively wielded.

SIGNIFICANCE

Henry is remembered as one of Castile's weakest monarchs. He was shy, introverted, and untrained in the ways of kingship. In addition, he was unassertive and gave way readily to those who were stronger than he. His seeming ineptitude, rumors of friendship with Jews and Moors, and his reputation as a lowlife raised grave questions of his leadership qualities. Still, he realized that Castile required more centralization to survive, surrounded as it was by Portugal, France, Navarre, Aragon, and Granada, and he did his best, however erratic, to accomplish this end. His efforts in this direction were often sensible and innovative and foretold the later work of Queen Isabella I and King Ferdinand II of Spain.

—Louis P. Towles

FURTHER READING

Doubleday, Simon, trans. "A Late-Medieval Spanish No-bleman: Don Juan Pacheco, Master of the Order of Santiago (1419-1474)." In *Medieval Sourcebook.* Bronx, N.Y.: Fordham University Center for Medieval Studies, 1971. Although tongue in cheek, this is the best source on Pacheco. The writer, a contemporary to the favorite, knew both his flaws and his virtues.

Lefseldt, E. A. "Ruling Sexuality: The Political Legitimacy of Isabel of Castile." *Renaissance Quarterly* 53, no. 1 (Spring, 2000): 31-56. Examines the gendered construction of power during the reign of Queen Isabella I. Argues that her legitimacy as a ruler was based on her ability to "transcend" her gender and thereby compensate for Henry's weaknesses.

Phillips, William D. *Enrique IV and the Crisis of Fifteenth Century Castile, 1425-1480.* Cambridge, England: Mediaeval Academy, 1978. Presents an excellent survey of works on Henry prior to 1975 and is the most readable account of his life. Lacks a detailed discussion of key aspects of Henry's life. No index.

Ruiz, Teofilio. *Spanish Society, 1400-1600.* Harlow, England: Longmans, 2001. Good commentary on Spanish society and customs; however, limited discussion of Henry IV.

SEE ALSO: Boabdil; Ferdinand II and Isabella I; Francisco Jiménez de Cisneros.

RELATED ARTICLES in *Great Events from History: The Renaissance & Early Modern Era, 1454-1600:* October 19, 1469: Marriage of Ferdinand and Isabella; 1474-1479: Castilian War of Succession; November 1, 1478: Establishment of the Spanish Inquisition.

HENRY VI
King of England (r. 1422-1461, 1470-1471)

As the realm recoiled from the confusion of a continental conflict and a civil war, Henry VI, the third and last Lancastrian king of England, abrogated his role as an effective monarch and became a pawn of his relatives and great nobles.

BORN: December 6, 1421; Windsor, Berkshire, England
DIED: May 21, 1471; London, England
ALSO KNOWN AS: Henry of Windsor
AREA OF ACHIEVEMENT: Government and politics

EARLY LIFE

Born at Windsor, and the only child of England's Henry V and Catherine of France, Henry of Windsor found himself to be a fated figure in the events of the Hundred Years' War between England and France and the subsequent Wars of the Roses, which pitted England's rival noble factions, the Lancastrians and Yorkists, against each other. After the death of Henry V on August 31, 1422, he ascended the throne as Henry VI, the third Lancastrian monarch of England. When his maternal grandfather, Charles VI, died a few weeks later, Henry was also acclaimed king of France. Henry's lifelong naïveté colored his almost forty-year rule, and his reign marked the pinnacle of royal impotence, giving credence to the well-known text from Ecclesiastes, "Woe to thee, O land, when the king is a child."

Head of a dual monarchy before his first birthday, Henry VI ruled for sixteen years under the regency of his father's brothers. John, duke of Bedford, an efficient administrator and capable soldier, oversaw France; the less competent Humphrey, duke of Gloucester, served as regent in England. A fierce rivalry erupted between Gloucester and the chancellor, Henry Beaufort, bishop of Winchester and the king's great-uncle. The two intrigued against each other, and their bickering disrupted the machinery of government and weakened the war effort abroad. Despite their differences, the uncles maintained the fiction of personal government, but the influence of an infant sovereign was negligible. At the age of two, Henry gave permission for his own chastisement, assuring his staff he would bear no grudges. The king's boyhood appearances, however, remained few and were confined to ceremonial acts, such as the opening of Parliament, his coronation at Westminster Abbey in 1429, and the French crowning in 1431. For the most part, he lived in comparative seclusion in the Thames Valley.

Although he hunted with falcon and hawk and had his own suits of armor, the bilingual young king preferred to spend his time reading religious tomes and the historical writings of English priests. A meek and devout boy whose piety bordered on smugness, Henry grew into a well-meaning but incapable recluse, better suited for the monastery than for the monarchy. His greatest oaths consisted of "forsooth and forsooth" and an occasional "St.

Jehan grant mercis," and nothing, not even stampeding horses and collapsed tents, roused him to profanity. Benevolent to the point of lunacy and oblivious to the sway of politics about him, the tall, studious Henry VI remained throughout his life the perfect pawn in the hands of his relatives and great nobles.

LIFE'S WORK

In the autumn of 1437, just before his sixteenth birthday, Henry VI ended his minority and began to issue warrants under his own seal. He traveled about the kingdom and involved himself in endowing a grammar school at Eton, establishing King's College at Cambridge, and authorizing a library for Salisbury Cathedral. The demands of the royal office rankled, and he soon allowed the nobles to resume the direction of affairs of state. As the power of the English monarchy declined, the prosecution of the war against France became a pivotal issue in politics. Beaufort, as well as his nephew Edmund Beaufort, duke of Somerset, and their ally William de la Pole, earl (later duke) of Suffolk, favored peace. Though Bedford had died in 1435, Gloucester and Richard, duke of York, next in line for the throne, wished to continue the war.

Ignoring Gloucester, Henry VI chose to end the conflict, which had gone badly after the 1429 French victory at Orléans, led by Joan of Arc. Since Beaufort was old and Somerset incompetent, Henry depended on Suffolk, whom he showered with offices and lands. Suffolk governed the court and in 1445 won a two-year truce in the war by arranging the marriage of Henry VI to Charles VII's niece, Margaret of Anjou. An assertive, capable beauty, the new queen assumed the necessary role of authority and persuaded her gentle husband to surrender Maine to the French and to reduce the English garrisons in Normandy. Gloucester and Beaufort both died in 1447, leaving Suffolk and Margaret in power and the duke of York biding his time. Losses in Normandy in 1449 and 1450 soon made Suffolk unpopular, and the House of Commons sought his impeachment. Six months later, Jack Cade led a force of thirty thousand discontented Kentsmen to London, yet their rout did not end the country's unrest.

Royal authority continued to decline throughout the 1450's. The year 1453 proved particularly traumatic. In July, England experienced its final military humiliation in the Hundred Years' War with the loss of all continental territory except the city of Calais; in August, Henry suffered a total mental and physical collapse. In the face of disaster, Parliament named the duke of York lord protector, but Yorkist control lasted only as long as the king's

Henry VI. (Library of Congress)

madness. When Henry regained his senses in December, 1454, Margaret, who had given birth to a son two months earlier, and her Lancastrian associates recovered their influence over royal administration. Confronted with an heir to the throne and a forceful queen, York, aided by his cousin Richard Neville, earl of Warwick, took action and the struggle for power erupted onto the battlefield.

At St. Albans in May, 1455, a Yorkist army defeated the Lancastrians in a battle that traditionally marks the beginning of the Wars of the Roses. Somerset died in the conflict, the king was wounded by an arrow in the neck, and York seized the opportunity to retake the protectorship as Henry suffered a second mental collapse. York did not hold power long, for the king regained a semblance of sanity in 1456 and the queen regained control at court. The next four years marked a period of Royalist reaction. Because of political tension in the countryside and growing tumult in London, the royal court resided primarily in the Midlands. Henry now became a pathetic shadow of a king, but he did strive intermittently for reconciliation with his opponents, offering them pardons. Morbidly preoccupied with death, Henry spent several months planning his vault and having workmen mark his exact measurements on the floor of Westminster Abbey.

The direction of the affairs of state lay with the masterful Margaret, who prepared for war with the Yorkists.

In 1460, York, disgusted by the puppet king, claimed the throne as his birthright—he was descended from Edward III's third son, while Henry's claim came from kinship with the fourth son. The civil conflict now began in earnest, with the fortunes of war fluctuating wildly. The Yorkists triumphed over the Lancastrians in July; Henry was taken prisoner and forced to acknowledge Richard to the exclusion of his young son. In December, the Lancastrians succeeded in a battle in which York met his death. In February, 1461, the Lancastrians won again, gaining for Henry his freedom, but in March, Warwick and the new duke of York, Edward, decisively defeated the Lancastrians in a savage seven-hour battle during a blinding snowstorm. The Lancastrians never recovered from this defeat, and Warwick the "kingmaker" successfully placed the duke of York on the throne as Edward IV. Henry VI spent the next three years in exile in Scotland; his movements during this period hardly reveal him to be a sane individual. He returned to take part in an abortive rising in 1464 but a year later was captured and taken as a prisoner to the Tower of London, where he remained until 1470.

As the Lancastrian menace lessened and peace appeared permanent, the friendship between Edward and Warwick paled. When Edward chose his own bride, ignoring his chief adviser's plans for a French marriage, Warwick joined the Lancastrian cause and aided Margaret in an attack on his former ally. Edward fled to the Continent. On October 3, 1470, Henry VI, a shuffling imbecile, left the Tower to be proclaimed monarch again by the kingmaker. Recaptured by Edward in April, 1471, Henry accompanied his Yorkist foe to Barnet, where the Lancastrians again tasted defeat and Warwick died. Another failure at Tewkesbury brought about the death of the prince of Wales, the capture of the queen, and the end of the Lancastrian cause. Henry VI died in the Tower, probably at the hands of an assassin, on May 21, 1471. His body was placed in an obscure grave in Chertsey Abbey and then reinterred at St. George Chapel, Windsor, in 1484.

SIGNIFICANCE

The reign of Henry VI, England's last Lancastrian monarch, has a number of dramatic ironies. Henry VI has the distinction of being the youngest ruler to ascend the English throne. He was also the only English ruler to be acknowledged by the French as the legitimate king of France and to receive coronation at Notre Dame Cathe-

dral in Paris. Because he was less than a year old at the time of his succession to two thrones, there was no time in Henry's memory when he was not a monarch, and he knew no effective role models for the task of governing. He also assumed his majority earlier than any of his predecessors and successors, and his thirty-nine-year reign provided ample opportunity for flaws to magnify themselves. Furthermore, Henry's rule coincided with, and contributed to, a debilitating civil war that cost him his throne. In the dynastic revolution that followed, he was briefly restored, thereby becoming the only British king to have two separate reigns.

Henry was well-intentioned, with some laudable aspirations for improving relations with France, fostering educational advantages, and rewarding friends and servants. As intelligent and as thoroughly schooled as his contemporaries, he never lost his youthful reliance on others to make decisions for him. He was also far too compassionate toward lawbreakers and lacked the ability to sense the implications of their activities. Henry VI's mental breakdown in 1453-1454, followed by his recovery and a subsequent relapse in 1455, vitiated any further possibility of effective leadership. An almost total dependence on others marked the last fifteen years of his life. Henry VI died a demented, pathetic figure who was denied even his fondest dream, burial at Westminster Abbey. Later efforts to canonize him provided posthumous praise. In death, Henry VI realized the potential he never achieved in life.

—Carol Crowe-Carraco

FURTHER READING

Chrimes, Stanley Bertram. *Lancastrians, Yorkists, and Henry VII*. New York: St. Martin's Press, 1965. General survey of the political and dynastic history of fifteenth century England with emphasis on constitutional issues. Denies that there was true war in the Wars of the Roses and insists that the conflict was a struggle for power based on dynastic rivalries. Makes an excellent supplement to William Shakespeare's historical plays.

Dockray, Keith, ed. *Henry VI, Margaret of Anjou, and the Wars of the Roses: A Source Book*. Stroud, Gloucestershire, England: Sutton, 2000. A collection of primary sources produced by and relating to Henry VI and his queen. Includes bibliographic references and index.

Gillingham, John. *The Wars of the Roses: Peace and Conflict in Fifteenth Century England*. Baton Rouge: Louisiana State University Press, 1981. Maintains that the Wars of the Roses were, in reality, three separate wars and that the first one (which the author dates from the 1450's to 1464) was caused by Henry VI's shortcomings and his inability to hold France or govern England. Suggests that Henry's mental collapses may have been a case of catatonic schizophrenia.

Griffiths, Ralph A. *The Reign of King Henry VI: The Exercise of Royal Authority, 1421-1461*. Rev. ed. Stroud, Gloucestershire, England: Sutton, 1998. The definitive study of Henry VI and the entire spectrum of political life during his reign. Discusses relations among political groups, financial concerns, administration of justice, and foreign affairs. Portrays the last Lancastrian king as a well-meaning incompetent, and questions if, after the mental collapse of 1454-1455, Henry VI ever again had the capacity to carry out his official responsibilities. A major contribution to fifteenth century English historiography.

Gross, Anthony. *The Dissolution of the Lancastrian Kingship: Sir John Fortescue and the Crisis of Monarchy in Fifteenth-Century England*. Stamford, Lincolnshire, England: P. Watkins, 1996. Set of three interrelated essays, together with a substantial introductory essay, on Fortescue's life and career. Attempts to understand the political instability and outbreaks of civil war during Henry VI's reign as a function of genuine philosophical differences between competing theoretical principles of government, and not merely as the Machiavellian maneuverings of self-interested nobles hungry for power. Includes illustrations, bibliographic references, and index.

Hicks, Michael. *The Wars of the Roses, 1455-1485*. New York: Routledge, 2004. Detailed history of the military campaigns of the Wars of the Roses, and the reasons behind them. Includes nine strategic maps, illustrations, bibliography, and index.

Jacob, Ernest Fraser. *The Fifteenth Century, 1399-1485*. Reprint. New York: Oxford University Press, 1993. Comprehensive and authoritative account of the fifteenth century in all its complexities and paradoxes. Provides more information than stimulus and has a detailed but dated bibliography. Contains no analysis of the character of Henry VI.

Kendall, Paul Murray. *Warwick the Kingmaker*. New York: W. W. Norton, 1957. Excellent and well-documented account of Warwick as a public figure. In a colorful format, follows the tangled relations between factions in fifteenth century England. Glimpses of Henry VI reveal an insane king who existed in an animal-like stupor. Presupposes extensive background knowledge.

Lander, Jack Robert. *Crown and Nobility, 1450-1509*. Montreal: McGill-Queen's University Press, 1986. Traces struggles for supremacy between the Crown and the nobility in the latter half of the fifteenth century and contains a historiographical essay on period studies. Questions the stories of Henry VI's 1455 mental breakdown as the reason for the duke of York's second protectorate and sees events in the light of York's possibly treasonable desire to have the throne.

Smith, Lacy Baldwin. *This Realm of England, 1399 to 1688*. Lexington, Mass.: D. C. Heath, 1976. A very readable, general account of English history from the fifteenth through the seventeenth centuries. Includes a basic narrative of the fifteenth century "curse of disputed succession" and identifies Henry VI as a cipher more qualified for the Church than the Crown.

Storey, Robin Lindsay. *The End of the House of Lancaster*. New York: Stein and Day, 1966. Finds the causes of the Wars of the Roses to be far more than conflicting hereditary claims to the throne. Places emphasis on the role of the nobility, who were concerned with getting and keeping real estate, not realms. Indicates that Henry VI had small capacity for kingship before his mental breakdown in 1454 and certainly none after that date.

Watts, John. *Henry VI and the Politics of Kingship*. New York: Cambridge University Press, 1996. Detailed structural analysis of the political system in place during Henry's reign. Attempts to understand how the chaotic civil wars broke out, and how Henry was able to stay on his throne for so long despite such intense political instability, and despite his own mental instability. Includes illustrations, bibliographic references, and index.

SEE ALSO: Lady Margaret Beaufort; Charles VII; Edward IV; Sir John Fortescue; Henry VII; Richard III; William Shakespeare; The Tudor Family; Earl of Warwick.

RELATED ARTICLE in *Great Events from History: The Renaissance & Early Modern Era, 1454-1600:* 1455-1485: Wars of the Roses.

HENRY VII
King of England (r. 1485-1509)

Henry's sense of caution, his flair for public relations, and his knowledge of the importance of timing allowed him to end the Wars of the Roses and lay the foundations of England's Tudor Dynasty.

BORN: January 28, 1457; Pembroke Castle, Pembrokeshire, Wales
DIED: April 21, 1509; Richmond, Surrey, England
ALSO KNOWN AS: Henry Tudor; earl of Richmond
AREA OF ACHIEVEMENT: Government and politics

EARLY LIFE

Henry Tudor spent his childhood and young adulthood in exile. The child who would one day found one of England's most illustrious dynasties became, at an early age, a pawn in that long, bitterly fought family squabble known as the Wars of the Roses. As the grandson of Catherine of France, King Henry V's widow, and Owen Tudor, a Welsh squire and courtier, young Henry was a relatively obscure Lancastrian claimant to the throne. On his mother's side, his blood was more legitimately royal and his claim to the throne was stronger. His mother, Lady Margaret Beaufort, was the great-great-granddaughter of King Edward III and therefore an undisputed Lancastrian princess. Henry's father, Edmund Tudor, earl of Richmond, died in 1456, only a few months before young Henry's birth, and the child was then adopted by his uncle Jasper Tudor, duke of Bedford, a diehard Lancastrian who was to defend the boy from Yorkist intrigue and advance his claim to the throne in the ensuing turbulent years.

The Lancastrian cause suffered a crushing blow at the Battle of Mortimer's Cross in 1461, and with it fell the fortunes of the Tudor family. Henry's grandfather, Owen Tudor, was captured by the Yorkists and publicly beheaded, while Jasper Tudor managed to escape and go underground. Young Henry fell into the hands of the Yorkists when they overtook Pembroke Castle in Wales, Jasper Tudor's stronghold. Taken from his mother, Henry was given over to the custody of Lord Herbert of Raglan, and he spent the next nine years of his life undergoing careful, but ultimately futile, Yorkist indoctrination. With King Henry VI imprisoned in the Tower of London and the Yorkist King Edward IV on the throne, the Lancastrian cause seemed lost forever. The unexpected restoration of Henry VI in 1470, however, brought the Lancastrians back to power and the Tudors back to royal favor. By then fourteen, Henry Tudor was taken

from the Herberts by his uncle Jasper and presented at King Henry's court. Yet another Yorkist uprising toppled Henry VI a mere six months after his restoration, however, and Edward IV reclaimed the throne. Jasper and Henry Tudor managed to escape the ensuing bloodbath and took refuge in Brittany, where they remained in relative seclusion for the next twelve years.

With the death of Edward IV in 1483, England again fell into political turmoil. Richard, duke of Gloucester (later King Richard III), the brother of the late king, installed the king's two young sons in the Tower, where they apparently died or were murdered by the ambitious Richard (though the facts in this case are still disputed). Meanwhile, however, Richard had declared them illegitimate and their claim to the throne invalid. In June of 1483, he seized power and claimed the throne. His reign, however, was to be relatively short-lived, for a Tudor conspiracy was brewing both in Brittany and among the dispossessed Lancastrian factions of England. Henry Tudor's mother, Margaret Beaufort, now married to the Yorkist Thomas, Lord Stanley, had apparently never given up hope of placing her son on the throne, and she was able to enlist the help of Queen Elizabeth Woodville, Edward IV's widow, as well as that of the powerful duke of Buckingham and, to a lesser extent, that of the seigneurial Stanley family. In August, 1485, a rebel army led by Jasper and Henry Tudor defeated the much larger but evidently less faithful army of Richard III at the Battle of Bosworth. Legend has it that the crown worn by the slain Richard III fell into a thornbush, from which it was retrieved by the man who then placed it on his head and proclaimed himself King Henry VII.

LIFE'S WORK

Almost at once, Henry VII began to exhibit the sure sense of public relations that would characterize his reign, that of his son, Henry VIII, and that of his granddaughter, Elizabeth I. His coronation, which took place on October 30, 1485, in Westminster Abbey, was a grand affair, full of the splendor, pomp, and pageantry that the English people expected from the monarchy. His marriage, on January 16, 1486, to Elizabeth of York, the daughter of Edward IV, was also a great and glamorous state ceremony, as was the christening of their first son, Prince Arthur, in September, 1486. Yet none of these showy and expensive public celebrations betrayed a mere love of luxury on the king's part; on the contrary, each of them bespoke Henry's characteristic political shrewdness.

The new king realized that his claim to the throne was more one of conquest than of birth, and that the greater the measures he took to make his reign appear legitimate, the better. Though his marriage is generally considered to have been a happy one, it was purely politically motivated: Elizabeth was the principal female heir of the House of York, and Henry's marriage to her went far toward healing the factious wounds inflicted by the seemingly endless Wars of the Roses. Even the infant Prince Arthur served his father's political purposes, since a new dynasty required a male heir to ensure a smooth succession. Arthur's birth was followed by those of Princess Margaret, Prince Henry (later King Henry VIII), Princess Elizabeth, Princess Mary, and Prince Edmund.

Despite Henry's surprisingly successful attempts to consolidate his power, however, Yorkist intrigue persisted, and at least two Yorkist plots seriously threatened to undermine his hold on the throne. In 1487, a man claiming to be the earl of Warwick, Edward IV's nephew and the principal Yorkist pretender to the throne, surfaced in Ireland and was given support by the Irish nobil-

ity and by the duchess of Burgundy, Edward IV's sister. Though it was obvious to Henry that the man was an impostor (the real Warwick had been imprisoned in the Tower since the Battle of Bosworth Field), he was no less a threat, especially after the Irish "crowned" him Edward VI in Dublin. Henry was able to thwart this plot, but only after a narrowly won battle at Stoke in the summer of 1487. The "earl of Warwick," in reality a commoner named Lambert Simnel, proved to be no more than a puppet of the duchess of Burgundy, and Henry, rather than executing him, put him to work in the royal kitchens.

In 1491, yet another "Warwick" appeared in Ireland, this time named Perkin Warbeck; once again, Margaret of Burgundy seems to have been responsible. Warbeck presented a greater threat to Henry's reign than had Simnel, for he was later recognized not as Warwick but as the duke of York, one of the presumably slain sons of Edward IV, by no less than King Charles VIII of France. The Warbeck affair continued to trouble Henry for some time, and before it was over, Henry had discovered that one of its sponsors was Sir William Stanley, his mother's brother-in-law, whom he then executed for treason in 1495. Warbeck was later supported by King James IV of Scotland, but, by 1497, popular support for the scheme had dwindled, and Warbeck was executed, along with the true earl of Warwick, in 1499.

When he was not occupied with putting down Yorkist plots against his reign, Henry sought to strengthen his international prestige through a series of matrimonial alliances, and in this area he was equally adept. In 1496, he successfully negotiated the betrothal of Prince Arthur to Princess Catherine of Aragon, daughter of Ferdinand and Isabella of Spain, and the two were married in 1501 (Arthur died in 1502, and Catherine later married Arthur's brother, Henry VIII, and became Queen Catherine, the first of the six wives of Henry VIII).

In 1503, Henry married his eldest daughter, Margaret, to King James IV of Scotland. Several other attempts at matrimonial diplomacy met with less success, including, after Queen Elizabeth's death in 1503, Henry's own attempts to marry Princess Margaret of Savoy (later Margaret of Austria), daughter of Emperor Maximilian I of the Holy Roman Empire and, later, Queen Joan of Naples, Isabella's niece. On the complicated political scene of medieval Europe, marriage was the preferred method of diplomacy, and Henry's matrimonial negotiations ensured a measure of peace between his island kingdom and the eternally warmongering Scottish to the north and a certain amount of strength through his association with the all-powerful Spanish and Austrians.

Henry VII. (Library of Congress)

Henry's domestic policies were less daring but equally as shrewd as his foreign policies. Justified or not, his reputation has often been that of a skinflint who kept the peace only because war was expensive, but his concern for financial stability is surely understandable in the light of the turmoil by which he came to power and of the comparative poverty in which he spent his youth. Through an aggressive trade policy and through vigorous taxation, he enriched a treasury that he had found sadly depleted. He showed considerable foresight in backing the explorer John Cabot, whose voyages cleared the way for the empire that would reach its height under Henry's granddaughter, Elizabeth I. Never a true innovator in the ways of government, Henry nevertheless valorized the virtues of caution and frugality by leaving an impressive budget surplus to his son, Henry VIII.

SIGNIFICANCE

When he died on April 21, 1509, Henry VII left behind an England much more powerful and prosperous than it had been when he had seized power nearly twenty-four years earlier, and it is by his effect on his country that he must be judged, especially in the light of the paucity of information about his private life and personality. Clearly, he was ruthless when his crown was at stake, as is evidenced by his execution of the innocent earl of Warwick in 1499. Yet though he was merciless to those who threatened or appeared to threaten his dynasty, he was unfailingly generous to those who helped him establish it, and he never forgot a favor.

In no way an intellectual, Henry contented himself with being crafty, and his ability to focus his attention on purely practical matters made possible the unparalleled patronage of the arts practiced by Henry VIII and Elizabeth I. Though he had little of the personal charisma enjoyed by his son and granddaughter, the great majority of his people revered him, but even here he was not overconfident and supplied them with lavish shows of royal pomp and ceremony whenever possible.

Modern interpretations of this first Tudor monarch differ vastly. To some historians, he was the ruthless and penurious king who overtaxed his subjects and used his marriageable children as mere instruments of statecraft, while to others, he was an innately kindly man who was ambitious and vengeful only because circumstances forced him to be. Perhaps Henry Tudor is best judged in the light of Niccolò Machiavelli's *Il principe* (wr. 1513, pb. 1532; *The Prince*, 1640), written just after Henry's death. Though Machiavelli had in mind the Borgia family of Italy while writing this masterpiece of political philosophy, his description of the pragmatic ruler whose morals must adapt themselves to the shifting political climate lends itself particularly well to this tough-minded Welshman who became king of England through sheer force of will.

—*J. D. Daubs*

FURTHER READING

Alexander, Michael Van Cleave. *The First of the Tudors: A Study of Henry VII and His Reign*. Totowa, N.J.: Rowman and Littlefield, 1980. This highly readable work, intended primarily for the general reader rather than the historian, seeks to supplement the rather scanty information about Henry's personality and to suggest how the political influenced the personal, and vice versa, in Henry's life. Alexander succeeds admirably in dispelling the myth of the dull and parsimonious king.

Bevan, Bryan. *Henry VII: The First Tudor King*. London: Rubicon Press, 2000. Emphasizes Henry's significant cunning and diplomacy, which enabled him to survive in his own treacherous court, as well as the deterioration of his character after his wife and son died. Includes illustrations, bibliographic references, index.

Chrimes, S. B. *Henry VII*. Berkeley: University of California Press, 1972. This book is probably the best available source of information about the changes in governmental policy brought about by Henry Tudor. Chrimes has drawn on rarely consulted government documents to create a comprehensive interpretation of Henry's relations with Parliament and with the European community. The result is solid and reliable, but the general reader may find it dry.

Elton, G. R. *England Under the Tudors*. 3d ed. New York: Routledge, 1991. Elton's study also focuses on the political and governmental but places Henry's reign in the larger context of the sixteenth century—what Elton calls "the Tudor century." Thus, his discussion of Henry VII is skillfully connected to those of Henry's successors. A good, if overdetailed, one-volume introduction to the Tudor dynasty.

Loades, David, ed. *Chronicles of the Tudor Kings*. Godalming, Surrey, England: Bramley Books, 1997. Anthology of eighty brief essays about all aspects of the culture and reign of the Tudor kings of England. Includes illustrations, genealogical table, maps, glossary, bibliography, and index.

Mackie, John D. *The Earlier Tudors, 1485-1558*. Rev. ed. Oxford, England: Clarendon Press, 1966. A heavily interpretive and consistently interesting account of nearly every conceivable facet of Henry's reign, and indeed of the reigns of all the Tudor rulers up to Elizabeth. This study also serves as a concise overview of European politics during the Tudor years. A lavishly detailed table of contents will aid the reader in finding what he or she seeks in this comprehensive account.

Simons, Eric N. *Henry VII: The First Tudor King*. New York: Barnes and Noble Books, 1968. Breezy and clearly written, this book often sacrifices rigor to romanticism, but the nonspecialist reader will find it an entertaining introduction to Henry's reign.

Tatton-Brown, Tim, and Richard Mortimer, eds. *Westminster Abbey: The Lady Chapel of Henry VII*. Rochester, N.Y.: Boydell Press, 2003. Details the history and importance of Henry VII's chapel in Westminster Abbey, the last masterpiece of medieval architecture and one of Henry's most concrete and lasting accomplishments as king. Includes photographic plates, illustrations, bibliographic references, index.

SEE ALSO: Lady Margaret Beaufort; Cesare Borgia; John Cabot; Catherine of Aragon; Charles VIII; Edward IV; Elizabeth I; Ferdinand II and Isabella I; Henry VI; Henry VIII; James IV; Niccolò Machiavelli; Maximilian I; Richard III; The Tudor Family; Earl of Warwick.

RELATED ARTICLES in *Great Events from History: The Renaissance & Early Modern Era, 1454-1600:* 1455-1485: Wars of the Roses; 1483-1485: Richard III Rules England; Beginning 1485: The Tudors Rule England; 1489: Yorkshire Rebellion; December 1, 1494: Poynings' Law; 1497: Cornish Rebellion; June 24, 1497-May, 1498: Cabot's Voyages.

HENRY VIII
King of England (r. 1509-1547)

Through administrative changes, a break with the Roman Catholic Church, and the subsequent establishment of the Church of England, Henry VIII strengthened the position of the monarch in English society. Furthermore, his chaotic and violent marital history revealed a side of Henry's character that is ambiguous and has led many scholars into the realm of psychological speculation.

BORN: June 28, 1491; Greenwich, near London, England
DIED: January 28, 1547; London
AREAS OF ACHIEVEMENT: Government and politics, religion and theology

EARLY LIFE

Henry VIII was the second son of the first Tudor king and the Lancastrian claimant to the throne, Henry VII, and Elizabeth, the daughter of the Yorkist Edward IV. Henry VII gained the Crown by defeating Richard III at Bosworth Field in 1485; Richard III was killed in the battle, and Henry Tudor, a Welshman, immediately assumed the throne. During his early years, Prince Henry was overshadowed by his older brother, Arthur, who was his father's heir. Little is known of Henry's education except that the poet John Skelton was involved; Skelton wrote *Speculum principis* (also known as *A Mirror for Princes*) in 1501 as a guidebook for Henry. It is also believed that Lady Margaret Beaufort, Henry VII's mother, was involved with her grandson's education. Whatever the nature and source of his education, Henry later demonstrated that he had a firm grasp of the classics, a limited knowledge of music, and fluency in three languages. Young Henry was interested in most forms of contemporary sport and was recognized for his athletic abilities.

Henry remained a secondary figure as long as his brother was alive. His father never assigned him any responsibility or seriously pursued any marriage arrangement for Henry. Henry VII did express some tentative interest in a marriage between Prince Henry and Eleanor, daughter of Philip, the duke of Burgundy, but it was not seriously considered. In April, 1502, Prince Arthur, earlier married to Catherine of Aragon, died in Wales from tuberculosis at the age of fifteen. Suddenly, the overlooked second son became the heir to the throne and the focus of great attention and interest. Henry VII became very protective of his only surviving son. Negotiations with Madrid were conducted in 1503, and on June 23 of that year a treaty was signed that provided for the marriage of Henry to the widow, Catherine of Aragon, on Henry's attainment of the age of fifteen. One obstacle that had to be overcome was acquiring a dispensation from Rome to permit the marriage. The need for the dispensation was based on a scriptural directive that prohibited one from marrying the widow of one's brother. Catherine argued that only a dispensation on the basis of the impediment of public honesty was required because the marriage had never been consummated. Both English and Spanish officials agreed, however, that a dispensation on the basis of the impediment of affinity in the first degree collateral should be obtained. Problems (financial, political, personal, and with the church) continued to plague the marriage treaty. On April 21, 1509, Henry VII died at Richmond Palace; six weeks later, on June 11, 1509, Henry VIII married Catherine of Aragon.

LIFE'S WORK

The thirty-six-year reign of one of the greatest monarchs in English history began with great expectations for a bright and progressive era in English affairs. Henry VIII, the eighteen-year-old king, was exceptionally handsome and stood slightly more than 6 feet in height. He was clearly different from his father: Whereas Henry VII was reserved and secretive, Henry VIII was open and frequently discussed matters of state freely. Henry VIII set out to create a public image of himself as a Renaissance prince in the tradition of Desiderius Erasmus and other notables of the Northern Renaissance. In fact, while he was familiar with the general scope of the literature, Henry VIII did not understand the ideals that motivated the writings of Erasmus, John Colet, and Sir Thomas More. On the second day of his reign, Henry ordered the arrest of two of his father's principal advisers and administrators, Richard Empson and Edmund Dudley, on charges of extortion. They were executed sixteen months later.

During the early years of his reign, Henry was content to pursue sports and court games. In 1512, in an effort to demonstrate that he was a warrior king, Henry entered into an alliance with Spain against France. While nothing of military substance emerged from the war, Henry gained popularity through the capture of Tournai. The most significant development of the war was Henry's recognition of the abilities of Thomas Wolsey. From 1515 to 1529, Wolsey served Henry as lord chancellor of England and as archbishop of York; Wolsey also became a cardinal of the Roman Catholic Church and entertained the ambition of becoming pope. In 1517, another able administrator, More, was named as a councillor to the king. More, who was considered one of the superior intellects of the age and who was the author of *De optimo reipublicae statu, deque nova insula utopia* (1516; *Uto-*

Henry VIII. (Library of Congress)

pia, 1551), observed that Henry compartmentalized his thoughts and discussions. Philosophic consideration of ideals had no impact on pragmatic situations; Henry did not allow these two separate concerns to intersect, for the result would be unpredictability, and with that, danger.

As Lutheranism developed on the Continent, Henry stood firm in his support of Rome. In 1520, Martin Luther wrote several pamphlets in which he denied or challenged several major tenets of Catholic theology. One of the most serious of Luther's assertions concerned sacramental theology; in response, Henry, in 1521, wrote *Assertio septem sacramentorum adversus Martinum Lutherum* (*Assertio septem sacramentorum: Or, An Assertion of the Seven Sacraments Against Martin Luther,*

1687), which denounced Luther's views and reaffirmed the traditional Catholic teaching on the Sacraments.

As the 1520's progressed, Henry's reign entered a period that became increasingly unsettled; this situation was a result of a number of factors. The public enthusiasm for the king that had greeted the new monarch and carried him through the early years of the reign was diminished significantly. Furthermore, Henry, as well as the other monarchs of Europe, ruled in the shadow of Charles V, the Holy Roman Emperor and unquestionably the most powerful individual in Europe during the first half of the sixteenth century. Finally, and most important for Henry, his marriage with Catherine had produced only one surviving child, Mary, and no male heir.

In 1527, Henry directed Wolsey to obtain an annulment of his marriage to Catherine so that he could be free to marry Anne Boleyn. Negotiations with Rome dragged on for years as Charles V, at the urging of his aunt, Catherine of Aragon, pressured Pope Clement VI not to grant the annulment. Henry's increasing frustration led to the fall of Wolsey in 1529 and the subsequent rise of Thomas Cromwell and Thomas Cranmer as the principal advisers to the king on state and religious matters. The influence of Protestants at the court became evident during the early 1530's. In 1533, a group of English bishops granted the king his annulment; Henry married Boleyn, who soon gave birth to Princess Elizabeth. In 1534, Henry and Cromwell pushed the Act of Succession and the Act of Supremacy from the Reformation Parliament, and the break with Rome was complete. In 1535-1536, the Henrician government suppressed opposition to these policies through the Pilgrimage of Grace in the northern counties. In 1536, the dissolution of the monasteries took place and the Ten Articles of Religion, which were sympathetic to the Protestants, appeared. In 1539, when it was perceived that the public did not support the changes, the Six Articles of Religion, which were Catholic in tenor, were pronounced. During the 1530's, Henry and Cromwell reorganized the administration of the government; the result was a primitive but effective bureaucracy.

In 1540, Cromwell was executed on the charge of treason. In 1536,

Boleyn was executed on the charge of adultery. Henry's next wife, Jane Seymour, provided him with a son, Edward, in 1537 and then died of natural causes associated with the birth. Marriages to Anne of Cleves, Catherine Howard, and Catherine Parr followed. Only Parr survived Henry.

During the 1540's, Henry's health declined steadily, but he retained his mental acumen. Before his death, he wrote a will that provided for a regency to rule the country during his son's minority. If Edward died without heirs, the crown would pass to Mary, and similarly, on to Elizabeth. Henry died on January 28, 1547.

SIGNIFICANCE

The impact of Henry VIII on the development of the English nation and constitution is extensive. Through the manipulation of Wolsey and Cromwell, Henry managed to expand his powers over church and state. Yet he appeared to do so in full cooperation with Parliament. From his personal perspective, the reign was a triumph because he succeeded in transferring the crown to his son, Edward Tudor, and, in so doing, maintained the Tudor Dynasty.

Bishop William Stubbs, a leading English historian of the late nineteenth century, once remarked that Henry was such a complex and immense historical figure that no biographer or historian should undertake to master all aspects of his turbulent life. Stubbs's caution has been accepted by some and rejected by others, but most historians credit Stubbs with making an astute observation.

—*William T. Walker*

HENRY VIII'S ACT OF SUCCESSION

King Henry VIII's Act of Succession proclaimed that his divorce from Queen Catherine to marry Anne Boleyn, despite Pope Clement VII's condemnation, was lawful in the eyes of God. Henry believed the pope had no authority over England's church and state affairs and, especially, no authority over the English monarch. Henry declared himself the head of the Church of England.

If any person or persons . . . maliciously, by writing, print, deed, or act, procure or do any thing or things to the prejudice, slander, or derogation of the said lawful matrimony solemnized between your Majesty and the said Queen Anne . . . every such person and persons, and their aiders and abettors, shall be adjudged high traitors, and every such offense shall be adjudged high treason, and their aiders and abettors, being lawfully convicted, shall suffer pain of death, as in cases of high treason.

Source: Excerpted from *Readings in European History*, by James Harvey Robinson, abridged ed. (Boston: Athenaeum Press, 1906), p. 306.

FURTHER READING

Byrne, Muriel St. Clare, and Bridget Boland, eds. *The Lisle Letters: An Abridgement*. Chicago: University of Chicago Press, 1983. In this collection of the letters of Lord Lisle (Arthur Plantagenet) and other members of his family between 1533 and 1540—when Lisle served as deputy of Calais—Henry is presented as an individual who was motivated by his determination to secure the continuance of the Tudor Dynasty and by his policy to establish an effective, centralized government.

Dickens, A. G. *The English Reformation*. 2d ed. University Park: Pennsylvania State University Press, 1991. Dickens's analysis of Henry's performance in the development of the English Reformation is generally sympathetic. By the late 1520's, Henry was viewed as sympathetic to many of Luther's concepts; the Henrician Reformation was part of a larger movement on the Continent.

Elton, Geoffrey R. *The Tudor Constitution, Documents, and Commentary*. 2d ed. Cambridge, England: Cambridge University Press, 1982. Elton stresses the impact of Cromwell on administrative changes. Through the use of primary documents relating to the Crown's approach to the Reformation, the council, finances, and the courts, the Henrician administration of the 1530's is interpreted as the work of a master political architect, Cromwell.

_____. *The Tudor Revolution in Government, Administrative Changes in the Reign of Henry VIII*. Reprint. Cambridge, England: Cambridge University Press, 1962. In this classic study the author argues that the policies and achievements of Cromwell during the 1530's constituted a revolution in the management of the English state. The beginnings of the modern bureaucratic English government can be traced to Cromwell.

Graves, Michael A. R. *Henry VIII: A Study in Kingship*. New York: Pearson/Longman, 2003. Attempts to separate myth from reality to better understand Henry's life. Good discussion of the relationship between king and Parliament and its historical precedents and effects. Includes bibliographic references and index.

Jensen, De Lamar. *Reformation Europe: Age of Reform and Revolution*. Lexington, Mass.: D. C. Heath, 1981. In this general survey of the Reformation, Henry is presented as a brilliant politician, clear in his purposes, who manipulated his ministers as well as situations in order to pursue his goals.

Loades, David, ed. *Chronicles of the Tudor Kings*. Godalming, Surrey, England: Bramley Books, 1997. Anthology of eighty brief essays about all aspects of the culture and reign of the Tudor kings of England. Includes illustrations, genealogical table, maps, glossary, bibliography, and index.

McEntegart, Rory. *Henry VIII, the League of Schmalkalden, and the English Reformation*. Rochester, N.Y.: Boydell Press, 2002. Study of Henry's alliance and consultation with the Protestant Schmalkaldic League, analyzing his partial incorporation of German religious ideology into his own theology and the nascent Church of England. Looks both at the evolution of Henry's religious thought and the wider political implications of that evolution. Includes bibliographic references and index.

Scarisbrick, J. J. *Henry VIII*. Berkeley: University of California Press, 1968. In this definitive study of Henry, the king emerges as being in control of the regime, a bright and clever politician, and a dedicated reformer in religion. The Scarisbrick thesis has become the standard interpretation of Henry VIII and has superseded the thesis advanced by A. F. Pollard in *Henry VIII* (1902), in which the king was viewed as a reluctant reformer who was loyal to Catholic doctrines.

Smith, Lacey Baldwin. *Henry VIII: The Mask of Royalty*. Boston: Houghton Mifflin, 1973. Henry is portrayed in this biography as an observant and effective administrator who was eccentric in his work habits. The eccentricity frequently led contemporaries to conclude that Henry was not interested in the administration of the realm.

Starkey, David. "After the 'Revolution.'" In *Revolution Reassessed: Revisions in the History of Tudor Government and Administration*, edited by Christopher Coleman and David Starkey. Oxford, England: Clarendon Press, 1986. In this chapter, the author summarizes the attacks which have dismantled the principal points of the Elton thesis.

Wilson, Derek. *In the Lion's Court: Power, Ambition, and Sudden Death in the Reign of Henry VIII*. New York: St. Martin's Press, 2002. Vivid study of the perils of Henry VIII's court that details the fates of six of its members. Thematically designed to suggest parallels between the lives of these "six Thomases" and Henry's six wives. Includes illustrations, maps, sixteen pages of plates, bibliographic references, and index.

SEE ALSO: Anne of Cleves; Lady Margaret Beaufort; Bess of Hardwick; Anne Boleyn; Catherine of Aragon; Charles V; John Colet; Thomas Cranmer; Thomas

Cromwell; Edward IV; Elizabeth I; Desiderius Erasmus; Henry VII; Catherine Howard; Martin Luther; Mary I; Sir Thomas More; Catherine Parr; Richard III; Jane Seymour; The Tudor Family; Cardinal Thomas Wolsey.

RELATED ARTICLES in *Great Events from History: The Renaissance & Early Modern Era, 1454-1600:* Early 1460's: Labor Shortages Alter Europe's Social Structure; July 16, 1465-April, 1559: French-Burgundian and French-Austrian Wars; Beginning 1485: The Tudors Rule England; August 22, 1513-July 6, 1560: Anglo-Scottish Wars; 1515-1529: Wolsey Serves as Lord Chancellor and Cardinal; 1516: Sir Thomas More Publishes *Utopia*; June 5-24, 1520: Field of Cloth of Gold; 1521-1559: Valois-Habsburg Wars; 1531-1540: Cromwell Reforms British Government; 1532: Holbein Settles in London; December 18, 1534: Act of Supremacy; July, 1535-March, 1540: Henry VIII Dissolves the Monasteries; October, 1536-June, 1537: Pilgrimage of Grace; May, 1539: Six Articles of Henry VIII; 1544-1628: Anglo-French Wars; February 27, 1545: Battle of Ancrum Moor; 1558-1603: Reign of Elizabeth I; April or May, 1560: Publication of the Geneva Bible.

JUAN DE HERRERA
Spanish architect

Herrera was Spain's most famous architect of the late sixteenth century. As the royal architect, he established classicism in Spanish architecture and was a symbol and defining presence of the Spanish golden age under King Philip II.

BORN: c. 1530; Mobellán, Spain
DIED: January 15, 1597; Madrid, Spain
AREAS OF ACHIEVEMENT: Architecture, science and technology, engineering

EARLY LIFE
Juan de Herrera (her-REHR-ah) was born to a gentry family of modest means in northern Spain. As a teenager, he studied Latin and philosophy at the University of Valladolid. In 1548, he left his studies and become a courtier of Prince Philip at the court in Valladolid. Herrera traveled to Italy and Flanders as part of the princely retinue, returning to Spain in 1551. Two years later, he joined the army of Charles V, king of Spain and Holy Roman Emperor. In 1556, he accompanied Charles V to the Hieronymite Monastery in Yuste, where the monarch retired. Herrera left Yuste for Madrid in 1558, after Charles V died.

LIFE'S WORK
In the late sixteenth century, Herrera was Spain's most famous architect, as well as a renowned mathematician and engineer. His career was inextricably linked to the reign of King Philip II, a knowledgeable and astute patron of the arts. Philip had an important influence on Spanish architecture, establishing Renaissance practices in Spain. Working together, Philip and Herrera created a recognizable royal building style that to this day is evocative of Spain's golden age.

Herrera seems to have had no formal architectural training until Philip appointed him assistant to the royal architect, Juan Bautista de Toledo, in 1563. In this role, Herrera helped with the design of the Escorial, the monumental palace, monastery, and royal tomb complex under construction outside Madrid. Herrera worked with Toledo, who himself had assisted Michelangelo in Rome in the 1540's, until 1567, when the older master died. By 1570, Herrera was in charge at the Escorial, although Philip II did not officially name him royal architect until 1579.

Herrera is most famous for the Escorial, one of the largest building complexes constructed in the sixteenth century. It was erected from 1563 to 1584. Although Toledo designed the initial ground plans, Herrera presided over most of its construction. Herrera was also responsible for the building's elevations, the design of the main facade, the imperial staircase, and the basilica. In addition, he directed the decoration of the immense complex, designing altarpieces, reliquaries, and furniture.

As Philip II's architect, Herrera worked at other Spanish royal palaces, including the Palace at Aranjuez, where he designed extensive gardens; in Granada, where he modified the sixteenth century Palace of Charles V; and in Toledo, where he redesigned the facade of the Alcázar. In the wake of Spain's annexation of Portugal in 1580, Herrera traveled to Lisbon with Philip II to renovate the Paço de Ribera, the Portuguese royal palace.

Herrera is credited with creating a distinctive form of Spanish classicism, called plain style. Abstract, simplified, and cerebral, Herrera's form of classicism virtually eliminated sculptural building decoration, relying only on the simplest classical order, the Doric, to enhance his structures. He thus rejected the elaborate late Gothic forms still fashionable in sixteenth century Spain. He combined an imported Italian classical vocabulary with certain Flemish traits, including high slate roofs, towers, and dormers, to create the new Spanish architectural style. In its rejection of ostentation and extravagance, this plain style gave perfect visual expression to Philip II's reign. Plain, sober, modest, and utilitarian, Herrera's style seemed to embody the king's virtues. In this way, Herrera's architecture, especially as seen at the Escorial, seems the perfect manifestation of the Spanish Counter-Reformation, the fervent Catholic reform movement of the sixteenth century, with which the fanatically religious Philip II is associated.

Scholars have suggested various sources for the genesis of Herrera's unique classicism. Some posit the influence of the Neoplatonic philosopher Raymond Lull (c. 1235-1316), whose emphasis on geometry and abstraction can be detected in Herrera's buildings. Another art historian has traced Herrera's style to the aesthetic ideas of Saint Augustine (354-430 C.E.)—order, unity, and consonance—a premise first suggested by the Escorial's official historian, friar José de Sigüenza, in the sixteenth century.

When Herrera employed his plain style, first used in royal commissions and in civic projects, public architecture became a royal symbol. This phenomenon can be seen in Herrera's urban design projects executed at Philip II's orders in Toledo, Madrid, Valladolid, Seville, and other Spanish cities.

Herrera's plans for the Plaza Mayor in Madrid, in 1580, demonstrate the flexibility of his architectural style. Using simple materials, Herrera planned a variable, additive plaza that could be extended to accommodate new construction but was unified by standardized ornament and repeated windows.

In Toledo, Herrera designed two new projects, a city hall in 1574 and the Plaza Zocodover in 1590. This plaza typifies Herrera's approach, combining classical orders in its four porticoes, Flemish roofing solutions, and indigenous Spanish medieval characteristics. In keeping with Hispanic tradition, Herrera's porticoes used columns and lintels, reserving the arch form for the major entrance. Similarly, he preserved the plaza's function as a commercial center.

Seville's Merchant's Exchange, planned by Herrera in 1582, exhibits the architect's inclination to classical order. The plan is strictly geometric, organized around an interior courtyard, and the building overall is very Italianate. In addition to these major projects of urban renewal, Herrera consulted on other more utilitarian structures, including a fountain in Ocaña and bridges in Madrid. He was also involved in drafting Philip II's Royal Ordinances for New Towns (1573), which provided guidelines for builders in the Americas.

Although Herrera built relatively few churches—the basilica at the Escorial, Valladolid Cathedral, plus others in Toledo, Granada, and Lisbon—his classical style had a profound impact on ecclesiastical architecture in Spain and the New World. Valladolid Cathedral, designed around 1580, encapsulates his unique approach. On first glance, the geometric double square plan is typical of Spanish Gothic cathedrals. Herrera, however, used the geometric plan to classical ends in this monumental structure. His other churches demonstrate a similar focus on geometry and are unified by the repetition of simple orders, windows, and towers. In the end, despite the Gothic genealogy of the plan, Herrera's churches leave an impression of majesty and classical abstraction.

While best known for his architecture, in his lifetime Herrera was also celebrated as a famous intellectual, mathematician, and engineer. One of his contemporaries described him as a "second Archimedes," and as a mathematician, Herrera served as the main consultant to Philip II's Academy of Mathematics in Madrid. His knowledge of engineering, science, and technology is demonstrated by the many machines he invented, most notably hoists and cranes to aid in building construction. He owned a significant library of scientific texts and a large collection of scientific instruments.

SIGNIFICANCE

Perhaps Herrera's most important legacy was his establishment of classicism as the dominant architectural language in Spain. In addition, Herrera's unique brand of classical architecture came to symbolize the Golden Age of Philip II. By skillfully combining Italian, Flemish, and indigenous Spanish traits, his buildings created an impression of order and authority. Herrera was also innovative in that he employed classical style in utilitarian structures. The numerous buildings at the Escorial, for example, from the main palace-monastery complex to the simplest outbuildings, are unified by the same sober classicism. Herrera's style can thus be appreciated not only in his major architectural monuments but also in his gardens, fountains, bridges, and commercial buildings. Conversely, he incorporated certain traits of functional architecture in his urban design, employing simple materials in an effort to make buildings economical and adaptable.

Herrera's influence was long lasting. His sober classicism remained the preferred style in Spanish architecture until the eighteenth century, enjoying revivals into the twentieth. Whether employed by Philip II, the Bourbons in the eighteenth century, or by the dictator Francisco Franco after the Spanish Civil War, Herrera's classicism came to represent what one architectural historian has described as "beneficent authority," demonstrating the power of architecture to create and uphold myths of political authority.

Finally, Herrera must be considered the first true Renaissance architect in Spain. In contrast to the Spanish medieval concept of the architect as a master of the works, directly supervising construction at the building site, Herrera dedicated himself solely to architectural design, leaving the day-to-day supervision to others. His innovative use of architectural drawings enabled him to do this. By creating very exact drawings of his buildings for others to follow, he was able to free himself from the manual labor involved in the actual building. Thus, he exemplified the architect as gentleman-scholar, as described by the Italian Renaissance theorist and architect Leon Battista Alberti.

—Charlene Villaseñor Black

FURTHER READING

Kubler, George. *Building the Escorial*. Princeton, N.J.: Princeton University Press, 1982. Detailed account of the actual building of Herrera's most important commission, including analysis of period documents. Includes important discussions of Herrera's distinctive architectural style and its possible sources, including the aesthetics of Saint Augustine.

Taylor, René. "Architecture and Magic: Considerations on the Idea of the Escorial." In *Essays in the History of Architecture Presented to Rudolf Wittkower*, edited by Douglas Fraser, Howard Hibbard, and Milton J. Lewine. London: Phaidon, 1967. Important early study of the iconography and meaning of the building. Introduces the notion that the Escorial was intended to represent a second Temple in Jerusalem (with Philip II then cast as Solomon). Also posits the influence of Raymond Lull on Herrera.

Trevor-Roper, Hugh. *Princes and Artists: Patronage and Ideology at Four Habsburg Courts, 1517-1633*. New York: Harper and Row, 1976. A more general, contextual study of Philip II as patron of architecture and the arts.

Wilkinson-Zerner, Catherine. *Juan de Herrera: Architect to Philip II of Spain*. New Haven, Conn.: Yale University Press, 1993. The definitive study of the architect and his work. Includes illustrations, bibliographical references, and index.

SEE ALSO: Leon Battista Alberti; Charles V; Philip II.

RELATED ARTICLE in *Great Events from History: The Renaissance & Early Modern Era, 1454-1600:* 1563-1584: Construction of the Escorial.

HIAWATHA
Mohawk chief

Hiawatha was instrumental in founding and organizing the Iroquois Confederacy with the prophetic peacemaker Deganawida. Through his skills of oratory and diplomacy, he helped establish peace among the Iroquois in precolonial North America.

BORN: c. 1525; Mohawk River Valley, New York
DIED: c. 1575; Mohawk River Valley
ALSO KNOWN AS: Hienwentha; Ayonwatha (He Who
    Combs); Heowenta; Aiionwatha; A-yo-went-ha;
    Hay-yonh-wa-tha
AREAS OF ACHIEVEMENT: Government and politics,
    law

EARLY LIFE

Not much is known about the life of Hiawatha (hi-eh-WAW-theh) before he became a chief. Some oral histories relate that he had another name before meeting the visionary Deganawida, and that it was the visionary who named him Hiawatha.

There are no written references to Hiawatha before the seventeenth century, and the first complete story of his life was written from oral tradition by the Mohawk chief and statesman Joseph Brant (1742-1807) shortly before his death. A more complete version by Seth Newhouse (1842-1921) in 1885 became the "official" version of the Iroquois Nations when the council of chiefs redacted it in 1900 and again in 1912. The story itself, however, suggests great antiquity. The exact date, or even century, of the founding of the Iroquois Confederacy might never be known, though recent archaeological evidence suggests a union of the five nations much earlier than the early sixteenth century date that has become standard.

Before his meeting with Deganawida, Hiawatha was a prosperous chief with seven beautiful daughters (in some versions of the story, three). An enemy of Hiawatha, Atotarho, whom some narratives describe as a wizard and a cannibal, killed the daughters, one at a time, when they would not marry him. Inconsolable with grief for his daughters, Hiawatha exiled himself in the woods. It was there that the meeting with Deganawida would change his life and make Hiawatha the first *royaneh* (chief) to accept the visionary's message of peace and consolation.

LIFE'S WORK

While recent historians and ethnographers have rightly emphasized the greater role of Deganawida in bringing peace to the five nations of the Iroquois (Mohawk, Cayuga, Oneida, Onandaga, and Seneca) and uniting them in a confederacy (to which the Tuscaroras were added in 1712 after their defeat by English colonial forces), one cannot overstate Hiawatha's role as the first tribal leader to embrace and have validated, because of his influence, Deganawida's vision of peace. Deganawida had been exiled from his own nation, the Huron, for his pacifist tendencies, and though he was presented in the narrative and religious tradition as divinely appointed, he met nothing but rebuffs until he met Hiawatha in the forest. The meeting of Deganawida and Hiawatha was mutually beneficial.

Deganawida had a message of peace to deliver to the warring tribes of Iroquoia (the geological term for central and western New York State), yet he was afflicted, some say, with a stutter or similar speech impediment. Hiawatha was gifted in eloquence, yet his debilitating grief isolated him from the people whom he should have served as hereditary leader. Deganawida healed Hiawatha by teaching him a series of rituals that remain part of the ceremonial life of the six nations: the sequential use of wampum, the condolence ceremony, and the requickening ceremony.

The use of wampum (Algonquian *wampumpeag*, white shell beads) represents a genuine collaboration between Hiawatha and Deganawida. The wampum were used for ceremonies, to record a treaty or other agreement, as tribute, and as gifts for exchange. The wampum in the case of Hiawatha came to represent his grief and reconciliation as he wandered through the forest. One story is as follows. On the third day of his exile (or perhaps the third leg of the journey), Hiawatha reached a deserted village on the Susquehanna River. He traced the river to its source and found a pond or lake filled with ducks. The ducks were startled by him, and then flew away, taking the water of the pond with them. Hiawatha then collected white and purple shells from the exposed dry bed of the pond and strung them on threads made from hemp to serve as reminders of the coming together of the Iroquois nations. Given the sacredness of the wampum to the Iroquois, and given that the wampum, by definition, is used to mark significant events, Hiawatha's collecting these sacred objects became legend.

On meeting Hiawatha on his journey to spread the gospel of peace, Deganawida used Hiawatha's strings of shells as a mnemonic (memory) device to guide his oration in a prototype of what would become the condolence ceremony. The concept of "condolence" is vital to the Iroquois concept of "peace." The warring nations, which had been familiar with an intricate system of retaliation and revenge that characterized their cultures at war, needed an alternate system of compensation to replace it. Hiawatha learned that by ritually mourning the deaths of his daughters, instead of seeking consolation through retaliation alone, he could return to the concerns of the living; he soon became an advocate of Deganawida's message of peace by mourning his daughters through a ritual of condolence.

The requickening ceremony takes the compensatory nature of condolence one step further by ritually adopting a member of another tribe as a re-embodiment of a slain member of one's own tribe. That these surrogates were often seized in raids on the tribe responsible for the death of a loved one (usually a chief or sachem) indicates that the Iroquois definition of "peace" is not necessarily

the cessation of all violence. It is, instead, a spiritual balance.

Hiawatha's total absorption of Deganawida's doctrine of peace is suggested by his reconciliation even with the evil Atotarho. The Onandaga shaman is depicted as having a crooked back and having snakes in his hair. In many cultures, including Iroquoian, straightness is an emblem of righteousness. Hiawatha straightened Atotarho's body and combed the snakes out of his hair. (Combs made of antlers are common archaeological finds at Iroquois sites, and a possible etymology of the word *hiawatha* is "he who combs.") The combing and straightening represented the re-formation of an evil wizard who would, as a now-righteous advocate of peace, become the first titular head of the Iroquois Confederacy.

The formation of the Iroquois Confederacy is the last great event of Hiawatha's life. Under his leadership, and that of the re-formed Atotarho, the five great nations—from east to west Seneca, Cayuga, Onandaga, Oneida, and Mohawk—became a loose confederacy with the

A Currier & Ives lithograph depicting Hiawatha's discovery of the death of his wife Minnehaha. (Hulton|Archive by Getty Images)

central nation, the Onondagas, having the final voice. The Onondaga's leadership was more spiritual than political, and all five (later six) nations still functioned independently.

The original wampum record of the confederacy—with four squares, two on either side of a central pine tree (which on the reverse appears as a heart), representing the union of five nations—can be seen in New York's state museum.

SIGNIFICANCE

As the primary carrier of Deganawida's message of peace, Hiawatha deserves a place not only in the history of the Iroquois but also in the history of world peace. As a Mohawk chief, he has come to stand for what was thought to be an unfamiliar (or unlikely) tolerance for peace, for like many Native American tribal names, the word "Mohawk" is derived from the slur of a neighboring tribe. In this case, "Mohawk" means "those who eat human flesh."

Some versions of the Hiawatha and the Iroquois Confederacy stories make Hiawatha a cannibal in a grieving phase—compounding his divorce from society—and other versions make Atotarho the cannibal. In either case, Hiawatha is the agent of reform, either himself repenting, or reforming another of cannibalism. For a great chief like Hiawatha to subordinate himself to a former enemy is the epitome of the humility that is necessary for peace to flourish.

The survival of Hiawatha's name and legend (though with a great deal of inevitable variation) across nearly half a millennium is itself indicative of his historical significance. As one of the facilitators of the Great Peace

and Power and Law that helped inspire the founders of American federalism, Hiawatha's historical importance goes beyond just Seneca or Native American history; he deserves to be an icon of democratic principles.

—*John R. Holmes*

FURTHER READING

Fenton, William N. *The Great Law and the Longhouse: A Political History of the Iroquois Confederacy.* Norman: University of Oklahoma Press, 1998. An exhaustive sourcebook on the Iroquois Confederacy from its inception to 1794. Chapters 2 through 6 deal with Hiawatha.

Hale, Horatio. *The Iroquois Book of Rites.* Toronto, Canada: University of Toronto Press, 1963. This reprint of Hale's 1883 classic preserves some of the earliest versions of the Hiawatha legend.

Parker, Arthur C. *Parker on the Iroquois.* Syracuse, N.Y.: Syracuse University Press, 1968. A reprint of three of an Iroquois ethnologist's early twentieth century monographs that includes the Newhouse text of the Hiawatha story.

Richter, Daniel K. *Ordeal of the Longhouse: The Peoples of the Iroquois League in the Era of European Colonization.* Chapel Hill: University of North Carolina Press, 1992. A thorough history of the Iroquois people and their confederacy before and after the arrival of the Europeans.

SEE ALSO: Jacques Cartier; Deganawida.
RELATED ARTICLE in *Great Events from History: The Renaissance & Early Modern Era, 1454-1600:* 16th century: Iroquois Confederacy Is Established.

HŌJŌ UJIMASA
Japanese warlord (r. 1560-1590)

The fourth generation ruler of much of eastern Japan, Hōjō Ujimasa, through skillful political and military maneuvering, maintained one of the largest independent domains in sixteenth century Japan. He was the last independent warlord of the Warring States period (1467-1600) at the time of his defeat in 1590.

BORN: 1538; Odawara, Japan
DIED: August 12, 1590; Odawara
ALSO KNOWN AS: Sagami no Kami
AREAS OF ACHIEVEMENT: Government and politics, warfare and conquest

EARLY LIFE

Hōjō Ujimasa (hoh-joh ew-gee-mah-sah) was the eldest son of Hōjō Ujiyasu (1515-1571). At the time of Hōjō Ujimasa's birth, Ujiyasu was already being prepared to take over the domain created by his grandfather Hōjō Sōun (1432-1519) and ruled by his father Hōjō Ujitsuna (1485-1541). The family succession was well established in the Hōjō domain, and Ujimasa's eventual move to family head and domain ruler was assumed. In this respect, the Hōjō domain was the most stable political unit in war-ravaged Japan.

The survival of the domain was dependent on the military and diplomatic genius of its rulers, as well as on internal coherence. Throughout most of Ujimasa's lifetime, the Hōjō core area of Izu and Sagami provinces (present-day Shizuoka and Kanagawa prefectures) was threatened by powerful neighbors to the north and northeast. Hōjō Ujiyasu, daimyo since 1541, was famously embroiled in a contest for control of the entire Kantō area (the eight provinces of eastern Japan) with warriors Takeda Shingen of Kai (now Yamanashi Prefecture) and Uesugi Kenshin of Echigo (now Niigata Prefecture). Across the domain's western border, the Imagawa family, daimyos of Suruga and Tōtōmi (now Shizuoka Prefecture), were traditional allies of the Hōjō since the days of Sōun.

Ujimasa thus grew up in an environment dominated by warfare, diplomatic maneuvering, and a bewildering complexity of alliances. In 1554, Imagawa Yoshimoto brokered an alliance between the Hōjō and the Takeda directed against Uesugi Kenshin. The resulting alliance was cemented by a series of marriages and adoptions. Ujimasa was married to Takeda Shingen's daughter; his brother, Ujihide, was sent to become Shingen's adopted son; and another sister of Ujimasa was married to Shingen's son Katsuyori.

Ujiyasu had groomed his son as heir apparent, involving him in military campaigns as well as in the important decisions affecting the situation inside the Hōjō domain. He was confident enough in the capabilities of his firstborn son to officially relinquish power to him in early 1560.

LIFE'S WORK

With his father alive and active for another eleven years, Ujimasa made decisions subject to the will of Ujiyasu. Crucial policy innovations that Ujiyasu had introduced, such as the rule that makes a vassal's obligation proportionate to the amount of land he owned, had strengthened the coherence of the domain and remained unchallenged. However, a sudden change occurred in the balance of power in eastern Japan at the very beginning of Ujimasa's tenure as daimyo. In June, 1560, Imagawa Yoshimoto, the most staunch of Hōjō allies, was killed in a battle with the powerful general Oda Nobunaga. Sensing opportunity, Takeda Shingen occupied the Imagawa domain, driving Yoshimoto's heir into exile. Thus, the Takeda were now occupying territories to the west and north of the Hōjō domain.

Perhaps sensing a certain discord in the Hōjō-Takeda alliance, Uesugi Kenshin attacked the following year (1561) and laid siege to Odawara, the domain capital. Yet the alliance held, and Kenshin was forced to withdraw after being attacked by Takeda forces. Eventually, however, Ujimasa thought it wise to counter the mounting Takeda strength by making a peace offering to Kenshin, and in 1567, the Hōjō-Takeda alliance came to an end. Ujimasa's brother, Ujihide, was sent home to Odawara by his adoptive father Takeda Shingen and was promptly sent to the Uesugi, where he was adopted by Kenshin.

It is not entirely clear whether Ujimasa was actually behind this shift in policy. The fact that his first diplomatic priority after his father's death in 1571 was to renew the alliance with the Takeda against the Uesugi suggests otherwise. The reaffirmed commitment to the Takeda in the early 1570's brought the Hōjō onto a collision course with the newly established power in the center of Japan: Oda Nobunaga and his lieutenants (and eventual successors) Toyotomi Hideyoshi and Tokugawa Ieyasu.

Partly because of three decades of administrative and fiscal reforms under Ujiyasu, Hōjō control over the domain had been institutionalized to an almost unprecedented degree. More than just a warlord, the Hōjō ruler had become the legitimate bearer of public authority, which could be delegated to officials and enforced by them. Hundreds of surviving documents bearing the "Tiger Seal" of the daimyo prove the degree to which Hōjō power relied on a bureaucratic pattern of administration. Continuing this trend initiated by his father, Ujimasa created a system in which the institution of the daimyo was ultimately more important than the person occupying it. While personal charisma continued to play a role in diplomacy and on the battlefield, it became an increasingly less important factor in internal affairs of the Hōjō domain. Ujimasa could thus relinquish the official reigns of power to his son Ujinao in 1577 without upsetting the internal stability of the domain. He remained, however, a powerful presence behind the scenes for the rest of his life.

In the years preceding this transition, the power balance in eastern Japan had once again shifted considerably. Takeda Shingen had died in 1573, and the fortunes of the Takeda had declined considerably after their defeat in the Battle of Nagashino in 1575. This created a favorable situation for the consolidation of Hōjō power. The death of Uesugi Kenshin in 1578 promised to make the Hōjō masters of all of eastern Japan, since Kenshin's chosen successor was the son he had adopted from the Hōjō, Ujimasa's brother Ujihide. However, Uesugi Kagekatsu took power after a bloody struggle, and in an astonishing reversal of decades of rivalry, the Takeda forged an alliance with the Uesugi. Thus put on the defensive, the Hōjō began a series of campaigns against their neighbors.

Partially as a consequence of these fights, Tokugawa Ieyasu managed to destroy the Takeda in 1582 and subsequently moved into Kai Province. Trying to secure his northern flank against this new threat, Ujimasa promptly moved his armies against Ieyasu. After several minor encounters, a truce was concluded, cemented with the marriage of Hōjō Ujinao to Tokugawa Ieyasu's daughter.

It was this alliance that most likely gave the Hōjō a false sense of security that eventually led to their downfall. During the 1580's, Toyotomi Hideyoshi, the new power in the capital after the death of Oda Nobunaga in 1582, had managed—by force or threat of force—to subjugate all the daimyos of Japan to his authority. By 1588, the Hōjō remained the only individually powerful daimyo house not to have pledged its allegiance to Toyotomi. A command to report to the capital was ignored, perhaps because Ujimasa, who claimed to be descended from a noble lineage, found it beyond his dignity to submit to demands of the upstart son of a peasant.

Sensing the danger they faced should Toyotomi resort to military action, Ujimasa and Ujinao requested the mediation of Tokugawa Ieyasu early in 1590. Unbeknownst to them, preparations for a major campaign were already well under way, and by late spring a huge army, including Tokugawa forces, descended on the Hōjō domain. By June, a garrison of 50,000 Hōjō warriors was under siege at Odawara by a force reported to have included 200,000 men. Both sides were well supplied, and Ujimasa in particular hoped to be able to outlast the besiegers. The Toyotomi camp had, however, the advantage of supply lines stretching the length of Japan, and the protracted siege ensued.

In this situation, two facts became clear. Ujimasa and Ujinao were not in agreement over how to proceed, and neither of them was able to gain a majority of supporters in the protracted discussions. Ujinao was ready to risk a pitched battle against impossible odds at the start of the campaign but argued in favor of surrender later in the summer. Ujimasa consistently argued for a sustained defense and against surrender. Finally, Ujinao prevailed and Odawara was surrendered without a fight. Hōjō Ujinao, daimyo of Sagami, was escorted under armed guard to a place of exile. He was spared a harsher fate because of his connection to Tokugawa Ieyasu. Ujimasa was not so fortunate. Ordered to commit suicide by Toyotomi Hideyoshi, he disemboweled himself on August 12, 1590.

SIGNIFICANCE

Hōjō Ujimasa is considered one of the most advanced territorial rulers of sixteenth century Japan. While his death can be considered the end of the Warring States period, the administrative system of his domain was a blueprint for the order that Tokugawa Ieyasu would establish in all of Japan.

—*Ronald K. Frank*

FURTHER READING

Birt, Michael P. *Warring States: A Study of the Go-Hōjō Daimyo and Domain, 1491-1590*. Ph.D. dissertation. Ann Arbor, Mich.: UMI Dissertation Information Services, 1983. This Princeton University doctoral dissertation was the first study in English exclusively devoted to the Hōjō.

Hall, John Whitney, Nagahara Keiji, and Kozo Yāmamura, eds. *Japan Before Tokugawa: Political Consolidation and Economic Growth, 1500 to 1650*. Princeton, N.J.: Princeton University Press, 1981. Collection of scholarly essays on the politics and economy of sixteenth century Japan.

Lamers, Jeroen Pieter. *Japonius Tyrannus: The Japanese Warlord Oda Nobunaga Reconsidered.* Leiden, the Netherlands: Hotei, 2000. A detailed scholarly account with ample quotations from primary sources. Includes bibliographical references and an index.

Turnbull, Stephen. *War in Japan, 1467-1615.* Oxford, England: Osprey, 2002. Turnbull, an expert on samurai warriors, analyzes samurai warfare in the Warring States period, with brief accounts of major battles.

SEE ALSO: Oda Nobunaga; Toyotomi Hideyoshi.

RELATED ARTICLE in *Great Events from History: The Renaissance & Early Modern Era, 1454-1600:* 1590: Odawara Campaign.

HANS HOLBEIN, THE YOUNGER
German artist

A master of portraits and an excellent draftsman, Holbein was an important transitional figure in European art. Holbein's portraits offer a revealing look at the personalities of his time.

BORN: 1497 or 1498; Augsburg, bishopric of Augsburg (now in Germany)
DIED: 1543; London, England
AREA OF ACHIEVEMENT: Art

EARLY LIFE

Hans Holbein (hahns HOHL-bin), the Younger, was born in the city of Augsburg, at that time an important commercial center of the Holy Roman Empire. The Holbein family was an artistic one: Hans Holbein, the Elder, was a widely known painter, much sought after for his skill in portraits, while his brother Sigmund was also an artist. The younger Holbein and his brother, Ambrosius, spent their early years learning the craft of painting from their father.

In 1515, Holbein moved to Basel, Switzerland, where he came to the attention of the noted printer and publisher Johann Froben, also known as Frobenius. Holbein was soon actively designing book illustrations and title-page borders for Froben and other printers in Basel. Since Froben was a publisher of Desiderius Erasmus, a noted Humanist scholar, Holbein came to know the internationally famous writer. Through Erasmus, Holbein was introduced to the circle of Humanist thinkers and leaders of the time. Holbein made other important contacts, including a 1516 commission to paint the portrait of Jacob Mayer, burgomaster of Basel, and his wife; this work is an early indication of Holbein's mastery of the portrait genre. During this time, he also produced several conventional religious paintings, a form of art popular at the time.

From 1517 to 1519, Holbein was away from Basel, perhaps traveling with his father on commissions in Switzerland, perhaps on a brief visit to northern Italy. By the fall of 1519, he had returned to Basel, for on September 25 of that year he was admitted as a master in the Painters' Guild. The next year, Holbein became a citizen of the town and married Elsbeth Schmid, the widow of a tanner; the couple had four children.

Holbein received a considerable amount of work in Basel, primarily designs and illustrations for printers but also a series of religious paintings influenced by his contemporary Albrecht Dürer; mural decorations for the Basel Town Hall; and more portraits, including his 1519 portrayal of the lawyer and scholar Bonifacius Amerbach. This portrait is the first showing Holbein's true genius in portraiture; fittingly, Amerbach later became the earliest collector of Holbein and preserved much of his work. In 1523, Holbein produced his first portrait of Erasmus; a second soon followed, which Erasmus sent to his friend Sir Thomas More in England. The English connection, so important in Holbein's life and career, was soon to be established.

A number of Holbein self-portraits have survived. They show him with a square, rather full face; a short, neatly trimmed beard but no mustache; and hair that was dark and worn moderately long. The most notable features are his mouth, firmly and tightly closed, and his eyes, which have a careful, wary expression. It is not the face of someone who revealed himself lightly or freely.

LIFE'S WORK

During the mid-1520's, the Protestant Reformation swept through Basel and the climate for the visual arts became much less favorable than before. In 1524, Holbein found it convenient to depart on an extended visit to France, where he was exposed to the influence of Italian painting, including the work of Leonardo da Vinci. In August of 1526, he left Basel again, this time for England. He carried with him a letter of introduction from Erasmus; once in England, he was welcomed into the household of Erasmus's good friend Sir Thomas More.

Through More, Holbein had an entry into the court of Henry VIII, then approaching the apogee of its brilliance. While Holbein did execute some decorations for court pageants, his initial relationship with the monarch was not as close as it would later become. Instead, he concentrated on portraits of prominent individuals and groups. One of his most striking works from this time, a group portrait of the More family (most likely painted in 1528) has been lost, but the preparatory drawings remain. As always, Holbein captures the character of his sitters with deft precision; equally important, this group portrait is the first known example in northern European art where the figures are shown sitting or standing in natural positions, rather than kneeling, a definite break with the religiously oriented art of the Middle Ages.

In 1528, Holbein returned to Basel, probably because of a previous agreement with the town council, since he promptly resumed his work of public commissions, devoting much time and energy to them over the next two years. The financial rewards seem to have been considerable, since he was able to purchase a new house and, in 1531, to buy the adjoining property as well. The same year as his return, Holbein was admitted into the Lutheran faith. Within two years, and certainly by late 1520, however, Holbein seems to have ceased all work in the area of religious painting, once a staple of any artist's career. Perhaps that reflected the preferences of the Reformation; it certainly allowed Holbein's talents to flow into paintings and portraits that favored his realistic and psychological technique.

Holbein's ability in portraiture reached its most profound and personal depths in his *Portrait of His Wife and Two Elder Children* (1528). In this searching, almost painful work, Holbein presents part of the family from which he was so long and so often absent. The painter's wife, Elsbeth, seems weary, perhaps sad; has this been caused by the absence of the artist who still records her features so faithfully? That is impossible to determine, but the technical mastery of the work is undoubted, as is its debt to Holbein's study of the works of Leonardo.

Leaving his wife and children in Basel, Holbein returned to England in 1532; he would remain there for the remainder of his life. His friend More had fallen from the king's favor over the matter of divorcing Queen Catherine of Aragon and the marriage to Anne Boleyn, so Holbein first concentrated on a series of portraits of German merchants living in London. Called the "Steelyard portraits," after the section of town where the sitters lived, these works marked a new development in Holbein's art. His acute perceptions of character increased, his draftsmanship acquired new and fluid power, and attention was focused on the person, because backgrounds and surroundings were greatly simplified.

Holbein also began to paint portraits of members of the court, including Thomas Cromwell, More's successor as lord chancellor; eventually, Holbein came to the attention of Henry himself. In 1537, Holbein executed a fresco for the royal palace of Whitehall, which brought him considerable fame (the work was destroyed in a 1698 fire). In 1538 came the first entry in the royal accounts of a salary paid to Holbein, indicating that he had officially entered the service of the king. Over the next five years, he would complete more than 150 portraits, in oils, chalk, and silverpoint, capturing some of the most influential and memorable figures from one of England's most turbulent periods. Holbein also remained active in preparing illustrations for printers, including the woodcut borders for the important English Bible of 1535, and he

Hans Holbein, the Younger. (Library of Congress)

designed costumes, jewelry, cups, and other art objects for the court.

Holbein's portraits remain his most important and enduring work. Among his sitters were Henry VIII and most of the major figures of his court, including several of Henry's wives. Most of these works have survived in chalk, or pen-and-ink studies, rather than completed oils, yet they all retain the vitality and insight that Holbein brought to his work. Some of them, such as the stunning full-length portrait *Christiana of Denmark, Duchess of Milan* (1538), rank among Holbein's supreme achievements.

The portrait of Christiana was painted for one of the frequent marriage negotiations engaged in by Henry; he often assigned Holbein to capture the likeness of a prospective bride. One of these, Holbein's study of Anne of Cleves (1539), seems to have been Holbein's downfall. Pleased by the portrait, Henry agreed to the marriage, but within six months he divorced the woman he called "the Flanders mare." After this, there were no more important royal commissions for Holbein.

Holbein continued to live in London, securing work from other patrons. His last portrait of Henry, for example, is that of the king granting a charter to the Barber-Surgeon's Company. The work was painted for that guild and was commissioned in 1541. Significantly, Holbein did not paint Henry from life but rather copied him from earlier works. Holbein did not live to complete the painting, for he died during an outbreak of the plague in London in 1543. His wife and children in Basel were attended to by his estate there and by a pension negotiated with the town council. In his last will in England, Holbein left funds for the keeping of two young children there. He was forty-five or forty-six years old when he died.

SIGNIFICANCE

Hans Holbein, the Younger, marks a turning point in the development of European art. His portraits show a decisive change from the older, religious orientation to the newer, more secular and worldly temper of the Renaissance and modern times. A number of critics have remarked on a lack of spiritual involvement by Holbein with his work, and perhaps Holbein did concentrate on the actual, the physical, and the immediate. That was appropriate, however, for his sitters were men and women of intense individuality, and often of supreme ambition; their concerns were often not spiritual but temporal. Holbein's portraits may lack piety, but they have psychological insight, an insight that he captured not by hands

clasped in prayer or holding a Bible but by hands fingering a jewel given by Henry VIII or the look of shrewd eyes calculating the latest events in the king's court. With Holbein, medieval painting departs and the art of the modern world begins.

Even in his religious paintings, Holbein took a new and sometimes disturbing stance. One of his most famous works, *The Body of the Dead Christ in the Tomb* (1521-1522), has intrigued and unsettled viewers since its creation. Some have complained that the painting dwells too closely on the material nature of Christ, slighting the spiritual side. While other religious paintings of the time used Christ's physical sufferings as an aid to devotion and meditation, Holbein's work is different and evokes different responses, because of the intense, unflinching realism in which it is rendered. There is no softening or evading the facts of brutal bodily injury and certain death.

Occupying a pivotal point in European artistic development, Holbein was not entirely a modern painter. The influence of older forms is seen most clearly in his woodcuts and illustrations, in particular the Dance of Death series, designed from 1522 through 1524, and executed by the brilliant woodblock carver Hans Lützelburger. Although not published until 1538, this series is one of the most famous variants on the "Dance macabre" theme so popular in the Middle Ages.

It is Holbein's portraits, however, which are the key to his work. His technical mastery is unmatched, and his ceaseless efforts at perfection allowed him to produce a series of masterpieces of psychological interpretation. Most famous are the portraits Holbein produced at the court of Henry VIII, which have left for later generations a true sense of the important and intriguing figures of the time, from the king himself to his friend and victim, Sir Thomas More. In these and other drawings, portraits, and paintings, Holbein captured the essence of the northern Renaissance and the men and women who created it. Through the works of Holbein, that world comes to life in all its vibrant energy.

—*Michael Witkoski*

FURTHER READING

Bätschmann, Oskar, and Pascal Griener. *Hans Holbein.* Translated by Cecilia Hurley and Pascal Griener. Princeton, N.J.: Princeton University Press, 1997. Important analysis of Holbein's entire corpus, ranging from general insights into the artist's place in political and artistic history to close readings of paintings to diverting anecdotes about specific incidents in Holbein's career. Includes illustrations, bibliographic references, and index.

Brooke, Xanthe, and David Crombie. *Henry VIII Revealed: Holbein's Portrait and Its Legacy.* London: Paul Holberton, 2003. Extremely detailed study of Holbein's portrait of Henry VIII, incorporating high-tech analysis of the physical paintings, historical research on Henry's court and the artist's workshop, and surveys of the effects of the painting, both on Holbein's contemporary culture and on subsequent portrayals of Henry in literature, film, and television. Includes illustrations, map, bibliographic references, index.

Buck, Stephanie, and Jochen Sander. *Hans Holbein the Younger: Painter at the Court of Henry VIII.* London: Thames and Hudson 2004. Monograph surveying Holbein's career in England provides biographical insight, analysis of the paintings, biographies of their subjects, and explications of the important movements and cultural influences on the artist's work. Includes 60 color and 120 black-and-white illustrations.

Holbein, Hans, the Younger. *Holbein.* Introduction by Roy Strong. New York: Rizzoli, 1980. This slender volume is part of the Every Painting series. Gives a rapid visual overview of Holbein's career. Especially useful in conjunction with the other readings suggested here.

Hueffer, Ford Madox. *Hans Holbein the Younger: A Critical Monograph.* New York: E. P. Dutton, 1905. A perceptive, if sometimes highly individual, study of Holbein's work by the famous English novelist, better known as Ford Madox Ford. The book does well in placing Holbein within the atmosphere of the Renaissance and provides a good, if idiosyncratic, overview of his achievement.

Roberts, Jane. *Holbein.* London: Oresko Books, 1979. A good study of Holbein's art, with particular emphasis on the drawings and portraits of his two English sojourns. There is a brief but generally informative biography.

Rowlands, John. *Holbein: The Paintings of Hans Holbein the Younger.* Oxford, England: Phaidon Press, 1985. Essentially a study of Holbein's works in oil, this book contains an excellent introductory biography. Very helpful in providing accessible critical commentary on the artist's work.

Strong, Roy. *Holbein and Henry VIII.* London: Routledge & Kegan Paul, 1967. A volume in the Studies in British Art series, this work provides an extensive review of Holbein's relationship with the Tudor court. In addition to the paintings and drawings, Holbein was productive in all aspects of decorations and embellishments.

Wilson, Derek. *Hans Holbein: Portrait of an Unknown Man.* London: Weidenfeld & Nicolson, 1996. Imaginative and frankly speculative biography of Holbein argues for the importance of his youth in Basel, the center of the Reformation, in influencing his later life and career.

SEE ALSO: Anne of Cleves; Thomas Cromwell; Albrecht Dürer; Desiderius Erasmus; Saint John Fisher; Henry VIII; Leonardo da Vinci; Aldus Manutius; Sir Thomas More.

RELATED ARTICLE in *Great Events from History: The Renaissance & Early Modern Era, 1454-1600:* 1532: Holbein Settles in London.

RICHARD HOOKER
English theologian

In his massive prose work, Of the Lawes of Ecclesiasticall Politie, *Richard Hooker drew on the ideas of earlier philosophers, theologians, and legal scholars to produce a solid rational justification for the form and practice of the Anglican church.*

BORN: March, 1554; Heavitree, Exeter, Devon, England
DIED: November 2, 1600; Bishopsbourne, near Canterbury, Kent, England
AREA OF ACHIEVEMENT: Religion and theology

EARLY LIFE

Richard Hooker's father, Roger Hooker, served as a religious leader in Ireland for some years and, though he had not been ordained, was appointed dean of Leighlen. Richard attended grammar school in Exeter, where he exhibited such devotion to his studies, along with so modest a demeanor, that the schoolmaster urged Richard's parents to keep him in school.

Hooker's biographer, Izaak Walton (1593-1683), argued that it was Roger's brother John Hooker, an eminent historian and a member of Parliament, who arranged for John Jewel, bishop of Salisbury, to meet young Richard. Jewel was so impressed with Richard that he helped him secure a place at Corpus Christi College, Oxford University, and helped him financially. In 1568, Richard arrived in Oxford. Assigned as his tutor was John Rainolds, a follower of the Protestant theologian John Calvin.

After Bishop Jewel died in 1571, Hooker supported himself by obtaining grants and by tutoring. In 1573, he became tutor to Edwin Sandys, whose father was bishop of London and later archbishop of York, and to George Cranmer, a great-nephew of the martyred Thomas Cranmer, Henry VIII's archbishop of Canterbury. The two young men would become lifelong friends of Hooker.

In 1573, Hooker was awarded his bachelor of arts degree and was named a scholar of the college. In 1577, he received his master of arts degree, and in 1579 he became a fellow. Hooker was highly respected at Oxford. He was a diligent scholar who was gifted with a sense of humor, though he was always restrained in his utterances. He took his faith seriously but maintained his composure even as religious controversies swirled around him. This judicious self-control would be reflected in his work.

LIFE'S WORK

By 1581, Richard Hooker had taken holy orders, for he had been asked to deliver a sermon at St. Paul's Cross on the grounds of St. Paul's Cathedral. In 1584, Hooker was appointed vicar of St. Mary's at Drayton Beauchamp Church in Buckinghamshire, but he probably remained at Oxford. Three months later, he was appointed master of the Temple Church in London.

Hooker's assistant, Walter Travers, a Puritan, began delivering afternoon sermons that denounced Hooker's morning sermons. Though Hooker did not ask him to intervene, John Whitgift, the archbishop of Canterbury, put an end to the controversy by ordering Travers to cease preaching, so Travers moved on. It is worth noting, however, that neither in their sermons nor in the pamphlets they issued later did either of the two men express anything other than mutual respect.

When he preached at St. Paul's Cross, Hooker may have spent a night or two at the nearby home of John Churchman, a well-to-do merchant, and he did take up residence there in 1584. In 1940, C. J. Sisson proved that what the early biographers, including Walton, had said about Hooker's wife, Joan Churchman, was untrue. Joan, the daughter of John Churchman, was not a penniless, ugly girl, foisted off by her mother onto a naive young divine. Moreover, since the marriage did not take place until February 13, 1588, the account of Hooker's miserable domestic life at Drayton-Beauchamp is patently untrue. In fact, Joan was neither ugly nor poor; her dowry was substantial, and the marriage, which produced two sons and four daughters, was evidently a happy one. Hooker's relationship with the Churchmans continued to be a harmonious one, for he and his family remained there at least until 1591.

It is thought that Hooker began his great work while he was living at the Churchman home, probably about 1586. *Of the Lawes of Ecclesiasticall Politie* (1594-1597, 1648, 1662) may have been inspired by the Travers conflict or perhaps by a 1577 publication by another Puritan, Thomas Cartwright, in an ongoing controversy with Whitgift. It seems likely that Whitgift intended to give Hooker more time for writing, for in 1591, he removed Hooker from the Temple and appointed him rector of Boscombe, near Salisbury. Thus, Hooker was assured of an income, but because his parish duties were assigned to someone else, he could spend most of his time in London, working on his treatise.

FROM HOOKER'S
OF THE LAWES OF ECCLESIASTICALL POLITIE

Richard Hooker attempted to persuade his contemporaries that deferring to human reason instead of to Church authority and the Scriptures was the means to understand and accept the Anglican faith and to resolve disputes and stifle dissent within the Church of England.

Nor is mine owne intent any other in these severall bookes of discourse, then to make it appeare unto you, that for the ecclesiasticall lawes of this land, we are led by great reason to observe them, and yee by no necessitie bound to impugne them. It is no part of my secret meaning to draw you hereby into hatred or to set upon the face of this cause any fairer glasse, then the naked truth doth afford: but my whole endevor is to resolve the conscience, and to shewe as neere as I can what in this controversie the hart is to thinke, if it will follow the light of sound and sincere judgement, without either clowd of prejudice, or mist of passionate affection.

. . . For whatsoever we believe concerning salvation by Christ, although the scripture be therein the ground of our beliefe; yet the authoritie of man is, if we marke it, the key which openeth the dore of entrance into the knowledge of the scripture. The scripture could not teach us the thinges that are of God, unlesse we did credite men who have taught us that the wordes of scripture doe signifie those things. Some way therefore, notwithstanding mans infirmitie, yet his authority may enforce assent.

Source: Quoted in "Richard Hooker and the Problem of Authority in the Elizabethan Church," by M. E. C. Perrott. *Journal of Ecclesiastical History* 49, no. 1 (January, 1998), pp. 36, 49.

---

ness, on November 2, 1600, he died. He was buried in his church at Bishopsbourne. Hooker left his masterpiece unfinished. Scholars agree, however, that only the sixth book was truly incomplete; the seventh and eighth books seem to lack only a final revision. The sixth and eighth books were published in 1648 and the seventh in 1662.

SIGNIFICANCE

Of the Lawes of Ecclesiasticall Politie provided a sound rational justification for the Anglican church that became known as a via media, a middle way between the extremes of Calvinistic Protestantism and Roman Catholicism. Hooker's work differed from many of the other treatises of his time in its sound scholarship, its impressive use of logic, its breadth of vision, its restrained tone, and its willingness to entertain other opinions. For all these reasons, it has not perished with the passage of time but continues to be a major sourcebook for Anglicans.

The work is read not merely for its theology. Hooker was a magnificent stylist, a writer who could move from voice to voice as the subject demanded. He also was an expert manipulator of the long, periodic sentence, a master of metaphor, and a skillful practitioner of such devices as repetition, alliteration, and antithesis. He was also a brilliant synthesizer. Like Dante Alighieri, Edmund Spenser, and John Milton, he united disparate elements to form a single, lucid, and memorable whole. For all these reasons, Hooker's *Of the Lawes of Ecclesiasticall Politie* is considered one of the highest achievements of human reason and one of the literary masterpieces of all time.

—*Rosemary M. Canfield Reisman*

By 1593, Hooker had the first four books of his treatise ready for publication, but no printer was interested in them. In the end, Edwin Sandys paid to have them printed, and they appeared the following year; Sandys also arranged for the publication of the fifth book in 1597.

In 1595, Hooker had been appointed rector of Bishopsbourne, near Canterbury. Although he continued to work on his fifth book and on the final three, for the first time Hooker was able to fulfill all the duties of a parish priest. His parishioners admired him for his kindliness, his meekness, and his humility. This unworldly individual became an easy mark for three Puritans, however, who over a period of several months extorted money from him by threatening him with scandal. Finally, Hooker confided in Sandys and Cranmer. Infuriated, his friends forced the culprits to admit their guilt and apologize for their actions. According to Walton, Hooker promptly forgave them.

In 1600, during a trip by water from London to Gravesend, Hooker caught a cold. After months of ill-

FURTHER READING

Archer, Stanley. *Richard Hooker*. Boston: Twayne, 1983. A chapter on Hooker's "Life and Times" is followed by a well-organized examination of the works. Includes a chronology.

Hooker, Richard. *The Folger Library Edition of the Works of Richard Hooker*. Vol. 6, Parts 1 and 2. Edited by W. Speed Hill. Binghamton, N.Y.: Medieval and

Renaissance Texts and Studies, 1993. The important final volume in a massive project. Includes essays by various scholars and extensive textual commentaries.

MacCulloch, Diarmaid. "Richard Hooker's Reputation." *English Historical Review* 117 (September, 2003): 773-813. Examines the attempts made over time by segments of the Anglican church to claim Hooker as a supporter of their various views.

McGrade, Arthur Stephen, ed. *Richard Hooker and the Construction of Christian Community.* Tempe, Ariz.: Medieval and Renaissance Texts and Studies, 1997. Essays on Hooker's life and his ideas.

Pollard, Arthur. *Richard Hooker.* London: Longmans, Green, 1966. A useful monograph, containing brief summaries of each book in *The Lawes of Ecclesiastical Politie.* Also includes sections on the historical context and on literary relationships.

Secor, Philip B. *Richard Hooker, Prophet of Anglicanism.* Tunbridge Wells, England: Burns & Oates, 2001. The first full biography since that of Izaak Walton, a carefully researched, highly readable book. Includes maps and illustrations.

Sisson, Charles Jasper. *The Judicious Marriage of Mr. Hooker and the Birth of The Laws of Ecclesiastical Polity.* 1940. Reprint. New York: Octagon Press, 1974. This crucial work corrects factual errors in Walton's biography, including false statements about Hooker's wife and her family.

Walton, Izaak. *The Lives of John Donne, Sir Henry Wotton, Richard Hooker, George Herbert, and Robert Sanderson.* 1670. Reprint. New York: Oxford University Press, 1973. Despite many errors, Walton's biography remains valuable as a character study of Hooker.

SEE ALSO: John Calvin; Thomas Cranmer; Edward VI; Elizabeth I; Henry VIII; Edmund Spenser.

RELATED ARTICLES in *Great Events from History: The Renaissance & Early Modern Era, 1454-1600:* 1499-1517: Erasmus Advances Humanism in England; January 28, 1547-July 6, 1553: Reign of Edward VI.

HOSOKAWA GRACIA
Japanese noblewoman and Christian martyr

Hosokawa Gracia was a prominent Japanese Christian, a symbol of wifely virtue, and the first Japanese individual on whom the Catholic Church conferred sainthood. As the wife of the important statesman Hosokawa Tadaoki, she also played a central role in the politics of Japan.

BORN: 1563; Japan
DIED: July 16, 1600; Osaka, Japan
ALSO KNOWN AS: Akechi Tama; Hosokawa Tama; Hosokawa Tamako
AREAS OF ACHIEVEMENT: Religion and theology, government and politics

EARLY LIFE

Very little is known concerning the early life of Akechi Tama, who later became prominent under the name of Hosokawa Gracia (hoh-sah-kah-wah grah-see-ah). She was the third daughter (some sources contend the second daughter) of Akechi Mitsuhide, whose origins are also obscure; he first appears in historical records as an important assistant to the warlord Oda Nobunaga in the city of Kyōto in the late 1560's. His first role was as a go-between working with Oda and the shogun Ashikaga Yoshiaki.

It is assumed that Tama was raised in the strict environment of an important samurai household and that she was groomed from an early age to take part in a strategic marriage. Akechi Mitsuhide later gained prominence as a general under Oda. Little is known about the life of his daughter during this period. It is believed that one of her maids had been converted to Christianity. It is likely, however, that she was thrust into an important role as a pawn in the political dealings between Oda and the shogun's court.

LIFE'S WORK

In 1578, under the instructions of Oda, Tama was married to Tadaoki, the son of the prominent daimyo (warlord or feudal baron) Hosokawa Yusai, and her name then changed to Hosokawa Tama. Oda, seeking to use the symbolic authority of the Ashikaga shoguns for his own purposes, enlisted Hosokawa as an important ally in Kyōto. Tama, as the daughter of one of Oda's most important lieutenants, served through her marriage to Tadaoki to cement the strategic connection between Oda and Hosokawa—an alliance that was strengthened when Oda awarded Hosokawa a small fief near Kyōto in 1580.

In 1582, however, Akechi Mitsuhide betrayed Oda when he cornered him at the Honnōji temple, where the would-be hegemon took his own life. Akechi was in turn defeated and killed by the forces of Toyotomi Hideyoshi after the Battle of Yamazaki, a mere eleven days later. Tama's father-in law had remained loyal to Oda, and her husband Tadaoki was instrumental in aiding Toyotomi in his fight against Akechi. Traditional Japanese standards of the day demanded absolute loyalty of a wife to her husband, even above ties of blood, and Tama's support of Tadaoki during this difficult affair resulted in part in her becoming an icon of traditional virtue.

Tradition testifies to the strong bond of love that existed between Tama and her husband, but because of her father's treachery and subsequent death, she was ordered by her new family to retire to Mitono. Toyotomi Hideyoshi was sympathetic to her situation, and she was allowed to return to Tadaoki when he intervened on her behalf in 1584. In fact, the main impact of her father's death on Tama was that it convinced her father-in-law to retire from public life in order to pursue his passion for the traditional Japanese poetry form known as *waka*. Tadaoki became the new ruler of his father's domains. His support of Hideyoshi during the campaign against Akechi Mitsuhide also guaranteed him an important place in the leader's new political order. He was a commander in Hideyoshi's campaigns during the 1580's, and Tama continued to support him through that period.

In 1587, Hosokawa Tama became a Christian and was given the name Gracia at the time of her baptism. Christianity, introduced into Japan in the 1540's by Jesuit missionaries, had made spectacular gains during the time in which Oda exercised power over Kyōto. The strongman was sympathetic to the faith mainly because it opened avenues of trade with the West. Gracia's conversion can be seen in terms of social trends at that time, but she also had a reputation as a passionate believer in her new faith.

After her baptism, Hosokawa Gracia became an important assistant of the Christian lord Takayama Ukon, another important ally of Toyotomi. Takayama received a number of holdings in Harima Province in what is now Hyogo Prefecture. He endeavored to convert the entire population there to the new faith. Gracia assisted him in this process. In that same year, however, as a result of fears of Spanish political influence entering Japan along with the new Christian religion, Hideyoshi issued edicts banning the new faith. Takayama lost his lands, and the first period of Christian persecution in Japanese history began. Destruction of churches was widespread, although practicing Christians such as Gracia were still able to worship.

While Gracia continued her religious efforts, her husband became a major player in the political developments of the day. The death of Toyotomi Hideyoshi in 1598 created a power vacuum in Japan. Two rivals vied for power: Tokugawa Ieyasu in the east of the country and Ishida Mitsunari in the west. Hosokawa Tadaoki decided to ally himself with Ieyasu. Gracia was in Osaka, the center of Ishida's sphere of power. As a result, Tadaoki left instructions with his retainers that Gracia should be killed if she were in danger of falling into Ishida's hands.

The situation came to a head in 1600, when Tadaoki proved to be an important ally of Ieyasu at the Battle of Sekigahara, which resulted in the defeat of Ishida's coalition. Before the battle, Ishida attempted to capture Gracia, who willingly accepted execution at the hands of one of Tadaoki's lieutenants. Tadaoki was well rewarded by Ieyasu, receiving a large fiefdom in the northern part of the island of Kyūshū, but was saddened by the death of his wife. Her selfless act has been celebrated in Japan's romantic tradition, and soon after her death she became a significant folk figure.

SIGNIFICANCE

While her life was tragically cut short as a result of the political machinations surrounding the Battle of Sekigahara, Gracia's reputation as a symbol of virtue and as a prominent Christian was secure. Her life became the subject of the 1975 book *Hosokawa Garasha Fujin* (the lady Hosokawa Gracia) by Miura Ayako, one of Japan's leading female novelists.

Her commitment to her Christian faith also resulted in her being recognized in the West when she was made the first Japanese saint by the Vatican in 1862. In Japan, her life is celebrated in the Nagaokakyo Gracia Festival, the main attraction of which is a reenactment of her wedding procession. There are also numerous monuments to her around the country, including a portrait in the Peace Museum in Nagasaki. Finally, to Western readers she may be most familiar as the historical figure on whom James Clavell based his character Mariko in *Shogun: A Novel of Japan* (1975).

—*Matthew Penney*

FURTHER READING

Breen, John, ed. *Japan and Christianity: Impact and Responses*. New York: Macmillan, 1995. A collection of essays concerning Japanese Christianity in a historical perspective. Contains information about Hosokawa Gracia and the nature of Japanese Christianity during her lifetime.

Francis, Carol B., and John Masaaki Nakajima. *Christians in Japan*. London: Friendship Press, 1991. Focuses on the unique elements of Japanese Christianity and provides biographical material on Hosokawa Gracia.

Laures, Johannes. *Two Japanese Christian Heroes: Justo Takayama Ukon and Gracia Hosokawa Tamako*. Rutland, Vt.: Bridgeway Press, 1959. Contains a brief, illustrated biography of Gracia.

Mullins, Mark. *Christianity Made in Japan: A Study of Indigenous Movements*. Honolulu: University of Hawaii Press, 1998. While the overwhelming majority of the material in this work deals with contemporary Japan, it is useful in assessing the importance of Hosokawa Gracia and her period of Japanese Christianity in the establishment of the Christian tradition in that country.

Natori, Jun'ichi. *The Life of Gracia Tama Hosokawa, a Great Christian Woman in Japan*. Tokyo: Hokuseido Press, 1956. At thirty-nine pages, a concise biography. Illustrated.

Sansom, George. *A History of Japan, 1334-1615*. Stanford, Calif.: Stanford University Press, 1961. Despite its age, Sansom's three-volume history of premodern Japan is still the most authoritative source in English. Includes detailed coverage of Japanese Christianity as well as the fighting and political dealings that surrounded Gracia's life.

Turnbull, Stephen. *Samurai Warfare*. London: Arms and Armour Press, 1996. The best English-language history of the Japanese wars of unification. Specifically addresses the political and military situation that resulted in Gracia's death.

SEE ALSO: Hōjō Ujimasa; Oda Nobunaga; Toyotomi Hideyoshi; Saint Francis Xavier.

RELATED ARTICLES in *Great Events from History: The Renaissance & Early Modern Era, 1454-1600:* 1457-1480's: Spread of Jōdo Shinshū Buddhism; 1467-1477: Ōnin War; 1477-1576: Japan's "Age of the Country at War"; March 5, 1488: Composition of the *Renga* Masterpiece *Minase sangin hyakuin*; Beginning 1513: Kanō School Flourishes; 1532-1536: Temmon Hokke Rebellion; 1549-1552: Father Xavier Introduces Christianity to Japan; 1550-1593: Japanese Wars of Unification.

FRANÇOIS HOTMAN
French church reformer, social reformer, and scholar

Hotman used his considerable knowledge and writing ability for the Protestant Huguenot cause of freedom of conscience and, in the process, developed a philosophy of limited constitutional monarchy and became one of the first modern revolutionaries.

BORN: August 23, 1524; Paris, France
DIED: February 12, 1590; Basel, Swiss Confederation (now in Switzerland)
ALSO KNOWN AS: Franciscus Hotomanus (Latin name)
AREAS OF ACHIEVEMENT: Law, government and politics, church reform, social reform, scholarship

EARLY LIFE
François Hotman (frah-swaw awt-mahn) was the son of Pierre Hotman, a successful lawyer and landowner who, in 1524, had just entered the king's service. He was to be rewarded after twenty years for his loyalty to the Crown with an appointment as conseiller in the Parlement de

Paris, which made him an important member of the feudal office-holding nobility. Little is known of François's mother, Paule, née de Marle, or of his early childhood, except that, as the eldest son who would inherit his father's fief and office, he grew up being prepared for a legal career.

In 1536, Hotman entered the University of Paris, where he was exposed to the new Humanistic learning and developed considerable enthusiasm for classical literature and languages. At fourteen, considered something of a prodigy, Hotman enrolled in the school of law at the University of Orléans. Although the teaching of law was dominated by the Scholastic method, Hotman was also exposed again to the new Humanist approach and learned the methodology of subjecting civil law to historical criticism. The curriculum was rigorous, but Hotman worked hard and received his license in civil law in only two years. Returning to Paris to begin his career, he soon made friends with several leading Humanist scholars, who increased his devotion to the historical school of interpreting the law. Within one year, he had published the first of his many books on law, and, in August of 1546, he assumed his first teaching position at the University of Bourges.

The Reformation, which in time would shake Western civilization to its foundations and profoundly affect Hotman, had begun in earnest only seven years before he was born. In 1536, the Reformation entered a new and more troubled phase with the publication of John Calvin's *Christianae religionis institutio* (*Institutes of the Christian Religion*, 1561). Little is known of when Hotman first came into contact with Reformation ideas. His conversion to Calvinism seems to have begun slowly during his years at the Universities of Paris and Orléans, quickened after his return to Paris, and culminated during his first visit to Switzerland in 1547.

Hotman returned from the University of Orléans to live at home with his parents for some months, but his father's work on a special tribunal of the Parlement de Paris, which was hearing the cases of Lutheran and Calvinist "heretics," apparently became more than he could tolerate. He fled in the spring of 1548, constantly afraid of pursuit by his father. He ended up in Geneva, where, for a short time, he was secretary to John Calvin, whom he now considered his spiritual father. Hotman's break with his home and parents was complete and painful. His father disinherited him, and the French government and French Catholic Church began to consider him dangerous because of his writings in support of the Protestant Huguenot cause. Hotman was never again either financially secure or able to return to France and Paris for any length of time. Geneva had become and remained the spiritual, intellectual, and often physical focus of Hotman's life.

Hotman was moderately attractive, with no outstanding or remarkable physical characteristics. His portrait shows penetrating, wide-set eyes and a high forehead and receding hairline that left him mostly bald by middle age. In the fashion of most Huguenots, he wore a beard and mustache but kept them relatively short, unlike many of his long-bearded colleagues. Within a year of arriving in Geneva, he married Claude Aubelin, the daughter of

François Hotman. (Library of Congress)

Sieur de la Rivière, formerly of Orléans, but who now was a fellow exile in Geneva for the Huguenot faith. Eleven children were born to them, eight of whom reached adulthood. Despite the frequent moves of the household, the uncertainty, and, occasionally, the fear of French reprisals, the marriage seems to have been a happy one.

LIFE'S WORK

Calvin took a deep interest in his followers. Now that Hotman was married, he needed a position with a larger income. Calvin found it for him at the Academy of Lausanne, where Hotman was to teach dialectic and Greek and Latin literature. The Lausanne Academy was the oldest Reformed (non-Catholic) school in a French-speaking area, and Hotman's salary was adequate. During these early years, he published a series of translations and commentaries on great Greek and Latin classical works. He also produced books and tracts on law, but only one of these won for him any particular recognition.

In 1551, Hotman published his *De statu primitivae ecclesiae* (1553; state of the primitive church), a Calvinist tract that attacked the Catholic Church for its deviations from original Christianity. His particular achievement with this work was to take standard Calvinist doctrine and support it with a wide selection of legal and historical authorities and precedents, a style he would perfect in the years to come.

In time, Hotman grew restless in Lausanne. In 1554, he returned to Geneva, which had granted him citizenship, and was soon involved in promoting the Huguenot cause. He did not stay long, however, moving to Strasbourg in October of 1555, where he remained eight years teaching at the academy there. Although not the oldest, it was the most famous and successful of all the Protestant schools and an important adjunct to the Calvinist church in Geneva. The new position had special significance for Hotman because he was taking the place of a rival legal scholar who had fallen out with Calvin, partly because of Hotman. In Strasbourg, Hotman was able to concentrate on teaching and studying civil law, especially the examination of Roman law from a historical point of view. His study of fifth century Roman Emperor Justinian's *Corpus juris civilis* led to a number of publications over the next five years and laid the foundations of his fame as a distinguished legal scholar of the Humanist school. These works also earned for him the doctoral degree from the University of Basel in 1558.

During this time, Hotman's vital interests in Calvinism and in legal scholarship combined, as his consciousness of politics awakened, into a career as a revolutionary propagandist. His central theme became the need to limit constitutionally the power of the French government, especially in religious matters. To this end, he built a case, based on legal and historical precedent, that it was legitimate to resist the exercise of unjustified authority by the French monarchy. Hotman discussed these matters with anyone who was interested and acquired a network of contacts with Protestant leaders all over Europe. He exchanged a large volume of letters with them over the years. He particularly admired the English and regarded Elizabeth I as one of the great hopes of the Protestant cause. He sent Jean, his eldest son, to study at the University of Oxford.

His first major propaganda pamphlet was published in 1560. It was a vigorous denunciation of the noble house of Guise, especially Charles, cardinal of Lorraine, who led the ultra-Catholic party in France. The cardinal and the Guise family had pressured King Henry II and his successors to increase the repression of Protestantism in France to counteract the increasing popularity of Calvinism, particularly among the French nobility and burgher classes. Following Hotman's lead, and in some cases undoubtedly with additional contributions written but not publicly acknowledged by him, a large number of Huguenot propaganda pamphlets were published attacking the cardinal of Lorraine and his faction, and presenting the Huguenot case. The Guises countered with claims that the Huguenots had attempted to murder the Catholic party's leaders and the king, and were also guilty of heresy and sedition. These were the opening salvos of what became a series of eight religious civil wars in France. Hotman had become the leading ideologist of the Huguenot cause for liberty of conscience, one of the trusted diplomatic agents and advisers of the Huguenot leadership, and a revolutionary.

By August of 1572, Hotman's reputation as a scholar and his list of texts and essays on legal subjects had grown considerably. His work for the Huguenots had brought him many friends and admirers among the Protestant leadership. His connections with important French nobles had made possible a return to France and a position at the University of Bourges. The St. Bartholomew's Day Massacre, however, caused him to leave again. In Paris on August 23, 1572, Hotman's forty-eighth birthday, the ultra-Catholics began slaughtering Huguenots. The king and the queen mother were parties to this butchery, which spread from Paris throughout France wherever there were concentrations of Huguenots. Suspicious of what could happen, Hotman walked out of town in disguise and without any of his possessions the instant he learned of the events in Paris. He and his family lost everything, although Hotman was later able to recover a few of his more important manuscripts. Once again, in mid-life, he sought asylum in Geneva, where after a few months he accepted a faculty position at the Geneva Academy.

The St. Bartholomew's Day Massacre resulted in the fourth of the French religious civil wars and in making Hotman an overtly declared revolutionary. In the propaganda tracts that were pouring from his pen, he no longer blamed the political tyranny and persecution of the Huguenots on the ultra-Catholic party but took aim directly at the king. Hotman spent much of the rest of his life developing his ideas on limited constitutional monarchy and freedom of religion and conscience.

Hotman's masterwork on these themes was *Franco-Gallia* (pb. 1573; English translation, 1711). Although he had been working on this project for at least six years, its publication was especially timely. Hotman's fundamental proposition, supported with a wide variety of evidence, was that the ancient and medieval Gauls and Franks had a constitution that limited the monarch's authority by requiring that the making of law be shared with a national council called the estates-general. This council also elected the king. In Hotman's description, the powers of the estates-general were remarkably similar to those of a modern-day legislature and not a medieval assembly. Hotman argued that the king did not rule by hereditary right but by the authority of the people as expressed in the estates-general. After equating royal absolutism with tyranny, Hotman suggested that the people have the right to depose a tyrant king. That was probably his most radical proposition. In an obvious reference to the Guise family of Lorraine, which was not considered an integral part of France at the time, Hotman also included the use of foreign mercenaries as typical of tyrants.

In *Franco-Gallia*, Hotman was clearly attempting to prove that ancient and medieval France had known a considerable degree of political and religious freedom that earlier national leaders, specifically the queen mother Catherine, her sons, and the Guise family, had distorted and corrupted for their own personal gain and at the people's expense. It was an enormously popular work among Protestants—infamous among the ultra-Catholics—and was translated into several other languages and went through several editions in Hotman's lifetime. It was a propaganda work and not entirely accurate historically but so impressive in its demonstrated learning and so brilliantly done that the Calvinist king, Henry of Navarre, who in time would end the French religious civil wars and become King Henry IV of France, enlisted Hotman's aid on numerous occasions. On the other hand, the Catholic party felt obliged to put their best talent to work in trying to refute Hotman.

Hotman's remaining years were not spent in comfort. When a temporary peace came in the French religious wars in 1576 and various offers came to return to France, Hotman was too fearful of another massacre of Huguenots and rejected all offers. His financial situation in Geneva was grim, and his health was deteriorating. To make matters worse, Geneva, which had been threatened by the duchy of Savoy periodically for years, entered a prolonged period of heightened anxiety over the possibility of being attacked and invaded. When the constant state of fear became more than he could bear, Hotman once again moved his family in August of 1578.

He had had numerous offers but decided to accept a teaching position at the University of Basel, where he

thought he could live and work in peace. While that proved to be true, his financial condition did not significantly improve and he found that his faith was tolerated but increasingly unpopular. Hotman's physical retreat to Basel, however, was only a semiretirement, not a full retreat from the Huguenot cause. He continued to be actively involved in the plots and schemes of his party, and in writing tracts and pamphlets. As something of a celebrity whose list of frequent correspondents contained the greatest minds of Protestant Europe, he also had many visitors, including the famous essayist Michel Eyquem de Montaigne.

Basel was not immune to the ravages of the plague, which, in February of 1583, swept through the region. Hotman's wife, who had always taken extraordinary measures to get herself and her family away whenever the plague broke out, caught the disease this time and died soon afterward. Hotman was even more deeply disturbed when Daniel, one of his sons, converted to Catholicism. As he had done so often before when distressed, he moved, this time back to Geneva, in late September, 1584, where he knew that a position at the academy was still available to him.

Besides the troubles in his personal life, the urging of his coreligionist Henry of Navarre to write in support of his claim to the French throne may also have influenced Hotman to return to Geneva. After Charles IX died in 1574, his brother became King Henry III. Henry III's only heir, however, had died in 1584, and the succession was between Henry of Navarre, now the most legitimate heir, and his uncle, the cardinal of Bourbon, who had the support of the ultra-Catholics. Hotman wrote and published several works on the question, basing the case for Henry of Navarre on fundamental constitutional law. The Guises were sufficiently disturbed by Hotman's work to set several of their best writers to work answering him. Henry of Navarre was sufficiently impressed and made Hotman a councillor and member of his Privy Council in 1585, a position Hotman held until his death.

In that same year, the ultra-Catholics virtually forced Henry III to provoke a war with Henry of Navarre and the Huguenots. This was the War of the Three Henrys, the eighth and final religious civil war in France. Apparently, the Guises hoped that the war would eliminate Henry of Navarre as a possible heir to the throne. The war, although not decisive, went more in favor of the Catholics than the Huguenots until 1589. In that year, Henry I of Lorraine, duke of Guise, seemed to be positioning himself to seize the throne and Henry III had him assassinated. The ultra-Catholics rose in rebellion, and

Henry III was forced to flee. On his way to Henry of Navarre for sanctuary, he was murdered by a Catholic monk. Meanwhile, the situation in Geneva was bleak. Savoy was once again threatening, and the city was in a virtual state of siege. In September of 1589, Hotman and his remaining three unmarried daughters escaped Geneva by water on Lake Lausanne to Basel. His health had been declining for some time and severe edema was added to his other health problems. On February 12, 1590, he died. In his will, he disinherited his son Daniel. To the end, his cause was the most important aspect of his life.

SIGNIFICANCE

Hotman was an uncompromising idealist and would have had mixed reactions to the immediate outcome of his cause. He would have been overjoyed when Henry of Navarre finally prevailed in the field of battle over the ultra-Catholics and became King Henry IV of France in 1589. He also would have applauded Henry IV's Edict of Nantes in 1598, which gave the Huguenots political and religious rights. He would have been appalled, however, by the high cost: the conversion of Henry IV to Catholicism. He would also have been disturbed by the failure of the estates-general to develop into an institution capable of limiting and controlling royal authority.

In the next century, Catholicism regained much of the ground lost to the Huguenots, sometimes by force, as in Louis XIV's Revocation of the Edict of Nantes in 1685. In 1789, during the reign of Louis XVI, the estates-general would emerge as a limiting force, but with such suddenness and violence as to create a great revolution.

Hotman, who wanted to restore religion and law to an idealized primitive perfection and thereby establish popular sovereignty and liberty of conscience, did not succeed in his own time. He did succeed, however, in raising issues and laying foundations on which later theorists of the seventeenth and eighteenth centuries would build a new vision of the state, which included not only concepts of popular sovereignty and religious freedom but also of social contract, individual freedom, and the rule of law.

—*Richard L. Hillard*

FURTHER READING

Bainton, Roland H. *The Reformation of the Sixteenth Century.* Boston: Beacon Press, 1952. For those interested in the religious issues of Hotman's era, this older but still quite useful work explains the development of Protestant thought and doctrine with sympathy and precision.

Conner, Philip. *Huguenot Heartland: Montauban and Southern French Calvinism During the Wars of Religion.* Burlington, Vt.: Ashgate, 2002. Study of the Wars of Religion, especially of the differences between the experiences of southern and northern France during the wars. Focuses on the southern town of Montauban as a case study of the larger religious, cultural, and political upheaval during Hotman's time. Includes maps, bibliographic references, and index.

Dunn, Richard S. *The Age of Religious Wars, 1559-1715.* 2d ed. New York: Norton, 1979. An excellent, readable, yet scholarly general history of Europe which includes the era of the wars between Protestants and Catholics that began in the latter half of the sixteenth century and lasted until the mid-seventeenth century. The Catholic-Huguenot wars of France and how they fit into the overall pattern of European history are well presented.

Kelly, Donald R. *François Hotman: A Revolutionary's Ordeal.* Princeton, N.J.: Princeton University Press, 1972. The only full-length biography of Hotman in English. A sympathetic treatment of Hotman's life, but it does not ignore his faults. Sometimes omits background that increases understanding of the significance of Hotman's work.

Major, J. Russell. *From Renaissance Monarchy to Absolute Monarchy: French Kings, Nobles, and Estates.* Baltimore: Johns Hopkins University Press, 1994. Study of the development and relative power of the French monarchy beginning in the Renaissance and ending with Louis XIV. Includes illustrations, map, bibliographic references, index.

Myers, A. R. *Parliaments and Estates in Europe to 1789.* New York: Harcourt Brace Jovanovich, 1975. A good general discussion of the origins and evolution of representative political assemblies and legislatures in Europe from their medieval origins to the French Revolution. Mentions Hotman in the discussion of the French estates-general and the impact of the religious wars.

Neale, J. E. *The Age of Catherine de Medici, and Essays in Elizabethan History.* London: Jonathan Cape, 1971. The title work is an excellent history of France during the latter half of the sixteenth century. Concentrates on political and legal issues, the collapse of the Valois Dynasty, and assumption of the French throne by Henry of Navarre.

Racaut, Luc. *Hatred in Print: Catholic Propaganda and Protestant Identity During the French Wars of Reli-*

gion. Burlington, Vt.: Ashgate, 2002. Study of those writing against Hotman and other Protestant propagandists. Analyzes the strategies, production, and impact of pro-Catholic propaganda of the period. Includes bibliographic references and index.

Reynolds, Beatrice. *Proponents of Limited Monarchy in Sixteenth Century France: François Hotman and Jean Bodin.* New York: Columbia University Press, 1931. Reprint. New York: AMS Press, 1968. An older but still-interesting, in-depth treatment of Hotman's ideas of constitutional monarchy. Not as clear as it could be on the relationship of Hotman's political ideas to his religious beliefs.

Skinner, Quentin. *The Foundations of Modern Political Thought.* 2 vols. Cambridge, England: Cambridge University Press, 1978. Perhaps the best scholarly study of the political philosophy of the Renaissance and Reformation. Volume 2 has numerous references to Hotman and the Huguenot cause. Particularly valuable in explaining the connections between religious doctrine and political philosophy.

SEE ALSO: John Calvin; Catherine de Médicis; Elizabeth I; Henry II; Henry III; Henry IV; Martin Luther; Michel Eyquem de Montaigne; Philippe de Mornay; Philip II; Joseph Justus Scaliger.

RELATED ARTICLE in *Great Events from History: The Renaissance & Early Modern Era, 1454-1600:* March, 1536: Calvin Publishes *Institutes of the Christian Religion.*

CATHERINE HOWARD
Queen of England (r. 1540-1542)

As fifth wife to King Henry VIII, Catherine Howard briefly reigned as queen of England until revelations about her personal life brought about her sudden downfall and execution.

BORN: c. 1521; probably at Horsham or Lambeth, England
DIED: February 13, 1542; London, England
AREA OF ACHIEVEMENT: Government and politics

EARLY LIFE

Catherine Howard was born into the English aristocracy, her father being Lord Edmund Howard, a younger son of Thomas Howard, second duke of Norfolk. Through her Howard connections, Catherine was a first cousin to Anne Boleyn, Henry VIII's second queen. Little is known about the future queen's childhood. She grew up in a large family of ten children and received little formal education. Her mother, Joyce Culpeper, died when Catherine was quite young. Her father, Lord Edmund Howard, subsequently married two more times, but he saw little of his daughter. Being a younger son, Lord Edmund did not inherit the considerable family estates, and he experienced continual financial difficulties, even after his appointment as controller of Calais in 1534. Never a major influence on his daughter's life, he died in 1539, a year before Catherine's dramatic rise to power.

The most significant development of Catherine's childhood occurred when her father sent her to live with his stepmother Agnes, the dowager duchess of Norfolk. One of the wealthiest and most influential women of her day, the duchess maintained a grand household at her country estate at Horsham in Sussex and her town house at Lambeth, across the River Thames from London. The duchess exercised only a loose supervision over her numerous charges; at Horsham, young Catherine soon engaged in a serious flirtation with Henry Manox, a musician hired to teach her to play the lute and virginal. Although the relationship did not become an actual affair, Manox followed Catherine to Lambeth and openly bragged to numerous people in the household of the liberties he had enjoyed with the duchess's charge.

While at Lambeth, probably in 1538, Catherine became sexually active with her next serious suitor, Francis Dereham, a distant kinsman of Duchess Agnes and a pensioner in her household. The two lovers openly exchanged gifts and were heard to call each other "husband" and "wife." Their clandestine nighttime meetings became something of a scandal and provoked the jealousy of Manox, who sent an anonymous note to the duchess informing her of the relationship. Discovering the two in an ardent embrace, she angrily struck both of them. Dereham soon left to seek his fortune in Ireland, leaving his life savings with his paramour. Catherine's passion for Dereham quickly cooled after her uncle Norfolk used his influence in 1540 to secure her a position at court, an event that drastically transformed the fortunes of this previously obscure young woman.

Catherine Howard. (Library of Congress)

LIFE'S WORK

The Howard family used Catherine as a pawn in the dangerous political game for dominance at the court of the aging Henry VIII. The duke stood as the representative of the conservative faction of old nobility who opposed the pro-Protestant policies of Thomas Cromwell, Henry's lord chancellor and the guiding genius behind the English Reformation. To cement an alliance with the German Protestants, Cromwell had just engineered the king's marriage to Anne of Cleves. From their first meeting in January, 1540, Henry had openly expressed his displeasure with his new foreign bride. Sensing Cromwell's vulnerability, the Norfolk faction brought Catherine to court and coached her on ways to attract the monarch's attention.

Henry evidently met Catherine at a banquet hosted by Norfolk's ally, Stephen Gardiner, bishop of Winchester; by April, the king was obviously smitten. On April 24, he granted her the lands of a convicted felon, and even more

lavish gifts followed the next month. Queen Anne's last public appearance with Henry occurred at the May Day festivities; soon thereafter, he sent her to the country so that he could court Catherine openly. On many spring nights, the royal barge crossed the Thames to visit Duchess Agnes's Lambeth residence so that Henry could enjoy Catherine's company.

Catherine's triumph came swiftly. On June 10, Henry ordered Cromwell's arrest on charges of heresy and treason. Facing death, the former chancellor agreed to supply information to enable Henry to divorce his German consort. Anne did not oppose Henry's schemes, and the grateful monarch offered her a generous settlement. Their divorce became final on July 9. Nineteen days later, ironically on the day Cromwell was beheaded, Henry summoned the bishop of London to the royal palace at Oatlands, where he secretly married Catherine. He publicly acknowledged her as his new queen at Hampton Court on August 8.

The aging, increasingly bloated monarch initially seemed besotted by his lively teenage bride. Catherine's youthful vigor, coupled with her submissiveness and outward virtue, rejuvenated her husband, who showered her with public caresses and worldly goods. He soon bestowed on her all the lordships and manors that had belonged to his beloved queen Jane Seymour, as well as some of Cromwell's former properties. The new queen chose "No other wish but his" as the motto above her new coat of arms.

Although Catherine's Howard relatives again found themselves in a position of preeminence at court, the new queen was far more naïve about court politics and factions than her two English predecessors, Anne Boleyn and Jane Seymour. Also unlike some of Henry's previous spouses, Catherine evidently made no real attempt to preoccupy herself with politics or interfere with state affairs, except for a handful of intercessions on behalf of prominent prisoners in the Tower. Throughout her brief reign, her main preoccupation seemed to be clothes and dancing, not political intrigue. The king appeared delighted with his young bride; the two remained constantly in each other's company until February, 1541.

Sometime in the spring of 1541, though, Catherine embarked on more dangerous behavior, which culminated in an affair with a distant cousin, Thomas Culpeper, an attractive young courtier who was several decades younger than her husband. The only surviving letter in Catherine's hand, written in April, 1541, is a love letter to Culpeper in which she recklessly pronounced herself "Yours as long as life endures."

Their affair evidently continued throughout the summer and autumn while Henry took his bride on a tour of northern England. Lavish ceremonies awaited the royal couple as they visited numerous towns. At Pontefract in Yorkshire, Francis Dereham reappeared in Catherine's life and demanded a post at court. On August 27, she unwisely appointed him her private secretary, perhaps to buy his silence about their previous relationship.

The royal entourage returned to Hampton Court on October 30, and Henry gave orders for a special thanksgiving service to be held celebrating his marriage. A sudden turn of events, though, brought an end to the marriage and death to the young queen. Shortly before their return, Archbishop Thomas Cranmer had received disturbing reports about Catherine's clandestine life before her marriage. The initial source of this news was John Lascelles, whose sister, Mary Hall, had been in the dowager duchess of Norfolk's service while Catherine lived with her. A zealous Protestant, Lascelles was not a personal enemy of the queen, but he did despise what she represented—the triumph of the Howard faction at court. After consultations with other leading men at court, Cranmer handed the king a note with the damning information while Henry was hearing a mass for the dead.

Initially astonished and unwilling to believe the charges, Henry nevertheless ordered the archbishop to conduct a thorough investigation and to confine the queen to her apartments pending its outcome. He never saw her again, as interrogation of numerous witnesses confirmed his worst fears. On being informed by his council that the allegations against Catherine had a sound basis, the king openly broke down and cried. Subsequently, increasingly outraged at being cuckolded, he furiously called for a sword so that he could execute his adulterous spouse personally.

Whereas Anne Boleyn had immediately been sent to the Tower after allegations of her infidelity, Catherine was instead placed under house arrest at the Abbey of Syon in Middlesex. The king allowed her to have four attendants and access to three chambers during this initial stage of her confinement. He also let Cranmer hold out some hope of royal mercy to Catherine if she would fully confess.

After initially denying the charges against her and changing her story several times, the queen eventually confessed her guilt to Cranmer. As evidence accumulated, it became obvious that Catherine had been not only indiscreet before her marriage to Henry, but also unfaithful to him afterward. On November 22, a royal proclamation announced that she had forfeited her rights as queen; two days later, she was formally indicted both for having concealed her relationship with Dereham before her marriage and for having committed adultery with Culpeper after becoming Henry's wife.

Culpeper and Dereham paid for their folly by being executed on December 1. The king decided against a public trial for his unfaithful wife. Instead, she was condemned by a special act of attainder passed by Parliament and approved by the king in early February. On two occasions, members of the council invited Catherine to come before Parliament to defend herself, but she refused, admitting her guilt and hoping for the king's mercy.

On February 10, Catherine was removed to the Tower, and on the evening of February 12, she was told she would die the following morning. She requested that the block on which she was to be executed be brought into her room in the Tower so that she could practice how to place herself. Early on February 13, guards escorted the prisoner to a spot within the Tower grounds, the same location where her cousin had been beheaded nearly six years earlier. Catherine made a brief speech admitting her sins to both God and king, after which the executioner severed her head with a single stroke from his axe. Like Anne Boleyn's before her, her body was interred in the chapel of St. Peter ad Vinicula within the Tower.

SIGNIFICANCE

Catherine Howard reigned only some eighteen months as Henry VIII's fifth queen, and fewer details about her brief life exist than for any of his other consorts. Except for a possible depiction in a stained-glass window in King's College Chapel, Cambridge, no contemporary portrait of her survived. Nor did Catherine play a significant role in determining policy during the tempestuous final years of Henry's reign. Rather, her powerful Howard relations used her as a pawn to forward their own ambitions at the volatile court of the second Tudor king.

Catherine became Henry VIII's final passion. His immediately preceding marriage with Anne of Cleves had been arranged, but Henry deliberately chose the young and seemingly innocent Catherine, some three decades his junior. For a few months, she succeeded in reinvigorating her prematurely aging husband. Her fall left him an increasingly embittered and dangerous sovereign and resulted in the temporary disgrace of her family. Her uncle Norfolk managed to save his life by abandoning Catherine and joining in her condemnation, as he had done with his other royal niece, Anne Boleyn, but Howard influence at Henry's court ended as the result of the scandal. An odd sequence of events had briefly turned this obscure young woman into the most prominent lady in the realm. Her indiscretions both before and after her marriage brought a tragically early end to her life.

—_Tom L. Auffenberg_

FURTHER READING

Fraser, Antonia. _The Wives of Henry VIII._ New York: Alfred A. Knopf, 1992. Part 4 of this well-written and well-researched collective biography by one of Britain's most popular writers provides a colorful portrait of Catherine and her contemporaries.

Lindsey, Karen. _Divorced, Beheaded, Survived: A Feminist Reinterpretation of the Wives of Henry VIII._ New York: Addison-Wesley, 1995. This lively collective biography examines the position of Catherine and Henry's other wives based on recent feminist interpretations of the role of women in Tudor society.

Loades, David. _Henry VIII and His Queens._ Stroud, Gloucestershire, England: Sutton, 2000. This short and highly readable work by a respected British historian provides a useful introduction to the topic.

Smith, Lacey Baldwin. _A Tudor Tragedy: The Life and Times of Catherine Howard._ London: Clay, 1961.

This sympathetic study by a leading Tudor-Stuart historian remains the standard biography.

Starkey, David. _Six Wives: The Queens of Henry VIII._ New York: HarperCollins, 2003. Emphasizes the religious and political complexities of Henry's court, and fleshes out many of the significant players in that milieu, in order better to understand the lives, careers, and deaths of each of Henry's wives.

Warnicke, Retha M. _The Marrying of Anne of Cleves: Royal Protocol in Early Modern England._ New York: Cambridge University Press, 2000. Extended study of Henry's fourth marriage, including its dissolution and the courtship of Catherine, Anne's replacement. Includes photographic plates, illustrations, map, bibliographic references, and index.

Weir, Alison. _The Six Wives of Henry VIII._ New York: Grove Press, 1991. Chapters 13 to 15 of this collective biography complement the work of Fraser. Weir asserts that Catherine was born around 1525, making her younger than other scholars assume.

SEE ALSO: Anne of Cleves; Anne Boleyn; Catherine of Aragon; Thomas Cranmer; Thomas Cromwell; Henry VIII; Catherine Parr; Jane Seymour.

RELATED ARTICLE in _Great Events from History: The Renaissance & Early Modern Era, 1454-1600:_ May, 1539: Six Articles of Henry VIII.

HUÁSCAR
King of the Inca Empire (r. 1525-1532)

Huáscar, the last ruler of the Incas, has the unenviable renown of losing the mightiest empire in pre-Columbian America.

BORN: c. 1495; Cuzco, Inca Empire (now in Peru)
DIED: 1532; Cajamarca, Inca Empire (now in Peru)
ALSO KNOWN AS: Inti Cusi Huallpa; Tupac Cusi Huallpa
AREAS OF ACHIEVEMENT: Military, government and politics

EARLY LIFE

Few details of the birth, childhood, and youth of Tupac Cusi Huallpa, known as Huáscar (WAHS-kahr), survive. His father, Huayna Capac, was called the Inca, eleventh in his line. From 1493 to 1525, he ruled Tahuantinsuyu (four quarters), the empire that stretched from northern

Chile to Ecuador's border with Colombia. Huáscar's mother, Ragua Ocllo, was Huayna Capac's sister, as custom required for a queen, or _qoya._ Huáscar was born in the capital, Cuzco, on the eastern slopes of the Andes mountains in southern Peru about 1495.

Huayna Capac celebrated Huáscar's weaning-and-hair-cutting ceremony, an initiation rite, by ordering craftspeople to fashion an immense golden chain. According to one account, the chain–_huasca_ in the Incan language—was seven hundred feet long and so heavy that two hundred men could not lift it. This extravagant gift is supposed to have inspired the name by which Huáscar is best known.

As a teenager, Huáscar remained behind in Cuzco when Huayna Capac left on extensive military campaigns, taking with him Huáscar's two elder half brothers, Ninan Cuyochi and Atahualpa. Huayna Capac was especially fond of the latter and spent the last twelve years of his reign with Atahualpa in Quito (now the capital of Ecuador).

LIFE'S WORK

Who was to succeed Huayna Capac appears to have been unsettled, as if the Inca could not make up his mind. Historical sources speak of Huáscar as if he were the heir, but his mother was Huayna Capac's second oldest sister, and Ninan Cuyochi, the son of the Inca's oldest sister, had the better claim. Furthermore, Atahualpa stood highest in his father's affection and had been groomed by the Inca to be a leader, although he could not hold supreme power because his mother was not of royal blood.

When Huayna Capac fell ill from smallpox in 1525, he had a premonition of death. He dispatched advisers to prepare Ninan Cuyochi to assume power, but the eldest son himself was already dead of smallpox. Huayna Capac then named Huáscar the heir, although with an important provision. He made Huáscar promise to treat the region around Quito as a semiautonomous province to be ruled by Atahualpa as a viceroy. Huáscar readily agreed. When Huayna Capac died, Huáscar received the *borla* in the official coronation ceremony in Cuzco. The *borla*, the insignia of the Inca, was a headband with a fringe in front that hung down to the wearer's eyebrows. With the assumption of power, Huáscar became a god in Incan religion, to be obeyed unquestioningly, on pain of death.

God or not, he was still subject to the intricate politics of the Cuzco court. Huayna Capac had left Huáscar with many half brothers, some loyal and some ambitious on their own behalf. The situation was ripe for intrigue, especially since Atahualpa commanded one-fifth of the realm from Quito, where the most experienced military officers lived and supported him. Moreover, an ancient division of Cuzco into Hanan and Hurin moieties had evolved into politically opposed factions; Huáscar was Hurin, while his mother and Atahualpa were Hanan. Huáscar could count on the loyalty of neither his capital nor his close kin.

Huáscar was aware of the dangers to his reign. He was far from stupid, but having been raised a royal heir in the narrow, elitist atmosphere of the Cuzco court, he was haughty, impulsive, and tactless. He may also have suffered from neuroses: Some contemporary sources call him "half mad" and argue that the ugliness of his short, swarthy physique proved that he was unfit to rule. Inexperience and willfulness, probably manipulated by the self-interested counsel of courtiers, soon made him disliked in the capital as arrogant and irresponsible. In any case, he quickly committed a series of major blunders.

The first occurred when he summoned Atahualpa to Cuzco. Atahualpa, Ragua Ocllo, and others of the royal court were to accompany the corpse of Huayna Capac to the capital for interment. While there, Atahualpa was to pledge his loyalty to the new Inca, as the law required. Atahualpa accompanied the group for a while but then turned back, sending a trusted friend of his father to assure Huáscar of his loyalty. When the dead Inca's entourage was near Cuzco, Huáscar learned that his half brother was still in Quito; he became enraged, interpreting Atahualpa's absence as disrespect. Deeply suspicious, he overreacted. He arrested the whole group, confined his mother, and tortured and executed Atahualpa's emissary.

If Atahualpa suspected that he was not safe in Huáscar's hands, as seems likely, he now had clear reason for his distrust. Worse for Huáscar, he had turned his mother into a political opponent. When he sought to take his eldest sister as his *qoya*, he needed Ragua Ocllo's formal permission. She refused it until he threatened her, hardening her enmity toward him.

Atahualpa sent another group of five noblemen to convey his loyalty to Huáscar. Before going to the Inca, however, the principal emissary visited Ragua Ocllo, who received him warmly. That meeting further inflamed Huáscar's suspicions. He executed four of the group and sent the last back to Atahualpa with a summons.

Atahualpa had no intention of delivering himself into Huáscar's power. With the support of his advisers, he gathered military forces, whereupon Huáscar declared Atahualpa to be a traitor. This was another blunder. Instead of coming to terms with his brother, Huáscar forced him into outright civil war.

Huáscar could not afford a civil war, politically or financially. Economics especially were a problem. Incan law devoted the income from areas conquered by previous rulers to supporting their households and the religious cults devoted to them. Each equal in size to Huáscar's court, the courts of the dead Incas drained off most state revenues. To support himself, Huáscar had to conquer new territory of his own. His attempts to do so in the south met with little success. The richest prizes lay to the north, in Colombia, but Atahualpa blocked the way. Huáscar tried to remedy the problem with reform: He moved to disband the cults of the dead Inca. Fierce opposition from the Incan priesthood stymied him, and all he achieved was to make the priests into political opponents.

Huáscar dispatched an army, commanded by a loyal half brother, to destroy Atahualpa in Quito. Although Atahualpa had far fewer resources to support a war, he had better troops and officers. In fact, his two top generals, Quizquiz and Chalicuchima, are thought to have been the ablest military leaders produced by the Inca Empire. The rebel army that met the Incan forces in southern Ecuador was seasoned from many campaigns under Huayna Capac. Atahualpa's generals won battle after battle, turned back the Incan army, and pushed it relentlessly toward Cuzco. Atahualpa followed well behind the main army, meeting with tribal leaders along the way and requiring them to swear allegiance to him. He ordered his troops to devastate the villages of those who refused.

Although Huáscar reinforced his army and changed commanders, Atahualpa's troops pressed on until they stood near Cuzco itself. At this point, Huáscar took personal command. He succeeded in punishing the enemy during a protracted battle, but his military inexperience showed. He was lured into an ambush and captured by Chalicuchima. Huáscar's army fell apart when it learned that he had been captured; soon afterward, Cuzco fell to Quizquiz with little resistance, almost certainly because the Hanan faction was happy to see Huáscar defeated.

On orders from Atahualpa, still well behind the army, Quizquiz massacred Huáscar's family and followers before his eyes, and he was publicly humiliated. Atahualpa donned the *borla* and deported himself as the new Inca, but he could not truly be the Inca until he was officially crowned in Cuzco.

On his way there, he heard news that a band of bearded strangers was advancing into the Andes from the coast. The new arrivals were the conquistador Francisco Pizarro and an army of fewer than two hundred Spaniards. Curious, Atahualpa turned aside to meet them in Cajamarca. He had heard of the Spaniards and, with tens of thousands of warriors around him, he intended to capture them. Pizarro tricked Atahualpa and captured him first. Still vastly outnumbered, the Spaniards held on to Atahualpa and bargained for a ransom. Fearing that Pizarro might use Huáscar to further weaken his bargaining power, Atahualpa secretly ordered Huáscar killed. The twelfth and last anointed Inca was put to death near or in Cajamarca, where Atahualpa was held prisoner. Pizarro killed him a few months later.

SIGNIFICANCE

With the last Inca, Huáscar, dead, as well as his rival, Atahualpa, the Inca armies fell into disarray, and the Spanish were able to conquer the Inca Empire, even though it was vastly superior in numbers of fighters and resources. Pizarro's astonishing success reveals several weaknesses in the Inca state.

First, succession of power from one Inca to the next was unfixed. The dying Inca, in fact, was responsible for naming his heir, who could be any of his pure-blood sons. Huayna Capac almost guaranteed trouble when he was indecisive about an heir and then apportioned part of his realm to a favorite not in line to succeed, Atahualpa.

Second, the Inca state relied precariously on one man, the Inca. Tahuantinsuyu had been blessed with a series of talented military leaders and administrators who held power firmly and expanded the empire's territories, but the state did not fare well without a dynamic Inca. The Inca Empire was vulnerable to the political intrigue among ambitious lieutenants that arises around a leader's incompetence.

Third, the Incas' own mythology worked against them. Although Huayna Capac, Atahualpa, and Huáscar knew about the invasion of South and Central America by white strangers, they thought it possible that these strangers were gods whose arrival had been prophesied. This uncertainty may have kept Huayna Capac from ensuring that the Spaniards could not threaten him.

Because they brought with them new diseases that were lethal to the Incas, the Spaniards may well have triumphed anyway. Smallpox, which was particularly virulent, reached the Incas even before Pizarro did, and it decimated the nobility and army. The civil war between Huáscar and Atahualpa, which by some estimates killed as many as 100,000 warriors, further crippled the Incas and prepared the way for the Spanish victory.

—*Roger Smith*

FURTHER READING

Betanzos, Juan de. *Narrative of the Incas*. Translated by Ronald Hamilton and Dana Buchanan. Austin: University of Texas Press, 1996. An example of the kind of contemporary source on which historians depend. Married to a royal Inca, Betanzos finished this somewhat slanted history in 1557.

Brundage, Burr Cartwright. *Empire of the Inca*. Norman: University of Oklahoma Press, 1963. Brundage relates, in a convoluted prose style, the rise of the Inca state, the careers of its twelve emperors, its social and religious organization, and its conquest by the Spanish.

D'Altroy, Terence N. *The Incas*. Malden, Mass.: Blackwell, 2002. Study of the Inca Empire from its beginnings to its fall. Reconsiders the social, political, and economic structure of the empire in the light of recent scholarship and archaeological discoveries. Includes illustrations, maps, bibliographic references, index.

Davies, Nigel. *The Incas*. Niwot: University Press of Colorado, 1995. A close analysis of the Spanish sources of Inca history, the archaeological evidence, and scholars' interpretations of both. Davies argues that little is known with certainty about the Inca rulers.

Hemmings, John. *The Conquest of the Incas*. New York: Harcourt Brace Jovanovich, 1970. This captivating, richly detailed book chronicles the conquest of the Inca Empire by Spaniards. The opening chapters describe Pizarro's encounter with Atahualpa and the fate of Huáscar.

Hyams, Edward, and George Ordish. *The Last of the Incas*. New York: Simon & Schuster, 1963. A provocative review of the rise and fall of the Incas that insists the empire was socialistic and the Inca skill for government was inherited. Hyams and Ordish find the Incas more benevolent than do other historians.

McIntyre, Loren. *The Incredible Incas and Their Timeless Land*. Washington, D.C.: National Geographic Society, 1975. Relates basic Inca history vividly and describes the society and its physical environment. Many lovely color drawings and photographs complement the text.

Malpass, Michael A. *Daily Life in the Inca Empire*. Westport, Conn.: Greenwood Press, 1996. Written for complete newcomers to pre-Columbian history, the text carefully defines Inca terms and anthropological concepts as it describes Inca culture and history. With illustrations and a handy glossary.

Stirling, Stuart. *The Last Conquistador: Mansio Serra de Lequizamón and the Conquest of the Incas*. Stroud, Gloucestershire, England: Sutton, 1999. Study of one of Pizarro's top lieutenants and his role in the conquest of the Incas. Includes illustrations, maps, bibliographic references, index.

SEE ALSO: Atahualpa; Pachacuti; Francisco Pizarro.

RELATED ARTICLES in *Great Events from History: The Renaissance & Early Modern Era, 1454-1600:* 1493-1525: Reign of Huayna Capac; 1525-1532: Huáscar and Atahualpa Share Inca Rule; 1532-1537: Pizarro Conquers the Incas in Peru.

BALTHASAR HUBMAIER
German church reformer and religious scholar

As an evangelical reformer, Hubmaier played a significant role in influencing Anabaptist beliefs, which include the believer's baptism, the refusal to baptize infants, and the role of free will as a catalyst for salvation. He also wrote one of the earliest pleas for religious tolerance.

BORN: c. 1480; Friedberg, near Augsburg, Bavaria (now in Germany)
DIED: March 10, 1528; Vienna, Austria
AREAS OF ACHIEVEMENT: Religion and theology, church reform, scholarship

EARLY LIFE
Balthasar Hubmaier (BAHL-tah-zahr HEWP-mi-ehr) was born five miles east of Augsburg. Scholars assume that his social class originated with the peasantry, yet he was well educated. After attending the Latin school in Augsburg, he entered the University of Freiburg in May of 1503, where he received his master's degree under theologian Johann Eck around 1505.

Ordained a priest in 1510, Hubmaier received his doc-

torate in theology from the University of Ingolstadt in 1512. He then became vice-rector of the university and then a preacher at the cathedral of Regensberg, playing a role in the expulsion of the city's Jews and promoting the cathedral as a pilgrimage center for local miracles.

LIFE'S WORK
With his adult baptism by Swiss religious leader Konrad Grebel in 1525, Hubmaier established himself as a radical Protestant reformer. His retreat from Catholicism emerged around 1522, after he began to study Paul's epistles in detail, conversed with other theologians, and witnessed the early stages of the Reformation.

Hubmaier was influenced by other reformers, such as Desiderius Erasmus, Martin Luther, Huldrych Zwingli, and the circle of early Anabaptists. Yet Hubmaier remained firmly individualistic, clearly differing from his peers on some issues. Having taken a position as a priest in the small town of Waldshut, near Zürich, Hubmaier forged a friendship with Zwingli and others, who had already begun to implement religious reform. Within this circle of friends, he privately debated the primacy of infant baptism, and at this point both Zwingli and Hubmaier began to express doubts about its efficacy. They criticized publicly the veneration of Catholic images and the sacrament of the Eucharist, especially at the Zürich disputation held in October of 1523.

Written in 1524 for a dispute among Waldshut clergymen, Hubmaier's "Eighteen Theses" (1976) reveals the evolution of his theology. His work sits squarely with that of other Protestant reformers of the era, particularly Zwingli. Hubmaier argued that faith alone brought salvation, that the Eucharist was a ceremony of remembrance, that church ceremony should be abandoned, and that promises of chastity likely were not kept. For his role in a 1524 peasant uprising and the Austrian attempt to re-Catholicize the community, Hubmaier left Waldshut.

At Schaffhausen in the Swiss confederacy, Hubmaier wrote his theses against Johann Eck, his former teacher, and wrote his well-known plea for tolerance, "Concerning Heretics and Those Who Burn Them" (1976). In this work he referred to inquisitors as heretics and condemned the practice of killing Turks and so-called heretics by sword and fire rather than patience and prayer. Even to a blind person, he argued, the burning of heretics was an invention of the devil. Still on the run, he chose Zürich as a possible safe haven. By this time, however, Zwingli had expressed his distaste for Hubmaier's disavowal of infant baptism, as it had "destroyed the peace of all Christians." Arrested soon after his arrival in Zürich, Hubmaier not only was forced to debate Zwingli but also was tortured on the rack and deprived of food, except bread, and water. He renounced his beliefs to save his life, but recanted after having left Zürich: "I may err—I am man—but heretic I not be." His wife, Elisabeth Hügline, played an important role in his struggle against those who sought to persecute him. Hubmaier was known for concluding his writings with the phrase "truth is immortal."

Hubmaier's most influential portion of his life was spent at Nikolsburg, a town in Moravia (now in the Czech Republic) that was well known for its religious diversity and toleration by the Moravian noblemen, the lords of Liechtenstein. It was here in 1526 that Hubmaier wrote more than seventeen major pamphlets and participated in large-scale adult baptisms.

Among his more important treatises, written in 1525, was "On the Christian Baptism of Believers" (1976), which described the believer's baptism as "a public confession and testimony of an inner faith." Hubmaier held that baptism should never come before faith, and, therefore, he argued against the baptism of infants, a practice he believed to be a harmful deception and one that was without biblical support. Although he considered baptism important, as it reflected one's commitment to Christ and as it was a promise to God to live according to his word, he believed that it did not save the individual or improve one's standing before God. In fact, Hubmaier argued that before and after baptism humans were poor and miserable sinners. Not being baptized did not damn a Christian, according to Hubmaier; much worse was not believing. His 1527 treatise "On Free Will" (1976) established his clear differences from Zwingli and Luther as he argued for the human role in salvation and the freedom of human choice in dictating one's salvation. According to Hubmaier, the responsibility for salvation rested in humans, not in God, as only humans decide whether to sin or not.

In comparison with some religious reformers in Moravia, his theology might be considered moderate; unlike Hans Hut, a radical reformer, he did not deny civic authority or disavow arms and taxes. He held a positive view on the role of government in society, and his 1527 tract "On the Sword" (1976) argued against "certain brothers" who held that "Christians should not sit in judgment, nor bear the sword." Unlike some Anabaptists, he rejected the doctrine of nonresistance and the notion of community of goods, although he advocated sharing one's wealth with the less fortunate.

Hubmaier died a martyr in the sixteenth century reform movement. Disliked by the secular authorities for his thwarting of political authority as well as his religious protests against Catholicism, and spurned by numerous Protestants who found his views on infant baptism disarming, Hubmaier was considered a potent enemy of religion. Ferdinand I of Austria began the formal process of condemnation, and Hubmaier was brought to Vienna in early July on charges of "doctrine mischief, ill-will, disturbance and rebellion." Hubmaier was held at a local castle and interrogated by old colleagues, including theologian Johannes Faber, the vicar-general to the archbishop of Constance and called the hammer of heretics. Hubmaier's words survive in the lengthy interview notes recorded over the course of several days. In these notes, Hubmaier thanks the king and argues that this was a great chance for him to be proved wrong.

In January of 1528, Hubmaier sent a formal statement of his beliefs to Ferdinand, hoping to show that he was "not stiff-necked." Scholars debate whether this statement reflected his actual beliefs or whether it was an attempt to appear conciliatory in the face of possible death.

Scholars have argued that Hubmaier recanted when persecuted by Zwingli earlier. Although Hubmaier did not appear heretical on issues of purgatory, free will, justification of faith, and the saints, and he made every effort to align himself with Catholicism, even offering to put off debate of his two controversial articles until a Church council could be called, he differentiated himself from orthodoxy with respect to infant baptism and the nature of the Eucharist. On March 10, 1528, Hubmaier was burned at the stake in Vienna, Austria. His wife was drowned three days later in the Danube River.

SIGNIFICANCE

Hubmaier was a prolific author and one of the few evangelical reformers who received a doctorate in theology. His theological message spread down the Danube into Moravia, where the Moravian Brethren, later known as the Hutterites, emerged. Although Anabaptism was still in its infancy and scholars debate whether Hubmaier was an Anabaptist, his theology clearly influenced Anabaptist doctrines, especially with respect to believers' baptism and the voluntary church in which humans dictate their role in salvation.

Although Hubmaier himself did not practice perfect toleration, his pleas for toleration and his untimely death provide ample opportunity to reflect on the ways in which government and society dictated religious orthodoxy in the sixteenth century.

—*Shelley Wolbrink*

FURTHER READING

Bergsten, Torgsten. *Balthasar Hubmaier: Anabaptist Theologian and Martyr.* Translated by Irwin J. Barnes and William R. Estep. Edited by William R. Estep. Valley Forge, Pa.: Judson Press, 1978. An excellent, detailed biography of Hubmaier, with critiques of scholarship and original research.

Estep, William R., ed. *Anabaptist Beginnings (1523-1533): A Source Book.* Bibliotheca Humanistica & Reformatorica 16. Nieuwkoop, the Netherlands: B. de Graaf, 1976. Contains translations of Hubmaier's major works. Includes a bibliography.

Mabry, Eddie Louis. *Balthasar Hubmaier's Doctrine of the Church.* Lanham, Md.: University Press of America, 1994. Explores Hubmaier's understanding of Church doctrines, including salvation, baptism, and the Lord's Supper.

_____. *Balthasar Hubmaier's Understanding of Faith.* Lanham, Md.: University Press of America, 1998. Addresses Hubmaier's understanding of faith and how it is reflected in medieval theological traditions and Anabaptist traditions.

Pipkin, H. Wayne, and John H. Yoder, eds. *Balthasar Hubmaier: Theologian of Anabaptism.* Scottdale, Pa.: Herald Press, 1989. Thorough collection of Hubmaier's writings, with introductory essays that prove especially useful.

Vedder, Henry C. *Balthasar Hubmaier: The Leader of the Anabaptists.* 1905. Reprint. New York: AMS Press, 1971. An older biography of Hubmaier that presents still-useful and interesting analysis and photographs from the surrounding area.

SEE ALSO: Anne Askew; Martin Bucer; John Calvin; Lucas Cranach, the Elder; Desiderius Erasmus; Martin Luther; Philipp Melanchthon; Menno Simons; Philip the Magnanimous; Huldrych Zwingli.

RELATED ARTICLE in *Great Events from History: The Renaissance & Early Modern Era, 1454-1600:* June, 1524-July, 1526: German Peasants' War.

HUMĀYŪN
Mughal emperor of India (r. 1530-1540, 1555-1556)

Humāyūn, faced with numerous trials and tribulations and with unrest in his realm, regained and solidified the Mughal Empire's control of North India.

BORN: 1508; Kabul, Mughal Empire (now in Afghanistan)
DIED: January, 1556; Delhi, Mughal Empire (now in India)
ALSO KNOWN AS: Nāṣin-ud-Dīn Muḥammad
AREAS OF ACHIEVEMENT: Government and politics, warfare and conquest, military

EARLY LIFE

Humāyūn (hoo-MAH-yoon) was the eldest son of Bābur, the first Mughal emperor of India. By all accounts, Humāyūn was also his father's favorite son. Although of Mughal descent, Humāyūn was born in Afghanistan and was influenced more by Afghan-Turk culture than by the Mughal nomadic culture of Asia.

At a young age, Humāyūn played significant roles in his father's victories over the Lodī sultans at the Battle of Panipat in 1526 and in his father's defeat of the Hindu Rajputs at Khauna in 1527, battles that established the Mughal Empire in North India. After these victories, Bābur sent Humāyūn back to Afghanistan with the goal of planning the conquest of Samarqand in Central Asia. After learning that Bābur had become seriously ill, Humāyūn returned to India in 1529. Bābur died in 1530 and Humāyūn became the second Mughal emperor at the age of twenty-two.

LIFE'S WORK

Although Humāyūn's reign as emperor of northern India began in 1530, he ruled the region successfully for just ten out of twenty-six years, through the year of his death. He showed considerable military talent like his father, but, unlike Bābur, Humāyūn was less disciplined, less driven, and more dedicated to a life of pleasure, including his possible use of opium. His several setbacks as ruler, however, did not come entirely from his own supposed weaknesses.

One of Humāyūn's earliest and most fateful decisions was to give power and responsibility to Bābur's other sons and to Humāyūn's three brothers. One brother was designated the ruler of Kabul in Afghanistan, but he also seized the Punjab area of North India, a crucial region of Bābur's legacy. When Humāyūn passively ac-

cepted the loss of the Punjab, the other two brothers believed that they, too, could defy the new emperor at will.

Humāyūn faced challenges from outside his family as well. Bābur had defeated the Lodī sultans of Delhi at Panipat, but there were other Afghan nobles eager to establish their own kingdoms in the region, notably Shēr Khan Sur from near Varanasi. Preparing to attack Shēr Khan Sur's fortress stronghold of Chunar, Humāyūn turned to the west instead to meet a challenge from the sultan of Gujarāt.

In the two years following 1534, Humāyūn defeated his opponents in the west successfully and brilliantly, leaving one of his brothers in charge. Instead of solidifying his rule, however, Humāyūn returned to Āgra and to a life of indulgence and pleasure. His victories became essentially meaningless when, predictably, his brother launched an aborted attempt to seize the Mughal Empire's throne.

More of a threat to Humāyūn was Shēr Khan Sur. In 1537, the emperor put his opium pipe aside and launched another campaign against Shēr Khan Sur, but in the interim Shēr Khan Sur had expanded his territory farther east into Bengal, and unlike Humāyūn, Shēr Khan Sur had consolidated his reign brilliantly. The crucial contest occurred in 1539, east of Varanasi at Chausa, where Humāyūn suffered a disastrous defeat and barely escaped with his life. The two opponents faced each again the following year near Kannauj, south of Delhi near Āgra. Even with an advantage in numbers and in the use of gunpowder, Humāyūn and his forces were overwhelmed by Shēr Khan Sur's cavalry. Once again, Humāyūn escaped death, but his brothers refused to come to his aid and he was forced to flee to the protection of Shāh Ṭahmāsp I of Iran's Ṣafavid Dynasty.

With Humāyūn in exile, Shēr Khan Sur became the dominant figure in North India, taking the title (and name) Shēr Shāh. Shēr Shāh was a Muslim like Bābur and Humāyūn, but he was less tolerant of India's Hindus and he attempted to eradicate Hinduism in regions under his control. He also instituted numerous governmental reforms in his dominions, and later Mughal emperors emulated his policy of greater centralization. After reigning for just five years (1540-1545), Shēr Shāh died in battle during a siege of the fortress of Kalinjar.

When Humāyūn fled into exile in Persia, he also managed to take with him a large diamond that had been

Humāyūn. (Hulton|Archive by Getty Images)

given to him by the family of the raja of Gwalior in the aftermath of Bābur's victory over the Delhi sultan at the Battle of Panipat. The weight of the diamond was 191 carats, and it became known as the Koh-i-noor diamond (mountain of light). Humāyūn took the diamond with him when he sought refuge at the court of Iran's Shāh Ṭahmāsp in 1542.

In northwest Iran in 1544, Shāh Ṭahmāsp and Humāyūn met and exchanged gifts. Humāyūn gave the Koh-i-noor diamond to the shah in exchange for the Ṣafavid Dynasty's support of Humāyūn when he was in exile there and for the military support of the Ṣafavids, which would allow the Mughals to regain their Indian throne.

In 1545, with twelve thousand Persian troops, Humāyūn left Ṣafavid Persia for Afghanistan, the original lands of the Mughals (Bābur was originally king of Kabul before his conquest of India). Shēr Shāh died about the time Humāyūn entered Afghanistan. His son and successor was Islam Shāh Sur, who was less able and less competent than his father. After Islam Shāh Sur's death in 1553, factional disputes erupted among members of the Sur family.

Humāyūn crossed into northwest India from his Af-

ghanistan sanctuary in 1555, with only three thousand warriors, according to one report. Others soon joined his army in the wake of Humāyūn's early victories. At Sirhind in the Punjab, Humāyūn's forces defeated the rebel Afghan governor Sikander Sur. Opposition faded, Humāyūn regained the throne in July, and he was once again in control of Delhi. During the next several months, Humāyūn consolidated his rule, extended his control in North India, and began to adopt some of the governmental policies developed by his old opponent, Shēr Shāh.

Humāyūn's reign and life ended in January, 1556, after he stumbled and fell down the steps of the observatory in his Delhi palace. In an often-quoted memorable comment, the emperor "stumbled out of life as he had stumbled through it."

SIGNIFICANCE

Among the Mughal emperors, Humāyūn is often overlooked, reigning as he did between Bābur, the founder of the dynasty, and Humāyūn's son, Akbar, perhaps the greatest Indian ruler. Humāyūn's accomplishments and significance, however, have been underestimated.

Although Humāyūn spent a good part of his reign in exile, he did regain India for the Mughals. After his father's death, Mughal rule had to establish itself fully, and any ruler would have been challenged by this. On Humāyūn's death, thirteen-year-old Akbar, though faced with opposition, was able to succeed to the Mughal throne.

Humāyūn's tomb in Delhi is one of the great architectural masterpieces in India and was the inspiration for the Tāj Mahal, built by Shāh Jahān, Humāyūn's great grandson.

—*Eugene Larson*

FURTHER READING

Burn, Sir Richard. *The Cambridge History of India.* Cambridge, England: Cambridge University Press, 1922-1937. One of the major multivolume histories of India. Vol. 4 explores the Mughal period and Humāyūn's reign.

Eraly, Abraham. *The Last Spring: The Lives and Times of the Great Mughals.* New Delhi, India: Viking Press, 1997. A long narrative of the lives and times of India's Mughal emperors, including Humāyūn.

Erskine, William. *A History of India Under the First Two Sovereigns of the House of Taimur, Bāber, and Humāyūn.* New York: Barnes & Noble Books, 1972. This classic work, first published in 1854, examines the reigns of Humāyūn and Bābur.

Streusand, Douglas E. *The Formation of the Mughal Empire*. New York: Oxford University Press, 1989. An important study of the early decades of the Mughal Empire, including the years of Humāyūn's rule.

Wolpert, Stanley. *A New History of India*. New York: Oxford University Press, 2000. This readily accessible and well-written text examines Mughal India and Humāyūn's accomplishments.

SEE ALSO: Akbar; Bābur; Ibrāhīm Lodī; Krishnadeva-raya.

RELATED ARTICLES in *Great Events from History: The Renaissance & Early Modern Era, 1454-1600:* April 21, 1526: First Battle of Panipat; December 30, 1530: Humāyūn Inherits the Throne in India; 1540-1545: Shēr Shāh Sūr Becomes Emperor of Delhi.

IBRĀHĪM LODĪ
Sultan of Delhi (r. 1517-1526)

Ibrāhīm Lodī, a greedy and tyrannical ruler, withdrew the power of his nobles and ministers, who then rebelled, resulting in the Mongol seizure of the Delhi sultanate.

BORN: Late fifteenth century; Delhi, Lodī Empire (now in India)
DIED: April 21, 1526; Panipat, Lodī Empire (now in India)
ALSO KNOWN AS: Ibrāhīm Hussain Lodī
AREAS OF ACHIEVEMENT: Government and politics, warfare and conquest

EARLY LIFE
Ibrāhīm Lodī (ihb-rah-HEEM law-DEE) was the eldest son of Delhi sultan Sikandar Lodī. Under Sikandar's rule, the sultanate of Delhi had expanded from the Punjab to Bihar, and the city of Āgra was founded and then named the sultanate's capital. Sikandar, a superb administrator who controlled ancient chiefdoms, delegated power to nobles to manage his vast and rapidly expanding kingdom more effectively. Ibrāhīm, however, would alter his father's success radically, to the detriment of the Delhi sultanate.

Ibrāhīm and his brothers were well-educated, but from an early age Ibrāhīm had demonstrated a demanding and uncompromising attitude, which would endure throughout his reign and would contribute to his and the sultanate's downfall.

LIFE'S WORK
Ibrāhīm Lodī succeeded his father as sultan in 1517 because of his seniority among his brothers, but it was not a peaceful succession. Ibrāhīm attempted to return the sultanate to absolute authority, thus removing the power that Sikandar had vested in the nobles. Also, Sikandar had moved the capital to Āgra, but Ibrāhīm returned it to Delhi. Greedy for power and money, Ibrāhīm intensified his quest for absolute power, signifying to the nobles a regression from the progressive rule of Sikandar. A number of nobles who had increased their power under Sikandar viewed Ibrāhīm as incompetent and headstrong, so they advocated a partition of the realm to two of Sikandar's sons. Ibrāhīm would rule from Delhi and his younger brother, Jalāl Khan, would rule Jaunpur. Ibrāhīm and his supporters did not condone this division, so they assassinated Jalāl Khan.

Darya Khan of Bihar also revolted against Ibrāhīm, striking his own coin to demonstrate his secession from the sultan.

In addition to political and economic conquest, Ibrāhīm made demands on the religious men of his kingdom. When Nānak, the founder of Sikhism, passed through Delhi, tradition states that he healed and revived a dead elephant belonging to Ibrāhīm. When the elephant died again, Ibrāhīm demanded that Nānak repeat the miracle, but the guru refused, telling Ibrāhīm that because he was a holy man, his healing powers were not subject to the whims of the emperor but to God. Also, Ibrāhīm discontinued the patronage of intellectual life characteristic of Sikandar's rule, fomenting great discontent among the learned populace.

Finally, Ibrāhīm's tyrannical ineptitude led his uncle, ʿĀlam Khan, and Daulat Khan, governor of Lahore, to plot against Ibrāhīm. They invited foreign invasion from Bābur, who was then the ruler of Kabul. Daulat Khan had hoped that Bābur would assist their coalition in deposing Ibrāhīm and then return to Kabul, allowing Daulat to become sultan in Delhi; this was not to be the case.

Bābur reached Panipat in early April of 1526, and Ibrāhīm's army had become aware of the engagement and had begun to advance toward Panipat as well. At a council of war, the coalition decided to give battle there, using the remaining days to plan carefully. As a barricade for his front lines, Bābur collected about seven hundred carts and bound them together with rawhide, repeating the same tactic that Afghan nomads had utilized against Roman expansion.

Bābur utilized a new technological innovation, field artillery, in this battle. Combining the old with the new, he situated the guns among the carts. After every two hundred yards, a gap for about two hundred horsemen remained. Panipat village would hide the location of Bābur's right flank, and his left flank was reinforced by a ditch and tree branches.

Ibrāhīm Lodī arrived on April 12 with 100,000 men and one thousand elephants. The armies faced each other for eight days. While Bābur's men were content and adept, Ibrāhīm's men were paid poorly and were unhappy. On the night of April 19, Bābur sent a raid of five thousand men to Ibrāhīm's camp, but this was an atypical movement for Bābur in that it was poorly accomplished. Nevertheless, the next morning, Ibrāhīm advanced, arrayed with grandeur and ceremony appropriate for battle.

Bābur eschewed military pageantry, but his complex strategy was in place. His son, Humāyūn, was on his right; on his left was his trusted commander. When Ibrāhīm's army advanced on Bābur's front, the flanks were to turn and attack Ibrāhīm from the rear.

At dawn on April 20, Ibrāhīm's army approached Bābur's right, so Bābur reinforced with his right reserve. Ibrāhīm continued the advance, but when his forces saw Bābur's reinforced front lines, they halted. Ibrāhīm was unable to make his men resume the advance. Bābur's center engaged, his artillery fired, and his flanks, as planned, turned and attacked Ibrāhīm's rear. Ibrāhīm attempted to break away from the assault but was trapped between the line of carts and artillery and the flanks. Ibrāhīm soon was defeated; sixteen thousand men were killed, among them Ibrāhīm.

SIGNIFICANCE

After the victory at Panipat, Bābur recognized the valor of his men and distributed money and gifts to his entire army. Bābur's act is symbolic of his success and of Ibrāhīm's failure. In his memoirs, Bābur recognized that Ibrāhīm's fatal flaw was his greed and wondered how Ibrāhīm could content his subjects when his own avarice had overpowered him. Bābur noted that Ibrāhīm's insatiable desire to grow his coffers superseded any concern for the welfare of his subjects.

Bābur's immense power prevented Daulat Khan from succeeding Ibrāhīm at Delhi; Bābur inaugurated his court there and, in doing so, began the process of consolidating India under Mongol authority, paving the way for a dynasty that would remain strong until 1707 and remain in power after. Ibrāhīm's incompetence and greed enabled both his own downfall and the demise of the Lodī Dynasty.

—Monica Piotter

FURTHER READING

Bābur. *The Baburnama: Memoirs of Babur, Prince and Emperor.* Translated by Wheeler Thackston. New York: Random House, 1996. This translation includes a preface by Salman Rushdie, historical background, a chronology, a glossary, and many more aids for the student.

Majumdar, R. C., ed. *The Delhi Sultanate.* Vol. 6 in *The History and Culture of the Indian People.* Bombay, India: B. V. Bhavan, 1960. Part of a superb eleven-volume set that covers India from the Vedic age to 1947. Covers the entire Delhi sultanate to the fall of Ibrāhīm and the Mongol possession.

Nigam, S. B. P. *Nobility Under the Sultans of Delhi, A.D. 1206-1398.* Delhi, India: Munshiram Manoharlal, 1967. A study of the evolution of the nobles throughout the Delhi sultanate that contextualizes their discontent under Ibrāhīm.

Qureshi, Ishtiaq Husain. *Administration of the Sultanate of Delhi.* 1942. Reprint. New Delhi, India: Oriental Books Reprint, 1996. Qureshi's study remains the foremost analysis of the administrative and political structures of the Delhi sultanate. Attempts at revising these structures led to Ibrāhīm's demise.

SEE ALSO: Akbar; Bābur; Humāyūn; Krishnadevaraya; Nānak.

RELATED ARTICLES in *Great Events from History: The Renaissance & Early Modern Era, 1454-1600:* 1451-1526: Lodī Kings Dominate Northern India; April 21, 1526: First Battle of Panipat.

İBRAHIM PAŞA
Grand vizier of the Ottoman Empire (1523-1536)

As grand vizier and trusted associate of Sultan Süleyman the Magnificent, İbrahim played leading political, military, and diplomatic roles in domestic and international events. İbrahim's death by strangulation and beating at the sultan's order marked a turning point for the Ottoman Empire.

BORN: 1493 or 1494; Parga, Republic of Venice (now in Greece)
DIED: March 15, 1536; Constantinople, Ottoman Empire (now in Turkey)
AREAS OF ACHIEVEMENT: Government and politics, warfare and conquest

EARLY LIFE

İbrahim Paşa (ihb-rah-HIM pah-SHAH) was born near the Greek town of Parga on the coast of the Ionian Sea. His parents were Christian and of common stock: His father labored as a sailor. As a young boy, İbrahim was kidnapped by corsairs, who commonly plied the coastal waters of the region. Following his capture, İbrahim apparently was sold to a wealthy Ottoman widow who, impressed by the young man's intellect, provided him with an education. He learned Italian, Persian, and Turkish, in addition to his native Greek, and became an excellent musician. At some point during his first years of slavery, he also embraced Islam.

Contemporary accounts disagree significantly on the genesis of İbrahim's relationship with Süleyman, son of Sultan Selim I and heir to the throne. Some accounts suggest Süleyman met İbrahim during his service as governor of Manisa, in eastern Anatolia, prior to acceding to the throne, and that because of İbrahim's intellect and charisma, and their similarity in age, they established an enduring relationship. Others suggest that İbrahim at some point was sent to Istanbul, where he was attached as a slave to the Imperial Serail and perhaps even attended the famed Palace School. According to this version, İbrahim accompanied Süleyman to Manisa. What is certain is that the close relationship between the heir to the throne and his slave flourished during the period in the provinces before Süleyman achieved the throne. The two became inseparable, and this set the stage for İbrahim's unprecedented ascent to the heights of power in the Ottoman Empire.

LIFE'S WORK

İbrahim Paşa accompanied his now close friend Süleyman to Istanbul on the death of Selim I in 1520. In very short order, the sultan made İbrahim his chief falconer, and then the master of his bedchamber, both desirable positions because they ensured close access to the ruler. Indeed, as master of the bedchamber, İbrahim slept next to the sultan in the private quarters of the palace to ensure his safety. Many contemporaries considered it scandalous that the ruler of the greatest Muslim empire should have such intimate ties with a slave and former Christian.

Less than three years later, in 1523, when İbrahim was barely thirty years old, Süleyman raised him to the highest position in the Ottoman hierarchy, the office of grand vizier, over a number of more experienced and senior officials. İbrahim would hold this position until his death in 1536. During this time, by all accounts, İbrahim ruled the day-to-day affairs of the empire effectively. Süleyman seems to have been content to give İbrahim nearly unlimited power and autonomy in running the Ottoman state, and all matters of any significance passed directly through his hands.

During his thirteen years as grand vizier, İbrahim enjoyed the complete confidence of Süleyman. Indeed, the sultan, perhaps to buttress the power and reputation of his young companion, granted him extraordinary titles and privileges. He was permitted to display six horsetails on his standard, one less than the sultan, and more than any other grand vizier had been granted previously. In 1524, İbrahim's relationship with the sultan was sealed through his marriage to Süleyman's sister, Hadice Hanim, with the sultan himself attending the opulent festivities.

If İbrahim's initial ascent was due to his personal ties to Süleyman, in his years as grand vizier, he proved himself a capable diplomat and an effective political and military leader. In 1524, Süleyman sent İbrahim to Egypt to restore order following an uprising led by a rebellious Ottoman official sent to rule the earlier conquered province. İbrahim reorganized legal and fiscal institutions, punished mutinous officials and subjects with severity, established schools, restored mosques, and, by all accounts, restored peace and order to the region.

Two years later, he joined Süleyman in leading the first Ottoman campaign in Hungary, which saw the Hungarians routed at the Battle of Mohács, and their young king, Louis II, killed on the battlefield. Because of his reliability and success in this first campaign, İbrahim was also charged with leading two subsequent military campaigns in Hungary: one in 1529, when he guided the unsuccessful Siege of Vienna, and another in 1532. A year later, İbrahim was supreme commander of an expedition against the shah of Persia, which culminated in the conquest of Baghdad in December, 1534. Contemporaries and subsequent writers have viewed Süleyman's reign as a golden era in Ottoman history, and while much credit goes to the sultan, İbrahim clearly played a central role.

If İbrahim's rise was unexpected and unprecedented, so too was his demise. Indeed, from the outset of his career, İbrahim had been unpopular among the Ottoman elite because of his unorthodox path to power, his favored position with the sultan, his wealth, and his reputation for arrogance. At the pinnacle of his power, with apparently no indication that he had fallen out of favor, İbrahim was strangled at the sultan's orders, during the season of Ramadan in March, 1536, and in the vizier's bedroom in the harem of Topkapi Palace. His body was buried in an unmarked grave that made no mention of the person who had gone from poor slave to nearly the sultan's equal.

The dramatic demise of İbrahim produced many theories attempting to explain his fall from grace. Some pointed to what was perceived as his questionable religious commitment, others to mismanagement of the Persian campaign, still other voices suggested he had betrayed his master to the Habsburgs. Certainly, important factors were palace intrigues. Süleyman's favorite consort, Roxelana, in her machinations to secure the throne for one of her sons, saw İbrahim as a potential threat. She gradually usurped his position with the sultan and played a central role in undermining the vizier's position. Following the death of İbrahim's primary defender in the harem, Süleyman's mother Hafsa, İbrahim was fatally exposed.

In the end, these intrigues alone were certainly not sufficient to force the sultan's hand. Rather, the best explanation for İbrahim's demise is that Süleyman perceived that his servant had become overly powerful and ambitious. İbrahim was reported to have stated publicly, "I can make a sultan of a stableboy. . . . And when [my master] orders me to do something I don't like, nothing is carried out. It is my will which is accomplished, not his." This imperiousness fed rumors that he aspired to Süleyman's throne, and it made him a liability to the ruler and to the empire.

That İbrahim was executed rather than simply dismissed or exiled testifies to the extent of his power and influence, and the possibility that even out of office he might remain a destabilizing threat to Süleyman's rule. The stains of İbrahim's blood, spilled as he tried to ward off his assassins' blows, were left on the walls for years as a reminder to all of the destiny of vainglorious and overly ambitious servants.

SIGNIFICANCE

In assessing İbrahim's brief life, it is difficult not to resort to superlatives. Born in poverty in an insignificant corner of the Mediterranean, his opportunities were quite limited. A stroke of misfortune opened opportunities for education and advancement, and in a relatively short time, İbrahim became the second most powerful man in the Ottoman Empire.

The tragic tale of İbrahim's life and death ensured his story's endurance. It provided great fodder for European novelists and playwrights, and was told in three seventeenth century dramas and a four-volume work by Madelaine de Scudéry called *İbrahim ou l'illustre bassa* (1641; *İbrahim: Or, The Illustrious Bassa*, 1652). Among Ottoman writers, İbrahim's life provided a cautionary tale, and indeed it came to be seen by some observers as a turning point in Ottoman history. One adviser to Sultan Murad IV, writing in 1630, maintained that Ottoman decline began when grand viziers ceased to be selected for their competence and experience. This led to the denigration of the office and to the rise of a destructive era of influential palace favorites, particularly women and eunuchs, who weakened the sultanate severely. While it may be too much to attribute the eventual decline of the empire to one man, İbrahim's rise to the summit of Ottoman power, his long, effective rule, and his dramatic end, seems the stuff of fiction.

—*Eric R. Dursteler*

FURTHER READING

Clot, André. *Suleiman the Magnificent: The Man, His Life, His Epoch*. London: Saqi Books, 1992. While devoted predominantly to the life of Süleyman the Magnificent, the work contains significant information on İbrahim, particularly his relationship with the sultan he served.

Gökbilgin, M. Tayyib. "İbrahim Paşa." *The Encyclopedia of Islam*. Vol. 3. Leiden, the Netherlands: E. J. Brill, 1971. A brief but useful overview that situates İbrahim Paşa more solidly in a Turkish documentary context.

Jenkins, Hester Donaldson. *İbrahim Pasha: Grand Vizier of Suleiman the Magnificent*. New York: Columbia University Press, 1911. This is still the only monograph dedicated to İbrahim Paşa's life and career.

While somewhat dated in its historical and historiographical context, it is nonetheless still important.

Shaw, Stanford J. *History of the Ottoman Empire and Modern Turkey: Empire of the Gazis.* Cambridge, England: Cambridge University Press, 1976. A general history of the Ottoman Empire in the premodern era that contains important contextual and biographical details on İbrahim Paşa's life.

SEE ALSO: Barbarossa; Pierre Belon; Mary of Hungary; Matthias I Corvinus; Mehmed II; Mehmed III; Süleyman the Magnificent; Vladislav II.

RELATED ARTICLES in *Great Events from History: The Renaissance & Early Modern Era, 1454-1600:* 1534-1535: Ottomans Claim Sovereignty Over Mesopotamia; 1536: Turkish Capitulations Begin.

SAINT IGNATIUS OF LOYOLA
Spanish religious leader

Ignatius of Loyola, a dynamic religious leader whose life and writings strongly influenced his times, was the founder of the Society of Jesus, better known as the Jesuits. His religious order was particularly notable in the field of education.

BORN: 1491; Loyola, Guipúzcoa Province, Castile (now in Spain)

DIED: July 31, 1556; Rome, Papal States (now in Italy)

ALSO KNOWN AS: Iñigo de Oñaz y Loyola (given name)

AREAS OF ACHIEVEMENT: Religion and theology, education

EARLY LIFE

The youngest son of a family known for its prowess in war, Ignatius (ihg-NAY-shyuhs) was given as an infant into the care of a nearby farm woman. During his childhood and youth, Ignatius was thus divided between his father's house, Casa Torre, and his foster mother's home, giving him a view of life from two sides—that of the rulers and that of the ruled. Of Basque descent, the Loyola family was deeply religious. Ignatius's father, Don Beltram, had close connections with the king for services rendered and received many privileges, both lay and clerical, in return. He had justifiably high aspirations for all his children.

Ignatius spent his early teens mostly at Casa Torre, taking school lessons from the village priest. At the age of sixteen, he was taken as a page into the house of Juan Velázquez de Cuéllar, a family relative who was treasurer of Castile and royal major domo at the court. In his service, Ignatius learned to sing, dance, and play musical instruments—skills he retained for the remainder of his life. For ten years, he lived as a courtier, traveling with his master and the royal court, visiting all

the towns of Castile. Thoroughly trained in formal manners and caught up in court life, Ignatius spent much time reading romances, tales featuring ghosts, dragons, princesses, and heroes engaged in impossible adventures.

On the death of King Ferdinand II in 1516, Juan Velázquez lost most of his estates and his position at court. He died in 1517, and a bereft Ignatius went to Pamplona, the capital of Navarre, to enlist in the viceroy's army, having decided to become a career soldier. From 1517 to 1521, a captain in the service of the duke of Najera, Ignatius fought the French, who were attempting to seize all Navarre by capturing the strategic city of Pamplona. In 1520, Ignatius participated in its defense, and in a fierce battle lasting six hours, he was struck by a cannon ball and suffered a broken right leg. The victorious French treated him well, returning him to Casa Torre for recuperation.

During his convalescence, a bored Ignatius, lacking his usual romances, read a life of Christ and a book on the lives of the saints. He was attracted by the sanctity of Christ and Christ's saints and wanted to imitate their virtues. Meditating on his past and on the future, he felt a need to do penance, which would culminate in a pilgrimage to Jerusalem. On recovery, he set about carrying out this goal.

LIFE'S WORK

In the spring of 1522, Ignatius visited Montserrat, the site of a famous shrine to the Black Virgin. From there, he went to Manresa, where he stayed about a year, undertaking a program of prayer and penance. During this period, Ignatius first conceived the idea of founding a "spiritual militia" for the service of the Church. At Manresa, he began writing his *Ejercicios espirituales* (1548; *The Spiritual Exercises*, 1736), for the use of directors of spiritual retreats. This famous book gives methods of freeing the soul to seek and to find the will of God. The practitioner goes through stages of meditation, examination of conscience, and methods of prayer; the exercises require thirty days to be completed. These exercises remain a vital part of the life of Jesuits.

From Manresa, Ignatius went to Barcelona in 1523, a stopover before continuing on to Rome. While in Barcelona, he occupied himself in prayer and good works, visiting hospitals and prisons. In March of 1523, he left for Rome, where he received Pope Adrian VI's blessing on his pilgrimage to Jerusalem. Leaving Venice, he was delayed for two months before finally sailing for Palestine. Ignatius and his fellow pilgrims arrived at Jerusalem in September, 1523, to be guided by Franciscan friars in their visits to the Holy Places. Although he wanted to stay permanently, converting the Muslims, Ignatius was refused permission by the Franciscan superiors. The pilgrims left Jerusalem and were back in Italy in October, 1523. Ignatius returned to Barcelona, arriving in March, 1524.

Wealthy friends paid for Ignatius's studies at the University of Barcelona, where he studied grammar. In 1526, he switched to Acalá University, studying logic, theology, and physics. Between classes, Ignatius begged alms for the poor and taught *The Spiritual Exercises* to any willing pupils. He gathered four like-minded companions about him and they went throughout the city teaching Christian doctrine. Thus were sown the seeds of the Society of Jesus.

In 1528, leaving his companions to follow at a later date, Ignatius went to France to attend the University of Paris. Dominican professors at both Barcelona and Salamanca judged him not ready to be a valid preacher. Needing a good foundation in systematic learning, Ignatius spent the next years studying Latin grammar, classical texts, theology, and philosophy. He obtained his licentiate in March, 1533, and his master's degree in 1534. In addition to his studies, Ignatius taught *The Spiritual Exercises* to fellow students. Among these was a roommate from Navarre, Francis Xavier, whom Ignatius eventually won to his way of life and who was destined to be the glory of Jesuit missionary work. By 1534, Ignatius had nine companions who agreed to unite in any needed spiritual enterprise.

The band of ten went to Rome in 1537, seeking the pope's approval of their new order. In 1539, Pope Paul III gave verbal approval to the society, and in September, 1540, they were granted canonical approval. That June, Ignatius and seven of his companions were ordained priests. They settled in Rome, living on alms and preach-

Saint Ignatius of Loyola. (Library of Congress)

ing sermons, catechizing children, and attending the sick.

Ignatius intended his Society of Jesus to be at the service of the pope and, thereby, of the universal church. The Renaissance church was in need of reform, being secularized by the prevailing educational and cultural milieu. Ignatius's society took a vow to obey the pope in all things and to go where and when he indicated a need for their services. In 1540, the first Jesuits were sent to the foreign missions. Two of them were chosen to work in India, one being Francis Xavier. From Goa, Xavier traveled to Japan, arriving in 1549. Later, he attempted to work in China but died before that desire could be fulfilled (1553). Jesuits fanned out all over the globe, with a concentration in Europe.

Ignatius and his society focused on education as the chief tool for reform within the Church, establishing many secondary schools and universities. Educated laypeople were needed to spread the Christian spirit. Martin

Luther's teachings were widespread in Europe in the sixteenth century, and Ignatius's society was in the vanguard of the Church's Counter-Reformation.

In 1541, Ignatius was elected the first general of the Society of Jesus—head for life. He began drafting the constitutions for the society, setting a solid foundation and structure on which his followers could build. The constitutions set down the qualities needed for the Jesuit general, among them a holy life, prayerfulness, humility, charity, and circumspection. There were also rules for admitting or expelling members, for the examination or formation of novices, and regulations for prayers. With some adaptation, *The Spiritual Exercises* and constitutions remain basic to Jesuit life.

In 1553, pressed by his friends, Ignatius began narrating his autobiography, completing it in early 1555. He spent the last year of his life overseeing the work of his far-flung order, which, by that time numbered about one thousand members. Ignatius died in 1556, confident that his society was fulfilling his hopes for it, revitalizing the spiritual life of the Church.

SIGNIFICANCE

Although Saint Ignatius of Loyola did not found his society expressly to combat the Protestant Reformation, his Jesuits are credited by his contemporaries and by later historians with having stemmed its tide. They were instrumental in winning back many who had fallen away from the Church and in opening vast new territories to the Church (for example, the Indies, China, Japan, South America, and North America).

A contemporary of such giants as Sir Thomas More, Desiderius Erasmus, Niccolò Machiavelli, Ferdinand Magellan, Michelangelo, Martin Luther, and the Tudors, Ignatius helped train and form men who became formidable theologians, lawyers, scientists, and mathematicians and who would be at home not only in the courts of European and Asian princes but also with Native Americans. The society's ultimate goal always remained the greater glory of God.

Because of strong criticism by opponents—chiefly within the Church—the Jesuit Order was suppressed in 1773 by Clement XIV. It dwindled in number but not in fervor, and on formal restoration in 1814, under Pius VII, it quickly regained its former vitality. Friends and foes alike acknowledge the tremendous effect of the Society of Jesus on the world, then and now. In 1622, the Catholic Church gave its highest seal of approval to Ignatius Loyola, canonizing him a saint.

—S. Carol Berg

FURTHER READING

Donnelly, John Patrick. *Ignatius of Loyola: Founder of the Jesuits*. New York: Longman, 2004. A thorough survey of Ignatius's life, work, and ideas; some chapters deal with biographical events while others focus on Ignatius's thought on a particular issue, such as education or women. Includes illustrations, maps, bibliographic references, glossary, and index.

Green, John D. *A Strange Tongue: Tradition, Language, and the Appropriation of Mystical Experience in Late Fourteenth-Century England and Sixteenth-Century Spain*. Dudley, Mass.: Peeters, 2002. A study of the Christian mystical notion of the "discernment of spirits," that is, the recognition of authentically divine inward promptings or stirrings, in the writings of St. John of the Cross, Ignatius of Loyola, Julian of Norwich, and Walter Hilton. Includes bibliographic references.

Lonsdale, David. *Eyes to See, Ears to Hear: An Introduction to Ignatian Spirituality*. Rev. ed. Maryknoll, N.Y.: Orbis Books, 2000. This classic introduction to Ignatius's spiritual theology and its applicability to contemporary life has been expanded to include a more thorough discussion of gender, and a consideration of the nature and meaning of the increase in modern interest in Ignatius. Includes bibliographic references and index.

Loyola, Ignatius. *The Autobiography of Saint Ignatius Loyola*. Edited by John C. Olin. Translated by Joseph F. O'Callaghan. New York: Harper & Row, 1974. Reprint. New York: Fordham Univerity Press, 1992. Contains an informative introduction. Sets the autobiography in the context of its time and gives a brief biography of Ignatius. The preface is by Father Luis Goncalves da Camara, to whom Ignatius narrated his life story. Contains reproductions of illustrations from a work published in Rome in 1609, footnotes expanding on the text, and appendices. Contains a short annotated bibliography.

Maynard, Theodore. *Saint Ignatius and the Jesuits*. New York: P. J. Kenedy and Sons, 1956. Examines the life of Ignatius in eight chapters, briefly, and gives the remaining seven to an analysis of the Jesuit Order and its experiences in the following centuries. Focuses on missionary activities, the suppression of the order, Jesuit education, and corporate achievement. Defends and admires the Society of Jesus. Contains a bibliography and an index.

Mitchell, David. *The Jesuits*. New York: Franklin Watts, 1981. A balanced, critical but respectful treatment of

Ignatius and his Jesuits. Covers beginnings to the late 1970's. Contains several illustrations. Appendices include a list of the generals and general congregations, common words used with reference to Jesuits, and a list of popes. Contains an extensive bibliography and a detailed index.

Purcell, Mary. *The First Jesuit*. Westminster, Md.: Newman Press, 1957. Based on contemporary evidence: the writings of Saint Ignatius and records of the first companions and fathers of the first generation of the Society of Jesus. Contains three appendices, a source list, notes, and an index.

Ravier, André, S. J. *Ignatius Loyola and the Founding of the Society of Jesus*. Translated by Joan Maura and Carson Daly. San Francisco, Calif.: Ignatian Press, 1987. An interpretation of Ignatius and his society. Begins with a chronology of Ignatius and his followers' activities; ends with an analysis of the message and mission of Ignatius. Based on Ignatius's correspondence and his autobiography, letters of some of his close collaborators, and several volumes of the Monumenta Historica Societatis Jesus. Contains a bibliography (primarily French sources) and an index.

Richter, Friedrich. *Martin Luther and Ignatius Loyola, Spokesmen for Two Worlds of Belief*. Translated by Leonard F. Zwinger. Westminster, Md.: Newman Press, 1960. A comparison/contrast of the careers of Luther and Ignatius. Analysis of Protestant and Catholic thought and teachings. No bibliography, but contains a brief index.

Tylenda, Joseph N., ed. and trans. *A Pilgrim's Journey: The Autobiography of St. Ignatius of Loyola*. Wilmington, Del.: Michael Glazier, 1985. A brief biography of Ignatius in the introduction. Contains a commentary on each page to flesh out allusions in the text. Contains appendices, select bibliography, and notes for each chapter.

SEE ALSO: Adrian VI; Desiderius Erasmus; Ferdinand II and Isabella I; Martin Luther; Niccolò Machiavelli; Ferdinand Magellan; Michelangelo; Sir Thomas More; Paul III; Sixtus V; The Tudor Family; Saint Francis Xavier.

RELATED ARTICLES in *Great Events from History: The Renaissance & Early Modern Era, 1454-1600:* August 15, 1534: Founding of the Jesuit Order; 1550's-c. 1600: Educational Reforms in Europe.

ISABELLA D'ESTE
Italian noblewoman

Isabella d'Este's collecting career is the best-documented of the Renaissance, and her extensive archive has provided much of what is known about the discovery, acquisition, export, and display of antiquities and other collectibles in private collections for this period.

BORN: May 18, 1474; Ferrara (now in Italy)
DIED: February 13, 1539; Mantua, Lombardy (now in Italy)
ALSO KNOWN AS: Marquise of Mantua
AREAS OF ACHIEVEMENT: Patronage of the arts, government and politics

EARLY LIFE

Isabella d'Este (ee-zah-BEHL-lah dih-ehs-TAY) was the daughter of Duke Ercole I d'Este and Eleanora of Aragon, a daughter of King Ferrante I of Naples. Isabella received a classical education at the court of Ferrara under the tutelage of Battista Guarini, son of the Greek scholar Guarino of Verona.

In 1490, she married the marquis Giovanni Francesco Gonzaga of Mantua. In the same year, her younger sister, Beatrice d'Este, married Ludovico Sforza, the duke of Milan. (A third, illegitimate daughter, Lucrezia d'Este, daughter of Ercole before his marriage to Eleanora, also enhanced the Este family's dynastic ties by marrying Annibale II Bentivoglio, lord of Bologna, in 1487.) Their brother, Alfonso II d'Este, inherited the title of duke of Ferrara on his father's death in 1505.

LIFE'S WORK

When she arrived in Mantua in 1490, Isabella immediately set to work renovating rooms in a tower of the medieval castle San Giorgio, the original building at the heart of the expanded Gonzaga Ducal Palace in Mantua. Her suite on the *piano nobile* (second story) of the castle included one of the corner circular towers and its attached, smaller tower called the Torretta di San Nicolò.

Two of the rooms in this smaller tower had formerly been used as a study and a treasury by Ludovico II Gonzaga, the previous marquis of Mantua. Starting in about 1493, Isabella turned the former study of the marquis into her own *studiolo* with the addition of intarsia wainscoting and painted decoration. The small room below this, accessible only through the *studiolo* and formerly used as a treasury, was modified to accommodate her growing collection of cameos, engraved gems, coins and medallions, miniature bronze sculptures, and various antique fragments. Probably because of its somewhat cavelike character, Isabella called this room, one of the first modern museum rooms, the Grotta (cave).

In about 1494, Isabella began to commission a series of painted allegorical scenes, on canvas, for the decoration of her *studiolo* space. Once again, her archive provides numerous letters regarding the commissioning, completion, and display of these paintings. The first of the allegories to be completed was *Parnassus* by Andrea Mantegna (1495-1497), followed by his *Pallas Expelling the Vices from the Garden of Virtue* (1499-1502). She then obtained two allegories from the Ferrarese artist Lorenzo Costa, one being *The Reign of Comus* (1506), which was based on a composition that was begun by Mantegna but left unfinished at his death in 1506. A fifth painting was completed by Pietro Perugino in 1505. As a group, the paintings allude to the war between virtue and vice, or the subjugation of the passions to reason. The program conveys the idea that the arts and intellectual pursuits, under the aegis of learned reason, flourished in Isabella's private study. Although united thematically, each painting was drawn by court Humanists from a variety of allegorical and mythological sources. They then devised written programs that were presented to the individual painters. Given this chain of transmission, the allegorical allusions are complex and occasionally baffling. Efforts to obtain a sixth allegory from such diverse artists as Giovanni Bellini, Francesco Francia, and Raphael were inconclusive. Her archive also makes references to negotiations with Leonardo da Vinci.

In the meantime, she also furnished her antiquities room, the Grotta, with a statue of cupid, attributed to the fourth century B.C.E. Athenian sculptor Praxiteles, and its modern counterpart fashioned by Michelangelo. In the true spirit of the Renaissance, the chief paradigm of the Grotta collection was this admixture of genuine antiquities with their modern counterparts. Several pieces that Isabella owned, including a celebrated antique cameo depicting a double profile portrait of Augustus and Livia (perhaps now in Vienna's Kunsthistorisches Museum) survive in modern collections.

Isabella spent two brief periods as de facto regent of Mantua: first when her husband was captured and held by the Venetians in 1509-1510 and again briefly after his death in 1519, when her eldest son and heir to the Mantuan Dynasty, Federigo II Gonzaga, was absent on military duty with the imperial forces.

Isabella had six children. Her eldest child, Eleanora, married Francesco Maria della Rovere and became duchess of Urbino. Other daughters—Ippolita and Livia—became nuns. There were three sons: Federigo, Ercole Gonzaga, who became a cardinal, and Ferrante Gonzaga, who became prince of Guastalla.

When Isabella became a widow in 1519, she moved out of the main palace at the center of the ducal complex to a new apartment on the ground floor of the Corte Vecchia wing. There she re-created her *studiolo* and Grotta, moving not only the collections but probably most of the fittings and fixtures to rooms that had been modified to the same dimensions as the originals. In the early 1530's, two more allegories—by Antonio Allegri, better known as Correggio—were added to the paintings in the *studiolo*.

In her later years, Isabella also continued to collect antiquities. She visited Rome for the first time in 1514 and again in 1527. Her 1527 trip coincided with the sack of the city by Holy Roman Emperor Charles V's troops, and she spent several days trapped in the palace of her son, Cardinal Ercole Gonzaga. Although she traveled to Mantua safely, many prized antiquities that she collected during this trip were lost in a disaster at sea.

Federigo was made the first duke of Mantua in 1530, and the next year he married Margherita Palaeologus (a princess of the last surviving branch of the final imperial family of Byzantium). Federigo died in 1540, leaving his widow in charge of three underage sons and one daughter. Isabella died in 1539. An inventory compiled of the Isabellalian collections in 1542 provides a detailed record of her extensive holdings and was probably drawn up because the deaths of Isabella and Federigo, occurring so close together, left the estate in the hands of guardians until Isabella's eldest grandson (Francesco) was ready to assume the role of duke.

As marquise of Mantua, Isabella was both the subject and the object of many literary dedications and literary portraits, most notably a tract called *I Ritratti* (1528), written by the Humanist Gian Giorgio Trissino, in which he celebrated her as one of the exemplars of female beauty and deportment in Italy. She was also the subject of several portraits: a celebrated medallic profile by Gian Cristoforo Romano, a pencil sketch by Leonardo da Vinci, and paintings by Lorenzo Costa, Francesco Francia (now lost), and the most famous by Titian (now in Vienna's Kunsthistorisches). Although not particularly famed for her physical beauty, contemporaries agreed that Isabella was a formidable cultural and social force, and she has become known as the first lady of the Renaissance.

SIGNIFICANCE

Isabella d'Este was a noted art patron and collector whose surviving archive has given scholars valuable insights into patronage and collecting patterns of this period. Her surviving letters, in which there are references to many other contemporary collectors, provide a history of collecting practices and insights into the display of art and collectibles. Her letters demonstrate also how art objects and antique fragments were translated into valuable cultural commodities. Isabella's life also is significant for studies on the cultural role that aristocratic women played at the northern Italian courts of the late fifteenth and early sixteenth centuries.

—Sally Hickson

FURTHER READING

Brown, Clifford M. "A Ferrarese Lady and A Mantuan Marchesa: The Art and Antiquities Collections of Isabella d'Este Gonzaga." In *Women and Art in Early Modern Europe: Patrons, Collectors, and Connoisseurs*, edited by Cynthia Lawrence. University Park: Pennsylvania State University Press, 1997. A brief but comprehensive overview of Isabella's career as patron and collector and a summary of her key cultural accomplishments.

_____. *"Per dare qualche splendore a la gloriosa città di Mantova": Documents for the Antiquarian Collection of Isabella d'Este.* Rome: Bulzoni, 2002. Brings together the complete file of documents pertaining to Isabella's antiquarian collections, with analysis in English. A second volume (forthcoming) will detail the physical fabric of Isabella's museum rooms.

Cartwright, Julia. *Isabella d'Este, Marchioness of Mantua, 1474-1539: A Study of the Renaissance.* 1903. Reprint. 2 vols. London: J. Murray, 1923. This is the first biography in English and the most complete, presenting in vivid detail Isabella's social, political, cultural, and family life with some complete documents and many excerpts from her letters translated into English.

Verheyen, Egon. *The Paintings in the Studiolo of Isabella d'Este at Mantua.* New York: College Art Association of America, 1971. A complete analysis and interpretation, in English, of the paintings completed by various artists for the decoration of Isabella's *studiolo*.

SEE ALSO: Giovanni Bellini; Vittoria Colonna; Correggio; Leonardo da Vinci; Andrea Mantegna; Michelangelo; Raphael; Ludovico Sforza; Titian.

RELATED ARTICLES in *Great Events from History: The Renaissance & Early Modern Era, 1454-1600:* 1481-1499: Ludovico Sforza Rules Milan; 16th century: Evolution of the Galleon.

IVAN THE GREAT
Grand prince of Moscow (r. 1462-1505)

Ivan united the Slavic independent and semi-independent principalities and cities under the aegis of the Muscovite rulers and began the long struggle with Poland-Lithuania and Sweden to recover the Ukraine, White Russia, and the Baltic States. Ivan also ended Russia's 240 years of Mongol or Tatar rule and proclaimed the independence of his country.

BORN: January 22, 1440; Moscow (now in Russia)
DIED: October 27, 1505; Moscow
ALSO KNOWN AS: Ivan III Vasilyevich
AREA OF ACHIEVEMENT: Government and politics

EARLY LIFE

Ivan III Vasilyevich, better known as Ivan (ee-VAHN) the Great, grand prince of Muscovy, was the son of Grand Prince Vasily II and Maria Yaroslavna. Vasily's reign was beset from the beginning by a series of savage civil wars with his rebellious uncles and cousins, who contested the throne of Muscovy. One of Vasily's uncles, Prince Yury, defeated him in 1433 and assumed the title of grand prince. When Yury died in 1434, one of his sons, Dmitri Shemyaka, claimed the throne, arrested Vasily, blinded him, and sent him into exile. The young Ivan, only six years old, was also seized by agents of Shemyaka and jailed with his father. Vasily, however, recovered his throne in 1447 and, despite being blind, ruled for another fifteen years.

Throughout the remainder of Vasily's reign, Ivan was closely associated with his father's administration. The blind Vasily assigned to him many of the daily duties and tasks of his government, providing him with valuable experience and political training in the affairs of the state. At the age of nine, Ivan was proclaimed grand prince and coruler in order to eliminate any question as to the succession to the throne. When Ivan was twelve years old, his father arranged, perhaps for political considerations, the marriage of his son to Maria, the daughter of the grand prince of Tver.

In 1452, Ivan was at the head of an army that defeated his father's enemy, Shemyaka. In 1458, Ivan was in charge of a successful military campaign against the Tatars to the south. On the death of his father on March 27, 1462, Ivan ascended the throne as grand prince and sovereign of Moscow at age twenty-two.

LIFE'S WORK

Ivan's reign was characterized by a series of foreign and domestic threats, all of which he was able to overcome. He proved to be a remarkable ruler of Russia, an individual with unusual political foresight and bold accomplishments. Ivan was endowed with extraordinary energy and native intelligence. He was persistent, calculating, and, at the same time, excessively cautious, secretive, and cunning in the extreme. He often avoided taking chances and was hesitant of drastic measures. Instead, he preferred to achieve his goal within the limits of his own power and resources. He employed discretion, calmly tolerated delays—often breaking his word—and used sinuous diplomacy, of which he proved to be a Machiavellian master. These attributes made him secure of himself and brought him many victories, for which he earned the appellation "the Great."

Ivan's major objective was to transform the small and often contested role of the principality of Moscow into the political center of a unified Russian state. He achieved this task through conquest, diplomacy, the purchase of land, annexation, and voluntary surrender of independent and semi-independent Russian principalities and free cities. He replaced the regional political fragmentation with a strong centralized administrative state. By the end of Ivan's reign, he had gathered all the Russian territories under the rule of the Muscovite grand prince and had incorporated them into the Muscovite state, increasing its territory from 150,000 square miles to nearly 400,000 square miles at the beginning of the sixteenth century.

At the time of Ivan's accession to the throne, there were four major principalities independent of Moscow—Yaroslavl', Rostov, Tver', and Ryazan'—and three city-states: the republic of Novgorod the Great, Vyatka, and Pskov. The principalities of Yaroslavl' and

Rostov were among the least independent Russian lands. By the treaties of 1463 and 1474, they were both formally annexed to Moscow.

Ivan's most important acquisition was the ancient city-republic of Novgorod the Great and its extensive colonies to the northeast. The republic cf Novgorod had preserved its independence for many centuries from both the Mongols and the Teutonic knights. Since the early fifteenth century, however, Novgorod had vacillated between Moscow and Poland-Lithuania. The Princes of Moscow viewed Novgorod's relations with these Catholic states with suspicion and distrust.

When a pro-Lithuanian party turned to Casimir IV, king of Poland and grand prince of Lithuania, seeking to select as their prince a Lithuanian, Ivan III turned against the Novgorodians. Accusing them of apostasy, he invaded the city in the spring of 1471 and imposed on them a treaty that bound the city closer to Moscow. Within a few years, however, the Novgorodians broke the terms of the treaty, and a pro-Polish party turned again to Poland-Lithuania. This new development forced Ivan to attack the city for a second time in 1478 and to order the annexation of its territory to Moscow and the confiscation of church lands. Finally, he ordered the deportation and exile of hundreds of prominent noble families, confiscation of their estates, and parceling out of these lands to individuals of lower classes conditional on military service. Ivan's acts signaled the end of Novgorod's independence.

The principality of Tver' was the second most important of Ivan's acquisitions. For centuries, Tver' had been Moscow's chief contender for control of Russia. When the grand prince of Tver', Mikhail, concluded a political alliance with Lithuania in 1483, Ivan used this act as an excuse to invade Tver' and officially annex it. The city of Vyatka, a former colony of Novgorod, was annexed in 1489. Finally, the principalities of Ryazan' and Pskov came under Moscow's control, but they were annexed by Ivan's son and successor, Vasily III, in 1521.

In the area of foreign affairs, Ivan was successful against both the Tatars to the east and the Poles and Lithuanians to the west. The Tatars, who established the Golden Horde in the southeastern part of Russia, remained potentially the most dangerous adversaries since the thirteenth century. Yet in the second half of the fifteenth century, the Golden Horde broke up into the independent khanates of Kazan, Astrakhan, and the Crimea. Ivan's goal was not only to terminate Moscow's nominal subservience to the khan of the Golden Horde but also to secure the southeastern boundaries of his realm from further attacks and incursions by the Tatar forces, allowing him to focus his attention on his principal task: the recovery of the Russian historical lands from Poland-Lithuania.

The friction between Moscow and the Golden Horde came to a head in 1480, when Khan Akhmed concluded an alliance with Poland-Lithuania and staged an attack on Moscow on the grounds that Ivan refused to pay him the customary annual tribute. The Russian and Tatar armies met on the opposite banks of the Ugra River in the fall of 1480. For more than two months, neither Akhmed nor the Russians attempted to attack each other. After waiting for the arrival of the Lithuanian and the Polish armies, who failed to appear, Akhmed suddenly withdrew his troops without giving a battle. In this rather unheroic manner, Ivan terminated Moscow's 240 years of Mongol domination.

Ivan also organized military campaigns against the Tatar khanate of Kazan to the southeast of Moscow. In 1487, Ivan captured the khanate and placed on its throne a Tatar vassal ruler, further stabilizing the southeastern

boundaries of his realm until the 1550's, when Kazan was finally annexed by Ivan IV.

Ivan III maintained friendly relations with the Tatar khan of Crimea and the Ottoman sultan. In 1480, he signed a treaty with the Crimean leader, Mengli Giray, against the Golden Horde and Poland. Though the Crimean Tatars remained unreliable allies, their hostility toward Lithuania and Poland helped Ivan in his plan to recover the ancient territory of Kievan Russia. In 1494, Ivan seized the town of Vyazma and annexed it to Moscow. A year later, he concluded a truce and entered into dynastic relations with the Grand Prince Alexander of Lithuania by offering his daughter in marriage. This arrangement, however, did not prevent Ivan from going to war with his son-in-law in 1500, on the grounds that his Orthodox subjects had allegedly been persecuted by the Catholic Church. When the war ended in 1503, Ivan captured much of the western Russian lands, except the cities of Kiev and Smolensk.

Finally, Ivan faced the growing power of Sweden, a perennial adversary of the Russians since the thirteenth

An engraved depiction of Ivan the Great (tearing document) defying the Tatar khan. (F. R. Niglutsch)

century. In 1493, Ivan and the king of Denmark signed an alliance against Sweden. The same year, Ivan went to war against Sweden, trying to gain control of Finland and the Baltic States. The Swedes, however, retaliated and attacked northern Russia, forcing Ivan to sign a truce in 1497. It was left to Peter the Great to break the power of Sweden in the eighteenth century.

Ivan's successes to the east against the Tatar khanates made Moscow the most powerful state on the Eurasia steppes, replacing the Golden Horde. His victories over Lithuania brought him into direct contact with Europe, and its sovereigns began to view him as a powerful and independent ruler. At the same time, Moscow gradually increased its economic and cultural ties with the West. In 1472, after the death of his first wife, Ivan married Sophia Palaeologus, the niece of the last Byzantine emperor.

The marriage of Sophia to Ivan was arranged, strangely enough, by Pope Paul II, who hoped to bring the Russian Orthodox Church under the orbit of the Roman Catholic Church. Ivan remained faithful to his orthodoxy, however, and used the marriage to the Byzantine princess to buttress the prestige and power of the office of the Muscovite ruler. To underscore the importance of his new position, he adopted the double-headed black eagle of Byzantium to his family coat of arms, called himself autocrat, or *samoderzhets*—an imitation of the Byzantine emperors—and added the complex Byzantine court ceremonies to his own. Ivan was also the first Russian ruler to use the title "czar" (Latin *caesar*) and "sovereign of all Russia." Moscow would henceforth claim to be the "Third Rome" after the fall of Constantinople in 1453, and the imperial idea became part of Russia's messianic tradition to modern times.

In his internal policy, Ivan was largely responsible for the administrative system he introduced, which lasted until the seventeenth century. He reformed the local government by introducing the system known as *kormlenie*, or the "feeding" system. This administrative innovation called for the appointment of district and provincial governors, who were charged with collecting taxes and custom duties for the grand prince, running the army and local militia, and administering justice. The governors were practically supported by taxes they extracted from the local population, thus the meaning of the term "feeding."

Ivan further suppressed and weakened the power of appanage princes, eliminated their separatist tendencies, and confiscated their lands. He replaced the hereditary aristocracy and created a new service system, known as *pomestie*. Under this system, the officials of the grand prince were granted land in return for military service. This new development led, in turn, to the formation of a new social class, the service gentry, or *dvorianstvo*. This service class became the core of Russia's military power and the staunch supporter of autocracy.

Ivan reformed the executive organs of the central government. At the end of the fifteenth century, the first bureaus, known as *prikazy*, were established. The *prikazy*, run by secretaries, were in charge of the various departments of the grand prince's government. Ivan also improved the system of justice. In 1497, he issued the first code of law, called *Sudebnik*. The code provided a uniform legal system and court procedure for the entire territory of the Muscovite realm. The law also outlined the rules and obligations of the peasants to their landlords, placing the first restrictions on their freedom to move about the land, as the growing gentry class demanded more peasant labor. These restrictions foreshadowed the beginning of serfdom in Russia.

During the last years of Ivan's reign, the Russian Orthodox Church underwent a serious inner crisis. There was growing opposition to the vast accumulation of wealth and land by the church and by monasteries. A group, called *strigolniki*, a religious sect known as Judaizers, and a minority of churchmen called the Trans-Volga Elders or "Non-Possessors," led by Nil Sorsky, criticized a range of practice within the church. These practices included the conduct of high prelates, monastic life, rituals, liturgy, and icon worship, as well as moral corruption, and simony. The majority of the conservative hierarchy of the church, led by Joseph of Volokolamsk defended the Church and monastic lands and condemned the reformers. Supporting the divine right of autocracy, they asked Ivan to suppress and persecute the reformers as heretics.

Ivan pondered for some time on the growing power of a church that appeared a rival of the state. He would have sided with the Trans-Volga Elders and secularized the church lands, but at the Church Council of 1503, he yielded to the demands of the Josephites and condemned the critics as heretics. At that point, Ivan was greatly concerned with family rivalry over the question of succession to the throne. He yielded to his wife, Sophia, and bestowed on his son Vasily the title of grand prince and asked the boyars to swear allegiance to him. In the meantime, the khanate of Kazan broke away from Moscow's subservience, and the Lithuanian War ended in 1503 rather inconclusively, as Ivan failed to recover all the Russian historical lands in the West. Two years later, on

October 27, 1505, Ivan died at the age of sixty-five, unlamented and apparently unloved by his own people. He was succeeded by his son Vasily.

SIGNIFICANCE

Ivan the Great was an outstanding ruler. His reign marked a turning point in the history of Russia from the medieval to the modern age. He created modern Russia. By gathering the Russian lands around the principality of Moscow, Ivan strengthened the power of the central government and increased the role and prestige of the Muscovite state and its ruler, both at home and abroad. Indeed, Ivan's diplomatic, political, military, and administrative achievements were comparable to those of his contemporaries Louis IX of France, Henry VII of England, and Ferdinand II and Isabella I of Spain.

Ivan was the first to encourage economic and cultural relations with the West and invited foreign craftspeople and artisans to Moscow, among them the noted Italian architect Aristotle Fioravanti, who built the famous Assumption (Uspenski) Cathedral in the Kremlin and other Italian-style palaces. Contacts with the Europeans convinced Ivan that Russia could learn from the West and that Russia could borrow its technical knowledge in order to strengthen its new position and compete successfully with other states. At the same time, Ivan protected and defended the Orthodox faith from Roman Catholicism and made the institution of the church the loyal supporter and advocate of Russian autocracy. In more ways than one, Ivan's accomplishments determined the course that Russia was to follow. He was the first to forge the great beginnings of Russia, which was destined to become a great European power. His appellation of "the Great" is deserved.

—James J. Farsolas

FURTHER READING

Fennel, J. L. I. "The Attitude of the Josephians and the Trans-Volga Elders to the Heresy of the Judaisers." *Slavonic and East European Review* 29 (June, 1951): 486-509. An inquiry into the different views of supporters of Sanin and the reformers of Sorsky toward the religious sect of the Judaizers.

_____. *Ivan the Great of Moscow.* New York: St. Martin's Press, 1962. The most complete and detailed study of all aspects of Ivan's reign in any language. The author emphasizes Ivan's foreign policy, diplomatic methods, and military campaigns in the Russo-Lithuanian War. Contains an extensive and valuable bibliography.

Grey, Ian. *Ivan III and the Unification of Russia.* New York: Collier, 1964. This is a well-written, detailed biography by a writer and biographer whose other work includes an account of Ivan the Terrible. Discusses the process of the unification of the Russian lands under the Muscovite princes, the wars and military campaigns against domestic and foreign enemies, and the emergence of the grand prince of Moscow as the leader of a strong and unified Russian state. Contains an index and brief bibliography.

Hunczak, Taras, ed. *Russian Imperialism from Ivan the Great to the Revolution.* Reprint. Lanham, Md.: University Press of America, 2000. Anthology of essays detailing the territorial expansion and imperial aspirations of Russia from the late fifteenth century to the early twentieth century. Includes maps, bibliographic references, and index.

Ostrowski, Donald. *Muscovy and the Mongols: Cross-Cultural Influences on the Steppe Frontier, 1304-1589.* New York: Cambridge University Press, 1998. A history of the development of Muscovy and the Russian state that focuses on its relationship to and interactions with other cultures, especially those of the Mongols. Looks at the extent to which external secular and religious practices were absorbed into, modified, or incorporated by Russian religious and political institutions, and the ways in which cross-cultural influence shaped the nation inherited and consolidated by Ivan. Includes glossary, chronology, bibliography, and index.

Riasanovsky, Nicholas V. *A History of Russia.* 6th ed. New York: Oxford University Press, 2000. Places Ivan's rule in the broader context of the formation of the Russian state. Includes photographic plates, illustrations, maps, bibliography, and index.

Soloviev, Sergei M. *History of Russia: The Reign of Ivan III the Great.* Edited and translated by John D. Windhausen. Gulf Breeze, Fla.: Academic International Press, 1979. A very important study of Ivan's reign by a great, "classic" Russian historian. Soloviev discusses Ivan's campaigns against Novgorod the Great, the acquisition of the various Russian principalities, his wars with the Eastern khanates, and Sophia and her influence in Russia.

_____. *History of Russia: Russian Society in the Age of Ivan III.* Translated and edited by John D. Windhausen. Gulf Breeze, Fla.: Academic International Press, 1979. A continuation of the previous work. Includes chapters on Ivan's wars with Lithuania and

Livonia and a discussion of Russian society under Ivan.

Vernadsky, George. *Russia at the Dawn of the Modern Age*. Vol. 4 in *A History of Russia*. New Haven, Conn.: Yale University Press, 1959. The most complete account and interpretation of Ivan's reign by an expert on the history of Russia. Vernadsky argues that Sophia had little influence in the court or on Ivan. Contains an extensive bibliography of Russian works.

SEE ALSO: Ferdinand II and Isabella I; Henry VII; Ivan the Terrible; Niccolò Machiavelli; Sophia Palaeologus; Vasily III.

RELATED ARTICLES in *Great Events from History: The Renaissance & Early Modern Era, 1454-1600*: 1478: Muscovite Conquest of Novgorod; 1480-1502: Destruction of the Golden Horde; After 1480: Ivan the Great Organizes the "Third Rome"; 1499-c. 1600: Russo-Polish Wars.

IVAN THE TERRIBLE
Czar of Russia (r. 1547-1584)

Of all Russian czars, Ivan contributed the most in giving shape to Russian autocracy as it would exist until the end of serfdom in 1861. He also conquered Kazan and Astrakhan, significantly reducing the Tatar threat and securing important trade routes in the Volga region, and took the first steps toward the incorporation of Siberia.

BORN: August 25, 1530; Moscow, Russia
DIED: March 18, 1584; Moscow
ALSO KNOWN AS: Ivan IV Vasilyevich
AREAS OF ACHIEVEMENT: Government and politics, warfare and conquest

EARLY LIFE

Ivan (ee-VAHN) the Terrible was born in the Kremlin Palace in Moscow. His father, Vasily III, had married Ivan's mother, Princess Elena Glinskaya, when his first wife failed to provide him an heir. Vasily died in 1533, leaving the three-year-old Ivan to be reared in the world of Kremlin politics, a world marked by violence, intrigues, and unashamed struggles for power among the hereditary nobles (boyar) and princely families. In order to forestall any threat to Ivan's succession, especially from his two uncles, Ivan was immediately declared as the next ruler. Under Muscovite law and custom, it was his mother who now exercised power as the regent. Although the next five years, until Elena's death in 1538, were normal years for Ivan, Kremlin politics were far from normal. Elena faced threats from her husband's two brothers, forcing her to order their arrest and imprisonment. Even her own uncle, Mikhail Glinsky, on whom she had relied in the beginning, appeared too ambitious; he suffered the same fate as the others.

Elena's death in 1538 opened a new chapter in young Ivan's life. Within a week of his mother's death, his nanny, Agrafena Chelyadina, who had provided him with loving care and affection, was taken away. The Kremlin now reverberated with intrigues and counterintrigues, especially those of two princely families, the Shuiskys and the Belskys. Power changed hands more than once. The first round went to the Shuiskys. Two brothers, Vasily and Ivan Shuisky, exercised power through the boyar Duma in succession. Ivan Shuisky in particular made a special point of neglecting and insulting both Ivan and his own brother. Ivan later recalled that Ivan Shuisky once "sat on a bench, leaning with his elbows on our father's bed and with his legs on a chair, and he did not even incline his head towards us . . . nor was there any element of deference to be found in his attitude toward us." Then, when power had passed to the Belskys and Ivan Shuisky was trying to regain it, Ivan had the horrifying experience of Shuisky's men breaking into his bedchamber in the night in search of the metropolitan.

Ivan thus developed deep hatred for the boyars, especially for the Shuiskys, who once again controlled power. Andrey Shuisky, who became the leader of this group after Ivan Shuisky's illness, imposed a reign of increased corruption and terror. Ivan, in a bold move in 1543, when he was only thirteen years old, ordered Prince Andrey to be arrested and brutally killed.

During these early years, Ivan not only witnessed cruel acts perpetrated around him that implanted fear and suspicion of boyars in his young heart but also engaged in such acts himself for fun and pleasure. Torturing all kinds of animals, riding through the Moscow streets knocking down the young and the old—men, women, and children—and engaging in orgies became his pastime.

Ivan, especially under the guidance of Metropolitan Makary, also read the Scriptures and became the first truly literate Russian ruler. Some scholars have cast doubt on this, challenging the authenticity of his corre-

Ivan the Terrible. (Library of Congress)

spondence with Prince Andrey Kurbsky after the defection of his once-trusted adviser to Lithuania, but most evidence suggests that Ivan became a well-read person. In Makary, Ivan also found support for his belief in his role as an absolute ruler whose power was derived from God.

Toward the end of 1546, when he was still sixteen, Ivan decided to have himself crowned as czar. He also decided to search for a bride from his own realm. Although his grandfather, Ivan III (Ivan the Great), had used the title of czar, Ivan IV was the first to be so crowned in a glittering ceremony in Moscow on January 16, 1547. On February 3, he was married to Anastasia Romanovna Zakharina, of a boyar family. She was to provide him many years of happy married life and to serve as a calming influence on his impulsive personality.

LIFE'S WORK

The first part of Ivan's rule as Russia's czar was marked by several important reforms. He hated the boyars but did not try to dismantle the boyar Duma at this time. Instead, he created a chosen council consisting of some of his close advisers that included Metropolitan Makary, Archpriest Silvester, and Aleksey Adashev, a member of the service-gentry class. He also called the *zemskii sobor*

(assembly of the land), representing the boyars and the service gentry as well as the townspeople, the clergy, and some state peasants.

A major drawback that adversely affected the fighting capacity of the Russian army was the system known as *mestnichestvo*, by which the appointments to top positions were based on the birth and rank of various boyars, not on their ability to command and fight. As he had done with the boyar Duma, Ivan did not end the system but provided for exceptions in case of special military campaigns. He also created regular infantry detachments known as the *streltsy*, to be paid by the state and to serve directly under the czar, and he regularized the terms and conditions under which a nobleman was expected to serve in the army. These steps greatly enhanced the army's fighting ability.

Some reforms in the system of local self-government were also undertaken in order to make it more efficient, especially for the purpose of tax collection. A collection and codification of laws resulted in the law code of 1550. A church council, the Hundred Chapters Council (for the hundred questions submitted to it), seriously undertook the question of reform in the Russian Orthodox Church. Ivan, though not successful in secularizing church lands, was able to limit the church's power to acquire new lands which, in the future, could be done only with the czar's consent.

This early period of reform saw the establishment of important trade links between Russia and England. In search of a northeastern passage to China, the English explorer Richard Chancellor found himself in the White Sea. Ivan warmly received him in Moscow and granted the English important trading privileges, hoping to acquire arms and support from the English against Ivan's European adversaries in his drive to find a foothold on the Baltic coast.

The early reform period was also marked by important successes in foreign policy. Although the long Mongolian domination over Russia had come to an end during the reign of Ivan's grandfather, Ivan the Great, the Mongolian khanates in the east and south still created problems. Their rulers undertook occasional raids against Moscow and the Muscovite territories. Ivan finally decided to undertake a military campaign to conquer the Kazan khanate in the upper Volga region. After some initial setbacks, he succeeded in capturing and annexing the whole khanate in 1557. While the Mongolian rule in Ivan III's time had ended without a major fight, the bloody battle at Kazan, with heavy casualties on both sides, came as a sweet revenge for the Russians. Ivan followed this by conquering Astrakhan in the south, thus acquiring the whole Volga region that now provided access to the Caspian Sea.

At this midpoint in his reign, Ivan experienced some unusual developments that reinforced his suspicion and hatred for the boyars. The result was the start of one of the bloodiest chapters in Russian history, during which thousands of people were tortured and executed. During his brief but serious illness in 1553, Ivan had asked various princes and boyars to take an oath of loyalty to his infant son, Dmitry. To his surprise and horror, he found that not everyone was ready to do so, including some of his closest advisers such as Silvester. Then, a dispute arose over Ivan's desire to engage in a war in the north to acquire territories on the Baltic coast from the Livonian Order of the German Knights. While Ivan decided to embark on the Livonian campaign in 1558, achieving some initial successes, the war was opposed by several members of the chosen council who noted the difficulties of fighting a two-front war. Finally, his beloved wife, Anastasia, died in 1560, removing a calming and restraining influence from his life.

Apparently deciding to destroy the power of the boyars once and for all, Ivan undertook a reign of terror. Some, like Adashev, were thrown in prison, where they died of torture and hunger. Others, like Prince Kurbsky, fled the country and joined Ivan's enemies, further intensifying the czar's suspicions about their loyalty. Ivan, in a well-planned move in December, 1564, suddenly decided to leave Moscow in full daylight with his belongings and to settle at nearby Alexandrovskaia Sloboda. In his message to the people of Moscow, he charged the boyars with disloyalty and treason but expressed faith in the ordinary people. As he had calculated, in asking him to return to Moscow, the people agreed to his condition that he should be allowed a free hand in punishing the boyars as well as in creating a separate state for himself that would be outside the jurisdiction of regular laws; this was to be known as *Oprichnina*.

Ivan took immediate steps to assign vast tracts of land in the Moscow region and other parts of Russia to the new autonomous state. As he did this, his objective seemed somewhat clearer. Much of the land belonged to the boyar families who were now forced to flee and seek land elsewhere. Ivan also selected a band of loyal guards, known as the *oprichniki*, whose number eventually rose to six thousand. They were assigned some of the newly vacated lands with the understanding that they would have the obligation to serve the czar. Thus, they became a part of the expanding service-gentry class.

While the aims of the *Oprichnina* seemed quite rational, what appeared incomprehensible was the excessive use of torture and murder by Ivan and his *oprichniki*. The job of the *oprichniki* was to clear the land of all possible traitors, but they themselves became a scourge of the land, killing and robbing innocent people. Anyone who criticized or opposed Ivan became his victim. Metropolitan Philip, who courageously castigated the czar for loosing these death squads on the Russian people, was thrown into a monastery and later strangled by one of Ivan's men. Ivan's cruelty, which bordered on insanity, was evident in the killings of thousands of innocent people that he personally undertook in Novgorod in 1570 on the suspicion that the territory was planning to defect to Lithuania.

In 1571, when the Crimean Tatars raided Moscow, the *oprichniki* failed to protect it. Instead, Moscow was saved when, in 1572, Russia's regular forces inflicted a crushing defeat on the Tatar army. Ivan then decided to disband *Oprichnina*. The Livonian War, however, did not go well for Ivan. After twenty-five years of fighting, Russia appeared exhausted. When the war ended in 1583, the country had lost all the gains it had made in the initial stages of the war. Indeed, Ivan had stretched himself too far. The end of the Livonian War also marked the end of his reign, as he died in 1584.

SIGNIFICANCE

Ivan the Terrible's reign remains one of the most controversial eras in Russian history. There is no doubt that his achievements were many. The victory over Kazan, which Ivan memorialized in the construction of the magnificent St. Basil's Cathedral in Moscow, and the conquest of Astrakhan, made available the whole Volga region for Russian trade and, because of the exploits of the Cossack leader Yermak Timofey, started Russia on its march into Siberia. Ivan's reforms, undertaken painstakingly and thoughtfully in the earlier period of his reign, provided for a more efficient civil administration and a better fighting force. Without these reforms, his victory over Kazan would not have been possible.

Even his struggle against the hereditary boyars and the resulting expansion of the service-gentry class, essential elements in the strengthening of Russian autocracy, constituted a continuation of the process that had already existed. What makes this period so puzzling is the excessive amount of force, including the use of inhumane torture, freely used by Ivan in order to weaken the power of the boyars. Providing a pathological interpretation, some historians find Ivan paranoid and his *Oprich-*

nina the work of a madman. Others, although acknowledging his excessive cruelty, see him not as a madman but as one who had lost his peace of mind and was haunted by an intense feeling of insecurity for himself and his family. Still others point to the fact that if Ivan used excessive force, it was not uncommon in a Europe dominated by the ideas of Niccolò Machiavelli. For them, Ivan, like some of his contemporaries, was a Renaissance prince. Whatever the final judgment may be, Ivan significantly expanded Russian frontiers and gave shape to a Russian autocracy that, in its essential contours, remained unchanged until the Great Reforms undertaken by Alexander II during the 1860's.

—*Surendra K. Gupta*

FURTHER READING

Cherniavsky, M. "Ivan the Terrible as Renaissance Prince." *Slavic Review* 27 (March, 1968): 195-211. This article argues that Ivan was no exception in using excessive force against his enemies in a Renaissance Europe dominated by Machiavellian ideas.

Grey, Ian. *Ivan the Terrible*. London: Hodder & Stoughton, 1964. A popular biography that presents an uncritical portrait of Ivan the Terrible. Blame for much of Ivan's cruelty is placed on his opponents. Contains a limited bibliography.

Keenan, Edward. *The Kurbskii-Groznyi Apocrypha*. Cambridge, Mass.: Harvard University Press, 1971. This book challenges the authenticity of Ivan's correspondence with Prince Kurbsky. Keenan's view remains controversial.

Kurbsky, A. M. *The Correspondence Between Prince A. M. Kurbsky and Tsar Ivan IV of Russia, 1564-1579*. Edited and translated by J. L. I. Fennell. Cambridge, England: Cambridge University Press, 1955. An excellent translation of a valuable but controversial historical source.

_____. *Prince A. M. Kurbsky's History of Ivan IV*. Edited and translated by J. L. I. Fennell. Cambridge, England: Cambridge University Press, 1965. Written by Prince Kurbsky after his defection, the book describes the events from 1533 to the early 1570's in a most critical manner. Though a valuable historical source, it is a highly partisan study of Ivan's reign.

Myerson, Daniel. *Blood and Splendor: The Lives of Five Tyrants, from Nero to Saddam Hussein*. New York: Perennial, 2000. Short but gripping and fully realized biography of Ivan, in a collection that also portrays Nero, Joseph Stalin, Adolf Hitler, and Saddam Hussein.

Pavlov, Andrei, and Maureen Perrie. *Ivan the Terrible*. London: Pearson/Longman, 2003. Major reassessment of Ivan's reign seeks to do away with the stereotypes of Cold War-era historians and achieve a balanced and accurate appraisal of Ivan as neither an evil genius nor a wise and benevolent statesman. Argues that Ivan's campaign of terror was motivated not merely by personal sadism but by a belief in the divine right of the monarch to punish treason on earth in a manner as extreme as the punishments of Hell. Includes maps, genealogical tables, bibliographic references, index.

Platonov, S. F. *Ivan the Terrible*. Edited and translated by Joseph L. Wieczynski. Gulf Breeze, Fla.: Academic International Press, 1974. An excellent translation of a work by a famous Russian historian of the old St. Petersburg school of Russian historiography, which emphasized facts in making historical interpretations. While Platonov does not accept the view of Ivan as paranoid, the book has an introductory part, "In Search of Ivan the Terrible," by Richard Hellie, that does.

Shulman, Sol. *Kings of the Kremlin: Russia and Its Leaders from Ivan the Terrible to Boris Yeltsin*. London: Brassey's, 2002. Ivan is the first of the major Russian leaders profiled in this history of the Kremlin. Includes photographic plates, illustrations, bibliographic references, and index.

Skrynnikov, Ruslan G. *Ivan the Terrible*. Edited and translated by Hugh F. Graham. Gulf Breeze, Fla.: Academic International Press, 1981. A serious and balanced study by a Soviet historian that presents Ivan and his *Oprichnina* in a nonideological framework. Contains a short bibliography of Russian-language books and articles.

SEE ALSO: Ivan the Great; Niccolò Machiavelli; Sophia Palaeologus; Vasily III.

RELATED ARTICLES in *Great Events from History: The Renaissance & Early Modern Era, 1454-1600:* 1499-c. 1600: Russo-Polish Wars; January 16, 1547: Coronation of Ivan the Terrible; January-May, 1551: The Stoglav Convenes; Summer, 1556: Ivan the Terrible Annexes Astrakhan; 1557-1582: Livonian War; c. 1568-1571: Ottoman-Russian War; November, 1575: Stephen Báthory Becomes King of Poland; 1581-1597: Cossacks Seize Sibir; July 21, 1582: Battle of the Tobol River; 1584-1613: Russia's Time of Troubles; 1589: Russian Patriarchate Is Established.

JAMES III
King of Scotland (r. 1460-1488)

James III was the first Scottish ruler to take an abiding interest in artistic and cultural matters, making him, in effect, Scotland's earliest Renaissance prince. His reign, however, was marred by his incapacity to prevent and control uprisings among his feudal nobility in a medieval environment that celebrated the masculine pursuits of war and stringent leadership.

BORN: July 10, 1451, or May, 1452; St. Andrews, Castle, Fife, Scotland
DIED: June 11, 1488; Milltown, near Bannockburn, Stirlingshire, Scotland
AREAS OF ACHIEVEMENT: Government and politics, patronage of the arts, warfare and conquest

EARLY LIFE

James was the eldest son of King James II, the fourth monarch of the House of Stuart, and his wife, Mary of Gueldres, niece of Philip the Good, duke of Burgundy. At the time of his birth, his father was in the process of successfully consolidating his power within the realm at the expense of some of the major feudal lords, notably the earls of Douglas, who were ultimately driven into exile. Younger sons, Alexander, duke of Albany, and John, earl of Mar, and two daughters, Mary and Margaret, were born to the royal couple and survived childhood.

On August 3, 1460, while laying siege to Roxburgh Castle on the border with England, King James II died instantly in the explosion of one of his own cannons. Mary assumed the regency, and after having the troops swear loyalty to her young son James III, she rallied the Scots to take Roxburgh. One week later, James III was officially crowned at Kelso Abbey.

During her period of regency, Queen Mary was able to frustrate the designs of King Edward IV of England, the earl of Douglas, and the McDonald Lord of the Isles to divide Scotland among them. She founded Holy Trinity Church in Edinburgh and generally kept intact her son's inheritance.

Mary died in December of 1463 and was succeeded as regent by James Kennedy, bishop of St. Andrews. Bishop Kennedy secured peace between Scotland and King Edward IV and governed the kingdom capably until his death on May 10, 1465. Thereafter, King James III, who was fourteen, began his personal rule.

LIFE'S WORK

Dark-complexioned and cultured, James III gained fame as a patron of poets, painters, musicians, and architects. His most famed art commission was an altarpiece by the Flemish painter Hugo van der Goes for Holy Trinity Church, Edinburgh, which contains the best likeness that has survived. Even more grandiose in conception, however, was the designing of the Great Hall of Stirling Castle by the architect Robert Cochrane, who became the most notorious of James's court favorites.

From the beginning, James III was to demonstrate an uncanny inability to exert effective leadership and to control his ambitious and often turbulent nobility. His apparent lack of interest in what were then considered kingly pursuits of warfare and hunting raised some eyebrows and led some to question both his manhood and his competence to govern. In some sense, the cultural achievements of his reign became political liabilities in what was still a very conservative medieval environment.

The first crisis of the reign occurred in 1466, when Lord Boyd of Kilmarnock engineered a coup by kidnapping the king and basically seizing control of the government for three years. Sir Thomas, Lord Boyd's son, even married the king's sister, Mary. In 1469, James III married Princess Margaret, whose father was King Christian I of Norway, Sweden, and Denmark. As a dowry, James obtained the Orkney and Shetland Islands, which he was to return to King Christian when the latter was able to raise 60,000 florins. When he failed to do so in the required time, James joyfully annexed the islands to the Scottish kingdom in 1472. Queen Margaret, who died in 1486, bore the king three sons. The monarch's marriage signaled, also, the downfall of the Boyds, who were forced into exile.

In 1479, another crisis broke, this time involving members of the royal family more closely. Discontent with the king's open-handed generosity to favorites such as Cochrane led to a gossip campaign, which in turn developed into support for the younger brothers, Alexander and John, who were better cast into the virile warlike role favored by much of the nobility. Suspicious, jealous of his brothers' growing popularity, and worried that control was slipping through his fingers, King James arrested his siblings. John died under mysterious circumstances, but Alexander escaped to England.

Promising to recognize Edward IV of England as his overlord in return for help in deposing his brother, Alexander invaded Scotland in 1482. While marching to confront Alexander, James was faced with a mutiny by his army at

Lauder Bridge. Resentment against Robert Cochrane and five other favorites reached the boiling point, and the unfortunate men were lynched in front of the king, who was further humiliated by becoming a prisoner of the mutineers. He was forced to come to a power-sharing agreement with Alexander. The next year, however, it was revealed that Alexander was once again plotting to deliver Scotland to Edward IV, and he was again forced to flee. Alexander would continue to attempt invasion and create disruption until his accidental death while participating in a jousting tournament in France in 1485.

Even after these unsettling series of events, which clearly demonstrated the king's unpopularity and the extent to which the discontented nobility might go in their opposition, James changed his ways, this time granting power, influence, offices, and titles to favorites who were even more obnoxious to the aristocracy—notably John Ramsey, earl of Bothwell. The Scottish parliament had also proved restive, criticizing the king time and again for his neglect in administering the law of the land and in his infrequent use of the death penalty for felons.

In 1488, rebellion erupted once more, led by Archibald Douglas, the fifth earl of Angus, and supported by half the nobles and bishops. The rebels captured the king's eldest son and heir to the throne, James, who (more or less) became an accomplice by agreeing to pose as the uprising's figurehead.

Both sides blundered into battle near Stirling Castle, on the old battleground of Bannockburn on June 11, 1488. The clash, which was called the Battle of Sauchieburn, was a series of confused skirmishes and encounters during which King James displayed inferior leadership. He was defeated and, either during the course of the melee, or shortly afterward, was killed.

The best-known account of James's death (which is somewhat suspect because it was written nearly a century later) relates that King James was thrown from his horse and injured while attempting to flee. He was taken to Beaton's Mill by the miller and his wife and had asked for a priest. They found a man who claimed to be a priest, but who instead of ministering to the king, stabbed him to death, fled, and evaded identification and capture.

SIGNIFICANCE

Though largely ignored and often dismissed as an insignificant ruler in historical terms, James III proved sufficiently able to hold the realm together so that his successor, James IV, was able to exert more effective control and bring to fruition the cultural advancements that his father had initiated. What James lacked in domestic political skills, too, can be balanced against some major foreign policy coups, especially in what proved to be the permanent addition of the Orkneys and the Shetlands.

—*Raymond Pierre Hylton*

FURTHER READING

Barrell, A. D. M. *Medieval Scotland*. New York: Cambridge University Press, 2000. A generally unfavorable depiction that argues that James III was a monarch who did not develop the martial and political qualities to survive in a medieval environment.

Bingham, Caroline. *The Stewart Kingdom of Scotland, 1371-1603*. New York: St. Martin's Press, 1974. Takes a very sympathetic view of the much-maligned monarch, stating that his art patronage and his diplomatic successes have been downplayed by historians. The same author puts forth much the same arguments, though more compactly, in *The Kings and Queens of Scotland* (New York: Taplinger, 1976).

Linklater, Eric. *The Royal House*. Garden City, N.Y.: Doubleday, 1970. Perceives in James the major tragic flaw of being too advanced for his own time, that is, as a king who neglected the masculine pursuits of hunting and war making.

James III. (Hulton|Archive by Getty Images)

MacDougall, Norman. *James III: A Political Study.* Edinburgh: John Donald, 1982. A definitive study on the subject of James's political shortcomings. The treatment is sympathetic and focuses on rashness as James's main flaw. Discounts the story of the priest responsible for his death.

Magnusson, Magnus. *Scotland: The Story of a Nation.* New York: Atlantic Monthly Press, 2000. Argues that James's mistakes were magnified by a particularly "bad press" and argues for a more balanced measure of his accomplishments and failures.

Mitchison, Rosalind. *A History of Scotland.* London: Methuen, 1982. Sees James as a victim of the attitudes of his time in a society that condemned artistic pursuits and extolled sport and horsemanship.

SEE ALSO: Edward IV; James IV; James V.
RELATED ARTICLES in *Great Events from History: The Renaissance & Early Modern Era, 1454-1600:* August 22, 1513-July 6, 1560: Anglo-Scottish Wars; February 27, 1545: Battle of Ancrum Moor; May, 1559-August, 1561: Scottish Reformation.

JAMES IV
King of Scotland (r. 1488-1513)

Unifying Scotland with internal peace and financial stability, the popular James IV promoted education, systematic justice, architecture, and literature, and negotiated the Treaty of Perpetual Peace with England. He also improved the standing of the Scottish within European politics through his skill and prestige.

BORN: March 17, 1473; Holyrood, Edinburgh, Scotland

DIED: September 9, 1513; Flodden, near Branxton, Northumberland, England

ALSO KNOWN AS: Duke of Rothesay; James Stewart; James Stuart

AREAS OF ACHIEVEMENT: Government and politics, warfare and conquest, diplomacy, education

EARLY LIFE

The eldest son of James III of Scotland and Margaret of Denmark, James was educated at his mother's charge in Latin and modern languages, French and Roman history, and the Bible. His interests included hunting, warfare, and surgery. He learned politics at age nine while experiencing the 1482 power struggle between his father and his uncle, Alexander, the duke of Albany.

When James was fifteen, aristocratic rebels fighting in his name defeated and assassinated James III at the Battle of Sauchieburn and crowned the prince King James IV at Scone in 1488. In penance for his part in the regicide, he thereafter wore an iron chain and made annual religious pilgrimages.

In James's minority, the earl of Bothwell's faction ruled initially, but soon another rebellion combined disaffected rebels with loyalists of the old regime under the *bludy serk* (bloody shirt) banner of James III, and

James IV rode to battle in 1489. Despite the royal victory under Lord Drummond, a conciliatory parliament appeased rebel demands, and in 1490, leaders of both factions joined Bothwell on James's new Privy Council. James gained military and diplomatic skills as well as a lifelong adviser, Bishop William Elphinstone of Aberdeen, his keeper of the privy seal for twenty-two years.

In 1493, James's new chancellor, the earl of Angus, extended crown authority with a show of naval power to enforce forfeiture of the lordship of the Isles, already weakened by internecine feuds. James made a rapid tour to the western Isles and to the south and the northeast, a public assertion of kingship.

LIFE'S WORK

Assuming personal rule in 1495 at age twenty-two, James was a popular and progressive monarch who consolidated his authority by balancing royal patronage among factions, finding income sources other than taxation, and very rarely calling Parliament. He toured his realm on pilgrimages and during hunting trips, and he enforced Crown law—especially in the Isles, which were finally secured by 1506.

James seized a pivotal role in European politics in 1495 by supporting Perkin Warbeck, who for four years convincingly masqueraded as Richard, duke of York, pretender to the English throne of Henry VII. Though England and Spain were unconvinced, Warbeck won the support of Charles VIII of France, Holy Roman Emperor Maximilian I, and Margaret, duchess of Burgundy, his supposed aunt. James treated Warbeck royally at the Scottish court. In 1496, he arranged and attended Warbeck's marriage to Lady Catherine Gordon, gave him a generous pension, and assembled artillery to invade England on his behalf. Meanwhile, Spanish ambassadors urged peace. In September, James led Scottish forces into Northumberland. When no English rose to Warbeck's support, Warbeck returned to Scotland, while James's army remained for five days of plundering before safely recrossing the Tweed River. Henry VII appropriated funds for a retaliatory strike, but tax revolts in Cornwall and Devonshire distracted him, and after another year of James's audacious border skirmishes, Henry initiated the process that would lead to the Treaty of Perpetual Peace between England and Scotland in 1502 and James's marriage to his daughter Margaret.

In August, 1503, the thirteen-year old Margaret, escorted by Henry Howard, the earl of Surrey, rode through triumphal arches into Edinburgh and married the king at Holyrood Abbey. Five days of music, dancing, feasts, and tournaments marked what court poet William Dunbar celebrated as the union of "the Thrissill and the Rois."

Scottish culture flourished during the peace. The education act of 1496, which had mandated literacy in Latin and the law for the eldest sons of nobles in order to professionalize the nation's judicial system, expanded lay interest in literature, Humanism, and literary patronage. In 1495, in his episcopal see at Aberdeen, Bishop Elphinstone already had founded Scotland's third university with Kings College. In 1505, James founded the Royal College of Surgeons, the first of its sort in Britain, and, in 1512, Elphinstone, with John Hepburn, founded St. Leonard's College at St Andrews. James licensed Scotland's first printing press in 1507. In 1509-1510, Elphinstone created a Scottish liturgy to replace the English Sarum use, or Sarum rite, and to honor more than seventy Scottish saints. Poets flourished during this time, including Robert Henryson—named the Scottish Geoffrey Chaucer—the aristocrats Sir David Lindsay and Gavin Douglas, and the eloquent and versatile Dunbar.

The king increased royal revenues, filled vacancies in the church with his relatives, enforced a succession tax on aristocratic sons as they succeeded their fathers, and introduced the feudal system to raise and fix rents on royal lands. He undertook elegant architectural projects at Linlithgow, Stirling, Falkland, and Holyrood. As he reformed the currency and standardized measures of weight and volume, guilds developed and merchants prospered in royal burghs, the only cities chartered for international trade.

James IV. (Hulton|Archive by Getty Images)

Meanwhile, James also expanded his navy. With brilliant if occasionally piratical sea captains and the financial and technical assistance of France, he built and armed a fleet, including in 1511 the thousand-ton *Great Michael*, the largest, most powerful warship afloat. The next year, England's young King Henry VIII copied it in building the ship *Henri Grâce à Dieu*.

The English peace lasted only a decade. In 1511, when Pope Julius II drew Henry into the Holy League against France, James assured Louis XII that he would uphold Scotland's auld alliance with France, and Louis supplied James with munitions and money. Except for Elphinstone and the queen, James's council was eager for war with England, and James drew forces from the whole of Scotland. The navy sailed for France and, in August of 1513, James led an infantry assault of more than twenty thousand men on Northumberland, achieving his objective, Norham Castle, in five days.

The earl of Surrey, who ten years earlier had escorted the king's bride, now hurried back north, this time with an English army. On September 9, on rough, marshy ground in a driving rain, he defeated James at Flodden Field, not far from the border. The English artillery, though smaller, was more accurate than the Scots' cannons, and the English halberds, though shorter, were at close range more deadly than the Scottish pikes. James died surrounded by ten thousand Scots, including nobles and churchmen from all parts of the nation he had unified. Edinburgh, in terror, prepared for an English invasion that never came. At sixteen months, James V inherited the Crown.

SIGNIFICANCE

Surrey's annihilation of the Scottish nobility and their strong, forty-year-old King James IV, was a greater English victory than anything Henry VIII achieved personally in his expensive French campaign. A musical lament composed for the fallen, "The Flowers of the Forest," is still piped at Scottish military funerals.

The divisive politics of James V's minority inhibited the diplomatic and cultural progress of his father's reign. In 1603, however, exactly a century after James's shrewdly contracted marriage joined the thistle and the rose, the last of Henry VIII's children—Elizabeth I—died without issue, and James's great grandson, James VI, became England's King James I.

—Gayle Gaskill

FURTHER READING

Bevan, Bryan. *Henry VII: The First Tudor King*. London: Rubicon, 2000. Bevan's brief and derivative but solid popular biography connects James's support for Perkin Warbeck to his marriage with Margaret.

Chrimes, S. B. *Henry VII*. New Haven, Conn.: Yale University Press, 1999. Chrimes's standard biography of Henry VII evaluates James's vacillating early foreign policy from an English perspective.

Macdougall, Norman. *James IV*. East Linton, Scotland: Tuckwell Press, 1997. Balanced, comprehensive, sympathetic, and corrective, Macdougall's work remains the standard biography.

_____. "Renewal: 1484-1517." In *An Antidote to the English: The Auld Alliance, 1295-1560*. East Linton, Scotland: Tuckwell Press, 2001. Macdougall assesses James's complex manipulation of conflicting French and English alliances within the context of two centuries of Franco-Scottish relations.

Mackie, R. L. *King James IV of Scotland*. Edinburgh: Oliver and Boyd, 1958. Now superseded by Macdougall's work, Mackie's entertaining narrative portrays James as a "Renaissance prince" and a "moonstruck romantic."

Mason, Roger A. "Regnum et Imperium: Humanism and Political Culture of Early Renaissance Scotland." In *Kingship and the Commonweal*. East Linton, Scotland: Tuckwell Press, 1998. Mason links Scotland's advances in education, law, diplomacy, architecture, and literature in James IV's reign to the king's imperial designs.

Scarisbrick, J. J. *Henry VIII*. New Haven. Conn.: Yale University Press, 1997. This revision of Henry VIII's standard biography represents Flodden as Henry's first great victory.

SEE ALSO: Catherine of Aragon; Charles VIII; Henry VII; Henry VIII; James III; James V; Julius II; Louis XII; Maximilian I.

RELATED ARTICLE in *Great Events from History: The Renaissance & Early Modern Era, 1454-1600:* August 22, 1513-July 6, 1560: Anglo-Scottish Wars.

JAMES V
King of Scotland (r. 1513-1542)

James V's effective fiscal and foreign policies kept a wealthy Scotland united and played key roles in international affairs. He was able to resist the Protestant Reformation's attempt to sweep into Catholic Scotland, but his invasion of England led to defeat and to a fractured political community for his lone heir to the throne, Mary, Queen of Scots.

BORN: April 10, 1512; Linlithgow, West Lothian, Scotland

DIED: December 14, 1542; Falkland Palace, Fife, Scotland

ALSO KNOWN AS: James Stewart (given name); James Stuart

AREAS OF ACHIEVEMENT: Government and politics, diplomacy, warfare and conquest

EARLY LIFE

In August, 1503, James Stewart's parents, James IV, king of Scotland, and Margaret Tudor, the eldest daughter of Henry VII, king of England, had contracted a marriage that was meant to establish peace between their perennially hostile realms. As James IV's effective financial administration and successful international diplomacy had brought great prestige to the Scottish crown, the infant James Stewart (and later James V) would have been born into a court characterized by relative political stability, teeming with material wealth and the newly imported notions of Renaissance culture.

The tranquility of the Scotland into which James was born, however, was soon disrupted, when James IV invited war with England by renewing, in 1512, Scotland's traditional alliance with France. In September, 1513, James IV's invasion of northern England led to a disastrous defeat at the Battle of Flodden Field, resulting in the death of James IV and much of the Scottish nobility. On September 21, 1513, the infant James found himself transformed into James V, after his coronation at the Chapel Royal in Stirling Castle.

For much of his youth, James V was subject to a chaotic political landscape, with various factions struggling for control of the king during the period of his minority. There had been much resistance to the regency of James's mother, Margaret, who remarried in 1514, to Archibald Douglas, the earl of Angus. The key disputants among the Scottish nobility, who each sought to control the young James V, included the powerful Douglas family, as well as factions allied to James's two closest relatives, who were both grandsons of James II—John, duke of Albany, who for some years governed Scotland, and James Hamilton, the earl of Arran.

LIFE'S WORK

In 1524, Margaret, again acting as regent of Scotland after the departure of Albany into France, enthroned James, providing him with the symbols of his power as king of Scotland and thereby ending the governorship of Albany. A compromise was made, whereby control of the young king would alternate among the key players in the Scottish nobility. The earl of Angus, who had earlier divorced Margaret, destroyed the delicate arrangements for the custody of James V when he kidnapped the young king in 1526 and proceeded to exploit James, whose period of minority he had declared over, enriching his own Red Douglas supporters for some two years. In 1528, James V escaped from the control of the earl of Angus and began to rally his supporters.

Over the next year, he and his adherents battled with the Douglases, eventually driving the earl of Angus into England. Over the next ten years, James pursued a vendetta against the Douglas family, which had exploited him during the tumultuous years of his minority. In July, 1537, Janet, lady of Glamis, the sister of the earl of Angus, was burned to death after being convicted of treason, while in August, 1540, James Hamilton of Finnart, a Douglas adherent, was also executed for treason. In December, 1540, James appears to have completed his vengeance against the Douglases, appropriating as Crown possessions the Angus estates, through the Act of Annexation. Apart from his harassment of the Douglases, however, James seems to have enjoyed relatively stable relations with the Scottish nobility throughout the period of his mature reign.

In 1536, James departed for France, appointing a committee of six nobles to rule in his absence. In January of 1537, James signaled his desire to maintain Scotland's traditional alliance with France by marrying, in Paris, Madeleine, the daughter of the French king Francis I. Madeleine died of consumption in July of that same year. In 1538, James married Mary of Guise, daughter of the duke of Guise, at St. Andrews, again using marriage to cement his realm's ties to France. James and Mary would have three children: two sons, James and Arthur, died in 1541, while James's sole surviving heir, Mary (the future Queen of Scots), was born on December 8, 1542.

James V. (Hulton|Archive by Getty Images)

James was successful in generating revenue from his subjects through taxation and fees, using the resources to fund numerous projects. Although James was not overly generous in distributing royal patronage, he succeeded in encouraging the cultivation of Renaissance pursuits, ensuring that his court was adorned by artistic and literary pursuits. James dedicated time and money to building projects at Falkland and Stirling, and he also devoted much of his realm's wealth to the stockpiling of artillery and to the strengthening of the Scottish navy.

In 1540, James led a naval expedition to Orkney and to the Hebrides, as part of a policy designed to extend royal presence and power even into the most peripheral parts of his realm. James also chose to take decisive action against the violent border reivers (raiders) such as the infamous Armstrongs, leading to the execution or imprisonment of many malefactors in the often lawless region. James's effective campaign against these border bandits led to his later vilification as a tyrant, in many popular ballads.

In 1542, James's realm was beset by belligerent moves made by the English king, Henry VIII, who feared

James's support of the French military. In October, 1542, after an invasion by the English duke of Norfolk, James gathered an army at Lauder; the army, bent on chasing Norfolk into Northumberland, soon disbanded, however. Another army was mustered, in order to invade the western border with England. The Scottish army was soundly defeated at Solway Moss on November 24, 1542. James V, dejected by the humiliating loss, died several weeks later, leaving his infant daughter, Mary, as his sole heir. James's death came at a time when Scotland was unstable politically, with James Hamilton, the earl of Arran, and Mary of Guise, competing for control of the government during the period of the infant Mary's minority.

SIGNIFICANCE

James V was successful in keeping the often fractious Scottish nobility relatively tranquil, despite his frequent taxation of his greater subjects. Though James was not overly generous in distributing the fruits of his financial success among his supporters, he did succeed in creating a court in which the culture of the Renaissance could continue to develop.

Through his effective fiscal policies and his cultivation of his realm's alliance with France, James managed to continue his father's policy of giving Scotland the prestige requisite for playing a key role in international affairs.

James also succeeded in resisting the pressures of the Reformation, keeping Scotland loyal predominantly to Catholicism, a policy that his wife, Mary of Guise, would pursue as regent, though his widow ultimately failed to stop the Reformation from gaining ascendancy in Scotland.

James's numerous illegitimate children—the fruits of at least six mistresses—would go on to contribute to the turbulent atmosphere of the reign of Mary, Queen of Scots, ensuring that his daughter, too, would face a political landscape peopled with competing claimants.

—*Randy P. Schiff*

FURTHER READING

Barrell, A. D. M. *Medieval Scotland.* New York: Cambridge University Press, 2000. Broad survey of the history of medieval Scotland, covering events from the earliest recorded history to the Reformation. Includes detailed discussion of the entirety of James V's reign. Challenges the conventional view of James as vindictive and arbitrary, details James's domestic programs, and details the background for his disastrous struggle with Henry VIII. Maps, genealogical tables.

Bingham, Caroline. *James V: King of Scots, 1512-1542*. London: Collins, 1971. A full biographical treatment of James V, featuring plates and genealogical tables.

Fradenburg, Louise Olga. *City, Marriage, Tournament: Arts of Rule in Late Medieval Scotland*. Madison: University of Wisconsin Press, 1991. Discusses the performative nature of political power in late medieval Scotland, analyzing the context in which James V and earlier kings exercised power. Includes plates.

Schama, Simon. *A History of Britain: At the Edge of the World? 3000 BC-AD 1603*. New York: Hyperion, 2000. A broad survey of British history through the sixteenth century, featuring numerous color plates, maps, and genealogical tables. Offers in-depth discussion of the background of James's conflict with England, pursuing James's resistance of the Reformation into the regency of Mary of Guise. Color maps, bibliography, index.

Thomas, Andrea. *Princelie Majestie: The Court of James V of Scotland, 1528-1542*. East Linton, Scotland: Tuckwell Press, 2004. Revises scholarly neglect of James V's patronage of the arts, focusing on the cultivation of various art forms in James's Scotland. Color plates.

Williams, Janet Hadley, ed. *Stewart Style, 1513-1542: Essays on the Court of James V*. East Linton, Scotland: Tuckwell Press, 1996. A collection of essays focusing on various aspects of cultural and political life in James's Scotland, surveying the entirety of his reign. Illustrations, bibliography, index.

SEE ALSO: George Buchanan; Francis I; Henry VII; Henry VIII; James III; James IV; Mary, Queen of Scots; Mary of Guise.

RELATED ARTICLE in *Great Events from History: The Renaissance & Early Modern Era, 1454-1600*: August 22, 1513-July 6, 1560: Anglo-Scottish Wars.

FRANCISCO JIMÉNEZ DE CISNEROS
Spanish scholar-official

Jiménez worked to maintain a united Spain at the beginning of the sixteenth century. He founded the University of Alcalá de Henares and sponsored the famous Polyglot Bible.

BORN: 1436; Torrelaguna, Castile (now in Spain)
DIED: November 8, 1517; Roa, Spain
ALSO KNOWN AS: Gonzalo Jiménez de Cisneros
AREAS OF ACHIEVEMENT: Government and politics, religion and theology, education

EARLY LIFE

Gonzalo Jiménez de Cisneros, the baptismal name of the future Francisco Jiménez de Cisneros (frahn-SEES-koh hee-MAY-nays day sees-NAY-rohs), was the first son of a family of esteemed lineage and humble means. His father, Alonso Jiménez de Cisneros, was trained in the law and made a modest living as collector and administrator of the papal tithe in the town of Torrelaguna. Young Gonzalo received his earliest training in Latin and reading at the household of an uncle, Alvaro, a priest in Roa. He then traveled to Alcalá and continued his studies of Latin and humanities in a school operated by the Franciscan order. He entered Spain's prestigious University of Salamanca in 1450 and remained there until he completed a degree in canon and civil law. He also became well versed in the philosophical currents of the day, showing particular affinity for biblical scholarship. Jiménez then traveled to Rome in search of more promising opportunities. In Italy, Jiménez made a living as a lawyer, representing cases before consistorial courts. He left Rome in 1465 and returned to his birthplace to care for his recently widowed mother.

LIFE'S WORK

Aside from his ordination and legal experience, Jiménez's most promising professional prospect on his return was the hope of fulfilling the terms of a *letrae expectativae*, a promissory papal letter appointing its possessor to any expected vacancy in a particular diocese. Jiménez had to wait years for a suitable opportunity. He lived in Torrelaguna until he received news of a vacancy in Úceda, in the diocese of Toledo. The Archpriest of Úceda had recently died, and Jiménez made a claim to that benefice in 1473. His ambitions were frustrated, however, when the powerful archbishop of Toledo, Alfonso Carrillo, blocked his candidacy. Jiménez's stubborn refusal to relinquish his right to Úceda so enraged Carrillo that he had Jiménez imprisoned. Jiménez was jailed for six years and was released in 1479, when influential relatives pleaded on his behalf. Once out of prison, Jiménez took possession of the Úceda post.

By now in his forties, Jiménez would soon enter the most productive and important stage of his career. He had the good fortune to come under the protection of the archbishop of Seville, Cardinal Pedro de Mendoza, and under his tutelage, Jiménez moved to the chaplaincy of the Cathedral of Sigüenza in the archdiocese of Seville. Mendoza, an enemy and rival of Carrillo, was the scion of one of Spain's most influential and accomplished families and a political ally and confidant of Queen Isabella I of Castile. Jiménez's advancement was now assured.

Mendoza promoted Jiménez once again, to the post of general vicar of Sigüenza, and even greater opportunities opened up when Mendoza succeeded Carrillo to the see of Toledo in 1483. Jiménez, however, opted for a different path. After his mother's death in 1486, he decided to set aside secular concerns and enter the Franciscan order. He took vows in 1486, changed his name from Gonzalo to Francisco—in honor of the order's founder—and began a new life devoted to prayer, fasting, and contemplation. The physical descriptions and portraits of Jiménez that have survived depict his slight build, weather-beaten skin, sharp profile, and thin body, features believed to have resulted from his rigid adherence to the physical rigors of monastic life.

Despite his attempt to withdraw from public life, Jiménez played a central role in the events that shaped the last quarter of the fifteenth century. His belated and somewhat surprising rise as a public figure began when, at the recommendation of Mendoza, he was invited to the royal court to serve as Isabella's confessor. Isabella became devoted to her confessor. In the fall of 1495, in a bold move, she selected Jiménez to the archbishopric of Toledo. Mendoza had died earlier that year, and Isabella secured papal approval to appoint Jiménez to preside over Spain's wealthiest and most important ecclesiastical see. She had to defend and impose her will over her husband, who wanted the prestigious post reserved for his illegitimate son. Jiménez accepted this great honor without hesitation and proceeded to reorganize the archiepiscopal see to reflect his religious convictions, tastes, and predilections.

A story associated with this period of Jiménez's career merits repetition. When Jiménez moved into his new quarters at the archiepiscopal palace in Toledo, the story goes, he ordered his staff to live, dress, and eat with the simplicity and austerity of Franciscan monks. Believing that such external signs of humility would undermine the prestige of the see, members of his staff appealed to the pope, asking him to help persuade Jiménez to recon-

sider. It seems that Jiménez heeded papal advice rather well. The Toledean ecclesiastical palace became once again the model of elegance and splendor it had always been.

Jiménez undertook a series of building projects such as the reconstruction of the main altar of the cathedral, contracting for that purpose the most accomplished architects, sculptors, and artists of the period. He also commissioned plans for the construction of his proudest achievement, the new University at Alcalá de Henares, which he foresaw as a center for Humanistic learning. He entrusted the project to Pedro Gumiel, after receiving approval in a papal bull issued in April, 1499. The plans would come to fruition when several of the university's many colleges opened in 1508.

A related project was Jiménez's wish to prepare the world's first edition of a Polyglot Bible, intended to contain parallel, annotated Hebrew, Aramaic, Greek, and Latin versions of the Old Testament, and a Greek and Latin version of the New Testament. Jiménez gathered lexicographers and biblical scholars at Alcalá and purchased and borrowed an impressive number of biblical manuscripts from libraries throughout Europe for his scholars to consult and compare. The resulting six-volume work, known as the Alcalá or Complutensian Polyglot Bible, was printed in 1517 and distributed for the first time three years later.

Jiménez's interest in learning, evident during his years at Salamanca and in his sponsorship of the university and important works of scholarship, contrasts with his harsh treatment of the Muslim population of Granada. According to the terms of Granada's surrender in 1492, Spain's new subjects were assured freedom of religion. Ferdinand II and Isabella I hoped, however, that all Spanish Muslims would eventually renounce their faith and adopt Christianity. Isabella had appointed her new confessor, Hernando de Talavera, to oversee this transition. In 1499, impatient with the pace of Talavera's methods, Jiménez traveled to Granada to inject fervor and zeal into the process. When the Muslim majority protested his intrusion, Jiménez retaliated by ordering all Arabic books, sacred and secular, burned in public squares. He spared three hundred medical works, a collection destined for the bookshelves at Alcalá de Henares.

Jiménez's harsh methods backfired and caused a number of serious and violent uprisings. He is held responsible for the unnecessary chaos, bloodshed, and distrust that ensued and for the wanton destruction of precious and irreplaceable Muslim books and manuscripts. This entire episode served to tarnish his image as a Humanist and lover of learning, although it did not affect his relationship with his patron, Isabella. He remained her trusted and respected adviser until her death in 1504.

Isabella's death produced a political crisis in Spain by jeopardizing the partnership of the two crowns, Castile and Aragon, which made up the nation. The union between the two had come about through marriage and personal agreement, and the death of one of the partners threatened this fragile arrangement. The question of inheritance was, then, crucial.

Isabella's choice of heir for the crown of Castile was her third daughter, Joan, who in 1496 had married Philip of Habsburg—archduke of Austria and son of Emperor Maximilian of the Holy Roman Empire. The couple lived in Flanders. Isabella, recognizing her daughter's incapacity to rule—Joan was emotionally unstable and is also known as "Joan the Mad"—intended for the couple to rule jointly and to be succeeded by their first son, Charles. Isabella had also appointed her husband Ferdinand regent; he was expected to govern the country until Joan and Philip made their way to Spain. Rivalry between Philip and Ferdinand soon developed, however, and each side tried to recruit supporters from the always quarrelsome Castilian nobility.

Joan and Philip arrived in Castile in 1505, but their rule was a brief one; Philip died mysteriously in the fall of 1506, and Joan's mental state took a turn for the worse. Jiménez, in the absence of Ferdinand, who had removed himself to Aragon and then to Italy, assumed the regency until Ferdinand's return in 1507. As regent, he acted to protect the interests of Castile, while keeping in check the ambitions of a number of restless courtiers. That same year, Jiménez was elevated to cardinal by the Holy See, and Ferdinand conferred on him the title of inquisitor general of Castile.

Jiménez the statesman and clergyman was also, for a brief time, a soldier. Using the rich rents of his archbishopric of Toledo, he persuaded Ferdinand to order a military campaign against the North African port of Oran, a favorite refuge of pirates who raided Spanish ships and ports. Jiménez planned and executed the military campaign that captured the city in 1509. Oran was to remain in Spanish hands until the eighteenth century.

After his military triumph, Jiménez returned to Alcalá de Henares to oversee the opening of the university and to attempt to recoup funds spent on the campaign. He remained in close contact with Ferdinand and might have been instrumental in persuading the king to cede the crowns of Aragon and of Navarre (annexed by Ferdinand in 1512) to his grandchild Charles, as Isabella had done

with Castile. Ferdinand's original choice had been his second grandchild and namesake who, unlike Charles, had been reared in Spain.

When Ferdinand died in 1516, Jiménez assumed the regency of Castile for a second time, in anticipation of the arrival and majority of Charles, who had remained in Flanders after his parents' return to Spain. Charles arrived on September 19, 1517, and was poised to claim the throne of a strong and united state composed of Castile, Aragon, and Navarre. The young king had intended to dismiss Jiménez, but Jiménez died on November 8, 1517, before receiving official notification of his dismissal. He was buried in the College of Saint Ildefonso at the University of Alcalá de Henares, and a magnificent marble monument was built over his grave two years later. The college fell into ill repair after the university moved to Madrid in 1836, and in 1857, the cardinal's remains were transferred to the Church of San Justo y Pastor in the city of Alcalá.

SIGNIFICANCE

Francisco Jiménez de Cisneros was, in many ways, the quintessential Spaniard of the Renaissance, embodying all the conflicts and contradictions of the period. Personally and intellectually devoted to rigid Christian observance, he nevertheless displayed great interest in scholarship and learning. He at once persecuted Muslims and collected their medical works. As inquisitor general, he investigated and intimidated some Jewish converts to Christianity, while employing others in his biblical project. A Franciscan by choice and training, he was committed to a life of austerity; yet his personal disregard for material comforts did not interfere with his sense of duty and the demands of the high office he occupied. As archbishop of Toledo, he was known to wear the coarse Franciscan hair shirt under the splendid robes of the office. Eager to devote himself to a life of contemplation, he led armies into battle more effectively than he led his own Franciscan monks to accept reform.

Jiménez's greatest achievement, however, might very well be his years of loyal service to Isabella and, after her death, to Ferdinand and the couple's heirs. As a statesman, he was dutiful and loyal, placing the interests of his patrons above his own and leading a life above reproach. While he did not introduce any significant new policies, through his patient and devoted service, he made possible the continued union of Castile and Aragon, which made Charles the most powerful king of his age.

—*Clara Estow*

FURTHER READING

Boruchoff, David A., ed. *Isabel la Católica, Queen of Castile: Critical Essays*. New York: Palgrave Macmillan, 2003. Anthology of essays that seek to penetrate the carefully crafted public self-image of Isabella to gain insight into the actual woman. Includes photographic plates, illustrations, maps, bibliographic references, and index.

Edwards, John. *The Spanish Inquisition*. Stroud, Gloucestershire, England: Tempus, 1999. Analysis of the motivations behind the Inquisition, its political and religious functions, and its cost in lives and suffering. Includes photographic plates, illustrations, maps, bibliographic references, and index.

Lyell, James P. R. *Cardinal Ximenes*. London: Grafton, 1917. A brief account of the cardinal's career, in which Lyell attributes to Jiménez a greater degree of cunning and deception than do most of his other biographers.

Lynch, John. *Spain, 1516-1598: From Nation State to World Empire*. Cambridge, Mass.: B. Blackwell, 1991. A serious and academic treatment of the first century of rule by the house of Austria; an excellent survey of all aspects of Spanish society during the 1500's.

Mariéjol, Jean Hippolyte. *The Spain of Ferdinand and Isabella*. Edited and translated by Benjamin Keen. New Brunswick, N.J.: Rutgers University Press, 1961. A favorable account of the role of Jiménez in the reign of the Catholic monarchs. The author praises Jiménez for undertaking the publication of the Polyglot Bible yet criticizes him for not requiring a more critical approach toward the material on the part of those who participated in the project.

Merton, Reginald. *Cardinal Ximenes and the Making of Spain*. London: Kegan Paul, Trench, Trubner, 1934. A fairly detailed biography of Jiménez. Merton believes that King Ferdinand and Jiménez were essentially rivals. In this account, Jiménez emerges as a paragon of virtue and statesmanship.

Prescott, William H. *History of the Reign of Ferdinand and Isabella, the Catholic*. 3 vols. 15th ed. Boston: Phillips, Sampson, 1859. Reprint. Abridged by C. Harvey Gardiner. Carbondale: Southern Illinois University Press, 1962. The third volume of this classic work is devoted to a detailed narrative account of the final period of the reign of the Catholic monarchs. Prescott, a liberal thinker, is critical of Jiménez's dogmatism and of his religious bigotry, assigning part of the blame to the society and period in which Jiménez lived.

Rummel, Erika. *Jiménez de Cisneros: On the Threshold of Spain's Golden Age*. Tempe: Arizona Center for Medieval and Renaissance Studies, 1999. Concise survey of Cisneros's life and influence, with a final chapter summarizing his posthumous image. Includes genealogical table, two appendices, bibliography of works cited, and index.

Starkie, Walter. *Grand Inquisitor*. London: Hodder & Stoughton, 1940. The author, whose interest in Spain is wide-ranging, approaches Jiménez as a cultural figure who embodies certain qualities associated with the national character, such as faith and the tragic sense of life.

SEE ALSO: Alexander VI; Charles V; Ferdinand II and Isabella I; Henry IV of Castile; Maximilian I.

RELATED ARTICLES in *Great Events from History: The Renaissance & Early Modern Era, 1454-1600*: Beginning c. 1495: Reform of the Spanish Church; January 23, 1516: Charles I Ascends the Throne of Spain.

SAINT JOHN OF THE CROSS
Spanish religious leader

Saint John of the Cross contributed to the renewal of monastic life and to the development of mystical theology during the golden age of the Catholic Reformation. His most lasting contribution has been to Western mysticism.

BORN: June 24, 1542; Fontiveros, Spain
DIED: December 14, 1591; Úbeda, Spain
ALSO KNOWN AS: Juan de Yepes y Álvarez
AREAS OF ACHIEVEMENT: Church reform, monasticism

EARLY LIFE

Juan de Yepes y Álvarez (later known as Saint John of the Cross) was born in a town of five thousand inhabitants situated on the Castilian tableland. His father, Gonzalo de Yepes, was the son of a prosperous local silk merchant. Gonzalo was disinherited for marrying Catalina Álvarez, an impoverished and orphaned Toledan, apprenticed to a weaver in Fontiveros. John was the third son born to this union. The death of his father following a prolonged illness when John was only two left John, his mother, and his siblings in dire poverty. Seeking help, Catalina left Fontiveros, going initially to the province of Toledo but later settling in Medina del Campo, a city of thirty thousand.

In Medina, there was a doctrine, or catechism, school. As much an orphanage as an educational institution for the poor, this school received John as a student. Children were fed, clothed, catechized, and given a rudimentary education. Apprenticeship in various trades was also part of the program of the doctrine school. Little is known of the four trades that John tried, except that his efforts were unsuccessful. Since in later life John was fond of painting and carving, his failure, perhaps, was one of premature exposure rather than of aptitude. John was next attached to the Hospital de la Concepción, where he worked as a nurse, begged alms for the poor, and continued his studies. Academic success caused him to be enrolled at the Jesuit College, situated barely two hundred yards from the hospital. Founded in 1551, this school enrolled forty students at the time John was in attendance, probably from 1559 to 1563. John's teachers recalled his passionate enthusiasm for books. With a good education in the humanities, John in 1563 found his life's vocation, taking the dark brown habit and white cloak of the Carmelites.

LIFE'S WORK

At the age of twenty-one, John entered the small community of the Carmelite brothers in Medina, then a fellowship of perhaps six members. The Order of Our Lady of Mount Carmel had been founded four centuries earlier, in 1156, in Palestine by Saint Berthold as one of extreme asceticism and of great devotion to Mary. By the sixteenth century, it admitted female as well as male members. The so-called Original or Primitive Rule of 1209 had been relaxed, the order following a Mitigated Observance.

Why John selected this order is not known. Perhaps it was his love of contemplation, his devotion to the Virgin, or his practice of extreme asceticism that attracted him to the Carmelites. John of Yepes now took the name Fray Juan de Santo Matia (Brother John of Saint Mathias), though, five years later, when, on November 28, 1568, he professed the Carmelite Primitive Rule, he would again change his name to Fray Juan de la Cruz (Brother John of the Cross). As a monastic reformer, John was to make a lasting contribution to Christianity.

Following his profession as a Carmelite, John continued his education at the College of San Andres, a school for sixteen years attached to the famed University of Salamanca. A good Latinist and an excellent grammarian, John took classes in the college of arts at Salamanca from 1564 to 1567. Perhaps seven thousand students were matriculated at the University of Salamanca at that time. Taught by a faculty known throughout Spain and the Habsburg lands, the young monk next turned his attention to theology, attending lectures in divinity in 1567-1568. At Salamanca, John was deeply immersed in the philosophy of Aristotle and the theology of Saint Thomas Aquinas. Concurrently, John was a master of students at San Andres.

Following his ordination as a priest in 1567, John met Saint Teresa of Ávila. Daughter of a noble Spanish family, Teresa had entered the Carmelite Convent of the Incarnation (Mitigated Observance) at Ávila in 1535. Teresa had become persuaded that discipline was too relaxed and that there ought to be a return to the Primitive Rule of the Carmelites. Her followers were called Discalced Carmelites, in opposition to the Calced Carmelites, who continued to follow the Mitigated rather than the Primitive Rule. Within a year of his meeting with the remarkable Mother Teresa, John was committed to the so-called Teresian Reforms of the Carmelite Order. For that reason, in November, 1568, John was made professor of the Primitive Rule of the Carmelites at Duruelo. Resolving "to separate himself from the world and hide himself in God," John sought a strictly contemplative life. That wish was never granted, for John was often sought as a counselor and confessor (for the laity and the religious) and as a popular and persuasive preacher.

Soon John became subprior, then novice master, and finally rector of a new house of studies founded at Alcalá. This was a creative time for John, who was able to integrate the intellectual and the spiritual life and who could combine contemplation with active service, including becoming Teresa's confessor after 1571. John found "the delights which God lets souls taste in contemplation," but he was advised by Teresa that "a great storm of trials" was on the horizon.

Disputes between the Carmelites who followed the Primitive Rule and those who held to the Mitigated Observance caused John to become a focus of attention. Following an initial imprisonment in 1576, John was seized on December 2, 1577, by some of the Calced Carmelites and taken to Toledo, where he was commanded by superiors to repent of his reforms. This was yet another step in the antireformist policies that had prevailed in the Carmelite Order since a general chapter meeting in 1575.

Because John refused to renounce the reforms, he was imprisoned for some nine months in a small cell. There was only one small opening for light and air. John's jailers were motivated by "vindictiveness . . . mingled with religious zeal," for they believed that his reforms of the order were a very great crime and revealed a stubborn pride and insubordination. John accepted his imprisonment, with its insults, slanders, calumnies, physical sufferings, and agonies of soul as a further labor by God to purify and refine his faith.

In August, 1578, John escaped from his captors and fled to southern Spain. The separation of the two branches of the Carmelite Order, the Calced and the Discalced, occurred in 1579-1580. John became the rector of a Discalced Carmelite college in Baeza in Andalusia, serving also as an administrator in the Reformed Carmelite Order, being prior of Granada in 1582 and of Segovia in 1588. Vicar provincial of his order's southern region, by 1588 John was major definitor and was a member of the governing body of the society.

John's contemporary, Eliseo de los Martires, described him as "a man in body of medium size" and one of "grave and venerable countenance." His complexion was "wheaty," or "somewhat swarthy," and his face was

Saint John of the Cross. (Library of Congress)

filled with "good features." Normally John wore a mustache and was often fully bearded. Dressed in "an old, narrow, short, rough habit," one so rough it was said that "the cloak seemed to be made of goat-hair," John reminded many of a latter-day John the Baptist. John impressed those he met with his purity of character, his intensity of spirit, his austerity of life, his profound humility, his fondness for simplicity, and his honesty and directness in speech. Contemporary biographers also recalled his sense of humor, noting that he delighted in making his friars laugh, often sprinkling his spiritual conversation with amusing stories.

Perhaps John's greatest legacy to the world community is his writing about the interior life. During his trials, tribulations, and travels, John wrote of his encounters with God. These extensive treatises on the mystical life are a unique combination of his poems and his commentaries on those poems. *Cántico espiritual* (1581; *A Spiritual Canticle of the Soul*, 1862), part of which was said to have been composed while John was on his knees in prayer, is such a synthesis of poetry and commentary.

That poetry is both didactic and symbolic, practical and devotional.

A Spiritual Canticle of the Soul describes the ancient threefold route of the soul to God. One moves from purgation (or confession of sin, the emptying of the self) to illumination (or instruction, revelation of God, filling with the divine) and then to union or perfection (going beyond a sense of separation to one of complete integration with God). This ongoing colloquy of Christ and the soul draws on the rich imagery of courtship and love, starting with the soul's search for the Beloved, continuing to an initial meeting, then describing the perfect union, and concluding with a discussion of the poignant desire for an everlasting intimacy with the Eternal, a longing that can only be fulfilled in eternity.

La subida del Monte Carmelo (1578; *The Ascent of Mount Carmel*, 1862) is also a discussion of how the soul can attain mystical union with God. The journey to God contains a "Dark Night," because the spirit must quite literally mortify, or put to death, sensory experience and sensible knowledge and then maintain itself by pure faith. Following such purgations, as well as those that come from the faith experience itself, the soul enters into a transforming union with God. This is truly a passion, for it combines both intense suffering and ecstatic pleasure, the two components of overwhelming love. In *Llama de amor viva* (1581; *Living Flame of Love*, 1862), the spiritual marriage, or divine union, is further described.

Though he longed only for contemplation, John once more was caught up in controversy. In 1591, he found himself banished to Andalusia. After some time in solitary life, John became extremely ill, going to Úbeda for medical attention. Following extreme pain, John died at Úbeda on December 14, 1591. In his dying moments, John requested the reading of the "Canticle of Canticles," the moving love poem of the Old Testament. Interpreting it as an allegory of the soul's romance of God, John commented, "What precious pearls."

SIGNIFICANCE

While controversial during his lifetime, Saint John of the Cross was commended by the Catholic Church, following his death, as both a saint and teacher. Beatified by Pope Clement X in 1675, John was canonized in 1726 by Benedict XIII. In 1926, Pius XI declared him a doctor of the church, one of perhaps thirty Catholics deemed a theologian of both outstanding intellectual merit and personal sanctity and to be received universally with appreciation.

John surely was a mighty doctor of the church, embodying the profound spirituality of the Catholic Reformation in Spain, drawing on the same religious energies that inspired Teresa; Ignatius of Loyola, the founder of the Society of Jesus; and Francis Xavier, a missionary-evangelist of Asia. He will forever be one of the treasures of the Roman Catholic tradition.

As reformer, master, saint, doctor, poet, and seer, John transcended the limits of any one country or creed. His significance is greater even than that of enriching the piety of Roman Catholicism and of enhancing the literature of his native Spain. John's profound mysticism causes him to be ranked alongside the great religious seekers of all human history—with the saints of Hinduism, the sages of Buddhism, the Sufis of Islam, the seekers of Daoism, the teachers of Confucianism, the visionaries of Protestantism, and the holy men and women of Orthodoxy and Oriental Christianity. As such, John of the Cross is one of the major figures of world religion, combining intellectual rigor with a vigorous work ethic, wrapping both in a profound and appealing spirituality.

—*C. George Fry*

FURTHER READING

Bruno de Jesus-Marie. *St. John of the Cross*. Edited by Benedict Zimmerman, with an introduction by Jacques Maritain. London: Sheed & Ward, 1936. Reprint. New York: Sheed & Ward, 1957. This extensively documented 495-page study by a Roman Catholic priest attempts to do justice to John as a reformer, theologian, and mystic, drawing on the insights of philosophy, history, and biography. The central thesis is that John was not simply a "Quietistic Mystic" who had mastered the interior life, but that he was also an "Activistic Churchman" who had a powerful impact on the external world of sixteenth century Catholicism.

Crisógono de Jesús. *The Life of St. John of the Cross*. Translated by Kathleen Pond. New York: Harper and Brothers, 1958. A thoroughly documented biography of John both as a person and as a monk. Illustrations, charts, notes, and references make this a useful starting point for further research.

Cugno, Alain. *Saint John of the Cross: Reflections on Mystical Experience*. Translated by Barbara Wall. New York: Seabury Press, 1979. This concise study in 153 pages contends that John was perhaps the greatest mystic produced by Christianity. Originally written for the University of Tours, this text attempts to understand John from a philosophical rather than a theological or mystical viewpoint. In six succinct and tightly written chapters, it explores such major themes in the philosophy of religion as the absence of God, the meaning of mysticism, the role of desire in religion, and the doctrine of the Kingdom of God.

Frost, Bede. *Saint John of the Cross, 1542-1591, Doctor of Divine Love: An Introduction to His Philosophy, Theology, and Spirituality.* London: Hodder & Stoughton, 1937. This classic study of John's thought attempts to do justice to the complexity and variety of the saint's writings. The author admits the inherent twofold difficulty of exploring John's thinking: mystical experiences in and of themselves are incommunicable and language proves inadequate to the description of such experiences, without the compounded problem of translation from Spanish to English.

Green, John D. *A Strange Tongue: Tradition, Language, and the Appropriation of Mystical Experience in Late Fourteenth-Century England and Sixteenth-Century Spain.* Dudley, Mass.: Peeters, 2002. A study of the Christian mystical notion of the "discernment of spirits," that is, the recognition of authentically divine inward promptings or stirrings, in the writings of St. John of the Cross, Ignatius of Loyola, Julian of Norwich, and Walter Hilton. Includes bibliographic references.

Howells, Edward. *John of the Cross and Teresa of Avila: Mystical Knowing and Selfhood.* New York: Crossroad, 2002. Study of the theology and philosophy of mind put forward by John and Teresa, demonstrating and analyzing their notion that the dynamic nature of the Holy Trinity bridges the gap between interior subjective experience and exterior objective reality. Includes bibliographic references and index.

John of the Cross, Saint. *The Ascent of Mount Carmel.* Translated by David Lewis, with a preface by Benedict Zimmerman. London: Thomas Baker, 1928. This indexed edition of John's major mystical work is useful as an introduction to a primary source for his thought. Indexed both by topic and by Scriptural references, the volume facilitates both the study of selected topics in John's piety and the identification of biblical sources for his themes.

Maio, Eugene A. *St. John of the Cross: The Imagery of Eros.* Madrid, Spain: Playor, 1973. In brief compass, the author introduces the reader to the mystical tradition of love, a theme central to John's life and thought. Chapters relate John to the poetic and mystical traditions of Spain, examine the role of Neoplatonism in Christian thought, and then explore the dynamics of John's spirituality. Contains an extensive bibliography.

May, Gerald G. *The Dark Night of the Soul: A Psychiatrist Explores the Connection Between Darkness and Spiritual Growth.* New York: HarperSanFrancisco, 2004. Psychological study of Saint John of the Cross and Teresa of Ávila, illuminating the positive and transformative aspects of spiritual darkness. Includes map, bibliographic references, and index.

Sencourt, Robert. *Carmelite and Poet: A Framed Portrait of St. John of the Cross, with His Poems in Spanish.* New York: Macmillan, 1944. This illustrated biography, in 253 pages, with an appended anthology of John's verse in Spanish, examines John from the standpoint of literature, providing the reader with "both the soul of poetry and the poetry of the soul." Extensive annotations compensate for the lack of a bibliography.

Thompson, Colin. *St. John of the Cross: Songs in the Night.* Washington, D.C.: Catholic University of America Press, 2003. Study of John's lyric poetry; devotes a full chapter to each of the major works, which are cited in the original Spanish with accompanying English translations. Includes bibliographic references and index.

SEE ALSO: Saint Catherine of Genoa; Saint Philip Neri; Saint Teresa of Ávila.

RELATED ARTICLE in *Great Events from History: The Renaissance & Early Modern Era, 1454-1600:* Beginning c. 1495: Reform of the Spanish Church.

JOHN II
King of Portugal (r. 1481-1495)

John II resumed exploration that took Portuguese seamen to the southern tip of Africa, confirming a southern route to the Indian Ocean. He also negotiated the Treaty of Tordesillas, thereby assuring future Portuguese preeminence in Indian trade and in Brazil. He is also recognized for his ruthless consolidation of royal authority by curbing the power of the Portuguese nobility.

BORN: March 3, 1455; Lisbon, Portugal
DIED: October 25, 1495; Alvor, Portugal
ALSO KNOWN AS: The Perfect Prince
AREAS OF ACHIEVEMENT: Government and politics, exploration, geography

EARLY LIFE

The only surviving son of King Afonso V, John II was immersed in Iberian politics from an early age. The Portuguese dynasty of Aviz was relatively young (John II was the grandson of its founder, John I), and it had been seeking to establish itself and to expand its territory.

John accompanied his father, King Afonso, a devout Christian, on North African crusades that conquered Arzila in Morocco. For his participation in this conquest, John was granted a knighthood. Afonso also had aspirations to the throne of Castile. In 1475, he went to war with Castile, challenging Isabella's claim to that throne. His son, acting as regent while his father was at war, sent troops to boost the Portuguese forces. They were, nonetheless, defeated, ending any hope of laying claim to the Spanish throne.

Early experiences with Iberian politics made John suspicious of the ultimate goals of Ferdinand of Aragon and Isabella of Castile. Although relinquishing claim to the crown of Castile through the Treaty of Alcáçovas (1479), Portugal gained formal acknowledgement that it had sole fishing and trading rights along the entire west African coast.

John II admired the work of his great-uncle, Prince Henry the Navigator, who had encouraged seamen to develop the skills and equipment necessary to sail into the Atlantic. His interest in voyages of trade and exploration increased after 1474, when his father granted him control of trade with African Guinea and the responsibility for Portuguese explorations.

LIFE'S WORK

John II is remembered first for having consolidated royal power in Portugal. It was his ability to subdue the nobility that later earned him recognition as the perfect prince, a ruler who embodied those political qualities Niccolò Machiavelli described in *Il principe* (wr. 1513, pb. 1532; *The Prince*, 1640). Learning of conspiracies against his authority, he did not hesitate to make examples of recalcitrant aristocrats. He was responsible for putting to death the duke of Bragança and also his brother-in-law, the duke of Viseu. With the nobility safely under royal control, John II turned to a rising merchant class for support in his most significant ventures, voyages of exploration in the Atlantic.

Like his great-uncle Prince Henry, John II became interested in the science of navigation. Shortly after coming to power, he convened a group of experts in mathematics to establish a scientific method for determining latitude by observing the sun. As Portuguese seamen pressed closer to the equator and then into southern equatorial waters, they found it increasingly difficult to rely on the guiding presence of the North Star. Calculation of latitude based on the sun thus allowed sailors to fix their position more accurately. The work of this group of mathematicians resulted in the early sixteenth century publication of the first European manual of navigation and the first nautical almanac.

Taking advantage of Portugal's right to explore and trade along the African coast, John II granted the right to Portuguese merchants to establish fortified trading posts in the region. In 1482, the fortress of São Jorge da Mina was constructed on the Guinea coast in order to protect Portuguese trade in slaves, gold, pepper, ivory, and palm oil, marking the southernmost point in the known world.

The king also outfitted caravels at crown expense to pursue voyages of discovery. What he hoped most to discover was a route that would make possible sea trade with India. He also hoped to make contact with the mythical Prester John, a Christian African king who, King John hoped, would facilitate trade with India. As a result of these Crown-sponsored voyages, Diogo Cão's expedition arrived at the mouth of the Congo River in 1483. Disappointed that Cão had not found a passageway around Africa into the Indian Ocean, John II commissioned the expedition of Bartolomeu Dias in 1487. Portuguese sailors on this voyage journeyed to the southernmost tip of Africa and realized there was indeed a sea route from the Atlantic into the Indian Ocean, providing access to the rich eastern trade.

During King John's reign, a number of Italian seamen settled in Portugal. Among them was the Genoese Christopher Columbus, who arrived in Portugal in 1476 and married a Portuguese woman. In 1484, he sought funding from the king to outfit a fleet that would seek a route to the Indies by sailing west rather than south. After consulting with some of his key maritime advisers, John II became convinced that Columbus's calculations underestimated the circumference of the globe; he therefore declined to fund the expedition.

Sailing for Spain in 1492, however, Columbus did indeed make landfall in a region he believed to be the East Indies. The Spanish kings quickly sought a papal bull granting them control over this newly discovered area. Pope Alexander VI, himself a Spaniard, issued the papal bull *Inter Caetera* (1493), giving to the monarchs of Spain authority over new lands discovered to the west of a meridian drawn 100 leagues west of the Cape Verde Islands. John, fearing this would give the Spaniards eventual authority over land and islands the Portuguese believed had come under their control in the Treaty of Alcáçovas, lobbied hard with the Spanish monarchs to establish another treaty placing the meridian line farther west. He succeeded in getting Ferdinand and Isabella to agree to a line 370 leagues west of the Cape Verde

Islands in the Treaty of Tordesillas (1494), which protected Portuguese rights to the more important sea lanes later used in the India trade. The treaty also allowed them to claim the South American territory that became Brazil.

SIGNIFICANCE

John II reestablished Portuguese power after his father's military loss to Spain and his attempt to claim the crown of Castile. By turning his attention to the Atlantic trade and Portuguese rights to that trade, John II funded the research into new navigational techniques and the voyages themselves, which demonstrated that trade with the East was possible by sailing around the southern tip of Africa. His savvy statesmanship and suspicion of Spanish ambitions allowed him to formulate the treaty that made possible Portuguese control of trade with the East during the first half of the sixteenth century.

—Joan E. Meznar

FURTHER READING

Anderson, James. *The History of Portugal*. Westport, Conn.: Greenwood Press, 2000. Succinct description of politics in the age of exploration, with a focus on the rise and fall of dynasties.

Catz, Rebecca. *Christopher Columbus and the Portuguese, 1476-1498*. Westport, Conn.: Greenwood Press, 1993. Describes the years Columbus lived in Portugal and the Portuguese influence on the admiral who claimed part of the Americas for Spain.

Livermore, H. V. *A History of Portugal*. 2d ed. Cambridge, England: Cambridge University Press, 1976. Classic discussion of Portuguese political history and an excellent overview of court intrigue in the fifteenth and sixteenth centuries.

Oliveira Marques, A. H. de. *History of Portugal*. New York: Columbia University Press, 1972. Sets the politics of the period into a cultural and demographic context, with an emphasis on broad changes in scientific ideas and in the population of Portugal.

Parry, J. H. *The Age of Reconnaissance: Discovery, Exploration, and Settlement, 1450 to 1650*. Berkeley: University of California Press, 1981. Describes John's instrumental role in the Portuguese voyages of exploration and the competition with Spain that resulted from Columbus's plan to reach the East by sailing west.

Russell, P. E. *Portugal, Spain, and the African Atlantic, 1343-1490: Chivalry and Crusade from John of Gaunt to Henry the Navigator and Beyond*. Brookfield, Vt.: Ashgate, 1995. Includes analysis of a con-

John II. (Hulton|Archive by Getty Images)

temporary account describing the visit made to Portugal by an African king during the reign of John II.

Russell-Wood, A. J. R. *Portuguese Empire, 1415-1808: A World on the Move*. Baltimore: Johns Hopkins University Press, 1998. A history of the expansion of the Portuguese empire, with particular attention to the individuals involved in the voyages that culminated in a Portuguese presence in the four corners of the world.

SEE ALSO: Alexander VI; Christopher Columbus; Pêro da Covilhã; Bartolomeu Dias; Juan Sebastián de Elcano; Ferdinand II and Isabella I; Vasco da Gama; John III; Ferdinand Magellan.

RELATED ARTICLES in *Great Events from History: The Renaissance & Early Modern Era, 1454-1600:* 1481-1482: Founding of Elmina; c. 1485: Portuguese Establish a Foothold in Africa; August, 1487-December, 1488: Dias Rounds the Cape of Good Hope; 1490-1492: Martin Behaim Builds the First World Globe; June 7, 1494: Treaty of Tordesillas; 1505-1515: Portuguese Viceroys Establish Overseas Trade Empire; 1565: Spain Seizes the Philippines.

JOHN III
King of Portugal (r. 1521-1557)

Heir to the Portuguese empire at its zenith, John III turned his attention to formalizing Portuguese settlement and government in Brazil. Known for his piety and religious devotion, he sought and received from the pope permission to establish a Portuguese inquisition in order to preserve orthodoxy in his vast domains, and he entrusted to the Jesuits missions to India, the Far East, and Brazil.

BORN: June 6, 1502; Lisbon, Portugal
DIED: June 11, 1557; Lisbon
ALSO KNOWN AS: John the Pious
AREAS OF ACHIEVEMENT: Government and politics, religion and theology, exploration

EARLY LIFE

Young Prince John witnessed dramatic transformations in Portugal as successful voyages of exploration increased Portuguese presence and influence abroad. African slaves and spices from the Far East sailed into Lisbon, and from there were sold throughout Europe. After 1500, a number of the indigenous peoples of Brazil were also brought to Portugal, as well as exotic birds and animals from the Americas.

John's father, King Manuel I, impressed on him the importance of maintaining solid diplomatic ties with neighboring Spain. The Portuguese royal House of Aviz tightened ties with the Habsburg rulers of Spain through marriage. After the death of his first two wives (both daughters of King Ferdinand II and Queen Isabella I of Spain), Manuel I married Eleanor of Austria, sister of King Charles I of Spain (later Holy Roman Emperor Charles V). John later married his new stepmother's sister, Catherine, and Charles, in turn, married John's sister Isabel. Thus, the rulers of Spain and Portugal solidified their alliance.

When John was a teenager, Catholicism was attacked by Martin Luther. During the first year of John's reign, the schism within Christendom became irrevocable, as Pope Leo X excommunicated Luther. Many of John's policies as king focused on preserving Christian orthodoxy within the lands he ruled.

LIFE'S WORK

John III inherited the difficult task of managing an empire that was increasingly unwieldy. Earlier Portuguese conquests in Morocco had become difficult and expensive to sustain. King John therefore chose to forgo Portuguese claims to the North African towns of Safi, Azamor, Alcácer, and Arzila. He focused, instead, on Portuguese interests in the Far East and in Brazil.

He strengthened the Portuguese position in Goa, thereby enlarging the Portuguese presence in the Indian Ocean, while at the same time encouraging Portuguese sea captains to continue exploring the Chinese coast to Japan.

For years, French pirates had been disrupting Portuguese trade routes in the South Atlantic. The French, furthermore, were poaching on the profitable brazilwood trade and making dangerous alliances with the indigenous peoples of Brazil against Portuguese traders. To curb the threat of permanent French claims to Brazil, John instituted a new system of settlement for that Portuguese colony. He divided the region into fifteen captaincies that were parceled out to Portuguese noblemen, who then became responsible for settling the land. Only two of these captaincies succeeded, however; in 1549, John reclaimed for the Crown the captaincies that had failed and sent a governor-general to rule Brazil in his stead. The arrival of the first governor, Tomé de Sousa, marked the beginning of significant Portuguese settlement in Brazil, where the trade in brazilwood came to be eclipsed by the planting and processing of sugarcane with the labor of slaves from Africa.

In Portugal, however, the king faced serious financial difficulties. Earlier profits from the spice trade dwindled as supply increased and prices fell. Losses to shipwrecks and piracy also cut into expected revenues from the India trade. Furthermore, Portugal had paid a large dowry when John's sister married Charles V and became empress. The Portuguese, in addition, had provided Spain with monetary compensation for recognizing Portuguese claims to the Moluccas, the Spice Islands in the Far East (which both Portugal and Spain had claimed under the provisions of the Treaty of Tordesillas in 1494). John thus ruled an empire facing ever-deeper financial troubles.

Concerned with the threat posed to Christian orthodoxy by converted Jews and Lutheran heretics, John petitioned Pope Clement VII to establish a Portuguese inquisition. The request was granted and the inquisition was instituted in 1536. Three years later, the king's brother Henrique became inquisitor general and moved with vigor to root out heresy. The first auto-da-fé, the burning of a heretic, occurred in Lisbon in 1541. Also in the 1530's, a new religious order, the Society of Jesus (the Jesuits), had been created. Impressed by the zeal of the Jesuits, John invited them to establish a university in Coimbra and to aid the Portuguese in conversion efforts in the Far East and in Brazil. From its earliest days, then, the Society of Jesus became an important force for religious orthodoxy in Portugal and in Portuguese possessions around the globe. Saint Francis Xavier, one of the founders of the Jesuits, went to India, China, and Japan in the service of God and of the Portuguese king. Jesuits also sailed to Brazil with Tomé de Sousa, where they became responsible for taking the Christian message to the indigenous peoples, for staffing schools, and for providing spiritual support for Portuguese settlers.

During the reign of John, Portugal witnessed a significant shift of population from the countryside to the cities, drawn in large part by hopes of participating in the boom generated from the transoceanic trade. Many peasant farmers moved to Lisbon, while others left for the colonies or to pursue new opportunities in the flourishing Spanish port of Seville. This migration led to food shortages and to rising costs for city dwellers, and discontent grew within the kingdom.

Despite a rising number of internal and external problems, John did succeed in keeping Portugal out of costly European wars. While his brother-in-law, Charles V, embarked on expensive military campaigns in Italy and in France, and the Wars of Religion exploded throughout the Holy Roman Empire, John refused to be drawn into the fray.

SIGNIFICANCE

Heir to an empire that had reached its prime, John III made important decisions to streamline costs and preserve at least some of Portugal's new possessions. He strengthened the Portuguese presence in Brazil and assured that the line drawn by the Treaty of Tordesillas would be extended around the globe to guarantee Portuguese rights in the Spice Islands.

Concerned with the threats facing Christendom, John brought the inquisition to Portugal, where it would have a lasting influence. He admired the work of the Jesuits, and invited them to participate in revamping the Portuguese educational system and in spearheading conversion efforts in Portugal's colonies.

The problems of ruling an overextended empire, however, were compounded by the early death of all ten of his children. His grandson, Sebastian, who inherited the crown, shared his grandfather's enthusiasm for preserving the Christian faith. Shortly after Sebastian died, leading a campaign against the Moors in North Africa, Philip II of Spain made good on his claim to the throne of Portugal, thereby ending the rule of the House of Aviz.

—Joan E. Meznar

FURTHER READING

Anderson, James. *The History of Portugal.* Westport, Conn.: Greenwood Press, 2000. Succinct description of politics in the age of exploration, with a focus on the rise and fall of Portuguese dynasties.

Livermore, H. V. *A New History of Portugal.* 2d ed. Cambridge, England: Cambridge University Press, 1976. Short but valuable descriptions of the accomplishments of Portuguese kings and the particular challenges each faced.

Oliveira Marques, A. H. de. *History of Portugal.* New York: Columbia University Press, 1972. Sets the politics of the period into a cultural and demographic context, with an emphasis on broad changes in science and in population size.

O'Malley, John W. *The First Jesuits.* Cambridge, Mass.: Harvard University Press, 1993. This outstanding work on the early years of the Society of Jesus provides an excellent account of the role of the Jesuits in Portugal and its territories during the reign of John.

Russell-Wood, A. J. R. *Portuguese Empire, 1415-1808: A World on the Move.* Baltimore: Johns Hopkins University Press, 1998. A history of the expansion of the Portuguese empire, with particular attention to the individuals who traveled from Portugal to the Far East and to Brazil. Less emphasis on dynastic policy and more on cultural exchange.

Saraiva, Joé Hermano. *Portugal: A Companion History.* Manchester, England: Carcanet Press, 1997. Focuses

on the significance of the Portuguese inquisition and the Jesuits for the reign of John.

SEE ALSO: Charles V; Clement VII; Ferdinand II and Isabella I; Saint Ignatius of Loyola; John II; Leo X; Martin Luther; Manuel I; Philip II; Sebastian; Tomás de Torquemada; Saint Francis Xavier.

RELATED ARTICLES in *Great Events from History: The Renaissance & Early Modern Era, 1454-1600:* 1500-1530's: Portugal Begins to Colonize Brazil; 1502: Beginning of the Transatlantic Slave Trade; 1580-1581: Spain Annexes Portugal.

JOSQUIN DES PREZ
Franco-Flemish musician

Josquin was a Renaissance composer whose works covered a great variety of musical genres, both sacred and secular (mostly chansons). He also was a singer in various royal and aristocratic chapels, including the Papal Chapel. Modern scholarship regards him as the quintessential Renaissance musician.

BORN: c. 1450-1455; possibly near Saint Quentin, France

DIED: August 27, 1521; Condé-sur-l'Escaut, Burgundian Hainaut (now in France)

ALSO KNOWN AS: Josquin Despres; Josquin Desprez; Jossequin Desprez; Josquin des Pres; Josquin des Près; Josquin des Prés; Josse des Pres; Gosse des Pres; Joskin des Prez; Josquinus Pratensis; Jodocus Pratensis; Judocus Pratensis; Juschino de Prato; Juschino a Prato

AREA OF ACHIEVEMENT: Music

EARLY LIFE

Almost no documents have survived that would shed light on the pre-1490's life and work of Josquin des Prez (zhaw-skan day pray). His exact date and place of birth are not known, and the chronology of his works is still a matter of debate. Some argue that his style of composition developed from one almost entirely based on canonical imitation to one allowing for a greater degree of freedom and a more expressive setting of the text. Others posit that, from very early in his career, Josquin manipulated both linear polyphony and vertical harmony with equal ease—which, in turn, makes it difficult to base a chronology of his works on style alone.

It has been hypothesized that Josquin was trained as a choirboy in Condé-sur-l'Escaut or its vicinity. From the evidence that has been preserved, it appears that Josquin spent most of his active musical life at various European courts: For instance, documents from 1475 place him in Aix-la-Chapelle, as a chapel singer for René I, duke of Anjou. From there Josquin might have been transferred, at the duke's death in 1480, to the service of King Louis XI of France.

LIFE'S WORK

Entering the service of Cardinal Ascanio Sforza in Milan shortly after 1483, Josquin is believed to have followed the cardinal to Rome in 1484. He is also mentioned as a *cantor duchalis* in documents issued by the house of Duke Gian Galeazzo Sforza. Recent research suggests he might have been at the court of Matthias Corvinus, king of Hungary, for a short period before 1490.

It is known that Josquin was a singer in the Papal Chapel under both Innocent VIII and Alexander VI—where, it is speculated, he remained perhaps until 1495. He spent one year (1503-1504) as the *maestro di cappella* for Duke Ercole d'Este in Ferrara, where he composed chiefly masses and motets. He left in the spring of 1504, fleeing the plague. Josquin returned to this native land to spend the last seventeen years of his life as provost of Condé, and he was entombed in the church of Notre Dame there.

Josquin was one of the several Renaissance composers who recrafted the motet as an all-purpose piece of texted, polyphonic, sacred music. The motet in his hands became perhaps the most progressive form of sacred choral composition. Josquin based his more than fifty motets on a wide range of Latin texts, both biblical and nonbiblical. Like other Renaissance composers, he took the Humanistic view that texted music should at least partially reflect the structure and organization of speech.

Josquin infused his motets with an amount of harmonic freedom, included moderate chromaticism for dramatic color, and used intervallic inflections suggestive of intense emotions. His music followed closely the denotations of individual words (a technique known as word painting), as well as the more subtle nuances and suggestions embedded in these words. Such depictions are found in *Dominus regnavit* (the Lord reigneth)—a four-part motet setting (music composed for a text) of Psalm 92 for the Office of Lauds, published posthumously in a 1539 Nuremberg anthology. Here Josquin conveyed the sense of ascension found in the words *elevaverunt flumina* (the floods have lifted up) through octave leaps, and he set the opening phrase *Dominus regnavit* to a series of repeated pitches to depict God sitting in majesty.

Formally, the Renaissance motet was divided into a *prima pars* and a *secunda pars* (the first part and the second part, respectively). Within this compositional frame, Josquin further divided each section into several subsections contrasted through meter and texture changes. This in turn caused such works to appear—both visually and aurally—as multisectional compositions based on clever interplays between polyphonic, imitative segments (with emphasis on imitative duets) and homophonic ones (where all the parts joined in simultaneously, in syllabic, declamatory music). *Tu solus, qui facis mirabilia*, a four-part motet printed in Venice in 1503 and perhaps one of Josquin's earlier Milanese works illustrates this approach: The opening statement in the *prima pars* and the closing phrase in the *secunda pars* are set to long values in declamatory style—thereby conferring a sense of architectural solidity on the whole structure. By contrast, the middle portions of both parts are more fluid and contrapuntal.

Josquin was at the forefront of Renaissance mass composition—a fact recognized in his lifetime, when the Venetian Ottaviano dei Petrucci (1466-1539), the first music printer, produced a volume of masses by Josquin (*Misse Josquin*) in 1502. Two more volumes followed, one printed in Venice (*Missarum Josquin liber secundus*, 1505), the other—in Fossombrone (*Missarum Josquin liber tertius*, 1514). Apart from settings of individual mass movements, Josquin completed eighteen

masses, some of which are known in more than one variant. These were settings of the Ordinary, and he was in agreement with all other Renaissance composers in using melodies from the traditional chant repertory as *canti firmi*. As the melodic line on which the whole composition was based, *cantus firmus* was the very foundation of the polyphonic mass, most frequently placed in the tenor, and subsequently imitated and developed in the other parts.

In addition to using chants, Josquin had a marked preference for incorporating secular songs, melodies borrowed from other composers, or melodic lines of his own invention as *canti firmi*. Such was the case, for instance, with the tune *L'Homme armé* (the armed man), of uncertain origin but very popular throughout the Middle Ages and Renaissance, which Josquin used as the *cantus firmus* for both the *Missa L'Homme armé sexti toni* (composed in the sixth tone or mode) and the *L'Homme armé super voces musicales* (where the tune was successively transposed to different degrees of the medieval/Renaissance six-step scale known as a hexachord). The mass *D'Ung aultre amer* takes its point of departure from a *chanson* by another famous Renaissance composer, Jean d'Ockeghem (c. 1420-1497), while the mass *Fortuna disperata* is based on a piece attributed to the Burgundian composer Antoine Busnoys (c. 1430-1492).

Josquin, like his predecessors and contemporaries, favored the canon (or *fuga*), which meant the writing of two or more parts in strict imitation. The canon—whether based on direct, inverted, or retrograde imitation, in rhythmic augmentation or diminution—could be utilized as one of several sections of a larger piece such as a mass, or as piece of smaller dimensions standing on its own. The tenor and *superius* (soprano) of Josquin's *Missa ad fugam* are written in strict imitation (canon) throughout, with the remaining two parts in a freer style, and his *Missa sine nomine* includes canons in paired voices.

In terms of secular music, Josquin's main contribution were his polyphonic chansons (songs)—many of which, like some of his masses and motets, employed pre-existing tunes. It is still a matter of speculation how many of the chansons were originally composed for instrumental performance rather than vocal. A very small number—of which the authenticity is still doubted—were based on Italian texts. The remaining ones were settings of French poetry. His earlier works in this group, like *Cela sans plus*, were conceived along the lines of the fifteenth century French and Burgundian *formes fixes*, such as the *rondeau* or *virelai*, with music rigorously adhering to the formal patterns of the poetry being set, and with canonic imitation being used extensively. *Mille regretz*, first published as a lute arrangement, represents a later stage in his treatment of the chanson, where the approach to form is much freer, and the number of parts is increased to four, five, and even six. One of Josquin's most famous chansons is his setting of *Nymphes des bois*, the elegy written by the French poet and historiographer Jean Molinet (1435-1507) at the death of Jean d'Ockeghem.

SIGNIFICANCE

Josquin's reputation as a brilliant composer was established after his death, but even during his lifetime he was held in esteem by his contemporaries: Thus the Humanist Paolo Cortese and the music theorists Franchino Gaffurio (1451-1522) and Pietro Aaron (c. 1480-1545), all writing during the first two decades of the sixteenth century, regarded Josquin as one of the most prominent composers of their time, and Martin Luther referred to him as "the master of notes." The Italian music publisher Ottaviano dei Petrucci began each of the four volumes of his first motet anthology with a piece by Josquin. In 1545, the Antwerp printer Tilman Susato printed a volume entirely devoted to Josquin, including about twenty-four chansons.

The composer's death was lamented by poetic luminaries of the period, and numerous musical tributes were paid by both contemporary and later composers who used quotations from Josquin's music and even incorporated titles of his motets in their own works. Two modern editions of Josquin's works were published in Amsterdam between 1921 and 1969.

—Luminita Florea

FURTHER READING

Elders, Willem, and Frits de Haen, eds. *Proceedings of the International Josquin Symposium, Utrecht 1986.* Utrecht, the Netherlands: Vereniging voor Nederlandse Muziekgeschiedenis, 1991. A collection based on papers given at a symposium, focusing on aspects of Josquin's life and works and discussing a variety of manuscripts in which these works have been preserved.

Merkley, Paul, and Lora L. M. Merkley. *Music and Patronage in the Sforza Court.* Turnhout, Belgium: Brepols, 1999. Discusses a large number of newly discovered documents relating to musical life at the chapel of Galeazzo Sforza in Milan, and presents the most recent scholarship on Josquin's life and works.

Reese, Gustave, and Jeremy Noble. "Josquin Desprez." In *Josquin, Palestrina, Lassus, Byrd, Victoria*, edited by Gustave Reese. New York: W. W. Norton, 1984. Represents the state of Josquin scholarship in the early 1980's, with informative discussions of selected masses, motets, and chansons.

Sherr, Richard. *The Josquin Companion.* New York: Oxford University Press, 2000. A collection of essays on Josquin's career, including detailed analytical studies of individual works by him. Includes one CD containing mass movements, motets, and chansons.

SEE ALSO: Louis XI; Matthias I Corvinus.

JULIUS II
Italian pope (r. 1503-1513)

Julius II, called Warrior Pope, was the first and only pontiff to command and lead a papal army into battle. His military exploits regained large amounts of territory lost to the Papal States in wars with France and small Italian republics. In addition to his attempts to strengthen church administration and reduce nepotism, he also was a patron to Michelangelo, Raphael, and Donato Bramante.

BORN: December 5, 1443; Albisola, Republic of Genoa (now in Italy)
DIED: February 21, 1513; Rome, Papal States (now in Italy)
ALSO KNOWN AS: Giuliano della Rovere
AREAS OF ACHIEVEMENT: Religion and theology, military, patronage of the arts

EARLY LIFE

Julius II was born Giuliano della Rovere in the small town of Albisola. When his father's brother, Francesco della Rovere, became head of the Franciscan order, Giuliano was educated under the direction of the Franciscans; soon after his studies were completed, he was ordained a priest. When his uncle became pope and took the name Sixtus IV in 1471, Giuliano was made a cardinal in the same year. Over the next few years, Cardinal della Rovere held eight bishoprics, controlled many more abbeys and benefices, and assumed the title of archbishop of Avignon.

From 1480 to 1482, della Rovere served as legate to France. In this capacity, he showed great diplomatic skill in reconciling the differences between Louis XI of France and Maximilian I of Austria. He returned to Rome when Sixtus IV died in 1484, and he bribed many cardinals into electing Batista Cibo as Pope Innocent VIII. Innocent was controlled rather easily; indeed, his policies were to a large extent determined and implemented by della Rovere.

Because of his strong influence over Innocent, della Rovere was opposed by Cardinal Rodrigo Borgia; in a short time, the two men became bitter rivals. Their disagreements escalated to such an extent that, when Innocent died in 1492 and Cardinal Borgia was elected Pope Alexander VI, della Rovere was forced to flee to France in order to save his life.

Della Rovere tried to convince King Charles VIII of France that church reforms in Italy could be achieved only with his personal support. In fact, della Rovere was seeking help in removing Alexander from the Papacy. When Charles VIII decided to invade Italy, della Rovere accompanied him and attempted to win his backing for the convocation of a council to depose the pope on the grounds of his having won the election of 1492 through bribery. Unfortunately for della Rovere, Charles negotiated and signed a conciliatory treaty with Alexander in 1495—all della Rovere's efforts to get rid of his enemy were frustrated.

In 1498, della Rovere was reconciled with Alexander when his diplomatic skills helped to arrange the marriage of Charlotte d'Albret, sister of the king of Navarre, to Cesare Borgia, a relative of the pope. When Borgia attacked the dukedom of Urbino, however, where della Rovere's nephew stood next in line to succeed the duke, the peace was over. Once again, della Rovere had to flee far from Rome. Only the death of Alexander in August of 1503 made it possible for the cardinal to return to Rome.

Believing that the way was now clear for him to become pope, della Rovere did everything in his power to assure the outcome of the election. Yet the Italian cardinals were divided as to which candidate to support and della Rovere, although he received a majority of the votes, fell two short of the required two-thirds. Realizing that he was not going to be elected to the Papacy, he threw his support to the cardinal of Siena, Francesco Piccolomini, who took the name Pius III. Yet della Rovere knew that the new pope's age and ill health meant a short tenure in office. When Pius died after only twenty-six days, della Rovere prepared for one last chance to wear the tiara.

LIFE'S WORK

By extensive promises to his opponents, and by resorting to bribery when necessary, della Rovere was unanimously elected pope on November 1, 1503, in the shortest conclave ever recorded, less than twenty-four hours. A proud and egotistical man, he changed two syllables of his given name, Giuliano, to come up with his papal name, Julius II. Extremely confident, impetuous, hot-tempered, and impatient, Julius soon gained the reputation of an activist pope, unable to listen to advice. He insisted on doing everything himself and was almost impossible to consult; when faced with a contrary opinion, he would stop the speaker with a little bell kept near him at all times. Although he was sixty years old at the time of his election to the Papacy and suffering from gout and kidney ailments, his spirit was indefatigable. He was large and had a tight mouth and dark eyes; the word most often used by Italians in describing him was *terribilitá*, or awesomeness.

Julius immediately began to repair the damage wrought on the Church by Alexander VI. He reorganized papal administration, planned to achieve financial solvency for the Church, promised to eliminate simony, and began to reduce nepotism. He established order in Rome by implementing harsh measures against bandits and hired assassins who had run rampant under Alexander; to serve as a bulwark against any foreign or domestic threat to himself, he hired mercenary Swiss guards as protectors of the Vatican.

Believing that the authority of the Papacy could be enhanced by the exercise of temporal power, Julius implemented a strategy of territorial conquest, expedient diplomacy, and the show of external pomp and glory. Accordingly, his first major decision as supreme pontiff was to recover the territories lost to the Papal States under the administration of and following the death of Alexander.

In the first year of his pontificate, Julius set out to regain the cities that Venice had seized from the Holy See and later occupied. Initially, he used diplomatic measures to isolate and pressure the Venetian republic to release its holdings. Venice did give back some of the land but continued to hold the cities of Rimini and Faenza. Frustrated by Venice's intransigence, the pope turned his attention to the recovery of Bologna and Perugia, two of the most important cities within the Papal States whose leaders ignored the authority of Rome. Impatient and reckless in his desire to recapture the land, Julius ignored the objections of many cardinals and shocked all Europe when he personally rode at the head of his army to conquer the cities in 1506. Shortly afterward, when the papal fief Ferrara turned against him, the white-bearded pope donned helmet, mail, and sword, and led his troops in an attack through a breach in the fortress wall. During these years of violent disputes, Julius was continually on horseback, encouraging his soldiers, directing their deployment, and making certain that they used the armaments of modern warfare correctly.

Still unable to subdue Venice, Julius sought the help of the Holy Roman Emperor Maximilian I and Louis XII of France. Julius convinced the two men to declare war on the republic and, with the added participation of Spain and Swiss mercenaries, formed the League of Cambrai to execute his plan. Julius also issued a bull of excommunication and interdict for the entire population of the city.

When the Venetians were finally defeated at the Battle of Agnadello in May of 1509, one of the bloodiest conflicts in the history of warfare, the pope's troops reclaimed Rimini, Faenza, and other territories previously held by the republic.

Only one year later, Julius received a formal confirmation of ecclesiastical rights and authority in the Venetian territory; with this reconciliation, he lifted the ban of excommunication. Yet neither Louis XII nor Maximilian I was ready to make peace and leave Italy; the expansion of their empires now dominated their strategy. Julius quickly recognized that there could be no consolidation of the Papal States as long as the French and the emperor remained in Italy. Convinced of the growing danger that foreign troops in Italy now posed, Julius made a complete about-face and formed an alliance in 1511 with Venice and Spain, along with Swiss mercenaries, against France. This new combination was called the Holy League, and Julius's new battle cry was, "Out with the barbarians!"

King Louis XII's resentment and animosity ran so deep as to label the war against himself illegal and to convene, with the support of Emperor Maximilian and prominent French cardinals, a synod at Tours intended to depose Julius from the Papacy; also in 1511, at the instigation of the French king, the rebel cardinals established their own antipapal council at Pisa. At the time, Julius was again waging war in person, on this occasion against the duke of Ferrara, who supported the French. When he received news of the attempts to remove him from office, however, the pope reacted swiftly: He excommunicated Louis and the rebellious cardinals, convinced England to join the Holy League, and convened the Fifth Lateran Council in 1512 to oppose the schismatic meeting at Pisa and reassert his own papal authority.

After a number of setbacks, Julius and the Holy League finally defeated the French at the Battle of Ravenna and drove them across the Alps. With a few concessions to Maximilian, the pope's campaign to oust foreign troops from Italy came to a successful conclusion. Yet, even though Julius had regained large tracts of land for the Papal States, the nature of Italian politics and diplomacy frustrated him in providing definite and long-lasting resolutions to many territorial problems.

Weary with war and in ill health, Julius turned his attention to the Lateran Council and church reform. Initially, the council was preoccupied with problems surrounding the French presence in Italy and with the illegitimate council at Pisa. With the defeat of the French and the dissolution of the assembly at Pisa, Julius pushed for needed reforms and the Lateran council responded. One of the most important of Julius's papal bulls confirmed by the council voided any papal election tainted with simony; any offender would suffer the loss of his office and endure large financial penalties. The council also confirmed Julius's renewal of a bull by Pius II, which prohibited switching an ecclesiastical appeal from a pope to a council.

One of Julius's last acts as pope, and one of the most far-reaching, was to grant a dispensation to Prince Henry of England, later King Henry VIII, enabling him to marry Catherine of Aragon. Julius II died on February 21, 1513, in Rome, but the Fifth Lateran Council he had convened remained in session for another four years.

SIGNIFICANCE

The goal of consolidating the Papal States, Julius II believed, could be attained only by keeping France and the Holy Roman Empire out of Italy. This strategy was achieved in three stages: the regaining of lost territories, the expelling of all so-called foreigners from the Italian peninsula, and the assuring of papal authority in Rome and throughout the Papal States. For these reasons, Julius is regarded by many historians as one of the earliest and most important proponents of Italian unification.

Yet because the great powers returned to plague Italian politics after the pope's death, it is arguable that Julius's more significant and lasting contribution to the Papacy involved his patronage of the arts. He beautified Rome and initiated a large amount of new construction, including new and rebuilt churches, such as Santa Maria del Popolo and Santa Maria della Pace, and he helped establish the Vatican Library. He commissioned Raphael to paint new frescoes for the papal apartments. Michelangelo, against his will, was browbeaten by the pope into painting the ceiling for the Sistine Chapel; working alone on a scaffold for almost four years, Michelangelo allowed no one but Julius to view his work.

Donato Bramante was one of the pope's favorite artists; Julius assigned Bramante the task of designing and building the courts of the Belvedere, where he started a collection of ancient sculpture. The monument to Julius's papacy was also given to Bramante to execute—the demolition of the old Basilica of St. Peter's and the construction of a new one. The cost of replacing the older building with a grander edifice significantly exceeded existing papal revenues and led Julius to implement a practice of dire consequence, the public sale of indulgences in Papal States. When the next pope extended the practice to Germany, it precipitated a revolt by a disillusioned and angry young cleric named Martin Luther.

—Thomas Derdak

FURTHER READING

Beck, James H. *Three Worlds of Michelangelo*. New York: W. W. Norton, 1999. One of these three interconnected studies of Michelangelo is an analysis of his relationship to Julius II. Includes illustrations, bibliographic references, index.

Chambers, D. S. *Cardinal Bainbridge in the Court of Rome, 1509 to 1514*. London: Methuen, 1965. An account of one cardinal's tenure in Rome and his eyewitness observations of the persons and events surrounding the Papacy during Julius's reign. Particularly good in relating the machinations involved in ecclesiastical politics.

Erasmus, Desiderius. *Julius Exclusus*. Translated by Paul Pascal. Bloomington: Indiana University Press, 1968. This work was completed after the pope's death. Julius is characterized as the embodiment of war and all its accompanying evils. An extremely hostile polemic against Julius. Not until the twentieth century was Erasmus's authorship verified.

Gilbert, Felix. *The Pope, His Banker, and Venice*. Cambridge, Mass.: Harvard University Press, 1980. A detailed examination of Julius's involvement in the League of Cambrai and his war against the republic of Venice. Stresses the financial arrangements made by both the pope and the Venetian republic to carry out the extended conflict. An excellent insight into the diplomatic and financial policies at work in the Papacy. Notes at the end of the book shed light on some of the more elusive historical problems during Julius's pontificate.

O'Malley, John W. "Fulfillment of the Christian Golden Age Under Pope Julius II: Text of a Discourse of Giles of Veterbo, 1507." *Traditio* 25 (1969): 265-338. A contemporary interpretation of Julius's policy that temporal power gives authority and prestige to the Church. Focuses on the interaction between secular and spiritual pursuits in war, diplomacy, and art.

Shaw, Christine. *Julius II: The Warrior Pope*. Cambridge, Mass.: Blackwell, 1996. Primarily a very useful political history of Julius's tenure as pope, this volume also contains a chapter on his patronage of the arts, but it is weak on theological analysis. Includes photographic plates, illustrations, bibliographic references, and index.

Stinger, Charles L. *The Renaissance in Rome*. Bloomington: Indiana University Press, 1998. Julius figures prominently in this study of the resurgence of Rome's cultural, religious, and political importance in the Renaissance. Includes maps, illustrations, bibliographic references, and index.

Tuchman, Barbara. *The March of Folly: From Troy to Vietnam*. New York: Alfred A. Knopf, 1984. A general overview of how the late Renaissance popes set the stage for Martin Luther's Reformation movement. More specifically, a character study of Julius II that raises questions about the propriety of his decision to lead an army into battle.

SEE ALSO: Alexander VI; Chevalier de Bayard; Cesare Borgia; Donato Bramante; Catherine of Aragon; Charles VIII; Henry VIII; James IV; Louis XI; Louis XII; Martin Luther; Niccolò Machiavelli; Maximilian I; Michelangelo; Pius III; Raphael; Sixtus IV.

KALICHO
Inuit interpreter and translator

Kalicho was an Inuit abducted by explorer Martin Frobisher's crew during the explorer's second voyage to the New World. Kalicho, an Inuit woman, and her child, were brought to England and exhibited as curiosities from the land Queen Elizabeth I designated meta incognita *or the unknown shore.*

BORN: c. mid-1500's; Arctic region (now Baffin, Nunavut, Canada)
DIED: Late 1577; Bristol, England
ALSO KNOWN AS: Calichough; Collichang; Callicho
AREA OF ACHIEVEMENT: Diplomacy

EARLY LIFE

Kalicho (kah-LEE-koh) probably belonged to one of the Baffin Inuit tribes, nomadic hunters and fishermen who moved throughout the region adjusting to the season and the animals they hunted. They lived traditionally in extended families of five or six members, which would band together in groups of six to ten families for hunting.

During the winter, the Baffin Inuit lived in coastal encampments, spearing seal and whale. They traveled by dog sled, often over great distances, and lived in igloos and homes of sod, stone, and whalebone. They moved inland during the summer in smaller groups, where they hunted caribou and caught fish in stone weirs. They lived in skin tents, traveled on foot, and subsisted on an all-meat diet.

Nothing is known of Kalicho's life prior to his abduction by British explorer Martin Frobisher's crew. His tribe had spent the summer on the outer islands at the northeast entrance to what came to be called Frobisher's Bay. A woman and child, who were captured later, came from a tribe on the southern shore, more than 62 miles (100 kilometers) away. The woman had a tattooed face—blue streaks down her cheeks and around her eyes—and would have carried her baby in her hood or under her coat in the traditional manner. It is unlikely that she and Kalicho had met prior to their captivity, but Frobisher's crew expected them to live as husband and wife.

LIFE'S WORK

Frobisher was one of the first English explorers to locate and navigate the Northwest Passage. The Inuit that Frobisher encountered on his first and subsequent voyages were familiar with explorers and their ships. The Inuit called them *qadlunaat*, which originally denoted the Norse explorers they had encountered during the pre-

vious three hundred years. The Inuit greeted Frobisher's crew and seemed to welcome the opportunity to trade with them. They traded fish, seal and bearskin coats, and received bells, mirrors, and other trinkets.

The language barrier proved to be a problem between the two groups, which might have led to the disappearance of five of Frobisher's men and their only landing boat. The men went ashore with an Inuit they believed to have been hired to be their guide but were never seen again.

Without a landing boat, Frobisher was unable to search for his missing crewmen. After several days, a group of Inuit came out to the ship, presumably to trade. The first to reach the ship was plucked from the ocean, kayak and all, and held as hostage against the return of the five missing men. When this failed, again because of the language barriers, Frobisher was forced to abandon his men and return to England, bringing with him the Inuit and his kayak as proof of the success of his mission. This Inuit's name is unknown, and he died shortly after they reached home.

During the second voyage in 1577, Frobisher and his men were more wary of the indigenous peoples they encountered, but still expected to rescue, or at least obtain word of, their missing crewmen. Frobisher decided to obtain an Inuit to use as an interpreter. The Englishmen pretended to discuss trade with two Inuit who had approached, then attempted to capture them. The Inuit escaped and fled to their boat, and Frobisher was wounded by an iron-bladed Inuit arrow in the struggle. The sailors ultimately succeeded in capturing one as an interpreter, an Inuit man named Kalicho.

They then sailed to the southwest, exploring the southern shore of Frobisher's Bay. Items of English clothing were found in an abandoned Inuit settlement, and despite being more than 125 miles (200 kilometers) from the place the men were last seen, the sailors believed they had found traces of their missing crewmen. They decided the men were being held captive and made plans to attack a nearby Inuit camp.

During the battle, the Englishmen found two Inuit women hiding among the rocks. Suspecting the older woman might be a witch, they left her behind and took the younger woman and her infant son hostage. The woman was known as Ignoth, a variation on the Baffin Island Eskimo word for "woman." Likewise, the infant Nutiok was called by the Inuit word for "child."

In later encounters with the Inuit, Kalicho acted as a translator for Frobisher, though he had been in captivity for a period of just weeks and could not have gained a full command of the English language in that time.

A group of Inuit attempted to rescue the hostages, presumably told of their plight by Kalicho during his translating sessions. The English responded by wounding the Inuit in order to show the power of their weapons. Hostility between the two groups prevented any further trading. At the end of August, Frobisher and his crew left the New World and sailed for home, carrying the three hostages with them.

Despite the severity of the situation, the hostages were not mistreated. The group was provided with a cabin and expected to live as a family. The English were surprised by the behavior of their Inuit captives because they had believed them to be savages. According to an account by George Best, Frobisher's second in command, the Inuit people were very eager to communicate with their captors and taught the seaman the names of things in their native language. They loved music and would keep time with their heads, hands, and feet, and they eventually grew attached to each other. According to Best, the woman acted as wife to Kalicho by caring for him or preparing his food, but the relationship was never consummated. Records indicate the Inuit killed and ate dogs (believed to have been stolen) while aboard the ship. Traditionally, Inuit ate dog only when nothing else was available; Kalicho and Ignoth may have found the English food unsuitable.

The trio arrived in Bristol, England, in the fall of 1577. The mayor of Bristol held a celebration in honor of the event. Kalicho demonstrated the use of his kayak and used his bird spear to hunt ducks on the Avon River. The Inuit were no longer considered hostages, and according to Best, they achieved a level of respect and admiration with their hosts.

During the first month, Kalicho fell ill but refused to have his blood let by a surgeon. His hosts, some of them Frobisher's people, supported his decision. The surgeon attributed Kalicho's death to their kindness in providing too much food and preventing medical care. The actual cause of death may have been pneumonia, aggravated by two broken ribs that had not healed properly and may have occurred during his initial capture. There was no burial ceremony because the English did not want to confuse Ignoth with the strange rituals; they feared that she would believe Kalicho had been sacrificed. They also had her watch him being buried, so she would know that he was not being used for food.

Ignoth died the following week. She had a skin rash, which may have been measles. Her child was sent to London in care of a nurse, where he died shortly thereafter, despite receiving medical care. Kalicho and Ignoth were buried at St. Stephen's Church in Bristol. Nutiok was buried in St. Olave's Church, in London, as was the unnamed Inuit from Frobisher's first voyage.

SIGNIFICANCE

Frobisher's disregard for the Inuit was typical of the period. For the most part, the indigenous peoples encountered by the early explorers were considered subhuman, without a society, religion, or even emotions. Kalicho and the other two hostages were brought to England to be displayed, like animals or like a mummy looted from an Egyptian tomb. Most such "visitors" died within weeks or months of their arrival because they lacked immunity to the diseases prevalent in crowded English seaports.

—*P. S. Ramsey*

FURTHER READING

McDermott, James. *Martin Frobisher: Elizabethan Privateer.* New Haven, Conn.: Yale University Press, 2001. A detailed biography of the explorer who brought Kalicho, Ignoth, and Nutiok to England and the circumstances of the expedition.

McGhee, Robert. *The Arctic Voyages of Martin Frobisher: An Elizabethan Adventure.* Seattle: University of Washington Press, 2001. A detailed account of Martin Frobisher's Arctic voyages. Includes maps, photographs, and replicas of historical documents.

Mason, Peter. *Infelicities: Representations of the Exotic.* Baltimore: Johns Hopkins University Press, 1998. A study of the text, paintings, drawings, photographs, and other displays that Europeans brought from the New World and the means they used to display the so-called exotic discoveries.

Ruby, Robert. *The Unknown Shore: The Lost History of England's Arctic Colony.* New York: H. Holt, 2001. A history of England's attempts to explore and colonize the Canadian Arctic, or *meta incognita* (unknown shore).

SEE ALSO: Elizabeth I; Sir Martin Frobisher.

RELATED ARTICLE in *Great Events from History: The Renaissance & Early Modern Era, 1454-1600:* June 7, 1576-July, 1578: Frobisher's Voyages.

JOSEPH BEN EPHRAIM KARO
Spanish-born Jewish scholar and rabbi

Karo codified Jewish law in a 1564-1565 work known as the Shulḥan arukh, *an abridgment of his more extensive major work, the* Bet yosef, *from 1542, which continues to be the authoritative source for Orthodox Judaism.*

BORN: 1488; Toledo, Castile (now in Spain)
DIED: March 24, 1575; Safed, Palestine (now Ẓefat, Israel)
ALSO KNOWN AS: Joseph Caro; Joseph Qaro; Maran (Our Master)
AREAS OF ACHIEVEMENT: Philosophy, religion and theology, scholarship

EARLY LIFE

Joseph ben Ephraim Karo (EE-fray-ehm KAHR-oh) and his family moved to Portugal around the period of the expulsion of Jews from Spain in 1492. Because of traditional religious prejudice and cultural and economic resentment, European countries began to expel Jews in the thirteenth century. In 1497, Jews were again subject to expulsion, this time from Portugal, and the Karo family moved to Constantinople (now Istanbul, Turkey). The Ottoman Empire during this period was somewhat open to Jewish immigration, and the family settled into their new homeland.

Karo's father, Ephraim, also was a noted Talmudic scholar, and Joseph spent a portion of his youth studying under his tutelage. On Ephraim's death, Joseph continued his studies with Isaac Karo, his father's brother.

During the ensuing years, Karo moved among several Turkish cities, including Salonika and Nikopol. In these travels, Karo became influenced by leading Kabbalists of the period, such as Solomon Alkabetz and Joseph Taitazak. Kabbalah, or Jewish mysticism and piety, included a doctrine of spiritual perfection and was common among scholars of the period. It was also while studying with Alkabetz that Karo developed the tradition of remaining up during the night to study Torah during the holiday of Shavuot, an all-night ritual known as Tikkun Leil Shavuot. Tradition includes the Kabbalistic belief that it was during one of these sessions that the maggid, a heavenly visitor not unlike an angel or a heavenly voice, first visited Karo. Karo considered such visits to be common during the remainder of his life.

LIFE'S WORK

Karo lived in Turkey approximately forty years. During this period of his life, and probably because of the influence of both Halachah (Jewish law) and Kabbalah, he began his most important work, the *Bet yosef*. Started in 1522, the work would require some twenty years to complete.

In 1536, Karo left Turkey and eventually made his way to Safed in Palestine. At the time, Safed was a center of Jewish life in the Ottoman Empire and a gathering point for the study of Kabbalah. Equally practical, it also contained one of the few printing presses in existence.

Soon after arriving in the Middle East, Karo began to study with Rabbi Jacob Berav. Berav at the time was involved in a controversy dealing with the proper procedure for ordination of rabbis, a process known as *semikhah*, or the laying on of hands. It was Berav's belief that the tradition had its origin with Moses, and that only by following the ritual properly could a person be considered properly ordained. Karo became one of the few scholars ordained by Berav. When Berav left Safed in 1538, Karo was acknowledged as the leading scholar in the city.

In addition to becoming head of the Safed yeshivah, or Jewish academy, Karo became the leading authority on questions concerning Halakhah. He also continued his work on the *Bet yosef*, which he completed in 1542.

The *Bet yosef* represented an update of Halakhic code and rulings in a way applicable to Karo's contemporaries. The first attempt to arrange Jewish law in a topical manner was carried out by Moses Maimonides in the twelfth century (*Mishneh Torah*, 1180; *The Code of Maimonides*, 1927-1965). As comprehensive as Maimonides' fourteen-volume work became, it was criticized by some for its lack of Talmudic references and its inability to address new disputes or legal questions. In the fourteenth century, Jacob ben Asher completed an update on the legal code known as the *Arba'a ṭurim* (1475; four rows). More popularly known simply as the *Ṭur*, Asher's work divided Jewish law into four sections that covered blessings, dietary law, marriage, and civil law. Karo followed Asher's model for the *Bet yosef*.

The *Bet yosef* was intended as a complete modernization and codification of Jewish law. Asher's work dealt with religious law in force during his own time. Karo's work was in part a commentary on the *Ṭur* and was a clarification of later rabbinic opinions and rulings. In addition, he attempted to explain the basis of Halakhic decisions described in the code. Karo followed the same chapter divisions used by Asher. It is in part Karo's use of reference material, however, which allowed this work to avoid much of the controversy associated with earlier codification of the law.

The *Bet yosef*, although completed in 1542, was published between 1550 and 1559. The major criticism of the work, however, lay in its very comprehensiveness. Karo continued with the writing of an abridged version in a manner accessible to persons who were not scholars. The result was the *Shulḥan arukh* (1565; *Code of Jewish Law*, 1927). The *Shulḥhan arukh* used the same format as the *Bet yosef*, but in a simpler fashion.

While clearly an important influence on Jewish law from its inception, the *Shulḥan arukh* nevertheless showed the Sephardic bias representative of its writer's origins; it failed to include Ashkenazy, or Eastern European, customs or law. In 1569, Moses ben Israel Isserles, a rabbi from Poland, attempted to address this problem by writing a commentary that dealt with Ashkenazy customs. Known as *Mapah* (pb. 1571), it became incorporated into the *Shulḥan arukh* as an appendix written in different script. Together, the works became the basis for Jewish law as it exists into the twenty-first century.

With the completion of his more famous work, Karo continued his scholarship with a commentary on Maimonides' *Mishneh Torah*. Karo's work, known as the *Kesef mishneh* (pb. 1574-1576), still represents the standard commentary on eight of the fourteen volumes from the *Mishneh Torah*, and includes Karo's analysis of commentaries by others concerning the other six volumes.

Karo's work was also influenced by his study of Kabbalah. He apparently kept a diary that described his visitations by the maggid and his views about mysticism and its effects on theology. The diary was published subsequent to Karo's death and provides insight into the Kabbalistic tradition extant at the time.

Karo was married either four or five times. While he apparently suffered the loss of several children over the course of his life, he was able to father at least one of his sons while in his eighties.

Significance

Prior to Karo's codification, Halachah, or Jewish law, was represented by a collection of decisions and interpretations of rabbis through the ages. The scholar Maimonides had brought a semblance of order to the understanding of the law in his legal work, but this work represented Sephardic laws and customs primarily, and it generally lacked Talmudic references. Legal questions and responses often fell outside the boundaries set by his

work. The *Ṭur* updated the law but still represented a period more than two hundred years before Karo.

The existence of an array of sources and commentaries on the law was also a source of frustration for rabbinic scholars. While Karo, in theory, was attempting to collate and correct errors found in the *Ṭur*, he hoped also to produce a definitive description of the law—what he believed would be represented as "one law and one Torah."

Karo's works therefore provided a contemporary discussion of Jewish law, in a format readily accessible to both scholars and laypersons. If someone wished to study the law in greater depth, however, the *Bet yosef* and its commentaries are best. Not surprisingly, Karo's legal decisions were always based on sources from the *Bet yosef*. Though several additional commentaries were added in subsequent years, more than four centuries after the work was published, the *Shulḥan arukh* remains the written authority for Jewish law.

—*Richard Adler*

Further Reading

Bridger, David, ed. *The New Jewish Encyclopedia*. New York: Behrman House, 1976. Contains a concise biography of Karo's life.

Encyclopedia Judaica. New York: Macmillan, 1972. Contains an extensive biography and describes the influence on Karo played by rabbis and scholars of the period.

Freedman, Benjamin, et al. *Duty and Healing: Foundations of a Jewish Bioethic*. New York: Routledge, 1999. Morality and ethical dilemmas in modern Judaism. Some examples delineated in the context of the *Shulḥan Arukh*.

Klein, Michele. *Not to Worry: Jewish Wisdom and Folklore*. Philadelphia: Jewish Publication Society, 2003. The author draws on Jewish tradition, philosophy, and folklore (Kabbalah) in the face of an uncertain world.

Telushkin, Joseph. *Jewish Literacy*. New York: William Morrow, 1991. Discussion of the role and significance of Karo in the evolution of an understanding of Halachah.

Werblosky, R. *Joseph Karo: Lawyer and Mystic*. Philadelphia: Jewish Publication Society, 1976. Biography of Karo that includes discussion of his use of Kabbalah and his belief that he was visited by a heavenly mentor.

See also: Isaac ben Judah Abravanel; Isaac ben Solomon Luria.

Related article in *Great Events from History: The Renaissance & Early Modern Era, 1454-1600:* 1492: Jews Are Expelled from Spain.

KENAU HASSELAER
Dutch social reformer

Kenau Hasselaer was the most celebrated heroine to emerge from the beginnings of Dutch revolt against Spain and its hold of the Netherlands. She led the defense of her native city, Haarlem, during the Spanish siege of 1572-1573.

BORN: 1526; Haarlem, Holland (now in the Netherlands)
DIED: 1588; Possibly at sea en route to Norway
ALSO KNOWN AS: Kenau Simonsdochter Hasselaer (full name); Kenau Simonsdochter van Haarlem; Kenau Hasselaar
AREA OF ACHIEVEMENT: Social reform

EARLY LIFE

Kenau Hasselaer (KAY-now HAWS-seh-lahr) was the second daughter of Guerte Coenendochter Hasselaer and Simon Gerritsz. Brouwer. Her parents were cousins who both came from Haarlem families of importance and distinction. Indeed, one of her ancestors was the legendary bailiff Claes van Ruyven, who was killed in a riot in 1492.

At the age of eighteen, in 1544, she married the shipbuilder Nanning Borst. The couple became parents of three, perhaps four, daughters and one son. Hasselaer was widowed in 1562, and, remarkably for the time, she took over her husband's business, with clients throughout the Dutch Republic.

LIFE'S WORK

One of the most famous sieges of the Dutch revolt against Spain took place at Haarlem. Prior to the arrival of the Spanish army, the Protestants in Haarlem had already gained control of the city. The siege, which began in December of 1572, dragged on for several months with the indefatigable citizens of Haarlem continually refortifying themselves and harassing the Spanish troops. The winter months took a heavy toll on the Spanish army and it was not until July of 1573 that they were able to elicit a surrender from the citizens of Haarlem.

A number of contemporary diaries, Dutch and German, recount the brave deeds of the Haarlem women who built and fortified the city wall during the siege. The women aided the fight also by pouring tar and pitch on the heads of the Spaniards and pelting them with stones. It is not known whether any of the women were actually armed during the struggle. Hasselaer was singled out, however, as the heavily armed "captain." Because of her bravery, which equaled, and even outshone, that of the men, she was described as a *manninne*, meaning half-man. In 1599, the historian Emanuel van Meteren praised Hasselaer for performing "manly" deeds as she attacked with spear, gun, and sword.

Van Meteran also wrote that Hasselaer looked like a man dressed as a woman. Increasingly, Hasselaer's deeds were expanded on and lauded in histories of the revolt. She and her legion of three hundred warrior women were called Amazons, and their fame became as legendary as that of their mythic predecessors.

The popular appeal of Hasselaer and her battalion of women is perhaps even more evident in the many visual images produced of her during the sixteenth and seventeenth centuries. As in male heroic images, Hasselaer was frequently depicted in a confident and swaggering hand-on-hip pose with an accompanying sash and medal. She is usually shown bearing a small arsenal of weapons, including pikes, swords, pistols, halberds, and powder horns. At times the image of decapitated heads of Spanish soldiers are included, thus linking Hasselaer to the biblical Judith, whose beheading of Holofernes saved her people.

Accompanying inscriptions in Latin, German, and Dutch identify the Dutch heroine as Captain Kenau, Amazon, and Judith, and they laud her bravery and proclaim her international fame. These images were often in the form of reproducible prints, thus greatly facilitating the spread of her heroic status and fame. A full-length image of Hasselaer in such a pose dominates the title plate of a mid-seventeenth century published play that reenacts Haarlem's struggle against Spain. Hasselaer is a primary character in the play who encourages everyone—men and women—to keep up the fight.

Another monumental image of Hasselaer supported by her legion of female soldiers is found in a 1661 text by Petrus de Lange on the glorious past of the Dutch Republic. He includes several engraved portraits of various Dutch heroes in his text—the first is of the prince, William the Silent, and the second is of Hasselaer. The place of honor allotted this image strikingly attests to the popularity and power of the Hasselaer legend.

Hasselaer continued to conduct her life and affairs independently after the revolt. She left Haarlem, and business and legal records indicate that she spent time in Delft, Arnemuiden, and Leiden, and that she was a rather tenacious businesswoman, pursuing her debtors even during the Siege of Haarlem. Her financial condition must have been quite satisfactory; she lent money for the acquisition of houses and she bought a farmhouse in Overveen. Even after the siege, it is evident that Hasselaer pursued her financial affairs vigorously, as her name appears in many legal and business documents.

In Arnemuiden in 1574, she was appointed to the post of weigh-master for the city. This position carried with it both wealth and status, and it was a highly unusual appointment for a single woman. It is not known whether her fame or her determination won her this post.

Eventually Hasselaer returned to Haarlem where she continued to deal in ships and lumber. It was on a trip by sea to Norway to buy lumber that Hasselaer disappeared. Her daughters claimed that her ship had fallen prey to pirates, but perhaps she was lost during a storm at sea. The heroine of Haarlem was declared dead in 1588.

SIGNIFICANCE

Hasselaer's deeds had an immediate impact on impressionable young female minds in the Dutch Republic after independence from Spain. Legal records indicate numerous instances of young women disguising themselves as men in order to go to war during the seventeenth century. Young women inspired by Hasselaer's bravery, and perhaps eager to achieve a similar fame, risked their lives and their reputations by following in Hasselaer's footsteps.

Some contemporaries praised Hasselaer's bravery but criticized this same behavior in other women. For most women, this type of role reversal was deemed unnatural. Hasselaer's fame, however, made it difficult to disparage her memory. Indeed, no other heroine of the Dutch revolt achieved the fame or status bestowed on Hasselaer. Despite the social stigma against so-called masculine behavior in women, the visual and written praise surrounding Hasselaer's heroism helped to eulogize other women who participated in the revolt.

The cities of Utrecht and Alkmaar used the images and descriptions of Hasselaer to praise their own heroines, Trijn van Leemput and Trijn Rembrands, but they never became household names. In contrast, Kenau's name became so familiar that it remains the Dutch term for an aggressive, assertive, or a so-called manly woman.

—*Martha Moffitt Peacock*

FURTHER READING

Dekker, Rudolf M., and Lotte C. van de Pol. *The Tradition of Female Transvestism in Early Modern Europe*. Translated by Judy Marcure and Lotte C. van de Pol. London: Macmillan Press, 1989. Dekker and van de Pol discuss the mixed reactions to and motivations of women dressing as men to enlist as sailors and soldiers. They investigate cases from the seventeenth and eighteenth centuries primarily, but they trace the tradition back to Kenau Hasselaer.

Kloek, Els. *Kenau: De heldhaftige zakenvrouw uit Haarlem (1526-1588)*. Hilversum, the Netherlands: Verloren, 2001. Although the text of this general biography of Hasselaer in the context of the revolt is in Dutch, the many reproduced images of the heroine are informative for readers not familiar with the Dutch language.

Peacock, Martha Moffitt. "Proverbial Reframing— Rebuking and Revering Women in Trousers." *Journal of the Walters Art Gallery* 57 (1999). This article links the general seventeenth century Dutch interest in images of powerful women to the early fame of Dutch heroines, particularly Kenau Hasselaer. It is argued that the attention given to these heroines caused a paranoia regarding female power, which manifested itself in satirical texts and ridiculing images of domineering women.

Schama, Simon. *The Embarrassment of Riches*. New York: Alfred A. Knopf, 1987. This already classic cultural history of the Dutch golden age briefly discusses Kenau Hasselaer in the general context of the revolt.

SEE ALSO: Duke of Alva; Alessandro Farnese; Margaret of Austria; Margaret of Parma; Johan van Oldernbarnevelt; Philip II; William the Silent.

JOHN KNOX
Scottish church reformer

The leading reformer and historian of the Protestant Reformation in Scotland, Knox gave to Calvinism its Presbyterian expression in both England and Scotland and found in covenant theology the rationale for political militancy.

BORN: c. 1514; Giffordgate, near Haddington, East Lothian, Scotland
DIED: November 24, 1572; Edinburgh, Scotland
AREAS OF ACHIEVEMENT: Church reform, religion and theology

EARLY LIFE

Although the exact date of his birth is still in dispute, John Knox (noks) was born probably at Giffordgate, near Haddington, a small town located eighteen miles east of Edinburgh in the coastal district of East Lothian. His father, William Knox, was a modest tradesman, and his mother's family name was Sinclair, but not much else is known about his family. He had a brother, William, who became a merchant at Prestonpans and traded goods between England and Scotland, but no other siblings are known.

Like most bright young men of humble birth, Knox was educated for the Catholic Church. He attended Latin school at Haddington, but his college training is far from certain. Historians once thought that he went to the University of Glasgow, but the judgment now is that he attended St. Andrews University in the late 1520's and early 1530's and studied under John Major, one of the leading Scholastic thinkers of the day. While his style of argumentation owed much to Scholasticism, Knox was not taken by the Aristotelian teachings of Major. Years later, he claimed to have been quite moved by church fathers such as Saint Augustine (354-430), Saint John Chrysostom (c. 354-407), and Saint Athanasius of Alexandria (c. 293-373). He also studied law. Thanks to a special dispensation, he was ordained into the priesthood before the canonical age of twenty-four. There were, however, many more priests than decent livings in the parishes of early sixteenth century Scotland, and Knox found employment as an apostolic notary, working in effect as a small country lawyer.

Except for his signature on several legal papers, almost nothing is known about Knox during the 1530's. Those documents, however, make clear that he dealt regularly not only with everyday people but also with the less-powerful lairds and nobility. He must have been

aware of the inroads being made by Protestant ideas and the ridicule being heaped on the Church for its wealth and for its many ignorant, venal, and immoral clergymen. By 1544, Knox was working as a tutor, instructing the sons of several Lothian lairds friendly toward George Wishart, a Lutheran preacher fleeing from James Beaton, cardinal and archbishop of St. Andrews. Much influenced by the charismatic Wishart, Knox traveled with him as he preached throughout East Lothian, reportedly brandishing a sword to protect Wishart. In January, 1546, however, Wishart was captured; quickly tried and convicted of heresy, he was burned at the stake the following March. In retaliation, Wishart's supporters murdered Cardinal Beaton in May, seized St. Andrews Castle, and sought the help of Scotland's ancient enemy, England, then undergoing religious reformation under Henry VIII.

Other Scottish Protestants took refuge in the castle of St. Andrews, including Knox and his pupils. After hearing the fiery Knox preach, the people gathered at the castle called him to be their minister. For more than a year, he served the congregation at St. Andrews, vigorously attacking the Papacy, the doctrine of purgatory, and the Mass. On July 31, 1547, the St. Andrews Protestants capitulated to a combined force of Scottish troops loyal to the queen regent Mary, the future queen of Scotland, and a fleet of French galleys. According to the terms of surrender, the prisoners, including Knox, were to be taken to France and there freed or transported to a country of their choice. Instead, they were either imprisoned in France or forced to labor as galley slaves. Knox remained in the galleys, probably chained much of the time to his oar, with little likelihood of ever being freed. The hardships deepened his commitment to Protestantism. After serving as a galley slave for nineteen months, Knox, along with several other prisoners, was freed, apparently through the diplomatic efforts of young Edward VI.

LIFE'S WORK

Making his way to England in early 1549, Knox was warmly received by the king's Privy Council, awarded a modest gratuity, and commissioned to preach in Berwick-upon-Tweed, located near the Scottish border. In late 1550, he removed to Newcastle, where he preached in the Church of St. Nicholas. The next year, he was among the six chosen as royal chaplains, thanks no doubt to his chief patron, the duke of Northumberland, a leading Protestant nobleman. Always vehement in his denunciations of the

Roman Catholic Church, Knox believed that the Church of England remained tainted by Catholic doctrine and ritual. He was among those who revised the Book of Common Prayer in 1552, contributing specifically the "black rubric," which denied that kneeling before the table implied adoration of the bread and wine. His inflexibility probably cost Knox the bishopric of Rochester, and even Northumberland grew weary of the opinionated preacher, though he never doubted Knox's utility and protected him from the mayor of Newcastle, who despised the irascible Scot. In June, 1553, Knox was sent to preach in Buckinghamshire. Mary Tudor (Mary I), a Roman Catholic, became queen in May, 1553, however, and English Protestants shortly found themselves facing persecution. Near the end of that year, Knox fled to France, joining a growing number of English Protestants known as the Marian exiles.

Accompanying him to France was his wife, Marjory, daughter of Elizabeth and Richard Bowes of Streatlam Castle, Durham. While preaching at Berwick, Knox had become good friends with Elizabeth Bowes. She encouraged Knox to marry her fifth daughter, though Knox was as old as Elizabeth Bowes herself. Her husband, Richard, did not approve of the match, and Elizabeth would later leave her husband and join Knox and her daughter in Geneva, where John Calvin provided refuge for the Marian exiles. At Calvin's urging, the Scotsman became the

John Knox. (Library of Congress)

preacher to the English congregation at Frankfurt am Main (now in Germany), but was forced to resign after a few months because the Anglican majority there objected to his strict Calvinism in church polity and liturgy. He was then called as pastor to the English congregation in Geneva. Thriving on controversy, he increasingly saw himself as a prophet of the Lord, calling both England and Scotland to repentance and right worship.

Knox returned to Scotland in late 1555. He felt secure enough to do so because Mary of Guise, the queen mother and regent for the young Mary, Queen of Scots, had found it expedient to tolerate Protestantism while she cultivated support for the marriage of her daughter to the dauphin of France. For almost nine months, Knox preached throughout the Lowlands, encouraging Protestant lords and the growing congregations of the faithful. He welcomed the support of John Erskine, Lord of Dun, and Lord Lorne, later the fifth earl of Argyll. He was also heartened that Protestantism could claim the prior of St. Andrews, Lord James Stewart, who later would become the regent, Lord Murray. Knox was well aware, however, that the nobility was largely self-serving and unreliable. His strongest support came from the lairds and the merchants and tradespeople of the towns and cities, where Protestantism was burgeoning. Around Easter, 1556, Knox and his followers, nobles and commoners alike, pledged themselves to advance "the true preaching" of the Gospel. This was the first of several "covenants" inspired by Knox, who was already looking to Calvin's federal theology to justify political resistance.

Protected by armed noblemen, Knox preached freely and dared to debate Catholic bishops. He was even bold enough to call on the queen regent herself to reform the Scottish Kirk (the Church of Scotland). After he returned to his congregation in Geneva in the fall of 1556, however, the Scottish bishops condemned him in absentia and burned his effigy, and the queen regent ridiculed his plea that she embrace Protestantism. The Protestant party in Scotland needed time to grow stronger, and Knox needed to refine his own thinking. Over the next three years, Knox learned much from and became close friends with John Calvin. He found Geneva under Calvin's rule "the greatest school of Christ" since the days of the Apostles. He longed for the triumph of Calvinism in both England and Scotland and prayed that both might be delivered from the Catholic women who ruled them. In fact, much to the chagrin of Calvin himself, Knox was hard at work developing a political theory justifying the revolution of godly subjects against ungodly rulers.

In a series of pamphlets published in 1558, Knox set forth his radical political ideas. He began by denouncing women rulers as monstrous and against the laws of God and nature. He then called on the Scottish nobility and the covenanted commoners to take up the sword and defend the faith against their Catholic rulers. Knox himself returned to Scotland in 1559 and became the central figure in its reformation. He wielded terrific political and religious influence, founding Presbyterianism and lecturing Mary, Queen of Scots, on the virtues of the good ruler. His first wife having died, Knox married for a second time in 1564. His bride was thirty-three years his junior and daughter to a laird of the powerful Stewart clan. Knox died in 1572, only two years before the disestablishment of the Roman Catholic Church in Scotland. His famous *The History of the Reformation of Religion Within the Realm of Scotland* was published posthumously in 1587.

SIGNIFICANCE

Knox was a popular preacher who contributed significantly to the Protestant triumph in both England and Scotland. The Presbyterian church of Scotland did not completely triumph until a few years after his death. Nevertheless, its congregational Calvinism clearly reflected Knox's views on church polity and would serve as a source of inspiration for the English Puritans, who grew increasingly restless with Anglicanism during the long reign of Elizabeth II.

Knox's Calvinism made him an internationalist in the faith, but he was first and last a Scotsman and infused Calvinism into Scottish nationalism. His writings did much to popularize the Scottish language. *The History of the Reformation of Religion Within the Realm of Scotland*, though extremely biased, is the fullest contemporary account of that upheaval. Inspired by Calvin's Geneva, Knox had plans for transforming his homeland into the City of God he detailed in *The First Book of Discipline* (1560), which the nobility refused to endorse. Those plans included a national system of poor relief and public education, both supervised by the Reformed Church of Scotland. The subsequent success of Scottish Calvinists in education owes no small debt to Knox's nationalistic vision.

As a political thinker, Knox is acknowledged as the best-known sixteenth century misogynist. In fact, *The First Blast of the Trumpet Against the Monstrous Regiment of Women* (1558) was a thoroughly uncompromising "complaint" against female rulers generally, though it was specifically directed against "Bloody Mary" Tudor

of England (Mary I). Knox also was thinking about Mary of Guise and her daughter, Mary, Queen of Scots. Ironically, shortly after the publication of his complaint, Mary I died, and Protestant Elizabeth I came to the throne. Elizabeth never forgave Knox for what he had written about the illegality of female rulers, and Knox, though he tried to flatter and encourage Elizabeth as the long-sought-after Protestant deliverer, never repudiated his views about women in politics. Knox's primary concern, however, was justifying the taking of power from Catholic rulers and giving it to Protestant leaders. He thought he had found ample justification in Calvin's covenant theology.

Not individuals, but the godly congregation covenanted together was the final authority for church polity. Should not the godly so covenanted resist an evil ruler? Passive resistance was as far as Calvin would ever go, fearing the political anarchy associated with Protestantism during the early years of the Reformation. By 1558, Knox was prepared to go much further. His attack on women rulers was less radical than what he had to say about the responsibility of godly nobility and even the commonalty to resist godless rulers. Shortly after *The First Blast of the Trumpet Against the Monstrous Regiment of Women*, in 1558, Knox published *The Appellation of John Knox . . . to the Nobility, Estates, and Commonalty* (of Scotland), in which he renounced the doctrine of Christian obedience to civil authority if the people in authority were ungodly. He told the nobility that it was their Christian duty to resist the ungodly queen regent. That was bold enough, but Knox had little confidence in the nobility. His most reliable support came from the commonalty, those sturdy farmers, merchants, and tradespeople of the congregations.

Appended to Knox's appeal was his *Letter to the Commonalty of Scotland*, in which Knox clearly stated that it was the duty of the common people to protect the true preaching of the Word. The congregations were to follow the nobility, if the lords would take the initiative and fight for reformation of church and state. If the nobility would not, the congregations must take matters into their own hands. It was their duty, as God's people, and to do less was to risk God's punishment on Earth and eternal damnation. It is important to note that, in speaking of the power of the people, Knox was referring to the people of God, under the discipline of the congregation, not to the people generally. Indeed, Knox believed that the godliness of the people justified their assumption of power, when all else failed.

Although surely no democrat in the modern sense of the word, Knox contributed mightily to the notion that the people who made the rules for the church could also rule the state. His thinking was widely endorsed by the English Puritans of the next century, who overthrew Charles I and who founded New England in North America. Indeed, Knox's legacy to both religion and politics has been a lasting one.

—Ronald William Howard

FURTHER READING

Graham, Roderick. *John Knox: Democrat*. London: R. Hale, 2001. Comprehensive if laudatory biography that seeks to defend Knox from modern charges of misogyny. Includes illustrations, bibliographic references, and index.

Greaves, Richard. *Theology and Revolution in the Scottish Reformation: Studies in the Thought of John Knox*. Grand Rapids, Mich.: Christian University Press, 1980. This is a fine analysis of Knox's theological and political thought by a leading scholar of the Reformation. It places Knox's ideas in historical perspective.

MacGregor, Geddes. *The Thundering Scot: A Portrait of John Knox*. London: Macmillan, 1958. A sympathetic portrayal of Knox, this popular biography reads like a novel and captures the hardships and triumphs of the Scottish reformer. It embellishes the facts somewhat but remains close to the secondary sources.

Marshall, Rosalind K. *John Knox*. Edinburgh: Birlinn, 2000. A portrait both of Knox and of the Scotland in which he lived, this study seeks to separate myth from reality to capture the complexities of Knox and his career. Includes illustrations, map, bibliographic references, and index.

Reid, W. Stanford. *Trumpeter of God: A Biography of John Knox*. New York: Charles Scribner's Sons, 1974. A scholarly study, this work examines the historiography on Knox, carefully separates Knox the individual from Knox the stereotype, and goes into some detail about the political and religious forces and the personalities that shaped the Scottish Reformation and its leading preacher

Ridley, Jasper. *John Knox*. New York: Oxford University Press, 1968. The most extensive biography of Knox to date, this study is drawn largely from the primary sources, especially Knox's own writings. It is especially strong on politics and Knox's political thought, but it does not neglect the theological or the personal faith of the reformer.

Walzer, Michael. *The Revolution of the Saints: A Study in the Origins of Radical Politics*. Cambridge, Mass.: Harvard University Press, 1965. This is a remarkable study that demonstrates how Calvinism provided the basis for a political ideology that sanctioned revolution as a positive duty. Walzer sees Knox as an early personification of that radical perspective that contributed much to the concept of popular sovereignty in the Western world.

Watt, Hugh. *John Knox in Controversy*. London: Thomas Nelson and Sons, 1950. An early scholarly study that challenged the traditional view of Knox as simply an obnoxious bigot. Watt explains the provocation for Knox's polemics and emphasizes his contribution to building the Scottish Kirk.

Wilkinson, John. *The Medical History of the Reformers: Martin Luther, John Calvin, John Knox*. Edinburgh: Handsel Press, 2001. Study of the privations and maladies Knox was inflicted with during his 19-month ordeal as a galley slave. Includes photographic plates, bibliographic references, and index.

SEE ALSO: John Calvin; Edward VI; Elizabeth I; Saint John Fisher; Henry VIII; Hugh Latimer; Mary, Queen of Scots; Mary of Guise; Mary I; William Tyndale.

RELATED ARTICLES in *Great Events from History: The Renaissance & Early Modern Era, 1454-1600:* August 22, 1513-July 6, 1560: Anglo-Scottish Wars; July, 1553: Coronation of Mary Tudor; May, 1559-August, 1561: Scottish Reformation.

KRISHNADEVARAYA
Emperor of the Vijayanagar Empire (r. 1509-1529)

Krishnadevaraya's reign was marked by a flowering of literature and a strong military. He was a patron of the arts and a poet but also a successful ruler, administrator, and military leader. He defeated hereditary chieftains, aspired to integrate international trade into the Vijayanagar economy, and worked to centralize the empire's administration.

BORN: Date unknown; place unknown
DIED: 1529; Vijayanagar, Vijayanagar Empire (now Hampi, India)
ALSO KNOWN AS: Kṛṣṇa Deva Rāya; Krishna-Deva-Raya; Krishnadeva Raya; Krsnadev Rai; Krishnadeva Raja
AREAS OF ACHIEVEMENT: Government and politics, patronage of the arts, military, warfare and conquest

EARLY LIFE

Krishnadevaraya (krish-nah-DAY-vah-ri-ah) was born into an empire whose throne would be usurped in 1505 by his brother, who established Tuluva dynastic rule. The Tuluvas reigned from the time of the usurpation until Rama Raja's defeat by the Mongols in the Battle of Talikot in 1565. This period was referred to as the third dynasty.

Prior to his accession as king in 1509, Krishnadevaraya was educated in languages, music, and religion. These years enabled him to maintain Telegu and Kannada as court languages written in a common script, known as Vijaya Lipi. He learned the arts of didactic poetry, which he later composed, resulting in one of the few extant Telegu *mahakavyas*, a particular style of epic poetry. These early years instilled in Krishnadevaraya an appreciation for the fine arts, which would last throughout his reign.

LIFE'S WORK

Krishnadevaraya experienced the greatest threats to a king's rule in the empire's history. Shortly after he succeeded his brother as king in 1509, his authority was threatened. The sultanate of Bijapur wanted the territory of Raichur in the northwest. In the northeast, the Gajapatis of Orissa wanted to expand their territory into Krishnadevaraya's realm. Karnataka chiefs had opposed the Tuluva accession, and under the leadership of the Ummatur, the chiefs worked to expand into Telegu areas. Gangaraja, the leader of the Ummatur chieftains, had built strongholds in the upper Kaveri. From Srirangapat-

tanam and Sivasamudram, Gangaraja discharged campaigns across the Andhra and Karnataka plains, to threaten Vijayanagar on western and southern fronts simultaneously. Gangaraja wished to inhibit communication within the Vijayanagar Empire's Telegu and Tamil domains.

Krishnadevaraya utilized similar yet overwhelmingly effective tactics against all three of these threats. He combined a series of military campaigns with a policy that reduced the power of the nobles and chiefs dramatically. Militarily, chiefs in the Tungabhadra-Krishna river basin were constrained by an arrangement of royal fortresses. These fortresses were commanded by Brahmans and garrisoned by a diverse array of troops. The troops included both Portuguese and Muslim mercenaries, and foot soldiers recruited from the "forest people" of the nonpeasant communities within the Vijayanagar dominions.

Additionally, Krishnadevaraya developed a system of lower-ranked chiefs, later called poligars by the British, who were dependent on military service under Krishnadevaraya. The poligars were keepers of the Vijayanagar forts and members of the infantry. Gangaraja and Sivasamudram were destroyed in 1512, but Gangaraja's successor was allowed to rule from Srirangapattanam. Later, this fortress would also fall to Krishnadevaraya. His successes in these territories demonstrated his intelligence as king and enhanced his subjects' confidence in him. In Virupaksha Temple, six months after his coronation, two titles were added to his monument: "Hindu Sultan" and "fever to the elephants of Gajapati."

The success of Krishnadevaraya's political, economic, and administrative strategies depended on areas rich in agriculture, population, and commerce. Resources from these areas made it possible for Krishnadevaraya to control the chiefdoms of the drier areas of Vijayanagar. Vijayanagar's environment divided into two types—soil-rich areas and drier plains—and the relationship between these categories provided difficulties and assistance to Krishnadevaraya's attempts at centralization.

To administer the newly centralized Vijayanagar Empire, Krishnadevaraya developed a system of command. Under Krishnadevaraya, nobles were entrusted with land, which they farmed to their own advantage but paid a fixed annual sum to the Crown. Several of Krishnadevaraya's military leaders served in this way. Nagama Nayaka, a trusted officer of Krishnadevaraya's, was not to be trusted, however. Nagama Nayaka's history survives in chronicles of the rise of the Nayaka kingdom of Madurai. According to these chronicles, Krishnadevaraya had commanded Nagama to perform a task that would defeat a challenge to the king's authority. After doing so, Nagama proclaimed himself sole ruler of Madurai. His son betrayed Nagama to Krishnadevaraya, displaying loyalty to his king over his father. Because of his honesty, Krishnadevaraya appointed Visvanatha governor of another part of Tamil country. This system was later misrepresented as akin to feudal Europe to support a theme of "backward" Indian history.

The richest provinces of Vijayanagar were not within the Tungabhadra-Krishna basin, which formed the core of the empire. Krishnadevaraya retained the resources of the rich Karnataka *maidan* (open plains) of the upper Kaveri under a system of tribute, but this wealth was lost by Krishnadevaraya's successors during the Wodeyar secession, in which the local chiefs separated from the Vijayanagar Empire. Telegu warrior-peasants resided on the agricultural frontiers of Vijayanagar during Krishnadevaraya's reign, as a result of decades of migrations. These farmers posed a challenge to Krishnadevaraya's revenue-seeking, regulated regime. Krishnadevaraya elected to rely on other sources for revenue, largely the wet zones of cultivation, which were richer in resources. The Tamil plains provided political assistance and monetary support to Krishnadevaraya but, as with the Wodeyar secession, did not extend greatly to the remaining Tuluvas. As a whole, though, rulers of the areas of cultivation were only slightly more amiable toward Krishnadevaraya.

Krishnadevaraya's Brahman minister attempted to gain from international trade along the coast, and Krishnadevaraya accorded great economic and ideological importance to this endeavor. His Telegu epic poem, *Āmuktamālyadā* (1520), conveyed these ideas and demonstrated his proficiency as a scholar and artist and his military and administrative talents. In this poem, he states that import and export are essential to the growth of a kingdom. Demonstrating considerable insight into the wider world, he recognized the need to care for foreign sailors in a manner suitable to their nationalities. Shrewdly, he promoted a need to monopolize elephant and horse trade on the peninsula with the Portuguese and Muslims. He did indeed interact with Portuguese and Muslim traders, as explorers' accounts show.

Unfortunately, despite his eloquent ideals, there is no evidence that Vijayanagar realized any great profits from international trade. Had the *Āmuktamālyadā* been actualized, Krishnadevaraya's plans for a centralized kingship

would have had sufficient resources to succeed. The only resources regularly utilized by Krishnadevaraya were in the Tungabhadra-Krishna basin, which had a population of about 2 million people and encompassed 30,000 square miles. It extended from the Kannada-speaking districts (modern Bellary) to the Telegu-speaking districts (modern Kurnool).

In the middle of dry fields were small pockets of production, which were derived from tank irrigation. The soil was ideal for cotton, and some of the best peninsular pasturages for cattle and sheep were also in the Vijayanagar heartland. These resources were enough to maintain an affluent kingdom and to build scores of temples and monuments but not to meet the lofty goals set forth in the *Āmuktamālyadā*. Krishnadevaraya's aspirations to a perfectly regulated, centralized Vijayanagar were not to be fully realized because of a need for greater resources.

SIGNIFICANCE

Krishnadevaraya's campaigns brought wealth and great honor to Vijayanagar. By defeating ancient chiefdoms surrounding Vijayanagar, he consolidated the power of the empire. His system of administration, while not wholly successful, was innovative and well organized, and it formed the basis for many of successor states after 1565. His successors were less competent than he, but Krishnadevaraya's systems of poligars endured well through the British Raj.

His poetry remains among the foundational texts of late medieval Telegu literature, and his ability to excel in a variety of areas contributed to his personal greatness and his ability to elevate Vijayanagar.

—Monica Piotter

FURTHER READING

Filliozat, Vasundhara. *The Vijayanagara Empire: As Seen by Domingos Paes and Fernao Nuniz, Two Sixteenth Century Chroniclers*. New Delhi, India: National Book Trust, 1977. Domingos Paes and Fernao Nuniz, Portuguese explorers who visited Vijayanagar during Krishnadevaraya's reign, offer an ample descriptive panegyric of Krishnadevaraya, depict the court, and report on the organization of the Krishnadevaraya government.

Karashima, Noboru. *Towards a New Formation: South Indian Society Under Vijayanagar Rule*. New York: Oxford University Press, 1997. Not strictly a biography of Krishnadevaraya, this work describes the social history of Vijayanagar.

Kulke, Hermann, ed. *The State in India, 1000-1700.* Delhi, India: Oxford University Press, 1995. This work depicts a variety of Indian states in the medieval and early modern period through 1700, including Vijayanagar at its zenith.

Rao, M. Rama. *Krishnadevaraya.* New Delhi, India: 1971. Rao's biography remains the foremost authority on Krishnadevaraya and is the clearest secondary source about his time.

Sarasvati, Rangasvami. "Political Maxims of the Emperor-Poet Krishnadeva Raya." *Journal of Indian History* 4, no. 3 (1925). This article remains among the foremost translations and analyses of Krishnadevaraya's own writings, especially the *Āmuktamālyadā.*

Sastri, K. A. Kilakanta, and N. Venkataramanayya. *Further Sources in Vijayanagara History.* Madras, India: University of Madras Press, 1946. This multivolume set includes translations of texts from and relating to Krishnadevaraya's reign and provides contextual documents for the reigns of other Vijayanagar rulers.

Stein, Burton. *The New Cambridge History of India.* New York: Cambridge University Press, 1989. Volume 1 of this multivolume set centers on the empire from 1509 to 1565 and the reigns of Krishnadevaraya and Rama Raja. Stein offers a valuable account of the state of the city and empire during Krishnadevaraya's reign and also a fairly detailed representation of Krishnadevaraya's political and military legacies.

Wagoner, Phillip B. *Tidings of the King: A Translation and Ethnohistorical Analysis of the "Rāyavācakamu."* Honolulu: University of Hawaii Press, 1993. The *Rāyavācakamu,* written about ninety years after Krishnadevaraya's reign, is one of the Nayaka epics chronicling his reign. Wagoner translates sixteenth century Telegu remarkably well, and he offers astute analyses of the climate in which the *Rāyavācakamu* was written, its communication of the memory of Krishnadevaraya, and the possible links between the epic and the actual history.

SEE ALSO: Akbar; Bābur; Humāyūn; Nānak.

RELATED ARTICLE in *Great Events from History: The Renaissance & Early Modern Era, 1454-1600:* 1509-1565: Vijayanagar Wars.

AEMILIA LANYER
English poet

One of the first women in England to publish a book of original poetry, Lanyer opposed the time's patriarchal conventions and social proscriptions. She also wrote the first country house poem published in England.

BORN: January 27, 1569; London, England
DIED: 1645; London
ALSO KNOWN AS: Aemelia Bassano (given name); Emilia Lanier
AREAS OF ACHIEVEMENT: Literature, women's rights

EARLY LIFE

Aemilia Lanyer (ih-MIHL-ee-ah LAN-yuhr) was born Aemilia Bassano. Her exact date of birth is unknown, but she was baptized January 27, 1569, in the church of St. Bardolph's, Bishopgate, England. Her father was Baptista Bassano, a musician in the court of Elizabeth I. Some historians have argued that the Bassano family was of Jewish origins, but the evidence is inconclusive. Lanyer herself seems to have been raised as a Protestant. Her father died when Lanyer was seven, and her mother, Margaret Johnson, died when Lanyer was eighteen.

Lanyer wrote that as a child she served in the household of Susan Bertie, dowager countess of Kent. Although little is known directly of Lanyer's education, she would most likely have learned Italian from her father, his family, and connections, and would have received an education in music. It is not known how long she served in the dowager countess's household, but there she would have been exposed to Protestant learning and devotion as well as a Humanist education. From her work, it seems that this education included Latin classical works and possibly some Greek.

At some point, most likely after her mother's death, Lanyer became the mistress of Henry Carey, lord Hunsdon (about forty-five years older than she). When she became pregnant, she was married to a court musician, Alfonso Lanyer, on October 10, 1592. A son born early the next year was named Henry. Based partly on these events, a case for identifying Lanyer as the "dark lady" of William Shakespeare's sonnets has not been accepted widely. A daughter, Odillya, was born December, 1598, and died in September, 1599. Although marriage most likely took Lanyer away from court circles, it does seem that she spent time with her patron Margaret Clifford, countess of Cumberland, and Margaret's daughter, Anne, at the country estate of Cookham perhaps between 1603 and 1605.

LIFE'S WORK

Lanyer is best known for a single book of poetry, *Salve Deus Rex Judæorum* (1611; *The Poems of Shakespeare's Dark Lady: Salve Deus Rex Judæorum*, 1978), which was entered in the Stationer's Register October 2, 1610. The volume begins with a number of dedications in verse and prose, followed by two poems: "Salve Deus" and "The Description of Cooke-ham." "Salve Deus," by far the most substantial piece in the volume, is a narrative poem written in ottava rima (stanza of eight lines of heroic verse) depicting Christ's Passion. The poem is presented in four parts: "The Passion of Christ," "Eves Apologie in Defence of Women," "The Teares of the Daughters of Jerusalem," and "The Salutation and Sorrow of the Virgine Marie." This single volume is all that is extant or known of Lanyer's poetry, but Lanyer's achievement is important from a number of perspectives.

The first notable feature of "Salve Deus" is the multiple dedications it contains in a variety of poetic forms and prose. Although multiple dedications were not unusual at a time when poets routinely dedicated their work to nobles from whom they sought patronage, Lanyer's dedications are exceptional in that all are to women, including Queen Anne, Princess Elizabeth, and Mary Sidney. Not all the extant copies of *Salve Deus Rex Judæorum*, however, contain the same dedications, which could indicate that Lanyer was conscious of the politically sensitive nature of some of her choices of dedicatees. The protofeminist nature of Lanyer's poems makes it clear that her decision to dedicate the work to women entirely was no coincidence. There is no evidence that the book won her the support she sought.

"Salve Deus," the longest poem in the volume, is noteworthy for its thoughtful exploration of the role of women in Christianity and particularly in the Passion. In the poem, Lanyer moves easily between biblical and classical allusions, suggesting something of the breadth of her own reading. She presents a feminized Christ betrayed and wronged by the men around him. In the poem's closely argued defense of Eve, Lanyer maintains that while Eve's fall was the result of ignorance, Eve's sin is vastly outweighed by the sins of men in condemning and crucifying Christ. She points out that Pilate's wife attempted to save Christ, only to be denied.

In the final two sections of the poem—"The Teares of the Daughters of Jerusalem" and "The Salutation and Sorrow of the Virgine Marie"—Lanyer depicts the women

---

LANYER'S APOLOGY FOR EVE

Aemelia Lanyer's longest poem, Salve Deus Rex Judæorum, *in part a defense of the biblical Eve, suggests in no uncertain terms in the stanza here that women should be the equals of men because it was men, and not women, who crucified Christ. Women, therefore, do not need to be redeemed.*

Then let us have our Libertie againe,
And challendge to your selves no Sov'raigntie;
You came not in the world without our paine,
Make that a barre against your crueltie;
Your fault beeing greater, why should you disdaine
Our beeing your equals, free from tyranny?
If one weake woman simply did offend,
This sinne of yours, hath no excuse, nor end.

Source: Excerpted from *Salve Deus Rex Judæorum* (1611), by Aemilia Lanyer. Renascence Editions, An Online Repository of Works Printed in English Between the Years 1477 and 1799. University of Oregon. http://darkwing .uoregon.edu/~rbear/ren.htm. Accessed September 23, 2004.

---

who mourn at Christ's suffering and death, while Mary's love is rewarded with an angelic visitation offering her comfort. Lanyer's opening and closing of the poem praise the virtues and chastity of Lanyer's main patrons, Margaret Clifford and her daughter, Anne, countess of Dorset. Some critics have found these passages intrusive, but they link the poem to its dedications and look forward to the final poem of the volume, "The Description of Cooke-ham."

Although Ben Jonson is usually credited with the first country house poem, Lanyer's "The Description of Cooke-ham" was the first country house poem published in England. Country house poems conventionally celebrate a family, their estate, and their creation of social order based in courtesy and aristocratic virtue. Some of these poems also sought to offer instruction on the mutual obligations of the estate's owners and the supporting community. Lanyer's poem praises the country house estate of Cookham where Margaret Clifford and her daughter lived for a time. Lanyer once again makes a community of women, including herself, the center of her poem. Cookham seems to have no lord, and men are absent from the poem. Unlike other examples of the genre, Lanyer's has an elegiac quality, and at the conclusion of the poem, the estate is imagined mourning the departure of the women.

It is assumed that Lanyer's poetry did not win the patronage she sought, because it seems she did not pub-

lish again, and one can catch only glimpses of the rest of her life. Her husband died in 1613. From 1617 to 1619, she opened and ran a school for the children of the wealthy. Her later life involved litigation against Alfonso's family as she sought income derived from a patent originally held by her husband. Lanyer was buried at St. James Clerkenwell on April 3, 1645.

SIGNIFICANCE

Lanyer's work is still being assessed, and her significance has yet to be fully appreciated. *Salve Deus Rex Judæorum* appeared in a first edition only, and there are no known contemporary references to her poetry.

Lanyer's work, however, enjoyed a substantial revival in the twentieth century, a revival that continues into the twenty-first century. She is widely studied in early modern literature courses and in courses on women's writing, and scholarship on her poetry suggests her work is valued both for what it adds to the knowledge of protofeminist thought of the early modern period and for its intrinsic value as the work of an original, thoughtful, and critical poet.

—*Christine Cornell*

FURTHER READING

Grossman, Marshall, ed. *Aemilia Lanyer: Gender, Genre, and the Canon.* Lexington: University Press of Kentucky, 1998. A collection of eleven essays by top scholars in the field, including David Bevington's critique of A. L. Rowse's case for Lanyer as Shakespeare's "dark lady."

Lamb, Mary Ellen. "Patronage and Class in Aemilia Lanyer's *Salve Deus Rex Judæorum.*" In *Women, Writing, and the Reproduction of Culture in Tudor and Stuart Britain*, edited by Mary E. Burke, Jane Donawerth, Linda L. Dove, and Karen Nelson. Syracuse, N.Y.: Syracuse University Press, 2000. Discusses the issue of class in the context of arts patronage in Lanyer's time, and includes a look at Lanyer's dedications to her patrons.

Lasocki, David. *The Bassanos: Venetian Musicians and Instrument Makers in England, 1531-1665.* Aldershot, England: Scolar Press, 1995. Helpful discussion of the evidence pointing to a Jewish background for the Bassano family. One chapter argues for the identification of Lanyer as the "dark lady."

McGrath, Lynette. *Subjectivity and Women's Poetry in Early Modern England: "Why on the Ridge Should She Desire to Go?"* Burlington, Vt.: Ashgate, 2002. Lanyer is one of three poets examined extensively in this feminist psychoanalytic study of women's writing in the early modern era.

Rowse, A. L., ed. *The Poems of Shakespeare's Dark Lady: "Salve Deus Rex Judæorum" by Emilia Lanier.* London: Jonathan Cape, 1978. Using the diaries of the astrologer Simon Forman, Rowse makes a case for identifying Lanyer as the "dark lady" of Shakespeare's sonnets.

Woods, Susanne. *Lanyer: A Renaissance Poet in Her Context.* New York: Oxford University Press, 1999. A careful and detailed examination of Lanyer's life and all that is known about her. Places Lanyer in the context of other poets of her day.

_____, ed. *The Poems of Aemilia Lanyer: Salve Deus Rex Judæorum.* New York: Oxford University Press, 1993. This annotated edition of Lanyer's poems begins with a helpful biography.

SEE ALSO: Elizabeth I; Marguerite de Navarre; William Shakespeare.

RELATED ARTICLE in *Great Events from History: The Renaissance & Early Modern Era, 1454-1600:* c. 1589-1613: Shakespeare Writes His Dramas.

BARTOLOMÉ DE LAS CASAS
Spanish historian and explorer

Las Casas wrote a history of the early Spanish conquests in the New World and participated in the Spanish conquest of the Caribbean. Concerned with the plight of the Caribbean Indians, he spent more than fifty years attempting to free them from their European oppressors, working to destroy the encomienda *system and finding peaceful ways of converting Indians to Christianity.*

BORN: August, 1474; Seville, Castile (now in Spain)
DIED: July 17, 1566; Madrid, Spain
AREAS OF ACHIEVEMENT: Religion and theology, social reform, exploration, warfare and conquest

EARLY LIFE

Bartolomé de Las Casas (bahr-toh-loh-MAY day lahs KAHS-ahs) was born into the family of a not very successful merchant, Pedro de Las Casas, who sailed with Christopher Columbus on his second voyage to the New World. Las Casas had witnessed the triumph of Columbus's return to Seville from his first voyage in March, 1493. He saw service in the militia against Moors in the Granada Rebellion (1497), studied Latin and theology at the cathedral academy in Seville, and became a lay teacher of Christian doctrine.

In 1502, Las Casas accompanied Nicolás de Ovando, the designated governor, to Española. There, he participated in putting down Caribbean Indian uprisings, for which he was rewarded with a royal grant of lands and Indians (*encomienda*). He was successful as a planter, and

he began to evangelize the Indians in his role as lay catechist. In 1506, he gave up his lands, going to Rome, where he took vows in the Order of Preachers (Dominicans). On his return to Española, in 1512, he was ordained a priest—probably the first in the Americas to receive Holy Orders. He was made chaplain with the forces that were engaged in the colonization of Cuba (begun in 1511 by Diego Velázquez de Cuéllar, although Las Casas was there only in the last year, 1513), for which he again received a grant of Indians and lands.

LIFE'S WORK

Perhaps it was his experiences and observations in the Cuban colonization (including the massacre of Caonao) and other military expeditions in Española, or the harsh realities of treatment of the Caribbean Indians in the mining and agricultural projects throughout the Spanish Antilles, where the number of indigenous was rapidly being depleted, or perhaps it was his position as priest and land grantee that led Las Casas to begin, at age forty, what would become his life's work. He attributed his change of lifestyle to his meditations on chapter 34 of Ecclesiastes. In any case, he gave his *encomienda* holdings to Diego Columbus and began to preach against the oppression of the Indians, calling for an end to the system of expropriating their land and enslaving them. He returned to Spain to lobby on behalf of the Indians in 1515. The cardinal archbishop of Toledo, Francisco Jiménez de Cisneros, supported him in this crusade, naming him priest-procurator of the Indies and appointing him to a commission to investigate the status of the Indians (1516).

Las Casas developed a plan for peaceful colonization and returned to Spain in July, 1517, to recruit farmers and obtain land for the experiment. The Holy Roman Emperor and king of Spain Charles V gave him permission to colonize an estate in Curmána, Venezuela (1510-1521). He later retracted a suggestion that slaves be imported for labor from West Africa. With an expression of shame, he regretted that he came so late to the realization that Africans had the same human rights as American Indians. The settlement was a failure, and Las Casas retired from public life to the Dominican monastery at Santo Domingo. It was during this time that he wrote the first draft of *Historia de las Indias* (wr. 1527-1561, pb. 1875-1876; partial translation, *History of the Indies*, 1971).

Las Casas was active in defense of the Indians in Mexico (1532) and in Nicaragua (1535-1536). During these years, he also visited and worked in defense of the Indians in Peru, Puerto Rico, and other settlements in the Spanish New World colonies. After Pope Paul III proclaimed the Indians' rationality and equality with other men to receive instructions and the faith (June 2, 1537), Las Casas renewed his activity to colonize and Christianize the Indians peacefully. His most notable success was in Guatemala.

In 1539, Las Casas returned to Spain. He continued his writings in defense of the Indians, including *Brevísima relación de la destruyción de las Indias* (1552; *The Tears of the Indians*, 1656; also known as *A Brief Account of the Devastation of the Indies*). In this treatise, he placed the desire for gold and material wealth at the center of motivation for all the injustice toward the Indians. Las Casas attributed the continued injustice to the greed of those in power. Because of this greed, those in power did not support just laws; rather, they opposed them in order to continue the system and institutions that would further their material gain.

Las Casas also began his struggle for the passage of the New Laws (1542 and 1543). These laws reorganized the Council of the Indies and prohibited the oppression of, exploitation of, and cruelty toward the Indians, against which Las Casas had long crusaded. These laws also prohibited the continuation of slavery for Indians of the second generation. Las Casas found support for his position in Spain at Court, in the Church, and in the Council of the Indies. In the colonies, however, the New Laws were received with great opposition and were largely unenforced. They were revoked in part, but later the key elements were reinstated.

Las Casas was named bishop of Chiapas in Guatemala and left Spain in July, 1544, with forty-four Dominicans to establish missions there for the peaceful Christianization of the Indians. He arrived in Guatemala after many interim stops in March, 1545. He proceeded with zeal rather than with practicality to enforce the New Laws, which led to protests and demonstrations against him in the colony. He was forced to return to Spain in 1547.

At the age of seventy-five, Las Casas renounced his bishopric and continued his life of tireless lobbying and protest in the cause of the Indians. He defended the equality and dignity of the Indians against all who were bent on their enslavement and oppression. In 1550 at Valladolid, he engaged in public debate with the Jesuit Juan Ginés de Sepúlveda, who had maintained that the Indians were inferior to the Spaniards. The controversy, which continued through the next year, has been debated anew through the centuries since. Las Casas organized missions to be staffed by learned and religious mendicants, who would Christianize and educate the Indians.

Bartolomé de Las Casas. (Library of Congress)

Las Casas continued to write. He also came to be an influential adviser to the Council of the Indies and at court on the many problems related to the colonies of the New World. He was a frequent witness at trials to free Indians, and much of his writing was directed to this end. He died in his early nineties in the Dominican convent of Nuestra Señora de Atocha in Madrid. The king of Spain, Phillip II, had all the works of Las Casas (published and unpublished) collected and preserved.

SIGNIFICANCE

Las Casas lived in the transitional period from the medieval to the modern age. He was traditional in his adherence to doctrine. His writings were based on the Gospel and teachings of the Church. Yet, he had an understanding of and sensitivity to the changing world about him. He was a Christian intellectual who became a prophet in the political and economic climate of his times; his society, however, was not ready and not eager to hear his message.

He anticipated many of the principles enunciated in the Charter of the United Nations (1945) and proclaimed by Vatican Council II (1963). His preaching, his planning, his colonial enterprises, and his writings were concerned with reforming the colonial practices of his day, with preaching the Gospel by peaceful persuasion, with abhorrence of violence and oppression, and with individual liberty and self-determination as the right of all peoples. He meant his *History of the Indies* to be a call for social and political change. He clearly inveighed against the injustice and immorality of the colonial system and institutions of the fifteenth and sixteenth centuries. Through his writings, he inspired the nineteenth century revolutionary, Simón Bolívar, and the leaders of the Mexican Revolution in which the independence of that people was won from Spain.

Las Casas's most important writings among the vast body of works he produced were *Del único modo* (wr. 1539, pb. 1942), which was on the theory of evangelization, *Apologética historia de las Indias* (wr. 1527-1560, pb. 1909), which was an analysis of the Indians' abilities, and his two histories of the Indies. The last of these, according to his instructions, was not to be published until forty years after his death, although the prologue was published in 1562. Nevertheless, a manuscript was circulated even before the publication by the Academy of Madrid, 1875-1876.

His writings, while they exaggerate the plight of the Indians and the cruelty of the Europeans, have fueled the "Black Legend" of Spanish cruelty in the New World promulgated by Spain's enemies and later taken up by nationalists and anticolonialists. His teachings concerning the equality of all peoples of the earth—the right of all people to determine their own destiny and to have their basic needs satisfied—were his most important legacy and have caused his writings to be debated throughout the world for more than four hundred years.

—Barbara Ann Barbato

FURTHER READING

Freide, Juan, and Benjamin Keen, eds. *Bartolomé de Las Casas in History: Toward an Understanding of the Man and His Work*. De Kalb: Northern Illinois University Press, 1971. A series of analytical essays on the life and ideology of Las Casas, on his activities and his impact on the Americas and history, and on his writings. The essays are written by authors of different nationalities and ideologies, thus bringing a variety of perspectives to bear on their subject. The text vindicates Las Casas and his ideals in the course that history has taken since his death.

González-Casanovas, Roberto J. *Imperial Histories from Alfonso X to Inca Garcilaso: Revisionist Myths of Reconquest and Conquest*. Potomac, Md.: Scripta Humanistica, 1997. Examines the political and ideological functions of official historiographies of Spanish conquest in the Americas and reconquest in Iberia. Reads Las Casas's critiques of colonialism alongside the pro-colonial writings of his contemporaries. Includes bibliographic references and index.

Hanke, Lewis. *Bartolomé de Las Casas: An Interpretation of His Life and Writings*. Philadelphia: University of Pennsylvania Press, 1959. Hanke's scholarly study is a sound biography of the life of Las Casas.

Helps, Arthur. *The Life of Las Casas: The Apostle of the Indies*. New York: Gordon Press, 1976. A standard biography of Las Casas.

Hodgkins, Christopher. *Reforming Empire: Protestant Colonialism and Conscience in British Literature*. Columbia: University of Missouri Press, 2002. Study of the ways in which Protestantism became a major discourse for both justifying and condemning the early modern English colonial project. Includes a study of English representations of Spanish conquistadores and the relationship between Las Casas's descriptions of Spanish conquest and Milton's portrayals of satanic Spaniards. Bibliographic references and index.

Keen, Benjamin. *Essays in the Intellectual History of Colonial Latin America*. Boulder, Colo.: Westview Press, 1998. This collection includes an essay surveying 460 years of Las Casas scholarship, and another essay evaluating Las Casas's legacy. Bibliographic references and index.

Las Casas, Bartolomé de. *History of the Indies.* Edited and translated by Andrée M. Collard. New York: Harper & Row, 1971. Collard's introduction provides a helpful analysis of Las Casas the man, the thinker, and the writer. Collard also answers criticisms of Las Casas.

Lupher, David A. *Romans in a New World: Classical Models in Sixteenth-Century Spanish America.* Ann Arbor: University of Michigan Press, 2003. Study of the influence of Roman models of empire on the Spanish imperial project. Discusses competing attitudes of Las Casas and Sepúlveda. Includes bibliographic references and indexes.

MacNutt, Francis A. *Bartholomew de Las Casas: His Life, His Apostolate, and His Writings.* New York: G. P. Putnam's Sons, 1909. Reprint. New York: AMS Press, 1972. This was the standard biography in English of Las Casas, but it has been superseded by the works of Lewis Hanke.

Remesal, Antonio de. *Bartolomé de Las Casas, 1474-1566, in the Pages of Father Antonio de Remesal.*

Translated and annotated by Felix Jay. Lewiston, N.Y.: Edwin Mellen Press, 2002. Translation and commentary on a life of Las Casas written sixty years after his death. Includes bibliographic references.

Wagner, Henry Raup, and Helen Rand Parish. *The Life and Writings of Bartolomé de Las Casas.* Albuquerque: University of New Mexico Press, 1967. A critical and detailed study of Las Casas. Wagner presents Las Casas as a prolific writer, and, equally, as one of action. Las Casas emerges with tremendous stature even among the giants of the sixteenth century. Wagner includes a narrative and critical catalog of Las Casas's writings.

SEE ALSO: Charles V; Christopher Columbus; Guacanagarí; Francisco Jiménez de Cisneros; Paul III; Philip II.

RELATED ARTICLES in *Great Events from History: The Renaissance & Early Modern Era, 1454-1600:* 1495-1510: West Indian Uprisings; 1502: Beginning of the Transatlantic Slave Trade; 1537: Pope Paul III Declares Rights of New World Peoples; 1542-1543: The New Laws of Spain; 1552: Las Casas Publishes *The Tears of the Indians.*

ORLANDO DI LASSO
Flemish composer

Lasso is often regarded as the most imaginative and influential of sixteenth century composers because of his mastery of virtually every Renaissance musical style, technique, and form, and because of his tremendous productivity, which included more than two thousand works.

BORN: 1532; Mons, Hainaut, Flanders (now in Belgium)

DIED: June 14, 1594; Munich, Bavaria (now in Germany)

ALSO KNOWN AS: Roland de Lassus; Orlandus Lassus; Orland Lassus

AREA OF ACHIEVEMENT: Music

EARLY LIFE

Born in Mons, situated in the region between France and the Spanish Netherlands, Orlando di Lasso was a singer of such skill and tonal purity as a child that myth says en-

terprising kidnappers targeted him three times to auction him to the highest "cultured" bidder.

Unlike so many obscure and impoverished composers throughout music history, Lasso became well known and affluent doing just as he pleased; that is, he traveled, enjoyed life, and composed music with enormous profusion and variety. His journeys across Europe and his rise to fame began at age twelve, when Ferrante Gonzaga, a Mantuan general in the army of Holy Roman Emperor Charles V, recruited him into his retinue in 1544.

In 1545, Gonzaga took Lasso to Sicily, Milan, Naples, and Rome. In Rome in 1553, Lasso landed the post of *maestro di cappella* (choir master) at San Giovanni Laterano (Saint John Lateran). Under ordinary circumstances, gaining this post would have made the career of most musicians, but for Lasso, it marked the inauguration of his climb to preeminence. At Rome, he probably met Giovanni Pierluigi da Palestrina, to whom he is often compared and with whom he is usually linked as one of the two greatest composers of the sixteenth century. Palestrina was master of the choir in the Julian Chapel and succeeded Lasso after his brief stint at San Giovanni Laterano.

LIFE'S WORK

Lasso began composing sometime during his Italian voyages. From the start, he displayed the inventiveness and economy of expression that would mark nearly all his compositions, one of the most notable of which, the *Prophetiae Sibyllarum* (1600), may have been composed, but not yet published, during this period. At an early stage of his career, he grasped the financial and professional value of publication, so he went north to Antwerp in 1555 and had published some of his earliest pieces.

Almost simultaneously, he brought out his first book of madrigals in Venice. By the end of his life, thirty-nine years later, he had published more work than any other composer of the century, distinguishing himself as an uncompromising artist and a thriving musical entrepreneur.

In 1556, Lasso left Antwerp for Munich to sing tenor in the chapel of Duke Albert V of Bavaria. Two years after his arrival, he married a well-to-do woman, Regina Wäckinger, whose father was a court official. The couple produced two daughters and four sons, two of whom, Ferdinand and Rudolph, became important musicians in their own right, which established the family as a Bavarian musical dynasty. Also, Ferdinand and Rudolph assembled for publication much of the work of their father.

Some writers have claimed that Lasso also visited England shortly after his marriage, and while his music was undeniably the rage at the court of Elizabeth I, no evidence supports the story of a visit. When a Protestant left Albert V's service in 1563, the duke placed Lasso, a Catholic, in charge of music for the chapel. From this time until his death in 1594, Lasso composed the greater part of his 60 masses, 4 passions, 101 magnificats, more than 500 motets and 200 madrigals, 150 French chansons, 90 German Lieder, and hundreds of other pieces. Erudite and well read, he composed vocal music in Latin, French, German, and Italian, choosing among the texts of the greatest poets of his day—Pierre de Ronsard, Joachim du Bellay, and Francesco Petrarch—and the finest poets of antiquity.

Of moderate religious disposition, he composed music of the profoundest spiritual sincerity; of boundless good humor, he spun out motets about compromised monks and nuns, the joys and repercussions of strong drink, and even a lamentation on flea infestation.

During the happy years of his employment in Bavaria, Lasso was free to compose much as he pleased and to travel widely to recruit musicians and perform diplomatic errands. In 1560, he searched for singers in Flanders and, in 1562, attended the coronation of Emperor Maximilian II in Frankfurt. After spending time in Ferrara and Venice in 1567, Lasso made the first of three trips to Paris (1570, 1573, 1574) and to the court of King Charles IX, where the worldly Valois courtiers reveled in both his sacred motets and his secular, often profane, chansons. Even the Huguenots, the enemies of the Catholic establishment, found his music irresistible.

Capitalizing on his popularity and always on the spy for profit, Lasso made lucrative publishing deals with a Parisian printing firm before returning home. His enjoyable interludes in France inspired yet another of the apocryphal stories adhering to his career: He was said to have been lured away from Bavaria and to be on the road to Paris in 1574, only to turn away when hearing of the French king's untimely demise.

True, however, are the stories that Emperor Maximilian ennobled him in 1570 and that Pope Gregory XIII awarded him the dignity of knight of the Golden Spur in 1574. In this period when musicians, regardless of their level of accomplishment, usually were thought of as servants, noble titles and memberships in papal societies were remarkable endorsements for the man often referred to as "the divine Lassus." With the Wars of Religion growing ever hotter and imperiling the roads and rivers of France, Lasso turned his attention south once more, and during the next five years, he journeyed to Italy (1574-1579), where he recruited the young and luminous Giovanni Gabrieli.

In 1579, Albert, the ideal Wittelsbach Dynasty patron with whom the composer enjoyed a close and productive friendship, died and was succeeded by his brother. More frugal than his predecessor, William V economized among his musicians, whose corps had once numbered seventy-three singers, keyboard players, and instrumentalists. Nevertheless, despite other offers, Lasso remained in Munich and continued to prosper, thanks to the late duke's provision of life-time employment at full pay.

In his last years, Lasso fell into deep depression and obsessed excessively over the fate of his children, whom he feared would languish after his death. (In fact, two sons and a grandson eventually succeeded to his office.) Lasso's productivity slowed with his declining health and the burden of age, but, despite his melancholia, the quality of his music reached a pinnacle of technical perfection and emotional depth, marked particularly by the astounding *Lagrime di San Pietro*, completed just three weeks before his death.

SIGNIFICANCE

Drawing on the writings of Plato, Aristotle, and many other ancient authors, who claimed for music the power to produce powerful ethical effects in listeners, Lasso and other Renaissance composers defined music as not only a cultured form of entertainment but also as a means of moving the passions of the mind and soul. Lasso sought to re-create the reputed ethical effects of ancient music in his own audiences, to move them to sadness, happiness, bellicosity, piety, or any other state of mind.

To achieve this lofty end, Lasso transformed many of the classical rhetorical devices familiar to any orator of the period into musical declamation. Primarily, he sought a union of poetry and music, sometimes through musical imitation of words (musical pictorialism and word painting), and at others by matching poetic meter to musical rhythm, an idea then current among the poets of the French group La Pléiade, which tried to revive the French language by using words from classical literature. Lasso loved to set the group's verse. The restoration of music's ancient moral ascendancy was not just a theory in the background to Lasso's music; both contemporary listeners and music theorists of later generations, including Joachim Burmeister and Marin Mersenne in the early seventeenth century, credited Lasso for carrying it off. He was, after all, "the prince of music."

—*David Allen Duncan*

FURTHER READING

Bergquist, Peter. *Orlando di Lasso Studies*. New York: Cambridge University Press, 1999. A renowned editor of Lasso's works, Bergquist brings together eleven authors whose essays constitute the first English-language attempt to survey all Lasso's music. Concentrating mainly on musical analysis, the essays also place Lasso's corpus in the context of the high Renais-

sance style, examine its influence, and locate the composer in his social context.

Crook, David. *Orlando di Lasso's Imitation Magnificats for Counter-Reformation Munich*. Princeton, N.J.: Princeton University Press, 1994. Argues that the musical sources of Lasso's parody magnificats tend to accentuate Marian themes in line with the renewed veneration of Mary at the post-Tridentine court of Albert V.

Erb, James. *Orlando di Lasso: A Guide to Research*. New York: Garland, 1990. Provides a brief biography, a compilation of Lasso's works, a valuable annotated bibliography, and a list of recordings.

Freedman, Richard. *The Chansons of Orlando di Lasso: Music, Piety, and Print in Sixteenth-Century France*. Rochester, N.Y.: University of Rochester Press, 2001. Explores the phenomenon whereby Protestant publishers transformed the French secular songs of Lasso into sacred music in order to publish them in collections of Protestant music.

Haar, James. "Orlando di Lasso, Composer and Print Entrepreneur." In *Music and the Culture of Print*, edited by Kate van Orden. New York: Garland, 2000. Examines the clever means by which Lasso managed to profit by the sale of his music in the days before the copyright protection of intellectual property.

Luoma, Robert. *Music, Mode, and Words in Orlando di Lasso's Last Works*. Lewiston, N.Y.: Edwin Mellen Press, 1989. A close analysis of Lasso's musical and rhetorical techniques in the *Lagrime de San Pietro*, with the purpose of establishing authentic performance practice.

SEE ALSO: Charles V; Joachim du Bellay; Elizabeth I; Giovanni Gabrieli; Gregory XIII; Luca Marenzio; Maximilian II; Thomas Morley; Giovanni Pierluigi da Palestrina; Pierre de Ronsard.

RELATED ARTICLES in *Great Events from History: The Renaissance & Early Modern Era, 1454-1600:* 1567: Palestrina Publishes the *Pope Marcellus Mass*; 1575: Tallis and Byrd Publish *Cantiones Sacrae*; 1588-1602: Rise of the English Madrigal; 1590's: Birth of Opera; October 31, 1597: John Dowland Publishes *Ayres*; 1599: Castrati Sing in the Sistine Chapel Choir.

HUGH LATIMER
English church reformer

With his powerful preaching, Latimer helped mobilize popular opinion to support the reformation of the English church.

BORN: Between 1485 and 1492; Thurcaston, Leicestershire, England
DIED: October 16, 1555; Oxford, England
AREAS OF ACHIEVEMENT: Church reform, religion and theology

EARLY LIFE

Hugh Latimer (LAHT-eh-mur) was born at Thurcaston, Leicestershire, England. His father, also named Hugh, was a yeoman farmer, and the son who rose to rank and influence in the Catholic Church never forgot his humble origins. Latimer's preaching reflected a social and political concern for the well-being of a class that endured the enclosure of its pastures and the pressure of rising rent. In later years, preaching before Edward VI, he would vigorously champion the cause of the oppressed worker.

Latimer was born into a large family. His mother, whose name is unrecorded, had six daughters and several other sons. She also oversaw the milking and care of a large dairy herd. When the father served under Henry VII in putting down an uprising in Cornwall, young Hugh helped buckle on his father's armor. The son also became an accomplished bowman.

Latimer was educated in the common schools and in 1506 went to Cambridge, where in 1510 he was elected a fellow at Clare Hall and in 1514 received a master of arts degree. Although Desiderius Erasmus came to Cambridge during Latimer's fellowship, there is no indication that Latimer had any enthusiasm for his insights into the Greek text of the New Testament. Latimer never learned Greek, and like most of his compatriots, he shared in the apathy for the new learning of Erasmus that eventually drove the discouraged Dutch scholar back to the Continent. The date of Latimer's ordination to the priesthood is unknown, but in 1522 he became one of twelve preachers licensed by Cambridge University to have the right to preach anywhere in England. A more important honor was his selection to be the cross-keeper to the university, a post that involved his serving as chaplain of New Chapel.

In his early years, Latimer seems to have held firmly to Roman Catholic orthodoxy. Although he grew up in an area strongly influenced by the Lollard tradition stemming from the heretical teaching of reformer John Wyclif (c. 1328-1384), there is no indication of its influence on Latimer. Since Lollardy especially appealed to the working classes and since Latimer closely identified with this group, it might be surmised that he had at least some acquaintance with the movement.

Latimer received a bachelor of divinity degree in 1524 and used the occasion to preach a vigorous sermon denouncing the Lutheran theologian Philipp Melanchthon. He had also ungraciously maligned George Stafford, a classmate who had deserted the traditions of the church fathers for the study of the New Testament. Latimer preached against Stafford to the people and warned his scholar friends not to hear him. It appeared that Latimer had been unaffected by either Lollardy, Martin Luther's teaching, or the influence of Erasmus.

Latimer's conversion to Protestant theology was in one sense a gradual movement. He was less of a theologian than a preacher, and he only reluctantly modified his views. The beginning of his drift toward Reformation theology began with an encounter with Thomas Bilney, whom Latimer affectionately called "little Bilney." In Latimer's own words, he had been, before his discussion with Bilney, "as obstinate a Papist as any was in England," but after Bilney had brought him to "smell the word of God" he had abandoned the "school-doctors and such fooleries." Bilney's discussion with Latimer occurred on the very day in 1524 that Latimer had made his bachelor of divinity degree oration against Melanchthon.

Latimer suffered from toothache and other maladies much of his life. A portrait shows him as a sallow-faced and weary scholar with a huge nose shaped like a parrot's beak. His large eyes look out with penetration but seem tired. Whatever his disabilities, Latimer was a tireless worker. He arose at two in the morning to begin his day's routine. He was also a gifted orator. His messages were emotional appeals couched often in colorful but blunt language. In his famous Sermon of the Plough, Latimer condemned unpreaching prelates for "pampering of their paunches, . . . munching in their mangers, . . . loitering in their lordships."

LIFE'S WORK

Bishop West of Ely suspected Latimer of harboring Lutheran ideas and in 1525 ordered him not to preach in the university or the diocese. A nearby Augustinian monastery, not being under diocesan control, invited Latimer to preach there. The bishop's charges led to a hearing at the court of the papal legate, Thomas Wolsey. Latimer argued before Wolsey's chaplains that he had not become a Lutheran and had not even read Luther's works. He was then again permitted to preach in all England. In 1529, he aroused resentment at the university by his two "sermons on the card" in which he questioned the value of pilgrimages as compared with works of charity. At the same time, he was gaining notice at the court of Henry VIII because of his expressed sympathy with the king's cause in the question of divorcing Catherine of Aragon. In 1530, the king invited Latimer to preach at Windsor during Lent. Latimer did not simply seek to curry favor at any cost. An anonymous letter from this period implored the king to allow William Tyndale to print and circulate the Scripture in English translation without restriction. Some scholars believe that the letter was from Latimer. Thomas Cranmer's good standing at the court and the favor of Thomas Cromwell, vicar general of the Church, brought him the living of West Kineton in Wiltshire.

Leaving the court in 1531, Latimer now gave himself to preaching against abuses in the Church. By 1533, he had accepted Luther's doctrine of justification by faith. "If I see the blood of Christ with the eye of my soul," he wrote in that year, "that is true faith that his blood was shed for me." His preaching aroused much opposition, and charges were made that he had denied the doctrines of purgatory, the sinlessness of Mary, and the value of pilgrimages. After appearing before the bishop of London and then the Convocation of Bishops on these charges, he was finally released on agreeing to submit to the teachings of the Church. He was made bishop of Worcester in 1535 but resigned the post four years later because he was unwilling to sign the Six Articles, a conservative expression of theology that indicated that Henry VIII believed that the Reformation had gone far enough and should be checked. Now out of favor, Latimer was held prisoner for nearly a year but was finally released. He was forbidden to preach, to visit the universities, or to return to his old diocese. From 1541 to 1546, his life is nearly a blank, but in the latter year, he was sent to the Tower of London because of his association with the condemned preacher Edward Crome. The next year, he was released as part of the general pardon given to prisoners at the accession of Edward VI.

Latimer refused an invitation to return to his old bish-

opric. Instead, he remained with the archbishop of Canterbury, Thomas Cranmer. Together they prepared the *Book of Homilies*. With England now turning strongly toward Reformation doctrines under Edward VI, Latimer in 1548 broke with the doctrine of transubstantiation, accepting instead the doctrine of the real mystical presence of Christ in the sacrament. With the Catholic Mary I's accession to the throne in 1553, the era of Protestant growth was checked temporarily. It had been clear that the coming of Catherine of Aragon's daughter to the throne would mean a return to papal supremacy in England. Latimer was among the three hundred reformers who perished as heretics during Mary's reign.

SIGNIFICANCE

Latimer's main claim to fame comes not from what he left behind, but from his ability as a shaper of popular opinion. He was not primarily a theologian such as John Calvin, who could leave behind a system of doctrine. His influence was as a preacher, and his effect was primarily on the people of his own time. He passionately drew their attention both to social injustice and to abuses of the clergy. Many among his hearers had experienced rural life and could identify with his pastoral allusions. He did not spare in his acid criticism the venality of clergymen, the sloth of nonresident bishops, or the hypocrisy of prelates. Latimer was a major influence in creating popular support for Protestant reform in England.

He is also remembered especially for his sacrifice of his own life for the faith he held dear. On September 4, 1553, he was summoned to London, charged with seditious behavior, and confined in the Tower of London. Although his treatment was not especially severe, his advancing age and poor health made the imprisonment very difficult to bear. An intentional warning that the summons was coming had given Latimer several hours to escape and save his life, but he chose to face his accusers. At Oxford, he and Nicholas Ridley and Thomas Cranmer were called on to argue before the bishops for their doctrine. The trial experienced numerous delays, in part caused by the need of reenacting a capital punishment act for heresy that had been annulled while Edward ruled. With the death penalty for heresy once again the law of England, Latimer finally went to the stake with his friend Ridley, on October 16, 1555. As the torch was being applied to the wood stacked around him, Latimer made the statement that has made him famous. According to John Foxe's *Actes and Monuments of These Latter and Perillous Dayes* (1563; better known as *Foxe's Book of Martyrs*), he turned to his fellow sufferer and said, "Be of good comfort, Master Ridley, and play the man. We shall this day light such a candle, by God's grace, in England, as I trust shall never be put out."

—*Richard L. Niswonger*

FURTHER READING

Carlyle, R. M., and A. J. Carlyle. *Hugh Latimer*. Boston: Houghton Mifflin, 1899. This is a fairly brief and readable account that is favorable to Latimer. It has no bibliography and little documentation.

Chester, Allan G. *Hugh Latimer: Apostle to the English*. Philadelphia: University of Pennsylvania Press, 1954. Although the author has been criticized for being too meticulous with providing details, this is an exciting and enjoyable book to read. It is also well documented and contains a useful bibliography. The author makes no secret of his admiration for Latimer yet provides a scholarly and cautious account.

Darby, Harold S. *Hugh Latimer*. London: Epworth Press, 1953. A biography written by one who deeply admired Latimer. Darby, himself a pulpiteer, sees Latimer as preeminently a preacher.

Demaus, Robert. *Hugh Latimer: A Biography*. London: Religious Tract Society, 1904. A very laudatory and fairly lengthy work. It was originally published in 1869, then revised slightly in 1881.

Foxe, John. *Actes and Monuments*. London: John Day, 1563. Reprint. New York: AMS Press, 1965. Along with Latimer's sermons, the contemporary account by Foxe is a major source of information. Foxe wrote from a pro-Protestant viewpoint at a time when religious viewpoints were expressed in strongly emotional terms.

Keeble, N. H. "'Take Away Preaching, and Take Away Salvation': Hugh Latimer, Protestantism, and Prose Style." In *English Renaissance Prose: History, Language, and Politics*, edited by Neil Rhodes. Tempe, Ariz.: Medieval & Renaissance Texts & Studies, 1997. Analysis of the relationship between style, faith, persuasion, and ideology in Latimer's sermons. Includes bibliographic references and index.

Latimer, Hugh. *The Works of Hugh Latimer*. Edited by George E. Corrie. 2 vols. Cambridge, England: Parker Society, 1844-1845. Reprint. New York: Johnson Reprint, 1968. Any serious investigation of Latimer should largely involve the study of his sermons as recorded by Corrie.

Marshall, Peter. *Reformation England, 1480-1642*. New York: Oxford University Press, 2003. Extremely detailed, meticulously supported argument that the English Reformation should be understood to begin in the late fifteenth century and to last well into the seventeenth century. Grapples with and explicates the specific meanings of Protestantism and Catholicism to the major players and to laypeople during the Renaissance. Includes bibliographic references and index.

Ryrie, Alec. *The Gospel and Henry VIII: Evangelicals in the Early English Reformation*. New York: Cambridge University Press, 2003. A close study of Protestant evangelicalism in England from 1539 to 1547. Includes bibliographic references and index.

SEE ALSO: Catherine of Aragon; Thomas Cranmer; Thomas Cromwell; Edward VI; Desiderius Erasmus; Saint John Fisher; Henry VII; Henry VIII; John Knox; Mary I; Philipp Melanchthon; Nicholas Ridley; William Tyndale; Cardinal Thomas Wolsey.

RELATED ARTICLES in *Great Events from History: The Renaissance & Early Modern Era, 1454-1600:* January 28, 1547-July 6, 1553: Reign of Edward VI; July, 1553: Coronation of Mary Tudor.

LE THANH TONG
Emperor of Vietnam (r. 1460-1497)

Le Thanh Tong expanded the Vietnamese Empire after battling the Kingdom of Champa. He also promulgated a progressive code of law based on the moral precepts of Confucius and instituted a Chinese-style centralized administration, which ordered Vietnamese society.

BORN: 1442; Thang Long (now Hanoi, Vietnam)
DIED: 1497; Vietnam
ALSO KNOWN AS: Tu Thanh (given name); Le Thanh Ton; Thuan Hoang De; Le Tu Thanh
AREAS OF ACHIEVEMENT: Warfare and conquest, law, government and politics, historiography

EARLY LIFE

Le Thanh Tong (lay-tahn-tawng) was born Prince Tu Thanh. His grandfather, Le Loi, had driven the Chinese out of Vietnam, winning Vietnamese independence from China. As Emperor Le Thai To, Le Loi founded the Le Dynasty (1428-1789). Le Thanh Tong's father was emperor Le Thai Tong, who came to the throne at age eleven. Ngo Tiop Du, Le Thai Tong's concubine, was Le Thanh Tong's mother.

Le Thanh Tong's father feared that there was a supernatural reason behind Ngo's delayed childbirth because she was ten months pregnant with the future Prince Tu Thanh, the fourth son of the emperor. Le Thai Tong ordered that she be tied to a stake and that arrows be shot into her womb by soldiers, but she was rescued by Nguyen Thi Lo, a poet and court lady. Ngo first was hid in the horse stables, then she gave birth to prince Tu Thanh in the house of the poet, who provided a place of escape from the emperor for mother and son.

When Tu Thanh was one year old, his father died at age twenty, under mysterious circumstances, after having spent the night with Nguyen Thi Lo. The court executed Nguyen Thi Lo, her husband, and their families. A half brother of the prince, Le Nhan Tong, became emperor at age two, but he and his mother were killed by his half brother, Le Nghi Dan; court officers rebelled. On June 24, 1460, the conspirators forced Nghi Dan to commit suicide after only eight months on the throne.

The conspirators then approached Prince Cung Vuong, the second son of Tu Thanh's father, to become emperor. After the prince declined, a majority of officials invited Tu Thanh, who accepted immediately.

LIFE'S WORK

On June 26, 1460, Prince Tu Thanh became Emperor Le Thanh Tong of Dai Viet, as the Vietnamese empire was then called. Le Thanh Tong ordered a state funeral for his half brother (and his half brother's mother), who had been killed eight months prior. After their bodies were transferred to a new tomb and their spirit names recorded on July 15, 1460, rain fell to end a drought. Le Thanh Tong interpreted this as heavenly approval of his reign, and his people concurred.

Also in July, he married his first two wives, daughters of men who had helped him. Of the two, it was Nguyen Thi Huyen who gave birth in 1461 to the son who would succeed his father as Emperor Le Hien Tong.

With the intelligence, energy, and determination that characterized his actions, Le Thanh Tong organized his administration. He appointed new key officials and generals, set clear responsibilities for high officials, and instituted an open court, where opinions and reports could be shared. He promoted governance by ability, demanded high morals of his administrators, and earned a reputation for both leniency and firmness.

Politically, he sought good relations with China. On October 16, 1460, he sent a diplomatic mission to his neighbor, and in October, 1462, the Ming court recognized his rule.

Le Thanh Tong also strengthened the Vietnamese army. He organized his forces of 70,000 soldiers into five regional armies. In 1467, he raised another 99,000 regional troops and instituted rigorous military training.

In the south, the Kingdom of Champa remained hostile. The Chams had been fighting with the Vietnamese to their north since the second century B.C.E. Through the centuries, the Vietnamese had pushed the Chams farther south and conquered their land in turn. In 1469, the Cham king, Ban La Tra Toan, raided a Vietnamese province. For Le Thanh Tong, it was time for a final reckoning.

In October of 1470, Tra Toan again invaded Vietnam. Le Thanh Tong responded immediately by sending a mission to China that won the neutrality of the Chinese. On November 28, 1470, Le Thanh Tong declared war on Champa, on the grounds that its king was an illegitimate usurper who had invaded Dai Viet. On December 6, 1470, the emperor led more than 100,000 foot soldiers on land and aboard 1,700 warships into Champa.

On December 28, the first Cham nobles surrendered, just before the Vietnamese navy had arrived. In desperation, Tra Toan ordered his brother to attack. On February 24, 1471, the Chams assembled five thousand war elephants near the River Sa Ky in central Vietnam, but they were discovered. When the Cham and their elephants attacked two days later, they ran into a strong defense, unable to break through the Vietnamese infantry. Their defeat was catastrophic.

Tra Toan's request for peace was refused. Instead, Le Thanh Tong assaulted the Champa capital of Vijaya. After four days of heavy fighting, the capital fell March 22, 1471. Le Thanh Tong had the Champa king caught alive with his wives and children. Between forty thousand and sixty thousand Chams died in battle, and Le Thanh Tong took some thirty thousand prisoners to Vietnam. There, he had their left ears cut off and deposited at a temple honoring his ancestors, and he then made them slaves. When Tra Toan died in captivity, Le Thanh Tong had Tra Toan's head cut off and displayed.

Le Thanh Tong annexed more than half of Champa territory, from the south and down the central Vietnamese coast for more than 500 miles, and then up to the Cu Mong pass, near the modern province of Phu Yen. The conquered territory became the new Vietnamese province of Quang Nam. He divided the remaining Champa lands into three different duchies, and he eventually recognized one of the dukes as vassal king.

In the west, in 1479, the Lao tribe of the Bon Man rebelled against Vietnamese rule. Their leader, Cam Cong, declared his allegiance to the king of Laos, Paya Sai Tiakapat, who sent Le Thanh Tong excrement from a white elephant and then attacked Vietnam. In the fall of 1479, Le Thanh Tong counter-attacked with a force of 180,000 soldiers, defeated the invaders, and captured the Laotian capital of Luang Prabang. Paya Sai Tiakapat was forced to abdicate in favor of King Suvarna Banlang, and Cam Cong was captured and executed. More than 80,000 Bon Man soldiers fell. Le Thanh Tong appointed a ruler over the defeated Bon Man, whose land was divided into nine districts.

Le Thanh Tong also worked as a lawgiver. In 1483, he promulgated the Hong Duc penal code, which would remain in effect until the nineteenth century. The code represented a genuine Vietnamese body of laws that corresponded to the needs of Vietnamese society and was based on Confucian moral principles. Its laws focused on agricultural society and also gave rules for marriage, divorce, and inheritance. The legal code was surprisingly progressive and improved the legal status of Vietnamese women significantly.

Le Thanh Tong also focused on historiography, commissioning the writing of an impressive history of Vietnam from its mythical origins to the reign of Le Thanh Tong's grandfather. In 1479, historian Ngo Si Lien completed the *Dai Viet su ky toan thu* (complete book of the historical record of Dai Viet). Also, the emperor supported the arts and education, did not favor Buddhism, ordered the accurate mapping of his empire, and strengthened civil administration.

When Le Thanh Tong died in 1497, he had fathered fourteen sons and twenty daughters. In an orderly transition, his oldest son, Le Hien Tong, succeeded him.

SIGNIFICANCE

Le Thanh Tong's victory over Champa greatly added to Vietnam's land. It also opened room for further expansion, which would continue into the nineteenth century. His defeat of the Chams marked the ultimate triumph of the Vietnamese in a struggle that had lasted more than a millennium. It is for this achievement that many Vietnamese consider him the most successful of their emperors.

Le Thanh Tong's other achievements are also impressive. His legal code would remain in effect for more than three hundred years and would shape the nature and jurisdiction of Vietnamese society, giving women many more rights than in neighboring China. His support for the writing of a comprehensive Vietnamese history bestowed on his people a sense of collective written memory that aided Vietnam in maintaining an independent cultural identity.

Le Thanh Tong, however, proved unable to provide Vietnam with able rulers to succeed him, once Le Hien Tong died in 1504. His second son, who came to the throne in 1505, was a serial killer who strangled at dawn the women with whom he had spent the night; he died in 1509. The Le Dynasty declined rapidly, and soon it would rule in name only. Thus, while Le Thanh Tong's military successes and legal reformation transformed Vietnam, his own dynasty was unable to cling to power.

—*R. C. Lutz*

FURTHER READING

Chapuis, Oscar. *A History of Vietnam*. Westport, Conn.: Greenwood Press, 1995. Describes the achievements and events of the emperor's reign in full detail. Very readable. Maps, bibliography, index.

Heidhues, Mary Somers. *Southeast Asia: A Concise History*. London: Thames and Hudson, 2000. Places Le

Thanh Tong's reign in the context of Vietnam's history. Illustrations, maps, index.

Huard, Pierre, and Maurice Durand. *Viet-Nam, Civilization, and Culture.* Rev. 2d ed. Hanoi: École Française d'Extrême Orient, 1994. A useful general history of Vietnam. Admires the emperor for his skills at ordering the administration. Rich illustrations, maps, bibliography, index.

Raj, Hans. *History of South-East Asia.* Delhi, India: Surjeet, 2002. Includes a brief account of the emperor's achievements. Maps, bibliography, index.

RELATED ARTICLES in *Great Events from History: The Renaissance & Early Modern Era, 1454-1600:* 1450's-1471: Champa Civil Wars; March 18-22, 1471: Battle of Vijaya.

JACQUES LEFÈVRE D'ÉTAPLES
French theologian

Lefèvre was an influential early French Humanist who admired and adhered to Desiderius Erasmus's methods of textual criticism. These methods laid the groundwork for one of the most heralded Renaissance accomplishments: a modern scholarly approach to secular and religious writings that constituted a rupture from common medieval practices of glossing, which neglected the actual text. This return to the source was instrumental in justifying the Reformation.

BORN: c. 1460; Étaples, Picardy, France
DIED: 1536; Nérac, France
ALSO KNOWN AS: Jacobus Faber Stapulensis
AREAS OF ACHIEVEMENT: Religion and theology, literature, scholarship

EARLY LIFE
Little is known about the early life of Jacques Lefèvre d'Étaples (leh-fehvruh day-tawpleh). He moved to Paris from Étaples at some point and enrolled at the Collège du Cardinal Lemoine. After obtaining his degree, he taught philosophy there until about 1509. At that time, Lefèvre was already well known in Humanist circles, and Guillaume Briçonnet, the abbot of Saint-Germain-des-Prés, invited him to live at the abbey and support his efforts of reformation there. This enabled the Humanist to concentrate exclusively on his studies. Lefèvre quickly became one of the most famous representatives of early French Humanism.

His intellectual development can be divided into three major parts: his studies and teaching position at the Collège du Cardinal Lemoine, which made him a student of philosophy, his interest in medieval spirituality and patristics, and his exclusive devotion to the Holy Scriptures.

LIFE'S WORK
In 1490, Lefèvre completed his first major work, an introduction to Aristotle's *Metaphysica* (335-323 B.C.E.; *Metaphysics*, 1801). The text aimed at renovating Aristotelianism by restoring Aristotle's original teachings (and thus rejecting the prevailing scholastic approach of preferring glosses and commentaries to the actual text).

Two main events in 1491-1492 opened new horizons for Lefèvre's thinking: first, he was deeply affected by the Spanish theologian Raymond Lull's *Contemplations*, and second, he took his first trip to Italy—two more were to follow in 1500 and 1507—which put him in touch with the Italian philosophers Ermolao Barbaro (an Aristotelian), Marsilio Ficino (a Platonist), and Giovanni Pico della Mirandola, whose work combined both schools of thought. These eminent Humanists introduced Lefèvre to ideas and concepts that would greatly determine the future direction of his work. He would study ancient texts (including the Holy Scriptures) using methods based on syncretism and contemplation, which were frequently informed by the works of the Syrian mystic and speculative theologian Dionysus Areopagite (c. 500). He also came to study the Hermetic writings and the Platonist school (although he quickly distanced himself from the latter).

In the light of such influences, it was not surprising that, on his return to Paris in 1492, Lefèvre decided to publish Aristotle's collected works. His modern critical edition—following Barbaro's method of providing new Humanist translations and scholarly comments based on a thorough Humanist education—was meant to contribute substantially to a better understanding of the philosopher's writings, especially for students, which underlines Lefèvre's pedagogical concerns. Editions of many other authors and texts were to follow. The most important of these were the works of Areopagite (1499), the *Hermetica* (1505), and Raymond Lull's work (1505).

In the first decade of the 1500's, a circle of intellectuals formed around Lefèvre, named the Fabristae. Two of them stood out at this juncture. The first was the editor and publisher Josse Bade, who collaborated on the edition of Aristotle's works, as well as on numerous other texts on music, mathematics, logic, mysticism, and patristics. The second was Charles de Bovelles, who rediscovered Nicholas of Cusa's work. Initially attracted by the mathematical grounding of Nicholas's thinking, it was in focusing on Nicholas's principle of *docta ignorantia*—"learned ignorance," which identifies God as the synthesis of all worldly contradictions and thus helps surpass the incompatibility of worldly appearances—that Lefèvre found the metaphysical framework for the syncretism of Greek wisdom and Christian faith for which he had been searching.

Lefèvre's oversight of a three-volume edition of Nicholas's works (1514) marked a highlight of his critical approach. It was also a clear indicator that Lefèvre would henceforth concentrate exclusively on biblical exegesis. All of his studies seemed to have been devoted to this final goal: to make use of modern scholarly methods to come to a better comprehension of the Bible, first as a commentator, then as a translator, and finally as a predicator.

One of the most important influences on Lefèvre in this domain was Desiderius Erasmus's *Enchiridion militis Christiani* (1503; *The Manual of the Christian Knight*, 1533), which proclaimed a purification of Christianity based on a return to its original source, the Bible. The great Dutch Humanist's method thus applied to the Scriptures what Lefèvre held to be the only acceptable means of scholarly textual criticism. Two years later, Erasmus edited Lorenzo Valla's *Annotations* on the New Testament and explained his ideas of textual criticism based on philological and historical methods. Even before Erasmus's *New Testament*, Lefèvre provided his own illustration of this approach in one of his main works, the critical edition of the *Quintuplex Psalterium* (1509; fivefold Psalter), a comment on five Latin translations of the Psalter. Then he turned his attention to the epistles of Saint Paul, which he edited and provided a new Latin translation based on the original text (1512).

Despite Lefèvre's penchant for mysticism, pure faith had regained its central position in his model, replacing the elaborate rituals of the contemporary Church. Following this logic, reformation was not only necessary but also inevitable to purify Christianity. This would lead to a reestablishment of the primitive Catholic Church, liberated from all the addenda of a millennium of falsification, a cleansing process that corresponded to Lefèvre's principles of textual purification.

The next significant event in Lefèvre's life was the publication of Erasmus's edition of the *New Testament* (1516), which clearly defined the rules of modern exegesis and therefore developed into a manifest for the Reformation movement. A struggle with the Dutch Humanist over the interpretation of a phrase from *Hebrews* 2:7 had somewhat alienated the two scholars, however. In Lefèvre's mind, modern scholarly methods reached their limits when they conflicted with faith, a conviction that he did not think Erasmus shared. The Dutch Humanist responded by pointing out his opponent's mediocre mastery of Greek, but tempers soon calmed down. Lefèvre's scholarly inferiority was obvious and his acknowledgment of Erasmus's major achievement confirmed his own personal convictions of the benefits of modern textual criticism. It was around that same time that he also began to admire Martin Luther's writings (1517). The condemnation of the new doctrines by the Faculty of Theology in Paris (1521) would not change these convictions, and Lefèvre left Paris that same year to help Briçonnet in his attempt to reform the diocese of Meaux.

Lefèvre was surrounded by friends and disciples in Meaux, particularly Gérard Roussel, and his work would take on a new dimension. Frequent attacks and attempts at censorship by the Faculty of Theology were usually thwarted by the benevolence of King Francis I, his sister Marguerite de Navarre, and the French scholar Guillaume Budé, who was Francis I's royal librarian. The call for the reestablishment of the primitive Catholic Church and the predominance of pure faith were strongly defended in Lefèvre's *Commentarii initiatorii in quartuor Evangelia* (1522; commentaries on the four Gospels) and repeated in his *Epistres et evangiles des cinquante-deux dimanches* (1525; Epistles and gospels for the fifty-two Sundays), the latter work openly proclaiming a break with ecclesiastical tradition in the name of purified faith. Conservative Catholicism saw its chance to deal a blow to the Reformation movement when Francis I was captured by Charles V (1525), which necessitated Marguerite's voyage to Spain to negotiate for her brother's release. Lefèvre and Roussel avoided capture by fleeing to Strasbourg. On his return to France (March, 1526), Francis I quickly ended the persecution and recalled the fugitives. He appointed Lefèvre head of the Royal Library in Blois and preceptor of his children. On his return trip, the Humanist stopped in Basle, where he met Erasmus, who had supported him during his exile.

It was toward the end of his stay in Blois that Lefèvre completed his translation of the Bible into French (based on the *Vulgate*). Its publication in 1530 coincided with an invitation to move to Marguerite de Navarre's court in Nérac, a haven for the evangelical and Reformation movements. He met John Calvin and Clément Marot there. He died in 1536.

SIGNIFICANCE

Lefèvre belonged to the first generation of French Humanists who prepared the ground for the movement's celebrated achievements in the following decades. His appeal for an objective scientific approach to textual criticism (as long as it did not contradict faith) and the return to original sources (following Erasmus's and Budé's lead) provided a theoretical foundation for the Reformation and became a principle of modern scholarship. The translation of the Bible into French was a significant milestone—French became the country's official administrative language in 1539—as it made the Scriptures available to many more people, an indispensable condition for the success of his call for a return to a purified Christian faith. The emancipated reading public was now able to make its own decisions in matters of faith based on an independent reading and interpretation of the Bible.

—*Bernd Renner*

FURTHER READING

Backus, Irena. "Renaissance Attitudes to New Testament Apocryphal Writings: Jacques Lefèvre d'Étaples and His Epigones." *Renaissance Quarterly* 51, no. 4 (1998): 1169-1198. Study of sixteenth century reception of New Testament Apocrypha; sheds light on Lefèvre's editorial approach.

Cottrell, Robert D. "Lefèvre d'Étaples and the Limits of Biblical Interpretation." *Œuvres & Critiques* 20, no. 2 (1995): 79-95. Useful essay explaining Lefèvre's attitude in the conflict between faith and reason.

Hughes, Philip Edgcumbe. *Lefèvre: Pioneer of Ecclesiastical Renewal in France*. Grand Rapids, Mich.: W. E. Eerdmans, 1984. First and only English book-length study on Lefèvre, which presents the Humanist's work as groundbreaking for the Reformation.

Lefèvre d'Étaples, Jacques. *The Prefatory Epistles of Jacques Lefèvre d'Étaples and Related Texts*, edited by Eugene F. Rice. New York: Columbia University Press, 1972. English edition of Lefèvre's theoretical texts; useful introduction.

SEE ALSO: John Calvin; Desiderius Erasmus; Marsilio Ficino; Francis I; Martin Luther; Marguerite de Navarre; Nicholas of Cusa; Giovanni Pico della Mirandola.

RELATED ARTICLE in *Great Events from History: The Renaissance & Early Modern Era, 1454-1600*: 1499-1517: Erasmus Advances Humanism in England.

MIGUEL LÓPEZ DE LEGAZPI
Spanish explorer

A distinguished civil servant, Legazpi led the expedition that conquered and colonized the Philippines. His navigator, Father Andrés de Urdaneta, discovered the all-important return route to Mexico, which made Spanish control of the islands possible.

BORN: c. 1510; Zumárraga, Guipúzcoa, Spain
DIED: August 20, 1572; Manila (now in the Philippines)
ALSO KNOWN AS: Miguel López de Legazpi y Gurruchátegui
AREAS OF ACHIEVEMENT: Geography, exploration, warfare and conquest

EARLY LIFE

Miguel López de Legazpi (mee-ghehl LOH-pehz day lay-GAHS-pee) was the son of Juan Martínez de Legazpi and Elvira de Gurruchátegui. Little is known of his youth. He was raised in a noble family that lived in a large house atop a hill dominating the valley of Zumárraga. The house still stands, and it contains a small museum devoted to Legazpi.

As the second son, Miguel had to seek his fortune beyond the confines of the family estate. On the recommendation of his Latin tutor, his family sent him to law school at the University of Alcalá, from which he graduated at a young age. This education prepared him to be a royal notary like his father, but like many Basques, he heard the call of the sea. In 1528, he set sail from Seville for New Spain (Mexico) with letters of introduction to Viceroy Antonio de Mendoza and Franciscan father Juan de Zumárraga. Not long after arriving in Mexico, he was named a royal notary. He then married Isabel Garcés, daughter of a wealthy Mexican family; they had nine children.

It did not take long for Legazpi's star to rise in New Spain's civil service. The positions he held included *intendente* (superintendent) of the treasury, principal secretary of the Mexico City council (1534-1557), secretary for Francisco Tello de Sandoval's *visita* (inspection) of Antonio de Mendoza's government (1544-1547), and local magistrate. Legazpi was regarded as intelligent, honorable, and of devout Christian character. His home was one of the principal residences in Mexico City and was always open to gentlemen and soldiers in need.

LIFE'S WORK

Legazpi's expedition to the Philippines was not the first for Spain, but it was the most carefully planned. The Portuguese explorer Ferdinand Magellan, sailing at the time in the service of Spain, had discovered the Philippines in 1521, but he did not succeed in signing a treaty with a local ruler, nor did he establish a permanent settlement. Thus, in 1557, when the Spanish crown decreed that the planning for the expedition be led later by Legazpi, it called for the discovery of the "Western islands" near the Moluccas and for the recording of the physical and human geography of those lands.

The Crown also wanted an expedition that would bring back spices for testing and one that would discover a return route to Mexico. Before year's end, Viceroy Velasco had initiated the construction of ships at Puerto de La Navidad (now Barra de Navidad) on Mexico's west coast. Philip II wanted only two ships for the expedition and as much secrecy as possible in order not to alarm the Portuguese, who vied with Spain for control of the east. Viceroy Velasco chose Legazpi to head the expedition, and the *audiencia* of Mexico gave him his instructions on September 1, 1564.

Legazpi was ordered to establish a settlement in the Philippines, but only if the islands were bountiful, and Father Urdaneta was to direct a return to Mexico as soon as possible. In any event, friars were to remain behind for conversion of the indigenous peoples. Although the initial instructions permitted Legazpi to set the outbound course, which was to include New Guinea, at one hundred leagues out to sea, Legazpi had to open secret, sealed instructions from the *audiencia* that ordered him to follow a direct route to the Philippines.

Legazpi was probably well into his fifties when he was made captain-general of the expedition to the Philippines. As captain-general, he was the representative of the king and in charge of military, judicial, and political operations. He could sign treaties with indigenous rulers and take possession of land in the king's name. He also was responsible for making sure that the men on the expedition were paid and properly clothed, fed, and armed; to meet this obligation, he sold most of his estate, impoverishing his own family.

The expedition finally set sail with 380 men on November 21, 1564, with two large galleons (*San Pedro* and *San Pablo*) and two small tenders (*San Juan* and *San Lucas*); the flagship *San Pedro* also carried a four-man brigantine for shallow water exploration. In January, 1565, on the way west, Legazpi took possession of the Ladrones (now the Marianas) and resupplied on Guam. The convoy arrived at what is thought to be the east coast of Samar on February 13, 1565. Finding little of value there, the expedition sailed on to Leyte, where the men took food by force from the islands' inhabitants. They hoped to continue to the north coast of Mindanao, but weather steered them to Bohol. In April, the expeditionaries held a conference in which they decided, at the urging of Legazpi, to establish a settlement on Cebu. This island seemed appealing because it was densely settled, had adequate food supplies, had many Christians (who converted after contact with Magellan), and had a local ruler recognizing the suzerainty of the king of Spain.

The convoy reached Cebu on April 27, 1565, and had to bombard the coast with artillery in order to force a landing. Occupying abandoned huts, the invaders laid out streets and built houses, a stockade, and a monastery, naming the place Villa San Miguel after Legazpi's patron saint.

As instructed, the *San Pedro* set sail for Mexico as soon as practicable, on June 1, 1565, with Felipe Salcedo, Legazpi's nephew, as captain and with Father Urdaneta as supervisor of the pilots. It arrived at Acapulco on October 10, 1565, which created great excitement in Mexico, leading Melchor de Legazpi, one of the captain-general's sons and principal secretary of Mexico City's city council, to a two-year leave of absence to sail to Spain to ask the king for favors for his family.

Legazpi had the right to take the return ship to Mexico, but he stayed, devoting the rest of his life to the conquest and colonization of the Philippines. Legazpi succeeded by acting graciously and judiciously with the islands' peoples and with his own men and by being willing to use lethal force as a last resort. By June, 1565, he controlled Cebu. Twice he had to put down revolts among some of his men, executing the leaders by hanging but pardoning their followers. Legazpi also had to confront Portuguese gun ships, which tried to intimidate him into abandoning the Philippines, but facing his refusal, they withdrew by the fall of 1568.

Eager to complete the conquest of the Philippines, Legazpi set sail for Panay and Masbate in mid-1569. The next year, he ordered a reconnaissance of Luzon, the most important Philippine island. One of the two rajas ruling the Manila area refused to submit to the Spaniards. In April, 1571, Legazpi sent a fleet of twenty-six vessels with three hundred soldiers to assault the rajas' forces. The rajas surrendered unconditionally, and Manila was formally founded on June 24, 1571. After establishing his residence and general quarters in Manila, Legazpi charged Martín de Goiti, the field master, and Captain Juan de Salcedo, Legazpi's grandson, with the pacification of Luzon. On August 21, 1572, one day after Legazpi's death, Salcedo returned to Manila, having completed the conquest of Luzon.

SIGNIFICANCE

Legazpi was an exemplary conquistador, forgoing riches and worldly adulation to devote his life to furthering the goals of his king and church. Four Spanish expeditions to the Philippines prior to Legazpi's had failed to reach the islands and find a return route to Mexico. Urdaneta's return route was used by the Manila galleons for some 250 years.

The thorough Christianization of the Philippines reflected the deepest desire of Legazpi, and it almost certainly prevented the expansion of Islam throughout the islands. The Spanish conquest of the Philippines also had geopolitical ramifications, as the Portuguese were forced to recognize Spanish suzerainty of the Philippines, China and Japan were prevented from colonizing the coveted islands, and Western interest in commerce with China was whetted as Spaniards in the Philippines devoted themselves to exporting Chinese goods to Mexico.

—*Steven L. Driever*

FURTHER READING

Gschaedler, Andre. *Mexico and the Pacific, 1540-1565: The Voyages of Villalobos and Legazpi and the Preparations They Made for Them.* Unpublished Ph.D. dissertation. Columbia University, 1954. An authoritative account of the complicated, secretive preparations for Legazpi's voyage to the Philippines.

Licuanan, Virginia Benitez, and José Llavador Mira, eds. *The Philippines Under Spain: A Compilation and Translation of Original Documents.* Manila: National Trust for Historical and Cultural Preservation of the Philippines, 1990. A unique collection of primary documents on the Spanish colonization of the Philippines, including Legazpi's 1564-1572 expedition.

Mahajani, Usha. *Philippine Nationalism: External Challenge and Filipino Response, 1565-1946.* St. Lucia, Australia: University of Queensland, 1971. Historical analysis of the roots of Philippine nationalism to the Spanish period. A good review of indigenous resistance to foreign subjugation.

Valdepenas, Edna-Anne. *Miguel López de Legazpi: Writings and the Colonization of the Philippines.* Unpublished Ph.D. dissertation. University of Michigan, 1996. Explores the conquest and settlement of the Philippines from Legazpi's arrival in 1565 to his death in 1572. Presents the introduction of Spanish authority in the Philippines as a relatively pacific endeavor.

SEE ALSO: Pedro de Alvarado; Vasco Núñez de Balboa; Álvar Núñez Cabeza de Vaca; Christopher Columbus; Francisco Vásquez de Coronado; Hernán Cortés; Juan Sebastián de Elcano; Ferdinand Magellan; The Pinzón Brothers; Francisco Pizarro; Juan Ponce de León; Hernando de Soto.

RELATED ARTICLE in *Great Events from History: The Renaissance & Early Modern Era, 1454-1600:* 1565: Spain Seizes the Philippines.

EARL OF LEICESTER
English nobleman

Robert Dudley, earl of Leicester, a key figure at Queen Elizabeth I's court, was very close to the monarch and was rumored to have been her lover. He became a strong leader of the Puritan cause at court and was appointed to lead the fight against the Spanish Armada in 1588, but he died before he saw much action.

BORN: June 24, 1532 or 1533; Kent, England
DIED: September 4, 1588; Cornbury, Oxfordshire, England
ALSO KNOWN AS: Robert Dudley (given name); Baron Denbigh; Sir Robert Dudley
AREAS OF ACHIEVEMENT: Government and politics, military

EARLY LIFE
Robert Dudley, later dubbed earl of Leicester (LEHS-tehr), was the grandson of Edmund Dudley, who had been executed by Henry VIII for crimes he had allegedly committed during his service to Henry VII years earlier. Robert's father, John Dudley, duke of Northumberland, also lost his life because of his involvement in politics.

After Edward VI's death in 1553, Northumberland and his two sons, Guildford and Robert, attempted to place Lady Jane Grey on the throne of England. For this, Queen Mary I sent all three men to the Tower of London and condemned them to death in 1554. Northumberland and Guildford were executed, but Mary pardoned Robert in early 1555. Despite the pardon from Mary, Dudley's later political life was tainted by his lineage, as his opponents often pointed out that he came from a line of traitors and so should not be trusted.

As a child, Dudley was taught by Roger Ascham, tutor also to Elizabeth I. In 1550, at age eighteen, he married Amy Robsart. Their relationship may have begun as a love match, but soon the couple grew apart because Dudley spent much of his time at the court of Mary's sister and successor, Queen Elizabeth I, while Amy lived with relations in the country. Tall, dark, handsome, and athletic, Dudley was favored by Elizabeth, who devoted much of her attention to the young man.

LIFE'S WORK
Robert Dudley's political and personal lives were always intimately linked. He is probably most famous for his controversial role as Queen Elizabeth's favorite. He had known Elizabeth since both were young children, and early in her reign, she named Dudley master of the horse.

This position allowed him to remain close to the queen. He had lodgings at court and rode directly behind Elizabeth during public ceremonies.

The two, very close in age, shared an intimate friendship, and many believed the relationship was more than platonic. Throughout Dudley's years at court, rumors about the nature of his involvement with the queen flourished. Dudley spent much of his time with Elizabeth, and the queen was clearly drawn to this handsome young man. Nicknamed "the gypsy" because of his dark eyes and hair, Dudley's attractiveness and his quick wit kept the queen in good humor.

Because Dudley was married, however, there was no hope of the two making a formal union. In 1559, however, his wife, Amy, became gravely ill (probably with breast cancer). This provoked a rumor at court that should she die, Dudley would probably marry the queen. Indeed, when Amy was found dead from a broken neck at the bottom of a staircase in 1560 at Cumnor Place in North Berkshire, many suspected foul play on Dudley's part because they believed he would do anything in order to marry the queen. So as to appear impartial, the queen set up a formal inquiry into Amy's death. After the investigation, Dudley was absolved of any wrongdoing and soon returned to court, apparently unaffected by his wife's death.

Elizabeth and Dudley might have pursued a serious relationship once he was single and proven innocent of his spouse's death. This never occurred, however, perhaps because Elizabeth knew that aligning herself with a questionable figure like Dudley would cause her to lose allies at home and abroad. Still, Dudley attempted to advance himself as a suitor to the queen by secretly joining forces with the Spanish. He was rumored to have promised that if Spain would encourage Elizabeth to take him as her husband, once he was king, he would restore England to Catholicism. Whether or not Dudley was sincere in his proposal to the Spanish is unclear, especially since later he would become a leader of the Puritan cause. Though this plan did not succeed in making Dudley Elizabeth's partner, it did not upset Elizabeth, who granted him apartments nearby the court. The ploy did, however, cultivate anti-Catholic feelings at court, and perhaps made Dudley decide that Protestantism was better suited to him.

In 1563, Elizabeth offered Dudley in marriage to Mary, Queen of Scots, probably in an effort to secure a

Protestant marriage for her Catholic cousin. In 1564 (perhaps to make the offer of Dudley more attractive to her cousin), Elizabeth named Dudley earl of Leicester. Mary, though, was not enthusiastic about accepting one of Elizabeth's old suitors, and she eventually stopped her cousin's plan by marrying Lord Darnley (Henry Stuart) in 1565.

About this time, Dudley surfaced as a strong supporter of the Puritan cause. This may seem strange because Dudley was a patron of one of the earliest acting companies, Leicester's Men, and the Puritans despised the theater. Dudley was full of contradictions, and endorsing the Puritans may have been yet another of his politic decisions. Though it is unclear whether he was sincere in his devotion to this religion, Dudley's association with the Puritans and his calculating behavior at court were the targets of a 1584 libel written by the Jesuits and most likely published in Antwerp. The book, soon outlawed by the queen, accused the earl of being evil and of killing anyone who got in his way. Although the libel was written by a group of extremists, Dudley's reputation for being arrogant and manipulative was widespread. His political savvy along with his desire and ability to remain close to the queen, contributed to his unpopularity among his contemporaries.

In spite of popular opinion, Elizabeth continued to favor Dudley until he married without asking her permission. In 1573, Dudley married a widow from Sheffield but later abandoned her in order to secretly marry Lettice Knolleys, cousin of Elizabeth and widow of Walter Devereux, first earl of Essex, in 1578. The marriage made him stepfather to Robert Devereux, second earl of Essex, a young man who would later replace Dudley as Elizabeth's favorite. Dudley's secret marriage greatly offended the queen, though the earl eventually managed to regain her favor and was appointed to command the Dutch campaign in 1585. Once in the Netherlands, however, the ambitious Dudley accepted the title of governor, which infuriated Elizabeth. She had instructed him clearly on the limits of his power there. Dudley eventually gave up the title and returned to England, where the queen, though upset, made up with her favorite.

In May, 1588, as the Spanish Armada approached, Elizabeth gave Dudley command of the main army. Dudley did not see much action, however, because by August he became ill and headed for the spas in Buxton at Derbyshire to regain his health. Though there have been speculations that he was murdered on his way to Buxton, it is most likely that the fifty-six-year-old earl died of natural causes on September 4 before he could reach the spas.

SIGNIFICANCE

Dudley's nearness to Queen Elizabeth set him apart from his contemporaries, many of whom were jealous of and nervous about the couple's relationship. Though the queen never chose a husband, Dudley was perhaps the suitor who came nearest to being Elizabeth's king.

The issue of Dudley's relationship with the queen was particularly important because all England was concerned about whom Elizabeth would marry. Dudley's contemporaries feared that because he was both favored and politic, he might persuade the queen to support him regardless of the cause, especially if he were king.

As a patron of the arts, a suitor to the queen, and a prominent man at court, Dudley was feared and admired by many. The earl was noted for being sometimes blithe and playful and at other times manipulative and ambitious. He remained an attractive and dangerous force at court for his entire life.

—Stephannie S. Gearhart

FURTHER READING

Adams, Simon. *Leicester and the Court: Essays on Elizabethan Politics*. Manchester, England: Manchester University Press, 2002. Sixteen chapters discuss the role Dudley played in the politics of Queen Elizabeth's court, and they provide a good introduction to Elizabeth, her court, Parliament, and early modern patronage.

Doran, Susan. *Monarchy and Matrimony: The Courtships of Elizabeth I*. New York: Routledge, 1996. This is the first comprehensive study of Queen Elizabeth I's courtships. In the book, Doran emphasizes both international and domestic issues as she examines the question of Elizabeth's marriage.

Rosenberg, Eleanor. *Leicester, Patron of Letters*. 1955. Reprint. New York: Columbia University Press, 1976. In this classic study of Dudley, Rosenberg examines the relationships between the earl and his many protégés closely while making larger generalizations about patronage in the English Renaissance.

Somerset, Anne. *Elizabeth I*. New York: Anchor Books, 2003. Somerset brings to life the queen of England as she explains the difficult political and personal choices faced by Elizabeth, including what to do with Dudley.

Weir, Alison. *The Life of Elizabeth I*. New York: Ballantine Books, 1998. The author explores the intersection of Elizabeth's political and personal lives, including her tumultuous relationship with Dudley.

Wilson, Derek. *Sweet Robin: A Biography of Robert Dudley, Earl of Leicester.* London: Hamish Hamilton, 1981. This biography presents Dudley not as a manipulative or evil politician, but rather as one doing his best to succeed professionally while remaining loyal to his queen.

SEE ALSO: William Cecil; Elizabeth I; Lady Jane Grey; Mary I; Sir Philip Sidney; Edmund Spenser.

RELATED ARTICLES in *Great Events from History: The Renaissance & Early Modern Era, 1454-1600:* 1576: James Burbage Builds The Theatre; July 26, 1581: The United Provinces Declare Independence from Spain; April, 1587-c. 1600: Anglo-Spanish War; July 31-August 8, 1588: Defeat of the Spanish Armada.

LEO AFRICANUS
Moroccan explorer and writer

Under the auspices of the Papacy, Leo Africanus wrote a detailed description of his travels through north and west Africa. His book—Descrittione dell' Africa—remained for Europeans the principal source for information on the geography of the Sudan until the nineteenth century.

BORN: c. 1485; Granada, Kingdom of Granada (now in Spain)

DIED: c. 1554; possibly Fez, Morocco, or Tunis (now in Tunisia)

ALSO KNOWN AS: al-Ḥasan ibn Muḥammad al-Wazzān al-Zaiyātī (given name); Jean-Leon d'African; John Leo; Johannes Leo de Medicis; Eliberitances; Leo de Grenade; Giovanni Leone; Leone the African

AREAS OF ACHIEVEMENT: Exploration, geography, historiography

EARLY LIFE

Scion of an Andalusian family that relocated to Fez, al-Ḥasan ibn Muḥammad al-Wazzān al-Zaiyātī, later called Leo Africanus (LEE-oh af-rih-KAY-nuhs), received a good education. While still in his teens he began to travel, seeking adventure and supporting himself in a variety of jobs, including clerk, trader, tax collector, diplomat, soldier, and poet. On his first trip out of Morocco, he visited Egypt, Syria, Iraq, Tartary, Armenia, and Constantinople.

Between 1507 and 1510, he accompanied his uncle on a diplomatic mission to Timbuktu. Deciding to see more of the West African interior, Leo returned in 1513 as a merchant. His final trip was to Constantinople on official business for the Moroccan sultan, during which time he took a side trip to Egypt. He traveled up the Nile River, crossed the Red Sea to Arabia, and probably made the pilgrimage to Mecca.

On his way home, his ship was captured by Christian pirates. They were so impressed by his knowledge of lands unknown to Europe that they brought him to Rome and presented him as a gift to Pope Leo X. The Moroccan was welcomed into the papal court, converted to Christianity, and given the pope's own name, Giovanni Leone (John Leo). His nickname became Leone the African and eventually Leo Africanus.

LIFE'S WORK

Leo had traveled to lands of which European geographers had only heard and to some lands that they had not even imagined. Pope Leo X provided him with a pension and encouraged him to work on his travel memoirs. The result was an opus divided into nine books called *Descrittione dell' Africa* (1550; *The History and Description of Africa and of the Notable Things Therein Contained*, 1600). Leo, however, did not set out to write a travel account; that was imposed on him by the pope, so it is highly possible that he was not especially careful with specific facts. He probably jumbled together various matters concerning people, places, and events. The stories Leo picked up from merchants and others were probably more gossip than information, and he might have misheard, misunderstood, or otherwise misconstrued them.

Error-prone documentation of the geography of little-known or even unknown lands was not unheard of for Leo's time, nor for earlier times. During the Middle Ages, Marco Polo's fourteenth century accounts of his travels to Asia and his closeness to Mongol ruler Kublai Khan have been questioned and even considered gross exaggerations. The Arab historian and geographer al-Masʿūdī (c. 890-956) has also been accused of misleading his readers, using folktales or anecdotes, for example, as facts. Nevertheless, Leo's work was critical to the early corpus of geographical knowledge, for it indicated, even with its errors and possible exaggerations, the intricacies of lands and peoples beyond the realm of the known world, details never-before documented in the languages of the West.

Also, Leo had to write in Arabic and then rely on Vatican-provided assistance to translate the text into Italian, providing ample opportunities for alteration, error, or both, which could only have increased the likelihood of mistakes. Before publication, his work was edited extensively by Venetian geographer Giovanni Battista Ramusio; others translated it into foreign languages in subsequent years. The original text is now lost.

The first book of Leo's *Descrittione dell'Africa* contains mostly general information and classifies peoples and lands by categories. Books 2 and 3 are devoted to Morocco and together make up 30 percent of the entire work. Book 3 focuses exclusively on the Kingdom of Fez, considered a separate entity from Morocco proper. Books 4 and 5 move quickly across the rest of North Africa to Tunis. Book 6 begins with the area around Tripoli, then plunges into the desert to include discussions of a number of oases and several of the important tribal groups of the Sahara. Book 7 covers the land below the Sahara, the savanna region known as the Sudan. Book 8 is devoted to Egypt, and book 9 concludes with a discussion on natural history.

Leo spent most of his life in Morocco, and much of his writing is devoted to it. Not surprisingly, this is the most accurate part of his work. The most influential section, however, is his discussion of Sudanic Africa, described as made up of fifteen adjoining countries west to east, beginning with Gualata (Walata) and ending with Nubia. Leo might have been intentionally misled by officials in Timbuktu. Most historians believe he visited that city but have varying degrees of doubt as to his travels in Sudanic Africa.

Timbuktu, described as a place where the inhabitants were very wealthy, receives great attention. Leo wrote that "The rich king of Tombuto hath many plates and scepters of gold, some whereof weigh 1300 poundes." Timbuktu, according to Leo, was the capital of a great state, by which he meant the Songhai Empire. This is an error. The real capital was Gao, about 200 miles down river, another place Leo claimed to have visited. Gao is just beyond the spot where the Niger River changes its eastward course and begins flowing southward. Leo, however, indicated that it continues ever eastward until finally meeting the Nile, which is another major error.

It is in the area beyond Gao that Leo's mistakes become more glaring. He discusses, for example, the Kingdom of Guangara, which he describes as very populous and rich. This was the mythical Wangara, which some medieval Arabs believed was the land of gold. Actually, the closest major gold-bearing region to Leo's Guangara was 600 miles away. His next stop, the Kingdom of Bornu near Lake Chad, did exist. It had long been in the Islamic fold, but Leo reports that the people there worshipped no form of religion. East of Bornu, occupying the huge territory between Lake Chad and the Nile, was the Kingdom of Gaoga, a state, like Guangara, which does not seem to have actually existed. Leo concluded his trip by arriving in Nubia on the Nile, from which he made his way north to Egypt and then back home.

Leo's most monumental mistake was indicating that the Niger River flows from east to west, when in fact it flows from west to east. Leo also claims to have followed the Niger clear across Sudanic Africa, which represents a lot of river watching. Unfortunately, the Niger does not flow across Sudanic Africa, not even halfway. In 1521, Pope Leo X died, and the next pope was not interested in such matters. So Leo left to teach Arabic at the University of Bologna, returning to Rome in 1526 to finish his manuscript.

Details of Leo's later life are somewhat hazy. Reports indicate either that he stayed in Rome or that he relocated in Tunis. Most likely, he returned to Fez in 1528 and converted back to Islam.

SIGNIFICANCE

Leo Africanus could have hardly imagined the impact of his work. To a Europe that was rediscovering geographical knowledge, his book suddenly and profoundly increased the available data on the African interior. William Shakespeare is said to have used Leo as his inspiration for writing *Othello, the Moor of Venice* (pr. 1604).

Leo's description of the Western Sudan remained a kind of geographical dogma until the explorations of Mungo Park, René-Auguste Caillié, and Heinrich Barth in the eighteenth and nineteenth centuries. In particular, Europeans never forgot Leo's descriptions of 1,300-pound plates and scepters of gold. Despite his inadequacies, however, and if handled with care, Leo's work still can be used profitably for a historical look at the geography of West Africa.

—Richard L. Smith

FURTHER READING

Andrea, Bernadette. "Assimilation or Dissimulation? Leo Africanus's 'Geographical Historie of Africa' and the Parable of Amphibia." *Ariel* 32, no. 3 (July, 2001): 7-29. Much of the work on Leo has been done in the field of literary criticism rather than history. Although somewhat burdened by jargon, this article is useful in providing a survey of the treatment of Leo in the study of postcolonial theory.

Fisher, Humphrey J. "Leo Africanus and the Songhay Conquest of Hausaland." *International Journal of African Historical Studies* 11, no. 1 (1978): 86-112. Perhaps the best critical examination of Leo's work from a skeptical point of view. Provides a good warning sign for those who might be tempted to use Leo's work without due care.

Leo Africanus. *The History and Description of Africa and of the Notable Things Therein Contained.* Translated by John Pory, edited by Robert Brown. 3 vols. New York: Burt Franklin, 1974. A full-length translation in English first published in 1600 and still in quaint Elizabethan linga. Pory has added much of his own information. The editor (from an 1896 edition) provides a lengthy introduction to Leo and his work.

Masonen, Pekka. *The Negroland Revisited: Discovery and Invention of the Sudanese Middle Ages.* Helsinki, Finland: Annales Academiae Scientiarun Fennicae Humaniora, 2000. Chapter 4 of this book provides the best summary in English of what is known and not known about the life of Leo.

Zhiri, Oumelbanine. "Leo Africanus, Translated and Betrayed." In *The Politics of Translation in the Middle Ages and the Renaissance*, edited by Renate Blumenfeld-Kosinski, Luise von Flotow, and Daniel Russell. Ottawa, Canada: University of Ottawa Press, 2001. This study shows how Leo's original work was changed and speculates on possible reasons for the changes.

SEE ALSO: Amina Sarauniya Zazzua; Askia Daud; Richard Hakluyt; Leo X; Muḥammad ibn ʿAbd al-Karīm al-Maghīlī; Gerardus Mercator; Mohammed I Askia; Sonni ʿAlī.

RELATED ARTICLES in *Great Events from History: The Renaissance & Early Modern Era, 1454-1600:* c. 1464-1591: Songhai Empire Dominates the Western Sudan; 1493-1528: Reign of Mohammed I Askia.

LEO X
Italian pope (1513-1521)

As a patron of the arts, Leo X turned Rome into the cultural center of the Western world. As pope, he engaged in secular politics and presided over the period in Catholic Church history that witnessed the beginning of the Protestant Reformation.

BORN: December 11, 1475; Florence (now in Italy)
DIED: December 1, 1521; Rome, Papal States (now in Italy)
ALSO KNOWN AS: Giovanni de' Medici
AREAS OF ACHIEVEMENT: Government and politics, religion and theology, patronage of the arts

EARLY LIFE

Pope Leo X was born Giovanni de' Medici, the second son of Lorenzo de' Medici and his wife, Clarice Orsini. Though brought up in the lap of Renaissance luxury, he was groomed for a career in the Catholic Church from an early age. Tonsured at age seven, he was appointed a cardinal at age thirteen, although he did not receive the insignia and the privileges of that office until 1492. As a youth, he was tutored by the famous Humanists Marsilio Ficino, Angelo Poliziano, and Giovanni Pico della Mirandola, who imparted to him a love of literature and the arts, which characterized his entire life.

From 1489 until 1491, Giovanni studied theology and canon law at the University of Pisa. Then, in 1492, he moved to Rome and assumed the responsibilities of a cardinal. He served on the conclave, which in that year elected Pope Alexander VI, although Giovanni did not vote for him.

After the death of his father in 1492, Giovanni returned to Florence, where he lived with his elder brother Pietro until the Medici family was exiled from their native city in 1494 during Girolamo Savonarola's reign of virtue. For the next six years, Giovanni traveled in France, the Netherlands, and Germany, and then returned in May of 1500 to Rome, where, for the next several years, he immersed himself in literature, music, and particularly the theater, interests that were the great loves of his life, taking precedence even over hunting, of which he was extremely fond.

When his elder brother died in 1503, Giovanni became the head of the Medici family, and much of his energy and his revenues from his many church benefices was expended in the ensuing years in his efforts to restore his family to prominence in Florence. After a bloodless revolution in that city in September of 1512, the Medicis were allowed to return, and Giovanni became the de facto ruler of Florence, although the nominal ruler would be his younger brother Giuliano. Then, when Pope Julius II died in February of 1513, the seven-day conclave that followed elected Giovanni his successor. Giovanni was crowned Pope Leo X on March 19.

LIFE'S WORK

The portrait of Leo by Raphael, which hangs in the Pitti Palace in Florence, depicts the pope as an unattractive man, with a fat, shiny, effeminate countenance and weak, bulging eyes. Yet, according to contemporaries, his kind smile, well-modulated voice, kingly bearing, and sincere friendliness ingratiated him with everyone he met. While his manner of life was worldly, he was unfeignedly religious and strictly fulfilled his spiritual duties—he knew how to enjoy life but not at the expense of piety. He heard Mass and read his Breviary every day and fasted three times a week. Contemporaries report that there was scarcely a work of Christian charity that he did not support, as he contributed more than six thousand ducats per month to worthy causes. He enjoyed banquets and spent lavishly on them but never over-indulged himself. Though his personal morality was impeccable, he sometimes attended scandalous theatrical presentations and seemed to enjoy the absurd and vulgar jokes of buffoons. Even during the very troubled period of 1520-1521, he amused himself during the Roman carnivals with masques, music, and theatrical performances.

Since Leo's love of literature and the arts was well known, soon after his elevation to the Papacy, Rome was flooded with Humanists, poets, musicians, painters, sculptors, and other talented individuals seeking the pope's patronage. The greatest among them, as well as the lesser accomplished, were not disappointed. Beneficiaries of his largess as patron were the Humanists Pietro Bembo and Jacopo Sadoleto, the artists Raphael and Michelangelo, the architect Donato Bramante, and hundreds of others. Leo collected books, manuscripts, and gems without regard to price. The construction of St. Peter's Basilica was greatly accelerated. So splendid was the cultural life of Rome during this period that it has been called the Leonine Age, for its patron. Leo is said to have spent 4.5 million ducats during his reign, leaving the papal treasury a debt of 400,000 ducats.

Although Leo showed little interest in theological matters, he did reconvene the Fifth Lateran Council, which had first opened its doors under Julius II but had

adjourned without accomplishment. Its objectives were to promote peace within the Christian world, proclaim a Crusade against the Turks, and reform the Church. The council was poorly attended, and most of the councillors were Italians so that it was not representative of Christendom as a whole. At its conclusion in March, 1517, the council issued decrees calling for stricter regulation of the conduct of cardinals and other members of the Curia and denouncing abuses such as pluralism and absenteeism; these decrees would largely be ignored in practice, however, even by Leo himself. Leo did preach a Crusade against the Turks in 1518, but the monarchs of Europe showed little interest.

As secular ruler of the Papal States and protector of the Medici interests in Florence, Leo found it necessary to engage in the balance-of-power politics characteristic of the age; it is for his political role that he is most severely criticized by modern writers. In this political capacity, he was frequently guilty of treachery and duplicity. For example, when he began his pontificate, he was part of an alliance aimed at thwarting the French king's territorial ambitions in Italy. After Francis I's smashing victory at Marignano (September, 1515), however, Leo secretly deserted his allies, met with Francis, and negoti-

Leo X. (Hulton|Archive by Getty Images)

ated the Concordat of Bologna (1516), whereby, in return for guarantees of the integrity of Leo's territory in Italy, Francis was granted the right to nominate all the bishops, abbots, and priors within his realm, a right French kings would retain until the French Revolution.

Leo's capriciousness in political affairs was again demonstrated when Holy Roman Emperor Maximilian I died in January of 1519. The two leading contenders for this position were Francis and Charles I, king of Spain. Leo at first supported Francis, since he feared the territorial ambitions of Charles in both northern and southern Italy; because Francis had similar claims in Italy, however, Leo attempted to persuade Frederick the Wise of Saxony to be a candidate. When Frederick refused, Leo reverted to his support of Francis. When Charles was eventually elected in June of 1519, Leo moved quickly to establish a papal alliance with him. In May of 1521, Leo secretly concluded a treaty with Charles, in which the pope agreed to join Charles in a renewed effort to drive the French from Milan, in return for which Charles promised to close the meeting of the Imperial Diet at Worms with the outlawing of the excommunicate Martin Luther.

Like most Renaissance popes, Leo was guilty of nepotism. In order to provide his nephew Lorenzo with a title, Leo, in 1516, declared the duke of the small papal state of Urbino deposed and conferred the duchy on his nephew. To carry out the deposition, Leo had to raise an army and commit it to an arduous winter campaign against the former ruler. Leo then supported Lorenzo, duke of Urbino, as the unofficial ruler of Florence. Among Leo's several relatives who enjoyed church appointments under that pontiff was his cousin, Giulio, whom Leo made a cardinal almost as soon as he himself had mounted the papal throne. Giulio would later be elevated to the Papacy as Clement VII.

Despite Leo's irenic disposition, he made enemies, and he did not shrink from retaliation against those who threatened him. In 1517, when a conspiracy aimed at poisoning the pope was uncovered, one of the leaders, Cardinal Petrucci, was executed, several other cardinals were imprisoned and heavily fined, and Leo appointed thirty-one new cardinals in rapid succession so that the pope would have a college in which the majority of cardinals would be loyal to him.

The greatest crisis that Leo faced as pope came toward the end of his pontificate, and he died without really understanding its severity. Leo's predecessor, Julius II, had promulgated a plenary Jubilee indulgence in an effort to raise money for the building of St. Peter's Basilica in Rome. The indulgence had not sold well, and its sale was discontinued until its revival by Leo in March of 1515. Arrangements had been made with Albrecht of Brandenburg for the sale of the indulgence in his archdioceses of Mainz and Magdeburg. When the sale of these indulgences by the Dominican Friar Johann Tetzel began in 1517, it was not long before the matter came to the attention of a young German monk, Martin Luther, who lodged a protest.

Pope Leo did not realize the seriousness of the protest and was preoccupied with the preparation for the upcoming imperial election and with his other worldly pursuits, and so the situation was allowed to deteriorate. In June of 1520, Leo issued the bull *Exsurge Domine*, in which Luther was accused of forty-one counts of heresy and ordered to recant on pain of excommunication. Luther's refusal to recant, together with his public burning of the bull, led to his formal excommunication on January 3, 1521. Within a short time after these events, Lutheranism had begun to win adherents among some of the northern German princes as well as in Denmark. Before the extent of the schism could be appreciated, Leo died, on December 1, 1521, from bronchitis.

SIGNIFICANCE

In early accounts of Leo X's reign, he was alleged to have remarked at the time of his coronation: "Let us enjoy the Papacy since God has given it to us." While there is strong evidence that Leo never actually said this, this remark does seem to reflect his attitude toward his high office. Within two years in office, Leo had exhausted the full treasury left him by Julius II, and, despite the additional revenues generated by the sale of church offices and papal favors as well as indulgences, Leo's extravagance bequeathed a debt of 400,000 ducats to his successor. While Roman cultural life had never been so splendid as it was during his pontificate, Leo's devil-may-care attitude and his capricious political activities, coupled with his failure to understand the religious intensity of men such as Luther or to respond to it, help to explain Protestantism's early success.

Leo's accession to the papal throne was accompanied by much celebration. Of his passing, a contemporary observed, "Never died Pope in worse repute." While it is no longer contended that he was the victim of poisoning, the circumstances of his burial were severe. The candles used in his obsequies were those left over from another funeral, and no monument was erected to his memory until the time of Paul III. With Leo's death, the age of the Renaissance popes was nearly at an end.

—*Paul E. Gill*

FURTHER READING

Bedini, Silvio A. *The Pope's Elephant*. Nashville, Tenn.: J. S. Sanders, 1998. Original, offbeat, and illuminating study; uses Hanno the elephant, a gift to Leo from King Manuel I of Portugal, as a lens through which to explore Leo and his place in Renaissance history.

Chamberlin, E. R. *The Bad Popes*. Stroud, Gloucestershire, England: Sutton, 2003. Leo's excesses and profligacy are portrayed in this study of papal corruption across the six hundred years leading up to the Reformation. Includes photographs, illustrations, genealogical tables, bibliographic references, and index.

Creighton, Mandell. *A History of the Papacy from the Great Schism to the Sack of Rome*. 6 vols. London: Longmans, Green, 1897. Provides a comprehensive survey of the pontificate of Leo. While Creighton gives recognition to Leo's importance as a patron of the arts, he is critical of Leo's reckless spending and his indifference toward spiritual matters. Concludes that Leo left a bitter heritage for his successors.

Mee, Charles L. *White Robe, Black Robe*. New York: G. P. Putnam's Sons, 1972. Presents an account of the early Reformation period through an examination of the lives, careers, and ideas of Leo and Luther, vividly contrasting the two protagonists. While it presents little new information on either figure, the work skillfully blends discussion of the political background to the Reformation with that of its theological significance. Contains a useful bibliography.

Pastor, Ludwig. *Leo X (1513-1521)*. Vol. 8 in *The History of the Popes from the Close of the Middle Ages*. Reprint. Wilmington, N.C.: Consortium, 1978. The entirety of this volume of this classic, monumental study of the modern Papacy is devoted to the pontificate of Leo. Provides an extensive treatment of the cultural life of Rome under Leo's patronage. Includes footnotes and English translations of many previously unpublished documents in the appendices.

Roscoe, William. *The Life and Pontificate of Leo the Tenth*. 6th ed. Rev. by Thomas Roscoe. 2 vols. London: H. G. Bohn, 1853. Reprint. New York: AMS Press, 1973. An excellent general history of the period of Leo's pontificate. Includes extensive notes and English translations of numerous documents relevant to the text. While mainly sympathetic to Leo, Roscoe maintains that criticism of Leo by contemporary and later writers is largely the result of Leo's duplicity and treacherousness as a political figure.

Rowe, Colin, and Leon Satkowski. *Italian Architecture of the Sixteenth Century*. New York: Princeton Architectural Press, 2002. Contains a study of Leo's architectural projects and legacy. Includes illustrations, bibliographic references, and index.

Schevill, Ferdinand. *The Medici*. New York: Harcourt, Brace, 1949. Reprint. New York: Harper, 1960. The chapter on Leo emphasizes how strongly he was motivated in most of his policies by his desire to advance the fortunes of the Medici family, both in Florence and in Italy as a whole. Schevill is critical of the artistic patronage of Leo, believing that he made poor use of the many talented persons in the papal employ.

Stinger, Charles L. *The Renaissance in Rome*. Bloomington: Indiana University Press, 1998. Leo is a central figure in this study of the resurgence of Rome's cultural, religious, and political importance in the Renaissance. Includes maps, illustrations, bibliographic references, and index.

Vaughan, Herbert M. *The Medici Popes*. New York: G. P. Putnam's Sons, 1908. This work is primarily devoted to an examination of the personal character and the strengths and weaknesses of Leo. The work's attention to unimportant details to the exclusion of the political realities faced by Leo necessitates consulting other works on the pontiff.

SEE ALSO: Alexander VI; Andrea del Sarto; Donato Bramante; Baldassare Castiglione; Catherine de Médicis; Clement VII; Marsilio Ficino; Francis I; Francesco Guicciardini; Julius II; Leo Africanus; Martin Luther; Maximilian I; Cosimo I de' Medici; Lorenzo de' Medici; Michelangelo; Giovannni Pico della Mirandola; Raphael.

RELATED ARTICLES in *Great Events from History: The Renaissance & Early Modern Era, 1454-1600:* Early 1460's: Labor Shortages Alter Europe's Social Structure; 1508-1520: Raphael Paints His Frescoes; 1515-1529: Wolsey Serves as Lord Chancellor and Cardinal; September 13-14, 1515: Battle of Marignano; August 18, 1516: Concordat of Bologna; October 31, 1517: Luther Posts His Ninety-five Theses; June 28, 1519: Charles V Is Elected Holy Roman Emperor; May 6, 1527-February, 1528: Sack of Rome.